ROBERT ALTHANN S.J.

ELENCHUS OF BIBLICA

1996

EDITRICE PONTIFICIO ISTITUTO BIBLICO

ROMA 2000

ROBERT ALTHANN S.J.

ELENCHUS OF BIBLICA

1996

EDITRICE PONTIFICIO ISTITUTO BIBLICO
ROMA 2000

EDITRICE PONTIFICIO ISTITUTO BIBLICO
Piazza della Pilotta, 35 - 00187 Roma, Italia

Urbes editionis — **Cities of publication**

AA	Ann Arbor	Lp	Leipzig
Amst	Amsterdam	LVL	Louisville KY
B	Berlin	Lv(N)	Leuven (L-Neuve)
Ba/BA	Basel/Buenos Aires	M/Mi	Madrid/Milano
Barc	Barcelona	Mkn/Mp	Maryknoll/Minneapolis
Bo/Bru	Bologna/Brussel	Mü/Müns('r)	München/Münster
C	Cambridge, England	N	Napoli
CasM	Casale Monferrato	ND	NotreDame IN
Ch	Chicago	Neuk	Neukirchen/Verlag
CinB	Cinisello Balsamo	NHv/Nv	New Haven/Nashville
CM	Cambridge, Mass.	NY	New York
ColMn	Collegeville MN	Oxf	Oxford
Da:Wiss	Darmstadt, WissBuchg	P/Pd	Paris/Paderborn
DG	Downers Grove	Ph	Philadelphia
Dü	Düsseldorf	R/Rg	Roma/Regensburg
E	Edinburgh	S/Sdr	Salamanca/Santander
ENJ	EnglewoodCliffs NJ	SF	San Francisco
F	Firenze	Shf	Sheffield
Fra	Frankfurt/M	Sto	Stockholm
FrB/FrS	Freiburg-Br/Schweiz	Stu	Stuttgart
Gö	Göttingen	T/TA	Torino/Tel Aviv
GR	Grand Rapids MI	Tü	Tübingen
Gü	Gütersloh	U/W	Uppsala/Wien
Ha	Hamburg	WL	Winona Lake IN
Heid	Heidelberg	Wmr	Warminster
Hmw	Harmondsworth	Wsb	Wiesbaden
J	Jerusalem	Wsh	Washington D.C.
K	København	Wsz	Warszawa
L/Lei	London/Leiden	Wu/Wü	Wuppertal/Würzburg
LA	Los Angeles	Z	Zürich

Punctuation: To separate a subtitle from its title, we use a COLON (:). The *semicolon* (;) serves to separate items that belong together. Hence, at the end of an entry a *semicolon* indicates a link with the following entry. This link may consist in the two entries having the same author or in the case of multiauthor works having the same book title; the author will be mentioned in the first entry of such a group, the common book title in the last entry, that is the one which concludes with a period [fullstop] (.).
Abbreviations: These follow S.M. Schwertner, **IATG**^{2} (De Gruyter; Berlin 1992) as far as possible.
Price of books: This is sometimes rounded off ($10 for $9.95).

Index systematicus — Contents

The present volume contains all the 1996 material of the Elenchus. I should like to thank Father Robert North S.J. for his ever willing help. The high standard set by him following in the footsteps of Father P. Nober S.J. presents a continuing challenge of excellence. The Catholic Biblical Association of America has once more granted a welcome subsidy towards defraying the cost of publication. Thanks are also due to the staff of the Editrice Pontificio Istituto Biblico which assures the publication of the Elenchus.

The materials for this volume were gathered from the libraries of the Pontifical Biblical Institute, the Pontifical Gregorian University and the University of Innsbruck. I should like here to express my gratitude to the staff of these libraries for their patience and willingness to help. The staff of the Department of Biblical Studies at the University of Innsbruck has again provided invaluable assistance in supplying information not only on books but also on many articles in periodicals and collected works. In return we are continuing to supply book reviews which may be accessed through BILDI on the internet. We are also planning to make the material of the Elenchus available on compact disk in association with the library of the Pontifical Biblical Institute.

Acronyms: Periodica - Series (small).
8 fig. = ISSN; *10 fig.* = ISBN.

A: in Arabic.
AcBib: Acta Pontificii Instituti Biblici; R.
ACPQ: American Catholic Philosophical Quarterly; Wsh.
Acta Patristica et Byzantina; Pretoria.
Acta Theologica; Bloemfontein.
ActBib: Actualidad Bibliográfica; Barc.
AETSC: Annales de l'Ecole Théologique Saint-Cyprien; Yaoundé, Cameroun.
AfR: Archiv für Religionsgeschichte; Stu.
AJPS: Asian Journal of Pentecostal Studies;
AJSR: Association for Jewish Studies Review; Waltham, MA.
Ä&L: Ägypten und Levante; Wien.
Alei Etzion; Alon Shvut.
Al-Mushir **[Urdu]**; Rawalpindi.
Alpha Omega; R.
AltOrF: Altorientalische Forschungen; B.
AnáMnesis; México.
AncB: Anchor Bible; NY.
Ancient Philosophy; Pittsburgh.
Annali Chieresi; Chieri.
Annals of Theology **[P.]**; Krakow.
AnnTh: Annales Theologici; R.
AnScR: Annali di Scienze Religiose; Mi.
Antologia Vieusseux; F.
Archaeology in the Biblical World; Shafter, CA.
ARET: Archivi reali di Ebla, testi; R.
ARJ: The Annual of Rabbinic Judaism; Lei.

ASJ: Acta Sumerologica; Kyoto, Japan.
ATT: Archivo teologico torinese; Leumann (Torino).
Atualizaçâo; Belo Horizonte.
AulOr: Aula Orientalis (**S**: Supplement); Barc.
Auriensia; Ourense, Spain [I, 1998].
BAIAS: Bulletin of the Anglo-Israel Archaeological Society; L.
Barnabiti Studi; R.
BBR: Bulletin for Biblical Research; WL.
BCSMS: Bulletin of the Canadian Society for Mesopotamian Studies; Toronto.
BEgS: Bulletin of the Egyptological Seminar; NY.
Bib(L): Bíblica; Lisboa.
Bibl.Interp.　　　**Bibl.Interp.**: Biblical Interpretation; Lei.
Biblioteca EstB: Biblioteca de Estudios Bíblicos; S.
BnS: La bibbia nella storia; Bo.
Bobolanum **[P.]**; Wsz.
Bogoslovni Vestnik **[S.]**; Ljubljana.
BolT: Boletín teológico; Buenos Aires.
BoSm: Bogoslovska Smotra; Zagreb.
BRT: The Baptist Review of Theology / La revue baptiste de théologie; Gormely, Ontario.
BSÉG: Bulletin de la Société d'Égyptologie; Genève.
BSLP: Bulletin de la Société de Linguistique de Paris; P.
BuBbgB: Bulletin de bibliographie biblique; Lausanne.
Bulletin of Judaeo-Greek Studies; C.
Bulletin of Research of Christian Culture; Okayama, Japan.
BurH: Buried History; Melbourne.
CAH: Cambridge Ancient History^2; Cambridge Univ.

Cahiers de l'Atelier; P.
CahPhRel: Cahiers de l'Ecole des Sciences philosophiques et religieuses; Bru.
CAL.N: Comprehensive Aramaic Lexicon, Newsletter; Cincinatti.
CamArch: Cambridge Archaeological Journal; C.
Carthaginensia; Murcia.
Catechisti parrocchiali; R.
Cathedra; Bogotá.
Cathedra [**H.**]; J.
Chemins de Dialogue; Marseille.
Choisir; Genève.
Chongshin Review; Seoul.
Chronology and Catastrophism Workshop; Luton.
Cias; Buenos Aires.
C: in Chinese.
CLEC: Common Life in the Early Church;
CLehre: Die Christenlehre; B.
CMAO: Contributi e Materiali di Archeologia Orientale; R.
Colloquium; Brisbane.
Comunidades; S.
ConAss: Convivium Assisiense; Assisi.
Confer; M.
Contacts; Courbevoie.
Contagion; Rocky Mount.
Convergência; São Paulo.
CoSe: Consacrazione e Servizio; R.
CredOg: Credereoggi; Padova.
CritRR: Critical Review of Books in Religion; Atlanta.
Crkva u Svijetu; Split.
Croire aujourd'hui; P.
Crux: Vancouver.
CTrB: Cahiers de traduction biblique; Pierrefitte, France.
CuesT: Cuestiones Teológicas; Medellin.
Cuestion Social, La; Mexico.
CurResB: Currents in Research: Biblical Studies; Shf.
Daphnis; Amst.
D.: Director dissertationis.
Diadokhē [ΔΙΑΔΟΧΗ]; Santiago de Chile.
Didascalia; Rosario, ARG.

Direction; Fresno, CA.
DiscEg: Discussions in Egyptology; Oxf.
DissA: Dissertation Abstracts International; AA/L. -A [= US *etc.*]: 0419-4209 [C = Europe. 0307-6075].
DosP: Les Dossiers de la Bible; P.
DQ: Documenta Q; Leuven.
DSBP: Dizionario di spiritualità biblico-patristica; R.
DSD: Dead Sea Discoveries; Lei.
E.: Editor, Herausgeber, a cura di.
Eccl(R): Ecclesia; R.
EfMex: Efemérides Mexicana; Tlalpan.
EgArch: Egyptian Archaeology, Bulletin of the Egypt Exploration Society; L.
Emmanuel; St. Meinrads, IN.
Encounters; Markfield, U.K.
ERSY: Erasmus of Rotterdam Society Yearbook; Lexington.
EscrVedat: Escritos del Vedat; Valencia.
Esprit; P.
Ethics & Medicine; Carlisle.
ETSI Journal; Igbaja, Nigeria.
EurJT: European Journal of Theology; Carlisle.
Evangel; E.
Evangelizzare; Bo.
EvV: Evangelio y Vida; León.
Exchange; Lei.
Faith & Mission; Wake Forest, NC.
Feminist Theology; Shf.
F.: Festschrift.
FgNT: Filologia Neotestamentaria; Córdoba.
Filosofia oggi; Genova.
Firmana; Fermo.
Florensia; S. Giovanni in Fiore (CS).
FolTh: Folia theologica; Budapest.
Forum. Sonoma, CA.
Forum Religion; Stu.
Franciscanum; Bogotá.
Fundamentum; Basel.
Furrow; Maynooth.

Gema; Yogyakarta.
Georgica; Konstanz.
G: in Greek.
Gnosis; SF.
Graphè; Lille.
Hagiographica; F.
Hamdard Islamicus; Karachi.
HBO: Hallesche Beiträge zur Orientwissenschaft; Halle.
Hekima Review; Nairobi.
Henoch; T.
H: in Hebrew.
History of European Ideas; Oxf.
HIL: Das Heilige Land; Köln.
Hokhma; Lausanne.
Holy Land; J.
Horeb; Pozzo di Gotto (ME).
Horizons; Villanova, PA.
HorWi: Horizonty Wiary; Kraków.
Ho Theológos; Palermo.
IAJS: Index of Articles on Jewish Studies; J.
Ichthys ΙΧΘΤΣ; Aarhus.
Igreja e Missão; Valadares, Cucujaes.
IHR: International History Review; Burnaby, Canada.
Iran; L.
Isidorianum; Sevilla.
IslChr: Islamochristiana; R.
ITBT: Interpretatie; Zoetermeer.
Iter; Caracas.
JAGNES: Journal of the Association of Graduates in Near Eastern Studies; Berkeley, CA.
Jahrbuch Politische Theologie; Mü.
Japan Mission Journal; Tokyo.
JEarlyC: Journal of Early Christian Studies; Baltimore.
Jeevadhara; Alleppey, Kerala.
JEGTFF: Jahrbuch der Europäischen Gesellschaft für theologische Forschung von Frauen; Mainz.
JHiC: Journal of Higher Criticism; Montclair, NJ.
Jian Dao; Hong Kong.
J: in Japanese.

JJTP: Journal of Jewish Thought & Philosophy; Ba.
JKTh: Jahrbuch für kontextuelle Theologien; Fra.
JNSL: Journal of Northwest Semitic Languages; Stellenbosch.
Journal of Medieval History; Amsterdam.
Journal of Psychology and Judaism; NY.
JPentec: Journal of Pentecostal Theology; Shf (S: Supplement).
JPersp: Jerusalem Perspective; J.
JProgJud: Journal of Progressive Judaism; Shf.
JRadRef: Journal from the Radical Reformation; Morrow, GA.
JRTR: Jahrbuch für Religionswissenschaft und Theologie der Religionen; FrB.
JSem: Journal for Semitics; Pretoria.
JSQ: Jewish Studies Quarterly; Tü.
JSSEA: Journal of the Society for the Study of Egyptian Antiquities; Toronto.
JTrTL: Journal of Translation and Textlinguistics; Dallas.
Jud.: Judaism; NY.
Kairos(G); Guatemala.
KaKe: Katorikku-Kenkyu [J.]; Tokyo.
Kerux; Escondido, CA.
K: in Korean.
Kwansei-Gakuin-Daigaku; Japan.
Landas; Manila.
Laós; Catania.
Living Light; Wsh.
LSDC: La Sapienza della Croce; R.
Luther-Bulletin; Amst.
Luther Digest; Crestwood, Miss.
M: Memorial.
MAI: Masters Abstracts International; AA: 0898-9095.
MastJ: Master's Seminary Journal; Sun Valley, CA.

Mayéutica; Marcilla (Navarra).
MEAH: Miscellánea de Estudios Árabes y Hebraicos **(MEAH.A (H)**: Árabe-Islam (Hebreo); Granada.
MethT: Method and Theory in the Study of Religion; Toronto.
Mid-Stream; Indianapolis.
MillSt: Milltown Studies; Dublin.
MissTod: Mission Today; Shillong, India.
Mitteilungen für Anthropologie und Religionsgeschichte; Saarbrücken.
Mondo della Bibbia, Il; T.
Moralia; M.
NABU: Nouvelles Assyriologiques; P.
NAC: New American Commentary; Nv.
NAOTS: Newsletter on African Old Testament Scholarship; Stavanger.
Naval Research Logistics; NY.
NEA(BA): Near Eastern Archaeology [BA]; Boston.
Neukirchener Theologische Zeitschrift; Neuk.
NewTR: New Theology Review; Ch.
NHMS: Nag Hammadi and Manichaean Studies; Lei.
NIBC: New International Biblical Commentary; Peabody.
Nicolaus; Bari.
NIntB: The New Interpreter's Bible; Nv.
NotesTrans: Notes on Translation; Dallas.
NTGu: New Testament Guides; Shf.
NTTRU: New Testament Textual Research Update; Ashfield NSW, Australia.
Nuova Umanità; R.
Omnis Terra; R.
OrBibChr: Orbis biblicus et christianus; Glückstadt.
OrExp: Orient-Express, Notes et Nouvelles d'Archéologie Orientale; P.
Orient; Tokyo.

Pacifica; Melbourne.
Paginas; Lima.
PaiC.: Paideia Cristiana; Rosario, ARG.
Parabola; NY.
Phase; Barc.
Philosophiques; Montréal.
P: in Polish.
PoeT: Poetics Today; Durham, NC.
PoST: Poznańskie studia teologiczne; Poznán.
PredOT: Prediking van het Oude Testament; Baarn.
Presbyteri; Trento.
Presbyterion; St. Louis.
PresPast: Presenza Pastorale, R.
Prism; St. Paul, MN.
ProcGLM: Proceedings of the Eastern Great Lakes and Midwest Bible Societies; Buffalo.
ProEc: Pro ecclesia; Northfield, MN.
Prooftexts; Baltimore.
Proverbium; Burlington, VT.
Proyección; Granada.
ProySal: Proyecto Centro Salesiano de Estudios; BA.
Prudentia [.S]; Auckland, NZ.
PzB: Protokolle zur Bibel; Klosterneuburg.
Qumran Chronicle; Kraków.
QVC: Qüestions de Vida Cristiana; Barc.
R: in Russian.
R: *recensio*, book-review.
RANL: Rendiconti dell' Accademia Nazionale dei Lincei; R.
RBBras: Revista Bíblica Brasileira; Fortaleza.
RCI: Rivista del clero italiano; R.
Reason and the Faith, The; Kwangju.
Recollectio; R.
Reformation, The; Oxf (Tyndale Soc.).
Religion. A Journal of Religion and Religions; L.
RelT: Religion and Theology; Pretoria.

Religion; L.
RelT: Religion and Theology; Pretoria.
ResB: Reseña Bíblica; Estella.
RevCT: Revista de cultura teológica; São Paulo.
Revista católica; Santiago de Chile.
Revue d'éthique et de théologie morale; P.
RGRW: Religions in the Graeco-Roman World; Lei.
Ribla: Revista de interpretação biblica latino-americana; Petrópolis.
RRT: Reviews in Religion and Theology; L.
R&T: Religion and theology = Religie en teologie; Pretoria.
S: Slovenian.
SAA Bulletin: State Archives of Assyria Bulletin; Padova.
SAAS: State Archives of Assyria, Studies; Helsinki.
Saeculum Christianum; Wsz.
San Juan de la Cruz; Sevilla.
SBL.SCSt: Society of Biblical Literature, Septuagint and Cognate Studies; Atlanta.
Science and Christian Belief; Carlisle.
Scriptura; Stellenbosch.
SdT: Studi di Teologia; R.
SEAP: Studi di Egittologia e di Antichità Puniche; Pisa.
Search; Dublin.
Sedes Sapientiae; Chéméré-le-Roi.
SeK: Skrif en Kerk; Pretoria.
Semeia; Atlanta.
Semiotica; Amst.
Sen.: Sendros; Costa Rica.
Servitium; CasM.
SetRel: Sette e Religioni; Bo.
Sevartham; Ranchi.
Sève; P.
Sewanee Theological Review; Sewanee, TN.
Shofar; West Lafayette, IN.
SIDIC: Service International de Documentation Judéo-Chrétienne; R.

Sinhak Jonmang; Kwangju, S. Korea.
Soleriana; Montevideo.
Sources; FrS.
Spiritual Life; Wsh.
Spiritus; P.
SPJMS: South Pacific Journal of Mission Studies; North Turramurra NSW.
St Mark's Review; Canberra.
Studia Textus Novi Testamenti; Osaka.
Studies in World Christianity; E.
Studi Fatti Ricerche; Mi.
Stulos; Bandung, Indonesia.
StWC: Studies in World Christianity; E.
SUBB: Studia Universitatis Babeş-Bolyai; Cluj-Napoca, Romania.
Synaxis; Catania.
T: Translator.
Teocomunicaçâo; Porto Alegre, Brasil.
TEuph: Transeuphratène; P.
Themelios; L.
Theologica & Historica; Cagliari.
Theologika; Lima.
Théologiques; Montréal.
Theologisches; Siegburg.
Theológos, Ho; Palermo.
Theology for Our Times; Bangalore.
Theotokos; R.
TrinJ: Trinity Journal; Deerfield, IL.
TTE: The Theological Educator; New Orleans.
Tychique; Lyon.
Umat Baru; Yogyakarta, Indonesia.
Una Voce-Korrespondenz; Köln.
Vie Chrétienne; P.
Vie, La: des communautés religieuses; Montréal.
Vita Sociale; F.
Vivarium; Catanzaro.
Vivens Homo; F.
VO: Vicino Oriente; R.
Vox Patrum; Lublin.

VoxScr: Vox Scripturae; São
Paulo.
WaW: Word and World; St.
Paul, Minn.
Way, The; L.
WBC: Word Biblical Commen-
tary; Waco.
WUB: Welt und Umwelt der

Bibel; Stu.
Yonsei Journal of Theology;
Seoul.
ZAR: Zeitschrift für altorienta-
lische und biblische Rechts-
geschichte; Wsb.
ZNT: Zeitschrift für Neues
Testament; Tü (1435-2249).

I. Bibliographica

A1 Opera collecta .1 **Festschriften**, memorials

1 ALBERIGO, Giuseppe: Cristianesimo nella storia, Saggi in onore
di..., EMelloni, Alberto (al): Testi e ricerche di scienze religiose 18:
[Bologna] 1996, Il Mulino 770 pp. L90.000. 88-15-05735-8.
2 AVIRAM, Joseph: Archaeological, historical and geographical studies: Joseph Aviram Volume, EBiran, Avraham: ErIs < vol.25 >: J
1996, Israel Exploration Society xvi; 108*; 551 pp. $108. 965-221-
032-3. H, Eng.
3 BADIAN, Ernst: Transitions to empire: essays in Greco-Roman history, 360-146 B.C., in honor of E. Badian, EWallace, Robert W.;
Harris, Edward Monroe: Oklahoma Series in Classical Culture: Norman 1996, Oklahoma University Press. x; 498 pp. Bibl. 0-8061-2863-
1.
4 BEAUCHAMP, Paul: Ouvrir les écritures: LeDiv 162: 1995,
⇒11/1,4. REeV 106 (1996) 547-549 (Cothenet, E.).
5 BELLONI, Gian Guido: Scritti di archeologia, storia e numismatica:
raccolti in occasione del 75. genetliaco dell'Autore, EPera, Rossella
(al): Mi 1996, Vita e Pensiero xxxi; 543 pp. 8-343-2455-2.
6 BERAN, Thomas: Vom Halys zum Ephrat: Thomas Beran zu Ehren.
Mit Beiträgen von Freunden und Schülern, EMagen, Ursula; Rashad,
Mahmoud: Altertumskunde des Vorderen Orients 7: Mü 1996,
Ugarit-Verlag x; 311 pp. 3-927120-41-3. RUF 28 (1996) 795-797
(Zwickel, Wolfgang).
7 BEYERLIN, Walter: Neue Wege der Psalmenforschung: für Walter
Beyerlin, ESeybold, Klaus; Zenger, Erich: Herders Biblische Studien
1: 1994, ⇒10,15. RBiLi 69 (1996) 53-54 (Kleer, Martin); ThRv 92
(1996) 222-225 (Oeming, Manfred); RivBib 44 (1996) 341-344
(Ravasi, Gianfranco).
8 BORCHARDT, Jürgen: Fremde Zeiten: Festschrift für Jürgen Borchhardt zum sechzigsten Geburtstag am 25. Februar 1996 dargebracht
von Kollegen, Schülern und Freunden, EBlakolmer, Fritz (al): Wien
1996, Phoibos 2 vols. 3-901232-13-3.
9 BORSE, Udo: Studien zur Entstehung und Auslegung des Neuen Testaments, EBörschel, Regina; Fischer, Wolfgang; Helfmeyer, Franz-
Josef: SBAB 21: Stuttgart 1996, Katholisches Bibelwerk 312 pp.
DM79. 3-460-06211-8. REThL 72 (1996) 438-439 (Neirynck, F.).
10 BROWNING, Robert: Philellen: studies in honour of Robert Browning, EConstantinides, Costas N.: Istituto Ellenico di Studi Bizantini
e Postbizantini di Venezia Bibliotheke 17: Venice 1996, Istituto Ellenico di Studi Bizantini e Postbizantini di Venezia xxiv; 419 pp. Bibl.
960-7743-00-8.

11 BROX, Norbert: ΦΙΔΟΦΡΟΝΗΣΙΣ für Norbert Brox, [E]Bauer, Johannes B.: GrTS 19: Graz 1995, RM 227 pp. [R]VetChr 33 (1996) 418-420 (*Veronese, Maria*).

12 BURGMANN, Hans: Mogilany 1993: papers on the Dead Sea Scrolls offered in memory of Hans Burgmann, [E]Kapera, Zdzislaw J.: Qumranica Mogilanensia 13: Kráków 1996, Enigma 229 pp. $38. 83-86110-18-X [ZAW 109,465].

13 BUTTRICK, David: Preaching as a theological task: word, gospel, scripture. In honor of David Buttrick, [E]Long, Thomas G.; Farley, Edward: Louisville 1996, Westminster x; 191 pp. $23. 0-664-25617-1 [ThD 45,86].

14 CASCIARO, José María: Biblia, exegesis y cultura, 1994, ⇒10,22a. [R]Muséon 109 (1996) 227-229 (*Auwers, J.-M.*); EstB 54 (1996) 117-118 (*Díez Merino, L.*).

15 ÇAMBEL, Halet: Prehistorya Yazilari: Halet Çambel İêin/ Readings in prehistory: studies presented to Halet Çambel, Istanbul 1995, Graphis ii; 268 pp. 128 fig.; 9 tab. 975-7783-03-X. [R]AJA 100 (1996) 608 (*Rosenberg, Michael*).

16 CHILDS, Brevard S.: Canon, theology, and Old Testament interpretation, 1988, ⇒4,25. [R]ThR 61 (1996) 123-126 (*Reventlow, Henning Graf*).

17 COSTE, René: Les combats de la paix: mélanges offerts à René Coste PSS, [E]Colombani, Pierre: Toulouse 1996, Institut Catholique de Toulouse 457 pp. 1 port.; Bibl. FF240. 2-227-315-96-2 .

18 COUTURIER, Guy: 'Où demeures-tu? (Jn 1,38)': la maison depuis le monde biblique, [E]Petit, Jean-Claude: 1994, ⇒10,30. [R]EeT 27 (1996) 410-412 (*Laberge, Léo*); ScEs 48 (1996) 347-348 (*Langevin, Paul-Émile*).

19 DASSMANN, Ernst: Stimuli: Exegese und ihre Hermeneutik in Antike und Christentum: Festschrift für Ernst Dassmann, [E]Schöllgen, Georg; Scholten, Clemens: JAC.E 23: Mü 1996, Aschendorff xix; 621 pp. Port.; 8 pl. DM213. 3-402-08107-5.

20 DELORME, Jean: Le temps de la lecture: exégèse biblique et sémiotique, LeDiv 155: 1993, ⇒9,39. [R]EstB 54 (1996) 553-556 (*Urbán, A.*).

21 DUPONT, Jacques: La parola edifica la comunità: liber amicorum offerto al Padre Jacques Dupont in occasione del suo 80. compleanno e del 60. anniversario di professione monastica, [E]Bianchi, Enzo: Magnano (Biella) 1996, Qiqajon 272 pp. Bibl. 88-85227-98-8.

22 EMERTON, John A.: Wisdom in ancient Israel, [E]Day, John (*al*): 1995, ⇒11/1,9. [R]ScrTh 28 (1996) 925-926 (*Aranda, G.*); RStT 15/2-3 (1996) 104-106 (*Landy, Francis*); JJS 47 (1996) 150-151 (*Mason, Rex*).

23 ERNST, Josef: Schrift und Tradition: Festschrift für Josef Ernst zum 70. Geburtstag, [E]Backhaus, Knut; Untergaßmair, Franz Georg: Pd 1996, Schöningh 508 pp. DM98. [R]SNTU.A 21 (1996) 225-227 *Fuchs, A.*).

24 FEIEREIS, Konrad: Von Gott reden in säkularer Gesellschaft: Festschrift für Konrad Feiereis zum 65. Geburtstag, [E]Coreth, Emerich; Ernst, Wilhelm; Tiefensee, Eberhard: EThSt 71: Leipzig 1996, Benno 361 pp. 3-7462-1163-8/-34-4.

25 FORESTI, Bruno: Il vescovo e la sua chiesa, [E]Montagnini, Felice: Quaderni teologici. Seminario di Brescia 6: Brescia 1996, Morcelliana 324 pp. L35.000. 88-372-1608-4.

26 FREDE, Hermann J.; Thiele, Walter: Philologia sacra: biblische und
patristische Studien, 1993, ⇒9,49. ᴿVetChr 33 (1996) 241-242
(*Veronese, Maria*); Aug. 36 (1996) 291-293 (*Studer, Basil*).

27 FURNISH, Victor Paul: Theology and ethics in Paul and his interpreters. Essays in honor of Victor Paul Furnish, ᴱLovering, Eugene H.;
Sumney, Jerry L.: Nv 1996, Abingdon x; 333 pp. 0-687-00767-4.

28 GARZETTI, Albino: Studi in onore di Albino Garzetti, ᴱStella,
Clara; Valvo, Alfredo: Brescia 1996, Ateneo di Brescia xii; 543 pp.

29 GENEST, Hartmut: Christi Leidenspsalm: Arbeiten zum 22. Psalm.
Festschrift zum 50. Jahr des Bestehens des Theologischen Seminars
"Paulinum" Berlin, Neuk 1996, Neuk 103 pp. 3-7887-1599-5.

30 GEORGI, Dieter: Religious propaganda and missionary competition in
the New Testament world, ᴱBormann, Lukas; Tredici, Kelly del;
Standhartinger, Angela: NT.S 74: 1994, ⇒10,40. ᴿCBQ 58 (1996)
372-374 (*Osiek, Carolyn*).

31 GIBSOB, John C.L.: Ugarit, religion and culture. Proceedings of the
International Colloquium on Ugarit, religion and culture Edinburgh,
July 1994: essays presented in honour of Professor John C.L. Gibson,
ᴱWyatt, N.; Lloyd, J.B.; Watson, Wilfred G.E.: Ugaritisch-
Biblische Literatur (UBL) 12: Mü 1996, UGARIT xiv; 448 pp. Port.
3-927120-37-5.

32 GIVERSEN, Søren: Apocryphon Severini, ᴱBilde, Per (*al*): 1993,
⇒11/2,67. ᴿBiOr 53 (1996) 189-192 (*Van Lindt, Paul*).

33 GUNDRY, Robert H.: To tell the mystery: essays on New Testament
eschatology, JSNT.S 100: 1994, ⇒10,46. ᴿCBQ 58 (1996) 393-394
(*Gaventa, Beverly R.*).

34 HAHN, Ferdinand: Die Verwurzelung des Christentums im Judentum: exegetische Beiträge zum christlich-jüdischen Gespräch. Zum 70.
Geburtstag, ᴱBreytenbach, Cilliers; collab. *Sönke, Stemm*: Neuk
1996, Neuk 205 pp. DM68. 3-7887-1577-4.

35 HARAN, Menahem: Texts, temples, and traditions. A tribute to Menahem Haran, ᴱFox, Michael Vass: WL 1996, Eisenbrauns xlii; 438,
(10), 133* pp. Port. $47.50. 1-57506-003-5.

36 HARL, Marguerite: KATA TOUS O': selon les Septante: trente études sur la Bible grecque des Septante, 1995, ⇒11/1,13. ᴿETR 71
(1996) 279-280 (*Bauks, Michaela*).

37 HARTMAN, Lars: Texts and contexts, 1995, ⇒11/1,14. ᴿSJOT 10
(1996) 140-142 (*Pilgaard, Aage*).

38 HASEL, Gerhard: Feet on level ground: a South African tribute of
Old Testament essays in honor of Gerhard Hasel, ᴱWyk, Koot van:
Berrien Center, Michigan 1996, Hester iv; xxvi; 378 pp. 0-9635837-2-
7. [RB 104,613].

39 HENGEL, Martin: Geschichte—Tradition—Reflexion. Festschrift für
Martin Hengel zum 70. Geburtstag, ᴱCancik, Hubert; Schäfer,
Peter; Lichtenberger, Hermann: Tü 1996, Mohr 3 vols. DM898. 3-
16-146401-X.

40 HIRSCH, Hans: Festschrift für Hans Hirsch zum 65. Geburtstag.
Gewidmet von seinen Freunden, Kollegen und Schülern, ᴱAmbros,
Arne A.; Kählbach, Markus: WZKM 86: Wien 1996, Institut für
Orientalistik 488 pp.

41 HOFFMAN, Michael Allen: The followers of Horus, 1992, ⇒8,84.
ᴿBiOr 53 (1996) 44-47 (*Caneva, Isabella*).

42 HOOD, Sinclair: Knossos: a labyrinth of history. Papers presented in
honour of Sinclair Hood, ᴱEvely, Don (*al*): London 1994, British

School at Athens 288 pp. £32.50. 0-904887-15-4. ^RAJA 100 (1996) 614-615 (*Hershenson, Carol R.*).

43 HOOKER, Morna Dorothy: Early Christian thought in its Jewish context, ^EBarclay, John M.G.; Sweet, John P.: C 1996, CUP xvii; 297 pp. Port. $60. 0-521-46285-1 [TD 44,165].

44 JAMIESON, Penelope: The call to serve: biblical and theological perspectives on ministry in honour of Bishop Penny Jamieson, ^ECampbell, Douglas A.: Shf 1996, Academic 299 pp. $58.50. 1-85075-625-2 [TD 44,159].

45 JERVELL, Jacob: Mighty minorities?, 1995, ⇒11/1,17. ^RSJOT 10 (1996) 143-145 (*Pilgaard, Aage*).

46 JUNGHANS, Helmar: Humanismus und Wittenberger Reformation: Festgabe anläßlich des 500. Geburtstages des Praeceptor Germaniae Philipp MELANCHTON am 16. Februar 1997: Helmar Junghans gewidmet, ^EBeyer, Michael; Wartenberg, Günther; Hasse, Hans-Peter: Lp 1996, Evangelische Verlagsanstalt 444 pp. 3-374-01623-5 [EThL 74,86*].

47 KAISER, Otto: 'Wer ist wie du, HERR, unter den Göttern?', 1994, ⇒10,61*. ^RThLZ 121 (1996) 137-139 (*Kratz, Reinhard G.*).

48 KERTELGE, Karl: Ekklesiologie des Neuen Testaments: für Karl Kertelge, ^EKampling, Rainer; Söding, Thomas: FrB 1996, Herder 492 pp. Bibl. DM68. 3-451-23830-6.

49 KING, Philip J.: Scripture and other artifacts: essays on the bible and archaeology in honor of Philip J. King, 1994, ⇒10,67a. ^RHebStud 37 (1996) 138-141 (*Laughlin, John C.*).

50 LAGA, Carl: Philohistôr, OLA 60: 1994, ⇒10,70. ^ROCP 62 (1996) 440-442 (*Ruggieri, V.*).

51 LEGASSE, Simon: L'Evangile exploré. Mélanges offerts à Simon Légasse à l'occasion de ses soixante-dix ans, ^EMarchadour, Alain: LeDiv 166: P 1996, Cerf 443 pp. Port. 2-204-05434-8.

52 LOHFINK, Norbert: Biblische Theologie und gesellschaftlicher Wandel, 1993, ⇒9,212. ^REstB 54 (1996) 116-117 (*Mielgo, C.*); CBQ 58 (1996) 374-376 (*Kselman, John S.*).

53 LUEDEMANN, Gerd: Historische Wahrheit und theologische Wissenschaft. Gerd Lüdemann zum 50. Geburtstag, ^EÖzen, Alf: Fra 1996, Lang 148 pp. 3-631-30427-7.

54 MACK, Burton L.: Reimagining christian origins: a colloquium honoring Burton L. Mack, ^ECastelli, Elizabeth Anne; Taussig, Hal: Valley Forge, PA 1996, Trinity xvii; 332 pp. 1-56338-171-0.

55 MARSHALL, I. Howard: Jesus of Nazareth: Lord and Christ: essays on the historical Jesus and NT christology, 1994, ⇒11/2,121. ^RCBQ 58 (1996) 385-386 (*Martin, Francis*).

56 MARTIN, Ralph P.: Worship, theology and ministry in the early church, JSNT.S 87: 1992, ⇒8,126. ^REvQ 68 (1996) 73-76 (*Warrington, Keith*).

57 MASON, Rex: After the exile: essays in honour of Rex Mason, ^EBarton, John; Reimer, David J.: [Macon, GA] 1996, Mercer Univ. Press xi; 293 pp. $40. 0-86554-524-3.

58 MCNAMARA, Martin: Targumic and cognate studies: essays in honour of Martin McNamara, ^ECathcart, Kevin J.; Maher, Michael J.: JSOT.S 230: Shf 1996, Academic 250 pp. £33. 1-85075-632-5.

59 METZGER, Bruce M.: The text of the New Testament in contemporary research, StD 46: 1995, ⇒11/2,126. ^RScrTh 28 (1996) 618-619 (*Chapa, J.*).

60 METZGER, Martin: Biblische Welten, OBO 123: 1993, ⇒9,105.
RPEQ 128 (1996) 85-87 (*Isserlin, B.S.J.*).
61 MEULENAERE, Herman De: Aegyptus museis rediviva, 1993,
⇒9,106. RBiOr 53 (1996) 398-400 (*Caluwe, Albert De*).
62 MEYENDORFF, John: New perspectives on historical theology: essays in memory of John Meyendorff, EBradley, Nassif; foreword by
Chadwick, Henry: GR 1996, Eerdmans xix; 377 pp. [OrChrP 63,583].
63 MEYER, Léon de: Cinquante-deux réflexions sur le Proche-Orient
Ancien, 1994, ⇒10,81. RBiOr 53 (1996) 737-742 (*Freydank, H.*).
64 MICHEL, Diethelm: 'Jedes Ding hat seine Zeit...': Studien zur
israelitischen und altorientalischen Weisheit: Diethelm Michel zum 65.
Geburtstag, EDiesel, Anja A.; Lehmann, Reinhard G.; Wagner,
Andreas: BZAW 241: B 1996, De Gruyter viii; 275 pp. Bibl. 3-11-
015052-2.
65 MILIK, Józef: Hommage à Józef Milik: EPuech, Émile; García
Martínez, F.: RdQ 17 (1996); iv; 676 pp. 0035-1725. RREJ 155
(1996) 523-525 (*Margain, Jean*).
66 MORAG, Shelomo: Studies in Hebrew and Jewish languagues presented to Shelomo Morag, J 1996, Center for Jewish Languages and Literatures, Hebrew University; Bialik 552 pp. [REJ 157/1-2,225ss—
Aslanov, Cyril]. H, Eng.
67 MOSCATI, Sabatino: Alle soglie della classicità: il Mediterraneo tra
tradizione e innovazione. Studi in onore di Sabatino Moscati,
EAcquaro, Enrico: Pisa 1996, Istituti Editoriali 3 vols. Port. 88-
8147-048-9.
68 NIELSEN, Eduard: History and traditions of early Israel, VT.S 50:
1993, ⇒9,112. RThLZ 121 (1996) 528-530 (*Niemann, Hermann Michael*).
69 PAPA, Benigno: Uniti nella carità: miscellanea in onore del 60° genetliaco di Mons. Papa nel 20° di fondazione dello Stip, EReho, Cosimo; Carucci, Massimiliano: Santa Fara 1996, Studio Teologico In-
terreligioso Pugliese 350 pp. RLASBF 46 (1996) 481-484
(*Paczkowski, Mieczysław Celestyn*).
70 PETRACEK, Karel: Studies in Near Eastern languages and literatures:
memorial volume of Karel Petrácek, EZemánek, Petr: Prague 1996,
Academy of Sciences 664 pp. 80-85425-23-8.
71 POLOTSKY, Hans J.: Semitic and Cushitic studies, 1994, ⇒10,94.
RLASBF 46 (1996) 432-434 (*Niccacci, Alviero*).
72 POPHAM, Mervyn: Minotaur and centaur: studies in the archaeology
of Crete and Euboea presented to Mervyn Popham, EEverly, Doniert;
Lemos, Irene S.; Sherratt, Susan: Oxf 1996, Tempus Reparatum 167
pp. 54 pl.; 21 fig.; 7 plans; 2 maps; 4 tables. £28. 0-86054-821-X.
73 PRIEST, John F.: Biblical and humane: a Festschrift for John F.
Priest, EElder, Linda Bennett; Barr, David L.; Malbon, Elizabeth
Struthers: Scholars Press Homage: Atlanta 1996, Scholars xiv; 313
pp. $40. 0-7885-0285-9 [BoL 1998,6—Grabbe, Lester L.].
74 RENAUD, Bernard: Ce Dieu qui vient, LeDiv 159: 1995, ⇒11/1,22.
RCBQ 58 (1996) 388-389 (*Vogels, Walter A.*).
75 RICHARDSON, H. Neil: Uncovering ancient stones, 1994, ⇒10,102.
RCBQ 58 (1996) 182-184 (*Burden, Terry L.*).
76 ROSENDAL, Bent: Lov og visdom: seks gammeltestamentlige studier
tilegnet Bent Rosendal, EHolt, Else K.; Lundager Jensen, Hans J.;
Jeppesen, Knud: Fredriksberg 1995, ANIS 104 pp. RSEÅ 61 (1996)
125-126 (*Ólafsson, Sverrir*).

77 SANDERS, James A.: A gift of God in due season: essays on scripture and community in honor of James A. Sanders, ᴱWeis, Richard D.; Carr, David McClain: JSOT.S 225: Shf 1996, Academic 302 pp. 1-85075-626-0.

78 SARNA, Nahum M.: Minḥah le-Naḥum: biblical and other studies presented to Nahum M. Sarna in honour of his 70th birthday, JSOT.S 154: 1993, ⇒9,135. ᴿDSD 3 (1996) 64-65 (Flint, Peter W.).

79 SAWYER, John F.A.: Words remembered, JSOT.S 195: 1995, ⇒11/1,24. ᴿCBQ 58 (1996) 785-787 (Ben Zvi, Ehud).

80 SCHMIDT, Günter Rudolf: Divinum et humanum: Günter R. Schmidt zum 60. Geburtstag: religions-pädagogische Herausforderungen in Vergangenheit und Gegenwart, ᴱAmbrosy, Markus; Lähnemann, Johannes; Grethlein, Christian: Fra 1996, Lang 322 pp. 3-631-30051-4.

81 SCHOTTROFF, Willy: Gott an den Rändern: sozialgeschichtliche Perspektiven auf die Bibel, ᴱBail, Ulrike; Jost, Renate: Gü 1996, Kaiser 168 pp. DM58. 3-579-01840-X [OTA 19,519]

82 SMITH, Dwight Moody: Exploring the gospel of John: in honor of D. Moody Smith, ᴱCulpepper, R. Alan; Black, C. Clifton: LVL 1996, Westminster xxxiv; 409 pp. $42. 0-664-22083-5. ᴿEThL 72 (1996) 456-457 (Neirynck, F.).

83 SPYCKET, Agnès: Collectanea orientalia: histoire, arts de l'espace et industrie de la terre. Études offertes en hommage, Civilisations du Proche-Orient I. Archéologie et environnement 3: Neuchâtel 1996, Recherches xvii; 406 pp. FS85. 2-940032-09-2.

84 STACHOWIAK, Lech: Światła prawdy bożej: Ksiedzu Profesorowi Kechowi Stachowiakowi w 70. rocznie urodzin [Lights of the Lord's truth: to the Rev. Professor Lech Stachowiak on his seventieth birthday], ᴱSzewc, Eugeniusz: Łódz 1996, Archidiecezjalne Wydawnictwo Łódzkie 271 pp. 83-85022-61-9.

85 STARR, Richard Francis Strong: Richard F.S. Starr Memorial Volume, ᴱOwen, David I.; Wilhelm, Gernot: Studies on the civilization and culture of Nuzi and the Hurrians 8: Bethesda, MD 1996, CDL viii; 474 pp. 1-883053-10-2.

86 STEINMETZ, David C.: Biblical interpretation in the era of the Reformation. Essays presented to David C. Steinmetz in honor of his sixtieth birthday, ᴱMuller, Richard A.; Thompson, John L.: GR 1996, Eerdmans xvi; 351 pp. Bibl. $35. 0-8028-3819-7.

87 STERN, Menahem: The Jews in the Hellenistic-Roman world: studies in memory of Menahem Stern, ᴱGafni, Isaiah M.; Oppenheimer, Aharon; Schwartz, Daniel R.: J 1996, Zalman Shazar Center for Jewish History 158*; 488 pp. 965-227-105-5.

88 STRECKER, Georg: Bilanz und Perspektiven gegenwärtiger Auslegung des NT, BZNW 75: 1995, ⇒11/2,536. ᴿSNTU.A 21 (1996) 223-225 (Fuchs, A.).

89 STUDER, Basil: Mysterium Christi, StAns 116: 1995, ⇒11/1,32. ᴿALW 38/39 (1996/97) 72-74 (Neunheuser, Burkhard).

90 Studi in onore del Kunsthistorisches Institut in Florenz per il suo centenario (1897-1997), ASNSP IV. 1-2: Pisa 1996, [Scuola Normale Superiore] xiii; 601 pp.

91 SUBILIA, Vittorio: Il pluralismo nelle origini cristiane, 1994, ⇒10,125. ᴿRivBib 44 (1996) 373-374 (Fusco, Vittorio).

92 TESTA, Emanuele: Early christianity in context: monuments and documents, 1993, ⇒9,150. ᴿED 49 (1996) 445-446 (Noce, Celestino).

93 THOMA, Clemens: Tempelkult und Tempelzerstörung, JudChr 15: 1995, ⇒11/1,33. ᴿJud. 52 (1996) 143-144 (*Jansen, Reiner*); FZPhTh 43 (1996) 489-491 (*Küchler, Max*); FrRu NF 1 (1996) 11-16 (*Ernst, Hanspeter*).

94 THUESING, Wilhelm: Der lebendige Gott: Studien zur Theologie des Neuen Testaments. Festschrift für Wilhelm Thüsing zum 75. Geburtstag, ᴱSöding, Thomas: NTA 31: Mü 1996, Aschendorff viii; 447 pp. DM98. 3-402-00000-0.

95 TUCKER, Gene Milton: Prophets and paradigms: essays in honor of Gene M. Tucker, ᴱReid, Stephen Breck: JSOT.S 229: Shf 1996, Academic 242 pp. £35. 1-85075-630-9.

96 VAN BEEK, Gus W.: Retrieving the past: essays on archaeological research and methodology in honor of Gus W. Van Beek, ᴱSeger, Joe D.: WL 1996, Eisenbrauns xxxi; 312 pp. Port. $39.50. 1-57506-012-4.

97 VAN DER TOORN, Karel: Kleine encyclopedie van de Toorn, 1993, ⇒11/2,198. ᴿBiOr 53 (1996) 174-177 (*Peels, H.G.L.*).

98 VAN DER WOUDE, Adam S.: Sacred history and sacred texts in early Judaism, 1992, ⇒8,504. ᴿBiOr 53 (1996) 803-806 (*Reasoner, M.*).

99 VAN DIJK-HEMMES, Fokkelien: On reading prophetic texts: gender-specific and related studies in memory of Fokkelien van Dijk-Hemmes, ᴱBecking, Bob; Dijkstra, Meindert: Bibl.Interp. 18: Lei 1996, Brill xiii; 295 pp. Port. ƒ145; $93.75. 90-04-10274-4.

100 VAN UCHELEN, Nico A.: Give ear to my words: Psalms and other poetry in and around the Hebrew Bible: essays in honour of Professor N.A. van Uchelen, ᴱDyk, Janet: Amst 1996, Societas Hebraica Amstelodamensis x; 268 pp. 90-390-0125-1.

101 VIA, Dan O.: Perspectives on New Testament ethics. Essays in honor of Dan O. Via, ᴱKea, Perry V.: PRSt 23, no. 2; NABPR Festschrift 14: Macon, GA 1996, National Association of Baptist Professors Religion 126 pp. [NThAR 1997/8,227].

102 WACHOLDER, Ben Zion: Pursuing the text, JSOT.S 184: 1994, ⇒10,133. ᴿCBQ 58 (1996) 391-392 (*Wright, John W.*).

103 WAGNER, Siegfried: Gottesvolk, 1991, ⇒7,163. ᴿThR 61 (1996) 97-98 (*Reventlow, Henning Graf*).

104 WASSERSTEIN, Abraham: Studies in memory of Abraham Wasserstein, ᴱCotton, Hannah M.; Price, Jonathan J.; Wasserstein, David J.: SCI 15: J 1996, Hebrew University v (4); 321 pp. Bibl.

105 WATTS, John D.W.: Forming prophetic literature: essays on Isaiah and the Twelve in honor of John D.W. Watts, ᴱWatts, James W.; House, Paul R.: JSOT.S 235: Shf 1996, Academic 324 pp. Port. £45. 1-85075-641-4.

106 YADIN, Yigael: Archaeology and history of the Dead Sea scrolls: the New York University conference in memory of Yigael Yadin, JSPE.S 8: 1990, ⇒6,554...10,9686. ᴿVT 46 (1996) 424-425 (*Emerton, John A.E.*).

107 YOUNG, Dwight W.: Go to the land I will show you: studies in honor of Dwight W. Young, ᴱColeson, Joseph E.; Matthews, Victor H.: WL 1996, Eisenbrauns xix; 428 pp. Bibl. $42.50. 0-93464-91-9.

108 ZUURMOND, Rochus: The power of right hermeneutics simply as entertainment. Vorträge aus Anlass der Emeritierung von Rochus

Zuurmond, Compiler **Diebner, B.J.**: DBAT.B 14a: Heid 1996, DBAT 56 pp. [DBAT 29,301];

109 YHWH—Kyrios—antitheism or: the power of the word. Festschrift für Rochus Zuurmond anlässlich seiner Emeritierung, **EDeurloo, Karel A.; Diebner, Bernd Jörg**: DBAT.B 14: Heid 1996, Wiss.-theol. Institut 224 pp. [DBAT 29,300].

A1.2 Miscellanea *unius* auctoris

110 **Albertz, Rainer** Zorn über das Unrecht: vom Glauben, der verändern will, Neuk 1996, Neuk 144 pp. DM24.80. 3-7887-1578-2.

111 **Barth, Gerhard** Neutestamentliche Versuche und Beobachtungen, Wechselwirkungen: Ergänzungsreihe 4: Waltrop 1996, Spenner 473 pp. 3-927718-71-8.

112 **Beckwith, Roger T.** Calendar and chronology, Jewish and christian: biblical, intertestamental and patristic studies, AGJU 33 Lei 1996, Brill xv; 333 pp. ƒ183. 90-04-10586-7 [NThAR 1997/7,191].

113 **Beilner, Wolfgang** Texte 1994-1995: unveröffentlichte Texte IV, Vermittlung 61: Salzburg 1996, n.p. 301 pp.

114 **Ben-Chorin, Sch.** Theologia Judaica: gesammelte Aufsätze 2, 1992, ⇒8,208. RSNTU.A 21 (1996,) 285-286 *(Fuchs, A.)*.

115 **Bonhoeffer, Dietrich** Life together: prayerbook of the bible, TBloesch, Daniel W.; Burtness, James H.; EKelly, Geffrey B.. Dietrich Bonhoeffer Works 5: Mp 1996, Fortress xiv; 218 pp. $30.

116 **Borgen, Peder** Early christianity and Hellenistic Judaism, E 1996, Clark xi; 376 pp. £25. 0-567-08501-5 [RB 104,313].

117 **Brin, Gershon** Issues in the bible and the Dead Sea scrolls, H, 1994, ⇒10,163. RCBQ 58 (1996,) 574-576 *(Ben Zvi, Ehud)*.

118 **Brueggemann, Walter** Old Testament theology: essays on structure, theme, and text, EMiller, Patrick D. 1992, ⇒8,220...10,7388. RCritRR 9 (1996) 144-146 *(Gladson, Jerry A.)*.

119 **Burchard, Christoph** Gesammelte Studien zu Josef und Aseneth, collab. Burfeind, Carsten. SVTP 13: Lei 1996, Brill xxiii; 463 pp. ƒ270. 90-04-10628-6 [JSJ 28,365].

120 **Cazelles, Henri** Études d'histoire religieuse et de philologie biblique, Sources bibliques: P 1996, Gabalda 325 pp. FF550. 2-85021-085-4.

121 **Crenshaw, James L.** Trembling at the threshold of a biblical text, 1994, ⇒10,167*. RCTJ 31 (1996) 234-236 *(Hoezee, Scott)*.

122 **Davies, Philip R.** Sects and scrolls: essays on Qumran and related topics, SFSHJ 134: Atlanta 1996, Scholars 187 pp. 0-7885-0213-1.

123 **Evans, Craig A.** Jesus and his contemporaries: comparative studies, AGJU 25: 1995, ⇒11/2,256. RSEÅ 61 (1996) 140-143 *(Caragounis, Chrys C.)*.

124 **Feldman, Louis H.** Studies in Hellenistic Judaism, AGJU 30: Lei 1996, Brill x; 677 pp. ƒ313.50. 90-04-10418-6.

125 **Fortin, Ernest L.** The birth of philosophic Christianity: studies in early christian and medieval thought, EBenestad, J. Brian. Ernest Fortin: Collected Essays 1: Lanham 1996, Rowman & L xxiii; (2) 349 pp. Bibl. 0-8476-8274-9.

126 **Grelot, Pierre** La tradition apostolique: règle de foi et de vie pour l'église, 1995, ⇒11/2,265. RScEs 48 (1996) 115-118 *(Thériault, Jean-Yves)*; ZKTh 118 (1996,) 109-111 *(Neufeld, Karl H.)*.

127 **Hengel, Martin** Studies in early christology. 1995. ⇒11/2,268(!).
ᴿEE 71 (1996) 302-303 (*Madangi Sengi, Jean de Dieu*)
[Psalms110,01];

128 Judaica et Hellenistica: kleine Schriften I. Collab. *Deines, Roland,*
(*al*), WUNT 90: Tü 1996, Mohr ix; 484 pp. Anhang von Hanswulf
Bloedhorn; DM278. 3-16-146588-1.

129 **Hoffmann, Paul** Studien zur Frühgeschichte der Jesus-Bewegung.
SBAB 17: 1994, ⇒10,185. ᴿActualidad Bibliográfica 33 (1996) 36-
37 (*Boada, J.*).

130 **Hübner, Hans** Biblische Theologie als Hermeneutik: gesammelte
Aufsätze. ᴱ*Labahn, Antje; Labahn, Michael.* 1995, ⇒11/2,272.
ᴿThLZ 121 (1996) 1028-1030 (*Söding, Thomas*).

131 **Janowski, Bernd** Gottes Gegenwart in Israel: Beiträge zur Theologie
des Alten Testaments. Neuk 1993, Neuk 352 pp. DM58. 3-7887-
1464-6. ᴿThR 61 (1996) 133-137 (*Reventlow, Henning Graf*).

132 **Klopfenstein, Martin A.** Leben aus dem Wort: Beiträge zum Alten
Testament. ᴱ*Dietrich, Walter.* BEAT 40: Fra 1996, Lang 354 pp.
DM74. 3-906756-65-3.

133 **Koch, Klaus** Vor der Wende der Zeiten: Beiträge zur apokalyptischen Literatur. Gesammelte Aufsätze 3. ᴱ*Gleßmer, Uwe; Krause,*
Martin. Neuk 1996, Neuk xii; 308 pp. DM98. 3-7887-1606-1.

134 **Kremer, Jacob** Die Bibel beim Wort genommen: Beiträge zu Exe-
gese und Theologie des Neuen Testaments. ᴱ*Kühschwelm, Roman;*
Stowasser, Martin. 1995, ⇒11/2,281. ᴿThGl 86 (1996) 630-631
(*Ernst, Josef*).

135 **Kunz, Claudia Edith** Schweigen und Geist: biblische und patristische Studien zu einer Spiritualität des Schweigens. FrB 1996, Herder
832 pp. 3-451-26118-9 [RTL 30,117s—Weber, Ph.].

136 **Kühnert, F.** Bildung und Redekunst in der Antike. Kleine Schriften.
ᴱ*Riedel, V..* Jena 1994, Friedrich-Schiller Universität 222 pp. ᴿClR
46 (1996) 61-62 (*Usher, S.*).

137 ᴱ**Levin, Meyer** Classic Chassidic tales. Northvale, NJ 1996, Jason
Aronson xvii; 357 pp. 1-56821-911-3.

138 **Marcadé, Jean** Études de sculpture et d'iconographie antiques:
scripta varia, 1941-1991. 1993, ⇒11/2,294. ᴿAnCl 65 (1996) 536-
538 (*Marc, Jean-Yves*).

139 **McKane, William** A late harvest. 1995, ⇒11/1,56. ᴿBib. 77 (1996)
266-269 (*Reventlow, Henning Graf*); Neotest. 30 (1996) 466-470
(*Snyman, Gerrie*).

140 ᴱ**Moreno Garcia, Abdon** Tras la huella de los humanistas extreme-
nos: manuscritos ineditos de Benito Arias Montano y Pedro de Valencia. Badajoz 1996, Universitas 208 pp. 84-88938-08-X [EstB
56,431s—Garcia Moreno, A.].

141 **Müller, Hans-Peter** Mythos—Kerygma—Wahrheit. BZAW 200:
1991, ⇒7,240. ᴿOLZ 91 (1996) 182-187 (*Otto, Eckart*).

142 **Neusner, Jacob** Formative Judaism: current issues and arguments 1.
SFSHJ 133: Atlanta, Georgia 1996 Scholars viii; 232 pp. 0-7887-
0232-8.

143 **Perlitt, Lothar** Allein mit dem Wort: theologische Studien. 1995,
⇒11/2,308. ᴿThLZ 121 (1996) 531 (*Smend, Rudolf*).

144 **Rad, Gerhard von** La acción de Dios en Israel: ensayos sobre el
Antiguo Testamento. ᴱ*Steck, Odil Hannes;* ᵀ*Mínguez, Dionisio.*
Estructuras y Procesos. Serie Religión: M 1996, Trotta 293 pp.
Pts2.300. 84-8164-078-6.

145 **Rendtorff, Rolf** Kanon und Theologie, 1991, ⇒7,252...9,1272. ^RThR 61 (1996) 130-133 (*Reventlow, Henning Graf*).

146 **Rist, John Michael** Man, soul and body: essays in ancient thought from PLATO to DIONYSIUS, Collected Studies CS 549: Aldershot 1996, Variorum x; 298 pp. £47.50. 0-86078-547-5.

147 **Rudolph, Kurt** Gnosis und spätantike Religionsgeschichte: gesammelte Aufsätze, Nag Hammadi studies 42: Lei 1996, Brill xii; 783 pp. DM425. 90-04-10625-1;

148 Register 66 pp.

149 **Schroer, Silvia** Die Weisheit hat ihr Haus gebaut: Studien zur Gestalt der Sophia in den biblischen Schriften, Mainz 1996, Grünewald 176 pp. DM46. 3-7867-1951-9.

150 **Smith, Morton** Studies in the cult of Yahweh: 1. Studies in historical method, ancient Israel, ancient Judaism, ^E*Cohen, Shaye J.D.* Religions in the Graeco-Roman World 130 no. 1: Lei 1996, Brill viii; 334 pp. f194; $125. 90-04-10477-1;

151 2. New Testament, early christianity, and magic, ^E*Cohen, Shaye J.D.* Religions in the Graeco-Roman world 130, no. 2: Lei 1996, Brill viii; 292 pp. f130; $84. 90-04-10479-8.

152 ^E**Swanson, Reuben J.** New Testament Greek manuscripts: variant readings arranged in horizontal lines against Codex Vaticanus, Shf 1995-1996, Academic 4 vols.

153 **Trakatellis, Dimitrios** Die Väter legen aus, G, Athen 1996, Apostoliki Diakonia 254 pp. ^ROrthFor 10/2 (1996) 273-274 (*Nikolakopoulos, Konstantin*).

154 **Vetter, Dieter** Das Judentum und seine Bibel: gesammelte Aufsätze, Religionswissenschaftliche Studien 40: Wü 1996, Echter 530 pp. DM84. 3-429-01843-9.

155 **Visotzky, Burton L.** Fathers of the world: essays in rabbinic and patristic literatures, WUNT 80: 1995, ⇒11/2,344. ^RRHE 91 (1996) 509-511 (*Zeegers, Nicole*); REAug 42 (1996) 160-161 (*Mopsik, Charles*); Jud. 52 (1996) 144-145 (*Schreiner, Stefan*).

156 **Wagner, Siegfried** Ausgewählte Aufsätze zum Alten Testament, ^E*Mathias, Dietmar.* BZAW 240: B 1996, De Gruyter viii; 294 pp. DM174. 3-11-014833-1.

157 **Westermann, Claus** Das mündliche Wort: Erkundungen im Alten Testament, ^E*Landau, Rudolf.* AzTh 82: Stu 1996, Calwer 264 pp. 3-7668-3425-8.

158 **Wohlmuth, Josef** Im Geheimnis einander nahe: theologische Aufsätze zum Verhältnis von Judentum und Christentum, Pd 1996, Schöningh 250 pp. [Ist. 43,350ss—Dupuy, B.].

A1.3 *Plurium compilationes* biblicae

159 ^E**Amphoux, Christian-Bernard; Margain, Jean** Les premières traditions de la Bible. Histoire du texte biblique 2: Lausanne 1996, Zèbre 304 pp. FS175. 2-9700088-2-3 [CBQ 59,419].

160 ^E**Augustin, Matthias; Schunck, Klaus-Dietrich** "Dort ziehen Schiffe dahin..." Collected communications to the...congress of the International organization for the Study of the Old Testament 14; BEAT 28: Fra 1996, Lang 229 pp. 3-631-48673-1 [NThAR 1997/2, 34].

161 ᴱ**Aus, Roger David** Barabbas and Esther and other studies in the Judaic illumination of earliest christianity. 1992, ⇒10,153. ᴿJSSt 41 (1996) 340-342 (*Van Henten, Jan Willem*).

162 ᴱ**Bail, Ulrike; Jost, Renate** Gott an den Rändern: sozialgeschichtliche Perspektiven auf die Bibel. Gü 1996, Gü'er 168 pp [FrRu 4,289s—Schwendemann, Wilhelm].

163 ᴱ**Bailey, Randall C.** Race, class, and the politics of biblical translation. Semeia 76: Atlanta 1996, Scholars 169 pp. [NThAR 1998,268].

164 ᴱ**Barbour, Robin S.** The kingdom of God and human society. 1993, ⇒9,257*...10,260. ᴿEvQ 68 (1996) 185-187 (*Peck, John*).

165 ᴱ**Berger, Klaus; Colpe, Carsten** Testi religiosi per lo studio del Nuovo Testamento. NT Suppl. 9: 1993, ⇒9,4010...10,3811. ᴿAnton. 71 (1996) 733-734 (*Nobile, Marco*).

166 **Bianchi, Enzo,** (*al*), La lectio divina nella vita religiosa. Magnano 1994, Qiqajon 384 pp. L40.000. 88-85227-60-0. ᴿPaVi 41/4 (1996) 59-60 (*Cappelletto, Gianni*).

167 **Bianchi, Enzo,** (*al*), Il giusto sofferente. PSV 34: Bo 1996, EDB 355 pp.

168 **Bianchi, Enzo,** (*al*), "La paura". PSV 33: Bo 1996, EDB 295 pp.

169 ᴱ**Boecker, Hans Jochen,** (*al*), Altes Testament. Neuk ⁵1996, Neuk x; 352 pp. DM49.80. 3-7887-1545-6.

170 ᴱ**Brenner, Athalya** A feminist companion to the Hebrew Bible in the New Testament. The Feminist Companion to the Bible 10: Shf 1996, JSOT 384 pp. £16.50; $24.50. 1-85075-754-2.

171 **Brett, Mark G.** Ethnicity and the bible. Bibl.Interp. 19: Lei 1996, Brill x; 509 pp. 90-04-10317-1.

172 ᴱ**Carter, Charles Edward; Meyers, Carol L.** Community, identity, and ideology: social science approaches to the Hebrew Bible. Sources for Biblical and Theological Study 6: WL 1996, Eisenbrauns xviii; 574 pp. 1-57506-005-1.

173 ᴱ**Casciaro, José María,** (*al*), Esperanza del hombre y revelación bíblica. XIV Simposio Internacional de Teología de la Universidad de Navarra. Simposios Internacionales de Teología 14: Pamplona 1996, EUNSA 569 pp. 84-313-1422-2.

174 ᴱ**Davies, Philip R.** The prophets. BiSe 42: Shf 1996, Academic 388 pp. £15; $20. 1-85075-788-7.

175 ᴱ**Den Boeft, J.; Hilhorst, A.** Early christian poetry. 1993, ⇒9,16047...11/2,668. ᴿRSLR 32 (1996) 450-458 (*Bona, Edoardo*).

176 ᴱ**Dunn, James D.G.** Paul and the Mosaic law. WUNT 89: Tü 1996, Mohr xi; 368 pp. DM248. 3-16-146573-3 [ThG 40,231].

177 **Fabris, Rinaldo,** (*al*), Introduzione generale alla bibbia; profeti e apocalittici; vangeli sinottici e Atti degli Apostoli; lettere paoline e altre lettere. Logos: corso di studi biblici I, III, V, VI. Leumann (Torino) 1994-1995, Elle Di Ci, ⇒10,722...11/2,1094. ᴿCivCatt 147 IV (1996) 512-513 (*Scaiola, D.*).

178 ᴱ**Filoramo, Giovanni** Storia delle religioni II: ebraismo e cristianesimo. R 1995, Laterza 704 pp. L75.000. ᴿSapDom 49 (1996) 466-468 (*Scilironi, Carlo*); CivCatt 147 II (1996) 217-219 (*Prato, G.L.*).

179 ᴱ**Finan, Thomas; Twomey, Vincent** Scriptural interpretation in the Fathers: letter and spirit. 1995, ⇒11/2,504. ᴿAng. 73 (1996) 602-603 (*Degórski, Bazyli*); Milltown Studies 37 (1996) 141-149 (*Clancy, Finbarr*); IBSt 18 (1996) 48-49 (*Kirkpatrick, Laurence S.*).

180 ᴱFitzgerald, John T. Friendship, flattery, and frankness of speech: studies on friendship in the New Testament world. NT.S 82: Lei 1996, Brill xiv; 291 pp. ƒ160; $103.25 90-04-10454-2 [RB 104,133].

181 ᴱFrankemölle, Hubert Sünde und Erlösung im Neuen Testament. QD 161: FrB 1996, Herder 223 pp. DM48. 3-451-02161-7.

182 ᴱGourgues, Michel; Laberge, Léo "De bien des manières": la recherche biblique aux abords du XXIe siècle. LeDiv 163: 1995, ⇒11/1,84. ᴿRSR 84 (1996) 478-482 (Guillet, Jacques).

183 ᴱHaase, Wolfgang ANRW 2.26/3. Teil II: Principat 37, 3. Teilband: Wissenschaften, B 1996, De Gruyter xiv; 1937-2735. DM590. 3-11-015006-9.

184 ᴱJüngel, Eberhard Theologie als gegenwärtige Schriftauslegung. ZThK.B 9: Tü 1995, Mohr 150 pp. 3-16-146428-1.

185 ᴱKeck, Leander E.; Petersen, David L.; Long, Thomas G. Maccabees, introduction to Hebrew poetry, Job, Psalms. NIntB 4: 1996, 1287 pp. $65. 0-687-27817-1. ᴿET 108 (1996-97) 99 (Rodd, C.S.).

186 ᴱKeck, Leander E.; Petersen, David L.; Long, Thomas G. Introduction to apocalyptic literature; Daniel; (Twelve Prophets). NIntB 7: Nv 1996, Abingdon 887 pp. $65. 0-687-27820-1.

187 ᴱLicharz, Werner; Schoneveld, Jacobus Neu auf die Bibel hören: die Bibelverdeutschung von BUBER/ROSENZWEIG: heute. Gerlingen 1996, Bleicher 184 pp. DM22. 3-7953-0935-2 [KuI 12/1,93].

188 ᴱLongenecker, Richard N. Patterns of discipleship in the New Testament. McMaster NT Studies: GR 1996, Eerdmans xi; 308 pp. $25; £17. 0-8028-4169-4.

189 ᴱLorenzani, Massimo La natura e l'ambiente nella bibbia. XVI corso biblico. Studio Biblico Teologico Aquilano: L'Aquila 1996, ISSRA xii; 262 pp.

190 Marconcini, Benito, (al), Profeti e apocalittici. LOGOS. Corso di Studi Biblici 3: Leumann (Torino) 1995, Elle Di Ci 459 pp. L55.000. 88-01-10472-3. ᴿRivBib 44 (1996) 478-480 (Scippa, Vincenzo); LASBF 45 (1995) 586-590 (Cortese, Enzo).

191 ᴱMargain, Jean; Amphoux, Christian-Bernard Les premières traditions de la Bible. Histoire du texte biblique 2: Lausanne 1996, Zébre 304 pp. 2-9700088-2-3.

192 ᴱMarguerat, Daniel Le déchirement: Juifs et chrétiens au premier siècle. MoBi: Genève 1996, Labor et F 296 pp. 2-8309-0788-4. ᴿBLE 97 (1996) 402-405 (Debergé, P.); EeV 106 (1996) 279-281 (Cothenet, E.).

193 ᴱMoor, Johannes C. de Synchronic or diachronic?: a debate on method in OT exegesis. OTS 34: 1995, ⇒11/1,99. ᴿThLZ 121 (1996) 824-826 (Schart, Aaron).

194 ᴱNatrup, Susanne Zehn Worte der Freiheit: aktuelle Bibelarbeiten zu den Zehn Geboten. Gütersloher Taschenbücher Siebenstern 1312: Gü 1996, Gü'er 160 pp. 3-579-01312-2.

195 ᴱNiccacci, Alviero Divine promises to the fathers in the three monotheistic religions. ASBF 40: 1995, ⇒11/1,100. ᴿIslamochristiana 22 (1996) 290-291 (Fitzgerald, Michael L.).

196 ᴱNiemann, Raul Von Pontius zu Pilatus: Pilatus im Kreuzverhör. Stu 1996, Kreuz 159 pp. 3-7831-1300-08.

197 ᴱPorter, Stanley E.; Carson, D.A. Discourse analysis and other topics in Biblical Greek. JSNT.S 113: 1995, ⇒11/1,102. ᴿCBQ 58 (1996) 584-585 (Parunak, H. Van Dyke).

198 EPorter, Stanley E.; Tombs, David Approaches to NT study.
JSNT.S 120: 1995, ⇒11/2,381. RRExp 93 (1996) 569-571
(Blomberg, Craig L.).

199 EPury, Albert de; Römer, Thomas; Macchi, Jean-Daniel Israël
construit son histoire: l'historiographie deutéronomiste à la lumière
des recherches récentes. MoBi 34: Genève 1996, Labor et F 539 pp.
FS55. 2-8309-0815-5.

200 ERegt, Lénart J. de; Waard, J. de; Fokkelman, J.P. Literary
structure and rhetorical strategies in the Hebrew Bible. Assen 1996,
Van Gorcum x; 270 pp. ƒ75. 90-232-2995-9.

201 EReventlow, Henning Graf; Farmer, William R. Biblical studies
and the shifting of paradigms 1850-1914. JSOT.S 192: 1995,
⇒11/2,383. RTheol. 99 (1996) 226-227 (Rogerson, J.W.).

202 ERogerson, John William The pentateuch. Sheffield Readers 6;
BiSe 39: Shf 1996, Academic 371 pp. £15; $20. 1-85075-785-2.

203 ESawyer, John F.A. Reading Leviticus: a conversation with Mary
DOUGLAS. Colloquium (1995: Lancaster). JSOT.S 227: Shf 1996,
Academic 290 pp. £50; $85. 1-85075-628-7.

204 ESchottroff, Luise; Wacker, Marie-Theres Von der Wurzel getragen: christlich-feministische Exegese in Auseinandersetzung mit Antijudaismus. Bibl.Interp. 17: Lei 1996, Brill viii; 283 pp. $87.25.
90-04-10336-8.

205 ESierra, Sergio J. La lettura ebraica delle Scritture. La Bibbia nella
Storia 18: 1995, ⇒11/2,388. RRasIsr 62/3 (1996) 191-194 (Bosco,
Gilberto).

206 Sorg, Theo; Stuhlmacher, Peter Das Wort vom Kreuz: zur Predigt
am Karfreitag. Calwer Taschenbibliothek 52: Stu 1996, Calwer 118
pp. 3-7668-3405-3.

207 ETrowitzsch, Michael Karl BARTHs Schriftauslegung. Tü 1996,
Mohr iv; 116 pp. 3-16-146615-2.

208 EUro, Risto Symbols and strata: essays on the sayings gospel Q.
SESJ 65: Helsinki 1996, The Finnish Exegetical Society (8) iii; 238
pp. 951-9217-20-7.

209 EVeijola, Timo Das Deuteronomium und seine Querbeziehungen.
Schriften der Finnischen Exegetischen Gesellschaft 62: Helsinki
1996, Finnische Exegetische Gesellschaft 296 pp. 951-9217-17-7.

210 EVesco, Jean-Luc L'Ancien Testament: cent ans d'exégèse à l'École
biblique. CRB 28: 1990, ⇒9,17272...11/2,q173. RMSR 53 (1996)
331-333 (Cannuyer, Christian).

211 EWest, Gerald Reading with: an exploration of the interface between
critical and ordinary readings of the bible. African Overtures. Semeia
73: Atlanta 1996, Scholars 284 pp. [NThAR 1998,300].

A1.4 *Plurium compilationes* theologicae

212 EBerlin, Adele Religion and politics in the ancient Near East. Studies and Texts in Jewish History and Culture. Bethesda, Md 1996,
University Press of Maryland 150 pp. 1-883053-24-2 [NThAR
1997,131].

213 EBillington, Sandra; Green, Miranda The concept of the goddess.
L 1996, Routledge 206 pp. 25 fig. $35. 0-415-14421-3 [AJA
101,631].

214 ^E**Fuchs, Gotthard** Angesichts des Leids an Gott glauben?: zur Theologie der Klage. Fra 1996, Knecht 267 pp. 3-7820-0742-5 [EThL 74,425*].

215 ^E**Goodman, Hananya** Between Jerusalem and Benares: studies in Judaism and Hinduism. NY 1994, State University of New York Press 344 pp. $22. 0-7914-1715-8. ^RNumen 43 (1996) 318-321 (*Katz, Nathan*).

216 ^E**Groß, Walter** Frauenordination: Stand der Diskussion in der katholischen Kirche. Mü 1996, Wewel 147 pp. DM29. 3-87904-126-1 [RTL 29,84ss—Dermience, Alice].

217 ^E**Haider, Peter W.** Religionsgeschichte Syriens: von der Frühzeit bis zur Gegenwart. Stu 1996, Kohlhammer 496 pp. DM149. 3-17-012533-8 [OTA 19,526].

218 ^E**Kampling, Rainer; Schlegelberger, Bruno** Wahrnehmung des Fremden: Christentum und andere Religionen. Schriften der Diözesanakademie Berlin 12: B 1996, Morus 318 pp. 3-87554-316-5.

219 ^E**Lane, Eugene N.** Cybele, Attis and related cults. Essays in memory of M.J. Vermaseren. Religions in the Graeco-Roman world 131; Lei 1996, Brill ix; 441 pp. f214; $138. 90-04-10196-9.

220 ^E**Lüdemann, Gerd** Die "religionsgeschichtliche Schule": Facetten eines theologischen Umbruchs. Studien und Texte zur religionsgeschichtlichen Schule 1: Fra 1996, Lang 298 pp. 3-631-30038-7.

221 ^E**Maier, Hans** Das Kreuz im Widerspruch: der Kruzifix-Beschluss des Bundesverfassungsgerichts in der Kontroverse. QD 162: FrB 1996, Herder 157 pp. 3-451-02162-5.

222 ^E**Patton, Laurie L.; Doniger, Wendy** Myth and method. Charlottesville 1996, University Press of Virginia xii; 416 pp. $57.50; $22.50 [JR 78,482ss—Alles, Gregory D.].

223 ^E**Wils, Jean-Pierre** Warum denn Theologie?: Versuche wider die Resignation. Tü 1996, Attempto 185 pp. 3-89308-238-7 [EThL 74,16*].

A1.5 *Plurium compilationes* philologicae *vel archaeologicae*

224 ^E**Calinescu, Adriana** Ancient jewelry and archaeology. Bloomington 1996, Indiana University Press 288 pp. 190 fig.; 7 maps. $60. 0-253-329-93-0 [AJA 101,631].

225 **Elsner, Jaś** Art and text in Roman culture. C 1996, CUP 401 pp. 44 fig. $75. 0-521-43030-5 [AJA 101,632].

226 ^E**Hoerth, Alfred J.; Mattingly, Gerald L.; Yamauchi, Edwin M.** Peoples of the Old Testament world: 1994, ⇒10,246*...11/2,c532. ^RCBTJ 12 (1996) 148-149 (*McLain, Charles E.*).

227 **Izre'el, Shlomo** Studies in modern Semitic languages. Israel oriental studies 16: Lei 1996, Brill 288 pp. 90-04-10646-4.

228 ^E**Kleiner, Diana E.E.; Matheson, Susan B.** I, Claudia: women in ancient Rome. NHv 1996, Yale University Art Gallery 240 pp. 11 col. fig.; 250 fig. $27. 0-89467-075-1 [AJA 101,431].

229 ^E**Lefkowitz, Mary R.; Rogers, Guy MacLean** Black Athena revisited. Chapel Hill 1996, University of North Carolina Press xxi; 522 pp. 0-8078-2246-9.

230 ^E**Loprieno, Antonio** Ancient Egyptian literature: history and forms. Probleme der Ägyptologie 10: Lei 1996, Brill xvi; 726 pp. 90-04-09925-5.

231 EMarcadé, Jean Sculptures déliennes. P 1996, De Boccard 225 pp. 104 fig. FF150. 2-7018-0100-1 [AJA 101,633].
232 EMenache, Sophia Communication in the Jewish diaspora: the premodern world. Jewish Studies 16: Lei 1996, Brill 426 pp. 90-04-10189-6.
233 EMikasa, Takahito Essays on ancient Anatolia and Syria in the second and third millennium B.C.. Bulletin of the Middle Eastern Culture Center in Japan 9: Wsb 1996, Harrassowitz 308 pp. DM128 3-447-03759-8 [OLZ 93,647s—Prechel, Doris].
234 Mitteilungen des Deutschen Archäologischen Instituts, Abt. Kairo 52: Mainz 1996, Deutsches Archäologisches Institut. Abt. Kairo 354 pp. 56 pl. 3-8053-1861-8.
235 ENeils, Jenifer Worshipping Athena: panathenaia and Parthenon. Wisconsin Studies in the Classics: Madison 1996, University of Wisconsin Press 261 pp. 36 fig.; 4 tables. $23. 0-299-15114-X [AJA 101,633].
236 EPoorthuis, Marcel; Safrai, Chana The centrality of Jerusalem: historical perspectives. Kampen 1996, Kok Pharos v; 244 pp. ƒ49. 90-390-0151-0. RATG 59 (1996) 363-364 (Verd, G.M.).
237 EPreucel, Robert W.; Hodder, Ian Contemporary archaeology in theory: a reader. Oxf 1996, Blackwell 692 pp. 101 fig.; 11 plans; 11 maps; 15 tables. $25. 0-631-19561-0 [AJA 101,634].
238 ESchmeling, Gareth The novel in the ancient world. Mn.S 159: Lei 1996, Brill x; 876 pp. $255; ƒ395. 90-04-09630-2 [TJT 14/1,100ss—Ascough, Richard S.].
239 Schoville, Keith N. Canaanites and Amorites. Peoples of the Old Testament world. C 1996, Lutterworth 400 pp. 0-7188-2953-0.
240 EShanks, Hershel Archaeology's publication problem. Wsh 1996, Biblical Archaeological Society 119 pp. 5 fig.; 7 tables. 1-880317-46-X [AJA 101,821].
241 EShipley, Graham; Salmon, John Human landscapes in classical antiquity: environment and culture. Leicester-Nottingham Studies in Ancient Society 6: L 1996, Routledge 358 pp. 17 fig.; 6 maps; 7 tables. $65. 0-415-10755-5 [AJA 101,432].
242 ESmall, David B. Methods in the Mediterranean: historical and archaeological views on texts and archaeology. 1995, ⇒11/2,478. RAJA 100 (1996) 415-416 (Bennet, John).
243 ESpencer, Jeffrey Aspects of early Egypt. L 1996, British Museum Press 216 pp. 4 col. pl.; 28 pl.; 26 fig.; 26 tables; 9 maps. £30. 0-7141-0999-1 [AJA 101,432].
244 ESpencer, N. Time, tradition and society in Greek archaeology: bridging the great divide. L 1995, Routledge 208 pp. 0-415-11412-8. RCIR 46 (1996) 344-345 (Boardman, John).
245 EStiros, S.; Jones, R.E. Archaeoseismology Fitch Laboratory Occasional Paper 7: Athens 1996, British School at Athens 268 pp. 115 fig.; 19 plans; 27 maps. £35. 0-904887-26-X [AJA 101,821].
246 EVirgilio, Biagio Studi ellenistici VIII. Pisa 1996, Istituti Editoriali e Poligrafici Internazionali [At. 86,584—Asheri, David].
247 EVitelli, Karen D. Archaeological ethics. Walnut Creek 1996, Altamira 272 pp. $17. 0-7619-0531-6 [AJA 101,200].
248 EWestenholz, Joan M. Goodnick Royal cities of the biblical world. J 1996, Bible Lands Museum xxii; (2) 334 pp. 965-7027-01-2.

249 EWright, Rita P. Gender and archaeology. Ph 1996, University of Pennsylvania Press 308 pp. 20 fig.; 23 tables. $17.50. 0-8122-1574-5 [AJA 101,634].

A2.1 Acta *congressuum* biblica

250 EAjamian, J.; Stone, M.E. Text and context: studies in the Armenian NT, 1994, ⇒11/2,481. RJAOS 116 (1996) 573-574 (*Greppin, John A.C.*).

251 EAugustin, Matthias; Schunck, Klaus-Dietrich "Dort ziehen Schiffe dahin...": collected communications to the XIVth Congress of the International Organization for the Study of the Old Testament, P 1992. BEAT 28: Fra 1996, Lang 229 pp. DM89. 3-631-48673-1.

252 EBorgen, Peder; Giversen, Søren The New Testament and Hellenistic Judaism. 1995, ⇒11/1,67. RStPhilo 8 (1996) 210-212 (*Runia, David T.*); CBQ 58 (1996) 573-574 (*Adler, William*).

253 EBorgonovo, Graziano Gesú Cristo, legge vivente e personale della Santa Chiesa. Atti del IX Colloquio Internazionale di Teologia di Lugano sul Primo capitolo dell'Enciclica "Veritatis Splendor"; Lugano, 15-17 giugno 1995. CasM 1996, Piemme 304 pp. 88-384-2574-4.

254 EBurchard, Christoph Armenia and the bible. 1993, ⇒9,374. RMuséon 109 (1996) 234-237 (*Coulie, B.*).

255 EDunn, James D.G. Paul and the Mosaic law: the third Durham-Tübingen Research Symposium on Earliest Christianity and Judaism (Durham, September, 1994). WUNT 89: Tü 1996, Mohr xi; 368 pp. 3-16-146573-3.

256 EEmerton, John Adney Congress Volume: Paris 1992 [IOSOT]. VT.S 6: 1995, ⇒11/1,135. RETR 71 (1996) 591-592 (*Macchi, Jean-Daniel*).

257 EHengel, Martin; Löhr, H. Schriftauslegung im antiken Judentum und im Urchristentum. WUNT 73: 1994, ⇒10,322*. RHenoch 18 (1996) 370-371 (*Chiesa, Bruno*).

258 EKertanova, L.S. Apokalipsis v russkoj kul'ture: materialy 3. R. Rosskijskoj naučnoj konferencii, posvjaščënnoj Pamjati Svjatitelja Makarija (6-8 ijunja 1995 goda). Makarievskie čtenija 3: Možajsk 1995, Možajska 2 vols; 171 + 169 pp. [NThAR 1998,335].

259 EMarin, Marcello; Girardi, Mario Retorica ed esegesi biblica: il rilievo dei contenuti attraverso le forme. Atti del II seminario di antichità cristiane, Bari 1991. QVetChr 24: Bari 1996, Edipuglia 272 pp. L40.000. 88-7228-122-9 [Asp. 45,292—Longobardo, Luigi].

260 Mednarodni simpozij o interpretaciji Svetega Pisma ob izidu novega slovenskega prevoda Svetega Pisma 17.- 20. september 1996 Slovenija, Ljubljana [International Symposium on the Interpretation of the Bible on the Occasion of the Publications of the New Slovenian Translation of the Bible Sept.17-20, 1996 Ljubljana. Ljubljana 1996, n.p. 197 pp.

261 EPadovese, Luigi Atti del I Simposio di Tarso su s. Paolo apostolo. R 1993, Pontificio Ateneo Antoniano 157 pp. RLaur. 37 (1996) 500-501 (*Martignani, Luigi*).

262 EPadovese, Luigi Atti del V Simposio di Efeso su S. Giovanni Apostolo. Turchia: la Chiesa e la sua storia 8: 1995, ⇒11/2,520. RGr. 77 (1996) 354-356 (*Ferraro, Giuseppe*).

263 EPadovese, Luigi Atti del IV Simposio di Tarso su S. Paolo Apostolo [1995]. Turchia: la Chiesa e la sua storia 10: R 1996, Pontificio Ateneo Antoniano 295 pp.
264 EPadovese, Luigi Atti del VI Simposio di Efeso su S. Giovanni Apostolo. Simposio di Efeso su S. Giovanni Apostolo 11. Turchia: la Chiesa e la sua storia 11: R 1996, Istituto Francescano di Spiritualità 359 pp.
265 EParker, D.C.; Amphoux, C.-B. Codex Bezae. Studies from the Lunel Colloquium June 1994. NTTS 22: Lei 1996, Brill xxx; 383 pp. ƒ195; $126. 90-04-10393-7 [ThLZ 122,674].
266 EPatlagean, Éveline: Le Boulluec, Alain Les retours aux Écritures: fondamentalismes présents et passés. AEPHER 1993, ⇒9,293; 10,329*. REThL 72 (1996) 248-249 (Verheyden, J.).
267 EPedersen, S. New directions in biblical theology. 1994, ⇒10,303a. RSNTU.A 21 (1996) 229-232 (Huber, K.).
268 EPorter, Stanley E.; Olbricht, Thomas H. Rhetoric, scripture and theology: essays from the 1994 Pretoria Conference. JSNT.S 131: Shf 1996, Academic 438 pp. £53; $79.50. 1-85075-607-4.
269 ERatzinger, Cardinal Josef Schriftauslegung im Widerstreit. QD 117:   1989,   ⇒5,591b...6,m203.   RThR   61   (1996)   138-140 (Reventlow, Henning Graf).
270 ERevell, Ernest John Proceedings of the Twelfth International Congress of the International Organization for Masoretic Studies. C 1995. SBL Masoretic Studies 8: [Alpharetta, GA] 1996, Scholars viii; 170 pp. $35. 0-7885-0180-1.
271 La Sagrada Familia en el Siglo XVIII: actas del tercer congreso internacional sobre la Sagrada Familia: en ocasión del LXXV Aniversario de la extensión de la fiesta litúrgica de la Sagrada Familia a la Iglesia Universal, Barc/Begues septiembre de 1996. Barc 1996, Hijos de la Sagrada Familia—Nazarenum 859 pp.
272 ESatterthwaite, Philip; Wright, David A pathway into the holy scripture. 1994 Swanwick conference. 1994, ⇒10,798. RRTR 55 (1996) 40-41 (Goldsworthy, Graeme).
273 ESchlosser, Jacques Paul de Tarse: congrès de L'ACFEB (Strasbourg, 1995). LeDiv 165: P 1996, Cerf 376 pp. FF255. 2-204-05384-8 [EThL 73,182].
274 Society of Biblical Literature 1996 Seminar Papers: One Hundred Thirty-Second Annual Meeting November 21-28, 1996 New Orleans. SBL.SPS 35: Atlanta, GA 1996, Scholars 504 pp. 0-7885-0292-1.
275 ETrublet, Jacques La sagesse biblique. Actes du 15e Congrès de l'ACFEB (1993). LeDiv 160: 1995, ⇒11/1,117. RTelema 22/1 (1996) 83-84 (Kipupu, Kafuti); NRTh 118 (1996) 107-108 (Luciani, D.); SR 25/1 (1996) 115-116 (Vogels, Walter); RevBib 58 (1996) 119-120 (Fernández, Victor M.); ETR 71 (1996) 442-443 (Cuvillier, Elian); ScrTh 28 (1996) 928-930 (Aranda, G.).
276 EVan Riel, Gerd; Steel, Carlos; McEvoy, James Johannes Scottus Eriugena, the bible and hermeneutics. Proceedings of the Ninth International Colloquium of the Society for the Promotion of Eriugenian Studies, Leuven and Louvain-La-Neuve, June 7-10, 1995. AMP 1/20: Lv 1996, University Press 408 pp.
277 EVanhoye, Albert La foi agissant par l'amour (Galates 4,12-6,16). Acta 14º Colloquio Ecumenico Paolino. SMBen.BE 13: R 1996, Abbaye de S. Paul 254 pp. L60.000.

A2.3 Acta congressuum theologica

278 ᴱBeltz, Walter Die Folgen der Kreuzzüge für die orientalischen Religionsgemeinschaften. Colloquium Halle 1996. HBO 22: Halle 1996, Martin-Luther-Universität 206 pp. [DBAT 29,324—Diebner, B.J.].

279 L'etica cristiana nei secoli III e IV: eredità e confronti. Atti del 23º Incontro di studiosi dell'antichità cristiana (4-6 maggio 1995). SEAug 53: R 1996, Augustinianum 685 pp. L120.000. 88-7961-044-9.

280 ᴱHelleman, Wendy E. Hellenization...christian response within the Greco-Roman world. 1994, ⇒11/2,587. ᴿCTJ 31 (1996) 551-552 (Gustafson, Mark); SR 25 (1996) 120-121 (Muir, Steven C.).

281 ᴱLoy, David Healing deconstruction: postmodern thought in Buddhism and Christianity. International Buddhist-Christian Dialogue Conference (4: 1992: Boston). Reflection and Theory in the Study of Religion 3: Atlanta, GA 1996, American Academy of Religion (6) 120 pp. 0-7885-0122-4.

A2.5 Acta philologica et historica

282 ᴱBasile, Corrado; Di Natale, Anna Atti del II Convegno Nazionale di Egittologia e Papirologia, Siracusa, 1-3 dicembre 1995. Quaderni dell'Istituto Internazionale del Papiro, Siracusa 7: [Siracusa] 1996, n.p. 237 pp.

283 ᴱBrenk, Beat Innovation in der Spätantike. Kolloquium Basel 6. und 7. Mai 1994. Spätantike—frühes Christentum—Byzanz: Reihe B, Studien und Perspektiven 1: Wsb 1996, Reichert 455 pp. 3-88226-879-4.

284 ᴱBriquel-Chatonnet, Françoise Mosaïque de langues, mosaïque culturelle: le bilinguisme dans le Proche-Orient Ancien. Actes de la Table-Ronde du 18 novembre 1995 organisée par l'URA 1062 "Études Sémitiques". Antiquités sémitiques 1: P 1996, Maisonneuve 221 pp. 2-2700-1104-5.

285 ᴱBunnens, Guy Cultural interaction in the ancient Near East: papers read at a symposium held at the University of Melbourne, Department of Classics and Archaeology (29-30 September 1994). Abr-n.S 5: Lv 1996, Peeters vii; 155 pp. 90-6831-786-5.

286 ᴱBühler, Pierre; Karakash, Clairette Quand interpréter c'est changer: pragmatique et lectures de la parole. 1994, ⇒11/2,673. ᴿETR 71 (1996) 460-463 (Bennahmias, Richard); RHPhR 76 (1996) 458-460 (Pfrimmer, Th.).

287 ᴱCassio, A.C.; Cerri, G. L'inno tra rituale e letteratura nel mondo antico. Atti di un colloquio, Napoli 1991. AION: R 1991, Gruppo Editoriale Internazionale 312 pp. ᴿCIR 46 (1996) 54-56 (Richardson, N.J.).

288 ᴱGill, Christopher; Wiseman, T.P. Lies and fiction in the ancient world. 1993, ⇒10,421. ᴿAt. 84 (1996) 273-281 (Nicolai, Roberto); JHS 116 (1996) 186-187 (Murray, Penelope).

289 ᴱGoldberg, Adele E. Conceptual structure, discourse, and language conference (1995 University of California, San Diego). Stanford, California 1996, CSLI xi; 503 pp. 1-57586-040-6.

290 ^E**Hellström, Pontus; Alroth, Brita** Religion and power in the ancient Greek world. Proceedings of the Uppsala Symposium 1993. BOREAS 24: Uppsala 1996, Almqvist & W 204 pp. SEK174. 91-554-3693-5 [JHS 117,222].

291 ^E**Isaac, B.; Oppenheimer, A.** Studies on the Jewish diaspora in the Hellenistic and Roman periods. Conference at Tel Aviv University, Jan. 1991. Teʿuda 12: Tel Aviv 1996, 254 pp.

292 ^E**Nicolet, Claude** Les littératures techniques dans l'antiquité romaine: statut, public et destination, tradition. Sept exposés...discussions. Entretiens sur l'antiquité classique (42: 1995: Vandoeuvres). Entretiens 42: Genève 1996, [Fondation Hardt] x; 260 pp.

293 ^E**Parry, Donald W.; Ricks, Stephen D.** Current research and technological developments on the Dead Sea Scrolls. Conference on the texts from the Judean desert, J, 30 April 1995. StTDJ 20: Lei 1996, Brill x; 279 pp. $93.75. 90-04-10662-6.

294 ^E**Willems, Harco** The world of the coffin texts. Proceedings of the symposium held on the occasion of the 100th birthday of Adriaan de Buck, Lei 1992. Egyptologische Uitgaven 9: Lei 1996, Nederlands Instituut voor het Nabije Osten viii; 209 pp. ^RRSO 70 (1996) 459-462 (*Ciampini, Emanuele M.*).

A2.7 *Acta* orientalistica

295 ^E**Allam, Schafik** Grund und Boden in Altägypten. Symposion Tü 1990. 1994, ⇒10,443. ^RAltOrF 23 (1996) 284-288 (*Haase, Richard*).

296 ^E**Bartl, Karin; Hauser, Stefan R.** Continuity and change in northern Mesopotamia from the Hellenistic to the early Islamic period. Proceedings of a colloquium held at the Seminar für Vorderasiatische Altertumskunde, Freie Universität Berlin, 6th-9th April, 1994. Berliner Beiträge zum Vorderen Orient 17: B 1996, Reimer xi; 452 pp. 8 pl. DM79. 3-496-02607-3.

297 ^E**Galter, Hannes D.** Die Rolle der Astronomie in den Kulturen Mesopotamiens. 3. Grazer Morgenländ. Symposion, 23-27.9.1991. 1993, ⇒9,3822. ^RBiOr 53 (1996) 744-749 (*Beaulieu, Paul-Alain*).

298 ^E**Taft, Robert F.** The Christian East: its institutions & its thought: a critical reflection. Papers of the International Scholars Congress for the 75th Anniversary of the Pontifical Oriental Institute, Rome, 30 May - 5 June 1993. OCA 251: R 1996, Pont. Istit. Orientale 704 pp. 88-7210-311-8.

299 ^E**Veenhof, Klaas R.** Houses and households in ancient Mesopotamia. Papers read at the 40e Rencontre Assyriologique Internationale Leiden, July 5-8, 1993. Uitgaven van het Nederlands Historisch-Archaeologisch Instituut te Istanbul 78: Lei 1996, Nederlands Historisch-Archaeologisch Instituut te Istanbul viii; 326 pp. ƒ70. 90-6258-079-3.

A2.9 *Acta* archaeologica

300 ^E**Andresen, Jens; Madsen, Torsten; Scollar, Irwin** Computing the past: computer applications and quantitative methods in archaeology.

Aarhus 1993, Aarhus University Press 464 pp. 87-7288-112-7. ^{R}AnCl 65 (1996) 530-532 (*Slachmuylder, Jean-Louis*).

301 ^{E}**Bietak, Manfred** House and palace in ancient Egypt: international symposium in Cairo, April 8-11, 1992. Untersuchungen der Zweigstelle Kairo des Österreichischen Archäologischen Instituts 14: W 1996, Österreichische Akademie der Wissenschaften 294 pp. 120 fig.; num. plans; 7 maps. 3-7001-2209-8 [AJA 101,631].

302 ^{E}**Biran, A.; Aviram, J.** Biblical archaeology today, 1990. 1993, ⇒9,554. ^{R}DSD 3 (1996) 58-61 (*Fröhlich, Ida*).

303 ^{E}**Cooper, Jerrold S.; Schwartz, Glenn M.** The study of the ancient Near East in the twenty-first century: The William Foxwell Albright Centennial Conference. WL 1996, Eisenbrauns x; 422 pp. $42.50. 0-931464-96-X [CBQ 59,420].

304 ^{E}**Dassmann, Ernst; Engemann, Josef** Akten des XII. Internationalen Kongresses für christliche Archäologie. Bonn 1991. SAC 52; JAC 20/1-2: Müns 1995, Aschendorff 2 vols. 3-402-08546-1. ALW 38/39 (1996/97) 428-429 (*Häußling, Angelus A.*).

305 ^{E}**Dimant, Devorah; Schiffman, Lawrence H.** Time to prepare the way in the wilderness. Papers on the Qumran Scrolls by Fellows of the Institute for Advanced Studies of the Hebrew University, J, 1989-1990. StTDJ 16: 1995, ⇒11/2,498. ^{R}CBQ 58 (1996) 383-384 (*Davila, James R.*); DSD 3 (1996) 217-219 (*Knibb, Michael A.*).

306 ^{E}**Durand, Jean-Marie** Mari, Ébla et les hourrites: dix ans de travaux: première partie. Actes du colloque international (Paris, mai 1993). Amurru 1: P 1996, Recherche sur les Civilisations 439 pp. FF230. 2-86538-251-6.

307 ^{E}**Fabry, Heinz-Josef; Lange, Armin; Lichtenberger, Hermann** Qumranstudien: Vorträge und Beiträge der Teilnehmer des Qumranseminars auf dem internationalen Treffen der Society of Biblical Literature, Müns, 25.-26. Juli 1993. Schriften des Institutum Judaicum Delitzschianum 4: Gö 1996, Vandenhoeck & R x; 252 pp. DM98. 3-525-54202-X.

308 ^{E}**Ferioli, Piera; Fiandra, Enrica; Fissore, Gian Giacomo** Administration in ancient societies. Proceedings of session 218 of the 13th International Congress of Anthropological and Ethnological Sciences Mexico City, July 29-Aug. 5, 1993. Centro Internazionale di Ricerche archeologiche, antropologiche e storiche 2: T 1996, Scriptorium 192 pp. 88-455-6113-5.

309 ^{E}**Gitin, Seymour; Dever, William G.** Recent excavations in Israel: studies in Iron Age archaeology. AASOR 49: NHv 1995, ASOR xii; 152 pp. 0-89757-049-9. ^{R}AJA 100 (1996) 610-611 (*Hoffman, Gail L.*).

310 ^{E}**Grundlach, Rolf; Rochholz, Matthias** Ägyptische Tempel, Struktur, Funktion und Programm. Akten der Ägyptologischen Tempeltagungen in Gosen 1990 und Mainz 1992. HÄB 37: Hildesheim 1994, Gerstenberg 342 pp. DM68. 3-8067-8131-1. ^{R}OLZ 91 (1996) 275-280 (*Lohwasser, Angelika*).

311 ^{E}**Hamma, Kenneth** Alexander and Alexandrianism: papers delivered at a symposium organized by the J. Paul Getty Museum and the Getty Center for the History of Art and the Humanities, the Museum April 22-25, 1993. Malibu 1996, Getty Museum 302 pp. 191 fig. $50. 0-89236-292-8 [AJA 101,632].

312 ^{E}**Herfort-Koch, Marlene; Mandel, Ursula; Schädler, Ulrich** Hellenistische und kaiserzeitliche Keramik des östlichen Mittelmeerge-

bietes: Kolloquium Frankfurt 24.-25. April 1995. Schriften des Arbeitskreises Frankfurt und die Antike: Fra 1996, Archäologisches Institut der Johann Wolfgang Goethe-Universität 151 pp. 30 pl; 5 fig. 3-9803946-3-8 [AJA 101,632].

313 ᴱHerrmann, Georgina The furniture of western Asia, ancient and traditional. Papers of the conference held at the Institute of Archaeology, University College London, June 28-30, 1993. Mainz 1996, Von Zabern xxviii; 301 pp. 92 pl.; 127 fig; 15 maps; 5 tables. DM268. 3-8053-1838-3 [AJA 102,642s—Lapatin, Kenneth D.S.].

314 ᴱHoepfner, Wolfram; Brands, Gunnar Basileia: die Paläste der hellenistischen Könige. Internationales Symposium in Berlin von 16.12.1992 bis 20.12.1992. Schriften des Seminars für klassische Archäologie der Freien Universität B: Mainz 1996, Von Zabern xii; 259 pp. 183 ill. DM140. 3-8053-1747-6.

315 ᴱHudson, Michael; Levine, Baruch A. Privatization in the ancient Near East and classical world. The International Scholars Conference on ancient Near Eastern economics: a colloquium held at the New York University November 17-18, 1994. Peabody Museum Bulletin 5: CM 1996, Peabody Museum of Archaeology and Ethnology Harvard University 308 pp. 0-87365-955-4.

316 ᴱIsmail, Farouk Proceedings of the international symposium on Syria and the ancient Near East 3000-300 BC. Univ. of Aleppo 17-20 Oct. 1992 in association with the University 'La Sapienza' of Rome. Aleppo 1996, University of Aleppo Publications. ᴿRA 90 (1996) 93-95 (Charpin, D.).

317 ᴱKarageorghis, V. Cyprus in the 11th century B.C.: proceedings of the international symposium held at Nicosia, 30-31 October, 1993. Nicosia 1994, Leventis xvi; 247 pp. 45 fig. Cyp£20. 9963-560-21-0. AJA 100 (1996) 181-182 (Muhly, J.D.).

318 ᴱKopcke, Günter; Takumaru, Isabella Greece between east and west: 10th-8th centuries B.C. 1992. ⟹11/2,741. ᴿAJA 100 (1996) 616-617 (Newton, Maryanne W.).

319 ᴱLesko, Barbara S. Women's earliest records from Ancient Egypt and Western Asia. BJSt 166: 1989, ⟹5,851. ᴿBiOr 53 (1996) 47-50 (Menu, Bernadette).

320 ᴱWinter, Nancy A. Proceedings of the international conference on Greek architectural terracottas of the classical and Hellenistic periods, 1991. Hesp.S 27: Princeton 1994, American School of Classical Studies at Athens xiv; 340 pp. 95 pl.; 97 fig. $120. 0-87661-527-2. ᴿAJA 100 (1996) 793-794 (Wescoat, Bonna D.).

A3.1 *Opera consultationis*—**Reference works** *plurium* infra

321 AncBD: ᴱFreedman, David Noël, (al), 1992   6 vols. ⟹8,741...11/2,754. ᴿThR 61 (1996) 103-107 (Perlitt, Lothar); HeyJ 37 (1996) 193-196 (Dines, Jennifer); IThQ 62 (1996) 75-77 (Drennan, Martin); SJTh 49 (1996) 245-246 (Joyce, Paul M.).

322 ANRW 2/27.1: ᴱHaase, Wolfgang Religion: Vorkonstantinisches Christentum: Apostolische Väter und Apologeten. 1993, ⟹9,581. ᴿOLZ 91 (1996) 44-51 (Tröger, Karl-Wolfgang); SNTU.A 21 (1996) 212-214 (Fuchs, A.).

323 **BiH** 2: Bible handbook: ^E**Van der Woude, A.S.** World of the OT, 1989, ⇒5,880...7,661. ^RJAOS 116 (1996) 137-138 (*Lutz, R. Theodore*).

324 **CAH VI:** ^E**Lewis, D.M.**, (*al*), The fourth century BC. ²1994, ⇒10,498. ^RPrudentia 28/2 (1996) 60-62 (*McKechnie, Paul*); ClR 46 (1996) 91-93 (*Harding, P.E.*).

325 **DBS** 12/69: ^E**Briend, Jacques; Cothenet, Edouard** Sermon sur la Montagne-Sexualité, 1994, ⇒10,515; 11/2,770. ^RRB 103 (1996) 121-122 (*Tournay, R.J.*).

326 **DBS** 12/70: Sexualité-Sichem ^E**Briend, Jacques**, (*al*), P 1996, Letouzey & A 1025-1280 col. FF352. 2-7063-0188-0. ^RRB 105 (1998) 131-133 (*Tournay, R.J.*).

327 **DSBP** 12: ^E**Panimolle, Salvatore A.** Culto divino, liturgia. R 1996, Borla 292 pp. L35.000. 88-263-1073-4.

328 **DSBP** 13: ^E**Panimolle, Salvatore A.** Dio—Signore nella bibbia. R 1996, Borla 266 pp. L37.000. 88-263-1119-6.

329 **D.S.:** ^E**Derville, A.**, (*al*), 1932-1995, 17 vols [⇒11/2,763]. ^RRSR 84 (1996) 483-485 (*Lamarche, Paul*); Ang. 73 (1996) 603-605 (*Lamarche, Paul*); EeV 106 (1996) 650-652 (*Lamarche, Paul*); ThPh 71 (1996) 619-620 (*Lamarche, P.*).

330 **LThK** 5: ^E**Kasper, Walter**, (*al*), Hermeneutik-Kirchengemeinschaft. FrB 1996, Herder 14*; 1514 Sp. 3-451-22005-9.

331 **NBL** 1: ^E**Görg, Manfred; Lang, Bernhard** 1991, ⇒10,511. ^RThR 61 (1996) 107-109 (*Perlitt, Lothar*).

332 **NBL** Lfg. 10: ^E**Görg, Manfred; Lang, Bernhard** Magier-Nymphas. Solothurn 1995, Benziger 685-950. DM39.80. 3-545-23061-9. ^RThLZ 121 (1996) 922-926 (*Stahl, Rainer*).

333 **ThWAT** 8/4, 5-7 [8. 1994s ⇒10,519] ^E**Ringgren, Helmer; Fabry, Heinz-Josef** 1994-1995. ^RThLZ 121 (1996) 932-934 (*Heller, Jan*); 10/1-3: Register/Literaturnachträge. Stu 1996, Kohlhammer 192 pp.

334 **TRE:** Theologische Realenzyklopädie 26: Paris-Polen ^E**Müller, Gerhard.** B 1996, De Gruyter 816 pp. 3-11-002218-4.

A3.3 *Opera consultationis* biblica *non excerpta infra*—not subindexed

335 ^E**Balz, Horst; Schneider, Gerhard** Exegetical dictionary of the NT 1: Ἀαρών-Ἑνώχ. 1990, ⇒9,611; 10,520. ^RHeyJ 37 (1996) 86-87 (*Upton, Bridget*).

336 ^E**Balz, Horst; Schneider, Gerhard** Diccionario exegético del Nuevo Testamento 1. ^T*Ruiz-Garrido, Constantino*. Biblioteca de Estudios Bíblicos 90: S 1996, Sígueme 575 pp. 84-301-1284-7 [Actualidad Bibliográfica 34,45].

337 ^E**Bauer, Johannes B.** Bibeltheologisches Wörterbuch ⁴1994, ⇒10,521; 11/2,777. ^REeT 27 (1996) 412-414 (*Laberge, Léo*); ThR 61 (1996) 112-115 (*Perlitt, Lothar*).

338 **Browning, W.R.F.** Oxford dictionary of the Bible. Oxf 1996, OUP xv; 415 pp. £17. 0-19-211691-6.

339 **Brownrigg, Ronald** Hvem er hvem i *Det nye testamentet*. Oslo 1996, Kolibri 280 pp. [NTT 99,263—Aasgaard, Reidar].

340 ^E**Buchwald, Albert** Alle Jesusworte von A bis Z: das praktische Handbuch zum Nachschlagen, Lesen und Zitieren. Stu 1996, Kreuz 478 pp. 3-7831-1450-0 [NThAR 1997/3,68].

341 **EBurkhardt, Helmut** Das große Bibellexikon. Wu 1996, Brockhaus 6 vols. 3-417-24614-8.
342 **Chasidah, Yishai** Encyclopedia of biblical personalities: anthologized from the talmud, midrash, and rabbinic writings. NY 1996, Shaar x; 548 pp. 0-89906-025-0 [NThAR 1997/3,66].
343 **Cocagnac, Maurice** I simboli biblici. 1994, ⇒11/2,783. RVetChr 33 (1996) 409-412 (*Infante, Renzo*).
344 **Comay, Joan** Hvem er hvem i *Det gamle testamentet*, med de apokryfiske skrifter. Oslo 1996, Kolibri 399 pp. [NTT 99,263—Aasgaard, Reidar].
345 **ECouch, Mal** Dictionary of premillennial theology: a practical guide to the people, viewpoints, and history of prophetic studies. GR 1996, Kregel 442 pp. $23 [BS 154,492—Witmer, John A.].
346 **EFilippi, Alfio** Le chiavi della Bibbia: vocabulario della Bibbia di Gerusalemme. Bo 1996, EDB 910 pp. L82.000. 88-20586-3 [Protest. 52,194].
347 **Gerard, A.-M.** Diccionario de la Biblia. M 1996, Anaya 1557 pp. [Carthaginensia 14,213s—Tamayo Acosta, J.J.].
348 **EGranerud, Svein; Kvalbein, Asbjørn; Sjaastad, Egil** Lundes bibelleksikon: viktige ord, begreper, navn og forhold i Bibelen. Oslo 1996, Lunde 429 pp. [NTT 99,263—Aasgaard, Reidar].
349 **Levine, Mark L.; Rachlis, Eugene** The complete book of Bible quotations from the Old Testament. NY 1996, Pocket Books (22) 375 pp. [0-671-53796-2].
350 **Lurker, Manfred** Diccionario de imágenes y simbolos de la biblia. 1994, ⇒11/2,794. RRevBib 58 (1996) 61-64 (*Serna, Eduardo de la*).
351 **Lurker, Manfred M.** Grande dizionario illustrato: dèi, angeli, demoni. ERoest Crollius, Arij A.: CasM 1994, Piemme 731 pp. RRSLR 32 (1996) 699 (*Pesce, Mauro*.
352 **Maier, Johann; Schäfer, Peter** Diccionario del judaísmo. Diccionarios Maior 3: Estella (Navarra) 1996, Verbo Divino 428 pp. 84-8169-058-9. RRET 56 (1996) 123 (*Barrado Fernández, P.*).
353 **Miquel, Pierre; Egron, Agnès; Picard, Paula** Les mots-clés de la bible: Révélation à Israël. Les Classiques Bibliques: P 1996, Beauchesne 347 pp. FF180. 2-7010-1337-2. RRSR 84 (1996) 477-478 (*Guillet, Jacques*).
354 **Mistrorigo, Antonio** Guida alfabetica alla bibbia. CasM ²1995, Piemme 720 pp. L45.000. RCivCatt 147 IV (1996) 612-613 (*Teani, M.*).
355 **ENeusner, J.; Green, W.S.** Dictionary of Judaism in the biblical period 450 BCE to 600 CE. NY 1996, MacMillan 2 vols; xxvi; 693 pp. $175. 0-02-897292-9. RBA 59 (1996) 243 (*Poirier, Paul-Hubert*).
356 **EPenna, Romano** Dizionario enciclopedico della bibbia. R 1995, Città Nuova 1380 pp. L230.000. 88-263-1050-5. RAnnTh 10 (1996) 553-554 (*Estrada, Bernardo*).
357 **ERienecker, Fritz** Lexikon zur Bibel. Rev. by *Maier, Gerhard*. 1994, ⇒10,535. RThR 61 (1996) 110-112 (*Perlitt, Lothar*).
358 **Rousseau, John J.; Arav, Rami** Jesus and his world: an archaeological and cultural dictionary. 1995, ⇒11/2,799. RCBQ 58 (1996) 359-361 (*Hoppe, Leslie J.*); BArR 22/2 (1996) 8, 67 (*Cole, Dan P.*); CritRR 9 (1996) 264-266 (*Edwards, Douglas R.*).

359 EVan der Toorn, Karel; Becking, Bob; Van der Horst, Pieter W.
Dictionary of deities and demons in the bible. 1995, ⇒11/2,800.
RThLZ 121 (1996) 928-930 (Gese, Hartmut).

360 EWood, D.R.W. New Bible dictionary. DG ³1996, InterVarsity xix;
1298 pp. $40. 0-8308-1439-6 [TD 44,81].

A3.5 Opera consultationis **theologica** non excerpta infra

361 EHanselmann, Johannes; Swarat, Uwe Fachwörterbuch Theologie.
Wu ²1996, Brockhaus 221 pp. DM20 [JETh 11,230—Eber, Jochen].

362 Hillerbrand, Hans J. The Oxford encyclopedia of the Reformation.
Oxf 1996, OUP 4 vols; 1584 pp. £260. [Reformation 3,370ss—
Collinson, Patrick].

363 EKazhdan, P. The Oxford dictionary of Byzantium. 1991, 3 vols.
⇒7,727...10,553. RBA 59 (1996) 132-133 (Krentz, Edgar).

364 ELatourelle, René; Fisichella, Rino Dictionary of fundamental
theology. NY 1995, Crossroad xxxviii; 1222 pp. $75. [AUSS
35,286ss—Hasel, Frank M.].

365 Leick, Gwendolyn A dictionary of ancient Near Eastern mythology.
1991, ⇒8,2086*. RJNES 55 (1996) 230-233 (Hoffner, Harry A.).

366 Marquardt, Manfred Kleines theologisches Fachwörterbuch. Stu
1996, Anker 112 pp. DM12.80 [JETh 11,230—Eber, Jochen].

367 McKim, Donald K. Westminster dictionary of theological terms.
LVL 1996, Westminster vii; 310 pp. $20. 0-664-25511-6 [ThD
44,371—Heiser, W. Charles].

368 EPanimolle, Salvatore A. Dio nei padri della chiesa. DSBP 14: R
1996, Borla 274 pp. 88-263-1120-X.

369 EProkurat, Michael; Golitzin, Alexander; Peterson, Michael D.
Historical dictionary of the Orthodox Church. L 1996, Scarecrow
xviii; 440 pp. [JRH 22,225—Doumanis, Nicholas].

370 ERussell, Letty M.; Clarkson, J. Shannon Dictionary of feminist
theologies. L 1996, Mowbray xxix; 351 pp. £20 [HeyJ 39,468—
Iozzio, M.J.].

371 EStuhlmueller, Carroll The Collegeville pastoral dictionary of biblical theology. ColMn 1996, Liturgical lv; 1120 pp. $75. 0-8146-
1996-7 [Gr. 78/1,209].

A3.6 Opera consultationis **generalia**

372 EBranigan, K., (al), Lexicon of the Greek and Roman cities and
place names in antiquity, ca. 1500 B.C.-ca. A.D. 500. Fasc. 1:
A...Ad Novas. 1992, ⇒9,14934. RGn. 68 (1996) 164-166 Prontera,
Francesco).

373 Damiano-Appia, Maurizio Dizionario enciclopedico dell'antico
Egitto e delle civiltà nubiane. Mi 1996, Mondadori 295 pp. Bibl. 88-
7813-611-5.

374 EDassmann, Ernst RAC 15/113-120: Hibernia-Hoffnung. RGn. 68
(1996) 674-677 (Betz, Hans Dieter);

375 16/121-128: Hofzeremoniell-Ianus. ⇒10,512. 1989-1994. RThLZ
121 (1996) 1067-1075 (Markschies, Christoph).

376 EDe Grummond, Nancy Thomson An encyclopedia of the history
     of classical archaeology. Westport, CONN 1996, Greenwood 2 vols:
     v.1, A-K; v.2, L-Z. $225. 0-313-22066-2.
377 Goffer, Zvi Elsevier's dictionary of archaeological materials and ar-
     chaeometry: in English with translations of terms in German, Spa-
     nish, French, Italian and Portuguese. Amst 1996, Elsevier xviii; 445
     pp. Bibl. 0-444-81949-5.
378 EStern, Ephraim The new encyclopedia of archaeological excava-
     tions in the Holy Land. 1993, ⇒9,669...11/2,853. RHR 36 (1996)
     81-83 (Collins, Adela Yarbro).

A4.0 Bibliographiae, computers biblicae

379 Bible [bibliography] QS 66 (1996) 299-323.
380 The Bible in English: a full-text database for literary, linguistic, and
     biblical studies. 1996, Chadwyck-Healey. CD-ROM. RReformation
     2 (1997) 345-351 (Westbrook, Vivienne).
381 BL: Book List. EGrabbe, Lester L. [Hull] 1996, Society for Old
     Testament Study c. 200 pp. 0309-0892.
382 Bulletin de bibliographie biblique. EKaestli, Jean-Daniel Lausanne
     1996, Institut des sciences bibliques. 3 issues a year.
383 ECamplani, Alberto; Perrone, Lorenzo Bibliografia generale di storia
     dell'interpretazione biblica: esegesi, ermeneutica, usi della bibbia [a
     general bibliography on the history of biblical interpretation: exege-
     sis, hermeneutics, uses of the bible] 13-14. ASEs 70 (1996) 393-430,
     659-705.
384 DAI: Dissertation Abstracts International. Ann Arbor, Michigan
     1996, Available on computer, ⇒10,582*.
385 Deyo, Steve The wired bible: software programs and internet resour-
     ces for bible study. BArR 22/6 (1996) 58-66, 75.
386 Elenchus Bibliographicus 1996. Scriptura Sacra: Veteris Testamenti:
     142*-248* (J. Lust); Novi Testamenti: 248*-319* (F. Neirynck; J.
     Verheyden). EThL 72. Lv 1996, Peeters. 0013-9513.
387 EHolleman, Joost An index to Vetus Testamentum volumes 1-45
     (1951-1995). Lei 1996, Brill viii; 451 pp. 90-04-10605.
388 Holter, Knut Tropical Africa and the Old Testament: a select and
     annotated bibliography. Bibliography 6: Oslo 1996, University of
     Oslo, Faculty of Theology 106 pp. 82-991913-7-8 [NThAR
     1997/4,98].
389 IZBG: ELang, Bernhard Internationale Zeitschriftenschau für Bibel
     und Grenzgebiete. Dü 1996-1997, Patmos xiv; 429 pp. 0074-9745.
390 Matras, Tadeusz Bibliografia prac publikowanych KS. Prof. Dra
     Hab. Stanisława Grzybka: część 1981-1995 [Bibliographia publica-
     tionum Prof. Stanislai Grzybek in annis 1981-1995]. RBL 49 (1996)
     63-67.
391 NTAb 40: New Testament Abstracts EHarrington, Daniel J. CM
     1996, Weston School of Theology vi; 612 pp. 0028-6877.
392 OTA 19: Old Testament Abstracts EBegg, Christopher Wsh 1996,
     Catholic Biblical Association of America 609 pp. 0364-8591.
393 Piñero, Antonio New Testament philology: Bulletin No. 17. FgNT 9
     (1996) 89-125;
394 Bulletin No. 18. FgNT 9 (1996) 227-259.

395 *Silberman, Neil Asher* Digitizing the ancient Near East: a survey of new software and internet resources. Arch. 49/5 (1996) 86-88.
396 **ThD** 43: Theology Digest: Book survey E*Heiser, W. Charles* Duluth, MN 1996, Theology Digest. 55-95; 155-196; 255-295; 353-394. 0040-5728.
397 E**Tiradritti, Francesco** Informatica ed egittologia all'inizio degli anni '90. Informatica e Discipline Umanistiche 7: R 1996, Bulzoni 264 pp. [Congresso Internazionale di Egittologia (6: 1991: Torino)].
398 E**Wagner, Günter** An exegetical bibliography of the New Testament 4: Romans and Galatians. Macon, GA 1996, Mercer University Press xiv; 379 pp. $40. 0-86554-468-9 [ThD 44,64].
399 **ZAW** 108: Zeitschrift für die alttestamentliche Wissenschaft: Zeitschriften und Bücherschau E*Schmitt, Hans-Christoph; Wanke, Gunther.* B 1996, De Gruyter. 108-160; 263-327; 441-493. 0044-2526/96.
400 **ZID**: Zeitschrifteninhaltsdienst Theologie. Tü 1996, Universitätsbibliothek, Theologische Abt. Monthly; Sep. Fasc. Indexes 1987-1996. 0340-8361.
401 **ZNW** 87: Zeitschrift für die neutestamentliche Wissenschaft: Zeitschriftenschau. E**Grässer, Erich**. B 1996, De Gruyter. 138-139; 296-298. 0044-2615/96.

A4.3 *Bibliographiae diversae*

402 *Acquaro, E.; Mazza, F.; Ribichini, S.* Bibliografia 24 (1.1.1995-31.12.1995). RSFen 24 (1996) 199-227.
403 *Balconi, Carla, (al),* Bibliografia metodica degli studi di egittologia e di papirologia. Aeg. 76 (1996) 205-255.
404 *Bergman, Diane; Gow, Mary* Review of Egyptological literature January 1993-December 1995. BEgS 12 (1996) 41-100.
405 *Chappaz, Jean-Luc; Poggia, Sandra* Ressources égyptologiques informatisées 2. BSÉG 20 (1996) 95-115.
406 *Daniluk, Mirosław* Indeks 'Vox Patrum' 1 (1981) - 12 (1992). Vox Patrum 16 (1996) 541-603. **P**.
407 *De Klerk, Peter* Calvin Theological Journal: index to volumes 1-30, 1966-1995. CTJ (1996) 1-148 [spec. fasc.].
408 *Deller, Karlheinz; Klengel, Horst; Schuster, A.* Keilschriftbibliographie 55: 1995 (mit Nachträgen aus früheren Jahren). Or. 65 (1996) 1*-124*.
409 **De Marco, Giuseppe** Contributo alla storia delle pubblicazioni periodiche dell'I.U.O.: Cento anni dopo (1894-1994); indici a Annali "Sex. Orientale," Annuario, L'Oriente, Memorie. Indices 1: N 1996, Istituto Universitario Orientale, Dipartimento di Studi Asiatici xviii; 433 pp. [CBQ 59,818].
410 *Durand, G.-M. de* Bulletin de Patrologie. RSPhTh 80 (1996) 113-142.
411 *Felber, Heinz* Demotistische Literaturübersicht XXIII. Enchoria 23 (1996) 150-176.
412 *Pomorska, Marzanna; Stachowski, Marek* Bibliography of *Folia Orientalia* 1-30 (1959-1994). FolOr 32 (1996) 203-256.
413 E**Rothschild, Jean-Pierre,** *(al),* Bibliographie annuelle du Moyen-Âge tardif: auteurs et textes latins 6. Turnhout 1996, Brepols vii; 631 pp. 2-503-50558-9.

II. Introductio

в1.1 *Introductio tota vel VT* — Whole Bible or OT

414 **Alonso Schökel, Luis** Lezioni sulla Bibbia. CasM 1996, Piemme 326 pp. L35.000 [RdT 37,719].

415 **Attinger, D.** 'La gloria di Dio è l'uomo vivente': percorso biblico sul tema della vita. Tracce 7: R 1995, Nuove Frontiere 132 pp. L18.000. ᴿClar. 36-37 (1996-97) 617-618 (*Sánchez Bosch, Jaime*).

416 **Barberá, Carlos** (*al*), Ver, oír, gustar y tocar a Dios. M 1996, Narcea 153 pp. [San Juan de la Cruz 21,131—Nicolás, Flori de].

417 **Baylis, Albert H.** From creation to the cross: understanding the first half of the Bible. GR 1996, Zondervan 392 pp. [revised and expanded edition of *On the Way to Jesus*]. 0-310-49080-4.

418 **Benetti, Santos** La bibbia tematica: Antico Testamento. ᴱ*Fillarini, C.; Cattazzo, S.* Padova 1996, Messagero 493 pp. L40.000. 88-250-0416-8 [RTL 29,373ss—Wénin, A.].

419 Bibbia per la formazione cristiana. Bo 1994, EDB 2,237 pp. L40.000. ᴿCivCatt 147 IV (1996) 198-199 (*Scaiola, D.*).

420 **Biblia** (Associazione Laica di Cultura Biblica) Vademecum per il lettore della Bibbia. Pref. *Soggin, J.A.*. Brescia 1996, Morcelliana 326 pp. L35.000 [RdT 37,574].

421 **Bloesch, Donald G.** Holy scripture: revelation, inspiration & interpretation. 1994, ⇒11/2,1086. ᴿEvQ 68 (1996) 173-176 (*Yates, John*).

422 *Bolin, Thomas M.* When the end is the beginning: the Persian period and the origins of the biblical tradition. SJOT 10 (1996) 3-15.

423 **Caird, George Bradford** The language and imagery of the Bible. Foreword *Wright, N.T.* GR 1996, Eerdmans xxviii; 280 pp. $24. 0-8028-4221-6.

424 ᴱ**Carey, George** The bible for everyday life. GR 1996, Eerdmans 400 pp. $20. 0-8028-4157-0.

425 **Ceresko, Anthony R.** Introduction to the Old Testament: a liberation perspective. 1992, ⇒8,1018*...11/2,1087. ᴿGr. 77 (1996) 350-352 (*Prato, Gian Luigi*);

426 Introdução ao Antigo Testamento numa perspectiva libertadora. ᵀ*Vidigal, José Raimundo*. São Paulo 1996, Paulus 352 pp. [REB 225,232].

427 *Choi, Jae-Sun* Wer sind unsere Nachbarn? Samok 213 (1996) 6-20 [ThIK 18/2,54]. K.

428 *Chopineau, Jacques* La bible symbolique: note sur l'apport hellénistique à la numérologie symbolique de la bible. Analecta Bruxellensia 1 (1996) 88-101 [ZID 24,343].

429 ᴱ**Dalla Vecchia, F.; Nepi, A.; Corti, G.L.** Introduzione generale allo studio della Bibbia. Brescia 1996, Queriniana 836 pp. L110.000 [RdT 37,719].

430 **Denver Catholic Biblical School Program** Old Testament continued: exile and restoration. Mahwah 1996, Paulist 99 pp. (Student Workbook, 100 pp., $4) $13 [BiTod 35,257].

431 **Dohmen, Christoph** Vom Umgang mit dem Alten Testament. Neuer Stuttgarter Kommentar—AT 27: 1995, ⇒11/2,1093. ᴿThR 61 (1996) 146-147 (*Reventlow, Henning Graf*).

432 Einleitung in das Alte Testament. KStTh 1,1: Stu [2]1996, Kohlhammer 447 pp. 3-17-014433-2.

433 **Elliger, Katharina** Paare in der Bibel: was damals alles möglich war. Mü 1996, Kösel 175 pp. DM34. 3-466-36447-7.

434 **Fischer, James A.** Interpreting the bible: a simple introduction. NY 1996, Paulist iv; 113 pp. $9. 0-8091-3653-8 [CBQ 59,421].

435 **Flanders, Henry Jackson** People of the covenant: an introduction to the Hebrew bible. NY [4]1996, OUP xiii; 562 pp. $35. 0-19-509370-4 [ThD 44,65].

436 **Fortosis, Stephen** Great men and women of the bible. NY 1996, Paulist xii; 157 pp. $12 [CBQ 59,421].

437 **Freedman, David Noel** The unity of the Hebrew bible. 1991, ⇒7,993...11/2,1097. [R]JNES 55 (1996) 142-143 (*Anderson, Gary A.*).

438 **Freudmann, Lillian C.** What's in the bible?: a concise look at the 39 books of the Hebrew Bible. Northvale, NJ 1996, Aronson xxii; 174 pp. Bibl. 1-56821-602-5.

439 **Gill, Ben** Stewardship: the biblical basis for living. Arlington 1996, Summit xxvi; 251 pp. $20. 1-56530-208-7 [ThD 44,169].

440 **Girard, Marc** Les symboles dans la bible. RFTP 26: 1991, ⇒8,1162...11/2,1297. [R]RivBib 44 (1996) 71-74 (*Ravasi, Gianfranco*).

441 **Girardet, Giorgio** Bibbia perché: il linguaggio e le idee guida. 1993, ⇒11/2,1166. [R]EstB 54 (1996) 115-116 (*Precedo, J.*).

442 **Gomes, Peter J.** The good book. NY 1996, Morrow xv; 383 pp. $25 [BiRe 14/1,10—Holbert, John C.].

443 Das große Buch der Bibel. Stu 1996, Kreuz 288 pp. Mit über 300 farbigen Abbildungen zu Ereignissen, Personen und Schauplätzen der biblischen Geschichte. 3-7831-1482-9.

444 **Herrmann, Siegfried; Klaiber, Walter** Die Schriften der Bibel: Entstehung und Botschaft. Introd. *Lohse, Eduard.* Stu 1996, Deutsche Bibelgesellschaft 239 pp. 3-438-06207-0 [NThAR 1997/2,33].

445 **Howard, David M.** An introduction to the Old Testament historical books. 1993, ⇒11/2,9,833...11/2,1102. [R]CTJ 31 (1996) 531-533 (*Knoppers, Gary N.*).

446 **Hueckel, Sharon** Stewardship by the book. Kansas City 1996, Sheed & W 17 pp. [BiTod 35,262].

447 *Hurowitz, Victor Avigdor* Three biblical expressions for being merciful in light of Akkadian and Aramaic. [F]Haran, M. ⇒35. 1996. 359-368.

448 *Hurvitz, Avi* The origins and development of the expression -מְגִלַּת סֵפֶ ר: a study in the history of writing-related terminology in biblical times. [F]Haran, M. ⇒35. 1996. 37*-46*. **H.**

449 **Kaiser, Walter C., Jr.** Hard sayings of the bible. DG 1996, InterVarsity 808 pp. 0-8308-1423-X [NThAR 1997,159].

450 *Karasszon, István* Heroism in the Acts of Paul and in the bible. The Apocryphal Acts of Paul and Thecla. [E]Bremmer, Jan N. Studies on the Apocryphal Acts of the Apostles 2: Kampen 1996, Kok. 179-190.

451 **Kissling, Paul J.** Reliable characters in the primary history: profiles of Moses, Joshua, Elijah and Elisha. JSOT.S 224: Shf 1996, Academic 220 pp. £45; $65. 1-85075-617-1.

452 **Klopfenstein, Martin A.** Friede (Schalom) im Alten Testament. Leben aus dem Wort ⇒132. BEAT 40: 1996, 217-222.

453 **Klopfenstein, Martin A.** Wunder im Alten Testament. Leben aus dem Wort ⇒132. BEAT 40: 1996, 191-198.
454 **Knauf, Ernst Axel** Die Umwelt des Alten Testaments. 1994, ⇒10,736; 11/2,1106. ᴿETR 71 (1996) 430-431 (*Balestier-Stengel, Guy*).
455 **Krahe, Susanne** Auf Maulbeerbäumen sitzt es sich nicht sehr bequem: biblische Anstößigkeiten. Dü 1996, Patmos 160 pp. DM29.80 [LM 36/8,43].
456 **LaSor, William Sanford; Hubbard, David Allan; Bush, Frederic William** Old Testament survey: the message, form, and background of the Old Testament. GR ²1996, Eerdmans xvii; 860 pp. $40. 0-8028-3788-3 [BiTod 35,257].
457 **MacCain, Danny** Notes on Old Testament introduction. Overland Parks 1996, International Institute for Christian Studies 206 pp. 978-2668-70-2 [NThAR 1997,192].
458 **Machet, Anne** La voie des nombres: comptes de la bible grecque. Lyon 1996, Presses Universitaires de Lyon 373 pp. 2-7297-0543-0 [REA 99/1-2,216].
459 *Mangold, Max* Die Aussprache der Bibelnamen. Mitteilungen für Anthropologie und Religionsgeschichte 9 (1994) 221-225 [IAJS 42,14].
460 *Mencej, Mirjam* [Meaning of water in Old Testament.]   Bogoslovni Vestnik 56 (1996) 269-284. Sum. 284. S.
461 **Miguel, Pierre; Egron, Agnès; Picard, Paula** Les mots-clés de la Bible: révélation à Israël. Classiques Bibliques: P 1996, Beauchesne 347 pp. [LTP 54,205s—Guindon, Henri-M.].
462 **Ortlund, Raymond C.** Whoredom: God's unfaithful wife in biblical theology. New Studies in Biblical Theology 2: [Leicester] 1996, Apollos 200 pp. $18. 0-85111-511-X.
463 *Pilch, John J.* Actions speak louder than words. BiTod 34 (1996) 172-176.
464 *Pilch, John J.* Singing in the bible. BiTod 34 (1996) 38-43.
465 *Pilch, John J.* Smells and tastes. BiTod 34 (1996) 246-251.
466 **Porter, J.R.** The illustrated guide to the bible. 1995, ⇒11/2,1125. ᴿTheol. 99 (1996) 380-381 (*Pickstone, Charles*).
467 **Rabinowitz, Isaac** A witness forever: ancient Israel's perception of literature and the resultant Hebrew bible. 1993, ⇒11/2,1127. ᴿAJSR 21 (1996) 125-127 (*Lund, Jerome A.*).
468 **Raurell, Frederic** 'I Déu digué...': la paraula feta història. 1995, ⇒11/2,1129. ᴿEstFr 97 (1996) 189-191 (*Fuentes i Grau, Joan Antoni*); RCatT 21 (1996) 250-251 (*Llopis, Joan*).
469 **Revell, Ernest John** The designation of the individual: expressive usage in biblical narrative. Contributions to Biblical Exegesis and Theology 14: Kampen 1996, Kok 432 pp. ƒ74.90. 90-390-0161-8 [OTA 19,528].
470 *Rogerson, John* Recent continental Old Testament literature. ET 107 (1996) 370-373.
471 **Salibi, Kamal** The bible came from Arabia. Beirut 1996, Naufal 223 pp. [ThRev 19,134ss—Gangloff, Frédéric].
472 **Service Biblique Évangile et Vie** Itinerario por el Antiguo Testamento. Estella 1996, Verbo Divino 200 pp. Ptas2.300.
473 **Severance, W. Murray** Pronouncing bible names. 1994, ⇒10,751. ᴿBA 59 (1996) 133 (*Phelps, Mark Anthony*).

474 **Sicre Diaz, José Luis** Introducción al Antiguo Testamento. Estella ³1996, Verbo Divino 299 pp. 84-7151-778-7.

475 **Simms, George Otto** Exploring the bible. Dublin 1996, Columba 141 pp. [Milltown Studies 42,166s—Byrne, Patrick].

476 **Smend, Rudolf** La formazione dell'Antico Testamento. 1993, ⇒9,850; 11/2,1135. ᴿPaVi 41/2 (1996) 53-54 (*Marocco, Giuseppe*).

477 *Smith, Morton* On the differences between the culture of Israel and the major cultures of the ancient Near East. Studies in...method. 1996 <1973>, ⇒150. 28-36.

478 **Stendebach, Franz-Josef** Einleitung in das Alte Testament. Leitfaden Theologie 22: 1994, ⇒11/2,1138. ᴿFrRu 3 (1996) 218-219 (*Beck, Monika*);

479 Introducción al Antiguo Testamento. BTeo 19: Pamplona 1996, Universidad de Navarra.

480 **Tarazi, Paul Nadim** The Old Testament: an introduction I: historical traditions. 1991, ⇒11/2,1140(!). ᴿOCP 62 (1996) 208-209 (*Farrugia, E.G.*).

481 *Tsau, Paul* Nebuchadnezzar II in the Old Testament. CTUF 110 (1996) 525-530 [ThIK 18/2,32]. C.

482 **Van Ligten, Alex** Wegwijzer voor de bijbel: een rondleiding vanuit het midden van een bijzonder boek. Kampen 1996, Kok 111 pp. ƒ20. 90-242-7840-6 [KeTh 49,156s—Van der Woude, A.S.].

483 **Verrecchia, Jean-Claude** La bible mode d'emploi. Dammarie-lès-Lys 1995, Vie et Santé 128 pp. FF30. 2-85300-910-6. ᴿHokhma 63 (1996) 68 (*Desplanque, Christophe*).

484 *Wagner, Andreas* Archäologie der mündlichen Kommunikation: auf der Suche nach gesprochener Sprache in der Bibel. Kognitive Aspekte der Sprache: Akten des 30. Linguistischen Kolloquiums Gdansk 1995 ᴱSroka , Kazimierz A. Linguistische Arbeiten 360: Tü 1996 Niemeyer. 273-280.

485 **Weisman, Ze'ēv** בַּסְ־מִקְרָה פּוֹלִיטִית סָטְרָה [Political satire in the bible]. J 1996, Mosad Beyaliq 287 pp. 965-342-667-2 [NThAR 1997/4,99]. H.

486 *Westermann, Claus* Vom Segen. Das mündliche Wort, 1996, ⇒157. 180-184.

487 ᴱZenger, Erich, (*al*), Einleitung in das Alte Testament. Studienbücher Theologie I 1: 1995, ⇒11/2,1147. ᴿETR 71 (1996) 431-433 (*Bauks, Michaela*); ThPQ 144 (1996) 317-318 (*Hubmann, Franz*).

488 **Zenger, Erich** Das erste Testament. ³1993 <1991>, ⇒8,1055...10,760. ᴿThR 61 (1996) 79-82 (*Reventlow, Henning Graf*).

489 ᴱZuck, Roy B. Vital Old Testament issues: examining textual and topical questions. Vital Issues 7: GR 1996, Kregel 272 pp. 0-8254-4073-4 [NThAR 1997,259].

B1.2 'Invitations' to Bible or OT

490 ᴱAbma, Richtsje Om het levende woord. Bijbels-theologische en dogmatische serie 6: Kampen 1996, Kok 142 pp. ƒ27.50 [GThT 97/2,99].

491 **Aitken, Anne-Marie; Kelly, Robert** La parole parmi nous: lire l'évangile avec les enfants pendant la messe, année liturgique B

(Marc). Centre National de l'Enseignement Religieux. P 1996, Brépols 272 pp.

492 *Baldermann, Ingo* Die Bibel—das Buch zum Film. Ein Interview mit Dr. Heinrich Krauss, Taurus-Film. JBTh 11 (1996) 213-223.

493 **Barton, John** Reading the Old Testament: method in biblical study. L ²1996 <1994>, Darton, L & T xviii; 294 pp. £16. 0-232-52201-4. ᴿET 108 (1996-97) 194-195 (*Rodd, C.S.*).

494 **Beck, Madeline** The rescue: the one story of the bible as told in the Old Testament. Lakeland ²1996, Pine Ridge 139 pp. [NThAR 1997,258].

495 **Bottigheimer, Ruth B.** The bible for children: from the age of GUTENBERG to the present. NHv 1996, Yale University Press xiv; 338 pp. $35. 0-300-06488-8 [ThD 44,158].

496 **Brown, Raymond E.** 101 preguntas y respuestas sobre la Biblia. ᵀ*Sánchez Bustamante, Damián*, S 1996, Sígueme 155 pp. Pts1.350. 84-301-1304-5. ᴿRET 56 (1996) 524-525 (*Barrado Fernández, P.*).

497 **Brueggemann, Walter** The bible and postmodern imagination: texts under negotiation. 1993, ⇒9,867; 11/2,1526. ᴿHeyJ 37 (1996) 83-84 (*Feeney, Joseph J.*).

498 **Buzzetti, Carlo** Giovani incontra alla Bibbia: cultura e preghiera. Giovani ed Educazione Religiosa: Leumann 1996, Elle Di Ci 176 pp. L17.000. 88-01-00705-1 [Itin. 5,247].

499 **Cipriani, Settimio** Primo incontro con la Bibbia: i libri dell'Antico Testamento. Leumann 1996, LDC 255 pp. L20.000. 88-01-00655-1 [Iter. 5,257].

500 **Comay, Joan; Brownrigg, Ronald** Who's who: the Old Testament, together with the Apocrypha. 1993, ⇒9,872; 10,775*. ᴿHebStud 37 (1996) 135-136 (*Lee, Archie C.C.*).

501 ᴱCottereau, **Philippe** Biblica: questions actuelles, éternelles paroles. P 1996, Fleurus 304 pp. FF189. 2-215-01542-X [BCLF 584 (1997) 1416].

502 **Courthial, Pierre** Le jour des petits recommencements: essai sur l'actualité de la parole. Lausanne 1996, Age d'homme [FV 96/3,71ss—*Martin, Alain G.*].

503 **Cratzius, Barbara** Meine große Bilderbibel: erzählt von... Ill. *Ferri, Giuliano.* FrB 1996, Herder 259 pp. DM39.80 [BiLi 70/1,84].

504 **Hari, Albert; Singer, Charles** Descubrir el Antiguo Testamento hoy: para tomar conciencia del pueblo de Dios, en el que estamos invitados a entrar. Estella 1996, Verbo Divino 248 pp. Ptas3.500. 84-7151-890-2.

505 **Josipovici, Gabriel** El libro de Dios: una respuesta a la Biblia. 1995, ⇒11/2,1177. ᴿCart. 12 (1996) 474 (*Cuenca Molina, J.F.*).

506 ᴱKlopfentstein, **Martin** Mitte der Schrift?: ein jüdisch-christliches Gespräch. 1987, ⇒3,549...7,975. ᴿThR 61 (1996) 76-78 (*Reventlow, Henning Graf*).

507 **Ko Ha Fong, Maria** Reading the bible in an Asian context. (*a*) WoWo 29/4 (1996) 131-152 [ThIK 18/2,47];

508 (*b*) Prodipon 19/3 (1996) 122-150 [ThIK 18/2,29].

509 **Magonet, Jonathan** Wie ein Rabbiner seine Bibel liest. 1994, ⇒11/2,1189. ᴿBiKi 51 (1996) 81-82 (*Baumann, Rolf*).

510 **Marín Heredia, Francisco** A Bíblia (palavra profética). ᵀ*Brunetta, Attilio.* Petrópolis 1996, Vozes 334 pp. [REB 225,225].

511 *Martini, Carlo Maria* 'Lectio divina' e pastorale. PaVi 41/4 (1996) 49-52.
512 **McKim, Donald K.** The bible in theology and preaching. 1994, ⇒10,1044; 11/2,1564. ᴿIBSt 18 (1996) 217-218 (*Sell, Alan P.F.*).
513 **Meynet, Roland** Lire la bible: un exposé pour comprendre: un essai pour réfléchir. P 1996, Flammarion 126 pp. 2-08-035419-1 [RTL 28,397].
514 **Miller, Gabrielle** Von Batseba—und andere Geschichten: biblische Texte spannend ausgelegt. ᴱ*Niehl, Franz W.* Mü 1996, Kösel 239 pp. DM36 [BiKi 52,147].
515 *Panimolle, Salvatore* I quattro gradi della 'Lectio divina' secondo GUIDO IL CERTOSINO. PaVi 41/6 (1996) 52-55.
516 **Para-Mallam, Gideon** Getting into scripture: a fresh approach to re-discovering biblical truth. Jos 1996, NIFES 149 pp. 978-33539-0-X [NThAR 1997,191].
517 **Porter, J.R.** Illustrert nøkkel til Bibelen. ᵀ*Larsen, Finn B.*; collab. *Askevold, Solveig.* Oslo 1996, Grøndahl 288 pp. [NTT 99,263— Aasgaard, Reidar].
518 **Porter, J.R.** Origines et histoires de la bible. P 1996, Bordas 286 pp. [RHPhR 77,196].
519 *Rad, Gerhard von* Es bueno leer el Antiguo Testamento. La acción de Dios, 1996 <1970>, ⇒144. 13-22.
520 *Raja, A. Maria Arul* Some reflections on a Dalit reading of the bible. ITS 33 (1996) 249-259 [1 Sam 17].
521 **Richards, Lawrence** International children's book. Dallas, TX 1996, Word 224 pp. $13 [BS 154,382].
522 **Roberts, Jenny** Bible then & now. NY 1996, Macmillan 135 pp. Num. ill. 0-02-861347-3 [NThAR 1997,159].
523 **Rösel, Martin** Bibelkunde des Alten Testaments: die kanonischen und apokryphen Schriften: Überblicke, Themakapitel, Glossar. Neuk 1996, Neuk 182 pp. DM29.80. 3-7887-1582-0 [BiKi 52,147].
524 **Schindler, Regine; Zavřel, Štěpán** Mit Gott unterwegs: die Bibel für Kinder und Erwachsene neu erzählt. Z 1996, Bohem 288 pp. Num. ill. ᴿThZ 52 (1996) 288 (*Neidhart, Walter*).
525 **Van Bruggen, Jakob** Het lezen van de bijbel: een inleiding. Kampen 1996, Kok 174 pp. 90-242-4612-1 [NThAR 1997,159].
526 **Vigée, Claude; Malka, Victor** Treize inconnus de la bible. P 1996, Albin M. [FV 96,79s—*Giniewski, Paul*].
527 *Wyssenbach, Jean P.* Nuestra lectura popular de la biblia. Iter 7 (1996) 117-130.

B1.3 *Paedagogia biblica* — Bible-teaching techniques

528 *Bach, Alice* Calling the shots: directing Salomé's dance of death. Semeia 74 (1996) 103-126.
529 *Bach, Alice* Film bibliography. Semeia 74 (1996) 199-206.
530 *Bach, Alice* Filmography: biblical and related subjects. Semeia 74 (1996) 207-214.
531 *Bach, Alice* "Throw them to the lions, Sire": transforming biblical narratives into Hollywood spectaculars. Semeia 74 (1996) 1-13.
532 BAKEB Informationen: 1996,1: Bibliodrama. W 1996, 28 pp.
533 **Baldermann, Ingo** Einführung in die biblische Didaktik. Da 1996, Primus xi; 239 pp. DM34. 3-89678-303-3 [ThRv 93,331].

534 *Baldermann, Ingo* Ungehört im Hearing: Religionsunterricht als gesellschaftliche Diakonie: Votum beim Hearing des Bildungsausschusses im Potsdamer Landtag am 19.10.95, ergänzt durch einen Kommentar des Verfassers. JBTh 11 (1996) 197-208.

535 **Baltzer, Dieter** Alttestamentliche Fachdidaktik: gesammelte Studien. Theologie 11: Mü 1996, Lit. 3-8258-3002-0. (*a*) Schöpfungsglaube und Umwelterziehung im Sachunterricht und Religionsunterricht in der Primarstufe. 233-256;

536 (*b*) Theorien alttestamentlicher Fachdidaktik vor dem Hintergrund der "zünftigen" Theologie. 203-231.

537 **Becker, Ulrich; Johannsen, Friedrich; Noormann,** Harry Neutestamentliches Arbeitsbuch für Religionspädagogen. UB 439: Stu 1993, Kohlhammer 292 pp. DM32. 3-17-010855-7. RThRv 92 (1996) 68-69 (*Dormeyer, Detlev*).

538 *Beilner, Wolfgang* Die Bibelbewegung: ihre Geschichte, ihre Bedeutung für das Konzil und ihre bleibenden Anliegen für Gegenwart und Zukunft. BiLi 69 (1996) 136-139.

539 **Biewald, Roland** Einblicke Religion: ein Studienbuch. Biblischtheologische Schwerpunkte 12: Gö 1996, Vandenhoeck & R 271 pp. 3-525-61294-X.

540 *Buschmann, Gerd* Der Sturm Gottes zur Neuschöpfung: biblische Symboldidaktik in Michael JACKSON's Mega-Video-Hit "Earth Song". KatBl 121 (1996) 187-196.

541 *Ceresko, Anthony R.* Reading and teaching the bible in India. BiTod 34 (1996) 311-315 [Mark 11,15-19].

542 *Demke,   Christoph*   Streitpunkt   Christenlehre-LER-Religionsunterricht: Randbemerkungen zu einer verwirrenden Diskussion aus der Sicht eines Bischofs. JBTh 11 (1996) 209-212.

543 **Eldridge, Daryl** The teaching ministry of the church: integrating biblical truth and contemporary application. Nv 1995, Broadman and H x; 326 pp. RFaith & Mission 14/1 (1996) 112-4 (*Buchanan, Edward A.*).

544 *Exum, J. Cheryl* Bathsheba plotted, shot, and painted. Semeia 74 (1996) 47-73.

545 *Falcke, Heino* Kirche und Öffentlichkeit in der DDR. JBTh 11 (1996) 3-13.

546 *Freeman, C.B.* Biblical principles for senior adults. TEd 53 (1996) 31-41 [NTAb 40,465].

547 *Fuchs, Ottmar* Kontextueller Bibelbezug in Tradition und Pastoral. BiLi 69 (1996) 150-155.

548 *Gabriel, Karl* Religion und Kirche im Spiegel- und Diskursmodell von Öffentlichkeit. JBTh 11 (1996) 31-51.

549 *Glancy, Jennifer* The mistress of the gaze: masculinity, slavery and representation. Semeia 74 (1996) 127-145.

550 *Gunn, David M.* Bathsheba goes bathing in Hollywood: word, images and social locations. Semeia 74 (1996) 75-101.

551 *Heidenreich, Hartmut* Varianten des Bibliodrama in der Literatur. BAKEB Informationen 1 (1996) 14-15.

552 *Hoegger, Martin* Une 'école de la parole', pour lire et prier la bible: les voies de la 'Lectio divina'. Hokhma 61 (1996) 37-49.

553 *Immich, Doris; Gremmels, Christian* Bibliodrama: Zwischenbilanz eines Fortbildungsangebotes. EvErz 48 (1996) 47-56.

554 *Kollmann, Roland* Bibliodrama in Praxis und Theorie. EvErz 48 (1996) 20-41.

555 *Koosed, Jennifer L.; Linafelt, Tod* How the west was not one: Delilah deconstructs the Western. Semeia 74 (1996) 167-181.

556 *Krax, Anja* Die Bibel entdecken: eine Unterrichtseinheit (mit Freiarbeitsmaterialien) in Klasse 5 des Gymnasiums. KatBl 121 (1996) 384-388.

557 *Louw, L.P.* Leerling- en leerkragvoorkeure ten opsigte van Bybelse inhoude. Tydskrif vir Christelike Wetenskap 32/3-4 (1996) 123-128 [ZID 23,242].

558 *Mense, Josef* Lakonischer Stil als Prinzip biblischen Erzählens: blickverändernde Impulse für Religionsunterricht und Predigt. KatBl 121 (1996) 374-383.

559 *Naranjo S., Gabriel* Formation for the reading of the scriptures and for the ministry of the word. Prodipon 19 (1996) 204-222 [ThIK 18/2,29].

560 *Naranjo S., Gabriel* Formation for the reading of the scriptures and for the ministry of the word. WoWo 29 (1996) 161-177 [ThIK 18/2,47].

561 *Nash, Kathleen S.* "Toto, we're not in Kansas anymore": from historical criticism to film theory. Semeia 74 (1996) 183-188.

562 *Panitz, Sunny James C.* Bibliodrama: Teilhabe an Wirkung und Inhalt der Heiligen Schrift. Wechselwirkungen 5: Waldrop 1996, Spenner 458 pp. 3-927718-77-7.

563 *Pardes, Ilana* Moses goes down to Hollywood: miracles and special effects. Semeia 74 (1996) 15-31.

564 **Pelikan, Jaroslav** The reformation of the bible: the bible of the Reformation. NHv 1996, Yale University Press. (*a*) The bible and the arts. 63-78. [AUSS 36,150—Strand, Kenneth A.];

565 (*b*) Bibles for the people. 41-62 [AUSS 36,150—Strand, Kenneth A.].

566 *Pohl-Patalong, Uta* Bibliodrama—zur gesellschaftlichen Relevanz eines Booms. PTh 85 (1996) 522-535.

567 **Printz, Markus** Grundlinien einer bibelorientierten Gemeindepädagogik: pädagogische und praktisch-theologische Überlegungen. Wu 1996, Brockhaus 335 pp. DM29 [JETh 11,348—Faix, Wilhelm].

568 *Richter, Klemens* Liturgie und Bibel für das Volk—biblische und liturgische Erneuerung als pastorale Bewegung. BiLi 69 (1996) 143-149.

569 *Rue, Victoria* Putting flesh on the bones of God: enacting sacred texts. Semeia 74 (1996) 189-198.

570 *Schaberg, Jane* Fast forwarding to the Magdalene. Semeia 74 (1996) 33-45.

571 *Schiefer, Franz* Erfahrungsbericht aus einem Bibliodramaseminar. BAKEB Informationen 1 (1996) 10-11.

572 *Schröer, Henning* Bibliodrama als theologische Herausforderung. EvErz 48 (1996) 42-46.

573 *Seils, Ruth Margarete* Bibliodrama als Befreiungsweg. REvErz 48 (1996) 95-104.

574 *Stöhr, Martin* Öffentliche Selbstdarstellung der Kirche—am Beispiel der Kirchentage: ein langer Weg in das noch nicht erreichte Land der Freiheit. JBTh 11 (1996) 167-180.

575 *Šabić, Ana Gabrijela* Književni interesi—važan kriterij u izboru književnoumjetničkih i biblijskih tekstova u katehezi [Literary interest—an important criterion in choosing literary-artistic and biblical texts in catechesis]. Sum. 492. BoSm 66 (1996) 469-493.

576 *Swain, Lionel* The use of the bible in 'Broad areas of attainment in religious education'. ScrB 26 (1996) 73-82.
577 *Tafferner, Andrea* Was trauen wir der Bibel in der Seelsorge zu? BiLi 69 (1996) 255-257.
578 *Thomas, Linda A.* Teaching with the bible in high school. BiTod 34 (1996) 45-49.
579 *Turniansky, Chava* La pedagogia dell'insegnamento della Bibbia nell'Europa orientale. La lettura ebraica. 1996, ⇒205. 329-347.
580 *Vetter, Dieter* Lernen und Lehren: Skizze eines lebenswichtigen Vorgangs für das Volk Gottes. Judentum. 1996 <1989>, ⇒154. 411-429.
581 *Warns, Eberhard* Weiterbildung in Bibliodrama-Leitung. BAKEB Informationen 1 (1996) 11-13.
582 **Weber, Hans-Ruedi** El libro que me lee: manual para formadores en el estudio de la Biblia. ᵀ*Amado Mier, Milagros*. Pastoral 54: Sdr 1996, Sal Terrae 110 pp. 84-293-1203-X [PerTeol 29,283].
583 *Westermann, Claus* Eine Bemerkung zur Reform des theologischen Studiums. Das mündliche Wort. 1996, ⇒157. 185-195.
584 *Westermann, Claus* Was kann das Alte Testament für die Praktische Theologie bedeuten? Das mündliche Wort. 1996, ⇒157. 202-232.

B2.1 **Hermeneutica**

585 *Arul Raja, A.M.* Some reflections on a Dalit reading of the bible. ITS 33 (1996) 249-259.
586 *Barr, James* Allegory and historicism. JSOT 69 (1996) 105-120.
587 *Barth, Gerhard* Kriterien theologischen Denkens und Urteilens im Neuen Testament. Neutestamentliche Versuche. 1996 <1989>, ⇒111. 385-421.
588 *Begley, J.* Modern theories of interpretation. ACR 73/1 (1996) 81-91.
589 *Berlin, Adele* A search for a new biblical hermeneutics: preliminary observations. Albright centennial conference. 1996, ⇒303. 195-207.
590 *Bertoli, Bruno* Scienze umane e interpretazione della bibbia: pastorale biblica in una chiesa locale. StPat 43 (1996) 101-105.
591 *Beuchot Puente, Mauricio* La hermenéutica y su fundamentación ontológica. EfMex 14 (1996) 219-229.
592 *Bey, Horst von der* Fundamentalist oder Spiritueller?: zum Schriftverständnis des hl. FRANZISKUS. WiWei 59 (1996) 307-316.
593 *Brett, Mark G.* The ethics of postcolonial criticism. Semeia 75 (1996) 219-228.
    ᴱ*Camplani, Alberto* Bibliografia generale di storia dell'interpretazione biblica. ⇒383.
594 *Cantilena, Mario* Scienze umane e interpretazione della bibbia: le perplessità di un filologo. StPat 43 (1996) 43-61.
595 *Chiappini, Azzolino* Leggere la scrittura: il testo e il lettore. RTLu 1 (1996) 61-78.
596 *Childs, Brevard S.* On reclaiming the bible for christian theology. Reclaiming the bible for the church [ᴱ**Braaten, Carl E.; Jenson, Robert W.** E 1996, Clark 137 pp. £10. 0-567-08533-3]. 1-17.
597 *Chmiel, Jerzy* Hermeneutyka i sens tekstów biblijnych [Hermeneutica et sensus biblici]. RBL 49 (1996) 44-49.

598 *Combet-Galland, Corina* Die Semiotik der Leidenschaften als ein Beitrag zur anthropologischen Reflexion. VF 41 (1996) 56-61.

599 *Combrink, H.J.* Dialogue in and with the bible. Scriptura 57 (1996) 193-200.

600 *Craffert, Pieter F.* On New Testament interpretation and ethnocentrism. Ethnicity. Bibl.Interp. 19: 1996, ⇒171. 449-468;

601 Reading and divine sanction: the ethics of interpreting the New Testament in the new South Africa. Rhetoric. JSNT.S 131: 1996, ⇒268. 54-71;

602 Relationships between social-scientific, literary, and rhetorical interpretation of texts. BTB 26 (1996) 45-55.

603 *Degner, G.W.* From text to context: hermeneutical principles for applying the word of God. 1996. CTQ 60 (1996) 259-278.

604 **Dohmen, Christoph; Stemberger, Günter** Hermeneutik der jüdischen Bibel und des Alten Testaments. KStTh 1/2: Stu 1996, Kohlhammer 216 pp. DM39.80. 3-17-012038-7 [ZKTh 119,72];

605 *Dohmen, Christoph* Hermeneutik des Alten Testaments. ⇒604. 133-209;

606 Das Konzept der doppelten Hermeneutik: eine Zusammenfassung. ⇒604. 211-213.

607 *Donaldson, Laura E.* Postcolonialism and biblical reading: an introduction. Semeia 75 (1996) 1-14.

608 *Donfried, Karl P.* Alien hermeneutics and the misappropriation of scripture. Reclaiming the Bible. 1996, ⇒596. 19-45.

609 *Draper, Jonathan A.* Confessional Western text-centered biblical interpretation and an oral or residual-oral context. Semeia 73 (1996) 59-77.

610 *Eskola, Timo* An era of apologetical hermeneutics—detecting a neo-Kantian paradigm of biblical interpretation. Sum. 343. EvQ 68 (1996) 329-344.

611 *Fiorenza, E.S.* The ethos of interpretation: biblical studies in a postmodern and postcolonial context. Theological Thought 95 (1996) 38-63 [ThIK 18/2,57].

612 *Fitzmyer, Joseph A.* The senses of scripture today. IThQ 62 (1996-97) 101-117.

613 *Fortin-Melkevik, Anne* Exégèse et théologie: le paradigme herméneutique comme lieu de réconciliation entre exégètes et théologiens. ScEs 48 (1996) 273-287.

614 *Franco, Francesco* Comprendere la parola di Dio: per una teologia ermeneutica. Ricerche Teologiche 7/1 (1996) 29-50.

615 *Franco, Francesco* Ermeneutica e verità. StPat 43 (1996) 165-175.

616 *Goosen, D.P.* The rhetoric of the scapegoat: a deconstructive view on postmodern hermeneutics. Rhetoric. JSNT.S 131: 1996, ⇒268. 383-392.

617 *Graham, Stephen R.* 'Thus saith the Lord': biblical hermeneutics in the early pentecostal movement. ExAu 12 (1996) 121-135.

618 *Heiligenthal, Roman* Methodische Erwägungen zur Analyse neutestamentlicher Gemeindekonflikte. ZRGG 48 (1996) 97-113.

619 *Hengel, Martin* Tasks of New Testament scholarship. BBR 6 (1996) 67-86.

620 *Hinga, Teresia M.* "Reading with": an exploration of the interface between "critical" and "ordinary" readings of the bible: a response. Semeia 73 (1996) 277-284.

621 *Horine, Steven C.* Bible translations: do we have the right models? CBTJ 12 (1996) 42-54.

622 *Jenson, Robert W.* Hermeneutics and the life of the church. Reclaiming the bible. 1996, ⇒596. 89-105.

623 *Joha, Zdenko* Hermeneutik-Methodik der theologischen Interpretation. JRTR 4 (1996) 120-134.

624 *Jonker, Louis C.* On plotting the exegetical-hermeneutical landscape. Scriptura 57 (1996) 397-411.

625 *Jospe, Raphael* Philosophic approaches to sacred scripture in Judaism. Adapted by *Pathrapankal, Joseph*. JDh 21/4 (1996) 345-363.

626 *Josuttis, Manfred* Für einen evangelischen Fundamentalismus. PTh 85 (1996) 74-85.

627 *Keck, Leander E.* The premodern bible in the postmodern world. Interp. 50 (1996) 130-141.

628 *Lategan, Bernard C.* Scholar and ordinary reader—more than a simple interface. Semeia 73 (1996) 243-255.

629 *Lee, Archie C.C.* Cross-textual hermeneutics on gospel and culture. AJTh 10/1 (1996) 38-48.

630 *Lespinasse, Francine* Le Roi-grenouille ou Henri-le-ferré. SémBib 82 (1996) 45-53.

631 *Lo, Chenfang* Chinese biblical interpretation in the eyes of a Chinese christian. Bibl.Interp. 4 (1996) 124-126.

632 *Maier, Gerhard* Wahrheit und Wirklichkeit im Geschichtsverständnis des Alten Testaments. Israel in Geschichte [und Gegenwart: Beiträge zur Geschichte Israels und zum jüdisch-christlichen Dialog. Bericht von der 9. Theologischen Studienkonferenz des Arbeitskreises für evangelikale Theologie (AfeT) vom 20.-23.8.1995 in Bad Blankenburg. EMaier, Gerhard. Wu 1996, Brockhaus 276 pp. 3-417-29415-0] 9-23.

633 *Makhloufi, Mustapha* Lecture sémiotique d'une nouvelle de D. BUZATTI: "Le K" SémBib 81 (1996) 35-52.

634 *Malina, Bruce J.* The bible: witness or warrant?: reflections on Daniel PATTE's ethics of biblical interpretation. BTB 26 (1996) 82-87.

635 *Mosala, Itumeleng J.* Race, class, and gender as hermeneutical factors in the African independent churches' appropriation of the bible. Semeia 73 (1996) 43-57.

636 *Murphy, Roland E.* The Old Testament and the New Catechism. BiTod 34 (1996) 253-259.

637 *Nolan, Albert* Work, the bible, workers, and theologians: elements of a workers' theology. Semeia 73 (1996) 213-220.

638 *Oeming, Manfred* Kanonische Schriftauslegung: Vorzüge und Grenzen eines neuen Zugangs zur Bibel. BiLi 69 (1996) 199-208.

639 *Otto, Eckart* "Wir wollen den Wald und fürchten dennoch seine Geister"—Beobachtungen zur Rezeption des Alten Testaments in Melanesien. Kontinuum [und Proprium: Studien zur Sozial- und Rechtsgeschichte des Alten Orients und des Alten Testaments EOtto, Eckart. Orientalia biblica et christiana 8: Wsb 1996, Harrassowitz x; 380 pp. 3-447-03835-7] <1988>. 59-71.

640 *Panier, Louis* L'analyse sémiotique d'un texte. SémBib 81 (1996) 5-18;

641 Lecture de "La Rempailleuse". SémBib 81 (1996) 19-34;

642 La Moitié de Poulet. SémBib 84 (1996) 40-51.

643 *Patte, Daniel* Biblical scholars at the interface between critical and ordinary readings: a response. Semeia 73 (1996) 263-276.

644 *Perez-Cotapos Larrain, Eduardo* El valor hermenéutico de la eclesialidad para la interpretación de la sagrada scritura. TyV 37/3 (1996) 169-185 [ThIK 18/2,72].
645 *Peskowitz, Miriam* Tropes of travel. Semeia 75 (1996) 177-196.
646 *Pippin, Tina* Ideology, ideological criticism, and the bible. CurResB 4 (1996) 51-78.
647 *Pobee, John S.* Bible study in Africa: a passover of language. Semeia 73 (1996) 161-179.
648 *Pudussery, Paul Savio* Christian approaches to the bible. JDh 21 (1996) 320-344.
649 *Pui-Lan, Kwok* Chinese christians and their bible. Bibl.Interp. 4 (1996) 127-129.
650 *Pui-lan, Kwok* Response to the Semeia volume on postcolonial criticism. Semeia 75 (1996) 211-217.
651 *Reid, Stephen Breck* Reading scripture as an African American. BiTod 34 (1996) 378-382 [Mark 11,15-19].
652 *Reventlow, Henning Graf* Theologie und Hermeneutik des Alten Testaments. ThR 61 (1996) 48-102, 123-176.
653 *Richard, Pablo* Biblical interpretation from the perspective of indigenous cultures of Latin America (Mayas, Kunas, and Quechuas);
654 *Riches, John* Cultural bias in European and North American biblical scholarship. Ethnicity. Bibl.Interp. 19: 1996, ⇒171. 297-314/431-448;
655 Interpreting the bible in African contexts: Glasgow consultation. Semeia 73 (1996) 181-188.
656 *Rogers, Eugene F.* How the virtues of an interpreter presuppose and perfect hermeneutics: the case of Thomas AQUINAS. JR 76 (1996) 64-81.
657 *Salazar, Philippe-Joseph* Beyond apologetics: mythology, rhetoric and the other in early eighteenth-century France. Rhetoric. JSNT.S 131: 1996, ⇒268. 369-382.
658 *Saye, Scott C.* The wild and crooked tree: BARTH, fish, and interpretive communities. MoTh 12 (1996) 435-458.
659 *Schmidt, Ludwig* Alttestamentliche Hermeneutik und biblische Theologie. Altes Testament. 1996, ⇒169. 323-344.
660 *Schöllgen, Georg* Pseudapostolizität und Schriftgebrauch in den ersten Kirchenordnungen: Anmerkungen zur Begründung des frühen Kirchenrechts. FDassmann, E., JAC.E 23: 1996, ⇒19. 96-121.
661 *Segalle, G.* Scienze umane e interpretazione della bibbia: introduzione: il convegno e la sua articolazione. StPat 43 (1996) 15-18.
662 *Snyman, Gerrie* Who is speaking?: intertextuality and textual influence. Neotest. 30 (1996) 427-449.
663 *Speelman, Willem Marie* Transformations discursives et énonciatives des objets narratifs. SémBib 82 (1996) 30-44.
664 *Stemberger, Günter* Hermeneutik der Jüdischen Bibel. Hermeneutik. 1996, ⇒604. 22-132.
665 *Sugirtharajah, R.S.* Plotting postcolonial biblical criticism. Theological Thought 95 (1996) 64-77 [ThIK 18/2,57]. **K.**
666 *Tamez, Elsa* The hermeneutical leap of today. Semeia 75 (1996) 203-205;
667 El salto hermenéutico de hoy. Semeia 75 (1996) 199-201.
668 *Underwood, Ralph L.* Primordial texts: an object relations approach to biblical hermeneutics. PastPsy 45 (1996-97) 181-192 [EThL 74,168*].

669 *VanZanten Gallagher, Susan* Mapping the hybrid world: three post-colonial motifs. Semeia 75 (1996) 229-240.
670 *Warrior, Robert Allen* Response. Semeia 75 (1996) 207-209.
671 *Weaver, Jace* From I-hermeneutics to we-hermeneutics: native Americans and the post-colonial. Semeia 75 (1996) 153-176.
672 *Weder, Hans* Kritik am Verdacht: eine neutestamentliche Erprobung der neueren Hermeneutik des Verdachts. ZThK 93 (1996) 59-83.
673 *Weems, Renita J.* Response to "'Reading with': an exploration of the interface between critical and ordinary readings of the bible". ⇒620. Semeia 73 (1996) 257-261.
674 *West, Gerald* Reading the bible differently: giving shape to the discourses of the dominated. Semeia 73 (1996) 21-41;
675 and *Dube, Musa W.* An introduction: how we have come to "read with". Semeia 73 (1996) 7-17.
676 *Westermann, Claus* (*a*) Ein Rückblick;
677 (*b*) Sechzig Jahre mit dem Alten Testament. Das mündliche Wort. 1996, ⇒157. 243-254/255-264.
678 *Wire, Antoinette* Chinese biblical interpretation since mid-century. Bibl.Interp. 4 (1996) 101-123.
679 *Zenger, E.* Überlegungen zu einem neuen christlichen Umgang mit dem sogenannten Alten Testament. JK 57 (1996) 137-151.

B2.4 *Analysis* **narrationis** *biblicae*

680 *Anderson, Janice Capel* Sermon and story. Treasures [new and old: recent contributions to Matthean studies. ᴱBauer, David R. ⇒F3.1]. 233-250.
681 *Bailey, Kenneth E.* "Inverted parallelism" and "encased parables" in Isaiah and their significance for OT and NT translation and interpretation. Literary structure. 1996, ⇒200. 14-30.
682 **Exum, J. Cheryl** Tragedy and biblical narrative: arrows of the Almighty. (*a*) 1992, ⇒8,1213...11/2,1374. ᴿSJTh 49 (1996) 500-501 (*Shields, Mary*);
683 (*b*) C ²1996, CUP xiv; 206 pp. £12. 0-521-56506-5.
684 **Glatt, David A.** Chronological displacement in biblical and related literatures. SBL.DS 139: 1993, ⇒9,12337; 11/2,1379. ᴿAJS Review 21 (1996) 367-369 (*Noegel, Scott B.*); CritRR 9 (1996) 148-150 (*Schley, Donald G.*).
685 **Gunn, David M.; Fewell, Danna Nolan** Narrative in the Hebrew bible. 1993, ⇒9,1043...11/2,1381. ᴿJAOS 116 (1996) 774-775 (*Edelman, Diana V.*); AJSR 21 (1996) 127-9 (*Prouser, Ora Horn*); SJTh 49 (1996) 512-513 (*Moberly, Walter*); HebStud 37 (1996) 141-145 (*Gottlieb, Isaac B.*).
686 **Healy, Joseph; Sybertz, Donald** Towards an African narrative theology. Nairobi 1996, Paulines 400 pp. DM168. 3-16-145828-1.
687 **Loughlin, Gerard** Telling God's story: bible, church and narrative theology. C 1996, CUP xv; 266 pp. £35; $55. 0-521-43285-5.
688 *Magonet, Jonathan* Character/author/reader: the problem of perspective in biblical narrative. Literary structure. 1996, ⇒200. 3-13.
689 **Magonet, Jonathan** Schöne, Heldinnen, Narren: von der Erzählkunst der Hebräischen Bibel. Gütersloher Taschenbücher Siebenstern 1444: Gü 1996, Gü'er 206 pp. 3-579-01444-7 [2 Samuel 12].

690 **Meier, Samuel** Speaking of speaking: marking direct discourse in the Hebrew Bible. VT.S 46: 1992, ⇒8,1219...11/2,1385. RJQR 86 (1996) 493-495 (*Savran, George*).

691 **Minette de Tillesse, Caetano** O Deus pelas costas: teologia narrativa da Bíblia. 1995, RBBras 12. ⇒11/2,1386. RThR 61 (1996) 59-60 (*Reventlow, Henning Graf*);

692 O Deus pelas costas: teologia narrativa da bíblia: Novo Testamento. RBBras 13: 1996, 790 pp.

693 *Nieuviarts, Jacques* D'Ulysse à la bible: les récits qui font le voyage. BLE.S 1 (1996) 75-88.

694 **Polak, Frank** Biblical narrative: aspects of art and design. 1994, ⇒11/2,1389. RCBQ 58 (1996) 131-133 (*Ben Zvi, Ehud*). **H.**

695 **Pratt, Richard J.** He gave us stories: the bible student's guide to interpreting Old Testament narratives. 1990, ⇒11/2,1206. RRTR 55 (1996) 96-98 (*McClean, John*).

696 **Prickett, Stephen** Origins of narrative: the romantic appropriation of the bible. C 1996 CUP xvi; 288 pp. $55. 0-521-44543-4 [NThAR 1997/2,33].

697 E**Rosenblatt, J.P.; Sitterson, J.C.** 'Not in heaven': coherence and complexity in biblical narrative. 1991, ⇒7,454b...11/2,1393. RJSSt 41 (1996) 320-322 (*Curtis, Adrian H.W.*).

698 *Schunack, Gerd* Neuere literaturkritische Interpretationsverfahren in der anglo-amerikanischen Exegese. VF 41 (1996) 28-55.

699 **Tertel, Hans Jürgen** Text and transmission. BZAW 221: 1994, ⇒10,926; 11/2,1397. ROLZ 91 (1996) 588-591 (*Stahl, Rainer*).

700 *Wenzel, Knut* Zu einer theologischen Hermeneutik der Narration. ThPh 71 (1996) 161-186.

701 *Westermann, Claus* (*a*) Erzählen und Erzählung;

702 (*b*) Der vorliterarische Bericht. Das mündliche Wort. 1996, ⇒157. 50-55/56-66.

703 *Zumstein, Jean* Narrative Analyse und neutestamentliche Exegese in der frankophonen Welt. VF 41 (1996) 5-27.

B2.6 *Critica reactionis lectoris* Reader response criticism

704 *Cahill, Michael* Reader-response criticism and the allegorizing reader TS 57 (1996) 89-96.

705 *Long, Tim* A real reader reading revelation. Semeia 73 (1996) 79-107.

706 *Noble, Paul R.* Fish and the bible: should reader-response theories 'catch on'? HeyJ 37 (1996) 456-467.

707 *Schnelle, Udo* Auf der Suche nach dem Leser. VF 41 (1996) 61-66.

B3.1 *Interpretatio ecclesiastica* Bible and Church

708 *Ardusso, Franco* La "Dei Verbum" a trent'anni di distanza. RdT 37 (1996) 29-45.

709 *Braaten, Carl E.; Jenson, Robert W.* Introduction: gospel, church, and scripture. Reclaiming the Bible. 1996, ⇒596. ix-xii.

710 *Dohmen, Christoph* Was Gott sagen wollte ... der sensus plenior im Dokument der Päpstlichen Bibelkommission. BiLi 69 (1996) 251-254.

711 **Farias, Domenico** La biblioteca di Gerusalemme: libri e documenti nella vita della Chiesa. Cultura e vita 1: [Soveria Mannelli (Catanzaro)] 1996, Rubbettino 103 pp. 88-7284-381-2.

712 **Fischer, Georg** Kann aus Rom etwas Gutes kommen? BiLi 69 (1996) 171-173.

713 **Fitzmyer, Joseph A.** Scripture, the soul of theology. 1994, ⇒10,959; 11/2,1423. ᴿScrB 26 (1996) 45-47 (*Swain, Lionel*);

714 The Biblical Commission's document *The interpretation of the Bible in the church*: text and commentary. SubBi 18: 1995, ⇒11/2,1424. ᴿCoTh 66/1 (1996) 191-192 (*Chrostowski, Waldemar*);

715 The interpretation of the bible in the church today. IThQ 62 (1996-97) 84-100.

716 **Fragnito, Gigliola** La bibbia al rogo: la censura ecclesiastica e i volgarizzamenti della scrittura (1471-1605). Bo 1996, Mulino 346 pp. L38.000. 88-15-05749-8 [BSSV 114,125].

717 *Franco, Francesco* Esegesi e metodo: riflessioni sul rapporto bibbia-chiesa-scienza. StPat 43 (1996) 107-121.

718 *Garrone, Daniele* Scienze umane e interpretazione della bibbia: riflessioni di un esegeta protestante. StPat 43 (1996) 93-99.

719 **Graziani, Domenico** Il primato della parola di Dio nella vita della chiesa secondo la *Dei verbum*. Vivarium 4 (1996) 51-62.

720 **Hopko, Thomas** The church, the bible, and dogmatic theology. Reclaiming the bible. 1996, ⇒596. 107-118.

721 ᴱ**Houlden, J.L.** The interpretation of the bible in the church, 1995, ⇒11/2,1443. ᴿSBET 14 (1996) 178-180 (*Graham, David*).

722 **Laghi, Card. Pio,** (*al*), Chiesa e sacra scrittura: un secolo di magistero ecclesiastico e studi biblici. 1994. ⇒10,977...11/2,1457. ᴿGr. 77 (1996) 349-350 (*Farahian, Edmond*).

723 ᴱ**Maggioni, Bruno** La sacra scrittura: i documenti ufficiali della chiesa. Mi 1996, Massimo 316 pp. 88-7030-734-4.

724 **Martins, José Saraiva** La sacra scrittura nella formazione teologica a trent'anni dalla "Dei Verbum". Seminarium 36 (1996) 314-327.

725 **McGrath, Alister E.** Reclaiming our roots and vision: scripture and the stability of the christian church. Reclaiming the Bible. 1996, ⇒596. 63-88.

726 **Murphy, Roland E.** Reflections on "actualization" of the bible. BTB 26 (1996) 79-81.

727 **Packer, James I.** Truth & power: the place of scripture in the christian life. Wheaton 1996, Shaw 251 pp. 0-87788-815-9 [NThAR 1999,2].

728 *Panimolle, Salvatore A.* La *Lectio divina* nella costituzione *Dei verbum* del Concilio Vaticano II. PaVi 41/5 (1996) 47-50.

729 **Pastore, Corrado; Wyssenbach, Jean-Pierre,** (*al*), Palabra que construye comunidad. Mes de la biblia 96: Caracas 1996, Iter 32 pp.

730 **Pelikan, Jaroslav** The reformation of the bible: the bible of the Reformation. NHv 1996, Yale University Press 208 pp. and catalog of the exhibition by Valerie R. Hotchkiss and David Price. $45. ᴿCTJ 31/2 (1996) 613-615 (*Blacketer, Raymond A.*).

731 **Ratzinger, Kard. Joseph** Evangelium—Katechese—Katechismus: Streiflichter auf den Katechismus der katholischen Kirche. 1995, ⇒11/2,1482. ᴿALW 38/39 (1996/97) 120-121 (*Neunheuser, Burkhard*).

732 **Ruppert, Lothar** Um Exegese und Bibelkommission: eine Kontroverse. Theologisches 26 (1996) 254-257.

733 **Ruppert, Lothar; Klauck, Jans-Josef** Die Interpretation der Bibel in der Kirche: das Dokument...mit einer kommentierenden Einführung und einer Würdigung. SBS 161: 1995, ⇒11/2,1489. RThLZ 121 (1996) 246-247 (*Kirchner, Hubert*).

734 *Segalle, Giuseppe* Scienze umane e interpretazione della bibbia: storia del documento. StPat 43 (1996) 19-23.

735 **Sieben, Hermann Josef** Sola traditione?: zur Rolle der Heiligen Schrift auf den Konzilien der Alten Kirche. FDassmann, E., JAC.E 23: 1996, ⇒19. 270-283.

736 **Steinmetz, David C.** The bible in the sixteenth century. DMMRS 11: Durham, NC 1996 <1990> Duke University Press viii; 263 pp. $17. 0-8223-1849-0 [BTB 27,120].

737 **Stravinskas, Peter M.J.** The catholic church and the bible. SF ²1996, Ignatius 135 pp. $10. 0-89870-588-6.

738 *Van den Brink, Hermann* Biblische Botschaft und Kirchenrecht: eine fruchtbare Spannung. Conc(D) 32 (1996) 383-388.

739 *Van der Ploeg, J.P.M.* Bemerkungen zu Prof. RUPPERTs Brief. Theologisches 26 (1996) 257-259;

740 Zur Abhandlung der Päpstlichen Bibelkommission über die Auslegung der Bibel in der Kirche. Theologisches 26 (1996) 117-130.

741 **Zaccaria, Giuseppe** Scienze umane e interpretazione della bibbia: pluralismo interpretativo e autorità del magistero. StPat 43 (1996) 63-65.

742 **Zenger, Erich** Weiße Flecken im neuen Dokument der Bibelkommission. BiLi 69 (1996) 173-176.

B3.2 *Homiletica* — The Bible in preaching

743 **Adam, Peter** Speaking God's words: a practical theology of preaching Leicester 1996, Inter-Varsity 173 pp. 0-85111-171-8 [ZNW 88,153].

744 **Allen, Ronald J.; Holbert, John C.** Holy root...christian preaching from the OT. 1995, ⇒11/2,1518. RBS 153 (1996) 501-502 (*Warren, Timothy S.*).

745 **Brueggemann, Walter** The threat of life: sermons on pain, power, and weakness. ECampbell, Charles L. Mp 1996, Fortress 163 pp. $15 [BiTod 35,255].

FButtrick, David Preaching as a theological task. 1996, ⇒13.

746 **Collins, Raymond F.** Preaching the epistles. Mahwah 1996, Paulist iii; 151 pp. 0-8091-3625-2.

747 *Grindal, G.* New sight, new life: Lenten gospels. WaW 16/1 (1996) 91-97.

748 *Klopfenstein, Martin A.* Erwägungen zur Predigt alttestamentlicher Texte. Leben aus dem Wort. BEAT 40: 1996, ⇒132. 297-308.

749 **Korenhof, Mieke** Mit Eva predigen. Ein anderes Perikopenbuch. Dü 1996, Presseverband der Evangelischen Kirche im Rheinland 229 pp. DM19.80.

750 **Lisher, Richard** The interrupted sermon. Interp. 50 (1996) 169-181.

751 ELong, G.; Farley, E. Preaching as a theological task: world, gospel, scripture. LVL 1996, Westminster 191 pp. 0-664-25617-1 [ETR 73,309].

752 **McCurley, Foster B.** Wrestling with the word of God: christian preaching from the Hebrew bible. Valley Forge, PA 1996, Trinity xii; 243 pp. $20. 1-56338-142-7 [OTA 19,548].
753 **McGrath, Alister E.** A passion for truth: the intellectual coherence of evangelicalism. Leicester 1996, Apollos 287 pp. 0-85111-447-4.
754 **Moloney, Francis J.** The gospel of the Lord: reflections on the gospel readings: year B. ColMn 1996, Liturgical 232 pp. 0-8146-2269-0.
755 [E]**Mühlenberg, E; Van Oort, J.** Predigt in der Alten Kirche. 1994, ⇒10,376. REAug 42 (1996) 195-197 (*Monaci Castagno, Adele*).
756 **Theissen, Gerd,** (*al*), Le défi homilétique, l'exégèse au service de la prédication. 1994, ⇒11/2,1578. [R]EeV 106 (1996) 397-398 (*Debarge, Louis*).
757 *Westermann, Claus* Zur Predigt alttestamentlicher Texte. Das mündliche Wort. 1996, ⇒157. 233-242.

B3.3 Inerrantia, inspiratio

758 **Artola Arbizu, Antonio M.** La escritura inspirada. 1994, ⇒11/2,1587. [R]Cart. 12 (1996) 511-512.
759 **Barton, John** People of the book?. 1993, ⇒9,1225. [R]SJTh 49 (1996) 381-382 (*Hodgetts, Pauline*).
760 **Beilner, Wolfgang** Das Wort Gottes. Vermittlung 57: Salzburg 1996, n.p. 249 pp.
761 *Bolognesi, Pietro* La dottrina della scrittura nella storia della chiesa. BeO 38 (1996) 239-267.
    [E]**Braaten, Carl E.**, (*al*), Reclaiming the Bible for the church. 1996, ⇒596.
762 **Bringas, Ernie** Going by the book: past and present tragedies of biblical authority. Charlottesville 1996, Hampton Roads 219 pp. Bibl.; 1-571-74022-8 [NThAR 1998,267].
763 *Delivuk, John Allen* Biblical authority and the proof of the regulative principle of worship in *The Westminster Confession*. WThJ 58 (1996) 237-256.
764 *Delorme, Jean* Vient de paraître. SémBib 83 (1996) 49-58.
765 **Dockery, David S.** Christian scripture: an evangelical perspective on inspiration, authority and interpretation. 1995, ⇒11/2,1594. [R]RExp 93 (1996) 438-439 (*Blomberg, Craig L.*).
766 *Edwards, Mark U.* Die Heilige Schrift als gedruckter Text. 1996, [F]Junghans, H. ⇒46. 33-52 [EThL 74,165*].
767 *Elders, Leo J.* Inspiración y revelación según Santo Tomas de Aquino. Esperanza del hombre. 1996, ⇒173. 181-198.
768 *Firmin, Gilles* Les controverses sur l'autorité du texte biblique à l'époque moderne. Les premières traditions. 1996, ⇒159. 241-290.
769 **Goldingay, John** Models for scripture. 1994, ⇒11/2,1599. [R]TS 57 (1996) 141-143 (*Fledderman, Harry T.*).
770 *Hargreaves, Mark* A new vocabulary of biblical authority: suggestions for the concept of narration. AThR 78 (1996) 290-307.
771 *Harrisville, Roy A.* The loss of biblical authority and its recovery. Reclaiming the Bible. 1996, ⇒596. 47-61.
772 **Hendrix, Scott H.** Tradition and authority in the Reformation. CStS: Aldershot, U.K. 1996, Ashgate xii; 330 pp. [ChH 67,148s—Pragman, James H.].

773 *Jacobson, Diane* Hosea 2: a case study on biblical authority. CThMi 23 (1996) 165-172.

774 *Jodock, Darrell* The American context and the authority of the bible. CThMi 23 (1996) 85-103.

775 *Juel, Donald* The authority of the scriptures: an assessment of a conversation. CThMi 23 (1996) 192-199.

776 *La Potterie, Ignace de* The spiritual sense of scripture. Com(US) (1996) 738-756.

777 **Lancaster, Sarah Heaner** The authority of biblical narrative: feminist reflections on the work of Hans FREI. DSouthern Methodist Univ. 1996, 306 pp. [EThL 74,169*].

778 **Martin, François** Pour une théologie de la lettre: l'inspiration des Écritures. CFi 196: P 1996, Cerf xii; 516 pp. FF190. 2-204-05371-6.

779 *Olson, Dennis T.* The lion, the itch and the wardrobe: Hosea 5:8-6:6 as a case study in the contemporary interpretation and authority of scripture. CThMi 23 (1996) 173-184.

780 **Ryrie, Charles C.** Irrtum ausgeschlossen!: Wahrheit und Inspiration der Bibel im Kreuzverhör. TReetnitz, Peter Schäfer von. Dillenburg 1996, Christliche Verl.-Ges. 108 pp. 3-89436-111-5 [NThAR 1997,98].

781 *Schott, Faye E.* Biblical authority and God—a theological reflection. CThMi 23 (1996) 119-125.

782 **Tischler, Gregor** Und Gott schrieb...: so verstehen Sie die Bibel. Mü 1996, Kösel 231 pp. 3-466-36461-2 [NThAR 1997,160].

783 **Wellum, Stephen Joel** An investigation of the interrelationship between the doctrines of divine action, sovereignty, omniscience, and scripture and its significance for contemporary debates on biblical authority. DFeinberg, J.S. 1996, 264 pp. Trinity Evang. Div. School [EThL 74,167*].

784 **Wenz, Armin** Das Wort Gottes—Gericht und Rettung: Untersuchungen zur Autorität der Heiligen Schrift in Bekenntnis und Lehre der Kirche. DSlenczka, R.. FSOTh 75: Gö 1996, Vandenhoeck & R 343 pp. DM98. 3-525-56282-9 [ThRv 93,406].

785 *Wood, Charles M.* Scripture, authenticity, and truth. JR 76 (1996) 189-205.

в3.4 Traditio

786 **Buckenmaier, Achim** 'Schrift und Tradition' seit dem Vatikanum II: Vorgeschichte und Rezeption. KKTS 62: Pd 1996, Bonifatius 560 pp. DM158. 3-87088-907-1 [ThLZ 124,119ss—Haudel, Matthias].

787 ECremascoli, Giuseppe; Leonardi, Claudio La bibbia nel Medioevo. La bibbia nella storia 16: Bo 1996, Dehoniane 486 pp. L62.000. 88-10-40262-6.

788 *Every, George* The bible in tradition. OiC 32 (1996) 323-328.

в3.5 Canon

789 *Achtemeier, Elizabeth* The canon as the voice of the living God. Reclaiming the bible. 1996, ⇒596. 119-130.

790 *Barthel, J.* Das Alte Testament als Kanon: Beobachtungen zur Ge-
    stalt der hebräischen Bibel und des christlichen Alten Testaments.
    ThFPr 22/1 (1996) 3-19.
791 *Barton, John* The significance of a fixed canon of the Hebrew bible.
    Antiquity [ESæbø, Magne 1996, ⇒Y1] 67-83.
792 **Barton, John** The spirit and the letter: studies in the biblical canon.
    L 1997, SPCK xiii; 210 pp. £17.50. 0-281-05011-2. RET 108 (1996-
    97) 289-290 (*Rodd, C.S.*.
793 *Berquist, Jon L.* Postcolonialism and imperial motives for canoniza-
    tion. Semeia 75 (1996) 15-35.
794 **Blanchard, Y.-M.** Aux sources du canon: le témoignage
    d'IRENEE. CFi 175: 1993, ⇒9,1259...11/2,1632. REThL 72 (1996)
    250-252 (*Verheyden, J.*).
795 **Bruce, Frederick Fyvie** The canon of scripture. DG ⁷1996, Inter-
    varsity 349 pp. 0-8308-1258-X.
796 *Buss, Martin J.* Hosea as a canonical problem: with attention to the
    Song of Songs. FTucker, G., JSOT.S 229: 1996, ⇒95. 79-93.
797 *Carr, David M.* Canonization in the context of community: an
    outline of the formation of the tanakh and the christian bible.
    FSanders, J., JSOT.S 225: 1996, ⇒77. 22-64.
798 *Cazelles, Henri* De la fixation du texte biblique à l'origine de son
    autorité. Études. 1996 <1995>, ⇒120. 181-192.
799 *Dohmen, Christoph* Wenn Texte Texte verändern: Spuren der Kano-
    nisierung der Tora vom Exodusbuch her. Die Tora als Kanon
    [EZenger, Erich ⇒E1.3]. Herders biblische Studien 10: 1996, 35-
    60.
800 **Dohmen, Christoph; Oeming, Manfred** Biblischer Kanon. QD
    137: 1992, ⇒8,1427...10,1082. RThR 61 (1996) 75-76 (*Reventlow,
    Henning Graf*).
801 *Elliott, J.K.* Manuscripts, the codex and the canon. JSNT 63 (1996)
    105-123.
802 **Ellis, Edward Earle** The Old Testament in early christianity.
    WUNT 54: 1991, ⇒7,198...11/2,1639. RThR 61 (1996) 151-153
    (*Reventlow, Henning Graf*).
803 *Fabry, Heinz-Josef* Der Umgang mit der kanonisierten Tora in
    Qumran. Die Tora als Kanon. Herders biblische Studien 10: 1996,
    ⇒E1.3. 293-327.
804 *Gisel, Pierre* Apocryphes et canon: leurs rapports et leur statut re-
    spectif. Sum. rés. 225. Apopocrypha 7 (1996) 225-234.
805 Zum Problem des biblischen Kanons. JBTh 3, 1988. RThR 61 (1996)
    163-166 (*Reventlow, Henning Graf*).
806 **Jasper, David** Readings in the canon of scripture. 1995,
    ⇒11/2,1643. RCritRR 9 (1996) 129-131 (*Britt, Brian*).
807 *Jeppesen, Knud* Biblia Hebraica—et Septuaginta: a response to Mo-
    gens MUELLER. SJOT 10 (1996) 271-281.
808 **Lienhard, Joseph T.** The bible, the church, and authority: the canon
    of the christian bible in history and theology. 1995, ⇒11/2,1649. In-
    terp. 50 (1996) 206, 208 (*McDonald, Lee Martin*).
809 *Luttikhuizen, Gerard* De veelvormigheid van het vroegste christen-
    dom: diversiteit binnen en buiten de canon van het Nieuwe Testa-
    ment. TTh 36 (1996) 331-347.
810 **McDonald, L.M.** The formation of the christian biblical canon.
    ²1995, ⇒11/2,1650. RRTR 55 (1996) 150-151 (*Peterson, David*).

811 *McDonald, Lee Martin* The integrity of the biblical canon in light of its historical development. BBR 6 (1996) 95-132.
812 **Miller, J.W.** The origins of the bible: rethinking canon history. 1994, ⇒10,1088; 11/2,1652. ᴿOTEs 9 (1996) 547-548 *(Helberg, J.L.)*.
813 *Nida, Eugene A.* Canonicity and bibles today. ᶠSanders, J., JSOT.S 225: 1996, ⇒77. 231-236.
814 **Noble, P.R.** The canonical approach. Lei 1996, Brill. 90-0410-1519 [NT 39,208].
815 *Otzen, Benedikt* Das Problem der Apokryphen. SJOT 10 (1996) 258-270.
816 *Parker, Kim I.* Speech, writing and power: deconstructing the biblical canon. JSOT 69 (1996) 91-103.
817 *Perkins, Pheme* Spirit and letter: poking holes in the canon. JR 76 (1996) 307-327.
818 **Rendtorff, Rolf** Kanon und Theologie. 1991, ⇒7,252...9,1272. ᴿThR 61 (1996) 130-133 *(Reventlow, Henning Graf)*.
819 *Rossin, Elena* Aɴꜰɪʟɪᴄʜɪᴏ di Iconio e il canone biblico "Contra Haereticos". StPat 43 (1996) 121-157.
820 **Sanders, James A.** From sacred story to sacred text. 1987, ⇒3,1466...6,1569. ᴿThR 61 (1996) 73-74 *(Reventlow, Henning Graf)*.
821 *Sierra, Sergio J.* Testo ebraico e canone masoretico. La lettura ebraica. 1996, ⇒205. 23-30.
822 *Skarsaune, Oskar* The question of Old Testament canon and text in the early Greek church. Antiquity. 1996, ⇒ʏ1. 443-450.
823 *Soupa, Anne* Les textes du canon. DosB 65 (1996) 5-7.
824 *Steins, Georg* Die Wiederentdeckung der Bibel als "Ein Buch": Chancen eines neuen Zugangs zur Bibel. BiLi 69 (1996) 237-243.
825 **Trebolle Barrera, Julio** La bíblia judía y la bíblia cristiana. 1993, ⇒9,851...11/2,1141. ᴿMEAH 42/2 (1993) 230-231 *(Pérez Fernández, Miguel)*.
826 **Trobisch, David** Die Endredaktion des Neuen Testaments: eine Untersuchung zur Entstehung der christlichen Bibel. NTOA 31: Gö 1996, Vandenhoeck & R 183 pp. FS52. 3-525-53933-9.

в4.1 *Interpretatio humanistica* **The Bible and man; health, toil, age**

827 **Bendor, Sônîʾa** The social structure of ancient Israel: the institution of the family (Beit ʾAb) from the settlement to the end of the monarchy. ᴰ*Malamat, A.*. Jerusalem Biblical Studies 7: J 1996, Simor 348 pp. Hebrew Univ. 1982. $29. 965-242-007-9 [EThL 74,241*].
828 *Blocher, Henri* La malattia secondo la bibbia. ᵀ*Corradini, G.* Studi di teologia 8 (1996) 101-115.
829 *Bohlen, Reinhold* Klagen—Leben—Hoffen—Trösten: die geistliche Rede angesichts von Sterben und Tod. TThZ 105 (1996) 275-284.
830 **Callahan, Rachel; McDonnell, Rea** God is close to the brokenhearted: good news for those who are depressed. Cincinnati 1996, St. Anthony Messenger 182 pp. $11 [BiTod 35,319].
831 *Dauphin, Claudine* Leprosy, lust and lice: health and hygiene in Byzantine Palestine. BAIAS 15 (1996-97) 55-80.
832 *Di Felice, F.* La dignità della vita umana nella tradizione neo-testamentaria. La natura. 1996, ⇒189. 135-154.

833 *Emlein, Günther* Menschen mit Behinderungen: biblisch-exegetische Gedanken. PTh 85 (1996) 239-255.
834 *Fontaine, Carole R.* Disabilities and illness in the bible: a feminist perspective on apocalypse and ancient Hebrew prophecy. A feminist companion. The feminist companion to the Bible 10: 1996 <1994>, ⇒170. 286-300.
835 *Gruson, Philippe* Le cœur dans la bible. Alliance 106-107 (1996) 74-77.
836 *Harrington, D.J.* Biblical contributions to a theology of aging. RevRel 55/2 (1996) 159-170 [NTAb 40,465].
837 *Klopfenstein, Martin A.* Die Stellung des alten Menschen in der Sicht des Alten Testamentes. Leben aus dem Wort. BEAT 40: 1996, ⇒132. 261-273.
838 *Kopciowski, Elia* La famiglia nella tradizione ebraica. Conferenza a Milano, 1995. Studi, Fatti, Ricerche 73 (1996) 3-6.
839 *Lee, Yeong-Heon* The humanism in the bible. Catholic Theology and Thought 17 (1996) 64-86 [ThIK 18/2 (1997) 51]. **K.**
840 **Longeaux, Jacques de** Amour, mariage et sexualité d'après la bible. Cahiers de l'École Cathédrale 22: P 1996, Mame 152 pp. 2-7289-0819-2. ᴿRThom 96 (1996) 676-678 (*Bonino, Serge-Thomas*).
841 **McAfee, Eugene Clifford** The patriarch's longed-for son: biological and social reproduction in Ugaritic and Hebrew epic. 1996, 337 pp. Diss. Harvard [EThL 74,192*].
842 **Ohler, Annemarie** Väter wie die Bibel sie sieht. FrB 1996, Herder 285 pp. DM39.80 [BiLi 70,239].
843 **Otto, Eckart** Sohnespflichten im antiken Syrien und Palästina. Kontinuum. Orientalia biblica et christiana 8: 1996, ⇒639. 265-282 [Exod 20,12; 21,17; Lev 19; Deut 5,16; Sir 3,1-16].
844 **Pauler, Norbert** Bibliodrama: Glauben erfahren mit Hand, Kopf und Herz. SHSJ 22: Stu 1996, Katholisches Bibelwerk 126 pp. DM20. 3-460-11022-8 [OrdKor 39,254].
845 **Rad, Gerhard von** Expresiones del Antiguo Testamento sobre la vida y la muerte. La acción de Dios. 1996 <1938>, ⇒144. 230-246.
846 *Ska, J.L.* La vita come benedizione. La natura. 1996, ⇒189. 13-40.
847 **Stordalen, Terje** Støv og livspust: mennesket i det gamle testamente. 1994, ⇒11/2,1698. ᴿSJOT 10 (1996) 145-146 (*Jeppesen, Knud*).
848 *Szymik, Stefan* Życie poczęte w świetle wypowiedzi biblijnych [La vie conçue et la bible]. AtK 126 (1996) 163-171.
849 **Van der Toorn, Karel** Family religion in Babylonia, Syria, and Israel: continuity and change in the forms of religious life. Studies in the History and Culture of the Ancient Near East 7: Lei 1996, Brill vii; 491 pp. $142. 90-04-10410-0. ᴿJQR 86 (1996) 519-522 (*Zevit, Ziony*).
850 *Vetter, Dieter* Leiden in der Bibel: Herausforderung zur Verantwortung. Judentum. 1996 <1988>, ⇒154. 510-514.
851 Il vocabolario della guarigione nel Nuovo Testamento. Studi di teologia 8 (1996) 159-160.
852 **Zuck, Roy B.** Precious in his sight: childhood and children in the bible. GR 1996, Baker 279 pp. $20 [BS 154,485].

B4.2 *Femina, familia;* Woman in the Bible [⇒H8.8s]

853 *Aleixandre, Dolores* Sara, Raquel y Miriam: tres mujeres en la tradición profética y en el *midrás*. MCom 54 (1996) 317-338.

854 *Azria, Régine* La femme dans la tradition et la modernité juives. ASSR 41 (1996) 117-132.

855 *Berlyn, P.J.* The great ladies. JBQ 24 (1996) 26-35.

856 *Bodi, Daniel* La tragédie de Mikal en tant que critique de la monarchie Israélite et préfiguration de sa fin. FV 95/2 (1996) 65-105.

857 **Brenner, Athalya; Van Dijk-Hemmes, Fokkelien** On gendering texts. 1993, ⇒10,1126; 11/2,1711. RJBL 115 (1996) 329-331 (*Pressler, Carolyn J.*).

858 **Bronner, Leila Leah** From Eve to Esther: rabbinic reconstructions of biblical women. 1994, ⇒10,1126; 11/2,1712. RHBT 18 (1996) 192-193 (*Day, Linda*); AJS Review 21 (1996) 376-379 (*Gruber, Mayer I.*); JR 76 (1996) 669-670 (*Menn, Esther*); HebStud 37 (1996) 210-212 (*Laffey, Alice L.*).

859 **Brooke, George J.** Women in the biblical tradition. SWR 31: 1992, ⇒9,373. RBibl.Interp. 4 (1996) 225-226 (*Shields, Mary E.*).

860 **Caspi, Mishael Maswari; Havrelock, Rachel S.** Women on the biblical road: Ruth, Naomi, and the female journey. Lanham 1996, University Press of America xiii; (2) 219 pp. 0-7618-0279-7.

861 **Dal Covolo, E.** Donna e matrimonio alle origini della chiesa. BSRel 122: R 1996, Lib. At. Salesiano 168 pp. L25.000 [Asp. 45,450—Longobardo, Luigi].

862 **Drewermann, Eugen** El mensaje de las mujeres: la ciencia del amor. TGancho, Claudio. Barc 1996, Herder 223 pp. 84-254-1926-3 [Actualidad Bibliográfica 34,48].

863 **Exum, J. Cheryl** Fragmented women: feminist (sub)versions of biblical narratives. JSOT.S 163: 1993, ⇒9,1320...11/2,1723. RSJTh 49 (1996) 384-386 (*Hodgetts, Pauline*).

864 **Exum, J. Cheryl** Plotted, shot and painted: cultural representations of biblical women. JSOT.S 215; Culture, Gender, Theory 3: Shf 1996, Academic 260 pp. $75/19.50; £46/15. 1-85075-592-2/-778-X [BTB 27,120].

865 **Fewell, Danna Nolan; Gunn, David M.** Gender, power and promise: the subject of the Bible's first story. 1993, ⇒9,1322...-11/2,1724. RBibl.Interp. 4 (1996) 237-239 (*Landy, Francis*).

866 EFiorenza, Elisabeth Schüssler A feminist introduction. Searching the Scriptures 1. 1993, ⇒9,1349...11/2,1767. RBTB 26 (1996) 58-59 (*Lillie, Betty Jane*).

867 *Jobes, Karen H.* 'For such a time as this': a defining moment in christian ministry. Faith & Mission 14/1 (1996) 3-13.

868 *Ko Ha Fong, Maria* Women: bestowers of the seed of life. WoWo 30/7 [sic (29/6)] 241-246 [ThIK 18/2,48].

869 EKroeger, Catherine Clark; Beck, James R. Women, abuse, and the bible: how scripture can be used to hurt or to heal. GR 1996, Baker 255 pp. 0-8010-5707-8.

870 **Lawler, Joy A.** Women. EHynson, Diana. Bible people: Nv 1996, Abingdon 80 pp. 0-687-01669-X.

871 **Logan, Morag Anne** Gender, literary characterization, and history: rewriting the stories of Deborah and Jezebel. 1996-97, Diss. Princeton [RTL 29,579].

872 *McKay, Heather A.* "Only a remnant of them shall be saved": women from the Hebrew Bible in New Testament narratives. A feminist companion. The feminist companion to the Bible 10: 1996, ⇒170. 32-61.

873 **McKenna, Megan** Not counting women and children: neglected stories from the bible. 1994, ⇒10,1152; 11/2,1751. ᴿAUSS 34 (1996) 132-133 (*Running, Leona Glidden*).

874 Frauen und Kinder nicht mitgezählt: die Verlorenen und Vergessenen der Bibel. ᵀ*Nugel, Wolfram*. Mü 1996, Claudius 227 pp. 3-532-62201-7 [NThAR 1997,129];

875 ᴱ**Navarro Puerto, Mercedes** Para comprender el cuerpo de la mujer: una perspectiva bíblica y ética. Para leer-comprender-vivir 58: Estella 1996, Verbo Divino 222 pp. 84-8169-081-3 [EstB 54,570].

876 *Navarro Puerto, Mercedes* Cuerpos invisibles, cuerpos necesarios: cuerpos de mujeres en la Biblia: exégesis y psicología. Para comprender el cuerpo. 1996, ⇒875. 137-186.

877 **Pardes, Ilana** Countertraditions in the Bible: a feminist approach. 1992, ⇒9,1343...11/2,1760. ᴿAJS Review 21 (1996) 379-381 (*Krook, Anne K.*).

878 *Pawlak, Leonard* Kobieta w Biblii [La femme dans la Bible]. AtK 127 (1996) 92-98.

879 **Plaskow, Judith** Und wieder stehen wir am Sinai: eine jüdisch-feministische Theologie. 1992, ⇒11/2,1761. ᴿBiKi 51 (1996) 83-84 (*Wehn, Beate*).

880 *Poorthuis, Marcel* Van helleveeg tot heilige: over de vrouw van Noach. Interpretatie 4/4 (1996) 12-15.

881 *Rabichev, R.* The Mediterranean concepts of honour and shame as seen in the depiction of the biblical women. R&T 3/1 (1996) 51-63.

882 **Rogers, O.; Hogg, S.** Does God expect less of women?: a series of bible studies. Partnership Study Guide 2: Carlisle 1996, Paternoster vii; 32 pp.

883 **Saunders, Ross** Outrageous women, outrageous God: women in the first two generations of christianity. Sydney 1996, Dwyer x; 182 pp. 0-8557-4278-X. ᴿGOTR 41/4 (1996) 402-403 (*Chryssavgis, John*).

884 **Sawyer, Deborah F.** Women and religion in the first christian centuries. Religion in the First Christian Centuries: L 1996, Routledge vii; 186 pp. £40/£13. 0-415-10748-2/-49-0 [RB 104,478].

885 *Schroer, Silvia* Abigajil—eine kluge Frau für den Frieden. Die Weisheit. 1996 <1988>, ⇒149. 90-95.

886 *Schroer, Silvia* Weise Frauen und Ratgeberinnen in Israel—Vorbilder der personifizierten Chokmah. Die Weisheit. 1996 <1991>, ⇒149. 63-79.

887 **Selvidge, Marla J.** Woman, violence, and the bible. Studies in Women & Religion 37: Lewiston, NY 1996, Mellen (8) 150 pp. 0-7734-8766-2.

888 *Troost, Arie* Elisabeth and Mary—Naomi and Ruth: gender-response criticism in Luke 1-2. A feminist companion. The feminist companion to the Bible 10: 1996, ⇒170. 159-196.

889 **Van der Toorn, Karel** From her cradle to her grave: the role of religion in the life of the Israelite and the Babylonian woman. 1994, ⇒10,1169; 11/2,1777. ᴿBArR 22/3 (1996) 9 (*Ackerman, Susan*).

B4.4 *Exegesis litteraria* — **The Bible itself as literature**

890 **Gabel, John B.; Wheeler, Charles B.; York, Anthony D.** The bible as literature: an introduction. NY ³1996, OUP xii; 330 pp. 0-19-509285-6 [NThAR 1997/2,33].

891 **Hamilton, William** A quest for the post-historical Jesus. 1994, ⇒11/2,1798. ᴿReligion 26 (1996) 385-386 (*Murphy, Tim*).

892 **Martin, Gerhard Marcel** Sachbuch Bibliodrama: Praxis und Theorie. 1995, ⇒11/2,1805. ᴿZKTh 118 (1996) 416-418 (*Meyer, Hans Bernhard*).

893 **Miles, J.** Dio: una biografia. Mi 1996, Garzanti 530 pp. L45.000 [RdT 38,286];

894 Dieu—une biographie. ᵀ*Dauzat, Emmanuel* P 1996, Laffont 462 pp. FF149. 2-221-08171-4;

895 'Gott': eine Biographie. Mü 1996, Hanser 499 pp. DM58. 3-446-17414-1. ᴿEK (1997/2) 112-113 (*Andric, Zoran*).

896 **Niditch, Susan** Oral world and written word: ancient Israelite literature. Library of Ancient Israel: LVL 1996, Westminster xi; 170 pp. $19. 0-664-21946-2.

897 **Norton, David** A history of the bible as literature I-II. 1993, ⇒9,1368...11/2,1807. ᴿEvQ 68 (1996) 364-366 (*Rosner, Brian S.*).

898 ᴱ**Olshen, Barry N.; Feldman, Yael S.** Approaches to teaching the Hebrew bible as literature in translation. 1989, ⇒7,1346. ᴿJAOS 116 (1996) 287-288 (*York, Anthony D.*).

899 *Pervo, Richard* The ancient novel becomes christian. The novel. Mn.S 159: 1996, ⇒238. 685-711.

900 *Rand, Harry* The potential of scripture's images: from Genesis to abstract expressionism. Religion and the Arts 1/3 (1996-97) 46-72 [EThL 74,161*].

901 ᴱ**Regt, Lénart J. de; Waard, J. de; Fokkelman, J.P.** Literary structure and rhetorical strategies in the Hebrew bible. Assen 1996, Van Gorcum x; 270 pp. *f*75. 90-232-2995-9.

902 ᴱ**Ryken, Leland; Longman, Tremper** A complete literary guide to the bible. 1993, ⇒9,1371; 11/2,1812. ᴿEvQ 68 (1996) 362-363 (*Rosner, Brian S.*).

903 **Tosaus Abadía, José Pedro** La biblia como literatura. El mundo de la Biblia 12: Estella 1996, Verbo Divino 283 pp. 84-8169-100-3. ᴿRET 56 (1996) 260-261 (*Barrado Fernández, P.*).

904 **Wierenga, Lambertus** De macht van de taal, de taal van de macht: over literatuurwetenschap en bijbelgebruik. Kampen 1996, Kok V 352 pp. *f*65. 90-297-1443-3 [NThAR 1997,160].

B4.5 Influxus biblicus in litteraturam profanam, *generalia*

905 ᴱ**Ebach, Jürgen; Faber, Richard** Bibel und Literatur. 1995, ⇒11/2,1823. ᴿBiKi 51 (1996) 86-87 (*Ruster, Thomas*).

906 **Garhammer, Erich** "Gebrannt und erfahren": Literaten als Bibelleser. ThGl 86 (1996) 39-48.

907 **González de Cardedal, Olegario** Cuatro poetas desde la otra ladera: UNAMUNO, JEAN PAUL, MACHADO, Oscar WILDE: prolegómenos para una cristología. M 1996, Trotta 659 pp. 84-8164-103-0 [EstB 55,365].

908 **Guandalini, Carlo** Biblicismi morfologici e sintattici nell'ebraico letterario della Rinascita. ᴰ*Zatelli, Ida.* Diss. Firenze 1996/97 [RivBib 46,3].

909 **Hansen-Löve, Aage A.** Der russische Formalismus: methodologische Rekonstruktion seiner Entwicklung aus dem Prinzip der Verfremdung. Veröffentlichungen der Kommission für Literaturwissenschaft / Österr. Akademie der Wissenschaften, Phil.-Hist. Kl. 5; Sitzungsberichte / Österr. Akad. der Wissenschaften, Phil.-Hist. Kl. 336: W 1996, Verl. d. Österr. Akad. d. Wiss. 636 pp. reissued. 3-7001-0251-8.

910 **Howlett, David** The Celtic Latin tradition of biblical style. Dublin 1996, Four Courts xix; 400 pp. £35. 1-85182-143-0 [JEH 48/3 (1997) 532].

911 **Jeffrey, David L.** People of the book: christian identity and literary culture. GR 1996, Eerdmans xx; 396 pp. £25/£17; $37/$25. 0-8028-4177-5/-7-0 [NThAR 1997,159].

912 **Kuklick, Bruce** Puritans in Babylon: the ancient Near East and American intellectual life. Princeton 1996, Princeton University Press xiii; 253 pp. $30. 0-691-02582-7. ᴿAntiquity 70 (1996) 973-974 (*Gathercole, Peter*).

913 *Langenhorst, Georg* Bibel und moderne Literatur: Perspektiven für Religionsunterricht und Religionspädagogik. rhs 39 (1996) 288-300.

914 **Muir, Lynette R.** The biblical drama of medieval Europe. 1995, ⇒11/2,1839. ᴿSCJ 27 (1996) 1109-1111 (*Glenn, Ehrstine*).

915 ᴱ**Nobel, Pierre** Poème anglo-normand sur l'Ancien Testament: édition et commentaire I: étude, notes, glossaire; II: texte et variantes. Nouvelle Bible moyen-âge: P 1996, Champion 608 + 968 pp. FF960. 2-85203-560-X [CCMéd 41,82ss—Short, Ian].

916 **Ritchie, Daniel E.** Reconstructing literature in an ideological age: biblical poetics and literary studies from MILTON to BURKE. GR 1996, Eerdmans ix; 302 pp. £20; $27. 0-8028-4140-6 [ET 108,191].

B4.6 *Singuli auctores* — **Bible-influence on individual authors**

917 **Hasel, Frank** Scripture in the theologies of W. PANNENBERG and D.G. BLOESCH: an investigation and assessment of its origin, nature and use. EHS.T 555: Fra 1996, Lang 337 pp. $58. 3-631-49264-2 [NThAR 1997,129].

918 *Neuss, Christina* HEINES Verhältnis zum Tod als Schlüssel zur Interpretation der "Lazarus"-Gedichte—sein Weg von Lazarus zu Hiob. BThZ 13 (1996) 111-132.

919 *Osten-Sacken, Peter von der* LESSINGs 'Nathan' und das Neue Testament. EvTh 56 (1996) 44-64.

920 *Rad, Gerhard von* Los diarios de Jochen KLEPPER. La acción de Dios. 1996 <1957>, ⇒144. 277-286.

921 **Rosenblatt, Jason P.** Torah and law in *Paradise Lost*. 1994, ⇒10,1239. ᴿAJSR 21 (1996) 174-176 (*Krook, Anne K.*).

B4.7 *Interpretatio* **psychiatrica**

922 **Berger, K.** Psicologia storica del Nuovo Testamento. Mi 1994, San Paolo 342 pp. ᴿRivBib 44 (1996) 371-372 (*Fabbro, Franco*).

923 **Drewermann, Eugen** Psicologia del profondo e esegesi 1: sogno, mito, fiaba, saga e legenda;

924 2: La verità delle opere e delle parole: miracolo, visione, profezia, apocalisse, storia, parabola. [T]*Danna, Carlo*. BTCon 86/87: Brescia 1996, Queriniana 494/600 pp;

925 Näher zu Gott—nah bei den Menschen: ein Gespräch mit Gwendoline Jarczyk. [T]*Stüer, Colette*. Mü 1996, Kösel 206 pp. DM36. 3-466-20410-0 [Actualidad Bibliográfica 34,56];

926 La palabra de salvación y sanación: la fuerza liberadora de la fe. [T]*Gancho, Claudio*. Barc 1996, Herder 331 pp. 84-254-1904-2 [Carthaginensia 14,246s—Tamayo Acosta, J.J.].

927 *Ellens, Harold J.* The bible and psychology, an interdisciplinary pilgrimage. PastPsy 45 (1996) 193-208 [EThL 74,168*].

928 **Farley, Edward** Deep symbols: their postmodern effacement and reclamation. Valley Forge, PA 1996 Trinity xii; 145 pp. 1-56338-185-0.

929 **Frey, Jörg** Eugen DREWERMANN und die biblische Exegese: eine methodisch-kritische Analyse. WUNT 2/71: 1995, ⇒11/2,1926. [R]Actualidad Bibliográfica 33 (1996) 33-34 (*Boada, J.*); ThLZ 121 (1996) 152-153 (*Leiner, Martin*); ZKTh 118 (1996) 270-271 (*Oberforcher, Robert*) [Mark 5,1-20; John 4,1-42; 20,1-10; 21,1-14].

930 **Klopfenstein, Martin A.** Was heißt Glauben? Versuch einer biblischen Typologie der Existenz aus Glauben, erarbeitet im Gespräch mit der Psychotherapie. Leben aus dem Wort. BEAT 40: 1996, ⇒132. 175-189.

931 **Lang, Bernhard** Die Bibel neu entdecken: DREWERMANN als Leser der Bibel. 1995, ⇒11/2,1935. [R]ThPQ 144 (1996) 319-320 (*Böhmisch, Franz*).

932 **Leiner, Martin** Psychologie und Exegese: Grundfragen einer textpsychologischen Exegese des Neuen Testaments. Gü 1995, Kaiser 349 pp. DM128. 3-579-01839-6. [R]BZ 40 (1996) 295-297 (*Klauck, Hans-Josef*).

933 *Meyer-Blank, Michael* Ursprung und Tiefe: einige religionspädagogische Anmerkungen zu Eugen DREWERMANNS Märchen- und Bibelauslegung. EvErz 48 (1996) 57-69.

934 *Raguse, Hartmut* Die Sehnsucht nach Unmittelbarkeit—eine Auseinandersetzung mit Eugen DREWERMANNS tiefenpsychologischer Bibelauslegung. ThZ 52 (1996) 54-72.

935 *Rollins, Wayne G.* The bible and psychology: new directions in biblical scholarship. PastPsy 45 (1996-97) 163-179 [EThL 74,168*].

936 **Sharkansky, Ira** Israel and its bible: a political analysis. GRL Social Sciences 1031: NY 1996, Garland xiii; 313 pp. $45. 0-8163-2021-3 [ThD 44,87].

937 *Smith, Morton* De superstitione (PLUTARCH, Moralia, 164E-171F). The New Testament [in its Hellenistic context. [E]Jónsson, Gunnlaugur A. ⇒F1.1] 1996 <1974>, 152-182.

938 **Sons, Rolf** Seelsorge zwischen Bibel und Psychotherapie. CThM.PT 24: Stu 1995, Calwer xi; 217 pp. DM48. 3-7668-3342-1. [R]ThRv 92 (1996) 430-433 (*Stollberg, Dietrich*).

939 *Stenger, Hermann M.* 53 Zeilen DREWERMANN: Analyse und Stellungnahme. ThG 39 (1996) 277-284.

940 *Süss, René* Eugen DREWERMANNS dieptepsychologische sleutel bij het 'openen der Schriften': mogelijkheden en gevaren. Analecta Bruxellensia 1 (1996) 66-87 [ZID 24,343].
941 *Wiersma, Jurjen* DREWERMANN systematisch-theologisch verkend: kanttekeningen bij angst, mens, God, kerk en bergrede. Analecta Bruxellensia 1 (1996) 48-56 [ZID 24,343].

B5 **Methodus exegetica** [⇒F2.1]

942 **Adam, A.K.M.** What is postmodern biblical criticism?. 1995, ⇒11/2,1969. ᴿCBQ 58 (1996) 740-741 (*Neufeld, Dietmar*); JBL 115 (1996) 721-722 (*Aichele, George*).
943 *Baena B., Gustavo* El método histórico-critico. Medellin 88 (1996) 19-47 [ThIK 18/2 (1997) 73].
     Barton, John Reading the Old Testament: method in biblical study. ⇒493.
944 **Braaten, Carl E.** Scripture, church, and dogma: an essay on theological method. Interp. 50 (1996) 142-155.
945 **Brouwer, Steve,** (*al*), Exporting the American gospel: global christian fundamentalism. NY 1996, Routledge viii; 344 pp. $19. 0-415-917-12-3 [ThD 44,158].
946 *Burdon, Christopher* The fathers and the birds: allegorical reading of the bible. Theol. 99 (1996) 443-452.
947 **Carson, D.A.** Exegetical fallacies. Carlisle ²1996, Paternoster 148 pp. 0-8010-2086-7.
948 ᴱ**Castelli, Elizabeth** The postmodern bible. 1995, ⇒11/2,359. ᴿJBL 115 (1996) 515-516 (*Farmer, Ronald L.*).
949 *De Jonge, H.J.* Joseph SCALIGER's historical criticism of the New Testament. NT 38 (1996) 176-193.
950 *Fishbane, Michael* Inner-biblical exegesis. Antiquity [ᴱ*Sæbø, Magne* 1996, ⇒Y1]. 33-48.
951 *Gallas, Alberto* 'Metodo storico' e 'metodo dogmatico' nel protestantesimo tedesco tra otto e novecento: sul dibattito tra HERRMANN e TROELTSCH. Sum. 8. AnScR 1 (1996) 203-218.
952 **Gargano, Innocenzo** Iniciación a la 'Lectio Divina': un itinerario para acercarse a la palabra de Dios. Biblioteca Básica del Creyente 35: M 1996, Sociedad de Educ. Atenas 125 pp. [RTLi 32/1-2,222—Kraft, Tomás].
953 *Garzya, Antonio* Appunti sulle *erotapocriseis*. Retorica. QVetChr 24: 1996, ⇒259. 45-55.
954 *Gitay, Yehoshua* Theories of literature and the question of (Hebrew) biblical theology: a prolegomenon. SJOT 10 (1996) 61-68.
955 *Hezser, Catherine* Die Verwendung der hellenistischen Gattung Chrie im frühen Christentum und Judentum. JSJ 27 (1996) 371-439.
956 **Hirshman, Marc G.** A rivalry of genius: Jewish and christian biblical interpretation in late antiquity. ᵀ*Stein, Batya.* SUNY series in Judaica: Hermeneutics, Mysticism, and Religion: Albany, NY 1996, State University of New York Press ix; 179 pp. $17. 0-7914-2727-7 [NThAR 1997,66].
957 **Johnstone, Christopher Lyle** Theory, text, context: issues in Greek rhetoric and oratory. Albany 1996, State University of New York Press 196 pp. [Rhetorica 16,227—*Pullman, George*].

958 **Jonker, Louis Cloete** Exclusivity and variety: perspectives on multi-dimensional exegesis. Contributions to Biblical Exegesis and Theology 19: Kampen 1996, Kok 408 pp. Diss. Stellenbosch. ƒ69.90. 90-390-0143-X [NThAR1997,99].

959 *Kampling, Rainer* Die Chance der Fremdheit: Anmerkungen zu einem Charakteristikum der Hl. Schrift und der historisch-kritischen Exegese. Wahrnehmung des Fremden. 1996, ⇒218. 299-316.

960 **Kennedy, G.A.** A new history of classical rhetoric. 1994, ⇒10,11187. RClR 46 (1996) 60-61 *(Too, Y.L.)*.

961 *Klement, Herbert H.* Die neueren literaturwissenschaftlichen Methoden und die Historizität des Alten Testaments. Israel in Geschichte. 1996, ⇒632. 81-101.

962 ELe **Boulluec, Alain; Patlagean, Évelyne** Les retours aux écritures: fondamentalismes présents et passés. BEHE.R 99: Louvain 1996, Peeters vi; 399 pp. 90-6831-540-4.

963 **Levenson, Jon D.** The Hebrew Bible, the OT, and historical criticism. 1993, ⇒9,1480...11/2,2014. RJThS 47 (1996) 555-560 *(Barr, James)*.

964 **Malbon, Elizabeth Struthers; McKnight, Edgar V.** The new literary criticism and the NT. JSNT.S. 109: 1994, ⇒10,139; 11/2,2017. RCBQ 58 (1996) 188-190 *(Watson, Duane F.)*.

965 *Mora P.* El método histórico-critico. Medellin 88 (1996) 19-47 [ThIK 18/2,73].

966 **Patte, Daniel** Structural exegesis for New Testament critics. Valley Forge, Pa. 1996, Trinity x; 134 pp. 1-56338-178-8.

967 *Pelikan, Jaroslav* Exegesis and hermeneutics. Reformation of the bible. 1996, ⇒730. 23-39 [AUSS 36,150—Strand, Kenneth A.].

968 *Pesce, Mauro* Scienze umane e interpretazione della bibbia: una rinnovata difesa dell'esegesi storica ed esigenza di una interpretazione teologica. StPat 43 (1996) 25-42.

969 *Raïsänen, H.* Liberating exegesis. BJRL 78/1 (1996) 193-204.

970 **Robbins, Vernon Kay** Exploring the texture of texts: a guide to socio-rhetorical interpretation. Valley Forge, PA 1996 Trinity x; 148 pp. $15. 1-56338-183-4 [NTS 43,622*].

971 *Rodríguez Carmona, Antonio* Los métodos histórico-críticos en el NT a la luz de un ejemplo: Jesús purifica un leproso (Mt 8,1-4). Sum. res. 15. MEAH 43/2 (1994) 15-48.

972 *Rutledge, David* Faithful reading: poststructuralism and the sacred. Bibl.Interp. 4 (1996) 270-287.

973 **Scharbert, Josef** Mit Gott "Deutsch reden": der Dialog zwischen Mensch und Gott in der Bibel. St. Ottilien 1996, EOS 119 pp. 3-88096-416-5.

974 *Smith, Morton* Historical method in the study of religion;

975 The present state of Old Testament studies. Studies in...method. 1996 <1968>/<1969>, ⇒150. 3-11/37-54.

976 *Sommer, Benjamin D.* Exegesis, allusion and intertextuality in the Hebrew Bible: a response to Lyle ESLINGER. VT 46 (1996) 479-489.

977 *Stipp, Hermann-Josef* 'Wenn du keine Fragen mehr stellst, kriegst du eine Eins': vom Nutzen und Frommen der Exegese. Warum denn Theologie? 1996, ⇒223. 109-132 [EThL 74,167*].

978 *Untergaßmair, Franz Georg* Bibelwissenschaft: Stand und Gegenwartsprobleme der biblischen Wissenschaften angesichts moderner

Bestreitungen der historisch-kritischen Exegese und des wachsenden Fundamentalismus inner- und außerhalb der Kirchen. BiLi 69 (1996) 139-143.
979 *Westermann, Claus* Skizze einer Formgeschichte des Alten Testaments. Das mündliche Wort. 1996, ⇒157. 9-49.
980 ᴱ**Worthington, Ian** Persuasion: Greek rhetoric in action. 1994, ⇒10,1342 [sic]. ᴿJHS 116 (1996) 198-199 (*Usher, S.*).

III. Critica Textus, Versiones

D1 Textual Criticism

981 *Albertz, Rainer* Bibelkritik als Selbst- und Kirchenkritik. Zorn. 1996, ⇒110. 24-43.
982 ᴱ**Barthélemy, Dominique** Ézéquiel, Daniel et les 12 prophètes. Critique textuelle de l'Ancien Testament 3. OBO 50/3: 1992. ⇒8,1689...11/2,2458. ᴿSef. 56 (1996) 199-204 (*Montaner, Luis Vegas*).
983 *Borse, Udo* Erwägungen zum "Urtext" und zur "Urfassung" der neutestamentlichen Geschichtsbücher. ᶠBORSE, U. SBAB 21: 1996, ⇒9. 61-94.
984 **Cox, Claude E.** Aquila, Symmachus and Theodotion in Armenia. SBL.SCSt 42: Atlanta, GA 1996, Scholars xxi; 472 pp. $50. 0-7885-0262-X.
985 *McLain, Charles E.* Variants: villainous or validating? CBTJ 12 (1996) 88-104.
986 *Ulrich, Eugene* Multiple literary editions: reflections toward a theory of the history of the biblical text. Current research...on the Dead Sea Scrolls. StTDJ 20: 1996, ⇒293. 78-105.

D2.1 *Biblia hebraica.* Hebrew text

987 **Brotzman, Ellis R.** Old Testament textual criticism: a practical introduction. 1994, ⇒10,1378; 11/2,2503. ᴿEvQ 68 (1996) 280-281 (*Brewer, David Instone*).
988 ᴱ**Disegni, Dario** Bibbia ebraica: profeti anteriori. Con traduzione e note. F 1996, La Giuntina 334 pp. L80.000 [StPat 45,197—Abbà, Maurizio].
989 **Dozio, Paolo** Fonetica e fonologia dell'ebraica tiberiense: principi per una lettura del 'materiale sonoro' della poesia biblica. R 1996, 295 pp. Diss. Antonianum; pars. publ. SBF 1997 [EThL 74,183*].
990 ᴱ**Elliger, Karl; Rudolph, Wilhelm** Biblica Hebraica Stuttgartensia. 1967-77. ⇒58s,1123...62,1925. ᴿRCB 77 (1996) 150-153 (*Merino, Luis Diez*).
991 *Fernández Tejero, Emilia* Masora or grammar revisited;
992 *Goerwitz, Richard L.* Is Tiberian segôl a phoneme?;
993 *Harviainen, Tapani* The Cairo genizot and other sources of the second Firkovich collection in St. Petersburg;
994 *Levin, Saul* The discrepancies between Moshe and Aharon BEN-ASHER;

995 *Lieberman, Abraham A.* Jedidiah Solomon NORZI and the stabilization of the textus receptus;

996 *Mashiah, Rachel* Parallel realizations of dichotomy patterns in biblical accentuation. Proceedings 12th Congress for Masoretic Studies. Masoretic studies 8: 1996, ⇒270. 11-23/155-170/25-36/49-57/37-47/59-69.

997 *Mynatt, Daniel S.* The sub loco notes in the Torah of Biblia Hebraica Stuttgartensia. BIBAL Dissertation Series 2: 1994, ⇒10,1381. RHebStud 37 (1996) 156-158 (*Cole, R. Dennis*).

998 *Ofer, Yosef* A Masoretic list of Babylonian origin of dotted words in the pentateuch. Proceedings 12th Congress for Masoretic Studies. 1996, ⇒270. 71-85.

999 *Ognibeni, Bruno* Biblia hebraica quinta: osservazioni ecdotiche. RivBib 44 (1996) 427-437.

1000 La seconde partie du sefer ʾoklah weʾoklah. Proceedings 12th Congress for Masoretic Studies. 1996, ⇒270. 87-103.

1001 *Pearl, Chaim* The bible: transmission—interpretation. JBQ 24 (1996) 74-81.

1002 **Richter, Wolfgang** Biblia Hebraica transcripta 1-3, 5 ATSAT 33, no. 1-3, 5: 1991, ⇒7,1505...10,1387. RCBQ 58 (1996) 133-135 (*Greenstein, Edward L.*).

1003 *Riepl, Christian* Satz- und Metasatzbezeichnung in BHt: Probleme, Lösungen und Änderungen. RB 103 (1996) 561-580.

1004 **Roth, Ernst; Prijs, Leo** Hebräische Handschriften 1B: Fra-Univ. 1990, ⇒7,1507. RBiOr 53 (1996) 180-181 (*Khan, Geoffrey*).

1005 *Scanlin, Harold P.* Erased gaʾyot in Codex Leningradensis. Proceedings 12th Congress for Masoretic Studies. 1996, ⇒270. 105-125.

1006 *Schenker, Adrian* Eine Neuausgabe der Biblia Hebraica. ZAH 9 (1996) 58-61.

1007 *Serfaty, Michel* Un guide massoretique de ponctuateur: les fragments TS-NS 287-21. Proceedings 12th Congress for Masoretic Studies. 1996, ⇒270. 127-153.

1008 *String, Tatiana C.* Henry VIII's illuminated 'Great Bible'. JWCI 59 (1996) 315-324.

1009 ETal, **Abraham** The Samaritan pentateuch. 1994, ⇒10,1393; 11/2,2523. RBiOr 53 (1996) 519-522 (*Crown, Alan D.*).

1010 **Tov, Emanuel** Textual criticism of the Hebrew bible. 1992, ⇒8,1761...11/2,2524. RSJTh 49 (1996) 259-260 (*Parker, D.C.*).

1011 *Tov, Emanuel* The history and significance of a standard text of the Hebrew Bible. Antiquity [ESæbø, *Magne* 1996, ⇒Y1]. 49-66.

1012 **Weil, Daniel Meir** The Masoretic chant of the Hebrew bible. J 1996, Mass 397 pp. (Eng.); 31 pp. (Heb.) [AJSR 23,112ss—Levin, Saul].

D2.2 Targum

1013 EBeattie, **D.R.G.; McNamara, M.J.** The Aramaic Bible: targums in their historical context. JSOT.S. 166: 1994, ⇒11/2,2532. RThLZ 121 (1996) 241-244 (*Bartelmus, Rüdiger*).

1014 *Cassuto, Philippe* La bible: langages d'Israël, langages des nations. FV 95/2 (1996) 107-111.

ᴱ**Cathcart, Kevin J.** Targumic and cognate studies.
ᶠMᴄɴᴀᴍᴀʀᴀ, M. ⇒58.

1015 *Díez Merino, Luis* Dos reglas de hermenéutica targúmica: traducción de topónimos y otros nombres comunes y nueva identificación. Sum. res. 19. MEAH 42/2 (1993) 19-36.

1016 *Flesher, Paul Virgil M.* The targumim. Judaism in Late Antiquity 1. 1995, ⇒11/2,376. 40-63 [Gen 34; Exod 22] [IAJS 42,15].

1017 ᴱ**Friedenthal, Ermanno** Nevi'im aharônîm: 'im targûm iṭalqî weheʿārôt [Profeti posteriori]. Tanak 3: F 1996, Giuntina 375 pp. Text hebr. und ital.; 88-8057-014-5 [NThAR 1997,99].

1018 **Glessmer, Uwe** Einleitung in die Targume zum Pentateuch. TSAJ 48: 1995, ⇒11/2,2541. ᴿJud. 52 (1996) 210-211 (*Schreiner, Stefan*).

1019 *Kasher, R.* Angelology and the supernal worlds in the Aramaic Targums to the Prophets. JSJ 27 (1996) 168-191.

1020 **Kaufman, Stephen A.; Sokoloff, Michael** A key-word-in context concordance to Targum Neofiti: a guide to the complete Palestinian Aramaic text of the torah. 1993, ⇒9,1558; 11/2,2544. ᴿHebStud 37 (1996) 202-204 (*Drazin, Israel*).

1021 **Levine, Étan** The targums: their interpretative character and their place in Jewish text tradition. Antiquity [ᴱ*Sæbø, Magne* 1996, ⇒ʏ1]. 323-331.

1022 **Margain, Jean** Les particules dans le targum samaritain de Génèse-Exode. 1993, ⇒10,1408; 11/2,2547. ᴿBiOr 53 (1996) 526-528 (*Bóid, I.R.M.*).

1023 *Somekh, Alberto* L'interpretazione ebraica della bibbia nei targumim. La lettura ebraica. 1996, ⇒205. 59-73.

ᴅ3.1 *Textus graecus—* **Greek NT**

1024 ᴱ**Aland, Barbara; Delobel, Joël** New Testament textual criticism. 1994, ⇒10,303b; 11/2,2556. ᴿEThL 72 (1996) 227-228 (*Neirynck, F.*).

1025 ᴱ**Ammassari, Antonio** Bezae Codex Cantabrigiensis: copia esatta del manoscritto onciale greco-latino dei quattro vangeli e degli Atti degli Apostoli scritto all'inizio del V secolo e presentato da Theodore Beza all'università di Cambridge nel 1581. Città del Vaticano 1996, LEV 949 pp. L95.000. 88-209-2227-4 [RB 104,468].

1026 *Amphoux, C.-B.* Le texte. Codex Bezae;

1027 *Auwers, Jean-Marie* Le texte latin des évangiles dans le Codex de Bèze;

1028 *Beatrice, P.F.* Traces du texte occidental chez le paien de Mᴀᴄᴀɪʀᴇ Mᴀɢɴᴇs;

1029 *Birdsall, J.N.* After three centuries of the study of Codex Bezae: the status quaestionis;

1030 *Callahan, A.D.* Again: the origin of the Codex Bezae. Codex Bezae. NTTS 22: 1996, ⇒265. 337-354/183-216/317-326/xix-xxx/56-64.

1031 **Chapman, Benjamin; Shogren, Gary Steven** Greek New Testament insert. Quakertown, PA ²1994 Stylus 63 pp. ᴿFaith & Mission 13/2 (1996) 112-114 (*Lanier, David E.*).

1032 *Ehrman, B.D.* The text of the gospels at the end of the second century. Codex Bezae. NTTS 22: 1996, ⇒265. 95-122.

^E**Ehrman, Bart D.**, (*al*), ^FMETZGER, B., ⇒59.

1033 **Ehrman, Bart D.** The orthodox corruption of scripture: the effects of early christological controversies on the text of the NT. 1993, ⇒9,1569...11/2,2561. ^RRSR 84 (1996) 601-604 (*Sesboüé, Bernard*).

1034 *Ellingworth, Paul* The UBS Greek New Testament, fourth revised edition: a user's response. NTS 42 (1996) 282-287.

1035 *Elliott, J.K.* Codex Bezae and the earliest Greek papyri. Codex Bezae. NTTS 22: 1996, ⇒265. 161-182.

1036 **Elliott, Keith** Manuscripts and the text of the NT: an introduction for English readers. 1995, ⇒11/2,2563. ^RBiTr 47 (1996) 352-353 (*Ellingworth, Paul*).

1037 *Emmel, Stephen* Greek biblical papyri in the Beinecke Library. ZPE 112 (1996) 289-294 [Gen 14,5-8; 14,12-15; Acts 8,26-32; 10,26-31; Eph 4,16-29.31-5,13].

1038 **Epp, Eldon Jay; Fee, Gordon D.** Studies in...NT textual criticism. 1993, ⇒9,193...11/2,2565. ^RJThS 47 (1996) 637-639 (*Birdsall, J. Neville*).

1039 *Guineau, B.; Holtz, L.; Vezin, J.* Étude comparée des tracés à l'encre bleue du ms. Lyon, B.M. 484 et du fol. 384v du Codex de Bèze;

1040 *Holmes, M.W.* Codex Bezae as a recension of the gospels;

1041 *Holtz, L.* L'écriture latine du Codex de Bèze;

1042 *Irigoin, J.* L'écriture grecque du Codex de Bèze. Codex Bezae. NTTS 22: 1996, ⇒265. 79-92/123-160/14-55/3-13.

1043 *Lovik, Gordon H.* The controversy over Greek texts. CBTJ 12 (1996) 55-87.

1044 *Marconot, J.-M.* Les marques de l'oralité dans le Codex de Bèze;

1045 *Martin, A.G.* Le palimpseste syriaque du Sinai et le Codex de Bèze;

1046 *Marucci, C.* Le comportement du Codex Bezae par rapport aux latinismes. Codex Bezae. NTTS 22: 1996, ⇒265. 65-73/248-254/296-302.

1047 **Metzger, Bruce M.** Il testo del Nuovo Testamento: trasmissione, corruzione e restituzione. Introduzione allo studio della bibbia, Suppl. 1: Brescia 1996, Paideia 289 pp. L40.000. 88-394-0537-2 [RTL 28,293].

1048 **O'Callaghan, José** Los primeros testimonios del Nuevo Testamento: papirologia neotestamentaria. 1995, ⇒11/2,2569. ^RActualidad Bibliográfica 33 (1996) 20-22 (*Puig Massana, Ramon*); Cart. 12 (1996) 480-481 (*Sanz Validvieso, R.*).

1049 *Outtier, B.* Les Prosermeneiai du Codex Bezae. Codex Bezae. NTTS 22: 1996, ⇒265. 74-78.

1050 **Panten, Kenneth E.** A history of research on Codex Bezæ, with special reference to the Acts of the Apostles: evaluation and future directions. ^D*Moore, Richard.* Diss. Murdoch 1995 [TynB 47,185ss].

1051 *Parker, D.C.* The palaeographical debate. Codex Bezae. NTTS 22: 1996, ⇒265. 329-336;

1052 Professor AMPHOUX's History of the New Testament text: a response. NTTRU 4 (1996) 41-45.

^E**Parker, D.C.**, (*al*), Codex Bezae. ⇒265;

1053 Codex Bezae: an early christian manuscript and its text. 1992, ⇒8,1792...10,1433. ^RJThS 47 (1996) 262-263 (*Delobel, Joël*).

1054 **Passioni dell'Acqua, Anna** Il testo del NT. 1994, ⇒11/2,2571.
      RAevum 70 (1996) 160-162 (*Troiani, Lucio*).
1055 *Petersen, William L.* A new testimonium to a Judaic-Christian go-
      spel fragment from a hymn of ROMANOS the Melodist. VigChr 50
      (1996) 105-116.
1056 *Pickering, Stuart R.* The "Electronic New Testament Manuscripts
      Project";
1057 A method for comparing manuscripts and variants: the Münster
      Institute system of categories;
1058 New Testament manuscripts and textual questions: a recent intro-
      duction;
1059 Piers Plowman and New Testament textual criticism. NTTRU 4
      (1996) 37-38//31-36/21-30/117-118.
1060 *Richards, W. Larry* Test passages or profiles: a comparison of two
      text-critical methods. JBL 115 (1996) 251-269.
1061 *Rouger, D.* CELSE et la tradition évangélique du Codex de Bèze.
      Codex Bezae. NTTS 22: 1996, ⇒265. 240-247.
1062 *Strothmann, Werner* Versio Harklensis-Codex D05 Cantabri-
      giensis. OrChr 80 (1996) 11-16.
      Swanson, Reuben J. New Testament Greek manuscripts. ⇒152.
1063 **Thiede, Carsten Peter; d'Ancona, Matthew** Témoin de Jésus: le
      papyrus d'Oxford et l'origine des évangiles. P 1996, Laffont 251
      pp. FF119. 2-221-08285-0. RCEv 96 (1996) 66-67 (*Cothenet, E.*).

D3.2 *Versiones graecae* — **VT, Septuaginta etc.**

1064 **Aejmelaeus, Anneli** On the trail of the Septuagint translators.
      1993, ⇒9,176; 11/2,2581. RTheol(A) 67 (1996) 907-910 (*Simotas,
      Pan.*).
1065 *Amir, Yehoshua* La letteratura giudeo-ellenistica: la versione dei
      LXX, FILONE e GIUSEPPE FLAVIO. La lettura ebraica. 1996,
      ⇒205. 31-58.
1066 **Cimosa, Mario** Guida allo studio della bibbia greca (LXX): sto-
      ria—lingua—testi. 1995, ⇒11/2,2583. RHenoch 18 (1996) 387-389
      (*Sacchi, Paolo*); Sal. 58 (1996) 739-742 (*Buzzetti, Carlo*).
1067 *Cook, Johann* Exodus 38 and Proverbs 31: a case of different order
      of verses and chapters in the Septuagint.   Studies in...Exodus.
      EVervenne, M. BEThL 126: 1996, ⇒E3.1. 537-549;
1068 Following the Septuagint translators. JNSL 22/2 (1996) 181-190.
1069 **Dogniez, Cécile** Bibliography of the Septuagint / Bibliographie de
      la Septante (1970-1993). VT.S 60: 1995, ⇒11/2,2586. RJBL 115
      (1996) 171-172 (*Bassler, Jouette M.*).
      EDorival, Gilles FHARL, M., 1995, ⇒36.
1070 *Galbiati, Enrico Rodolfo* La versione dei LXX: influsso sui Padri e
      sulla liturgia greca e latina. Sum. 6. AnScR 1 (1996) 57-70.
1071 *Haber, Heriberto* The LXX and the bible: matter for thought. JBQ
      24 (1996) 260-261.
1072 EHengel, Martin; Schwemer, Anna Maria Die Septuaginta zwi-
      schen Judentum und Christentum. WUNT 72: 1994, ⇒10,1446;
      11/2,2591. RHenoch 18 (1996) 367-369 (*Chiesa, Bruno*).
1073 *Joosten, Jan* Elaborate similes—Hebrew and Greek: a study in Sep-
      tuagint translation technique. Bib. 77 (1996) 227-236.

1074 *Montevecchi, Orsolina* La lingua dei papiri e quella della versione dei LXX: due realtà che si illuminano a vicenda. Sum. 6. AnScR 1 (1996) 71-80.

1075 **Müller, Mogens** The first bible of the church: a plea for the Septuagint. JSOT.S 206: Copenhagen International Seminar 1: Shf 1996, Academic 163 pp. £25; $37. 1-85075-571-X.

1076 *Olofsson, Staffan* The Septuagint and earlier Jewish interpretative tradition—especially as reflected in the targums;

1077 Studying the word order of the Septuagint: questions and possibilities. SJOT 10 (1996) 197-216/217-237.

1078 *Passoni Dell'Acqua, Anna* I LXX: punti d'arrivo e di partenza per diversi ambiti di ricerca. Sum. 5. AnScR 1 (1996) 17-31;

1079 La versione dei LXX testimonianza di istituzioni tolemaiche documentate nei papiri. Conv. di Egittologia e Papirologia. 1996, ⇒282. 193-197.

1080 **Salvesen, Alison** SYMMACHUS in the pentateuch. JSSt.M 15: 1991, ⇒7,1551...10,1454. ᴿEstB 54 (1996) 123-124 (*Trebolle, J.*); BiOr 53 (1996) 800-801 (*Van der Kooij, Arie*).

1081 *Sipilä, Seppo* The Tetrapla—is it all Greek to us?. SJOT 10 (1996) 169-182.

1082 **Sollamo, Raija** Repetition of the possessive pronouns in the Septuagint. SBL.SCS 40: 1995, ⇒11/2,2600. ᴿCBQ 58 (1996) 727-728 (*Cox, Claude*); EThL 72 (1996) 212-214 (*Lust, J.*).

1083 *Sollamo, Raija* The origins of LXX studies in Finland. SJOT 10 (1996) 159-168.

1084 **Veltri, Giuseppe** Eine Tora für den König Talmai. 1994, Diss., ⇒10,1458; 11/2,2602. ᴿRCatT 21 (1996) 249-250 (*Raurell, Frederic*); Henoch 18 (1996) 369-370 (*Chiesa, Bruno*).

1085 *Voitila, Anssi* What the translation of tenses tells about the Septuagint translators. SJOT 10 (1996) 183-196.

1086 *Wasserstein, Abraham* On donkeys, wine and the uses of textual criticism: Septuagintal variants in Jewish Palestine. ᶠSTERN, M., ⇒87. 119*-142*.

1087 *Wevers, John William* The interpretative character and significance of the Septuagint version. Antiquity [ᴱSæbø, Magne 1996 ⇒Y1]. 84-107.

D4 **Versiones orientales**

1088 *Boud'hors, Anne; Nakano, C.; Werner, P.* Fragments coptes de l'Ancien Testament au Musée du Louvre. Muséon 109 (1996) 17-58.

1089 *Joosten, Jan* La Peshitta de l'Ancien Testament dans la recherche récente. RHPhR 76 (1996) 385-395.

1090 **Kiraz, George Anton** Comparative edition of the Syriac gospels, aligning the Sinaiticus, Curetonianus, Peshîttâ & Harklean versions. NTTS 21,1-4: Lei 1996, Brill 4 vols. 90-04-10419-4.

1091 *Metzger, Bruce M.* Bible hype: the saga of the Yonan Codex. BiRe 12/6 (1996) 26-30, 56.

1092 *Pickering, Stuart R.* The importance of the Diatessaron for reconstructing the text of the New Testament;

1093 Old Georgian evidence for the New Testament text;

1094 Works and manuscripts attesting readings of the Diatessaron. NTTRU 4 (1996) 1-7/93-98/8-18.
1095 *Polliack, Meira* Medieval Karaite views on translating the Hebrew bible into Arabic. JJS 47 (1996) 64-84.
1096 *Weitzman, Michael* The interpretative character of the Syriac Old Testament. Antiquity [ᴱ*Sæbø, Magne* 1996 ⇒ɤ1]. 587-611.

D5.0 Versiones latinae

1097 *Bogaert, Pierre-Maurice* Bulletin de la Bible latine: VII: deuxième série. RBen 106 (1996) 386-412.
1098 *Brown Tkacz, Catherine* Labor tam utilis: the creation of the Vulgate. VigChr 50 (1996) 42-72.
1099 ᴱ**Frede, Hermann Josef** Vetus Latina-Fragmente zum Alten Testament: die pelagianische Epistula ad quandam matronam Christianam. AGLB 28: FrB 1996, Herder 229 pp. 3-451-21937-9.
1100 ᴱ**Gameson, Richard** The early medieval bible: its production, decoration, and use. 1994, ⇒10,1482; 11/2,2637. ᴿJEarlyC 4 (1996) 257-258 (*Cahill, Michael*).
1101 **Gibson, Margaret T.** The bible in the Latin West. 1993, ⇒10,1483. ᴿNT 38 (1996) 86-87 (*Parker, D.C.*).
1102 *Haelewyck, Jean-Claude* Les premières versions latines de la bible. Les premières traditions. 1996, ⇒159. 122-136.
1103 **Marsden, Richard** The text of the Old Testament in Anglo-Saxon England. CSASE 15: 1995, ⇒11/2,2645. ᴿRHE 91 (1996) 537-538 (*Bogaert, P.-M.*).
1104 *Reynolds, Roger E.* Visigothic-script remains of a pandect Bible and the Collectio Canonum Hispana in Lucca. MS 58 (1996) 305-311.
1105 *Rickert, Franz* Beobachtungen an den Quedlinburger Itala-Fragmenten. ᶠDassmann, E., JAc.E 23: 1996, ⇒19. 575-581.
1106 ᴱ**Sánchez-Prieto Borja, Pedro; Horcajada Diezma, Bautista** Libros de Salomón: Cantar de los Cantares, Proverbios, Sabiduría y Eclesiastés. Alfonso el Sabio: general estoria, part 3. BiRoHi.T 23: M 1993, Gredos 413 pp. ᴿCBQ 58 (1996) 306-307 (*Lavoie, Jean-Jacques*).
1107 Tobie, Judith, Esther. BVLI 40 (1996) 20-21.
1108 Travaux du Centre de recherches sur la bible latine [Hieronymus, Jesajabuch]. BVLI 40 (1996) 19-20.
1109 Vetus Latina: Arbeitsbericht der Stiftung. Vetus Latina. Bericht des Instituts 29: FrB 1996, 32 pp.
1110 Vier neue Bände in der Reihe "Aus der Geschichte der lateinischen Bibel" [Hieronymus, Jesajabuch, Origenes]. BVLI 40 (1996) 13-17.
1111 Zuwuchs zur Vetus Latina-Edition: 480 Seiten in 5 Lieferungen [Rom, Song, 1 Cor, Sir, Isa]. BVLI 40 (1996) 11-13.

D5.5 *Citationes apud Patres* — the Patristic Bible

1112 *García de la Fuente, Olegario* Latín bíblico y latín cristiano. RechAug 29 (1996) 25-41.

1113 Biblia patristica: index des citations et allusions bibliques dans la littérature patristique 6: HILAIRE de Poitiers, AMBRIISE de Milan, AMBROSIASTER. P 1995, CNRS 374 pp. 2-271-05326-9. [R]RHE 91 (1996) 465-473 (*Gryson, R.*).

D6 Versiones modernae .1 *romanicae*, romance

1114 **Alonso Schökel, Luis** Nuevo Testamento. Biblia del peregrino 3. Estella 1996, Verbo Divino 670 pp. Edición de estudio. 84-8169-089-9. [R]RET 56 (1996) 405-406 (*Barrado Fernández, P.*).

1115 *Cuomo, Luisa* Traduzioni bibliche giudeo-italiane ed umanistiche. ZRP 111/2 (1995) 206-243 [IAJS 42,17].

1116 [E]**Disegni, Dario** Bibbia ebraica: profeti anteriori. 334 pp. L80.000;

1117 Profeti posteriori. Con traduzione e note. F 1996, La Giuntina 376 pp. L88.000 [StPat 45,197—Abbà, Maurizio].

1118 La bibbia. [E]**Pacomio, Luciano**; collab. *Dalla Vecchia, Flavio; Pitta, Antonio*. CasM 1995, Piemme 3392 pp. Dir. AT: F. Dalla Vecchia; dir. NT: A. Pitta. [R]PaVi 41/2 (1996) 54-56 (*Marocco, Giuseppe*).

1119 [T]**Hurault, Bernard; Hurault, Louis; Van der Meersch, Jean** La bible des communautés chrétiennes. 1994, ⟹10,1504. [R]FV 95/5 (1996) 47-69 (*Macina, M.R.*).

1120 [E]**Lazar, Moshe** Biblia de Ferrara. M 1996, Biblioteca Castro xxvii; 1303 pp. 84-7506-461-2.

1121 **Péter-Contesse, René** La révision de la bible en français courant. CahTrB 25 (1996) 15-20.

1122 *Rodríguez, Isidoro* Traducciones bíblicas españolas deficientes (Dan 3,57-88, 56 [sic]; Jn 1,1). Helmantica 139-141 (1995) 201-264 [IAJS 42,18].

[E]**Sánchez-Prieto Borja, Pedro**, (*al*), Libros de Salomón. ⟹1106.

1123 La sacra bibbia: nuova riveduta sui testi originali. Genève 1994, Società biblica di Ginevra xiv; 1282 pp. [R]Protest. 51 (1996) 296-297 (*Soggin, J.A.*).

1124 Sagrada Biblia. Pamplona [4]1986-1996. Trad. y anot. por Prof. de la Fac. de Teol. de la Univ. de Navarra. Ed. Univ. de Navarra 12 vols. 84-313-0433-2.

D6.2 *Versiones anglicae* — English Bible Translations

1125 *Banz, Clint* A seventeenth century English bible controversy. CBTJ 12 (1996) 116-134.

1126 **Barker, Kenneth Lee** The accuracy of the NIV. GR 1996, Baker 126 pp. 0-8010-5639-X.

1127 *Carroll, Robert P.* He-bibles and she-bibles: reflections on the violence done to texts by productions of English translations of the bible. Bibl.Interp. 4 (1996) 257-269.

1128 [E]**Daniell, David** TYNDALE's New Testament, translated by William Tyndale: a modern-spelling edition of the 1534 edition. NHv 1995, Yale University Press xxxvi; 429 pp. Bibl. $15. 0-300-06580-9. [R]SCJ 27 (1996) 1236-1237 (*Werrell, Ralph S.*).

1129 **France, Richard Thomas** Translating the bible: choosing and using an English version. With an additional chapter by Philip Jenson. C 1996, Grove 24 pp. £2. 1-85174-338-3 [BiTr 49,352— Ellingworth, Paul].

1130 [E]**Gillquist, Peter E.** The Orthodox Study Bible: New Testament and Psalms. Nv 1993, Nelson xii; 1054 pp. $25. 0-8407-8391-4. [R]CTJ 31 (1996) 218-220 (*Payton, James B.*).

1131 [E]**Gold, Victor R.**, (*al*), The NT and Psalms: an inclusive version. 1995, ⇒11/2,2684. [R]CritRR 9 (1996) 215-217 (*Ehrman, Bart D.*); CThMi 23 (1996) 291-295 (*Linss, Wilhelm C.*).

1132 *Ham, Young Y.* A linguistic study of biblical English with special reference to the King James Bible (1611). Chongshin Review 1 (1996) 149-184.

1133 *LaGrand, James* Proliferation of the "gentile" in the New Revised Standard Version. BR 41 (1996) 77-87.

1134 *Lindström, Bengt* Notes on the Middle English 'Genesis and Exodus'. NPM 96/1 (1995) 67-79 [IAJS 42,17].

1135 **Milton, Ralph** The family story bible. Ill. *Kyle, Margaret.* LVL 1996, Westminster 289 pp. $19 [BiTod 36,261—Bergant, Dianne].

1136 [T]**Murphy, Conor** The New Testament. The African Bible. 1995, ⇒11/2,2692. [R]Ter. 47 (1996) 690-691 (*Tauro, Joe*).

1137 The new Oxford annotated bible with the Apocrypha. Oxf 1995, OUP Electronic edition, version 1.0 for MS Windows. $80. [R]SJTh 49 (1996) 118-119 (*Good, Deirdre*).

1138 [E]**Poling, Judson** The journey: a bible for seeking God & understanding life: New International Version. Notes. GR 1996, Zondervan xxi; 1706 pp. 0-310-91949-5 [NThAR 1997,191].

1139 **Remley, Paul G.** Old English biblical verse: studies in Genesis, Exodus and Daniel. CSASE 16: C 1996, CUP xvii; 476 pp. $75. 0-521-47454-X.

1140 *Smith, Abraham* The productive role of English bible translators. Semeia 76 (1996) 55-68.

D6.3 *Versiones germanicae* — **Deutsche Bibelübersetzungen**

1141 *Das Alte Testament: 3. Jesaja—Jeremia—Ezechiel.* Neuhausen-Stu 1996, Hänssler xvi; 1167 pp. 3-7751-1275-8.

1142 *Bubenheimer, Ulrich* Eine unechte Lutherreliquie in der Württembergischen Landesbibliothek Stuttgart. "Was Christum treibet". Bibel im Gespräch 4: 1996, ⇒1149. 140-144.

1143 *Die Evangelien nach Matthäus, Markus, Lukas, Johannes: die Psalmen.* Zürcher Bibel. Z 1996, Zürcher Bibel 303 pp. 3-85995-221-8.

1144 *Fricke, Klaus Dietrich* "Dem Volk aufs Maul sehen": Bemerkungen zu LUTHERS Verdeutschungsgrundsätzen. "Was Christum treibet". Bibel im Gespräch 4: 1996 <1978>, ⇒1149. 24-37.

1145 **Harjung, J. Dominik** Die genaueste und zuverlässigste deutsche Bibel: woran erkennt man eine gute Bibelübersetzung?. Schwengeler-Sachbuch 379: Berneck 1996, Schwengeler 415 pp. 3-85666-379-7 [NThAR 1999,1].

1146 *Haubrichs, Wolfgang* Die Sprache Martin LUTHERS. "Was Christum treibet". Bibel im Gespräch 4: 1996 <1983>, ⇒1149. 52-69.

1147 ᴱLicharz, Werner; Schoneveld, Jacobus Neu auf die Bibel hören: die Bibelverdeutschung von Buber/Rosenzweig: heute. Gerlingen 1996, Bleicher 184 pp. DM22. 3-7953-0935-2 [KuI 12/1,93].

1148 *Lohse, Eduard* Martin Luthers Übersetzung der Bibel: Sprache, Theologie und Schriftverständnis. "Was Christum treibet". Bibel im Gespräch 4: 1996 <1983>, ⇒1149. 38-51.

1149 ᴱMeurer, Siegfried 'Was Christum treibet': Martin Luther und seine Bibelübersetzung. Jahrbuch der Deutschen Bibelgesellschaft. Bibel im Gespräch 4: Stu 1996, Deutsche Bibelgesellschaft. 3-438-06225-9 [NThAR 1997,66].

1150 *Schat, Andrea* 'Nicht gegen die Tradition': die Entstehung einer Pentateuch-Übersetzung aus dem Streit zwischen Orthodoxie und Reform. FJB 22 (1995) 77-103 [IAJS 42,18].

1151 *Schloemann, Martin* Die zwei Wörter: Luthers Notabene zur "Mitte der Schrift". "Was Christum treibet". Bibel im Gespräch 4: 1996 <1994>, ⇒1149. 89-99.

1152 *Schreiber, Hannes* Ökumenische Bibelausgaben und deren Verwendung in der Liturgie und kirchlichem Leben in Mitteleuropa. BiLi 69 (1996) 97-100.

1153 ᴱSplett, Jochen Das Bremer Evangelistar. Collab. *Brockelmann, Marion; Kerstan, Andreas*. QFSKG 110: B 1996, De Gruyter. DM232. 3-110-14548-0.

1154 ᴱSteurer, Rita Maria Jesaja, Jeremia, Ezechiel. Das Alte Testament: Interlinearübersetzung Hebräisch-Deutsch und Transkription des hebräischen Grundtextes nach der Biblia Hebraica Stuttgartensia 3. Neuhausen-Stu ²1996, Hänssler xvi; 1167 pp. 3-7751-1275-8.

1155 **Strohm, Stefan** Deutsche Bibeldrucke 1601-1800. 1993, ⇒10,1532. ᴿLutherjahrbuch 63 (1996) 140-141 (*Junghans, Helmar*).

1156 *Tschirch, Fritz* Luthers Septembertestament: eine Wende in der Übersetzung der Bibel ins Deutsche. "Was Christum treibet". Bibel im Gespräch 4: 1996 <1973>, ⇒1149. 11-23.

1157 *Wagner, Andreas* Von splittenden 'Superintendenten', geschlechtsneutralen 'Gemeindegliedern' und integrativen 'HebräerInnen': zur Gleichbehandlung von Frauen und Männern im Deutschen der Gegenwart und in Bibelübersetzungen. EvTh 56 (1996) 214-239.

1158 ᴱWetzel, Christoph Die Bibel: Stuttgarter Bibel der Buchmalerei: die Einheitsübersetzung mit Meisterwerken mittelalterlicher Buchkunst. Stu 1996, Belser 1392 pp. Bildauswahl, Bilderläuterungen und Register: Christoph Wetzel mit Hieke Drechsler. ÖS2.200. 3-460-32046-X. ᴿZKTh 118 (1996) 543-544 (*Meyer, Hans Bernhard*).

D6.4 **Versiones nordicae** *et variae*

1159 **Bakker, Hette Popke S.** Towards a critical edition of the old Slavic New Testament; a transparent and heuristic approach. Diss. 1996, Amsterdam xii; 188 pp. [NThAR 1997,162].

1160 *Balabán, Milan* Der Kralitzer Kurzkommentar zum Hohenlied: zur theologischen Bedeutung der Kralitzer Bibel—Anmerkungen. Kralitzer Bibel. 1995, ⇒1170. 243-269 [IAJS 42,xxxvi].

1161 *Bohatcová, Mirjam* Die tschechischen gedruckten Bibeln des 15. bis 18. Jahrhunderts. Kralitzer Bibel. 1995, ⇒1170. 1-182 [IAJS 42,17].

1162 **Ejrnæs, Bodil** Skriftsynet igennem den danske bibels historie. Forum for bibelsk eksegese 6: Köbenhamm 1995, Museum Tusculanum 270 pp. ᴿSEÅ 61 (1996) 132-133 (*Åsberg, Christer*).

1163 *Gimbatov, Magomed-Kamil; Testelets, Yakov* Translating the New Testament into the Avar language. BiTr 47 (1996) 434-443.

1164 *Heller, Jan* Die Theologie der Kralitzer Bibel und ihre Erforschung in den letzten zwei Jahrhunderten. Kralitzer Bibel. 1995, ⇒1170. 215-242 [IAJS 42,17].

1165 *Hong, Joseph* Translating and revising *Today's Khmer New Testament*. BiTr 47 (1996) 233-239.

1166 *Kang, Wi J.* Introduction, translation and application of the bible in Korean history. JAAAT 1/1 (1996) 47-62 [ZID 23,445].

1167 ᴱ**Kocijančič, Gorazd** Biblije na Slovenskem. Ljubljana 1996, NUK 230 pp. 19.9.1996-2.1.1997 Narodna Galerija, Ljubljana; num. ill. 961-6162-11-X [NThAR 1998,365].

1168 **Koole, J.A.** Het Oude Testament in de NBG-vertaling 1951: ontstaansgeschiedenis, receptie en revisie van een Nederlandse vertaling van het Oude Testament. Haarlem 1996, Nederlands Bijbelgenootschap 235 pp. ƒ42.90. 90-6126-726-9 [Streven 64,569].

1169 *Michálek, Emanuel* Philologischer Kommentar zu der sechsteiligen Kralitzer Bibel. Kralitzer Bibel. 1995, ⇒1170. 183-214 [IAJS 42,18].

1170 ᴱ**Rothe, Hans; Scholz, Friedrich** Kralitzer Bibel—Kralická Bible. Pd 1995, Schöningh.

1171 *Safran, Gabriella* Love songs between the sacred and the vernacular: PUSHKIN's 'Podrazhaniia' in the context of bible translation. Slavic and East European Journal 39/2 (1995) 165-183 [IAJS 42,18].

1172 **Sun, Xiao-Ping** Dao für Logos: ein evangeliumsgemäßes Äquivalent?: eine Untersuchung der Inkulturationsprobleme des Christentums bei der Bibelübersetzung in China am Beispiel der Übersetzung des Logosbegriffs im Johannesprolog in der chinesischen Unionsübersetzung (1890-1919). Diss. Hamburg 1996, ᴰ*Ahrens, T.*, 374 pp. [EThL 74,278*].

1173 *Timm, Erika* Forme di trasmissione della bibbia nello yiddish antico: a proposito degli studi yiddish negli ultimi settanta anni. ᵀ*Mantovan, Daniela.* RasIsr 62/1-2 (1996) 19-44.

1174 **Van Capelleveen, Jan J.** Het woord gaat zijn weg: een geschiedenis van bijbelvertalen en van de invloed van bijbelvertalingen op de samenleving. Haarlem 1996, Vlaams Bijbelgenootschap 362 pp. ƒ54.90. 90-6126-916-4 [Streven 64,570].

1175 ᵀ**Warren, Hans; Molegraaf, Mario** Het evangelie volgens Markus, Mattheus, Lukas en Johannes. Amst 1996, Prometheus 256 pp. ƒ39.90. 90-5333-444-0 [Interpretatie 5/7,32].

1176 *Wendland, E.R.* A review of "relevance theory" in relation to bible translation in south-central Africa. JNSL 22/1 (1996) 91-106.

1177 ᵀ**Wujek, Jakub** Ewangelia wedlug Lukasza. Poznan 1996, Kapitula Kolegiacka w Poznaniu xxii; 85 pp. w przekladzie ksiedza Ja-

kuba Wujka z roku 1593, z ilustracjami Grzegorza Bednarskiego. 83-904881-4-0. **P.**
1178 *Yilibuw, Dolores* Tampering with bible translation in Yap. Semeia 76 (1996) 21-38.

D7 *Problemata vertentis* — Bible translation technniques

1179 *Babut, Jean-Marc* Déchiffer et traduire les expressions idiomatiques. CahTrB 25 (1996) 8-14.
1180 ᴱ**Bailey, Randall C.** Race, class, and the politics of biblical translation. Semeia 76: Atlanta 1996, Scholars 169 pp. [NThAR 1998,268].
1181 *Bailey, Randall C.* "They shall become as white as snow": when bad is turned into good. Semeia 76 (1996) 99-113 [Isa 1,18];
1182 *Bailey, Randall C.; Pippin, Tina* Race, class, and the politics of bible translation: introduction. Semeia 76 (1996) 1-7.
1183 *Bammer, Angelika* On being faithful and disloyal. Semeia 76 (1996) 135-146.
1184 **Buber, Martin; Rosenzweig, Franz** Scripture and translation. 1994, ⇒10,1540...11/2,2718. ᴿCritRR 9 (1996) 396-397 (*Rumscheidt, Martin*).
1185 *Burggraff, David L.* Paradigm shift: translations in transition: we've been here before. CBTJ 12 (1996) 105-115.
1186 *Caroll, Robert P.* Cultural encroachment and bible translation: observations on elements of violence, race and class in the production of bibles in translation. Semeia 76 (1996) 39-53.
1187 *Clark, David J.* Vocative displacement in the gospels: lexico-syntactic and sociolinguistic influences. BiTr 47 (1996) 313-321.
1188 *Ettien, Koffi Nda* Translating the term 'but'—unsuspected challenges. BiTr 47 (1996) 218-226.
1189 *Fite, Frances* Translating for the guy with the Gideon Bible. Semeia 76 (1996) 119-121.
1190 *Greenstein, Edward L.* On the ethics of translation: a response. Semeia 76 (1996) 127-134.
1191 *Gross, Carl D.* Translation by omission. BiTr 47 (1996) 211-217.
1192 *Handy, Lowell K.* One problem involved in translating to meaning: an example of acknowledging time and tradition. SJOT 10 (1996) 16-27 [Ps 82].
1193 *Hermanson, Eric A.* Recognising Hebrew metaphors: conceptual metaphor theory and bible translation. JNSL 22/2 (1996) 67-78.
1194 *Kinukawa, Hisako* The politics of race and class in bible translation: a response. Semeia 76 (1996) 123-125.
1195 **Kuen, Alfred** Une bible...et tant de versions!. Saint-Legier 1996, Emmaüs 206 pp. 2-8287-0056-9 [NThAR 1997,159].
1196 *Lim, Seung-Phil* Entwurf der Transskription von biblischen Eigennamen. Samok 212 (1996) 71-82 [ThIK 18/2 (1997) 54]. **K.**
1197 *Lincoln, Lucy* Translating Hebrew and Greek terms for sheep and goats. BiTr 47 (1996) 322-335.
1198 *McClenney-Sadler, Madeline* Retroubling biblical waters. Semeia 76 (1996) 115-118.
1199 *Mitchell, William* Sacred scripture in early colonial Peru: rationale, translation and use. BiTr 47 (1996) 301-313.

1200 *Newman, Barclay M.* Grace under pressure to be understood;
1201 A message in terms that most people can understand. BiTr 47 (1996) 401-407/201-207.
1202 *Noss, Philip A.* The stain of blood. BiTr 47 (1996) 139-141.
1203 *Omanson, Roger L.* Translation as communication. BiTr 47 (1996) 407-413.
1204 **Ortega Arjonilla, Emilio** Apuntes para una teoría hermenéutica de la traducción. Málaga 1996, Universidad de Málaga 177 pp. Bibl. 84-7496-590-X.
1205 *Ortiz V., Pedro* Translating terms of measurement. ᵀ*Omanson, Roger L.*, BiTr 47 (1996) 413-419.
1206 *Pagán, Samuel* Poor amd poverty: social distance and bible translation. Semeia 76 (1996) 69-79.
1207 *Phillips, Gary A.* Translation: postmodern passage to ethical fragments. Semeia 76 (1996) 147-158.
1208 *Pippin, Tina; Vaughan, Cynthia V.* Readings in translation theory and practice: a bibliography. Semeia 76 (1996) 159-169.
1209 *Pope, Kathrin* Les propositions subordonnées en *waama*: comment leur utilisation affecte-t-elle la traduction?. CahTrB 26 (1996) 3-11.
1210 *Regt, Leendert J. de* Domains of Biblical Hebrew discourse as a translation problem. JOTT 8 (1996) 50-72.
1211 *Ross, L. Ronald* Brief note on form and meaning. BiTr 47 (1996) 137-138.
1212 *Schneider, Théo* Contenu et contenant: un essai d'équivalence fonctionnelle. CahTrB 26 (1996) 12-20.
1213 *Smit, D.J.* "Pidgin or pentecost"?: on translation and transformation. Scriptura 57 (1996) 305-328.
1214 *Soesilo, Daud H.* Sir, teacher, master, lord. BiTr 47 (1996) 335-340.
1215 *Sugirtharajah, R.S.* Textual cleansing: a move from the colonial to the postcolonial version. Semeia 76 (1996) 7-20.
1216 *Thomas, Kenneth J.* Study bibles for religious audiences. BiTr 47 (1996) 207-211.
1217 **Venuti, Lawrence** The translator's invisibility: a history of translation. NY 1995, Routledge 353 pp. $19 [BiTr 49,148ss—Wilt, Timothy].
1218 *Wendland, Ernst R.* On the relevance of 'relevance theory' for bible translation. BiTr 47 (1996) 126-137.
1219 *Wilson, W.A. André* A question of standing. BiTr 47 (1996) 346-351.

D8 *Concordantiae*—Synopses

1220 **Goodrick, Edward W.; Kohlenberger, John R.** The NIV exhaustive concordance. 1990, ⇒8,1934. ᴿNT 38 (1996) 304-306 (*Elliott, J.K.*).
1221 **Kohlenberger, John R.; Goodrick, Edward W.; Swanson, James A.** The exhaustive concordance to the Greek New Testament. 1995, ⇒11/2,2743. ᴿNT 38 (1996) 307-309 (*Elliott, J.K.*).
1222 **Schierse, Franz Josef** Neue Konkordanz zur Einheitsübersetzung der Bibel. Dü 1996, Patmos 2048 pp. 3-491-71106-1 [NThAR 1997,130].

1223   *Valdes, Jorge L.* Reclaiming the lost tradition: JIMENEZ and the
       Complutensian Polyglot. ProcGLM 16 (1996) 59-71 [EThL
       74,160*].
1224   **Wigram, George V.; Strong, James**   The Englishman's Greek
       concordance of the New Testament: coded with the numbering sy-
       stem from STRONG's *Exhaustive concordance of the bible.*
       Peabody 1996, Hendrickson xxxix; 1021 pp. 1-56563-207-9.

IV. Exegesis generalis VT vel cum NT

D9 Commentaries on the whole Bible or OT

1225   *Best, Ernest* The reading and writing of commentaries. ET 107
       (1996) 358-362.
1226   **Currie, James Daniel** Bread and the recipe: a prescription for
       seeing and hearing the hidden word of God as seen by the blind and
       heard by the deaf. Valley Forge 1996, Trinity xix; 588 pp. $25
       [CBQ 59,818].
1227   ᴱ**Felder, Cain H.** The original African heritage study bible: King
       James version with special annotations relative to the Afri-
       can/Edenic perspective. Nv 1996, Winston 1893 pp. 1-55523-674-
       X [NThAR 1997,65].
1228   ᴱ**Fiorenza, Elisabeth Schüssler** A feminist commentary. Searching
       the Scriptures 2: 1994, ⇒10,1166; 11/2,2760. ᴿBTB 26 (1996) 58-
       59 (*Lillie, Betty Jane*); Horizons 23 (1996) 332-333 (*Laffey, Alice
       L.*); JES 33 (1996) 589-590 (*Reumann, John*); ScrB 26 (1996) 43-
       44 (*Grey, Mary*); CBQ 58 (1996) 578-580 (*Gillman, Florence
       Morgan*).
1229   ᴱ**Keck, Leander E.** NIntB 4: the first book of Maccabees, the se-
       cond book of Maccabees, introduction to Hebrew poetry, the book
       of Job, the book of Psalms. Nv 1996, Abingdon xviii; 1287 pp.
       $65. 0-687-27817-1.
1230   *McEvenue, Sean* Commentaire biblique: un genre littéraire spécial.
       BEAT 28: IOSOT 1992. 1996, ⇒160. 131-134.
1231   ᴱ**Mills, Watson B.; Wilson, Richard F.** Mercer commentary on
       the bible. 1994, ⇒10,1573; 11/2,2756. ᴿInterp. 50 (1996) 412,
       414, 416 (*Ramsay, William M.*).
1232   ᴱ**Newsom, Carol A.; Ringe, Charon H.** Da Genesi a Neemia. La
       bibbia delle donne: un commentario 1. T 1996, Claudiana 248 pp.
       L30.000. ᴿItin. 4/7 (1996) 235-236 (*Varagona, Francesco*).
1233   ᴱ**Tukker, C.A.** 1 Kronieken-Hooglied van Salomo. De kantteke-
       ningen van het Oude en Nieuwe Testament 2. Utrecht 1996, De
       Banier 726 pp. 90-336-0346-2 [NThAR 1997,130].

V. Libri historici VT

E1.1 Pentateuchus, Torah *Textus, commentarii*

1234   **Blenkinsopp, Joseph** The pentateuch. AnchorBRef: 1992,
       ⇒8,1952...10,1579. ᴿCBQ 58 (1996) 100-102 (*Ska, Jean Louis*);
       ThR 61 (1996) 332-337 (*Otto, Eckart*).

1235 **Boorer, Suzanne** The promise of the land as oath: a key to the formation of the Pentateuch. BZAW 205: 1992, ⇒9,1729...11/1,141. ᴿBZ 40 (1996) 109-110 (*Scharbert, Josef*); ThLZ 121 (1996) 433-435 (*Kreuzer, Siegfried*).

1236 *Breuer, Mordechai* Il commento al Pentateuco di Samson Raphael HIRSCH. La lettura ebraica. 1996, ⇒205. 381-400.

1237 **Crüsemann, Frank** Die Tora. 1992, ⇒8,229...11/1,143. ᴿBZ 40 (1996) 116-119 (*Grünwaldt, Klaus*); EvTh 56/1 (1996) 83-92 (*Janowski, Bernd*).

1238 *Dorival, Gilles* 'Dire en grec les choses juives': quelques choix lexicaux du pentateuque de la Septante. REG 109 (1996) 527-547.

1239 Le pentateuque grec de la Septante. Les premières traditions. 1996, ⇒159. 104-119.

1240 ᵀ**Fox, Everett** The five books of Moses...a new translation with introduction, commentary, and notes. The Schocken Bible 1: 1995, ⇒11/1,144. ᴿBiRe 12/5 (1996) 10, 14 (*Propp, William H.C.*).

1241 **Frankel, Ellen** The five books of Miriam: a woman's commentary on the Torah. NY 1996, Grosset xxv; (2) 354 pp. 0-399-14195-2.

1242 ᴱ**Gorenberg, Gershon** Seventy facets: a commentary on the torah: from the pages of the Jerusalem report. Northvale 1996, Aronson xvii; 309 pp. 1-56821-904-0 [NThAR 1997,162].

1243 *Gorman, Michael* The commentary on the pentateuch attributed to BEDE in PL 91.189-394. RBen 106 (1996) 61-108, 255-307.

1244 *Harl, Marguerite* Problèmes de traduction du pentateuque de la Septante dans une lange moderne. Sum. 5. AnScR 1 (1996) 33-56.

1245 ᴱ**Haudebert, P.** Le pentateuque. 1992, ⇒8,474...11/1,146. ᴿGr. 77 (1996) 149-152 (*Prato, Gian Luigi*).

1246 ᴱ**Keck, Leander E.**, (*al*), General and Old Testament articles: Genesis, Exodus, Leviticus. NIntB 1. 1994, ⇒10,1575; 11/1,147. ᴿInterp. 50 (1996) 297-299 (*Lemke, Werner E.*); ET 108 (1996-97) 97-98 (*Rodd, C.S.*); CBQ 58 (1996) 326-327 (*Boadt, Lawrence*).

1247 ᴱᵀ**Langermann, Yitzhak Tzvi** Yemenite midrash: philosophical commentaries on Torah. Sacred Literature: SF 1996, HarperSanFrancisco xxx; (2) 351 pp. 0-06-065391-4.

1248 *Margain, Jean* Les Samaritains et le texte du pentateuque. Les premières traditions. 1996, ⇒159. 58-64.

1249 ᵀ**Munk, Eliyahu** Rabbi Chayim ben ATTAR: Or hachayim: commentary on the Torah. J 1995, Munk 5 vols. Bibl.

1250 ᴱ**Nodet, Étienne** Le pentateuque. La bible de Josephe 1. Josèphe et son temps 1,1: P 1996, Cerf 240 pp. FF150. 2-204-05394-5. ᴿNRTh 118 (1996) 911 (*Ska, Jean Louis*).

1251 **Oussoren, Pieter** De stem uit het vuur: de eerste vijf bijbelboeken naar het Hebreeuws. Zoetermeer 1993, Boekencentrum 605 pp. ƒ95. 90-2391-122-9. ᴿNedThT 50 (1996) 158-159 (*Tromp, Nico*).

1252 **Price, James D.** Concordance of the Hebrew accents used in the pentateuch. Concordance of the Hebrew accents in the Hebrew Bible 1. Studies in the Bible and early Christianity 34A: Lewiston, NY 1996, Mellen xiv; 274 pp. 0-7734-2395-8.

1253 ᴱ**Rogerson, John William** The pentateuch. A Sheffield Reader. BiSe 39: Shf 1996, Academic 371 pp. £15; $20. 1-85075-785-2.

E1.2 *Pentateuchus* **Introductio; Fontes JEDP**

1254 **Achermann, Dirck** August KLOSTERMANN und der Pentateuch: ein forschungsgeschichtlicher Beitrag zum Pentateuchproblem. Diss. Kiel 1996, 250 pp. [EThL 74,191*].

1255   *Albrecht, Ralf* Pentateuchkritik im Umbruch. Israel in Geschichte [ᴱMaier, Gerhard 1996, ⇒Q1]. 61-79.

1256   *Atkinson, Dick* The patchwork pentateuch. Chronology and Catastrophism Workshop 1 (1995) 18-22 [IAJS 42,20].

1257   *Blenkinsopp, Joseph* An assessment of the alleged pre-exilic date of the priestly material in the pentateuch. ZAW 108 (1996) 495-518.

1258   **Blenkinsopp, Joseph** Il pentateuco: introduzione ai primi cinque libri della bibbia. BiBi(B) 21: Brescia 1996, Queriniana 307 pp. L45.000. 88-399-2021-8 [RdT 38,141].

1259   **Campbell, Antony F.; O'Brien, Mark A.** Sources of the pentateuch: texts, introductions, annotations. 1993, ⇒9,1743; 10,1589. ᴿTTK 67 (1996) 145-146 (*Sæbø, Magne*).

1260   *Carmichael, Calum M.* Ancient academic activity and the origin of the pentateuch. Jewish Education and Learning (1994) 23-35 [Gen 34; Exod 22] [IAJS 42,13].

1261   ᴱ**Carmy, Shalom** Modern scholarship in the study of torah: contributions and limitations. Orthodox Forum. Northvale, NJ 1996, Aronson xvii; 297 pp. 1-56821-450-2 [NThAR 1997,259].

1262   *Dionne, Christian* Réflexions sur les débats entourant la composition du pentateuque. EeT(O) 27 (1996) 181-198.

1263   **Fretheim, Terence E.** The pentateuch. Interpreting Biblical Texts. Nv 1996, Abingdon 183 pp. $16. 0-687-00842-5.

1264   *Friedman, Richard Elliot* Some recent non-arguments concerning the documentary hypothesis. ᶠHARAN 1996, ⇒35. 87-101.

1265   ᴱ**García López, Félix** El pentateuco. Estella 1996, Verbo Divino 72 pp. Ptas1.200 [RB 103,635].

1266   **Hiebert, Theodore** The Yahwist's landscape: nature and religion in early Israel. NY 1996, OUP xv; 210 pp. $45. 0-19-509205-8.

1267   **Houtman, Cees** Der Pentateuch: die Geschichte seiner Erforschung neben einer Auswertung. Contributions to Biblical Exegesis and Theology 9: 1994, ⇒10,1584; 11/1,157. ᴿJR 76 (1996) 456-458 (*Dozeman, Thomas B.*); ThR 61 (1996) 337-341 (*Otto, Eckart*).

1268   *Hurowitz, Victor* P—understanding the Priestly source. BiRe 12/3 (1996) 30-37, 44-47.

1269   *Ibañez Arana, Andrés* Peter WEIMAR y la obra del Jehovista;
1270   Crisis de la crítica literaria del pentateuco?. ScrVict 43 (1996) 237-296/41-116.

1271   **King, Thomas John** The priestly literature and its northern component. Diss. Graduate Theol. Union 1996, 368 pp. [EThL 74,191*].

1272   **Krapf, Thomas M.** Die Priesterschrift und die vorexilische Zeit: Yehezkiel KAUFMANNS vernachlässigter Beitrag zur Geschichte der biblischen Religion. OBO 119: 1992, ⇒8,1971...11/1,158. ᴿCritRR 9 (1996) 152-155 (*Ehrlich, Carl S.*).

1273   *LaCocque, André* The land in 'D' and 'P'. BEAT 28: IOSOT 1992. 1996, ⇒256. 91-100.

1274   **Levin, Christoph** Der Jahwist. FRLANT 157: 1993, ⇒9,1747...-11/1,159. ᴿBib. 77 (1996) 425-428 (*Ska, Jean Louis*); OTEs 9 (1996) 155-160 (*Oosthuizen, M.J.*).

1275   **Lohfink, Norbert** Les traditions du pentateuque: autour de l'exil. CEv 97: P 1996, Cerf 67 pp. F33.

1276   **Owczarek, Susanne** Die Vorstellung vom Wohnen Gottes inmitten seines Volkes in der Priesterschrift: zur Heiligtumstheologie der priesterlichen Grundschrift. Diss. Erlangen-Nürnberg 1996-1997. ^D*Schmitt, H.-Ch.* [ThLZ 122,761].

1277 *Propp, William H.C.* The priestly source recovered intact?. VT 46 (1996) 458-478.

1278 **Pury, Albert de** O pentateuco em questão. ^T*Orth, Lúcia Mathilde E..* Petrópolis 1996, Vozes 324 pp. 85-326-1589-9 [PerTeol 29,137].

1279 *Rendtorff, Rolf* Welche Folgerungen hat der Wandel in der Pentateuchforschung für unsere Sicht der Geschichte Israels?. Israel in Geschichte [^E**Maier, Gerhard** 1996, ⇒Q1]. 43-59;

1280 The 'Yahwist' as theologian?: the dilemma of pentateuchal criticism. The pentateuch. BiSe 39: 1996 <1977>, ⇒202. 15-23.

1281 *Ricciardi, Alberto* Modelos alternativos para la hipotesis de los documentos a partir de la historia patriarcal. RevBib 58 (1996) 193-210.

1282 *Römer, Thomas* La formation du pentateuque selon l'exégèse historico-critique. Les premières traditions. 1996, ⇒159. 17-55 [[OTA 20,54].

1283 **Rymanover, Menahem Mendel** The torah discourses of the holy Tzaddik Reb Menachem MENDEL of Rimanov. ^T*Levine, Dov.*, Hoboken, NJ 1996, KTAV xxxiii; 775 pp. 0-88125-540-8.

1284 *Schmid, H.H.* In search of new approaches in pentateuchal research. The pentateuch. BiSe 39: 1996 <1977>, ⇒202. 24-32.

1285 *Schmidt, Ludwig* Pentateuch. Altes Testament. 1996, ⇒169. 88-109;

1286 Weisheit und Geschichte beim Elohisten. 'Jedes Ding hat seine Zeit...'. ^FMICHEL, D. BZAW 241: 1996, ⇒64. 209-225.

1287 **Schwantes, Milton** Pentateuco. Petrópolis 1996, Vozes 200 pp. [REB 225,225].

1288 *Schwartz, Baruch J.* La critica del Pentateuco nell'ebraismo e negli studiosi ebrei moderni. La lettura ebraica. 1996, ⇒205. 433-463;

1289 The priestly account of the theophany and lawgiving at Sinai. ^FHARAN 1996, ⇒35. 103-134.

1290 *Seebaß, Horst* Pentateuch. TRE 26. 1996, ⇒334. 185-209.

1291 **Seidel, Bodo** Karl David ILGEN und die Pentateuchforschung im Umkreis der sogenannten älteren Urkundenhypothese: Studien zur Geschichte der exegetischen Hermeneutik in der späten Aufklärung. 1993, ⇒9,1755; 11/1,167. ^ROLZ 91 (1996) 432-436 (*Oßwald, Eva*); ThR 61 (1996) 472-474 (*Perlitt, Lothar*).

1292 *Ska, Jean Louis* Le Pentateuque: état de la recherche à partir de quelques récentes "Introductions". Bib. 77 (1996) 245-265.

1293 *West, G.* J, E, D, P and the RDP: biblical sources for translation and transformation. Scriptura 57 (1996) 251-261.

1294 **Whybray, R. Norman** Introduction to the pentateuch. 1995, ⇒11/1,171. ^RThLZ 121 (1996) 351-352 (*Schmidt, Ludwig*); ABR 44 (1996) 74-76 (*Brett, Mark*); HebStud 37 (1996) 158-161 (*McKay, Heather A.*).

E1.3 *Pentateuchus,* **themata**

1295 *Chien, Lin-Ju [Ling-Chu]* Pentateuch in the reading of the paschal triduum. CTUF 108 (1996) 235-246 [ThIK 18/1,'28]. C.

1296 *Christensen, Duane L.* The pentateuchal principle within the canonical process. JETS 39 (1996) 537-548.

1297 **Duranti, Gian Carlo** Codici nel Pentateuco e matematica egizioplatonica. Biblioteca di filosofia oggi 5: 1994, ⇒10,1599. [R]Ang. 73 (1996) 438-439 (*Lamoureux, Françoise*).

1298 *Gorman, Frank H.* Ritualizing, rite and pentateuchal theology. [F]TUCKER, G., JSOT.S 229: 1996, ⇒95. 173-186.

1299 **Grünwaldt, Klaus** Exil und Identität: Beschneidung, Passa und Sabbat in der Priesterschrift. BBB 85: 1993, ⇒8,1984...11/1,181. [R]BZ 40 (1996) 122-124 (*Willmes, Bernd*).

1300 *Hayward. Robert* Shem, Melchizedek, and concern with christianity in the pentateuchal targumim. [F]MCNAMARA, JSOT.S 230: 1996, ⇒58. 67-80.

1301 **Jenson, Philipp Peter** Graded holiness: a key to the priestly conception of the world. JSOT.S 106: 1992, ⇒8,1988...11/1,182. [R]BZ 40 (1996) 101-103 (*Scharbert, Josef*).

1302 **Meir, Amira** Medieval Jewish interpretation of pentateuchal poetry. 218 pp. Diss. McGill 1995 [JQR 87,265].

1303 **Murphy, Roland Edmund** Responses to 101 questions on the biblical Torah: reflections on the pentateuch. Mahwah 1996, Paulist x; 126 pp. $13. 0-8091-3630-9 [OTA 19,530].

1304 *Shinan, Avigdor* Post-pentateuchal figures in the pentateuchal Aramaic targumim. [F]MCNAMARA, JSOT.S 230: 1996, ⇒58. 122-138.

1305 *Stemberger, Günter* Öffentlichkeit der Tora im Judentum: Anspruch und Wirklichkeit. JBTh 11 (1996) 91-101.

1306 **Sysling, Harry** Tehiyyat Ha-Metim: the resurrection of the dead in the Palestinian targums of the pentateuch and parallel traditions in classical rabbinic literature. TSAJ 57: Tü 1996, Mohr xxi; 329 pp. DM228. 3-16-146583-0.

1307 *Watts, James W.* The legal characterization of God in the pentateuch. HUCA 67 (1996) 1-14.

1308 [E]**Zenger, Erich** Die Tora als Kanon für Juden und Christen. Herder's Biblical Studies 10: FrB 1996, Herder (6) 419 pp. DM94. 3-451-26128-6.

1309 *Zenger, Erich* Der Pentateuch als Tora und als Kanon. ⇒1308. 5-34.

E1.4 **Genesis;** *textus, commentarii*

1310 **Alter, Robert** Genesis: translation and commentary. L 1996, Norton li; 324 pp. $25. 0-393-03981-1 [TD 44,155].

1311 **Berman, Samuel A.** Midrash Tanhuma-Yelammedenu: an English translation of Genesis and Exodus from the printed version of Tanhuma-Yelammedenu with an introduction, notes, and indexes. Hoboken, NJ 1996, KTAV xvi; 702 pp. 0-88125-400-2.

1312 **Bianchi, Enzo** Adamo, dove sei?: commento esegetico-spirituale ai capitoli 1-11 della Genesi. [2]1994, ⇒10,1660; 11/1,192. [R]CivCatt 147 I (1996) 301-302 (*Scaiola, D.*); Ter. 47 (1996) 352-353 (*Pasquetto, Virgilio*).

1313 [E]**Brenner, Athalya** A feminist companion to Genesis. Feminist Companion to the Bible 2: 1993, ⇒9,1769; 10,1615. [R]TJT 12/1 (1996) 80-81 (*Becker, Dennis*).

1314   **Chrostowski, Waldemar** Ogród Eden: zapoznane swiadectwo asyryjskiej diaspory [Gen 1-11]. Wsz 1996, Oficyna Wydawnicza "Vocatio" 342 pp. Bibl. 83-7146-057-0.

1315   *Cohn, Robert L.* Narrative structure and canonical perspective in Genesis. The pentateuch. BiSe 39: 1996 <1983>, ⇒202. 89-102.

1316   *Feldman, Louis H.* The Jewish sources of Peter COMESTOR's commentary on Genesis in his Historia Scholastica. Studies in Hellenistic Judaism. AGJU 30: 1996 <1993>, ⇒124. 317-347.

1317   **Feyerick, Ada; Gordon, Cyrus Herzl; Sarna, Nahum M.** Genesis: world of myths and patriarchs. NY 1996, New York University Press 256 pp. $56. 0-8147-2668-2 [NThAR 1997,258].

1318   **Hamilton, Victor P.** The book of Genesis: chapters 18-50. NIC.OT. 1995, ⇒11/1,196. RAUSS 34 (1996) 340-342 (*Miller, James E.*).

1319   ET**Harl, Marguerite** La Genèse: traduction du texte grec, introduction et notes. P ²1994, Cerf 336 pp. RIgreja Missão 48/1 (1996) 87-88 (*Couto, A.*).

1320   **Horton, Stanley M.** Genesis: the promise of blessing = Be-rêšît. Complete Biblical Library Commentary. Springfield 1996, World Library 207 pp. Bibl. 1-88464-209-8 [NThAR 1998,268].

1321   **Jagersma, H.** Genesis 1:1-25:11. 1995, ⇒11/1,197. RKeTh 47/3 (1996) 245-246 (*Van der Woude, A.S.*);

1322   Genesis 25:12-50:26. Verklaring van de Hebreeuwse Bijbel: Nijkerk 1996, Callenbach 280 pp. ƒ44.90. 90-266-0877-2 [Streven 64,668].

1323   **Kamesar, Adam** JEROME, Greek scholarship and the Hebrew bible: a study of the *Quaestiones Hebraicae in Genesim*. Oxford Classical Monographs: 1993, ⇒9,1777...11/1,198. RASEs 13 (1996) 374-378 (*Pieri, Francesco*); JAOS 116 (1996) 556-557 (*Wevers, John Wm.*).

1324   T**Korsak, Mary Phil** At the start: Genesis made new: a translation of the Hebrew text. 1992, ⇒8,2008...11/1,200. RNBl 77 (1996) 304-307 (*Edwards, Sara Dudley*).

1325   *Kvam, Bjørn Olva Grümer* Targum Onkelos til Genesis 4,7B. Sum.; Nordisk Judaistik 16/1-2 (1995) 41-55 [IAJS 42,15].

1326   *Marin, Marcello L'elocutio* della scrittura nei due primi commenti agostiniani alla *Genesi*. Retorica ed esegesi biblica. QVetChr 24: 1996, ⇒259. 127-160.

1327   **Mathews, Kenneth A.** Genesis 1-11:26. NAC 1A: Nv 1996, Broadman & H. 528 pp. $37. 0-8054-0101-6. RRevBib 58 (1996) 247-249 (*Croatto, J. Severino*).

1328   T**Mitchell, Stephen** Genesis: a new translation of the classical biblical stories. NY 1996, Harper C. lvi; 161 pp. 0-06-017249-5.

1329   T**Moraldi, Luigi; Barzaghi, Alessandro,** (*al*), Nuovo Testamento: con commenti ai vangeli tratti dai padri, santi e mistici della Chiesa e con la prima parte della Genesi [1,1-12,9]. n.p. 1996, Verità e Vita (6) 1718 pp.

1330   **Petit, Françoise** La chaîne sur la Genèse: édition intégrale: chapîtres 29 à 50. Traditio Exegetica Graeca 4: Lv 1996, Peeters xiv; 505 pp. 90-6831-817-9 [EThL 74,176*].

1331   *Petit, Francoise* La chaîne grecque sur la Genèse, miroir de l'exégèse ancienne. FDASSMANN, E., JAC.E 23: 1996, ⇒19. 243-253.

1332 **Ravasi, Gianfranco** El libro del Génesis (12-50). Guía Espiritual del AT. 1994, ⇒11/1,207. ᴿScrTh 28/1 (1996) 299-300 (*Jarne, J.*); PerTeol 28 (1996) 260-261 (*Gottardo, Roberto J.*).

1333 ᵀ**Rottzoll, Dirk U.** Abraham Iʙɴ Esʀᴀs Kommentar zur Urgeschichte: mit einem Anhang: Rᴀsᴄʜʙᴀᴍs Kommentar zum ersten Kapitel der Urgeschichte. SJ 15: B 1996, De Gruyter xxxiii; 243 pp. DM164. 3-11-015068-9.

1334 **Rösel, Martin** Übersetzung als Vollendung der Auslegung: Studien zur Genesis Septuaginta. BZAW 223: 1994, ⇒10,1551; 11/1,208. ᴿThLZ 121 (1996) 544-547 (*Willi-Plein, Ina*); VT 46 (1996) 131-134 (*Schaper, J.L.W.*).

1335 **Ruppert, Lothar** Genesis: 1. Teilband: Gen 1,1-11,26. FzB 70: 1992, ⇒8,2015...11/1,211. ᴿBZ 40 (1996) 304-307 (*Mosis, Rudolf*).

1336 ᴱ**Savoca, Gaetano** Traduzione interlineare della Genesi sul testo della BHS. 1995, ⇒11/1,213. ᴿCivCatt 147 II (1996) 517-518 (*Scaiola, D.*); NRTh 118 (1996) 908-909 (*Ska, Jean Louis*); Teol. 33 (1996) 254-256 (*Briglia, Sergio*).

1337 *Talmon, Shemaryahu* Masada 1045-1350 and 1375: fragments of a Genesis apocryphon. IEJ 46 (1996) 248-255.

1338 *Van Uchelen, Niek A.* Rᴀsʜɪ's commentary on Genesis I-V: some rhetorical aspects. FJB 23 (1996) 15-22.

1339 **Vegas Montaner, Luis** Génesis Rabbah I (Génesis 1-11): comentario midrásico al libro del Génesis. Biblioteca Midrásica 15: 1994, ⇒10,1634. ᴿMEAH 43/2 (1994) 188-189 (*Pérez Fernández, Miguel*).

1340 **Wenham, Gordon J.** Genesis 16-50. WBC 2: 1994, ⇒10,1635. ᴿNRTh 118 (1996) 909-910 (*Ska, Jean Louis*); ThLZ 121 (1996) 1140-1141 (*Zobel, Hans-Jürgen*); AUSS 34 (1996) 340-342 (*Miller, James E.*); JETh 10 (1996) 197-200 (*Hilbrands, Walter*).

E1.5 *Genesis*, topics

1341 *Armogathe, Jean-Robert* Lectures de la Genèse aux origines de la science classique. RICP 60 (1996) 53-63.

1342 **Armstrong, Karen** In the beginning: a new interpretation of Genesis. NY 1996, Knopf viii; 195 pp. £15. 0-679-45089-0.

1343 *Baumgart, Norbert Clemens* Das Ende der biblischen Urgeschichte in Gen 9,29. BN 81 (1996) 27-58.

1344 **Bauval, Robert; Hancock, Graham** Keeper of Genesis: a quest for the hidden legacy of mankind. L 1996, Heinemann xiii; 362 pp. 0-434-00302-6.

1345 **Carr, David M.** Reading the fractures of Genesis: historical and literary approaches. LVL 1996, Westminster 388 pp. $39. 0-664-22071-1.

1346 **Dutourd, Jean** La Genesi come un romanzo. ᵀ*Ferrara, Maurizio.* Vicenza 1996, Neri Pozza 175 pp. 88-7305-574-8.

1347 *Gitay, Yehoshua* Geography and theology in the biblical narrative: the question of Genesis 2-12. ᶠTᴜᴄᴋᴇʀ, G. JSOT.S 229: 1996, ⇒95. 205-216.

1348 *Gutiérrez, Miguel* En busca de un titulo para Génesis 1-11. 1996, Theologika 11/1 (1996) 84-101 [ZID 23,321].

1349 **Hamming, G.** Het sumerisch testament: wat is de werkelijkheid van Genesis?. Milieufilosofie 6: Utrecht 1996 Van Arkel 176 pp. *f*29.50 [GThT 97/2,99].

1350 ᵀHayward, C.T.R. JEROME's *Hebrew questions on Genesis*. 1995, ⇒11/1,225. ᴿJJS 47 (1996) 162-164 *(Edwards, M.J.)*; JThS 47 (1996) 698-702 *(Kamesar, Adam)*.

1351 Minear, Paul Sevier Christians and the new creation: Genesis motifs in the New Testament. 1994, ⇒10,1645. ᴿPSB 17/1 (1996) 95-96 *(Greene-McCreight, Kathryn)*; CBQ 58 (1996) 559-560 *(Boer, Martinus C. de)*; JBL 115 (1996) 534-536 *(Meyer, Paul W.)*.

1352 Moyers, Bill D.; ᴱFlowers, Betty Sue Genesis: a living conversation [Discussion]. NY 1996, Doubleday xxxvii; 361 pp. 0-385-48345-7.

1353 Rashkow, Ilona N. The phallacy of Genesis: a feminist-psychoanalytic approach. 1993, ⇒9,1345...11/1,232. ᴿHebStud 37 (1996) 161-163 *(Bauer, Angela)*.

1354 *Rendsburg, Gary A.* Biblical literature as politics: the case of Genesis. Religion and politics. 1996, ⇒212. 47-70.

1355 ᴱRosenberg, David Genesis: as it is written: contemporary writers on our first stories. SF 1996 Harper SF vii; 215 pp. 0-06-066706-0.

1356 Ross, Allen P. Creation and blessing: a guide to the study and exposition of Genesis. GR 1996, Baker 744 pp. 0-8010-2107-3.

1357 Saltzman, Steven A small glimmer of light: reflections on the book of Genesis. Hoboken, NJ 1996, KTAV xix; 202 pp. $25. 0-88125-549-1.

1358 Syrén, Roger The forsaken first-born: a study of a recurrent motif in the patriarchal narratives. JSOT.S 133: 1993, ⇒9,1801...-11/1,234. ᴿBZ 40 (1996) 107-109 *(Maier, Johann)*; JQR 87 (1996) 215-218 *(Schwartz, Baruch J.)*.

1359 Van der Zee, William R. Ape or Adam?: our roots according to the book of Genesis. North Andover, MA 1995, 107 pp. $19.50. 1-886670-03-X [ThD 44,390—Heiser, W. Charles].

1360 *Van Exem, Albert* Genesis 1-11 as living tradition. Sevartham 21 (1996) 3-29.

1361 Van Wolde, Ellen Words become worlds: semantic studies of Genesis 1-11. BIS 6: 1994, ⇒10,1692. ᴿSJOT 10/1 (1996) 152-153 *(Jeppesen, Knud)*; Synaxis 14/1 (1996) 351-364 *(Aliotta, Maurizio)*.

1362 Zornberg, Avivah Gottlieb Genesis: the beginning of desire. 1995, ⇒11/1,237. ᴿJR 76 (1996) 611-612 *(Frymer-Kensky, Tikva)*.

E1.6 **Creatio,** *Genesis 1s*

1363 *Albertz, Rainer* Segen Gottes: wo ist er erfahrbar?: wie gehen wir damit um?. Zorn. 1996, ⇒110. 85-113.

1364 *Allchin, A.M.* The worship of the whole creation: MERTON and the Eastern Fathers. Sobornost 18/2 (1996) 28ff [ThD Index Feb. 1997,13].

1365 Amsler, Samuel Le secret de nos origines: étrange actualité de Genèse 1-11. 1993, ⇒9,1805. ᴿEstB 54 (1996) 126-127 *(Pérez Escobar, J.)*.

1366 Bazelaire, Thomas-M. de Quelques réflexions sur les récits bibliques de la création du monde. Sedes Sapientiae 56 (1996) 39-54.

1367 *Beauchamp, Paul* Un entretien avec Paul BEAUCHAMP: la première page de la Bible. *Boyer, Frédéric <interviewer>*. MoBi 96 (1996) 24-27.

1368 *Beckwith, Roger T.* The day: its divisions and its limits in biblical times. Calendar and chronology. AGJU 33: 1996, ⇒112. 1-9.

1369 **Bof, Giampiero** Al principio dell'essere umano. Istituto Siciliano di Bioetica, Moralis 3: R 1994, Armando 355 pp. RLat. 62 (1996) 383-384 (*Sanna, Ignazio*).

1370 **Bossard, Franz; Bossard, Paul** Die Welt als Gottes Schöpfung. 1995, ⇒11/1,243. RKiHe 4 (1996) 36-37 (*Hüntelmann, Rafael*).

1371 *Boyce, Richard N.* Genesis 1:1-5. Interp. 50 (1996) 394-397.

1372 *Briend, Jacques* Les deux récits de la Genèse. MoBi 96 (1996) 20-22.

1373 **Carmichael, Calum M.** The story of creation: its origin and its interpretation in PHILO and the fourth gospel. Ithaca 1996, Cornell University Press xii; (2) 136 pp. £19.50. 0-8014-3261-8 [JJS 48/2,368].

1374 **Cassidy, Sheila** The creation: the story of how God created the world. NY 1996, Crossroad 28 pp. $10 [BiTod 35,256].

1375 *Castro, José Acácio* O homem como 'imagem de Deus' na antropologia boaventuriana. Sum. 355. HumTeo 17/3 (1996) 253-275 [Gen 1,26].

1376 *Chapalain, Claude* "Tradition et création" devant le retable dit de Sainte ANNE à Commana (Finistère). SémBib 83 (1996) 33-48.

1377 EColzani, Gianni Creazione e male del cosmo: scandalo per l'uomo e sfida per il credente. 1995, ⇒11/1,247. Il Futuro dell'Uomo 23/2 (1996) 79-81 (*Bisio, Franco*).

1378 *De Benedetti, Paolo* 'A immagine e somiglianza': la natura teofanica dell'uomo in Genesi 1,26-27. Humanitas 51 (1996) 765-774.

1379 *Domergue, Marcel* Genèse 1 et 2: Adam. Croire aujourd'hui 1 (1 Feb. 1996) 34-35.

1380 *Feldman, Louis H.* The enigma of HORACE's thirtieth sabbath. Studies in Hellenistic Judaism. AGJU 30: 1996 <1989/90>, ⇒124. 351-376.

1381 *Guiteras, J.* La creación, fuente nutricia de la plegaria. Liturgia y Espiritualidad 27/5 (1996) 193-197 [Comunidades 89,145].

1382 **Haag, Herbert** Am Morgen der Zeit: das Hohelied der Schöpfung. Fotografien von *Richter, Werner*. 1995, ⇒11/1,255. RThPh 71 (1996) 280-281 (*Koltermann, R.*) [Ps 113; 2 Cor 5,17].

1383 *Hill, Edmund* Creation and creator:; knowing and glorifying God. NBl 77 (1996) 390-400.

1384 *Hudson, Don Michael* From chaos to cosmos: sacred space in Genesis. ZAW 108 (1996) 87-97.

1385 *Jaki, Stanley L.* Le sabbat du créateur de l'univers. Sum. RQSc 167 (1996) 355-373 [Gen 2,2-3].

1386 *Klopfenstein, Martin A.* Was heißt:"Macht euch die Erde untertan"?: Überlegunge zur Schöpfungsgeschichte der Bibel in der Umweltkrise heute. Leben aus dem Wort. BEAT 40: 1996, ⇒132. 275-283 [Gen 1,28].

1387 ELifschitz, Daniel Uomo e donna, immagine di Dio: il sabato: l'aggadah su Genesi 2. Israele racconta: R 1996, Dehoniane 158 pp. 88-396-0472-3.

1388 *Lubszyk, Hans* Ursprünge und Aktualität des Schöpfungsglaubens in Israel. IOSOT 1992. BEAT 28: 1996, ⇒256. 101-118.

1389 *Maillet, Henri* Quatorze variations sur la création de l'homme à l'image de Dieu. FV 95/1 (1996) 57-73.

1390 **Maranesi, Pietro** Verbum inspiratum, chiave ermeneutica dell'Hexaëmeron di San BONAVENTURA. BSC 51: R 1996, Istituto Storico dei Cappuccini 430 pp.

1391 ^TMartin, Christopher F.J. Robert GROSSETESTE: on the six days of creation: a translation of the *Hexaëmeron*. ABMA 6/2: Oxf 1996, OUP ix; 373 pp. $55. 0-19-726150-7 [[ThD 44,364— Heiser, W. Charles].

1392 *Moore, Stephen D.* Gigantic God: Yahweh's body. JSOT 70 (1996) 87-115 [Gen 1,26-27].

1393 *Morales, José* Solidaridad de la creación con el destino humano. Esperanza del hombre. 1996, ⇒173. 271-286.

1394 *Mutius, Hans-Georg von* Die Masoreten als Textverfälscher?: neue Üerlegungen zu einem bekannten Problem in Genesis 1,20. BN 81 (1996) 15-20.

1395 **Pannenberg, Wolfhart** SCHLEIERMACHERS Schwierigkeiten mit dem Schöpfungsgedanken. Bayerische Akad. der Wissenschaften Phil.-hist. Kl. Sitzungsberichte 1996, no. 3: Mü 1996, Bayerische Akad. der Wissenschaften 17 pp. 3-7696-1587-5.

1396 *Pozo Abejón, Gerardo del* Dios creador y la creación en teología: presentación y valoración de la interpretación de C. WESTERMANN. Sum. 201. RET 56 (1996) 201-257.

1397 *Rad, Gerhard von* El relato bíblico de la creación. La acción de Dios. 1996 <1970>, ⇒144. 99-108.

1398 *Raha, R.J.* 'In the beginning...' (ecolological considerations in the creation narratives: Gen 1-3). Vaiharai 1 (1996) 219-232 [ThIK 18/1,39].

1399 **Rappel, Simone** 'Macht euch die Erde untertan': die ökologische Krise als Folge des Christentums?. ASE 39: Pd 1996 Schöningh 436 pp. DM52. 3-506-70239-4. ^RTTh 36 (1996) 431 (*Manenschijn, G.*) [Gen 1,26-28].

1400 *Renaud, Bernard* Procréation humaine et mystère de la vie selon la bible. RDC 45 (1995) 229-244 [IAJS 42,23].

1401 **Rüterswörden, Udo** Dominium terrae: Studien zur Genese einer alttestamentlichen Vorstellung. BZAW 215: 1993, ⇒9,1863; 10,1710. ^RCBQ 58 (1996) 722-724 (*Daniels, Dwight, R.*) [Gen 1,28].

1402 **Sailhamer, John H.** Genesis unbound: a provocative new look at the creation account. Sisters, Or. 1996, Multnomah 257 pp. 0-88070-868-9 [NThAR 1997,225].

1403 *Schindler, David L.* Christology and the *imago Dei*: interpreting *Gaudium et Spes*. Com(US) 23/1 (1996) 156-184 [Gen 1,26].

1404 *Schmidt, Ludwig* Schöpfung: Natur und Geschichte. Altes Testament. 1996, ⇒169. 267-289.

1405 **Scholten, Clemens** Antike Naturphilosophie und christliche Kosmologie in der Schrift *De opificio mundi* des Johannes PHILOPONOS. PTS 45: B 1996, De Gruyter xi; 488 pp. DM268. 3-11-014834-X.

1406 *Scholten, Clemens* Titel-Gattung-Sitz im Leben: Probleme der Klassifizierung antiker Bibelauslegung am Beispiel der griechischen Hexaemeronschriften. ^FDASSMANN, E. JAC.E 23: 1996, ⇒19. 254-269.

1407 *Schrader, W.* Schöpfung und Geburt: mit Stift und Papier schaffen sich Kinder ihre Welt. Ren. 52 (1996) 101-112.

1408 **Seebaß, Horst** Genesis 1: Urgeschichte (1,1-11,26). Neuk 1996, Neuk viii; 292 pp. DM78. 3-7887-1517-0.

1409 *Signorini, Rodolfo* The creation of Adam: a detail in MANTEGNA's *Madonna della vittoria*. JWCI 59 (1996) 303-304 [Gen 2,7].

1410 **Simkins, Ronald A.** Creator and creation: nature in the worldview of ancient Israel. 1994, ⇒10,1685; 11/1,269. ᴿCBQ 58 (1996) 135-136 (*Schmitz, Philip C.*); BA 59 (1996) 133-134 (*Embree, David*).
1411 *Smith, Morton* On the shape of God and the humanity of gentiles. Studies in...method. 1996 <1968>, ⇒150. 150-160 [Gen 1,26].
1412 *Speyer, Wolfgang* Der Bibeldichter Dʀᴀᴄᴏɴᴛɪᴜs als Exeget des Sechstagewerkes Gottes. ᶠDᴀssᴍᴀɴɴ, E. JAC.E 23: 1996, ⇒19. 464-484.
1413 *Terra, João Evangelista Martins* A imagem de Deus. 1996, RCB 79/80 (1996) 150-154 [Gen 1,26].
1414 *Turner, Joseph* Franz Rᴏsᴇɴᴢᴡᴇɪɢ's interpretation of the creation narrative. JJTP 4/1 (1994) 23-37 [IAJS 42,24].
1415 **Van de Beek, Abraham** Schepping: de wereld als voorspel voor de eeuwigheid [Creation: the world as a prelude to eternity]. Baarn 1996, Callenbach 459 pp.
1416 **Van Soest, H.J.** 'Welk is het voortreffelijkste schepsel op aarde'?: de interpretatie van een omstreden bijbelse voorstelling in het 19e en 20e eeuwse Nederland. Diss. Kampen. Delft 1996, Eburon [BMGN 112,554] [Gen 1,26-27].
1417 **Van Wolde, Ellen** Stories of the beginning: Genesis 1-11 and other creation stories. L 1996, SCM xi; 273 pp. £15. 0-334-02637-7.
1418 *Van Wolde, Ellen J.* The text as an eloquent guide: rhetorical, linguistic and literary features in Genesis 1. Literary structure. 1996, ⇒200. 134-151.
1419 *Varo, Francisco* Naturaleza, trabajo y dignidad del hombre: Gen 2,4b-5 y su inserción en el canon judío. Esperanza del hombre. 1996, ⇒173. 333-350.
1420 **Vernier, J.M.** Théologie et métaphysique de la création chez saint Tʜᴏᴍᴀs d'Aquin. P 1995, Téqui 348 pp. ᴿEstTrin 30/2 (1996) 293-294 (*Ofilada Macario, Mina*).
1421 *Vetter, Dieter* Lernen mit dem Judentum: des Menschen Verantwortung für die Schöpfung. Judentum. 1996 <1988>, ⇒154. 273-281.
1422 *Viciano, Albert* El hombre, imagen de Dios (Gen 1,26), en las obras exegéticas de Tᴇᴏᴅᴏʀᴇᴛᴏ de Ciro. Esperanza del hombre. 1996, ⇒173. 199-214.
1423 *Yasuda, Harno* Ökologie und Schöpfung aus japanischer Sicht. ZMiss 21/1 (1996) 34-42 [ThIK 18/1,84].
1424 *Zenger, Erich* Die Erschaffung der Welt: der Kosmos als Haus für alle [Rev 21-22];
1425 Die Erschaffung des Menschen als Mann und Frau. WUB 2 (1996) 25-29/30-33.

E1.7 *Genesis 1s:* Bible and myth [⇒ᴍ3.8]

1426 *Albertz, Rainer* Schöpfungsmythos und Umweltethik. Zorn. 1996, ⇒110. 65-84.
1427 *Anderson, Bernhard W.* The persistence of chaos in God's creation. BiRe 12/1 (1996) 19, 44-45.
1428 *Baines, John* Myth and literature. Ancient Egyptian literature. Probleme der Ägyptologie 10: 1996, ⇒230. 361-377.
1429 *Bammel, Caroline P.* Der Tod, die Gestirne und die Jahreszeiten in antiker und christlicher Dichtung. JAC 39 (1996) 5-12.

1430 **Bickel, Susanne** La cosmogonie égyptienne avant le nouvel empire. OBO 134: 1994, ⇒10,1718. ᴿWO 27 (1996) 140-145 (*Quack, Joachim Friedrich*); Or. 65 (1996) 166-171 (*Derchain, Philippe*).

1431 *Boespflug, François* Die Harmonie der Schöpfung: die Genesis in der Kunst des Mittelalters. WUB 2 (1996) 34-43.

1432 *Bonnafé, Annie* Die Ordnung der Welt nach griechischer Vorstellung. WUB 2 (1996) 16-19;

1433 La mise en ordre du monde grec. MoBi 96 (1996) 16-19.

1434 *Bottéro, Jean* La naissance du monde en Mésopotamie. MoBi 96 (1996) 9-11;

1435 Mesopotamische Schöpfungsvorstellungen. WUB 2 (1996) 9-11.

1436 **Clifford, Richard J.** Creation accounts in the ancient Near East and in the bible. CBQ.MS 26: 1994, ⇒10,1721*; 11/1,284. ᴿHebStud 37 (1996) 150-153 (*Maier, John*); CBQ 58 (1996) 702-704 (*Batto, Bernard F.*); JBL 115 (1996) 120-122 (*Simkins, Ronald A.*); BiRe 12/5 (1996) 15-16 (*Hendel, Ronald S.*).

1437 **Diakonoff, Igor M.** Archaic myths of the orient and the occident. Orientalia Gothoburgensia: 1995, ⇒11/1,285. ᴿRSO 70 (1996) 227-228 (*Garbini, Giovanni*).

1438 *Hess, Richard S.* Genesis 1-2 and recent studies of ancient texts. Science and Christian Belief 7/2 (1995) 141-149 [IAJS 42,22].

1439 *King, Karen L.* Mackinations on myth and origins. ᶠMACK, B., 1996, ⇒54. 157-172.

1440 *Lacarrière, Jacques* Nous ne sommes pas les enfants du hasard. MoBi 96 (1996) 5-6;

1441 Keine Kinder des Zufalls. WUB 2 (1996) 4-6.

1442 *Lang, B.* Mythos und soziale Kontrolle: der muythologische Rahmen gesellschaftlichen Handelns im antiken Judentum. Mythologica. ᴱTepe, Peter, (*al*), Düsseldorfer Jahrbuch für interdisziplinäre Mythosforschung 4: Essen 1996, Blau Eule. 11-24 [ZAW 110,474—Köckert, M.].

1443 **Lefkowitz, Mary R.** Not out of Africa: how afrocentrism became an excuse to teach myth as history. NY 1996, Basic xvii; 222 pp. 0-465-09837-1.

1444 *Morales, José* Mito y misterio. ScrTh 28 (1996) 77-95.

1445 **Nejrotti, Chiara** Sotto il segno di Hermes: i percorsi del mito e la narrativa dell'immaginario. Fantàsia Rimini 1996, Il Cerchio 143 pp. 88-86583-24-9.

1446 **Niditch, Susan** Folklore and the Hebrew Bible. 1993, ⇒9,1879...-11/2,2444. ᴿCBQ 58 (1996) 129 (*Culley, Robert C.*).

1447 **Okwueze, Malachy Ikechukwu** Myth: the Old Testament experience. ᴰEbo, D.J.I. Diss. University of Nigeria, Nsukka 1995 [NAOTS 3,15—Holter, Knut].

1448 **Page, Hugh R.** The myth of cosmic rebellion: a study of its reflexes in Ugaritic and biblical literature. VT.S 65: Lei 1996, Brill xvi; 232 pp. ƒ140; $90.50. 90-04-10563-8 [CBQ 59,423].

1449 **Pitzele, Peter** Our fathers' wells: a personal encounter with the myths of Genesis. 1995, ⇒11/1,289. ᴿJRHe 35/1 (1996) 75-76 (*Cook, Catherine E.*).

1450 *Rad, Gerhard von* Conocimiento de la naturaleza y del mundo en el Antiguo Testamento. La acción de Dios. 1996 <1967>, ⇒144. 109-129.

1451 *Sauer, James A.* The river runs dry—creation story preserves historical memory. ᴿBArR 22/4 (1996) 52-57, 64.

1452 ᴱSchabert, Tilo; Hornung, Eerik Strukturen des Chaos. Ascona 1994, Eranos 298 pp. FS52.80; 3-7705-2830-1. ᴿBiOr 53 (1996) 685-690 (*Englund, Gertie*).

1453 *Sjöberg, Åke W.* Bibel och Babel: en assyriolog läser Genesis 1-3. SEÅ 61 (1996) 7-32.

1454 Wyatt, Nick Myths of power: a study of royal myth and ideology in Ugaritic and biblical tradition. UBL 13: Müns 1996, Ugarit-Verlag vii; 492 pp. Bibl. 3-927120-43-X.

1455 *Yoyotte, Jean* Ägyptische Vorstellungen von der Entstehung der Welt. WUB 2 (1996) 12-15;

1456 La cosmogonie des anciens Égyptiens. MoBi 96 (1996) 12-15.

1457 *Zenger, Erich* Die Schöpfungsgeschichten der Genesis im Kontext des Alten Orient. WUB 2 (1996) 20-24.

E1.8 *Gen 1s, Jos 10,13...:* The Bible, the Church and Science

1458 *Arcidiacono, Salvatore* El darwinismo entre la ciencia y el mito [Darwinism: science and myth]. Folia Humanistica 34 (1996) 409-418.

1459 Barbour, Ian Religion in an age of science. 1990, ⇒6,2195...-11/2,10,1752. ᴿRStR 22/1 (1996) 36-43 (*Gerhart, Mary; Russell, Allan Melvin; Cole-Turner, Ronald*);

1460 Religion in an age of technology. SF 1993, HarperSanFrancisco xix; 312 pp. Gifford Lectures 1989, 1991, vol. 2. $19. ᴿ⇒1459.

1461 *Bauks, M.* Big bang ou création ex nihilo?: à propos de la relation entre un état préexistant du monde et la création en Gn 1/1-3. ETR 71 (1996) 481-493.

1462 Bosinski, Gerhard Les origines de l'homme en Europe et en Asie. Archéologie aujourd'hui. P 1996, Errance 176 pp. Atlas des sites du Paléolithique inférieur. 2-87772-125-6.

1463 Boyd, Robert Boyd's handbook of practical apologetics. GR 1997, Kregel 251 pp. ᴿFaith & Mission 14/1 (1996) 125-6 (*Bush, L. Russ*).

1464 ᴱBrandmüller, Walter, (*al*), COPERNICO, GALILEI e la chiesa. 1992, ⇒10,1756. ᴿRSLR 32 (1996) 673-683 (*Motta, Franco*).

1465 Drees, W.B. Van niets tot nu: een wetenschappelijke scheppings-vertelling. Interacties: Kampen 1996, Kok 88 pp. *f*20 [GThT 98,137].

1466 *Elbert, Paul* Biblical creation and science: a review article. JETS 39 (1996) 285-289.

1467 Eliezer, Christie J. Evolution, creation or what?. Delhi 1996, SPCK x; 125 pp. Rs50. 81-7214-216-1 [VJTR 60,703].

1468 Gilkey, Langdon Nature, reality, and the sacred: the nexus of science and religion. 1993, ⇒10,1796; 11/2,2332. ᴿInterp. 50 (1996) 92, 94 (*Nash, James A.*).

1469 Gillispie, Charles Coulston Genesis and geology: a study in the relations of scientific thought, natural theology, and social opinion in Great Britain. Foreword by *Rupke, Nicolaas A.,* HHS 58: CM 1996, Harvard University Press xxxiii; (2) 315 pp. 0-674-34481-2.

1470 Granada, Miguel El debate cosmológico en 1588: BRUNO, BRAHE, ROTHMANN, URSUS, ROESLIN. Istituto Italiano per gli Studi Filosofici, Lezioni della Scuola di Studi Superiori in Napoli 18: N 1996, Bibliopolis.

1471 *Granada, Miguel A.* Il problema astronomic-cosmologico e le Sacre Scritture dopo COPERNICO: Christoph ROTHMANN e la 'teoria dell'accomodazione'. RSF 51 (1996) 789-828.

1472 **Haught, John F.** Science and religion: from conflict to conversation. 1995, ⇒11/1,295. RHorizons 23/2 (1996) 349-351 (*Barnes, Michael H.*).
1473 **Jaki, Stanley L.** Bible and science. Front Royal, Va 1996, Chri-
stendom (6) 222 pp. 0-931888-63-8.
1474 *Lachièze-Rey, Marc* Die Urknall-Theorie ist kein Schöpfungsbe-
richt. WUB 2 (1996) 7.
1475 **Lattis, James M.** Between COPERNICUS and GALILEO: Christoph CLAVIUS and the collapse of Ptolemaic cosmology. Ch
1994, University of Chicago Press 320 pp. £43.25/£18. 0-226-
46927-1/-9-8. RASEs 13 (1996) 656-657 (*Motta, Franco*).
1476 **Mazhar, Noor Giovanni** Catholic attitudes to evolution in
nineteenth-century Italian literature. 1995, ⇒11/1,298. RIl Futuro
dell'Uomo 23/2 (1996) 81-83 (*Mantovani, Fabio*).
1477 **Midgley, Mary** Science as salvation: a modern myth and its
meaning. 1992, ⇒9,1994; 10,1829. RRStR 22/1 (1996) 36-40
(*Gerhart, Mary; Russell, Allan Melvin*).
1478 **Moss, Jean Dietz** Novelties in the heavens: rhetoric and science in
the Copernican controversy. 1993, ⇒9,1959; 10,1834. RRHS 49
(1996) 602-603 (*Hallyn, Fernand*).
1479 **Pannenberg, Wolfhart** Toward a theology of nature: essays on
science and faith. EPeters, Ted. 1993, ⇒9,228a; 11/2,2375.
RInterp. 50 (1996) 88, 90 (*Santmire, H. Paul*).
1480 **Pelt, Jean-Marie** Dieu de l'univers: sciences et foi. 1995,
⇒11/1,299. REeV 106 (1996) 447-448 (*Jay, Pierre*).
1481 **Poupard, P.** La nuova immagine del mondo. CasM 1996, Piemme
163 pp. [AnnTh 11,281ss—Vitoria, María Angeles].
1482 **Ratzsch, Del** The battle of beginnings: why neither side is winning
the creation-evolution debate. DG 1996, Inter-Varsity 248 pp. $15
[BS 154,233].
1483 **Saget, Henri** La science et la foi. Langres 1996, Guéniot 184 pp.
1484 **Schwarz, Hans** Schöpfungsglaube im Horizont moderner Naturwissenschaft. Apologetische Themen 7: Neuk 1996 Bahn 256 pp.
DM29.80.
1485 **Tipler, Frank J.** The physics of immortality: modern cosmology,
God, and the resurrection of the dead. NY 1994, Doubleday 528
pp. $25. RRStR 22 (1996) 36-40 (*Gerhart, Mary; Russell, Allan
Melvin*).
1486 **Wilkinson, David** God, the big bang and Stephen HAWKING. L
²1996 <1993>, Monarch 176 pp. £6.
1487 **Wilkinson, David; Frost, Rob** Thinking clearly about God and
science. L 1996, Monarch 224 pp. £6. 1-85424-333-0.
1488 **Worthing, Mark William** God, creation, and contemporary physics. Theology and the Sciences: Mp 1996, Fortress vii; 260 pp.
£13. 0-8006-2906-X. RTS 57 (1996) 762-763 (*Doughty, Mark*); ET
108 (1996-97) 33-35 (*Rodd, C.S.*).

E1.9 Peccatum originale, **The Sin of Eden**, *Genesis 2-3*

1489 *Ademiluka, S. Sola* The fall of man: a critical study of Genesis 3 in
an African background. TBasileiade, P.; Keramida-Giannopoulou,
Ph. DBM 15 (1996) 52-59.
1490 *Altner, H.* Gut und Böse aus der Sicht eines Biologen. Glaube und
Denken 9 (1996) 145-155 [Gen 2,16-17].

1491 *Askani, H.C.* Quand Adam et Eve ont-ils péché?. ETR 71 (1996) 361-377.

1492 **Associazione Teologica Italiana** Questioni sul peccato originale. Padova 1996, Messaggero 264 pp. L30.000. [R]Il Futuro dell'Uomo 23/2 (1996) 77-79 (*Mantovani, Fabio*).

1493 **Barr, James** Éden et la quête de l'immortalité. LiBi 107: 1995, ⇒11/1,307. [R]BLE 97/2 (1996) 187 (*Monloubou, L.*); RET 56/1 (1996) 119-120 (*Barrado Fernández, P.*).

1494 **Basset, Lytta** Le pardon originel: de l'abîme du mal au pouvoir de pardonner. LiTh 24: 1995 <1994>, ⇒11/1,308. [R]NRTh 118 (1996) 439-440 (*Pottier, B.*).

1495 **Berzosa Martínez, Raúl** Angeles y demonios: sentido de su retorno en nuestros días. BAC Popular 115: M 1996, BAC 188 pp. 84-7914-215-4 [Isidorianum 6,296].

1496 *Bettiolo, Paolo* Adamo in Eden: il difficile discernimento della vita perfetta. ASEs 13 (1996) 509-527.

1497 *Bianchi, Daniela* L'amore in paradiso: il caso di MILTON. ASEs 13 (1996) 597-612.

1498 *Bonola, Gianfranco* Il paradiso dei nomi: BENJAMIN interprete di Genesi 1-3 (1916). ASEs 13 (1996) 623-654.

1499 *Bori, Pier Cesare* I tre giardini nella scena paradisiaca del *De hominis dignitate* di PICO DELLA MIRANDOLA ASEs 13 (1996) 551-564.

1500 *Burns, Dan E.* Dream form in Genesis 2.4B-3:24: asleep in the garden. The pentateuch. BiSe 39: 1996 <1987>, ⇒202. 150-160.

1501 *Busi, Giulio* L'architettura mistica dell'Eden nella tradizione ebraica. ASEs 13 (1996) 465-475.

1502 *Cristiani, Marta* Paradiso e natura in SCOTO ERIUGENA. ASEs 13 (1996) 529-537.

1503 *Daly, Gabriel* Interpreting original sin. PrPe 10/3 (1996) 87-91.

1504 *Destro, Alberto* Il paradiso nella scena finale del *Faust II*. ASEs 13 (1996) 613-622.

1505 **Dohmen, Christoph** Schöpfung und Tod: die Entfaltung theologischer und anthropologischer Konzeptionen in Gen 2/3. SBB 35: Stu 1996, Katholisches Bibelwerk 366 pp. Aktualisierte Neuausgabe. DM89. 3-460-00351-0.

1506 **Drewermann, Eugen** Le mal: approche psychanalytique du récit yahviste des origines 2. [T]*Bagot, Jean-Pierre*. P 1996, Desclée de B. 674 pp. FF350. 2-220-03755-X.

1507 *Duff, Paul; Hallman, Joseph* Murder in the garden?: the envy of the gods in Genesis 2 and 3. Contagion 3 (1996) 183-200.

1508 *Ellens, Harold J.* A psychodynamic hermeneutic of the Fall story: Genesis 2:25-3:24 through a psychological lens. PastPsy 45 (1996-97) 221-236 [EThL 74,193*].

1509 **Engammare, Max** Portrait de l'exégète en géographie: la carte du paradis comme instrument herméneutique chez CALVIN et ses contemporains. ASEs 13 (1996) 565-581.

1510 *Fernández Sanchez, Francisco-Cristóbal* Eva y la libertad sexual de la mujer. Communio 18/1 (1996) 58-77.

1511 *Ginzburg, Lisa* Adamiti, nuovi adamiti nella morale del seicento francese. ASEs 13 (1996) 583-596.

1512 **Gottfried, Robert R.** Economics, ecology and the roots of western faith: perspectives from the garden. 1995, ⇒11/1,319. [R]ThTo 53 (1996) 418, 420-422 (*Rolston, Holmes*).

1513 *Görg, Manfred* Der "Satan"—der "Vollstrecker" Gottes?. BN 82 (1996) 9-12.

1514 *Jones, M.J.* Toward a theology of origins: a partnership in peril. ABQ 15/1 (1996) 42-45 [Gen 3,1-9].
1515 *Judisch, D.M.* The protoevangelium and Concordia Theological Seminary. CTQ 60 (1996) 75-93 [Gen 3,15].
1516 *Katz, Jack* The social psychology of Adam and Eve. Theory and Society 25 (1996) 545-582.
1517 *Kennedy, James M.* Peasants in revolt: political allegory in Genesis 2-3. The pentateuch. BiSe 39: 1996 <1990>, ⇒202. 161-172.
1518 *Kessler, Rainer* Das kollektive Schuldbekenntnis im Alten Testament. EvTh 56 (1996) 29-43 [1 Kgs 8,46; Ps 106,6; Ezek 18,20; Lam 5,7].
1519 *Kimelman, Reuven* The seduction of Eve and the exegetical politics of gender. Bibl.Interp. 4 (1996) 1-39.
1520 *Kinsella, Sean Edward* Tangled thread of creation: Eve and Mary in the *Adversus Haereses*. Magistra 2/2 (1996) 92ff [ThD Index, Feb. 1997,8].
1521 *Koch, Klaus* "Adam, was hast du getan?": Erkenntnis und Fall in der zwischentestamentlichen Literatur. Wende der Zeiten. 1996 <1982>, ⇒133. 181-217.
1522 **Kruck, Gustav** Das Böse: die Bibelkritik eines Ex-Protestanten. Hasliberg-Wasserwendi 1996, Kruck 308 pp. 3-9521237-0-6 [NT-hAR 1999,2].
1523 **Ladaria, Luis F.** Teología del pecado original y de la gracia: antropología teológica especial. Manuales de Teología 1: 1993, ⇒10,1919. ᴿRET 56/3 (1996) 408-410 (*Navarro Girón, Mᵃ Angeles*).
1524 **Laurentin, René** Der Teufel: Mythos oder Realität?: die Lehre und die Erfahrungen Christi und der Kirche. Hauteville/Schweiz 1996, Parvis 399 pp. DM39. 3-907523-72-5 [ThGl 87, 674].
1525 **Lavatori, Renzo** Satana un caso serio: studio di demonologia cristiana. Nuovi Saggi Teologici 38: Bo 1996, Dehoniane 476 pp. 88-10-40540-4 [Isidorianum 6,300].
1526 *Maddox, Alana* Genesis 3:20: names of suffering and name of grace. RExp 93 (1996) 521-527.
1527 **Martinek, Manuela** Wie die Schlange zum Teufel wurde: die Symbolik in der Paradiesgeschichte von der hebräischen Bibel bis zum Koran.StOR 37: Wsb 1996, Harrassowitz 197 pp. 3-447-03752-0.
1528 **Messadié, Gerald** A history of the devil. ᵀ*Romano, Mare*. NY 1996, Kodansha vi; 377 pp. 1-56836-081-9.
1529 **Miller, James E.** The Western paradise: Greek and Hebrew traditions. SF 1996, International Scholars (8) 143 pp. 1-573-09127-8.
1530 ᴱ**Monaci Castagno, Adele** Il diavolo e i suoi angeli: testi e tradizioni (secoli I-III). BPat 28: F 1996, Nardini 507 pp. 88-404-2019-3.
1531 *Navarro Puerte, Mercedes* Gen 3,20 "...y el ꜣAdam llamó a su mujer Eva". Rés. 40. EphMar 46/1 (1996) 9-40.
1532 *Neufeld, Ernest* The anatomy of the first lies. JBQ 24/2 (1996) 112-114 [Gen 3,6-13].
1533 *Otto, Eckart* Die Paradieserzählung Genesis 2-3: eine nachpriesterschriftliche Lehrerzählung in ihrem religionshistorischen Kontext. ᶠMichel, D., BZAW 24: 1996, ⇒64. 167-192.
1534 **Page, Sydney H.T.** Powers of evil: a biblical study of Satan. 1995, ⇒11/1,333. ᴿRExp 93 (1996) 572-574 (*Arnold, Clinton E.*).
1535 **Pagels, Elaine** The origin of Satan. 1995, ⇒11/1,334. ᴿParabola 21/1 (1996) 106, 107 (*Frisardi, Andrew*); ThTo 53 (1996) 398,

400-401 (*Williams, James G.*); RStR 22/1 (1996) 3-9 (*TeSelle, Eugene*);

1536 As origens de Satanás: um estudo sobre o poder que as forças irracionais exercem na sociedade moderna. Rio de Janeiro 1996, Ediouro [Atualidade Teológica 1/1,97— Cavalcanti, Tereza];

1537 Satans Ursprung. B 1996, Berlin-Verl. 287 pp. 3-8270-0199-4.

1538 **Panier, Louis** Le péché originel: naissance de l'homme sauvé. Théologies: P 1996, Cerf 147 pp. F125. 2-204-05396-1 [EeV 107/3,22].

1539 **Peacock, Kevin Curtis** The covenant promises in their canonical relationship to the Eden narrative. 270 pp. Diss. Southwestern Bapt. Theol. Sem. 1995 [EThL 74,194*].

1540 *Perani, Mauro* Il giardino dell'Eden in NAHMANIDE. ASEs 13 (1996) 477-491.

1541 *Pochon, Martin* Adam et Eve: la mémoire d'un avenir. Vie Chrétienne Suppl. 413: P 1996, Vie Chrétienne 106 pp. FF65.

1542 *Poorthuis, M.* Who is to blame: Adam or Eve?: a possible Jewish source for AMBROSE's *De Paradiso* 12,56. VigChr 50 (1996) 125-135.

1543 **Pottier, Bernard** Le péché originel selon HEGEL: commentaire et synthèse critique. 1990, ⇒6,2336. ᴿZKTh 118 (1996) 529-530 (*Kern, Walter*).

1544 *Psaki, Regina* The sexualized body in DANTE and the medieval context. ASEs 13 (1996) 539-550.

1545 ᴱ**Resnick, Irven M.** ODO of Tournai: on original sin and a disputation with the Jew, LEO, concerning the advent of Christ, the son of God. 1994, ⇒10,1938. ᴿMedieval Encounters 2 (1996) 385-389 (*Saperstein, Marc*).

1546 *Rota Scalabrini, Patrizio* Ho avuto paura perché sono nudo (Gen 3,10). PSV 33/1 (1996) 21-37.

1547 **Santos Vaz, Armindo dos** A visâo das origens em Génesis 2,4b-3,24: coerência temática e unidade literária. Fundamenta 14: Lisbon 1996, Carmelo 605 pp. 927-651-246-8. ᴿTer. 47 (1996) 663-667 (*Báez, Silvio José*).

1548 *Savasta, Carmelo* Gen. 3,20-24; 4,1-4a,26g. BeO 38 (1996) 65-77.

1549 *Sola Ademiluka, S.* The fall of man: a critical study of Genesis 3 in an African background. DBM 15/1 (1996) 52-59.

1550 **Spaemann, Heinrich** Il maligno, conoscerlo e vincerlo secondo la bibbia. ᵀ*Pessa, G.*, R 1993, Città Nuova 64 pp. L4.500. 88-311-3943-6. ᴿAnime e Corpi 187 (1996) 703-704 (*Casera, Antonio*).

1551 *Spiazzi, R.* Meditazione sul Genesi: la pena. Collegamento pro fidelitate (2 February 1996) 16-18 [Gen 3,8-9].

1552 *Stadelmann, Luís* The serpent in paradise. Month 29 (7 July 1996) 263-265 [Gen 3].

1553 *Starke, Robert* The tree of life: protological to eschatological. Kerux 11/2 (1996) 15-31.

1554 **Stratton, Beverly J.** Out of Eden: reading, rhetoric, and ideology in Genesis 2-3. JSOT.S 208: 1995, ⇒11/1,340. ᴿCritRR 9 (1996) 170-172 (*Donaldson, Mara E.*).

1555 **Suchocki, Marjorie Hewitt** The fall to violence: original sin in relational theology. 1994, ⇒11/1,341. ᴿRStR 22/2 (1996) 124-128 (*Farley, Wendy*).

1556 *Van Ruiten, J.* The Garden of Eden and Jubilees 3:1-31. Bijd. 57 (1996) 318-336.

1557   **Vaz, Armindo dos Santos** A visão das origens em Gen 2,4b-3,24 como coerência temática e unidade literária. Diss. PUG 1995, ᴰ*Costacurta, Bruna*. Pref. by *Prato, Gian Luigi*. Lisboa 1996, Didaskalia 605 pp. 972-651-246-8 [RB 103,480].

1558   ᴱ**Verdegaal, C.** Stromen uit Eden: Genesis 1-11: ꟳPᴏᴜʟssᴇɴ, N., 1992, ⇒8,148b. ᴿNedThT 49/1 (1996) 73-74 (*Van Soest, H.-J.*).

1559   *Vogels, Walter* The power struggle between man and woman (Gen 3,16b). Bib. 77 (1996) 197-209.

1560   *Wagner, Siegfried* Anmerkungen eines Alttestamentlers zur Erbsündenlehre der Confessio Augustana (Artikel II). Ausgewählte Aufsätze. BZAW 240: 1996 <1980>, ⇒156. 169-181.

1561   *Wright, David P.* Holiness, sex, and death in the garden of Eden. Bib. 77 (1996) 305-329.

1562   *York, Anthony* The maturation theme in the Adam and Eve story. ꟳYᴏᴜɴɢ, D., 1996, ⇒107. 393-410.

1563   *Zilio-Grandi, Ida* Adamo in Paradiso nel Corano e nella tradizione esegetica musulmana. ASEs 13 (1996) 493-507.

ᴇ2.1 **Cain et Abel**; *gigantes, longaevi; Genesis 4s*

1564   *Alvarez Valdés, Ariel* Cain y Abel y el pecado original 'social'. RevBib 58 (1996) 237-243.

1565   *Bailey, Lloyd R.* Biblical math as *Heilsgeschichte?*. ꟳSᴀɴᴅᴇʀs, J., JSOT.S 225: 1996, ⇒77. 84-102 [Gen 5; 11].

1566   *Choi, Chang-Moh* The structure and meaning of Cain and Abel story in Genesis 4. Theological Thought 95 (1996) 139-160 [ThIK 18/2 (1997) 57]. **K.**

1567   *Clines, David J.A.* The significance of the 'sons of God' episode (Genesis 6.1-4) in the context of the 'primaeval history' (Genesis 1-11). The pentateuch. BiSe 39: 1996 <1979>, ⇒202. 75-88.

1568   **Delaney, David Kevin** The sevenfold vengeance of Cain: Genesis 4 in early Jewish and christian interpretation. Diss. Virginia 1996, ᴰ*Wilken, R.L.*, 239 pp. [EThL 74,193*].

1569   '*Eisses, Karel Th.* Een ernstig spel met getallen: de Godsnaam in Genesis 5. Interpretatie 4/1 (1996) 19-21.

1570   *Garrone, Daniele* Abele il giusto. Som. 11. PSV 34 (1996) 11-23 [Gen 4].

1571   *Kass, Leon R.* Farmers, founders, and fratricide: the story of Cain and Abel. First Things 62 (1996) 19-26 [Gen 4].

1572   *Külling, S.R.* Genesis 59: Teil: Gen 5,4-24. Fundamentum 1 (1996) 8-16;

1573   Genesis 60: Teil: Gen 5,24b. Fundamentum 2 (1996) 15-19 [OTA 19,409].

1574   *Lee, Jeong Woo (James)* A glimmer of hope: Genesis 5. Kerux 11/2 (1996) 7-14.

1575   *Moster, Julius B.* Cain: why is he featured so prominently in the bible?. JBQ 24 (1996) 233-240.

1576   *Paul, M.J.* Genesis 4:17-24: a case-study in eisegesis. TynB 47 (1996) 143-162.

1577   *Perani, Mauro* Abele nella tradizione ebraica. Som. 113. PSV 34 (1996) 113-133 [Gen 4].

1578   *Soggin, J. Alberto* Sons of God(s), heroes, and *nephilim*: remarks on Genesis 6:1-4. ꟳHᴀʀᴀɴ 1996, ⇒35. 135-136.

1579 *Tillard, J.-M.R.* 'Ecclesia ab Abel justo': la chiesa del martirio. Som. 299. PSV 34 (1996) 299-322 [Gen 4].

E2.2 *Diluvium*, **The Flood;** Gilgameš (Atraḫasis); **Genesis 6...**

1580 *Afanasieva, Veronika* Der irdische Lärm des Menschen (nochmals zum Atramḫasīs-Epos). ZA 86 (1996) 89-96.
1581 *Bowley, James E.* Ur of the Chaldees in Pseudo-EUPOLEMUS. JSPE 14 (1996) 55-63 [Gen 11,28; 15,7; Neh 9,7].
1582 *Castillo Castillo, Concepción* El *arca* de Noé en las fuentes árabes. MEAH 40-41/1 (1991-1992) 67-78.
1583 *Ciná, Giuseppe* 'Domanderò conto...a ognuno di suo fratello' (Gen 9,5): la responsabilità per la vita degli operatori sanitari alla luce della 'Evangelium vitae'. Camillianum 14/2 (1996) 195-217.
1584 **Cohn, Norman** Noah's flood: the Genesis story in western thought. NHv 1996, Yale University Press xiv; 154 pp. £20. 0-300-06823-9.
1585 *Croatto, José Severino* El relato de la torre de Babel (Génesis 11:1-9): bases para una nueva interpretación. RevBib 58 (1996) 65-80.
1586 **Davis, J. David** Finding the God of Noah: the spiritual journey of a Baptist minister from christianity to the laws of Noah. Hoboken, NJ 1996, KTAV xv; 224 pp. 0-88125-535-1.
1587 **Harland, Peter J.** The value of human life: a study of the story of the flood (Genesis 6-9). Diss. Durham, ᴰ*Moberly, R.W.L.*, VT.S 64: Lei 1996, Brill xiii; 245 pp. *f*150; $97. 90-04-10534-4.
1588 **Katz, Dina** Gilgamesh and Akka. 1993, ⇒9,2084. ᴿBiOr 53 (1996) 107-110 (*Lafont, Bertrand*); OLZ 91 (1996) 27-31 (*Böck, Barbara*).
1589 *Kilmer, Anne Draffkorn* Crossing the waters of death: the "stone things" in the Gilgamesh epic. WZKM 86 (1996) 213-217.
1590 *Kübel, Paul* Eva, Pandora und Enkidus "Dirne". BN 82 (1996) 13-20.
1591 **Louyot, Yves** La longue 'marche' de Noé. Saint-Maurice 1996, Saint-Augustin. FS24.80.
1592 *Loza Vera, José* Genesis 9,18-27. EfMex 14 (1996) 155-168.
1593 *Mendecki, Norbert* Tablica narodów w Rdz 10 [De tabula nationum in Gen 10]. RBL 49 (1996) 104-107. **P.**
1594 *Messina, J.P.* La bible et le destin du peuple noir: essai de réflexion critique sur le mythe de la malédiction de Cham. MSR 53 (1996) 183-199 [Gen 9,25].
1595 *Munday, John C.* Eden's geography erodes flood geology. WThJ 58 (1996) 123-154.
1596 **Müller, Klaus** Tora für die Völker: die noachidischen Gebote und Ansätze zur ihrer Rezeption im Christentum. SKI 15: 1994, ⇒10,1989; 11/1,371. ᴿCritRR 9 (1996) 352-354 (*Segal, Alan*) [Gen 9,1-7].
1597 *Prandi, Carlo* Il tema del diluvio nella storia delle religioni: un modello. Humanitas 51 (1996) 867-882.
1598 *Ska, J.L.* Nel segno dell'arcobaleno: il racconto biblico del diluvio (Gen 6-9). La natura. 1996, ⇒189. 41-66.
1599 *Smith, David* What hope after Babel?: diversity and community in Gen 11:1-9; Exod 1:1-14; Zeph 3:1-13 and Acts 2:1-3. HBT 18 (1996) 169-191.
1600 **Sölle, Dorethee** Wider den Gottesimperialismus: eine sozialgeschichtliche Interpretation von Gen 8,1-12. ᶠSCHOTTROFF, W., 1996, ⇒81. 11-16 [OTA 19,409].

1601 ᵀᴱTournay, Raymond Jacques; Shaffer, Aaron L'épopée de Gilgamesh. LAPO 15: 1994, ⇒10,1989. ᴿCBQ 58 (1996) 336-337
(*Moran, William L.*); EstB 54 (1996) 261-262 (*García Recio, J.*);
WO 27 (1996) 171-173 (*Röllig, Wolfgang*).
1602 **Uehlinger, Christoph** Weltreich und 'eine Rede'...Gen 11,1-9.
OBO 101: 1990, ⇒5,2238...10,2013. ᴿBiOr 53 (1996) 28-38 (*Van
der Kooij, Arie*).
1603 *Van der Kooij, Arie* The story of Genesis 11:1-9 and the culture of
ancient Mesopotamia. BiOr 53 (1996) 28-38.
1604 **Woodmorappe, John** Noah's ark: a feasibility study. Santee,
Calif. 1996, Institute for Creation Research xiv; 306 pp. 0-932766-
41-2 [NThAR 1997,259].
1605 **Young, Davis A.** The biblical flood: a case study of the church's
response to extrabiblical evidence. 1995, ⇒11/1,374. ᴿBS 153
(1996) 241-242 (*Pyne, Robert A.*); CTJ 31 (1996) 302-305 (*Cook,
Harry*); WThJ 58 (1996) 155-157 (*Futato, Mark*); SBET 14/2
(1996) 168-169 (*Graham, David*); ThTo 53 (1996) 401-402, 404
(*Haas, J.W.*).

E2.3 **Patriarchae, Abraham;** *Genesis 12s*

1606 *Alonso Schökel, Luis* Les cercles de la promesse et du don.
ᵀ*Chanet, Laurence Breysse*. MoBi 100 (1996) 51-55.
1607 *Ben-Gurion, David* The patriarchs <1964>. JBQ 24 (1996) 213-
220.
1608 *Berton, Raymond* Abraham est-il un modèle?: l'opinion des Pères
dans les premiers siècles de l'Église. BLE 97 (1996) 349-373.
1609 **Brunette, Pierre** Sur les pas d'Abraham. P 1996, Médiaspaul 108
pp.
1610 *Ego, Beate* Abraham als Urbild der Toratreue Israels: traditionsgeschichtliche Überlegungen zu einem Aspekt des biblischen Abra-
hambildes. Bund und Tora. WUNT 92: 1996, ⇒1645. 25-40.
1611 *Eitz, A.* Theater, Theater—welcher Abraham wird gespielt?: ein
Stückchen episches Theater. Forum Religion 3 (1996) 31-33 [ZID
22,428].
1612 *Eitz, A.; Göttling-Fuchs, M.* Der Blick zurück: perspektivische
Erzählungen zu Abraham, Sara und Hagar. Forum Religion 3
(1996) 33-36 [ZID 22,428].
1613 **Fischer, Irmtraud** Die Erzeltern Israels: feministisch-theologische
Studien zu Genesis 12-26. BZAW 222: 1994, ⇒10,2027; 11/1,388.
ᴿETR 71 (1996) 271-273 (*Römer, Thomas*); CBQ 58 (1996) 114-
116 (*Moore, Michael S.*); ThRv 92 (1996) 217-221 (*Kaiser, Otto*);
ThLZ 121 (1996) 1044-1047 (*Blum, Erhard*).
1614 *Futterlieb, H.* Du bist Abraham. Forum Religion 3 (1996) 3-7
[ZID 22,428].
1615 **Gossai, Hemchand** Power and marginality in the Abraham narrative. 1995, ⇒11/1,392. ᴿCBQ 58 (1996) 315-316 (*Pilch, John J.*).
1616 *Habas Rubin, Ephrat* A poem by the empress EUDOCIA: a note on
the patriarch. IEJ 46 (1996) 108-119.
1617 **Habel, Norman C.** The land is mine: six biblical land ideologies.
1995, ⇒11/1,393. ᴿBTB 26 (1996) 88 (*Hobbs, T.R.*); CBQ 58
(1996) 708-709 (*Scott, William R.*).
1618 *Habel, Norman C.* The indigenous and the immigrant ancestors and
the land. Al-Liqa³ 9-10 (1996) 14-33.

1619 *Härterich, H.* Aufbrechen—wandern—segnen: Abraham—ein Thema nicht nur für den Religionsunterricht. Forum Religion 3 (1996) 8-13 [ZID 22,428].

1620 *Henke, E.* Abrahams 'Versuchung': Versuch einer mythologisch-religiösen Deutung der Abrahamgeschichte. Forum Religion 3 (1996) 37-42 [ZID 22/11, 428].

1621 *Horner, T.J.* The problem with Abraham: JUSTIN Martyr's use of Abraham in the "Dialogue with Trypho a Jew". ChM 110 (1996) 230-250.

1622 **Jaffin, David** Abraham und die Erwählung Israels. Bad Liebenzell 1996, Liebenzeller Mission 127 pp. 3-88002-600-9 [NThAR 1997,67].

1623 *Kolb, D.* Abraham—Urbild des Glaubens. Forum Religion 3 (1996) 22-30 [ZID 22,428].

1624 *Lenhardt, Pierre* La terre d'Israël, Jérusalem, le temple: leur valeur pour les juifs et pour les chrétiens. Som., sum. 140. Cahiers Ratisbonne 1 (1996) 106-140. 0793-7229.

1625 *Leveen, Adriane B.* Memory and reflection: Jacob's story. JAGNES 5/2 (1995) 70-81 [IAJS 42,23].

1626 *Nicol, George G.* Jacob as Oedipus: Old Testament narrative as mythology. ET 108 (1996) 43-44.

1627 **Nielsen, Eduard** Abrahams historie. 1992, ⇒8,2341. RSEÅ 61 (1996) 117-118 (*Krantz, Eva Strömberg*).

1628 **Peinado Munñoz, Miguel** Abrahán y el libro del Génesis: (reflexiones sobre los relatos patriarcales: Gn 12-50). Granada 1996, Facultad de Teología 65 pp. Discurso inaugural del curso académico 1996-1997 [NThAR 1997,290].

1629 *Ravasi, Gianfranco* La espera de Abrahán y la esperanza del pueblo judío: el Cristo esperado. T*Padilla, Juan*. Communio 18 (1996) 427-435/Com(F) 21/5 (1996) 23-36.

1630 *Spero, Shubert* Was Abram born in Ur of the Chaldees?. JBQ 24/3 (1996) 156-159.

1631 *Thompson, Thomas L.* The background of the patriarchs: a reply to William DEVER and Malcolm CLARK. The pentateuch. BiSe 39: 1996 <1978>, ⇒202. 33-74.

1632 *Tournay, Raymond Jacques* Genèse de la triade "Abraham-Isaac-Jacob". RB 103 (1996) 321-336.

1633 *Van der Toorn, Karel* Ancestors and anthroponyms: kinship terms as theophoric elements in Hebrew names. ZAW 108 (1996) 1-11.

1634 *Vogelaar, H.* Abraham the archetype of faith: "there is no God but God!". WaW 16/2 (1996) 169-172.

1635 **Vogels, Walter A.** Abraham et sa légende: Genèse 12,1-25,11. LiBi 110: P 1996, Cerf 355 pp. FF98. 2-204-05546-8.

1636 *Wallace, Howard* On account of Sarai: Gen 12:10-13:1. ABR 44 (1996) 32-41.

1637 *Washington, Harold C.* Abraham's family as a prototype for interfaith dialogue: Judaism, Christianity, and Islam. RelEd 90 (1995) 286-301 [IAJS 42,24].

1638 *Weiß, I.* 'Es muß im Leben mehr als alles geben': eine Unterrichtseinheit für die Grundschule zur Geschichte Abrahams und Saras—nicht nur für den Religionsunterricht. Forum Religion 3 14-21 [ZID 22,428].

1639 *Wesselius, Jan Wim* De bedrogen bedrieger als oorsprong van het geschiedverhaal bij HERODOTUS en in het Oude Testament. Schurken en schelmen. 1995, F*BREMER, J.*, 33-43 [IAJS 42,24]

[Schurken en schelmen: culturhistorische verkenningen rond de Middellandse Zee. ᴱVan Erp Taalman Kip, A. Maria; Jong, Irene J.F. de. Amst 1995, Amsterdam University Press].

1640 *Westermann, Claus* Gebete in den Vätergeschichten. Das mündliche Wort. 1996, ⇒157. 67-79.

E2.4 Melchisedech, Sodoma; *Genesis 14...19*

1641 *Collin, Matthieu* Sodoma e Gomorra nel ciclo di Abramo. Il Mondo della Bibbia 34/4 (1996) 38-43.
1642 *Davila, James R.* Melchizedek, Michael, and war in heaven. SBL.SPS 35. 1996, ⇒274. 259-272 [Rev 12].
1643 *Gosse, Bernard* Melchisedech et le messianisme sacerdotal. Rés. 89. BeO 38 (1996) 79-89.
1644 **Letellier, Robert Ignatius** Day in Mamre, night in Sodom: Abraham and Lot in Genesis 18 and 19. Bibl.Interp. 10: 1995, ⇒11/1,437. ᴿScriptB 26 (1996) 84-86 (*Greenhalgh, Stephen*); CritRR 9 (1996) 155-156 (*Britt, Brian*).

E2.5 The Covenant (alliance, Bund): *Foedus, Genesis 15...*

1645 ᴱ**Avemarie, Friedrich; Lichtenberger, Hermann** Bund und Tora: zur theologischen Begriffsgeschichte in alttestamentlicher, frühjüdischer und urchristlicher-Tradition. WUNT 92: Tü 1996, Mohr x; 346 pp. DM218. 3-16-146627-6.
1646 **Elazar, Daniel J.** The covenant tradition in politics 2: covenant and commonwealth: from christian separation through the Protestant Reformation. L 1996, Transaction xix; 389 pp. $55 [RP 60,168s—Gross, George M.].
1647 *Ellis, Marc H.* Restoring the ordinary: an inquiry into the Jewish covenant at the end of Auschwitz. AJTh 10 (1996) 377-413 [ThIK 18/2,34].
1648 *Hermisson, Hans-Jürgen* Bund und Erwählung. Altes Testament. 1996, ⇒169. 244-267.
1649 **Kim, Tai-Il** The biblical foundations of mission in the Abrahamic covenant. Diss. Reformed Theological Seminary 1996, 220 pp. DAI-A 57/09, p. 3983; AAC 1382068.
1650 *Krasovec, Joze* Two types of unconditional covenant. HBT 18 (1996) 55-77 [Gen 15,7-21; 17,1-19; 2 Sam 7,1-17; Ps 89,20-38].
1651 *Levison, John R.* Torah and covenant in Pseudo Philo's Liber Antiquitatum Biblicarum;
1652 *Neef, Heinz-Dieter* Aspekte alttestamentlicher Bundestheologie. Bund und Tora. WUNT 92: 1996, ⇒1645. 111-127/1-23.
1653 *Olyan, Saul M.* Honor, shame, and covenant relations in ancient Israel and its environment. JBL 115 (1996) 201-218.
1654 **Rendtorff, Rolf** Die "Bundesformel". SBS 160: 1995, ⇒11/1,425. ᴿCBQ 58 (1996) 332-333 (*Gnuse, Robert*); Bib. 77 (1996) 432-433 (*Buis, Pierre*).
1655 *Wodecki, Bernard* Les aspects sotériologiques de l'alliance sinaïtique. IOSOT 1992. BEAT 28: 1996, ⇒256. 211-229.

1656 *Abécassis, Armand* Le rire des patriarches. LV(L) 45/5 (1996) 7-14 [Gen 18].

1657 **Hagelia, Hallvard** Numbering the stars...Gen 15. CB.OT 39: 1994, ⇒10,2041; 11/1,430. ^RCBQ 58 (1996) 116-117 *(Mandell, Sara)*.

1658 *Kaddari, Menahem Z.* Ma ra^ʾita ki...(Genesis 20,10). IOSOT 1992. BEAT 28: 1996, ⇒256. 79-84.

1659 **Kunin, Seth Daniel** The logic of incest: a structuralist analysis of Hebrew mythology. JSOT.S 185: 1995, ⇒11/1,443. ^RCBQ 58 (1996) 516-518 *(Moore, Michael S.)*.

1660 **Kwakkel, G.** De gerechtigheid van Abram: exegese van Genesis 15:6. KaBi 35: Barneveld 1996, De Vuurbaak 67 pp. f16. 90-5560-059-8 [NThAR 1997,259].

1661 *Pelletier, Anne-Marie* Mères et enfants dans l'Ancien Testament. MoBi 101 (1996) 7-10 [Gen 16].

1662 *Weis, Richard D.* Stained glass window, kaleidoscope or catalyst: the implications of difference in readings of the Hagar and Sarah stories. ^FSANDERS J., JSOT.S 225: 1996, ⇒77. 253-273 [Gen 16; 21].

E2.6 The ʿAqedâ; Isaac, Genesis 22...

1663 *Cardellino, Lodovico* Jahweh contro gli elohim per il sacrificio di Isacco. BeO 38 (1996) 91-110.

1664 **Caspi, Mishael Maswari; Cohen, Sascha Benjamin** The Binding [Aqedah] and its transformations in Judaism and Islam: the lambs of God. Lewiston, NY 1995, Mellen vi; 175 pp. £40; $80. ^RCritRR 9 (1996) 189-191; *(Kinlaw, Pamela)*.

1665 **Gellman, Jerome I.** The fear, the trembling, and the fire: KIERKEGAARD and Hasidic masters on the Binding of Isaac. 1994, ⇒10,2058. ^RHeyJ 37 (1996) 500-501 *(Watkin, Julia)*.

1666 **Krupp, Michael** Den Sohn opfern?: die Isaak-Überlieferung bei Juden, Christen und Muslimen. Nes Ammim Buch: Gü 1995, Kaiser 91 pp. DM38. 0-579-00289-9 [BL 1996,82].

1667 *Kunin, Seth Daniel* The death of Isaac: structuralist analysis of Genesis 22. The pentateuch. BiSe 39: 1996 < 1994 >, ⇒202. 319-343.

1668 *Lambert, Jean* La ligature d'Isaac et la non-confusion des générations. FV 95/4 (1996) 53-66.

1669 *Maltz, M.A.H.* The dynamics of intertextuality: the 'Akedah' and other biblical allusions in Henry ABRAMOVITCH's *Psalms of the jealous God* and Matti MEGGED's *The Akedah*. Sum. 79. JSem 8/1 (1996) 79-95.

1670 ^E**Manns, Frédéric** The sacrifice of Isaac in the three monotheistic religions. Symposium J 1995. ASBF 41: 1995, ⇒11/1,448. IslChr 22 (1996) 289 *(Fitzgerald, Michael L.)*.

1671 **Mbachu, Hilary** Abraham, offer your only beloved son as holocaust!: narrative-inculturation study of Gen 22,1-19. Deutsche Hochschulschriften 1100: Egelsbach 1996, Hänsel-Hohenhausen 301 pp. 3-8267-1100-9 [NThAR 1997,161].

1672 **Parmentier, M.F.G.** Isaak gebonden—Jezus gekruisigd: oudchristelijke teksten over Genesis 22. Christelijke Bronnen 9: Kampen 1996, Kok 143 pp. f27.50. 90-242-2489-6.

1673 *Pöhlmann, Wolfgang* Die Opferung Isaaks—die 'Bindung' Isaaks: ein umstrittener Bibeltext in vielfacher Auslegung. ᶠSᴄʜᴍ ɪᴅᴛ, G., 1996, ⇒80. 249-265.
1674 *Prolow, S.; Orel, Vladimir* Isaac unbound. BZ 40 (1996) 84-91.
1675 *Schlichting, W.* Ein schwerer Weg: (1.Mose 22,1-14). ThBeitr 27 (1996) 249-252.
1676 *Tilliette, Xavier* Bible et philosophie: le sacrifice d'Abraham. Gr. 77 (1996) 133-146.
1677 *Vermes, Geza* New light on the sacrifice of Isaac from 4Q225. JJS 47 (1996) 140-146.
1678 *Vetter, Dieter* Die Bindung Jizchacks: das sprachliche Werk—"ein mit den Lippen geschlossener Bund". Judentum. 1996 <1990>, ⇒154. 430-453;
1679 Rechtfertigung im Gericht: die Bedeutung von Genesis 22 für Rosch Ha-Schana und Jom Kippur. Judentum. 1996 <1988>, ⇒154. 364-368.

1680 *Hurowitz, Victor Avigdor kaesaep ʿober lassoḥer* (Genesis 23,16). ZAW 108 (1996) 12-19.
1681 *Lauwers, Michel* La sépulture des patriarches (Genèse, 23): modèles scripturaires et pratiques sociales dans l'occident médiéval ou du bon usage d'un récit de fondation. StMed 37 (1996) 519-547.
1682 *Teugels, Lieve* 'A strong woman, who can find?': a study of characterization in Genesis 24, with some perspectives on the general presentation of Isaac and Rebekah in the Genesis narratives. The pentateuch. BiSe 39: 1996 <1994>, ⇒202. 281-295.

ᴇ2.7 **Jacob** and Esau: ladder dream; *Jacob, somnium, Gen 25...*

1683 **Couture, André; Allaire, Nathalie** Ces anges qui nous reviennent. Rencontres Aujourd'hui 23: Montréal 1996, Fides 178 pp. ᴿScEs 48/3 (1996) 351-352 (*Archambault, Jean-Marie*).
1684 **Crüsemann, Frank** Dominion, guilt, and reconciliation: the contribution of the Jacob narrative in Genesis to political ethics. Semeia 66 (1994) 67-77.
1685 **Curzon, David** The view from Jacob's ladder: one hundred midrashim. Ph 1996, Jewish Publication Society of America xviii; 161 pp. 0-8276-0568-4.
1686 **Dresner, Samuel** Rachel. 1994, ⇒10,2088. ᴿJdm 45 (1996) 502-506 (*Schein, Andrew*).
1687 **Faes de Mottoni, Barbara** Bᴏɴᴀᴠᴇɴᴛᴜʀᴀ e la scala di Giacobbe: letture di angelologia. 1995, ⇒11/1,474. ᴿRThPh 128 (1996) 285-286 (*Suarez-Nani, Tiziana*).
1688 **Garcia de Fleury, Maria** Emisarios celestiales, los angeles. Caracas 1996, Panapo 110 pp.
1689 **Jeremiah, David** What the bible says about angels: powerful guardians, a mysterious presence, God's messengers. Sisters, Or. 1996, Multnomah 237 pp. 0-88070-902-2.
1690 *Malul, M.* ʿaqeb "Heel" and ʿaqab "to supplant" and the concept of succession in the Jacob-Esau narratives. VT 46 (1996) 190-212 [Gen 25,26].

1691 *Massonnet, Jean* Targum, midrash et Nouveau Testament: le songe de Jacob (Gn 28,10-22). Les premières traditions. 1996, ⇒159. 68-101 [John 1,51].

1692 **Miller, Patricia Cox** Dreams in late antiquity: studies in the imagination of a culture. 1994, ⇒10,9508*. ᴿChH 65 (1996) 445-446 (*Kelly, Joseph, F.*); JRS 86 (1996) 242-243 (*Price, S.R.F.*); JR 76 (1996) 469-470 (*Strousma, Guy G.*).

1693 *Nicol, George G.* The chronology of Genesis: Genesis xxvi 1-33 as "flashback";

1694 The narrative structure and interpretation of Genesis xxvi 1-33. VT 46 (1996) 330-338/339-360.

1695 *Ojore, Aloys Otieno* An African reading of the Jacob—Esau story, Gen. 25:19-34 and Gen. 27:1-45. African Christian Studies 12/4 (1996) 18-29.

1696 **Olyan, Saul M.** A thousand thousand served him: exegesis and the naming of angels in ancient Judaism. TSAJ 36: 1993, ⇒9,2205...11/2,3798. ᴿAJS Review 21 (1996) 384-386 (*Reeves, John C.*); CritRR 9 (1996) 162-163 (*Wacholder, Ben Zion*).

E2.8 Jacob's wrestling; the Angels; *Gen 31-36 & 38*

1697 *Amit, Yairah* Implicit redaction and latent polemic in the story of the rape of Dinah. ꟳHARAN M., 1996, ⇒35. 11*-28* [Gen 34]. H.

1698 **Bechtel, Lyn M.** What if Dinah is not raped? (Genesis 34). The pentateuch. BiSe 39: 1996 <1994>, ⇒202. 263-280.

1699 **Berzosa Martínez, Raúl** Ángeles y demonios: sentido de su retorno en nuestros días. BAC Popular 115: M 1996, BAC 188 pp. 84-7914-215-4 [Isidorianum 6,296].

1700 *Capuchin, Bona Marcel* Jacob at Jabbok: a close reading of Genesis 32:23-33. BiBh 22/1 (1996) 5-21.

1701 *Feld, Gerburgis* "... Wie es eben Frauen ergeht" (Gen 31, 35): Kulturgeschichtliche Überlegungen zum gegenwärtigen Umgang mit der Menstruation der Frau in Gesellschaft und Theologie. Von der Wurzel getragen. 1996, ⇒204. 29-42.

1702 **Garrett, Duane A.** Angels and the new spirituality. Nv 1995, Broadman & H. 272 pp. $13. 0-8054-6176-0. ᴿRExp 93 (1996) 574-575 (*Arnold, Clinton E.*).

1703 *Guardini, Romano* L'angelo: cinque meditazioni. Brescia 1994, Morcelliana 76 pp. ᴿLat. 62 (1996) 418-419 (*Sanna, Ignazio*).

1704 *Hatzapoulos, Athanasios* The struggle for a blessing: reflections on Genesis 32:24-31. ER 48 (1996) 507-512.

1705 *Hernández, Lucía Victoria* Los ángeles en el Antiguo Testamento y en las culturas del oriente medio. Cuestiones Teológicas y Filosóficas 60/2 (1996) 41-59.

1706 **Hoekveld-Meijer, Gerda** Esau: salvation in disguise: Genesis 36: a hidden polemic between our teacher and the prophets about Edom's role in post-exilic Israel through Leitwort names. Kampen 1996, Kok xiii; 461 pp. ƒ74.90. 90-390-0133-2.

1707 *Kasher, R.* Angelology and the supernal worlds in the Aramaic Targums to the Prophets. JSJ 27 (1996) 168-191.

1708 *Lesses, Rebecca* Speaking with angels: Jewish and Greco-Egyptian revelatory adjurations. HThR 89 (1996) 41-60.

1709 *Lewis, Naphtali* In the world of P. YADIN: where did Judah's wives live?. IEJ 46 (1996) 256-257 [Gen 38].
1710 **Lockyer, Herbert** All the angels in the bible. Peabody, MASS 1996, Hendrickson xv; 175 pp. 1-56563-198-6.
1711 *Mor, Menachem* עיון מחודש—תיאודוטוס, האפוס על שכם והשומרונים [THEODOTOS, the epos of Schechem and the Samaritans: a new interpretation]. ᶠSTERN M., 1996, ⇒87. Sum. 153*. 345-359 [Gen 33,8-34,13].
1712 *Noble, Paul* A "balanced" reading of the rape of Dinah: some exegetical and methodological observations. Bibl.Interp. 4 (1996) 173-204 [Gen 34].
1713 **Salm, Eva** Juda und Tamar: eine exegetische Studie zu Gen 38. Diss., FzB 76: Wü 1996, Echter x; 284 pp. DM39. 3-429-01748-3 [RB 103,638].
1714 *Samaha, John* Angels: their meaning for our world. Holy Land 16 (1996) 198-202.
1715 *Sarmiento, Victor J.* Los ángeles en las religiones no cristianas. Cuestiones Teológicas y Filosóficas 60/2 (1996) 25-40.
1716 **Scholz, Susanne** Rape plots: a feminist cultural study of Genesis 34. Diss. NY Union 1996-97 [RTL 29,580].
1717 *Smith, Morton* A note on some Jewish assimilationists: the angels. New Testament, 1996 <1984>, ⇒151. 235-241.
1718 *Snell, Robert T.* Genesis 32:22-32. Interp. 50 (1996) 277-280.
1719 *Zwickel, Wolfgang* Pnuel. BN 85 (1996) 38-43 [Gen 32,23-33].

E2.9 **Joseph;** Jacob's blessings; *Genesis 37; 39-50*

1720 *Bohak, Gideon* From fiction to history: contextualizing Joseph and Aseneth. SBL.SPS 35: 1996, ⇒274. 273-284.
1721 *Burchard, Christoph* Bibliographie zu Joseph und Aseneth. 437-459;
1722 The importance of Joseph and Aseneth for the study of the New Testament: a general survey and a fresh look at the Lord's supper. <1987>. 263-295 [Luke 2,15-17; John 6; 1 Cor 10-11];
1723 Joseph et Aséneth: questions actuelles. <1974>. 224-261;
1724 Joseph und Aseneth 25-29 armenisch. <1979>. 93-102;
1725 Joseph und Aseneth neugriechisch. <1977/78>. 35-51;
1726 Joseph und Aseneth serbisch -kirchenslawisch: Text und Varianten. <1980>. 53-91;
1727 Der jüdische Asenethroman und seine Nachwirkung: von EGERIA zu Anna Katharina EMMERICK oder von MOSES aus Aggel zu Karl KERENYI. <1987>. 321-436;
1728 Neues von Joseph und Aseneth auf armenisch. <1990/91>. 139-159;
1729 The present state of research on Joseph and Aseneth. <1987>. 297-320.
1730 Ein vorläufiger griechischer Text von Joseph und Aseneth. <1982>. 161-209.
1731 Zum Text von "Joseph und Aseneth". <1970>. 3-34;
1732 Zur armenischen Übersetzung von Joseph und Aseneth. Collab. *Burfeind, Carsten.* Gesammelte Studien. SVTP 13: 1996, ⇒119. 103-137.

1733 *Carmichael, Calum M.* Joseph, Moses, and the institution of the Israelite judicature. FYOUNG D., 1996, ⇒107. 15-25.

1734 *Chesnutt, Randall D.* From text to context: the social matrix of Joseph and Aseneth. SBL.SPS 35: 1996, ⇒274. 285-302.

1735 *Cruz Hernández, M.* Las 'novelas' egipcias de José y del joven Moisés. Sum. res. 5. MEAH 41/2 (1992) 5-33.

1736 *Deist, Ferdinand* A note on the narrator's voice in Gen 37,20-22. ZAW 108 (1996) 621-622.

1737 *Deselaers, Paul* "Fruchtbar im Lande meines Elends" (Gen 41,52): Josef und seine Brüder. GuL 69 (1996) 112-122.

1738 *Fokkelman, Jan P.* Genesis 37 and 38 at the interface of structural analysis and hermeneutics. Literary structure. 1996, ⇒200. 152-187.

1739 *Görg, Manfred* Potifar und Potifera. BN 85 (1996) 8-10 [Gen 37,36; 39,1; 41,45; 46,20].

1740 *Matthews, Victor H.* The anthropology of clothing in the Joseph narrative. The pentateuch. BiSe 39: 1996 <1995>, ⇒202. 344-355.

1741 *Mello, Alberto* Giuseppe e i suoi fratelli. Som. 25. PSV 34 (1996) 25-37.

1742 *Mizuno, Ryuichi* Put him under my control: power game of Reuben and Judah in the Joseph novelle. Kwansei-Gakuin-Daigaku 1 (1996) 1-21.

1743 *Opeloye, Muhib Omolayo* The account of Joseph (Yusuf) in the Qur'an and the bible. Hamdard Islamicus 18/3 (1995) 85-96 [IAJS 42,23].

1744 *Péter-Contesse, René* Was Potiphar a eunuch (Genesis 37,36; 39,1)?. BiTr 47 (1996) 142-146.

1745 *Rad, Gerhard von* El ciclo de José. <1970>;

1746 La historia bíblica de José y su versión novelística por Thomas MANN. La acción de Dios. 1996 <1965>, ⇒144. 23-39/260-276.

1747 *Remaud, Michel* Prophétesse et fille d'Asher. Rias., sum. 46. Cahiers Ratisbonne 1 (1996) 31-46 [Gen 46,17; Num 26,47].

1748 *Sacchi, Paolo* Il problema della datazione della storia di Giuseppe (Gen 37-50). Henoch 18 (1996) 357-364.

1749 *Shupak, Nili* The Joseph story: legend or history?. FHARAN M., 1996, ⇒35. 125*-133*. H.

1750 *Soggin, J. Alberto* Uno sguardo alla narrazione di Giuseppe Genesi cc. 37-50. FMOSCATI S., 1996: I, ⇒67. 393-401.

1751 *Standhartinger, Angela* From fictional text to socio-historical context: some considerations from a textcritical perspective on Joseph and Aseneth. SBL.SPS 35: 1996, ⇒274. 303-318.

1752 *Storniolo, I.* A história de José do Egito. Vida Pastoral 187 (1996) 2-6 [Strom. 52,345].

1753 *Wesselius, Jan Wim* Biblical poetry through targumic eyes: Onkelos' treatment of Genesis 49:8-12. FVAN UCHELEN. 1996, ⇒100. 131-145 [OTA 19,413].

E3.1 **Exodus event and theme;** *textus, commentarii*

1754 **Bräumer, Hansjörg** Das zweite Buch Mose: Kap. 1 bis 18. WStB.AT: Wu 1996, Brockhaus 304 pp. DM38. 3-417-25229-6/-329-2 [NThAR 1997,192].

1755 EBrenner, Athalya A feminist companion to Exodus to Deutero-
      nomy. Feminist Companion to the Bible 6: 1994, ⇒11/1,525.
      RScrB 26 (1996) 86-87 (Dines, Jennifer).
1756 Childs, Brevard S. Il libro dell'Esodo. 1995, ⇒11/1,526. RNRTh
      118 (1996) 913-914 & RdT 37 (1996) 562-564 (Ska, Jean Louis).
1757 Houtman, Cornelis Exodus 2: chapters 7:14-19:25. Historical
      Commentary on the OT: Kampen 1996, Kok 466 pp. 90-242-6194-
      5. RETR 72 (1997) 128 (Macchi, Jean-Daniel);
1758 Exodus 3: Exodus 20-40. Commentaar op het OT: Kampen 1996,
      Kok 715 pp. f99. 90-242-6234-8.
1759 Martínez Sáiz, Teresa Mekilta de Rabbí ISMAEL: comentario
      rabínico al libro del Éxodo. Biblioteca Midrásica 16: Estella 1995,
      Verbo Divino iv; 534 pp. 84-8169-054-6. RMEAH.H 44 (1995)
      174-175 (Pérez Fernández, Miguel).
1760 McNamara, Martin; Hayward, Robert; Maher, Michael
      Targum Neofiti 1 and Pseudo-Jonathan: Exodus. The Aramaic
      Bible: 1994, ⇒10,2146. RHebStud 37 (1996) 204-207 (Lund, Je-
      rome A.); CBQ 58 (1996) 716-717 (Bernstein, Moshe J.).
1761 Spreafico, Ambrogio El libro del Éxodo. Guía espiritual del AT:
      1995, ⇒11/1,533. RPerTeol 28 (1996) 261-262 (Gottardo, Roberto
      J.).
1762 EWevers, John William; Quast, U. Exodus. Septuaginta 2/1:
      1991, ⇒7,2155...11/1,534. RTheol(A) 67 (1996) 568-570
      (Simotas, P.).

1763 Alonso Schökel, Luis Salvezza e liberazione: l'Esodo. Epifania
      della Parola 8: Bo 1996, Dehoniane 222 pp. L33.000. 88-10-
      40232-4 [RTL 29,121].
1764 Anati, Emmanuel Exodus et Sinai: une reconsideration. IOSOT
      1992. BEAT 28: 1996, ⇒256. 11-25.
1765 Cazelles, Henri Peut-on circonscrire un événement Exode?. Études.
      1996 <1990>, ⇒120. 195-217.
1766 Choi, Baek Sung Exodus: how big was the population?. JBQ 24
      (1996) 115-118.
1767 Davies, Graham I. The composition of the book of Exodus: reflec-
      tions on the theses of Erhard BLUM. FHARAN, 1996, ⇒35. 71-85.
1768 Dohmen, Christoph Wenn Texte Texte verändern: Spuren der Ka-
      nonisierung der Tora vom Exodusbuch her. Die Tora als Kanon.
      1996, ⇒1308. 35-60.
1769 Dozeman, Thomas B. God at war: power in the Exodus tradition.
      NY 1996, OUP xv; 222 pp. £35.50. 0-19-510217-7.
1770 Ellis, Carl F. Free at last?: the gospel in the African-American
      experience. DG 21996, InterVarsity 285 pp. $13 [AUSS 36,122—
      Mulzac, Kenneth D.].
1771 Eslinger, Lyle Freedom or knowledge?: perspective and purpose in
      the Exodus narrative (Exodus 1-15). The pentateuch. BiSe 39:
      1996 <1991>, ⇒202. 186-202.
1772 Fischer, Georg Exodus 1-15: eine Erzählung. Studies in...Exodus.
      BEThL 126: 1996, ⇒1794. 149-178.
1773 Fontana, Raniero Sinai e Sion. ED 49 (1996) 211ff [ThD Index
      Feb. 1997,4].
1774 Fretheim, E. Terence "Because the whole earth is mine": theme and
      narrative in Exodus. Interp. 50 (1996) 229-239.

1775 **Genuyt, François** La sortie d'Égypte. Bible-Sciences du Langage: Lyon 1996, Profac-Cadir 162 pp. FF75 [EeV 107,274].

1776 **Gowan, Donald E.** Theology in Exodus: biblical theology in the form of a commentary. 1994, ⇒10,2139. [R]Pro Ecclesia 5 (1996) 370-371 (*Williamson, Clark M.*); CBQ 58 (1996) 515-516 (*Nagel, Elizabeth M.*).

1777 *Klopfenstein, Martin A.* Auszug, Wüste, Gottesberg: biblische Überlieferungen vom Sinaigebiet. Leben aus dem Wort. BEAT 40: 1996, ⇒132. 137-158.

1778 **Knohl, Israel** The sanctuary of silence: the priestly torah and the holiness school. 1995, ⇒11/1,545. LASBF 46 (1996) 442-448 (*Cortese, Enzo*).

1779 *Kreuzer, Siegfried* Die Exodustradition im Deuteronomium. SESJ 62 (1996) 81-106.

1780 *Levenson, Jon D.* The Exodus and biblical theology: a rejoinder to John J. COLLINS. BTB 26 (1996) 4-10.

1781 **Loewenstamm, Samuel E.** The evolution of the Exodus tradition. 1992, ⇒8,2469*; 10,2145. [R]JAOS 116 (1996) 288-289 (*Propp, William H.C.*).

1782 *Moor, Johannes C. de* Egypt, Ugarit and Exodus. [F]GIBSON J., 1996, 213-247.

1783 *Ostinelli, Caterina* Tra paura e timore nell'Esodo. PSV 33/1 (1996) 39-53.

1784 **Oswald, Wolfgang** Gottesberg—Wüste Sinai—Berg Sinai: eine Untersuchung zur Literargeschichte der vorderen Sinaiperikope Ex 19-24 und ihrem historischen Hintergrund. Diss. Zürich 1996-1997 [D]*Krüger, T.* [ThLZ 122,765].

1785 *Otto, Eckart* Die nachpriesterschriftliche Pentateuchredaktion im Buch Exodus. Studies in...Exodus. BEThL 126: 1996, ⇒1794. 61-111.

1786 **Owens, J. Edward** Narrative criticism and theology in Exodus 1-15. Diss. Cath. Univ. of America 1996, 255 pp. DAI-A 57/03, p. 1183; AAC 9629249.

1787 *Polak, Frank* Theophany and mediator: the unfolding of a theme in the book of Exodus. Studies in...Exodus. BEThL 126: 1996, ⇒1794. 113-147.

1788 *Regt, Lénart J. de* Aspects of the syntax and rhetoric of participant reference in Exodus. Studies in...Exodus. BEThL 126: 1996, ⇒1794. 515-522.

1789 *Schäfer, Peter* The Exodus tradition in pagan Greco-Roman literature. [F]STERN M., 1996, ⇒87. 9*-38*.

1790 *Schenker, Adrian* Drei Mosaiksteinchen: "Königreich von Priestern", "und ihre Kinder gehen weg", "wir tun und wir hören" (Exodus 19,6; 21,22; 24,7). Studies in...Exodus. BEThL 126: 1996, ⇒1794. 367-380.

1791 *Smith, Mark S.* The literary arrangement of the priestly redaction of Exodus: a preliminary investigation. CBQ 58 (1996) 25-50.

1792 *Trublet, Jacques* Les effets pervers de l'Exode. LV(L) 45/1 (1996) 19-41.

1793 **Utzschneider, Helmut** Gottes langer Atem: die Exoduserzählung (Ex 1-14) in ästhetischer und historischer Sicht. SBS 166: Stu 1996, Kath. Bibelwerk 134 pp. DM39.80. 3-460-04661-9 [BiKi 52,147].

1794 ^E**Vervenne, Marc** Studies in the book of Exodus: redaction—
reception—interpretation. BEThL 126: Lv 1996, University Press
xi; 660 pp. FB2.400. 90-6186-755-X.

1795 *Vervenne, Marc* Current tendencies and developments in the study
of the book of Exodus. Studies in...Exodus. ⇒1794. 21-59.

1796 **Zakovitch, Yair** 'And you shall tell your son...': the concept of
the Exodus in the bible. 1991, ⇒7,2159...10,2156. ^RHenoch 18/1-
2 (1996) 213-217 (*Marquis, Galen*); ThR 61 (1996) 147-148
(*Reventlow, Henning Graf*).

E3.2 Moyses — Pharaoh, Goshen — *Exodus 1...*

1797 *Beauchamp, Paul* Exode 2: Moïse entre deux peuples. Croire 19
(1996) 34-35.

1798 *Boecker, Hans Jochen* Mose. Altes Testament. 1996, ⇒ 169. 1-10.

1799 **Bucaille, Maurice** Moïse et Pharaon: les hébreux en Egypte: quel-
les concordances des livres saints avec l'histoire?. P 1995, Seghers
264 pp. 2-232-10466-4.

1800 **Butler, John G.** Moses: the emancipator of Israel. Bible Biography
12: Clinton, Iowa 1996, LBC 810 pp. [NThAR 1997,192].

1801 *Cogan, Mordechai* The other Egypt: a welcome asylum. ^FHARAN
M., 1996, ⇒35. 65-70 [Deut 23,4-9].

1802 **Cohen, Jonathan** The origin and evolution of the Moses nativity
story. SHR 58: 1993, ⇒9,2288. ^RStPhilo 8 (1996) 187-189
(*Sterling, Gregory E.*).
Cruz Hernández, M. Las 'novelas' egipcias de José y del joven
Moisés. ⇒1735.

1803 **Davies, Gordon F.** Israel in Egypt: reading Exodus 1-2. JSOT.S
135: 1992, ⇒8,2489...11/1,563. ^RAUSS 34/1 (1996) 112-114
(*Hasel, Michael G.*).

1804 **Dörrfuß, Ernst Michael** Mose in den Chronikbüchern: Garant
theokratischer Zukunftserwartung. BZAW 219: 1994, ⇒10,2162;
11/1,567. ^RThRev 92 (1996) 304-305 (*Oeming, Manfred*); BiOr 53
(1996) 499-502 (*Dirksen, Piet B.*).

1805 *Gelernter, David* Who is the man beneath the veil?. CJud 47/3
(1995) 13-23 [IAJS 42,25].

1806 **Greenberg, Gary** The Moses mystery: the African origins of the
Jewish people. Secaucus, NJ 1996, Birch Lane x; (2) 308 pp. 1-
55972-371-8.

1807 **Hertog, C. den** Het zonderlinge karakter van de godsnaam: lite-
raire, psychoanalytische en theologische aspecten van het roepings-
verhaal van Mozes (Exodus 2.23-4.17). Zoetermeer 1996, Boekencentrum 263 pp. *f*42.50. 90-239-0549-0 [GThT 97/2,99].

1808 *Hughes, Paul Edward* Kings without privilege: Graeme AULD's
interpretation of the bible's presentation of David and Moses. BBR
6 (1996) 153-157.

1809 **Lenzen, Verena** Moses. Augsburg 1996, Pattloch 144 pp. DM68
[BiLi 70,327].

1810 **MacQuarrie, John** Mediators between human and divine: from
Moses to MUHAMMAD. NY 1996, Continuum viii; 171 pp. $20.
0-8264-0887-7 [ThD 44,77].

1811 *Maher, Michael* Targum Pseudo-Jonathan of Exodus 2.21.
^FMcNAMARA M., JSOT.S 230: 1996, ⇒58. 81-99.

1812 *Muffs, Yochanan* Moses for the defense. Parabola 21/1 (1996) <1992> 67-68.
1813 **Nataf, Georges** Moïse, autobiographie. Anamorphoses: P 1996, Berg 228 pp. FF98. 2-911289-06-4 [BCLF 582,807].
1814 *Noegel, Scott B.* Moses and magic: notes on the book of Exodus. JANES 24 (1996) 45-59.
1815 **Nohrnberg, James** Like unto Moses: the constituting of an interruption. 1995, ⇒11/1,576. RCBQ 58 (1996) 520-521 (*Walsh, Jerome T.*).
1816 **Paul, Robert A.** Moses and civilization: the meaning behind FREUD's myth. NHv 1996, Yale University Press (10) 268 pp. 0-300-06428-4.
1817 **Pinnick, Avital Kobayashi** The birth of Moses in Jewish literature of the Second Temple period. Diss. Harvard 1996, DStone, M.E., 244 pp. [EThL 74,244*].
1818 *Remus, Harold* Moses and the thaumaturges: PHILO's De vita Mosis as a rescue operation. LTP 52 (1996) 665-680.
1819 **Rohl, David M.** Pharoahs and kings: a biblical quest. NY 1995, Crown 425 pp. RFaith & Mission 14/1 (1996) 96-98 (*Patterson, Paige*).
1820 *Römer, Thomas* Les sages-femmes du pharaon et la 'crainte de Dieu' (Exode 1,15-22);
1821 *Siebert-Hommes, Jopie* Hebräerinnen sind חיות [Exod 1,19]. IOSOT 1992. BEAT 28: 1996, ⇒160. 183-190/191-199.
1822 **Smend, Rudolf** Mose als geschichtliche Gestalt. Schriften des Historischen Kollegs, Dokumentationen 11: Mü 1995, Stiftung Historisches Kolleg 23 pp. Theodor-Schieder-Gedächtnisvorlesung, 5 [NThAR 1998,335].
1823 *Van Seters, John* The life of Moses: the Yahwist as historian in Exodus-Numbers. 1994, ⇒10,2177; 11/1,580. RETR 71 (1996) 273-274 (*Macchi, Jean-Daniel*); SJOT 10 (1996) 146-148 (*Willesen, Søren*); Interp. 50 (1996) 295-297 (*Balentine, Samuel E.*); CBQ 58 (1996) 140-141 (*Ska, Jean Louis*).
1824 *Weimar, Peter* Exodus 1,1-2,10 als Eröffnungskomposition des Exodusbuches. Studies in...Exodus. BEThL 126: 1996, ⇒1794. 179-208.

E3.3 Nomen divinum, Tetragrammaton; *Exodus 3,14...*Plagues

1825 *Cazelles, Henri* Yahwisme, ou Yahwé en son peuple. Études. 1996 <1995>, ⇒120. 35-47.
1826 *Diebner, Bernd Jorg* Verkörperung des Wortes Gottes im TNK. FZUURMOND R., YHWH. DBAT.B: 1996, ⇒109. 143-164 [OTA 19,486].
1827 *Dijkstra, Meindert* Yahwe-El or El Yahweh?. IOSOT 1992. BEAT 28: 1996, ⇒160. 43-52.
1828 *Eslinger, Lyle* Knowing Yahweh: Exod 6:3 in the context of Genesis 1 - Exodus 15. Literary structure. 1996, ⇒200. 188-198.
1829 **Faivre, Daniel** L'idée de Dieu chez les hébreux nomades: une monolâtrie sur fond de polydémonisme. Pref. by *Rose, Martin.* P 1996, L'Harmattan 293 pp. FF160. 2-7384-4909-3 [RTL 28,292].
1830 *Frolov, Serge* The hero as bloody bridegroom: on the meaning and origin of Exodus 4,26. Bib. 77 (1996) 520-523.

1831 *Gruenwald, Ithamar* God the 'stone/rock': myth, idolatry, and cultic fetishism in Ancient Israel. JR 76 (1996) 428-449.
1832 **Kowalski, Vesta Marie H**. Rock of ages: a theological study of the word 'Tsur' as a metaphor for Israel's God. Diss. Jewish Theol. Sem. of America 1996, 334 pp. [JQR 87,264].
1833 *Kunin, Seth D*. The bridegroom of blood: a structuralist analysis. JSOT 70 (1996) 3-16 [Exod 4,20-26].
1834 *Lehane, Terry John* Zipporah and the Passover. JBQ 24/1 (1996) 46-50 [Exod 4,22-26].
1835 *Lewis, Theodore J*. The identity and function of El/Baal Berith. JBL 115 (1996) 401-423.
1836 *Lim, Seung-Pil* Wie kann der Name Gottes übersetzt werden?. Samok 204 (1996) 84-99 [ThIK 18/1,52]. **K.**
1837 *Lust, Johan* Exodus 6,2-8 and Ezekiel.   Studies in...Exodus. BEThL 126: 1996, ⇒1794. 209-224 [Exod 6,2-8; 20,5-6.42].
1838 *Macchi, J.D.* Exode et vocation (Ex 3/1-12). ETR 71 (1996) 67-74.
1839 *Mafico, T.L.J.* The divine compound name יְהוָה אֱלֹהִים and Israel's monotheistic polytheism. JNSL 22/1 (1996) 155-173.
1840 **Mettinger, Tryggve N.D.** Buscando a Dios: significado y mensaje de los nombres divinos en la Biblia. 1994, ⇒10,2195; 11/1,595. ᴿRBíbArg 58/1 (1996) 56-58 (*Mendoza, Claudia*); Cart. 12 (1996) 478-479 (*Cuenca Molina, J.F.*).
1841 **Niehaus, Jeffrey J.** God at Sinai: covenant and theophany in the bible and ancient Near East. 1995, ⇒11/1,655. ᴿBS 153 (1996) 495-496 (*Chisholm, Robert B.*).
1842 *Richter, Hans-Friedemann* Gab es einen "Blutbräutigam"?: Erwägungen zu Ex 4,24-26.;
1843 **Scriba, Albrecht** Die Geschichte des Motivkomplexes Theophanie. FRLANT 167: 1995, 11/1,598. ᴿOrdKor 37 (1996) 488-489 (*Giesen, Heinz*).
1844 *Siebert-Hommes, Jopie* 'ICH WERDE SEIN' oder 'ICH WERDE DA SEIN': eine Untersuchung zu Exodus 3,14. ᶠZUURMOND R.: YHWH. DBAT.B: 1996, ⇒109. 59-67 [OTA 19,415].
1845 **Smith, Robert C.** Hebrew names for God: a series of bible studies. Nv 1996, Townsend 80 pp. Diss. M.Div. 1987. 0-910683-33-6 [NThAR 1998,367].
1846 *Taylor, J. Glen* A response to Steve A. WIGGINS, 'Yahweh: the God of sun?'. JSOT 71 (1996) 107-119.
1847 **Tournier, Michel** Eléazar ou la source et le buisson. P 1996, Gallimard 140 pp. F78. ᴿStr. 64/1 (1996) 38-47 (*Pelckmans, Paul*).
1848 *Wiggins, Steve A*. Yahweh: the God of sun?. JSOT 71 (1996) 89-106.

1849 *Lemmelijn, Bénédicte* Transformations in biblical studies: the story of the history of research into the "plague narrative" in Exod 7:14-11:10. JNSL 22/2 (1996) 117-127;
1850 'Zoals het nog nooit was geweest en ook nooit meer zou zijn' (Ex. 11,6): de 'plagen von Egypte' volgens Ex. 7-11: historiciteit en theologie. TTh 36 (1996) 115-131.
1851 *Poorthuis, Marcel* De staf van Mozes in de tuin van Tsippora. Interpretatie 4/2 (1996) 17-20 [Exod 4].

1852 Schmidt, Werner H. Die Intention der beiden Plagenerzählungen (Exodus 7-10) in ihrem Kontext. Studies in...Exodus. BEThL 126: 1996, ⇒1794. 433-441/225-243.

E3.4 Pascha, sanguis, sacrificium: Passover, blood, sacrifice, Ex 11...

1853 Ahuis, Ferdinand Exodus 11,1-13,16 und die Bedeutung der Trägergruppen für das Verständnis des Passa. FRLANT 168: Gö 1996, Vandenhoeck & R. 126 pp. DM54. 3-525-53851-0. ^RZAR 2 (1996) 183-189 (Gertz, Jan Christian).
1854 Anderson, Gary A. Sacrifices and offerings in ancient Israel: an introduction. Community. 1996 <1987>, ⇒172. 182-200.
1855 Andrei, Osvalda The 430 years of Ex. 12:40, from DEMETRIUS to JULIUS Africanus: a study in Jewish and Christian chronography. Henoch 18 (1996) 9-67.
1856 Ansaldi, Jean Le sacrifice comme séduction du 'Dieu obscur'. FV 95/4 (1996) 77-91.
1857 Banon, David Une lecture midrachique d'Exode 14 et 15;.
1858 Batista, Israël Lire la bible avec les yeux de la foi: libération, rationalisme et utopie. BCPE 48/7-8 (1996) 18-27/28-39.
1859 Baumgarten, Albert I. ḥaṭṭaʾt sacrifices. RB 103 (1996) 337-342.
1860 Berger, Gedalyah A study of 'Shirat Hayam'. Alei Etzion 2 (1995) 75-84 [Exod 15,1-18] [IAJS 42,25].
1861 Bernardini, P. GIUSTINO, Cartagine e il Tophet. RSFen 24 (1996) 27-45.
1862 Briend, Jacques Sinai, Oreb: dov'è la "montagna di Dio"?. Il Mondo della Bibbia 33/3 (1996) 30-31.
1863 Bulas, Ryszarda Représentation du passage de la Mer Rouge dans l'ensemble des mosaïques de la Basilique Santa Maria Maggiore à Rome. Som. 40. Vox Patrum 11-12 (1991-92) 33-40. P.
1864 Burden, Terry L. The kerygma of the wilderness traditions in the Hebrew Bible. AmUSt.TR 163: 1994, ⇒10,2227. ^RCBQ 58 (1996) 103-104 (Nagel, Elizabeth M.).
1865 Cantalamessa, Raniero La montée au Sinaï: à la rencontre du Dieu vivant. ^TDovetta, Jean. Versailles 1996, Saint-Paul 214 pp. 2-85049-664-2.
1866 Charcosset, Jean-Pierre Des choses cachées aux intelligents et aux 'sages': René GIRARD et le sacrifice. FV 95/4 (1996) 93-107.
1867 Ciasca, Antonia, (al), Saggio preliminare sugli incinerati del tofet di Mozia. VO 10 (1996) 317-346.
1868 Cohen, Jeffrey M. 1001 questions and answers on Pesach. Northvale, NJ 1996, Aronson xv; 363 pp. 1-56821-523-1.
1869 Dietzfelbinger, Rudolf Ex 17,8-16 in der frühchristlichen Exegese: einige Anmerkungen. Studies in...Exodus. BEThL 126: 1996, ⇒1794. 603-607.
1870 Dozeman, Thomas B. The yam-sûp in the Exodus and the crossing of the Jordan river. CBQ 58 (1996) 407-416 [Exod 15,4; Josh 4,21-24].
1871 Engstrom, Paul Lee Deliverance at the sea: a reading of Exodus 15 in light of ancient Near Eastern literature and its implications for The Assemblies of God. Diss. Luther Seminary 1996, ^DNysse, Richard. 233 pp. DAI-A 57/08, p. 3541; AAC 9634273.

1872 *Fischer, Georg* Das Schilfmeerlied Exodus 15 in seinem Kontext. Bib. 77 (1996) 32-47.
1873 **Goodhart, Sandor** Sacrificing commentary: reading the end of literature. Baltimore 1996, Johns Hopkins Univ. Press xiv; 362 pp. $54 [JR 78,496ss—Britt, Brian].
1874 *Johnstone, William* From the sea to the mountain, Exodus 15,22-19,2: a case study in editorial techniques. Studies in...Exodus. BEThL 126: 1996, ⇒1794. 245-263.
1875 *Krüger, Thomas* Erwägungen zur Redaktion der Meerwundererzählung (Exodus 13,17-14,31). ZAW 108 (1996) 519-533.
1876 **Kvarme, Ole Kristian** Åtte dager i Jerusalem: en bok om Jesu påske, om jødisk og kristen påskefeiring. Oslo 1996, Verbum [TTK 69,236-237—Kullerud, O.F.].
1877 *Lemmelijn, Bénédicte* Setting and function of Exod 11,1-10 in the Exodus narrative. Studies in...Exodus. BEThL 126: 1996, ⇒1794. 443-460.
1878 *Limet, Henri* Le sacrifice sanglant. WZKM 86 (1996) 251-262.
1879 *Macchi, Jean-Daniel* Le sacrifice samaritain de la Pâque. FV 95/4 (1996) 67-76.
1880 *Malina, Bruce J.* Mediterranean sacrifice: dimensions of domestic and political religion. BTB 26 (1996) 26-44.
1881 *Mann, Thomas W.* Passover: the time of our lives. Interp. 50 (1996) 240-250 [Exod 12].
1882 *Marx, Alfred* Le sacrifice dans l'Ancien Testament: regard impressionniste sur un quart de siècle de recherches. FV 95/4 (1996) 3-17.
1883 *Milbank, John* Stories of sacrifice. MoTh 12 (1996) 27-56.
1884 *Milgrom, Jacob* Further on the expiatory sacrifices. JBL 115 (1996) 511-514.
1885 *Molina, Jean-Pierre* Le sacrifice, désir de payer, besoin d'être pardonnée. FV 95/4 (1996) 109-121.
1886 *Moscati, S. Tofet* e necropoli I. RSFen 24 (1996) 73-76.
1887 *Remaud, Michel* Le pronom 'moi': interprété comme nom propre de Dieu dans quelques midrashim sur l'Exode. Som., sum. 148. Cahiers Ratisbonne 1 (1996) 141-148 [Exod 18,6; 3,11-12].
1888 *Ribichini, S. Tofet* e necropoli II. RSFen 24 (1996) 77-83.
1889 **Rooze, E.** Amalek geweldig verslagen: een bijbelstheologisch onderzoek naar de vijandschap Israël-Amalek. Gorinchem 1995, Narratio 248 pp. ƒ39.50. 90-5263-902-7. ᴿKeTh 47 (1996) 246-247 (*Van der Woude, A.S.*).
1890 *Rösel, Martin* Pesach: Altes Testament. TRE 26 (1996) 231-236.
1891 *Sarianidi, Viktor* The biblical lamb and the funeral rites of Margiana and Bactria. Mes. 31 (1996) 33-47.
1892 *Schenker, Adrian* 'Ein Königreich von Priestern' (Ex 19,6): welche Priester sind gemeint?. IKaZ 25 (1996) 483-490;
1893 Un regno di sacerdoti (Es 19,6). 1996. Com(I) 150,9-16; Com(F) 21/6, 33-41; Commmunio 18,488-494.
1894 *Schnider, Franz* Pesach: Judentum. TRE 26 (1996) 236-240.
1895 *Ska, Jean Louis* Exode 19,3b-6 et l'identité de l'Israël postexilique. Studies in...Exodus. BEThL 126: 1996, ⇒1794. 289-317.
1896 *Stein, Dominique* Histoire d'un passage: réflexions psychanalytiques à propos d'Exode 14-15. BCPE 48/7-8 (1996) 40-51.
1897 *Tabory, Joseph* The crucifixion of the paschal lamb. Sum. 395. JQR 86 (1996) 395-406.

1898 *Teugels, Lieve* Did Moses see the chariot?: the link between Exod 19-20 and Ezek 1 in early Jewish interpretation. Studies in...Exodus. BEThL 126: 1996, ⇒1794. 595-602.

1899 *Vervenne, Marc* Exodus expulsion and Exodus flight: the interpretation of a crux critically re-assessed. JNSL 22/2 (1996) 45-58 [Exod 14,5].

1900 *Vetter, Dieter* Brauchtum und Bedeutung des Pesach-Festes: "Warum unterscheidet sich diese Nacht von allen Nächten?". Judentum. 1996 <1988>, ⇒154. 345-353.

1901 *Wagenaar, Jan* Crossing the Sea of Reeds (Exod 13-14) and the Jordan (Josh 3-4): a priestly framework for the wilderness wandering;

1902 *Wénin, André* La théophanie au Sinaï: structures littéraires et narration en Exode 19,10-20,21;

1903 *Zenger, Erich* Wie und wozu die Tora zum Sinai kam: literarische und theologische Beobachtungen zu Exodus 19-34. Studies in...Exodus. BEThL 126: 1996, ⇒1794. 461-470/471-480/265-288.

E3.5 Decalogus, *Ex 20 = Dt 5; Ex 21ss;* Ancient Near East Law

1904 *Anderson, Gary A.* Torah before Sinai: the do's and don'ts before the Ten Commandments. BiRe 12/3 (1996) 39-44.

1905 ᴱ**Barker, William S.; Godfrey, W. Robert** Theonomy. 1990, ⇒9,11502. ᴿTrinJ 17/1 (1996) 105-109 (*Brand, Chad*).

1906 *Benecchi, Valdo* Il decalogo: dono e responsabilità. Servitium 30/108 (1996) 15-23.

1907 *Boecker, Hans Jochen* Recht und Gesetz: der Dekalog. Altes Testament. 1996, ⇒169. 110-127.

1908 *Braun, Carola von; Martiny, Anke* Von der Scham in der Politik. Zehn Worte. 1996, ⇒194. 124-144.

1909 *Bruni, Giancarlo* Le dieci parole, perché?: introduzione al quaderno. Servitium 30/108 (1996) 9-14.

1910 *Crüsemann, Frank* Die zehn Worte. Zehn Worte. 1996, ⇒194. 20-37.

1911 *Devaux, Michaël* The truth of love, the lie of death. ᵀ*Schindler, David Louis.* Com(US) 23/1 (1996) 110-121.

1912 **Douma, Jochem** The ten commandments: a manual for the christian life. ᵀ*Kloosterman, Nelson D.*, Phillipsburg, NJ 1996, P&R xiv; 410 pp. $25. 0-87552-237-8 [ThD 45,169—Heiser, W. Charles].

1913 *Ebach, Jürgen* Keine Engel, keine Sklaven—Gebote für befreite Menschen. Zehn Worte. 1996, ⇒194. 52-72.

1914 *Ehrlich, Carl S.* Die Zehn Gebote im jüdischen Rahmen. Orien. 60/17 (1996) 185-187.

1915 *Heid, Stefan* Die Tora als Staatsgesetz in der jüdisch-christlichen Apologetik. ᶠDASSMANN, E., JAC.E 23: 1996, ⇒19. 49-65.

1916 *Hirschler, Horst* Konkretionen der Freiheit. Zehn Worte. 1996, ⇒194. 84-102.

1917 **Howe, Frederic R.** Witnesses in stone: landmarks and lessons from the living God. GR 1996, Kregel 144 pp. 0-8254-2869-6 [NThAR 1997,259].

1918 **Jiménez Hernández, Emiliano** Las alas de la Torá: comentarios rabínicos del decálogo. Biblioteca Catecumenal: Bilbao 1996, Desclée de B. 178 pp. 84-330-1150-2 [NThAR 1998,268].

1919 *Klein, Christoph* Die Zehn Gebote—Ordnungen der Liebe. Zehn Worte. 1996, ⇒194. 38-51.

1920 **Koch, Traugott** Zehn Gebote für die Freiheit. 1995, ⇒11/1,652. ᴿZEE 40 (1996) 313-316 (*Lincoln, Ulrich*); ThLZ 121 (1996) 1197-1199 (*Kern, Udo*).

1921 **Krawczyk, Roman** Dekalog: Kodeks etyki społecznej Starego Testamentu. Siedlce 1994, Siedleckie Wydawnictwo Diecezjalne 148 pp. ᴿAtK 126 (1996) 298-299 (*Dziuba, Andrzej*). P.

1922 **Lehmann, Paul L.** The decalogue and a human future: the meaning of the commandments for making and keeping human life human. 1995, ⇒11/1,653. ᴿTS 57 (1996) 373-375 (*Spohn, William C.*); Interp. 50 (1996) 328, 330 (*Jersild, Paul*).

1923 *Mahrenholz, Ernst Gottfried* Gesetzgeber Gott? oder: Freiheit, die ich meine. Zehn Worte. 1996, ⇒194. 103-123.

1924 **Marshall, Jay W.** The 10 commandments & christian community. Scottdale, PA 1996, Herald 128 pp. 0-8361-9027-0.
ᴱ**Natrup, Susanne** Zehn Worte der Freiheit. ⇒194.

1925 *Natrup, Susanne* Zehn Worte der Freiheit. Zehn Worte. 1996, ⇒194. 7-19.

1926 *Otto, Eckart* Alte und neue Perspektiven in der Dekalogforschung;

1927 Der Dekalog als Brennspiegel israelitischer Rechtsgeschichte. Kontinuum. 1996, ⇒2002. 285-292/293-303.

1928 *Renaud, Bernard* Al Sinai, Dio dà la sua legge. Il Mondo della Bibbia 33/3 (1996) 32-34.

1929 *Rizzi, Armido* Lettura 'laica': un tentativo [Decalogo]. Servitium 30/108 (1996) 24-30.

1930 **Schmidt, Werner H.** I dieci comandamenti e l'etica veterotestamentaria. Collab. *Delkurt, Holger; Graupner, Axel*, CSB 114: Brescia 1996, Paideia 235 pp. L35.000. 88-394-0539-9.

1931 *Steyn, Gert J.* Pretexts of the second table of the decalogue and early christian intertexts. Neotest. 30 (1996) 451-464.

1932 ᴱ**Trotta, Giuseppe** Sul Monte Sinai: etica o rivelazione?. Attendendo l'aurora: Brescia 1996, Morcelliana 172 pp. L25.000. 88-372-1591-6 [RdT 38,287].

1933 *Ullmann, Wolfgang* Die Zehn Worte der Menschlichkeit Gottes. Zehn Worte. 1996, ⇒194. 145-158.

1934 *Venema, René* YHWH or Moses?: a question of authorship: Exodus 34:28; Deuteronomy 10:4; 31:9,24. ᶠZuurmond R.: YHWH. DBAT.B. 1996, ⇒109. 69-76 [OTA 19,418].

1935 *Vicente Valtueña, Juan Miguel* Ex 20,1-17: la experiencia del éxodo en el Decálogo. EstFr 97/1 (1996) 93-119 [Exod 20,1-17].

1936 *Wartenberg-Potter, Bärbel* Die belebende Kraft glücklicher Erinnerungen—die Weisungen vom Sinai. Zehn Worte. 1996, ⇒194. 73-83.

1937 *Neudecker, Reinhard* 'Ich bin der Herr, dein Gott...' (Ex 20,2=Dtn 5,6): das erste Gebot des Dekalogs in rabbinischer Auslegung. (*a*) Bulletin of Research of Christian Culture 18 (1996) 1-22 [APIB 10/3,265]. J.;

1938 (*b*) Jud. 52 (1996) 179-189.

1939 *Stefani, Piero* Io sono. Servitium 30/108 (1996) 33-41 [Exod 20,2].

1940 *Bodrato, Aldo* Non avere altri dèi: monoteismo biblico e politeismo contemporaneo. Servitium 30/108 (1996) 42-49 [Exod 20,3].

1941 **Mettinger, Tryggve N.D.** In search of God. 1988, ⇒4,2477...-7,2179. ᴿThR 61 (1996) 87-88 (*Reventlow, Henning Graf*).

1942 *Rad, Gerhard von* El enigma del Israel veterotestamentario. <1970> [Exod 20,3-6];

1943 Origen del monoteísmo mosaico. <1958> [Exod 20,3]. La acción de Dios. 1996, ⇒144. 83-98/150-159.

1944 **Mettinger, Tryggve N.D.** No graven image?: Israelite aniconism in its ancient Near Eastern context. CB.OT 42: 1995, ⇒11/1,672. ᴿZAW 108 (1996) 477-478 (*Köckert, M.*); RHR 213 (1996) 93-95 (*Caquot, André*); ThRv 92 (1996) 215-216 (*Dohmen, Christoph*); NTT 97 (1996) 172-173 (*Thelle, Rannfrid I.*); RB 103 (1996) 605-606 (*Tarragon, J.-M. de*); RSO 70/1-2 (1996) 233-236 (*Peri, Chiara*).

1945 **Keel, Othmar** Das Recht der Bilder gesehen zu werden: drei Fall-studien zur Methode der Interpretation altorientalischer Bilder. OBO 122: 1992, ⇒8,2558*...10,2251. OTEs 9 (1996) 152-155 (*Boshoff, W.S.*).

1946 **Podella, Thomas** Das Lichtkleid JHWH's: Untersuchungen zur Gestalthaftigkeit Gottes im Alten Testament und seiner altorientali-schen Umwelt. FAt 15: Tü 1996, Mohr xvi; 338 pp. DM258. 3-16-146-598-9 [RB 105,157].

1947 *Uehlinger, Christoph* Israelite aniconism in context. Bib. 77 (1996) 540-549.

1948 *Van der Plas, Dirk* L'image divine et son interdiction dans les reli-gions monothéistes. BSÉG 20 (1996) 71-84 [Exod 20,3].

1949 *Bierma, Lyle D.* Remembering the Sabbath Day: URSINUS'S expo-sition of Exodus 20:8-11. ᶠSTEINMETZ D., 1996, ⇒86. 272-291.

1950 *Klopfenstein, Martin A.* Sabbattag-Feiertag. Leben aus dem Wort. BEAT 40: 1996, ⇒132. 255-257.

1951 *Mackiewicz, Marie-Claude* Le sabbat: le temps sanctifié. DosB 64 (1996) 6-8.

1952 *Maggiani, Silvano* Riposo sabatico e festa. Servitium 30/108 (1996) 88-98 [Exod 20,8].

1953 *Vetter, Dieter* Der Schabbat ist von der Art der kommenden Welt: die Bedeutung des siebenten Tages im jüdischen Leben. Judentum. 1996 <1988>, ⇒154. 339-344.

1954 *De Benedetti, Paolo* Onora il padre e la madre: anche il cattivo padre e la cattiva madre?. Servitium 30/108 (1996) 84-87 [Exod 20,12].

1955 **Ojo, Anthony Adewale** "Honour your father and your mother" (Ex 20,12): the dignity of parents and the duties of children in the pentateuch. Pars Diss. Pont. Univ. Urbaniana, R 1996, xli; 68 pp.

1956 *Otto, Eckart* Sohnespflichten im antiken Syrien und Palästina. Kon-tinuum. 1996, ⇒2002. 265-282 [Exod 20,12; 21,17; Lev 19; Deut 5,16; Sir 3,1-16].

1957 **Seifert, Elke** Die Verfügungsgewalt der Väter über ihre Töchter im Alten Testament. Diss. Marburg 1996, ᴰ*Gerstenberger, E.S.* [EThL 74,242*].

1958 *Gaudemet, Jean* 'Non occides' (Ex 20,13). ᶠALBERIGO G., CrSt: 1996, ⇒1. 89-99.

1959 *Peyretti, Enrico* Non fare omicidio: comandamento ed eccezioni.
Servitium 30/108 (1996) 50-63 [Exod 20,13].
1960 *Garrone, Daniele* Non fare adulterio: disciplina della sessualità.
Servitium 30/108 (1996) 64-72 [Exod 20,14].
1961 *Tognoni, Gianni* Non rubare: la disciplina dell'avere. Servitium
30/108 (1996) 73-76 [Exod 20,15].
1962 *Levi, Abramo* Non dire falsa testimonianza: ovvero la disciplina del
dire. Servitium 30/108 (1996) 77-83 [Exod 20,16].

1963 *Ausloos, Hans* Deuteronomi(sti)c elements in Exod 23,20-33?:
some methodological remarks. Studies in...Exodus. BEThL 126:
1996, ⇒1794. 481-500.
1964 *Ausloos, Hans* The Septuagint version of Exod 23:20-33: a "Deuteronomist" at work?. JNSL 22/2 (1996) 89-106.
1965 **Barbiero, Gianni** L'asino del nemico: Es 23,4-5; Dt 22,1-4; Lv
19,17-18. AnBib 128: 1991, ⇒7,2224...11/1,679. ᴿCrSt 17/1
(1996) 173-176 (*Tosato, Angelo*).
1966 *Barbiero, Gianni* Lo straniero nel Codice dell'Alleanza e nel Codice di Santità: tra separazione e accoglienza. RStB 8 (1996) 41-69
[Lev 17-26].
1967 **Bultmann, Christoph** Der Fremde im antiken Juda. FRLANT
153: 1992, ⇒8,2581...10,2272. ᴿBZ 40 (1996) 112-115
(*Grünwaldt, Klaus*).
1968 *Cazelles, Henri* Histoire et institutions dans la place et la composition d'Ex 20,22-23,19. Études. 1996 <1991>, ⇒120. 127-138.
1969 *Houtman, C.* Der Altar als Asylstätte im Alten Testament: Rechts-
bestimmung (Ex. 21,12-14) und Praxis (I Reg. 1-2). RB 103
(1996) 343-366;
1970 Eine schwangere Frau als Opfer eines Handgemenges (Exodus
21,22-25): ein Fall von stellvertretender Talion im Bundesbuch?.
Studies in...Exodus. BEThL 126: 1996, ⇒1794. 381-397.
1971 **Marshall, Joy Wade** Israel and the book of the covenant: an
anthropological approach to biblical law. SBL.DS 140: 1993,
⇒9,2364...11/1,687. ᴿEThL 72 (1996) 220 (*Schoors, A.*).
1972 *Nardoni, Enrique* Normas de justicia en las leyes de la alianza.
RevBib 58 (1996) 81-116.
1973 *Olson, Dennis T.* The jagged cliffs of Mount Sinai: a theological
reading of the Book of the Covenant (Exod. 20:22-23:19). Interp.
50 (1996) 251-263.
1974 *Olyan, Saul M.* Why an altar of unfinished stones?: some thoughts
on Ex 20,25 and Dtn 27,5-6. ZAW 108 (1996) 161-171.
1975 *Otto, Eckart* Diachronie und Synchronie im Depositenrecht des
'Bundesbuches': zur jüngsten literatur- und rechtshistorischen Diskussion von Ex 22,6-14. ZAR 2 (1996) 76-85;
1976 Die Aktualität des biblischen Fremden-Rechts. Kontinuum. 1996,
⇒2002. 317-321;
1977 Die Geschichte der Talion im Alten Orient und Israel. <1991>.
224-245;
1978 The pre-exilic Deuteronomy as a revision of the covenant code.
112-122;
1979 Die rechtshistorische Entwicklung des Depositenrechts in altorientalischen und altisraelitischen Rechtskorpora. <1988>. 139-163
[Exod 22,6-14];

1980 Zur Stellung der Frau in den ältesten Rechtstexten des Alten Testaments (Ex 20,14; 22,15f.)—wider die hermeneutische Naivität im Umgang mit dem Alten Testament. <1982>. Kontinuum. 1996, ⇒2002. 30-48.

1981 **Van Houten, Christiana** The alien in Israelite law. JSOT.S 107: 1991, ⇒7,2231...11/1,701. ᴿBZ 40 (1996) 112-115 (*Grünwaldt, Klaus*).

1982 *Van Seters, John* The law of the Hebrew slave. ZAW 108 (1996) 534-546 [Exod 21,2-11; Lev 25,39-46; Deut 15,12-18; Neh 5,1-13];

1983 Cultic laws in the covenant code (Exodus 20,22-23,33) and their relationship to Deuteronomy and the Holiness Code. Studies in...Exodus. BEThL 126: 1996, ⇒1794. 319-345;

1984 *Vetter, Dieter* "Auge um Auge, Zahn um Zahn": der Mißbrauch mit einem Bibelwort. Judentum. 1996 <1988>, ⇒154. 232-237 [Exod 21,23-25].

1985 *Zakovitch, Yair* The Book of the Covenant interprets the Book of the Covenant: the 'boomerang phenomenon'. ᶠHARAN M., 1996, ⇒35. 59*-64*. H.

1986 *Zevit, Ziony* The earthen altar laws of Exodus 20:24-26 and related sacrificial restrictions in their cultural context. ᶠHARAN M., 1996, ⇒35. 53-62 [Exod 20,24-26].

1987 **Brin, Gershon** Studies in biblical law: from the Hebrew Bible to the Dead Sea Scrolls. JSOT.S 176: 1994, ⇒10,163*; 11/1,697. ᴿScrTh 28 (1996) 297-299 (*Ausín, S.*).

1988 **Carmichael, Calum M.** The spirit of biblical law. Athens, GA 1996, Univ. of Georgia Press xviii; (2) 238 pp. 0-8203-1845-0.

1989 **Crüsemann, Frank** The torah: theology and social history of Old Testament law. ᵀ*Mahnke, Allan W.*, E 1996, Clark xv; 460 pp. £25. 0-567-08524-4. ᴿET 108 (1996-97) 321-322 (*Rodd, C.S.*).

1990 **Falk, Ze'ev** Religious law and ethics. 1991, ⇒7,2227; 9,2384. ᴿZAR 2 (1996) 189-191 (*Otto, Eckart*).

1991 ᴱ**Gehrke, Hans-Joachim** Rechtskodifizierung und soziale Normen im interkulturellen Vergleich. ScriptOralia 66, A., Altertumswiss. 15: Tü 1994, Narr iv; 183 pp. DM96. 3-8233-4556-7. ᴿZAR 2 (1996) 192-196 (*Otto, Eckart*) [Exod 11,1-13,16].

1992 *Hruby, Kurt* Das Reich der Tora. Aufsätze [ᴱ**Osten-Sacken, P. von der**]. ANTZ 5: 1996 <1974>, ⇒ĸ5. 51-70.

1993 *Jackson, Bernard S.* The ceremonial and the judicial: biblical law as sign and symbol. The pentateuch. BiSe 39: 1996 <1984>, ⇒202. 103-127.

1994 Gesetz als Thema biblischer Theologie. JBTh 4, 1989. ThR 61 (1996) 166-168 (*Reventlow, Henning Graf*).

1995 *Janowski, Bernd* Israels Weg zur Tora: zu Frank CRUESEMANNS "Theologie und Sozialgeschichte des alttestamentlichen Gesetzes". ⇒8,2544*. EvTh 56/1 (1996) 83-92.

1996 **Lasserre, Guy** Synopse des lois du pentateuque. VT.S 59: 1994, ⇒10,2283; 11/1,702. ᴿCTrB 25 (1996) 22-23 (*Péter-Contesse, René*); NRTh 118 (1996) 740-741 (*Luciani, D.*).

1997 ᴱ**Levinson, Bernard M.** Theory and method in biblical and cuneiform law. JSOT.S 181: 1994, ⇒11/1,714. ᴿZAR 2 (1996) 201-207 (*Lohfink, Norbert*); HebStud 37 (1996) 153-156 (*Avalos, Hector*).

1998   *Löhr, Winrich A.* Die Auslegung des Gesetzes bei MARKION, den Gnostikern und den Manichäern. ^FDASSMANN E., JAC.E 23: 1996, ⇒19. 77-95.
1999   ^E**Machado Siqueira, Tércio** A lei. Petrópolis 1996, Vozes 70 pp. [REB 225,225].
2000   ^E**Mainville, Odette,** *(al),* Loi et autonomie dans la bible et la tradition. CTHP 53: 1994, ⇒10,255. ^RCBQ 58 (1996) 790-791 *(Frizzell, Lawrence E.).*
2001   *Otto, Eckart* Town and rural countryside in ancient Israelite law: reception and redaction in cuneiform and Israelite law. The pentateuch. BiSe 39: 1996 <1993>, ⇒202. 203-221.
2002   **Otto, Eckart** Kontinuum und Proprium: Studien zur Sozial- und Rechtsgeschichte des Alten Orients und des Alten Testaments. Orientalia Biblica et Christiana 8: Wsb 1996, Harrassowitz x; 380 pp. 3-447-03835-7. See:
2003   Gerechtigkeit und Erbarmen im Recht des Alten Testaments und seiner christlichen Rezeption. 342-357;
2004   Gewaltvermeidung und -überwindung in Recht und Religion Israels: rechtshistorische und theologische Anmerkungen eines Alttestamentlers zu R. SCHWAGERs Entwurf einer biblischen Erlösungslehre. <1992>. 246-264;
2005   Homosexualität im Alten Orient und im Alten Testament. 322-330 [Gen 19,5; Exod 22,18; Lev 18,22; 20,13; Judg 19,22];
2006   Körperverletzung im hethitischen und israelitischen Recht: Rechts- und religionshistorische Aspekte. <1993>. 192-223 [Exod 21,18-32];
2007   Interdependenzen zwischen Geschichte und Rechtsgeschichte des antiken Israels. <1988>. 75-93;
2008   Sozial- und rechtshistorische Aspekte in der Ausdifferenzierung eines altisraelitischen Ethos aus dem Recht. <1987>. 94-111.
2009   **Porten, Bezalel** The Elephantine papyri in English: three millennia of cross-cultural continuity and change. Collab. *Farber, J. Joel,* DMOA 22: Lei 1996, Brill xvii; 621 pp. ƒ402. 90-04-101977 [NT 39,415].
2010   *Preiser, Wolfgang* Zur Ausbildung einer völkerrechtlichen Ordnung in der Staatenwelt des Alten Orients. ^FBERAN T., 1996, ⇒6. 227-239.

2011   **Dombradi, Eva** Die Darstellung des Rechtsaustrags in den altbabylonischen Prozessurkunden 1: Halbband I: die Gestaltung der altbabylonischen Prozessurkunden: der altbabylonische Zivilprozess; Halbband II: Appendix: die Organe der Rechtsprechung: Anmerkungen—Exkurse—Indices. FAOS 20: Wsb 1996, Steiner. DM196. 3-515-05513-4 [Or. 68,122ss— Westbrook, Raymond].
2012   ^E**Foxhall, Lin; Lewis, Andrew D.E.** Greek law in its political setting: justifications not justice. Oxf 1996, Clarendon 172 pp. £25 [HZ 265,746].
2013   **Freydank, Helmut** Mittelassyrische Rechtsurkunden und Verwaltungstexte III. 1994, ⇒10,12584. ^ROr. 65 (1996) 177-180 *(Cancik-Kirschbaum, Eva).*
2014   *Haase, Richard* Anmerkungen zum sogenannten Lehensrecht der Hethiter. ZAR 2 (1996) 135-139;
2015   Überlegungen zur erlaubten Tötung eines Menschen in der hethitischen Rechtssammlung. WO 27 (1996) 36-44;

2016 Über allgemeine Rechtsregeln in den keilschriftlichen Rechtscor-
pora. ZAR 2 (1996) 131-134.

2017 ᴱHalpern, Bruce; Hobson, D. Law, politics and society in the
ancient Mediterranean world. 1993, ⇒10,471. ᴿSR 25 (1996) 357-
358 (*Westerholm, Stephen*).

2018 Hurowitz, Victor A. *Inu Anum sīrum*: literary structures in the
non-juridical sections of Codex Hammurabi. Occasional Publications of the Samuel Noah Cramer Fund 15: Ph 1994, xiv; 198 pp.
ᴿZAR 2 (1996) 196-201 (*Arneth, Martin*).

2019 ᴱJakob-Rost, Liane; Fales, Frederick Mario Neuassyrische
Rechtsurkunden I. Collab. *Klengel-Brandt, Evelyn*. WVDOG 94: B
1996, Mann 76 pp. hrsg. von der Deutschen Orient-Gesellschaft
und dem Vorderasiatischen Museum der Staatlichen Museen zu
Berlin. 3-7861-1751-9.

2020 Jas, Remko Neo-Assyrian judicial procedures. State Archives of
Assyria Studies 5: Helsinki 1996, The Neo-Assyrian Text Corpus
Project x; 116 pp. $26. 951-45-7287-4.

2021 *Kienast, Burkhart* Mündlichkeit und Schriftlichkeit im keilschriftlichen Rechtswesen. ZAR 2 (1996) 114-130.

2022 *Limet, H.* Traditions juridiques en contact dans le Proche-Orient
achéménide. TEuph 12 (1996) 163-179.

2023 *Neumann, Hans* Zum privaten Werkvertrag im Rahmen der neusumerischen handwerklichen Produktion. AltOrF 23 (1996) 254-264.

2024 *Otto, Eckart* Der reduzierte Brautpreis: Ehe- und Zinsrecht in den
Paragraphen 18 und 18a des Kodex Ešnunna. Kontinuum. 1996
<1992>, ⇒2002. 164-171.

2025 *Rems, Renate* Eine Kleinigkeit zum altassyrischen Eherecht.
WZKM 86 (1996) 355-367.

2026 Selb, Walter Antike Rechte im Mittelmeerraum. 1993, ⇒10,2299.
ᴿZAR 2 (1996) 212-214 (*Yaron, Reuven*).

2027 *Smith, Morton* East Mediterranean law codes of the early Iron Age.
Studies in...method. 1996 <1978>, ⇒150. 84-92.

2028 *Starke, Frank* Zur 'Regierung' des hethitischen Staates. ZAR 2
(1996) 140-182.

E3.6 Cultus, *Exodus 24-40*

2029 ᴱAnderson, G.A.; Olyan, S.M. Priesthood and cult in ancient
Israel. JSOT.S 125: 1991, ⇒7,288...10,2309. ᴿBZ 40 (1996) 103-
107 (*Albertz, Rainer*); JNES 55 (1996) 139-140 (*Handy, Lowell
K.*).

2030 *Bird, Phyllis* The place of women in the Israelite cultus. Community. 1996 <1987>, ⇒172. 515-536.

2031 *Blum, Erhard* Das sog. "Privilegrecht" in Exodus 34,11-26: ein
Fixpunkt der Komposition des Exodusbuches?;

2032 *Bogaert, Pierre-Maurice* L'importance de la Septante et du "Mona-
censis" de la Vetus Latina pour l'exégèse du livre de l'Exode
(chap. 35-40). Studies in...Exodus. BEThL 126: 1996, ⇒1794.
347-366/399-428.

2033 Brinkman, J. The perception of space in the Old Testament. 1992,
⇒8,2604; 10,2306. ᴿJNSL 22/2 (1996) 144-146 (*Odendaal,
D.H.*).

2034 **Brown, William** The tabernacle: its priests and its services. Peabody, MASS 1996, Hendrickson xi; 220 pp. Updated ed. 1-565-63195-1.

2035 *Chong Kyoon Shin, Samuel* Centralization and singularization: official cult and royal politics in ancient Israel. Diss. Richmond 1996-97 [RTL 29,577].

2036 *Contessa, Andreina* 'Arbor bona': dalla menorah alla Vergine: la metafora arborea, segno della redenzione. Som., sum. 74. Cahiers Ratisbonne 1 (1996) 47-85 [Exod 25,31-40].

2037 *Dearman, J.A.* The tophet in Jerusalem: archaeology and cultural profile. JNSL 22/1 (1996) 59-71.

2038 *Ellingworth, Paul* Who did what?: reference and meaning in Exodus 28, 39, and 16. BiTr 47 (1996) 340-346.

2039 A festa e as festas na Bíblia e na vida. Bíblica: série científica 4: Lisboa 1995, Difusora Bíblica 160 pp. RHumTeo 17 (1996) 374-375 *(Alves, Herculano)*.

2040 *González, J.* Símbolo y figura de los querubines. Liturgia y Espiritualidad 27 (1996) 333-336 [Exod 25].

2041 *Gosse, Bernard* Transfert de l'onction et de marques royales au profit du Grand Prêtre en Ex 25 ss. Henoch 18 (1996) 3-8. [Isa 22,15-25; 61,1; Ezek 21,30-31].

2042 **Heger, Paul** The development of the incense cult in Israel. Diss. Toronto 1996, DFox, Harry. 353 pp. DAI-A 57/08, p.3541; AAC 9631845.

2043 **Henshaw, Richard A.** Female and male: the cultic personnel: the bible and the rest of the ancient Near East. PTMS 31: 1994, ⇒11/2,1736. RJAOS 116 (1996) 286-287 *(Smith, Mark S.)*; AJS Review 21 (1996) 369-372 *(Hurowitz, Victor Avigdor)*.

2044 *Horbury, William* Land, sanctuary and worship. FHOOKER M., 1996, ⇒43. 207-224.

2045 *Klein, Ralph W.* Back to the future: the tabernacle in the book of Exodus. Interp. 50 (1996) 264-276.

2046 *Levine, Lee I.* The nature and origin of the Palestinian synagogue reconsidered. JBL 115 (1996) 425-448.

2047 *Maggioni, Bruno* Il culto nell'Antico Testamento. DSBP 12 (1996) 30-63. ⇒327.

2048 *Meyers, Carol* Realms of sanctity: the case of the 'misplaced' incense altar in the tabernacle texts of Exodus. FHARAN M., 1996, ⇒35. 33-46.

2049 *Monloubou, Louis* Culte et eschatologie: 'les cœurs purs verront Dieu'. FLEGASSE S., LeDiv 166: 1996, ⇒51. 41-48.

2050 *Moore, Michael S.* Role pre-emption in the Israelite priesthood. VT 46 (1996) 316-329.

2051 **Pham, Xuan Huong Thi** Lamentations 1 and 2, Isa 51:9-52:2, and their mourning ceremony setting. Diss. Washington, DC, Cath. Univ. 1996, x; 319 pp. [NThAR 1999,4].

2052 **Pigott, Susan Marie** God of compassion and mercy: an analysis of the background, use, and theological significance of Exodus 34:6-7. Diss. Southwestern Bapt. Theol. Sem. 1995. 223 pp. [EThL 74,198*].

2053 *Ritmeyer, Leen* The ark of the covenant: where it stood in Solomon's temple. BArR 22/1 (1996) 46-55, 70-73.

2054 **Rooke, D.W.** The role and development of the high priesthood with particular reference to the post-exilic period. Diss. Oxf 1996 [RTL 29,580].

2055 **Rubenstein, Jeffrey L.** The history of Sukkot in the Second Temple and rabbinic periods. BJSt 302: 1995, ⇒11/1,734. RJSJ 27/1 (1996) 91-95 & SFSHJ 133 (1996) 183-187 (*Neusner, Jacob*).

2056 *Sievers, Joseph* Il culto e la liturgia nel giudaismo antico. DSBP 12 (1996) 64-79. ⇒327.

2057 *Silva, Carlos Alberto da Costa* A festa de Pentecostes, festa da nova aliança. RevCuBíb 38 (1996) 37-70.

2058 **Songate, John Lalrosem** The re-discovery of the tabernacle. Delhi 1996, SPCK xxxii; 284 pp. Rs60. 81-7214-178-5 [VJTR 60,704].

2059 *Stefani, Piero* Il volto di Mosè era raggiante (Es 34,29-39). Humanitas 51 (1996) 775-796.

2060 *Talstra, Eep* Reconstructing the Menorah on disk: some syntactic remarks [Exod 25,31-40; 37,17-24; Num 8,1-4];

2061 *Van Den Eynde, S.* Keeping God's Sabbath: 'wt and brjt (Exod 31,12-17);

2062 *Van Ruiten, J.T.A.G.M.* The relationship between Exod 31,12-17 and Jubilees 2,1.17-33. Studies in...Exodus. BEThL 126: 1996, ⇒1794. 523-533/501-511/567-575.

2063 *Vetter, Dieter* Allein dem Schutz des Himmels vertrauen: "das Fest der Hütten ..., freue dich an deinem Fest";

2064 "Das Fest der Lichter": Ursprung und Bedeutung des Chanukka-Festes. <1988>;

2065 "Freude an der Tora": Grundlage jüdischer Existenz vergegenwärtigt;

2066 "Kehrt heim zu mir, so kehr ich heim zu euch": die Botschaft des jüdischen Versöhnungstages Jom Kippur;

2067 Rosch Ha-Schana: das jüdische Neujahrsfest und die Einheit der Menschheit. Judentum 1996 <1988>, ⇒154. 383-389/394-402 /390-393/377-382/369-376.

2068 *Vriezen, Karel J.H.* Cakes and figurines: related women's cultic offerings in ancient Israel?. MVan Dijk-Hemmes F., 1996, ⇒99. 251-264 [Jer 7,17-19].

2069 **Willi-Plein, Ina** Opfer und Kult im alttestamentlichen Israel: Textbefragungen und Zwischenergebnisse. SBS 153: 1993, ⇒9,2420; 11/1,738. RZRGG 48 (1996) 81-84 (*Herr, Bertram*); ThLZ 121 (1996) 1050-1053 (*Janowski, Bernd*).

2070 **Yang, Kon Hwon** Theological significance of the motif of the vineyard in the Old Testament. Diss. Golden Gate Bapt. Theol. Sem., DEakins, J.K., 1996, 237 pp. [EThL 74,239*].

E3.7 Leviticus

2071 *Auld, Graeme* Leviticus at the heart of the Pentateuch?. Reading Leviticus. JSOT.S 227: 1996, ⇒203. 40-51.

2072 *Berger, Michael S.* The 'moadim' of 'parashat Emor'. Alei Etzion 3 (1995) 7-23 [IAJS 42,26].

2073 *Bettiolo, Paolo* Appunti sul seminario 'Purità e culto nell'esegesi ebraica e cristiana del *Levitico*'. ASE 13/1 (1996) 291-294.

2074 *Braulik, Georg* Weitere Beobachtungen zur Beziehung zwischen dem Heiligkeitsgesetz und Deuteronomium 19-25. Das Deuteronomium. 1996, ⇒209. 23-55.

2075 **Budd, Philip J.** Leviticus. NCBC: GR 1996, Eerdmans 395 pp. $26. 0-8028-4197-X.
2076 **Chirichigno, Gregory C.** Debt slavery in Israel and the ancient Near East. JSOT.S 141: 1993, ⇒9,2466...11/1,744. ᴿWThJ 58 (1996) 157-159 (*Whitekettle, Richard*).
2077 *Coelho Dias, Geraldo* As festas na Bíblia. Theologica 31/2 (1996) 245-260.
2078 **Cortese, Enzo; Kaswalder, Pietro** Il fascino del sacro: alla riscoperta del libro del Levitico. Narrare la Bibbia 3: CinB 1996, San Paolo 119 pp. L24.000. 88-215-3084-1. ᴿAng. 73 (1996) 435-436 (*Jurič, Stipe*).
2079 *Davies, Philip R.* Leviticus as a cultic system in the Second Temple period: responses to Hannah K. HARRINGTON. Reading Leviticus. JSOT.S 227: 1996, ⇒203. 230-237.
2080 *Destro, Adriana* The witness of times: an anthropological reading of Niddah. Reading Leviticus. JSOT.S 227: 1996, ⇒203. 124-138.
2081 *Destro, Adriana; Pesce, Mauro* La normativa del *Levitico*: interpretazioni ebraiche e protocristiane. ASEs 13 (1996) 15-37.
2082 *Douglas, Mary* The abominations of Leviticus. Community. 1996 <1966>, ⇒172. 119-134;
2083 The forbidden animals in Leviticus. The pentateuch. BiSe 39: 1996 <1993>, ⇒202. 242-262.
2084 **Finkelstein, Louis** Sifra on Leviticus. 1991, ⇒9,2436. ᴿJQR 86 (1996) 422-425 (*Basser, Herbert W.*).
2085 **Gerstenberger, Erhard S.** Das dritte Buch Mose: Leviticus. ATD 6: ²1993, ⇒9,2437...11/1,750. ᴿOTEs 9 (1996) 541-543 (*Wyk, W.C. van*);
2086 Leviticus: a commentary. OTL: LVL 1996, Westminster xiv; 450 pp. $34. 0-664-22064-9.
2087 *Girardi, Mario* Puro/impuro in BASILIO di Cesarea: da categoria cultuale a discrimine paolino di fraternità. ASEs 13 (1996) 159-177.
2088 *Gutzwiller, Kathryn* Comments on Rolf RENDTORFF. Reading Leviticus. JSOT.S 227: 1996, ⇒203. 36-39.
2089 **Harrington, Hannah K.** The impurity systems of Qumran and the rabbis: biblical foundations. SBL.DS 143: 1993, ⇒9,2633...-11/1,752. ᴿAJSR 21 (1996) 142-144 (*Jaffee, Martin S.*) [Exod 12; Lev 11].
2090 *Harrington, Hannah K.* Interpreting Leviticus in the Second Temple period: struggling with ambiguity. Reading Leviticus. JSOT.S 227: 1996, ⇒203. 214-229.
2091 *Hartley, John E.; Dwyer, Timothy* An investigation into the location of the laws on offerings to Molek in the book of Leviticus. ᶠYOUNG D., 1996, ⇒107. 81-93.
2092 **Houston, Walter** Purity and monotheism: clean and unclean animals in biblical law. JSOT.S 140: 1993, ⇒9,2455; 11/1,754. ᴿBZ 40 (1996) 101-103 (*Scharbert, Josef*) [Lev 11; Deut 14].
2093 *Jackson, Bernard* Talion and purity: some glosses on Mary DOUGLAS [Exod 21,22-25];
2094 *Johnstone, William* The use of Leviticus in Chronicles. Reading Leviticus. JSOT.S 227: 1996, ⇒203. 107-123/243-255.
2095 *Joosten, J.* Moïse a-t-il recelé le Code de Sainteté?. BN 84 (1996) 75-86 [Lev 21,24; 23,44; Deut 5,25-6].
2096 **Lane, David J.** The Peshitta of Leviticus. MPIL 6: 1994, ⇒10,2322; 11/1,761. ᴿCBQ 58 (1996) 120-121 (*Mathews, Edward G.*).

2097 *Maccoby, Hyam* Holiness and purity: the holy people in Leviticus and Ezra-Nehemiah. Reading Leviticus. JSOT.S 227: 1996, ⇒203. 153-170.

2098 *Maier, Johann* La *Torah* di purità nel *Levitico* e sua trattazione nella letteratura giudaica del periodo del Secondo Tempio e nei primi secoli cristiani. ᵀ*Miletto, Gianfranco*, ASEs 13 (1996) 39-66.

2099 *Manns, Frédéric* Il giubileo secondo la bibbia. ᵀ*D'Amato, F. David*, TS(I) 72 (lug.-ago. 1996) 18-21.

2100 *Melcher, Sarah J.* The holiness code and human sexuality. Biblical ethics [ᴱ**Brawley, R.L.**]. 1996, ⇒H3.7. 87-102.

2101 **Milgrom, Jacob** Leviticus 1-16. AncB 3: 1991, ⇒7,2270...-11/1,765. ᴿBZ 40 (1996) 301-303 (*Seidl, Theodor*); JNES 55 (1996) 300-301 (*Pardee, Dennis*).

2102 *Rendtorff, Rolf* Is it possible to read Leviticus as a separate book?. Reading Leviticus. JSOT.S 227: 1996, ⇒203. 22-35.

2103 *Rogerson, John* Response to Jacob MILGROM's concept of holiness. Reading Leviticus. JSOT.S 227: 1996, ⇒203. 76-78.

2104 *Sawyer, John F.A.* The language of Leviticus. Reading Leviticus. JSOT.S 227: 1996, ⇒203. 15-20.

2105 *Scorza Barcellona, Francesco* Le norme veterotestamentarie sulla purità nell'*Epistola di Barnaba*. ASEs 13 (1996) 95-111.

2106 *Segal, Robert A.* Response to Hyam MACCOBY's holiness and purity. Reading Leviticus. JSOT.S 227: 1996, ⇒2109. 171-173.

2107 *Smith, Christopher R.* The literary structure of Leviticus. JSOT 70 (1996) 17-32.

2108 **Staubli, Thomas** Die Bücher Levitikus, Numeri. Neuer Stuttgarter Kommentar. AT 3: Stu 1996, Kath. Bibelwerk 400 pp. DM68. 3-460-07031-5.

2109 *Stefani, Piero* Un anno di riposo e di liberazione sulla terra. Studi, Fatti, Ricerche 76 (1996) 3-4.

2110 *Tampellini, Stefano* L'esegesi del *Levitico* di ESICHIO di Gerusalemme: osservazioni introduttive e sondaggi preliminari. ASEs 13 (1996) 201-209.

2111 **Tidball, Derek J.** Leviticus. Crossway Bible Guide: Leicester 1996, Crossway 224 pp. 1-85684-140-5.

2112 *Vian, Giovanni M.* Purità e culto nell'esegesi giudaico-ellenistica. ASEs 13 (1996) 67-84.

2113 *Whitekettle, Richard* Levitical thought and the female reproductive cycle: wombs, wellsprings, and the primeval world. VT 46 (1996) 376-391;

2114 **Wright, Christopher J.H.** God's people in God's land: family, land and property in the OT. 1990, ⇒6,2762...8,2645. ᴿSBET 14 (1996) 152-154 (*Hess, Richard*).

2115 *Zocca, Elena* La lebbra e la sua purificazione nel *Commentario al Levitico* di ESICHIO: un tentativo di confronto con la tradizione esegetica precedente e contemporanea. ASEs 13 (1996) 179-199.

2116 *Utzschneider, Helmut* Vergebung im Ritual: zur Deutung des חַטָּת Rituals (Sündopfer) in Lev 4,1-5,13. Abschied von der Schuld?: zur Anthropologie und Theologie von Schuldbekenntnis, Opfer und Versöhnung [ᴱ**Riess, Richard** Theologische Akzente 1: Stu 1996, Kohlhammer 272 pp. DM34.80. 3-17-013908-8]. 99-119 [Lev 4,1-5,13].

2117 *Budd, Philip* מַעַל in Leviticus 5,14-19 and other sources: response to William JOHNSTONE. Reading Leviticus. JSOT.S 227: 1996, ⇒203. 256-259.

2118 *Klingbeil, Gerald A.* La unción de Aarón: un estudio de Lev 8:2 en
      su contexto veterotestamentario y antiguo cercano-oriental. Theolo-
      gika 11/1 (1996) 64-83 [ZID 23,320];
2119 The syntactic structure of the ritual of ordination (Lev 8). Bib. 77
      (1996) 509-519.
2120 *Goerwitz, Richard L.* What does the priestly source mean by פרע
      את הראש?. Sum. 377. JQR 86 (1996) 377-394 [Lev 10,06].
2121 *Harris, Marvin* The abominable pig. Community. 1996 <1987>,
      ⇒172. 135-151 [Lev 11].
2122 *Magonet, Jonathan* "But if it is a girl, she is unclean for twice
      seven days ...": the riddle of Leviticus 12,5. Reading Leviticus.
      JSOT.S 227: 1996, ⇒203. 144-152.
2123 **Willis, G.C.** La ley del leproso: [immundo; estará impuro, y habi-
      tará solo; fuera del campamento, Levítico 13:46]. Perroy ³1996,
      Biblicas 70 pp. 2-88208-112-X [NThAR 1997,162].
2124 *Whitekettle, Richard* Leviticus 15.8 reconsidered: chiasm, spatial
      structure and the body. The pentateuch. BiSe 39: 1996 <1991>,
      ⇒202. 173-185.
2125 **Deiana, Giovanni** Il giorno dell'espiazione: il *kippur* nella tradi-
      zione biblica. RivBib.S 30: 1994, ⇒10,2338. ᴿPaVi 41/2 (1996)
      56-57 (*Ciccarelli, Michele*); Bib. 77 (1996) 111-113 (*Cortese, E.*);
      EstTrin 30 (1996) 456-457 (*Pikaza, Xabier*) [Lev 16].
2126 *Rodriguez, Angel M.* Leviticus 16: its literary structure. AUSS 34
      (1996) 269-286.
2127 **Joosten, Jan** People and land in the holiness code: an exegetical
      study of the ideational framework of the law in Leviticus 17-26.
      VT.S 67: Lei 1996, Brill xiii; 223 pp. ƒ135. 90-04-10557-3.
2128 *Xella, Paolo* Il 'capro espiatorio' a Ebla: sulle origini storiche di
      una antico rito mediterraneo. SMSR 62 (1996) 677-684 [Lev 16].
2129 *Schwartz, Baruch J.* "Profane" slaughter and the integrity of the
      priestly code. HUCA 67 (1996) 15-42 [Lev 17,3-7].
2130 *Ziskind, Jonathan R.* The missing daughter in Leviticus xviii. VT
      46 (1996) 125-130.
2131 *Cohen, Jeffrey M.* Love of neighbor and its antecedent verses. JBQ
      24/1 (1996) 18-21 [Lev 19,18].
2132 *Milgrom, Jacob* Law and narrative and the exegesis of Leviticus
      xix 19. VT 46 (1996) 544-548.
2133 *Carmichael, Calum* A strange sequence of rules: Leviticus 19,20-
      26. Reading Leviticus. JSOT.S 227: 1996, ⇒203. 182-205.
2134 *Milgrom, Jacob* The changing concept of holiness in the pentateu-
      chal codes with emphasis on Leviticus 19. Reading Leviticus.
      JSOT.S 227: 1996, ⇒203. 65-75.
2135 *Douglas, Mary* Sacred contagion. Reading Leviticus. JSOT.S 227:
      1996, ⇒203. 86-106 [Exod 21,23-25; Lev 24,19-20.
2136 *Le Saux, Madeleine* La grâce du jubilé. DosB 64 (1996) 9-10 [Lev
      25].
2137 *Fox, Mary K.* Leviticus 26: elevating or terrifying?. JOTT 8 (1996)
      73-88.

E3.8 *Numeri;* Numbers, Balaam

2138 **Berlinerblau, Jacques** The vow and the 'popular religious groups'
      of ancient Israel: a philological and sociological inquiry. JSOT.S
      210: Shf 1996, Academic 219 pp. $58.50. 1-85075-578-7 [OTA
      19,547].

2139 **Cartledge, Tony W.** Vows in the Hebrew Bible and the ANE. JSOT.S 147: 1992, ⇒8,2655...11/1,795. RBZ 40 (1996) 298-300 (*Schäfer-Lichtenberger, Christa*); JNES 55 (1996) 219-220 (*Handy, Lowell K.*) [Num 6; 15; 30].

2140 **Davies, Eryl W.** Numbers. NCeB: 1995, ⇒11/1,782. RAnton. 71 (1996) 567-568 (*Nobile, Marco*); Bib. 77 (1996) 550-552 (*Seebass, Horst*).

2141 EDorival, **Gilles** Les Nombres: traduction du texte grec de la Septante, introduction et notes. La Bible d'Alexandrie 4: 1994, ⇒10,2350; 11/1,783. REstB 54 (1996) 557-558 (*Díez Merino, L.*); FZPhTh 43 (1996) 488 (*Barthelemy, Jean-Dominique*); StPhilo 8 (1996) 167-172 (*Van den Hoek, Annewies*); StMon 38 (1996) 423-424 (*Ribera-Mariné, R.*).

2142 **Douglas, Mary** In the wilderness: the doctrine of defilement in the book of Numbers. JSOT.S 158: 1993, ⇒9,2477...11/1,799. RETR 71/1 (1996) 104-105 (*Römer, Thomas*); Review Colloquium in Religion 26/1 (1996) 69-89.

2143 EDoutreleau, **Louis** ORIGENE: homélies sur les Nombres 1: homélies I-X. SC 415: P 1996, Cerf 327 pp. Texte latine de W.A. Baehrens; d'après l'édition d'André Méhat et les notes de Marcel Borret. FF191. 2-204-05337-6.

2144 **Levine, Baruch A.** Numbers 1-20. AncB 4A: 1993, ⇒9,2479...-11/1,786. RGr. 77 (1996) 572-576 (*Prato, Gian Luigi*); EstB 54 (1996) 558-559 (*Mielgo, C.*); JNES 55 (1996) 301-302 (*Pardee, Dennis*).

2145 **Licht, Jacob** פירוש על ספר במדבר [A commentary on the book of Numbers (XXII-XXXVI)]. 1995, ⇒11/2,787. RJQR 86 (1996) 462-463 (*Hurowitz, Victor Avigdor*). H.

2146 *Ogden, Graham S.* The design of Numbers. BiTr 47 (1996) 420-428.

2147 **Olson, Dennis T.** Numbers. Interpretation: LVL 1996, Knox vi; (6) 196 pp. $23. 0-8042-3104-4.

2148 *Pike, Dana M.* The book of Numbers at Qumran: texts and context. Current research. StTDJ 20: 1996, ⇒293. 166-193.

2149 **Sakenfeld, Katharine Doob** Journeying with God: a commentary on the book of Numbers. ITC: 1995, ⇒11/1,790. RPSB 17 (1996) 268-269 (*Brueggemann, Walter*).

2150 **Schenker, Adrian** La profession religieuse comme proclamation de la foi et édification de l'Église: contribution de théologie biblique à la théologie des vœux. VieCon 6 (1996) 368-376.

Staubli, Thomas Die Bücher Levitikus, Numeri. ⇒2108.

2151 *Vetter, Dieter* Brauchen Menschen, was sie wollen?: die Erzählung in 4. Mose 11. Judentum. 1996 <1990>, ⇒154. 497-509.

2152 **Rabe, Norbert** Vom Gerücht zum Gericht: die Kundschaftererzählung Num 13.14. THLI 8: 1994, ⇒9,2494. RTZ 52 (1996) 272-274 (*Bartelmus, Rüdiger*).

2153 *Levine, Baruch A.* Offerings rejected by God: Numbers 16:15 in comparative perspective. FYOUNG D., 1996, ⇒107. 107-116.

2154 *Lim Teng Kok, Johnson* Whose staff is it, anyway?. BN 85 (1996) 17-21 [Num 20,9; 17].

2155 *Dorival, Gilles* 'Un astre se lèvera de Jacob': l'interprétation ancienne de *Nombres* 24,17. ASEs 13 (1996) 295-352.

2156 *Frankel, David* The Deuteronomic portrayal of Balaam. VT 46 (1996) 30-42 [Deut 24,4-6; 24,10].

2157 *Goodnick, Benjamin* Balaam: some aspects of his character. JBQ 24/3 (1996) 167-172.
2158 *Kaiser, Walter C.* Balaam son of Beor in light of Deir ʿAllā and scripture: saint or soothsayer?. FYOUNG D., 1996, ⇒107. 95-106.
2159 *Rad, Gerhard von* La historia de Balaán. La acción de Dios. 1996 <1970>, 40-43.
2160 *Savran, G.* Beastly speech: intertextuality, Balaam's ass and the garden of Eden. The pentateuch. BiSe 39: 1996 <1994>, ⇒202. 296-318.
2161 *Vuilleumier, René* Bileam zwischen Bibel und Deir ʿAlla. ThZ 52 (1996) 150-163.
2162 *Wagner, Siegfried* Offenbarungsphänomenologische Elemente in den Bileam-Geschichten von Numeri 22-24. Ausgewählte Aufsätze. BZAW 240: 1996 <1975>, ⇒156. 83-108.

E3.9 Liber Deuteronomii

2163 **Bovati, Pietro** Il libro del Deuteronomio (1-11). 1994, ⇒10,2380; 11/1,819. RThPh 71 (1996) 575-577 (*Lohfink, N.*).
2164 TDogniez, Cécile; Harl, Marguerite Le Deutéronome: traduction du texte grec. Bible d'Alexandrie 5: 1992, ⇒8,2673...10,2385. RGr. 77 (1996) 152-153 (*Farahian, Edmond*); EstB 54 (1996) 123-124 (*Trebolle, J.*); Theol(A) 67 (1996) 380-382 (*Simota, Panagiotou*).
2165 **Merrill, Eugene H.** Deuteronomy. NAC 4: 1994, ⇒10,2390; 11/1,823. REvQ 68 (1996) 347-348 (*McConville, Gordon*).
2166 **Nielsen, Eduard** Deuteronomium. HAT 1/6: 1995, ⇒11/1,824. REstAg 31/1 (1996) 126-127 (*Mielgo, C.*); KeTe 47 (1996) 163-164 (*Van der Woude, A.S.*); JThS 47 (1996) 174-177 (*Mayes, A.D.H.*); ThPh 71 (1996) 573-575 (*Lohfink, N.*); Bib. 77 (1996) 428-432 (*Laberge, Léo*); ThLZ 121 (1996) 1136-1138 (*Perlitt, Lothar*); ZAR 2 (1996) 86-113 (*Achenbach, Reinhard*).
2167 **Rose, Martin** 5. Mose 12-25. ZBK.AT 5/1;
2168 5. Mose 1-11 und 26-34. ZBK.AT 5/2: 1994, ⇒10,2392. RZAR 2 (1996) 86-113 (*Achenbach, Reinhard*).
2169 **Tigay, Jeffrey H.** Deuteronomy. JPS Commentary on the Torah 5. Ph 1996, Jewish Publication Society xlvii; 548 pp. The traditional Hebrew text with the new JPS translation. $60. 0-8276-0330-4 [ThD 44,91].
2170 **Weinfeld, Moshe** Deuteronomy 1-11. AncB 5: 1991, ⇒7,2337...- 11/1,825. RHebStud 37 (1996) 164-166 (*Matthews, Victor H.*).
2171 **Wright, Christopher J.H.** Deuteronomy. NIBC.OT 4: Peabody 1996, Hendrickson xiv; 350 pp. $12. 0-85364-725-9.

2172 *Aejmelaeus, Anneli* Die Septuaginta des Deuteronomiums. Das Deuteronomium. 1996, ⇒209. 1-22.
2173 **Ashmore, James Philip** The social setting of the law in Deuteronomy. Diss. Duke 1995, DMeyers, C.L., 207 pp. [EThL 74,199*].
2174 EBraulik, Georg Bundesdokument und Gesetz: Studien zum Deuteronomium. 1995, ⇒11/1,828. RThLZ 121 (1996) 539-541 (*Nielsen, Eduard*).
2175 *Braulik, Georg* Das Deuteronomium und die Bücher Ijob, Sprichwörter, Rut: zur Frage früher Kanonizität des Deuteronomiums. Die Tora als Kanon. 1996, ⇒1308. 61-138;

2176 "Weisheit" im Buch Deuteronomium. Weisheit außerhalb der kanonischen Weisheitsschriften [EJanowski, B.]. 1996, ⇒E7.5. 39-69.

2177 *Cazelles, Henri* Les milieux du Deutéronome;

2178 Sur l'origine du mouvement deutéronomique. Études. 1996
<1993>, ⇒120. 157-170/171-179.

2179 *Clements, Ronald E.* The Deuteronomic law of centralisation and
the catastrophe of 587 B.C. FMASON R., 1996, ⇒57. 5-25 [Deut
12,2-28].

2180 **Dahmen, Ulrich** Leviten und Priester im Deuteronomium: lite-
rarkritische und redaktionsgeschichtliche Studien. Diss. Bonn. BBB
110: Bodenheim 1996, Philo xiv; 458 pp. 3-8257-0039-9 [NThAR
1997,224].

2181 **Dangl, Oskar** Methoden im Widerstreit: sprachwissenschaftliche
Zugänge zur deuteronomischen Rede von der Liebe Gottes. THLI
6: 1993, ⇒9,2524; 10,2397. RThZ 52 (1996) 271-272 (*Bartelmus,
Rüdiger*).

2182 *Deist, Ferdinand E.* Conservative rebound in Deuteronomy: a case
study in social values. JNSL 22/2 (1996) 17-30.

2183 **Elnes, Eric Eugene** Discerning the difference: the distinctiveness
of Yahweh and Israel in the book of Deuteronomy. Diss. Princeton
1996-97 [RTL 29,577].

2184 **Eynikel, Erik** The reform of King Josiah and the composition of
the deuteronomistic history. Diss. Louvain 1989, ⇒5,2874.
DBrekelmans, C., OTS 33: Lei 1996, Brill xix; 411 pp. ƒ184;
$119. 90-04-10266-3 [NThAR 1996,87].

2185 **Gertz, Jan Christian** Die Gerichtsorganisation Israels im deuteronomischen Gesetz. FRLANT 165: 1994, ⇒10,2400. RJThS 47
(1996) 563-566 (*McConville, J.G.*); ThLZ 121 (1996) 1130-1133
(*Otto, Eckart*); CBQ 58 (1996) 707-708 (*Gnuse, Robert*).

2186 *Hausmann, Jutta* "Weisheit" im Kontext alttestamentlicher Theologie: Stand und Perspektiven gegenwärtiger Forschung. Weisheit
außerhalb der kanonischen Weisheitsschriften [EJanowski, B.].
1996, ⇒E7.5. 1996, 9-19.

2187 **Jeffers, Ann** Magic and divination in Ancient Palestine and Syria.
Studies in the History and Culture of the Ancient Near East 8: Lei
1996, Brill xviii; 277 pp. ƒ146; $94.50. 90-04-10513-1.

2188 **Keller, Martin** Untersuchungen zur deuteronomisch-deuterono-
mistischen Namenstheologie. Diss. Bonn. DSeybold, K., BBB 105:
Bonn 1996, Beltz A. xiii; 235 pp. DM88. 3-89547-105-4.

2189 *Knoppers, Gary N.* The deuteronomist and the deuteronomic law of
the king: a reexamination of a relationship. ZAW 108 (1996) 329-
346 [Deut 17,14-20].

2190 *Levin, Christoph* Über den "Color Hieremianus" des Deuteronomiums. Das Deuteronomium. 1996, ⇒209. 107-126.

2191 **Lohfink, Norbert** Studien zum Deuteronomium und zur deuteronomistischen Literatur 3. SBAB.AT 20: 1995, ⇒11/1,54. RNRTh
118 (1996) 912 (*Ska, Jean Louis*).

2192 *Lohfink, Norbert* The laws of Deuteronomy: a utopian project for a
world without any poor. ScrB 26 (1996) 2-19;

2193 *Lundbom, Jack R.* The inclusio and other framing devices in Deuteronomy i-xxviii. VT 46 (1996) 296-315.

2194 *Mayes, A.D.H.* On describing the purpose of Deuteronomy. The
pentateuch. BiSe 39: 1996 <1993>, ⇒202. 222-241.

2195 **McConville, J. Gordon** Grace in the end: a study in Deuteronomic
theology. 1993, ⇒9,2532...11/1,848. RThLZ 121 (1996) 541-542
(*Lohfink, Norbert*); EvQ 68 (1996) 238 (*Evans, Mary J.*).

2196 **McConville, J. Gordon; Millar J.G.** Time and place in Deuteronomy. JSOT.S 179: 1994, ⇒10,2405; 11/1,849. [R]Reviews in Religion and Theology 1996/2, 49-51 (*Gillingham, Sue*); CritRR 9 (1996) 159-161 (*Burns, John Barclay*).

2197 *Mendoza, González* La Biblia paso a paso: el libro del Deuteronomio (II). EvV 38 (1996) 30-31.

2198 **Olson, Dennis T.** Dt and the death of Moses. 1994, ⇒10,2450; 11/1,854. [R]New Theology Review 9/1 (1996) 88-89 (*Harrelson, Walter*); CritRR 9 (1996) 161-162 (*Clements, Ronald E.*).

2199 *Oosthuizen, Martin J.* The deuteronomic code as a resource for christian ethics. JTSA 96 (1996) 44-58 [ThIK 18/2,23].

2200 *Otto, Eckart* The pre-exilic Deuteronomy as a revision of the covenant code. Kontinuum. 1996, ⇒2002. 112-122;

2201 Treueid und Gesetz: die Ursprünge des Deuteronomiums im Horizont neuassyrischen Vertragsrechts. ZAR 2 (1996) 1-52.

2202 **Perlitt, Lothar** Deuteronomium-Studien. FAT 8: 1994, ⇒10,214; 11/1,858. [R]OTEs 9 (1996) 165-169 (*Oosthuizen, M.J.*).

2203 *Rofé, Alexander* The laws of warfare in the book of Deuteronomy: their origins, intent and positivity. The pentateuch. BiSe 39: 1996 <1985>, ⇒202. 128-149.

2204 *Sonnet, Jean-Pierre* Le Deutéronome et la modernité du livre. NRTh 118 (1996) 481-496.

2205 **Sonnet, Jean-Pierre** 'When Moses had finished writing' (Deut 31:24): communication in Deuteronomy, Deuteronomy as communication. Diss. Indiana 1996. [D]*Ackerman, James S.; Sternberg, Meir*. 360 pp. DAI-A 57/03, p. 1183; AAC 9629580.
      [E]**Veijola, Timo** Das Deuteronomium und seine Querbeziehungen. ⇒209.

2206 *Veijola, Timo* Bundestheologische Redaktion im Deuteronomium. Das Deuteronomium. 1996, ⇒209. 242-276 [Deut 7; 15,1-11].

2207 *Weinfeld, Moshe* Deuteronomy's theological revolution. BiRe 12/1 (1996) 38-41, 44-45.

2208 **Yu, Suee Yan** Tithes and firstlings in Deuteronomy. Diss. Richmond 1996-97 [RTL 29,581].

2209 *Westermann, Claus* Mahnung, Warnung und Geschichte: die Paränese 5. Mose 1-11. Das mündliche Wort. 1996, ⇒157. 80-97.

2210 *Holter, Knut* Literary critical studies of Deut 4: some criteriological remarks. BN 81 (1996) 91-103.

2211 *Otto, Eckart* Deuteronomium 4: die Pentateuchredaktion im Deuteronomium. Das Deuteronomium. 1996, ⇒209. 196-222.

2212 *Avril, Anne-Catherine* "Écoute, Israël": réflexions sur la vie consacrée. NRTh 118 (1996) 709-726 [Deut 6,4-5].

2213 **Gerhardsson, Birger** The Shema in the New Testament: Deut 6:4-5 in significant passages. Lund 1996, Novapress 324 pp. £39; $59. 91-7137-003-X. [R]EThL 72 (1996) 437-438 (*Neirynck, F.*).

2214 *Bascom, Robert A.* Adaptable for translation: Deuteronomy 6.5 in the synoptic gospels and beyond. [F]SANDERS J., JSOT.S 225: 1996, ⇒77. 166-183.

2215 *Schäfer-Lichtenberger, Christa* JHWH, Israel und die Völker aus der Perspektive von Dtn 7. BZ 40 (1996) 194-218.

2216 *Zipor, Moshe A.* The Deuteronomic account of the Golden Calf and its reverberation in other parts of the book of Deuteronomy. ZAW 108 (1996) 20-33 [Deut 9; 10,1-11; 31,14-30; 4].

2217 *Lohfink, Norbert* Fortschreibung?: zur Technik von Rechtsrevisionen im deuteronomischen Bereich, erörtert an Deuteronomium

12, Ex 21,2-11 und Dtn 15,12-18. Das Deuteronomium. 1996,
⇒209. 127-171.

2218 **Reuter, Eleonore** Kultzentralisation: Entstehung und Theologie
von Dtn 12. BBB 87: 1993, ⇒9,2549; 11/1,884. RJBL 115 (1996)
336-338 *(Morrow, William S.)*.

2219 *Levinson, Bernard M.* Recovering the lost original meaning of ולא
תכסה עליו (Deuteronomy 13:9). JBL 115 (1996) 601-620.

2220 **Morrow, William S.** Scribing the center...Dt 14:1-17:13. SBLMS
49: 1995, ⇒11/1,887. RZAR 2 (1996) 208-212 *(Otto, Eckart)*.

2221 *Kessler, Rainer Gôjim* in Dtn 15,6; 28,12: 'Völker' oder 'Heiden'?. IOSOT 1992. BEAT 28: 1996, ⇒160. 85-89.

2222 *Veijola, Timo* The history of the passover in the light of Deuteronomy 16,1-8. ZAR 2 (1996) 53-75.

2223 *Otto, Eckart* Soziale Verantwortung und Reinheit des Landes: zur
Redaktion der kasuistischen Rechtssätze in Deuteronomium 19-25.
Kontinuum. 1996 <1991>, ⇒2002. 123-138.

2224 *Otto, Eckart* Das Eherecht im Mittelassyrischen Kodex und im
Deuteronomium: Tradition und Redaktion in den Paragraphen 12-
16 der Tafel A des Mittelassyrischen Kodex und in Dtn 22,22-29.
Kontinuum. 1996 <1993>, ⇒2002. 172-191.

2225 *Leonhard, Clemens* Halakha und Haggada als Kontext der Targume
zu Dtn 24,16. WZKM 86 (1996) 235-249.

2226 *Kruger, Paul A.* The removal of the sandal in Deuteronomy xxv 9:
"a rite of passage"?. VT 46 (1996) 534-539.

2227 *Fuhs, Hans F.* Aus der Befreiung Leben: Erwägungen zum ge-
schichtlichen Credo in Dtn 26,1-11. FERNST J., 1996, ⇒23. 3-18
[OTA 19,422].

2228 **Steymans, Hans Ulrich** Deuteronomium 28 und die *Adê* zur
Thronfolgeregelung Asarhaddons: Segen und Fluch im Alten
Orient und in Israel. OBO 145: 1995, ⇒11/1,902. RZAR 2 (1996)
214-221 *(Otto, Eckart)*.

2229 **Knight, George A.F.** The song of Moses: a theological quarry.
1995, ⇒11/1,905. RCBQ 58 (1996) 318-319 *(Olson, Dennis T.)*;
RExp 93 (1996) 431-432 *(Drinkard, Joel F.)*; HebStud 37 (1996)
166-168 *(Watts, James W.)* [Deut 32].

2230 *Nigosian, Solomon A.* The song of Moses (Dt 32): a structural analysis. EThL 72 (1996) 5-20.

2231 **Sanders, Paul** The provenance of Deuteronomy 32. OTS 37: Lei
1996, Brill ix; 468 pp. ƒ258; $166.50. 90-04-10648-0.

2232 **Wiebe, John Merritt** Deuteronomy 32, the deliberative rîb tradition, and Hosea's concept of hope. Diss. Fuller 1995, DAllen,
L.C., 460 pp. [EThL 74,201*].

2233 *Tournay, R.J.* Le psaume et les bénédictions de Moise. RB 103
(1996) 196-212 [Deut 33].

2234 *Steiner, Richard C.* דָּת and עַיִן: two verbs masquerading as nouns
in Moses' blessing (Deuteronomy 33:2, 28). JBL 115 (1996) 693-
698.

2235 *Lohfink, Norbert* Moses Tod, die Tora und die alttestamentliche
Sonntagslesung. ThPh 71 (1996) 481-494 [Deut 34].

2236 *Tigay, Jeffrey H.* The significance of the end of Deuteronomy
(Deuteronomy 34:10-12). FHARAN M., 1996, ⇒35. 137-143.

E4.1 *Origo Israelis in Canaan: Deuteronomista*; **Liber Josue**

2237 **Bieberstein, Klaus** Josua—Jordan—Jericho...Josua 1-6. OBO 143: 1995, ⇒11/1,948. ᴿJNSL 22/1 (1996) 175-177 (*Stipp, Hermann-Josef*).
2238 *Boecker, Hans Jochen* Die Landnahme;
2239 Das vorstaatliche Israel. Altes Testament. 1996, ⇒169. 11-23/23-37.
2240 *Catastini, Alessandro* Le notizie degli autori classici sulle origini degli Ebrei: considerazioni generali. ᶠMoscᴀᴛɪ S., 1, 1996, ⇒67. 81-88.
2241 *Coote, Robert B.; Whitelam, Keith W.* The emergence of Israel: social transformation and state formation following the decline in late Bronze Age trade. Community. 1996 <1986>, ⇒172. 335-376.
2242 *Dever, William G.* The identity of early Israel: a rejoinder to Keith W. Wʜɪᴛᴇʟᴀᴍ. JSOT 72 (1996) 3-24.
2243 *Flanagan, James W.* Chiefs in Israel. Community. 1996 <1981>, ⇒172. 311-334.
2244 **Fritz, Volkmar O.** Die Entstehung Israels im 12. und 11. Jahrhundert v. Chr. Biblische Enzyklopädie 2: Stu 1996, Kohlhammer 223 pp. DM39. 3-17-012331-9.
2245 *Gottwald, Norman K.* Domain assumptions and societal models in the study of pre-monarchic Israel. Community. 1996 <1974>, ⇒172. 170-181.
2246 *Kugel, James* The holiness of Israel and the land in Second Temple times. ᶠHᴀʀᴀɴ M., 1996, ⇒35. 21-23.
2247 **Lemche, Niels Peter** Die Vorgeschichte Israels. Biblische Enzyklopädie 1: Stu 1996, Kohlhammer 231 pp. DM39. 3-17-021330-0 [Protest. 52,196].
2248 *Mendenhall, George E.* The Hebrew conquest of Palestine. Community. 1996 <1962>, ⇒172. 152-169.
2249 *Nibbi, Alessandra* Some remarks on the Merenptah stela and the so-called name of Israel. DiscEg 36 (1996) 79-102.
2250 **Sarna, Nahum M.** Exploring Exodus: the origins of biblical Israel. NY 1996, Schocken xx; 277 pp. 0-8052-1063-6.
2251 ᴱ**Shanks, Hershel** The rise of ancient Israel. 1992, ⇒9,408. ᴿIEJ 46 (1996) 142-143 (*Cogan, Mordechai*); JNES 55 (1996) 210-212 (*Tomasino, Anthony J.*).
2252 *Van Cangh, Jean-Marie* Les origines d'Israël et du monothéisme: institution et/ou charisme?. ᶠAʟʙᴇʀɪɢᴏ G., 1996, ⇒1. 35-88.
2253 **Younger, K. Lawson** Ancient conquest accounts. JSOT.S 19: 1990, ⇒6,b404...10,2484(!). ᴿJAOS 116 (1996) 289-291 (*Meltzer, Tova*).

2254 *Albertz, Rainer* Le milieu des deutéronomistes. Israël construit son histoire. 1996, ⇒199. 377-407 [OTA 19,422].
2255 *Briend, Jacques* Les sources de l'histoire deutéronomique: recherches sur Jos 1-12. Israël construit son histoire. 1996, ⇒199. 345-374 [OTA 19,425].
2256 *Dietrich, Walter* Histoire et loi: historiographie deutéronomique et loi deutéronomique à l'exemple du passage de l'époque des Juges à l'époque royale. Israël construit son histoire. 1996, ⇒199. 297-323 [OTA 19,423].
2257 **Doorly, W.D.** Obsession with justice...the deuteronomists. 1994, ⇒10,2459; 11/1,922. ᴿRivBib 44 (1996) 227-229 (*Bovati, Pietro*); JNSL 22/2 (1996) 149-151 (*Terblanche, M.D.*).

2258 *Knauf, Ernst Axel* L''historiographie deutéronomiste' (STRG) existe-t-elle?. Israël construit son histoire. 1996, ⇒199. 409-418 [OTA 19,423].

2259 *Mayes, Andrew D.H.* De l'idéologie deutéronomiste à la théologie de l'Ancien Testament. Israël construit son histoire. 1996, ⇒199. 477-508 [OTA 19,423].

2260 **Mullen, E. Theodore** Narrative history...the deuteronomistic historian. 1993, ⇒9,2583...11/1,928. RVT 46 (1996) 421-422 (*Satterthwaite, P.E.*).

2261 **O'Brien, Mark A.** The Deuteronomistic History hypothesis. OBO 92: 1989, ⇒5,2602...11/1,930. RRStR 22/1 (1996) 22-27 (*Schniedewind, William*).
   EPury, **Albert de** Israël construit son histoire. ⇒199.

2262 *Rose, Martin* L'idéologie deutéronomiste et théologie de l'Ancien Testament. Israël construit son histoire. 1996, ⇒199. 445-476 [OTA 19,424].

2263 *Römer, Thomas; Pury, Albert de* L'historiographie deutéronomiste (HD): histoire de la recherche et enjeux du débat. Israël construit son histoire. 1996, ⇒199. 9-120 [OTA 19,424].

2264 *Schmidt, Ludwig* Deuteronomistisches Geschichtswerk. Altes Testament. 1996, ⇒169. 127-141.

2265 *Sicre, José Luis* La investigación sobre la historia deuteronomista: desde Martin NOTH a nuestros días. EstB 54 (1996) 361-415.

2266 *Spreafico, A.* Lo straniero e la difesa delle categorie più deboli come simbolo di giustizia e di civiltà nell'opera deuteronomicodeuteronomistica. RStB 8 (1996) 117-134.

2267 **Stone, Ken** Sex, honor, and power in the deuteronomistic history. JSOT.S 234: Shf 1996, Academic 170 pp. £35; $50. 1-85075-640-6 [ET 108,278].

2268 *Wessels, J.P.H.* 'Postmodern' rhetoric and the former prophetic literature. Rhetoric. JSNT.S 131: 1996, ⇒268. 182-194.

2269 *Westermann, Claus* Satzparallelismus in den Geschichtsbüchern. Das mündliche Wort. 1996, ⇒157. 113-132.

2270 **Würthwein, Ernst** Studien zum Deuteronomistischen Geschichtswerk. BZAW 227: 1994, ⇒10,233; 11/1,936. RRStR 22/1 (1996) 22-27 (*Schniedewind, William*); OTEs 9 (1996) 173-177 (*Oosthuizen, M.J.*).

2271 EAtanasova, **Diljana** Das Buch Josua. Die Methodbibel. Die Slawischen Sprachen 49: Salzburg 1996, Institut für Slawistik der Univ. Salzburg 290 pp. Kritische Ausgabe altbulgarischer Texte [NThAR 1997,289].

2272 **Cate, Robert L.** An introduction to the historical books of the Old Testament. Nv 1994, Broadman & H. 175 pp. RAUSS 34 (1996) 109-110 (*Pröbstle, Martin*).

2273 **Curtis, Adrian H.W.** Joshua. OTGu: Shf 1994, Academic 89 pp. £6. 1-85075-706-2. RETR 71 (1996) 105-106 (*Macchi, Jean-Daniel*).

2274 **Fritz, Volkmar** Das Buch Josua. HAT 1/7: 1994, ⇒10,2467; 11/1,939. RThPh 71 (1996) 577-578 (*Lohfink, N.*); ZDPV 112 (1996) 61-66 (*Bieberstein, Klaus*).

2275 **Görg, Manfred** Josua. Neue Echter Bibel. 1991, ⇒7,2377...-9,2590. RNedThT 50 (1996) 67-68 (*Noort, E.*).

2276 **Hertog, Cornelis den** Studien zur griechischen Übersetzung des Buches Josua. Diss. Giessen 1995-96, DFritz, V. [RTL 27,528].

2277   *Hertog, Cornelis G. den* Drei Studien zur Übersetzungstechnik des
       griechischen Josuabuches. BIOSCS 29 (1996) 22-52.
2278   **Hess, Richard Samuel** Joshua: an introduction and commentary.
       Tyndale OT Commentaries: Leicester 1996, Inter-Varsity 320 pp.
       0-85111-849-6.
2279   [T]**Moatti-Fine, Jacqueline** Jésus (Josué). La Bible d'Alexandrie 6:
       P 1996, Cerf 258 pp. FF185. 2-204-05429-1 [RTL 28,290].
2280   **Navarro Puerto, Mercedes** Los libros de Josué, Jueces y Rut.
       1995, ⇒11/1,945. [R]PerTeol 28 (1996) 270 (*Lima, Marco Antônio
       Morais*); Iter 7/2 (1996) 152-153 (*Wyssenbach, Jean Pierre*).
2281   **Winther-Nielsen, Nicolai** A functional discourse grammar of Jos-
       hua. CB.OT 40: 1995, ⇒11/1,962. [R]SEÅ 61 (1996) 118-122
       (*Norin, Stig*); CBQ 58 (1996) 736-738 (*Miller, Cynthia L.*).

2282   *Boer, Roland* Green ants and Gibeonites: B. WONGAR, Joshua 9,
       and some problems of postcolonialism. Semeia 75 (1996) 129-152.
2283   **Getz, Gene A.** Joshua: living as a consistent role model. Foreword
       Minirth, Frank, Nv 1995, Broadman & H. x; 193 pp. 0-8054-
       6163-9 [NThAR 1998,98].
2284   *Hess, Richard S.* Joshua 1-12 as a centrist document. IOSOT 1992.
       BEAT 28: 1996, ⇒160. 53-67;
2285   Non-Israelite personal names in the book of Joshua. CBQ 58
       (1996) 205-214;
2286   A typology of West Semitic place name lists with special reference
       to Joshua 13-21. BA 59 (1996) 160-170.
2287   *Jericke, Detlef* Josuas Tod und Josuas Grab: eine redaktionsge-
       schichtliche Studie. ZAW 108 (1996) 347-361 [Josh 24,28-31;
       Judg 2,6-9].
2288   **Koorevaar, H.J.** De opbouw van het boek Jozua. 1990, ⇒6,2868-
       ...9,2593. [R]NedThT 50 (1996) 66-67 (*Noort, E.*).
2289   **Merling, David** The book of Joshua: its theme and use in discus-
       sions of the Israelite conquest and settlement and the relationship of
       archaeology and the bible. Diss. Andrews, [D]*Shea, William H.*,
       1996, 343 pp. DAI-A 57/05, p. 2083; AAC 9630651.
2290   **Mitchell, Gordon** Together in the land: a reading of...Joshua.
       JSOT.S 134: 1993, ⇒10,2470; 11/1,954. [R]CBQ 58 (1996) 126-127
       (*Matties, Gordon H.*).
2291   *Reiner, Elchanan* מקומי למיתוס מקראי מסיעור לישוע: יהושע בין
       (הגלילי היהודי של הדתי בעולמו פרק) [From Joshua to Jesus—the
       transformation of a biblical story to a local myth (a chapter in the
       religious life of the Galilean Jew)]. Sum. xxii. Zion 61 (1996) 281-
       316.
2292   **Rowlett, Lori L.** Joshua and the rhetoric of violence: a new histo-
       ricist analysis. JSOT.S 226: Shf 1996, Academic 197 pp. $40. 1-
       85075-627-9.
2293   **Schäfer-Lichtenberger, Christa** Josua und Salomo: eine Studie zu
       Autorität und Legitimität des Nachfolgers im AT. VT.S 58: 1995,
       ⇒11/1,959. [R]IBSt 18/1 (1996) 49-52 (*McConville, Gordon*).
2294   *Schibler, Daniel* L'enjeu du livre de Josué et du livre des Juges.
       Hokhma 61 (1996) 1-14.
2295   *Shiryon, Michael* Joshua—the underestimated leader: the use of
       psychology in the book of Joshua. Journal of Psychology and Ju-
       daism 19 (1995) 205-225 [IAJS 42,29].
2296   *Stricher, Joseph* Au temps de Josué et des Juges. DosB 62 (1996)
       3-4.

2297 **Wolf, Joh. de** Jozua en Richteren: het beloofde land een bedreigd bezit. Bijbel en Kerk: Barneveld 1996, De Vuurbaak 117 pp. 90-5560-057-1 [NThAR 1997,259].

E4.2 *Liber Judicum:* Richter, Judges

2298 **Amit, Yairah** The book of Judges: the art of editing. 1992, ⇒8,2776. RBiOr 53 (1996) 167-170 *(Schoors, Antoon).* H.
2299 **Arnold, Daniel** Ces mystérieux héros de la foi: une approche globale du livre des Juges. St-Légier 1995, Emmaüs 384 pp. 2-8287-0053-4. RHokhma 63 (1996) 69-71 *(Desplanque, Christophe).*
2300 **Holland, Martin; Steinhoff, Volker** Das Buch der Richter und das Buch Rut. WStB.AT: 1995, ⇒11/1,981. RJETh 10 (1996) 188-192 *(Bluedorn, Wolfgang)*; OTEs 9 (1996) 543-544 *(Roux, M. le).*
2301 **Lindars, Barnabas** Judges 1-5 EMayes, *A.D.H.,* 1995, ⇒11/1,982. RReviews in Religion and Theology (1996/4) 71-73 *(Norton, Gerard J.).*
2302 *Malamat, Abraham* Charismatic leadership in the book of Judges. Community. 1996 <1976>, ⇒172. 293-310.
2303 **O'Connell, Robert H.** The rhetoric of the book of Judges. VT.S 63: Lei 1996, Brill xxi; 541 pp. ƒ257.25. 90-04-10104-7.
2304 *Roux, Magdel le* 'n Reënbooggod vir 'n reënboognasie?: 'n Ou Testamentiese perspektief op 'n multireligieuse samelewing. OTEs 9 (1996) 400-422.
    Schibler, Daniel L'enjeu du livre de Josué et du livre des Juges ⇒2296.
2305 **Smelik, Willem F.** A bilingual concordance to the Targum of the Prophets 2: Judges. Diss. Kampen 1995, DMoor, *J.C. de,* OTS 36: Lei 1996, Brill xi; 681 pp. ƒ278.50; $180. 90-04-10365-1/-284-1 [set] [NTAb 41,190].

2306 *Oded, Bustenai* Cushan-Rishathaim (Judges 3:8-11): an implicit polemic. FHARAN M., 1996, ⇒35. 89*-94*. H.
2307 *Miller, Geoffrey P.* Verbal feud in the Hebrew Bible: Judges 3:12-30 and 19-21. JNES 55 (1996) 105-117.
2308 *Deist, Ferdinand* 'Murder in the toilet' (Judges 3:12-30): translation and transformation. Scriptura 58 (1996) 263-272 [OTA 19,426].
2309 *Van der Kooij, Arie* On male and female views in Judges 4 and 5;
2310 *Van Wolde, Ellen* Deborah and Ya'el in Judges 4. MVAN DIJK-HEMMES F., 1996, ⇒99. 135-152/283-295.
2311 *Tournay, Raymond J.* Le cantique de Déborah et ses relectures. FHARAN M., 1996, ⇒35. 195-207 [Judg 5].
2312 **Becker-Spörl, Silvia** 'Und Debora sang an jenem Tag': Untersuchungen zu Sprache und Intention des Deboraliedes (Ri 5). Diss. Wü 1995/96, DSeidl [BZ 42,319].
2313 *Becker-Spörl, Silvia* Krieg, Gewalt und die Rede von Gott im Deboralied (Ri 5). BiKi 51 (1996) 101-106.
2314 *Claassens, L. Julie M.* Notes on characterisation in the Jephtah narrative. JNSL 22/2 (1996) 107-115 [Judg 11; 12].
2315 *Rad, Gerhard von* Jueces 12,5-7;
2316 El ciclo de Sansón [Judg 13-16]. La acción de Dios. 1996 <1970>, ⇒144. 44-45/46-49.
2317 **Bader, Winfried** Simson bei Delila. TTHLLI 3: 1991, ⇒7,2434; 11/1,1015. REThL 72 (1996) 217-218 *(Vervenne, M.)* [Judg 13-16].

2318   *Jost, Renate* Der Gott der Liebe—der Gott der Rache oder: Simons "Rachegebet". Von der Wurzel getragen. 1996, ⇒204. 103-113 [Judg 16,28].
2319   *Bauer, Uwe F.W.* Zum Problem des Handelns Gottes nach Ri 17-18. FZuurmond R., YHWH. DBAT.B: 1996, ⇒109. 77-84 [OTA 19,427].
2320   *Jost, Renate* Der Fluch der Mutter: feministischsozialgeschichtliche Überlegungen zu Ri 17,1-6. FSchottroff W., 1996, ⇒81. 17-23 [OTA 19,427].
2321   *Brooks, Simcha Shalom* Was there a concubine at Gibeah?. BAIAS 15 (1996-97) 31-40 [Judg 19-21].
2322   **Lawrie, Douglas Gordon** The rhetoric of royalism: persuasion history and imagination in Judges 19-21 and the book of Ruth. Diss. Western Cape, South Africa 1996, DEls, P.J.J.S., 662 pp. [EThL 74,203*].
2323   *Müllner, Ilse* Tödliche Differenzen: sexuelle Gewalt als Gewalt gegen Andere in Ri 19. Von der Wurzel getragen. 1996, ⇒204. 81-100.

E4.3 **Liber Ruth,** '*V Rotuli*', the Five Scrolls

2324   *Avalos, H.I.* A Ladino version of the Targum of Ruth. EstB 54 (1996) 165-182.
2325   *Berlin, Adele* Ruth: big theme, little book. BiRe 12/4 (1996) 40-43, 47-48.
2326   **Bush, Frederic William** Ruth, Esther. WBC 9: Dallas 1996, Word xiv; 514 pp. $30. 0-8499-0208-8.
2327   *Coleson, Joseph E.* The peasant woman and the fugitive prophet: a study in biblical narrative settings. FYoung D., 1996, ⇒107. 27-44.
2328   **Deurloo, Karel A.** YHWH in den Büchern Ruth und Jona. FZuurmond R.: YHWH, DBAT.B: 1996, ⇒109. 105-116 [OTA 19,427].
2329   **Deurloo, Karel A.; Van Duin, Kees** Beter dan zeven zonen: de feestrol Rut als messiaanse verwijzing. Baarn 1996, Ten Have 164 pp. 90-259-4587-2.
2330   *Fischer, Irmtraud* Rut—das Frauenbuch der Hebräischen Bibel. rhs 39 (1996) 1-6.
2331   *Gosse, Bernard* Le livre de Ruth et ses liens avec II Samuel 21,1-14. ZAW 108 (1996) 430-433.
2332   *Grelot, Pierre* Ruth et Noémi. Alliance 103 (1996) 30-31.
2333   **Hamlin, E. John** Ruth: surely there is a future. Internat. Theol. Comm.: GR 1996, Eerdmans xi; 82 pp. $10. 0-8028-4150-3. RKerux 11/3 (1996) 34-35 (*Dennison, James T.*).
       Holland, Martin, (*al*), Das Buch der Richter und das Buch Rut ⇒2300.
2334   **Larkin, Katrina J.A.** Ruth and Esther. OTGu: Shf 1996, Academic 106 pp. 1-85075-755-0.
       Lawrie, D.G. The rhetoric of royalism: persuasion history and imagination in Judges 19-21 and the book of Ruth ⇒2322.
2335   *Luter, A.B.; Rigsby, R.O.* An adjusted symmetrical structuring of Ruth. JETS 39 (1996) 15-28.
2336   *Magonet, Jonathan* Character/author/reader: the problem of perspective in biblical narrative. Literary structure. 1996, ⇒200. 3-13.

2337 **Masini, Mario** "Lectio divina" del libro di Rut. 1994, ⇒10,2530; 11/1,1028. RBen. 43/1 (1996) 190-192 (*Ranzato, Agostino*); Civ-Catt 147 II (1996) 312-313 (*Scaiola, D.*); Laur. 36 (1995) 517-519 (*Dalbesio, Anselmo*).

2338 *Mensing, Roman* Die biblischen Bücher Rut, Ester und Judit im Religionsunterricht: ein Arbeitsbericht. rhs 39 (1996) 37-46.

2339 **Neusner, Jacob** The mother of the Messiah in Judaism: the book of Ruth [Rabbah]. 1993, ⇒9,2663. RBibl.Interp. 4 (1996) 245-247 (*Bach, Alice*).

2340 *Rebera, Ranjini* Naomi, Ruth and the women of Bethlehem: faithfulness in commitment. PJT 15 (1996) 30-42 [ThIK 18/1,61].

2341 **Silva, Aldina da** Ruth: un évangile pour la femme aujourd'hui. P 1996, Médiaspaul 79 pp. [EeV 106,351].

2342 *Vílchez, José* De Belen a Moab: Rut 1,1-6. EE 71 (1996) 441-449.

2343 *Dray, Stephen* Ruth 2:1-23 grace for today. Evangel 14/1 (1996) 2-4.

2344 *Martel, G. de* Le sermon d'EUDES de Châteauroux sur Ruth 2,14. SE 36 (1996) 363-380.

2345 *Dray, Stephen* Ruth 3:1-4:22: living in grace. Evangel 14/2 (1996) 35-37.

2346 *Pollack, Aharon* Notes on Megillat Ruth—chapter 4. JBQ 24 (1996) 183-185.

2347 *Rofé, Alexander* Ruth 4:11 LXX: a midrashic dramatization. FHARAN M., 1996, ⇒35. 119*-124*. H.

2348 *Bush, Frederic William* Ruth 4:17: a semantic wordplay. FYOUNG D., 1996, ⇒107. 3-14.

E4.4 1-2 Samuel

2349 **Bar-Efrat, Shimon** I and II Samuel: introduction and commentary. Mikra Leyisra'el: a bible commentary for Israel: J 1996, Magnes 2 vols. H.

2350 **Brock, Sebastian Paul** The recensions of the Septuagint version of I Samuel. Foreword *Fernández Marcos, Natalio*, Quaderni di Henoch 9: T 1996, Zamorani 23*; 364 pp. 88-7158-053-2.

2351 **Caquot, André; Robert, Philippe de** Les livres de Samuel. 1994, ⇒10,2535; 11/1,1051. REstB 54 (1996) 267-268 (*Precedo, J.*); RThPh 128 (1996) 401-402 (*Bühlmann, Alain*); REJ 155 (1996) 250-259 (*Rouillard-Bonraisin, Hedwige*).

2352 **Cohen, Menachem** Mikra'ot gedolot 'haketer' 2: Samuel I-II. Ramat-Gan 1993, Bar-Ilan University Press 282 pp. 965-266-166. RJSSt 41 (1996) 153-154 (*McCarthy, Carmel*).

2353 **Davis, Dale Ralph** Looking on the heart: expositions of the book of 1 Samuel. 1994, ⇒10,2538. RTrinJ 17 (1996) 260-263 (*Hurst, Larry*).

2354 *Gordon, Robert P.* Translational features of the Peshitta in 1 Samuel. FMCNAMARA M., JSOT.S 230: 1996, ⇒58. 163-176.

2355 **Koster, Albert** Samuel, Saul en David: een woord-voor-woord vertaling uit het Hebreeuws van 1 en 2 Samuel. Eindhoven 1995, Aproges 170 pp. ƒ29.50. 90-800961-5-6 [Bijdr. 59,453—Van Wieringen, A.L.H.M.].

2356 **Schroer, Silvia** Die Samuelbücher. 1992, ⇒8,2824...10,2544. RThRv 92 (1996) 139-140 (*Schäfer-Lichtenberger, Christa*).

2357 **Sicre, José Luis** El primer libro de Samuel. Guia espiritual del
      Antiguo Testamento: Barc 1996, Herder 187 pp. Bibl. 84-254-
      1999-9 [Mayéutica 24,298—Almeida, Washington].
2358 *Taylor, Bernard* The Lucianic text of 1 Reigns: three texts compa-
      red and contrasted. BIOSCS 29 (1996) 53-66.
2359 **Taylor, Bernard A.** The Lucianic manuscripts of 1 Reigns: (*a*)
      majority text. HSM 50: 1992;
2360 (*b*) Analysis. HSM 51: 1993, ⇒9,2682; 10,2546. RJAOS 116
      (1996) 551-553 (*Tov, Emanuel*).
2361 EVan Liere, Franciscus A. Andreas de Sancto Victore, opera 2:
      expositio hystorica in librum Regum. CChr.CM 53A: Turnhout
      1996, Brepols cxxx; 158 pp. 2-503-03533-7.
2362 EVan Staalduine-Sulman, Eveline A bilingual concordance to the
      Targum of the Prophets 3: Samuel I: א-ו. Lei 1996, Brill vi; 360
      pp. ƒ184; $118.75. 90-04-10492-9;
2363 A bilingual concordance...4: Samuel II: ח-ס. Lei 1996, Brill 337
      pp. 90-04-10491-7;
2364 A bilingual concordance...5: Samuel III: ע-ת. Lei 1996, Brill iv;
      369 pp. ƒ180; $116.25. 90-04-10492-5.

2365 *Auld, Graeme* Re-reading Samuel (historically): 'etwas mehr Nicht-
      wissen'. Origins...Israelite states [EFritz, V.O.]. JSOT.S 228:
      1996, ⇒Q1. 160-169.
2366 **Barsotti, Divo** Meditazione sui due libri di Samuele. Bibbia e Li-
      turgia 39: Brescia 1996, Queriniana 349 pp. L37.000. 88-399-
      1639-3 [RdT 38,141].
2367 *Brettler, Marc Z.* Biblical literature as politics: the case of Samuel.
      Religion and politics. 1996, ⇒212. 71-92.
2368 **Fokkelman, J.P.** Vow and desire (1 Sam 1-12). SSN 31: 1993,
      ⇒9,2684...11/1,1069. RTJT 12/1 (1996) 85-86 (*Harvey, John E.*).
2369 La lettura profetica della storia. Conferenza dei religiosi del Bra-
      sile. 1995, ⇒11/1,1056. RPaVi 41/4 (1996) 61-62 (*Lopasso, Vin-
      cenzo*).
2370 *Parry, Donald W.* 4QSam[a] and the tetragrammaton. Current re-
      search...on the Dead Sea Scrolls. StTDJ 20: 1996, ⇒293. 106-125.
2371 *Parry, Donald W.* Retelling Samuel: echoes of the books of Samuel
      in the Dead Sea scrolls. RdQ 17 (1996) 293-306.
2372 **Sturhahn, Herbert** An investigation of the literary artistry of the
      final composer of the narrative of 1 Samuel 1-8. Diss. Fuller 1995,
      339 pp. [EThL 74,203*].
2373 *Tsumura, David Toshio* Coordination interrupted, or literary inser-
      tion: AX&B pattern in the books of Samuel. Literary structure.
      1996, ⇒200. 117-132.
2374 **Wénin, André** Samuel, juez y profeta: lectura narrativa. Pref. *Gru-
      son, Philippe*, CuaBi 89: Estella 1996, Verbo Divino 71 pp. 84-
      8169-094-5.

2375 *Kauffmann, C. Michael* Elkanah's gift: texts and meaning in the
      Bury Bible miniature. JWCI 59 (1996) 279-285 [1 Sam 1,4-8].
2376 *Frolov, Serge; Orel, Vladimir* Was the lad a lad?: on the interpreta-
      tion of I Sam. 1:24. BN 81 (1996) 5-7.
2377 *Meyers, Carol* The Hannah narrative in feminist perspective.
      FYOUNG, D., 1996, ⇒107. 117-126 [1 Sam 1].
2378 **Becker-Spörl, Silvia** "Und Hanna betete". 1992, ⇒8,2840...-
      11/1,1070. ROLZ 91 (1996) 436-440 (*Stahl, Rainer*) [1 Sam 2,1-
      10].

2379 *Duarte Castillo, Raúl* De la comunidad a la comunidad (1 Sam 2,12-26). EfMex 14/1 (1996) 5-24.

E4.5 *1 Sam 7...Initia potestatis regiae,* **Origins of kingship**

2380 *Boecker, Hans Jochen* Die Entstehung des Königtums. Altes Testament. 1996, ⇒169. 38-48.
2381 *Brooks, Simcha Shalom* Saul and the Samson narrative. JSOT 71 (1996) 19-25 [Judg 13,2; 1 Sam 1,1; 9,1].
2382 *Cazelles, Henri* Royauté, prophétisme et identité de l'Israël biblique. RICP 59 (1996) 147-156.
2383 *Chang, Sok C.* Kingship and royal ideology. Yonsei Journal of Theology 1 (1996) 35-53 [ZID 23,414].
2384 *Edelman, Diana* Saul ben Kish in history and tradition. Origins... Israelite states [EFritz, V.O.]. JSOT.S 228: 1996, ⇒Q1. 142-159.
2385 *Finkelstein, Israel* The emergence of the monarchy in Israel: the environmental and socio-economic aspects. Community. 1996 <1989>, ⇒172. 377-403.
2386 **Goodblatt, David** The monarchic principle. TSAJ 38: 1994, ⇒10,2571(!). RJJS 47 (1996) 167-169 (*Schwartz, Seth*).
2387 *Hanson, K.C.* When the king crosses the line: royal deviance and restitution in Levantine ideologies. BTB 26 (1996) 11-25 [1 Sam 5,1-7,1; 2 Sam 21,1-14; 24,1-25; 1 Kgs 16,29-18,45].
2388 *Hawk, L. Daniel* Saul as sacrifice: the tragedy of Israel's first monarch. BiRe 12/6 (1996) 20-25, 56.
2389 *Kessler, Rainer* Gott und König, Grundeigentum und Fruchtbarkeit. ZAW 108 (1996) 214-232.
2390 *McKenzie, Steven L.* Cette royauté qui fait problème. Israël construit son histoire. 1996, ⇒199. 267-295 [OTA 19,430].
2391 **Moenikes, Ansgar** Die grundsätzliche Ablehnung des Königtums in der Hebräischen Bibel: ein Beitrag zur Religionsgeschichte des Alten Israel. BBB 99: 1995, ⇒11/1,1060. RThLZ 121 (1996) 253-255 (*Schmidt, Ludwig*); CBQ 58 (1996) 325-326 (*McKenzie, Steven L.*); BiOr 53 (1996) 774-776 (*Dirksen, P.B.*).
2392 **Niemann, Hermann Michael** Herrschaft, Königtum und Staat. FAT 6: 1993, ⇒9,2705... 11/1,1078. ZAW 108 (1996) 149-150 (*Köckert, M.*); JThS 47 (1996) 566-569 (*Whitelam, Keith W.*).
2393 **Van der Spek, W.** 1 Samuël: een koningschapsboek: analyse en alternatief. Zoetermeer 1996, Boekencentrum 122 pp. ƒ22.50. 90-239-1482-1. Interpretatie 4/7 (1996) 32-33 (*Hofstra, Dussie*).
2394 *Wyatt, N.* Les mythes des Dioscures et l'idéologie royale dans les littératures d'Ougarit et d'Israël. RB 103 (1996) 481-516.
2395 **Wyatt, Nick** Myths of power: a study of royal myth and ideology in Ugaritic and biblical tradition. UBL 13: Münster 1996, Ugarit-Verlag vii; 492 pp. Bibl. 3-927120-43-X.
2396 *Zwickel, Wolfgang* Der Beitrag der Ḥabiru zur Entstehung des Königtums. UF 28 (1996) 751-766.

2397 *Van der Jagt, Krijn A.* What did Saul eat when he first met Samuel?: light from anthropology on biblical texts. BiTr 47 (1996) 226-230 [1 Sam 9,24].

2398 *Venturini, Simone* 1 Sam 10,27-11,1: Testo Masoretico e 4QSamᵃ: le posizioni di alcuni autori e un tentativo di soluzione. RivBib 44 (1996) 397-425.

2399 *Kreuzer, Siegfried* "Saul war noch zwei Jahre König ...": textge-schichtliche, literarische und historische Beobachtungen zu 1 Sam 13,1. BZ 40 (1996) 263-270.

2400 *Jacobson, Howard* Nonnulla onomastica. VigChr 50 (1996) 210-211 [1 Sam 14,4].

2401 *Kio, Stephen Hre* What did Saul ask for: ark or ephod? (1 Samuel 14.18). BiTr 47 (1996) 240-246.

2402 *Smelik, Klaas A.D.* Saul's mercy and God's mercilessness: a reappraisal of 1 Samuel 15:6. ᶠZUURMOND R.: YHWH. DBAT.B: 1996, ⇒109. 85-88 [OTA 19,431].

2403 *Frisch, Amos* "For I feared the people, and I yielded to them" (1 Sam 15,24)—is Saul's guilt attenuated or intensified?. ZAW 108 (1996) 98-104.

E4.6 *1 Sam 16...2 Sam: Accessio Davidis.* **David's Rise**

2404 **Auld, A. Graeme** Kings without privilege: David and Moses. 1994, ⇒10,2583; 11/1,1089. ᴿPEQ 128 (1996) 71-72 *(Bartlett, J.R.)*; BBR 6 (1996) 153-157 *(Hughes, Paul Edward)*; VT 46 (1996) 553-555 *(Williamson, H.G.M.)*.

2405 *Boecker, Hans Jochen* Das Großreich Davids und Salomos. Altes Testament. 1996, ⇒169. 48-58.

2406 **Byamungu, Gosbert T.M.** Stronger than death: David's winning story in an intertextual perspective of 1 Sam 13-2 Sam 6. Diss. ex-cerpt PUG, ᴰ*Conroy, Charles,* R 1996, 95 pp.

2407 *Çazelles, Henri* La mère du roi-messie dans l'Ancien Testament. Études. 1996 <1959>, ⇒120. 109-124.

2408 *Eggenberger, Christoph* David als Psalmist im Lichte mittelalterli-chen Bilderpsalterien. BiKi 51/1 (1996) 23-27.

2409 **Flanagan, James W.** David's social drama. JSOT.S 73: 1988, ⇒4,2855...9,2712. ᴿBiKi 51 (1996) 38-39 *(Knauf, Ernst Axel)*.

2410 *Gavron, Daniel* King David and Jerusalem: myth and reality. Ariel 102 (1996) 6-11.

2411 **Gelander, Shamai** David and his God. JBS 5: 1991, ⇒7,2512... 10,2615. ᴿBiOr 53 (1996) 506-507 *(Haag, Herbert)* [2 Sam 6].

2412 *Halpern, Baruch* The construction of the Davidic state: an exercise in historiography. Origins...Israelite states [ᴱFritz, V.O.]. JSOT.S 228: 1996, ⇒Q1. 44-75.

2413 *Hughes, Paul Edward* Kings without privilege: Graeme AULD's interpretation of the bible's presentation of David and Moses. BBR 6 (1996) 153-157.

2414 **Kleer, Martin** "Der liebliche Sänger der Psalmen Israels": Un-tersuchungen zu David als Dichter und Beter der Psalmen. BBB 108: Bodenheim 1996, Philo (4) 353 pp. 3-8257-0037-2.

2415 *Knauf, Ernst Axel* Das "Haus Davids" in der alt-aramäischen Inschrift vom Tel Dan. BiKi 51/1 (1996) 9-10.

2416 *Langlamet, François* Le cadre alphabétique du 'Livre de Jonathan' (1 Sam 16:14-2 Sam 1:27). ᶠHARAN M., 1996, ⇒35. 163-186.

2417 *Lemche, Niels Peter* From patronage society to patronage society. Origins... Israelite states [EFritz, V.O.]. JSOT.S 228: 1996, ⇒Q1. 106-120.

2418 *Livingston, Michael E.* Remembering David. PSB 17 (1996) 351-352.

2419 *Malul, Meir* Was David involved in the death of Saul on the Gilboa mountain?. RB 103 (1996) 517-545 [1 Sam 31,3; 1 Chr 12].

2420 *Montero, Domingo* Aprender a leer la Biblia: el imperio davídico-salmónico: los orígenes de David y su acceso al poder (I Sm 16-II Sm 5). EvV 38 (1996) 5-6;

2421 El imperio davídico-salomónico. EvV 38/2 (1996) 37-38.

2422 *Na'aman, Nadav* Sources and composition in the history of David. Origins... Israelite states [EFritz, V.O.]. JSOT.S 228: 1996, ⇒Q1. 170-186 [1 Kgs 4,2-19; 9,15-18].

2423 **Oegema, Gerbern S.** The history of the shield of David: the birth of a symbol. JudUm 62: Fra 1996, Lang 223 pp. 50 ill.; Bibl. 0-8204-3182-6.

2424 *Ohler, Annemarie* Herrscher in einer Umbruchszeit: nach dem historischen David fragen. BiKi 51 (1996) 2-8.

2425 **Ollenburger, Ben C.** Zion. JSOT 41: 1987, ⇒3,2718... 7,2515. RThR 61 (1996) 89-91 (*Reventlow, Henning Graf*).

2426 **Pomykala, Kenneth E.** The Davidic dynasty tradition in early Judaism: its history and significance for Messianism. 1995, ⇒11/1,1111. RCBQ 58 (1996) 330-332 (*Basser, Herbert W.*); NT 38 (1996) 402-406 (*Collins, Nina L.*); HebStud 37 (1996) 193-196 (*Jossa, Giorgio*).

2427 *Prouser, Ora Horn* Suited to the throne: the symbolic use of clothing in the David and Saul narratives. JSOT 71 (1996) 27-37.

2428 *Rand, Herbert* David and Ahab: a study of crime and punishment. JBQ 24 (1996) 90-97 [2 Sam 11,2-26; 12,1-15; 1 Kgs 21,1-29].

2429 *Schroer, Silvia; Staubil, Thomas* Saul, David und Jonatan—eine Dreiecksgeschichte?: ein Beitrag zum Thema "Homosexualität im Ersten Testament". BiKi 51 (1996) 15-22 [2 Sam 1,26].

2430 *Soupa, Anne* David et Salomon, entre guerre et paix. DosB 62 (1996) 7-8.

2431 *Zhao, Qiusheng* The story of David and Jonathan. CTR 11/1 (1996) 121-127 [ThIK 18/2,30].

2432 *Daly-Detnon, Margaret* Shades of David in the Johannine presentation of Jesus. PIBA 19 (1996) 9-47 [1 Sam 15-17].

2433 *Abir, Peter A.* The literary character of 1 Samuel 17. ITS 33 (1996) 232-248.

2434 *Dietrich, Walter* Die Erzählungen von David und Goliat in I Sam 17. ZAW 108 (1996) 172-191.

2435 *Vargon, Shmuel* The blind and the lame. VT 46 (1996) 498-514 [1 Sam 20; 2 Sam 4; 9; 16; 19].

2436 **Riepl, Christian** Sind David und Saul berechenbar?... 1 Sam 21 u. 22. ATSAT: 1993, ⇒9,2728... 11/1,1122. RThR 92 (1996) 410-411 (*Schäfer-Lichtenberger, Christa*); JSSt 41 (1996) 322-323 (*Tomes, Roger*).

2437 **Cryer, Frederick** Divination in ancient Israel. JSOT.S 142: 1994, ⇒10,2602. RCBQ 58 (1996) 109-111 (*Simkins, Ronald A.*); ThLZ 121 (1996) 631-633 (*Nissinen, Martti*) [1 Sam 28,8].

2438 **Kleiner, Michael** Saul in En-Dor Wahrsagung oder Totenbeschwö-
rung?... 1 Sam 28. EThSt 66: 1995, ⇒11/1,1125. REThL 72
(1996) 431 (*Lust, J.*).
2439 **Schmidt, Brian B.** Israel's beneficent dead: ancestor cult and
necromancy in ancient Israelite religion and tradition. Diss. Oxf
DDay, John, WL 1996, Eisenbrauns xiv; 400 pp. $37.50. 1-57506-
008-6 [1 Sam 28].

2440 **Bietenhard, Sophia** Des Königs General: die Heerführertradi-
tionen in vorstaatlicher und staatlicher Zeit und die Joabgestalt in 2
Sam 2-20; 1 Kön 1-2. Diss. Bern 1996-97 DDietrich, W., [ThLZ
122,760].
2441 **Hentschel, Georg** 2 Samuel. NEB: 1994, ⇒10,2540. RLebZeug
51/1 (1996) 77-78 (*Frevel, Christian*).
2442 **Keys, Gillian** The wages of sin: a reappraisal of the 'Succession
Narrative'. Diss. JSOT.S 221: Shf 1996, Academic 244 pp. £27;
$40. 1-85075-621-X [ET 108,278].

2443 *Auffret, Pierre* Comment sont tombés les héros?: étude structurelle
de 2Sm 1,19-27. JANES 24 (1996) 1-8.
2444 *Pisano, Stephen* 2 Samuel 5-8 et le deutéronomiste: critique textuelle ou critique littéraire. Israël construit son histoire. 1996,
⇒199. 237-263 [OTA 19,433].
2445 *Keel, Othmar* Davids "Tanz" vor der Lade. BiKi 51/1 (1996) 11-14
[2 Sam 6].
2446 *Frolov, Serge; Orel, Vladimir* The house of Yhwh. ZAW 108
(1996) 254-257 [2 Sam 7,13].
2447 *Knoppers, Gary N.* Ancient near eastern royal grants and the Davidic covenant:a parallel?. Sum. 670. JAOS 116 (1996) 670-697 [2
Sam 7].
2448 *Arackal, George* David's fall and redemption: a study of 2 Samuel
10-12 as a unit of biblical narrative literature. Diss. excerpt PUG
1996, DConroy, Charles. R 1996, 91 pp.
2449 *Smelik, Klaas A.* De moord op Uria: een literair-theologische analyse van 2 Samuël 11. Analecta Bruxellensia 1 (1996) 102-114
[ZID 24,343].
2450 **Pyper, Hugh S.** David as reader: 2 Samuel 12:1-15 and the poetics
of fatherhood. Bibl.Interp. 23: Lei 1996, Brill xi; 238 pp. $79. 90-
04-10581-6.
2451 *Derby, Josiah* A biblical Freudian slip: II Samuel 12:6. JBQ 24
(1996) 107-111.
2452 *Cole, Lois* The church's neglect of Tamar's story. Focus 16/1
(1996) 61-65 [ThIK 18/2,60] [2 Sam 13,1-21].
2453 **Lyke, Larry Lewis** 'And the two of them struggled in the field':
intertextuality and the interpretation of the mashal of the wise
woman of Tekoa in 2 Samuel 14:1-20. Diss. Harvard DLevenson,
Jon D., 1996, 225 pp. DAI-A 57/06, p. 2528; AAC 9704833.
2454 *Costen, James H.* Running with the right message: II Samuel 18:9-
33. JITC 24 (1996-97) 215-221 [ZID 23,406].
2455 *Schroer, Silvia* Und als der nächste Krieg begann...: die weise Frau
von Abel-Bet-Maacha (2 Samuel 20,14-22). Die Weisheit. 1996
<1992>, ⇒149. 80-89.

2456 *Gourgues, Michel* 'Desde su templo él escuchó mi voz': ecos del 'cántico de David' en el Nuevo Testamento. Anamnesis 6/2 (1996) 5-21 [2 Sam 22; Ps 18].

2457 *Naéh, Shlomo* A new suggestion regarding 2 Samuel xxiii 7. VT 46 (1996) 260-265.

2458 *Adler, Joshua J.* David's census: additional reflection. JBQ 24 (1996) 255-257 [2 Sam 24].

E4.7 *Libri Regum:* Solomon, Temple: 1 Kings...

2459 **Cogan, Mordechai; Tadmor, Hayim** II Kings. AncB 11: 1988, ⇒4,2952... 8,2907. ᴿEstB 54 (1996) 128-129 (*Zamora, P.*).

2460 ᴱ**Dunkov, Dimitär** Die Bücher der Könige: das erste Buch der Könige. Die Methodbibel. Die Slawischen Sprachen 47: Salzburg 1996, Institut für Slawistik der Univ. Salzburg 412 pp. Kritische Ausgabe altbulgarischer Texte [NThAR 1997,289].

2461 **Fernández Marcos, Natalio** Scribes and translators: LXX and Old Latin in... Kings. VT.S 54: 1994, ⇒10,2636; 11/1,1149. ᴿCBQ 58 (1996) 514-515 (*Pisano, Stephen*); JAOS 116 (1996) 553-555 (*Pietersma, Albert*); JBL 115 (1996) 520-521 (*Davila, James R.*).

2462 **Fritz, Volkmar** Das erste Buch der Könige. ZBK.AT 10/1: Z 1996, Theologischer 207 pp. 3-290-14757-6 [NThAR 1997,161].

2463 **Smelik, Klaas A.D.** 1 Koningen; 2 Koningen. 1993-94, 2 vols, ⇒10,2641. ᴿCBQ 58 (1996) 725-726 (*Vogels, Walter A.*).

2464 *Vogüé, Adalbert de* L'auteur du commentaire des Rois attribué à Saint GREGOIRE: un moine de Cava?. RBen 106 (1996) 319-331.

2465 **Walsh, Jerome T.** 1 Kings. Berit Olam, Studies in Hebrew Narrative & Poetry. ColMn 1996, Liturgical xxi; 393 pp. $40. 0-8146-5044-9 [RB 103,639].

2466 *Barrick, W. Boyd* On the meaning of בֵּית־הַבָּמוֹת and בָּתֵּי־הַבָּמוֹת and the composition of the Kings history. JBL 115 (1996) 621-642.

2467 **Galil, Gershon** The chronology of the kings of Israel and Judah. Studies in the History and Culture of the Ancient Near East 9: Lei 1996, Brill xix; 180 pp. *f*96; $62. 90-04-10611-1.

2468 *Koch, Klaus* Die mysteriösen Zahlen der judäischen Könige und die apokalyptischen Jahrwochen. Wende der Zeiten. 1996 <1978>, ⇒133. 135-142.

2469 *Łach, Józef* Jak ujmować w nowy sposób teologię w 1-2 Królów? [De theologia 1-2 Regum in nova luce]. RBL 49 (1996) 249-255. **P.**

2470 **McKenzie, Steven L.** The trouble with Kings. VT.S 42: 1991, ⇒7,2534... 11/1,1159. ᴿRStR 22/1 (1996) 22-27 (*Schniedewind, William*).

2471 *Schniedewind, William* The problem with Kings: recent study of the Deuteronomistic History. RStR 22/1 (1996) 22-27.

2472 *Talshir, Ziporah* Towards the structure of the book of Kings: formulaic synchronization and story synchronism (1 Kings 12-2 Kings 17). ᶠHARAN M., 1996, 73*-87*. **H.**

2473 **Wallace, Ronald S.** Readings in 1 Kings: an interpretation arranged for personal and group bible study: with questions and notes. GR 1996, Eerdmans xvi; 174 pp. £7.50. 0-8028-4200-3 [EvQ 69,366].

2474 *Ahituv, Shmuel* King Solomon's designation for kingship in biblical historiography. ^FH ARAN M., 1996, ⇒35. 1*-10*. **H.**

2475 *Bose, Mishtooni* From exegesis to appropriation: the medieval Solomon. MAe 65/2 (1996) 187-210 [1 Kgs 11].

2476 *Fritz, Volkmar* Monarchy and re-urbanization: a new look at Salomon's kingdom. Origins...Israelite states [^E**Fritz, V.O.**]. JSOT.S 228: 1996, ⇒Q1. 187-195.

2477 **Jost, Franklyn Loren** 'Why is 1 Kings 3-11 lying to me?': literary and homiletic analysis. Diss. Vanderbilt 1996 ^D*Buttrick, D.G.*, 444 pp. [EThL 74,205*].

2478 **Knoppers, Gary N.** The reign of Solomon and the rise of Jeroboam. HSM 52: 1993, ⇒9,2807... 11/1,1163. ^RRStR 22/1 (1996) 22-27 (*Schniedewind, William*); Interp. 50 (1996) 293-295 (*DeVries, Simon J.*); JThS 47 (1996) 569-72 (*Gordon, Robert P.*); EstB 54 (1996) 560-561 (*García Santos, A.*).

2479 **Rappe, Claude** Σολομών, ο Βασιλιάς των Γυναικών [Solomon, the king of women]. Nea Synora: Athens 1996, Livanis 378 pp. [DBM 16/1,81]. **G.**

2480 *Särkiö, Pekka* Die Struktur der Salomogeschichte (1 Kön 1-11) und die Stellung der Weisheit in ihr. BN 83 (1996) 83-106.

2481 **Steller, Hans-Ernest** Giv'on: Solomon's dream or ask what I shall give thee: a study in midrash texts and their interrelations. Diss. Rijksuniv. 1996, xxvii; 510 pp. [1 Kgs 3,5-15] [NThAR 1997,99].

2482 *Tomes, Roger* 'Our holy and beautiful house': when and why was 1 Kings 6-8 written?. JSOT 70 (1996) 33-50.

2483 *Hirth, Volkmar* Die Königin von Saba und der Kämmerer aus dem Mohrenland oder das Ende menschlicher Weisheit vor Gott: ein Versuch biblischer Theologie. BN 83 (1996) 13-15 [1 Kgs 10,1-10; Acts 8,26-40].

2484 *Bissoli, Giovanni* La regina di Saba. TS(I) 72 (Gen-feb 1996) 7-10 [1 Kgs 10,1-13; 2 Chr 9,1-12].

2485 **Lassner, Jacob** Demonizing the Queen of Sheba. 1994, ⇒9,2798; 10,2675. ^RJAOS 116 (1996) 158-160 (*Brinner, William M.*) [1 Kgs 10,1-13].

2486 *Schenker, Adrian* Un cas de critique narrative au service de la critique textuelle (1 Rois 11,43-12,2-3.20). Bib. 77 (1996) 219-226.

2487 *Schenker, Adrian* Jéroboam et la division du royaume dans la Septante ancienne LXX 1 R 12,24a-z, TM 11-12; 14 et l'histoire deutéronomiste. Israël construit son histoire. 1996, ⇒199. 193-236 [OTA 19,435].

2488 **Talshir, Zipora** The alternative story of the division of the kingdom: 3 Kingdoms 12:24a-z. JBS 6: 1993, ⇒9,2802; 11/1,1216. ^RJAOS 116 (1996) 550-551 (*Wevers, John Wm.*); CritRR 9 (1996) 172-174 (*Wright, John W.*).

Templum

2489 *Amitzur, Hagi* JUSTINIAN's Solomon's temple in Jerusalem. Centrality of Jerusalem. 1996, ⇒236. 160-175.

2490 **Backhouse, Robert** The Kregel pictorial guide to the temple. ^E*Dowley, Tim*, GR 1996, Kregel 32 pp. $8. 0-8254-3039-9 [ThD 44,156].

2491 *Bar-Kochva, Bezalel* An ass in the Jerusalem Temple—the origins and development of the slander;

2492 *Bauckham, Richard* Josephus' account of the temple in Contra Apionem 2.102-109. Josephus' Contra Apionem [E**Feldman, L.H.**]. AGJU 34: 1996, ⇒Q7. 310-326/327-347.

2493 *Berlejung, Angelika* Der Handwerker als Theologe: zur Mentalitäts- und Traditionsgeschichte eines altorientalischen und alttestamentlichen Berufstands. VT 46 (1996) 145-168.

2494 *Davies, Philip R.* The ideology of the temple in the Damascus document. Sects and scrolls. SFSHJ 134: 1996 <1982>, ⇒122. 45-60.

2495 *Fine, Steven* Did the synagogue replace the temple?. BArR 22/2 (1996) 18-26, 41.

2496 **Gibson, Shimon; Jacobson, David M.** Below the Temple Mount in Jerusalem: a sourcebook on the cisterns, subterranean chambers and conduits of the Haram al Sharif. BArR International Series 637: Oxf 1996, Tempus Reparatum xxv; 301 pp. 130 fig. £40. 0-86054-820-1 [PEQ 130,76—Murphy-O'Connor, Jerome].

2497 *Gilboa, R.* Cherubim: an inquiry into an enigma. BN 82 (1996) 59-75.

2498 E**Hayward, Robert C.** The Jewish temple: a non-biblical sourcebook. L 1996, Routledge xvi; 211 pp. £45/£15. 0-415-10239-2/-40-5 [JSJ 28,366].

2499 **Hurowitz, Victor** I have built you an exalted house: temple building... JSOT.S 115: 1992, ⇒8,2929... 11/1,1197. R BZ 40 (1996) 308-310 (*Thiel, Winfried*).

2500 **Junco, Carlos** La crítica profética ante el templo: teología veterotestamentaria. 1994, ⇒10,2669; 11/1,1200. R EfMex 14/1 (1996) 114-116 (*Carrillo Alday, Salvador*); CBQ 58 (1996) 317-318 (*Gossai, Hemchand*).

2501 *Knohl, Israel* Between voice and silence: the relationship between prayer and temple cult. JBL 115 (1996) 17-30.

2502 *Monson, J.H.* Solomon's temple and the temple at ᶜAin Dārā. Qad. 29 (1996) 33-38. **H**.

2503 *Parmentier, Martin* No stone upon another?: reactions of Church Fathers against the Emperor JULIAN's attempt to rebuild the Temple. Centrality of Jerusalem. 1996, ⇒236. 143-159.

2504 *Robert, Philippe de* Pour ou contre le second temple. IOSOT 1992. BEAT 28: 1996, ⇒160. 179-182.

2505 **Schmidt, Francis** La pensée du temple: de Jérusalem à Qoumrân. 1994, ⇒10,2668; 11/1,1206. R REJ 155 (1996) 259-261 (*Petit, Madeleine*).

2506 *Schwartz, Joshua* The temple in Jerusalem: Birah and Baris in archaeology and literature. Centrality of Jerusalem. 1996, ⇒236. 29-49.

2507 *Taran, Anat* התלמודית בספרות החורבן ותיאורי פלוויוס יוספוס [Remarks on JOSEPHUS Flavius and the destruction of the Second Temple]. Sum. xiii. Zion 61 (1996) 141-157.

2508 *Taylor, N.H.* Palestinian christianity and the CALIGULA: part I, social and historical reconstruction. JSNT 61 (1996) 101-124.

2509 **Weinberg, Joel** The citizen-temple community. JSOT.S 151: 1992, ⇒10,2670. R VDI 217 (1996) 225-227 (*Sventsitskaya, I.S.*).

2510 **Zwickel, Wolfgang** Der Tempelkult in Kanaan und Israel: Studien zur Kultgeschichte Palästinas von der Mittelbronzezeit bis zum

Untergang Judas. FAT 10: 1994, ⇒10,2671; 11/1,1208. ᴿJThS 47 (1996) 173-174 (*Watson, W.G.E.*); ThLZ 121 (1996) 655-658 (*Conrad, Diethelm*).

1 Regum 12ss

2511 **Boer, Roland** JAMESON and Jeroboam. SBL Semeia Studies: Atlanta 1996, Scholars xviii; 367 pp. $30. 0-7885-0117-8 [1 Kgs 11-14; 2 Chr 10-13].
2512 *Etz, Donald V.* The genealogical relationships of Jehoram and Ahaziah, and of Ahaz and Hezekiah, kings of Judah. JSOT 71 (1996) 39-53.
2513 *Harvey, John E.* Jeroboam I as a second Moses gone awry. CSBS annual meeting 26 May 1996. Sum. BCSBS 55 (1995/96) 7-8.
2514 **Knoppers, Gary N.** The reign of Jeroboam, the fall of Israel and the reign of Josiah. HSM 53: 1994, ⇒10,2637; 11/1,1210. ᴿRStR 22/1 (1996) 22-27 (*Schniedewind, William*); CBQ 58 (1996) 117-118 (*Rogers, Jeffrey S.*); Interp. 50 (1996) 293-295 (*DeVries, Simon J.*); JThS 47 (1996) 569-72 (*Gordon, Robert P.*); EstB 54 (1996) 560-561 (*García Santos, A.*); JBL 115 (1996) 732-734 (*Klein, Ralph W.*).
2515 **Toews, Wesley I.** Monarchy and religious institution in Israel under Jeroboam I. SBL.MS 47: 1993. ⇒9,2806... 11/1,1209. ᴿTJT 12/1 (1996) 92-93 (*McLaughlin, John L.*); JAOS 116 (1996) 548-549 (*Hurowitz, Victor Avigdor*).

2516 *Slusser, Michael* Golden calves and church divisions. ET 107 (1996) 141-142 [1 Kgs 12,25-32].
2517 *Van Winkle, D.W.* 1 Kings xii 25-xiii 34: Jeroboam's cultic innovations and the man of God from Judah. VT 46 (1996) 101-114.
2518 *Fox, Nili* Royal officials and court families: a new look at the jldjm (yeladîm) in 1 Kings 12. BA 59 (1996) 225-232.
2519 *Klopfenstein, Martin A.* 1. Könige 13: vom Erwählen und Verwerfen Gottes. Leben aus dem Wort. BEAT 40: 1996, ⇒132. 75-116.
2520 *Conroy, Charles* Hiel between Ahab and Elijah-Elisha: 1 Kgs 16,34 in its immediate literary context. Bib. 77 (1996) 210-218.

E4.8 *1 Regum 17-22: Elias,* Elijah

2521 **Àlvarez Barredo, Miguel** Las narraciones Elías y Eliseo en los libros de los Reyes: formación y teología. Publicaciones Instituto Teológico Franciscano Serie Mayor 21: Murcia 1996, Espigas 139 pp. 84-86042-30-5 [OTA 19,536] [=Carthaginensia 12 (1996) 1-123].
2522 **Granowski, Janis Jaynes** Polemics and praise: the deuteronomistic use of the female characters of the Elijah-Elisha stories. Diss. Baylor 1996, ᴰ*Bellinger, W.H.*, 253 pp. [EThL 74,201*].
2523 *Oeming, Manfred* Das Alte Testament als Buch der Kirche?: exegetische und hermeneutische Erwägungen am Beispiel der Erzählung von Elija am Horeb (I Kön 19), alttestamentlicher Predigttext am Sonntag Okuli. ThZ 52 (1996) 299-325.

2524 *Overholt, Thomas W.* Elijah and Elisha in the context of Israelite religion. ᶠTUCKER G., JSOT.S 229: 1996, ⇒95. 94-111.

2525 **Poirot, Soeur Éliane** Élie, archétype du moine: pour un ressourcement prophétique de la vie monastique. SpOr 65: 1995, ⇒11/1,1252. ᴿOCP 62 (1996) 257-258 (*Poggi, V.*).

2526 *Raske, Michael* JHWH oder Baal: zur Unduldsamkeit eines Propheten. Gott an den Rändern. 1996, ⇒162. 24-31 [OTA 19,385].

2527 **Roberts, Kathryn Lee** Elijah and ninth century Israelite religion. Diss. Princeton Theological Seminary 1996, ᴰ*Miller, Patrick D.*, 188 pp. DAI-A 57/05, p. 2084; AAC 9629100.

2528 *Siebert-Hommes, Jopie* The widow of Zarephath and the great woman of Shunem: a comparative analysis of two stories. ᴹVAN DIJK-HEMMES F., 1996, ⇒99. 231-250 [1 Kgs 17,8; 2 Kgs 4,8-37].

2529 *Vorndran, Jürgen* Elijas Dialog mit Jahwes Wort und Stimme (1 Kön 19,9b-18). Bib. 77 (1996) 417-424.

2530 *Wagner, Siegfried* Elia am Horeb: methodologische und theologische Überlegungen zu I Reg 19. Ausgewählte Aufsätze. BZAW 240: 1996 <1991>, ⇒156. 213-225.

2531 **Woods, Fred E.** Water and storm polemics against Baalism in the deuteronomic history. 1994, ⇒10,2704. ᴿBS 153 (1996) 244-245 (*Chisholm, Robert B.*).

E4.9 **2 Reg 1...** *Elisaeus, Elisha...* Ezechias, Josias

2532 *Begg, C.* The end of King Jehoiakim: the afterlife of a problem. Sum. 12. JSem 8/1 (1996) 12-20.

2533 *Ben Zvi, Ehud* Prelude to a reconstruction of the historical Manassic Judah. BN 81 (1996) 31-44.

2534 **Dunkov, Dimităr** Die Methodbibel: die Bücher der Könige: das zweite Buch der Könige. Die Slawischen Sprachen 48: Salzburg 1996, Institut für Slawistik der Univ. Salzburg 189 pp. Kritische Ausgabe altbulgarischer Texte [NThAR 1997,289].

2535 **Dutcher-Walls, Patricia N.** Narrative art, political rhetoric: the case of Athaliah and Joash. JSOT.S 209: Shf 1996, Academic 198 pp. [2 Kgs 11].

2536 **Lowery, Richard H.** The reforming kings: cults and society in First Temple Judah. JSOT.S 120: 1991, ⇒7,2583... 10,2644. ᴿJJS 47 (1996) 356-357 (*Knoppers, Gary N.*); JNES 55 (1996) 55-57 (*Holloway, Steven*).

2537 *Marocco, Giuseppe* Studi storici e letterari sull'epoca di Ezechia. ATT 2 (1996) 254-266.

2538 **Nakanose, Shigeyuki** Josiah's passover: sociology and the liberating bible. 1993, ⇒9,2851... 11/1,1290. ᴿJThS 47 (1996) 178-180 (*Rogerson, J.W.*).

2539 **Provan, Iain W.** Hezekiah. BZAW 172: 1988, ⇒4,2979... 8,2989. ᴿRStR 22/1 (1996) 22-27 (*Schniedewind, William*).

2540 *Talshir, Zipora* The three deaths of Josiah and the strata of biblical historiography (2 Kings xxiii 29-30; 2 Chronicles xxxv 20-5; 1 Esdras i 23-31). VT 46 (1996) 213-236.

2541 **Van Keulen, Percy S.F.** Manasseh through the eyes of the deuteronomists: the Manasseh account (2 Kings 21:1-18) and the final chapters of the deuteronomistic history. OTS 38: Lei 1996, Brill viii; 249 pp. ƒ135; $87.25. 90-04-10666-9.

2542 *Sternberger, Jean-Pierre* L'holocauste à la frontière: une lecture de 2 Rois 3. FV 95/4 (1996) 19-32.

2543 *Becking, Bob* "Touch for health...": magic in II Reg 4,31-37 with a remark on the history of Yahwism. ZAW 108 (1996) 34-54.

2544 *O'Brien, D.P.* "Is this the time to accept ...?" (2 Kings v 26b): simply moralizing (LXX) or an ominous foreboding of Yahweh's rejection of Israel (MT)?. VT 46 (1996) 448-457.

2545 *Rad, Gerhard von* Naamán: ensayo de crítica narrativa. La acción de Dios. 1996 <1970>, ⇒144. 50-59 [2 Kings 5].

2546 *Mulzer, Martin; Krieger, Klaus-Stefan* Die Jehuerzählung bei Josephus (Ant.Jud. IX.105-139.159f.). BN 83 (1996) 54-82 [2 Kgs 8,25-10,36].

2547 **Mulzer, Martin** Jehu schlägt Joram... 2 Kön 8,25-10,36. ATSAT 37: 1992, ⇒8,2978... 10,2729. ᴿOLZ 91 (1996) 311-314 (*Stahl, Rainer*).

2548 **Jong, Stephen de** Het verhaal van Hizkia en Sanherib: een synchronische en diachronische analyse van II Kon. 18,13-19,37 (par. Jes. 36-37). 1992, ⇒8,2987; 9,2844. ᴿBZ 40 (1996) 314-315 (*Becker, Joachim*).

2549 *Van Keulen, P.S.F.* The meaning of the phrase *wn'spt 'l-qbrtyk bšlwm* in 2 Kings xxii 20. VT 46 (1996) 257-259.

2550 *Smyth, Françoise* Quand Josias fait son oeuvre ou le roi bien enterré: une lecture synchronique de 2 R 22,1-23,28. Israël construit son histoire. 1996, ⇒199. 325-339 [2 Kgs 22,1-23,28] [OTA 19,436].

2551 *Na'aman, Nadav* The dedicated treasures buildings within the house of YHWH where women weave coverings for Asherah (2 Kings 23,7). BN 83 (1996) 17-18.

2552 *Luciani, Ferdinando* 2 Re 23,18b nel Targum di Jonathan e nella Pᵉšittā'. Sum. 396. RivBib 44 (1996) 385-396 [2 Kgs 23,18].

E5.2 *Chronicorum libri* — **The books of Chronicles**

2553 *Augustin, Matthias* Neue territorialgeschichtliche Überlegungen am Beispiel rubenitischer Texte in 1 Chronik 1-9. IOSOT 1992. BEAT 28: 1996, ⇒160. 27-30.

2554 **Bowman, Craig Douglas** An analysis of the Chronicler's use of sources: methodological concerns and criteria. Diss. Princeton 1996-97 [RTL 29,576].

2555 **Dörrfuß, Ernst Michael** Mose in den Chronikbüchern. BZAW 219: 1994, ⇒10,2162; 11/1,567. ᴿThRev 92 (1996) 304-305 (*Oeming, Manfred*); BiOr 53 (1996) 499-502 (*Dirksen, Piet B.*).

2556 *Dyck, Jonathan E.* The ideology of identity in Chronicles. Ethnicity. Bibl.Interp. 19: 1996, ⇒171. 89-116.

2557 **Fernández Marcos, Natalio; Busto Saiz, José Ramón** El texto antioqueno de la biblia griega 3: 1-2 Crónicas. Collab. *Spottorno Díaz-Caro, María Victoria; Cowe, S. Peter*, TEstCisn 60: M 1996, Instituto de Filología, C.S.I.C. lxv; 162 pp. 84-00-07585-4 [OTA 19,536].

2558 *Gelston, Anthony* The end of Chronicles. SJOT 10 (1996) 53-60.

2559 *Glatt-Gilad, David A.* The role of Huldah's prophecy in the Chronicler's portrayal of Josiah's reform. Bib. 77 (1996) 16-31 [2 Chr 22-23].

2560 *Gosse, Bernard* Les citations de Psaumes en 1 Ch 16,8-36 et la conception de relations entre Yahvé et son peuple dans la rédaction des livres des Chroniques. EeT(O) 27 (1996) 313ff [ThD Index Feb. 1997,3].

2561 *Höffken, Peter* Der Prophet Jesaja beim Chronisten. BN 81 (1996) 82-90.

2562 **Japhet, Sara** I and II Chronicles. OTL: 1993, ⇒9,2861... 11/1,1299. ᴿBiOr 53 (1996) 170-173 (*Dirksen, P.B.*); Interp. 50 (1996) 195 (*Schuller, Eileen*); ZAW 108 (1996) 471-472 (*Köckert, M.*).

2563 *Japhet, Sara* The distribution of the priestly gifts according to a document of the Second Temple period. ᶠHARAN M., 1996, ⇒35. 3-20 [2 Chr 31,4-19].

2564 **Kelly, Brian E.** Retribution and eschatology in Chronicles. JSOT.S 211: Shf 1996, Academic 279 pp. £35; $50. 1-85075-579-5.

2565 *Knoppers, Gary N.* "Yhwh is not with Israel": alliances as a topos in Chronicles. CBQ 58 (1996) 601-626.

2566 *Lorenzin, Tiziano* L'uso della regola ermeneutica *gezerah shawah* nel Cronista. RivBib 44 (1996) 65-70.

2567 **Peltonen, Kai** History debated: the historical reliability of Chronicles in pre-critical and critical research. Diss. Helsinki. SESJ 64: Helsinki 1996, Finnish Exegetical Society 2 vols. 951-9217-19-3 [EThL 73,159].

2568 **Ravasi, Gianfranco** I libri delle Cronache. Ciclo di conferenze tenute al Centro culturale S. Fedele di Milano. Conversazioni bibliche: Bo 1996, EDB 112 pp. 88-10-70957-8.

2569 *Rendtorff, Rolf* Chronicles and the priestly torah. ᶠHARAN M., 1996, ⇒35. 259-266.

2570 **Riley, William** King and cultus in Chronicles: worship and the reinterpretation of history. JSOT.S: 160: 1993, ⇒9,2877... 11/1,1313. ᴿEThL 72 (1996) 221 (*Schoors, A.*); JAOS 116 (1996) 541-543 (*Knoppers, Gary N.*).

2571 *Steins, Georg* Die Bücher der Chronik als Schule der Bibellektüre. BiLi 69 (1996) 36-40, 105-109, 166-170, 247-251.

2572 *Steins, Georg* Torabindung und Kanonabschluß: zur Entstehung und kanonischen Funktion der Chronikbücher. Die Tora als Kanon. 1996, ⇒1308. 213-256.

2573 **Weinberg, Joel** Der Chronist in seiner Mitwelt. BZAW 239: B 1996, De Gruyter x; 334 pp. DM218. 3-11-014675-4 [CBQ 59,209].

2574 *Witczyk, Henryk* Historyczno-Prorockie tło dzieła Kronikarskiego [De opere Chronistae eiusque historico ac prophetico fondo]. RBL 49/1 (1996) 1-14. **P.**

2575 *Levin, Schneir* Zerubbabel: a riddle. JBQ 24/1 (1996) 14-17 [1 Chr 3,19].

2576 *Snyman, Gerrie* Who is responsible for Uzzah's death?: rhetoric in 1 Chronicles 13. Rhetoric. JSNT.S 131: 1996, ⇒268. 203-217.

2577 *Dirksen, P.B.* I Chronicles 16:38: its background and growth. JNSL 22/1 (1996) 85-90.
2578 *Dirksen, Piet B.* Why was David disqualified as temple builder?: the meaning of 1 Chronicles 22.8. JSOT 70 (1996) 51-56 [1 Kgs 5,17].
2579 *Dirksen, P.B.* 1 Chronicles xxviii 11-18: its textual development. VT 46 (1996) 429-438.
2580 **Vaughn, Andrew G.** The chronicler's account of Hezekiah: the relationship of historical data to a theological interpretation of 2 Chronicles 29-32. Diss. Princeton Theological Seminary 1996 ᴰ*Miller, Patrick D.*, 342 pp. DAI-A 57/05, p. 2086; AAC 9701749.
2581 *Schniedewind, William M.* A Qumran fragment of the ancient "Prayer of Manasseh"?. ZAW 108 (1996) 105-107 [2 Chr 33,1-19].

E5.4 *Esdrae libri* — **Ezra, Nehemiah**

2582 **Breneman, Mervin** Ezra, Nehemiah, Esther. NAC 10: 1993, ⇒9,2895... 11/1,1327. ᴿTJT 12/1 (1996) 79 (*Davies, Gordon*).
2583 **Koster, Albert** Daniël, Ezra, Nechemja: een woord-voor-woord vertaling uit de grondtekst. Eindhoven 1996, Aproges 120 pp. *f*29. 90-800961-9-9 [Bijdr. 59,453—Van Wieringen, Archibald L.H.M.].

2584 **Abadie, Philippe** Le livre d'Esdras et de Néhémie. CEv 95: P 1996, Cerf 68 pp. F33.
2585 *Bergren, Theodore A.* Christian influence on the transmission history of 4, 5, and 6 Ezra. The Jewish apocalyptic heritage in early christianity [ᴱVanderKam, J.C..]. CRI 3: 1996, ⇒G2.4. 102-127.
2586 *Demsky, Aaron* Who returned first—Ezra or Nehemiah?. BiRe 12/2 (1996) 28-33, 46-48.
2587 *Littman, Robert J.* Athens, Persia and the book of Ezra. TPAPA 125 (1995) 251-259 [IAJS 42,51].
2588 **Mathys, Hans-Peter** Dichter und Beter: Theologen aus spätalttestamentlicher Zeit. OBO 132: 1994, ⇒10,2807. JBL 115 (1996) 331-333 (*Creach, Jerome F.D.*); AuOr 14 (1996) 289-291 (*Olmo Lete, G. del*).
2589 **Sack, Ronald H.** Images of Nebuchadnezzar. 1991, ⇒7,2645. ᴿJNES 55 (1996) 135-138 (*Weisberg, David B.*).
2590 *Smith, Daniel L.* The politics of Ezra: sociological Indicators of postexilic Judaean society. Community. 1996 <1991>, ⇒172. 537-556.
2591 *Uffenheimer, Benjamin* Zerubbabel: the messianic hope of the returnees. ᵀ*Bakon, Shimon*, JBQ 24 (1996) 221-228.
2592 *Wagner, Siegfried* Exegetische Betrachtungen zu Nehemia. Ausgewählte Aufsätze. BZAW 240: 1996 <1994>, ⇒156. 239-246.
2593 *Williamson, H.G.M.* The problem with First Esdras. ᶠMᴀsoN R., 1996, ⇒57. 201-216.

2594 *Wyk, W.C. van* The enemies in Ezra 1-6: interaction between text and reader. Sum. 34. JSem 8/1 (1996) 34-48.

2595 *Briend, Jacques* L'édit de Cyrus et sa valeur historique. TEuph 11 (1996) 33-44 [Ezra 1,2-4; 6,2-5].
2596 *Sérandour, Arnaud* Remarques sur le bilinguisme dans le livre d'Esdras. Mosaïque de langues. Antiquités sémitiques 1: 1996, ⇒284. 131-144 [Ezra 4,8-6,18; 7,12-26].
2597 *Kegler, Jürgen* Die Fürbitte für den persischen Oberherrn im Tempel von Jerusalem (Esra 6,10): ein imperiales Herrschaftsinstrument. ^FSCHOTTROFF W., 1996, ⇒81. 73-82 [OTA 19,439].
2598 *Benn, W.* The bible and the church. ChM 110 (1996) 156-164 [Neh 8].
2599 *Boda, M.J.* Chiasmus in ubiquity: symmetrical mirages in Nehemiah 9. JSOT 71 (1996) 55-70.

2600 ^T**Klijn, A. Frederik J.** Die Esra-Apokalypse (IV. Esra). GCS: 1992, ⇒8,3060; 10,2811. ^RZRGG 48 (1996) 189-190 (*Horn, Friedrich W.*).

E5.5 Libri Tobiae, Judith, Esther

2601 ^E**Brenner, Athalya** A feminist companion to Esther, Judith and Susanna. 1995, ⇒11/1,1343. ^RReviews in Religion and Theology (1996/2), 36-38 (*Hodgetts, Pauline*).
2602 **Craghan, John** Ester, Giuditta, Tobia, Giona. LoB.AT 11: 1995, ⇒11/1,1344. ^RPaVi 41/3 (1996) 64 (*Carrucola, Maurilio*).
Mensing, Roman Die biblischen Bücher Rut, Ester und Judit im Religionsunterricht: ⇒2338.

2603 *Cook, Edward M.* Our translated Tobit. ^FMcNAMARA M., JSOT.S 230: 1996, ⇒58. 153-162.
2604 *Grelot, Pierre* Les noms de parenté dans le livre de Tobie. RdQ 17 (1996) 327-337.
2605 **Moore, Carey A.** Tobit: a new translation with introduction and commentary. AncB 40A: NY 1996, Doubleday xxx; 336 pp. $35. 0-385-18913-3 [NThAR 1997,161].
2606 *Nickelsburg, George W.E.* The search for Tobit's mixed ancestry: a historical and hermeneutical odyssey. RdQ 17 (1996) 339-349.
2607 **Rabenau, Merten** Studien zum Buch Tobit. BZAW 220: 1994, ⇒10,2818. ^RZKTh 118 (1996) 97-98 (*Oesch, Josef M.*).
2608 *Schmitt, Armin* Die Achikar-Notiz bei Tobit 1,21b-22 in aramäischer (pap4QToba ar-4Q196) und griechischer Fassung. BZ 40 (1996) 18-38.
2609 *Weitzman, Steven* Allusion, artifice, and exile in the hymn of Tobit. JBL 115 (1996) 49-61.

2610 *Zenger, Erich* "Wir erkennen keinen anderen als Gott an ..." (Jdt 8,20): Programm und Relevanz des Buches Judit. rhs 39 (1996) 23-36.

2611 *Arzt, Silvia* "Absurd, daß die Frauen so niedergemacht werden": zur geschlechtsspezifischen Rezeption der Erzählung vom Widerstand der Waschti in Ester 1. KatBl 121 (1996) 370-373.

2612 **Baum-Sheridan, Jutta** Studien zu den westjiddischen Estherdich-
tungen. Jidische Schtudies 5: Hamburg 1996, Buske viii; 328 pp.
3-87548-139-9 [NThAR 1997,98].

2613 [E]**Bekhor, Shlomo** Meghilla di Estèr. [T]*Levi, Mosè;* collab. *Tchilibon, Giuseppe,* Mi 1996, DLI 78 pp. 88-86674-04-X.

2614 *Blumenthal, David R.* Where God is not: the book of Esther and
Song of Songs. Jdm 44 (1995) 80-92 [IAJS 42,47].
    Bush, F.W. Ruth, Esther. 1996, ⇒2326.

2615 *Butting, Klara* Das Esterbuch. rhs 39 (1996) 7-16.

2616 *Cohen, Jeffrey M.* Vashti—an unsung heroine. JBQ 24/2 (1996)
103-106.

2617 **Craig, Kenneth M.** Reading Esther. 1995, ⇒11/1,1366. [R]ThLZ
121 (1996) 1043-1044 *(Hermann, Wolfram).*

2618 [TE]**Ego, Beate** Targum Scheni zu Ester: Übersetzung, Kommentar
und theologische Deutung. TSAJ 54: Tü 1996, Mohr xvi; 383 pp.
DM248. 3-16-146480-X.

2619 **Grossfeld, Bernard** The targum Sheni to the book of Esther. 1994,
⇒10,2827. [R]BiOr 53 (1996) 801-803 *(Martínez-Borobio, Emiliano);* AJSR 21 (1996) 139-142 *(Rendsburg, Gary A.).*

2620 **Jobes, Karen H.** The Alpha-text of Esther: its character and rela-
tionship to the Masoretic Text. Diss. [D]*Silva, M.,* SBL.DS 153:
Atlanta 1996, Scholars 256 pp. $45/$30. 0-7885-0202-6/-3-4
[NTAb 41,178].

2621 *Jobes, Karen H.* 'For such a time as this': a defining moment in
christian ministry. Faith & Mission 14/1 (1996) 3-13.
    Larkin, K. Ruth and Esther ⇒2334.

2622 *Manns, Frédéric* Le Targum d'Esther: manuscrit Urbinati 1.
SBFLA 46 (1996) 101-166.

2623 *Snyman, Gerrie* Bybelless en wedestrewigheid—leserreaksie op
God en Esther [Bible reading and recalcitrance—reader reaction to
God and Esther]. Koers 61 (1996) 37-55 [OTA 19,441].

2624 *Vetter, Dieter* Purim erinnert an die Erhaltung des Lebens: das Fest
gegenseitiger Geschenke und unbedingter Wohltätigkeit. Judentum.
1996 <1989>, ⇒154. 403-408.

2625 *White Crawford, Sidnie* Has Esther been found at Qumran?:
4QProto-Esther and the Esther corpus. RdQ 17 (1996) 307-325.

E5.8 *Machabaeorum libri,* 1-2[3] **Maccabees**

2626 **Abadie, Philippe** Lecture des livres des Maccabés: études historiques et littérature sur la crise maccabéenne. Profac: Lyon 1996,
Université Catholique 140 pp. FF75. 2-85317-063-2 [RTL
28,290].

2627 *Autané, Maurice* La guerre des Maccabées. DosB 62 (1996) 13-14.

2628 *Davies, Philip R.* Ḥasidim in the Maccabean period. Sects and
scrolls. SFSHJ 134: 1996 <1977>, ⇒122. 5-21.

2629 *Deiana, G.* Lo straniero nel periodo qumranico. RStB 8 (1996)
173-182.

2630 *Flusser, David* חנוכת הבית של ההיסטוריות הנסיבות—?"חנוכה "מאי
השמונאי בית בידי [The dedication of the temple by Judas Maccabaeus: story and history]. [F]STE RN M., 1996, ⇒87. Sum. 144*.
55-82. **H.**

2631 *Frede, Hermann Josef* Libri Macchabeorum Veteris Latinae versionis. Vetus Latina-Fragmente zum AT. AGLB 28: 1996, ⇒1099. 225-229 [RBen 106,396, 400].

2632 *Gruen, Erich S.* The purported Jewish-Spartan affiliation. ᶠBADIAN E., 1996, ⇒3. 254-269.

2633 *Horowitz, Wayne* HALLEY's comet and Judaean revolts revisited. CBQ 58 (1996) 456-459.

2634 Libri I-II Macchabeorum. Biblia Sacra iuxta Latinam Vulgatam versionem 18: 1995, ⇒11/1,1390. ᴿRBen 106 (1996) 400-402 (*Bogaert, P.-M.*).

2635 *Smith, Morton* Were the Maccabees priests?. Studies in...method. 1996, ⇒150. 320-325.

2636 *Doran, Robert* The first book of Maccabees: introduction, commentary, and reflections. NIntB 4: 1996, ⇒185. 1-178.

2637 *Gera, Dov* קרב בית זכריה בראי ספרות יוון [The battle of Beth Zachariah and Greek literature]. 1996, ᶠSTERN M., Sum. 143*. 25-50. **H**. [1 Macc 6,39-42.47].

2638 *Van Henten, Jan Willem* The song of praise of Judas Maccabaeus: some remarks on I Maccabees 3:3-9. ᶠVAN UCHELEN N., 1996, ⇒100. 199-206 [OTA 19,441].

2639 *Doran, Robert* The second book of Maccabees: introduction, commentary, and reflections. NIntB 4: 1996, ⇒185. 179-299.

2640 *Van Henten, Jan Willem* ΠΑΝΤΟΚΡΑΤΩΡ ΘΕΟΣ in 2 Maccabees. ᶠZUURMOND R., DBAT.B: 1996, ⇒109. 117-126 [OTA 19,442].

VI. Libri didactici VT

E6.1 *Poesis metrica,* Biblical and Semitic versification

2641 **Alter, Robert** The art of biblical poetry. 1990 <1985>, ⇒1,2978... 9,2969. ᴿITS 33/1 (1996) 70 (*Ambrose, M. Devadass*).

2642 *Attridge, Derek* Beyond metrics: Richard CURETON's *Rhythmic phrasing in English verse*;

2643 A note on Richard CURETON's response. Poetics Today 17/1 (1996) 9-27/51-54.

2644 *Berlin, Adele* Introduction to Hebrew poetry. NIntB 4: 1996, ⇒1229. 301-315.

2645 **Ceresko, Anthony R.** Psalmists and sages: studies in OT poetry and religion. ITS.S: 1994, ⇒10,166. ᴿVJTR 60 (1996) 637-638 (*Meagher, P.M.*).

2646 *Cureton, Richard* A response to Derek ATTRIDGE. Poetics Today 17/1 (1996) 29-50.

2647 **Gillingham, S.E.** The poems and psalms of the Hebrew bible. 1994, ⇒10,2872; 11/1,1407. ᴿBEL 97 (1996) 87-88 (*Rochettes, J. des*); JR 76 (1996) 100-101 (*Richards, Kent Harold*); Bibl.Interp. 4 (1996) 239-242 (*Johnston, Philip*).

2648 *Gutenberg, Norbert* Die 'Eierschalen' der Rhetorik: Argumente für eine Rekonstruktion kulturspezifischer Unterschiede zwischen

'Rhetorik' und 'rhetorike techne'. Sum. 113. Rhetorica 14/2 (1996) 113-149.

2649 *Macht, S.* 'Mein Psalm': ein subjektiver Zugang zur Poesie des Alten Testaments. ReHe 27 (1996) 196-203 [ZID 22,434].

2650 ᴱMoor, Johannes C. de; Watson, Wilfred G.E. Verse in ancient Near Eastern prose. AOAT 42: 1993, ⇒9,291. ᴿTJT 12/1 (1996) 82-84 (*Williams, Tyler F.*).

2651 Nagy, Gregory Poetry as performance: Homer and beyond. C 1996, CUP 254 pp.

2652 *Paul, Shalom M.* Polysemous pivotal puntuation: more Janus double entendres. ᶠHaran M., 1996, ⇒35. 369-374 [Song 7,6; Isa 49,7.17].

2653 Pernot, Laurent La rhétorique dans le monde gréco-romain. EAug.Antiquité 136: P 1993, Institut d'études augustiniennes. 2-85121-135-8. ᴿRhetorica 14 (1996) 347-351 (*Reardon, B.P.*).

2654 Petersen, David L.; Richards, Kent Harold Interpreting Hebrew poetry. 1992, ⇒8,3121; 10,2875. ᴿHeyJ 37 (1996) 85-86 (*Mulrooney, Joseph*).

2655 *Raurell, Frederic* La poesia come funzione ermeneutica della bibbia nella lettura di Venanzio Agostino Reali. Laur. 36 (1995) 433-476.

2656 *Schenk, Wolfgang* Poesie, biblische: Neues Testament;
2657 *Seybold, Klaus* Poesie, biblische: Altes Testament. TRE 26 (1996) 748-752/743-748 ⇒334.

2658 Tromp, Nico Vruchten in overvloed: poëzie en perspectief in de psalmen. Averbode 1996, Altiora 253 pp. 90-317-1167-5 [Collationes 27/1,108].

2659 *Tsur, Reuven* Rhyme and cognitive poetics. Sum. 55. Poetics Today 17/1 (1996) 55-87.

2660 *Waldman, Nahum M.* Some aspects of biblical punning. Shofar 14 (1996) 38-52 [Num 5,11-31; 6,1-21; 11,10-15] [OTA 19,385].

2661 *Walker, Jeffrey* Before the beginnings of 'poetry' and 'rhetoric': Hesiod on eloquence. Sum. 243. Rhetorica 14/3 (1996) 243-264.

2662 Watson, Wilfred G.E. Traditional techniques in classical Hebrew verse. JSOT.S 170: 1994, ⇒10,230c. ᴿCBQ 58 (1996) 142-143 (*Collins, Terence*).

2663 Watson, Wilfred G.E. Verse patterns in KTU 1.199:26-36. SEL 13 (1996) 25-30.

E6.2 Psalmi, textus

2664 Alonso Schökel, Luis Salmi e cantici. Itinerari biblici: R 1996, Borla 520 pp. L40.000. 88-263-1142-0.

2665 Alonso Schökel, Luis; Carniti, Cecilia Salmos I (Salmos 1-72). ᵀCosta, Joao Rezende; Dalbosco, H.; Nascimento, M., Grande Comentário Bíblico: São Paulo 1996, Paulus 919 pp. 85-349-0155-4.

2666 ᴱBekhor, Shlomo Salmi di Davide. ᵀSierra, S.J., Collab. tec. *Tchilibon, Giuseppe*, Mi 1996, DLI 406 pp. 88-86674-01-5.

2667 ᴱBlum-Cuny, Pascale Le psaultier de David torné en prose mesurée ou vers libres, 2. *Vignère, Blaise de* <aut.>. P 1996, Miroir Volant 576 pp. Bibl. FF280. 2-9510044-0-0 [BHR 59,746].

2668 ^E**Davie, Donald Alfred** The Psalms in English. Penguin classics: Poets in translation: L 1996, Penguin lviii; 389 pp. 0-14-044618-4.

2669 ^E**Defaux, Gérard** Clément MAROT: cinquante pseaumes de David mis en françoys selon la vérité hébraïque: édition critique sur le texte de l'édition publiée en 1543 à Genève par Jean GERARD: introduction, variantes et notes. Textes de la Renaissance 1: P 1995, Champion 345 pp.

2670 *Flint, Peter W.* Of psalms and psalters: James SANDERS's investigation of the Psalms scrolls. ^FSANDERS J., JSOT.S 225: 1996, ⇒77. 65-83.

2671 **Mele, Giampaolo** Hymni Psalterium—Hymnarium Arborense, 1. 1994, ⇒11/1,1423. ^RMF 96 (1996) 657-659 (*Costa, Francesco*).

2672 *Monloubou, Louis* Les psaumes: texte et théologie. EeV 106 (1996) 284-288.

2673 *Montecchi, Giorgio* La bozza de uno *Psalterium* (1499-1500?) dell'officina tipografica di Giovanni EMERICO da Spira. Il Bibliotecario 13/2 (1996) 201-221.

2674 **Nicole, Émile; Johnston, Philip; Blanchard, Thomas** Les psaumes: aide à la lecture cursive du texte hébreu. 1995, ⇒11/1,1424. ^RFV 95/5 (1996) 89 (*Keller, Bernard*).

2675 *Schenke, Hans-Martin* Die Psalmen im mittelägyptischen Dialekt des Koptischen. Enchoria 23 (1996) 86-144.

2676 *Schippers, Arie* Medieval opinions on the difficulty of translating the Psalms: some remarks on Ḥafṣ al-Qūṭi's Psalms in Arabic *rajaz* metre. ^FVAN UCHELEN N., ⇒100. 219-226.

2677 ^T**Slavitt, David R.** Sixty-one psalms of David. NY 1996, OUP xvi; 120 pp. $19. 0-19-510711-X.

E6.3 Psalmi, introductio

2678 *Bacon, Julien* Les Psaumes. PenCath 51 (1996) 5-11.

2679 *Boecker, Hans Jochen* Psalmen. Altes Testament. 1996, ⇒169. 179-199.

2680 ^E**Heine, Ronald E.** GREGORIUS NYSSENUS: in iscriptiones Psalmorum. 1995, ⇒11/1,1440. ^RJThS 47 (1996) 691-693 (*Meredith, A.*); ScrTh 28 (1996) 900-902 (*Mateo-Seco, Lucas F.*).

2681 *Kratz, Reinhard Gregor* Die Tora Davids: Psalm 1 und die doxologische Fünfteilung des Psalters. ZThK 93 (1996) 1-34.

2682 **Levine, Herbert J.** Sing unto God a new song: a contemporary reading of the Psalms. 1995, ⇒11/1,1441. ^RTS 57 (1996) 338-339 (*Moriarty, Fred L.*).

2683 **Mays, James Luther** The Lord reigns: a theological handbook to the Psalms. 1994, ⇒10,2897. ^RPSB 17/1 (1996) 91-93 (*Lemke, Werner E.*); Interp. 50 (1996) 185-187 (*Limburg, James*); JBL 115 (1996) 523-524 (*Bellinger, W.H.*); CBQ 58 (1996) 581-582 (*Ceresko, Anthony R.*).

2684 **Millard, Matthias** Die Komposition des Psalters. FAT 9: 1994, ⇒10,2901*; 11/1,1446. ^{RT}ThLZ 121 (1996) 143-146 (*Albertz, Rainer*); ETR 71 (1996) 589-591 (*Hüllstrung, Wolfgang*); ThR 61 (1996) 272-273 (*Seybold, Klaus*).

2685 **Raguer, Hilari** Para comprender los salmos. Estella 1996, Verbo Divino 180 pp. Ptas2.000. 84-8169-105-4.

2686   **Ravasi, Gianfranco** I salmi. Testimonianza iniziale e conclusiva di David Maria Turoldo. I Triangoli 32: CasM 1996, Piemme 191 pp. 88-384-2327-X [NThAR 1997,131].

2687   *Rose, André* Les psaumes de l'Ancien Testament et leur interprétation dans la tradition chrétienne. Sedes Sapientiae 14/3 (1996) 19-33.

2688   *Seybold, Klaus* Beiträge zur neueren Psalmenforschung. ThR 61 (1996) 247-274.
       ᴱSeybold, K., Neue Wege der Psalmenforschung ⇒7.

2689   **Smith, James E.** The wisdom literature and Psalms. Old Testament Survey: Joplin, Mo. 1996, College 873 pp. 0-89900-439-3 [1997,162].

2690   *Steinberg, Theodore L.* The SIDNEYS and the Psalms. SP 92/1 (1996) 1-17 [IAJS 42,18].

2691   **Synowiec, Juliusz Stanislaw** Wprowadzenie do Ksiegi Psalmów. Kraków 1996, Wydanictwo OO. Franciszkanów "Bratni Zew" 328 pp. 83-86991-11-9. **P.**

2692   *Whealey, Alice* Prologues on the Psalms: ORIGEN, HIPPOLYTUS, EUSEBIUS. RBen 106 (1996) 234-245.

2693   **Whybray, R. Norman** Reading the psalms as a book. JSOT.S 222: Shf 1996, Academic 137 pp. £24.50; $36.50. 1-85075-622-8 [ET 108,277].

2694   **Wolff, Kurt** Leben bist du: die Psalmen persönlich genommen: 150 'einseitige' Texte. Neuk 1996, Aussaat 150 pp. 3-7615-5603-9 [NThAR 1997,35].

ᴇ6.4 Psalmi, commentarii

2695   ᴱᵀ**Alobaidi, Joseph** Le commentaire des Psaumes par le qaraïte SALMON BEN YERUHAM: Psaumes 1-10. La bible dans l'histoire, textes et études 1: Fra 1996, Lang 509 pp. 3-906754-29-4. **H.**

2696   **Alonso Schökel, Luis; Carniti, Cecilia** Salmos. 1992-93, ⇒8,3147*... 10,2903. ᴿEstB 54 (1996) 423-424 (*Contreras, F.*).

2697   **Blaumeiser, Hubertus** Martin LUTHERs Kreuzestheologie... Operationes in Psalmos. KKTS 60: 1995, ⇒11/1,1458. ᴿThGl 86 (1996) 229-230 (*Schmidt, Axel*); SCJ 27 (1996) 796-798 (*Alfsvag, Knut*).

2698   **Centre d'Analyse et de Documentation Patristiques.** Le Psautier chez les Pères. *Maraval, Pierre* <prés.>. CBiPa 4: 1994, 11/2,1460. ᴿREAug 42 (1996) 172-173 (*Wolinski, Joseph*).

2699   **Cimosa, Mario** Con te non temo alcun male: Salmi 1-25. Lettura esegetica e spirituale della Bibbia 1: R 1995, Dehoniane 342 pp. L28.000. 88-396-0573-8. ᴿRivBib 44 (1996) 476-477 (*Boschi, Bernardo Gianluigi*).

2700   ᵀᴱ**Coppa, Giovanni** ORIGENE—GEROLAMO, 74 omelie sul libro dei Salmi. 1993, ⇒10,2908; 11/1,1462. ᴿRSLR 32/3 (1996) 702-703 (*Pieri, Francesco*).

2701   **Girard, Marc** Les psaumes redécouverts, 2-3. 1994, ⇒11/1,1467. ᴿBib. 77 (1996) 121-124 (*Ska, Jean Louis*).

2702   **Girard, Marc** Les psaumes redécouverts: de la structure au sens, 1: 1-50. Montréal ²1996 <1984>, Bellarmin 814 pp. 2-89007-

803-5. ⇒65,2642... 4,3157. ^RSR 25 (1996) 356-357 (*Lavoie, Jean-Jacques*).

2703 **Gross-Diaz, Theresa** The Psalms: commentary of GILBERT of Poitiers: from Lectio Divina to the lecture room. Brill's Studies in Intellectual History 68: Lei 1996, Brill xv; 193 pp. 90-04-10211-6.

2704 **Hirsch, Samson Raphael** Psalmen. 1995, ⇒11/1,1468. ^RFrRu NF 3/4 (1996) 286-287 (*Sonnevelt, Nico*).

2705 *Jeudy, Colette* Un relevé carolingien des schèmes extraits du commentaire de CASSIODORE sur les Psaumes. [On cod. 3303, Hessische Landes- und Hochschulbibliothek Darmstadt.] MLJb 29 (1995) 1-20 [IAJS 42,43].

2706 **Lampartner, Helmut** Köstlich ist es, den Herrn zu preisen: ausgewählte Psalmen. Stu 1996, Calwer 216 pp. 3-7668-3352-9 [NThAR 1997,161].

2707 *McCann, J. Clinton* The book of Psalms. NIntB 4: 1996, ⇒185. 639-1280.

2708 *Morard, Martin* A propos du Commentaire des Psaumes de saint THOMAS d'Aquin. RThom 96 (1996) 653-670.

2709 ^{TE}**Orazzo, Antonio** Sanctus HILARIUS Pictaviensis: tractatus super psalmos: i salmi delle ascensioni: cantico del pellegrino. Cultura cristiana antica, Testi: R 1996, Borla 238 pp. 88-263-1150-1.

2710 **Palmer, Alan** Psalms 1-72. Crossway Bible Guide: Leicester 1996, Crossway 223 pp. 1-85684-149-9.

2711 ^{TE}**Ruggiero, Andrea** PROSPER Aquitanus: la poesia davidica, profezia di Cristo: commento ai Salmi 100-150. CTePa 131: R 1996, Città Nuova 299 pp. 88-311-3131-1 [EThL 74,179*].

2712 **Schneider, Dieter** Das Buch der Psalmen, 1: Psalm 1-50. WStB.AT: 1995, ⇒1472. ^RJETh 10 (1996) 195-197 (*Pehlke, Helmuth*);

2713 Buch 2: Psalm 51-100. WStB.AT: Wu 1996, Brockhaus 256 pp.

2714 **Seybold, Klaus** Die Psalmen. HAT I/15: Tü 1996, Mohr viii; 548 pp. DM169. 3-16-146664-0.

2715 ^{TE}**Stroobant de Saint-Éloy, Jean-Éric** THOMAS d'Aquin: commentaire sur les psaumes. Pref. *Jordan, Mark D.*, P 1996, Cerf 796 pp. Introd., trad., notes. FF490. 2-204-05267-1. ^RCTom 123 (1996) 629-630 (*Celada, Gregorio*).

2716 ^T**Tronina, Antoni** Psałterz Biblii greckiej: przełożył według septuaginty, wprowadz i kom. Lublin 1996, Wydawnictw Katolikkiego Uniwersytetu Lubelskiego 272 pp. 83-228-0460-1 [NThAR 1998,99].

E6.5 Psalmi, themata

2717 *Alonso Schökel, Luis* True language of the human spirit: the language of the psalms. Way.S 87: L 1996, Way. 45-57.

2718 **Avishur, Yitzhak** Studies in Hebrew and Ugaritic psalms. 1994, ⇒10,2926. ^RJSSt 41 (1996) 314-316 (*Watson, Wilfred G.E.*); CBQ 58 (1996) 698-700 (*Miller, Patrick D.*); REJ 155 (1996) 248-249 (*Margain, Jean*).

2719 **Bader, Günter** Psalterium affectuum palaestra: prolegomena zu einer Theologie des Psalters. HUTh 33: Tü 1996, Mohr ix; 266 pp. DM178. 3-16-146505-9 [ThLZ 122,645].

2720 **Ballard, Harold Wayne** The divine warrior motif in the Psalms. Diss. Southern Bapt. Theol. Sem. 1995 DTate, M.E., 200 pp. [EThL 74,223*].

2721 Barthélemy, Dominique L'appropriation juive et chrétienne du psautier. FSANDERS J., JSOT.S 225: 1996, ⇒77. 206-218.

2722 Beckwith, Roger T. The Qumran psalter: the courses of the Levites and the use of the Psalms at Qumran. Calendar and chronology. AGJU 33: 1996, ⇒112. 141-166.

2723 **Beyerlin, Walter** Im Licht der Traditionen: Psalm LXVII und CXV. VT.S 45: 1992, ⇒8,3271; 9,3131. RJBL 115 (1996) 340-342 (Kselman, John S.).

2724 Blank, Andreas Trinität und Geschichte in JOACHIM von Fiores: psalterium decem chordarum. Sum. 170. Florensia 10 (1996) 155-170.

2725 **Bouzard, Walter C.** We have heard with our ears, O God: sources of the communal laments in the Psalms. Diss. Princeton Theol. Sem. 1996 DMiller, Patrick D., 256 pp. DAI-A 57/05, p. 2080; AAC 9629097.

2726 **Box, Reginald** Make music to our God: how we sing the Psalms. L 1996, SPCK xi; 143 pp. £16. 0-281-04932-7 [ET 108,318].

2727 **Cameron, Glenn Michael** AUGUSTINE's construction of figurative exegesis against the Donatists in the Enarrationes in psalmos. Diss. Fac. of Div. School, Chicago DMcGinn, B., Ann Arbor 1996, 456 pp. UMI 1998 [REAug 44,377].

2728 Christensen, Duane L. The book of Psalms within the canonical process in ancient Israel. JETS 39 (1996) 421-432.

2729 Cimosa, Mario Dio nel salterio. Dio—Signore nella bibbia. DSBP 13: 1996, ⇒328. 76-101.

2730 Clark, Mary T. St AUGUSTINE's use of the psalms. Way.S 87: L 1996, Way 91-101.

2731 Collins, Mary Psalms in the daily office. Way.S 87: L 1996, Way 67-78.

2732 Cotter, Jim Modern psalms. Way.S 87: L 1996, Way 111-123.

2733 **Creach, Jerome F.D.** Yahweh as refuge and the editing of the Hebrew psalter. JSOT.S 217: Shf 1996, Academic 156 pp. £35. 1-85075-601-5.

2734 Custer, John S. The psaltery, the harp and the Fathers: a biblical image and its interpreters. DR 114 (1996) 19-31.

2735 **Dhanaraj, Dharmakkan** Theological significance of the motif of enemies in selected psalms of individual lament. OrBibChr 4: 1992, ⇒8,3177; 11/1,1495. RCBQ 58 (1996) 308-310 (Smith, Mark S.).

2736 **Emmendörffer, Michael** Der ferne Gott: Israels Ringen um die Abwesenheit JHWSs in tempelloser Zeit: eine Untersuchung der alttestamentlichen Volksklagelieder auf dem Hintergrund der altorientalischen Literatur. Diss. Hamburg 1995-96 DSpieckermann, H. [RTL 27,528].

2737 Endres, John C. Cry out to God in our need: psalms of lament. Way.S 87: L 1996, Way 34-44.

2738 **Firth, David G.** Responses to violence in lament psalms of the individual. Diss. Pretoria 1996 DPrinsloo, W.S. [EThL 74,223*].

2739 García Cordero, Maximiliano Los salmos mesiánico-imperialistas. Salm. 43 (1996) 177-207.

2740 *Gerstenberger, Erhard S.* Welche Öffentlichkeit meinen das Klage-
und das Danklied?. JBTh 11 (1996) 69-89.
2741 *Gibbons, Robin* To curse is to pray. Way.S 87: L 1996, Way 102-
110.
2742 **Gillette, Gertrude** The glory of God in AUGUSTINE's Enarrationes in psalmos. Diss. Cath. Univ. of America, Ann Arbor 1996,
448 pp. UMI 1996 [REAug 44,377].
2743 *Gillingham, S.* Messianic prophecy and the psalms. Theol. 99
(1996) 114-124.
2744 *Gillingham, Susan* Psalmody and apocalyptic in the Hebrew bible:
common vision, shared experience. ^FMASON R., 1996, ⇒57. 147-
169.
2745 **Girard, Marc** The Psalms: mirror of the poor. Montreal 1996,
Médiaspaul 139 pp. [Spiritual Life 42/4,250].
2746 **Goulder, Michael D.** Studies in the Psalter, 3: the psalms of
Asaph and the pentateuch. JSOT.S 233: Shf 1996, Academic 378
pp. £47.50; $70. 1-85075-639-2 [ET 108,277].
2747 **Hauge, Martin Ravndal** Between Sheol and temple: motif structure and function in the I-Psalms. JSOT.S 178: 1995, ⇒11/1,1507.
^RSJOT 10 (1996) 142-143 *(Jeppesen, Knud)*; ScrTh 28 (1996) 577-
579 *(Aranda, G.)*; CBQ 58 (1996) 709-710 *(Nasuti, Harry P.)*.
2748 *Hossfeld, Frank-Lothar; Zenger, Erich* Neue und alte Wege der
Psalmenexegese: Antworten auf die Fragen von M. MILLARD und
R. RENDTORFF. Bibl.Interp. 4 (1996) 332-343 [Resp. M. Millard 344-345].
2749 *Houtman, C.* Die Aktualisierung der Geschichte in den Psalmen.
^THilbrands, Walter, ^FVAN UCHELEN N., 1996, ⇒100. 107-114.
2750 **Ishikawa, Ritsu** Der Hymnus im Alten Testament und seine kritische Funktion. Diss.-Habil 1995-96 Mü ^DBaltzer, K. [RTL
27,529].
2751 *Jauss, Hannelore* Fluchpsalmen beten?: zum Problem der Feind-
und Fluchpsalmen. BiKi 51 (1996) 107-115.
2752 *Jeffers, Ann* The earth is full of your creatures. Way.S 87: L 1996,
Way 24-33.
2753 **Keel, Othmar** Die Welt der altorientalischen Bildsymbolik und das
Alte Testament: am Beispiel der Psalmen. Gö 1996, Vandenhoeck
& R. 390 pp. 3-525-53638-0 [OLZ 93,499s—Zwickel, Wolfgang].
2754 *Kennedy, Philip* The psalms and the prayer of praise. Way.S 87: L
1996, Way 4-14.
       Kleer, Martin "Der liebliche Sänger der Psalmen Israels"
⇒2414.
2755 **Koenen, Klaus** Gottesworte in den Psalmen: eine formgeschichtli-
che Untersuchung. BThSt 30: Neuk 1996, Neuk (10) 82 pp. 3-
7887-1607-X.
2756 **Kraus, Hans-Joachim** Theology of the Psalms. 1986, ⇒2,2288...
4,3186. ^RVJTR 60 (1996) 422-424 *(Meagher, P.M.)*.
2757 *Kselman, John S.* The psalms and modern biblical studies. Way.S
87: L 1996, Way 15-23.
2758 **Lindström, Fredrik** Suffering and sin: interpretations of illness in
the individual complaint psalms. CB.OT 37: 1994, ⇒10,2937;
11/1,1518. ^RDialog 35 (1996) 229-230 *(Frerichs, Wendell W.)*;
ZAW 108 (1996) 474-475 *(Spieckermann, H.)*; Bibl.Interp. 4
(1996) 239-242 *(Johnston, Philip)*; CritRR 9 (1996) 156-158
(Barré, Michael L.).

2759 *Masini, Mario* Il giusto sofferente dei salmi. Som. 39. PSV 34 (1996) 39-58.

2760 *Millard, Matthias* Von der Psalmenexegese zur Psalterexegese: Anmerkungen zum Neuansatz von Frank-Lothar HOSSFELD und Erich ZENGER. Bibl.Interp. 4 (1996) 311-328 ⇒2748.

2761 *Mouhanna, Antoine* La crítica de los dioses en el libro de los salmos. RevBib 58 (1996) 161-171.

2762 **Pedersen, Kirsten Stofregen** Traditional Ethiopian exegesis of the book of Psalms. Diss. Hebrew University 1990. ÄthF 36: Wsb 1995, Harrassowitz ix; 302 pp. DM98. 3-447-03443-2 [JSSt 43,163—Ullendorff, Edward].

2763 *Rendtorff, Rolf* Anfragen an Frank-Lothar HOSSFELD und Erich ZENGER aufgrund der Lektüre des Beitrages von Matthias MILLARD. Bibl.Interp. 4 (1996) 329-331 ⇒2760.

2764 **Schaper, Joachim** Eschatology in the Greek Psalter. WUNT 2/76: 1995, ⇒11/1,1526. ᴿRHPhR 76 (1996) 227-228 (*Joosten, J.*); JThS 47 (1996) 580-583 (*Salvesen, Alison*).

2765 *Seybold, Klaus* Jerusalem in the view of the psalms. The centrality of Jerusalem. 1996, ⇒236. 7-14 [OTA 19,444].

2766 **Starbuck, Scott Richard Austin** And what had Kings?: the reappropriation of court oracles among the royal psalms of the Hebrew psalter. Diss. Princeton Theol. Sem. ᴰ*Roberts, J.J.M.* 1996, 286 pp. DAI-A 57/05, p. 2085; AAC 9629102.

2767 *Stricher, Joseph* Les ennemis dans les Psaumes. DosB 62 (1996) 19-20.

2768 **Sylva, Dennis** Psalms and the transformation of stress. LThPM 16: 1995, ⇒11/1,1530. ᴿJRHe 35 (1996) 263-264 (*Cook, Stephen L.*); EThL 72 (1996) 433 (*Lust, J.*); CBQ 58 (1996) 729-730 (*Romero, C. Gilbert*).

2769 ᵀᴱ**Traverso, Alberto** Gregorio di Nissa: sui titoli dei Salmi. 1994, ⇒10,2891. ᴿCivCatt 147 I (1996) 406-408 (*Cremascoli, G.*).

2770 **Tronina, Antoni** Teologia Psalmów. 1995, ⇒11/1,1455. ᴿAtK 127 (1996) 305-307 (*Warzecha, Julian*).

2771 *Wagner, Siegfried* Das Reich des Messias: zur Theologie der alttestamentlichen Königspsalmen. Ausgewählte Aufsätze. BZAW 240: 1996 <1984>, ⇒156. 199-212.

2772 **Waite, Terry** The wisdom of the psalms. GR 1996, Eerdmans 47 pp. $8 [BiTod 35,321].

2773 **Weems, Ann B.** Psalms of lament. Foreword *Brueggemann, Walter*, LVL 1995, Westminster xvii; 104 pp. $12. 0-664-22074-6 [BL 1996,70].

2774 *Willcock, Christopher* 'With lute and harp'. Way.S 87: L 1996, Way 58-66.

2775 **Wilson, Gnanamuthu S.** A descriptive analysis of creation concepts and themes in the book of Psalms. Diss. Andrews 1996 ᴰ*Shea, W.H.* 250-373 [EThL 74,224*].

2776 *Wright, Alexandra* Whose language? Way.S 87: L 1996, Way 79-90.

2777 *Zamagni, Claudio* Sui salmi nel Nuovo Testamento. RivBib 44 (1996) 439-454.

2778 **Zenger, Erich** Ein Gott der Rache?. 1994, ⇒10,2952; 11/1,1537. ᴿGuL 69/1 (1996) 77-78 (*Klein, Ralf*); FrRu NF 3 (1996) 300-301 (*Beck, Monika*);

2779 A God of vengeance?: understanding the psalms of divine wrath.
^T*Maloney, Linda M.*, LVL 1996, Westminster 104 pp. $13. 0-664-
25637-6. ^RSvTK 72 (1996) 138-139 (*Lindström, Fredrik*); WThJ
58 (1996) 331-333 (*Belcher, Richard P.*); ET 108 (1996-97) 65-66
(*Rodd, C.S.*).

E6.6 *Psalmi: oratio, liturgia*—Psalms as prayer

2780 **Alonso Schökel, Luis** "Contempladlo y quedaréis radiantes": salmos y ejercicios. El Pozo de Siquem 74: Santander 1996, Sal Terrae 222 pp. 84-293-1186-6;
2781 "Contemplatelo e sarete raggianti": salmi ed esercizi. Bibbia e
Preghiera 27: R 1996, ADP 300 pp. 88-7357-164-6.
2782 **Aparicio, A.; Rey Garcia, J.C.** I salmi, preghiera della commu-
nità: per celebrare la liturgia delle ore. 1995, ⇒11/1,1540. ^RTer.
47/1 (1996) 307-308 (*Castellano, J.*).
2783 **Bonhoeffer, Dietrich** Life together: prayerbook of the bible.
Dietrich Bonhoeffer Works 5: Mp 1996, Fortress 218 pp. $30.
^RCritRR 9 (1996) 375-378 (*Frick, Peter*).
2784 **Chittister, Joan** The Psalms: meditations for every day of the
year. NY 1996, Crossroad 141 pp. $13 [Spiritual Life 42,250].
2785 *Delhougne, Henri* ¿Rezar los Salmos?. CuadMon 31 (1996) 352-
371.
2786 ^T**Donnelly, John Patrick** PETER Martyr Vermigli: sacred prayers
drawn from the psalms. SCES 34: Peter Martyr Library 3: Kirksville, Mo. 1996, SCJ xxviii; 164 pp. [ChH 67,151—Boyd, Ste-
phen].
2787 *Felten, Gustavo* Orando los Salmos. La Revista Católica 96/1
(1996) 57-64 [Ps 95].
2788 **Jossua, Jean-Pierre** Mon amour vient à moi: lectures des psaumes.
Épiphanie: Initiations: P 1996, Cerf 144 pp. FF88. 2-204-05471-2.
2789 **Kaiser, Walter C.** Psalms, heart to heart with God. Great Books
of the Bible: GR 1995, Zondervan 96 pp. $5. 0-310-49871-6 [BL
1996,82].
2790 ^E**Lardon, Sabine** JEAN de Sponde: méditations sur les pseaumes.
P 1996, Champion 517 pp.
2791 *Lohfink, Norbert* El salterio y la meditación cristiana: importancia
de la última redacción para la comprensión del salterio. ^T*Casañas,
Francesc de P.*, SelT 35 (1996) 299-306 [< BiKi 47 (1992) 195-
200].
2792 **Peltz, Carl F.** Psalms for all occasions: with accompanying
prayers. Boston 1996, Pauline 71 pp. $4 [BiTod 34,393].
2793 *Raguer, Hilari* Los salmos como problema. Phase 36 (1996) 313-
322.
2794 *Ramshaw, Gail* Symposium: liturgical language, III: the Psalter in
the Book of Common Worship. StLi 26 (1996) 140-143.
2795 *Redmont, Jane* From lamentation to jubilation: praying the psalms
in daily life. Way.S 87: L 1996, Way 124-132.
2796 **Rougier, Stan** Montre-moi ton visage: variations sur les Psaumes.
1995, ⇒11/1,1428. Revue internationale de catéchèse et de pastorale 51/1 (1996) 112-113 (*L. Escoyez, A. Fossion*).

2797 ᴱSueldo, Gerardo Los Salmos en la liturgia romana... Conferencia
      Episcopal Argentina. 1994, ⇒11/1,1565. Phase 36 (1996) 265-266
      (*Aroztegui, F. Xavier*).
2798 Taulé, Alberto Salmos para cantar: 30 salmos responsoriales y 3
      cántos bíblicos. Barc 1996, Centre de Pastoral Litúrgica 91 pp.
      ᴿRTLi 30 (1996) 371-372 (*Jiménez Sanz, Donato*).
2799 *Thienpont, J.C.* Un livre pour chanter: le Psautier français, les 150
      Psaumes versifiés en français contemporain, mélodies originales du
      16. siècle, harmonisées à quatre voix. RRef 47 (1996) 17-24.
2800 Vincent, Monique Saint Aᴜɢᴜsᴛɪɴ maître de prière... EnPs.
      1990, ⇒6,3338... 9,3074. ᴿALW 38-39 (1996/97) 76-77
      (*Klöckener, Martin*).

E6.7 *Psalmi: versiculi—*Psalms by number and verse

2801 *Taylor, J. Glen* Psalms 1 and 2 as introduction to the Hebrew Psal-
      ter. CSBS annual meeting 27 May 1996; sum.   BCSBS 55
      (1995/96) 11-12.
2802 *Safrai, C.* Über die Grenzen der Toleranz: sozialgeschichtliche
      Bibelauslegung zu Psalm 1. JK 57 (1996) 551-559.
2803 *Gitay, Yehoshua* Psalm 1 and the rhetoric of religious argumenta-
      tion. Literary structure. 1996, ⇒200. 232-240.
2804 *Schneck, Richard* El salmo 1 y 'los caminos de la vida'. ThX 46
      (1996) 425-431.
2805 *Deurloo, Karel A.* Die Klage in der Mitte von Psalm 6. ᶠVᴀɴ
      Uᴄʜᴇʟᴇɴ N., 1996, ⇒100. 3-9.
2806 *Korting, Georg* Gott als Baumeister (Ps 8,2). BN 84 (1996) 41-45.
2807 *Jeong, Hak-Keun* Was ist der Mensch?. Samok 211-212 (1996)
      111-130; 98-113. K. [ThIK 18/2,54: Literarische, linguistische
      und theologische Studie von Psalm 8,5].
2808 *Kolb, Robert* The doctrine of Christ in Nikolaus Sᴇʟɴᴇᴄᴋᴇʀ's
      interpretation of Psalms 8, 22 and 110. ᶠSᴛᴇɪɴᴍᴇᴛᴢ D., 1996,
      ⇒86. 313-332.
2809 *Talstra, Eep* Singers and syntax: on the balance of grammar and
      poetry in Psalm 8. ᶠVᴀɴ Uᴄʜᴇʟᴇɴ N., 1996, ⇒100. 11-22.
2810 Urassa, Wenceslaus Mkeni A christological interpretation of
      Psalm 8 in the New Testament: a case study in biblical hermeneu-
      tics. Diss. excerpt PUG, R 1996 ᴰ*Grech, Prosper*, xiv; 104 pp.
2811 *Arambarri, Jesús* Zu einem gelungenen Leben: Psalm 1,2.
      ᶠMɪᴄʜᴇʟ D., BZAW 241: 1996, ⇒64. 1-17.
2812 *Butting, K.* Das Ächzen wird zu Worten. JK 57 (1996) 27-30 [Ps
      12].
2813 *Crüsemann, Frank* Gottes Ort, Israel—und Armentheologie in Ps
      14. Gott an den Rändern. 1996, ⇒81. 32-41 [OTA 19,445].
2814 *Zenger, E.* Einsatz für die Gerechtigkeit: sozialgeschichtliche Bibe-
      lauslegung zu Psalm 15. JK 57 (1996) 93-96.
2815 *Auffret, Pierre* C'est pourquoi se rejouit mon coeur: étude structu-
      relle du Psaume 16. BZ 40 (1996) 73-83.
2816 *Albertz, Rainer* "Birg mich im Schatten deiner Flügel!" (Psalm
      17,8): Kirchenasyl—wieder eine Christenpflicht?. Zorn. 1996,
      ⇒110. 114-129.
2817 *Franssens, Th.* De metafoor van de leeuw in Psalm 17. Interpreta-
      tie 4/4 (1996) 10-11.

2818 *Auwers, Jean-Marie* La rédaction du psaume 18 dans le cadre du premier livre des Psaumes. EThL 72 (1996) 23-40.

2819 **Denninger, David** The creator's fiat and the creature's witness: a literary study of the structure, dynamics, and meaning of psalm 19. Diss. Trinity Evangelical Divinity School 1996 DHoward, David M., 322 pp. DAI-A 57/05, p. 2082; AAC 9631855.

2820 *Wrede, Gisela* Überlegungen zu einem Unterrichtsentwurf zu Psalm 22. Leidenspsalm 95-103;

2821 *Hirth, Volkmar* Psalm 22 als zeitumspannendes Gebet. Leidenspsalm 13-25;

2822 *Genest, Hartmut* Der Tod des Gottmenschen und das Leben des menschlichen Gottes: HEGELs Christologie als Paraphrase des 22. Psalms. Leidenspsalm 56-68;

2823 *Genest, Hartmut* Predigt über Psalm 22. Leidenspsalm 88-94;

2824 *Heidler, Johannes* Die Verwendung von Psalm 22 im Kreuzigungsbericht des Markus: ein Beitrag zur Frage nach der Christologie des Markus. Leidenspsalm 26-34;

2825 *Bunners, Christian* Jesu Kreuzeswort aus Psalm 22 in Predigtdeutungen (J. ARNDT, Fr.D.E. SCHLEIERMACHER, A. THOMAS, P. ALTHAUS, K. RAHNER, M. MARTIN). Leidenspsalm 35-55 [Mark 15,24];

2826 *Heidler, Johannes* Die Verwendung von Psalm 22 im Kreuzigungsbericht des Markus: ein Beitrag zur Frage nach der Christologie des Markus. Christi Leidenspsalm. 1996, ⇒29. 26-34.

2827 *Klopfenstein, Martin A.* Predigt über Psalm 24: von Hoffnung und Erfüllung. Leben aus dem Wort. BEAT 40: 1996, ⇒132. 313-318.

2828 *Leeman, Saul* The atbash-acrostic. JBQ 24/1 (1996) 43-45 [Pss 25; 34].

2829 *Grol, Harm W.M. van* Psalm 27:1-6: a literary stylistic analysis. FVAN UCHELEN N., 1996, ⇒100. 23-38.

2830 *Kelm, Christian K.* The presence of YHWH: psalm 27 and the audience's horizon of expectation. Arc 24 (1996) 87-96 [ZID 23,267].

2831 *Cohn, Herbert* Hinds in Psalm 29. JBQ 24 (1996) 258-259.

2832 *Wagner, Andreas* Ist Ps 29 die Bearbeitung eines Baal-Hymnus?. Bib. 77 (1996) 538-539.

2833 *Scruggs, G. Christopher* Psalm 31:9-16. Interp. 50 (1996) 398-402.

2834 TEDonnelly, **John Patrick** Girolamo SAVONAROLA: prison meditations on Psalms 51 and 31. 1994, ⇒10,3020. RSCJ 27 (1996) 561-562 (*Nugent, Don Christopher*).

2835 **Bons, Eberhard** Psalm 31—Rettung. FTS 48: 1994, ⇒10,3003. RNRTh 118 (1996) 920-921 (*Ska, Jean Louis*); Bib. 77 (1996) 553-557 (*Tate, Marvin E.*).

2836 *Heubach, J.* Mein liebster Luthertext. ZdZ 50/1 (1996) 12 [Ps 32,8].

2837 **Willmes, Bernd** Freude über die Vergebung der Sünden: Synchrone und diachrone Analyse von Psalm 32. FHSS 28: Fra 1996, Knecht 108 pp. 3-7820-0736-0.

2838 *Wang, Agnes* A reading of Ps 34 with praising and thankful heart. CTUF 108 (1996) 247-256 [ThIK 18/1,28]. C.

2839 **Eriksson, Lars Olov** 'Come...' Psalm 34. CB.OT 32: 1991, ⇒7,2834... 11/1,1608. REvQ 68 (1996) 153 (*Alexander, T.D.*); VT 46 (1996) 570-571 (*Dell, Katharine J.*).

2840 ᵀᴱCrouzel, Henri; Brésard, Luc ORIGENE: homélies sur les psaumes 36 à 38. SC 411: 1995, ⇒11/1,1610. ᴿThLZ 121 (1996) 1066-1067 (*Haendler, Gert*); POC 46/1-2 (1996) 283-284 (*Ternant, P.*).

2841 *Westermann, Claus* Aufbau und Absicht von Psalm 37. Das mündliche Wort. 1996, ⇒157. 176-179.

2842 *González, Jesús* Salmo a salmo: Salmo 42-43 (41-42) "¿Cuándo entraré a ver el rostro de Dios?". EvV 38 (1996) 12-14.

2843 *Hemelsoet, Ben* Abyssus abyssum invocat: word for word, grace for grace. ᶠVAN UCHELEN N., 1996, ⇒100. 39-46 [Ps 42,7-8].

2844 *González, Jesús* Salmo 44 (43): "Despierta, Señor, ¿por qué duermes?". EvV 38 (1996) 44-46.

2845 *Hoftijzer, J.* Some remarks on Psalm 45:2. ᶠVAN UCHELEN N., 1996, ⇒100. 47-59.

2846 **Grünbeck, Elisabeth** Christologische Schriftargumentation des 44. (45.) Psalms. SVigChr 26: 1994, ⇒10,3013; 11/1,1615. ᴿJThS 47 (1996) 306-307 (*Wickham, L.R.*); ChH 65/1 (1996) 64-65 (*Kolp, Alan*); EThL 72 (1996) 462-463 (*Verheyden, J.*); ThLZ 121 (1996) 376-378 (*Markschies, Christoph*).

2847 *Schroeder, Christoph* "A love song": Psalm 45 in the light of ancient Near Eastern marriage texts. CBQ 58 (1996) 417-432.

2848 *Vattioni, Francesco* Domus aeterna. Aug. 36/1 (1996) 231-236 [Ps 49,12].

2849 *Pleins, J. David* Death and endurance: reassessing the literary structure and theology of Psalm 49. JSOT 69 (1996) 19-27.

2850 *Reid, Stephen Breck* Psalm 50: prophetic speech and God's performative utterances. ᶠTUCKER G., JSOT.S 229: 1996, ⇒95. 217-230.

2851 *Auffret, Pierre* L'étude structurelle des Psaumes: réponses et compléments I (Pss. 51, 57, 63, 64, 65, 86, 90, 91, 95). ScEs 48 (1996) 45-60.

2852 *Leene, Henk* Personal penitence and the rebuilding of Zion: the unity of Psalm 51. ᶠVAN UCHELEN N., 1996, ⇒100. 61-77.

2853 *Bail, Ulrike* Die Klage einer Frau: zu sprechen gegen das Schweigen: eine feministisch-sozialgeschichtliche Auslegung von Psalm 55. JK 57 (1996) 154-157 [= BiKi 51 (1996) 116-118].

2854 *Doyle, B.* Psalm 58: curse as voiced disorientation. Bijdr. 57 (1996) 122-148.

2855 *Wright, D.P.* Blown away like a bramble: the dynamics of analogy in Psalm 58. RB 103 (1996) 213-236.

2856 **Bellinger, W.H.** A hermeneutic... Psalm 61. 1995, ⇒11/1,1624. ᴿCBQ 58 (1996) 500-501 (*Holladay, William L.*).

2857 *Barré, Michael L.* A proposal on the crux of Psalm LXIV 9A. VT 46 (1996) 115-118.

2858 *Weber, Dorothea* Gedanken zur Textgestaltung von AUGUSTINUS: *Ennarationes in psalmos* 64 und 68. AugSt 27/2 (1996) 47-58.

2859 *Auffret, Pierre* "Dieu sauvera Sion": étude structurelle du Psaume LXIX. VT 46 (1996) 1-29.

2860 *Auwers, Jean-Marie* Les psaumes 70-72: essai de lecture canonique. TDL.T 16/1 (1996): Philologie biblique [Sum. diss. = RB 101 (1994) 242-257].

2861 *Auffret, Pierre* 'Toutes les nations le diront bienheureux': étude structurelle du psaume 72. SEL 13 (1996) 41-58.

2862 *Brueggemann, Walter; Miller, Patrick D.* Psalm 73 as a canonical marker. JSOT 72 (1996) 45-56.

2863 *Auffret, Pierre* Quand Dieu se lève pour le jugement: étude structurelle du Psaume 76. BN 84 (1996) 5-10.

2864 *Loretz, Oswald* Baal und Jammu/Tiamat in Psalm 77,17-20. WZKM 86 (1996) 263-276.

2865 **Weber, Beat** Psalm 77 und sein Umfeld. BBB 103: 1995, ⇒11/1,1635. [R]JETh 10 (1996) 192-194 (*Klement, Herbert H.*).

2866 *Weiss, Meir* 'And I will tell of all your work': faith and belief in Psalm 77. [F]HARAN M., 1996, ⇒35. 47*-58*. H.

2867 *Lee, Archie C.C.* The recitation of the past: a cross-textual reading of Ps.78 and the Odes. ChFe 39 (1996) 173-200.

2868 *Hieke, Thomas* Der Exodus in Psalm 80: Geschichtstopik in den Psalmen. Studies in...Exodus. BEThL 126: 1996, ⇒1794. 551-558.

2869 *Talmon, Shemarayahu* Fragments of a Psalms Scroll-MasPs/a Ps 81:2b-85:6a (1039-160; Masle; final photo 5255). DSD 3 (1996) 296-314.

2870 *Human, Dirk* Die teks en sitz im leben van psalm 83 [The text and life-setting of psalm 83]. NGTT 37 (1996) 3-18 [OTA 19,449].

2871 *Van Midden, Piet* The peoples in Psalm 83. [F]VAN UCHELEN N., 1996, ⇒100. 79-90.

2872 *Ebach, Jürgen* 'Gerechtigkeit und Frieden küssen sich' oder: 'Gerechtigkeit und Frieden kämpfen' (Ps 85:11): über eine biblische Grundwertedebatte. Gott an den Rändern. 1996, ⇒81. 42-52 [OTA 19,449].

2873 *Merwe, C.H.J. van der* 'n donker psalm 88: moontlike lig vanuit sy taalhandelinge [A dark psalm: can it be illuminated by means of speech acts?]. NGTT 37 (1996) 27-38 [OTA 19,450].

2874 **Isaac, Gordon Lincoln** In public defense of the ministry of Moses: LUTHER's *Enarratio* on Psalm 90, 1534-1535. Diss. Marquette 1996 [D]*Hagen, K.G.*, 321 pp. [EThL 74,180*].

2875 *Rad, Gerhard von* El salmo 90. La acción de Dios. 1996 <1963>, ⇒144. 247-259.

2876 *Avril, Anne* Psaume 92,1 selon l'interprétation du Midrash Tehillim. Som., sum. 30. Cahiers Ratisbonne 1 (1996) 14-30.

2877 *Albertz, Rainer* "Gott der Rache, erscheine!" Predigt über Psalm 94,1-23. Zorn. 1996, ⇒110. 130-144.

2878 *Sedlmeier, Franz* Psalm 102,13-23: Aufbau und Funktion. BZ 40 (1996) 219-235.

2879 **Brunert, Gunhild** Ps 102 im Kontext des vierten Psalmenbuches. Diss. SBS 30: Stu 1996, Katholisches Bibelwerk 328 pp. DM79. 3-460-00301-49.

2880 *Auffret, Pierre* "Avec sagesse tu les fis": étude structurelle du Psaume 104: réponses et compléments. EeT(O) 27 (1996) 5-19.

2881 *Ahrens, M.* Natur pur?: Probleme mit Psalm 104. JK 57 (1996) 348-353.

2882 **Davis, Barry Craig** A contextual analysis of psalms 107-118. Diss. Trinity Evangelical Divinity School 1996 [D]*Howard, David M.*, 592 pp. DAI-A 57/05, p. 2081; AAC 9631850.

2883 *Zenger, Erich* Komposition und Theologie des 5. Psalmenbuchs 107-145. BN 82 (1996) 97-116.

2884 *Booij, Thijs* Psalm 109:6-19 as a quotation: a review of the evidence. [F]VAN UCHELEN N., 1996, ⇒100. 91-106.

2885 *Görg, Manfred* Thronen zur Rechten Gottes: zur altägyptischen Wurzel einer Bekenntnisformel. BN 81 (1996) 72-81 [Ps 110,1].

2886 *Nel, P.J.* Psalm 110 and the Melchizedek tradition. JNSL 22/1 (1996) 1-14.

2887 **Güntner, Diana** Das Gedenken mittels Psalmen im Neuen Testament: zum Psalmengebrauch der frühen Kirche am Modell des Psalms 110. Diss. Benediktbeuern 1995/96 ᴰ*Häußling* [BZ 42,315].

2888 *Prinsloo, G.T.M.* Yahweh and the poor in Psalm 113: literary motif and/or theological reality?. OTEs 9 (1996) 465-485.

2889 *Hagen, Kenneth Omnis homo mendax*: Lᴜᴛʜᴇʀuther on Psalm 116. ᶠSᴛᴇɪɴᴍᴇᴛᴢ D., 1996, ⇒86. 85-102.

2890 *Dupont, Jacques* Le '*suscipe me*' d'un vieux moine. ᶠDᴜᴘᴏɴᴛ J., 1996, ⇒21. 257-263 [Ps 118,116].

2891 **Berder, Michel** "La pierre rejetée par les bâtisseurs": psaume 118,22-23 et son emploi dans les traditions juives et dans le Nouveau Testament. EtB 31: P 1996, Gabalda 473 pp. FF390. 2-85021-089-7.

2892 *Schröten, Jutta* Das Spiel mit Anspielungen—Ps 118 im Neuen Testament. BiLi 69 (1996) 228-237.

2893 *Pizzolato, Luigi F.* Un'analisi retorica del prologo dell'*Expositio psalmi cxviii* di Aᴍʙʀᴏɢɪᴏ. Retorica. QVetChr 24: 1996, ⇒259. 57-71.

2894 *McLain, Charles E.* The function of the preposition בְּ in Psalm 119:89. CBTJ 12 (1996) 135-146.

2895 *Vetter, Dieter* 'Zeit zu handeln...' (Ps 119,126): ein Orientierungsversuch. JRTR 4 (1996) 102-119 [EThL 74,171*].

2896 *Sellier, Philippe* Pᴀꜱᴄᴀʟ et le psaume 118. VS 76 (1996) 269-277.

2897 ᵀ**Van Bavel, T.J.** Aurelius Aᴜɢᴜꜱᴛɪɴᴜꜱ: Commentar op psalm 118/119. Antwerpen 1996, Baarn 180 pp. [REAug 44,370].

2898 **Auffret, Pierre** Voyez... vingt psaumes, dont le psaume 119. VT.S 48: 1993, ⇒9,3165; 11/1,1673. ᴿBiOr 53 (1996) 173-174 *(Botha, Phil J.)*.

2899 **Crow, Loren D.** The Songs of Ascents (Psalms 120-134): their place in Israelite history and religion. SBL.DS 148: Atlanta 1996, Scholars xiii; 226 pp. $30/$20. 0-7885-0128-2/9-0. ᴿSJOT 10 (1996) 310-312 *(Knudsen, Mia D.)*.

2900 ᵀ*Solms, Elisabeth de* [Aᴜɢᴜꜱᴛɪɴᴜꜱ] Psaumes de pèlerinage (les 'Psaumes des montées'). PenCath 51 (1996) 12-21.

2901 ᵀᴱ**Orazzo, A.** Iʟᴀʀɪᴏ di Poitiers: i salmi delle ascensioni: cantico del pelegrino. R 1996, Borla 238 pp. L32.000.

2902 **Cuënot, Michel** Jérusalem joie pour toute la terre: psaumes des montées. Pref. *Dancourt, Gérard*, Troyes 1996, Fates 239 pp.

2903 *Creach, Jerome F.D.* Psalm 121. Interp. 50 (1996) 47-51.

2904 *Weiss, Meir* Psalm 130. Sum. v. Tarbiz 65 (1996) 203-208. **H.**

2905 *Dray, Stephen* Psalm 130: out of the depths. Evangel 14/3 (1996) 66-67.

2906 *Felten, Gustavo* Orando los salmos: Salmo 131 (130). La Revista Católica 96 (1996) 309-311.

2907 *Auwers, Jean-Marie* Le psaume 132 parmi les graduels. RB 103 (1996) 546-560.

2908 *Holman, Jan* Psaume 138 de la Septante. SémBib 84 (1996) 25-39.

2909 *Costen, James H.* Viewing life from high places: Psalm 139:1-18, Luke 19:1-10. JITC 24 (1996) 183-188.
2910 *Wagner, Siegfried* Zur Theologie des Psalms cxxxix. Ausgewählte Aufsätze. BZAW 240: 1996 <1978>, ⇒156. 131-150.
2911 *Brown, William P.* Psalm 139: the pathos of praise. Interp. 50 (1996) 280-284.
2912 *Chinitz, Jacob* Psalm 145: its two faces. JBQ 24 (1996) 229-232.
2913 **Sedlmeier, Franz** Jerusalem—Jahwes Bau: Untersuchungen zu Komposition und Theologie von Psalm 147. FzB 79: Wü 1996, Echter 395 pp. DM48. 3-429-01792-0.
2914 **Risse, Siegfried** Gut ist es... Untersuchungen zu Ps 147. MThA 37: 1995, ⇒11/1,1692. ᴿNRTh 118 (1996) 416-417 (*Ska, Jean Louis*); ThLZ 121 (1996) 1138-1139 (*Oeming, Manfred*).
2915 *Brüning, Christian* Psalm 148 und das Psalmenbeten. MThZ 47 (1996) 1-12.

E7.1 **Job**, *textus, commentarii*

2916 **Bonora, Antonio** Giobbe. Sussidi biblici 50: Reggio Emilia 1996, San Lorenzo (4) 75 pp. 88-8071-057-5.
2917 ᴱ**Brünnel, Gabriele** Avrāhām Ben-Šemûʾēl (Piqartei) [Die 'Hiob'-Paraphrase. Jidische Schtudies 6: Hamburg 1996, Buske xlix; 313 pp. NThAR 1997,98. 3-87548-107-0.
2918 Centre d'Analyse et de Documentation Patristiques. Le livre de Job chez les Pères. CBiPa 5: Strasbourg 1996, Brepols 284 pp. F158. 2-906805-04-1.
2919 **Clines, David J.A.** Job 1-20. WBC 17: 1989, ⇒5,3173... 10,3077. ᴿEstB 54 (1996) 272-274 (*Zamora, P.*).
2920 **Gentry, Peter John** The asterisked materials in the Greek Job. SCSt 38: 1995, ⇒11/1,1696. ᴿCBQ 58 (1996) 313-314 (*Cox, Claude*); HebStud 37 (1996) 207-210 (*Hiebert, Robert J.V.*).
2921 **Good, Edwin M.** In turns of tempest: a reading of Job, with a translation. 1990, ⇒6,3432... 9,3182. ᴿJNES 55 (1996) 140-142 (*Pardee, Dennis*).
2922 ᴱᵀ**Hagedorn, Dieter; Hagedorn, Ursula** Johannes CHRYSOS-TOMOS: Kommentar zu Hiob. PTS 35: 1990, ⇒6,3435a... 9,3185. ᴿJAC 39 (1996) 274-277 (*Schatkin, Margaret A.*).
2923 *Newsom, Carol A.* The book of Job: introduction, commentary, and reflections. NIntB 4: 1996, ⇒185. 317-637.
2924 *Pazzini, Domenico* ORIGENE commenta Giobbe. 1996, Som. 289. PSV 34 (1996) 289-298.
2925 ᵀ**Ravasi, Gianfranco** Il libro di Giobbe. Pref. *Luzi, Mario,* I classici 4: Locarno (CH) 1996, Armando D. 137 pp. 88-86315-56-2.
2926 **Rignell, G.** The Peshitta to the book of Job, critically investigated with introduction, translation, commentary and summary. ᴱ*Rignell, K.-E.*, Stockholm 1994, Almqvist & W. 382 pp. ᴿHenoch 18/1-2 (1996) 217-218 (*Dirksen, Piet*).
2927 ᴱ**Stec, David M.** The text of the targum of Job. AGJU 20: 1994, ⇒10,3086. ᴿJAOS 116 (1996) 555 (*Bernstein, Moshe J.*).
2928 **Szpek, Heidi M.** Translation technique in the Peshitta to Job. SBL.DS 137: 1992, ⇒8,3332... 11/1,1702. ᴿJThS 47 (1996) 584-587 (*Weitzman, Michael*); BSL 91 (1996) 381-383 (*Margain, Jean*).

2929 **Vattioni, Francesco** Per il testo di Giobbe. AION.S 89: N 1996, Istituto Universitario Orientale vii; 155 pp.

E7.2 *Job: themata,* **Topics...** *Versiculi,* **Verse numbers**

2930 *Begheyn, Paul* Job: visies van twintig hedend aagse kunstenaars. Str. 63 (1996) 928-931.

2931 **Ben-Chorin, Schalom; Langer, Michael** Die Tränen des Hiob. Ill. *Kaufmann, Hans-Günther,* Innsbruck 1994, Tyrolia 84 pp. 20 ill. RFrRu (1996/1) 41-42 *(Plünnecke, Elisabet).*

2932 *Bertrand, Daniel A.* Le bestiaire de Job: notes sur les versions grecques et latines. Le Livre de Job chez les Pères. 1996, ⇒2918. 215-258.

2933 EBeuken, Willem A.M. The book of Job. BEThL 114: 1994, ⇒10,305; 11/1,134. RETR 71 (1996) 107-108 *(Römer, Thomas)*; ThLZ 121 (1996) 250-252 *(Strauß, Hans).*

2934 *Bezuidenhout, L.C.* A context to frame the book of Job. OTEs 9 (1996) 9-19.

2935 *Bommel, Jan P.* De raamvertelling van het boek Job. Interpretatie 4/2 (1996) 23-24.

2936 *Boorer, Suzanne* A matter of life and death: a comparison of Proverbs 1-9 and Job. FTucker G., JSOT.S 229: 1996, ⇒95. 187-204.

2937 *Borgonovo, Gianantonio* La paura del disfacimento: il libro di Giobbe come itinerario dall'angoscia alla consolazione. PSV 33/1 (1996) 55-67.

2938 *Brottier, Laurence* L'actualisation de la figure de Job chez Jean Chrysostome. Le Livre de Job chez les Pères. 1996, ⇒2918. 63-110.

2939 *Carpentier, Jean-Marie* L'interrogation de Job sur la toute-puissance de Dieu et la conversion de cette interrogation dans *Le guide des égarés* de Maimonide. MélSR 53 (1996) 39-50.

2940 **Cazier, Pierre** Le cri de Job: approche biblique, mythologique et littéraire du problème de la souffrance du juste. Arras 1996, Artois Presse Université 292 pp. FF150 [Graphè 6,178ss—Sys, Jacques].

2941 **Champy, Harry Doyle** The meaning of the book of Job: a literary approach. Diss. New Orleans Bapt. Theol. Sem. 1995 DCole, R.D., 212 pp. [EThL 74,226*].

2942 **Course, John E.** Speech and response... Job 4-24. CBQ.MS 25: 1994, ⇒10,3127; 11/1,1715. RCBQ 58 (1996) 509-510 *(Gladson, Jerry A.)*; HebStud 37 (1996) 182-185 *(Oosthuizen, M.J.)*; JBL 115 (1996) 342-344 *(Szpek, Heidi M.)*; LASBF 46 (1996) 448-452 *(Niccacci, Alviero).*

2943 *Dailey, Thomas F.* Job as an icon for theology. PRSt 23 (1996) 247-254.

2944 *Daube, David* Reflections on Job and Greek tragedy. ICS 15 (1996) 72-81.

2945 **Déclais, Jean-Louis** Les premiers musulmans face à la tradition biblique: trois récits sur Job. Pref. *Tarot, Camille,* P 1996, L'Harmattan 318 pp. FF180. 2-7384-4136-X.

2946 *Doignon, Jean* "Rengaines" origéniennes dans les Homélies sur Job d'Hilaire de Poitiers. Le Livre de Job chez les Pères. 1996, ⇒2918. 7-11.

2947 **Ebach, Jürgen** Streiten mit Gott—Hiob, 2: Hiob 21-42. Kleine Biblische Bibliothek: Neuk 1996 Neuk'er vi; 169 pp. DM34. 3-7887-1495-6 [ZAW 109,452].

2948 *Flecha Andrés, José-Román* Buscadores de Dios: Elifaz, o el defensor de Dios. EvV 38 (1996) 27-29.

2949 **Fuchs, Gisela** Mythos und Hiobdichtung. 1993, ⇒9,3201... 11/1,1724. RBiOr 53 (1996) 502-504 (*Müller, Hans-Peter*).

2950 **Fyall, Robert** How does God treat his friends: learning from the book of Job. Fearn 1995, Christian Focus 157 pp. £4.50. 1-85792-115-1 [BL 1996,79].

2951 *Goldin, Paul Rakita* Job's transgressions: Luis ALONSO SCHOEKEL and José LUZ OJEDA. ZAW 108 (1996) 378-390.

2952 *Greenstein, Edward L.* A forensic understanding of the speech from the whirlwind. FHARAN M., 1996, ⇒35. 241-258.

2953 *Guinot, Jean-Noël* Regard sur l'utilisation du Livre de Job dans l'oeuvre de THEODORET de Cyr. Le Livre de Job chez les Pères. 1996, ⇒2918. 111-140.

2954 *Hayashi, Tadayoshi* KIERKEGAARD über Hiob. Kwansei-Gakuin-Daigaku 1 (1996) 71-81.

2955 **Hoffman, Yair** A blemished perfection: the book of Job in context. JSOT.S 213: Shf 1996, Academic 360 pp. £51; $77.50. 1-85075-583-3.

2956 *LaCocque, André* Job and religion at its best. Bibl.Interp. 4 (1996) 131-153.

2957 **Leduc-Fayette, Denise** PASCAL et le mystère du mal: la clef de Job. Diss. Sorbonne 1993. CFi 198: P 1996, Cerf v; 396 pp. FF190. 2-204-05428-3 [NThAR 1997,290].

2958 *Mangan, Céline* The attitude to women in the prologue of Targum Job. FMCNAMARA M., JSOT.S 230: 1996, ⇒58. 100-110.

2959 *Maraval, Pierre* Job dans l'oeuvre de ZENON de Vérone. Le Livre de Job chez les Pères. 1996, ⇒2918. 23-30.

2960 **Mathew, Geevarughese** The role of the epilogue in the book of Job. Diss. Drew 1995 DHuffmon, H.B., 133 pp. [EThL 74,227*].

2961 *Meves, Christa* Vom Sinn des Leidens—Lebenshilfe durch Hiob. Theologisches 26 (1996) 172-178.

2962 **Moore, Richard K.** The psalms of lamentation and the enigma of suffering. Mellen 50: Lewiston, NY 1996, Mellen 136 pp. 0-7734-2416-4 [NThAR 1997,131].

2963 *Morriston, Wesley* God's answer to Job. RelSt 32 (1996) 339-356.

2964 **Müller, Hans-Peter** Das Hiobproblem. EdF 84: ³1995, ⇒11/1,1739. RThLZ 121 (1996) 146-148 (*Van Oorschot, Jürgen*).

2965 *Noegel, Scott B.* Janus parallelism in Job and its literary significance. JBL 115 (1996) 313-320.

2966 **Noegel, Scott B.** Janus parallelism in the book of Job. Diss. DRendsburg, Gary A., JSOT.S 223: Shf 1996 Academic 223 pp. £30; $45. 1-85075-624-4.

2967 *Noegel, Scott B.* Wordplay and translation technique in the Septuagint of Job. Sum. 33. AuOr 14 (1996) 33-44.

2968 **O'Connor, Donald** Job. 1995, ⇒11/1,1744. RStudies in World Christianity 2/1 (1996) 122-123 (*Gibson, John C.L.*).

2969 EPieretti, **Antonio** Giobbe: il problema del male nel pensiero contemporaneo. Incontri: Assisi 1996, Cittadella 232 pp. 88-308-0601-3.

2970 *Polak, Frank H.* On prose and poetry in the book of Job. JANES
      24 (1996) 61-97.
2971 *Rad, Gerhard von* Discusión de las miserias de Job;
2972 Presentación de las miserias de Job. La acción de Dios. 1996
      <1970>, ⇒144. 77-82/72-82.
2973 *Ravasi, Gianfranco* 'Le lacrime da nessuno consolate': il giusto
      sofferente in Giobbe e Qohelet. Som. 85. PSV 34 (1996) 85-95.
2974 *Renoux, Charles* La chaîne arménienne sur le Livre de Job. Le
      Livre de Job chez les Pères. 1996, ⇒2918. 141-161.
2975 *Rohr, Richard* Job and the mystery of suffering: spiritual reflec-
      tions. NY 1996, Crossroad 189 pp. 0-8245-1474-2 [NThAR
      1997,259].
2976 *Sarna, Nahum M.* Notes on the use of the definite article in the
      poetry of Job. ᶠHARAN M., 1996, ⇒35. 279-284.
2977 **Schreiner, Susan E.** "Where shall wisdom be found?": CALVIN's
      exegesis of Job. 1994, ⇒10,3084; 11/1,1750. ᴿBibl.Interp. 4
      (1996) 251-252 (*Walker, Robert*); JR 76 (1996) 639-640 (*Wright,
      David F.*); Pro Ecclesia 5 (1996) 504-507 (*Farmer, Craig S.*).
2978 *Schultz, Carl* The cohesive issue of *mišpāṭ* in Job. ᶠYOUNG D.,
      1996, ⇒107. 159-175.
2979 *Sciumbata, Maria Patrizia* Gli usi e i valori di *ḥkyr* in Giobbe: un
      contributo dell'analisi paradigmatica alla datazione della lingua del
      testo. Quaderni del Dipartimento di Linguistica, Università di Fi-
      renze 7: 213-225.
2980 **Siertsema, Bettine** Job: steen des aanstoots?. Kampen 1996, Kok
      163 pp. ƒ32.50. 90-242-7875-0 [KeTh 49,157—Van der Woude,
      A.S.].
2981 *Steinmann, Andrew E.* The structure and message of the book of
      Job. VT 46 (1996) 85-100.
2982 **Susaimanickam, Jebamalai** Commitment to the oppressed: a Dalit
      reading of the book of Job. Diss. excerpt PUG, ᴰ*Conroy, Charles*,
      R 1996, x; 88 pp.
2983 **Susman, Margarete** Das Buch Hiob und das Schicksal des jüdi-
      schen Volkes. Pref. *Goldschmidt, Hermann Levin*, Fra 1996 Jüdi-
      scher Verlag im Suhrkamp 168 pp. DM38 [Soziologische Revue
      20,307].
2984 **Terrien, Samuel** The iconography of Job through the centuries:
      artists as biblical interpreters. University Park, PA 1996, Pennsyl-
      vania State Univ. Press xxxv; 308 pp. $65. 0-271-01528-4.
2985 **Turoldo, David Maria** La parabola di Giobbe. ᴱ*Levi, Abramo*,
      QRCSE 41: Sotto il Monte ²1996, Servitium 347 pp.   L35.000
      [RAMi 67,122—Spera, Salvatore].
2986 **Van der Lugt, Pieter** Rhetorical criticism and the poetry of the
      book of Job. OTS 32: 1995, ⇒11/1,1735. ᴿThLZ 121 (1996) 350-
      351 (*Strauß, Hans*); Bib. 77 (1996) 557-560 (*Lévêque, Jean*); CBQ
      58 (1996) 730-732 (*Irwin, William H.*).
2987 **Vogels, Walter** Job. LiBi 104: 1995, ⇒11/1,1755. ᴿNRTh 118
      (1996) 125-126 (*Ska, Jean Louis*); EeV 106 (1996) 14-15
      (*Monloubou, Louis*); ScEs 48 (1996) 343-345 (*Duhaime, Jean*).
2988 *Wagner, Siegfried* Leiderfahrung und Leidbewältigung im bibli-
      schen Ijobbuch. <1994>;
2989 'Schöpfung' im Buche Hiob. <1980>. Ausgewählte Aufsätze.
      BZAW 240: 1996, ⇒156. 247-277/183-189.

2990 *Wilson, Lindsay* The role of the Elihu speeches in the book of Job. RTR 55 (1996) 81-94.

2991 *Wolfers, David* The book of Job: its true significance. JBQ 24 (1996) 3-8.

2992 *Yeager, Janet; Dailey, Thomas F.* Job's world: a chaotic conundrum!. Encounter 56 (1995) 175-187 [IAJS 42,47].

2993 *Doignon, Jean* Versets de Job sur le péché de notre origine selon HILAIRE de Poitiers. Le Livre de Job chez les Pères. 1996, ⇒2918. 13-21 [Job 1-2; 42,10-17].

2994 *Linafelt, Tod* The undecidability of ברך in the prologue to Job and beyond. Bibl.Interp. 4 (1996) 154-172 [Job 1,5].

2995 *Klopfenstein, Martin A.* ḥnm (ḥinnam) im Hiobbuch. Leben aus dem Wort. BEAT 40: 1996, ⇒132. 117-121 [Job 1,9].

2996 **Egger-Wenzel, Renate** 'Von der Freiheit Gottes, anders zu sein': die zentrale Rolle der Kapitel 9 und 10 für das Ijobbuch. Diss. Benediktbeuern 1996/97 ᴰWahl [BZ 42,315].

2997 *Doukhan, Jacques* Radioscopy of a resurrection: the meaning of *niqqepu zoʾt* in Job 19:26. AUSS 34 (1996) 187-193.

2998 **Witte, Markus** Vom Leiden zur Lehre... (Hiob 21-27). BZAW 230: 1994, ⇒10,3134; 11/1,1765. ᴿThRev 92 (1996) 305-306 (*Oeming, Manfred*); CBQ 58 (1996) 144 (*Gladson, Jerry A.*); JBL 115 (1996) 522-523 (*Durlesser, James A.*).

2999 **Witte, Markus** Philologische Notizen zu Hiob 21-27. BZAW 234: 1995, ⇒11/1,1764. ᴿCBQ 58 (1996) 338-339 (*Vall, Gregory*).

3000 *Hermisson, Hans-Jürgen* Von Gottes und Hiobs Nutzen: zur Auslegung von Hiob 22. ZThK 93 (1996) 331-351.

3001 *Brüning, Christian* Der Hymnus auf den Schöpfergott in Ijob 26,5-14. TThZ 105 (1996) 151-156.

3002 *Hermisson, H.J.* Ein Bibeltext für Fortgeschrittene: (Hiob 26). ThBeitr 27 (1996) 137-144.

3003 *Fiddes, Paul S.* 'Where shall wisdom be found?': Job 28 as a riddle for ancient and modern readers. ᶠMASON R., 1996, ⇒57. 171-190.

3004 *Fournier, Christian* AUGUSTIN, Adnotationes in Job I, 29-31 (traduction d'après CSEL 28). Le Livre de Job chez les Pères. 1996, ⇒2918. 49-61.

3005 *Doucet, Dominique* Job: l'église et la tribulation: Augustin Adnotationes in Job 29-31. Le Livre de Job chez les Pères. 1996, ⇒2918. 31-48.

3006 **Wahl, Harald-Martin** Der gerechte Schöpfer... Elihureden—Hiob 32-37. BZAW 207: 1993, ⇒9,3245... 11/1,1770. ᴿCBQ 58 (1996) 141-142 (*Vall, Gregory*); ThRv 92 (1996) 221-222 (*Oeming, Manfred*).

3007 *Oeming, Manfred* 'Kannst du der Löwin ihren Raub zu jagen geben?' (Hi 38,39): das Motiv des 'Herrn der Tiere' und seine Bedeutung für die Theologie der Gottesreden Hi 38-42. IOSOT 1992. BEAT 28: 1996, ⇒160. 147-163 [Job 38-42].

3008 *Gounelle, Rémi* Le frémissement des portiers de l'Enfer à la vue du Christ: Jb 38, 17b et trois symboles de foi des années;

3009 *Vinel, Françoise* Job 38: le commentaire de JULIEN l'arien et les interprétations cappadociennes. Le Livre de Job chez les Pères. 1996, ⇒2918. 177-214/163-175.

3010 *Wagner, Siegfried* Theologischer Versuch über Ijob 42,7-9(10a).
Ausgewählte Aufsätze. BZAW 240: 1996 <1992>, ⇒156. 227-
238.

E7.3 *Canticum Canticorum*, Song of Songs, Das Hohelied, *textus, comm.*

3011 *Albrektson, Bertil* Singing or pruning. BiTr 47 (1996) 109-114.
3012 **Ben-Chorin, Schalom**, (*al*), Das Hohelied der Liebe: ein einziger
Blick deiner Augen. Innsbruck 1996, Tyrolia 96 pp. OS348.
3013 **Bloch, Ariel; Bloch, Chana** The Song of Songs. 1995,
⇒11/1,1781. BR 12/1 (1996) 14-15 (*Pope, Marvin H.*); HebStud
37 (1996) 185-187 (*Renn, Stephen*).
3014 [T]**Bonato, Vincenzo** GREGORIO di Nissa: omelie sul Cantico dei
cantici. 1995, ⇒11/1,1782. [R]Hum(B) 51 (1996) 990-991
(*Moreschini, Claudio*).
3015 *Cotterell, Peter* The greatest song: some linguistic considerations.
BiTr 47 (1996) 101-108.
3016 *Dove, Mary* Sex, allegory and censorship: a reconsideration of
medieval commentaries on the Song of Songs. JLT 10 (1996) 317ff
[ThD Index Feb. 1997,7].
3017 [T]**Dünzl, Franz** GREGOR von Nyssa: in Canticum Canticorum
Homiliae: Homilien zum Hohenlied. FC 16/1-3: FrB 1994, Herder
875 pp. 3 Teilbände. 3-451-22123-3/24-1/26-0. [R]ZKG 107/1
(1996) 129-131 (*Böhm, Thomas*).
3018 **Dünzl, Franz** Braut und Bräutigam: die Auslegung des Canticum
durch GREGOR von Nyssa. BGBE 32: 1993, ⇒9,3259...
11/1,1785. [R]JThS 47 (1996) 311-313 (*Meredith, Anthony*); ThRv
92 (1996) 505-507 (*Drecoll, Volker Henning*); ThR 61 (1996) 297-
298 (*Mühlenberg, Ekkehard*).
3019 *Fernández Marcos, N.* La lectura helenística del Cantar de los cantares. Sum., res. 282. Sef. 56 (1996) 265-282.
3020 [T]**Fernández Tejero, Emilia** El cantar más bello. 1994, ⇒10,3162;
11/1,1789. [R]EstB 54 (1996) 274-275 (*Mayoral, J.A.*).
3021 **Girón Blanc, Luis-Fernando** Midrás Cantar. 1991, ⇒7,2943...
10,3164. [R]Gr. 77 (1996) 147-148 (*Prato, Gian Luigi*).
3022 **Giudici, Maria Pia** 'Lectio divina' del Cantico dei Cantici. Leggere le Scritture 3: Padova 1996, Messaggero 126 pp. L13.000.
88-250-0490-7. [R]RAMi 65 (1996) 509-510 (*Fozzer, Giovanna*).
3023 [E]**Guérard, Marie-Gabrielle** NIL d'Ancyre: commentaire sur le
Cantique, 1. SC 403: 1994, ⇒10,3166; 11/1,1792. [R]REAug 42/1
(1996) 187-188 (*Brottier, Laurence*).
3024 *Guérard, Marie-Gabrielle* Éléments de romanesque dans le *Commentaire sur le Cantique* de NIL d'Ancyre. RechAug 29 (1996)
127-139.
3025 *Kellner, Menachem* Communication or the lack thereof among
thirteenth-fourteenth century Provençal Jewish philosophers: Moses
IBN TIBBON and GERSONIDES on Song of Songs. Communication in the Jewish diaspora. Jewish studies 16: 1996, ⇒232. 227-
255.
3026 **Mathieu, Bernard** La poésie amoureuse de l'Égypte ancienne: recherches sur un genre littéraire au Nouvel Empire. BEt 115: Cairo
1996, Institut Français vii; 267 pp. 2-7247-0182-8.

3027 *Montanari, Antonio* Sulle tracce profumate dello sposo: elementi di un metodo esegetico nell'*Expositio super Cantica Canticorum* di GUGLIELMO di Saint-Thierry. RiCi 13 (1996) 205-255.

3028 **Pelletier, Anne-Marie** El Cantar de los cantares. CuaBi 84: 1995, ⇒11/1,1800. RScrTh 28 (1996) 930-931 (*Aranda, G.*).

3029 **Quaglia, Rocco** Fiamma di eternità: Cantico 'dei Cantici. Spiritualità Biblica: Moncalvo 1996, Sharòn 184 pp. L25.000. 88-86965-02-8 [Iter. 5/8,258].

3030 TE**Richter-Ushanas, Egbert** Eros und Mythos: das Hohelied Salomos. Bremen 1996, Richter 76 pp. 3-92442-19-6f [NThAR 1997, 161].

3031 *Sáenz-Badillos, Angel* En torno a dos comentarios al Cantar de los Cantares. Helm. 139-141 (1995) 159-176 [IAJS 42,48].

3032 E**Sánches-Prieto, Pedro; Horcajada Diezma, Bautista** Libros de Salomón: Cantar de los Cantares, Proverbios, Sabiduría y Eclesiastés. Alfonso el Sabio: General estoria, 3. BRoHi.T IV 23: M 1994, Gredos 413 pp. RCBQ 58 (1996) 306-307 (*Lavoie, Jean-Jacques*).

3033 E**Schulz-Flügel, Eva** GREGORIUS Eliberritanus: epithalamium sive explanatio in Canticis Canticorum. Diss. Tü 1996 [EThL 74,178*].

3034 **Treat, Jay Curry** Lost keys: text and interpretation in Old Greek 'Song of Songs' and its earliest manuscript witnesses. Diss. Pennsylvania 1996 DKraft, Robert Alan, 535 pp. DAI-A 57/04, p. 1677; AAC 9629088.

3035 **Turner, Denys** Eros and allegory: medieval exegesis of the Song of Songs. CiSt: 1995, ⇒11/1,1810. RTS 57 (1996) 533-535 (*Matter, E. Ann*); CistC 58/4 (1996) [99]-[101]; ChH 65 (1996) 680-681 (*Madigan, Kevin*).

E7.4 **Canticum,** *themata, versiculi*

3036 *Alexander, Philip S.* The Song of Songs as historical allegory: notes on the development of an exegetical tradition. FMcNAMARA M., JSOT.S 230: 1996, ⇒58. 14-29.

3037 *Alexeev, Anatoly A.* The Song of Songs in the Slavonic bible tradition. BiTr 47 (1996) 119-125.

3038 *Aparicio Rodríguez, Ángel* Su diestra me abraza: la mujer del Cantar y María. Sum., rés. 194. EphMar 46 (1996) 169-194.

3039 *Blok, Hanna* Allegoric geography in the Song of Songs. FVAN UCHELEN N., 1996, ⇒100. 173-182 [OTA 19,461].

Blumenthal, David R. Where God is not: the book of Esther and Songs of Songs ⇒2614.

3040 *Bosshard-Nepustil, Erich* Zu Struktur und Sachprofil des Hohenlieds. BN 81 (1996) 45-71.

3041 *Buss, Martin J.* Hosea as a canonical problem: with attention to the Song of Songs. FTUCKER G., JSOT.S 229: 1996, ⇒95. 79-93.

3042 **Elliott, M. Timothea** The literary unity of the Canticle. EHS.T 23 371: 1989, ⇒5,3259... 8,3429. RBiOr 53 (1996) 504-505 (*Goulder, Michael*).

3043 **Engammare, Max** Qu'il me baise... le Cantique des cantiques à la Renaissance. 1993, ⇒8,3430... 11/1,1787. RRHPhR 76 (1996) 368-369 (*Arnold, M.*).

3044 Equipo de Animacion Biblica. Una poesía de amor: el Cantar de los Cantares. Biblia y Vida 22: México 1996, Dabar 77 pp. [Ef-Mex 15,392].

3045 *Henry, Nathalie* The lily and the thorns: AUGUSTINE's refutation of the Donatist exegesis of the Song of Songs. REAug 42 (1996) 255-266.

3046 *Kellner, Menachem* GERSONIDES on the Song of Songs and the nature of science. JJTP 4/1 (1994) 1-21 [IAJS 42,19].

3047 *Morfino, Mauro Maria* Il *Cantico dei cantici* e il patto elettivo: possibili connessioni. Theologica & Historica 5 (1996) 7-42 [Gen 15].

3048 *Payne, Robin* The Song of Songs: song of woman, song of man, song of God. ET 107 (1996) 329-333.

3049 *Pledel, Agneta* Author and translator: the stylist's work with the Song of Songs. BiTr 47 (1996) 114-118.

3050 *Sæbø, Magne* On the canonicity of the Song of Songs. FHARAN M., 1996, ⇒35. 267-277.

3051 TEVerdeyen, Paul; Fassetta, Raffaele, (al), BERNARD de Clairvaux: sermons sur le Cantique, 1: 1-15. SC 414: P 1996, Cerf 366 pp. Oeuvres complètes, X. FF237. 2-204-05350-3. RCCist 58/4 (1996) [110]-[112] (*Martel, Gérard de*).

3052 *Hostetter, E. C.* Mistranslation in Cant 1:5. AUSS 34 (1996) 35-36.
3053 *Ogden, Graham* 'Black but beautiful' (Song of Songs 1.5). BiTr 47 (1996) 443-445.

3054 *Hunt, Patrick* Sensory images in Song of Songs 1:12-2:16. IOSOT 1992. BEAT 28: 1996, ⇒160. 69-78.

3055 *Girón Blanc, Luis F.* Notas a Cantar de los Cantares Rabbah 4,8. MEAH 43/2 (1994) 7-14.

3056 *Long, Gary Alan* A lover, cities, and heavenly bodies: co-text and the translation of two similes in Canticles (6:4c; 6:10d). JBL 115 (1996) 703-709.

E7.5 *Libri sapientiales*—Wisdom literature

3057 *Assmann, Jan* Die Wende der Weisheit im Alten Ägypten. Weisheit. 1996, ⇒3071. 20-38.

3058 **Brown, William P.** Character in crisis: a fresh approach to the wisdom literature of the Old Testament. GR 1996, Eerdmans xi; 179 pp. $17. 0-8028-4135-X [OTA 19,537].

3059 *Collins, John J.* Wisdom, apocalypticism and the Dead Sea scrolls. FMICHEL D., BZAW 241: 1996, ⇒64. 19-32.

3060 *D'Alario, V.* Qualità della vita e armonia con l'ambiente nella pedagogia sapienziale. La natura. 1996, ⇒189. 67-100.

EDay, John Wisdom in ancient Israel ⇒22.

3061 EGammie, John G., (al), The sage. 1990, ⇒6,336... 8,3467. RBiOr 53 (1996) 162-168 (*Van Henten, J.W.*); JNES 55 (1996) 215-216 (*Jasnow, Richard*).

3062 **Golka, Friedemann W.** The leopard's spots. 1993, ⇒9,3312... 11/1,1873. RJSSt 41 (1996) 328-330 (*Crenshaw, James L.*);

3063 Die Flecken des Leoparden. 1994, ⇒10,3210. RBiOr 53 (1996) 779-783 (*Cook, Johann*).

3064 *Gundlach, Rolf* Ägyptische Weisheit in der politischen 'Lebenslehre': König Amenemhet I. ᶠMɪᴄʜᴇʟ D., BZAW 241: 1996, ⇒64. 91-105.

3065 **Heaton, E.W.** The school tradition of the OT. 1994, ⇒10,730; 11/1,1878. CBQ 58 (1996) 316-317 (*Hoppe, Leslie J.*); JR 76 (1996) 102-103 (*Crenshaw, James L.*).

3066 *Heerden, Willie van* A bright spark is not necessarily a wise person: Old Testament and contemporary perspectives on wisdom and intelligence. OTEs 9 (1996) 512-526.

3067 *Hembrom, T.* Economic policy in the wisdom literature of the Old Testament. BiBh 22 (1996) 232-237.

3068 *Hermisson, Hans-Jürgen* Weisheit. Altes Testament. 1996, ⇒169. 200-225.

3069 **Hill, Robert Charles** Wisdom's many faces. Glazier: ColMn 1996, Liturgical xii; 121 pp. $12. 0-8146-5515-7.

3070 *Iversen, Erik* Amenemope. ZÄS 123 (1996) 41-45.

3071 ᴱ**Janowski, Bernd** Weisheit außerhalb der kanonischen Weisheitsschriften. Veröffentlichungen der Wissenschaftlichen Gesellschaft für Theologie 10: Gü 1996 Gü'er 171 pp. DM54. 3-579-01812-4.

3072 *Kottsieper, Ingo* Die alttestamentliche Weisheit im Licht aramäischer Weisheitstraditionen. Weisheit ⇒3071. 128-162.

3073 **Lévêque, Jean** Sabidurías de Mesopotamia. Documentos en torno a la Biblia 26: Estella 1996, Verbo Divino 130 pp. 84-8169-096-1.

3074 *Lefebure, Leo D.* The wisdom tradition in recent christian theology. JR 76 (1996) 338-348.

3075 *Lichtheim, Miriam* Didactic literature. Ancient Egyptian literature. PÄ 10: 1996, ⇒230. 243-262.

3076 **McKinlay, Judith E.** Gendering wisdom the host: biblical invitations to eat and drink. JSOT.S 216; Gender, Culture, Theory 4: Shf 1996, Academic 280 pp. £40/$60; £15/$20. 1-85075-602-3/776-3 [ET 108,278].

3077 *Michel, Diethelm* Weisheit im Alten Testament. EvErz 48 (1996) 145-157.

3078 *Milazzo, Maisa* Timore Dei: principio della sapienza, sapienza del principio. Servitium 103 (1996) 12-26.

3079 *Morla, Víctor* La fascinación de la sabiduría. ᵀ*Capmany, Tomás*, SelT 35 (1996) 307-314 [< Sal Terrae 83 (1995) 843-857].

3080 **Murphy, Roland E.** The tree of life: an exploration of biblical wisdom literature. GR ²1996, Eerdmans xii; 233 pp. $22. 0-8028-4192-9 [JSJ 28,367].

3081 *Nel, Philip* The voice of Ms Wisdom: wisdom as intertext. OTEs 9 (1996) 423-450.

3082 **Neu, Erich** Das hurritische Epos der Freilassung I: Untersuchungen zu einem hurritisch-hethitschen Textensemble aus Ḫattuša. StBT 32: Wsb 1996, Harrassowitz.

3083 **Niccacci, Alviero** La casa della sapienza. 1994, ⇒10,3221; 11/1,1888. ᴿCBQ 58 (1996) 127-128 (*Bernas, Casimir*).

3084 ᴱ**Perdue, Leo G.** In search of wisdom. ᴹGᴀᴍᴍɪᴇ J., 1993, ⇒9,50; 11/1,1870. ᴿTJT 12/1 (1996) 89-90 (*McLaughlin, John L.*); Bibl.Interp. 4 (1996) 248-250 (*Johnston, Philip*);

3085 Wisdom and creation. 1994, ⇒10,3224; 11/1,1891. ᴿCBQ 58 (1996) 329-330 (*Clifford, Richard J.*); JR 76 (1996) 612-614 (*Kolarcik, Michael*).

3086 **Ponchia, Simonetta** La palma e il tamarisco e altri dialoghi mesopotamici. Collana di classici del Vicino Oriente antico: Venezia
1996, Marsilio 168 pp. RRSO 70 (1996) 228-230 (*Garbini,
Giovanni*).
3087 **Quack, Joachim Friedrich** Die Lehren des Ani. OBO 141: 1994,
⇒10,3226. RDiscEg 36 (1996) 147-150 (*Sturtewagen, Christian*).
3088 *Rad, Gerhard von* Sabiduría en Israel. La acción de Dios. 1996
<1970>, ⇒144. 212-217.
3089 ERoccati, **Alessandro** Sapienza egizia. TVOA 1/4: 1994,
⇒11/1,1895. RAsp. 43 (1996) 568-569 (*Scippa, V.*).
3090 *Sauer, Georg* Weisheit und Tora in qumranischer Zeit. Weisheit.
1996, ⇒3071. 107-127.
3091 *Schroer, Silvia* Die göttliche Weisheit und der nachexilische Monotheismus;
3092 Weise Frauen und Ratgeberinnen in Israel—Vorbilder der personifizierten Chokmah. Die Weisheit. 1996 <1991>, ⇒149. 27-
62/63-79.
      Schroer, Silvia, Die Weisheit ⇒149.
3093 **Shupak, Nili** Where can wisdom be found... Bible and ancient
Egyptian literature. OBO 130: 1993, ⇒9,3328... 11/1,1897.
RJAOS 116 (1996) 175-176 (*Bleiberg, Edward*); DiscEg 36 (1996)
145-147 (*Sturtewagen, Christian*).
      Smith, J. The wisdom literature and Psalms ⇒2689.
3094 **Urbach, Ephraïm E.** Les sages d'Israël: conceptions et croyances
des maîtres du talmud. TJolivet, *Marie-José*, Patrimoines, Judaïsme: P 1996, Cerf 1051 pp. FF450. 2-204-005505-0 [RB
104,317].
3095 *Volk, Konrad* Methoden altmesopotamischer Erziehung nach Quellen der altbabylonischen Zeit. Saec. 47 (1996) 178-216.
3096 **Weeks, Stuart** Early Israelite wisdom. 1994, ⇒10,3236;
11/1,1901. RInterp. 50 (1996) 196 (*Morgan, Donn F.*); JAOS 116
(1996) 138-139 (*Fox, Michael V.*).
3097 *Westermann, Claus* Grenzen der Weisheit;
3098 Weisheit und Theologie. Das mündliche Wort. 1996, ⇒157. 140-
159/160-175.

E7.6 **Proverbiorum liber,** *themata, versiculi*

3099 *Cook, J.* Aspects of the translation technique followed by the
translator of LXX Proverbs. JNSL 22/1 (1996) 143-153;
3100 The Hexaplaric text, double translations and other textual pheno-
mena in the Septuagint (Proverbs). JNSL 22/2 (1996) 129-140.
3101 *Frede, Hermann Josef* Zuwachs zur Handschrift 165. Vetus Latina-
Fragmente zum AT. 1996, ⇒1099. 9-34.
3102 **Koster, Albert** Spreuken: een woord-voor-woord vertaling uit het
Hebreeuws. Eindhoven 1996, Aproges 92 pp. ƒ28. 90-800961-7-2
[Bijdr. 59,453—Van Wieringen, A.L.H.M.].
3103 **Lelièvre, André; Maillot, Alphonse** Commentaire des Proverbes,
2: chapitres 19-31. LeDiv: Commentaires 4: P 1996, Cerf 377 pp.
F230. 2-204-05364-3.
3104 **Tuinstra, Evert Willem** Spreuken I. De prediking van het OT:
Baarn 1996, Callenbach 320 pp. ƒ99.50. 90-266-0193-X.

3105 **Whybray, R. Norman** Proverbs. NCeB: 1994, ⇒10,3245. [R]ThLZ
121 (1996) 1047-1050 (*Krispenz, Jutta*); CBQ 58 (1996) 735-736
(*McCreesh, Thomas P.*).

3106 **Atkinson, David J.** The message of Proverbs: wisdom for life.
The Bible Speaks Today: Leicester 1996, Inter-Varsity 173 pp. 0-
85111-166-1.

3107 *Clements, R.E.* The concept of abomination in the book of Proverbs. [F]HARAN M., 1996, ⇒35. 211-225.

3108 Consejos de la Sabiduría de Salomón: libro de máximas. Barc
1996, Humanitas 206 pp. 84-7910-207-1.

3109 **Dennis, Carlton Alexander** Proverbs and the people: a comparative study of Afri-Caribbean and biblical proverbs. Diss. Drew
1995 [D]*Huffmon, H.*, 142 pp. [EThL 74,229*].

3110 *Forti, Tova* Animal images in the didactic rhetoric of the book of
Proverbs. Bib. 77 (1996) 48-63.

3111 *Fox, Michael V.* The social location of the book of Proverbs.
[F]HARAN M., 1996, ⇒35. 227-239.

3112 **Hausmann, Jutta** Studien zum Menschenbild der älteren Weisheit:
(Spr 10ff.). FAT 7: 1995, ⇒11/1,1958. [R]ThLZ 121 (1996) 639-
641 (*Krispenz, Jutta*); JAOS 116 (1996) 771-772 (*Murphy, Roland
E.*).

3113 **Kaiser, Walter C.** Proverbs: wisdom for every day life. Great
Books of the Bible: GR 1995, Zondervan 45 pp. $5. 0-310-49861-
9 [BL 1996,82].

3114 *Kamugisha, J.M.* African proverbs and resources of wisdom. African Christian Studies 12/4 (1996) 1-17.

3115 *Loader, J.A.* Learning in the indicative. Sum. 21. JSem 8/1 (1996)
21-33.

3116 *McKenzie, Alyce M.* The preacher as subversive sage: preaching on
biblical proverbs. Proverbium 12 (1995) 169-193 [IAJS 42,46].

3117 **McKenzie, Alyce M.** Preaching Proverbs: wisdom for the pulpit.
LVL 1996, Westminster xxii; 170 pp. $15. 0-664-25653-8 [ThD
44,371—Heiser, W. Charles].

3118 *Overland, Paul* Structure in *The Wisdom of Amenemope* and Proverbs. [F]YOUNG D., 1996, ⇒107. 275-291.

3119 **Reich, Rachel** Stylistic editorial and linking devices in the book of
Proverbs. Diss. Bar-Ilan 1996 [D]*Vargon, S.* [EThL 74,229*].

3120 **Sneed, Mark** The class culture of Proverbs: eliminating stereoty-
pes. SJOT 10 (1996) 296-308.

3121 **Snell, Daniel C.** Twice-told proverbs and the composition of the
book of Proverbs. 1993, ⇒9,3358... 11/1,1926. [R]OLZ 91 (1996)
440-443 (*Meinhold, Arndt*); JAOS 116 (1996) 543-544 (*Crenshaw,
James L.*).

3122 [TE]**Visotzky, Burton L.** The midrash on Proverbs. 1992,
⇒10,3243. [R]HebStud 37 (1996) 212-214 (*Sarason, Richard S.*).

3123 *Waltke, Bruce* Does Proverbs promise too much?. AUSS 34 (1996)
319-336.

3124 **Washington, Harold C.** Wealth and poverty in the instruction of
Amenemope and the Hebrew Proverbs. SBL.DS 142: Atlanta, 1994
Scholars xii; 242 pp. $30/$20. [R]JBL 115 (1996) 734-736
(*Crenshaw, James L.*); CBQ 58 (1996) 337-338 (*Burns, Camilla*).

3125 **Wehrle, Josef** Sprichwort und Weisheit. AOtt 38: 1993,
⇒8,3510... 10,3244. [R]EstB 54 (1996) 270-271 (*Arambarri, J.*).

3126 **Westermann, Claus** Roots of wisdom. 1995, ⇒11/1,1929.
RTheol. 99/787 (1996) 68-69 (*Coggins, Richard*); ScrTh 28 (1996)
926-927 (*Aranda, G.*); HebStud 37 (1996) 177-179 (*Fredericks, Daniel C.*); BiRe 12/3 (1996) 14, 16-17 (*Fontaine, Carole R.*).
3127 **Whybray, R. Norman** The composition of the book of Proverbs.
JSOT.S 168: 1994, ⇒10,3255; 11/1,1930. RScrTh 28 (1996) 579-582 (*Aranda, G.*); JAOS 116 (1996) 544-545 (*Forti, Tova*);
3128 *Wyse, R.R.; Prinsloo, W.S.* Faith development and proverbial wisdom. OTEs 9 (1996) 129-143.

3129 *Whybray, Roger Norman* City life in Proverbs 1-9. FMICHEL D., BZAW 241: 1996, ⇒64. 243-250.
3130 **Baumann, Gerlinde** Die Weisheitsgestalt in Proverbien 1-9: traditionsgeschichtliche und theologische Studien. FAT 16: Tü 1996, Mohr xi; 374 pp. DM198. 3-16-146597-0.
3131 **Maier, Christl Margarethe** Die "fremde Frau"... Prov. 1-9. OBO 144: 1995, ⇒11/1,1936. RCBQ 58 (1996) 714-715 (*Murphy, Roland E.*).
3132 *Baumann, Gerlinde* "Zukunft feministischer Spiritualität" oder "Werbefigur des Patriarchats"?: die Bedeutung der Weisheitsgestalt in Prov 1-9 für die feministisch-theologische Diskussion. Von der Wurzel getragen. 1996, ⇒204. 135-152.
3133 *Harris, Scott L.* 'Figure' and 'riddle': Prov 1:8-19 and innerbiblical interpretation. BR 41 (1996) 58-76 [Gen 37].
3134 *Klopfenstein, Martin A.* Auferstehung der Göttin in der spätisraelitischen Weisheit von Prov 1-9?. Leben aus dem Wort. BEAT 40: 1996, ⇒132. 123-135.
3135 *Bellis, Alice Ogden* The gender and motives of the wisdom teacher in Proverbs 7. BBR 6 (1996) 15-22.
3136 *Maier, Christl* Im Vorzimmer der Unterwelt: die Warnung vor der "fremden Frau" in Prov 7 in ihrem historischen Kontext. Von der Wurzel getragen. 1996, ⇒204. 179-198.
3137 *Schroer, Silvia* Weisheit auf dem Weg der Gerechtigkeit (Spr 8,20). Die Weisheit. 1996 <1986>, ⇒149. 12-25.
3138 *Fox, Michael V.* ᵓAmon again. JBL 115 (1996) 699-702 [Prov 8,30];
3139 The strange woman in Septuagint Proverbs. JNSL 22/2 (1996) 31-44 [Prov 9,13-18; 7,1-27; 2,16-22; 5,1-23; 6,20-35].
3140 **Lelièvre, André; Maillot, Alphonse** Les proverbes de Salomon 10-18. LDComm 1: 1993, ⇒10,3241. REstBíb 54 (1996) 269-270 (*Flor, G.*).
3141 *Dyk, Janet W.* Rhythm and sense in Proverbs 14:2. FVAN UCHELEN N., 1996, ⇒100. 161-171 [OTA 19,458].
3142 *Vanoni, Gottfried* "Was verursacht Reichtum?" und weitere Fragen zu Spr 15,16—mit Hilfe der BHt-Software zu beantworten versucht. BN 85 (1996) 70-88.
3143 *Luke, K.* The seven sages (Proverbs 26:16). ITS 33/1 (1996) 54-67.
3144 *Georgi, Dieter* Weisheitliche Skepsis und charismatische Weisheit. FSCHOTTROFF W., 1996, ⇒81. 53-63 [Prov 30,1-4] [OTA 19,458].
3145 *Strömberg Krantz, Eva* "A man not supported by God": on some crucial words in Proverbs xxx 1. VT 46 (1996) 548-553.

3146 *Hawkins, Tom R.* The wife of noble character in Proverbs 31:10-31. BS 153 (1996) 12-23.
3147 *Gous, Ignatius G.P.* Proverbs 31:10-31—the A to Z of woman wisdom. OTEs 9 (1996) 35-51.
3148 **Masenya, Madipoane J.** Proverbs 31:10-31 in a South African context: a *Bosadi* (womanhood) perspective. Diss. UNISA 1996 ᴰ*Burden, J.J.* [NAOTS 2,15—Holter, Knut].

E7.7 *Ecclesiastes*—Qohelet; *textus, themata, versiculi*

3149 **Boira Sales, José** El 'Commentarius in Ecclesiasten' de San JERONIMO. Diss. Ath. S. Crucis, R 1996, xv; 481 pp. [EThL 74,179*].
3150 **Bonora, Antonio** El libro de Qohélet. 1994, ⇒10,3277. ᴿPerTeol 28 (1996) 262-263 (*Mondoni, Danilo*); EfMex 14 (1996) 394-395 (*Anízar, Humberto Encarnación*); NatGrac 43 (1996) 477-479 (*Ramos, Felipe F.*).
3151 **D'Alario, Vittoria** Il libro del Qohelet. RivBib.S 27: 1993, ⇒9,3399; 10,3288. ᴿEThL 72 (1996) 436-437 (*Schoors, A.*).
3152 ᴱ**Géhin, Paul** ÉVAGRE le Pontique: scholies à l'Ecclésiaste. SC 397: 1993, ⇒9,3385... 11/1,1977. ᴿContacts 48 (1996) 317-318 (*Lépine, Jacques-Jude*).
3153 ᵀᴱ**Gómez Aranda, Mariano** El comentario de Abraham IBN EZRA. TextEstCisn 56: 1994, ⇒10,3280. ᴿJThS 47 (1996) 194-197 (*Loewe, Raphael*); MEAH 43/2 (1994) 159-161 (*Pérez Fernández, Miguel*).
3154 **Vílchez Líndez, José** Ecclesiastes. Nueva Biblia Española. 1994, ⇒10,3284; 11/1,1984. ᴿNRTh 118 (1996) 741-742 (*Ska, Jean Louis*); CBQ 58 (1996) 530-531 (*Kaltner, John*).

3155 *Brzegowy, Tadeusz* Czy warto być uczciwym?: wskazania etyczne mędrca Koheleta [De honestate quid dicit Qohelet?]. RBL 49 (1996) 221-230. **P.**
3156 *D'Alario, V.* L'enigma del mondo e della vita nel Qohelet. La natura. 1996, ⇒189. 101-133.
3157 **Fischer, Alexander Achilles** Skepsis oder Furcht Gottes: Studien zur Komposition und Theologie des Buches Kohelet. Diss. Marburg 1996 ᴰ*Kaiser, O.* [NThAR 1997,130].
3158 **Fischer, Stephan** Die Aufforderung zur Lebensfreude im Buch Kohelet und seine Rezeption der ägyptischen Harfnerlieder. Diss. Pretoria 1996 ᴰ*Loader, J.A.*, 464 pp. [EThL 74,230*].
3159 *Gómez Aranda, Mariano* Teorías astronómicas y astrológicas en el 'Comentario de Abraham IBN EZRA al libro del Eclesiastés'. Sef. 55 (1995) 257-272.
3160 *Heard, R. Christopher* The *dao* of Qoheleth: an intertextual reading of the *daode jing* and the book of Ecclesiastes. Jian Dao 5 (1996) 65-93 [OTA 19,458].
3161 *Klopfenstein, Martin A.* Kohelet und die Freude am Dasein;
3162 Die Skepsis des Kohelet. Leben aus dem Wort. BEAT 40: 1996, ⇒132. 27-39/13-26.
3163 *Krüger, Thomas* Dekonstruktion und Rekonstruktion prophetischer Eschatologie im Qohelet-Buch. ᶠMICHEL D., BZAW 241: 1996, ⇒64. 107-129.

3164 **Lavoie, Jean-Jacques** La pensée du Qohélet. CTHP 49: 1992, ⇒8,3553; 10,3293. ᴿScEs 48 (1996) 230-232 (*Faucher, Alain*).

3165 **Miller, Douglas B.** The symbolic function of *hebel* in the book of Ecclesiastes (Qohelet). Diss. Princeton Theol. Sem. 1996 ᴰ*Seow, C.L.* 239 pp. DAI-A 57/05, p. 2083; AAC 9629097.

3166 **Raurell, Frederic** Dimensión ético-pedagógica de la provocación en el Qohélet. ᵀ*Casas, Josep*, SelT 35 (1996) 315-323 [<Laur. 33 (1992) 375-402].

   Ravasi, Gianfranco 'Le lacrime...': il giusto sofferente in Giobbe e Qohelet ⇒2973.

3167 ᴱ**Ridderbos, J.** Mens, durf te leven!: Prediker: een postmoderne denker uit de derde eeuw voor Christus. Kampen 1996, Kok 120 pp. ƒ25. 90-242-7831-7 [Str. 64,470].

3168 *Rochettes, Jacqueline des* Qohélet ou l'humour noir à la recherche de Dieu dans un contexte hébraïco-hellénique. ᶠLEGASSE S., LeDiv 166: 1996, ⇒51. 49-71.

3169 *Schoors, Antoon* Qoheleth: a book in a changing society. OTEs 9 (1996) 68-87;

3170 The verb ראה in the book of Qoheleth. ᶠMICHEL D., BZAW 241: 1996, ⇒64. 227-241.

3171 *Schùermans, Marie-Philippe* Qohélet le controversé. ᶠDUPONT J., 1996, ⇒21. 31-53.

3172 *Sciumbata, M. Patrizia* Peculiarità e motivazioni della struttura lessicale dei verbi della "conoscenza" in Qohelet: abbozzo di una storia dell'epistemologia ebraico-biblica. Henoch 18 (1996) 235-249.

3173 *Seow, C.L.* Linguistic evidence and the dating of Qohelet. JBL 115 (1996) 643-666.

3174 *Shead, Andrew G.* Ecclesiastes from the outside in. RTR 55 (1996) 24-37.

3175 *Spangenberg, Izak J.J.* Irony in the book of Qohelet. JSOT 72 (1996) 57-69.

3176 *Taylor, J.P.* A time to dance: reflections on the book of Ecclesiastes. IBSt 18 (1996) 114-135.

3177 ᵀᴱ**Vinel, Françoise** GREGORIUS Nyssenus: in Ecclesiasten homiliae VIII [Grégoire de Nysse: homélies sur l'Ecclésiaste]. Texte grec *Alexander, P.*, SC 416: P 1996, Cerf 446 pp. Introd., trad., notes. FF298. 2-204-05355-4. ᴿScEs 48 (1996) 349-350 (*Poirier, Paul-Hubert*).

3178 *Vioque, Guillermo Galán* ERASMO en España: *Ecclesiastes y De Rationes Dicendi* de Alfonso GARCIA MATAMOROS. HL 45 (1996) 372-384.

3179 ᴱ**Zuck, Roy B.** Reflecting with Solomon. 1994, ⇒10,3299; 11/1,2016. ᴿOTEs 9 (1996) 178-180 (*Viviers, H.*).

3180 *Verheij, Arian J.C.* Words speaking for themselves: on the poetics of Qohelet 1:4-7. ᶠVAN UCHELEN N., 1996, ⇒100. 183-188 [OTA 19,459].

3181 *Müller, Hans-Peter* Kohelet und Amminadab. ᶠMICHEL D., BZAW 241: 1996, ⇒64. 149-165 [Qoh 2,1-11].

3182 *Schwienhorst-Schönberger, Ludger* Nicht im Menschen gründet das Glück. 1994, ⇒10,3302; 11/1,2009. ᴿThLZ 121 (1996) 149-151 (*Schreiner, Stefan*) [Qoh 2,24].

3183   *Tita, Hubert* Ist die thematische Einheit Koh 4,17-5,6 eine Anspie-
lung auf die Salomoerzählung?: Aporien der religionskritischen Interpretation. BN 84 (1996) 87-102.

3184   *Riesener, Ingrid* Frauenfeindschaft im Alten Testament?: zum
Verständnis von Qoh 7,25-29. FMICHEL D., BZAW 241: 1996,
⇒64. 193-207.

3185   *Richter, Hans-Friedemann* Kohelets Urteil über die Frauen: zu Koh
7,26.28 und 9,9 in ihrem Kontext. ZAW 108 (1996) 584-593.

3186   **Pahk, Johan Yeong-Sik** Il canto della gioia in Dio: l'itinerario
sapienziale espresso dall'unitá letteraria in Qohelet 8,16-9,10 e il
parallelo di Gilgames Me. iii. Diss. Pont. Ist. Biblico 1994-95
DGilbert, Maurice, IUO.S Maior 52: N 1996, Istituto Universitario
Orientale xv; 366 pp.

3187   *Lavoie, Jean-Jacques* Temps et finitude humaine: étude de Qohélet
ix 11-12. VT 46 (1996) 439-447.

3188   *Salters, Robert B.* A gloss in RASHBAM on Qohelet. JQR 86
(1996) 407-408 [Qoh 12,5].

3189   *Lohfink, Norbert* Zu einigen Satzeröffnungen im Epilog des Kohe-
letbuches. FMICHEL D., BZAW 241: 1996, ⇒64. 131-147 [Qoh
12,9.12].

E7.8   *Liber Sapientiae*—Wisdom of Solomon

3190   EHübner, Hans Die Weisheit Salomos. 1993, ⇒10,324a. RThRv
92 (1996) 497-500 (*Engel, Helmut*).

3191   TEScarpat, Giuseppe Libro della Sapienza, 2. Biblica, Testi e
studi 3: Brescia 1996, Paideia 546 pp. 88-394-0530-5.

3192   **Vílchez Líndez, José** Sabedoria. 1995, ⇒11/1,2029. RREB 56
(1996) 1001-1005 (*Gruen, Wolfgang*).

3193   **Boiten, Gerda Jeannette** Wijsheid in context: een onderzoek naar
de retorische opbouw van het boek Wijsheid van Salomo en de betekenis van Vrouwe Wijsheid. Diss. Groningen 1996, 210 pp.
[EThL 74,232*].

3194   *Castro, J. Mendes* Influência helenística no livro da Sabedoria.
Sum. 355. HumTeo 17 (1996) 277-282.

3195   *Hug, Joseph* Sabiduría y condición humana: reflexión sobre el libro
de la Sabiduría. TSala, Màrius, SelT 35 (1996) 324-326 [< Choisir
429 (1995) 9-12].

3196   *Nielsen, Donald A.* La misura divina: creazione e retribuzione nel
libro della Sapienza in FILONE: aspetti dell'incontro fra giudaismo
ed ellenismo. TStein, Elisabeth, ReSo 11/1 (1996) 9-21.

3197   **Premstaller, Volkmar M.** "Gericht" und "Strafe" im Buch der
Weisheit: alttestamentliche Vorstellungen und griechisch-
hellenistische Terminologie. St. Georgen an der Gusen 1996, St.
Georgs vii; 158 pp. DM38.

3198   *Schroer, Silvia* Die personifizierte Sophia im Buch der Weisheit.
Die Weisheit. 1996 <1994>, ⇒149. 110-125.

3199   **Fabri, Marco Valerio** Creazione e salvezza nel libro della Sapienza: esegesi di Sap. 1,13-15. Diss. Pamplona 1996 DAranda,
G., 505 pp. [EThL 74,232*].

3200 *Miller, Robert J.* Immortality and religious identity in Wisdom 2-5.
      F MACK B., 1996, ⇒54. 199-213.
3201 *Massinghi, Luca* Il giusto oppresso perché scomodo (Sap 2,10-20).
      Som. 97. PSV 34 (1996) 97-111.
3202 *Gignac, Alain* Quel sens donner à la mort prématurée du juste?: la
      pédagogie éthique d'un texte biblique (Sg 4,7-20). EeT(O) 27
      (1996) 199-227.
3203 *Mazzinghi, Luca* 'Un improvviso e inatteso timore si era riversato
      su di loro': la paura dei malvagi in Sap 7. PSV 33/1 (1996) 81-92.
3204 *Dumoulin, Pierre* Le livre de la Sagesse à la charnière des deux te-
      staments: l'actualité du "midrash" de Sg 11-19. RTLu 1 (1996)
      227-255.
3205 *De Carlo, Giuseppe* 'Ami, infatti, gli esistenti, tutti': studio di
      Sap 11,24. Laur. 36 (1995) 391-432.
3206 **Dumoulin, Pierre** Entre la manne...Sg 16,15-17,1a. AnBib 132:
      1994, ⇒10,3325; 11/1,2041. R RdT 37 (1996) 414-416 (*D'Alario,
      Vittoria*); CBQ 58 (1996) 310-311 (*Kolarcik, Michael*).
3207 *Poniży, Bogdan* Manna biblijna zapowiedzią eucharystii [Manna
      biblica sicut praefiguratio eucharistiae]. RBL 49 (1996) 73-85 [Wis
      16,20-28].
3208 **Mazzinghi, Luca** Notte... Sap 17,1-18,4. AnBib 134: 1995,
      ⇒11/1,2042. R RevAg 37 (1996) 856-857 (*Salugal, Santos*); CBQ
      58 (1996) 715-716 (*Winston, David*).
3209 *Schenker, Adrian* La loi de la divinité: le rachat des fils premieres-
      nés et le sens de la pâque en Sagesse XVIII,9. RevSR 70 (1996)
      183-187.
3210 *Poniży, Bogdan* Logos in the book of Wisdom 18:14-16. IOSOT
      1992. BEAT 28: 1996, ⇒160. 169-177.

              E7.9 *Ecclesiasticus, Siracides;* **Wisdom of Jesus Sirach**

3211 **Minissale, Antonino** La versione greca del Siracide. 1995,
      ⇒11/1,2043. R RevAg 37 (1996) 856-857 (*Salugal, Santos*); ScrTh
      28 (1996) 617 (*Jarne, J.*); Henoch 18/1-2 (1996) 218-219 (*Sacchi,
      Paolo*); ATG 59 (1996) 315-316 (*Vílchez, José*).
3212 E **Thiele, Walter** Vetus Latina 11/2: Sirach (Ecclesiasticus). Fasc.
      6: FrB 1996, Herder 80 pp. 3-451-00429-1 [Sir 11,35-16,21].

3213 *Alonso Schökel, Luis* Notas exegéticas al Eclesiástico (Ben Sira).
      EstB 54 (1996) 299-312.
3214 *Botha, P.J.* Through the figure of a woman many have perished:
      Ben Sira's view of women. OTEs 9 (1996) 20-34.
3215 *Calduch-Benages, Nuria* Elementos de inculturación helenista en el
      libro de Ben Sira: los viajes. EstB 54 (1996) 289-298.
3216 **Corley, Jeremy** Ben Sira's teaching on friendship. Diss. Cath.
      Univ. of America 1996 D *Di Lella, Alexander A.*, 374 pp. DAI-A
      57/05, p. 2081; AAC 9629881.
3217 *DeSilva, David A.* The wisdom of Ben Sira: honor, shame, and the
      maintenance of the values of a minority culture. CBQ 58 (1996)
      433-455.
3218 *Dewsnap, Molly* The twins and the scholar: how two Victorian si-
      sters and a rabbi discovered the Hebrew text of Ben Sira. BArR
      22/5 (1996) 54-62.

3219 *Di Lella, Alexander A.* The wisdom of Ben Sira: resources and recent research. CurResB 4 (1996) 161-181.

3220 *Harrington, Daniel J.* Two early Jewish approaches to wisdom: Sirach and Qumran Sapiential Work A. SBL.SP 35: 1996, ⇒274. 123-132.

3221 *Hengel, Martin* Ben Sira und der Hellenismus. Judaica et Hellenistica. WUNT 90: 1996 <1974>, 252-257.

3222 *Kraft, Thomas* Justicia y liturgia: la maravillosa síntesis de Sirácida. RTLi 30 (1996) 307-318.

3223 **Marböck, Johannes** Gottes Weisheit. 1995, ⇒11/1,55. ᴿThRv 92 (1996) 225-227 (*Kaiser, Otto*).

3224 ᴱ**Reiterer, Friedrich Vinzenz** Freundschaft bei Ben Sira. BZAW 244: B 1996, De Gruyter viii; 264 pp. Symposion zu Ben Sira (1: 1995: Salzburg). DM158. 3-11-015261-4.

3225 *Schroer, Silvia* Der eine Herr und die Männerherrschaft im Buch Jesus Sirach: Frauenbild und Weisheitsbild in einer misogynen Schrift. Die Weisheit. 1996, ⇒149. 96-109.

3226 **Wischmeyer, Oda** Die Kultur des Buches Jesus Sirach. BZNW 77: 1995, ⇒11/1,2061. ᴿThLZ 121 (1996) 166-168 (*Sauer, Georg*); JThS 47 (1996) 188-190 (*Schaper. J.L.W.*); ThRv 92 (1996) 496-497 (*Marböck, Johannes*); CBQ 58 (1996) 531-532 (*Winston, David*); CrSt 17 (1996) 631-633 (*Westermann, Claus*).

3227 *Wright, Benjamin G.* Putting the puzzle together: some suggestions concerning the social location of the wisdom of Ben Sira. SBL.SP 35: 1996, ⇒274. 133-149.

3228 *Yifrach, Esther* The construct infinitive in the language of Ben Sira. Sum. I. Leš. 59 (1996) 275-294. **H.**

3229 *Frede, Hermann Josef* Ein Sirachtext aus Cruas. Vetus Latina-Fragmente. AGLB 28: 1996, ⇒1099. 191-203 [Sir 1,1-2,23(18)] [RBen 106,405].

3230 **Kondracki, Andrzej** La zedaqah che espia i peccati: studio esegetico di Sir 3,1-4,10. Diss. excerpta Pont. Inst. Biblicum ᴰ*Gilbert, Maurice*, 1996, xviii; 110 pp.

3231 *Stendebach, Franz Josef* Weisheitlische Mahnung zu mitmenschlichen Verhalten: eine Auslegung zu Sir 4,1-10. ᶠSsʜoᴛᴛʀoғғ W., 1996, ⇒81. 83-90 [OTA 19,463].

3232 *Di Lella, Alexander A.* Use and abuse of the tongue: Ben Sira 5,9-6,1. ᶠMɪcʜᴇʟ D., BZAW 241: 1996, ⇒64. 33-48.

3233 *Krammer, Ingrid* Scham im Zusammenhang mit Freundschaft. Freundschaft bei Ben Sira. BZAW 244: 1996, ⇒3224. 171-201 [[Sir 5,14-6,1; 20,21-23; 22,25; 29,14; 41,18; 41,22].

3234 *Corley, Jeremy* Caution, fidelity, and the fear of God: Ben Sira's teaching on friendship in Sir 6:5-17. EstB 54 (1996) 313-326.

3235 *Beentjes, Pancratius* "Ein Mensch ohne Freund ist wie eine linke Hand ohne die Rechte": Prolegomena zur Kommentierung der Freundschaftsperikope Sir 6,5-17;

3236 *Schrader, Lutz* Unzuverlässige Freundschaft und verläßliche Feindschaft: Überlegungen zu Sir 12,8-12;

3237 *Kieweler, Hans Volker* Freundschaft und böse Nachrede: exegetische Anmerkungen zu Sir 19,6-19. BZAW 244: 1996, ⇒3224. 1-18/19-59/61-85.

3238 *Weber, Kathleen* Wisdom false and true (Sir 19,20-30). Bib. 77 (1996) 330-348.

3239 *Marböck, Johannes* Gefährdung und Bewährung: Kontexte zu Freundschaftsperikope Sir 22,19-26. Freundschaft bei Ben Sira: BZAW 244: 1996, ⇒3224. 87-106.

3240 *Rogers, Jessie F.* Wisdom and creation in Sirach 24. JNSL 22/2 (1996) 141-156.

3241 *Reiterer, Friedrich V.* Gelungene Freundschaft als tragende Säule einer Gesellschaft: exegetische Untersuchung von Sir 25,1-11;

3242 *Kaiser, Otto* Was ein Freund nicht tun darf: eine Auslegung von Sir 27,16-21;

3243 *Sauer, Georg* Freundschaft nach Ben Sira 37,1-6. Freundschaft bei Ben Sira. BZAW 244: 1996, ⇒3224. 107-122/133-169/123-131.

3244 *Botha, P.J.* The ideology of shame in the Wisdom of Ben Sira: Ecclesiasticus 41:14-42:8. OTEs 9 (1996) 353-371.

3245 **Hildesheim, Ralph** Bis daß ein Prophet aufstand wie Feuer: Untersuchungen zum Prophetenverständnis des Ben Sira in Sir 48,1-49,16. TThSt 58: Trier 1996, Paulinus (8) 279 pp. DM48. 3-7902-1286-5.

3246 *Dalla Vecchia, Flavio* Gloria del sacerdozio. FFORESTI B., 1996, ⇒25. 33-49 [Sir 50].

VII. Libri prophetici VT

E8.1 Prophetismus

3247 **Abrego de Lacy, José Maria** I libri profetici. Introduzione allo studio della Bibbia 4: Brescia 1996, Paideia 261 pp. L38.000. 88-394-0520-8.

3248 *Andrew, Maurice E.* The prophetic example: referentiality or textuality?. FJAMIESON P., 1996, ⇒44. 32-50.

3249 **Aune, David Edward** La profezia nel primo cristianesimo e il mondo mediterraneo antico. BSSTB 10: Brescia 1996, Paideia 725 pp. L142.000. 88-394-0531-3.

3250 *Baltzer, Dieter* Didaktik alttestamentlicher Prophetie im Licht der neueren Prophetenforschung—Versuch einiger Grundbestimmungen. Alttestamentliche Fachdidaktik. 1996, ⇒535. 107-126.

3251 *Ben Zvi, Ehud* Studying prophetic texts against their original backgrounds: pre-ordained scripts and alternative horizons of research. FTUCKER G., JSOT.S 229: 1996, 125-135.

3252 *Bird, Phyllis* Poor man or poor woman: gendering the poor in prophetic texts. MVAN DIJK-HEMMES F., 1996, ⇒99. 37-51.

3253 *Bony, Paul* Prophètes et dissentiment. LV(L) 45/4 (1996) 7-25.

3254 *Bovati, Pietro* La parola come atto profetico. RCI 77/1 (1996) 33-51.

3255 **Brauer, Bernd** Das Bild der Unheilsprophetie Israels in der frühen soziologisch orientierten Forschung. Diss. Mü 1996-97 DMüller, H.-P. [ThLZ 122,764].

3256 **Bravo, Arturo** Y dios perdio paciencia: estudios sobre crítica profética al culto. Diss. Tü 1995 DGross, W., 249 pp. [RTL 29,576].

3257 **Brensinger, Terry L.** Simile and prophetic language in the Old Testament. Mellen 43: Lewiston, NY 1996, Mellen vi; 203 pp. $90. 0-7734-2413-X [TD 44,158].

3258 **Bryan, Timothy** Prophets. ᴱ*Jacobs, Victor*, Bible people: Nv 1996, Abingdon 80 pp. 0-687-05528-8.

3259 *Burr, David* Oʟɪ ᴠɪ on prophecy. Sum. 391. CrSt 17 (1996) 369-391.

3260 ᴱ**Cagni, Luigi** Le profezie di Mari. TVOA 2/2: 1995, ⇒11/1,2096. ᴿBib. 77 (1996) 451-453 (*Conroy, Charles*).

3261 *Cazelles, Henri* Bible et politique. Études. 1996 <1971>, ⇒120. 49-73.

3262 *Childs, Brevard S.* Retrospective reading of the Old Testament prophets. ZAW 108 (1996) 362-377.

3263 **Clements, Ronald E.** Old Testament prophecy: from oracles to canon. LVL 1996, Westminster x; 278 pp. $29. 0-664-22082-7.

3264 **Collins, Terence** The mantle of Elijah. BiSe 20: 1993, ⇒9,3466... 11/1,2105. ᴿBiOr 53 (1996) 764-766 (*Becking, Bob*).

3265 **Cook, Albert Spaulding** The burden of prophecy: poetic utterance in the prophets of the Old Testament. Carbondale 1996, Southern Illinois University Press ix; 163 pp. 0-8093-2083-5.

3266 **Dassmann, Ernst** Frühchristliche Prophetenexegese. Westfälische Akademie der Wissenschaften; Geisteswissenschaften, G. 339: Opladen 1996, Westdeutscher 49 pp.
ᴱ**Davies, P.R.** The prophets ⇒174.

3267 *Davies, Philip R.* The audiences of prophetic scrolls: some suggestions. ᶠTᴜᴄᴋᴇ ʀ G., JSOT.S 229: 1996, 48-62.

3268 ᴱ**Davies, Philip R.; Clines, David J.A.** Among the prophets. 1993, ⇒9,265. ᴿBiOr 53 (1996) 496-497 (*Corrie, S.J.*).

3269 *Deist, Ferdinand* Prophetic discourse: dialogue, disaster or opportunity. Scriptura 57 (1996) 179-192 [OTA 19,463].

3270 **DeVries, Simon J.** From old revelation to new. 1995, ⇒11/1,2109. ᴿPacifica 9 (1996) 210-212 (*Jobb, Joseph*); ETR 71 (1996) 434-435 (*Macchi, Jean-Daniel*); JThS 47 (1996) 577-580 (*Mason, Rex*); Bib. 77 (1996) 434-438 (*Beuken, Willem A.M.*); CBQ 58 (1996) 511-512 (*Redditt, Paul L.*).

3271 **Eynikel, Erik; Van Wieringen, Archibald** Toez zond de Heer een profeet naar Israël: het voor-exilische profetisme van het Oude Testament. Baarn 1996 Gooi en Sticht 131 pp. ƒ29.50; FB590. 90-304-0844-8 [Streven 64,375].

3272 *Ghisalberti, Alessandro* Il lessico della profezia in s. Tᴏᴍᴍᴀsᴏ d'Aquino. Sum. 368. CrSt 17 (1996) 349-368.

3273 *Gitay, Yehoshua* The realm of prophetic rhetoric. Rhetoric. JSNT.S 131: 1996, ⇒268. 218-229.

3274 *Gottwald, Norman K.* Ideology and ideologies in Israelite prophecy. ᶠTᴜᴄᴋᴇ ʀ G., JSOT.S 229: 1996, ⇒95. 136-149.

3275 **Heaton, E.W.** A short introduction to the Old Testament prophets. Oxf 1996, Oneworld xi; 202 pp. $14. 1-85168-114-0.

3276 *Heschel, Abraham J.* What manner of man is the prophet?. Parabola 21/1 (1996) <1962> 6-9.

3277 *Johnston, Ann* Prophetic leadership in Israel. BiTod 34 (1996) 83-88.

3278 **Kaiser, Otto** Die prophetischen Werke 2: Grundriß der Einleitung in die kanonischen und deuterokanonischen Schriften des Alten

Testaments. Gü 1994, Gü'er 198 pp. DM38. ᴿJBL 115 (1996) 125-127 (*Strong, John T.*).

3279 *Klopfenstein, Martin A.* Das Gesetz bei den Propheten. Leben aus dem Wort. BEAT 40: 1996, ⇒132. 41-57.

3280 **Koch, Klaus** Die Profeten: Assyrische Zeit. UB 280: ³1995, ⇒11/1,2127. ᴿThPh 71 (1996) 578-579 (*Sebott, R.*).

3281 **Koenen, Klaus** Heil den Gerechten. BZAW 229: 1994, ⇒10,3361; 11/1,2128. ᴿZKTh 118 (1996) 101-102 (*Hubmann, Franz David*).

3282 **Laato, Antti J.** History and ideology in the Old Testament prophetic literature: a semiotic approach to the reconstruction of the proclamation of the historical prophets. CB.OT 41: Stockholm 1996, Almqvist & Wiksell x; 435 pp. SEK266. 91-22-01701-1 [OTA 19,541].

3283 *Laras, Giuseppe* La dottrina di MAIMONIDE sulla profezia. Sum. 347. CrSt 17 (1996) 335-347.

3284 **Law, G.V.C.** The hermeneutics of mythology in biblical prophecy. Diss. Oxf 1996 [RTL 29,578].

3285 **Lehnart, Bernhard** Prophet und König im Nordreich Israel: Studien zur sogenannten vorklassischen Prophetie im Nordreich Israel anhand der Samuel-, Elija- und Elischaüberlieferung. Diss. St. Georgen 1996/97 ᴰ*Lohfink, Norbert*.

3286 *Lemaire, André* Les textes prophétiques de Mari dans leurs relations avec l'Ouest. Amurru 1. 1996, ⇒306. 427-438.

3287 **Loza Vera, José** Los profetas de la antigua alianza: carateristicas y mensaje: ¿Que es un profeta?: los profetas del siglo VIII a.C.. Material Académico UPM 16: Tlalpan México D.F. 1996, Universidad Pontificia de México 352 pp. [RB 104,315].

3288 *Mackiewicz, Marie-Claude* Les prophètes devant la guerre. DosB 62 (1996) 11-12.

3289 **Marcus, David** From Balaam to Jonah. BJSt 30: 1995, ⇒11/1,2134. ᴿCBQ 58 (1996) 321-322 (*Person, Raymond F.*).

3290 *Melugin, Roy F.* Prophetic books and the problem of historical reconstruction. ᶠTUCKER G., JSOT.S 229: 1996, ⇒95. 63-78.

3291 **Mills, Watson Early; Wilson, Richard Francis** The prophets. Mercer Commentary on the Bible 4: Macon, GA 1996, Mercer University Press xxii; 359 pp. 0-86554-509-X.

3292 *Nissinen, Martti* Falsche Prophetie in neuassyrischer und deuteronomistischer Darstellung. Das Deuteronomium und seine Querbeziehungen. 1996, ⇒209. 172-195.

3293 *Overholt, Thomas W.* Prophecy: the problem of cross-cultural comparison. Community. 1996 <1982>, ⇒172. 423-447.

3294 **Peckham, Brian** History and prophecy. 1993, ⇒9,3483; 11/1,2143. ᴿAJSR 21 (1996) 132-134 (*Ben Zvi, Ehud*).

3295 **Potestà, Gian Luca** Progresso della conoscenza teologica e critica del profetismo in GIOACCHINO da Fiore. Sum. 334. CrSt 17 (1996) 305-334.

3296 **Prévost, Jean-Pierre** Pour lire les prophètes. 1995, ⇒11/1,2146. ᴿEeV 106 (1996) 558-559 (*Walter, Louis*);

3297 How to read the prophets. ᵀ*Bowden, John*, L 1996, SCM iv; 140 pp. £10. 0-334-02592-3.

3298 *Rad, Gerhard von* Los caminos de Dios en la historia universal, según el testimonio de los profetas. La acción de Dios. 1996, ⇒144. 196-211.

3299 *Reventlow, Henning Graf* Participial formulations: lawsuit, not wisdom: a study in prophetic language. ^FHARAN M., 1996, ⇒35. 375-382.

3300 *Robinson, Gnana* The new economic order in the light of the message of the pre-exilic prophets. BiBh 22 (1996) 238-254.

3301 **Rofé, Alexander** Introduzione alla letteratura profetica. StBi 111: 1995, ⇒11/1,2151. ^RPaVi 41/3 (1996) 63-64 *(Rolla, Armando)*; Asp. 43 (1996) 420-422 *(Scippa, V.)*.

3302 *Schmidt, Johann Michael* Prophetie. Altes Testament. 1996, ⇒169. 141-178.

3303 *Secondin, Bruno* "Ha parlato per mezzo dei profeti". Horeb 5/3 (1996) 18-22.

3304 **Sicre Diaz, José Luís** Profetismo em Israel. ^T*Baraúna, João Luís*, Petrópolis 1996, Vozes 540 pp. 85-326-1588-0;

3305 Profetismo. 1995, ⇒11/1,2157. ^RAsp. 43 (1996) 563-564 *(Di Palma, G.)*.

3306 **Smith, Gary V.** The prophets as preachers. 1994, ⇒10,3368. ^RAUSS 34/1 (1996) 143-145 *(Pröbstle, Martin)*.

3307 *Sommer, Benjamin D.* Did prophecy cease?: evaluating a reevaluation. JBL 115 (1996) 31-47.

3308 **Spreafico, Ambrogio** I profeti. LPastB 27: 1993, ⇒9,3495... 11/1,2158. ^RRivBib 44 (1996) 229-230 *(Scippa, Vincenzo)*.

3309 **Steck, Odil Hannes** Die Prophetenbücher und ihr theologisches Zeugnis: Wege der Nachfrage und Fährten zur Antwort. Tü 1996, Mohr xiv; 226 pp. DM58. 3-16-146619-5.

3310 **Vogels, W.** I profeti. 1994, ⇒10,3374. ^RAsp. 43/1 (1996) 118 *(Scippa, V.)*.

   ^E**Watts, J.** Forming prophetic literature ⇒105.

3311 *Westermann, Claus* Sprüche in den Prophetenbüchern. Das mündliche Wort. 1996, ⇒157. 133-139.

3312 **Whitelam, Keith W.** Prophetic conflict in Israelite history: taking sides with William G. DEVER. JSOT 72 (1996) 25-44.

3313 **Wilson, Robert R.** Prophecy and ecstasy: a reexamination. Community. 1996 <1979>, ⇒172. 404-422.

3314 **Witaszek, Gabriel** Moc Slowa prorockiego: przewodnik po literaturze prorockiej Starego Testamentu. Jak Rozumiec Pismo Swiete 7: Lublin 1996, Katolickiego Uniwersytetu 330 pp. 83-228-0528-40. P.

3315 **Zucker, David J.** Israel's prophets. 1994, ⇒10,3376; 11/1,2173. ^RNew Theology Review 9/1 (1996) 103-104 *(Perelmuter, Hayim)*.

E8.2 **Proto-Isaias,** *textus, commentarii*

3316 *Carr, David M.* Reading Isaiah from beginning (Isaiah 1) to end (Isaiah 65-66): multiple modern possibilities. New visions of Isaiah. JSOT.S 214: 1996, ⇒3331. 188-218.

3317 *Clements, Ronald E.* A light to the nations: a central theme of the book of Isaiah. Forming prophetic literature. JSOT.S 235: ^FWATTS J., 1996, ⇒105. 57-69.

3318 *Coggins, Richard J.* New ways with old texts: how does one write a commentary on Isaiah?. ET 107 (1996) 362-367.

3319 Conrad, Edgar W. Prophet, redactor and audience: reforming the notion of Isaiah's formation. New visions of Isaiah. JSOT.S 214: 1996, ⇒3331. 306-326.

3320 TEDanieli, Maria Ignazia ORIGENES: omelie su Isaia. CTePa 132: R 1996, Città Nuova 186 pp. 88-311-3132-X.

3321 TEGoshen-Gottstein, Moshe R. Judah IBN BALcAM's commentary on Isaiah. 1992, ⇒8,3648; 10,3379. RJQR 86 (1996) 468-476 (Maman, Aharon); VT 46 (1996) 408-409 (Polliack, Meira). H.

3322 EGryson, Roger Esaias 1-39; 40,1-54,17. Die Reste der altlateinischen Bibel nach Petrus Sabatier 12: I, II Fasc. 1-7. FrB 1987-1996, Herder;

3323 Commentaires de JEROME sur le prophète Isaïe I-IV. AGLB 23: 1993, ⇒9,3505... 11/1,2178. RAug. 36/1 (1996) 295-296 (Studer, Basil); Latomus 55 (1996) 418-420 (Duval, Y.-M.).

3324 Gummelt, Volker Lex et evangelium... J. BUGENHAGEN. 1994, ⇒10,3382. RChH 65 (1996) 481-482 (Lehmann, Helmut T.).

3325 Holman, Jan De kernboodschap van Jesaja: omvang en betekenis van de inclusie van Jes. 1-2, 4 met 65-66. TTh 36 (1996) 3-17.

3326 Kilian, Rudolf Jesaja II: 13-39. NEB 32: 1994, ⇒10,3385. RBiOr 53 (1996) 769-771 (Höffken, Peter).

3327 Lohfink, Norbert; Zenger, Erich Der Gott Israels. SBS 154: 1994, ⇒10,3402. RThQ 176/1 (1996) 80-81 (Groß, Walter); ThLZ 121 (1996) 821-824 (Oeming, Manfred); CBQ 58 (1996) 712-713 (Limburg, James).

3328 McMichael, Steven J. Did Isaiah fortell Jewish blindness and suffering for not accepting Jesus of Nazareth as messiah?: a medieval perspective. BTB 26 (1996) 144-151.

3329 Marconcini, Benito El libro de Isaías (1-39). 1995, ⇒11/1,2185. RPerTeol 28 (1996) 271 (Lima, Marco Antônio Morais); Iter 7/2 (1996) 149-150 (Wyssenbach, Jean Pierre).

3330 Melugin, Roy F. Reading the book of Isaiah as christian scripture. SBL.SP 35: 1996, ⇒274. 188-203.

3331 EMelugin, Roy F.; Sweeney, Marvin Alan New visions of Isaiah. JSOT.S 214: Shf 1996, Academic 344 pp. £39; $58.50. 1-85075-584-1.

3332 Motyer, J. Alec The prophecy of Isaiah. 1993, ⇒9,3512... 11/1,2188. BS 153 (1996) 123-124 (Chisholm, Robert B.); ScotBEv 14/1 (1996) 76-78 (Middleton, Jeremy R.H.).

3333 Oswalt, John N. The kerygmatic structure of the book of Isaiah. FYOUNG D., 1996, ⇒107. 143-157.

3334 Rendtorff, Rolf The book of Isaiah: a complex unity: synchronic and diachronic reading. New visions of Isaiah. JSOT.S 214: 1996, ⇒3331. 32-49.

3335 Ruppert, Lothar Crítica a los dioses en el libro de Isaías. RevBib 58 (1996) 129-159;

3336 Die Kritik an den Göttern im Jesajabuch. BN 82 (1996) 76-96.

3337 Sawyer, John F.A. The fifth gospel: Isaiah in the history of christianity. C 1996, CUP xvii; 281 pp. £35/$50; £13/$18. 0-521-44007-6/56596-0. RET 107 (1995-96) 353-355 (Rodd, C.S.).

3338 Seitz, Christopher R. Isaiah 1-39. 1993, ⇒9,3518... 11/1,2189. RBS 153 (1996) 248-249 (Chisholm, Robert B.); OLZ 91 (1996) 309-311 (Waschke, E.-J.).

3339 Sheppard, Gerald T. Isaiah as scroll or codex within Jewish and Christian scripture. SBL.SP 35: 1996, ⇒274. 204-224.

3340 *Sheppard, Gerald T.* The 'scope' of Isaiah as a book of Jewish and Christian scriptures. New visions of Isaiah. JSOT.S 214: 1996, ⇒3331. 257-281.
3341 **Simian-Yofre, Horacio** Testi isaiani dell'Avvento: esegesi e liturgia. CSB 29: Bo 1996, Dehoniane 255 pp. L35.000. 88-10-40731-8.
3342 *Sommer, Benjamin D.* Allusions and illusions: the unity of the book of Isaiah in light of Deutero-Isaiah's use of prophetic tradition. New visions of Isaiah. JSOT.S 214: 1996, ⇒3331. 156-186;
3343 The scroll of Isaiah as Jewish scripture, or, why Jews don't read books. SBL.SP 35: 1996, ⇒274. 225-242.
3344 *Sweeney, Marvin A.* The book of Isaiah as prophetic torah. New visions of Isaiah. JSOT.S 214: 1996, ⇒3331. 50-67;
3345 Reevaluating Isaiah 1-39 in recent critical research. CurResB 4 (1996) 79-113.
3346 **Sweeney, Marvin Alan** Isaiah 1-39: with an introduction to prophetic literature. FOTL 16: GR 1996, Eerdmans xix; 547 pp. $45; £33. 0-8028-4100-7.
3347 *Tate, Marvin E.* The book of Isaiah in recent study. ᶠWATTS J., JSOT.S 235: 1996, ⇒105. 22-56.
3348 *Trakatellis, Dimitrios* THEODORET's commentary on Isaiah: a synthesis of exegetical traditions. Die Väter legen aus. 1996, ⇒153. 95-145. G.
3349 **Webb, Barry G.** The message of Isaiah: on eagles' wings. The Bible Speaks Today: Leicester 1996, Inter-Varsity 252 pp. 0-85111-167-X.
3350 **Williamson, H.G.M.** The book called Isaiah: Deutero-Isaiah's role. 1994, ⇒10,3397; 11/1,2261. ᴿJThS 47 (1996) 573-575 (*Clements, R.E.*); HebStud 37 (1996) 171-175 (*Laato, Anti*); JR 76 (1996) 99-100 (*Sommer, Benjamin D.*).

E8.3 Proto-**Isaias 1-39,** themata, versiculi

3351 *Bailey, Kenneth E.* "Inverted parallelism" and "encased parables" in Isaiah and their significance for OT and NT translation and interpretation. Literary structure. 1996, ⇒200. 14-30.
3352 **Darr, Katheryn Pfisterer** Isaiah's vision. 1994, ⇒10,3400; 11/1,2176. ᴿAThR 78/1 (1996) 158-159 (*Bauer, Angela*); CBQ 58 (1996) 307-308 (*Polan, Gregory J.*); Interp. 50 (1996) 423-424 (*Everson, A. Joseph*); HebStud 37 (1996) 168-171 (*Sweeney, Marvin A.*); JSSt 41 (1996) 324-325 (*Clements, Ronald E.*).
3353 **Fischer, Irmtraud** Tora... Konzept des Jesajabuches. SBS 164: 1995, ⇒11/1,2200. ᴿTLS 121/12 (1996) 1129-1130 (*Kilian, Rudolf*).
3354 *Fischer, Irmtraud* Die Bedeutung der Tora Israels für die Völker nach dem Jesajabuch. Die Tora als Kanon. 1996, ⇒1308. 139-167.
3355 **Foulkes, Pamela A.** God in Isaiah. Homebush, NSW 1996, St Paul's 91 pp. AUS$15 [ACR 74,376].
3356 **Pfaff, Heide-Marie** Die Entwicklung des Restgedankens in Jesaja 1-39. Diss. FrB 1995 ᴰ*Ruppert, L.*, EHS.T 561: Fra 1996, Lang 271 pp. DM79. 3-631-49913-2.
3357 **Veen, Wilken** Hizkia. Verklaring van een Bijbelgedeelte: Kampen 1996, Kok 88 pp. f22.50. 90-242-7847-3 [KeTh 48/2,160].

3358 *Melugin, Roy F.* Figurative speech and the reading of Isaiah 1 as scripture. New visions of Isaiah. JSOT.S 214: 1996, ⇒3331. 282-305.

3359 *Blum, Erhard* Jesajas prophetisches Testament: Beobachtungen zu Jes 1-11, I. ZAW 108 (1996) 547-568.

3360 *Polan, Gregory J.* The prophetic voice: linking liturgy to life. BiTod 34 (1996) 276-281 [Isa 1,10-20].

3361 *Fischer, Irmtraud* Schwerter oder Pflugscharen?: Versuch einer kanonischen Lektüre von Jesaja 2, Joël 4 und Micha 4. BiLi 69 (1996) 208-216.

3362 **Bartelt, Andrew H.** The book around Immanuel: style and structure in Isaiah 2-12. Biblical and Judaic Studies from the Univ. of California, San Diego 4: WL 1996, Eisenbrauns xi; 287 pp. $32.50. 1-57506-006-X.

3363 *Virgili, Rosanna* Una vigna eletta e negletta: lettura di Is 5,1-7. Firmana 12-13 (1996) 61-75.

3364 *Lee, Ki-Rak* The announcement of judgement concerning Judah and Israel. Catholic Theology and Thought 15 (1996) 148-180 [Isa 5,1-30] [ThIK 18/1,50]. **K.**

3365 *Olivier, J.P.J.* Rendering יריד as benevolent patron in Isaiah 5:1. JNSL 22/2 (1996) 59-65.

3366 *Toloni, Giancarlo* ἀγαπάω come rilettura dei LXX di šᶜăšûᶜîm (Is 5,7) e šaᶜaᶜ (Sal 94[93],19). Sum. 156. RivBib 44 (1996) 129-156.

3367 *Bauer, Dieter* Jesaja und der "Rinderwahnsinn": eine Glosse zum Thema "Inspiration" in der Bibel. BiKi 51 (1996) 182-183 [Isa 5,18].

3368 *Korpel, Marjo C.A.* Structural analysis as a tool for redaction criticism: the example of Isaiah 5 and 10.1-6. JSOT 69 (1996) 53-71.

3369 *Jeanlin, Françoise* Un exemple d'exégèse spirituelle: ORIGENE à propos d'Esaïe 6,1-13. UnChr 124 (1996) 16-18.

3370 **Waters, Kenneth L.** I saw the Lord: a pilgrimage through Isaiah 6. Nv 1996, Upper Room 112 pp. 0-8358-0784-3 [NThAR 1997,193].

3371 **Werlitz, Jürgen** Studien...Jesaja 7,1-17 und 29,1-8. BZAW 204: 1992, ⇒8,3691... 11/1,2221. ᴿBZ 40 (1996) 111-112 (*Willmes, Bernd*).

3372 *Werlitz, Jürgen* Noch einmal Immanuel—gleich zweimal!. BZ 40 (1996) 254-263 [Isa 7,1-17; Mic 5,2].

3373 *Dearman, J. Andrew* The son of Tabeel (Isaiah 7.6). ᶠTUCKER G., JSOT.S 229: 1996, ⇒95. 33-47.

3374 *Otasso, Giovanni* Il segno dell'Emmanuele nella tradizione dell'Antico Testamento. Sum. 187. Theotokos 4/1 (1996) 151-188 [Isa 7,14].

3375 **Lepore, Luciano** Dal re Giosia al messia: problemi letterari, redazionali e teologici di Isaia 8,23b; 9,1-6. Diss. excerpt Pont. Univ. Urbaniana ᴰ*Spreafico, Ambrogio*, R 1996, 111 pp.

3376 *Gosse, Bernard* Isaiah 8.23b and the three great parts of the book of Isaiah. JSOT 70 (1996) 57-62.

3377 *Brandscheidt, Renate* Ein großes Licht (Jes 9,1-6): Standortbestimmung zur Stärkung des Glaubens. TThZ 105 (1996) 21-38.

3378 *Sweeney, Marvin A.* Jesse's new shoot in Isaiah 11: a Josianic reading of the prophet Isaiah. ᶠSANDERS J., JSOT.S 225: 1996, ⇒77. 103-118.

3379 *Franke, Chris A.* Reversals of fortune in the ancient Near East: a study of the Babylon oracles in the book of Isaiah. New visions of Isaiah JSOT.S 214: 1996, ⇒3331. 104-123 [Isa 13-14; 47-48].

3380 **Zapff, Burkard M.** Schriftgelehrte Prophetie—Jes 13. fzb 74: 1995, ⇒11/1,2226. ᴿBiOr 53 (1996) 766-768 (*Höffken, Peter*).

3381 **Jones, Brian C.** Howling over Moab: irony and rhetoric in Isaiah 15-16. SBL.DS 157: Atlanta, GA 1996, Scholars xi; 292 pp. $30. 0-7885-0257-3.

3382 *Smothers, Thomas G.* Isaiah 15-16. ᶠWATTS J., JSOT.S 235: 1996, ⇒105. 70-84.

3383 *Schenker, Adrian* Universalismo y reconciliación de los pueblos (Is 19,16-25). ᵀ*Sala, Màrius*, SelT 35 (1996) 279-282 [<RivBib 43 (1995) 321-329].

3384 *Ellington, John* A swimming lesson (Isaiah 25.11). BiTr 47 (1996) 246-247.

3385 *Gryson, Roger* "Enfanter un esprit de salut": histoire du texte de Isaïe 26,17.18. RTL 27 (1996) 25-46.

3386 *Stansell, Gary* Isaiah 28-33: blest be the tie that binds (Isaiah together). New visions of Isaiah. JSOT.S 214: 1996, ⇒3331. 68-103.

3387 *Asen, Bernhard A.* The garlands of Ephraim: Isaiah 28.1-6 and the marzeah. JSOT 71 (1996) 73-87.

3388 *Wong, G.C.I.* Isaiah's opposition to Egypt in Isaiah xxxi 1-3. VT 46 (1996) 392-401.

3389 *Kruger, H.A.J.* 'Gods', for argument's sake: a few remarks on the literature and theological intention of Isaiah 36-37. OTEs 9 (1996) 52-67, 383-399.

3390 *Darr, Katheryn Pfisterer* No strength to deliver: a contextual analysis of Hezekiah's proverb in Isaiah 37.3b. New visions of Isaiah. JSOT.S 214: 1996, ⇒3331. 219-256 [Isa 36-37].

3391 *Seijas de los Ríos-Zarzosa* La aplicación de la sintaxis textual en el apéndice histórico de Isaías. Sum. res. 5. MEAH 42/2 (1993) 5-17 [Isa 36-39].

3392 *Williamson, H.G.M.* Hezekiah and the temple. ᶠHARAN M., 1996, ⇒35. 47-52 [Isa 36-39].

E8.4 **Deutero-Isaias 40-52:** *commentarii, themata, versiculi*

3393 **Cajot, Rodel M.** Salvation in Deutero-Isaiah. Diss. Pont. Univ. S. Thomae 1996 ᴰ*Agius, J.*, Romae 1996, xiii; 205 pp.

3394 *Hinlicky, Paul R.* Isaianic texts in Advent, Christmas and Epiphany. ProEc 5 (1996) 488-495.

3395 **Hudson, Matthew Howard** Creation theology in Isaiah 40-66: an expression of confidence in the sovereignty of God. Diss. Southwestern Bapt. Theol. Sem. 1996, 204 pp. [EThL 74,213*].

3396 *Leene, Hendrik* Auf der Suche nach einem redaktionskritischen Modell für Jesaja 40-55. ThLZ 121 (1996) 803-818.

3397 **Marconcini, Benito** Il libro di Isaia (40-66). Guide spirituali all'Antico Testamento: R 1996, Città Nuova 200 pp. L20.000. 88-311-3741-7. ᴿPaVi 41/3 (1996) 56-57 (*Carrucola, Maurilio*).

3398 *Rooker, Mark F.* Dating Isaiah 40-66: what does the linguistic evidence say?. WThJ 58 (1996) 303-312.

3399   *Seitz, Christopher R.* How is the prophet Isaiah present in the latter
       half of the book?: the logic of chapters 40-66 within the book of
       Isaiah. JBL 115 (1996) 219-240.
3400   *Smith, Morton* II Isaiah and the Persians. Studies in...method.
       1996 <1963>, ⇒150. 73-83.
3401   *Turner, E.A.* The foreign idols of Deutero-Isaiah. OTEs 9 (1996)
       111-128.
3402   **Van den Berg, M.R.** (Niet) ter wille van Israël: een uitleg van Je-
       saja 40-55. Zicht op de Bijbel 47: Amst 1996, Buijten & S. 160
       pp. 90-6064-918-4 [NThAR 1997,130].
3403   **Van Oorschot, Jürgen** Von Babel zum Zion. BZAW 206: 1993,
       ⇒9,3594; 10,3453. [R]ThRv 92 (1996) 138-139 *(Beuken, Willem
       A.M.)*; ZAW 108 (1996) 479-480 *(Wegner, A.-C.)*; OLZ 91 (1996)
       314-316 *(Kellenberger, Edgar)*; CBQ 58 (1996) 733-734 *(Melugin,
       Roy E.)*.
3404   *Van Wieringen, Archibald L.H.M.* Parallel clauses between Third
       and Second Isaiah: a new kind of computer-concordance. BN 82
       (1996) 21-26.
3405   **Williamson, H.G.M.** The book called Isaiah: Deutero-Isaiah's
       role. 1994, ⇒10,3397; 11/1,2261. [R]JThS 47 (1996) 573-575
       (Clements, R.E.); HebStud 37 (1996) 171-175 *(Laato, Anti)*; JR 76
       (1996) 99-100 *(Sommer, Benjamin D.)*.

3406   *Ska, Jean Louis* Spiritualità dell'Avento: lettura dal Deuteroisaia.
       Firmana 12-13 (1996) 305-323 [Isa 40,1-11; 54].
3407   *Małecki, Zdzisław* Struktura literacka prologu księgi Deuteroizajasza
       [De structura litteraria prologi Deutero-Isaiae (Is 40,1-11)]. RBL
       49 (1996) 14-18. **P.**
3408   *Holter, Knut* Zur Funktion der Städte Judas in Jesaja XL. VT 46
       (1996) 119-121 [Isa 40,9].
3409   **Farfán Navarro, Enrique** El desierto transformado. AnBib 130:
       1992, ⇒7,3192... 11/1,2267. [R]BZ 40 (1996) 307-308 *(Becker,
       Joachim)* [Isa 41,17-20].
3410   *Klopfenstein, Martin A.* Predigt über Jes 42,1-4: das Recht des
       Schwachen. Leben aus dem Wort. BEAT 40: 1996, ⇒132. 309-
       312.
3411   *Vieweger, Dieter; Böckler, Annette* "Ich gebe Ägypten als Lösegeld
       für dich": Mk 10,45 und die jüdische Tradition zu Jes 43,3b.4.
       ZAW 108 (1996) 594-607.
3412   *Małecki, Zdzisław* Krytyka pogańskich bóstw u Deuteroizajasza
       44,9-20 [Plastae idolorum confundentur apud Dt-Is 44,9-20]. RBL
       49 (1996) 149-154. **P.**
3413   **Franke, Chris** Isaiah 46, 47, and 48: a new literary-critical
       reading. 1994, ⇒10,3463. [R]JBL 115 (1996) 338-339 *(Polley, Max
       E.)*; CBQ 58 (1996) 311-313 *(Webster, Edwin C.)*.
3414   [E]**Gryson, Roger** Esaias. Fasc. 6. Collab. *Auwers, Jean Marie;
       Baise, Ignace,* Vetus Latina 12/2. FrB 1996, Herder. 3-451-00124-
       6 [Isa 46,13-50,3].
3415   *Biddle, Mark E.* Lady Zion's alter egos: Isaiah 47.1-15 and 57.6-
       13 as structural counterparts. New visions of Isaiah. JSOT.S 214:
       1996, ⇒3331. 124-139.
3416   *Goldingay, John* What happens to Ms Babylon in Isaiah 47, why,
       and who says so?. TynB 47 (1996) 215-243.

E8.5 *Isaiae 53ss, Carmina Servi YHWH:* **Servant Songs**

3417 *Abma, Richtsje* Terms of endearment: YHWH and Zion in Isaiah 54. ^FZuurmond R.: YHWH. DBAT.B: 1996, ⇒109. 97-104 [OTA 19,469].

3418 **Bastiaens, Jean Charles** Interpretaties van Jesaja 53. TFT-Studies 22: 1993, ⇒9,3607... 11/1,2280. ^RThLZ 121 (1996) 247-250 (*Noort, Ed*) [Luke 22,14-38; Acts 3,12-26; 4,23-31; 8,26-40].

3419 *Booy, G.M.* Jesaja 52:13-53:12: voorspelling of trooswoord [Isaiah 52:13-53:12: prediction or word of comfort?]. SeK 17 (1996) 1-14 [OTA 19,468].

3420 *Carra de Vaux Saint-Cyr, Bruno* La théologie de la rédemption (1100-1250). Collab. *Chardonnens, Denis*, CEv.S 97 (1996) 112-132.

3421 ^E**Carra de Vaux Saint-Cyr, Bruno; Defélix, Chantal; Guinot, Jean-Noël** Le serviteur souffrant (Isaïe 53). CEv.S 97. P 1996, Cerf 147 pp. FF60. 0222-9706.

3422 *Costen, James H.* Doing the right thing: Isaiah 53:1-12, Luke 23:13-25. JITC 24 (1996-97) 207-213 [ZID 23,406].

3423 *Cousin, Hugues* Le Serviteur souffrant dans le Nouveau Testament. CEv.S 97 (1996) 19-25.

3424 *Defélix, Chantal* Lectures juives. ⇒3421. 27-68.

3425 *Grelot, Pierre* Le Serviteur souffrant dans le Premier Testament: une lecture diachronique. CEv.S 97 (1996) 5-14.

3426 *Guinot, Jean-Noël* Lectures patristiques. ⇒3421. 69-111.

3427 *Haag, Ernst* Stellvertretung und Sühne nach Jesaja 53. TThZ 105 (1996) 1-20.

3428 *Hengel, Martin* Zur Wirkungsgeschichte von Jes 53 in vorchristlicher Zeit [Zech 13,7; 12,9-13,1];

3429 *Hermisson, Hans-Jürgen* Das vierte Gottesknechtslied im deuterojesajanischen Kontext;

3430 *Hofius, Otfried* Das vierte Gottesknechtslied in den Briefen des Neuen Testaments;

3431 *Janowski, Bernd* Er trug unsere Sünden: Jes 53 und die Dramatik der Stellvertretung. Der leidende Gottesknecht. FAT 14: 1996, ⇒3432. 49-91/1-25/107-127/27-48.

3432 ^E**Janowski, Bernd; Stuhlmacher, Peter** Der leidende Gottesknecht: Jesaja 53 und seine Wirkungsgeschichte mit einer Bibliographie zu Jes 53. FAT 14: Tü 1996, Mohr vi; 286 pp. DM228. 3-16-146499-0.

3433 *Korpel, Marjo C.A.* The female servant of the LORD in Isaiah 54. ^Mvan Dijk-Hemmes F., 1996, ⇒99. 153-167 [Isa 54,1-17].

3434 *Korpel, Marjo C.A.* Metaphors in Isaiah lv. VT 46 (1996) 43-55.

3435 **Lavilla Martín, M.A.** La imagen del Siervo en el pensamiento de san Francisco de Asís, según sus escritos. Diss. Antonianum. Valencia 1995, Asís 424 pp. [Comunidades 26,22s—Anxo Pena, Miguel].

3436 *Marconcini, Benito* Il servo giusto e sofferente (Is 52,13-53,12). Som. 59. PSV 34 (1996) 59-72.

3437 *Markschies, Christoph* Der Mensch Jesus Christus im Angesicht Gottes: zwei Modelle des Verständnisses von Jesaja 52,13-53,12 in der patristischen Literatur und deren Entwicklung. Der leidende Gottesknecht. FAT 14: 1996, ⇒3432. 197-249.

3438 *Nicholls, Bruce J.* The servant songs of Isaiah in dialogue with Muslims. ERT 20 (1996) 168-177 [OTA 19,468].
3439 **Remaud, Michel** Israël serviteur de Dieu. Préf. *Lovsky, Fadiey,* J 1996, CCEJ-Ratisbonne 167 pp. 965-398-014-9.
3440 *Ruppert, Lothar* "Mein Knecht, der gerechte, macht die Vielen gerecht, und ihre Verschuldungen—er trägt sie" (Jes 53,11): univèrsales Heil durch das stellvertretende Strafleiden des Gottesknechtes?. BZ 40 (1996) 1-17.
3441 *Schreiner, Stefan* Jes 53 in der Auslegung der Sepher Chizzuq Emunah von R. Isaak ben Avraham aus Troki. Der leidende Gottesknecht. FAT 14: 1996, ⇒3432. 159-195.
3442 *Sekine, Seizo* Identity and authorship in the Fourth Song of the Servant: a redactional attempt at the Second Isaianic theology of redemption, II. AJBI 22 (1996) 3-30.
3443 *Sion, Danièle* L'expérience spirituelle de Madame Guyon. ⇒3421. 133-137.
3444 *Sorg, Theo* Stellvertretung: Jesaja 52,13-53,12. Das Wort vom Kreuz. 1996, ⇒206. 93-101.
3445 *Stuhlmacher, Peter* Jes 53 in den Evangelien und in der Apostelgeschichte. Der leidende Gottesknecht. FAT 14: 1996, ⇒3432. 93-105.
3446 **Varo, Francisco** Los cantos del siervo. 1993, ⇒9,3619... 11/1,2289. RScrB 26 (1996) 87-88 (*Dines, Jennifer*); RCatT 21 (1996) 461-462 (*Ferrer i Costa, Joan*); MEAH 42/2 (1993) 233-234 (*Pérez Fernández, Miguel*).

E8.6 [Trito-]Isaias 56-66

3447 *Bedyche, Malgorzata* Jerozolima w przepowiadaniu Trito-Izajasza [Jerusalem in Trito-Isaia]. RBL 49 (1996) 170-177. **P.**
3448 *Kipper, João Balduíno* El mensaje social de los profetas postexílicos. TSuñol, Miguel, SelT 35 (1996) 289-298 [<RCB 15 (1991) 77-104].
3449 **Lau, Wolfgang** Schriftgelehrte prophetie in Jes 56-66. BZAW 225: 1994, ⇒10,3481; 11/1,2297. RCBQ 58 (1996) 319-321 (*Sweeney, Marvin A.*).
3450 **Schramm, Brooks** The opponents of Third Isaiah. JSOT.S 193: 1995, ⇒11/1,2298. RCBQ 58 (1996) 333-334 (*Strong, John T.*); JR 76 (1996) 614-615 (*Sommer, Benjamin D.*).
3451 **Smith, Paul A.** Rhetoric and redaction in Trito-Isaiah. VT.S 62: 1995, ⇒11/1,2299. RThLZ 121 (1996) 547-548 (*Wallis, Gerhard*); ETR 71 (1996) 588-589 (*Macchi, Jean-Daniel*).
3452 *Wells, Roy D. Jr* 'Isaiah' as an exponent of torah: Isaiah 56.1-8. New visions of Isaiah. JSOT.S 214: 1996, ⇒3331. 140-155.

E8.7 Jeremias

3453 **Fischer, Georg** El libro de Jeremías. TVillanueva Salas, Marciano, Guía espiritual del AT: Barc 1996, Herder 256 pp. 84-254-1927-1. REspiritu 45 (1996) 258-259 (*Forment, E.*).

3454 Il libro di Geremia: le Lamentazioni. Introd. *Ravasi, Gianfranco;* T*Moraldi, Luigi,* Classici della BUR: Mi 1996, Rizzoli 366 pp. Testo ebraico a fronte; note di Luigi Moraldi; Bibl. 88-17-17112-3.

3455 **McKane, William** Commentary on Jeremiah XXVI-LII. Jeremiah 2. ICC: E 1996, Clark cxxiii-clxxiv; 659-1396 pp. $70. 0-567-09732-3.

3456 *Perani, Mauro* Frammenti del commento perduto a Geremia ed Ezechiele di Abraham IBN EZRA o di un suo discepolo dalla "genizah" di Bologna. Henoch 18 (1996) 283-325.

3457 **Thompson, Henry O.** The book of Jeremiah: an annotated bibliography. ATLA.BS 41: Lanham, MD 1996, Scarecrow xxxii; 745 pp. $92. 0-81083178-3 [EThL 74,215*].

3458 *Bogaert, Pierre-Maurice* 'Vie et paroles de Jérémie selon Baruch': le texte court de Jérémie (LXX) comme œuvre biographique. FDUPONT J., La parola. 1996, ⇒21. 15-29.

3459 *Callaway, Mary Chilton* Exegesis as banquet: reading Jeremiah with the rabbis. FSANDERS J., JSOT.S 225: 1996, ⇒77. 219-230.

3460 *Carroll, R.P.* Jeremiah, intertextuality and Ideologiekritik. JNSL 22/1 (1996) 15-34;

3461 Surplus meaning and the conflict of interpretations: a dodecade of Jeremiah studies (1984-95). CurResB 4 (1996) 115-159.

3462 EGroß, **Walter** Jeremia und die 'deuteronomistische Bewegung'. BBB 98: 1995, ⇒11/1,86. RThLZ 121 (1996) 1133-1136 (*Thiel, Winfried*).

3463 **Habel, Norman C.** The God of Jeremiah. Australian Biblical Project 3: Homebush 1996, St Paul's 103 pp. AUS$14.

3464 **Jun-Hee, Cha** Micha und Jeremia. Athenäums Monografien, Theologie: BBB 107: Weinheim 1996; Beltz ix; 151 pp. 3-89547-107-0.

3465 *King, Philip J.* Jeremiah and idolatry. FAVIRAM J., ErIs 25: 1996, ⇒2. 31*-36*.

3466 **McConville, J. Gordon** Judgment and promise. 1993, ⇒9,3666... 11/1,2322. RJSSt 41 (1996) 325-328 (*Wilson, Ian*).

3467 *Mulzac, Kenneth* The remnant and the new covenant in the book of Jeremiah. AUSS 34 (1996) 239-248.

3468 *Quacquarelli, Antonio* Il genere omiletico in ORIGENE: le *Omelie su Geremia.* Retorica. QVetChr 24: 1996, ⇒259. 31-43.

3469 *Römer, Thomas* Y a-t-il une rédaction deutéronomiste dans le livre de Jérémie. Israël construit son histoire. 1996, ⇒199. 419-441 [OTA 19,470].

3470 **Seybold, Klaus** Der Prophet Jeremia. 1993, ⇒9,3670... 11/1,2329. RKeTh 47 (1996) 339-340 (*Van der Woude, A.S.*).

3471 *Shanks, Hershel* Fingerprint of Jeremiah's scribe. BArR 22/2 (1996) 36-38.

3472 *Steiner, Richard C.* The two sons of Neriah and the two editions of Jeremiah in the light of two atbash code-words for Babylon. VT 46 (1996) 74-84.

3473 **Stipp, Hermann-Josef** Das masoretische und alexandrinische Sondergut des Jeremiabuches. OBO 136: 1994, ⇒10, 3516; 11/1,2330. RCBQ 58 (1996) 728-729 (*Michael, Tony S.L.*).

3474 *Stipp, Hermann-Josef* Zedekiah in the book of Jeremiah: on the formation of a biblical character. CBQ 58 (1996) 627-648.

3475 *Virgulin, Stefano* Geremia: il giusto perseguitato. Som. 73. PSV 34 (1996) 73-84.
3476 *Wanke, Gunther* Weisheit im Jeremiabuch. Weisheit. 1996, ⇒3071. 87-106.

3477 *Ruprecht, Eberhard* Das Zepter Jahwes in den Berufungsvisionen von Jeremia und Amos. ZAW 108 (1996) 55-69 [Num 17,16-26; Jer 1,11-14; Amos 7,1-8; 8,1-2; 9,1-4].
3478 *Mello, Alberto* 'Terrore da ogni parte': paura degli uomini e timore di Dio in Geremia. PSV 33/1 (1996) 69-79 [Jer 1,14-15; 17; 20].
3479 *Diamond, Pete A.R.; O'Connor, Kathleen M.* Unfaithful passions: coding women coding men in Jeremiah 2-3 (4:2). Bibl.Interp. 4 (1996) 288-310.
3480 *Hardmeier, Christof* Geschichte und Erfahrung in Jer 2-6: zur theologischen Notwendigkeit einer geschichts- und erfahrungsbezogenen Exegese und ihrer methodischen Neuorientierung. EvTh 56 (1996) 3-29.
3481 *Bozak, Barbara A.* Heeding the received text: Jer 2,20a, a case in point. Bib. 77 (1996) 524-537.
3482 *Kruger, Paul A.* The psychology of shame and Jeremiah 2:36-37. JNSL 22/2 (1996) 79-88.
3483 **Biddle, Mark E.** Polyphony and symphony in prophetic literature: rereading Jeremiah 7-20. Studies in OT Interpretation 2: Macon, GA 1996, Mercer University Press x; 136 pp. $30. 0-86554-503-0 [OTA 19,543].
3484 *Kang, Sa-Moon* The authentic sermon of Jeremiah in Jeremiah 7:1-20. FHARAN M., ⇒35. 147-162.
3485 **Jost, Renate** Frauen, Männer und die Himmelskönigin. 1995, ⇒11/2,2351. RThLZ 121 (1996) 542-544 (*Balz-Cochois, H.*) [Jer 7,17-18; 44,15-25].
3486 *Vriezen, Karel J.H.* Cakes and figurines: related women's cultic offerings in ancient Israel?. MVAN DIJK-HEMMES F., 1996, 251-264 [Jer 7,17-19].
3487 *Noegel, Scott B.* atbash (אתב"ש) in Jeremiah and its literary significance, II. JBQ 24/3 (1996) 160-166 [Jer 20,10; 25,10-26.30.38; 34,14].
3488 *Costen, James H.* A new agenda for the nineties: Jeremiah 23:25-40. JITC 24 (1996-97) 167-173; 175-182 [ZID 23,406].
3489 *Gosse, Bernard* La terminologie de Jér 25,15-18 et l'histoire de la rédaction du recueil d'Oracles contre les Nations du livre de Jérémie. BN 85 (1996) 11-13.
3490 *Noegel, Scott B.* atbash (אתב"ש) in Jeremiah and its literary significance, I. JBQ 24/2 (1996) 82-89 [Jer 25,26; 51,1; 51,41].
3491 *Smelik, Klaas A.D.* Letters to the exiles: Jeremiah 29 in context. SJOT 10 (1996) 282-295.
3492 *Van der Wal, A.J.O.* Themes from Exodus in Jeremiah 30-31. Studies in...Exodus. BEThL 126: 1996, ⇒1794. 559-566.
3493 *McKane, William* The composition of Jeremiah 30-31. FHARAN M., 1996, ⇒35. 187-194.
3494 *Sweeney, Marvin A.* Jeremiah 30-31 and King Josiah's program of national restoration and religious reform. ZAW 108 (1996) 569-583.
3495 **Schmid, Konrad** Buchgestalten des Jeremiabuches: Untersuchungen zur Redaktions- und Rezeptionsgeschichte von Jer 30-33 im

Kontext des Buches. Diss. DSteck, O.H., WMANT 72: Neuk 1996, Neuk xiii; 446 pp. DM148. 3-7887-1608-8. RThQ 176 (1996) 358-359 (Groß, Walter).

3496 Van der Wal, A.J.O. "Opdat Jakob weer Gods dienaar kan zijn": opbouw en achtergrond van Jeremia 30:5-11. ACEBT 15 (1996) 77-93, 139-143.

3497 Marafioti, Domenico Sant'AGOSTINO e la nuova alleanza. Aloi. 26: 1995, ⇒11/1,2371. RAng. 73/1 (1996) 118-120 (Degórski, Bazyli); EstAg 31/1 (1996) 149 (Luis, P. de); RTL 27 (1996) 215-216 (Auwers, J.-M.); CDios 209 (1996) 502-503 (Gutiérrez, J.); RdT 37 (1996) 710-713 (Orazzo, Antonio).

3498 Lichtenberger, Hermann; Schreiner, Stefan Der neue Bund in jüdischer Überlieferung. ThQ 176 (1996) 272-290.

3499 Becking, Bob Text-internal and text-external chronology in Jeremiah 31:31-34. SEÅ 61 (1996) 33-51.

3500 Gosse, Bernard Jérémie 31,37 dans la rédaction du livre de Jérémie. BN 85 (1996) 14-16.

3501 Groß, Walter Der neue Bund in Jer 31 und die Suche nach übergreifenden Bundeskonzeptionen im Alten Testament. ThQ 176 (1996) 259-272.

3502 Brueggemann, Walter A 'characteristic' reflection on what comes next (Jeremiah 32.16-44). FTUCKER G., JSOT.S 229: 1996, ⇒95. 16-32.

3503 Migsch, Herbert Jeremias Ackerkauf: eine Untersuchung von Jeremia 32. ÖBS 15: Fra 1996, Lang 455 pp. $70. 3-631-49152-2 [OTA 19,544].

3504 Gamberoni, Johann '...Jonadab, unser Vater, hat uns geboten...' (Jer 35,6): die Rechabiter—am Rand und in der Mitte. FERNST J., 1996, ⇒23. 19-31 [OTA 19,472].

3505 Knights, Chris 'Standing before me for ever': Jeremiah 35:19. ET 108 (1996) 40-42;

3506 Who were the Rechabites?. ET 107 (1996) 137-140.

3507 Noegel, Scott B. atbash (ש"אתב) in Jeremiah: its literary significance, III. JBQ 24 (1996) 247-250 [Jer 36,27; 48,2].

3508 Hoffman, Yair Aetiology, redaction and historicity in Jeremiah xxxvi. VT 46 (1996) 179-189.

3509 Carroll, Robert P. Manuscripts don't burn—inscribing the prophetic tradition: reflections on Jeremiah 36. IOSOT 1992. BEAT 28: 1996, ⇒160. 31-42.

3510 Gershenson, Daniel E. A Greek myth in Jeremiah. ZAW 108 (1996) 192-200 [Jer 46,20].

3511 Huwyler, Beat Jeremia und die Völker: politische Prophetie in der Zeit der babylonischen Bedrohung (7./6. Jh. v. Chr.). ThZ 52 (1996) 193-205 [Jer 46].

E8.8 Lamentationes, Threni; Baruch

3512 EBartoli, Marco Pietro di Giovanni OLIVI: la caduta di Gerusalemme...Lamentazioni. Nuovi Studi Storici 12: 1991, ⇒8,3827; 11/1,2384. RWiWei 59 (1996) 334-337 (Schlageter, Johannes).

3513 Freedman, David N.; Fange, Erich A. von Metrics in Hebrew poetry: the book of Lamentations revisited. CTQ 60 (1996) 279-305.

3514 *Gous, Ignatius G.P.* Mind over matter: Lamentations 4 in the light of the cognitive sciences. SJOT 10 (1996) 69-87.
3515 *Heikens, Henk* The alphabet in Lamentations: a 'dagmaat' contribution. ^FVAN UCHELEN N., 1996, ⇒100. 189-196 [OTA 19,472].
3516 **Hunter, Johannes Henderson (Jannie)** Faces of a lamenting city: the development and coherence of the book of Lamentations. BEÀT 39: Fra 1996, Lang 155 pp. $36. 3-631-48397-X.
3517 **Koster, Albert** Ach Hoe: de Klaagliederen, gedichten naar het Hebreeuws. Eindhoven 1995, Aproges 67 pp. *f*21.50. 90-800961-6-4 [Bijdr. 59,453—Van Wieringen, A.L.H.M.].
      Il libro di Geremia: le Lamentazioni ⇒3454.
3518 **Mayoral, Juan Antonio** Sufrimiento y esperanza: la crisis exílica en Lamentaciones. ISJTM 29: Estella 1994, Verbo Divino 381 pp. 84-7151-990-9. ^REstB 54 (1996) 275-276 (*Barrado, P.*).
3519 **Miller, Charles William** Poetry and personae: the use and functions of the changing speaking voices in the book of Lamentations. Diss. Iliff 1996, 245 pp. DAI-A 57/09, p. 3983; AAC 9623887.
3520 **Neusner, Jacob** Israel after calamity. 1995, ⇒11/1,2390. ^RCTJ 31 (1996) 589-590 (*VanderKam, James C.*).
3521 **Provan, Iain W.** Lamentations. NCent: 1991, ⇒7,3290... 9,3724. ^RThR 61 (1996) 349-350 (*Seybold, Klaus*).
3522 **Shute, Daniel** PETER Martyr and the Rabbinic Bible in the interpretation of Lamentations. Diss. McGill 1996, ^D*McLelland, J.C.* [EThL 74,180*].
3523 *Wagner, S.* Güte, Gnade und Garaus. JK 57 (1996) 2-4 [Lam 3,22].
3524 **Westermann, Claus** Lamentations. 1995, ⇒11/1,2394. ^RBSOAS 59 (1996) 339-340 (*Becking, Bob*); Pacifica 9 (1996) 208-210 (*Moss, Alan*); Kerux 11/2 (1996) 32-37 (*Dennison, James T.*).
3525 *Wright, J. Edward* Baruch, the ideal sage. ^FYOUNG D., 1996, ⇒107. 193-210.
3526 **Yuen, Shing-Chung Royan** Qing-hen in the book of Lamentations: a rhetorical analysis of Lamentations from Chinese perspectives. Diss. Graduate Theol. Union 1996, 258 pp. DAI-A 57/09, p.3985; AAC 9631645.

3527 *Herzer, Jens* Alttestamentliche Traditionen in den Paralipomena Jeremiae als Beispiel für den Umgang frühjüdischer Schriftsteller mit 'Heiliger Schrift'. Schriftauslegung. WUNT 73: 1994, ⇒257. 114-132 [IAJS 42,19].
3528 *Philonenko, Marc* Simples observations sur les Paralipomènes de Jérémie. RHPhR 76 (1996) 157-177.
3529 *Raurell, F.* "Doxa" and nationalistic particularism. Laur. 37 (1996) 121-147 [Bar 4-5].

3530 *Roddy, Nicolae* 'Two parts: weeks of seven weeks': the end of the age as terminus ad quem for 2 Baruch. JSPE 14 (1996) 3-14.

E8.9 **Ezekiel:** *textus, commentarii; themata, versiculi*

3531 **Allen, Leslie C.** Ezekiel 1-19. WBC 28: Dallas 1994, Word xxxvi; 306 pp. $29. 0-8499-0830-2. ^RJThS 47 (1996) 180-181 (*Joyce, Paul M.*); CritRR 9 (1996) 143-144 (*Block, Daniel I.*).

3532 **Biggs, Charles R.** The book of Ezekiel. Epworth Commentaries: L 1996, Epworth xxi; 147 pp. 0-7162-0505-X.
3533 **Clements, Ronald Ernest** Ezekiel. Westminster Bible Companion: LVL 1996, Westminster x; 211 pp. $17. 0-664-25272-9.
3534 **Craven, T.** I libri di Ezechiele e Daniele. BT 16: Brescia 1996, Queriniana 204 pp. L24.000 [RdT 37,428].
3535 **Feist, Udo** Ezechiel. BWANT 138: 1995, ⇒11/1,2407. RAnton. 71 (1996) 566-567 (*Nobile, Marco*); ThLZ 121 (1996) 820-821 (*Krüger, Thomas*).
3536 T**Izumi, Yasuhiro** The book of Ezechiel. Tokyo 1996, Studium Biblicum Franciscanum vi; 351 pp. The Holy Bible: annotated critical translation from the original languages by the Studium Biblicum Franciscanum; ¥5.000. 4-8056-1007-7 [RB 103,636].
3537 **Lind, Millard C.** Ezekiel. Believers Church Bible Commentary: Scotdale, Pa. 1996 Herald 416 pp. $20. 0-8361-9016-5.
3538 **McKeating, Henry** Ezekiel. 1993, ⇒9,3752; 10,3578. RVJTR 60 (1996) 639-640 (*Meagher, P.M.*).
    Perani, Mauro Frammenti del commento perduto a Ger. ed Ezech. ⇒3456.
3539 **Pohlmann, Karl-Friedrich** Das Buch des Propheten Hesekiel (Ezechiel) Kap. 1-19. ATD 22/1: Gö 1996, Vandenhoeck & R. 297 pp. DM54. 3-525-51210-4.

3540 *Boadt, Lawrence* Mythological themes and the unity of Ezekiel. Literary structure. 1996, ⇒200. 211-231.
3541 *Chevillard, Jean* La gloire de Dieu, du temple aux exilés. DosB 63 (1996) 12-14.
3542 *Dubreucq, Marc* Ézéchiel: un prêtre devient prophète. DosB 63 (1996) 3-5.
3543 **Duguid, Iain M.** Ezekiel and the leaders of Israel. VT.S 56: 1994, ⇒10,3576; 11/1,2406. RJBL 115 (1996) 127-128 (*Tuell, Steven S.*).
3544 **Ehrlich, Carl Stephan** "Anti-Judäismus" in der Hebräischen Bibel: der Fall: Ezechiel. VT 46 (1996) 169-178.
3545 **Halperin, David** Seeking Ezekiel. 1993, ⇒9,3735... 11/1,2403. RJThS 47 (1996) 182-188 (*Morray-Jones, C.R.A.*).
3546 *Lust, J.* Jhwh 'dnj in Ezekiel and its counterpart in the Old Greek;
3547 The Septuagint of Ezekiel according to Papyrus 967 and the pentateuch. EThL 72 (1996) 138-145/131-137.
3548 **McBride, Gregory Joseph** The nature of God's judgment against Israel in Ezekiel 1-24. Diss. New Orleans Bapt. Theol. Sem., DMosley, H.R., 1995, 160 pp. [EThL 74,218*].
3549 ERecchia, **Vincenzo** San GREGORIO Magno: omelie su Ezechiele: libro secondo. Roma 1993, Città Nuova 333 pp. L50.000. RCivCatt 147 I (1996) 525-526 (*Cremascoli, G.*).
3550 *Recchia, Vincenzo* I moduli espressivi dell'esperienza contemplativa nelle *Omelie su Ezechiele* di GREGORIO Magno: schemi tropi e ritmi. Retorica. QVetChr 24: 1996, ⇒259. 163-200.
3551 *Ribera, Josep* The image of Israel according to Targum Ezekiel. FMCNAMARA M., JSOT.S 230: 1996, ⇒58. 111-121.
3552 *Schüngel-Straumann, Helen* Ruaḥ und Gender-Frage am Beispiel der Visionen beim Propheten Ezechiel. MVAN DIJK-HEMMES F., 1996, ⇒99. 201-215.

3553 *Stricher, Joseph* L'aigle, le dragon et la marmite. DosB 63 (1996) 9-11.
3554 *Talmon, S.* Fragments of an Ezekiel scroll from Masada (Ezek 35:11-38:14) 1043-2220, Mas 1D. OLoP 27 (1996) 29-49.
3555 *Turner, P.D.M.* The Greek translator(s) of Ezekiel revived: new light on an old question. Sum. BCSBS 55 (1995/1996) 15-16.
3556 **Ulrich, Dean R.** Proleptic intrusions in the final judgment in Eze-kiel's oracles against the nations. Diss. Westminster Theol. Sem. 1996, ^D*Longman, T.*, 210 pp. [EThL 74,218*].
3557 **Wündrich, Rosemarie** 'Du sollst erfahren, dass ICH der Herr BIN...': das Buch Hesekiel und die Geschichte des Nahen Ostens. Fra 1996, Haag und H. 127 pp. 3-86137-469-2 [NThAR 1997,193].

3558 **Groh, Verena** Traditionsgeschichtliche Untersuchung zu der Be-rufungsvision Hesekiels (1,1-3,15 und 10,1-22). Diss. Wien 1996-97 ^D*Sauer, G.* [ThLZ 122,765].
3559 *Schnocks, Johannes* Eine intertextuelle Verbindung zwischen Eze-chiels Eifersuchtsbild und Sacharjas Frau im Efa. BN 84 (1996) 59-63 [Ezek 8,1-6; Zech 5,5-11.
3560 *Lutzky, H.C.* On "the image of jealousy" (Ezekiel VIII 3,5). VT 46 (1996) 121-124 [Ezek 8,3-5].
3561 *Dijkstra, Meindert* Goddess, gods, men and women in Ezekiel 8. ^MVAN DIJK-HEMMES F., 1996, ⇒99. 83-114.
3562 *Joyce, Paul M.* Dislocation and adaptation in the exilic age and after. ^FMASON R., 1996, ⇒57. 45-58 [Ezek 11,16].
3563 *Korpel, Marjo C.A.* Avian spirits in Ugarit and Ezekiel 13. ^FGIBSON J., 1996, ⇒31. 99-113.
3564 *Carroll, Robert P.* Whorusalamin: a tale of three cities as three si-sters. ^MVAN DIJK-HEMMES F., 1996, ⇒99. 67-82 [Ezek 16,1].
3565 **Gravett, Sandra** That all women may take warning: reading the sexual ethnic violence in Ezekiel 16 and 23. Diss. Duke 1996 ^D*Crenshaw, J.* [EThL 74,218*].
3566 *Autané, Maurice* Jérusalem, l'infidèle (Ez 16). DosB 63 (1996) 19-21.
3567 *Witaszek, Gabriel* Sprawiedliwość społeczna a odpowiedzialność indywidualna (Ez 18) [De iustitia sociali et responsabilitate indivi-duali apud Ez 18]. RBL 49 (1996) 154-164. **P.**
3568 *Beentjes, Panc C.* What a lioness was your mother: reflections on Ezekiel 19. ^MVAN DIJK-HEMMES F., 1996, ⇒99. 21-35.
3569 *Patton, Corrine* "I myself gave them laws that were not good": Ezekiel 20 and the Exodus traditions. JSOT 69 (1996) 73-90.
3570 *Terrien, Samuel* Ezekiel's dance of the sword and prophetic theonomy. ^FSANDERS J., JSOT.S 225: 1996, ⇒77. 119-132 [Ezek 21,14-22].
3571 *Gosse, Bernard* Le temple dans le livre d'Ézéchiel en rapport à la rédaction des livres des Rois. BTB 26 (1996) 40-47 [1 Kgs 6-8; 2 Kgs 25; Ezek 24,1-2; 40].
3572 *Lewis, Theodore J.* CT 13.33-34 and Ezekiel 32: lion-dragon myths. Sum. 28. JAOS 116 (1996) 28-47.
3573 *Brin, Gershon* The data and the meaning of the prophecy against 'those who live in these ruins in the land of Israel' (Ezekiel 33:23-29). ^FHARAN M., 1996, ⇒35. 29*-36*. **H.**

3574 **Fikes, Barry Alan** A theological analysis of the shepherd-king motif in Ezekiel 34. Diss. Southwestern Bapt. Theol. Sem. 1995 D*Hunt, H.B.* 200 pp. [EThL 74,218*].

3575 *Eid, Volker* Ezechielvision 37,1-14: eine Reliefdarstellung aus dem 6. Jahrhundert in Dara-Anastasioupolis, Türkisch-Nordmesopotamien. BN 83 (1996) 5-8.

3576 *Gonsalves, Michael* Dry bones—spotlight on Devadasis: an adaptation of Ez 37:1-14: a dramatized liturgical celebration. WoWo 29/2 (1996) 76-79 [ThIK 18/1,44].

3577 *Wagner, Siegfried* Geist und Leben nach Ezechiel 37,1-14. Ausgewählte Aufsätze. BZAW 240: 1996 <1979>, ⇒156. 151-168.

3578 *Costen, James H.* How can these bones live?: Ezekiel 37. JITC 24 (1996-97) 51-65 [ZID 23,406].

3579 *Tanner, J.P.* Rethinking Ezekiel's invasion by Gog. JETS 39 (1996) 29-45 [Ezek 38; 39].

3580 *Mendecki, Norbert* Deuteronomistische Redaktion von Ez 39,23-29?. IOSOT 1992. BEAT 28: 1996, ⇒160. 135-145.

3581 *Tuell, Steven S.* Ezekiel 40-42 as verbal icon. CBQ 58 (1996) 649-664.

3582 *Sharon, Diane M.* A biblical parallel to a Sumerian temple hymn?: Ezekiel 40-48 and Gudea. JANES 24 (1996) 99-109.

3583 *Gruson, Philippe* La Jérusalem idéale (Ez 40-48). DosB 63 (1996) 23-24.

3584 **Tuell, Steven Shaun** The law of the temple in Ezekiel 40-48. HSM 49: 1992, ⇒8,3893... 11/1,2431. R*IEJ* 46/1-2 (1996) 143-144 (*Greenberg, Moshe*); BiOr 53 (1996) 497-499 (*Lust, J.*).

3585 **Stevenson, Kalinda Rose** Vision of transformation: the territorial rhetoric of Ezekiel 40-48. Diss. D*Chaney, M.*, SBL.DS 154: Atlanta, GA 1996, Scholars xxiv; 192 pp. $30/$25. 0-7885-0242-5/3-3 [EThL 73,161].

3586 *Le Saux, Madeleine* La source du temple (Ez 47,1-12). DosB 63 (1996) 25-26.

3587 *Engelhard, David H.* Ezekiel 47:13-48:29 as royal grant. F*YOUNG D.*, 1996, ⇒107. 45-56.

E9.1 Apocalyptica VT

3588 E*Bull, Malcolm* Apocalypse theory. 1995, ⇒11/1,2436. R*RRT* 1996/2, 33-36 (*Bryan, David*).

3589 **Cohn, Norman** Cosmos, chaos, and the world to come. 1993, ⇒9,3782... 11/1,2348. R*HR* 36 (1996) 79-81 (*Dimant, Devorah*).

3590 *Gillingham, Susan* Psalmody and Apocalyptic in the Hebrew bible: common vision, shared experience. F*MASON R.*, 1996, ⇒57. 147-169.

3591 *Ibáñez Ramos, Miguel Antonio* El renacer de la esperanza en el judaísmo en crisis: el reino de Dios en la literatura apocalíptica. Esperanza del hombre. 1996, ⇒173. 453-460.

3592 *Koch, Klaus* Die Anfänge der Apokalyptik in Israel und die Rolle des astronomischen Henochbuchs;

3593 Esras erste Vision: Weltzeiten und Weg des Höchsten <1978>;

3594 Monotheismus und Analogie <1984>;

3595 Die mysteriösen Zahlen der judäischen Könige und die apokalyptischen Jahrwochen <1978>;

3596 Sabbatstruktur der Geschichte: die sogenannte Zehn-Wochen-Apokalypse (1Hen 93,1-10; 91,11-17) und das Ringen um die alttestamentlichen Chronologien im späten Israelitentum <1983>;
3597 Vom profetischen zum apokalyptischen Visionsbericht <1983> [Dan 8; Amos 7,1-3]. Wende der Zeiten. 1996, ⇒133. 3-44/77-106/219-234/135-142/45-76/143-178.
3598 *Marcheselli-Casale, Cesare* Rassegna di studi sull'Apocalittica. Asp. 43 (1996) 67-78 [Mark 6,52-53].
3599 *Murphy, Frederick J.* Introduction to apocalyptic literature. NIntB 7: 1996, ⇒186. 1-16.
3600 *Russell, David S.* Apocalyptic imagery as political cartoon?. FMASON R., 1996, ⇒57. 191-200.
3601 **Sacchi, Paolo** L'apocalittica giudaica. BCR 55: 1990, ⇒6,3984... 11/1,2446. RRSLR 32 (1996) 173-178 (*Martone, Corrado*);
3602 Jewish apocalyptic and its history. TShort, William J., JSPE.S 20: Shf 1996, Academic 288 pp. £30. 1-85075-585-X [JSJ 28,368].
3603 *Schmidt, Johann Michael* Apokalyptik. Altes Testament. 1996, ⇒169. 226-243.
3604 **Schmidt, Thomas** Das Ende der Zeit: Mythos und Methaphorik als Fundamente einer Hermeneutik biblischer Eschatologie. BBB 109: Bodenheim 1996, Philo 467 pp. 3-8257-0038-0.

E9.2 **Daniel:** *textus, commentarii; themata, versiculi*

3605 **Bauer, Dieter** Das Buch Daniel. Neuer Stuttgarter Kommentar, AT 22: Stu 1996, Katholisches Bibelwerk 261 pp. DM48. 3-460-07221-0.
3606 **Collins, John J.** Daniel. Hermeneia: 1993, ⇒9,3794... 11/1,2447. RInterp. 50 (1996) 66-68 (*LaCocque, André*); JR 76 (1996) 458-460 (*Wills, Lawrence M.*); SJTh 49 (1996) 367-368 (*Gosling, F.A.*); Bib. 77 (1996) 560-564 (*Davies, Philip R.*).
    Craven, T. I libri di Ezech. e Dan. ⇒3534.
    Koster, Albert Daniël, Ezra...⇒2583.
3607 **Miller, Stephen R.** Daniel. NAC 18: 1994, ⇒10,3614; 11/1,2451. RWThJ 58 (1996) 339-343 (*Schwab, George M.*).
3608 *Smith-Christopher, Daniel L.* The additions to Daniel;
3609 The book of Daniel. NIntB 7: 1996, ⇒186. 153-194/17-152.
3610 **Taylor, Richard A.** The Peshitta of Daniel. MPIL 7: 1994, ⇒10,3620; 11/1,2455. RCBQ 58 (1996) 121-122 (*Mathews, Edward G.*).
3611 *Trakatellis, Dimitrios* Λόγοι 'Αγωνισικός [Hippolytus' commentary on Daniel]. Die Väter legen aus. 1996, ⇒153. 23-61. G.

3612 **Aaron, Charles Lynn** Loosening a knot: theological development in the book of Daniel. Diss. Union Theol. Sem. in Virginia 1996, 137 pp. [EThL 74,218*].
3613 *Adler, William* The apocalyptic survey of history adapted by christians: Daniel's prophecy of 70 weeks. Apocalyptic heritage [EVanderKam, J.]. CRI 3: 1996, ⇒G2. 201-238.
3614 **Anderson, Lewis O.** The Michael figure in the book of Daniel. Diss. Andrews 1995 DShea, William H., 515 pp. [AUSS 35,241 (Abstr.)].

3615 *Asurmendi, J.* Les deux sagesses du livre de Daniel. Chemins de Dialogue 8 (1996) 169-179 [ZID 22,482].

3616 **Bombeck, Stefan** Die Verwendung der Präformativkonjugation im Aramäischen des Buches Daniel. BN 83 (1996) 5-8.

3617 **Cole, H. Ross** The sacred times prescribed in the pentateuch: Old Testament indicators of the extent of their applicability. Diss. Andrews 1996 ^D*Davidson, Richard M.* [Abstr. AUSS 35,242-244].

3618 *Davies, Philip R.* Eschatology in the book of Daniel. Sects and scrolls. SFSHJ 134: 1996 <1980>, ⇒122. 24-44.

3619 *Hubeňák, Florencio* Historia política y profecía: Roma y los grandes imperios antiguos a la luz de las predicciones del profeta Daniel. Sum. 95. Historia Sacra 48/1 (1996) 95-119.

3620 **Lieth, Norbert** Zukunftsaussichten: Perspektiven aus dem Daniel-Buch. Pfäffikon 1996, Mitternachtsruf 187; 181 pp. 3-85810-196-4/8-2 [NThAR 1997,130].

3621 **McLay, Tim** The OG and Th versions of Daniel. SCSt 43: Atlanta, GA 1996, Scholars xvii; 286 pp. $40. 0-7885-0269-7.

3622 *McLay, Tim* Syntactic profiles and the characteristics of revision: a response to Karen JOBES. BIOSCS 29 (1996) 15-21.

3623 **Stahl, Rainer** Von Weltengagement... Danielbuch. 1994, ⇒10,3629; 11/1,2469. ^RBib. 77 (1996) 275-278 (*LaCocque, André*); OLZ 91 (1996) 39-41 (*Seidel, Hans*); CBQ 58 (1996) 334-335 (*Wolters, Al*).

3624 *Rouillard-Bonraisin, Hedwige* Problèmes du bilinguisme en Daniel. Mosaïque de langues. Antiquités sémitiques 1: 1996, ⇒284. 145-170 [Dan 2,4-7,27].

3625 *Pfandl, Gerhard* Interpretation of the kingdom of God in Daniel 2:44. AUSS 34 (1996) 249-268.

3626 **Miegge, Mario** Il sogno del re di Babilonia: profezia e storia da Thomas MUENTZER a Isaac NEWTON. 1995, ⇒11/1,2476. ^RSdT 8 (1996) 76-77 (*Bernardi, Valerio*) [Dan 2].

3627 **Burnier-Genton, Jean** Le rêve... Daniel 7. MoBi 27: 1993, ⇒9,3824... 11/1,2490. ^REThL 72 (1996) 221-223 (*Lust, J.*).

3628 *Bissoli, Giovanni* S. Gabriele. TS(I) 72 (maggio 1996) 8-10 [Dan 8,16].

3629 ^E**Bader, Winfried** 'Und die Wahrheit wurde hinweggefegt': Dan 8. THLI 9: 1994, ⇒10,3645. ^RThZ 52 (1996) 274-276 (*Bartelmus, Rüdiger*).

3630 *Chazan, Robert* Daniel 9:24-27: exegesis and polemics. Contra ludaeos [^E*Limor, O.*]. TSMJ 10: 1996, ⇒κ8. 143-159.

3631 **Rigger, Hansjörg** Die Jahrwochenweissagung des Buches Daniel: Untersuchungen zu Text, Textgenese, Form und Tradition von Daniel 9. Diss. Trier 1996, 382 pp. [EThL 74,219*].

3632 *Bissoli, Giovanni* San Michele. TS(I) 72 (luglio 1996) 16-17 [Dan 12,1].

3633 **Stele, Artur A.** Resurrection in Daniel 12 and its contribution to the theology of the book of Daniel. Diss. Andrews 1996 ^D*Doukhan, Jacques B.* [Abstr. AUSS 35,246].

3634 *Stump, Eleonore* Susanna and the elders: wisdom and folly. 85-100 [Dan 13];

3635 *Spolsky, Ellen* Law or the garden: the betrayal of Susanna in pastoral painting. 101-117 [Daniel 13];

3636   ᴱ**Spolsky, Ellen** The judgment of Susanna: authority and witness. SBL Early Judaism and Its Literature 11: Atlanta, GA 1996 Scholars viii; 145 pp. $35. 0-7885-0181-X [Dan 13].

3637   *Sered, Susan; Cooper, Samuel* Sexuality and social control: anthropological reflections on the book of Susanna. Judgment of Susanna. 1996, ⇒3636. 43-55 [Dan 13].

3638   *Pearce, S.J.* Echoes of Eden in the Old Greek of Susanna. Feminist Theology 11 (1996) 11-31 [Dan 13].

3639   *Jeffrey, David Lyle* False witness and the just use of evidence in the Wycliffite "Pistel of swete Susan";

3640   *Halpern-Amaru, Betsy* The journey of Susanna among the church fathers;

3641   *Fisch, Harold* Susanna as parable: a response to Piero Bᴏɪᴛᴀɴɪ;

3642   *Deykin Baris, Sharon* Hosannas to an American Susanna;

3643   *Boitani, Piero* Susanna in excelsis. Judgment of Susanna. 1996, ⇒3636. 57-71/21-34/35-41/119-138/7-19.

3644   *Bail, Ulrike* Susanna verlässt Hollywood: eine feministische Auslegung von Dan 13. ᶠScʜᴏᴛᴛʀᴏꜰꜰ W., 1996, ⇒81. 91-98 [OTA 19,475].

3645   *Kaplan, M. Lindsay* Sexual slander and the politics of the erotic in Gᴀʀᴛᴇʀ's "Susanna". Judgment of Susanna. 1996, ⇒3636. 73-84.

3646   **Wysny, Andreas** Die Erzählungen von Bel und dem Drachen: Untersuchungen zu Dan 14. SBB 33: Stu 1996, Katholisches Bibelwerk 366 pp. DM89. 3-460-00331-6 [Dan 14].

ᴇ9.3   *Prophetae Minores,* **Dōdekaprophēton...Hosea, Joel**

3647   **Achtemeier, Elizabeth** Minor Prophets I. New International Biblical Commentary, OT 17: Peabody, MASS 1996, Hendrickson xiii; 390 pp. Hosea, Joel, Amos, Obadiah, Jonah, Micah; based on the New International Version. $12; 0-85364-809-3 [ThD 44,81].

3648   *Barton, John* The canonical meaning of the Book of the Twelve. ᶠMᴀsᴏɴ R., 1996, ⇒57. 59-73.

3649   **Brown, William P.** Obadiah through Malachi. Westminster Bible Companion: LVL 1996, Westminster xii; 209 pp. $17. 0-664-25520-5 [NThAR 1997,258].

3650   **Gordon, Robert P.** Studies in the Targum to the Twelve Prophets: from Nahum to Malachi. VT.S 51: 1994, ⇒10,3651; 11/1,2496. ᴿCBQ 58 (1996) 314-315 (*Aufrecht, Walter E.*).

3651   *House Paul R.* Dramatic coherence in Nahum, Habakkuk, and Zephaniah. ᶠWᴀᴛᴛs J., JSOT.S 235: 1996, ⇒105. 195-208.

3652   **House, Paul R.** The unity of the twelve. JSOT.S 97: 1990, ⇒6,4030... 9,3836. ᴿZKTh 118 (1996) 65-67 (*Oesch, Josef M.*).

3653   **Jones, Barry Alan** The formation of the Book of the Twelve. SBL.DS 149: 1995, ⇒11/2,2498. ᴿEThL 72 (1996) 223-224 (*Lust, J.*); CBQ 58 (1996) 710-711 (*Person, Raymond F.*).

3654   **Maeijer, Floor** Klein en fijn: twaalf kleine profeten. Baarn 1996, Gooi en Sticht 85 pp. ƒ19.50. 90-304-08561-1.

3655   **Nogalski, James** Literary precursors to the book of the Twelve. BZAW 217: 1993, ⇒9,3839... 11/1,2501. ᴿZKTh 118 (1996) 65-

67 (*Oesch, Josef M.*); CBQ 58 (1996) 130-131 (*O'Brien, Julia M.*); ThLZ 121 (1996) 645-649 (*Schart, Aaron*); BO 53 (1996) 493-496 (*Wolters, A.*);

3656 Redactional processes in the book of the Twelve. BZAW 218: 1993, ⇒9,3839... 11/1,2502. ᴿZKTh 118 (1996) 65-67 (*Oesch, Josef M.*); CBQ 58 (1996) 130-131 (*O'Brien, Julia M.*); ThLZ 121 (1996) 645-649 (*Schart, Aaron*).

3657 *Nogalski, James D.* Intertextuality and the Twelve. ᶠWᴀᴛᴛs J., JSOT.S 235: 1996, ⇒105. 102-124.

3658 **Pazdan, Mary M.** I libri di Gioele, Abdia, Aggeo, Zaccaria e Malachia. BT 17: Brescia 1996, Queriniana 188 pp. L25.000 [RdT 37,576].

3659 *Redditt, Paul L.* Zechariah 9-14, Malachi, and the redaction of the book of the Twelve. ᶠWᴀᴛᴛs J., JSOT.S 235: 1996, ⇒105. 245-268.

3660 **Smith, Billy K.; Page, Frank S.** Amos, Obadiah, Jonah. NAC 19B: 1995, ⇒11/1,2503. ᴿRExp 93 (1996) 295-296 (*Drinkard, Joel F.*).

3661 *Steck, Odil Hannes* Zur Abfolge Maleachi-Jona in 4Q76 (4QXII/a). ZAW 108 (1996) 249-253.

3662 **Stuhlmueller, C.** I libri di Amos, Osea, Michea, Naum, Sofonia, Abacuc. BT 15: Brescia 1996, Queriniana 171 pp. L22.000 [RdT 37,431].

3663 *Zvi, Ehud ben* Twelve prophetic books or 'The Twelve': a few preliminary considerations. ᶠWᴀᴛᴛs J., JSOT.S 235: 1996, ⇒105. 125-156.

3664 **Bons, Eberhard** Das Buch Hosea. Neuer Stuttgarter Kommentar, AT 23.1: Stu 1996, Katholisches Bibelwerk 186 pp. DM39. 3-460-07231-8.

3665 *Buss, Martin J.* Hosea as a canonical problem: with attention to the Song of Songs. ᶠTᴜᴄᴋᴇʀ G., JSOT.S 229: 1996, 79-93.

3666 **Davies, Graham I.** Hosea. NCBC: 1992, ⇒8,3964... 11/1,2506. ᴿThR 61 (1996) 474-475 (*Seybold, Klaus*).

3667 **Holt, Else Kragelund** Prophesying the past... Hosea. JSOT.S 194: 1995, ⇒11/1,2513. ᴿSJOT 10 (1996) 151-152 (*Nielsen, Kirsten*).

3668 **Hynniewta, Maksal Jones** The integrity of Hosea's future hope: a study of the oracles of hope in the book of Hosea. Diss. Union Theol. Sem. in Virginia 1996, 276 pp. DAI-A 57/03, p. 1182; AAC 9625233.

3669 **Jeremias, Jörg** Hosea und Amos: Studien zu den Anfängen des Dodekapropheton. FAT 13: Tü 1996, Mohr vii; 287 pp. DM178. 3-16-146477-X.

3670 *Jeremias, Jörg* The interrelationship between Amos and Hosea. ᶠWᴀᴛᴛs J., JSOT.S 235: 1996, ⇒105. 171-186.

3671 **Morris, Gerald** Prophecy, poetry and Hosea. JSOT.S 219: Shf 1996, Academic 167 pp. £30; $45. 1-85075-599-X.

3672 *Odell, Margaret S.* The prophets and the end of Hosea. ᶠWᴀᴛᴛs J., JSOT.S 235: 1996, ⇒105. 158-170;

3673 Who were the prophets in Hosea?. HBT 18 (1996) 78-95.

3674 *Pinto, C.O.* O contexto político e social de Oséias. VoxScr 6/1 (1996) 15-32.

3675 **Seifert, Brigitte** Metaphorisches Reden von Gott im Hoseabuch. FRLANT 166: Gö 1996, Vandenhoeck & R. 285 pp. DM98. 3-525-53848-0 [ThLZ 122,663].

3676 **Simian-Yofre, Horacio** Il deserto... Osea. 1994, ⇒10,3666. ᴿRivBib 44 (1996) 357-360 (*Marconcini, Benito*).

3677 **Walker, Thomas Worth** The metaphor of healing and the theology of the book of Hosea. Diss. Princeton 1996-97 [RTL 29,580].
      Wiebe, John Merritt Deut 32... and Hosea's concept of hope ⇒2232.

3678 *Yee, Gale A.* The book of Hosea. NIntB 7: 1996, ⇒186. 195-297.

3679 **Gangloff, Frédéric** La figure de la 'mère' dans le livre prophétique d'Osée: étude exégétique et iconographique d'Os 1-3; 4,1-5,7; 11; 14,6-9. Diss. Strasbourg 1996 ᴰ*Heintz, J.-G.*, 409 pp. [EThL 74,219*].

3680 *Priebe, Duane* A holy God, an idolatrous people, and religious pluralism: Hosea 1-3. CThMi 23 (1996) 126-133.

3681 **Wacker, Marie-Theres** Figurationen des Weiblichen im Hoseabuch. Diss.-habil. ᴰ*Zenger, E.*, Herders Biblische Studien 8: FrB 1996, Herder ix; 384 pp. 3-451-23951-5. ᴿUF 27 (1995) 729-730 (*Loretz, O.*) [Hos 1-3].

3682 *MacKinlay, J.* Bringing the unspeakable to speech in Hosea. Pacifica 9 (1996) 121-133 [Hosea 1-3].

3683 **Sherwood, Yvonne** The prostitute and the prophet: Hosea's marriage in literary-theoretical perspective. JSOT.S 212: Gender, culture, theory 2: Shf 1996, JSOT 357 pp. £43/$64. 1-85075-581-7/777-1 [Hosea 1-3].

3684 *Farthing, John L.* Holy harlotry: Jerome ZANCHI and the exegetical history of Gomer (Hosea 1-3). ꟳSTEINMETZ J., 1996, ⇒86. 292-312 [Hosea 1-3].

3685 *West, G.* The effect and power of discourse: a case study of a metaphor in Hosea. Scriptura 57 (1996) 201-212 [Hosea 1-3].

3686 *Haag, Ernst* 'Söhne des lebendigen Gottes' (Hos 2,1). ꟳTHUESING W., NTA 31: 1996, ⇒94. 3-24.

3687 *Frede, Hermann Josef* Reste einer Prophetenhandschrift. Vetus Latina-Fragmente. AGLB 28: 77-189 [Hos 2,12-4,8; 10,5-11,9; Amos 1,11-3,2; Joel 2,3-25] [RBen 106,407].

3688 *Díaz Mateos, Manuel* "Le hablaré al corazón" (Os. 2,16). ᵀ*García Plaza, Elisa*, SelT 35 (1996) 272-278 [< Paginas 21/2,9-20].

3689 *Ambrose, M. Devadass* New marriage in Hosea: an Indian look (Hos 2:18-25: Heb; 2:16-23: Eng.). Vaiharai 1/2 (1996) 134-149 [ThIK 18/1,39].

3690 *Haag, Ernst* Der Ehebund Jahwes mit Israel in Hosea 2. ꟳKERTELGE K., 1996, ⇒48. 9-32.

3691 **Eidevall, Göran** Grapes in the desert: metaphors, models, and themes in Hosea 4-14. CB.OT 43: Sto 1996, Almqvist & W. xii; 274 pp. SEK192. 91-22-01709-7. ᴿSvTK 72/4 (1996) 177-178 (*Tångberg, Arvid*).

3692 *Pfeiffer, Henrik* Zechen und Lieben: zur Frage einer Göttin-Polemik in Hos 4,16-19. UF 28 (1996) 495-511.

3693 *Meadowcroft, T.J.* καταστροφή: a puzzling LXX translation choice in Hosea viii 7a. VT 46 (1996) 539-543.

3694 **Lacerda, Ronald Ayres** A função social do conceito de Deus em Oséias 11. Diss. MA UMESP 1996 [D]*Schwantes, Milton* [REB 58,995 som.].

3695 *Wacker, Marie-Theres* Gendering Hosea 13. [M]VAN DIJK-HEMMES F., 1996, ⇒99. 265-282.

3696 *Achtemeier, Elizabeth* The book of Joel. NIntB 7: 1996, ⇒186. 299-336.

3697 *Coggins, Richard* Interbiblical quotations in Joel. [F]MASON R., 1996, ⇒57. 75-84.

3698 **Crenshaw, James L.** Joel. AncB 24C: 1995, ⇒11/1,2548. [R]ArOr 64 (1996) 285-286 (*Segert, Stanislav*).

3699 **McQueen, Larry R.** Joel and the spirit: the cry of a prophetic hermeneutic. JPentec.S 8: Shf 1995, Academic 125 pp. £11; $13. 1-85075-736-4 [BL 1996,85].

3700 **Van Leeuwen, C.** Joël. De prediking van het OT: 1993, ⇒9,3872; 10,3686. [R]BiOr 53 (1996) 772-774 (*Van der Wal, Adri*).

3701 *Strong, John T.* Joel 2:1-2, 12-17. Interp. 50 (1996) 51-54.

E9.4 Amos

3702 **Bovati, Pietro; Meynet, Roland** Le livre du prophète Amos. 1994, ⇒10,3690. [R]Bib. 77 (1996) 114-117 (*McLaughlin, John L.*);

3703 Il libro del profeta Amos. 1995, ⇒11/1,2564. SdT 8/2 (1996) 173-174 (*Radici, Giuseppe*); Ang. 73 (1996) 594-595 (*Jurič, Stipe*); Sal. 58 (1996) 777-778 (*Cimosa, Mario*); RdT 37 (1996) 559-562 (*Prato, Gian Luigi*).

3704 **Carbone, Sandro Paolo; Rizzi, Giovanni** Il libro di Amos. 1993, ⇒9,3880... 11/1,2565. [R]RivBib 44 (1996) 360-362 (*Deiana, Giovanni*).

3705 *Gowan, Donald E.* The book of Amos. NIntB 7: 1996, ⇒186. 337-431.

3706 **Jeremias, Jörg** Der Prophet Amos. ATD 24/2: 1995, ⇒11/1,2566. [R]JThS 47 (1996) 572-573 (*Auld, Graeme*).

3707 **Álvarez Barredo, M.** Relecturas deuteronomísticas de Amós, Miqueas y Jeremías. 1993, ⇒9,3884; 10,3698. [R]ScrTh 28/1 (1996) 295-297 (*Ausín, S.*); Ben. 43 (1996) 409-410 (*Ranzato, Agostino*).

3708 **Bovati, Pietro; Meynet, Roland** La fin d'Israël: paroles d'Amos. LiBi 101: 1994, ⇒10,3691; 11/1,2563. [R]CBQ 58 (1996) 501-503 (*Dempsey, Carol J.*).

3709 *Carroll, M. Daniel* The prophetic text and the literature of dissent in Latin America: Amos, GARCIA MARQUEZ, and CABRERA INFANTE dismantle militarism. Sum. 100. Bibl.Interp. 4/1 (1996) 76-100.

3710 *Hasel, Michael G.* La ubicación de la Tecoa de la época de hierro y los estudios de Amos. Theologika 11/1 (1996) 138-159 [ZID 23,321].

3711 *Noble, Paul R.* The function of $n^{\jmath}m$ Yhwh in Amos. ZAW 108 (1996) 623-626.

3712 *O'Connell, Robert H.* Telescoping N + 1 patterns in the book of Amos. VT 46 (1996) 56-73.

3713 **Park, Sang Hoon** Eschatology in the book of Amos: a text-linguistic analysis. Diss. Trinity Evang. Div. School 1996 ᴰ*VanGemeren, W.*, 292 pp. [EThL 74,220*].

3714 *Passaro, Angelo* Profezia e denuncia dei mali sociali nel libro del profeta Amos. Synaxis 14/2 (1996) 7-25.

3715 *Ramírez, Guillermo* The social location of the prophet Amos in light of the group/grid cultural anthropological model. ꟳTᴜᴄᴋᴇʀ G., JSOT.S 229: 1996. 112-124.

3716 **Rottzoll, Dirk U.** Studien zur Redaktion und Komposition des Amosbuchs. Diss. ᴰ*Kaiser, O.*, BZAW 243: B 1996, De Gruyter x; 319 pp. DM168. 3-11-015240-1.

3717 *Strijdom, P.D.F.* What Tekoa did to Amos. OTEs 9 (1996) 273-293.

3718 *Tawil, Hayim* Amos' oracles against the nations: a new interpretation. Beit Mikra 147 (1996) 388-375.

3719 *Urbrock, William J.* The book of Amos: the sounds and the silences. CThMi 23 (1996) 245-253.

3720 *Wagner, Siegfried* Überlegungen zur Frage nach den Beziehungen des Propheten Amos zum Südreich. Ausgewählte Aufsätze. BZAW 240: 1996 <1971>, ⇒156. 57-82.

3721 *Widbin, Bryan R.* Center structure in the center oracles of Amos. ꟳYᴏᴜɴɢ D., 1996, ⇒107. 177-192.

3722 **Witaszek, Gabriel** Amos: prorok sprawiedliwosci spolecznej. Lublin 1996, Katolickiego Uniwersytetu 277 pp. 83-228-0419-9. P.

3723 *Carroll R., M.D.* God and his people in the nations' history: a contextualised reading of Amos 1-2. TynB 47 (1996) 39-70.

3724 *Pfeifer, Gerhard* Amos I 1: Worte des Amos?. IOSOT 1992. BEAT 28: 1996, ⇒160. 165-168.

3725 **Siqueira, Reinaldo W.** The presence of the covenant motif in Amos 1:2-2:16. Diss. Andrews 1996 ᴰ*Davidson, Richard M.*, 355 pp. DAI-A 57/05, p. 2084; AAC 9638070.

3726 *Kim, In H.* A study of the legitimacy of Yahweh in judging the nations in the oracles of Amos (Am 1:3-2:16). Chongshin Review 1 (1996) 31-67.

3727 *Bons, Eberhard* Das Denotat von *kzbjhm* "ihre Lügen" im Judaspruch Am 2,4-5. ZAW 108 (1996) 201-213.

3728 **Subagyo, Yohanes** Amos 2:6-16: Israel's moral transgressions. Diss. extract Pont. Univ. Urbaniana ᴰ*Spreafico, Ambrogio*, R 1996, 77 pp.

3729 *Kleven, Terence* The cows of Bashan: a single metaphor at Amos 4:1-3. CBQ 58 (1996) 215-227.

3730 *Snyman, S.D.* Towards a theological interpretation of *HMS* in Amos 6:1-7. IOSOT 1992. BEAT 28: 1996, ⇒160. 201-209.

     Ruprecht, Eberhard Das Zepter Jahwes in den Berufungsvisionen von Jer. und Amos ⇒3477.

3731 *Schullerus, Konrad* Überlegungen zur Redaktionsgeschichte des Amosbuches anhand von Am 9,7-10. BN 85 (1996) 56-69.

3732 *Viberg, Å.* Amos 7:14: a case of subtle irony. TynB 47 (1996) 91-114.

3733 *Mulzer, Martin* Amos 8,14 in der LXX: ein Einwurf in die Tel Dan-Text Debatte. BN 84 (1996) 54-58.

3734 *Firth, David G.* Promise as polemic: levels of meaning in Amos 9:11-15. OTEs 9 (1996) 372-382.

E9.5 **Jonas:** *commentarii; themata; versiculi*

3735 **Deurloo, K.A.** Jona. 1995, ⇒11/1,2618. RKeTh 47 (1996) 249-251 (*Van der Woude, A.S.*).

3736 A Jewish Greek version of the book of Jonah. On Bodl. MS Opp. Add. 8°.91. Bulletin of Judaeo-Greek Studies 16 (1995) 29-31 [IAJS 42,40].

3737 **Limburg, James** Jonah. 1993, ⇒9,3915... 11/1,2620. Evangel 14/3 (1996) 87-88 (*McConville, Gordon*); HebStud 37 (1996) 175-177 (*Marcus, David*).

3738 **Lux, Rüdiger** Jona. FRLANT 162: 1994, ⇒10,3732; 11/1,2631. RKeTh 47 (1996) 75-77 (*Van der Woude, A.S.*).

3739 **Simon, Uriel** Jona. SBS 157: 1994, ⇒10,3726. RITS 33/1 (1996) 80-83 (*Ceresko, Anthony R.*).

3740 **Struppe, Ursula** Die Bücher Obadja, Jona. Neuer Stuttgarter Kommentar, AT 24.1: Stu 1996, Katholisches Bibelwerk 155 pp. DM36. 3-460-07241-5.

3741 ETchilibon, **Giuseppe** Libro di Giona. TGentili, Meir; Bekhor, rav Shlomo, Mi 1996, DLI 107 pp. Testo ebraico con la traduzione...commenti esplicativi tratti dal Talmud e dalla tradizione ebraica. 88-86674-05-8.

3742 *Trible, Phyllis* The book of Jonah. NIntB 7: 1996, ⇒186. 461-529.

3743 **Bauer, Olivier** Le jeu de Dieu et de Jonas: grille de lecture pour un livre déroutant. Poliez-le-Grand 1996, Du Moulin 84 pp. FF56. REeV 106 (1996) 671 (*Paillerets, M. de*).

3744 **Bouthors, J.-F.** Jonas l'entêté. P 1996, DDB 136 pp. FF82 [VieCon 69,337].

3745 *Coleson, Joseph E.* The peasant woman and the fugitive prophet: a study in biblical narrative settings. FYOUNG D., 1996, ⇒107. 27-44.

3746 **Craig, Kenneth M.** A poetics of Jonah. 1993, ⇒9,3925; 10,3727. RCritRR 9 (1996) 146-148 (*Bland, Dave*).

3747 *Dell, Katharine J.* Reinventing the wheel: the shaping of the book of Jonah. FMASON R., 1996, ⇒57. 85-101.

3748 *Della Rocca, Roberto* Giona ben Amitai—Giona figlio delle mie verità. RasIsr 61 (1995) 179-188 [IAJS 42,40].

3749 *Flipo, Claude* ¿Comó usar bien de la ciudad?. SalTer 84 (1996) 235-241.

3750 *Hamel Gildas* Taking the Argo to Nineveh: Jonah and Jason in a Mediterranean context. Jdm 44 (1995) 341-359 [IAJS 42,40].

3751 *Hoheisel, Karl* Jonas im Koran. FDASSMANN E., JAC.E 23: 1996, ⇒19. 611-621.

3752 *Kaplan, Kalman J.* Jonah versus Narcissus: a biblical approach to suicide prevention. Journal of Psychology and Judaism 19 (1995) 143-151 [IAJS 42,40].

3753 *Krašovec, Jože* Salvation of the rebellious prophet Jonah and of the penitent heathen sinners. SEÅ 61 (1996) 53-75.

3754 *Maggioni, Bruno* Giona, profeta controvoglia. RCI 77 (1996) 182-191.

3755   *Niccacci, Alviero* Syntactic analysis of Jonah. SBFLA 46 (1996) 9-32.
3756   **Person, Raymond Franklin, Jr.** In conversation with Jonah: conversation analysis, literary criticism, and the book of Jonah. JSOT.S 220: Shf 1996, Academic 204 pp. £30; $45. 1-85075-619-8.
3757   *Rad, Gerhard von* El profeta Jonás. La acción de Dios. 1996 <1970>, ⇒144. 60-71.
3758   **Trible, Phyllis** Rhetorical criticism...Jonah. 1994, ⇒10.2740; 11/1,2637. ᴿNewTR 9/2 (1996) 88-89 *(Wimmer, Joseph F.)*; CBQ 58 (1996) 527-528 *(Craig, Kenneth M.)*.
3759   *Wendland, Ernst R.* Text analysis and the genre of Jonah, 1. JETS 39 (1996) 191-206.
3760   *Zenger, Erich* Was wir Christen von der jüdischen Schriftauslegung lernen können: am Beispiel des Jonabuchs. BiKi 51 (1996) 46-53.

3761   *Smelik, K.A.D.* The literary function of poetical passages in biblical narrative: the case of Jonah 2:3-10. ᶠᵛᴬᴺ Uchelen N., 1996, ⇒100. 147-151 [OTA 19,479].
3762   *Schriver, Ragan* Jonah's growth in relationship to God. BiTod 34 (1996) 289-294 [Jonah 2,3-10].
3763   *Ferguson, Paul* Who was the "king of Nineveh" in Jonah 3:6?. TynB 47 (1996) 301-314.
3764   *Spangenberg, I.J.J.* Jonah and Qohelet: satire versus irony. OTEs 9 (1996) 495-511 [Qoh 7,1-4; 9,1-10; Jonah 4,1-3; 2,3-10].
3765   *Antoniotti, Guido* La libertà di Dio: la confessione di fede di Gn 4,2 alla luce della sua relazione con Gl 2,13. Sum. 277. RivBib 44 (1996) 257-277.

E9.6 *Micheas,* Micah

3766   **Carbone, Sandro Paolo; Rizzi, Giovanni** Il libro di Michea: secondo il testo ebraico Masoretico, secondo la versione greca della LXX, secondo la parafrasi aramaica targumica. La Parola e la sua tradizione 3: Bo 1996, Dehoniane 237 pp. L39.000. 88-10-20584-7.
3767   **Jun-Hee, Cha** Micha und Jeremia. Athenäums Monografien, Theologie: BBB 107: Weinheim 1996, Beltz, Athenäum ix; 151 pp. 3-89547-107-0.
3768   *Oberforcher, Robert* Das Buch Micha. 1995, ⇒11/1,2641. ᴿBiKi 51 (1996) 192-194 *(Reuter, Eleonore)*.
3769   *Oberforcher, Robert* Entstehung, Charakter und Aussageprofil des Michabuches. BiKi 51 (1996) 150-154.
3770   *Simundson, Daniel J.* The book of Micah. NIntB 7: 1996, ⇒186. 531-589.
3771   **Tavares Zabatiero, Júlio Paulo** Miquéias: voz dos sem-terra. Petrópolis 1996 Vozes 140 pp. [REB 225,226].

3772   *Wagenaar, Jan A.* The hillside of Samaria: interpretation and meaning of Micha 1:6. BN 85 (1996) 26-30.
3773   *Hentschel, Georg* Enteignung: die soziale Frage in Micha 2. BiKi 51 (1996) 155-158.

3774 *Gerstenberger, Erhard S.* Kritik an Autoritäten (Mi 3,9-12). BiKi 51 (1996) 159-162.

3775 *Schwendemann, Wilhelm* Weisung vom Zion (Mi 4,1-5). BiKi 51 (1996) 163-165.

3776 *Kriener, Tobias* Völkerwallfahrt zum Zion—heute—praktisch. BiKi 51 (1996) 166-167 [Mic 4,5].

3777 *Michel, Diethelm* Das Ende der "Tochter der Streifschar" (Mi 4,14). ZAH 9 (1996) 196-198.

3778 *Albertz, Rainer* "Aufrechten Ganges mit Gott wandern ...": Bibelarbeit über Micha 6,1-8. Zorn. 1996, ⇒110. 44-64.

3779 *Kessler, Rainer* Mirjam und die Prophetie der Perserzeit. ᶠScHOTTROFF W., 1996, ⇒81. 64-72 [Mic 6,4] [OTA 19,480].

3780 *Ebach, Jürgen* Was bei Micha "gut sein" heißt. BiKi 51 (1996) 172-181 [Mic 6,8].

E9.7 *Abdias, Sophonias...* Obadiah, Zephaniah, Nahum

3781 **Ben Zvi, Ehud** A historical-critical study of the book of Obadiah. BZAW 242: B 1996, De Gruyter x; 309 pp. DM198. 3-11-015225-8.

3782 *Meinhold, Arndt* Weisheitliches in Obadja. Weisheit. 1996, ⇒3071. 70-86.

3783 *Pagán, Samuel* The book of Obadiah. NIntB 7: 1996, ⇒186. 433-459.

3784 **Raabe, Paul R.** Obadiah: a new translation with introduction and commentary. AncB 24D: NY 1996, Doubleday xxvi; 310 pp. 0-385-41268-1 [NThAR 1997,67].
    Struppe, Ursula Die Bücher Obadja, Jona ⇒3740.

3785 *Wendland, Ernst R.* Obadiah's "day": on the rhetorical implications of textual form and intertextual influence. JOTT 8 (1996) 23-49.

3786 *Bennett, Robert A.* The book of Zephaniah. NIntB 7: 1996, ⇒186. 657-704.

3787 **Berlin, Adele** Zephaniah. AncB 25A: 1994, ⇒10,3758. ᴿGr. 77 (1996) 352-354 (*Conroy, Charles*); Bib. 77 (1996) 117-121 (*Spreafico, Ambrogio*); Interp. 50 (1996) 424, 426 (*King, Greg A.*); ArOr 64 (1996) 286-287 (*Segert, Stanislav*).

3788 *Crüsemann, Frank* Israel, die Völker und die Armen: Grundfragen alttestamentlicher Hermeneutik am Beispiel des Zefanjabuches. Der Tag. ⇒3789. 123-133.

3789 ᴱ**Dietrich, Walter; Schwantes,** Milton Der Tag wird kommen: ein interkontextuelles Gespräch über das Buch des Propheten Zefanja. SBS 170: Stuttgart 1996, Katholisches Bibelwerk 173 pp. DM43.80. 3-460-04701-1:

3790 *Dietrich, Walter* Die Kontexte des Zefanjabuches ⇒3789. 19-37;

3791 *Hunziker-Rodewald, Regine* Zum Verhältnis von Wahrheit und Gerechtigkeit: aus den Tonbandprotokollen der Kolloquiumsverhandlungen ⇒3789. 154-164.

3792 *King, Greg A.* The message of Zephania: an urgent echo. AUSS 34 (1996) 211-222.

3793 **King, Greg A.** The theological coherence of the book of Zephaniah. Diss. Union Theol. Sem. in Virginia 1996 ᴰ*Towner, W. Sibley,* 223 pp. DAI-A 57/03, p. 1182; AAC 9625235.

3794 *Neef, H.D.* Glaube als Demut: zur Theologie des Propheten Zephanja. ThBeitr 27 (1996) 145-158.
3795 *Schwantes, Milton* "Jhwh" hat Schutz gewährt": theologische Anmerkunge zum Buch des Propheten Zefanja ⇒3789. 134-153;
3796 *Veijola, Timo* Zefanja und Joschija ⇒3789. 9-18.
3797 **Vlaardingerbroek, J.** Sefanja. COT: 1993, ⇒9,3957. ᴿOTEs 9 (1996) 552-553 (*Tonder, C.A.P. van*).
3798 *Weigel, Michael* Hacia los orígenes de la teología bíblica de los pobres. ᵀ*Sala, Màrius*, SelT 35 (1996) 283-288 [< BiKi 50 (1995) 6-11].
3799 **Weigl, Michael** Zefanja und das "Israel der Armen". ÖBS 13: 1994, ⇒10,3763; 11/1,2671. ᴿZKTh 118 (1996) 102-103 (*Hubmann, Franz David*); ThLZ 121 (1996) 934-936 (*Otto, Ekkart*).

3800 *Reimer, Haroldo* Sozialkritik und Zukunftsperspektiven in Zef 1-2 ⇒3789. 38-48;
3801 *Schroer, Silvia* Das "Kommen des Tages" und unsere Zeitrechnung-ein Einwurf ⇒3789. 84-87 [Zeph 1,14-16];
3802 *Uehlinger, Christoph* Astralkultpriester und Fremdgekleidete, Kanaanvolk und Silberwäger: zur Verknüpfung von Kult- und Sozialkritik in Zef 1 ⇒3789. 49-83;
3803 *Schäffer, Dario* Über den Tag Gottes und wer-vielleicht-überleben wird: Predigt über Zef 2,1-3 ⇒3789. 88-92;
3804 *Salgado, Josué Mello* Über die Versklavung und Befreiung der 'Kuschiten': Assoziation und Überlegungen eines dunkelhäutigen Lesers von Zef 3,10 ⇒3789. 113-122.
3805 *Spreafico, Ambrogio* Il resto d'Israele: l'annuncio di una nuova comunità (Sof 3,12-13). ᶠDUPONT J., 1996, ⇒21. 55-65.
3806 *Sharp, D.B.* The remnant of Zephaniah: identifiying "A people humble and lowly". IBSt 18 (1996) 2-15 [2 Kgs 21; Zeph 3,12].
3807 *Gerstenberger, Erhard S.* Der Hymnus der Befreiung im Zefanjabuch ⇒3789. 102-112 [Zeph 3,14-18].
3808 *Kessler, Rainer* "Ich rette das Hinkende, und das Versprengte sammle ich": zur Herdenmetaphorik in Zef 3 ⇒3789. 93-101.

3809 *Becking, Bob* Passion, power, protection: interpreting the God of Nahum. ᴹVAN DIJK-HEMMES F., 1996, ⇒99. 1-20.
3810 *Christensen, Duane L.* The book of Nahum: a history of interpretation. ᶠWATTS J., JSOT.S 235: 1996, ⇒105. 187-194.
3811 *García-Treto, Francisco O.* The book of Nahum. NIntB 7: 1996, ⇒186. 591-619.
3812 *Toloni, Giancarlo* Σῶμα / gᵉwiyyâ (Na 3,3b) alla luce delle versioni antiche. AION 56/1 (1996) 1-13.

E9.8 *Habacuc,* **Habakkuk**

3813 *Hiebert, Theodore* The book of Habakkuk. NIntB 7: 1996, ⇒186. 621-655.
3814 *MacCabe, D.* How long?: not long! ABQ 15/1 (1996) 28-35 [Hab 1,1-4].
3815 **O'Neal, Guy Michael** Interpreting Habakkuk as scripture: an application of the canonical approach of Brevard S. CHILDS. Diss.

Southern Bapt. Theol. Sem. 1996 ^D*Tate, M.*, 269 pp. [EThL 74,222*].

3816 *Tsumura, D.T.* The 'word pair' *qšt and *mt in Habakkuk 3:9 in the light of Ugaritic and Akkadian. ^FYOUNG D., 1996, ⇒107. 353-361.

3817 *Tuillén Torralba, Juan* Yahvé, mi salvador: Habacuc, 3. Sum. 95. Isidorianum 5 (1996) 95-123.

3818 **Van Leeuwen, C.** Habakuk: een praktische bijbelverklaring. Tekst en Toelichting: Kampen 1996, Kok 73 pp. *f*25. 90-242-7791-4.

3819 *Watts, James W.* Psalmody in prophecy: Habakkuk 3 in context. ^FWATTS J., JSOT.S 235: 1996, ⇒105. 209-223.

E9.9 *Aggaeus,* **Haggai**—*Zacharias,* **Zechariah**—*Malachias,* **Malachi**

3820 **Amsler, Samuel** Los últimos profetas: Ageo, Zacarías, Malaquías y algunos otros. Pref. *Gruson, Philippe,* CuaBi 90: Estella 1996, Verbo Divino 64 pp. 84-8169-095-3.

3821 **Bauer, Lutz** Zeit des Zweiten Tempels... Haggai-Sacharja-Maleachi-Korpus. 1992, ⇒8,4080... 10,3772. ^RBZ 40 (1996) 303-304 (*Maier, Johann*).

3822 *Craig, Kenneth M.* Interrogatives in Haggai-Zechariah: a literary thread. ^FWATTS J., JSOT.S 235: 1996, ⇒105. 224-244.

3823 **James, John** Haggai, Zechariah, Malachi. Crossway Bible Guide: Leicester 1996, Crossway 166 pp. 1-85684-150-2.

3824 **Petersen, David L.** Zechariah 9-14 and Malachi. 1995, ⇒11/1,2687. ^RJThS 47 (1996) 575-577 (*Tollington, Janet*); CBQ 58 (1996) 525-527 (*Wolters, Al*).

3825 **Redditt, Paul L.** Haggai, Zechariah and Malachi. NCeB: 1995, ⇒11/1,2688. ^RThLZ 121 (1996) 826-827 (*Kratz, Reinhard G.*); CBQ 58 (1996) 525-527 (*Wolters, Al*); CritRR 9 (1996) 166-168 (*Floyd, Michael H.*).

3826 **Sykes, Seth** Time and space in Haggai—Zechariah 1-8: a Bakhtinian analysis of a prophetic chronicle. Diss. Richmond 1996-97 [RTL 29,580].

3827 *March, W. Eugene* The book of Haggai. NIntB 7: 1996, ⇒186. 705-732.

3828 **Larkin, Katrina J.A.** The eschatology of Second Zechariah. 1994, ⇒10,3787; 11/1,2707. ^RSal. 58/1 (1996) 186 (*Vicent, R.*); SJTh 49 (1996) 369-370 (*Love, Mark*).

3829 *Meyers, Eric M.* Messianism in First and Second Zechariah and the 'end' of biblical prophecy. ^FYOUNG D., 1996, ⇒107. 127-142.

3830 **Monshouwer, D.; Vreekamp, H.** Zacharja: een profeet om te gedenken: van Loofhutten naar Pasen. Zoetermeer 1994, Boekencentrum 204 pp. *f*34. 90-239-1052-4. ^RKeTh 47/1 (1996) 72-75 (*Van der Woude, A.S.*).

3831 **Nurmela, Risto** Prophets in dialogue: inner-biblical allusions in Zechariah 1-8 and 9-14. Åbo 1996, Åbo Akademis Förlag; Åbo University Press 263 pp. [NTT 97,254].

3832 *Ollenburger, Ben C.* The book of Zechariah. NIntB 7: 1996, ⇒186. 733-840.

3833 **Thompson, Henry O.** Zechariah: a bibliography. Delhi 1996, SPCK 165 pp. Rs25. 81-7214-123-8 [VJTR 60,640].

3834 **Tidiman, Brian** Le livre de Zacharie. Commentaire Évangélique de la Bible 18: Vaux sur Seine 1996, Edifac 301 pp. FF150. 2-904407-17-0 [NThAR 1997,193].

3835 **Tigchelaar, Eibert J.C.** Prophets of old and the day of the end: Zechariah and the Book of Watchers and Apocalyptic. Diss. ᴰ*Van der Woude, A.S.*, OTS 35: Lei 1996, Brill viii; 278 pp. *f*147; $95.50. 90-04-10356-2 [NTAb 41,192].

3836 **Marinkovic, Peter** Stadt ohne Mauern: die Neukonstitution Jerusalems nach Sacharja 1-8. Diss.-habil Mü 1996 ᴰ*Baltzer, K.* [RTL 27,529].

3837 *Lemaire, André* Zorobabel et la Judée à la lumière de l'épigraphie (fin du VI/e S. AV. J.-C.). RB 103 (1996) 48-57 [Zech 3,8; 6,12].

3838 *Floyd, Michael H.* The evil in the ephah: reading Zechariah 5:5-11 in its literary context. CBQ 58 (1996) 51-68.

3839 *Kline, Meredith G.* Marana Tha. Kerux 11/3 (1996) 10-28 [Zech 6,1-8].

3840 **Hanhart, Robert** Sacharja (6,1-7,14). BKAT 14/7: Fasc. 6.: Neuk 1996, Neuk, DM33. 401-480.

3841 *Nagel, Elizabeth M.* A sowing of peace. BiTod 34 (1996) 282-287 [Zech 8].

3842 **Kunz, Andreas** Auch heute sage ich—eine Wiederholung verkünde ich dir: Untersuchung zur literarischen Kontinuität und Diskontinuität in Sach 9,1-10; 11-17; 10,3b-12 und zum soziokommunikativen Hintergrund der Textentstehung. Diss. Leipzig 1996-97 ᴰ*Lux, R.*, 347 pp. [ThLZ 122,764].

3843 *Hobbs, T.R.* The language of warfare in Zechariah 9-14. ᶠMᴀꜱᴏɴ R., 1996, ⇒57. 103-128.

3844 **Tai, Nicholas Ho Fai** Prophetie als Schriftauslegung in Sacharja 9-14: traditions- und kompositionsgeschichtliche Studien. Diss. Mü 1993 ᴰ*Specht, H.*, CThM.BW 17: Stu 1996, Calwer ix; 309 pp. 3-7668-3426-6.

3845 *Wolters, Al* Targumic כרובת (Zechariah 14:20) = Greek κορυφαία?. JBL 115 (1996) 710-713.

3846 *Rubenstein, J.L.* Sukkot, eschatology and Zechariah 14. RB 103 (1996) 161-195.

3847 *Berry, Donald K.* Malachi's dual design: the close of the canon and what comes afterward. ᶠWᴀᴛᴛꜱ J., JSOT.S 235: 1996, ⇒105. 269-302.

3848 *O'Keefe, John J.* Christianizing Malachi: fifth-century insights from Cyril of Alexandria. VigChr 50 (1996) 136-158.

3849 *Oesch, Josef M.* Die Bedeutung der Tora für Israel nach dem Buch Maleachi. Die Tora. 1996, ⇒1308. 169-211.

3850 *Schuller, Eileen M.* The book of Malachi. NIntB 7: 1996, ⇒186. 841-877.

3851 *Habets, Goswin* "Ich habe Euch lieb": die Grundsatzerklärung: eine Exegese von Maleachi 1,2-5. Ter. 47 (1996) 431-465.

3852 *Kugler, Robert A.* A note on the Hebrew and Greek texts of Mal 2,3aA. ZAW 108 (1996) 426-429.

3853 Snyman, S.D. A structural approach to Malachi 3:13-21. OTEs 9 (1996) 486-494.
3854 Van den Brom, L.J. Tijdsleer. KeTh 47 (1996) 90-92 [Mal 3,22-24].

VIII. NT Exegesis generalis

F1.1 New Testament Introduction

3855 [E]Aguirre Monasterio, Rafael; Rodríguez Carmona, Antonio La investigación de los evangelios sinópticos y Hechos de los Apóstoles en el siglo XX. Introducción al estudio de la Biblia, Instrumentos de trabajo 1: Estella (Navarra) 1996, Verbo Divino 397 pp. 84-8169-029-5.
3856 Aguirre Monasterio, Rafael; Rodríguez Carmona, Antonio Vangeli sinottici e Atti degli Apostoli. Introduzione allo Studio della Bibbia 6: Brescia 1995, Paideia 339 pp. [R]Ter. 47 (1996) 658-660 (Borrell, Agustí).
3857 Ahn, Byeung-Cheol A study on the notion of christian solidarity in the New Testament. Catholic Theology and Thought 18 (1996) 5-28 [ThIK 18/2,51]. K.
3858 Bartolomé, Juan José El evangelio y Jesús de Nazaret. 1995, ⇒11/2,2090. [R]Sal. 58 (1996) 776-777 (Buzetti, Carlo).
3859 Beatrice, Pier Franco L'eredità delle origini: saggi sul cristianesimo primitivo. Genova 1992, Marietti 298 pp. L40.000. 88-211-6816-6. [R]At. 84 (1996) 320-323 (Jucci, Elio).
3860 Beker, J. Christiaan The NT: a thematic introduction. 1994, ⇒10,3808. [R]CritRR 9 (1996) 181-182 (McCane, Byron R.).
3861 Benz, Ernst Descrição do cristianismo. [T]Almeida Pereira, Carlos, Petrópolis 1995, Vozes 460 pp. [R]REB 56 (1996) 992-995 (Lepargneur, Hubert).
3862 Best, Ernest Recent continental New Testament literature. ET 107 (1996) 237-240.
3863 Borgen, Peder Early christianity and Hellenistic Judaism. E 1996, Clark xi; 376 pp. £25. 0-567-08501-5 [RB 104,313].
3864 Brown, Schuyler The origins of christianity: a historical introduction to the NT. 1984, ⇒54,3433... 4,4077. [R]RBL 49 (1996) 207-209 (Wojciechowski, Michał).
3865 Cabellaro, José Maria Panorámica del Nuevo Testamento. Dabar 6: Madrid 1996, San Pablo 247 pp. 84-285-1914-5 [NThAR 1998,270].
3866 Castelli, Elizabeth A.; Taussig, Hal Introduction: drawing large and startling figures: reimagining christian origins by painting like PICASSO. 1996, ⇒54. 3-20.
3867 Chilton, Bruce; Neusner, Jacob Judaism in the New Testament: practices and beliefs. NY 1996, Routledge xix; 203 pp. $55/$18. 0-415-11843-3/4-1 [ThD 44,61].
3868 Czerski, Janusz Wprowadzenje do Ksjag Nowego Testamentum [Einführung in das Buch des Neuen Testaments]. Podreczniki i skriypty 1: Opole 1996, 188 pp. 83-86865-02-4 [DBAT 29,313— Diebner, B.J.].

3869 **Dale, Robert D.** Leading edge: leadership strategies from the New Testament. Nv 1996, Abingdon 137 pp. $13. 0-687-01506-5 [RExp 94,474].

3870 **Dietl-Zeiner, Johannes** Das kastrierte Evangelium: die falsch übersetzte Bibel und die Wiederentdeckung der Lust. Kreuzlingen 1996, Ariston 283 pp. 3-7205-1941-4 [NThAR 1997,163].

3871 **Flaminio, Marco Antonio** Apologia del beneficio di Cristo e altri scritti inediti. E*Marcatto, Dario*, Studi e Testi 5: F 1996, Olschki 225 pp. 88-222-4412-5 [NThAR 1997,163].

3872 **Flusser, David** Il giudaismo e le origini del cristianesimo. Radici 15: Genova 1995, Marietti 246 pp. L33.000. RSIDIC 29/2-3 (1996) 63 (*Di Sante, Carmine*).

3873 **Gibert, Pierre,** (*al*), Pour enseigner les origines chrétiennes. Histoire des religions: P 1996, Cerf 206 pp. Extraits des actes de l'université académique d'automne de Caen-Houlgate, 23-25 oct. 1995; FF139. 2-84093-051-X [BCLF 587-9,2058].

3874 **Giesriegl, Richard** Die Juden und die Tora im Neuen Testament. Thaur 1996, Kulturverlag 232 pp. 3-85400-013-8 [NThAR 1997,100].

3875 **Gloer, W. Hulitt** As you go: an honest look at the first followers of Jesus. Macon, Ga. 1996, Peake Road viii; 117 pp. 1-57312-007-3 [NThAR 1997,163].

3876 T**Guyot, Peter;** E**Klein, Richard** Das frühe Christentum bis zum Ende der Verfolgungen: eine Dokumentation, Bd. 1: Die Christen im heidnischen Staat; Bd. 2: Die Christen in der heidnischen Gesellschaft. TzF 60, 62: Da 1996, WissBuchg xii; 516; xii; 412 pp. Kommentar von R. Klein. DM112 + 112 3-534-11451-5 [Latomus 57,939ss—Inglebert, H.].

3877 **Harrington, Daniel** How to read the gospels: answers to common questions. Hyde Park, NY 1996, New City 95 pp. $7. 1-56548-076-7 [ThD 44,171].

3878 *Hengel, Martin* Zum Thema "Die Religionsgeschichte und das Urchristentum". Judaica et Hellenistica. WUNT 90: 1996 <1967/69>, ⇒128. 131-150.

3879 **Hinson, E. Glenn** The early church: origins to the dawn of the Middle Ages. Nv 1996, Abingdon 365 pp. $19 [JEarlyC 6,327—Gustafson, Mark].

3880 **Hoornaert, Eduardo** El movimento de Jésus. México 1996, Dabar 192 pp. [EfMex 15,400].

3881 **Jacobi, Ernst** Kennen Sie das Neue Testament wirklich?: ein Leitfaden. Fra 1996, Haag u. H. 243 pp. 3-86137-439-0 [NThAR 1997,100].

3882 E**Jónsson, Gunnlaugur A.** The New Testament in its Hellenistic context. Ritröd Gudfraedistofnunar 10: Reykjavík 1996, Háskóli Islands Gudfraedistofnun 185 pp. Proceedings of a Nordic conference of NT scholars, held in Skálholt. 9979-826-52-5 [NThAR 1997,227].

3883 **Karris, Robert J.** A symphony of New Testament hymns: commentary on Philippians 2:5-11, Colossians 1:15-20, Ephesians 2:14-16, 1 Timothy 3:16, Titus 3:4-7, 1 Peter 3:18-22, and 2 Timothy 2:11-13. ColMn 1996, Liturgical 181 pp. $15. 0-8146-2425-1.

3884 **Keener, Craig S.** The IVP bible background commentary: NT. 1993, ⇒11/2,2147. RBiTr 47 (1996) 445-447 (*Ellington, John*).

3885 *Knox, R.B.* Christianity and classical culture. IBSt 18 (1996) 194-204.

3886 *Konstan, David* Friendship, frankness and flattery. Friendship. NT.S 82: 1996, ⇒180. 7-19.

3887 **Law, Philip** The wisdom of Jesus. GR 1996, Eerdmans 48 pp. $8 [BiTod 35,262].

3888 ˙**Lea, Thomas D.** The New Testament: its background and message. Nv 1996, Broadman and H. 630 pp. RFaith & Mission 14/1 (1996) 94-96 (*Michael, Thomas*).

3889 **Lorenzen, Thorwald** Resurrection and discipleship. 1995, ⇒11/1,3278. RTS 57 (1996) 549-550 (*Johnson, Luke T.*).

3890 **Luter, Boyd; McReynolds, Kathy** Disciplined living: what the New Testament teaches about recovery and discipleship. GR 1996, Baker 213 pp. 0-8010-5243-2.

3891 **Lüdemann, Gerd** Die Ketzer: die andere Seite des frühen Christentums. Studienausgabe: Stu 1996, Radius 264 pp. 3-87173-078-5 [ActBib 34,49].

3892 **MacCain, Danny** Notes on New Testament introduction. Jos 1996, African Christian Textbooks xii; 335 pp. 978-2668-66-4 [NThAR 1997,292].

3893 **Malina, Bruce J.** The social world of Jesus and the gospels. Mp 1996, Fortress xvi; 256 pp. $50. 0-415-14628-3-629-1 [NThAR 1997,163].

3894 **McEleney, Neil J.** Gospel simplicity. Spiritual Life 42/4 (1996) 195-200.

3895 **Merklein, Helmut** La signoria di Dio nell'annuncio di Gesù. 1994, ⇒10,3849*. RPaVi 41/1 (1996) 57-59 (*Vallauri, Emiliano*).

3896 **Patzia, Arthur G.** The making of the NT. 1995, ⇒11/2,2177. RBiTr 47 (1996) 154-156 (*Omanson, Roger L.*).

3897 E**Piñero, Antonio** Orígenes del cristianismo. 1991, ⇒7,453... 10,3857. MEAH 41/2 (1992) 156-158 (*Ramón Ayaso, José*);

3898 Fuentes del cristianismo. 1993, ⇒9,4063... 11/2,2181. RSal. 58 (1996) 380-381 (*Bartolomé, J.J.*).

3899 **Piñero, Antonio; Peláez, Jesús** El Nuevo Testamento: introducción. 1995, ⇒11/2,2182. RBLE 97/2 (1996) 189 (*Légasse, S.*); EE 71 (1996) 476-477 (*Vargas Machuca, Antonio*); ΕΠΙΜΕΛΕΙΑ 5 (1996) 143-146 (*García Bazán, Francisco*); Cart. 12 (1996) 479-480 (*Sanz Valdivieso, R.*).

3900 **Popkes, Wiard** Paränese und Neues Testament. SBS 168: Stu 1996, Katholisches Bibelwerk 208 pp. DM59. 3-460-04681-3 [NTAb 41,166].

3901 **Pronzato, Alessandro** Vangeli scomodi. Mi ^{25}1996, Gribaudi 341 pp. 88-7152-228-1.

3902 **Raja, Retchaganathan Jesu** The gospels with an Indian face. Madras 1996, Christian Literature Society viii; 81 pp. [NThAR 1998,368].

3903 **Ravasi, Gianfranco** La buona novella: le storie, le idee, i personaggi del Nuovo Testamento. Saggi: Mi 1996, Mondadori (8) 331 pp. L30.000. 88-04-41052-3.

3904 **Rhoads, David** The challenge of diversity. Mp 1996, Fortress x; 172 pp. $12 [BiTod 35,326].

3905 **Riches, John** El mundo de Jesús: el judaísmo del siglo I, en crisis. Córdoba 1996, El Almendro 195 pp. Pts1.600.

3906   *Sabatino, C.J.* Disenpowering judgement. Encounter 57/2 (1996) 127-138 [NTAb 41,24].

3907   *Saddington, D.B.* Roman military and administrative personnel in the New Testament. Religion. ANRW II.26.3: 1996, ⇒183. 2409-2435.

3908   ^E**Salwak, Dale** The words of Christ. Novato, Calif. 1996, New World Library x; 161 pp. 1-880032-84-8 [NThAR 1997,262].

3909   **Schnelle, Udo** Einleitung in das NT. UTB.W 1830: 1994, ⇒11/2,2199. ^RThLZ 121 (1996) 358-363 (*Broer, Ingo*); CritRR 9 (1996) 269-270 (*Kahl, Werner*);

3910   Einleitung in das Neue Testament. UTB.W 1830: Gö ²1996, Vandenhoeck & R. 639 pp. DM54. 3-525-53633-X.

3911   *Schuster, Ildefonso* Gesù Cristo nella storia: condizioni per un accurato studio della storia della chiesa antica: discorso d'introduzione al corso di storia ecclesiastica. Ben. 43/1 (1996) 7-14.

3912   **Schweitzer, Albert** Conversations sur le Nouveau Testament. ^T*Kemner, Pierre,* P 1996, Brepols 185 pp. FF85. 2-503-83024-2.

3913   **Schweizer, Eduard** A theological introduction to the NT. 1991, ⇒8,4188; 9,4074. ^RSBET 14 (1996) 175-176 (*Adams, Edward*).

3914   **Simmons, William S.** A theology of inclusion in Jesus and Paul: the God of outcasts and sinners. Diss. St. Andrews 1990. Mellen 39: Lewiston, NY 1996, Mellen xv; 193 pp. 0-7734-2430-X [NThAR 1997,262].

3915   *Smith, Morton* How magic was changed by the triumph of christianity. New Testament. 1996 <1983>, ⇒151. 208-216;

3916   Terminological boobytraps and real problems in Second-Temple Judaeo-Christian studies. Studies in...method. 1996 <1983>, ⇒150. 95-103.

3917   *Soards, M.L.* Key issues in biblical studies and their bearing on mission studies. Miss. 24/1 (1996) 93-109 [NTA 40,462].

3918   **Stark, Rodney** The rise of christianity: a sociologist reconsiders history. Princeton 1996, Princeton University Press xiv; 246 pp. $25 [JEarlyC 5,306].

3919   **Stott, John** Imágenes del predicador en el Nuevo Testamento. BA 1996, Nueva Creación 120 pp. [Mayéutica 23,559—Oliveira, Milton C. de].

3920   **Strecker, Georg** Literaturgeschichte des NT. 1992, ⇒8,4192... 11/2,2211. ^RBiLi 69 (1996) 49-50 (*Söding, Thomas*).

3921   **Thüsing, Wilhelm** Die neutestamentlichen Theologien und Jesus Christus: Grundlegung einer Theologie des Neuen Testaments I: Kriterien aufgrund der Rückfrage nach Jesus und des Glaubens an seine Auferweckung. Müns ²1996, Aschendorff 405 pp. 3-402-03408-5.

3922   **Troiani, Lucio** A proposito delle origini del cristianesimo. At. 84 (1996) 7-22.

3923   **Ulonska, Herbert** Streiten mit Jesus: Konfliktgeschichten in den Evangelien. BTSP 11: 1995, ⇒11/2,2216. ^RThLZ 121 (1996) 164-166 (*Zager, Werner*).

3924   **Winkelmann, Friedhelm** Geschichte des frühen Christentums. Mü 1996, Beck 125 pp. DM15 [HZ 266/1,167—Molthagen, Joachim].

3925   *Wong, T(h)eresa* The disciples of Christ in the gospels, 1-2. CTUF 109, 110 (1996) 323-332, 467-482 [ThIK 18/2,31, 32]. C.

3926 ᴱZuck, Roy B. Vital New Testament issues: examining New Testament passages and problems. Vital Issues 8: GR 1996, Kregel 288 pp. 0-8254-4074-2 [NThAR 1997,262].

F1.2 *Origo Evangeliorum*, the Origin of the Gospels

3927 ᴱAlberto, Stefano Vangelo e storicità. 1995, ⇒11/2,2088. ᴿVetChr 33/1 (1996) 226-229 (*Infante, Renzo*); PaVi 41/3 (1996) 54-56 (*Làconi, Mauro*).

3928 Benjamin, David Eugene The identification of the genre 'gospel' and its hermeneutical significance for the canonical gospels. Diss. Southwestern Bapt. Theol. Sem. 1995. 284 pp. [EThL 74,288*].

3929 Brown, Raymond E. Reading the gospels with the Church: from Christmas through Easter. Cincinnati, OH 1996, St. Anthony Messenger vi; 90 pp. $8. 0-86716-268-6 [NTAb 41,143].

3930 Burridge, Richard A. Four gospels, one Jesus?. 1994, ⇒10,3889. ᴿClR 46 (1996) 265-266 (*Duff, Tim*).

3931 Delorme, Jean Au risque de la parole: lire les évangiles. 1991, ⇒7,195; 10,3892. ᴿSEÁ 61 (1996) 143-144 (*Kieffer, René*).

3932 Los evangelios. Grupo Notre Histoire. Bilbao 1996, Desclée de B. 155 pp. [Proyección 44,162].

3933 *Girard, René* Are the gospels mythical?. First Things 62 (1996) 27-31 [Gen 4].

3934 Gundry, Robert H. ΕΥΑΓΓΕΛΙΟΝ: how soon a book?. JBL 115 (1996) 321-325.

3935 Schulz, Hans-Joachim Die apostolische Herkunft der Evangelien. QD 145: 1994, ⇒10,3906; 11/2,2200. ᴿNT 38 (1996) 298-299 (*Stenschke, Christoph*).

3936 Stanton, Graham N. The gospels and Jesus. 1989, ⇒5,4016... 8,4232. ᴿRBL 49 (1996) 209-211 (*Wojciechowski, Michał*).

3937 Thiede, Carsten Peter; D'Ancona, Matthew Testimone oculare di Gesù: la nuova sconvolgente prova sull'origine del vangelo. CasM 1996, Piemme 238 pp.

F1.4 *Jesus historicus*—The human Jesus

3938 *Adam, A.K.M.* Docetism, KAESEMANN, and christology: why historical criticism can't protect christological orthodoxy. SJTh 49 (1996) 391-410.

3939 Aers, David; Staley, Lynn The powers of the holy: religion, politics, and gender in late medieval English culture. University Park, Penn. 1996, Pennsylvania State University 310 pp. $45 [TS 58,542].

3940 Aguirre, R. Aproximación actual al Jesús de la historia. Cuadernos de Teología Deusto 5: Bilbao 1996, Universidad de Deusto 44 pp. 84-7485-424-5 [NTAb 41,142].

3941 *Aguirre, Rafael* Estado actual de los estudios sobre el Jesús histórico después de BULTMANN. EstB 54 (1996) 433-463.

3942 *Allison, Dale C.* The contemporary quest for the historical Jesus. IBSt 18 (1996) 174-193.

3943 Alt, Franz Jesús, el primer hombre nuevo. 1993, ⇒9,4129; 11/2,2089. ᴿRevBib 58 (1996) 124-127 (*Levoratti, A.J.*).

3944 **Barry, William A.** Who do you say I am?: meeting the historical Jesus in prayer. Notre Dame, IN 1996, Ave Maria 148 pp. 0-87793-575-0.

3945 *Barth, Gerhard* Spekulationsobjekt Jesus oder der vermarktete Jesus. Neutestamentliche Versuche. 1996 <1994>, ⇒111. 455-473.

3946 **Bartley, Peter** The gospel Jesus: fact or fiction?. Dublin 1996, Veritas 107 pp. 1-85390-335-3.

3947 **Beaude, Pierre Marie** Jésus. P 1996, Casterman 160 pp. FF42.

3948 **Becker, Jürgen** Jesus von Nazareth. B 1996, De Gruyter xi; 461 pp. DM74/38. 3-11-014881-1/2-X. ᴿSynaxis 14 (1996) 366-368 (*Osculati, Roberto*).

3949 **Berger, Klaus** Wer war Jesus wirklich?. Stu 1995, Quell 232 pp. DM29.80. 3-7918-1950-X. ᴿBiKi 51 (1996) 144-146 (*Hoppe, Rudolf*).

3950 *Berger, Klaus* Der "brutale" Jesus: Gewaltsames in Wirken und Verkündigung Jesu. BiKi 51 (1996) 119-127.

3951 **Berger, Klaus** Wie was Jezus werkelijk?. Kampen 1996, Kok 247 pp. *f*35. 90-242-7907-0.

3952 *Boomershine, Thomas E.* Jesus of Nazareth and the watershed of ancient orality and literacy. Semeia 65/2 (1994) 7-36;

3953 ᴱ**Borg, Marcus** Jesus at 2000. Boulder 1996, Westview xiv; 177 pp. $21. 0-860-78557-2 [JEarlyC 5,315].

3954 **Borg, Marcus J.** Meeting... the historical Jesus. 1994, ⇒10,3930; 11/2,2096. ᴿCThMi 23 (1996) 450-451 (*Conrad, Robert*);

3955 Un nouveau regard sur Jésus. ᵀ*Perrottet, Claude; Guyénot, Laurent*, Le Kremlin-Bicêtre 1996, La Pierre d'Angle 277 pp. [RHPhR 77,201].

3956 *Boring, M. Eugene* The "third quest" and the apostolic faith. Interp. 50 (1996) 341-354.

3957 *Cameron, Ron* The sayings gospel Q and the quest of the historical Jesus: a response to John S. KLOPPENBORG. HThR 89 (1996) 351-354.

3958 **Chilton, Bruce D.** Pure kingdom: Jesus' vision of God: studying the historical Jesus. GR 1996, Eerdmans x; 178 pp. $15. 0-8028-4187-2.

3959 ᴱ**Chilton, Bruce; Evans, Craig A.** Studying the historical Jesus. NTTS 19: 1994, ⇒10,239b. ᴿCBQ 58 (1996) 380-382 (*Scroggs, Robin*).

3960 **Cook, M.L.** E voi chi dite che io sia?: 101 domande su Gesù Cristo. CinB 1996, San Paolo 190 pp. L16.000 [RdT 38,142].

3961 **Cothenet, Édouard** Jésus: 70 ans de recherches. EeV 106 (1996) 353-362.

3962 **Crossan, Dominic** Der historische Jesus. ²1995 <1994>, ⇒11/2,2119. ᴿZKTh 118 (1996) 262-263 (*Oberforcher, Robert*);

3963 The essential Jesus. ⇒10,3939. ᴿABR 44 (1996) 81-84 (*Stewart, William R.*);

3964 Jesus: a revolutionary biography. 1994, ⇒10,3938; 11/2,2120. ᴿETR 71 (1996) 113-115 (*Rakotoharintsifa, Andrianjatovo*); IBSt 18 (1996) 44-48 (*Campbell, Denis*); CritRR 9 (1996) 191-192 (*Allison, Dale C.*);

3965 Jesus: ein revolutionäres Leben. ᵀ*Hahlbrock, Peter*, Mü 1996, Beck 264 pp. DM19.80. 3-406-39244-X [ThRv 93,167].

3966 *Crossan, John Dominic* Why christians must search for the historical Jesus. BiRe 12/2 (1996) 34-38, 42-45.

3967 **Crotty, Robert** The Jesus question: the historical search. Blackburn 1996, Harper Collins Religious 228 pp. AUS$25. 1-86371-681-5 [ACR 74,254].

3968 ᵀ**Davenport, Guy; Urrutia, Benjamin** The logia of Yeshua: the sayings of Jesus. Wsh 1996, Counterpoint xxi; 67 pp. Bibl. 1-887178-18-X.

3969 *Davies, Stevan* The historical Jesus as a prophet/healer: a different paradigm. Neotest. 30 (1996) 21-38.

3970 *Davies, Stevan* The historical Jesus as a prophet/healer: a different paradigm. Neotest. 30 (1996) 21-38.

3971 **De Rosa, Giuseppe** Gesù di Nazaret: la vita il messaggio, il mistero. Leumann 1996, Elle Di Ci 344 pp. L30.000. ᴿPalCl 75 (1996) 861-862 (*Lavarda, Girolamo*).

3972 *Denaux, A.* Did Jesus found the church?. LouvSt 21 (1996) 25-45.

3973 **Di Mura, Francesco** La storia di Gesù: quel tempo: le persone: i luoghi. Salerno 1994, Palladio 536 pp. L32.000. ᴿCivCatt 147 I (1996) 621-622 (*Scaiola, D.*).

3974 ᴱ**Dupuy, Michel**, (*al*), Pierre de BE RULLE: narré, vie de Jésus, élévations, mémorial sur sainte Madeleine. Œuvres complètes 8: P 1996, Cerf 512 pp. F250. ᴿEeV 106 (1996) 301-303 (*Oury, G.-M.*).

3975 **Duquesne, Jacques** Jésus. 1994, ⇒10,3943; 11/2,2127. ᴿSalm. 43/1 (1996) 43-50 (*González de Cardedal, Olegario*); Positief 265 (1996) 237-238 (*La Potterie, Ignace de*);

3976 Jesús. ᵀ*Figueres, Anna*, Barc 1996, Empúries 322 pp. [TE 42,276—Gelabert, Martín].

3977 *Ebner, Martin* Kynische Jesusinterpretation—"disciplined exaggeration"?: eine Anfrage. BZ 40 (1996) 93-100.

3978 *Echlin, Edward P.* James [sic] and sensate creatures of Palestine and of the earth. IThQ 62 (1996-97) 269-283.

3979 *Eddy, Paul Rhodes* Jesus as DIOGENES?: reflections on the Cynic Jesus thesis. JBL 115 (1996) 449-469.

3980 **Evans, C. Stephen** The historical Christ and the Jesus of faith: the incarnational narrative as history. Oxf 1996, Clarendon xiv; 386 pp. £40/13. 0-19-826382-1/97-X.

3981 **Evans, Craig A.** Life of Jesus research: an annotated bibliography. NTTS 24: Lei 1996, Brill xvii, 335 pp. Rev. ed. ƒ172; $111. 90-04-10282-5.

3982 **Fiensy, David A.** The message and ministry of Jesus: an introductory textbook. Lanham, Md. 1996, Univ. Press of America xiii; 331 pp. 0-7618-0502-2/6-0 [NThAR 1997,194].

3983 **Freyne, Sean** A Galiléia, Jesus e os evangelhos. ᵀ*Noble, Tim*, Bíblica Loyola 16: São Paulo 1996, Loyola 254 pp. 85-15-011859-9 [PerTeol 29,134].

3984 *Freyne, Sean* Jesus, der Pilger. Conc(D) 32 (1996) 315-321.

3985 **Frickenschmidt, Dirk** Vier antike Jesusbiographien: die kanonischen Evangelien im Rahmen antiker biographischer Erzählkunst. Diss. Heidelberg 1996/7, ᴰ*Berger, K.* [ThLZ 122,762].

3986 **Funk, Robert W.** Honest to Jesus: Jesus for a new millennium. San Francisco 1996, HarperSanFrancisco x; 342 pp. $24. 0-06-062757-3 [RExp 94,465].

3987 **Funk, Robert Walter; Hoover, Roy W.** The five gospels: the search for the authentic words of Jesus. The Jesus Seminar, new translation and commentary. NY 1996, Scribner xxii, 553 pp. 0-02-541949-8.

3988 **Galbiati, Gilberto** Gesù e il suo vangelo. Mercator 16: F 1996, Atheneum 237 pp. 88-7255-111-0.

3989 *Galvin, John P.* "I believe... in Jesus Christ, his only son, our Lord": the earthly Jesus and the Christ of faith. Interp. 50 (1996) 373-382.

3990 *García Bazán, Francisco* Los 'parientes del Señor' en la tradición cristiana primitiva y sus proyecciones religiosas. Res. 167. ΕΠΙΜΕΛΕΙΑ 5 (1996) 167-182.

3991 **Gnilka, Joachim** Gesù di Nazaret. CTNT.S 3: 1993, ⇒9,4162. RAsp. 43/1 (1996) 118-119 (*Di Palma, G.*); Anton. 71 (1996) 358 (*Nobile, Marco*).

3992 **Goldenberg, David M.** Retroversion to Jesus' ipsissima verba and the vocabulary of Jewish Palestinian Aramaic: the case of *mata'* and *quarta'*. Bib. 77 (1996) 64-83.

3993 **Green, Barbara** 'What profit for us?': remembering the story of Jesus. Lanham 1996 Univ. Press of America vi; 234 pp. $28.50. 0-7618-0510-9/1-7 [NThAR 1997,260].

3994 TGreiner, **Susanne; Gisi, Martha** Ludolf von Sachsen: Das Leben Jesu Christi. CMe 47: FrB 1994, Johannes 228 pp. ÖS195. 3-89411-324-3. RZKTh 118 (1996) 538-539 (*Batlogg, Andreas*).

3995 *Grelot, Pierre* Jésus et ses témoins. RSR 84 (1996) 413-423.

3996 *Guillet, Jacques* La promesse accomplie, Jésus Christ Omega. RSR 84 (1996) 177-190.

3997 **Gutierrez Martin, Darío** La humanidad de Jesus de Nazaret. M 1995, San Pablo 240 pp. RRICP 59 (1996) 295-296 (*Soriano, M.-E.*).

3998 **Heyer, C.J. den** Jesus matters: 150 years of research. L 1996, SCM xiv; 193 pp. 0-334-02659-8;

3999 *Opnieuw: wie is Jezus?*: balans van 150 haar onderzoek naar Jezus. Zoetermeer 1996, Meinema 232 pp. ƒ35; FB700. 90-211-3632-5 [TTh 36,414—*Van de Sandt, Huub*].

4000 **Hoppe, Rudolf** Jesus: von der Krippe an den Galgen. Stu 1996, Katholisches Bibelwerk 164 pp. DM24.80.

4001 *Horsley, Richard A.* What has Galilee to do with Jerusalem?: political aspects of the Jesus movement. HTS 52/1 (1996) 88-104 [NTAb 41,26].

4002 *Jacobs, Maretha M.* The relation between Jesus, Christ and Christian faith in current historical Jesus scholarship. Neotest. 30 (1996) 103-119.

4003 **Jeremias, Joachim** Théologie du Nouveau Testament: la prédication de Jésus. TAizin, J.; Liefooghe, A., Initiations Bibliques: P 1996, Cerf 420 pp. FF148. 2-204-05560-3 [RB 104,474].

4004 **Johnson, Luke Timothy** The real Jesus: the misguided quest for the historical Jesus and the truth of the traditional gospels. San Francisco 1996, HarperSanFrancisco 182 pp. $22/12. RATR 78/2 (1996) 335-337 (*Deakle, David W.*).

4005 *Kealy, Seán P.* The third quest for the historical Jesus. PIBA 19 (1996) 84-98.

4006 *Kee, Howard Clark* Jesus: a glutton and a drunkard. NTS 42 (1996) 374-393.

4007 *Kelber, Werner H.* Jesus and tradition: words in time, words in space. Semeia 65/2 (1994) 139-167.

4008 **Kieffer, R.** Jésus raconté: théologie et spiritualité des évangiles. LiBi 108: P 1996, Cerf 209 pp. FF90. 2-204-05328-7.

4009 *Kloppenborg, John S.* The sayings gospel Q and the quest of the historical Jesus. HThR 89 (1996) 307-344.

4010 *Koester, Helmut* The sayings gospel Q and the quest of the historical Jesus: a response to John S. KLOPPENBORG. HThR 89 (1996) 345-349.

4011 *Kozhamthadam, Job* SOCRATES vs Christ: dichotomy vs integration. Sum. 641. VJTR 60 (1996) 641-653.

4012 *Lannert, Berthold* "Wer war Jesus von Nazareth?": eine Artikelserie von Johannes WEISS in Naumanns Zeitschrift "Die Hilfe". Die "religionsgeschichtliche Schule". 1996, ⇒220. 107-148.

4013 **Laudert-Ruhm, Gerd** Jesus von Nazareth: das gesicherte Basiswissen: Daten, Fakten, Hintergründe. Stu 1996, Kreuz 137 pp. 3-7831-1449-7.

4014 **Laurentin, René** Vie authentique de Jésus-Christ: fondements, preuves et justification. P 1996, Fayard 236 pp. F130. 2-213-59664-6 [NThAR 1997,163].

4015 *Lémonon, J.-P.* Exégèse et lecture dans la foi: Jésus de Nazareth au regard de l'historien. Bulletin de l'Institut Catholique de Lyon 114 (1996) 57-74.

4016 *Legrand, Lucien* Biblical scholarship on the historical Jesus. Jeevadhara 26 (1996) 87-106.

4017 *Lobo Gajiwala, Astrid* Gospel leadership, 1. Sum. 155. VJTR 60/3 (1996) 155-166.

4018 **Loew, Jacques** Ce Jésus qu'on appelle Christ: retraite au Vatican (1970). Foi vivante—Vie spirituelle 371: P 1996, Cerf xv (2) 9-286 pp. 2-204-05373-2.

4019 **Lövestam, Evald** Jesus and 'this generation': a New Testament study. [T]*Linnarud, M.*, CB.NT 25: Sto 1995, Almqvist & W. 130 pp. SK132. 91-22-01668-6. [R]CritRR 9 (1996) 241-242 (*Powery, Emerson B.*).

4020 **Maass, Fritz** Der historische Jesus. Denzlingen 1996, Maass 38 pp. [DBAT 29,307ss—Diebner, B.J.].

4021 **Maillot, Alphonse** Un Jésus 'Vous, qui dites-vous que je suis?'. P 1995, Lethielleux 318 pp. F140. [R]FV 95/5 (1996) 87-88 (*Leplay, Michel*).

4022 *Manicardi, E.* Gesù e gli stanieri. RStB 8 (1996) 197-231.

4023 *Martin, A.G.* Jésus dans l'Évangile et dans le Coran. RRef 47 (1996) 5-14.

4024 **Mattioli, Anselmo** Quel no del giudaismo a Gesù: i motivi e le cause di un grande fatto storico. R 1996, Città Nuova 363 pp. L68.000. [R]Mar. 58 (1996) 301-302 (*Stern, Jean*); Ter. 47 (1996) 695-698 (*Pasquetto, Virgilio*).

4025 *Meagher, Patrick M.* Jesus of history and Jesus of faith. Jeevadhara 26 (1996) 107-118.

4026 *Meier, John P.* Dividing lines in Jesus research today: through dialectical negation to a positive sketch. Interp. 50 (1996) 355-372.

4027 **Men', Aleksandr** Gesú maestro di Nazaret: la storia che sfida il tempo. [E]*Guaita, Giovanni*, R 1996, Città Nuova 375 pp. L48.000. 88-311-5207-6.

4028 **Mesters, Carlos** Jesús nuestro hermano. Biblia y Vida: México 1996, Dabar 3 vols; 77; 77; 72 pp. [EfMex 15,407].

4029 **Monjardet, André** Jesús de Nazareth, autobiographie. Anamorphoses: P 1996, Berg 175 pp. Texte établi et commenté; suivi de réflexions sur l'évolution historique des relations de l'homme avec Dieu. F98. 2-911289-03-X. RLV(L) 45/5 (1996) 88 (*Duquoc, Christian*).

4030 **Morse, Mary Katherine** The relationship of wisdom to transformational leadership: illustrated by the historical Jesus. Diss. Gonzaga 1996, DWilson, S.M., 327 pp. [EThL 74,291*].

4031 *Mulloor, Augustine* Jesus the Christ of the gospels. Jeevadhara 26 (1996) 119-130.

4032 *Murphy-O'Connor, Jerome* Why Jesus went back to Galilee. BiRe 12/1 (1996) 20-29, 42-43.

4033 **Ng, Eng Eng** Jesus and the other sex. CTUF 108 (1996) 179-199 [ThIK 18/1,28]. C.

4034 **Nolan, Albert** Jesus before christianity. 1976, ⇒58s,6039; 60,5460. RDoLi 46/5 (1996) 271-278 (*O'Leary, P.*);

4035 Jesus vor dem Christentum. 1993, ⇒10,3993. RThLZ 121 (1996) 160-162 (*Zager, Werner*).

4036 **Omodeo, Adolfo** Gesù il Nazoreo. 1992, ⇒8,4324; 10,3997. RAt. 84 (1996) 316-320 (*Jucci, Elio*).

4037 **Pacomio, L.** Gesù: i 37 anni che venti secoli fa cambiarono il senso della storia e i nostri destini. Giubileo 2000: CasM 1996, Piemme 334 pp. L20.000 [RdT 38,287].

4038 *Patterson, S.J.* Shall we teach what Jesus taught?. Prism 11/1 (1996) 40-57 [NTAb 41/1 (1997) 27].

4039 **Perry, John Michael** Exploring the identity and mission of Jesus. Exploring Scripture: Kansas City, MO 1996, Sheed & W. xiv; 280 pp. $20. 1-55612-820-7.

4040 **Phipps, William E.** The sexuality of Jesus. Cleveland, Ohio 1996, Pilgrim 250 pp. $17. 0-8298-1144-3 [NThAR 1997,261].

4041 *Pieterse, H.* Bybelwetenskaplike navorsing en die geloof van de gemeentes [Biblical scholarship and the faith of the church]. RelT 3/1 (1996) 64-71 [NTAb 41,28].

4042 **Piñero, A.** L'altro Gesù: vita di Gesù secondo i vangeli apocrifi. TeVi 24: Bo 1996, EDB 200 pp. [RivBib 45,493];

4043 L'autre Jésus: vie de Jésus selon les évangiles apocryphes. TMaldonado, Oscar, P 1996, Seuil 200 pp. F130. 2-02-025801-3 [BCLF 584,1420].

4044 **Pixner, Bargil** With Jesus in Jerusalem: his first and last days in Judea. Rosh Pina 1996, Corazin 184 pp. $20. 965-434-004-6 [RB 105,304s—Murphy-O'Connor, J.].

4045 **Powell, Robert** Chronicle of the living Christ: the life and ministry of Jesus Christ: foundations of cosmic christianity. Hudson, NY 1996, Anthroposphic 495 pp. 0-88010-407-4 [NThAR 1997,164].

4046 *Ri, Jemin* Jesus als Mensch, der unser 'Ich' gefunden hat. Samok 213 (1996) 38-47 [ThIK 18/2,54]. K.;

4047 Jesus—ein freier Mensch. Samok 215 (1996) 58-68 [ThIK 18/2,55]. K.

4048 *Riches, John K.* The social world of Jesus. Interp. 50 (1996) 383-393.

4049 *Riesner, Rainer* Wurden in Jerusalem die Särge Jesu und seiner Familie gefunden?. BiKi 51 (1996) 133-137.

4050 ᴱRietveld, Jan Essays over Jezus: gedachten aan het einde van de twintigste eeuw. Kampen 1996, Kok 96 pp. ƒ17.50. 90-242-7977-1 [Str. 64,451].

4051 Rizzacasa, Aurelio Il tema di Lᴇssɪɴɢ. CinB 1996, San Paolo 166 pp. L20.000 [Cultura & Libri.S 112,70—Scalabrin, Sandro].

4052 Rogers, Patrick Wanted: the real historical Jesus. Milltown Studies 37 (1996) 108-119.

4053 Sandelin, Karl-Gustav The Jesus-tradition and idolatry. NTS 42 (1996) 412-420.

4054 Sanders, E.P. Jezus: mythe en werkelijkheid. Baarn 1996, Callenbach 352 pp. ƒ49.50. 90-266-0489-0 [Bijdr. 59,460s—Koet, Bart J.];

4055 Sohn Gottes: eine historische Biographie Jesu. ᵀEnderwitz, Ulrich, Stu 1996, Klett-Cotta 452 pp. DM48. 3-608-91721-7 [NThAR 1997,70].

4056 Schnackenburg, Rudolf La persona di Gesù Cristo nei quattro vangeli. CTNT.S 4: 1995, ⇒11/2,2197. ᴿAnton. 71 (1996) 357 (Nobile, Marco).

4057 Schröter, Jens The historical Jesus and the sayings tradition: comments on current research. Neotest. 30 (1996) 151-168.

4058 Schürmann, Heinz Jesus—Gestalt und Geheimnis. ᴱScholtissek, Klaus, 1994, ⇒10,224a. ᴿThLZ 121 (1996) 559-562 (Walter, Nikolaus); ThRv 92 (1996) 32-34 (Giesen, Heinz).

4059 Schweizer, Eduard Jesus, das Gleichnis Gottes: was wissen wir wirklich vom Leben Jesu?. Kleine Vandenhoeck-Reihe 1572: Gö 1995, Vandenhoeck & R. 120 pp. DM18.80. 3-525-33596-2. ᴿThLZ 121 (1996) 162-164 (Becker, Jürgen); JETh 10 (1996) 257-259 (Hörster, Gerhard);

4060 Gesú, la parabola di Dio: il punto sulla vita di Gesù. Giornale di teologia 246: Brescia 1996, Queriniana 175 pp. L24.000. 88-399-0746-7 [RdT 37/6 (1996) 850].

4061 Shamon, Albert Joseph Mary A graphic life of Jesus the Christ. Milford, OH 1996, Faith xix; 188 pp. 1-877678-41-4 [NThAR 1997,228].

4062 Siebel, W.A.; Winkler, T. Das Kerygma Jesu: eine andere Rekonstruktion der Worte Jesu und ihre religionsgeschichtliche Bedutung. Glasers Sozialanthropologische Reihe 8: Wsb ²1996, Glaser xiii; 410 pp. 3-89379-128-0 [NThAR 1997,36].

4063 Stanton, Graham Gospel truth?: new light on Jesus and the gospels. 1995, ⇒11/2,2208. ᴿRRT 3/2 (1996) 8-16 (Need, Stephen W.); CritRR 9 (1996) 278-279 (Evans, Craig A.).

4064 Stegemann, Ekkehard "Ich habe öffentlich zur Welt gesprochen": Jesus und die Öffentlichkeit. JBTh 11 (1996) 103-121.

4065 Stein, Robert H. Jesus the Messiah: a survey of the life of Christ. DG 1996, InterVarsity 290 pp. $25. 0-8308-1884-7 [BiTod 35,264].

4066 Suau, Teodor Algunes reflexions sobre el llibre De Cafarnaüm a Jerusalem. QVC 184 (1996) 63-72.

4067 Tamayo-Acosta, Juan José Imágenes de Jesús: condicionamientos sociales, culturales, religosos y de género. Hacia la comunidad 4: M 1996, Trotta 158 pp.

4068 Theißen, Gerd; Merz, Annette Der historische Jesus: ein Lehrbuch. ᶠBᴜʀᴄʜᴀʀᴅ Christoph, Gö 1996, Vandenhoeck & R. 557 pp. DM58. 3-525-52143-X.

4069 *Theißen, Gerd* Historical scepticism and the criteria of Jesus research or my attempt to leap across LESSING's yawning gulf. SJTh 49 (1996) 147-176.

4070 **Theissen, Gerd** The shadow of the Galilean. 1987, ⇒4,3969... 6,4330, ᴿSBET 14 (1996) 72-73 (*Wilson, Alistair*).

4071 *Thissen, Werner* Schöpfungsbejahung und Kreuzesnachfolge: Christsein in Spannungseinheit von Nähe und Distanz zur Welt. ᶠTHUESING W., NTA 31: 1996, ⇒94. 361-367.

4072 **Tully, Mark** God, Jew, rebel, the hidden Jesus: an investigation into the lives of Jesus. L 1996, BBC Books 224 pp. 0-563-37148-X.

4073 *Twycross, Stephen* Was Jesus married?. ET 107 (1996) 334.

4074 *Ukpong, Justin S.* Jesus and the exercise of authority. C.U.E.A. African Christian Studies 12/3 (1996) 1-16 [ThIK 18/2,17].

4075 *Viviano, B.T.* The historical Jesus in the doubly attested sayings: an experiment. RB 103 (1996) 367-410.

4076 *Wanamaker, Charles* The historical Jesus today: a reconsideration of the foundation of christology. JTSA 94 (1996) 3-17 [ThIK 18/1,19].

4077 *Weiser, Alfons* Jesus und die neutestamentliche Theologie: zur Frage nach dem Einheitsgrund des Neuen Testaments. ZNW 87 (1996) 146-164.

4078 **Wells, George Albert** The Jesus legend. Foreword *Hoffman, R. Joseph*, Ch 1996, Open Court xxxii; 287 pp. 0-8126-9334-5.

4079 ᴱ**Wilkins, Michael J.; Moreland, J.P.** Jesus under fire...the historical Jesus. 1995, ⇒11/2,390. ᴿTrinJ 17 (1996) 98-101 (*Copan, Paul*).

4080 **Wilson, A.N.** Jesus. 1992, ⇒8,4346. ᴿJdm 45 (1996) 373-376 (*Goldberg, Michael*).

4081 **Witherington, Ben** Jesus the sage: the pilgrimage of wisdom. E 1995, Clark 436 pp. ᴿRRT 3/2 (1996) 8-16 (*Need, Stephen W.*); ScrTh 28 (1996) 927-928 (*Aranda, G.*); CritRR 9 (1996) 307-309 (*Evans, Craig A.*);

4082 The Jesus quest: the third search for the Jew of Nazareth. DG ²1996, InterVarsity 304 pp. 0-8308-1861-8.

4083 **Wojciechowski, Michał** Jezus Jako święty: w pismach Nowego Testamentu. Rozprawy i Studia Biblijne 2: Wsz 1996, Oficyna Wydawnicza "Vocatio" 244 pp. 83-7146-058-9.

4084 *Wright, N.T.* How Jesus saw himself. BiRe 12/3 (1996) 22-29.

4085 **Wright, Tom** The original Jesus: the life and vision of a revolutionary. GR 1996, Eerdmans 160 pp. 0-8028-3837-5.

4086 *Yamauchi, Ichiro* The problem of the historical Jesus and christian mission. Kwansei-Gakuin-Daigaku 1 (1996) 23-40.

4087 *Young, Pamela Dickey* Encountering Jesus through the earliest witnesses. TS 57 (1996) 513-521.

4088 **Zahrnt, Heinz** Jésus de Nazareth: une vie. ᵀ*Rey, François; Guého, Marie-Thérèse*, P 1996, Seuil. F125. 2-02-011423-2.

F1.5 *Jesus et Israel*—**Jesus the Jew**

4089 *Bodendorfer, Gerhard* Jüdische Stimmen zu Jesus. PzB 5 (1996) 95-107.

4090 ^E**Charlesworth, James H.** Jesus' Jewishness. 1991, ⇒7,294...
9,4229. ^REE 71 (1996) 107-108 (*Pastor, F.*).

4091 **Charlesworth, James H.** Gesù nel giudaismo. 1994, ⇒10,4038.
^RDiv. 40 (1996) 183-184 (*Stramare, Tarcisio*); RivBib 44 (1996)
113-115 (*Fabbro, Franco*); VetChr 33 (1996) 233-234 (*Aulisa,
Immacolata*); Teol. 33 (1996) 253-254 (*Hubeňák, Florencio*).

4092 *Dautzenberg, Gerhard* Jesus und die Tora. Die Tora. 1996,
⇒1308. 345-378.

4093 **Horsley, Richard A.** Jesus and...popular Jewish resistance in
Roman Palestine. 1993, ⇒9,4242. ^RRB 103 (1996) 134-135
(*Viviano, B.T.*).

4094 **Meier, John P.** A marginal Jew: rethinking the historical Jesus 2:
mentor, message, and miracles. AncB Ref. Lib. 1994, ⇒10,4069.
^RCBQ 58 (1996) 758-760 (*Donahue, John R.*).

4095 *Moltmann, Jürgen* Jesus between Jews and christians. Arc 24
(1996) 61-76 [ZID 23,267].

4096 **Neusner, Jacob** Are there really tannaitic parallels to the gospels?:
a refutation of Morton SMITH. 1993, ⇒9,4256. ^RJAOS 116 (1996)
85-89 (*Cohen, Shaye J.D.*);

4097 Rabbinic literature and the NT. 1994, ⇒10,4075. ^RCritRR 9 (1996)
246-248 (*Fonrobert, Charlotte*);

4098 Disputa immaginaria tra un rabbino e Gesù: quale maestro se-
guire?. CasM 1996, Piemme 185 pp. L30.000. ^RStudi, Fatti, Ricerche 74 (1996) 12 (*Abbà, Maurizio*).

4099 **Pixner, Bargil** With Jesus through Galilee according to the fifth
gospel. ^T*Botha, Christa; Foster, David*, ColMn 1996, Liturgical
136 pp. $25. 0-8146-2427-8 [NTAb 41,151].

4100 **Potin, Jacques** Jésus en son pays. Domaine Biblique: P 1996,
Bayard 125 pp. F195 [EeV 106,277].

4101 ^E**Sauerbier, Edith** Auf der Suche nach einer neuen Christologie:
von Jesus, dem Juden, erzählen. Bendorf 1994, Hedwig-Dransfeld-
Haus 103 pp. ^RFrRu NF (1996/1) 63-64 (*Ahl, Ruth*).

4102 **Schwartz, Daniel R.** Studies in the Jewish background of christianity. 1992, ⇒8,4405; 10,4092. ^RNT 38 (1996) 406-407
(*Collins, Nina L.*).

4103 *Sievers, Joseph* Gesù e l'ebraismo. Unità e Carismi 6/6 (1996) 33-
38 [APIB 10/3 (1997) 268].

4104 **Spong, John Shelby** Liberating the gospels: reading the Bible with
Jewish eyes: freeing Jesus from 2,000 years of misunderstanding.
SF 1996, HarperSanFrancisco xviii; 361 pp. £11. 0-06-067556-X.

4105 **Vermes, Geza** The religion of Jesus the Jew. 1993, ⇒9,4284...
11/2,3426. ^RJThS 47 (1996) 201-208 (*Riches, John K.*).

4106 *Vermes, Geza* Jesus the Jew and his religion. Expl. 10/2 (1996) 7-8
[NTAb 41,29].

4107 **Vermes, Geza** La religión de Jesús el judío. M 1996, Muchnick
341 pp. ^RRF 234 (1996) 359-360 (*Vallarino, Jesús M.^a*).

4108 **Vidal, Marie** Un juif nommé Jésus: une lecture de l'évangile à la
lumière de la Torah. Pref. *Dujardin, Jean; Abécassis, d'Armand*,
Paroles vives: P 1996, Albin M. 326 pp. FF120. 2-226-08788-5.

4109 **Willems, Gerard F.** Jezus en de chassidim van zijn dagen: een
godsdienst-historische entdekking. Baarn 1996, Ten Have 219 pp.
ƒ35. 90-259-4663-1 [Bijdr. 58,240].

4110 *Wright, N.T.* Jesus. ^FHOOKER M., 1996, ⇒43. 43-58.

4111 **Wylen, Stephen M.** The Jews in the time of Jesus: an introduction. Mahwah 1996, Paulist viii; 215 pp. $15. 0-8091-3610-4.
4112 *Yancey, P.* Unwrapping Jesus: my top ten surprises. ChristToday 40/7 (1996) 29-32, 34 [NTAb 41,30].
4113 **Young, Brad H.** Jesus the Jewish theologian. 1995, ⇒11/2,2279. RJRH 20 (1996) 248-249 (*Lieu, Judith M.*); CritRR 9 (1996) 312-313 (*Howard, George*).

F1.6 *Jesus in Ecclesia*—The Church Jesus

4114 **Alfonso de Liguori** Jésus, amour des hommes. Pref. *Mermet, Rey*, Versailles 1996, Saint-Paul 174 pp. F79.
4115 **Alunno, Luigi** La vita di Gesù Cristo—croce e martirio: meditazioni. Pref. *Brovetto, Costante*, S. Gabriele (Te) 1996, Eco 285 pp. L18.000.
4116 *Amaladoss, Michael* 'Who do you say that I am?': speaking of Jesus in India today. Sum. 782. VJTR 60 (1996) 782-794.
4117 **Bockmuehl, Markus N.A.** This Jesus: martyr, Lord, messiah. DG 1996, InterVarsity xi; 242 pp. $18. 0-8308-1875-8 [ThD 44,59].
4118 **Bonte, N.** Weerbaren: Jezusboek voor jongeren. Bru 1996, Licap 301 pp.
4119 **Dehau, Thomas** L'apostolat de Jésus. Pref. *Philippe, M.-D.*, Versailles 1995, Saint-Paul 285 pp. F110. REeV 106 (1996) 165-166 (*Jay, Pierre*); Sedes Sapientiae 14/4 (1996) 85-88 (*Bazelaire, Thomas-M. de*).
4120 **Depoortere, K.** Wie is die Jezus?. Tielt 1996, Lannoo 224 pp.
4121 **Fernández, B.** El Cristo del seguimiento. M 1995, Claretianas 324 pp. 84-7966-114-3. RClar. 36-37 (1996-97) 630 (*D'Ors, Pablo Juan*).
4122 **Hari, Albert; Singer, Charles** Encontrar a Jesucristo hoy: para encontrar y conocer a Jesús. Estella 1996, Verbo Divino 248 pp. Ptas3.100.
4123 *Okure, Teresa* Word of God—word of life: an African perspective. WoWo 29/5 (1996) 178-200 [ThIK 18/2,47].
4124 *Rayan, Samuel* Jesus: a flesh-translation of divine compassion;
4125 Jesus today: steadfastness of love and life. Jeevadhara 26 (1996) 212-229/146-162.
4126 **Schuster, Ildefonso** Gesù Cristo nella storia: lezioni di storia ecclesiastica. SMBen 9: R 1996, Benedictina 121 pp. L22.000. RBen. 43 (1996) 420-423 (*Valli, Annamaria*).
4127 **Spicacci, Virginio** Gesù di Nazareth: una buona notizia?: una proposta di iniziazione all'esperienza cristiana. Mi 1995, L'Àncora 620 pp. L33.000. RCivCatt 147 II (1996) 92-93 (*Simone, M.*).
4128 **Stuhlmacher, Peter** Jesús de Nazaret, Cristo de la fé. TRuiz-Garrido, Constantino, VeIm 138: S 1996, Sígueme 124 pp. 84-301-1297-9. RREsp 55 (1996) 567-568 (*Castro, Secundino*); EstTrin 30 (1996) 299-300 (*Ofilada Macario, Mina*); Communio 29 (1996) 395-399 (*Burgos, M. de*).
4129 **Tupper, Frank E.** A scandalous providence: the Jesus story of the compassion of God. Macon 1995, Mercer University Press 468 pp. $35. RThTo 53 (1996) 408, 410-411 (*Cooper, Burton*).

4130 *Van der Horst, P.W.* Korte notities over het godsbegrip bij Grieken en Romeinen en de vergoddelijking van Jezus in het Nieuwe Testament. Bijd. 57 (1996) 149-157.

F1.7 *Jesus 'anormalis':* **to atheists, psychoanalysts, romance...**

4131 **Borrmans, Maurice** Jésus et les musulmans d'aujourd'hui. CJJC 69: P 1996, Desclée [Cahiers de l'Atelier 478,100s—Guillaud, Michel].

4132 **Burkhalter, Carmen** Un prince à Nazareth: une biographie littéraire de Jésus-Christ. Autres Temps 3: Genève 1996, Labor et Fides 141 pp. FF88. 2-8309-0785-X [RHPhR 78,96—Pfrimmer, T.].

4133 **Claes, Paul** Die zoon van de panter. Amst 1996, De Besige Bij 119 pp. BF490 [Str. 64,451].

4134 **De Vincenzis, Franco** SOCRATE e Gesù in *Volksreligion und Christentum* di G.W.F. HEGEL: oltre l'omologia e la correlazione. Paradigma 14 (1996) 593-609.

4135 **Drewermann, Eugen** Glauben in Freiheit. Jesus von Nazareth: Befreiung zum Frieden, 2: Z 1996, Walter 819 pp. 3-530-16897-1 [NThAR 1997,36].

4136 [E]**Elliott, J.K.** The apocryphal Jesus: legends of the early church. NY 1996, OUP 220 pp. $35/13. 0-19-826385-6/4-4. [R]RRt 3/2 (1996) 8-16 (*Need, Stephen W.*).

4137 **Garske, Volker** Jesus von Nazareth in den Romanen Heinrich BOELLS. Diss. Paderborn 1996, [D]*Frankemölle* [BZ 42,317].

4138 **Hurth, Elisabeth** Der literarische Jesus: Studien zum Jesusroman. 1993, ⇒10,4141. [R]MThZ 47 (1996) 421-422 (*Stettberger, Herbert*).

4139 **Jacomuzzi, Stefano** Cominciò in Galilea. CasM 1995, Piemme 230 pp. L28.000. [R]RdT 37 (1996) 714 (*Castelli, Ferdinando*).

4140 **Kersten, Holger** Jesus lebte in Indien: sein geheimes Leben vor und nach der Kreuzigung. B [2]1996, Ullstein 325 pp. 3-548-335490-4 [Biblos 47,324s—Förster, Hans].

4141 **Parrinder, Geoffrey** Jesus in the Qur'an. Oxf 1996, One World 187 pp. 1-85168-094-2.

4142 **Phipps, William E.** MUHAMMED and Jesus: a comparison of the prophets and their teachings. L 1996, SCM xii; 304 pp. £15. 0-334-02630-X. [R]IslChr 22 (1996) 293 (*Fitzgerald, Michael L.*).

4143 *Singh, David Emmanuel* Role of Jesus in Ibn al-ᶜARABI's spirituality. AJTh 10/1 (1996) 118-153.

4144 **Urbina, Pedro Antonio** Dios, el hijo de María. M 1995, Rialp 518 pp. [R]ScrTh 28 (1996) 962-963 (*Odero, J.M.*).

4145 **Vallet, Odon** Jésus et Bouddha: destins croisés du christianisme et du bouddhisme. Spiritualités: P 1996, Albin M. 265 pp. FF98. 2-226-08789-3 [BCLF 587-9,2064s].

F2.1 *Exegesis creativa*—**innovative methods**

4146 **Amador, James David H.** 'Not with excess of word or wisdom...': power and rhetorical criticism of the New Testament.

Diss. Graduate Theol. Union 1995, ^D*Waetjen, H.*, 433 pp. [EThL 74,275*].

4147 **Andreotti, Mario** Traditionelles und modernes Drama. Bern 1996, Haupt. ^RZeitschrift für Semiotik 18 (1996) 483-484 (*Hafner, Heinz*).

4148 **Bailey, James L.; Vander Broek, Lyle D.** Literary forms in the NT. 1992, ⇒8,4465... 10,4159. ^RSBET 14 (1996) 170-171 (*Still, Todd D.*).

4149 *Beentjes, Pancratius C.* Discovering a new path of intertextuality: inverted quotations and their dynamics. Literary structure. 1996, ⇒200. 31-50.

4150 *Botha, Pieter J.J.; Vorster, Johannes N.* Introduction. Rhetoric. JSNT.S 131: 1996, ⇒268. 17-26.

4151 **Byrskog, Samuel** Nya testamentet och forskningen: några aktuella tendenser inom den nytestamentliga exegetiken. Religio 39: 1992, ⇒8,4471; 10,14774. ^RSEÅ 61 (1996) 158-159 (*Ericsson, Bengt*).

4152 *Combrink, H.J. Bernard* The rhetoric of sacred scripture. Rhetoric. JSNT.S 131: 1996, ⇒268. 102-123.

4153 **Egger, Wilhelm** How to read the New Testament: an introduction to linguistic and historical-critical methodology. ^E*Boers, Hendrikus*, Peabody, MASS 1996, Hendrickson lxix; 232 pp. 1-56563-149-8.

4154 **Henderson, Ian H.** Jesus, rhetoric and law. Bibl.Interp. 20: Lei 1996, Brill vii; 437 pp. ƒ233.50. 90-04-10377-5.

4155 **Hens-Piazza, Gina** Of methods, monarchs, and meanings: a sociorhetorical approach to exegesis. Studies in OT Interpretation 3: Macon, GA 1996, Mercer University Press x; 199 pp. 0-86554-514-6.

4156 *Hinze, Bradford E.* Reclaiming rhetoric in the christian tradition. TS 57 (1996) 481-499.

4157 **Keßler, Hildrun** Bibliodrama und Leiblichkeit: leibhafte Textauslegung im theologischen und therapeutischen Diskurs. Geleitwort *Passauer, Ruth*, PTHe 20: Stu 1996, Kohlhammer 208 pp. DM59.80. 3-17-03714-X [ThLZ 122,655].

4158 *Malina, Bruce J.* Rhetorical criticism and social-scientific criticism: why won't romanticism leave us alone?. Rhetoric. JSNT.S 131: 1996, ⇒268. 72-101.

4159 *Mayes, Andrew D.H.* Idealism and materialism in WEBER and GOTTWALD. Community. 1996 <1988>, ⇒172. 258-272.

4160 *Meynet, Roland* I frutti dell'analisi retorica per l'esegesi biblica. Gr. 77 (1996) 403-436.

4161 **Minor, M.** Literary-critical approaches to the bible: a bibliographical supplement. West Cornwall, CT 1996, Locust Hill xvii; 310 pp. 0-933951-69-8 [NTAb 41,137].

4162 *Muthuraj, J. Gnanaseelan* New Testament and methodology: an overview. AJTh 10/2 (1996) 253-277 [ThIK 18/2,33].

4163 *Nerlich, Brigitte* Einführung in die Geschichte der Pragmatik;

4164 Sprachliche Darstellung als Prozeß: die Pragmatisierung eines Begriffs von KANT bis BUEHLER. Zeitschrift für Semiotik 18 (1996) 413-421/423-440.

4165 **Page, Hugh Rowland** Exploring new paradigms in biblical and cognate studies. Mellen 48: Lewiston, NY 1996, Mellen (6) 107 pp. 0-7734-2407-5.

4166 **Robbins, Vernon Kay** The tapestry of early christian discourse: rhetoric, society and ideology. L 1996, Routledge xiii; 278 pp. $20. 0-415-13997-X.

4167 *Schüssler Fiorenza, Elisabeth* Challenging the rhetorical half-turn: feminist and rhetorical biblical criticism. Rhetoric. JSNT.S 131: 1996, ⇒268. 28-53.

4168 *Smit, Dirk J.* Theology as rhetoric?: or: guess who's coming to dinner. Rhetoric. JSNT.S 131: 1996, ⇒268. 393-422.

4169 *Staley, Jeffrey L.* The father of lies: autobiographical acts in recent biblical criticism and contemporary literary theory. Rhetoric. JSNT.S 131: 1996, ⇒268. 124-160.

4170 *Vonk, Frank* Ausdruck als Mitteilung und Steuerung: pragmatische Kritik an WUNDTs völkerpsychologischem Forschungsprogramm. Semiotik 18 (1996) 441-460.

4171 *Vonk, Frank* Geballte Zeichen: das Symbol und seine Deutungen. Zeitschrift für Semiotik 18 (1996) 461-482.

4172 *Waard, Jan de* Hebrew rhetoric and the translator. Literary structure. 1996, ⇒200. 242-251.

4173 *Wessels, J.P.H.* 'Postmodern' rhetoric and the former prophetic literature. Rhetoric. JSNT.S 131: 1996, ⇒268. 182-194.

F2.2 *Unitas VT-NT:* The Unity of the Two Testaments

4174 **Boccara, Elia** Il peso della memoria: una lettura ebraica del Nuovo Testamento. 1994, ⇒10,4031; 11/2,2230. [R]Studi, Fatti, Ricerche 74 (1996) 11 (*Ballabio, Fabio*).

4175 *Borgen, Peder* 'In accordance with the scriptures'. [F]HOOKER M., 1996, ⇒43. 193-206.

4176 *Dohmen, Christoph* Die zweigeteilte Einheit der christlichen Bibel. Hermeneutik. 1996, ⇒604. 11-22.

4177 *Fuller, Daniel P.* The unity of the bible. 1992, ⇒8,4502. [R]ThR 61 (1996) 72-73 (*Reventlow, Henning Graf*).

4178 *Kertelge, Karl* Das Alte und das Neue Testament—die eine Heilige Schrift. [F]ERNST J., 1996, ⇒23. 159-171 [OTA 19,489].

4179 *Kogler, Franz* Das Verhältnis von AT-NT in jüngeren römischen Dokumenten. PzB 5 (1996) 109-143.

4180 **Liebers, Reinhold** 'Wie geschrieben steht': Studien zu einer besonderen Art frühchristlichen Schriftbezuges. 1993, ⇒9,4383... 11/2,2251. [R]JBL 115 (1996) 349-351 (*Stanley, Christopher D.*).

4181 **Robertson, A.W.** El Antiguo Testamento en el Nuevo. BA 1996, Nueva Creación xviii; 262 pp. 0-8028-0941-3 [NThAR 1998,98].

4182 **Trevijano Etcheverria, Ramón** Orígenes del cristianismo: el trasfondo judío del cristianesimo primitivo. 1995, ⇒11/2,2276. [R]Ang. 73 (1996) 598-602 (*Degórski, Bazyli*).

4183 [E]**Zenger, Erich** Der neue Bund im Alten: zur Bundestheologie der beiden Testamente. QD 146: 1993, ⇒9,421... 11/2,2281. [R]ThGl 86 (1996) 195-200 (*Sedlmeier, Franz*); ThR 61 (1996) 83-85 (*Reventlow, Henning Graf*).

4184 *Zmijewski, Josef* "Weg-Weisung" für das Christusgeschehen: Gebrauch und Verständnis der Schrift in der urkirchlichen Christusverkündigung. SNTU.A 21 (1996) 146-187.

F2.3 *Unitas interna*—NT—**Internal unity**

4185 **Aletti, Jean-Noël** Jesús-Christ fait-il l'unité du Nouveau Testament?. 1994, ⇒10,4215. [R]RSR 84 (1996) 604-606 (*Sesboüé, Bernard*).
4186 **Rolland, Philippe** Présentation du Nouveau Testament: selon l'ordre chronologique et la structure littéraire des écrits apostoliques. P 1996, Éd. de Paris. [R]EeV 106 (1996) 549-550 (*Cothenet, Édouard*); POC 46 (1996) 484 (*Ternant, P.*); EThL 72 (1996) 232-233 (*Neirynck, F.*).

F2.5 *Commentarii*—**Commentaries on the whole NT**

4187 Comentario al Nuevo Testamento. M 1995, Estella. La Casa de la Biblia. [R]Seminarios 42 (1996) 255-257 (*Casero, Hernández*).
4188 **Kiliphe, Timothy K.** Τὸ κατὰ Ματθαῖον εὐαγγέλιο, τὸ κατὰ Μᾶρκον εὐαγγέλιο, τὸ κατὰ Λουκᾶν εὐαγγέλιο, τὸ κατὰ Ἰωάννην εὐαγγέλιο. Κείμενο, Ἑρμηνεία, Σχόλια ᾿Αθήνα 1996-1997. [R]ΘΕΟΛΟΓΙΑ 68 (1997) 614-615 (*Moutsoulas, Elias D.*).
4189 **Mills, Watson Early; Wilson, R.F.** The gospels. Mercer Commentary on the Bible 6: Macon, GA 1996, Mercer University Press xlix; 224 pp. $17. 0-86554-511-1 [NTAb 41,149].

IX. Evangelia

F2.6 **Evangelia Synoptica;** *textus, synopses, commentarii*

4190 **Aland, Kurt** Synopsis quattuor Evangeliorum locis parallelis evangeliorum locis parallelis evangeliorum apocryphorum et patrum adhibitis. Stu [15]1996, Deutsche Bibelgesellschaft xxxvi; 606 pp. 3-438-05130-3.
4191 **Daniel, Orville E.** A harmony of the four gospels: the New International Version. GR [2]1996, Baker 224 pp. 0-8010-5642-X.
4192 **Díaz, José Alonso; Vargas Machuca, Antonio** Sinopsis de los evangelios. M 1996, Universidad Pontificia Comillas 331 pp. 84-87840-96-5. [R]MCom 54 (1996) 479-480 (*Vargas-Machuca, Antonio*).
4193 *Guillet, Jacques* Exégèse synoptique. RSR 84 (1996) 425-442.
4194 **Hobbs, Herschel H.** An exposition of the four gospels: v.1, the gospel of Matthew, the gospel of Mark; v.2, the gospel of Luke; the gospel of John. GR 1996, Baker 2 vols. 0-8010-5696-9.
4195 **Kudasiewicz, Joseph** The synoptic gospels today. Staten Island, NY 1996, Alba 342 pp. $19. 0-8189-0726-6 [HPR 97/8,75].
4196 **Lasserre, Guy** Les synopses: élaboration et usage. SubBi 19: R 1996, Pont. Ist. Biblico viii; 136 pp. L20.000. 88-7653-607-8. [R]EThL 72 (1996) 439-442 (*Neirynck, F.*).
4197 **Malina, Bruce J.; Rohrbaugh, Richard L.** Los evangelios sinopticos y la cultura mediterranea del siglo I: comentario desde las ciencias sociales. Estella 1996, Verbo Divino 424 pp. Ptas5.500. 84-8169-048-1.

4198 TMoraldi, Luigi; Barzaghi, Alessandro Nuovo Testamento: con commenti ai vangeli tratti dai padri, santi e mistici della Chiesa e con la prima parte della Genesi [1,1-12,9]. n.p. 1996, Verità e Vita (6) 1718 pp.

4199 Price, Reynolds Three gospels: the good news according to Mark: the good news according to John: an honest account of a memorable life. NY 1996, Scribner 288 pp. $23. 0-684-80336-4.

4200 Rozman, Francè Evangelijska harmonija. Ljubljana 1993, DZS 357 pp. RBog.Smo. 66 (1996) 147-148 (Rebić, Adalbert). S.;

4201 Sinopsa štirih evangelijev. Ljubljana 1993, DZS 242 pp. RBog.Smo. 66 (1996) 148-150 (Rebić, Adalbert). S.

4202 Sanders, Ed P.; Davies, Margaret Studying the synoptic gospels. L 51996, SCM ix; 374 pp. 0-334-02341-6. 0-334-02342-4.

4203 Sicre, José Luis El cuadrante: introducción a los evangelios. Estella 1996, Verbo Divino 304 pp. Ptas2.000.

F2.7 Problema synopticum: The Synoptic Problem

4204 Baik, Woon Chul La christologie de la source Q. Diss. 1996, DPerrot, Charles, 359 pp. RRICP 61 (1997) 348-350 (Perrot, Charles).

4205 Borgen, Peder The independence of the gospel of John: some observations <1992>;

4206 John and the synoptics <1990>. Early christianity. 1996, ⇒116. 183-204/121-182.

4207 Bultmann, Rudolf La storia dei vangeli sinottici. EGiordano, L., Cosenza 1996, Giordano 120 pp. L20.000. [Divinitas 40/2,188].

4208 Carruth, Shawn; Garsky, Albrecht Documenta Q: reconstructions of Q through two centuries of gospel research excerpted, sorted and evaluated. EAnderson, Stanley D., Lv 1996, Peeters xii; 206 pp. The database of the international Q project: Q11:2b-4. BEF800; $27. 90-6831-788-1. RATG 59 (1996) 306-308 (Rodríguez Carmona, A.); CTom 123 (1996) 618-619 (Espinel, J.L.).

4209 Crossan, John Dominic Itinerants and householders in the earliest Kingdom movement. FMACK L., 1996, ⇒54. 113-129.

4210 Downing, F. Gerald Word-processing in the ancient world: the social production and performance of Q. JSNT 64 (1996) 29-48.

4211 Engelbrecht, J. Challenging the two-source hypothesis: how successful are the commentaries?. Neotest. 30 (1996) 89-101.

4212 Erlemann, Kurt Papyrus Egerton 2: "Missing Link" zwischen synoptischer und johanneischer Tradition. NTS 42 (1996) 12-34.

4213 Farmer, William R. The gospel of Jesus... synoptic problem. 1994, ⇒10,4255; 11/1,2766. RInterp. 50 (1996) 308, 310 (Ellis, E. Earle); HBT 18/1 (1996) 101-102 (Collins, Raymond F.).

4214 Fleddermann, Harry T. Mark and Q. BEThL 122: 1995, ⇒11/1,2735. SNTU.A 21 (1996) 237-241 (Niemand, Chr.).

4215 EFocant, Camille The synoptic gospels. BEThL 110: 1993, ⇒9,382; 11/1,2736. REstB 54 (1996) 131-133 (González García, F.).

4216 Goodman, Daniel Eugene Heretical discourse: prophecy, symbolic forms, and the critique of ideology in Q. Diss. Drew 1996, DStroker, W.D., 287 pp. [EThL 74,293*].

4217   *Goulder, Michael D.* Is Q a juggernaut?. JBL 115 (1996) 667-681.
4218   ᴱ**Heil, Christopher** Documenta Q: reconstructions of Q through two centuries of gospel research excerpted, sorted and evaluated: Q 4:1-13,16: the database of the International Q Project: the temptations of Jesus Nazara. Lv 1996, Peeters xviii; 479 pp. 90-6831-880-2.
4219   **Hoffmann, Paul** Tradition und Situation. NTA 28: 1995, ⇒11/1,2737. ᴿJThS 47 (1996) 597-599 *(Tuckett, C.M.)*; CritRR 9 (1996) 231-233 *(Kloppenborg, John S.)* [Matt 5,38-48; Luke 6,27-36].
4220   *Hutchinson, R.J.* The Jesus Seminar unmasked. ChristToday 40/5 (1996) 28-30 [NTAb 41/1,27].
4221   **Jacobson, Arland D.** The first gospel... Q. 1992, ⇒10,4237. ᴿSNTU.A 21 (1996) 243-246 *(Fuchs, A.)*.
4222   ᴱᵀ**Kiwiet, John L.** Meijboom... Marcan hypothesis 1835-1866. 1993, ⇒9,4413. ᴿTJT 12/1 (1996) 104-105 *(Kloppenborg, John S.)*.
4223   ᴱ**Kloppenborg, John S.** Conflict and invention...Q. 1995, ⇒11/1,94. ᴿEThL 72 (1996) 442-443 *(Neirynck, F.)*.
4224   *Kloppenborg, John S.* The sayings gospel Q: literary and stratigraphic problems. Symbols and strata. SESJ 65: 1996, ⇒208. 1-66.
4225   *Krämer, Michael* Welches ist das erste Evangelium?. Sal. 58 (1996) 3-19.
4226   *Linnemann, E.* The lost gospel of Q—fact or fantasy?. TrinJ 17 (1996) 3-18.
4227   ᴱ**McNicol, Allan James** Beyond the Q impasse: Luke's use of Matthew: a demonstration by the research team of the International Institute for Gospel Studies. Collab. *Dungan, David L.; Peabody, David Barrett*; Pref. *Farmer, William R.*, Valley Forge, PA 1996, Trinity xvi; 333 pp. $25. 1-56338-184-2.
4228   *Myllykoski, Matti* The social history of Q and the Jewish War. Symbols and strata. SESJ 65: 1996, ⇒208. 143-199.
4229   *Neirynck, F.* Documenta Q: Q 11,2b-4. EThL 72 (1996) 418-424;
4230   The first synoptic pericope: the appearance of John the Baptist in Q?. EThL 72 (1996) 41-74.
4231   **Neirynck, Frans** Q-Synopsis. SNTA 13: 1995 <1988>, ⇒11/1,2746. ᴿRivBib 44 (1996) 367-368 *(Poppi, Angelico)*.
4232   *Pettem, Michael* Luke's Great Omission and his view of the law. NTS 42 (1996) 35-54.
4233   *Poppi, Angelico* La questione sinottica oggi e la neutralità delle sinossi. RivBib 44 (1996) 75-112.
4234   ᴱ**Powelson, Mark; Riegert, Ray** The lost gospel Q: the original sayings of Jesus. Collab. *Moore, Thomas; Borg, Marcus J.*, Berkeley, Calif. 1996, Ulysses 128 pp. Bibl. 1-56975-100-5.
4235   *Räisänen, Heikki* Exorcisms and the kingdom: is Q 11:20 a saying of the historical Jesus?. Symbols and strata. SESJ 65: 1996, ⇒208. 119-142 [Matt 12,28; Luke 11,20].
4236   *Reed, Jonathan L.* The Sign of Jonah (Q 11:29-32) and other epic traditions in Q;
4237   *Robinson, James M.* Building blocks in the social history of Q. ᶠMACK B., 1996, ⇒54. 130-143/87-112.
4238   *Schlosser, J.* L'utilisation des écritures dans la source Q. ᶠLEGASSE S., LeDiv 166: 1996, 123-146.

4239 *Scholer, David M.* Q bibliography supplement VII: 1996. SBL.SPS
35: 1996, ⇒274. 1-7.
4240 **Schröter, Jens** Erinnerung an Jesu Worte: Studien zur Rezeption
der Logienüberlieferung in Markus, Q und Thomas. Diss.-Habil.
Humboldt 1996/7 ᴰ*Breytenbach, C.* [ThLZ 122,759].
4241 *Seeley, David* Futuristic eschatology and social formation in Q.
ᶠMᴀᴄᴋ B., 1996, ⇒54. 144-153.
4242 *Thomas, R.L.* Evangelical responses to the Jesus Seminar. Master's
Seminary Journal 7/1 (1996) 75-105 [NTAb 41,29].
4243 *Uro, Risto* Apocalyptic symbolism and social identity in Q.
Symbols and strata. SESJ 65: 1996, ⇒208. 67-118.
4244 **Williams, Matthew Clark** Is Matthew a scribe?: an examination
of the text-critical argument for the synoptic problem. Diss. Trinity
Evang. Div. School 1996 ᴰ*McKnight, Scot*, 357 pp. DAI-A 57/05,
p. 2086; AAC 9631864.

F2.8 *Synoptica:* **themata**

4245 *Barth, Gerhard* Glaube und Zweifel in den synoptischen Evangelien. Neutestamentliche Versuche. 1996 <1975>, ⇒111. 135-167.
4246 **Bartnicki, Roman** Ewangelie synoptyczne: Geneza i interpretacja.
Wsz ²1996, Akad. Teologii Katol. 455 pp. 83-7072-070-6 [NT-
hAR 1997,226].
4247 **Barton, Stephen C.** Discipleship and family ties in Mark and
Matthew. MSSNTS 80: 1994, ⇒10,4736; 11/1,2763. ᴿRB 103
(1996) 100-103 (*Guijarro, Santiago*); JThS 47 (1996) 212-213
(*Best, Ernest*); EThL 72 (1996) 238-239 (*Neirynck, F.*); CBQ 58
(1996) 532-534 (*Balch, David L.*).
4248 ᴱ**Carruth, Shawn; Robinson, James M.; Heil, Christopher** Q
4:1-13,16: the temptations of Jesus—Nazara. Documenta Q: the
database of the International Q Project. Lv 1996, Peeters xviii; 479
pp. BEF1.800. 90-6831-880-2 [LouvSt 23,283—Verheyden, Jo-
seph].
4249 *Chalendar, Xavier de* Corps et cœur dans l'évangile. Alliance 106-
107 (1996) 78-81.
4250 **Ennulat, Andreas** Die "Minor Agreements". WUNT 2/62. 1993,
⇒10,4253; 11/1,2765. ᴿThG(B) 39 (1996) 155-156 (*Giesen,
Heinz*); CBQ 58 (1996) 153-155 (*Mowery, Robert L.*); ThLZ 121
(1996) 831-834 (*Walter, Nikolaus*); CritRR 9 (1996) 199-201
(*Dungan, David*).
4251 **Giesen, Heinz** Herrschaft Gottes. BU 26: 1995, ⇒11/1,2768.
ᴿBiKi 51 (1996) 89-90 (*Porsch, Felix*).
4252 *Grilli, M.* L'universalismo nei sinottici. RStB 8 (1996) 297-315.
4253 **Grisi, Francesco** Lettere di Luca e Matteo: evangelisti di verità.
Rerum agmina ac itinera 16: N 1996, D'Auria 61 pp. 88-7092-118-
7.
4254 **Habbe, Joachim** Palästina zur Zeit Jesu: die Landwirtschaft in
Galiläa zur Zeit Jesu und ihr Niederschlag im Zeugnis der synoptischen Evangelien. Diss. Erlangen-Nürnberg ᴰ*Merk, O.*, Neuk
Theologische Diss. u. Habil. 6: Neuk 1996, Neuk 126 pp.
DM39.80. 3-7887-1579-0 [NThAR 1997,36].
4255 *Hiers, R.H.* The kingdom of God in the synoptic tradition, 1.
JRadRef 5/3 (1996) 3-11 [NTAb 41,32].

4256 **Merklein, Helmut** Die Jesusgeschichte—synoptisch gelesen. SBS
156: 1994, ⇒10,4260; 11/1,2784. ^RCritRR 9 (1996) 244-246
(*Arnal, William*).

4257 ^E**Piper, Ronald A.** The gospel behind the gospels... Q. NT.S 75:
1995, ⇒11/1,101. ^RNT 38 (1996) 194-196 (*Goulder, Michael*);
ThLZ 121 (1996) 552-554 (*März, Claus-Peter*); EThL 72 (1996)
443-444 (*Neirynck, F.*).

4258 **Sevenich-Bax, Elisabeth** Israels Konfrontation mit den letzten
Boten der Weisheit... Logienquelle. MThA 21: 1993, ⇒9,4437;
10,4263. ^RThLZ 121 (1996) 941-943 (*Niebuhr, Karl-Wilhelm*).

4259 *Stock, Klemens* L'incontro con Cristo e la strada della perfezione.
Gesù Cristo, legge vivente. 1996, ⇒253. 71-93.

4260 **Tuckett, Christopher M.** Q and the history of early christianity:
studies on Q. E 1996 Clark xv; 492 pp. £30; 0-567-09742-0.
^RTheol. (1996) 470-471 (*Houlden, Leslie*); ET 108 (1996-97) 305-
306 (*Telford, W.R.*); SNTU.A 21 (1996) 188-210 (*Fuchs, Albert*).

4261 **Vaage, Leif E.** Galilean upstarts: Jesus' first followers according
to Q. 1994, ⇒10,4266; 11/1,2802. ^RSR 25 (1996) 504-505
(*Kloppenborg, John S.*); JBL 115 (1996) 136-138 (*Denaux, Adelbert*).

F3.1 Matthaei evangelium: *textus, commentarii*

4262 ^E**Ammassari, Antonio** Il vangelo di Matteo nella colonna latina
del Bezae Codex Cantabrigiensis: note di commento sulla struttura
letteraria, la punteggiatura, le lezioni e le citazioni bibliche. Città
del Vaticano 1996, Libreria Editrice Vaticana 239 pp. L32.000.
88-209-2209-6.

4263 ^{ET}**Amphoux, Christian-Bernard** L'Evangile selon Matthieu:
Codex de Bèze. L'Isle-sur-la-Sorgue 1996, Le Bois d'Orion 279
pp. Introd., texte, trad. et notes. FF125. 2-909201-13-9.

4264 **Barton, Bruce B.** Matthew. Life Application Bible Commentary:
Wheaton, Ill. 1996, Tyndale xix; 597 pp. 0-8423-3034-8 [NThAR
1997,261].

4265 ^E**Bauer, David R.; Powell, Mark Allan** Treasures new and old:
recent contributions to Matthean studies. SBL.Symposium 1:
Atlanta, GA 1996, Scholars xiv; 454 pp. $50/35. 0-7885-0220-4/1-
2. ^REThL 72 (1996) 446-447 (*Neirynck, F.*).

4266 ^T**Benyik, György; Lázár, István Dávid; Nagy, László** S.
T HOM A S Aquinas: gyermekkor evangéliuma Máté szerint. Szeged
1996, JATE 159 pp. H.

4267 **Buchanan, George Wesley** The gospel of Matthew. Mellen Biblical Commentary, NT 1: Lewiston, NY 1996, Mellen 2 vols. 0-
7734-2373-7/421-0.

4268 **Calloud, Jean; Genuyt, François** Lecture sémiotique des chapitres
1 à 10. L'évangile de Matthieu, 1. La Tourette 1996, Centre Thomas More 112 pp. FF70. 2-905600-14-4. ^RScEs 48 (1996) 341-343
(*D'Aragon, Jean-Louis*).

4269 *Cuvillier, E.* Chronique matthéenne (2). ETR 71 (1996) 81-94.

4270 **Galizzi, Mario** Vangelo secondo Matteo. 1995, ⇒11/1,2813.
^RPaVi 41/3 (1996) 59-60 (*Vallauri, Emiliano*).

4271 **Hagner, Donald A.** Matthew 1-13. WBC 33A: 1993, ⇒9,4452...
11/1,2818. ^RJThS 47 (1996) 209-211 (*Head, Peter*); AnnTh 10

(1996) 555-559 (*Estrada, Bernardo*); JBL 115 (1996) 354-356 (*Levine, Amy-Jill*);

4272 Matthew 14-28. WBC 33B: 1995, ⇒11/1,2819. [R]Anton. 71 (1996) 569-570 (*Alvarez Barredo, Miguel*); Annales Theologici 10 (1996) 555-559 (*Estrada, Bernardo*).

4273 **Harrington, Daniel J.** Matthew. 1991, ⇒7,3838... 11/1,2821. [R]HeyJ 37 (1996) 197-198 (*Duckworth, J.R.*).

4274 [E]**Howard, George** Hebrew Gospel of Matthew. 1995, ⇒11/1,2824. [R]JJS 47 (1996) 382-384 (*Horbury, William*).

4275 **Joosten, Jan** The Syriac language of the Peshitta and Old Syriac versions of Matthew: syntactic structure, inner-Syriac developments and translation technique. Diss. [D]*Goshen-Gottstein, M.H.*, SStLL 22: Lei 1996, Brill xii; 223 pp. ƒ190; $122.75. 90-04-10036-9 [NTAb 41,146].

4276 **Kiraz, George Anton** Matthew. Comparative edition of the Syriac gospels, aligning the Sinaiticus, Curetonianus, Peshîttâ & Harklean versions, 1. NTTS 21/1: Lei 1996, Brill l-lxxxv; 454 pp. 7 pl. ƒ820 [4 vols]. 90-04-104194 [NT 39,405].

4277 **Leiva-Merikakis, Erasmo** Fire of mercy, heart of the word: meditations on the gospel according to Saint Matthew, 1: chapters 1-11. Foreword *Bouyer, Louis*, SF 1996, Ignatius 746 pp. 0-89870-558-4.

4278 **Loski, Taduesza** Ewangelia według św. Mateusza. 1995, ⇒11/1,2825. [R]RBL 49/3 (1996) 214-216 (*Grzybek, Stanisław*). **P.**

4279 **Mali, Franz** Das "Opus imperfectum in Matthaeum". 1991, ⇒8,4585; 11/1,2828. [R]ZKG 107 (1996) 124-127 (*Bammel, Caroline*).

4280 **Mello, Alberto** Evangelo secondo Matteo. 1995, ⇒11/1,2829/. [R]Henoch 18/1-2 (1996) 228-230 (*Sacchi, Paolo*).

4281 *Morton, Andrew Q.* A new look at the gospel of Matthew. JHiC 3 (1996) 267-283.

4282 **Overman, J. Andrew** Church and community in crisis: the gospel according to Matthew. NT in Context: Valley Forge, PA 1996, Trinity x; 437 pp. $28. 1-56338-101-X.

4283 **Patte, Daniel** The gospel according to Matthew: a structural commentary on Matthew's faith. Valley Forge, Pa. [5]1996, Trinity xvi; 432 pp. 1-56338-179-6.

4284 *Pickering, Stuart R.* The Greek text of Matthew in Codex Bezae: a new edition and French translation;

4285 Readings of the Codex Bezae in the gospel of Matthew. NTTRU 4 (1996) 101-107/61-66.

4286 **Riches, John K.** Matthew. NTGu: Shf 1996, Academic 113 pp. 1-85075-741-0.

4287 **Thiede, Carsten Peter** Jésus selon Matthieu: la nouvelle datation du papyrus Magdalen d'Oxford et l'origine des évangiles: examen et discussion des dernières objections scientifiques. Paris 1996, De Guibert 119 pp. 10 pl. FF120. 2-86839-384-5 [RB 105,589—Grelot, Pierre].

4288 **Thiede, Carsten Peter; D'Ancona, Matthew** Der Jesus-Papyrus: die Entdeckung einer Evangelien-Handschrift aus der Zeit der Augenzeugen [P64+67]. Mü 1996, Luchterhand 303 pp. ÖS295. 3-630-87983-7 [ZThK 119,220];

4289 The Jesus papyrus. L 1996, Weidenfeld & N. xiv; 193 pp. 0-297-81658-6. [R]ActBib 33 (1996) 186-187 (*Puig Massana, R.*).

4290 **Weren, Wim** Matteüs. 1994, ⇒10,4295. RBijdr. 57 (1996) 341-343 (*Lambrecht, Jan*).

F3.2 **Themata** *de Matthaeo*

4291 **Allison, Dale C.** The new Moses. 1993, ⇒9,4470... 11/1,2839. RRB 103 (1996) 137-138 (*Viviano, Benedict T.*); NewTR 9/2 (1996) 92-93 (*Senior, Donald*); CBQ 58 (1996) 145-146 (*Barta, Karen A.*); SBET 14/2 (1996) 146-147 (*Hingle, N.N.*); Neotest. 30 (1996) 470-472 (*Botha, Pieter J.J.*); JBL 115 (1996) 356-358 (*Kingsbury, Jack Dean*).

4292 **Anderson, Janice Capel** Matthew's narrative web. JSNT.S 91: 1994, ⇒10,4299. RCBQ 58 (1996) 146-147 (*Wainwright, Elaine M.*); JBL 115 (1996) 141-143 (*McKnight, Scot*).
Anderson, Janice Capel Sermon and story ⇒680.

4293 *Barth, Gerhard* Auseinandersetzungen um die Kirchenzucht im Umkreis des Matthäusevangeliums <1978>;

4294 Jüngerschaft und Kirche im Matthäusevangelium <1965>. Neutestamentliche Versuche. 1996, ⇒111. 217-245/195-216.

4295 *Brant, Jo-Ann A.* Infelicitous oaths in the gospel of Matthew. JSNT 63 (1996) 3-20.

4296 *Bredin, Mark* Gentiles and the Davidic tradition in Matthew. A feminist companion. 1996, ⇒170. 95-111.

4297 **Breukelman, Frans** De theologie van de evangelist Matteüs, 2: het evangelie naar Matteüs als 'Die Heilsbotschaft vom Königtum'. Bijbelse Theologie 3: Kampen 1996, Kok 286 pp. ƒ59. 90-242-6195-3 [Streven 64,375].

4298 **Byrskog, Samuel** Jesus the only teacher...Mt. CB.NT 24: 1994, ⇒10,4301; 11/1,2845. RJSJ 27/1 (1996) 75-76 (*Neusner, Jacob*); Bib. 77 (1996) 438-441 (*Marguerat, Daniel*).

4299 **Carter, Warren** Matthew: storyteller, interpreter, evangelist. Peabody 1996, Hendrickson xii; 322 pp. $17. 1-56563-153-6. ROCP 62/2 (1996) 431-433 (*Nedungatt, G.*).

4300 *Charette, B.* 'Never has anything like this been seen in Israel': the Spirit as eschatological sign in Matthew's gospel. Journal of Pentecostal Theology 8 (1996) 31-51 [NTAb 41,33].

4301 *Combrink, H.J.* Translating or transforming: receiving Matthew in Africa. Scriptura 57 (1996) 273-284.

4302 *Combrink, H.J.B.* The reception of Matthew in Africa. Scriptura 58 (1996) 285-303 [NTAb 41,34].

4303 **Deutsch, Celia M.** Lady Wisdom, Jesus, and the sages: metaphor and social context in Matthew's gospel. Valley Forge, PA 1996 Trinity x; 260 pp. $20. 1-56338-163-X.

4304 *Donaldson, Terence L.* Guiding readers—making disciples: discipleship in Matthew's narrative strategy. Patterns of discipleship. 1996, ⇒188. 30-49.

4305 *Doyle, B.R.* Position of leadership: some reflections from Matthew's gospel. Pacifica 9 (1996) 135-144 [Matt 20,21-28; 16,17-19; 28,34; 28,16-20].

4306 *Dunn, James D.G.* The significance of Matthew's eschatology for biblical theology. SBL.SPS 35: 1996, ⇒274. 150-162.

4307 **Eltrop, Bettina** Denn solchen gehört das Himmelreich: Kinder im Matthäusevangelium: eine feministisch-sozialgeschichtliche Untersuchung. Wendlingen 1996, Grauer iii; 227 pp. 3-86186-147-X.

4308 *Frankemölle, Hubert* Johannes der Täufer und Jesus im Matthäusevangelium: Jesus als Nachfolger des Täufers. NTS 42 (1996) 196-218;

4309 Die matthäische Kirche als Gemeinschaft des Glaubens. [F]KERTELGE K., 1996, ⇒48. 85-132;

4310 Die Tora Gottes für Israel, die Jünger Jesu und die Völker nach dem Matthäusevangelium. Die Tora. 1996, ⇒1308. 379-419.

4311 *Gabriel, K.J.* Economic perspective as presented in Matthew. BiBh 22 (1996) 200-209.

4312 **González, Justo L.** Tres meses en la escuela de Mateo: estudios sobre el evangelio de Mateo. Nv 1996, Abingdon v; 170 pp. 0-687-02176-6 [NThAR 1997,226].

4313 **Grasso, Santi** Gesù e i suoi fratelli...Matteo. RivBib.S 29: 1994, ⇒9,4481... 11/1,2855. [R]LASBF 46 (1996) 458-461 (*Chrupcała, Lesław Daniel*); RSR 84 (1996) 608-609 (*Sesboüé, Bernard*).

4314 *Hagner, Donald A.* The *Sitz im Leben* of the gospel of Matthew. Treasures. 1996, ⇒4265. 27-68.

4315 *Hemelsoet, Ben; Monshouwer, Dirk* Het evangelie volgens Matteüs. Interpretatie 4/4 (1996) 31-32.

4316 *Jones, Ivor* Matthew. [F]HOOKER M., 1996, ⇒43. 59-69.

4317 *Kealy, S.P.* On reading Matthew. Scripture in Church 26 (1996) 348-352 [NTAb 41,34].

4318 **Klein, H.** Bewährung im Glauben: Studien zum Sondergut des Evangelisten Matthäus. Biblisch-theologische Studien 26: Neuk 1996, Neuk 223 pp. DM68. 3-7887-1408-5. [R]SNTU.A 21 (1996) 235-236 (*Fuchs, A.*).

4319 **Knowles, Michael** Jeremiah in Matthew's gospel. JSNT.S 68: 1993, ⇒9,4487... 11/1,2869. [R]JThS 47 (1996) 602-604 (*Jones, Ivor H.*).

4320 **Kupp, David D.** Matthew's Emmanuel: divine presence and God's people in the first gospel. MSSNTS 90: C 1996, CUP xx; 292 pp. £37.50; $60. 0-521-57007-7.

4321 **Leiva-Merikakis, Erasmo** Fire of mercy, heart of the word: meditations on the gospel according to Saint Matthew, 1: chapters 1-11. Foreword *Bouyer, Louis*, SF 1996, Ignatius 746 pp. $30. 0-89870-558-4. [R]Crisis (Nov. 1996) 45-46 (*Saward, John*).

4322 **Luomanan, Petri** Entering the kingdom of heaven: a study of the structure of Matthew's view of salvation. Diss. Helsinki. Gummerus 1996, Saarijärvi [StTh 51/1,86].

4323 **Luz, Ulrich** The theology of the gospel of Matthew. 1995, ⇒11/1,2874. [R]Reviews in Religion and Theology (1996/1) 87-88 (*Parker, D.C.*); HBT 18 (1996) 201-202 (*Hare, Douglas R.A.*).

4324 *Luz, Ulrich* Le problème historique et théologique de l'antijudaïsme dans l'évangile de Matthieu. [T]*Jaillet, Ira*, Le déchirement. MoBi 32: 1996, ⇒192. 127-150.

4325 *Martin, R.T.* Ideology, deviance, and authority in the gospel of Matthew: the political functioning of performative writing. LitTheol 10/1 (1996) 20-32 [NTAb 40,416].

4326 **Martini, Carlo Maria** Aus dem Herzen handeln: christliche Lebenspraxis nach dem Matthäusevangelium. FrB 1996, Herder 195 pp. 3-451-23253-7[NThAR 1997,163].

4327 **Mathavadian, Christudhas** The exousia of Jesus in the gospel of Matthew. Diss. extract Pont. Univ. Urbaniana. R 1995, vi; 112 pp.

4328 **Menninger, Richard E.** Israel and the church in the gospel of Matthew. 1994, ⇒10,4321. RCritRR 9 (1996) 242-244 (*Carter, Warren*).

4329 *Morton, Andrew W.* A new look at the gospel of Matthew. Journal of Higher Criticsm 3/2 (1996) 267-283 [ZID 23,168].

4330 *Neusner, Jacob* BYRSKOG's Jesus the only teacher: didactic authority and transmission in ancient Israel, ancient Judaism, and the Matthean community. Formative Judaism. SFSHJ 133: 1996, ⇒142. 193-195.

4331 *Pacomio, L.* Contemplazione della natura: inno alla vita. La natura. 1996, ⇒189. 155-169.

4332 **Powell, Mark Allan** God with us: a pastoral theology of Matthew's gospel. 1995, ⇒11/1,2882. RNewTR 9/2 (1996) 93-94 (*Okoye, James C.*).

4333 *Powell, Mark Allan* Characterization on the phraseological plane in the gospel of Matthew;

4334 *Pregeant, Russell* The wisdom passages in Matthew's story. Treasures. 1996, ⇒4265. 161-177/197-232.

4335 **Rapinchuk, Mark Edward** The end of the exile: a neglected aspect of Matthean christological typology. Diss. Trinity Evang. Div. School DMcKnight, Scot, 1996, 335 pp. DAI-A 57/05, p. 2084; AAC 9631863.

4336 *Robouam, Thierry Jean* The visions of the seven mountains. KaKe 65 (1996) 107-134 [ThIK 18/1,50]. **J.**

4337 **Saldarini, Anthony J.** Matthew's Christian-Jewish community. 1994, ⇒10,4335; 11/1,2885. RHBT 18/1 (1996) 103-105 (*Hare, Douglas R.A.*); HebStud 37 (1996) 196-199 (*Cotter, Wendy*).

4338 **Schachl-Raber, Ursula** Aufgespürte Frauenarbeit in Männerberichten: explizite und implizite Frauenarbeit im Matthäusevangelium auf dem Hintergrund einer sozialgeschichtlich-feministischen Analyse. Diss. Salzburg 1996 DBeilner [BZ 42,318].

4339 **Scheuermann, Georg** Gemeinde im Umbruch: eine sozialgeschichtliche Studie zum Matthäusevangelium. FzB 77: Wü 1996, Echter xi; 279 pp. DM39. 3-429-01764-5.

4340 *Schnackenburg, Rudolf* Matthew's gospel as a test case for hermeneutical reflections. TWitherup, Ronald D., Treasures. 1996, ⇒4265. 251-269.

4341 *Schwarz, Hans* The significance of Matthew's eschatology for systematic theology. SBL.SPS 35: 1996, ⇒274. 182-187.

4342 **Senior, Donald P.** What are they saying about Matthew?. Mahwah, NJ 21996, Paulist iii; 136 pp. $10. 0-8091-3624-4. REThL 72/4 (1996) 444-445 (*Neirynck, F.*).

4343 **Sim, David** Christianity and ethnicity in the gospel of Matthew. Ethnicity. Bibl.Interp. 19: 1996, ⇒171. 171-195.

4344 **Sim, David C.** Apocalyptic eschatology in the gospel of Matthew. Diss. DStanton, G., MSSNTS 88: C 1996, CUP xvii; 282 pp. $55. 0-521-55365-2 [NTAb 41,153].

4345 *Snodgrass, Klyne* Matthew and the law. Treasures. 1996, ⇒4265. 99-127.

4346 *Stanton, Graham N.* Ministry in Matthean christianity. FJAMIESON P., ⇒44. 142-160.

4347 *Stock, Klemens* Giusto e ingiusto nell'insegnamento di Gesù. Som. 137. PSV 34 (1996) 137-149.
4348 **Trilling, W.** Il vero Israele...Mt. 1992, ⇒8,4640... 11/1,2897. RStPat 43 (1996) 210-211 (*Segalla, Giuseppe*); LASBF 46 (1996) 452-454 (*Chrupcała, Lesław Daniel*).
4349 *Weaver, Dorothy Jean* Power and powerlessness: Matthew's use of irony in the portrayal of political leaders. Treasures. 1996, ⇒4265. 179-196.
4350 *Weber, Kathleen* Plot and Matthew. SBL.SPS 35: 1996, ⇒274. 400-431.
4351 *Weiss, Hans-Friedrich* Kirche und Judentum im Matthäusevangelium: zur Frage des 'Antipharisäismus' im ersten Evangelium. Religion. ANRW II.26.3: 1996, ⇒183. 2038-2098.
4352 *Weren, Wim* Los niños en Mateo: un estudio semántico. Conc(D) 32/2 (1996) 147-154; Conc(S) 264 (1996) 79-91.
4353 **Wong, Kun-Chun** Interkulturelle Theologie... im Matthäusevangelium. NTOA 22: 1992, ⇒8,4643; 9,4507. RJThS 47 (1996) 599-602 (*Jones, Ivor H.*).
4354 **Wouters, Armin** "...wer den Willen meines Vaters tut": eine Untersuchung zum Verständnis vom Handeln im Matthäusevangelium. BU 23: 1992, ⇒8,4644... 11/1,2903. RThG(B) 39/2 (1996) 156-158 (*Giesen, Heinz*); Sal. 58/2 (1996) 383-384 (*Bartolomé, J.J.*).

F3.3 *Mt 1s (Lc 1s ⇒*F7.5) Infantia Jesu*—*Infancy Gospels

4355 *Beckwith, Roger T.* The date of Christmas and the courses of the priests. Calendar and chronology. AGJU 33: 1996, ⇒112. 71-92.
4356 *Bolewski, Jacek* Protest(anci) wobec znaku dziewiczego poczęcia [Protest(anten) angesichts der Jungfrauengeburt]. Zsfg. 125. Bobolanum 7 (1996) 107-125. **P.**
4357 *Brändle, Francisco* San José: consideraciones en torno a su misterio en la revelación cristiana. EstJos 50 (1996) 355-371.
4358 *Canal, José María* Doctrina josefina de San BUENAVENTURA: el matrimonio de María y José. EstJos 50 (1996) 25-32.
4359 *Delenda, Odile* L'enfance du Christ dans l'art, présage de la Rédemption. Sedes Sapientiae 14/1 (1996) 37-48.
4360 *Farin, Michel* Le couple, l'ange et l'enfant. MoBi 101 (1996) 12-17.
4361 *Gutiérrez, José Ignacio* La mejor de las familias humanas. EstJos 50 (1996) 33-42.
4362 *Juan Pablo II* San José, testigo insuperable del silencio contemplativo. EstJos 50 (1996) 65-68.
4363 *Kirwan, Michael* The man nearest to Christ: St Joseph, 'glorious patriarch'. Month 29 (1996) 88-91.
4364 *Marcos, Juan A.* San José y la novela contemporánea. EstJos 50 (1996) 3-24.
4365 *Mimouni, Simon C.* Les origines de Jésus en débat. MoBi 101 (1996) 25-26.
4366 *Paul, André* Comment lire les évangiles de l'enfance. MoBi 101 (1996) 19-24.
4367 *Rigato, Maria-Luisa* Giuseppe, sposo di Maria, in Mt 1-2. Sum. 218. Theotokos 4/1 (1996) 189-218.

4368 *Sanabria, José Rubén* La explicación 'cientifica' de la paternidad de San José. EstJos 50 (1996) 327-339.
4369 *Schweitzer, Albert* Nazareth. FV 95/2 (1996) 1-5.
4370 *Sorg, Jean-Paul* SCHWEITZER, lecteur de Pierre LOTI. FV 95/2 (1996) 7-22.
4371 *Stöhr, Johannes* Die Verehrung der Hl. Familie—theologisch begründet. KiHe (1996/3) 39-42.
4372 *Thraede, Klaus* Epiphanien bei JUVENCUS: Ausgangstext: Evangeliorum Libri 1,1/26. ᶠDASSMANN E., JAC.E 23: 1996, ⇒19. 499-511.
4373 *Timms, M.* The birth stories about Jesus. Friends Quarterly 30/1 (1996) 17-24 [NTAb 41,35].
4374 *Valdivieso Ramos, Sofía* Buscó vivir come José vivía (Bonifacia RODRIGUEZ. EstJos 50 (1996) 53-64.
4375 *Verd Conradi, Gabriel María* Jesús Bar-José Bar-David. EstJos 50 (1996) 315-325.
4376 *Vilar, Johannes* Josef im Leben der Christen. KiHe (1996/3) 17-20, 37-38.

4377 *Nolland, J.* Genealogical annotation in Genesis as background for the Matthean genealogy of Jesus. TynB 47 (1996) 115-122 [Matt 1,1-17].
4378 *Luther, Martin* Mein Gesell und mein Bruder, mein Fleisch und mein Blut. Martin Luthers theologische Interpretation des Geschlechtsregisters nach Matthäus. ᴱ*Hövelmann, Hartmut*, Luther 67/3 (1996) 106-108 [Matt 1,1-17].
4379 *Bauer, David R.* The literary and theological function of the genealogy in Matthew's gospel. Treasures. 1996, ⇒4265. 129-159 [Matt 1,1-17].
4380 *Schaberg, Jane* The foremothers and the mother of Jesus. A feminist companion. 1996, ⇒170. 149-158 [Isa 7,14; Matt 1,1-17].
4381 *Nolland, J.* What kind of Genesis do we have in Matt 1.1?. NTS 42 (1996) 463-471;
4382 A text-critical discussion of Matthew 1:16. CBQ 58 (1996) 665-673;
4383 No son-of-God christology in Matthew 1.18-25. JSNT 62 (1996) 3-12.
4384 *Fauquex, Jacques* Matthieu 1: une généalogie à surprises. Hokhma 61 (1996) 15-26.
4385 *Viviano, Benedict T.* The movement of the star, Matt 2:9 and Num 9:17. RB 103 (1996) 58-64.
4386 *Böttge, Bernhard* Der Stern von Bethlehem: Informationen und Materialien zur Geschichte von den Weisen und dem Stern (Mt 2,1-12) für 6.-10. Schuljahr. Forum Religion 4 (1996) 4-11 [ZID 23,28].
4387 *Pierini, Franco* Mariologia patristica di Mt 2,11. Sum. 58. Theotokos 4/1 (1996) 41-58.
4388 *Erickson, Richard J.* Divine injustice?: Matthew's narrative strategy and the slaughter of the innocents (Matthew 2.13-23). JSNT 64 (1996) 5-27.
4389 *Stramare, Tarcisio* Il pianto di Rachele e la strage degli innocenti. BeO 38 (1996) 209-225 [Matt 2,16-18].
4390 *Bukas-Yakabuul, B.* Étude de Matthieu 2.16. CahTrB 25 (1996) 3-7.

4391 *Segalla, Giuseppe* Il bambino con Maria sua madre in Matteo 2. Sum. 27. Theotokos 4/1 (1996) 15-27.
4392 *Van Reisen, Hans* Op zoek nar een koningskind: AUGUSTINUS' verkondiging op Epifanie, 1. Interpretatie 4/8 (1996) 11-13 [Matt 2].
4393 *Cavalletti, Sofia* Sfondo giudaico e tradizioni nel capitolo secondo di Matteo. Sum. 39. Theotokos 4/1 (1996) 29-39.
4394 *Gharib, Georges* Mt 2 in alcune tradizioni liturgiche. Sum. 93. Theotokos 4/1 (1996) 59-93.

F3.4 Mt 3...Baptismus Jesus, Beginning of the Public Life

4395 **Bentivegna, Giuseppe** Le baptême de l'Esprit Saint: témoignage de l'église des Pères. ^T*Peyrode, Henri*, Chemins ouverts: P 1996, Desclée de B. 128 pp. 2-220-03831-9.
4396 *Brasil Pereira, Ney* O batismo no espírito. RCB 77/78 (1996) 71-80 [Matt 3,11].
4397 *Cheung, T.-M.* Understandings of spirit-baptism. JPentec 8 (1996) 115-128 [NTAb 41,93].
4398 *Dunn, J.D.G.* Born again: baptism and the spirit: a Protestant response. Conc(US) (1996/3) 109-115 [NTAb 41,93].
4399 *Giesen, Heinz* Die Johannestaufe: religions- bzw. traditionsgeschichtliche Einordnung und Bedeutung für die christliche Taufe. ThG 39 (1996) 114-127.
4400 **Guyénot, Laurent** Le roi sans prophète: l'enquête historique sur la relation entre Jésus et Jean-Baptiste. Le Kremlin-Bicêtre 1996, Pierre d'Angle 308 pp. FF139. 2-9115-00-0 [RB 103,636];
4401 *Guyénot, Laurent* A new perspective on John the Baptist's failure to support Jesus. DR 114 (1996) 129-152.
4402 **Kazmierski, Carl R.** John the Baptist: prophet and evangelist. Glazier: ColMn 1996, Liturgical 126 pp. $11. 0-8146-5851-2 [EeT(o) 28/1,116].
4403 *Kvalbein, Hans* The baptism of Jesus as a model for christian baptism: can the idea be traced back to New Testament times?. StTh 50 (1996) 67-83.
4404 **McDonnell, Kilian** The baptism of Jesus in the Jordan: the trinitarian and cosmic order of salvation. ColMn 1996, Liturgical 256 pp. $25. 0-814-65307-3 [Worship 72,371s—Wilken, Robert Louis].
4405 *Moingt, Joseph* L'Homme qui venait de Dieu. CFi 176: P 1996, Cerf 725 pp. 2-204-04782-1.
4406 *Pereira, Ney Brasil* O batismo no espírito. RevCuBíb 38 (1996) 71-80.
4407 *Piccirillo, Michele* Il luogo di Giovanni il Battista. TS(I) 72 (gen.-feb. 1996) 40-43.
4408 *Schroer, Silvia* Der Geist, die Weisheit und die Taube: feministisch-kritische Exegese eines zweittestamentlichen Symbols auf dem Hintergrund seiner altorientalischen und hellenistisch-frühjüdischen Traditionsgeschichte. Die Weisheit. 1996 <1986>, ⇒149. 144-175.
4409 *Soares-Prabhu, George M.* The God experience of Jesus. WoWo 29/1 (1996) 1-5 [ThIK 18/1,44].

4410 *Taylor, Joan E.* John the Baptist and the Essenes. JJS 47 (1996) 256-285.
4411 **Vigne, Daniel** Christ au Jourdain. EtB 16: 1992, ⇒8,4699... 11/1,2960. [R]JEarlyC 4 (1996) 394-396 (*O'Keefe, John J.*).
4412 **Webb, Robert L.** John the baptizer and prophet. JSNT.S 62: 1991, ⇒7,3919... 10,4394. [R]EvQ 68 (1996) 240-241 (*Brewer, David Instone*).
4413 *Yildiz, Efrem* El bautismo de Jesucristo como teofanía trinitaria. Sum. 106. DiEc 31/1 (1996) 81-106.

4414 **Gibson, Jeffrey B.** The temptations of Jesus in early Christianity. JSNT.S 112: 1995, ⇒11/1,2963. [R]ThLZ 121 (1996) 659-660 (*Pokorný, Petr*); JThS 47 (1996) 617-619 (*Best, Ernest*); CritRR 9 (1996) 213-215 (*Donelson, Lewis R.*) [Mk 1,9-13; 8,1-13].
4415 *Tilliette, Xavier* I filosofi leggono il vangelo: la tentazione di Cristo. RdT 37 (1996) 293-311.
4416 *Wagner de Reyna, Alberto* La tentación de Jesús. RTLi 30/3 (1996) 294-306.

F3.5 MT 5...Sermon on the Mount [...plain, Lk 6,17]

4417 *Anderson, Janice Capel* Matthew: sermon and story. Treasures. 1996, ⇒4265. 233-250.
4418 **Betz, Hans Dieter** The Sermon on the Mount. 1995, ⇒11/1,2966. [R]CCen 113 (1996) 270-274 (*Paul, G.E.*); ThTo 53 (1996) 392-394 (*Carter, Warren*); TS 57 (1996) 736-738 (*Dillon, Richard J.*); BiRe 12/4 (1996) 14, 16 (*Cahill, Lisa G. Sowle*).
4419 *Carter, Warren* Some contemporary scholarship on the Sermon on the Mount. CurResB 4 (1996) 183-215.
4420 *Clark, David J.* The Sermon on the Plain: structure and theme in Luke 6.20-49. BiTr 47 (1996) 428-434.
4421 **Dumais, Marcel** Le sermon sur la montagne... interprétation. 1995, ⇒11/1,2972. [R]FV 95/5 (1996) 78-79 (*Amphoux, C.-B.*); POC 46/1-2 (1996) 280-281 (*Ternant, P.*); LASBF 46 (1996) 455-458 (*Chrupcała, Lesław Daniel*);
4422 Le sermon sur la montagne (Matthieu 5-7). CEv 94: 1995, ⇒11/1,2973. [R]EeV 105 (1996) 78-79 (*Cothenet, E.*).
4423 **Giavini, Giovanni** Ma io vi dico: esegesi e vita attorno al discorso della montagna. 1993, ⇒10,4404. [R]Ben.43/1 (1996) 187-189 (*Ranzato, Agostino*).
4424 **Krämer, Michael** Überlieferungsgeschichte der Bergpredigt. [3]1994, ⇒10,4408; 11/1,2977. [R]FKTh 12 (1996) 312-313 (*Stimpfle, Alois*).
4425 *Leitner, Rupert; Schrettle, Anton* Die Ethik der Bergpredigt als Herausforderung für eine christliche Erziehung. CPB 109 (1996) 40-44.
4426 **Lenz, Johannes** 'Ihr seid das Salz der Erde': die Bergpredigt heute. Phoenix 2: Stu 1996, Urachhaus 169 pp. 3-8251-7058-6/9-4 [NThAR 1997/2,37].
4427 **Patte, Daniel** Discipleship according to the Sermon on the Mount: four legitimate readings, four plausible views of discipleship, and their relative values. Valley Forge, PA 1996, Trinity xiii; 416 pp. 1-56338-177-X.

4428 *Paul, G.E.* Jesus' ethic of perfection. ChristCent 113 (1996) 270-274 [NTAb 40,417].

4429 *Piryns, Ernest D.* The encounter of the message of Jesus with Japanese culture. Japan Mission Journal 50 (1996) 160-177 [ThIK 18/2,50].

4430 **Rohr, Richard** Jesus' plan for a new world: the Sermon on the Mount. Collab. *Feister, John Bookser,* Cincinnati 1996, St. Anthony Messenger x; 175 pp. 0-86716-203-1 [NThAR 1997,101];

4431 *Vision einer neuen Welt: die Bergpredikt des Jesus von Nazaret.* FrB 1996, Herder 237 pp. 3-451-26097-2 [NThAR 1997,70].

4432 *Scott, Bernard Brandon; Dean, Margaret E.* A sound map of the Sermon on the Mount. Treasures. 1996, ⇒4265. 311-378.

4433 *Slatinek, Stanislav* Kanonsko pravo in Sveto pirmo Nove zaveze [Canon Law and the New Testament]. Sum. 152. Bogoslovni Vestnik 56/2 (1996) 139-152. **S.**

4434 **Stoutenburg, Dennis** With one voice: the Sermon on the Mount and rabbinic literature. SF 1996, International Scholars ix; 163 pp. 1-883255-051-4.

4435 **Watson, Alan** Jesus and the law. Athens 1996, Univ. of Georgia Press xi; (2) 166 pp. 0-8203-1813-2.

4436 *Quilici, Alain* Vous êtes le sel de la terre. Sources 22/1-2 (1996) 25-33 [Matt 5,13].

4437 *Ruzer, Serge* The technique of composite citation in the Sermon on the Mount (Matt 5:21-22, 33-37). RB 103 (1996) 65-75.

4438 *Wick, Peter* Die erste Antithese (Mt 5,21-26): eine Pilgerpredigt. ThZ 52 (1996) 236-242.

4439 *Wick, Peter* Die Antithesen der Bergpredigt als paränetische Rhetorik: durch scheinbaren Widerspruch zu einem neuen Verständnis. Jud. 52 (1996) 156-178 [Matt 5,21-48].

4440 *Pak, Tae-Sik* 'Ihr habt gehört, daß zu den Alten gesagt worden ist: du sollst keinen Meineid schwören, und du sollst halten, was du dem Herrn geschworen hast... Ich aber sage euch: schwört überhaupt nicht'. Sinhak Jonmang 112 (1996) 104-118 [Matt 5,33-37] [ThIK 18/1,54]. **K.**

4441 *Kollmann, Bernd* Das Schwurverbot Mt 5,33-37 / Jak 5,12 im Spiegel antiker Eidkritik. BZ 40 (1996) 179-193.

4442 *Hartin, Patrick J.* Call to be perfect through suffering (James 1,2-4): the concept of perfection in the epistle of James and the Sermon on the Mount. Bib. 77 (1996) 477-492 [Matt 5,48; James 1,2-4].

4443 **Carter, Warren** What are they saying about Matthew's Sermon on the Mount?. 1994, ⇒10,4400; 11/1,2968. RPSB 17/1 (1996) 100-101 *(Adam, A.K.M.)*.

4444 *Koch, Klaus* Der Schatz im Himmel. Wende der Zeiten. 1996 <1968>, ⇒133. 267-279 [Matt 6,19-21; Mark 10].

4445 **Vaz, Harold A.** 'Do not be anxious': human concerns and Christian pursuit of God's kingdom and righteousness in Mt. 6:25-34. Diss. Inst. Cath. de Paris 1996, DQuesnel, Michel, 261 pp. Sum. RICP 60,218-223.

4446 *Parrott, J.* See ye first... ModBelieving 37/1 (1996) 30-36 [NTAb 40,418] [Matt 6,33].

4447 **Wattles, Jeffrey Hamilton** The golden rule. NY 1996 OUP viii; 257 pp. $45/$19. 0-19-510187-1/1036-6 [Matt 7,12] [ThD 44,388—Heiser, W. Charles].

F3.6 **Mt 5,3-11** (Lc 6,20-22) **Beatitudines**

4448 *Baroffio, Bonifacio G.* Le beatitudini (7): beati i puri di cuore, perché vedranno Dio. Presbyteri 30/1 (1996) 61-66 [Matt 5,8].
4449 *Bravo L., Carlos* Las bienaventuranzas como contracultura. Christus(Mexico) 697 (1996) 14-17 [ThIK 18/2,76].
4450 **Easwaran, Eknath** Original goodness: Eknath EASWARAN on the beatitudes of the Sermon on the Mount. Classics of Christian Inspiration: Tomales, Calif. [2]1996, Nilgiri 286 pp. 0-915132-92-3/1-5 [NThAR 1997,194].
4451 *Etchegaray, Card. Roger* Pauvreté économique et pauvreté évangélique: le témoignage des religieux et ses enjeux. Telema 22/3-4 (1996) 57-59.
4452 **Ghidelli, C.** Beatitudini evangeliche e spiritualità laicale. Spiritualità 49: Brescia 1996, Queriniana 232 pp. L25.000 [RdT 37,428].
4453 *Jacquet, Pierre* La vraie richesse, c'est Dieu. Telema 22/3-4 (1996) 69-70.
4454 *Jivan, Jennifer Jag* Beatitudes: a reflection. Al-Mushir 38/2 (1996) 66-76 [ThIK 18/1 (1997) 56]. **Urdu.**
4455 **Madre, Philippe** Beati i misericordiosi. Mi 1996, Ancora [Anime e Corpi 192,586s—Casera, Antonio].
4456 *Powell, Mark Allan* Matthew's beatitudes: reversals and rewards of the kingdom. CBQ 58 (1996) 460-479.
4457 *Whitters, M.* The beatitudes: glimpses of heaven for those stuck on earth. Emmanuel 102/4 (1996) 223-229 [NTAb 41,37].

4458 *Barth, Heinz-Lothar* Zeugnisse aus Schrift und Tradition zum Sakramentenempfang wiederverheirateter Geschiedener, 3. Una Voce-Korrespondenz 26 (1996) 13-63.
4459 *Ilan, Tal* On a newly published divorce bill from the Judaean desert. HThR 89 (1996) 195-202.
4460 *Okorie, A.M.* Divorce and remarriage among the Jews in the time of Jesus. DBM 15/2 (1996) 64-73.

F3.7 *Mt 6,9-13 (Lc 11,2-4)* **Oratio Jesu,** Pater Noster, **Lord's Prayer**

4461 **Bittlinger, A.** Padrenostro: la più conosciuta preghiera cristiana alla luce della meditazione sui chakra. Mi 1996, Red 133 pp. L24.000 [RdT 37,574].
4462 *Boismard, Marie-Émile* La sixième demande du 'Pater'. [F]LEGASSE S., LeDiv 166: 1996, ⇒51. 187-194.
4463 *Cadwallader, Alan H.* An embolism in the Lord's prayer?. NTTRU 4 (1996) 81-86.
4464 [E]**Charlesworth, James** The Lord's Prayer and other prayer texts from the Greco-Roman era. 1994, ⇒10,4440. [R]PSB 17/1 (1996) 88-90 (*Chesnutt, Randall D.*).
4465 [E]**Cibotto, Gian Antonio; Merlo, Bernardino** Il 'Padre Nostro'— ieri e oggi. Vicenza 1996, Neri Pozza xii; 116 pp. L15.000. [R]PalCl 75 (1996) 558 (*Lavarda, Girolamo*).
4466 **Gentili, Antonio; Camici, Alberto** Il Padre Nostro. Dentro il mistero 2: Mi 1994, Ancora 120 pp. L12.000. 88-7610-497-6. [R]Unitas(R) 51/3-4 (1996) 168-169 (*Mangiavacchi, Sergio*).

4467 *Gomà Civit, Isidro* 'Santificado sea tu nombre': la primera petición del Padrenuestro. Sum. 332. RCatT 21 (1996) 289-332 [Matt 6,9].

4468 *Guarducci, Margherita* Qualche osservazione sul testo evangelico del *Pater Noster*. Summ. 243. AANL.R 7 (1996) 243-246.

4469 *Haacker, K.* Stammt das Vater-Unser nicht von Jesus?. ThBeitr 27 (1996) 176-182.

4470 *Healy, Jack* To pray as Jesus taught us. Carmel 35/3 (1996) 164-168.

4471 **Hinnebusch, Paul** The Lord's Prayer in the light of our Lord's life and preaching. Boston, Mass. 1996, St. Paul's 189 pp. 0-8198-4480-2 [NThAR 1997,227].

4472 **Jiménez Hernández, Emiliano** Padrenuestro: fe, oración y vida. Biblioteca para la nueva evangelización: M 1996, Caparrós 244 pp. 84-87943-31-4 [NThAR 1998,336].

4473 *Kalonga, Joachim* La guérison dans quelques récits bibliques. RASM 3 (1996) 61-68.

4474 *Kasser, Rodolphe* La 'Prière de Jésus' kelliote réexaminée en quelques points. OCP 62 (1996) 407-410.

4475 *Lienhard, Marc* LUTHER et CALVIN: commentateurs du Notre Père [Luther and Calvin: commentators on the Our Father]. Abstr. *Posset, Franz*, ⇒8,4768. Luther Digest 6 (1996) 125-129.

4476 **Martín Nieto, Evaristo** El Padre Nuestro: la oración de la utopía. M 1996, San Pablo 243 pp. RRevAg 37 (1996) 1215-1216 (*Domínguez Sanabria, Jesús*).

4477 *Marucci, Corrado* Il Padre Nostro e la sua traduzione. CivCatt 147 II (1996) 338-350.

4478 **Ségalen, Jean-Marie** Prier avec Jésus. 1995, ⇒11/1,3043. REeV 106 (1996) 126-127 (*Oury, G.-M.*).

4479 **Wright, Nicholas Thomas** The Lord and his prayer. GR 1996, Eerdmans 89 pp. $8. 0-8028-4320-4 [BiTod 35,327].

4480 **Yoo, Sang Sub** Matthew's concept of Jesus' Holy War against Satan with special reference to the Gadarene demoniac story (Matthew 8:28-34). Diss. Westminster Theol. Sem. 1996, DPoythress, V.S., 551 pp. [EThL 74,299*].

4481 *Nun, Mendel* Gergesa: site of the demoniac's healing. JPersp 50 (1996) 18-25 [Matt 8,28-34].

4482 **Nun, Mendel** Land of the Gadarenes: new light on an old Sea of Galilee puzzle. Sea of Galilee Series: Kibbutz Ein Gev 1996, [Author] 32 pp.

4483 *Rodríguez Carmona, Antonio* Los métodos histórico-críticos en el NT a la luz de un ejemplo: Jesús purifica un leproso (Mt 8,1-4). Sum. rés. 15. MEAH 43/2 (1994) 15-48.

4484 *Umeagudosu, Margaret A.* The healing of the Gerasene demoniac from a specifically African perspective. African Christian Studies 12/4 (1996) 30-37 [Matt 8,28-34].

F4.1 *Mt 9-12; Miracula Jesu*—The Gospel miracles

4485 *Arboleda, Carlos* Posesión diabólica, brujería y sectas satánicas. CuesT 60/2 (1996) 105-117.

4486 *Berceville, Gilles* Les miracles comme motifs de crédibilité chez THOMAS d'Aquin. MélSR 53 (1996) 51-64.

4487 **Berger, Klaus** Darf man an Wunder glauben?. Stu 1996, Quell 174 pp. DM29.80 [BiLi 70,237].
4488 *Cantalamessa, Raniero* La force de guérison de l'Esprit Saint. ᵀ*Maire, R.*, Séminaire sur la Guérison 3-7 Oct. 1995. Tychique 121 (1996) 9-21. ·
4489 ᴱ**Cohn-Sherbok, Dan** Divine intervention and miracles in Jewish theology. Jewish Studies 16: Lewiston, NY 1996, Mellen viii; 214 pp. 0-7734-9093-0.
4490 **Davies, Stevan L.** Jesus the healer. 1995, ⇒11/1,3056. ᴿRRT 3/2 (1996) 8-16 (*Need, Stephen W.*); CBQ 58 (1996) 743-744 (*Gallagher, Eugene V.*).
4491 *Dowse, S.* Miracles. JLT 10 (1996) 212-215 [ZiD 22,406].
4492 *Hengel, Martin; Deines, Roland* E.P. SANDERS' "Common Judaism", Jesus und die Pharisäer. Judaica. WUNT 90: 1996, ⇒128. 392-479.
4493 **Houston, J.** Reported miracles: a critique of HUME 1994, ⇒10,4465; 11/1,3060. ᴿEvQ 68 (1996) 176-178 (*Brown, Colin*); SJTh 49 (1996) 364-366 (*Helm, Paul*); JThS 47 (1996) 790-792 (*Hebblethwaite, Brian*).
4494 **Imbach, Josef** Wunder. 1995, ⇒11/1,3061. ᴿCoTh 66/1 (1996) 196-200 (*Tomczak, Ryszard*).
4495 *Jiménez, Humberto* Ángeles, diablos, y demonios en el Nuevo Testamento. CuesT 60/2 (1996) 61-80.
4496 **Kahl, Werner** NT miracle stories. FRLANT 163: 1994, ⇒10,4466. ᴿThLZ 121 (1996) 835-837 (*Kollmann, Bernd*).
4497 **Kee, Howard Clark** Medicina, miracolo e magia nei tempi del Nuovo Testamento. StBi 102: Brescia 1993, Paideia 245 pp. ᴿPaVi 41/2 (1996) 59-60 (*Mazzucco, Clementina*).
4498 **Kollmann, Bernd** Jesus und die Christen als Wundertäter: Studien zu Magie, Medizin und Schmanismus in Antike und Christentum. FRLANT 170: Gö 1996, Vandenhoeck & R. 438 pp. DM138. 3-525-53853-7. ᴿSNTU.A 21 (1996) 257-263 (*Fuchs, A.*).
4499 **Latourelle, René** Du prodige au miracle. 1995, ⇒11/1,3065. ᴿSR 25 (1996) 359-360 (*Poirier, Paul-Hubert*).
4500 **Mullin, Robert Bruce** Miracles and the modern religious imagination. New Haven 1996, Yale University Press 322 pp. $30 [ThTo 54,545ss—Moorhead, James H.].
4501 **Myre, André** Gesù e i malati: i miracoli, segni del suo amore. ᵀ*Rossi Ferrini, D.*, R 1992, Città Nuova 64 pp. L4.500. 88-311-3942-8. Anime e Corpi 187 (1996) 685-686 (*Casera, Antonio*).
4502 *Perlewitz, Miriam F.* Jesus Christ the healer: hope of the suffering people of Bangladesh. Prodipon 19/2 (1996) 79-81 [ThIK 18/1,26].
4503 **Perrot, Charles; Souletie, Jean-Louis; Thévenot, Xavier** Les miracles. 1995, ⇒11/1,3067. ᴿRICP 57/1 (1996) 253-254 (*Baudoz, Jean-François*); RevSR 70 (1996) 421-422 (*Thiel, Marie-Jo*).
4504 *Smith, Morton* On the history of the divine man < 1978 >;
4505 Prolegomena to a discussion of aretalogies, divine men, the gospels and Jesus < 1971 >. New Testament. 1996, ⇒151. 28-38/3-27.
4506 **Twelftree, Graham H.** Jesus the exorcist. WUNT 2/54: 1993, ⇒10,4647; 11/1,3070. ᴿJR 76 (1996) 103-105 (*Lanpher, James E.*); CritRR 9 (1996) 296-297 (*Stanton, Graham*).

4507 *Elas, José Eugenio* La vocación de Leví (Mt 9,9-13). Diálogo 3 (1996) 149-151.
4508 *Levine, Amy-Jill* Discharging responsibility: Matthean Jesus, biblical law, and hemorrhaging woman. Treasures. 1996, ⇒4265. 379-397 [Matt 9,18-26].
4509 *Veitch, James* The making of a myth: the case of Judas Iscariot and the rise of anti-Semitism. AJTh 10 (1996) 363-376 [Matt 10,4] [ThIK 18/2,34].
4510 **Lohmeyer, Monika** Der Apostelbegriff im NT. SBB 29: 1995, ⇒11/1,3082. RSNTU.A 21 (1996) 246-247 (*Fuchs, A.*).
4511 *Schwarz, Günther* "Ein Rohr, vom Wind bewegt"? (Matthäus 11,7 par. Lukas 7,24). BN 83 (1996) 19-21.
4512 *Merkelbach, Reinhold* Wir haben euch geflötet und ihr habt nicht getanzt. RMP 139 (1996) 365-367 [Matt 11,16-17].
4513 *Jarvis, Cynthia A.* Matthew 11:16-30. Interp. 50 (1996) 284-288.
4514 **Mulloor, Augustine** Jesus' prayer of praise: a study of Mt 11:25-30 and its communicative function in the first Gospel. New Delhi 1996, Intercultural Publications xliv; 370 pp. Rs300. 81-85574-17-0.
4515 *Payne, John B.* ERASMUS's influence on ZWINGLI and BULLINGER in the exegesis of Matthew 11:28-30. FSTEINMETZ D., 1996, ⇒86. 61-81.
4516 *González, L.* Jesus e o templo. Itaici 24 (1996) 85-88 [Matt 12,6] [Comunidades 89,145].
4517 **Chow, Simon** The sign of Jonah reconsidered. CB.NT 27: 1995, ⇒11/1,3092. RTTK 67/1 (1996) 64-66 (*Kvalbein, Hans*); NRTh 118 (1996) 919-920 (*Ska, Jean Louis*) [Matt 12,39-41; Luke 11,29-32].
4518 **Álvarez Gómez, J.** '...y El los curó' (Mt 15,30): historia e identidad evangélica de la acción sanitaria de la iglesia. M 1996, Claretianas 182 pp. RClar. 36-37 (1996-97) 614-615 (*Gonzales Silva, Santiago Mª*).

F4.3 Mt 13... *Parabolae Jesu*—the Parables

4519 *Autané, Maurice* Pourquoi Jésus parlait en paraboles?. DosB 61 (1996) 25-26.
4520 *Battaglia, Oscar* Parabole dell'amore, parabole del dialogo. ConAss 4 (1996) 9-50.
4521 *Blomberg, Craig L.* Poetic fiction, subversive speech, and proportional analogy in the parables: are we making any progress in parable research?. HBT 18 (1996) 115-132.
4522 **Cocagnac, Maurice** La parole et son miroir: les symboles bibliques. LiBi 102: 1994, ⇒10,4504. RRHPhR 76 (1996) 224-225 (*Pfrimmer, Th.*).
4523 **Culbertson, Philip Leroy** A word fitly spoken... parables of Jesus. 1995, ⇒11/1,3096. RATR 78 (1996) 341, 343-344 (*Townsend, John T.*); HBT 18 (1996) 108-109 (*Macky, Peter W.*); CritRR 9 (1996) 194-197 (*Modica, Joseph B.*).
4524 *Dubreucq, Marc* Le langage des paraboles. DosB 61 (1996) 6-8.
4525 **Fernández Ramos, Felipe** El reino en parábolas. S 1996, Universidad Pontificia 362 pp. [EstTr 31,188].

4526 *Fickett, Harold* Stories that will get you killed. Image 15 (1996) 95-103.

4527 **Harnisch, Wolfgang** Die Mitte der Botschaft: Gleichnisse Jesu und das Problem ihrer Auslegung. Praktische Theologie 31 (1996) 31-43.

4528 **Hedrick, Charles W.** Parables as poetic fiction. 1994, ⇒10,4510. RCBQ 58 (1996) 549-550 (*Doran, Robert*); Neotest. 30 (1996) 220-221 (*Hunter, J.H.*).

4529 **Herzog, William R.** Parables as subversive speech. 1994, ⇒10,4511; 11/1,3102. RCBQ 58 (1996) 348-349 (*Reid, Barbara E.*); ABR 44 (1996) 84-85 (*Pritchard, Norman M.*); HBT 18 (1996) 110-111 (*Priest, Paul*).

4530 **Kähler, Christoph** Jesu Gleichnisse. WUNT 2/78: 1995, ⇒11/1,3106. RThLZ 121 (1996) 153-156 (*Harnisch, Wolfgang*).

4531 *Le Saux, Madeleine* Images et paraboles. DosB 61 (1996) 3-5.

4532 **McKenna, Megan** Parables. 1994, ⇒10,4516. RHBT 18 (1996) 106-107 (*Kelley, Robert L.*).

4533 **Parker, Andrew** Painfully clear: the parables of Jesus. BiSe 37: Shf 1996, Academic 166 pp. £10.50/$15. 1-85075-771-2.

4534 **Pérez-Cotapos Larraín, Eduardo** Parábolas / Dupont. 1991, ⇒8,4861... 10,4521. REstB 54 (1996) 427-428 (*Contreras, F.*).

4535 **Pronzato, Alessandro** Parabole di Gesù: I: 'Uscì il seminatore a seminare....' Marco e Matteo. Mi 1996, Gribaudi 251 pp. L28.000. 88-7152-418-7 [Iter. 5,258].

4536 **Ramos, Felipe Fernández** El reino en parábolas. S 1996, Publicaciones de la Univ. Pontificia 361 pp. PTA2.700. 84-7299-371-X. RRET 56 (1996) 525-527 (*Barrado Fernández, P.*).

4537 *Reid, B.* Preaching justice parabolically. Emmanuel 102 (1996) 342-347 [NTAb 41,28].

4538 **Royster, Dmitri** The parables: biblical, patristic and liturgical interpretation. Crestwood, NY 1996 St. Vladimir's Seminary Press 143 pp. 0-88141-067-5 [NThAR 1997,195].

4539 *Schottroff, Luise* Unsichtbarer Alltag und Gottes Offenbarung: die Öffentlichkeit des "Privaten" in Gleichnissen Jesu. JBTh 11 (1996) 123-133.

4540 **Scott, Bernard Brandon** Hear then the parable: a commentary on the parables of Jesus. Mp ⁴1996, Fortress xii; 465 pp. 0-8006-0897-6.

4541 **Thomson, Clarence** Parables & the enneagram. NY 1996, Crossroad x; 144 pp. 0-8245-1583-8 [NThAR 1997,293].

4542 **Torres, V.** Enseñar en parábolas: actualidad pedagógicas y didáctica de un estilo sin tiempo. Cuadernos de Teología Deusto 6: Bilbao 1996, Univ. de Deusto 68 pp. 84-7485-425-3 [NTAb 41,153].

4543 **Valavanolickal, Kuriakose Antony** The use of the gospel parables in the writings of APHRAHAT and EPHREM. Diss. Oxf 1995, DBrock, S.P. Studies in the Religion and History of Early Christianity 2: Fra 1996, Lang xvii; 380 pp. $64. 3-631-30333-5.

4544 *Zincone, Sergio* Parlare in parabole: osservazioni sull'esegesi chrisostomiana di Mt. 13,10 sgg. SMSR 62 (1996) 685-690.

4545 *Khatri, R.* The authenticity of the parable of the darnel. ATA Journal 4 (1996) 3-40 [Matt 13,24-30; Mark 4,26-29].

4546 *Strelan, R.E.* A ripping yarn: Matthew 13:24-30. LTJ 30/1 (1996) 22-29 [NTAb 41,38].

4547 *Martin, Vincent* L'ancien et le nouveau. NRTh 118 (1996) 59-65 [Matt 13,52].

4548 *Simonetti, Manlio* Cenni sull'interpretazione patristica di Mt 15,11. ASEs 13/1 (1996) 113-122.

4549 *Iacopino, Giuliana* Mt 15,11 e Lc 11,39-40 nel *Vangelo di Tommaso*. ASE 13/1 (1996) 85-93.

4550 *Graue, J.M.* A problem... or a moonbeam?: sermon study on Matthew 15:21-28. LTJ 30/2 (1996) 75-80 [NTAb 41,38].

4551 *Czerny, Michaël* 'Même les petits chiens...': la justice du Royaume à la veille du jubilé. VieCon 68 (1996) 352-367 [Matt 15,21-28; Mark 7,24-30].

4552 **Baudoz, Jean-François** Les miettes de la table: étude... de Mt 15,21-28 et de Mc 7,24-30. EtB 27: 1995, ⇒11/1,3123. RThLZ 121 (1996) 452-453 (*Rebell, Walter*); CBQ 58 (1996) 534-535 (*Mangan, Celine*); CritRR 9 (1996) 178-180 (*Graham, David J.*).

4553 *Scott, J. Martin C.* Matthew 15.21-28: a test-case for Jesus' manners. JSNT 63 (1996) 21-44.

4554 *Dube, Musa W.* Readings of Semoya: Batswana women's interpretations of Matt 15:21-28. Semeia 73 (1996) 111-129.

4555 *Choi, Hye-Yeong* Untersuchung über das Gebet Jesu vor seinem Tod am Kreuz. Sinhak Jonmang 113 (1996) 2-26 [Matt 15,34; 27,46] [ThIK 18/1,55]. K.

F4.5 **Mt 16...** *Primatus promissus*—**The promise to Peter**

4556 **Dentin, Pierre** Les privilèges des papes devant l'Écriture et l'histoire. 1995, ⇒11/1,3124. RRThom 96 (1996) 682-685 (*La Soujeole, Benoît-Dominique de*).

4557 **Dschulnigg, Peter** Petrus im Neuen Testament. Stu 1996, Katholisches Bibelwerk xiv; 230 pp. DM59. 3-460-33122-4.

4558 *Froehlich, Karlfried* Petrus, Apostel: II. Alte Kirche. TRE 26/1-2 (1996) 273-278 ⇒334.

4559 **Garuti, Adriano** S. Pietro unico titolare del primato: a proposito del decreto del S. Ufficio del 24 gennaio 1647. 1993, ⇒9,4723. RBLE 97/1 (1996) 99-102 (*Bonnet, L.*).

4560 **Grappe, Christian** Images de Pierre aux deux premiers siècles. EHPR 75: 1995, ⇒11/1,3127. RCrSt 17 (1996) 415-419 (*Claudel, Gérard*); RHR 213 (1996) 97-98 (*Méhat, André*); CBQ 58 (1996) 749-750 (*Turro, James C.*).

4561 **Guerriero, Elio** Il sigillo di Pietro. T 1996, SEI 160 pp. L22.000. RCom(I) 149 (1996) 95-99 (*Ravasi, Gianfranco*) & 99-102 (*Vigini, Giuliano*).

4562 **Minnerath, Roland** De Jérusalem à Rome: Pierre et l'unité de l'Église apostolique. ThH 101: 1994, ⇒10,4546. RFKTh 12/2 (1996) 156-157 (*Imkamp, Wilhelm; Vesperbild, Maria*); RBen 106 (1996) 203-204 (*Rapp, Francis*); RHR 213 (1996) 350-352 (*Méhat, André*).

4563 **Perkins, Pheme** Peter. 1994, ⇒10,4549; 11/1,3130. RInterp. 50 (1996) 410-412 (*Cousar, Charles B.*).

4564 **Powell, Ivor** Simon Peter: fisherman from Galilee. GR 1996, Kregel 224 pp. 0-8254-3548-X [NThAR 1997,195].

4565 **Schatz, Klaus** Das päpstliche Primat: seine Geschichte von den Ursprüngen bis zur Gegenwart. 1990, ⇒6,4947... 9,4734. ᴿThRv 92 (1996) 38-39 (*Rivinius, Karl Josef*);

4566 Papal primacy: from its origins to the present. ᵀ*Otto, John A.; Maloney, Linda M.*, ColMn 1996, Liturgical x; 197 pp. $20 [TS 58,565].

4567 **Wehr, Lothar** Petrus und Paulus—Kontrahenten und Partner: die beiden Apostel im Spiegel des Neuen Testaments, der Apostolischen Väter und früher Zeugnisse ihrer Verehrung. NTA 30: Mü 1996, Aschendorff viii; 416 pp. DM145. 3-402-04778-0.

4568 *Hoet, Hendrik* Sous le signe de Jonas. ᶠDᴜᴘᴏɴᴛ J., 1996, ⇒21. 67-94 [Matt 16,1-4].

4569 *Leth, Carl M.* Balthasar Hᴜʙᴍᴀɪᴇʀ's 'catholic' exegesis: Matthew 16:18-19 and the power of the keys. ᶠSᴛᴇɪɴᴍᴇᴛᴢ D., 1996, ⇒86. 103-117.

4570 *Frankovic, Joseph* Stewards of God's keys. JPersp 50 (1996) 26-34 [Matt 16,19].

4571 *Galot, Jean* La trasfigurazione. VitaCon 32 (1996) 351-362 [Matt 17,1-9].

4572 *MacClister, David* "Where two or three are gathered together": literary structure as a key to meaning in Matt 17:22-20:19. JETS 39 (1996) 549-558.

4573 *Garland, David E.* The temple text in Matthew 17:24-25 and the principle of not causing offense;

4574 Matthew's understanding of the Temple tax [17,24]. Treasures. 1996, ⇒4265. 69-98/69-98.

4575 *Horn, Friedrich W.* Die synoptischen Einlaßsprüche. ZNW 87 (1996) 187-203 [Matt 18,3; Mark 10,23].

4576 *Doignon, Jean* Hɪʟᴀɪʀᴇ sur Matth. 18,3: la "simplicité des enfants" ou un programme fragile pour croyants. RevSR 70 (1996) 307-312.

4577 *Genuyt, François* Matthieu 18. SémBib 82 (1996) 3-15.

4578 *Hermant, Dominique* Structure littéraire du "Discours communautaire" de Matthieu 18. RB 103 (1996) 76-90.

4579 **Ulrich, Daniel Warren** True greatness: Matthew 18 and its literary context. Diss. Richmond 1996-97 [RTL 29,588].

4580 **Carter, Warren** Households and discipleship... Mt 19-20. JSNT.S 103: 1994, ⇒10,4565. ᴿCBQ 58 (1996) 540-542 (*Balch, David L.*); CritRR 9 (1996) 185-189 (*Weaver, Dorothy Jean*).

4581 **Carver, Stephen Scot** Finding a new voice for Matthew 19:16-30. Diss. Luther Sem. 1996, ᴰ*Koester, Craig R.*, 309 pp. DAI-A 57/05, p. 2081; AAC 9701750.

4582 *Genuyt, François* Matthieu 19. SémBib 83 (1996) 3-16.

F4.8 **Mt 20...** *Regnum eschatologicum*—**Kingdom eschatology**

4583 *Allison, Dale* The eschatological Jesus: did he believe the end was near?. BiRe 12/5 (1996) 34-41, 54-55.

4584 *Cho, Kyu-Man* Jesus Christ and the kingdom of God. Catholic Theology and Thought 18 (1996) 78-121 [ThIK 18/2,51]. **K.**

4585 **Clifford, Paul R.** The reality of the Kingdom. GR 1996, Eerdmans 133 pp. [Studies in World Christianity 3/2,268].

4586 **Fudge, Edward William** The fire that consumes: the biblical case for conditional immortality. [E]*Cousins, Peter,* Carlisle [2]1994, Paternoster xii; 226 pp. £10. 0-85364-587-6. [R]EvQ 68 (1996) 274-275 (*Colwell, John E.*).

4587 **Fuellenbach, John** The kingdom of God: the message of Jesus today. 1995, ⇒11/1,3160. [R]Irénikon 69 (1996) 145-146.

4588 *Gubler, Marie-Louise* Die Auferstehung der Toten und das Weltgericht: zur Entstehung der neutestamentlichen Zentralbotschaft. Diak. 27 (1996) 150-161.

4589 *Hagner, Donald A.* Matthew's eschatology. SBL.SP 35: 1996, 163-181.

4590 **Schürmann, Heinz** Regno di Dio e destino di Gesù: la morte di Gesù alla luce del suo annuncio del regno. Già e non ancora 303: Mi 1996, Jaca 158 pp. 88-16-30303-4.

4591 *Soupa, Anne* Une invitation aux noces: les paraboles du jugement. DosB 61 (1996) 19-20 [Matt 20-25].

4592 *Busse, Ulrich* In Souveränität—anders: verarbeitete Gotteserfahrung in Mt 20,1-16. BZ 40 (1996) 61-72.

4593 *Genuyt, François* Matthieu 20. SémBib 84 (1996) 3-13.

4594 *Langley, Wendell E.* The parable of the two sons (Matthew 21:28-32) against its Semitic and rabbinic backdrop. CBQ 58 (1996) 228-243.

4595 *Gruson, Philippe* Les vignerons révoltés (Mt 21,33-46). DosB 61 (1996) 9-10.

4596 *Evans, Craig A.* Jesus' parable of the tenant farmers in light of lease agreements in antiquity. JSPE 14 (1996) 65-83 [Matt 21,33-46].

4597 *Bauckham, Richard* The parable of the royal wedding feast (Matthew 22:1-14) and the parable of the lame man and the blind man (Apocryphon of Ezekiel). JBL 115 (1996) 471-488.

4598 **Vögtle, Anton** Gott und seine Gäste: das Schicksal des Gleichnisses Jesu vom grossen Gastmahl (Lukas 14,16b-24; Matthäus 22,2-14). Biblisch-theologische Studien 29: Neuk 1996, Neuk 94 pp. 3-7887-1575-8.

4599 *Kombos, Antonios G.* Σύντομος ἑρμηνεία τῆς ἐν Ματθαίου 22,21 ἀποκρίσεως τοῦ Κυρίου πρὸς τοὺς ἀπεσταλμένους τοῦ Ἰουδαϊκοῦ συνεδρίου [A brief interpretation of our Lord's answer to the messengers of the Jewish sanhedrin found in Matth. 22,21]. Theol(A) 67 (1996) 211-229. G.

4600 *Luz, Ulrich* Überlegungen zum Verhältnis zwischen Liebe zu Gott und Liebe zum Nächsten (Mt 22,34-40). [F]THUESING W., NTA 31: 1996, ⇒94. 135-148.

4601 **Meisinger, Hubert** Liebesgebot und Altruismusforschung: ein exegetischer Beitrag zum Dialog zwischen Theologie und Naturwissenschaft. NTOA 33: Gö 1996, Vandenhoeck & R. (12) 320 pp., DM122. 3-525-53935-5 [Matt 22,35-40].

4602 *Miles, Delos* Evangelism and personal renewal through loving God with our minds. Faith & Mission 13/2 (1996) 35-59 [Matt 22,37].

4603 *Deddo, Gary W.* Jesus' paradigm for relating human experience and language about God. Sum. 33. EvQ 68 (1996) 15-33 [Matt 23,9].

4604 **Lunde, Jonathan M.** The salvation-historical implications of Matthew 24-25 in light of Jewish apocalyptic literature. Diss. Trinity

Evang. Div. School 1996, ᴰ*McKnight, Scot*, 342 pp. DAI-A 57/05, p. 2082; AAC 9631858.

4605 **Friedl, Alfred** Das eschatologische Gericht in Bildern aus dem Alltag: eine exegetische Untersuchung von Mt 24,40f par Lk 17,34f. ÖBS 14: Fra 1996, Lang 355 pp. 3-631-48533-6.

4606 **McNicol, Allan J.** Jesus' directions for the future: a source and redaction-history study of the use and eschatological traditions in Paul and the synoptic accounts of Jesus' last eschatological discourse. New Gospel Studies 9: Macon, Ga. 1996, Mercer xiii; 219 pp. $35. 0-86554-497-2 [Matt 24] [NThAR 1997,195].

4607 *Le Saux, Madeleine* Les dix jeunes filles (Mt 25,1-12). DosB 61 (1996) 15-18.

4608 *Martin, François* La parabole des talents: Matthieu 25,14-30. SémBib 84 (1996) 14-24.

4609 *Stricher, Joseph* Des talents à gérer (Mt 25; Lc 19). DosB 61 (1996) 11-12.

4610 *Luz, Ulrich* The final judgment (Matt 25:31-46): an exercise in "history of influence" exegesis. Treasures. 1996, ⇒4265. 271-310.

F5.1 *Redemptio*, Mt 26, *Ultima coena;* The Eucharist [⇒H7.4]

4611 *Barth, Gerhard* Das Herrenmahl in der frühen Christenheit. Neutestamentliche Versuche. 1996, ⇒111. 67-134.

Burchard, Christoph The importance of Joseph and Aseneth for the study of the NT: a general survey and a fresh look at the Lord's supper ⇒1722.

4612 **Chilton, Bruce** A feast of meanings: eucharistic theologies from Jesus through Johannine circles. NT.S 72: 1994, ⇒10,4589; 11/1,3186. ᴿCBQ 58 (1996) 542-544 (*Jacobson, Arland D.*).

4613 **Coda, P.** El ágape como gracia y libertad: en la raíz de la teología y praxis de los cristianos. M 1996, Ciudad Nueva 191 pp. ᴿComunidades 89 (1996) 126-127 (*Gómez, Enrique*).

4614 *Commission Théologique Internationale* Le Dieu rédempteur: questions choisies. EeV 106/44-47 (1996) 577-588; 593-601; 618-623; 634-638.

4615 *Driscoll, Jeremy* The eucharist and fundamental theology. EO 13 (1996) 407-434.

4616 **FitzPatrick, P.J.** In breaking the bread: the Eucharist and ritual. C 1993, CUP xxiii; 407 pp. £40. ᴿNedThT 50/2 (1996) 168-169 (*Rikhof, H.*); SJTh 49 (1996) 510-511 (*Spinks, Bryan D.*).

4617 *Fuchs, Guido* "... gleichsam als Agape": zur Fortführung der Eucharistie im Mahl. LJ 46 (1996) 23-38.

4618 **Gerrish, Brian A.** Grace... the eucharistic theology of John CALVIN. 1993, ⇒9,4811; 10,4596. ᴿScotBEv 14/1 (1996) 70-71 (*Wright, David F.*); EvQ 68 (1996) 251-253 (*Lane, Tony*).

4619 *Grelot, Pierre* L'institution du 'Repas du Seigneur': pour une lecture des textes parallèles. EeV 106 (1996) 474-479.

4620 ᴱHilberath, B.J.; Sattler, D. Vorgeschmack: Ökumenische Bemühungen um die Eucharistie. ᶠSCHNEIDER T., 1995, ⇒11/2,177. ᴿTTh 36 (1996) 429 (*Witte, Henk*).

4621 *Jammo, Sarhad Y.H.* Die Qudasha nach Addai und Mari und der eucharistische Einsetzungsbericht. HlD 50 (1996) 204-218.

4622 **Jaouen, René** L'Eucharistie du mil. 1995, ⇒11/1,3190. ᴿRET 56/2 (1996) 267-268 (*Gesteira, Manuel*); RASM 3/4 (1996) 220-223 (*Kabasele Lumbala, François*); MD 207 (1996) 154-156 (*Béguerie, Ph.*).

4623 **Jones, Paul H.** Christ's eucharistic presence: a history of the doctrine. 1994, ⇒10,4602. ᴿTS 57 (1996) 169-170 (*Empereur, James L.*).

4624 *Kim, S.Y.* Jesus' teaching on salvation and suffering. ERT 20/1 (1996) 49-59 [NTAb 41,96].

Kvarme, Ole Kristian Åtte dager i Jerusalem: en bok om Jesu påske, om jødisk og kristen påskefeiring ⇒1876.

4625 **LaVerdiere, Eugene** The Eucharist in the New Testament and the early church. ColMn 1996, Liturgical xi; 202 pp. $18. 0-8146-6152-1 [CBQ 59,422].

4626 **Libambu Muaso, Michel-Willy** L'eucharistie, annonce de la nouvelle alliance: quelques implication pour l'Église d'Afrique. Préf. *Nlandu, Daniel*, Théologie et Pastorale 2: 1996, Le Sénévé Séminaire Jean XXIII 47 pp. [EeV 106,351].

4627 *Lozupone, Francesco* Cenacolo, cuore della chiesa. TS(I) 72 (nov-dic 1996) 24-27.

4628 **Marinelli, F.** L'eucaristica presenza del Risorto: per la chiesa e la storia degli uomini. Bo 1996, EDB 215 pp. EstTrin 30/2 (1996) 311-312 (*Miguel, José María de*).

4629 **Moloney, Francis J.** A body broken for a broken people. 1990, ⇒7,4141... 10,4609. ᴿABR 44 (1996) 79-81 (*Lee, Dorothy A.*).

4630 *Navarro Girón, María Ángeles* El banquete eucarístico, sacramentel del sacrificio de Cristo en la primera controversia eucarística (s.IX). RET 56 (1996) 5-34, 149-200.

4631 *Neuner, J.* Listen to the Spirit: the sacred mystery of the eucharist. Sum. 770. VJTR 60 (1996) 770-773, 740.

4632 *Nicolas, Jean-Hervé* Le Christ est mort pour nos péchés selon les écritures. RThom 96 (1996) 209-234.

4633 *Nikolakopoulos, Konstantin* Autokephaliesystem und eucharistische Einheit: orthodoxe Ekklesiologie mit neutestamentlichen Fundamenten. Theol(A) 67 (1996) 361-371.

4634 **O'Brien, Kevin** But the gates were shut: operation of Jerusalem's perimeter gates within new evidence and a new methodology for dating and locating the last supper and identifying the beloved disciple in John 13:25 project, 1. SF 1996, Internat. Scholars Publ. xxxix; 508 pp. 1-57309-078-6/9-4.

4635 *Pahl, Irmgard* The Paschal mystery in its central meaning for the shape of christian liturgy. StLi 26 (1996) 16-38.

4636 **Paillard, Jean** Broder Judas. 1995, ⇒11/1,3199. ᴿNTT 97/2-3 (1996) 169 (*Opsahl, Carl Petter*).

4637 *Pickstock, Catherine* Necrophilia: the middle of modernity: a study of death, signs, and the Eucharist. Modern Theology 12 (1996) 405-433.

4638 **Piolanti, Antonio** Il mistero eucaristico. Città del Vaticano ⁴1996, Pontificia Accademia Teologica Romana; Libreria Editrice Vaticana 681 pp. L60.000 [EThL 72,495].

4639 *Polag, Athanasius* Der treue Zeuge: zur Deutung der Todes Jesu im Lichte der Abendmahlstradition. ᶠTHUESING W., NTA 31: 1996, ⇒94. 61-70.

4640 *Rordorf, Willy* A response to the paper of Irmgard PAHL. StLi 26 (1996) 39-48.

4641 *Rossé, Gérard* La spiritualità di comunione e il testamento di Gesù. Nuova Umanità 18/1 (1996) 19-32.

4642 *Rouet, Albert* Présence de corps et de cœur: l'eucharistie. Alliance 106-107 (1996) 84-86.

4643 *Traets, Cor* Les paroles sur la coupe pendant la prière eucharistique: trois considérations bibliques et liturgico-pastorales. QuLi 77 (1996) 135-151, 213-228.

4644 *Van Cangh, Jean-Marie* Les origines de l'eucharistie: le cas des Actes des Apôtres apocryphes. ^FLEGASSE S., LeDiv 166: 1996, ⇒51. 393-414.

4645 *Welker, Michael* What happens in the Lord's Supper?. Dialog 35 (1996) 209-217.

4646 **Woungly-Massaga, Lucette** Judas mon ami: la foi dans l'impasse. Aubonne 1993, Moulin 81 pp. ^RProtest. 51/1 (1996) 76 (*Conte, Gino*).

4647 **Thiede, Carsten Peter; D'Ancona, Matthew** Eyewitness to Jesus: amazing new manuscript evidence about the origin of the gospels. NY 1996, Doubleday xi; 206 pp. $24. 0-385-48051-2. ^RBiRe 12/4 (1996) 12, 14 (*Metzger, Bruce M.*) [Matt 26,6-7].

4648 *Vocke, Harald* Papyrus Magdalen 17: weitere Argumente gegen die Frühdatierung des angeblichen Jesus-Papyrus. ZPE 113 (1996) 153-157.

4649 *Thiede, Carsten Peter* The Magdalen papyrus: a reply. ET 107 (1996) 240-241.

F5.3 **Mt 26,30...// *Passio Christi;* Passion narrative**

4650 **Alfonso María de Ligorio** Meditaciones sobre la pasión de Jesucristo. M 1996, Palabra 403 pp. [EstTr 31,230}.

4651 *Battaglia, Vincenzo* La passione di Cristo nei commenti al Cantico dei Cantici, 1. LSDC 11 (1996) 325-338.

4652 *Beckwith, Roger T.* The date of the crucifixion: the misuse of calendars and astronomy to determine the chronology of the passion. Calendar. AGJU 33: 1996, ⇒112. 276-296.

4653 *Berder, Michel* La passione nei quattro vangeli. Il Mondo della Bibbia 7/2 (1996) 45-49.

4654 *Biser, Eugen* Bindet ihn los!: zur Frage nach dem Sinn des Todes Jesu. LebZeug 51 (1996) 54-66.

4655 *Bösen, Willibald* Der letzte Tag des Jesus von Nazareth. 1994, ⇒10,4632; 11/1,3213. ^RBiKi 51 (1996) 39-40 (*Baur, Wolfgang*); ZKTh 188 (1996) 263-264 (*Oberforcher, Robert*).

4656 *Broadhead, Edwin K.* Form and function in the Passion Story: the issue of genre reconsidered. JSNT 61 (1996) 3-28.

4657 **Brown, Raymond E.** The death of the Messiah, 1-2. 1994, ⇒10,4634; 11/1,3214. ^RLTP 52/1 (1996) 225-227 (*Racine, Jean-François*); RTL 27 (1996) 99-100 (*Focant, C.*); LouvSt 21 (1996) 87-90 (*Harrington, Jay M.*); RB 103 (1996) 135-137 (*Murphy-O'Connor, Jerome*); Interp. 50 (1996) 187-189 (*Green, Joel B.*); AUSS 34 (1996) 102-104 (*Shepherd, Tom*); Bijdr. 57 (1996) 343-

344 (*Denaux, Adelbert*); HBT 18 (1996) 194-200 (*Gagnon, Robert A.J.*).

4658 *Brown, Raymond E.* Los relatos de la pasión de Jesús y el antijudaísmo. Crit. 49 (1996) 45-48 [Strom. 52,346].

4659 *Coda, Piero* Il Cristo crocifisso e abbandonato: redenzione della libertà e nuova creazione. Som. 105. Nuova Umanità 18 (1996) 365-400.

4660 **Crossan, John Dominic** Who killed Jesus?. 1995, ⇒11/1,3217. RBBR 6 (1996) 159-165 (*Evans, Craig A.*); CritRR 9 (1996) 193-194 (*Sanders, Jack T.*).

4661 **Derbes, Anne** Picturing the Passion in late medieval Italy. NY 1996, CUP xvi; 270 pp. $75 [ChH 67,138s—Byrne, Joseph P.].

4662 *Evans, Craig A.* The passion of Jesus: history remembered or prophecy historicized?. BBR 6 (1996) 159-165.

4663 **Fenton, John C.** The Matthew Passion: a Lenten journey to the cross and resurrection. Mp 1996, Augsburg 158 pp. 0-8066-2986-X.

4664 **Flieger, Manfred** Interpretationen zum Bibeldichter IUVENCUS: Gethsemane, Festnahme Jesu und Kaiphasprozeß. Beiträge zur Altertumskunde 40: Stu 1993, Teubner 245 pp. DM74. 3-519-07489-3. RGn. 68 (1996) 461-462 (*Roberts, Michael*).

4665 *Florio, Mario* La morte di Cristo come luogo di speranza. Quaderni di Scienze Religiose 5 (1996) 11-19.

4666 *Ford, Josephine M.* The crucifixion of women in antiquity. JHiC 3 (1996) 291-309 [ZID 23,168].

4667 *Fornberg, Tord* Deicide and genocide: Matthew, the death of Jesus, and Auschwitz. SEÅ 61 (1996) 97-104.

4668 *Fricke, Weddig* Ein biblischer Biedermann. Pontius zu Pilatus. 1996, ⇒196. 46-56.

4669 **Georgeot, J.-M.** Pilate. De Saint-Marc jusqu'à Tertullien 16: n.p. 1996, n.p. 192 pp.

4670 *Herrmann, Horst* Römer bin ich, Richter: über eine leicht zu behebende Störung in der Realpolitik. Pontius zu Pilatus. 1996, ⇒196. 107-114.

4671 **Holtz, Gudrun** Der Herrscher und der Weise im Gespräch: Studien zu Form, Funktion und Situation der neutestamentlichen Verhörgespräche und der Gespräche zwischen jüdischen Weisen und Fremdherrschern. Diss. Berlin 1993 DOsten-Sacken, P. von der, ANTZ 6: B 1996, Institut Kirche und Judentum xi; 392 pp. DM37.80. 3-923095-88-0.

4672 **Hooker, Morna D.** Not ashamed of the gospel: NT interpretations of the death of Christ. 1994, ⇒10,4675. RCBQ 58 (1996) 552-553 (*Green, Joel B.*); JBL 115 (1996) 741-742 (*Cousar, Charles B.*).

4673 *Huidekoper, Ellen* Leben mit dem ungewissen: Zukunftshoffnung in der Ölbergapokalypse. THolberg, Marianne, Phoenix ie: Stu 1996, Urachhaus 212 pp. 3-8251-7058-6 [NThAR 1997,36].

4674 *Kiepe-Fahrenholz, Stephan* Das letzte Verhör. Pontius zu Pilatus. 1996, ⇒196. 131-138.

4675 **Klassen, William** Judas: betrayer or friend of Jesus?. L 1996, SCM xiv; 238 pp. $19/£13. 0-334-02636-9.

4676 *Krahe, Susanne* Pilatus wird verhört. Pontius zu Pilatus. 1996, ⇒196. 123-130.

4677 *Lapide, P.* Der Mut des Tapferen: Gedanken eines Juden zu Jesu Tod. LM 35/5 (1996) 35.

4678 **Légasse, Simon** Le procès de Jésus, 1: l'histoire. LeDiv 156: 1994, ⇒10,4666; 11/1,3230. RTer. 47/1 (1996) 328-330 (*Borrell, Agustí*);

4679 Le procès de Jésus, 2: la passion dans les quatre évangiles. 1995, ⇒11/1,3231. RETR 71 (1996) 284-285 (*Cuvillier, Élian*); Ter. 47/1 (1996) 328-330 (*Borrell, Agustí*); ScrTh 28 (1996) 935-936 (*García-Moreno, A.*);

4680 El proceso de Jesús, 1: la historia. Bilbao 1995, Desclée 189 pp. Eccl(R) 10/1 (1996) 178-179 *Izquierdo, A.*;

4681 El proceso de Jesús, 2: la Pasión en los cuatro evangelios. Bilbao 1996, DDB 581 pp. RRevAg 37 (1996) 1186-1187 (*Sabugal, Santos*); Teol. 33 (1996) 251-252 (*Hubeňák, Florencio*).

4682 **Lentini, S.** Passione e morte di Gesù Cristo: figure, profezie e vangelo. Vigodarzere 1996, Carroccio 158 pp. L22.000. 88-7974-183-1.

4683 *Luisier, Philippe* De Pilate chez les coptes. OCP 62 (1996) 411-425.

4684 *Maier, Paul L.* The inscription on the cross of Jesus of Nazareth. Hermes 124/1 (1996) 58-75.

4685 **Martin, Ernest L.** Secrets of Golgotha: the lost history of Jesus' crucifixion. Portland, OR ²1996, Associates for Scriptural Knowledge 455 pp. $19. 0-945657-86-2 [TD 44,179].

4686 *Martin, Gerhard Marcel* Ecce homo: ein Gespräch zwischen Pontius Pilatus und einem Gerichtspsychiater am Hofe des Prokurators. Pontius zu Pilatus. 1996, ⇒196. 115-122.

4687 **Martinelli, Paolo** La morte di Cristo come rivelazione dell'amore trinitario nella teologia di Hans Urs VON BALTHASAR. Pref. *Fisichella, Rino*, Già e non ancora 301: Mi 1996, Jaca 443 pp. L44.000. 88-16-30301-8.

4688 *Märtin, Ralf-Peter* Von Pontius zu Pilatus: auf den Spuren des Präfekten durchs Heilige Land. Pontius zu Pilatus. 1996, ⇒196. 32-45.

4689 **Meester, Paul de** Redécouvrir le Sacré-Coeur. P 1996, Médiaspaul 154 pp. FF85 [EeV 106,180].

4690 *Mendt, Dietrich* Das Testament des Pilatus. Pontius zu Pilatus. 1996, ⇒196. 147-155.

4691 **Myllykoski, Matti** Die letzten Tage Jesu, 2: Markus, Johannes... AASF B 272: 1994, ⇒10,4644; 11/1,3235. RRHPhR 76 (1996) 234-235 (*Grappe, Ch.*).

4692 *Niemann, Raul* Ein umstrittener Römer: Vorbemerkungen des Herausgebers. Pontius zu Pilatus. 1996, ⇒196. 7-8.

4693 **Noll, Mark A.** Adding cross to crown: the political significance of Christ's passion. GR 1996, Baker 95 pp. $10 [BS 154,490].

4694 **O'Brien, Kevin** But the gates were shut, 2: New Testament rediscoveries: extramural paradigm applied to the Jewish arraignment of Jesus. SF 1996, Internat. Scholars Publ. xxvi; 540 pp. 1-57309-076-X/7-8.

4695 **Obeid, Mona Aghnatios** La passione del Signore e il 'giusto sofferente' del salmo 21 (22). Diss. Pont. Univ. Urbaniana, DFederici, Tommaso, R 1996, xlvi; 287 pp.

4696 *Okorie, A.M.* Who crucified Jesus?. RelT 3/3 (1996) 289-296.

4697 *Pawlikowski, J.T.* Reflections on the BROWN-CROSSAN debate. Explorations 10/2 (1996) 2-3 [NTAb 41,30].

4698 *Pelli, Anna* L'apporto di un carisma all'approfondimento teologico dell'abbandono di Gesù: il pensiero di Chiara Lubich. Nuova Umanità 18/2 (1996) 137-153.

4699 *Provera, Mario* The Via Crucis in documents and tradition. Holy Land 16 (1996) 27-34.

4700 **Reinbold, Wolfgang** Der älteste Bericht über den Tod Jesu. BZNW 69: 1994, ⇒10,4649; 11/1,3238. ᴿNT 38 (1996) 77-86 (*Telford, W.R.*); NT 38 (1996) 411-413 (*Stenschke, Christoph*); JBL 115 (1996) 138-141 (*Senior, Donald*).

4701 *Salles, Catherine* La crucifixion chez les Romains. MoBi 97 (1996) 6-8.

4702 *Schlosser, Jacques* La passione di Gesù: le domande poste allo storico. Il Mondo della Bibbia 7/2 (1996) 50-55.

4703 **Schürmann, Heinz** Regno di Dio e destino di Gesù: la morte di Gesù alla luce del suo annuncio del regno. Mi 1996, Jaca 158 pp. L25.000.

4704 *Schwelien, Maria* Mit Krone, Helm und Lorbeerkranz: die Gestalt des Pilatus in der Kunst. Pontius zu Pilatus. 1996, ⇒196. 69-81.

4705 **Sloyan, Gerard S.** The crucifixion of Jesus. 1995, ⇒11/1,3244. Worship 70 (1996) 381-383 (*Murphy, Francis X.*).

4706 **Speyr, Adrienne von** Au coeur de la passion. Adrienne von Speyr 14: P 1996, Brépols 127 pp. [EeV 106,383].

4707 *Spitzing, Günter* Auch sie haben ihm die Hände gewaschen... Pontius Pilatus in der apokryphen Überlieferung. Pontius zu Pilatus. 1996, ⇒196. 57-68.

4708 *Stuhlmacher, Peter* Zur Predigt am Karfreitag. Das Wort vom Kreuz. 1996, ⇒206. 11-49.

4709 *Szczypiorski, Andrzey* Pilatus;

4710 *Uthmann, Jörg von* In dieser Weltgegend fühlt sich jeder Dritte zum Religionsstifter berufen: Fragmente aus dem verschollenen Briefwechsel des Präfekten Pontius Pilatus;

4711 *Webers, Thomas* Morituri te salutant: die unglaubliche Geschichte des Pontius Pilatus. Pontius zu Pilatus. 1996, ⇒196. 82-92/93-106/139-146.

4712 *Zhangí, Giuseppe Maria* Alcuni cenni su Gesù abbandonato. Nuova Umanità 18/1 (1996) 33-39.

4713 *Derrett, J. Duncan M.* Sleeping at Gethsemane. DR 114 (1996) 235-245 [Matt 26,36-46].

4714 *Légasse, Simon* Le coup d'épée de Gethsémani. ᶠCoste R., 1996, ⇒17. 285-291 [Matt 26,50-51].

4715 *Jepsen, Maria* Pilatus verheiratet: Gedanken zu einer kleinen Notiz (Mt 27,19). Pontius zu Pilatus. 1996, ⇒196. 24-31 [Matt 27,19].

4716 *Sorg, Theo* Welt-bewegendes Sterben: Matthäus 27,33-54. Das Wort vom Kreuz. 1996, ⇒206. 83-92 [Matt 27,33-54].

4717 *Geiger, Joseph* Titulus crucis. ICS 15 (1996) 202-207 [Matt 27,37].

4718 *Painchaud, Louis* Le Christ vainqueur de la mort dans l'évangile selon Philippe: une exégèse valentinienne de Matt. 27:46. NT 38 (1996) 382-392.

4719 *Nieuviarts, Jacques* Le cri de Jésus en croix en Mt 27,46: éclairage par les citations psalmiques du récit de la passion. ᶠLegasse S., LeDiv 166: 1996, ⇒51. 195-215.

F5.6 **Mt 28//: Resurrectio**

4720 *Aleixandre, Dolores* Les femmes au tombeau: une histoire qui est la nôtre. Christus 43 (1996) 152-158.

4721 **Andrews, Richard; Schellenberger, Paul** The tomb of God: the body of Jesus and the solution to a 2000-year-old mystery. L 1996, Little xii; 513 pp. Bibl. $25. 0-316-87997-5. ᴿCritRR 9 (1996) 340-342 (*Culbertson, Philip*).

4722 ᴱ**Avis, Paul** The resurrection of Jesus Christ. 1993, ⇒10,4683. ᴿSJTh 49 (1996) 388-389 (*Fergusson, David A.S.*).

4723 *Balthasar, Hans Urs von* Kreuz und Kirche: Begegnung mit dem Auferstandenen. KiHe 4 (1996) 30-33.

4724 **Barišić, Marin** Galilea e Gerusalemme negli studi recenti: il problema nei racconti pasquali. Diss. 1979, excerpt Pont. Univ. Gregoriana 1996, ᴰ*Dhanis, Édouard*, 102 pp.

4725 **Barker, Margaret** The risen Lord. E 1996, Clark xvii; 166 pp. £12. 0-567-08537-6 [ET 108,377].

4726 *Beckwith, Roger T.* Easter and Whitsun: the origin of the church's earliest annual festivals. Calendar. AGJU 33: 1996, ⇒112. 51-70.

4727 **Boismard, Marie-Émile** Faut-il encore parler de "résurrection"?. 1995, ⇒11/1,3261. ᴿCarthaginensia 12 (1996) 485-486 (*Sanz Valdivieso, R.*); BEL 97 (1996) 88-90 (*Légasse, S.*); NRTh 118 (1996) 258-265 (*Masset, Pierre*); MSR 53 (1996) 201-203 (*Van Toan, A. Tran*); RTL 27 (1996) 228-230 (*Ponthot, J.*); StRel 25/1 (1996) 118-119 (*Michaud, Jean-Paul*); Telema 22/3-4 (1996) 77-78 (*Haes, René de*); RB 103 (1996) 443-446 (*Murphy-O'Connor, Jerome*); POC 46/1-2 (1996) 277-280 (*Ternant, P.*);

4728 ¿Es necesario aún hablar de 'resurrección'?: los datos bíblicos. Bilbao 1996, Desclée de B. 159 pp. [Studium 37,337].

4729 **Cacitti, Remo** Grande sabato: il contesto pasquale quartodecimano nella formazione della teologia del martirio. SPMed 19: Mi 1994, Vita e P. lx; 207 pp. L48.000. 88-343-0180-3. ᴿJThS 47 (1996) 279-281 (*Frend, W.H.C.*); Sal. 58 (1996) 790-792 (*Amata, Biagio*); CrSt 17 (1996) 633-634 (*Rordorf, Willy*).

4730 ᵀ**Cerbelaud, Dominique** ᴇᴘʜʀᴇᴍ: célébrons la Pâques. CPF 58: P 1995, Migne 200 pp. Guide thématique de A.-G. Hamman. 2-908587-18-1. ᴿFV 95/2 (1996) 116-117 (*Vahanian, Gabriel*).

4731 ᴱ**D'Costa, Gavin** Resurrection reconsidered. n.p. 1996, Oneworld 227 pp. £12. 1-85168-113-2. ᴿTablet 250 (1996) 1204-1205 (*O'Collins, Gerald*); ET 108 (1996-97) 1-2 (*Rodd, C.S.*).

4732 **Essen, Georg** Historische Vernunft und Auferweckung Jesu. TSTP 9: 1995, ⇒11/1,3269. ᴿZKTh 188 (1996) 246-249 (*Neufeld, Karl H.*).

4733 **Federici, Tommaso** Resuscitò Cristo!: commento alle letture bibliche della divina liturgia bizantina. Quaderni di Oriente Cristiano 8: Palermo 1996, Eparchia di Piana degli Albanesi 1836 pp. L170.000 [RdT 38,285].

4734 **Gubler, Marie-Louise** Wer wälzt uns den Stein vom Grab?: die Botschaft von Jesu Auferweckung. Bibelkompaß: Mainz 1996, Grünewald 96 pp. 3-7867-1903-9.

4735 *Hill, W.* Und sei's ein zerissener Leichnam;

4736 *Hille, R.* Übermacht der Auferstehung. LM 35/7 (1996) 3-4/5-6.

4737 **Intrigillo, G.** Indagine nel sepolcro 'vuoto': 'venite a vedere il luogo dove era deposto'. Udine 1996, Segno 54 pp. L8.000 [RdT 38,286].

4738 *Janicki, Jan* Misterium paschalne Chrystusa centralnym wydarzeniem życia kościoła [De mysterio paschali Christi sicut centrali eventu vitae ecclesiae]. RBL 49 (1996) 236-248. **P.**

4739 *Kent, J.A.* The psychological origins of the resurrection myth. FaF 49/1 (1996) 5-22 [NTAb 41,31].

4740 *Lalleman, Pieter J.* The resurrection in the Acts of Paul. Apocryphal Acts of Paul. 1996, ⇒450. 126-141.

4741 **Lüdemann, Gerd** Die Auferstehung Jesu. ²1994 Radius, ⇒11/1,3279. RCart. 12 (1996) 486-487 (*Sanz Valdivieso, R.*); BiLi 69 (1996) 266-267 (*Schubert, Kurt*);

4742 Die Auferstehung Jesu. 1994, ⇒10,4695; 11/1,3280. RJThS 47 (1996) 255-256 (*Morgan, Robert*);

4743 The resurrection of Jesus. 1994, ⇒10,4697; 11/1,3281. RTheol. 99 (1996) 154-156 (*O'Neill, J.C.*); Gr. 77 (1996) 357-359 (*O'Collins, Gerald*); PSB 17/1 (1996) 98-100 (*Fuller, Reginald H.*); TS 57 (1996) 341-343 (*O'Collins, Gerald*);

4744 What really happened to Jesus: a historical approach to the resurrection. 1995, ⇒11/1,3282. REE 71 (1996) 323-324 (*Madangi Sengi, Jean de Dieu*).

4745 **Lüdemann, Gerd; Özen, A.** De opstanding van Jezus: een historische benadering. Baarn 1996, Averbode 199 pp. [Coll. 27,221].

4746 **März, Claus-Peter** Hoffnung auf Leben: die biblische Botschaft von der Auferstehung. Begegnung mit der Bibel: Stu 1995, Katholisches Bibelwerk 124 pp. DM39. RThPQ 144 (1996) 435-436 (*Niemand, Christoph*).

4747 **Mørstad, Erik M.** Jesus—den oppstandne: et kulturfilosofisk og teologisk oppgjør om Jesus fra Nasarets og menneskets minne. Oslo 1996, Apostrof 402 pp. 82-579-0154-7.

4748 *Myre, André* La résurrection selon le Catéchisme de l'Église Catholique: perspectives exégétiques. ScEs 48 (1996) 327-340.

4749 *Ouellet, Marc* The mystery of Easter and the culture of death. TSchindler, David Louis, Com(US) 23/1 (1996) 5-15.

4750 **Pikaza, Xabier** Camino de Pascua: misterios de gloria. Nueva Alianza 139: S 1996, Sígueme 198 pp. 84-301-1308-8.

4751 *Poets, K.* Die Auferstehung Jesu Christi von den Toten: Frühjahrstagung der Reformierten Konferenz Bentheim-Steinfurt-Tecklenburg. RKZ 137 (1996) 249-250.

4752 **Riley, Gregory John** Resurrection reconsidered: Thomas and John in controversy. 1995, ⇒11/1,3296. RCBQ 58 (1996) 766-768 (*Attridge, Harold W.*).

4753 **Sawicki, Marianne** Seeing the Lord: resurrection and early Christian practices. 1994, ⇒11/2,2195. RWorship 70/1 (1996) 85-87 (*Perkins, Pheme*); CBQ 58 (1996) 771-773 (*Carroll, John T.*).

4754 *Smith, Morton* Ascent to the heavens and the beginning of christianity < 1981 >;

4755 Two ascended to heaven—Jesus and the author of 4Q491.11.1 < 1992 >. New Testament. 1996, ⇒151. 47-67/68-78.

4756 **Swain, Lionel** Reading the Easter gospels. GNS 35: 1993, ⇒9,4889. RRB 103 (1996) 618-619 (*Patella, Michael*).

4757   ^E**Verweyen, Hansjürgen** Osterglaube ohne Auferstehung?: Diskussion mit Gerd LUEDEMANN. QD 155: 1995, ⇒11/1,118. ^ROrdKor 32 (1996) 254-255 (*Giesen, Heinz*).

4758   *Welker, Michael* Die Wirklichkeit des Auferstandenen: Gerd LUEDEMANNS aufklärerischer Fundamentalismus. EK 29 (1996) 206-207.

4759   *Wilckens, Ulrich* Die Auferstehung Jesu: historisches Zeugnis—Theologie—Glaubenserfahrung: eine Auseinandersetzung mit Gerd LUEDEMANN. PTh 85 (1996) 102-120.

4760   **Wilckens, Ulrich** Hoffnung gegen den Tod: die Wirklichkeit der Auferstehung Jesu. Lehre und Leben: Stu 1996, Hänssler 128 pp. 3-7751-2735-6.

4761   *Woodward, K.L.* Rethinking the resurrection. Newsweek (8 April 1996) 60-70 [NTAb 40,414].

4762   *Carter, Warren* "To see the tomb": Matthew's women at the tomb. ET 107 (1996) 201-205 [Matt 28,1].

4763   **Lodu Kose, Lawrence** 'Make disciples of all nations' (Mt. 28,16-20). Diss. extract Pont. Univ. Urbaniana, ^D*Virgulin, Stefano,* R 1996, 98 pp.

4764   *Kirschner, E.F.* Mateus 28:18-20: missao conforme Jesus Cristo. VoxScr 6/1 (1996) 33-48.

F6.1   **Evangelium Marci**—*Textus, commentarii*

4765   ^E**Ammassari, Antonio** Il vangelo di Marco nella colonna latina del Bezae Codex Cantabrigiensis: note di commento sulla struttura letteraria, la punteggiatura, le lezioni e le citazioni bibliche. Città del Vaticano 1996, Libreria Editrice Vaticana 157 pp. L24.000. 88-209-2274-6.

4766   **Black, Allen** Mark. NIV commentary: Joplin, Mo. 1995, College 295 pp. Bibl. 0-89900-629-9 [NThAR 1998,100].

4767   **Bodrato, Aldo** Il vangelo delle meraviglie: commento al vangelo di Marco. Foreword *Ravasi, Gianfranco,* Bibbia per tutti: Assisi 1996, Cittadella 256 pp. L25.000. 88-308-0593-9. ^RHum(B) 51 (1996) 983-985 (*Stefani, Piero*).

4768   **Boismard, Marie-Émile** L'évangile de Marc: sa préhistoire. EtB 26: 1995, ⇒10,4740; 11/1,3330. ^RRB 103 (1996) 277-279 (*Kloppenborg, John S.*); CBQ 58 (1996) 535-536 (*Evans, Craig A.*).

4769   **Drewermann, Eugen** Il vangelo di Marco: immagini di redenzione. BTCon 78: 1994, ⇒10,4718; 11/1,3346. ^RAnime e Corpi 187 (1996) 689-690 (*Casera, Antonio*).

4770   **Fabris, Rinaldo** Marco. LoB.NT 2: Brescia 1996, Queriniana 141 pp. L18.000. 88-399-1578-8 [RdT 38,142].

4771   **Frinking, Bernard** La parole est tout près de toi: apprendre l'évangile pour apprendre à le vivre. P 1996, Bayard 250 pp. FF120.

4772   **Gundry, Robert H.** Mark. 1993, ⇒8,5144... 11/1,3311. ^RAUSS 34 (1996) 124-127 (*Terian, Abraham*).

4773   **Hare, Douglas R.A.** Mark. Westminster Bible Companion: LVL 1996, Westminster x; 230 pp. $17. 0-664-25551-5 [NTAb 41,146].

4774 **Heil, John Paul** The gospel of Mark as a model for action. 1992, ⇒8,5098; 10,4723. [R]BTB 26/1 (1996) 56-57 (*McVann, Mark*).

4775 *Hendriks, W. M. A.* Leçons pré-alexandrines du Codex Bezae dans Marc (illustrées par Mc 10,1 et 1,4 et 5,21). Codex Bezae. NTTS 22: 1996, ⇒265. 232-239.

4776 *Horman, John* Is there a common Greek source for Thomas and Mark?. CSBS annual meeting 27 May 1996. Sum. BCSBS 55 (1995/96) 10-11.

4777 **Kiraz, George Anton** Comparative edition of the Syriac gospels, aligning the Sinaiticus, Curetonianus, Peshîttâ & Harklean versions, 2: Mark. NTTS 21/2: Lei 1996, Brill 257 pp. ƒ820 [4 vols]. 90-04-104194 [NT 39,405].

4778 **Lamarche, Paul** Évangile de Marc: commentaire. EtB 33: P 1996, Gabalda 431 pp. FF450. 2-85021-093-5.

4779 **MacBride, Denis** The gospel of Mark: a reflective commentary. Dublin 1996, Dominican 270 pp. 1-87155-255-9 [NThAR 1998,271].

4780 **Mateos, Juan; Camacho Acosta, Fernando**. Marco. Bibbia per tutti: Assisi 1996, Citadella 408 pp. 88-308-0602-1.

4781 **Mosconi, Luis** Evangelho de Jesus Cristo segundo Marcos: para cristãos e cristãs rumo ao novo milênio. São Paulo 1996, Loyola 128 pp. 85-15-01508-0 [PerTeol 29,134].

4782 *Pickering, Stuart R.* Readings of the Codex Bezae in the gospel of Mark. NTTRU 4 (1996) 67-78.

4783 **Pikaza Ibarrondo, Xabier** Il vangelo di Marco. Itinerari biblici 2: R 1996, Borla 464 pp. 88-263-1143-9. [R]PaVi 41/5 (1996) 56-57 (*Bagni, Arcangelo*);

4784 El evangelio: vida y pascua de Jesús. Biblioteca de Estudios Bibli-cos 75: S [2]1993, Sígueme 440 pp. [R]NatGrac 43 (1996) 496-497 (*Pena, Miguel Auxo*).

4785 **Robinson, Geoffrey** A change of mind and heart: the good news according to Mark. Revesby, N.S.W. 1994, Parish Ministry 579 pp. AUD$25. 1-8754-6304-6. [R]Pacifica 9/1 (1996) 106-108 (*Doyle, B. Rod*); VJTR 60 (1996) 687-688 (*Meagher, P.M.*).

4786 *Robinson, Maurice A.* Two passages in Mark: a critical text for the Byzantine-priority hypothesis. Faith & Mission 13 (1996) 66-111 [Matt 22,37; Mark 1,2; 13,14].

4787 *Rodd, C.S.* Reading the book, 1: the gospel according to Mark. ET 108 (1996) 4-7.

4788 **Smith, Stephen H.** A lion with wings: a narrative-critical approach to Mark's Gospel. BiSer 38: Shf 1996, Academic 258 pp. £20/$25. 1-85075-784-4 [NTS 43,622].

4789 *Tarocchi, Stefano* Marco evangelista. PaVi 41/5 (1996) 6-9.

4790 *Verheyden, J.* Mark and Q. EThL 72 (1996) 408-417.

4791 *Vironda, Marco* Dall'"evangelo" ai vangeli. PaVi 41/1 (1996) 6-9.

F6.2 *Evangelium Marci*, **Themata**

4792 **Aichele, George** Jesus framed: biblical limits. L 1996, Routledge x; 204 pp. £45/£14. 0-415-13862-0/3-9. [R]RRT (1996/4) 63-64 (*Jones, Gareth*).

4793 *Baltzer, Dieter* Alttestamentliche Motive als Verstehensschlüssel der Christologie markinischer Wundergeschichten: Exempel gesamtbiblischer Didaktik. Alttestamentliche Fachdidaktik. Theologie 11: 1996, 169-201.

4794 **Beck, Robert R.** Nonviolent story: narrative conflict in the gospel of Mark. Maryknoll 1996, Orbis xviii; 206 pp. $16 [AThR 79.264].

4795 **Black, C. Clifton** Mark: images of an apostolic interpreter. 1994, ⇒10,4738; 11/1,3329. REvQ 68 (1996) 154-156 (*Smith, Stephen H.*); CBQ 58 (1996) 147-149 (*Hurtado, Larry W.*); SJTh 49 (1996) 112-113 (*Best, Ernest*).

4796 **Boismard, Marie-Émile** Jésus, un homme de Nazareth: raconté par Marc l'évangéliste. Théologies: P 1996, Cerf 216 pp. 2-204-05361-9.

4797 **Bryan, Christopher** A preface to Mark. 1993, ⇒9,4925... 11/1,3332. RSJTh 49 (1996) 225-226 (*Burridge, Richard A.*).

4798 **Camery-Hoggatt, Jerry** Irony / Mk. MSSNTS 72: 1992, ⇒8,2129... 10,4744. RSJTh 49 (1996) 223-225 (*Telford, W.R.*).

4799 *Catchpole, David R.* Mark. FHOOKER M., 1996, ⇒43. 70-83.

4800 **Collins, Adela Yarbro** The beginning of the gospel: probings of Mark in context. 1992, ⇒8,5131... 10,4747. RJR 76 (1996) 618-619 (*Gibson, Jeffrey B.*).

4801 **Cook, John Granger** The structure and persuasive power of Mark. SBL Semeia Studies 28: 1995, ⇒11/1,3337. REThL 72 (1996) 447-448 (*Neirynck, F.*).

4802 **Davidsen, Ole** The narrative Jesus: a semiotic reading of Mark's gospel. 1993, ⇒9,4902; 10,4750. RThLZ 121 (1996) 548-550 (*Niebuhr, Karl-Wilhelm*); SJTh 49 (1996) 380 (*Paraphilippopoulos, Rosalind*).

4803 *Davies, Stevan* The use of the gospel of Thomas in the gospel of Mark. Neotest. 30 (1996) 307-334.

4804 **Dwyer, Timothy** The motif of wonder in the gospel of Mark. JSNT.S 128: Shf 1996, Academic 243 pp. £39/$58.50. 1-85075-603-1.

4805 *Elliott, J.K.* The position of the verb in Mark with special reference to chapter 13. NT 38 (1996) 136-144.

4806 *Focant, Camille* Le rapport à la loi dans l'évangile de Marc. RTL 27 (1996) 281-308.

4807 **Georgeot, J.-M.** Lexique [v.1] Lettre A; [v.2] Lettres B-C; [v.3] Lettres D-E; [v.4] Lettres F-K. De Saint-Marc jusqu'à Tertullien 2 A- n.p. 1996-, n.p. 5 vols.

4808 **Goins, Kevin Dale** The narrative function of the women in Mark. Diss. Southern Bapt. Theol. Sem. DBlevins, J.L., 1995, 327 pp. [EThL 74,301*].

4809 *Gruson, Philippe* Les combats de Jésus. DosB 62 (1996) 21-22.

4810 **Hamerton-Kelly, Robert G.** The gospel... violence in Mark. 1994, ⇒10,4761; 11/1,3355. RJBL 115 (1996) 358-360 (*Malbon, Elizabeth Struthers*).

4811 **Hanson, James Steven** The endangered promises: conflict in Mark. Diss. Princeton Sem. 1996-97 [RTL 29,585].

4812 **Harrington, Wilfrid J.** Mark: realistic theologian: the Jesus of Mark. Dublin 1996, Columba 149 pp. £9. 1-85607-169-3.

4813 *Heidler, Johannes* Die Verwendung von Psalm 22 im Kreuzigungsbericht des Markus: ein Beitrag zur Frage nach der Christologie des Markus. Christi Leidenspsalm. 1996, ⇒29. 26-34.

4814 *Hilgert, Earle* The Son of Timaeus: blindness, sight, ascent, vision in Mark. [F]MACK B., ⇒54. 185-198.

4815 **Huber, Konrad** Jesus in Auseinandersetzung. FzB 75: 1995, ⇒11/1,3357. [R]ZKTh 188 (1996) 258-259 (*Hasitschka, Martin*); ThLZ 121 (1996) 550-552 (*Fenske, Wolfgang*).

4816 *Hurtado, Larry W.* Following Jesus in the gospel of Mark—and beyond. Patterns of discipleship. 1996, ⇒188. 9-29.

4817 **Jensen, Richard A.** Preaching Mark's gospel: a narrative approach. Lima, Ohio 1996, CSS 200 pp. 0-7880-0833-1 [NThAR 1997,194].

4818 **Juel, Donald H.** A master of surprise: Mark interpreted. 1994, ⇒10,4768. [R]Pacifica 9/1 (1996) 104-106 (*Moloney, Francis D.*).

4819 **Kinukawa, Hisako** Women and Jesus in Mark: a Japanese feminist perspective. 1994, ⇒10,8738; 11/1,3366. [R]CBQ 58 (1996) 158-159 (*Love, Stuart L.*).

4820 *Kowalczyk, Andrzej* Dlaczego Marek napisał drugą ewangelię? [Cur Marcus secundum evangelium scripsit?]. RBL 49 (1996) 107-120. **P.**

4821 **Küster, Volker** Jesu und das Volk im Markusevangelium: ein Beitrag zum interkulturellen Gespräch in der Exegese. BThSt 28: Neuk 1996, Neuk x; 98 pp. 3-7887-1581-2 [NThAR 1997,36].

4822 **La Casa de la Biblia** El auténtico rostro de Jesús: guía para una lectura comunitaria del evangelio de Marcos. Estella [3]1996, Verbo Divino 136 pp. Ptas675 [Comunidades 89,125].

4823 [E]**Lattea, Karen** "Say to this mountain": Mark's story of discipleship. Maryknoll, NY 1996, Orbis xv; 240 pp. 1-57075-100-5.

4824 *Le Boulluec, Alain* La lettre sur l'"Évangile secret' de Marc et le 'Quis dives salvetur?' de CLEMENT d'Alexandrie. Sum. rés. 27. Apocrypha 7 (1996) 27-41 [Mark 10,17-31].

4825 *Loader, William* Challenged at the boundaries: a conservative Jesus in Mark's tradition. JSNT 63 (1996) 45-61 [Mark 7,24-31; 1,39-45; 5,1-43].

4826 *Manns, Frédéric* Egli lo guardò. TS(I) 72 (sett.-ott. 1996) 19-22.

4827 **Marcus, Joel** The way of the Lord: christological exegesis in... Mark. 1992, ⇒8,5156... 11/1,3372. [R]SJTh 49 (1996) 111-112 (*France, R.T.*); Bibl.Interp. 4 (1996) 244-245 (*Hooker, Morna D.*).

4828 **Marshall, Christopher D.** Faith as a theme in Mark's narrative. 1989, ⇒5,4920... 11/1,3373. [R]ABR 44 (1996) 85-87 (*Trebilco, Paul*).

4829 *Marucci, Corrado* Spunti ecclesiologici nel vangelo di Marco. RdT 37 (1996) 169-199.

4830 **Mazzocchi, Luciano; Forzani, Jiso** Il vangelo secondo Marco e lo Zen. Vangelo e Zen: Bo 1996, EDB 252 pp. 88-10-80793-6.

4831 **Meadors, Edward P.** Jesus the messianic herald of salvation. WUNT 2/72: 1995, ⇒9,4958; 11/1,3378. [R]NT 38 (1996) 296-297 (*Tuckett, C.M.*); JThS 47 (1996) 595-597 (*Catchpole, David*); ATG 59 (1996) 306-308 (*Rodríguez Carmona, A.*).

4832 **Minor, Mitzi** The spirituality of Mark. LVL 1996, Westminster xi; 141 pp. $15. 0-664-25679-1 [ThD 44,373—Heiser, W. Charles].

4833 **Morton, Andrew Queen** The making of Mark. Mellen Biblical Press 41: Lewiston, NY 1996, Mellen (8) 108 pp. 0-7734-2393-1.

4834 **Müller, Peter** 'Wer ist dieser?': Jesus im Markusevangelium. BThSt 27: 1995, ⇒11/1,3382. ᴿLuThK 20/4 (1996) 203 (*Stolle, Volker*); ThLZ 121 (1996) 1158-1160 (*Mell, Ulrich*).

4835 **Myers, Ched** Who will roll away the stone?: discipleship queries for first world christians. 1994, ⇒10,4781. ᴿRRel 55 (1996) 440-441 (*Chaffee, Pat*).

4836 **Myers, Ched**, (*al*), Say to this mountain: Mark's story of discipleship. Maryknoll 1996, Orbis 240 pp. $14 [Miss. 26,105s— Arias, Mortimer].

4837 *Onuki, Takashi* The Minjung theology of Mark—a dialogue with Ahn Byung Mu. AJBI 22 (1996) 31-85.

4838 *Orchard, Bernard* Revelación bíblica y evangelio según San Marcos. Esperanza del hombre. 1996, ⇒173. 469-479.

4839 **Peterson, Dwight Norman** The origins of Mark: the Marcan community in current debate. Diss. Duke 1995, ᴰ*Smith, D.M.*, 321 pp. [EThL 74,302*].

4840 *Pikaza, X.* Jesús y los enfermos en el evangelio de Marcos. EstTrin 30 (1996) 151-247.

4841 **Pikaza, Xabier** Para viver o evangelho: leitura de Marcos. Coimbra 1996, Gráfica 300 pp. [Brot. 146,234].

4842 *Ramelli, Ilaria* Pᴇᴛʀᴏɴɪᴏ e i cristiani: allusioni al vangelo di Marco nel *Satyricon*?. Aevum 70 (1996) 75-80.

4843 *Schmahl, Günther* Die erste Bestimmung der Zwölf im Markusevangelium. ꜰKᴇʀᴛᴇʟɢᴇ K., 1996, ⇒48. 133-138.

4844 **Schneck, Richard** Isaiah in the gospel of Mark, 1-8. 1994, ⇒10,4790. ᴿJThS 47 (1996) 213-215 (*Watts, R.E.*); AUSS 34/1 (1996) 140-142 (*Shepherd, Tom*).

4845 *Scholtissek, Klaus* 'Er ist nicht ein Gott der Toten, sondern der Lebenden' (Mk 12,27): Grundzüge der markinischen Theo-logie. ꜰTʜᴜᴇsɪɴɢ W., NTA 31: 1996, ⇒94. 71-100.

4846 **Servotte, H.** Marcus literair: de dubbele focus in het tweede evangelie. Averbode 1996, Altiora 162 pp.

4847 **Shiner, Whitney Taylor** Follow me!: disciples in Markan rhetoric. Diss., ᴰ*Meeks, W.*, SBL.DS 145: Atlanta 1995, Scholars xviii; 334 pp. $30/$20. ᴿCBQ 58 (1996) 774-775 (*Vaage, Leif E.*).

4848 *Smith, Stephen H.* The function of the Son of David tradition in Mark's gospel. NTS 42 (1996) 523-539.

4849 **Smith, Stephen H.** A lion with wings: a narrative-critical approach to Mark's Gospel. BiSer 38: Shf 1996, Academic 258 pp. £20/$25. 1-85075-784-4 [NTS 43,622].

4850 **Suau, Teodor** Mujeres en el evangelio de Marcos. Emaús 20: Barc 1996, Centre de Pastoral Litúrgica 75 pp. [EfMex 15,419].

4851 *Taracchi, Stefano* La geografia del vangelo di Marco. PaVi 41/3 (1996) 6-10;

4852 L'"Euanghélion" di Marco. PaVi 41/1 (1996) 35-39.

4853 **Tate, W. Randolph** Reading Mark from the outside: Eᴄᴏ and Isᴇʀ leave their marks. 1995, ⇒11/1,3407. ᴿJBL 115 (1996) 542-544 (*Moore, Stephen D.*).

4854 ᴱTelford, **William R.** The interpretation of Mark. ²1995, ⇒11/1,116. ᴿScrB 26 (1996) 53-54 (*Wansbrough, Henry*).

4855 ᴱ**Van Oyen, G.** De tijd is rijp: Marcus en zijn lezers toen en nu. Verslagboek Vliebergh-Sencie-Leergang Afedling Bijbel 1995: Lv 1996, Vlaamse Bijbelstichting [VBS] 216 pp. 90-334-3570-5 [NT-hAR 1997,293].

4856 **Wansbrough, Henry J.** The lion and the bull: the gospels of Mark and Luke. L 1996, Darton, L. & T. xi; 195 pp. 0-232-52162-X.

4857 *Watson, Alan* Leviticus in Mark: Jesus' attitude to the law. Reading Leviticus. JSOT.S 227: 1996, ⇒203. 263-271.

4858 **Williams, Joel F.** Other followers of Jesus... Mk. JSNT.S 102: 1994, ⇒10,4802; 11/1,3420. ᴿBZ 40 (1996) 271-273 (*Ebner, Martin*); CBQ 58 (1996) 173-174 (*Powell, Mark Allan*); CritRR 9 (1996) 305-307 (*Webb, Robert L.*).

4859 **Zager, Werner** Gottesherrschaft und Endgericht in der Verkündigung Jesu: eine Untersuchung zur markinischen Jesusüberlieferung einschliesslich der Q-Parallelen. BZNW 82: B 1996, De Gruyter xiii; 420 pp. DM188. 3-11-015263-0.

F6.3 Evangelii Marci versiculi

4860 *Malbon, Elizabeth Struthers* The beginning of a narrative commentary on the gospel of Mark. SBL.SPS 35: 1996, ⇒274. 98-122 [Mark 1-3].

4861 *Hock, Ronald F.* Social experience and the beginning of the gospel of Mark [1,1-15];

4862 *Vaage, Leif E.* Bird-watching at the baptism of Jesus: early christian mythmaking in Mark 1:9-11. ᶠMACK B., 1996, ⇒54. 311-326/280-294.

4863 *Dell'Orto, Giuseppe* Il battesimo di Gesù: Mc 1,9-11. PaVi 41/1 (1996) 10-14.

4864 *Van Eck, Ernest* The baptism of Jesus in Mark: a status transformation ritual. Neotest. 30 (1996) 187-215 [1,9-13].

4865 *Mell, Ulrich* Jesu Taufe durch Johannes (Markus 1,9-15)—zur narrativen Christologie vom neuen Adam. BZ 40 (1996) 161-178.

4866 *Perroni, Marinella* I primi discepoli: Mc 1,16-20;

4867 *Mazzucco, Glementina* Gesù nella sinagoga di Cafarnao: Mc 1,21-28;

4868 *Bagni, Arcangelo* La guarigione della suocera di Pietro [1,29-31];

4869 *Orsatti, Mauro* "Ti sono rimessi i tuoi peccati": Mc 2,1-12. PaVi 41/1 (1996) 15-20/21-25/40-43/26-29.

4870 *Mickiewicz, Franciszek* 'Synu, odpuszczają ci się twoje grzechy' ['Fili, dimittuntur tibi peccata tua' (Mc 2,1-12)]. RBL 49 (1996) 28-38. P.

4871 *Derrett, J. Duncan M.* Why 'bed'? (Mark 2,9d; John 5,8b). BeO 38 (1996) 111-116.

4872 *Graziani, Domenico* Mc 2,18-20: la gioia incompiuta dell'incontro nell'attesa. Vivarium 4 (1996) 361-390.

4873 *Mell, Ulrich* "Neuer Wein (gehört) in neue Schläuche" (Mk 2,22c): zur Überlieferung und Theologie von Mk 2,18-22. ThZ 52 (1996) 1-31.

4874 *Ginami, Corrado* "Il Figlio dell'uomo è signore anche del sabato": Mc 2,23-28. PaVi 41/1 (1996) 31-34.

4875 *Grün, Anselm* Der Mann mit der verdorrten Hand (Mk 3,1-6). LS 47 (1996) 68-69.

4876 *Gamba, Giuseppe Giov.* A proposito di Marco 3,20-21 (ricerca e definizione del senso). Sal. 58 (1996) 223-268.

4877 *Montagnini, Felice* Il peccato contro lo Spirito Santo: Mc 3,20-30. PaVi 41/2 (1996) 14-17.

4878 *Neufeld, Dietmar* Eating, ecstasy, and exorcism (Mark 3:21). BTB 26 (1996) 152-162.
4879 *Umeagudosu, Margaret A.* The healing of the Gerasene demoniac from a specifically African perspective. C.U.E.A. African Christian Studies 12/4 (1996) 30-37 [4,1-20] [ThIK 18/2 (1997) 17].
4880 *Boismard, M.-E.* De JUSTIN à l'harmonie de PEPYS: la parabole de la semence. RB 103 (1996) 433-440 [4,3-9].
4881 *Chempakassery, Philip* Dhvani (implied) meaning of the Markan parable of the sower. ITS 33/1 (1996) 5-16 [4,5].
4882 *Estrada, Bernardo* La esperanza de salvación de Israel según Mc 4,11-12. Esperanza del hombre. 1996, ⇒173. 511-525.
4883 *Orsatti, Mauro* Il seme che cresce da solo: Mc 4,26-29. PaVi 41/2 (1996) 18-22.
4884 *Hirth, Volkmar* Die baumgroße Senfstaude—Bild der wahren Königsherrschaft: ein Versuch biblischer Theologie. BN 83 (1996) 15-16 [4,30-32; Ezek 17,23].
4885 *Schwarz, Alois* Jede Zeit hat ihre Bedrängnis: Seesturmgeschichten ermutigen, mit Widerständen zurechtzukommen. LS 47 (1996) 240-242 [4,35-41].
4886 *Matjaž, Maksimilijan* Die Sturmstillung als markinische Wundererzählung [The calming of the storm as a Marcan miracle story]. Sum. 189. Bogoslovni Vestnik 56/2 (1996) 169-189 [4,35-41] **S.**
4887 *Mosetto, Francesco* "Chi è costui...?": Mc 4,35-41. PaVi 41/2 (1996) 23-26.
4888 *Cilia, Lucio* Fede e paura (Mc 4,35-41). PSV 33/1 (1996) 95-107.
4889 *MacInerny, William F.* An unresolved question in the gospel called Mark: "Who is this whom even wind and sea obey?" (4:41). PRSt 23 (1996) 255-268.
4890 **Henaut, Barry W.** Oral tradition... Mk 4. JSNT.S 82: 1993, ⇒9,5002... 11/1,3449. [R]ThRv 92 (1996) 227-229 (*Scholtissek, Klaus*).
4891 *Gabriel, A.* The Gerasene demoniac (Mk 5:1-20): a socio-political reading. BiBh 22 (1996) 167-174.
4892 *Raja, A. Maria Arul* Exorcism and the Dalit self-affirmation: a reinterpretation of Mk 5:1-20. Sum. 843. VJTR 60 (1996) 843-851.
4893 *Kahl, Brigitte* Jairus und die verlorenen Töchter Israels: sozioliterarische Überlegungen zum Problem der Grenzüberschreitung in Mk 5,21-43. Von der Wurzel getragen. 1996, ⇒204. 61-78.
4894 *Heller, Karin* Nella sinagoga di Nazaret: Mc 6,1-6a. PaVi 41/2 (1996) 27-30.
4895 *Cuvillier, Elian* Coopération interprétative et questionnement du lecteur dans le récit d'envoi en mission (Mc 6:6b-13.30-32//Mt 10:1-11:1). RHPhR 76 (1996) 139-155.
4896 *Ostinelli, Caterina* La missione dei dodici: Mc 6,6b-32. PaVi 41/3 (1996) 11-15.
4897 *Couffignal, Robert* Le conte merveilleux du martyre de Jean-Baptiste: étude littéraire de Marc 6,14-29. [F]LEGASSE S., LeDiv 166: 1996, ⇒51. 147-165.
4898 *Dell'Orto, Giuseppe* La sezione dei pani: Mc 6,30-8,26. PaVi 41/3 (1996) 16-20.
4899 *Rolland, Philippe* La véritable préhistoire de Marc (Mc 6,30-34 et parallèles). RB 103 (1996) 244-256.

4900 *Orsatti, Mauro* Il miracolo dei pani: Mc 6,33-44; cf 8,1-9. PaVi 41/3 (1996) 21-24.
4901 *Smith, Stephen H.* Bethsaida via Gennesaret: the enigma of the sea-crossing in Mark 6,45-53. Bib. 77 (1996) 349-374.
4902 *Massana, Ramón Puig* Acerca de una reciente publicacion de Jose O'CALLAGHAN sobre los papiros de la cueva 7 de Qumran [7Q5]. FgNT 9 (1996) 51-59 [6,52-53].
4903 *Mosetto, Francesco* La controversia sulla tradizione: Mc 7,1-23. PaVi 41/3 (1996) 25-28.
4904 *Poirier, John C.* Why did the pharisees wash their hands?. JJS 47 (1996) 217-233 [7,1-23].
4905 *Chilton, Bruce* A generative exegesis of Mark 7:1-23. JHiC 3 (1996) 18-37.
4906 *Perkinson, Jim* A Canaanitic word in the Logos of Christ; or the difference the Syro-Phoenician woman makes to Jesus. Semeia 75 (1996) 61-85 [7,23-30].
4907 *Taussig, Hal* Dealing under the table: ritual negotiation of women's power in the Syro-Phoenician woman pericope. FMACK B., 1996, ⇒54. 264-279 [7,24-30; Matt 15,22-28].
4908 *Pellegrini, Rita* 'Tu sei il Cristo': Mc 8,27-30. PaVi 41/3 (1996) 29-32.
4909 *Tremolada, Pierantonio* L'annuncio del destino del Figlio dell'uomo. PaVi 41/4 (1996) 11-15 [8,31-33].
4910 **Seebadduka, George William** 'Rabbi, it is good that we are here': Moses, Elijah, and John in Mark's transfiguration story (9:2-8). Diss. Marquette 1995, 239 pp. [EThL 74,303*].
4911 *Zeller, Dieter* La métamorphose de Jésus comme épiphanie (Mc 9,2-8). FLEGASSE S., LeDiv 166: 1996, ⇒51. 167-186.
4912 *Simonetti, Manlio* Alcune antiche interpretazioni della Trasfigurazione (Marco 9,2-9). SMSR 62 (1996) 599-608.
4913 *Smith, Morton* The origin and history of the transfiguration story. New Testament. 1996 <1980>, ⇒151. 79-86 [9,2-10].
4914 *Paul VI, Pope* Il mistero della Trasfigurazione: riflessione di PAOLO VI [9,2-10];
4915 *Bottini, Giovanni Claudio* La trasfigurazione in Marco 9,2-10;
4916 *Jerome* Dal *Commento al vangelo di S. Marco* di S. GIROLAMO (Mc 9,5-8);
4917 *Bagni, Arcangelo* L'uomo non separi ciò che Dio ha unito Mc 10,1-12. PaVi 41/4 (1996) 46-48/16-21/45-46/22-25.
4918 **Drewermann, Eugen** Psicoanálisis y teología moral II: caminos y rodeos del amor [10,1-12]. Bilbao 1996, Desclée de B. 314 pp. [Carthaginensia 14,247s—Tamayo Açosta, J.J.].
4919 *Le Boulluec, Alain* La lettre sur l''Évangile secret' de Marc et le 'Quis dives salvetur?' de CLEMENT d'Alexandrie. Sum. rés. 27. Apocrypha 7 (1996) 27-41 [10,17-31].
4920 *Bagni, Arcangelo* Sequela di Cristo e beni terreni Mc 10,17-31. PaVi 41/4 (1996) 26-31.
4921 **Leal Salazar, Gabriel** El seguimiento de Jesús según la tradición del rico: estudio redaccional y diacrónico de Mc 10,17-31. EMISJ 31: Estella 1996, Verbo Divino 279 pp. PTA2.500. 84-8169-136-4 [EstB 55,569].
4922 *McHardy, W.D.* Mark 10:19: a reference to the Old Testament?. ET 107 (1996) 143.

4923   *Prete, Benedetto* Il logion di Gesù: "Dare la propria vita in riscatto
       per molti" (Mc 10,45). Sum. 335. RivBib 44 (1996) 309-335.
4924   *Cramarossa, Lydia* Il cieco di Gerico Mc 10,46-52. PaVi 41/4
       (1996) 32-36.
4925   *Flores, José Prado* Jésus guérit et sauve. ᵀ*Maire, R.*, Séminaire sur
       la Guérison 3-7 Oct. 1995. Tychique 121 (1996) 3-8 [10,46-52].
4926   *Eckstein, Hans-Joachim* Markus 10,46-52 als Schlüsseltext des
       Markusevangeliums. ZNW 87 (1996) 33-50.
4927   *Pellegrini, Rita* L'ingresso del Messia in Gerusalemme. PaVi 41/5
       (1996) 10-15 [11,1-11].
4928   *Botha, J.* The bible in South African public discourse—with special
       reference to the right to protest. Scriptura 58 (1996) 329-343 [11,1-
       33] [NTAb 41,45].
4929   *Ferrari, Pier Luigi* Il fico senza frutti e il tempio. PaVi 41/5 (1996)
       16-20 [11,12-25].
4930   **Krause, Deborah Davies** Seeing the fig tree anew: the exegesis of
       Hosea 9:10-17 in Mark 11:12-25. Diss. Emory 1996, ᴰ*O'Day,
       Gail R.*, 301 pp. DAI-A 57/04, p. 1674; AAC 9625953.
4931   *Pilch, John J.* Slow to anger and long of nose. BiTod 34 (1996)
       305-310 [11,15-19].
4932   **Mell, Ulrich** Die "anderen" Winzer... Mk 11,27-12,34. WUNT
       2/77: 1994, ⇒10,4850; 11/1,3501. ᴿOrdKor 37 (1996) 129-130
       (*Giesen, Heinz*); ThLZ 121 (1996) 158-160 (*Karrer, Martin*);
       ZKTh 188 (1996) 243-246 (*Huber, Konrad*); Neotest. 30 (1996)
       225-228 (*Strijdom, J.M.; Bosman, P.R.*); CBQ 58 (1996) 761-762
       (*Evans, Craig A.*).
4933   *Huber, Konrad* Zur Frage nach christologischen Implikationen in
       den "Jerusalemer Streitgesprächen" bei Markus. SNTU.A 21
       (1996) 5-19 [11,27-12,37].
4934   **Navarro Puerto, Mercedes** Ungido para la vida: exégesis narrativa
       y teología de Mc 14,3-9 y 12,1-8. Diss. excerpt Pont. Univ. Gre-
       goriana, ᴰ*Aletti, Jean-Noël*, R 1996, vi; 118 pp.
4935   **Aus, Roger David** The wicked tenants and Gethsemane: Isaiah in
       the wicked tenants' vineyard, and Moses and the high priest in
       Gethsemane: Judaic traditions in Mark 12:1-9 and 14:32-42. Uni-
       versity of South Florida, International Studies in Formative Chri-
       stianity and Judaism 4: Atlanta, GA 1996 Scholars xii; 199 pp. 0-
       7885-0261-1.
4936   *Schottroff, Willy* Das Gleichnis von den bösen Weingärtnern (Mk
       21,1-9 parr.): ein Beitrag zur Geschichte der Bodenpacht in Palä-
       stina. ZDPV 112 (1996) 18-48.
4937   *Mosetto, Francesco* 'Un uomo piantò una vigna...'. PaVi 41/5
       (1996) 21-24 [12,1-12].
4938   *Huber, Konrad* Vom "Weinberglied" zum "Winzergleichnis": zu
       einem Beispiel innerbiblischer relecture. PzB 5 (1996) 71-94 [12,1-
       12; Ps 80,9-16; Isa 27,2-6; 5,1-7; Jer 12,7-13].
4939   *Barraclough, Ray* Jesus' response to reputation: a study of Mark
       12:14 and parallels. Colloquium 28 (1996) 3-11 [Matt 22,16-17;
       Luke 20,21-22].
4940   *Main, Emmanuelle* Les Sadducéens et la résurrection des morts:
       comparaison entre Mc 12,18-27 et Lc 20,27-38. RB 103 (1996)
       411-432.
4941   *Ghidelli, Carlo* Il Dio dei viventi. PaVi 41/5 (1996) 25-29 [12,18-
       27].

4942 *Tremolada, Pierantonio* Il ritorno del Figlio dell'Uomo. PaVi 41/5 (1996) 30-36 [13,1-37].
4943 *Van Iersel, Bas M.F.* Failed followers in Mark: Mark 13:12 as a key for the identification of the intended readers. CBQ 58 (1996) 244-263.
4944 *Such, W.A.* The "crux criticorum" of Mark 13:14. RestQ 38 (1996) 93-108.
4945 *Hatina, Thomas R.* The focus of Mark 13:24-27: the parousia, or the destruction of the temple?. BBR 6 (1996) 43-66.
4946 *Taylor, N.H.* Palestinian christianity and the CALIGULA crisis, II: the Markan eschatological discourse. JSNT 62 (1996) 13-41 [13].
4947 *Collins, Adela Yarbro* The apocalyptic rhetoric of Mark 13 in historical context. BR 41 (1996) 5-36.

F6.8 **Passio secundum Marcum, 14,1...[⇒5.3]**

4948 *Baecher, Claude* La fin du monde: levée d'un coin de voile sur la continuité entre le monde présent et le royaume à venir. Ḥokhma 62 (1996) 41-67.
4949 *Bammel, E.* The trial of Jesus in the gospel of Mark. HTS 52/1 (1996) 48-67 [NTAb 41,40].
4950 *Bergeson, Bob* Buried in the church, raised in the bread: literary observations in Mark's gospel. BTB 26 (1996) 64-69 [1,32-39; 14,17-41; 16,7].
4951 **Bourquin, Yvan** La confession du centurion: le Fils de Dieu en croix selon l'évangile de Marc. Poliez-le-Grand 1996, Du Moulin 76 pp. FF56 [FV 96/3,73].
4952 **Cuvillier, Élian** La fin du monde... et puis après?: témoignage de quelques auteurs du Nouveau Testament. Ḥokhma 62 (1996) 17-34.
4953 *LaVerdiere, E.* The passion-resurrection according to Mark: act III: crucifixion, death and resurrection (15:21-16:8): scene two: crucifixion and death at Golgotha (15:21-41): part one: the way of the cross, the crucifixion, and the final mockery (15:21-32). Emmanuel 102/3 (1996) 136-147 [NTAb 40,424].
4954 *Maggioni, Bruno* Passione e croce nel vangelo di Marco. RCl 77 (1996) 726-736.
4955 **Myllykoski, Matti** Die letzten Tage Jesu, 2: Markus, Johannes... AASF B 272: 1994, ⇒10,4644; 11/1,3235. RRHPhR 76 (1996) 234-235 (*Grappe, Ch.*).
4956 **Schreiber, Johannes** Die Markuspassion. BZNW 68: [2]1993 <1969>, ⇒9,5047... 11/1,3528. RNT 38 (1996) 77-86 (*Telford, W.R.*).
4957 **Sommer, Urs** Die Passionsgeschichte des Markusevangeliums. WUNT 2/58: 1993, ⇒9,5048... 11/1,3529. RNT 38 (1996) 77-86 (*Telford, W.R.*).
4958 *Strickert, Fred* With wide open arms: the passion according to Mark. CThMi 23 (1996) 416-420.

4959 **Lücking, S.** Mimesis der Verachteten... Mk 14,1-11. SBS 152: 1993, ⇒9,5401. RSNTU.A 21 (1996) 242-243 (*Fuchs, A.*).
4960 *Bagni, Arcangelo* Si racconterà ciò che ella ha fatto (Mc 14,3-9);
4961 *Ostinelli, Caterina* L'ultima cena (Mc 14,17-25). PaVi 41/6 (1996) 46-49/6-11.

4962 **Cha, Jung Sik** Confronting death: the story of Gethsemane in Mark 14:32-42 and its historical legacy. Diss. Chicago 1996, DBetz, Hans Dieter, 416 pp. DAI-A 57/05, p. 2081; AAC 9703842.

4963 Galizzi, Mario Getsemani (Mc 14,32-42). PaVi 41/6 (1996) 12-17.

4964 **Dhas, T. Arul** The prayer of Jesus at Gethsemane with reference to other prayers and speeches before death and martyrdom. Diss. E 1996, 291 pp. [14,35-36] [EThL 74,304*].

4965 Walsh, J.E. The two linen cloths. HPR 96/10 (1996) 63-66 [14,51-52] [NTAb 41,46].

4966 Manicardi, Ermenegildo Gesù davanti al sinedrio (Mc 14,53-65). PaVi 41/6 (1996) 18-22.

4967 **Borrel i Viader, Agusti** Il rinnegamento di Pietro e i discepoli nella passione secondo Marco: la funzione narrative e retorica di Mc 14,54.66-72. Diss. Pont. Inst. Biblicum 1996, DAletti, Jean-Noël [AcBib 10/2,228].

4968 Grillo, Margherita Il Cireneo. TS(I) 72 (luglio-agosto 1996) 8-10 [15,20].

4969 Tremolada, Pierantonio Il figlio di Dio crocifisso (Mc 15,21-39). PaVi 41/6 (1996) 23-30.

4970 Borse, Udo Der Mehrheitstext Mk 15,27f.32c: die Kreuzigung Jesu zwischen zwei Räubern als Schrifterfüllung. FBORSE U., SBAB 21: 1996 <1992>, ⇒9. 11-38.

4971 Thatcher, Tom (Re)mark(s) on the cross. Bibl.Interp. 4 (1996) 346-361 [15,33-34; Ps 22].

4972 Trainor, Michael The women, the empty tomb, and that final verse. BiTod 34 (1996) 177-182 [15,40-16,8].

4973 Danove, Paul The characterization and narrative function of the women at the tomb (Mark 15,40-41.47; 16,1-8). Bib. 77 (1996) 375-397.

4974 Barnouin, M. Marie, mère de Jacques et de José (Marc 15.40). NTS 42 (1996) 472-474.

4975 Bolt, P.G. Mark 16:1-8: the empty tomb of a hero?. TynB 47 (1996) 27-37.

4976 Vignolo, Roberto Il sepolcro di Gesù nel vangelo di Marco (Mc 16,1-8). PaVi 41/6 (1996) 31-35.

4977 Frankemölle, Hubert Theodizee-Problematik im Markusevange-lium?: Anmerkungen zu Mk 16,1-8 im Kontext. FThUESING W., NTA 31: 1996, ⇒94. 101-134.

4978 Schwarz, Günther Sie "kauften .. Kräuteröle"? (Markus 16,1). BN 85 (1996) 22-23.

4979 De Virgilio, Giuseppe La finale canonica del vangelo di Marco (Mc 16,9-20). PaVi 41/6 (1996) 36-40.

4980 Davies, R.E. The great commission from CALVIN to CAREY. Evangel 14/2 (1996) 44-49 [16,15].

X. Opus Lucanum

F7.1 Opus Lucanum—Luke-Acts

4981 Agua, Agustín del La interpretación del 'relato' en la doble obra lucana. EE 71 (1996) 169-214.

4982 **Aletti, Jean-Noël** Il racconto come teologia: studio narrativo del terzo vangelo e del libro degli Atti degli Apostoli. CBi: R 1996, Dehoniane 229 pp. L28.000. 88-396-0686-6.

4983 *Ascough, Richard S.* Narrative technique and generic designation: crowd scenes in Luke-Acts and in CHARITON. CBQ 58 (1996) 69-81.

4984 **Awwad, Johnny B.** The significance of the death of Jesus in the plan of God in Luke-Acts: a door and a model for the gentile mission. Diss. Princeton Theol. Sem. 1996, ^D*Mauser, U.*, 226 pp. DAI-A 57/05, p. 2079; AAC 9629088.

4985 *Barrett, C.K.* The first New Testament?. NT 38 (1996) 94-104;

4986 Luke-Acts. ^FHOOKER M., 1996, ⇒43. 84-95.

4987 *Baum, Armin D.* Hat Lukas Jesus und die Apostel genau zitiert?: die oratio recta im lukanischen Werk zwischen antiker Profan- und Kirchengeschichtsschreibung. Israel in Geschichte. 1996, ⇒632. 105-145.

4988 **Bergholz, Thomas** Der Aufbau des lukanischen Doppelwerkes. 1995, ⇒11/1,2554. ^RSNTU.A 21 (1996) 265-267 (*Schreiber, S.*).

4989 **Bibb, Charles Wade** The characterization of God in Luke-Acts. Diss. Southern Bapt. Theol. Sem. 1996, ^D*Polhill, John*, 324 pp. DAI-A 57/04, p. 1671; AAC 9628672.

4990 **Bonz, Marianne Palmer** The best of times, the worst of times: Luke-Acts and epic tradition. Diss. Harvard 1996, ^D*Polhill, J.*, 240 pp. [EThL 74,305*].

4991 **Bosetti, Elena** Luca: il cammino dell'evangelizzazione. 1995, ⇒11/1,3556. ^RQuaderni di Scienze Religiose 5 (1996) 103 (*Marconi, Gilberto*).

4992 **Brawley, Robert L.** Centering on God: method and message in Luke-Acts. 1990, ⇒6,5304... 8,5262. ^RVJTR 60 (1996) 688 (*Durack, Jerome F.*).

4993 *Buckwalter, H. Douglas* Luke as a writer of sacred history. EvJo 14/2 (1996) 86ss [ThD Index Feb. 1997,5].

4994 *Caballero Cuesta, José M^a* Esperanza y 'más allá' en la obra de Lucas. Esperanza del hombre. 1996, ⇒173. 139-153.

4995 *Casalegno, Alberto* O discípulo e a metáfora da luz nos escritos lucanos. PerTeol 28/1 (1996) 65-81.

4996 **Crump, David** Jesus the intercessor. 1992, ⇒8,5264. ^REQ 68/1 (1996) 67 (*Graham, D.J.*).

4997 **Dollar, Harold E.** St. Luke's missiology: a cross-cultural challenge. Pasadena, CA 1996, Carey Library 197 pp. $10 [BS 154,383].

4998 *Fusco, Vittorio* Luke-Acts and the future of Israel. NT 38 (1996) 1-17.

4999 *Gérard, Jean-Pierre* Les riches dans la communauté lucanienne. Sum. diss., TDL.T 16, fasc. 7, sect. philologie biblique ⇒11/1,3576.

5000 *Ghidelli, Carlo* Alla ricerca dello specifico lucano. ^FDUPONT J., 1996, ⇒21. 95-113.

5001 *Green, Joel B.* Internal repetition in Luke-Acts: contemporary narratology and Lucan historiography. History in Acts. 1996, ⇒5223. 283-299.

5002 *Kampling, Rainer* Erinnernder Anfang: eine bibeltheologische Besinnung zur Relevanz der lukanischen Kirchenkonzeption für eine christliche Israeltheologie. ^FKERTELGE K., 1996, ⇒48. 139-160.

5002 *Kampling, Rainer* Erinnernder Anfang: eine bibeltheologische Besinnung zur Relevanz der lukanischen Kirchenkonzeption für eine christliche Israeltheologie. ^FKERTELGE K., 1996, ⇒48. 139-160.

5003 *Kawamura-Hanaoka, Eiko* The significance of Luke-Acts for Zen Buddhism. BudCS 16 (1996) 79-85.

5004 **Kayama, Hisao** Believers who belonged to the sect of the pharisee (Acts 15:5)—towards an understanding of Luke's picture of the pharisees. AJBI 22 (1996) 86-109.

5005 **Kim, Hee-Song** Geisttaufe des Messias. StKlasPg 81: 1993, ⇒8,5273; 9,5080. ^RThRv 92 (1996) 229-230 (*Radl, Walter*).

5006 **Lane, Thomas Joseph** Luke and the gentile mission: gospel anticipates Acts. Diss. Pont. Univ. Gregoriana 1994, ^D*Kilgallen, John J.*, EHS.T 571: Fra 1996, Lang 240 pp. $53. 3-631-49999-X.

5007 **Leroy, Thierry** Le testament de saint Luc. P 1996, Albin Michel 319 pp. F120.

5008 *Longenecker, Richard N.* Taking up the cross daily: discipleship in Luke-Acts. Patterns of discipleship. 1996, ⇒188. 50-76.

5009 *Marguerat, Daniel* Juifs et chrétiens selon Luc-Actes. Le déchirement. MoBi 32: 1996, ⇒192. 151-178.

5010 *Mealand, David L.* Luke-Acts and the verbs of DIONYSIUS of Halicarnassus. JSNT 63 (1996) 63-86.

5011 **O'Toole, Robert F.** L'unità della teologia di Luca. 1994, ⇒10,4900. ^RCivCatt 147 III (1996) 91-92 (*Scaiola, D.*).

5012 **Ray, Jerry Lynn** Narrative irony in Luke-Acts: the paradoxical interaction of prophetic fulfillment and Jewish rejection. Mellen 28: Lewiston, NY 1996, Mellen xi; 188 pp. $90. 0-7734-2359-1 [NTAb 41,152].

5013 **Reinhardt, Wolfgang** Das Wachstum des Gottesvolkes. 1995, ⇒11/1,3589. ^ROrdKor 37 (1996) 489-490 (*Giesen, Heinz*).

5014 **Reinmuth, Eckart** Pseudo-Philo und Lukas. WUNT 2/74: 1994, ⇒10,4907; 11/1,3590. ^RBZ 40 (1996) 135-137 (*Heininger, Bernhard*); ZRGG 48 (1996) 187-188 (*Horn, Friedrich W.*); ThLZ 121 (1996) 1160-1162 (*Vollenweider, Samuel*); RB 103 (1996) 606-608 (*Taylor, Justin*).

5015 *Rossé, Gérard* Il giusto sofferente nell'opera di Luca. Som. 151. PSV 34 (1996) 151-167.

5016 *Sampathkumar, P.A.* The rich and the poor in Luke-Acts. BiBh 22 (1996) 175-189.

5017 **Seim, Turid Karlsen** The double message... in Luke-Acts. 1994, ⇒10,4909; 11/1,3592. ^RNTT 97 (1996) 52-53 (*Gilhus, Ingvild Sælid*); JBL 115 (1996) 746-748 (*Corley, Kathleen E.*).

5018 **Shepherd, William H.** The narrative function of the Holy Spirit as a character in Luke-Acts. SBL.DS 147: 1994, ⇒10,4913. ^RCBQ 58 (1996) 168-169 (*Montague, George T.*); JBL 115 (1996) 744-745 (*Karris, Robert J.*).

5019 **Sluda, Tomasz** Die Theologie des Geistes im lukanischen Doppelwerk. Diss. Mü 1996, ^D*Gnilka, J.*, 323 pp. [EThL 74,306*].

5020 *Stenschke, Christoph W.* Die Bedeutung der Propheten und des Prophetenwortes der Vergangenheit für das lukanische Menschenbild. JETh 10 (1996) 123-148.

5021 **Sterling, Gregory E.** Historiography... Luke-Acts. NT.S 64: 1992, ⇒8,5292; 9,5109. ^RJQR 86 (1996) 452-455 (*Gray, Rebecca*).

5022 **Strauss, Mark L.** The Davidic messiah in Luke-Acts. JSNT.S 110: 1995, ⇒9,5110; 11/1,3595. ^RCBQ 58 (1996) 775-777 (*Ascough, Richard S.*) [Luke 4,16-30; Acts 2,14-41; 13,16-41].

5023 *Stricher, Joseph* Le milieu du temps: Luc et la théologie de l'histoire. DosB 64 (1996) 21-23.

5024 **Stricher, Joseph** La parité hommes-femmes dans l'oeuvre de Luc. P 1996, ACGF. F65.

5025 *Taylor, Justin* St Luke: architect of Christian unity. Holy Land 16 (1996) 140-144.

5026 **Turner, Max** Power from on high: the spirit in Israel's restoration and witness in Luke-Acts. JPentec.S 9: Shf 1996, Academic 511 pp. £30/$45. 1-85075-756-9.

5027 **Weatherly, John A.** Jewish responsibility for the death of Jesus in Luke-Acts. JSNT.S 106: 1994, ⇒10,4920; 11/1,3601. ^RJThS 47 (1996) 511-612 (*Franklin, E.*); EvQ 68 (1996) 357 (*Marshall, I. Howard*); JBL 115 (1996) 360-361 (*Setzer, Claudia*).

F7.3 **Evangelium Lucae**—*Textus, commentarii*

5028 ^E**Ammassari, Antonio** Il vangelo di Luca nella colonna latina del Bezae Codex Cantabrigiensis: note di commento sulla struttura letteraria, la punteggiatura, le lezioni e le citazioni bibliche. Città del Vaticano 1996, Vaticana 190 pp. L27.000. 88-209-2244-4.

5029 **Bock, Darrell L.** Luke, 1: 1:1-9:50. 1994, ⇒10,4921; 11/1,3603. ^RWThJ 58 (1996) 170-173 (*Green, Joel B.*); TrinJ 17 (1996) 248-252 (*Hurst, Larry*);

5030 Luke, 2: 9:51-24:53. GR 1996, Baker 1162 pp. $50. 0-8010-1052-7.

5031 **Bovon, François** Lc 1-9. 1995, ⇒11/1,3604. ^RRevAg 37 (1996) 853-854 (*Salugal, Santos*); REspir 55 (1996) 366-367 (*Castro, Secundino*); EE 71 (1996) 475-476 (*Castro, Secundino*).

5032 **Bovon, François** L'évangile selon saint Luc (9,51-14,35). Commentaire du NT 3B: Genève 1996, Labor et F. 492 pp. FS78. 2-8309-0830-9 [ZNW 88,153];

5033 Das Evangelium nach Lukas, 2: Lk 9,51-14,35. Evangelisch-Katholischer Kommentar zum NT 3/2: Solothurn 1996, Benziger viii; 556 pp. ÖS1081. 3-787-1549-9 [ZThK 119,229].

5034 **Cousin, H.** Vangelo di Luca. 1995, ⇒11/1,3607. ^RREsp 55 (1996) 555-556 (*Castro, Secundino*).

5035 **Hendrickx, Herman** Preface and infancy narrative (Luke 1:1-2:52). The third gospel for the third world 1: ColMn 1996, Liturgical xiv; 285 pp. 0-8146-5870-9 [NThAR 1997,260].

5036 **Just, Arthur A.** Luke 1:1-9:50. Concordia Commentary: Saint Louis 1996, Concordia xxxi; 416 pp. $30. 0-570-04254-2 [NThAR 1997,292].

5037 **Kiraz, George Anton** Luke. Comparative edition of the Syriac gospels, aligning the Sinaiticus, Curetonianus, Peshîttâ & Harklean versions, 3. NTTS 21/3: Lei 1996, Brill 514 pp. ƒ820 [4 vols]. 90-04-104194 [NT 39,405].

5038 **Kunduru, Joji** Sandhata: Jesus the liberator—unifier. Secunderabad 1996, Andhra Jesuit Publ. xvi; 287 pp. Rs20. **Telugu**.

5039 *Manns, Frédéric* Un document judéo-chrétien: la source propre à Luc. BeO 38 (1996) 43-62.

5040 **Menichelli, Ernesto** Il vangelo di Luca: lectio su brani scelti. Verucchio (Rimini) 1995, Pazzini 94 pp. 88-85124-25-9.
5041 **Nolland, John** Luke 9:21-18:34. WBC 35B: 1993, ⇒10,4930; 11/1,3611. REvQ 68 (1996) 157-159 (*Weatherly, Jon*).
5042 *Pickering, Stuart R.* Readings of the Codex Bezae in the gospel of Luke. NTTRU 4 (1996) 87-92.
5043 **Romaniuk, Kazimierz** Czwarty rozdzial ewangelii Lukasza: komentarz biblijny dla potrzeb ekumenicznych obchodów Jubileuszu 2000 lecia chrzescijanstwa. Wsz 1996, Wydawnictwo AKCES 80 pp. 83-903394-7-1. **P.**
5044 **Spinetoli, Ortensio da** Lukács: a szegények evangéliuma. Szeged 1996, Agape 770 pp. 963-458-039-4. **Hungarian.**
5045 **Swanson, Reuben J.** Luke. New Testament Greek manuscripts: variant readings arranged in horizontal lines against Codex Vaticanus, 3. Shf 1996, Academic xx; 420 pp. £25. 1-85075-774-7 [NT 39,286].
5046 **Tannehill, Robert C.** Luke. Abingdon NT Commentaries: Nv 1996, Abingdon 378 pp. 0-687-06132-6.
5047 **Tuckett, Christopher M.** Luke. NTGu: Shf 1996, Academic 122 pp. 1-85075-751-8.

F7.4 *Lucae themata*—Luke's Gospel, topics

5048 **Bohuytrón Solano, José Antonio** ¿En qué modo es significativo el termino *paz* para el retrato lucano de *Jesús*?. Diss. excerpt Pont. Univ. Gregoriana 1996, DO'*Toole, Robert F.*, xi; 110 pp.
5049 **Buckwalter, H. Douglas** The character and purpose of Luke's christology. MSSNTS 89: C 1996, CUP xxii; 342 pp. £37.50. 0-521-56180-9 [NTS 43,620].
5050 **Cárdenas Pallares, José** Ternura de Dios ternura de mujer: la mujer en el evangelio de San Lucas. EstB 2: México 1992, Dabar. REfMex 14 (1996) 396-397 (*Cepeda Salazar, Antonino*).
5051 *Casalegno, Alberto* Salvação e corporeidale no evangelho de Lucas. PerTeol 28 (1996) 191-208.
5052 **Conzelmann, Hans** Il centro del tempo: la teologia di Luca. TGatti, Enzo; EPitta, Antonio, Theologica: CasM 1996, Piemme 282 pp. L45.000. 88-384-2462-4. RLASBF 46 (1996) 461-465 (*Chrupcała, Lesław Daniel*).
5053 **Diefenbach, Manfred** Die Komposition des Lukas-Evangeliums unter Berücksichtigung antiker Rhetorikelemente. FTS 43: 1993, ⇒9,5136; 10,4941. RThPh 71 (1996) 268-269 (*Wucherpfennig, A.*); FKTh 12 (1996) 311-312 (*Stimpfle, Alois*).
5054 **Doble, Peter** The paradox of salvation: Luke's theology of the cross. MSSNTS 87: C 1996, CUP xiv; 272 pp. £35. 0-521-55212-5.
5055 **Dornisch, L.** A woman reads the gospel of Luke. ColMn 1996, Liturgical 232 pp. $20. 0-8146-2307-7 [NTAb 41,144].
5056 **García Pérez, José M.** San Lucas... sustrato arameo en Lc 1,39; 8,26-39; 21,36; 22,28-30; 23,39-43. 1995, ⇒11/1,3625 [οἰκουμένη]. RREsp 55 (1996) 141-144 (*Castro, Secundino*); EE 71 (1996) 299-301 (*Castro, Secundino*); ScrTh 28 (1996) 931-932 (*Balaguer, V.*).

5057 **Graumann, Thomas** Christus interpres: die Einheit von Auslegung und Verkündigung in der Lukaserklärung des AMBROSIUS
von Mailand. PTS 41: 1994, ⇒10,4943. [R]RHE 91 (1996) 521-524
(*Savon, Hervé*); ChH 65 (1996) 448-450 (*Rusch, William G.*).

5058 **Green, Joel B.** The theology of the gospel of Luke. 1995,
⇒11/1,3626. [R]RRT (1996/1) 94-96 (*Parker, D.C.*); CritRR 9
(1996) 219-221 (*Powell, Mark Allan*).

5059 **Huizing, Klaas** Lukas malt Christus: ein literarisches Porträt. Dü
1996, Patmos 191 pp. DM36.80. [R]BiLi 69 (1996) 267-268
(*Geiger, Georg*).

5060 [T]**Lienhard, Joseph** ORIGEN: homilies on Luke. FaCh 94: Wsh
1996, Cath. Univ. of America Press xxxix; 246 pp. $32. 0-8132-
0094-6 [JEarlyC 5,452].

5061 *Liu, P.* Political rivalry and parables. Jian Dao 5 (1996) 153-174
[NTA 40,424]. C.

5062 *Mayer, E.* Sell everything and become 'rich': dealing with posses-
sions according to Luke. LTJ 30/2 (1996) 58-65 [NTAb 41,48].

5063 **Moxnes, Halvor** A economia do reino... Lc. 1995, ⇒11/1,3637.
[R]REB 56 (1996) 489-490 (*Comblin, José*); RCB 38 (1996) 155-157
(*Ribeiro, Ari L. do Vale*).

5064 **Noël, Filip** De compositie van het Lucasevangelie in zijn relatie tot
Marcus. VAW.L 56; VVAW.L 150: 1994, ⇒10,4952. [R]EThL 72
(1996) 240-241 (*Verheyden, J.*).

5065 *Okorie, A.M.* Meals as type-scenes in the third gospel. MTh 47/1
(1996) 17ss [ThD Index Feb. 1997,8].

5066 *Plessis, Isak J. du* Applying the results of social-historical research
to narrative exegesis: Luke as case study. Neotest. 30 (1996) 335-
358.

5067 **Prieur, Alexander** Die Verkündigung der Gottesherrschaft: exegetische Studien zum lukanischen Verständnis von βασιλεια του θεου.
Diss. Tü 1993, [D]*Jeremias, G.*, WUNT 2/89: Tü 1996, Mohr viii;
336 pp. DM118. 3-16-146574-1.

5068 *Prior, Michael* Jesus and the evangelization of the poor. ScrB 26
(1996) 34-41.

5069 **Qualls, Paula Fontana** Isaiah in Luke: a study of comparative
midrash. Diss. Southern Bapt. Theol. Sem. 1996, [D]*Smothers,
T.G.*, 270 pp. [EThL 74,307*].

5070 **Reid, Barbara E.** Choosing the better part?: women in the gospel
of Luke. ColMn 1996, Liturgical xiv; 245 pp. $18. 0-8146-5494-0
[NTAb 41,152].

5071 **Rius-Camps, Josep** El éxodo del hombre libre... Lucas. 1991,
⇒8,5356. [R]ThLZ 121 (1996) 556-559 (*Stenschke, Christoph*).

5072 **Seland, Torrey** Establishment violence in PHILO and Luke. 1995,
⇒11/1,3649. [R]StPhilo 8 (1996) 208-210 (*Pervo, Richard I.*) [Acts
6,8-7,60; 21,15-36; 23,12-15].

5073 *Simmer-Brown, Judith* Suffering and social justice: a Buddhist response to the gospel of Luke. Bud[C]S 16 (1996) 99-112.

5074 **Wasserberg, Günter** Aus Israels Mitte—Heil für die Welt: eine
narrativ-exegetische Studie zur Theologie des Lukas. Diss. Kiel
1996/97, [D]*Becker, J.* [ThLZ 122,763].

F7.5 *Infantia, cantica*—Magnificat, Benedictus: Luc. 1-3

5075 **Drewermann, Eugen** Tu nombre es como el sabor de la vida: el
relato de la infancia de Jesús según el evangelio de Lucas: una interpretación psicoanalítica. 1995, ⇒11/1,3655. ᴿActBib 33 (1996)
3,2-33 (*Patuel, J.*).

5076 **Hendrickx, Herman N.** Preface and infancy narrative (Luke 1:1-
2:52). Third gospel for the third world, 1: ColMn 1996, Glazier
xiv; 285 pp. Bibl. $20. 0-8146-5870-9.

5077 *Kampling, Rainer* 'Gepriesen sei der Herr, der Gott Israels': zur
Theozentrik von Lk 1-2. ᶠТHUESING W., NTA 31: 1996, ⇒94.
149-179.

5078 **Kaut, Thomas** Befreier... Magnifikat, Benediktus. BBB 77: 1990,
⇒6,5392... 8,5379. ᴿThPh 71 (1996) 269-271 (*Meissner, J.*).

5079 *Leroy, Chantal* Images d'Annonciation. Vie Chrétienne (mars
1996) 1-4.

5080 **O'Fearghail, Fearghus** The introduction to Luke-Acts... Lk 1:1-
4:44. AnBib 126: 1994, ⇒7,4486... 9,5177. ᴿBiBh 22/2-3 (1996)
157-158 (*George, Gabriel*).

5081 **Radl, Walter** Der Ursprung Jesu: traditionsgeschichtliche Untersuchungen zu Lukas 1-2. Biblische Studien 7: FrB 1996, Herder 397
pp. DM88. 3-451-23940-X.

5082 **Sebastiani, L.** Maria ed Elisabetta. Cammini nello Spirito 1: Mi
1996, Paoline 208 pp. ᴿMiles Immacolatae 32 (1996) 708-709
(*Patrizi, M. Elisabetta*).

5083 *Troost, Arie* Elisabeth and Mary-Naomi and Ruth: gender-response
criticism in Luke 1-2. A feminist companion. 1996, ⇒170. 159-
196.

5084 **Muñoz Nieto, Jesús María** Tiempo de anuncio: estudio de Lc 1,5-
2,52. 1994, ⇒10,4970; 11/1,3659. ᴿRET 56 (1996) 406-408
(*Barrado Fernández, P.*); JBL 115 (1996) 544-545 (*Brown,
Raymond E.*).

5085 *Manicardi, Ermenegildo* L'annuncio a Maria: Lc 1,26-38 nel contesto di Lc 1,5-80. Sum. 331. Theotokos 4 (1996) 297-331.

5086 *Ferreira-Martins, J.M.* Anunciação a Maria: um relato de José?:
contributos para o estudo das fontes de Lc. 1,26-38a. Sum. 356.
HumTeo 17 (1996) 283-307.

5087 *Gargano, Guido Innocenzo* Lectio divina su Lc 1,26-38;

5088 *Morante, Giuseppe* Catechesi sull'Annunciazione (Lc 1,26-38).
Theotokos 4 (1996) 577-588/543-575.

5089 *LaVerdiere, E.* The annunciation to Mary: a story of faith, II: the
greeting. Emmanuel 102 (1996) 4-13 [1,28-29] [NTAb 40,425].

5090 *Cimosa Mario* Il senso del titolo κεχαριτωμένη. Theotokos 4
(1996) 589-59 [1,28].

5091 *LaVerdiere, E.* The annunciation to Mary: a story of faith, III: the
announcement;

5092 IV: the question. Emmanuel 102 (1996) 215-222/290-297 [1,30-
33] [NTAb 41,49].

5093 **Martini, Carlo Maria** Sui sentieri della Visitazione. Mi 1996, ÀÌ-
cora 116 pp. L14.000 [1,39-56] [CiVi 52,415].

5094 *Pikaza, Xabier* La madre de mi Señor (Lc 1,43). EphMar 46/4
(1996) 395-432.

5095 **Richert, Ulrike** Magnifikat und Benediktus: die ältesten Zeugnisse der judenchristlichen Tradition von der Geburt des Messias. Diss. D*Hengel, M.*, WUNT 2/90: Mohr 1996, Tü viii; 303 pp. 3-16-146590-3 [1,46-55.68-79] [NThAR 1997,101].

5096 *Schneider, Hans* Zw ing lis Marienpredigt und Luthe rs Magnifikat—Auslegung. Zwing. 23 (1996) 105-141 [1,46-55].

5097 *Marucci, Corrado* Notizie di storia e di amministrazione romana nel Nuovo Testamento. Religion. ANRW II.26.3: 1996, ⇒322. 2178-2220 [2,1-5].

5098 *Stimpfle, Alois* "Und Hirten waren in dieser Gegend ...": hermeneutische und exegetische Überlegungen zum Verständnis der Geburtsverkündigung Lk 2,8-20. SNTU.A 21 (1996) 20-41.

5099 *Janssen, Claudia* Hanna—Prophetin der Befreiung: sozialgeschichtliche Bibelauslegung zu Lukas 2,25-38. JK 57 (1996) 686-689.

5100 **Simón Muñoz, Alfonso** El Mesías y la hija de Sion: teología de la redención en Lc 2,29-35. 1994, ⇒10,4983; 11/1,3680. RRivBib 44 (1996) 368-371 (*Valentini, Alberto*); CBQ 58 (1996) 169-170 (*Branick, Vincent P.*); Mar. 58 (1996) 239-242 (*Pikaza, Xabier*); StLeg 37 (1996) 272-273 (*Ramos, Felipe F.*).

5101 **Hendrickx, Herman** Ministry in Galilee (Luke 3:1-6:49). The third gospel for the third world, 2A: ColMn 1996, Liturgical 376 pp. $20 [Mayéutica 24,251—Doyle, John].

F7.6 Evangelium Lucae 4,1...

5102 *Paffenroth, Kim* The testing of the sage: 1 Kings 10:1-13 and Q 4:1-13 (Lk 4:1-13). ET 107 (1996) 142-143.

5103 *Gibson, Jeffrey B.* A turn on "turning stones to bread": a new understanding of the devil's intention in Q 4.3. BR 41 (1996) 37-57.

5104 **Prior, Michael Patrick** Jesus the liberator... Lk 4:16-30. BiSe 26: 1995, ⇒11/1,3698. RMonth 29 (1996) 114-115 (*Casalegno, Alberto*); ScrB 26 (1996) 91-92 (*Rowland, Christopher*); CritRR 9 (1996) 255-258 (*Pilgrim, Walter E.*).

5105 **Mielcarek, Krzysztof** Jezus: ewangelizator ubogich (Łk 4,16-30). 1994, ⇒10,4987. RCoTh 66/3 (1996) 202-205 (*Szymik, Stefan*). P.

5106 *Basset, L.* La culpabilité paralysie du coeur: réinterprétation du récit de la guérison du paralysé (Lc 5/17-26). ETR 71 (1996) 341-345.

5107 *Klein, Hans* Am ersten Sabbat: eine Konjektur zu Lk 6,1. ZNW 87 (1996) 290-293.

5108 *Klein, Hans* Gerichtsankündigung und Liebesforderung: Lk 6.24-6 und 27 innerhalb der Botschaft des frühen Christentums. NTS 42 (1996) 421-433.

5109 *Swaeles, Romain* Un guide clairvoyant, un disciple bien formé (Lc 6,39-40). FDupont J., 1996, ⇒21. 115-126.

5110 *Terrinoni, Ubaldo* Cristo, "un grande profeta", risuscita un giovane di Nain: Lc 7,11-17. RVS 50 (1996) 622-640.

5111 *Schottroff, Luise* Through German and feminist eyes: a liberationist reading of Luke 7.36-50. A feminist companion. 1996, ⇒170. 332-341.

5112   *Friedrichsen, Timothy A.* Luke 9,22—a Matthean foreign body?.
       EThL 72 (1996) 398-407.
5113   *Manus, Chris U.* Lk 9,46-50: biblical theological reflections on an
       All-African war against indiscipline, corruption and political inep-
       titude. Scriptura 57 (1996) 451-460.

F7.7   *Iter hierosolymitanum—Lc 9,51...*—Jerusalem journey

5114   **Mayer, Edgar** Die Reiseerzählung des Lukas (Lk 9,51-19,10):
       Entscheidung in der Wüste. EHS.T 554: Fra 1996, Lang 358 pp.
       3-631-49638-9.

5115   *Hövelmann, Hartmut* Wer ist der Barmherzige Samaritaner?: eine
       ungewohnte Perspektive in LUTHE RS Auslegung von Lk 10,23-37
       [Who is the Good Samaritan?: an unusual perspective in Luther's
       commentary on Luke 10,23-37] ⇒9,5224. Abstr. *Rossol, Heinz D.*,
       Luther Digest 4 (1996) 70-71.
5116   *Kilgallen, John J.* The plan of the 'νομικός' (Luke 10.25-37). NTS
       42 (1996) 615-619.
5117   *Miller, Merrill P.* Parable and myth, argument and pronouncement
       in Luke 10:25-37. FMACK B., 1996, ⇒54. 214-228.
5118   *Combet-Galland, C.* L'amour, au jeu de la loi et du hasard: la pa-
       rabole du "Bon samaritain" et le débat qu'elle bouscule (Lc 10/25-
       37). ETR 71 (1996) 321-330.
5119   *Rodet, Chantal* La parabole du Samaritain: un indû pour la vie.
       SémBib 83 (1996) 17-32 [10,25-37].
5120   *Talmon, Shemaryahu* The 'Good Samaritan': a 'good Israelite'?.
       Sum. 239. Cathedra 80 (1996) 19-30 [10,25-37]. **H.**
5121   *Durand, Alain* Le bon samaritain (Lc 10,25-37). DosB 61 (1996)
       21-22.
5122   *Rivera, Enrique* Sabiduría y vida cristiana: "díjole Jesús: vete y haz
       tú lo mismo" (Lc 10,37). EvV 38 (1996) 18-19 [10,29-37].
5123   *Vanhoye, Albert* Le bon samaritain: herméneutique biblique de la
       parabole. Dolentium hominum: église et santé dans le monde, 11.
       1996, 198-202 [10,30-36] [APIB 10/3,269].
5124   **Fornari-Carbonell, Isabel M.** La escucha del huésped (Lc 10,38-
       42). EMISJ 30: 1995, ⇒11/1,3726. RTer. 47/1 (1996) 331-332
       (Borrell, Agustí).
5125   **Constable, Giles** Three studies in medieval religious and social
       thought: the interpretation of Mary and Martha [10,38-42]. 1995,
       ⇒11/1,3728. RHorizons 23/2 (1996) 334-336 *(Principe, Walter
       H.)*.
5126   *Carter, Warren* Getting Martha out of the kitchen: Luke 10:38-42
       again. CBQ 58 (1996) 264-280.

5127   *Landes, George M.* Jonah in Luke: the Hebrew bible background
       to the interpretation of the 'sign of Jonah' pericope in Luke 11.29-
       32. FSANDE RS J., JSOT.S 225: 1996, ⇒77. 133-163 [Matt 12,38-
       42].
5128   *Bissoli, Giovanni* Occhio semplice e occhio cattivo in Lc 11,34 alla
       luce del Targum. SBFLA 46 (1996) 45-51.
5129   *Malherbe, Abraham* The christianization of a topos (Luke 12:13-
       34). NT 38 (1996) 123-135.

5130 *Terrinoni, Ubaldo* Il primato dell'uomo: la polemica sul sabato: Lc 13,10-17. RVS 50 (1996) 125-147.

5131 *Söding, Thomas* Das Gleichnis vom Festmahl (Lk 14,16-24 par Mt 22,1-10): zur ekklesiologischen Dimension der Reich-Gottes-Verkündigung Jesu. ᶠKERTELGE K., 1996, ⇒48. 56-84.

5132 **Vögtle, Anton** Gott und seine Gäste: das Schicksal des Gleichnisses Jesu vom grossen Gastmahl (Lukas 14,16b-24; Matthäus 22,2-14). BThSt 29: Neuk 1996, Neuk 94 pp. DM19.80. 3-7887-1575-8 [BiKi 52,147].

5133 **Amisi, Kaobo** Renoncer à tout pour suivre Jésus: lectures exégétiques de Lc 14,25-33. Diss. extract Pont. Univ. Urbaniana 1996, ᴰ*Virgulin, Stefano*, 84 pp.

5134 **Braun, Willi** Feasting and social rhetoric in Luke 14. MSSNTS 85: 1995, ⇒11/1,3741. ᴿNT 38 (1996) 408-409 (*Muir, Steven C.*); EThL 72 (1996) 449-452 (*Neirynck, F.*); Bib. 77 (1996) 564-567 (*Tannehill, Robert*); CritRR 9 (1996) 183-185 (*Brawley, Robert L.*).

5135 *Leonardi, Mauro* Il Figlio Prodigo. StCatt 420 (1996) 100-103 [15,11-32].

5136 *Giertych, Wojciech* The glory of God is man fully alive. Sum. 9. Zycie Duchowe 5/3 (1996) 113-131 [15,11-32]. **P**.

5137 *Borghi, Ernesto* Lc 15,11-32: linee esegetiche globali. Sum. 308. RivBib 44 (1996) 279-308.

5138 *Schwarz, Günther* "Er hängte sich an einen Bürger"? (Lukas 15,15a). BN 85 (1996) 24-25.

5139 *Harrill, J. Albert* The indentured labor of the prodigal son (Luke 15:15). JBL 115 (1996) 714-717.

5140 *Parsons, Mikeal C.* The prodigal's elder brother: the history and ethics of reading Luke 15:25-32. PRSt 23 (1996) 147-174.

5141 **Basset, Lytta** La joie imprenable: pour une théologie de la prodigalité [15]. LiTh 30: Genève 1996, Labor et F. 371 pp. FF168. 2-8309-0818-X [RHPhR 78,112s—Pfrimmer, T.].

5142 *Chevillard, Jean* "Il fallait bien se réjouir..." (Luc 15). DosB 61 (1996) 23-24.

5143 *Kurz, Paul Konrad* Der verlorene Sohn—die verlorenen Väter: literarische Spiegelungen und Verfremdungen. StZ 214 (1996) 621-628 [15].

5144 *Wendland, E.R.* Finding some lost aspects of meaning in Christ's parables of the lost-and-found (Luke 15). TrinJ 17 (1996) 19-65.

5145 *Combrink, Hans J.B.* A social-scientific perspective on the parable of the 'unjust' steward (Lk 16:1-8a). Neotest. 30 (1996) 281-306.

5146 *Ukpong, Justin S.* The parable of the shrewd manager (Luke 16:1-13): an essay in inculturation: biblical hermeneutic. Semeia 73 (1996) 189-210.

5147 *Bivin, David* "And" or "in order to" remarry. JPersp 50 (1996) 10-17, 35-38 [16,18].

5148 *Wielenga, Bastiaan* The rich man and Lazarus. RW 46/3 (1996) 109-116 [16,19-31] [ZID 23,32].

5149 **Zúñiga Zúñiga, Miguel Angel** El hombre rico y el pobre Lazaro: investigación exegética sobre Lc 16,19-31. Diss. St. Georgen 1996, ᴰ*Beutler, Johannes* [BZ 42,316].

5150 **Oh, Duck-ho** Faith and wealth: a literary-historical study of Luke 16. Diss. Union Theol. Sem. in Virginia 1996, 463 pp. [EThL 74,309*].

5151 *Sorensen, Randall Lehmann* 'Where are the nine?';
5152 The tenth leper. JPsT 24/3 (1996) 179-196/197-211 [17,17].
5153 *Holmén, Tom* The alternatives of the kingdom: encountering the semantic restrictions of Luke 17,20-21 (ἐντὸς ὑμῶν). ZNW 87 (1996) 204-229.
5154 *Derrett, J. Duncan M.* 'On that night': Luke 17,34. Sum. 46. EvQ 68 (1996) 35-46.
5155 *Kolvenbach, Peter-Hans* Responsables religieux: au miroir du pharisien et du publicain (Lc 18,9-14). Telema 22/2 (1996) 3-4.
5156 *Raguer, H.* Postparábola del fariseo y el publicano. Liturgia y Espiritualidad 27/7-8 (1996) 282-284 [18,9-14] [Comunidades 89,146].
5157 *Costen, James H.* Viewing life from high places: psalm 139:1-18, Luke 19:1-10. JITC 24 (1996-97) 183-188 [ZID 23,406].
5158 *D'Sa, Thomas* Exploiter evangelized: reflections based on the episode of Zacchaeus and pastoral practice. VJTR 60 (1996) 194-206 [19,1-10].
5159 **Grangaard, Blake R.** Conflict and authority: a narrative-critical study of Luke 19:47-21:4, Jesus' encounter with the Jerusalem leadership. Diss. Union Theol. Sem. in Virginia 1996, ᴰ*Kingsbury, Jack Dean*, 261 pp. DAI-A 57/03, p. 1182; AAC 9625231.
5160 *Sebastian, V.* Jesus' teaching on offering: Lk. 21:1-4. BiBh 22 (1996) 108-119.
5161 **Smuts, Peter Webster** Luke and the Olivet discourse: a redaction-critical study of Luke 21:5-36. Diss. Westminster Theol. Sem. 1996, ᴰ*McCartney, Dan G.*, 279 pp.

F7.8 **Passio**—*Lc 22...*

5162 **Ledrus, Michel** Alla scuola del "ladrone" penitente. R 1993, Apostolato Della Preghiera 168 pp. L15.000. ᴿLSDC 11/1 (1996) 80-82 (*Zecca, Tito Paolo*).
5163 *Morell Baladrón, Fernando* El relato de la pasión según san Lucas: de STREETER a BROWN: 70 anos de investigación de la composición de Lc 22-23. EstB 54 (1996) 79-114, 225-260.
5164 **Prete, Benedetto** I racconti della passione, 1: l'arresto. La passione e la morte di Gesù nel racconto di Luca. StBi 112: Brescia 1996, Paideia 244 pp. L32.000. 88-394-0534-8.

5165 **Nelson, Peter K.** Leadership and discipleship... Lk 22:24-30. SBL.DS 138: 1994, ⇒10,5042. ᴿHebStud 37 (1996) 199-202 (*Squires, John T.*); JBL 115 (1996) 147-150 (*Chance, J. Bradley*).
5166 *Costen, James H.* Doing the right thing: Isaiah 53:1-12, Luke 23:13-25. JITC 24 (1996/97) 207-213 [ZID 23,406].
5167 *Sorg, Theo* Den Gekreuzigten vor Augen haben: Lukas 23,33-46. Das Wort vom Kreuz. 1996, ⇒206. 67-73.

5168 *Kellermann, Ulrich* Elia als Seelenführer der Verstorbenen oder Elia-Typologie in Lk 23,43 "Heute wirst du mit mir im Paradies sein". BN 83 (1996) 35-53.

5169 *Neirynck, F.* A supplementary note on Lk 24,12. EThL 72 (1996) 425-430.

5170 *Borse, Udo* Der Evangelist als Verfasser der Emmauserzählung. F BORSE U., SBAB 21: 1996 <1987>, ⇒9. 175-210 [24,13-35].

5171 *Derrett, J.D.M.* The walk to Emmaus (Lk 24,13-35): the lost dimension. EstB 54 (1996) 183-193 [Exod 33,14; 24,3-11; Mal 3,16-17].

5172 *Houyvet, P.J.* Regards sur un chef-d'oeuvre. NV 71 (1996) 70-76 [24,13-35].

F8.1 *Actus Apostolorum*, Acts—*text, commentary, topics*

5173 T**Abbolito Simonetti, Giuseppina** BEDA Venerabilis: esposizione e revisione degli Atti degli Apostoli. CTePa 121: 1995, ⇒11/1,3779. RComp. 41 (1996) 259-260 (*Romero Pose, Eugenio*).

5174 **Arens, Eduardo** Serán mis testigos: historia, actores y trama de Hechos de Apósteles. CEP 170: Lima 1996, CEP 374 pp. [PerTeol 29,281].

5175 *Arnold, Bill T.* Luke's characterizing use of the Old Testament in the book of Acts. History in Acts. 1996, ⇒5223. 300-323.

5176 *Barrett, C.K.* How history should be written. History in Acts. 1996, ⇒5223. 33-57.

5177 **Barrett, Charles K.** Acts I-XIV. ICC: 1994, ⇒10,5059. RTS 57 (1996) 145-146 (*Fitzmyer, Joseph A.*).

5178 E**Bateman, John J.** In Acta apostolorum paraphrasis [Paraphrase on the Acts of the Apostles]. Collected works of Erasmus 50: 1995, ⇒11/1,3783. REHR 111 (1996) 971-972 (*Scribner, R.W.*); JThS 47/2 (1996) 755-758 (*Brooks, Peter Newman*); Milltown Studies 37 (1996) 150-152 (*O'Loughlin, Thomas*).

5179 E**Bauckham, Richard** The book of Acts in its Palestinian setting. 1995, ⇒11/1,3784. RBS 153 (1996) 251-252 (*Constable, Thomas L.*).

5180 *Bauckham, Richard* Kerygmatic summaries in the speeches of Acts. History in Acts. 1996, ⇒5223. 185-217.

5181 *Boismard, Marie-Émile* Le Codex de Bèze et le texte Occidental des Actes. Codex Bezae. NTTS 22: 1996, ⇒265. 257-270.

5182 *Borse, Udo* Die Wir-Stellen der Apostelgeschichte und Timotheus. F BORSE U., SBAB 21: 1996 <1985>, ⇒9. 141-173.

5183 **Bossuyt, Philippe; Radermakers, Jean** Témoins de la parole de la grâce: Actes des Apôtres, 1, texte 2: lecture continue. IET 16: Bru 1995, Institut d'Études Théologiques 2 vols, 116; 782 pp. FB1680. 2-930067-15-2/6-0. RNRT 118 (1996) 273-274 (*Faux, J.-M.*).

5184 *Carrón Pérez, Julián* La permanencia de la experiencia cristiana en el libro de los Hechos. Communio 18 (1996) 270-284.

5185 *Childers, J.W.* The Old Georgian Acts of the Apostles: a progress report. NTS 42 (1996) 55-74.

5186 **Cipriani, Settimio** Missione ed evangelizzazione negli Atti degli Apostoli. T 1994, Elle Di Ci 246 pp. L22.000. RHum(B) 51/1 (1996) 135-136 (*Grassi, Piergiorgio*).

5187 **Compton, Michael Bruce** Introducing the Acts of the Apostles: a study of John CHRYSOSTOM's 'On the beginning of Acts'. Diss. Virginia 1996. 249 pp. [EThL 74,271*].

5188 **Dunn, J.D.G.** The Acts of the Apostles. L 1996, Epworth xxvi; 357 pp. £13. 0-7162-0506-8 [ET 108,343].

5189 *Elliott, J.K.* The Greek manuscript heritage of the book of Acts. FgNT 9 (1996) 37-50.

5190 **Geer, Thomas C.** Family 1739 in Acts. SBL.MS 48: 1994, ⇒10,5063; 11/1,3793. RCBQ 58 (1996) 346-348 (*Cody, Aelred*); CritRR 9 (1996) 209-212 (*Petersen, William L.*).

5191 EGill, David W.J.; Gempf, Conrad The book of Acts in its Graeco-Roman setting. 1994, ⇒10,5064; 11/1,3796. RJEarlyC 4 (1996) 255-256 (*Pervo, Richard I.*); AUSS 34 (1996) 155-156 (*Coutsoumpos, Panayotis*); Bijdr. 57 (1996) 452-454 (*Koet, Bart J.*); RB 103 (1996) 609-610 (*Taylor, Justin*).

5192 *Jervell, Jacob* The future of the past: Luke's vision of salvation history and its bearing on his writing of history. History in Acts. 1996, ⇒5223. 104-126.

5193 **Jervell, Jacob Stephan** The theology of the Acts of the Apostles. NT Theology: C 1996, CUP xiii; 142 pp. $35/$13. 0-521-41385-0/2447-X. RWThJ 58 (1996) 333-335 (*Cara, Robert J.*).

5194 **Klauck, Hans-Josef** Magie und Heidentum in der Apostelgeschichte des Lukas. SBS 167: Stu 1996, Kath. Bibelwerk 147 pp. DM39.80. 3-460-04671-6.

5195 **L'Éplattenier, Charles** Atti degli Apostoli: commento pastorale. Fame e sete della parola 22: CinB 1996, San Paolo 333 pp. 88-215-3314-X.

5196 **Larsson, Edvin** Apostlagärningarna. Kommentar till Nya Testamentet 5C: U 1996, EFS 469-640. 91-7085-100-X [NThAR 1997,261].

5197 **Levinskaya, Irina** The book of Acts in its diaspora setting. The book of Acts in its first century setting, 5. GR 1996, Eerdmans 450 pp. $37.50/£30. 0 8028 2434 X [AUSS 33,332].

5198 **Luzzi, Giovanni** Fatti degli apostoli. Commentario esegetico-pratico del NT: T 1996, Claudiana 270 pp. 88-7016-074-2 [ristampa].

5199 **Marconcini, Benito** Atti degli Apostoli. 1994, ⇒10,5075. RCivCatt 147 II (1996) 216-217 (*Scaiola, D.*).

5200 *Marguerat, Daniel* Le Dieu du livre des Actes. FLEGASSE S., LeDiv 166: 1996, ⇒51. 301-331.

5201 **McCoy, W.J.** In the shadow of THUCYDIDES. History in Acts. 1996, ⇒5223. 3-32.

5202 **Mills, Watson Early** The Acts of the Apostles. Bibliographies for Biblical Research, NT 5: Lewiston, NY 1996, Mellen xx; 323 pp. 0-7734-2432-6.

5203 *Moessner, David P.* The "script" of the Scripture in Acts: suffering as God's "plan" (βουλή) for the world for the "release of sins". History in Acts. 1996, ⇒5223. 218-250.

5204 *Rius-Camps, J.* Le substrat grec de la version latine des Actes dans le Codex de Bèze. Codex Bezae. NTTS 22: 1996, ⇒265. 271-295.

5205 **Rius-Camps, Josep** Jerusalem... Ac 1.1-5.42. Comentari als Fets dels Apòstols, 1. CStP 43: 1991, ⇒8,5498... 11/1,3818. RFgNT 9 (1996) 77-80 (*Heimerdinger, Jenny*); Laur. 36 (1995) 515-517 (*Dalbesio, Anselmo*);

5206 Judea i Samaria... Ac 6.1-12.25. Comentari als Fets dels Apòstols, 2. CStP 47: 1993, ⇒9,5304... 11/1,3818. RFgNT 9 (1996) 77-80 (*Heimerdinger, Jenny*);

5207 "Fins als confins de la terra"... Ac 13,1-18,23. CStP 54: 1995, ⇒11/1,3902. RFgNT 9 (1996) 77-80 (*Heimerdinger, Jenny*).

5208 *Rius-Camps, Josep* Las variantes de la recensión occidental de los Hechos de los Apóstoles, 7-8. FgNT 9 (1996) 61-76/201-216 [3,1-26/4,1-22].

5209 *Rivas, Luis Heriberto* Algunas cuestiones historiográficas en torno al libro de los Hechos de los Apóstoles. Teol. 33 (1996) 221-235.

5210 *Smith, Morton* The reason for the persecution of Paul and the obscurity of Acts. New Testament. 1996 <1967>, ⇒151. 87-94.

5211 *Spottorno, M.V.* Le Codex de Bèze et le texte antiochien dans les Actes des Apôtres. Codex Bezae. NTTS 22: 1996, ⇒265. 311-316.

5212 **Steyn, Gert Jacobus** Septuagint quotations... Acts. 1995, 11/1,3823. RBib. 77 (1996) 567-570 (*Bock, Darrell L.*); RB 103 (1996) 619-620 (*Taylor, J.J.*); SNTU.A 21 (1996) 267-269 (*Schreiber, S.*); CritRR 9 (1996) 279-281 (*Soards, Marion L.*).

5213 *Talbert, Charles H.* The Acts of the Apostles: monograph or "bios"?. History in Acts. 1996, ⇒5223. 58-72.

5214 **Taylor, Justin** Commentaire historique (Act. 9,1-18,22). EtB 23: 1994, ⇒10,5092; 11/1,3827. RJBL 115 (1996) 750-752 (*Parsons, Mikeal C.*); RB 103 (1996) 97-100 (*Blanchetière, François*); JThS 47 (1996) 239-245 (*Heimerdinger, J.*);

5215 Commentaire historique (Act. 18,23-28,31). Les Actes des deux apôtres, 6. EtB 30: P 1996, Gabalda xxvii; 294 pp. FF210. 2-85021-084.

5216 *Taylor, Justin* The Roman Empire in the Acts of the Apostles. Religion. ANRW II.26.3. 1996, ⇒183. 2436-2500.

5217 *Taylor, Justin* St. Luke, architect of christian unity. Holy Land 16 (1996) 140-144.

5218 *Thompson, Richard Paul* Christian community and characterization in the book of Acts: a literary study of the Lukan concept of the church. Diss. Southern Methodist Univ. 1996, DTyson, Joseph B., 498 pp. DAI-A 57/04, p. 1677; AAC 9623748.

5219 *Valentino, Timothy R.* The homiletical charge in the book of Acts: does Luke reveal an anti-Semitism?. EvJo 14/2 (1996) 62ss [ThD Index Feb. 1997, 5].

5220 *Varickasseril, Jose* Response to the word: a study in the Acts of the Apostles. IMR 19/2 (1996) 78-89 [ThIK 18/1,34].

5221 EWinter, Bruce W.; Clarke, Andrew D. The book of Acts in its ancient literary setting. 1993, ⇒9,5310; 11/1,3832. RBijdr. 57 (1996) 452-454 (*Koet, Bart J.*); RB 103 (1996) 608-609 (*Taylor, Justin*).

5222 *Winter, S.C.* παρρησία in Acts. Friendship. NT.S 82: 1996, ⇒180. 185-202.

5223 EWitherington, Ben History, literature and society in the book of Acts. C 1996, CUP xx; 374 pp. £40; $60. 0-521-49520-2 [NTAb 41,154]. RIrén. 69 (1996) 288-289.

5224 *Witherington, Ben* Finding its niche: the historical and rhetorical species of Acts. SBL.SPS 35: 1996, ⇒265. 67-97;

5225 Editing the Good News: some synoptic lessons for the study of Acts. History in Acts. 1996, ⇒5223. 324-347.

5226 *Yamada, Kota* A rhetorical history: the literary genre of the Acts of the Apostles. Rhetoric. JSNT.S 131: 1996, ⇒268. 230-250.
5227 **Zedda, Silverio** Teologia della salvezza negli Atti degli Apostoli. CSB 20: 1994, ⇒10,5093; 11/1,3833. RCivCatt 147 II (1996) 206-207 (*Scaiola, D.*).
5228 **Zmijewski, J.** Die Apostelgeschichte. 1994, ⇒10,5095. SNTU.A 21 (1996) 263-265 (*Schreiber, S.*).

F8.3 *Ecclesia primaeva Actuum:* **Die Urgemeinde**

5229 **Goulder, Michael** St. Paul versus St. Peter: a tale of two missions. 1994, ⇒10,5108a. RHeyJ 37 (1996) 526-527 (*Upton, Bridget*); CritRR 9 (1996) 217-219 (*Muir, Steven C.*).
5230 **Manns, Frédéric** L'Israël de Dieu: essais sur le christianisme primitif. ASBF 42: J 1996, Franciscan Printing Press 339 pp. $45. RCDios 209 (1996) 763-765 (*Gutiérrez, J.*).
5231 **Nouailhat, R.** Les premiers christianismes. 1988, ⇒5,5284. RVetChr 33 (1996) 235-236 (*Infante, Renzo*).
5232 **Rius-Camps, Josep** De Jerusalén a Antioquía... Hch 1-12. 1989, ⇒5,5246... 8,5529. RThLZ 121 (1996) 556-559 (*Stenschke, Christoph*).
5233 **Taylor, Nicholas** Paul, Antioch and Jerusalem. JSNT.S 66: 1992, ⇒8,5534... 10,5116. RRB 103 (1996) 292-293 (*Murphy-O'Connor, Jerome*).
5234 **Testa, Emanuele** La fede della chiesa madre di Gerusalemme. 1995, ⇒11/1,3844. RED 49 (1996) 446-448 (*Noce, Celestino*).

F8.5 **Ascensio, Pentecostes; ministerium Petri**—*Act 1...*

5235 *Bartolini, Elena* Dalla torre di Babele alla Pentecoste. Horeb 5/2 (1996) 22-29 [ZID 23,3].
5236 *Costa Silva, Carlos Alberto da* A festa de Pentecostes, festa da nova aliança. RCB 77/78 (1996) 37-70.
5237 *Figura, Michael* Martyrdom and the following of Jesus. Com(US) 23/1 (1996) 101-109.
5238 **Matson, David L.** Household conversion narratives in Acts: pattern and interpretation. JSNT.S 123: Shf 1996, Academic 224 pp. £43. 1-85075-586-8.
5239 *Murawski, Roman* Katecheza czasów apostolskich [Catéchèse des temps apostoliques]. Rés. 78. Bobolanum 7 (1996) 58-78. **P.**

5240 *Kock, Wynand J. de* Empowerment through engagement: pentecostal power for a pentecostal task. ExAu 12 (1996) 136-146 [1-2].
5241 *Alexander, Loveday C.A.* The preface to Acts and the historians. History in Acts. 1996, ⇒5223. 73-103 [1,1].
5242 *Zwiep, A.W.* The text of the Ascension narratives (Luke 24.50-3; Acts 1.1-2,9-11). NTS 42 (1996) 219-244.
5243 *Valentini, Alberto* Una comunità orante in attesa dello Spirito (At 1,14). FDUPONT J., 1996, ⇒21. 127-157.
5244 *Schott, Faye E.* Acts 2:1-21. Interp. 50 (1996) 406-408.
5245 *Kilgallen, John J.* A rhetorical and source-traditions study of Acts 2,33. Bib. 77 (1996) 178-196.

5246 *McIntyre, Luther B.* Baptism and forgiveness in Acts 2:38. BS 153 (1996) 53-62.

5247 *Cowton, Christopher J.* The alms trade: a note on identifying the Beautiful Gate of Acts 3.2. NTS 42 (1996) 475-476.

5248 **Carrón Pérez, Julián** Jesús, el Mesías manifestado... Hch 3,19-26. 1993, ⇒8,5549*... 11/1,3865. ᴿStLeg 37 (1996) 271-272 (*Ramos, Felipe F.*).

5249 **Moehn, W.H.Th.** God roept ons tot zijn dienst: een homiletisch onderzoek naar de verhouding tussen God en hoorder in CALVIJNS preken over Handelingen 4:1-6:7. Kampen 1996, Kok 391 pp. ƒ49.90. [GThT 97,100].

5250 *Wahlde, Urban C. von* Acts 4,24-31: the prayer of the apostles in response to the persecution of Peter and John—and its consequences. Bib. 77 (1996) 237-244.

5251 *Armellini, Fernando* Atti degli Apostoli/16: un angelo libera Pietro. Evangelizzare 22 (1996) 365-368 [5,17-21].

5252 *Penner, Todd C.* Narrative as persuasion: epideictic rhetoric and scribal amplification in the Stephen episode in Acts. SBL.SPS 35: 1996, ⇒265. 352-367 [6-7].

5253 *Watson, Alan* The trial of Stephen: the first christian martyr. Athens 1996, Univ. of Georgia Press xiii; (2) 156 pp. 0-8203-1855-8 [6-7].

5254 *Hill, Craig C.* Acts 6.1-8.4: division or diversity?. History in Acts. 1996, ⇒5223. 129-153.

5255 *Borse, Udo* Der Rahmentext im Umkreis der Stephanusgeschichte (Apg 6,1-11,26). ᶠBORSE U., SBAB 21: 1996 <1973>, ⇒9. 97-117.

5256 *Cabié, Robert* Quand les "Sept" deviennent des diacres. BLE 97 (1996) 219-226 [6,1-7].

5257 *Panning, A.J.* Acts 6: the 'ministry' of the Seven. WLQ 93/1 (1996) 11-17 [NTAb 40,436].

5258 *Litke, Wayne* Acts 7,3 and Samaritan chronology. NTS 42 (1996) 156-160.

5259 *Ferreiro, Alberto* Simon Magus: the patristic-medieval traditions and historiography. Sum. rés. 147. Apocrypha 7 (1996) 147-165 [8,9-24].

5260 **Rafanambinana, Jean Romain** Ac 8,26-40: le récit, la catéchèse et la théologie: essai de lecture sémiotique. Diss. excerpt Pont. Univ. Gregoriana. ᴰ*Rasco, Emilio*, R 1996, xi; 197 pp.

5261 *Cannuyer, Christian* Aux origines de l'église éthiopienne: à propos d'un ouvrage récent. RHE 91 (1996) 863-871 [8,26-40].

5262 *Schreiber, Stefan* "Verstehst du denn, was du liest?": Beobachtungen zur Begegnung von Philippus und dem äthiopischen Eunuchen (Apg 8,26-40). SNTU.A 21 (1996) 42-72.

5263 *Smith, Morton* The account of Simon Magus in Acts 8. New Testament. 1996 <1965>, ⇒151. 140-151.

5264 **Kohlbrugge, Hermann Friedrich** De bekering van Paulus: verklaringen van Handelingen 9:1-22. Houten 1996, Den Hertog 83 pp. 90-331-1174-8 [NThAR 1997,163].

5265 *Reymond, Sophie* Paul sur le chemin de Damas (Ac 9,22 et 26): temps et espace d'une expérience. NRTh 118 (1996) 520-538.

5266 *Monferrer Sala, Juan Pedro* La conversión de Saulo, según IBN KATIR. Sum. res. 147. MEAH.A 45 (1996) 147-159 [9].

5267 *Barbi, A.* Cornelio (At 10,1-11,18): percorsi per una piena integrazione dei pagani nella chiesa. RStB 8 (1996) 277-295.
5268 *O'Toole, Robert F.* Εἰρήνη, an underlying theme in Acts 10,34-43. Bib. 77 (1996) 461-476.
5269 *Heimerdinger, J.* The seven steps of Codex Bezae: a prophetic interpretation of Acts 12. Codex Bezae. NTTS 22: 1996, ⇒265. 303-310.

F8.7 Act 13...*Itinera Pauli;* Paul's Journeys

5270 **Breytenbach, Cilliers** Paulus und Barnabas in der Provinz Galatien: Studien zu Apostelgeschichte 13f.; 16,6; 18,23 und den Adressaten des Galaterbriefes. AGJU 38: Lei 1996, Brill xvi; 215 pp. $91.75. 90-04-10693-6.
5271 **Carrez, Maurice** Le parcours christologique des discours de Paul dans le livre des Actes coïncide-t-il avec celui de l'apôtre dans ses épîtres authentiques?. FLEGASSE S., LeDiv 166: 1996, ⇒51. 357-374.
5272 **Economou, Christos K.** The beginnings of Christianity in Cyprus: historical-philological-theological and religions-historical analysis. Studies in the beginnings of Christianity 3: Paphos 1996, n.p. 483 pp. G.
5273 **McCormick, Larry** Paul's addresses to Jewish audiences in the Acts of the Apostles. Diss. Fordham 1996, DDillon, R.J., 380 pp. [RTL 29,586].
5274 *Neyrey, Jerome H.* Luke's social location of Paul: cultural anthropology and the status of Paul in Acts. History in Acts. 1996, ⇒5223. 251-279.
5275 **Rapske, Brian** The book of Acts and Paul in Roman custody. 1994, ⇒10,5191. RRB 103 (1996) 151-152 *(Taylor, Justin)*; CTJ 31 (1996) 559-563 *(DeBoer, Willis P.)*.
5276 *Robinson, Bernard P.* Paul and Barnabas in Cyprus. ScrB 26 (1996) 69-72.
5277 **Rosenblatt, Marie-Eloise** Paul the accused: his portrait in... Ac. 1995, ⇒11/1,3900. RRB 103 (1996) 147-149 *(Taylor, Justin)*; CBQ 58 (1996) 358-359 *(Danker, Frederick W.)*; CritRR 9 (1996) 260-261 *(Given, Mark D.)*.
5278 **Schreiber, Stefan** Paulus als Wundertäter: redaktionsgeschichtliche Untersuchungen zur Apostelgeschichte und den authentischen Paulusbriefen. BZNW 79: B 1996, De Gruyter xii; 329 pp. DM164. 3-11-015021-2. RSNTU.A 21 (1996) 269-271 *(Schreiber, Stefan)*.
5279 **Schwartz, Daniel R.** Agrippa I: the last king of Judaea. TSAJ 23: 1990, ⇒10,5190. RGn. 68 (1996) 126-134 *(Strobel, Karl)*.
5280 *Silberman, Neil Asher* The world of Paul. Arch. 49/6 (1996) 30-36.
5281 **Tajra, Harry W.** The trial of St. Paul. WUNT 2/35: 1989, ⇒5,5341... 7,4717. RRB 103 (1996) 149-151 *(Taylor, Justin)*.
5282 **Thornton, Claus-Jürgen** Der Zeuge... Paulusreisen. WUNT 2/56: 1991, ⇒7,4711... 11/1,3897. RBijdr. 57 (1996) 214-216 *(Koet, Bart J.)*.

5283 *Bauckham, Richard* James and the gentiles (Acts 15.13-21). History in Acts. 1996, ⇒5223. 154-184.

5284 **Johnson, L.T.** Scripture & discernment: decision making in the church. Nv 1996, Abingdon 166 pp. $20. 0-687-01238-4 [15] [NTAb 41,165].

5285 *Horn, Friedrich Wilhelm* Der Verzicht auf die Beschneidung im frühen Christentum. NTS 42 (1996) 479-505 [15].

5286 **Hilary, Mbachu** Inculturation theology of the Jerusalem Council in Acts 15. EHS.T 520: 1995, ⇒11/1,3911. RCBQ 58 (1996) 556-557 (*Okoye, James C.*).

5287 *Gianotto, Claudio* L'interpretazione di Atti 15 nei primi secoli cristiani. ASE 13/1 (1996) 123-141.

5288 *Simonetti, Manlio* Eresia e ortodossia ad Antiochia nei primi tre secoli. Sal. 58 (1996) 645-659 [15].

5289 *Stefano, Piero* Il concilio di Gerusalemme. Horeb 5/2 (1996) 30-34 [15] [ZID 23,3].

5290 *Borse, Udo* Kompositionsgeschichtliche Beobachtungen zum Apostelkonzil. FBORSE U., SBAB 21: 1996 <1980>, ⇒9. 119-139 [15].

5291 *Borgen, Peder* Catalogues of vices, the apostolic decree, and the Jerusalem meeting. Early christianity. 1996 <1988>, ⇒116. 233-251 [15].

5292 *Yoo, Sang H.* Paul à Jérusalem. Yonsei Journal of Theology 1 (1996) 67-96 [15] [ZID 23,414].

5293 **Barnes, Jeffrey Allen** Honor and shame: a sociological model for understanding Acts 16:11-40. Diss. Golden Gate Bapt. Theol. Sem. 1995, DHarrop, C.K., 260 pp. [EThL 74,319*].

5294 *Winter, B.W.* On introducing gods to Athens: an alternative reading of Acts 17:18-20. TynB 47 (1996) 71-90.

5295 *Geraghty, Gerard* Paul before the Areopagus: a new approach to priestly formation in the light of (*Ecclesia in Africa*). African Christian Studies 12/3 (1996) 32-41 [17].

5296 *Van der Meulen, H.C.* Met BARTH en THIELICKE op de Areopagus. KeTh 47/1 (1996) 22-40 [17].

5297 *Koet, Bart J.* As close to the synagogue as can be: Paul in Corinth (Acts 18,1-18). The Corinthian correspondence [EBieringer, Reimund]. BEThL 125: 1996, ⇒G5.1. 397-415.

5298 *Koet, Bart J.* Why did Paul shave his hair (Acts 18,18)?. The centrality of Jerusalem [EPoorthuis, M.] 1996, ⇒T4.3. 128-142.

5299 *Armellini, Fernando* Terzo viaggio missionario di Paolo. Evangelizzare 22 (1996) 621-624 [20].

5300 *Brown, H. Stephen* Paul's hearing at Caesarea: a preliminary comparison with legal literature of the Roman period [24,1-23];

5301 *Crouch, Frank* The persuasive moment: rhetorical resolutions in Paul's defense before Agrippa [25,23-26,32]. SBL.SPS 35: 1996, ⇒265. 319-332/333-342.

5302 *Gilchrist, J.M.* The historicity of Paul's shipwreck. JSNT 61 (1996) 29-51 [27,1-28,16].

5303 *Aletti, Jean-Noël* Le naufrage d'Actes 27: mort symbolique de Paul?. FLEGASSE S., LeDiv 166: 1996, ⇒51. 375-392.

5304 *Brosend, Wm. F.* The means of absent ends. History in Acts. 1996, ⇒5223. 348-362 [28,30-31].

XI. Johannes

G1.1 *Corpus johanneum:* **John and his community**

5305 **Augenstein, Jörg** Das Liebesgebot im Johannesevangelium und in den Johannesbriefen. BWANT 134: 1993, ⇒9,5489; 11/1,4021. ᴿSNTU.A 21 (1996) 250-252 *(Giesen, H.)*.

5306 *Blasi, Anthony* La dinamica non-sincretistica nel cristianesimo giovanneo. ᵀ*Stein, Elisabeth*, ReSo 11/1 (1996) 40-47.

5307 **Blasi, Anthony J.** A sociology of Johannine christianity. TSR 69: Lewiston, NY 1996, Mellen xv; 444 pp. 0-7734-8753-0.

5308 **Boismard, Marie-Émile** Le martyre de Jean l'apôtre. CRB 35: P 1996, Gabalda 88 pp. FF120. 2-85021-086-2. ᴿRThom 96 (1996) 474-478 *(Devillers, Luc)*; EThL 72 (1996) 459-460 *(Neirynck, F.)*; ScEs 48 (1996) 346 *(Langevin, Paul-Émile)*.

5309 **Culpepper, R. Alan** John, the son of Zebedee. 1994, ⇒10,5199; 11/1,3939. ᴿCThMi 23/1 (1996) 48-49 *(Linss, Wilhelm C.)*; EeT(O) 27 (1996) 279-282 *(Gourgues, Michel)*; Interp. 50 (1996) 410-412 *(Cousar, Charles B.)*.

5310 *Devillers, Luc* Etudes sur les écrits johanniques. RThom 96 (1996) 453-478.

5311 *Hillmer, Melvyn R.* They believed in him: discipleship in the Johannine tradition. Patterns of discipleship. 1996, ⇒188. 77-97.

5312 **Kobayashi, M.** The Johannine writings. ᵀ*Ohnuki, T.*, ᴿKaKe 65 (1996) 224-229 *(Momose, F.)*. **J.**

5313 **Maloney, Francis J.** Reading John. 1995, ⇒11/1,3946. ᴿVJTR 60 (1996) 689 *(Meagher, P.M.)*.

5314 *Morgen, Michèle* La littérature johannique. RSR 84 (1996) 277-303.

5315 **Nkulu-Kankote, Kusla** L'être chrétien dans les écrits johanniques. Diss. Bru 1996 [EThL 74,313*].

5316 *Otranto, Giorgio* Note sulla presenza della tradizione giovannea a Roma nel II secolo: CLEMENTE e Il Pastore di Erma. Retorica ed esegesi biblica. QVetChr 24: 1996, ⇒259. 13-30.
ᴱ**Padovese, Luigi** Atti del VI Simposio di Efeso su S. Giovanni Apostolo ⇒264.

5317 ᴱ**Padovese, Luigi** Atti del III Simposio di Efeso su S. Giovanni apostolo. 1993, ⇒9,401. ᴿOCP 62 (1996) 502-503 *(Farrugia, E.G.)*; StFr 93 (1996) 533-535 *(Giovannetti, Ottaviano)*;

5318 Atti del IV Simposio di Efeso su S. Giovanni apostolo. 1994, ⇒10,329; 11/1,3948. ᴿStFr 93 (1996) 535-538 *(Giovannetti, Ottaviano)*.

5319 **Panthapallil, Mary** Mary, the type of the church in the Johannine writings: a biblico-theological analysis. Kottayam 1996, Oriental Inst. of Relig. Studies India Publ. 274 pp. 81-86063-17-X. ᴿBiBh 22 (1996) 156-157 *(Nereparampil, Lucius)*; JDh 21 (1996) 298 *(Nereparampil, Lucius)*.

5320 *Pasquetto, Virgilio* Il lessico antropologico del vangelo e delle lettere di Giovanni. Ter. 47 (1996) 103-137.

5321 *Phidas, Vlassios I.* Ἡ Ἰωάννειος ἀποστολικότης τοῦ θρόνου τῆς Κωνσταντινουπόλεωσ [The Johannine apostolicity of the throne of Constantinople]. Theol(A) 67 (1996) 230-267.

5322 **Powell, Evan** The unfinished gospel: notes on the quest for the historical Jesus. 1994, ⇒10,5207. ᴿJR 76 (1996) 619-620 (*Stamos, Colleen*).

5323 **Rossé, Gérard** La spiritualità di comunione negli scritti giovannei. R 1996, Città Nuova 126 pp. L15.000. 88-311-3620-8 [RdT 37,850].

5324 **Schwankl, Otto** Licht und Finsternis. 1995, ⇒11/1,4096. ᴿBib. 77 (1996) 442-445 (*Horn, Friedrich Wilhelm*); RivBib 44 (1996) 484-487 (*Segalla, Giuseppe*).

5325 **Smalley, Stephen S.** Thunder and love: John's Revelation and John's community. 1994, ⇒10,5210; 11/1,3952. ᴿEvQ 68 (1996) 244-246 (*Marshall, I. Howard*).

5326 **Tuñi, Josep Oriol; Alegre, Xavier** Escritos joánicos y cartas católicas. 1995, ⇒11/1,3955. ᴿScrTh 28 (1996) 932 (*García-Moreno, A.*).

5327 *Zumstein, Jean* Der Prozess der Relecture in der johanneischen Literatur. NTS 42 (1996) 394-411.

G1.2 Evangelium Johannis: *textus, commentarii*

5328 ᴱᵀ**Accorinti, Domenico** NONNUS PANOPOLITANUS: parafrasi del vangelo di S. Giovanni: canto XX. Pubblicazioni della Classe di Lettere e Filosofia 15: Pisa 1996, Scuola Normale Superiore 240 pp. 88-7642-055-X.

5329 ᴱ**Ammassari, Antonio** Il vangelo di Giovanni nella colonna latina del Bezae Codex Cantabrigiensis: note di commento sulla struttura letteraria, la punteggiatura, le lezioni e le citazioni bibliche. Città del Vaticano 1996, Libreria Editrice Vaticana 130 pp. L22.000. 88-209-2210-X.

5330 **Arminjon, Blaise** Nous voudrions voir Jésus: Jean 12-21. Christus, Essais 85: P 1996, DDB 203 pp. F115. 2-220-03796-7 [EeV 106,223].

5331 ᴱᵀ**Blanc, Cécile** ORIGENE: commentaire sur Saint Jean: livres 1-5. SC 120/2: Paris ²1996, Cerf 420 pp. FF290. 2-204-05382-1 [NThAR 1997,133].

5332 **Blanchard, Yves-Marie** Des signes pour croire?... évangile de Jean. LiBi 106: 1995, ⇒11/1,3960. ᴿEeV 106 (1996) 277-278 (*Cothenet, Édouard*); Cahiers de l'Atelier 470 (1996) 100-101 (*Lanchier, Jean*).

5333 **Boismard, Marie-Émile; Lamouille, A.** Un évangile pré-johannique, 1: Jean 1,1-2,12. EtB 17-18: 1993, ⇒9,5468... 11/1,3995. ᴿRThom 96 (1996) 467-478 (*Devillers, Luc*); RSR 84 (1996) 287-289 (*Morgen, Michèle*).

5334 **Boismard, Marie-Émile** Un évangile pré-johannique, 2: Jean 2,13-4,54. EtB 24-25: 1994. ⇒10,5261; 11/1,3996. ᴿRB 103 (1996) 91-97 (*Taylor, Justin*); RThom 96 (1996) 467-478 (*Devillers, Luc*); ABR 44 (1996) 87-88 (*Moloney, Francis J.*); RSR 84 (1996) 289-290 (*Morgen, Michèle*).

5335 **Brodie, Thomas L.** The gospel according to John. 1993, ⇒9,5423; 11/1,3961. ᴿBib. 77 (1996) 281-285 (*Zevini, Giorgio*); LouvSt 21 (1996) 289-292 (*Verheyden, Joseph*); RSR 84 (1996) 280-282 (*Morgen, Michèle*).

5336 **Fabris, Rinaldo** Giovanni. 1992, ⇒8,5645... 10,5223. RScrTh 28 (1996) 932-933 (*García-Moreno, A.*).

5337 **García Moreno, Antonio** El evangelio según San Juan: introducción y exegesis. Badajoz 1996, 524 pp. REE 71 (1996) 652-654 (*Castro, S.*); REsp 55 (1996) 541-546 (*Castro, Secundino*); Ter. 47 (1996) 701-702 (*Pasquetto, Virgilio*).

5338 **Hobbs, Herschel H.** An exposition of the four gospels: v.1, the gospel of Matthew, the gospel of Mark; v.2, the gospel of Luke; the gospel of John. GR 1996, Baker 2 vols. 0-8010-5696-9.

5339 **Jonge, M. de** Johannes: een praktische bijbelverklaring. Tekst en Toelichting: Kampen 1996, Kok 250 pp. f45. 90-242-7792-2.

5340 **Kiraz, George Anton** Comparative edition of the Syriac gospels, aligning the Sinaiticus, Curetonianus, Peshîttâ & Harklean versions, 4: John. NTTS 21/4: Lei 1996, Brill 375 pp. f820 [4 vols]. 90-04-104194 [NT 39,405].

5341 **L'Éplattenier, Charles** L'évangile de Jean. La Bible, Porte-Parole: Genève 1996, Labor et F. 423 pp. FS42 [CBQ 59,422].

5342 **Léon-Dufour, Xavier** Jn 5-12. 1992, ⇒8,5658; 9,5436. RActBib 33/2 (1996) 163-165 (*Tuñi, Josep Oriol*);

5343 Leitura do evangelho segundo João (II: capítulos 5-12). TKonings, Johan; Ferreira, Isabel Leao Fontes, Bíblica Loyola 14: São Paulo 1996, Loyola 349 pp. 85-15-01265-0 [PerTeol 28,274].

5344 *Lee, Yeong-Heon* Kommentar zum Johannesevangelium, 1-2. Sinhak Jonmang 112 (1996) 119-143 & 113 (1996) 27-52 [ThIK 18/1,54, 55]. K.

5345 **Mannucci, Valerio** Giovanni. LoB.NT 2/4: 1995, ⇒11/1,3971. RRdT 37 (1996) 279-280 (*Casalegno, Alberto*).

5346 **Moloney, Francis J.** Signs and shadows: reading John 5-12. Mp 1996, Fortress xiv; 231 pp. Bibl. $22. 0-8006-2936-1.

5347 **Morris, Leon** The gospel according to John. NICNT: 21995, ⇒11/1,3973. RSNTU.A 21 (1996) 248-249 (*Fuchs, A.*).

5348 *Pickering, Stuart R.* Papyri of the gospel of John with 'Hermeneiai'. NTTRU 4 (1996) 57-58;

5349 Texts of the gospel of John on papyrus. NTTRU 4 (1996) 46-56.

5350 TERettig, John W. Augustine: tractates on the gospel of John 112-24: tractates on the first epistle of John. FC 92: 1995, ⇒11/1,3977. RJEH 47 (1996) 556-558 (*Bonner, Gerald*).

5351 **Schwank, Benedikt** Evangelium nach Johannes, erläutert für die Praxis. St. Ottilien 1996, EOS 521 pp. DM70. 3-88096-260-X. RFKTh 12 (1996) 313-315 (*Schulz, Hans Joachim*).

5352 **Smith, Dennis E.** John. The storyteller's companion to the bible 10: Nv 1996, Abingdon 202 pp. 0-687-05585-7.

5353 **Swanson, Reuben J.** New Testament Greek manuscripts: variant readings arranged in horizontal lines against Codex Vaticanus, 4: John. Shf 1996, Academic xix; 302 pp. £20. 1-85075-775-5 [NT 39,286].

5354 **Witherington, Ben** John's wisdom: a commentary on the fourth gospel. C 1996, Lutterworth 488 pp. £25 [ScrB 26,57].

5355 **Zevini, Georges** Commentaire spirituel de l'évangile de Jean, 2: ch. 11-21. TRoyer, Madeleine, P 1996, Médiaspaul 238 pp. FF120 [EeV 106,279].

G1.3 **Introductio** *in Evangelium Johannis*

5356 **Ashton, John** Studying John. 1994, ⇒10,5244; 11/1,3986. ᴿJThS
47 (1996) 218-219 (*Grayston, K.*); Carthaginensia 12 (1996) 483-
484 (*Sanz Valdivieso, R.*); RRT (1996/1) 83-84 (*Paget, James
Carleton*); NBl 77 (1996) 303-304 (*Green, H. Benedict*); JR 76
(1996) 620-622 (*Wahlde, Urban C. von*); CritRR 9 (1996) 176-178
(*Staley, Jeffrey L.*).

5357 **Barnhart, Bruno** The good wine: reading John from the center.
1993, ⇒9,5455... 11/1,3988. ᴿRivBib 44 (1996) 239-240 (*Segalla, Giuseppe*).

5358 **Brodie, Thomas L.** The quest for the origins of John's gospel.
1993, ⇒9,5469... 11/1,3997. ᴿLouvSt 21 (1996) 289-292
(*Verheyden, Joseph*); Bibl.Interp. 4 (1996) 224-225 (*Bauckham,
Richard*); IThQ 62 (1996-97) 331-332 (*Nolan, Brian*); RSR 84
(1996) 278-280 (*Morgen, Michèle*).

5359 **Dunderberg, Ismo** Johannes und die Synoptiker... Joh 1-9.
AASF.DHL 69: 1994, ⇒10,5249; 11/1,4001. ᴿSEÅ 61 (1996)
138-139 (*Kieffer, René*); EThL 72 (1996) 454-456 (*Neirynck, F.*);
JBL 115 (1996) 150-153 (*Smith, D. Moody*).

5360 **Fenton, John C.** Finding the way through John. L 1995, Mowbray
xi; 146 pp. 0-264-67402-2.

5361 **Gadecki, Stanislaw** Wstep do Pism Janowych: (Wydanie drugie
poprawione i uzupelnione). Gniezno 1996, Prymasowskie Wydawnictwo Gaudentinum. 251 pp. 83-85654-48-8. **P**.

5362 **Hengel, Martin** Die johanneische Frage. WUNT 2/67: 1993,
⇒9,5477; 11/1,4006. ᴿRHPhR 76 (1996) 236-237 (*Grappe, Ch.*).

5363 **Koester, Craig R.** Symbolism in the fourth gospel. 1995,
⇒11/1,4059. ᴿCritRR 9 (1996) 236-239 (*Thompson, Marianne
Meye*).

5364 **Korting, Georg** Die esoterische Struktur des Johannesevangeliums,
I-II. BU 25: 1994, ⇒10,5265; 11/1,4008. ᴿNRT 118 (1996) 267
(*Simoens, Yves*); CBQ 58 (1996) 159-160 (*Moloney, Francis J.*);
RSR 84 (1996) 282-284 (*Morgen, Michèle*); CivCatt 147 III (1996)
543-544 (*Scaiola, D.*).

5365 **Kysar, Robert** The contribution of D. Moody SMITH to Johannine scholarship. ᶠSMITH D., 1996, ⇒82. 3-17.

5366 **Mannucci, Valerio** Giovanni, il vangelo narrante. 1993,
⇒9,5486... 11/1,4012. ᴿAsp. 43 (1996) 423-425 (*Rolla, A.*).

5367 **Marrow, Stanley B.** The gospel of John. 1995, ⇒11/1,4013.
ᴿBTB 26 (1996) 174 (*Bode, Edward L.*); RB 103 (1996) 413-414
(*Devillers, Luc*).

5368 **Mees, Michael** Die frühe Rezeptionsgeschichte des Johannesevangeliums. ᴱ*Scheuermann, Georg; Alkofer, Andreas-P.*, FzB 72:
1994, ⇒10,207b. ᴿBZ 40 (1996) 138-140 (*Kühscheim, Roman*).

5369 **Ravasi, Gianfranco** Das Evangelium nach Johannes: eine erste
Hinführung. Neue Stadt—NT: Mü 1996, Neue Stadt 164 pp.
DM27. 3-87996-330-4 [OrdKor 39,253].

5370 *Rigato, Maria-Luisa* Convergenze e divergenze con Claude
TRESMONTANT sull'autore del quarto vangelo. RivBib 44 (1996)
193-204.

5371 **Ruckstuhl, Eugen; Dschulnigg, Peter** Stilkritik und Verfas-
serfrage: die johanneischen Sprachmerkmale. NOrb 17: 1991,
⇒7,4790... 10,5266. ᴿRHPhR 76 (1996) 237-238 (*Grob, F.*).

5372 *Sloyan, Gerard S.* The gnostic adoption of John's gospel and its canonization by the church catholic. BTB 26 (1996) 125-132.
    ᶠ**Smith, D. Moody** Exploring the gospel of John ⇒82.

G1.4 *Themata de evangelio Johannis*—**John's Gospel, topics**

5373 **Aejmelaeus, Lars J.T.** Jeesuksen ylösnousemus: Osa III: Johanneksen Evankeliumi ja systemaattinen tarkastelu. Suomen Eksegeettisen Seuran Julkaisuja 66: Helsinki 1996, Suomen Eksegeettisen Seuran Julkaisuja (8) 351 pp. 951-9217-21-5.

5374 *Agurides, Sabbas C.* Authority in the church of the fourth gospel. DBM 15/2 (1996) 98-109.

5375 **Anderson, Paul N.** The christology of the fourth gospel: its unity and disunity in the light of John 6. WUNT 2/78: Tü 1996, Mohr 329 pp. DM128. 3-16-145779-X.

5376 **Ball, David Mark** 'I Am' in John's gospel: literary function, background and theological implications. JSNT.S 124: Shf 1996, Academic 309 pp. £35.50/$52. 1-85075-587-6.

5377 *Barnard, Willem* De mare van God-bewaar: me volgens Johannes; enkele dagboekaantekeningen—deel 2. ITBT 4/7 (1996) 19-22.

5378 *Barrett, C.K.* The parallels between Acts and John. ᶠSмɪтн D., 1996, ⇒82. 163-178.

5379 **Benedetti, Ugolino** Il vangelo secondo Giovanni alla fine dell'epoca moderna. 1994, ⇒10,5268. ᴿRdT 37 (1996) 277-279 (*Casalegno, Alberto*); PaVi 41/3 (1996) 58-59 (*Migliasso, Secondo*).

5380 *Beutler, Johannes* L'emploi de 'l'Écriture' dans l'évangile de Jean. RICP 60 (1996) 133-153;

5381 The use of 'scripture' in the gospel of John. ᶠSмɪтн D., 1996, ⇒82. 147-162.

5382 **Bittner, W.J.** Jesu Zeichen im Johannesevangelium. WUNT 2/26: 1987, ⇒3,5274... 6,5661. ᴿSEA 61 (1996) 139-140 (*Caragounis, Chrys C.*).

5383 *Black, C. Clifton* 'The words that you gave to me I have given to them': the grandeur of Johannine rhetoric. ᶠSмɪтн D., 1996, ⇒82. 220-239.

5384 *Boer, Martinus C. de* L'évangile de Jean et le christianisme juif (Nazoréen). ᵀ*Voilley, Pascale*, Le déchirement. MoBi 32: 1996, ⇒192. 179-202.

5385 **Booth, Steve** Selected peak marking features in the gospel of John. AmUSt.TR 178: NY 1996, Lang xiii; 183 pp. 0-8204-2474-9.

5386 *Borgen, Peder* The gospel of John and Hellenism: some observations. ᶠSмɪтн D., 1996, ⇒82. 98-123.

5387 *Brant, Jo-Ann A.* Husband hunting: characterization and narrative art in the gospel of John. Bibl.Interp. 4 (1996) 205-223.

5388 **Burkett, Delbert** The Son of Man in the gospel of John. JSNT.S 56: 1991, ⇒7,4806... 11/1,4027. ᴿThLZ 121 (1996) 453-454 (*Schnelle, Udo*).

5389 *Cardellino, Lodovico* Leggere Giovanni. BeO 38 (1996) 129-201.

5390 **Casey, Maurice** Is John's gospel true?. L 1996, Routledge xii; 268 pp. $75. 0-415-14630-5.

5391 *Charlesworth, James H.* The Dead Sea scrolls and the gospel according to John. ᶠSмɪтн D., 1996, ⇒82. 65-97.

5392 **Chatelion Counet, P.J.E.** De sarcofaag van het woord: postmoderniteit, deconstructie en het Johannesevangelie [Le sarcophage de la parole: postmodernité, déconstruction et l'évangile de Jean]. Diss. ^D*Van Tilborg, S.*, Kampen 1996, Kok. 90-242-7801-5 [RTL 27,534].

5393 *Cilia, Lucio* Gesù straniero tra i suoi nel vangelo di Giovanni. RStB 8/1-2 (1996) 233-250.

5394 *Cocchini, Francesca* Presenza e funzione del IV vangelo nel Perì euches di Origene. Atti del VI Simposio. 1996, ⇒264. 215-221.

5395 **Crouch, Frank** Everyone who sees the Son: signs, faith, Peirce's semiotics and the gospel of John. Diss. Duke 1996, ^D*Via, D.* [RTL 29,583].

5396 *Culpepper, R. Alan* The gospel of John as a document of faith in a pluralistic culture. "What is John?", 1. 1996, ⇒5470. 107-127;

5397 Reading Johannine irony. ^FSmith D., 1996, ⇒82. 193-207.

5398 *Dalbesio, Anselmo* La concezione giovannea di 'comandamento' quale anima della morale cristiana. Atti del VI Simposio. 1996, ⇒264. 81-89.

5399 *Daly-Denton, Margaret* Shades of David in the Johannine presentation of Jesus. PIBA 19 (1996) 9-47 [1 Sam 15-17].

5400 *Dunn, James D.G.* John and the synoptics as a theological question. ^FSmith D., 1996, ⇒82. 301-313.

5401 *Dupleix, André* La lumière de l'amour: méditation sur la spiritualité de saint Jean. BLE.S 1 (1996) 105-116.

5402 *Edwards, Ruth B.* Ministry and church leadership in the gospel of John. ^FJamieson P., 1996, ⇒44. 117-141.

5403 **Ensor, Peter W.** Jesus and his 'works': the Johannine sayings in historical perspective. Diss. Aberdeen. WUNT 2/85: Tü 1996, Mohr x; 237 pp. DM98. 3-16-146564-4 [ThG 40,233].

5404 **Fehribach, Adeline** A feminist literary analysis and interpretation of the female characters in the fourth gospel. Diss. Vanderbilt 1996, ^D*Tolbert, Mary Ann,* 322 pp. [RTL 29,584].

5405 **Ferrando, Miguel Angel** Dios padre en el evangelio según san Juan. Anales de la Facultad de Teología 47/1: Santiago 1996, Pont. Univ. Católica de Chile 179 pp. $50.

5406 **Ferraro, Giuseppe** Mio-tuo: teologia del possesso reciproco del Padre e del Figlio nel vangelo di Giovanni. 1994, ⇒10,5302; 11/1,4039. ^RAng. 73 (1996) 592-593 (*Marcato, Giorgio*);

5407 Lo Spirito Santo nel quarto vangelo. OCA 246: 1995, ⇒11/1,4040. ^REThL 72 (1996) 253-254 (*Van Belle, G.*); ALW 38-39 (1996/97) 69-70 (*Olivar, Alexander*);

5408 Il Paraclito, Cristo, il Padre nel quarto vangelo. Città del Vaticano 1996, Libreria Editrice Vaticana 196 pp. L29.000. 88-209-2308-4;

5409 Lo spirito e l'"ora" di Cristo: l'esegesi di san Tommaso d'Aquino sul quarto vangelo. Città del Vaticano 1996, Libreria Editrice Vaticana 222 pp. L30.000. 88-209-2139-1. ^RCivCatt 147 II (1996) 306-307 (*Mucci, G.*); EstTrin 30/1 (1996) 111-113 (*Ofilada Mina, Macario*).

5410 **Fower, William Glenn** The influence of Ezekiel in the fourth gospel: intertextuality and interpretation. Diss. Golden Gate Bapt. Theol. Sem. 1995, ^D*Harrop, C.K.,* 248 pp. [EThL 74,311*].

5411 **García Moreno, Antonio** El cuarto evangelio: aspectos teológicos. 'Cienpuertas, ciencaminos' 2: Pamplona 1996, Eunate 532 pp. 84-

7768-070-1. ᴿRevAg 37 (1996) 1185-1186 (*Sabugal, Santos*);
RET 56 (1996) 527-528 (*Barrado Fernández, P.*).
5412 *García-Moreno, Antonio* Signo joanneo en la esperanza de salvación. Esperanza del hombre. 1996, ⇒173. 489-501.
5413 *Gawlick, Matthias* Mose im Johannesevangelium. BN 84 (1996) 29-35.
5414 *Grech, Prosper* Le confessioni di fede in Giovanni. Atti del VI Simposio. 1996, ⇒264. 29-37.
5415 **Grelot, Pierre** Les juifs dans l'évangile selon Jean. CRB 34: 1995, ⇒11/1,4044. ᴿEeV 106 (1996) 279-283 (*Cothenet, Édouard*); BLE 97 (1996) 293-294 (*Légasse, S.*).
5416 *Hasitschka, Martin* Befreiung und Sünde nach dem Johannesevangelium. Sünde und Erlösung im NT. QD 161: 1996, ⇒181. 92-107.
5417 **Hawkin, David J.** The Johannine world: reflections on the theology of the fourth gospel and contemporary society. SUNY Series in Religious Studies: Albany, NY 1996, SUNY xiv; 183 pp. $49.50/$17. 0-7914-3065-0/0-9 [NTAb 41,146].
5418 **Hemmerle, Klaus** Linien des Lebens: Meditationsimpulse zum Johannesevangelium. Hilfen zum Christlichen Leben. Mü 1996, Neue Stadt 80 pp. DM19.80. 3-87069-348-7.
5419 **Hergenröder, Clemens** Wir schauten seine Herrlichkeit: das johanneische Sprechen vom Sehen im Horizont von Selbsterschliessung Jesu und Reaktion des Menschen. FzB 80: Wü 1996, Echter 772 pp. DM80. 3-429-01826-9.
5420 **Hofius, Ottfried Friedrich; Kammler, Hans-Christian** Johannesstudien: Untersuchungen zur Theologie des vierten Evangeliums. WUNT 2/88: Tü 1996, Mohr vii; 256 pp. DM168/DM88. 3-16-146572-5/1-7 [NT 39,394].
5421 **Howard-Brook, Wes** Becoming children of God: John's gospel and radical discipleship. 1994, ⇒10,5290; 11/1,4049. ᴿAUSS 34/1 (1996) 127-130 (*Maynard-Reid, Pedrito U.*); CritRR 9 (1996) 233-235 (*Segovia, Fernando F.*).
5422 *Infante, Renzo* Lo sposo e la sposa: contributo per l'ecclesiologia del quarto vangelo. RdT 37 (1996) 451-481.
5423 **Jerumanis, Pascal-Marie** Réaliser la communion avec Dieu: croire, vivre et demeurer dans l'évangile selon S. Jean. Diss. Fribourg 1995, ᴰRouiller, G., EtB 32: P 1996, Gabalda 601 pp. FF490. 2-85021-091-9.
5424 *Kammler, Hans-Christian* Jesus Christus und der Geistparaklet: eine Studie zur johanneischen Verhältnisbestimmung von Pneumatologie und Christologie. Johannesstudien. WUNT 88: 1996, ⇒5420. 87-190.
5425 *Kanagaraj, Jey J.* Jesus the king, Merkabah mysticism and the gospel of John. TynB 47 (1996) 349-366.
5426 *Keck, Leander E.* Derivation as destiny: 'of-ness' in Johannine christology, anthropology, and soteriology. ᶠSᴍɪᴛʜ D., 1996, ⇒82. 274-288.
5427 *Kelber, Werner H.* Metaphysics and marginality in John. "What is John?", 1. 1996, ⇒⇒5470. 129-154.
5428 **Kelleher, Sean B.** Praying with St John. Bangalore ²1996 <1988>, IJA xvi; 174 pp. Rs70. 81-86778-03-9 [VJTR 60, 704].
5429 *Koester, Craig R.* The spectrum of Johannine readers. "What is John?", 1. 1996, ⇒5470. 5-19.

5430 *Köstenberger, Andreas J.* The challenge of a systematized biblical theology of mission: missiological insights from the gospel of John. Missiology 23 (1995) 445-464.

5431 *Kysar, Robert* Coming hermeneutical earthquake in Johannine interpretation. "What is John?", 1. 1996, ⇒5470. 185-189.

5432 *La Potterie, Ignace de* La figliolanza divina del cristiano secondo Giovanni. Atti del VI Simposio. 1996, ⇒264. 53-80.

5433 *Lieu, Judith* Scripture and the feminine in John. A feminist companion. 1996, ⇒170. 225-240.

5434 **Lim, Lilian Hui-Kiau** Christ and community in the fourth gospel: pastoral symbols as symbolic relationship. Diss. Southern Bapt. Theol. Sem. 1996, 191 pp. [EThL 74,312*].

5435 **Lindars, Barnabas** Essays on John. ᴱ*Tuckett, C.M.*, 1992, ⇒8,271... 10,5320. ᴿRHPhR 76 (1996) 238-239 (*Grob, F.*).

5436 **Lorenzini, Ezio** Il vangelo di Giovanni: tre studi linguistico-letterari. Lyceum, saggi e ricerche 5: Cesena 1996, "Il Ponte Vecchio" 101 pp. Bibl. L15.000.

5437 **Maccini, Robert Gordon** Her testimony is true: women as witnesses according to John. JSNT.S 125: Shf 1996, Academic 278 pp. £39; $58.50. 1-85075-588-4 [NTAb 41,148].

5438 *Martyn, J. Louis* A Gentile mission that replaced an earlier Jewish mission. ᶠSмɪтʜ D., 1996, ⇒82. 124-144.

5439 *Mathai, Varghese* Paraclete and Johannine christology. BiBh 22 (1996) 120-138.

5440 **Mbachu, Hilary** Cana and Calvary revisited in the fourth gospel: narrative mario-christology in context. Deutsche Hochschulschriften 1102: Egelsbach 1996, Hänsel-Hohenhausen 109 pp. 3-8267-1102-5 [NThAR 1997,161].

5441 *McKay, K.L.* "I am" in John's gospel. ET 107 (1996) 302-303.

5442 *Meeks, Wayne A.* The ethics of the fourth evangelist. ᶠSмɪтʜ D., 1996, ⇒82. 317-326.

5443 *Menken, Maarten J.J.* Conclusion. Old Testament quotations ⇒5445. 205-212;

5444 Introduction. Old Testament quotations ⇒5445. 11-19.

5445 **Menken, Maarten J.J.** Old Testament quotations in the fourth gospel: studies in textual form. Contributions to Biblical Exegesis and Theology 15: Kampen 1996, Kok 255 pp. ƒ65/£26. 90-390-0181-2. ᴿEThL 72/4 (1996) 452-454 (*Neirynck, F.*).

5446 *Merklein, Helmut* Gott und Welt: eine exemplarische Interpretation von Joh 2,23-3,21; 12,20-36 zur theologischen Bestimmung des johanneischen Dualismus. ᶠTʜᴜᴇѕɪɴɢ W., NTA 31: 1996, ⇒94. 287-305.

5447 *Meyer, Paul W.* 'The Father': the presentation of God in the fourth gospel. ᶠSмɪтʜ D., 1996, ⇒82. 255-273.

5448 *Michaels, J. Ramsey* The gospel of John as a kinder, gentler apocalypse for the 20th century. "What is John?", 1. 1996, ⇒5470. 191-197.

5449 *Morgen, Michèle* Afin que le monde soit sauvé: Jésus révèle sa mission de salut dans l'Evangile de Jean. LeDiv 154: 1993, ⇒9,5508... 11/1,4076. ᴿRSR 84 (1996) 141-142 (*Simoens, Yves*); RB 103 (1996) 279-282 (*Boismard, M.-É.*).

5450 **Muller, Jean-Jacques** Le quatrième évangile et la gnose: les témoignages du christianisme ancien: les études johanniques du

milieu du XIXe siècle jusque vers 1990. Diss. Strasbourg 1996,
^DTrocmé, É., 346 pp. [EThL 74,313*].

5451 Muñoz León, Domingo El acceso a la verdad en san Juan. Communio 18 (1996) 285-296.

5452 Newheart, Michael Willett Toward a psycho-literary reading of the
fourth gospel. "What is John?", 1. 1996, ⇒5470. 43-58.

5453 Obermann, Andreas Die christologische Erfüllung der Schrift im
Johannesevangelium: eine Untersuchung zur johanneischen Herme-
neutik anhand der Schriftzitate. Diss. ^DKarrer, M., WUNT 2/83:
Tü 1996, Mohr xi; 479 pp. DM128. 3-16-146530-X.

5454 Pacomio, Luciano Il vangelo secondo Giovanni: unità del cuore
unità nella storia. 1993, ⇒10,5236. ^RBen. 43 (1996) 414-415
(Ranzato, Agostino).

5455 Pacomio, Luciano 'Servire', il Cristo e lo Spirito, nel vangelo di
Giovanni. Atti del VI Simposio. 1996, ⇒264. 91-100.

5456 Painter, John Inclined to God: the quest for eternal life—
Bultmannian hermeneutics and the theology of the fourth gospel.
^FSmith D., 1996, ⇒82. 346-368.

5457 Peterson, Norman R. The gospel of John and the sociology of
light. 1993, ⇒9,5532; 11/1,4085. ^RBiTr 47 (1996) 353-355
(Hodgson, Robert).

5458 Philippe, Marie-Dominique Suivre l'Agneau. ²1995, ⇒11/1,4086.
^REeV 105 (1996) 125-126 (Tort, Fernand).

5459 Pippin, Tina "For fear of the Jews": lying and truth-telling in
translating the gospel of John. Semeia 76 (1996) 81-97.

5460 Rand, Jan A. du Repetitions and variations—experiencing the
power of the gospel of John as literary symphony. Neotest. 30
(1996) 59-70.

5461 Ravindra, Ravi Mystisches Christentum: das Johannesevangelium
im Licht östlicher Weisheit. ^TTürstig, Hans-Georg, Fra 1996,
Fischer-Taschenbuch 282 pp. 3-596-13029-8 [NThAR 1997,70].

5462 Rese, Martin Das Selbstzeugnis des Johannesevangeliums über seinen Verfasser. EThL 72 (1996) 75-111.

5463 Riedl, Hermann Zeichen und Herrlichkeit: die christologische
Relevanz der Semeiaquelle in den Kanawundern Joh 2,1-11 und Joh
4,46-54. Diss. Regensburg 1996, ^DRitt, H., RSTh 51: Fra 1996,
Lang 362 pp. 3-631-30451-X [NThAR 1997,164].

5464 Rissi, Mathias "Die Juden" im Johannesevangelium. Religion.
ANRW II.26.3: 1996, ⇒183. 2099-2141.

5465 Santos, Bento Silva Fe e sacramentos no evangelho de Sao Joao.
Aparecida-SP 1995, Santuario 134 pp. [REB 58,993—Voigt, Si-
mao].

5466 Schlütter, Astrid Die Selbstauslegung des Wortes: Selbstreferenz
und Fremdreferenzen in der Textwelt des Johannesevangeliums.
Diss. Heidelberg 1996, 298 pp. [EThL 74,313*].

5467 Scholtissek, Klaus Kinder Gottes und Freunde Jesu: Beobachtungen
zur johanneischen Ekklesiologie. ^FKertelge K., 1996, ⇒48,
184-211.

5468 Schottroff, Luise Important aspects of the gospel for the future.
"What is John?", 1. 1996, ⇒5470. 205-210.

5469 Schweizer, Eduard What about the Johannine 'parables'?. ^FSmith
D., 1996, ⇒82. 208-219.

5470 ^ESegovia, Fernando F. 'What is John?', 1,: readers and readings
of the fourth gospel. SBL.Symposium 3: Atlanta, GA 1996, Scho-

lars xii; 293 pp. $50/$30. 0-7885-0239-5/40-9. [R]EThL 72 (1996) 457-458 (*Neirynck, F.*).

5471 *Segovia, Fernando F.* The gospel at the close of the century: engagement from the diaspora. "What is John?", 1. 1996, ⇒5470. 211-216;

5472 Reading readers of the fourth gospel and their readings: an exercise in intercultural criticism. "What is John?", 1. 1996, ⇒5470. 237-277;

5473 The tradition history of the fourth gospel. [F]SMITH D., 1996, ⇒82. 179-189.

5474 *Sinoir, Michel* Le progrès du mal dans le coeur de Judas, selon l'évangile de saint Jean. Sedes Sapientiae 14/4 (1996) 53-83.

5475 *Smalley, Stephen S.* 'The Paraclete': pneumatology in the Johannine gospel and Apocalypse. [F]SMITH D., 1996, ⇒82. 289-300.

5476 *Smith, D. Moody* John. [F]HOOKER M., 1996, ⇒43. 96-111;

5477 Prolegomena to a canonical reading of the fourth gospel. "What is John?", 1. 1996, ⇒5470. 169-182;

5478 What have I learned about the gospel of John?. "What is John?", 1. 1996, ⇒5470. 217-235.

5479 **Smith, Moody D.** The theology of the gospel of John. 1995, ⇒11/1,4098. [R]RRT (1996/1) 36-38 (*Bryan, David*); CBQ 58 (1996) 564-565 (*Kiley, Mark*); RSR 84 (1996) 290-291 (*Morgen, Michèle*); CritRR 9 (1996) 273-275 (*Carson, D.A.*).

5480 *Soeting, A.G.* Jezus was ook een jood: ioudaîos in het Evangelie naar Johannes. ITBT 4/1 (1996) 17-18.

5481 **Suh, J.S.** The glory in the gospel of John. 1995, ⇒11/1,4101. [R]CritRR 9 (1996) 282-284 (*Draper, Jonathan*).

5482 **Thatcher, Thomas William** The riddles of Jesus in the fourth gospel. Diss. Southern Bapt. Theol. Sem. 1996, [D]*Borchert, G.*, 263 pp. [EThL 74,314*].

5483 *Thompson, Marianne Meye* The historical Jesus and the Johannine Christ. [F]SMITH D., 1996, ⇒82. 21-42.

5484 **Trumbower, Jeffrey A.** Born from above: the anthropology of the gospel of John. HUTh 29: 1992, ⇒8,5741... 11/1,4105. [R]ThLZ 121 (1996) 455-457 (*Schnelle, Udo*).

5485 **Van 't Riet, Peter** Het evangelie uit het leerhuis van Lazarus: een speurtocht naar de joodse herkomst van het vierde evanglie. Baarn 1996, Ten Have 356 pp. ƒ49.90. 90-259-4666-6.

5486 **Van Belle, Gilbert** The signs source in the fourth gospel. BEThL 116: 1994, ⇒10,5259; 11/1,3993. [R]RThom 96 (1996) 449-462 (*Devillers, Luc*); CBQ 58 (1996) 780-781 (*Segovia, Fernando F.*); RSR 84 (1996) 296-298 (*Morgen, Michèle*); Cart. 12 (1996) 483-484 (*Sanz Valdivieso, R.*).

5487 **Van der Merwe, Dirk Gysbert** Discipleship in the fourth gospel. Diss. Pretoria 1996, [D]*Van der Watt, J.G.* [EThL 74,314*].

5488 **Van Tilborg, Sjef** Reading John in Ephesus. NT.S 83: Lei 1996, Brill vii; 232 pp. ƒ132/$85.25. 90-04-10530-1 [NTAb 41,153].

5489 *Vellanickal, Mathew* The historical Jesus in the Johannine christological vision. Sum. 131. Jeevadhara 26 (1996) 131-145.

5490 **Vignolo, Roberto** Personaggi del quarto vangelo. 1994, ⇒10,5329; 11/1,4107. [R]NRT 118 (1996) 270-271 (*Simoens, Yves*); ScrTh 28 (1996) 303-305 (*García-Moreno, A.*).

5491 *Viviano, Benedict T.* The spirit in John's gospel: a Hegelian perspective. FZPhTh 43 (1996) 368-387.

5492 *Weder, Hans Deus incarnatus*: on the hermeneutics of christology in the Johannine writings. ^{F}SMITH D., 1996, ⇒82. 327-345.

5493 **Welck, Christian** Erzählte Zeichen: die Wundergeschichten des Johannesevangeliums literarisch untersucht: mit einem Ausblick auf Joh 21. WUNT 2/69: Tü 1994, Mohr xvi; 377 pp. DM98. ^{R}OrdKor 37 (1996) 130-131 (*Giesen, Heinz*); CBQ 58 (1996) 782-783 (*Wahlde, Urban C. von*); CritRR 9 (1996) 302-304 (*Köstenberger, Andreas J.*).

5494 **Westermann, Claus** Das Johannesevangelium aus der Sicht des Alten Testaments. AzTh 99: 1994, ⇒10,5295; 11/1,4112. ^{R}BZ 40 (1996) 137-138 (*Reim, Günther*).

5495 **Winsor, Ann Roberts** A king is bound in the tresses: allusions to the Song of Songs in the fourth gospel. Diss. Grad. Theol. Union 1996, ^{D}*Maloney, Linda M.*, 218 pp. DAI-A 57/07, p. 3077; AAC 9706669.

5496 *Xavier, Aloysius* Andrew in the fourth gospel: first disciple of Jesus. ITS 33/2 (1996) 139-146 [ThIK 18/1,35].

5497 *Zevini, Giorgio* Il giusto sofferente glorificato nel vangelo di Giovanni. Som. 169. PSV 34 (1996) 169-182.

5498 **Zing, Jörg** Die sieben Zeichen: die Wunder im Johannesevangelium als Zeichen zum Heilwerden. FrB 1996, Herder 159 pp. DM14.80. 3-451-04407-2 [RB 103,480].

G1.5 **Johannis Prologus 1,1...**

5499 **Cholin, M.** Le prologue et la dynamique de l'évangile de Jean. 1995, ⇒11/1,4118. ^{R}RSR 84 (1996) 284-285 (*Morgen, Michèle*).

5500 **Harris, Elizabeth** Prologue and gospel. JSNT.S 107: 1994, ⇒10,5339; 11/1,4119. ^{R}JThS 47 (1996) 215-218 (*Smalley, Stephen S.*); Irén. 69 (1996) 287-288.

5501 *Hofius, Otfried* Struktur und Gedankengang des Logos-Hymnus in Joh 1,1-18. Johannesstudien. WUNT 88: 1996 <1987>, ⇒5420. 1-23.

5502 Logos di Dio e Sofia moderna: storia dell'interpretazione del Prologo di Giovanni. Bologna 1994, EDB 408 pp. ASEs 11. ^{R}FilTeo 10/1 (1996) 175-177 (*Sorrentino, Sergio*).

5503 *Merklein, Helmut* Geschöpf und Kind: zur Theologie der hymnischen Vorlage des Johannesprologs. ^{F}KERTELGE K., 1996, ⇒48. 161-183.

5504 *Muñoz León, Domingo* Trinidad inmanente e interpretación del NT: preexistencia y encarnación del verbo (Jn 1,1.14) según J.A.T. ROBINSON. EstB 54 (1996) 195-223.

5505 **Schwankl, Otto** Auf der Suche nach dem Anfang des Evangeliums: von 1 Kor 15,3-5 zum Johannes-Prolog. BZ 40 (1996) 39-60.

5506 *Valentine, Simon Ross* The Johannine prologue—a microcosm of the gospel. Sum. 304. EvQ 68 (1996) 291-304.

5507 *Hofius, Otfried* Struktur und Gedankengang des Logos-Hymnus in Joh 1,1-18. Johannesstudien. WUNT 88: 1996 <1987>, ⇒5240. 1-23.

5508 *Amato, Carmelo* Il Λόγος vita e luce degli uomini: l'essere e il suo manifestarsi. Itinerarium 4 (1996) 223-226 [1,1].

5509 *Theiss, Norman C.* John 1:6-8, 19-28. Interp. 50 (1996) 402-405.
5510 *Kirchhevel, Gordon D.* The children of God and the glory that John 1:14 saw. BBR 6 (1996) 87-93.
5511 *Hofius, Otfried* "Der in des Vaters Schoß ist" Joh 1,18. Johannesstudien. WUNT 88: 1996 <1989>, ⇒5240. 24-32.
5512 *Menken, Maarten J.J.* "I am the voice of one crying in the wilderness ..." (John 1:23). OT quotations. 1996 <1985>, ⇒5445. 21-35 [Isa 40,3].
5513 *Nortjé, S.J.* Lamb of God (John 1:29): an explanation from ancient christian art. Neotest. 30 (1996) 141-150.
5514 *Sieg, Franciszek* IV Ewangelia o powotanui pierwszych uczniów (J 1,35-51) [The fourth gospel about the vocation of the first disciples (John 1:35-51)]. Sum. 152. Bobolanum 7 (1996) 126-152 **P**.
5515 *McGowan, Andrew* Ecstasy and charity: AUGUSTINE with Nathaniel under the fig tree. AugSt 27/1 (1996) 27-38 [1,48].

5516 *Bechtel, Lyn M.* A symbolic level of meaning: John 2.1-11 (the marriage in Cana). A feminist companion. 1996, ⇒170. 241-255.
5517 **Lütgehetmann, Walter** Die Hochzeit von Kana. 1990, ⇒6,5796... 11/1,4140. RRHPhR 76 (1996) 240-241 (*Grob, F.*) [2,1-11].
5518 **Deines, Roland** Jüdische Steingefässe und pharisäische Frömmigkeit... Joh 2,6. WUNT 2/52: 1993, ⇒9,5561. RJSJ 27 (1996) 78-81 (*Reed, J.L.*); JETh 10 (1996) 251-252 (*Riesner, Rainer*).

5519 *Alonso Alonso, Florentino* El verdadero templo: la persona de Jesucristo, auténtico 'lugar' de encuentro del hombre con Dios (Jn 2,13-22 y par.). StLeg 37 (1996) 197-268 [2,13-22].
5520 *Schnelle, Udo* Die Tempelreinigung und die Christologie des Johannesevangeliums. NTS 42 (1996) 359-373 [2,13-22].
5521 *Menken, Maarten J.J.* "Zeal for your house will consume me" (John 2:17). OT quotations. 1996 <1994>, ⇒5445. 37-45.

G1.6 Jn 3ss...Nicodemus, Samaritana

5522 **Létourneau, Pierre** Jésus, fils de l'homme et fils de Dieu: Jean 2,23-3,36. RFTP 27: 1993, ⇒8,5786... 11/1,4145. RScrTh 28 (1996) 938-939 (*García-Moreno, A.*); RSR 84 (1996) 600-601 (*Sesboüé, Bernard*).
5523 *Kysar, Robert* The making of metaphor: another reading of John 3:1-15. "What is John?", 1. 1996, ⇒5470. 21-41.
5524 *Hofius, Otfried* Das Wunder der Wiedergeburt: Jesu Gespräch mit Nikodemus Joh 3,1-21. Johannesstudien. WUNT 88: 1996, ⇒5240. 33-80.
5525 *Brug, J.F.* The son of man who is in heaven. WLQ 93 (1996) 140-141 [3,13] [NTAb 40,431].
5526 *Bang, Sang-Man* Exegetical analysis of Jn 3:14-21. The Reason and the Faith 11 (1996) 210-284 [ThIK 18/1,51] **K**.
5527 *Benoit, Camille* Le signe à Nicodème: quelle image de la Croix?. Sources 22/1-2 (1996) 23-24 [3,14].
5528 *MacArthur, J.F.* The love of God for humanity. MastJ 7/1 (1996) 7-30 [3,16] [NTAb 41,57].
5529 *Infante, Renzo* La voce dello sposo: Gv 3,29. VetChr 33 (1996) 301-308.

5530 *Asakawa, Toru* L'expérience de Nicodème à la lumière des Exercices. Cahiers de Spiritualité Ignatienne 77/1 (1996) 51-60 [3; 7; 19].

5531 *Dube, Musa W.* Reading for decolonization (John 4:1-42). Semeia 75 (1996) 37-59.

5532 *Han, Bide* Jesus' attitude and manner of work (John 4:1-42). CTR 11/1 (1996) 51-60 [ThIK 18/2,30].

5533 *Mesters, Carlos* Word of God—source of life: John 4,1-42. WoWo 29 (1996) 213-227; 252-258 [ThIK 18/2,48].

5534 *Cuvillier, Élian* La figure des disciples en Jean 4. NTS 42 (1996) 245-259.

5535 *Cho, Tae-Yeon* A feministic reflection on the narrative of a Samaritan woman. Theological Thought 92 (1996) 96-124 [4,3-42] [ThIK 18/1,55]. **K.**
      Ska, J.-L., Jésus et la Samaritaine ⇒6934.

5536 *Galot, Jean* Le 'don de Dieu' dans le dialogue évangélique. EeV 106 (1996) 385-391 [4,10].

5537 *Hahn, Ferdinand* "Weder auf diesem Berg noch in Jerusalem" (Joh 4,21): zur Unverfügbarkeit Gottes <1986>:

5538 "Das Heil kommt von den Juden": Erwägungen zu Joh 4,22b <1976>. FHAHN, F. 1996, ⇒34. 144-159/99-118.

5539 EBori, Pier Cesare In spirito e verità: letture di Giovanni 4,23-24. Epifania della Parola 6: Bo 1996, EDB 336 pp. L40.000. 88-10-40230-8.

5540 *Legrand, L.* Rencontres kénotiques de Jésus. Spiritus 37 (1996) 40-49 [4,41-42] [NTAb 40,431].

5541 **Landis, Stephan** Das Verhältnis des Johannesevangeliums zu den Synoptikern... Mt 8,5-13; Lk 7,1-10; Jo 4,46-54. BZNW 74: 1994, ⇒10,5367. RThLZ 121 (1996) 665-666 (*Becker, Jürgen*); RB 103 (1996) 614-615 (*Boismard, M.-É.*); CritRR 9 (1996) 239-240 (*Matson, Mark*).

5542 *Farmer, Craig S.* Changing images of the Samaritan woman in early reformed commentaries on John. ChH 65 (1996) 365-375 [4].

5543 *Backus, Irena* The chronology of John 5-7: Martin BUCER's commentary (1528-36) and the exegetical tradition. FSTEINMETZ D., 1996, ⇒86. 141-155.

5544 *Borgen, Peder* The Sabbath controversy in John 5:1-18 and analogous controversy reflected in PHILO's writings. Early christianity. 1996 <1991>, ⇒116. 105-120.

5545 EBoismard, Marie-Émile; Lamouille, A. Un évangile préjohannique, 3/1-2: Jean 5,1-47. EtB 28-29: P 1996, Gabalda 176; 168 pp. 2-85021-082-X/3-8. RRThom 96 (1996) 467-478 (*Devillers, Luc*).

5546 *Casto, Lucio* Ma tu vuoi guarire? (cf Gv 5,6). Presbyteri 30 (1996) 679-690 [Matt 18,12-14].

5547 **Lozada-Smith, Frank** A literary reading of John 5: text as construction. Diss. Vanderbilt 1996, DSegovia, Fernando F., 251 pp. [EThL 74,315*].

5548 *Venema, Jon Roger* An apologetic role for agency in John five. Diss. Golden Gate Bapt. Theol. Sem. 1996, DBrooks, O., 299 pp. [EThL 74,315*].

G1.7 **Panis Vitae**—*Jn 6...*

5549 *Vassiliadis, Petros* The understanding of eucharist in St. John's gospel. Atti del VI Simposio. 1996, ⇒264. 39-52 [6,22-71].

5550 *Menken, Maarten J.J.* "He gave them bread from heaven to eat" (John 6:31). OT quotations. 1996 <1988>, ⇒5445. 47-65 [Ps 78,24].

5551 *Hofius, Otfried* Erwählung und Bewahrung: zur Auslegung von Joh 6,37. WUNT 88: 1996 <1977>, 81-86.

5552 *Mongillo, Dalmazio* L'attrazione alla fede in Gesù Cristo nel commento di AGOSTINO e TOMMASO su Gv. 6,44. Atti del VI Simposio. 1996, ⇒264. 311-332.

5553 *Menken, Maarten J.J.* "And they shall all be taught by God" (John 6:45). OT quotations. 1996 <1988>, ⇒5445. 67-77 [Isa 54,13].

5554 *Theobald, Michael* Häresie von Anfang an?: Strategien zur Bewältigung eines Skandals nach Joh 6,60-71. [F]KERTELGE K., 1996, ⇒48. 212-246.

5555 *Stephens, W.P.* ZWINGLI on John 6:63: 'Spiritus est qui vivificat, caro nihil prodest'. [F]STEINMETZ D., 1996, ⇒86. 156-185.

5556 *Borgen, Peder* John 6: tradition, interpretation and composition. Early christianity. 1996 <1993>, ⇒116. 205-229.

5557 *Caba, José* Pan de vida... estudio exegético de Jn 6. BAC 531: 1993, ⇒9,5582... 11/1,4193. [R]RThom 96 (1996) 453-455 *(Devillers, Luc)*.

5558 *Menken, Maarten J.J.* "Rivers of living water shall flow from his inside" (John 7:38). OT quotations. 1996, ⇒5445. 187-203 [Ps 77,16.20; Zech 14,8];

5559 The origin of the Old Testament quotation in John 7:38. NT 38 (1996) 160-175.

5560 *Sedlmeier, Franz* Und keiner warf den Stein: theologische Meditation zur Perikope von der Ehebrecherin. Prisma 8/2 (1996) 14-17 [7,53-8,11].

5561 *Neyrey, Jerome H.* The trials (forensic) and tribulations (honor challenges) of Jesus: John 7 in social science perspective. BTB 26 (1996) 107-124.

5562 *Schöndorf, Harald* Jesus schreibt mit dem Finger auf die Erde: Joh 8,6b.8. BZ 40 (1996) 91-93 [Exod 31,18].

5563 *Lane, Tom* Making our home in God's word. DoLi 46 (1996) 592-599 [8,31].

5564 *Baarda, Tjitze* John 8:57b: the contribution of the Diatessaron of TATIAN. NT 38 (1996) 336-343.

5565 *Farmer, Craig S.* Wolfgang MUSCULUS's commentary on John: tradition and innovation in the story of the woman taken in adultery. [F]STEINMETZ D., 1996, ⇒86. 216-240 [8].

5566 *Poirier, John C.* "Day and night" and the punctuation of John 9.3. NTS 42 (1996) 288-294.

5567 *Humphries, Michael L.* The physiognomy of the blind: the Johannine story of the blind man. [F]MACK B., 1996, ⇒54. 229-243 [9].

5568 *Farmer, David Albert* John 9. Interp. 50 (1996) 59-63.

5569 **Rein, Matthias** Die Heilung des Blindgeborenen (Joh 9). WUNT 2/73: 1995, ⇒11/1,4204. ᴿOrdKor 37 (1996) 490-491 (*Giesen, Heinz*); ThR 92 (1996) 414-418 (*Labahn, Michael*).
5570 *Tite, Philip L.* A community in conflict: a literary and historical reading of John 9. RStT 15/2-3 (1996) 77-100.
5571 *Lawless, George* The man born blind: AUGUSTINE's tractate 44 on John 9. AugSt 27/2 (1996) 59-77.

5572 **Kowalski, Beate** Die Hirtenrede (Joh 10,1-18) im Kontext des Johannesevangeliums. Diss. ᴰ*Dschulnigg, P.*, SBB 31: Stu 1996, Kath. Bibelwerk v; 378 pp. DM89. 3-460-00311-1.
5573 *Owan, Kris J.N.* Jesus, justice and Jn 10:10: liberation hermeneutics in the Nigerian context. NJT 10/1 (1996) 18-42 [ThIK 18/1,21].
5574 *Schenke, Ludger* Das Rätsel von Tür und Hirt: wer es löst, hat gewonnen!. TThZ 105 (1996) 81-100 [10].

5575 *Dennison, James T.* Jesus and Lazarus. Kerux 11/2 (1996) 3-6 [11].
5576 **Partyka, J.S.** La résurrection de Lazare dans les monuments funéraires... à Rome. 1993, ⇒10,5395. ᴿVetChr 33 (1996) 229-231 (*Felle, Antonio Enrico*) [11].
5577 **Rouvière, Jean-Marc** Le silence de Lazare: méditation sur une résurrection. Voie spirituelle: P 1996, Desclée de B. 96 pp. F58 [11] [EeV 106 (1996) 399].
5578 **Baltz, Frederick W.** Lazarus and the fourth Gospel community. Mellen 37: Lewiston, NY 1996, Mellen ix; 109 pp. $60. 0-7734-2428-8 [11] [NTAb 41,142].
5579 **Koumaglo, Joseph Kossivi** Tod als Verherrlichung: eine exegetische Untersuchung zur Perikope Joh 12,20-36 im Blick auf die johanneische Christologie und Soteriologie. Diss. Innsbruck 1996/97, ᴰ*Hasitschka, Martin* [BZ 42,316].
5580 *Galot, Jean* Il turbamento del Cristo di fronte all'ora della Passione. CivCatt 147 I (1996) 446-459 [12,27].
5581 *Menken, Maarten J.J.* "He has blinded their eyes ..." (John 12:40). OT quotations. 1996 <1988>, ⇒5545. 99-122 [Isa 6,10].

G1.8 Jn 13...Sermo sacerdotalis et Passio

5582 *Bender, Jorge Alberto* El evangelio de Juan 'alimento' para las comunidades cristianas: notas sobre la historia joánica de la pasión. NuMu 52 (1996) 3-21.
5583 **Boer, Martinus C. de** Johannine perspectives on the death of Jesus. Contributions to Biblical Exegesis and Theology 17: Kampen 1996, Kok 360 pp. ƒ69.90. 90-390-0191-X.
5584 *Bourgeois, Daniel* El sacerdocio único de Jesucristo, el sacerdocio real de los bautizados y el sacerdocio ministerial. ᵀ*Rosón Alonso, Antonio-Gabriel*, Communio 18 (1996) 495-508; Fr. 21/6,15-32.
5585 **Carver, Frank G.** When Jesus said good-bye: John's witness to the Holy Spirit. Kansas City, Mo. 1996 Beacon Hill 134 pp. 0-8341-1570-0 [NThAR 1997,226].

5586 **Derrett, J. Duncan M.** The victim—the Johannine passion narrative re-examined. 1993, ⇒8,5849... 10,5429. ^REvQ 68 (1996) 68-69 (*Ensor, Peter*).

5587 *Ghiberti, Giuseppe* Tradizione giovannea ·e tradizione sinottica sulla cena 'pasquale' di Gesù. Atti del VI Simposio. 1996, ⇒264. 101-109.

5588 **Hoegen-Rohls, Christina** Der nachösterliche Johannes: die Abschiedsreden als hermeneutischer Schlüssel zum vierten Evangelium. Diss. Mü 1993, ^D*Hahn, F.*, WUNT 2/84: Tü 1996, Mohr xi; 349 pp. DM118. 3-16-146271-8. ^RSNTU.A 21 (1996) 255-257 (*Fuchs, A.*).

5589 *Klauck, Hans-Josef* Der Weggang Jesu: neue Arbeiten zu Joh 13-17. BZ 40 (1996) 236-250.

5590 **La Potterie, Ignace de** La passione di Gesù secondo il vangelo di Giovanni: testo e spirito. CinB ³1996, 171 pp. [APIB 10/3,266].

5591 **Léon-Dufour, Xavier** L'heure de la glorification. Lecture de l'évangile selon Jean, 4. Parole de Dieu 34: P 1996, Seuil 270 pp. FF190. 2-02-030411-2.

5592 *Raurell, Frederic* Èxode i resurrecció διὰ τῆς δόξης θεοῦ. Sum. 17. RCatT 21 (1996) 1-17.

5593 **Winter, Martin** Das Vermächtnis Jesu... Joh. 13-17. FRLANT 161: 1994, ⇒10,5410; 11/1,4232. ^ROrdKor 37 (1996) 131-132 (*Giesen, Heinz*); Neotest. 30 (1996) 221-223 (*Tolmie, D.F.*); JBL 115 (1996) 546-548 (*Kurz, William S.*).

5594 *Gangemi, Attilio* La lavanda dei piedi: il coinvologimento dei discepoli nell'esodo di Gesù mediante l'amore, 1. Synaxis 14/2 (1996) 27-120 [13,1-5].

5595 *Marcel, P.* Jésus lave les pieds de ses disciples. RRef 47 (1996) 55-60 [13,1-11].

5596 *Destro, Adriana; Pesce, Mauro* La lavanda dei piedi nel vangelo di Giovanni: un rito di inversione. Atti del VI Simposio. 1996, ⇒264. 9-27 [13,1-20].

5597 *Connell, Martin F.* Nisi pedes: except for the feet: footwashing in the community of John's gospel. Worship 70 (1996) 517-530 [13,2-20].

5598 *Menken, Maarten J.J.* "He who eats my bread, has raised his heel against me" (John 13:18). OT quotations. 1996 <1990>, ⇒5545. 123-138 [Ps 41,10].

5599 **O'Brien, Kevin** But the gates were shut: operation of Jerusalem's perimeter gates within new evidence and a new methodology for dating and locating the last supper and identifying the beloved disciple in John 13:25 project. SF 1996, Int. Scholars Publ. 2 vols (xxxix+508 pp.; xxvi+540 pp.). $75/$55. 1-57309-077-8/9-4; 1-57309-076-X/8-6.

5600 **Dettwiler, Andreas** Die Gegenwart des Erhöhten... Joh 13,31-16,33. FRLANT 169: 1995, ⇒11/1,4240. ^RThLZ 121 (1996) 1054-1055 (*Becker, Jürgen*); SNTU.A 21 (1996) 254-255 (*Fuchs, A.*).

5601 **Niemand, Christoph** Fußwaschungserzählung. StAns 114: 1993, ⇒9,5612... 11/1,4243. ^RTPQ 144 (1996) 196-198 (*Frey, Jörg*); ZKTh 188 (1996) 259-260 (*Hasitschka, Martin*); RHPhR 76 (1996) 241-242 (*Grappe, Ch.*) [13].

5602 **Thomas, John Christopher** Footwashing in John 13 and the Johannine community. JSNT.S 61: 1991, ⇒7,4943... 10,5416. ᴿRSR 84 (1996) 293-294 (*Morgen, Michèle*).

5603 *Derickson, Gary W.* Viticulture and John 15:1-6. BS 153 (1996) 34-52.

5604 *Manns, Frédéric* Je vous appelle mes amis. BeO 38 (1996) 227-238 [15,1-17].

5605 *Stimpfle, Alois* "Ihr seid schon rein durch das Wort" (Joh 15,3a). Sünde und Erlösung im NT. QD 161: 1996, ⇒181. 108-122.

5606 *Manjaly, Thomas* 'Love one another as I have loved you' (John 15:12): some reflections in the context of a youth convention. IMR 18 19 [sic]/1 (1996) 87-91 [ThIK 18/1,34].

5607 *Barth, Gerhard* Schutz des Lebens und Liebesgebot: theologische Erwägungen für Seelsorger und Berater. Neutestamentliche Versuche. 1996 <1977>, ⇒111. 283-297 [15,12].

5608 *Menken, Maarten J.J.* "They hated me without reason" (John 15:25). OT quotations. 1996, ⇒5545. 139-145 [Ps 35,19; 69,05].

5609 *Angelt, Kurt* Gottes Verborgenheit als "Gerechtigkeit": eine theologische Studie zu Joh 16,10. ThPh 71 (1996) 12-32.

5610 *Pasquetto, Virgilio* La preghiera di Gesù al Padre in Gv 17,1-26. RVS 50/1 (1996) 9-22.

5611 *Weber, Laura Ann* 'That they may all be one': John 17:21-23 and a Plotinian application of unity. Diss. Marquette 1996, ᴰ*Kurz, William S.*, 355 pp. DAI-A 57/06, p. 2531; AAC 9637724.

5612 **Van Kaam, Adrian** The tender farewell of Jesus: meditations on chapter 17 of John's gospel. Hyde Park, NY 1996, New City 128 pp. [CBQ 59,424].

5613 *Weren, Wim* 'Het is volbracht': structuur en betekenis van het lijdensverhaal van Johannes (Joh. 18-19). TTh 36 (1996) 132-154.

5614 *Staley, Jeffrey Lloyd* Reading myself, reading the text: the Johannine passion narrative in postmodern perspective. "What is John?", 1. 1996, ⇒5470. 59-104 [18-19].

5615 **Heil, John Paul** Blood and water: the death and resurrection of Jesus in John 18-21. CBQMS 27: 1995, ⇒11/1,4257. ᴿThLZ 121 (1996) 834-835 (*Klauck, Hans-Josef*); JThS 47 (1996) 612-617 (*Carson, D.A.*); ATG 59 (1996) 311-312 (*Contreras Molina, F.*); CBQ 58 (1996) 754-755 (*Koester, Craig R.*); CritRR 9 (1996) 229-231 (*Marrow, Stanley B.*).

5616 *Diebold-Scheuermann, Carola* Jesus vor Pilatus: eine Gerichtsszene: Bemerkungen zur joh. Darstellungsweise. BN 84 (1996) 64-74 [18,28-19,16].

5617 *Söding, Thomas* Die Macht der Wahrheit und das Reich der Freiheit: zur johanneischen Deutung des Pilatus-Prozesses (Joh 18,28-19,16). ZThK 93 (1996) 35-58.

5618 *Baudler, Georg* Gott zwischen staatlicher Exekutionsgewalt und archaischer Tötungswut: die Gottesoffenbarung Jesu im Prozeß vor Pilatus (Jh 18,28-19,16b). Pontius zu Pilatus. 1996, ⇒196. 15-23.

5619 *Zahrnt, Heinz* Der Prozeß: nach dem Johannesevangelium 18,28-19,16. Pontius zu Pilatus. 1996, ⇒196. 9-14.

5620 *Sorg, Theo* Das Kreuz-Fixpunkt im Leben: Johannes 19,16-30. Das Wort vom Kreuz. 1996, ⇒206. 53-59.

5621 *Trimaille, Michel* Le partage des vêtements de Jésus en Jean 19,23-24 et l'ecclésiologie paulinienne. [F]LEGASSE S., LeDiv 166: 1996, ⇒51. 251-264.

5622 *Schöni, Marc* The mother at the foot of the cross: the key to the understanding of St. John's account of the death of Jesus. ThRev 17 (1996) 71-95 [19,25-27].

5623 *Léon-Dufour, Xavier* Jésus constitue sa nouvelle famille Jn 19,25-27;

5624 *Zumstein, Jean* Jean 19,25-27. [F]LEGASSE S., LeDiv 166: 1996, ⇒51. 265-281/219-249.

5625 *Wilckens, Ulrich* Maria, Mutter der Kirche (Joh 19,26f). [F]KERTELGE K., 1996, ⇒48. 247-266.

5626 *Witkamp, L. Th.* Jesus' thirst in John 19:28-30: literal or figurative?. JBL 115 (1996) 489-510.

5627 **Leone, Cosimo** La morte di Gesù e il dono dello spirito (Gv 19,28-37). Diss. excerpt Pont. Univ. Gregoriana 1996 <1992>, [D]*Rasco, Emilio*, R 217 pp.

5628 *Sorg, Theo* "Es ist vollbracht!" Johannes 19,30. Das Wort vom Kreuz. 1996, ⇒206. 103-108.

5629 *Menken, Maarten J.J.* "Not a bone of him shall be broken" (John 19:36) <1992> [Exod 12,10.46; Num 9,12; Ps 34,21];

5630 "They shall look on him whom they have pierced" (John 19:37) [Zech 12,10] <1993>. OT quotations. 1996, ⇒5545. 147-166/167-185.

5631 *Borse, Udo* Joh 20,8: österlicher oder vorösterlicher Glaube?. [F]BORSE U., SBAB 21: 1996 <1989>, ⇒9. 211-221.

5632 *Schneiders, Sandra M.* John 20:11-18: the encounter of the easter Jesus with Mary Magdalene—a transformative feminist reading. "What is John?", 1. 1996, ⇒5470. 155-168.

5633 *Faessler, Marc* Kérygme et imaginaire. Sum. rés. 235. Apocrypha 7 (1996) 235-241 [20,11-18].

5634 *Antoniotti, Louise-Marie* L'apparition de Jésus à Marie de Magdala. RThom 96 (1996) 302-311 [20,17].

5635 *Haag, E.* Aus Angst zur Freude, aus Resignation zu Perspektiven, aus Müdigkeit zu Vollmacht (Joh. 20,19-23). ThBeitr 27/2 (1996) 57-60.

5636 *Aizpurúa, Fidel* 'Cum esset sero die illo' (Jn 20,19): una valoración actual de la exégesis antoniana [Antonio di Padua]. EstFr 97 (1996) 281-298.

5637 *Kammler, Hans-Christian* Die "Zeichen" des Auferstandenen: Überlegungen zur Exegese von Joh 20,30+31. Johannesstudien. WUNT 88: 1996, ⇒5240. 191-211.

5638 *Hennessy, A.* The formation of adult disciples: a reading of John 20-21. Emmanuel 102/3 (1996) 173-179 [NTAb 40,434].

5639 *Gaventa, Beverly Roberts* The archive of excess: John 21 and the problem of narrative closure. [F]SMITH D., 1996, ⇒82. 240-252.

G2.1 Epistulae Johannis

5640 **Burge, Gary M.** The letters of John. NIV Application Commentary: GR 1996, Zondervan 264 pp. 0-310-48620-3.

5641 **Edwards, Ruth B.** The Johannine epistles. NTGu: Shf 1996, Academic 121 pp. £7/$10. 1-85075-750-X.
5642 **Nieuwenhuis, Jan** Het laatste uur: brieven van Johannes voor de gemeente van nu. Kampen 1996, Kok 186 pp. ƒ44.50. 90-242-8749-9 [ITBT 5/5,34].
5643 **Strecker, Georg** The Johannine letters: a commentary on 1, 2, and 3 John. [T]*Maloney, Linda M.*, Hermeneia: Mp 1996, Fortress xliv; 319 pp. $46. 0-8006-6047-1 [TS 58,352].

5644 **Barsotti, Divo** Méditation sur la première épître de saint Jean. P 1996, Téqui 220 pp. FF98 [EeV 107,23].
5645 **Dalbesio, Anselmo** "Quello...": l'esperienza cristiana nella prima lettera di Giovanni. RivBib.S 22: 1990, ⇒6,5912... 10,5448. [R]Anton. 71/1 (1996) 123-124 (*Alvarez Barredo, Miguel*).
5646 *De Simone, Giuseppe* Il 'vangelo della carità' nel commento di Sant'AGOSTINO all prima lettera di Giovanni. Vivarium 4 (1996) 331-337.
5647 **Gelnnie Graue, Enrique** La primera carta de S. Juan, un llamado a la comunión: estudio analítico-espiritual. Material Académico UPM 14: México 1996, Universidad Pontificia de México 161 pp. [EfMex 15,396].
5648 **Griffith, Terry** 'Little children, keep yourselves from idols' (1 John 5:21): the form and function of the ending of the first epistle of John. Diss. L, King's College 1996, [D]*Lieu, Judith*, 294 pp. [TynB 48,187-190].
5649 **Monari, L.** 'La vita si è fatta visibile': commento alla prima lettera di Giovanni. Sussidi biblici 51-52: Reggio Emilia 1996, San Lorenzo 218 pp. L18.000 [Asp. 45,448s—Rolla, Armando].
5650 **Moriconi, B.** "Lectio divina" della prima Lettera di Giovanni. 1995, ⇒11/1,4302. [R]PaVi 41/3 (1996) 57-58 (*Migliasso, Secondo*); RdT 37 (1996) 707-708 (*Casalegno, Alberto*).
5651 **Renoux, Charles** La chaîne sur la première épitre de Jean. La chaîne arménienne sur les Épitres Catholiques, 3. 1994, ⇒10,5462. [R]Muséon 109 (1996) 237-239 (*Coulie, B.*).
      [TE]**Rettig, John W.** AUGUSTINE:... tractates on the first epistle of John ⇒5350.
5652 *Söding, Thomas* 'Gott ist Liebe': 1Joh 4,8.16 als Spitzensatz biblischer Theologie. [F]THUESING W., NTA 31: 1996, ⇒94. 306-357.
5653 *Standaert, Benoît* 'Dieu est amour': la première épître de Jean: une parole de vie pour une communauté en état de choc. [F]DUPONT J., 1996, ⇒21. 197-213.
5654 *Studer, Basil* ORIGENE e la prima lettera di Giovanni. Atti del VI Simposio. 1996, ⇒264. 223-236.
5655 *Turek, Waldemar* La prima lettera di Giovanni negli scritti di TERTULLIANO. Atti del VI Simposio. 1996, ⇒264. 199-213.
5656 **Veerkamp, Ton** Weltordnung und Solidarität oder Dekonstruktion christlicher Theologie: Auslegung des ersten Johannesbriefes und Kommentar. TeKo 19/3-4: B 1996, Lehrhaus 141 pp. [NThAR 1997,228].
5657 *Wyller, E.A.* Johannes' fårste brev, hans håysang, henologisk fortolket. TTK 67 (1996) 3-19.

5658 **Barbuto, Gennaro Maria** Il principe e l'Anticristo: Gesuiti e ideologie politiche. N 1994, Guida 323 pp. [R]ASEs 13 (1996) 367-369 (*Motta, Franco*).

5659 **Guadalajara Medina, José** Las profecías del Anticristo en la Edad Media. M 1996, Gredos 506 pp. 84-249-1792-8.

5660 **Heid, Stefan** Chiliasmus und Antichrist-Mythos. 1993, ⇒9,5674; 11/1,4310. [R]JThS 47 (1996) 658-665 (*Hill, Charles E.*); ThRv 92 (1996) 237 (*Stritzky, Maria-Barbara von*) [1 John 2,18].

5661 **Lietaert Peerbolte, Lambertus J.** The antecedents of antichrist: a traditio-historical study of the earliest christian views on eschatological opponents. Diss. [D]*Jonge, M. de*, JStJudS 49: Lei 1996, Brill xi; 381 pp. *f*190/$122.75. 90-04-10455-0 [NTAb 41,166].

5662 **McGinn, Bernard** Antichrist. 1994, ⇒10,5466; 11/1,4313. [R]TS 57 (1996) 140-141 (*Guinan, Michael D.*); JR 76 (1996) 623-624 (*Emmerson, Richard K.*).

5663 **Nietzsche, Friedrich** L'antéchrist. [T]*Blondel, Éric*, P 1994, Flammarion 215 pp. 2-08-070753-1. [R]RPFE (1996) 536-537 (*Wotling, Patrick*).

5664 *Renoux, Charles* La chaîne sur 2-3 Jean et Jude. La chaîne arménienne sur les Épitres Catholiques, 4. PO 47/2,210: Turnhout 1996, Brepols. 81-191.

5665 *Rigato, Maria Luisa* La testimonianza di PAPIA de Gerapoli sul 'secondo' Giovanni e il contesto eusebiano: riscontri nel Nuovo Testamento. Atti del VI Simposio. 1996, ⇒264. 237-272.

G2.3 *Apocalypsis Johannis*—Revelation: text, introduction

5666 **Burr, David** OLIVI's peaceable kingdom: a reading of the Apocalypse Commentary. 1993, ⇒9,5682. [R]EHR 111 (1996) 682-683 (*Leff, Gordon*); ChH 65 (1996) 462-463 (*Madigan, Kevin*); Florensia 10 (1996) 183-187 (*Solvi, Daniele*).

5667 *Dubreucq, Marc* Espérer la paix: l'Apocalypse. DosB 62 (1996) 25-26.

5668 *Giesen, Heinz* Ermutigung zur Glaubenstreue in schwerer Zeit: zum Zweck der Johannesoffenbarung. TThZ 105 (1996) 61-76.

5669 [ET]**González Echegaray, Joaquin**, (*al*), Obras completas de BEATO de Liébana. 1995, ⇒11/1,4324. [R]Lumen 45 (1996) 91-92 (*Ortiz de Urtaran, Félix*); RevAg 37 (1996) 880-881 (*Viuda, Isidro de la*); ScrTh 28 (1996) 587-590 (*Tineo, P.*).

5670 **Grünberg, Karsten** Die kirchenslavische Überlieferung der Johannes-Apokalypse. Diss. Heidelberg, 1995. Heidelberger Publikationen zur Slavistik: A. Linguistische Reihe 9: Fra 1996, Lang xi; 223 pp. 3-631-30177-4 [EThL 74,338*].

5671 **Harrington, Wilfrid J.** Revelation. 1993, ⇒9,5688... 11/1,4328. [R]TJT 12 (1996) 100-101 (*Fox, Kenneth*).

5672 **Ironside, Henry A.** Revelation. Ironside Commentaries: Neptune, NJ [2]1996, Loizeaux 233 pp. 0-87213-407-5 [NThAR 1997,260].

5673 **Kraft, H.** Die Bilder der Offenbarung des Johannes. 1994, ⇒10,5507. [R]SNTU.A 21 (1996) 277-278 (*Fuchs, A.*).

5674 *MacDonald, P.M.* Lion as slain lamb: on reading Revelation recursively. Horizons 23/1 (1996) 29-47.

5675 TEMamiani, M. NEWTON: trattato sull'Apocalisse. 1994
      <1733>, ⇒11/1,4329. RPhysis 33/1-3 (1996) 376-378 (Cleri-
      cuzio, Antonio).
5676 EMcGinn, Sheila E. The book of Revelation. Bibliographies for
      biblical research. Lewiston 1996, Mellen xii; 520 pp. 0-7734-
      2438-5 [NThAR 1998,335].
5677 Panzeri, Fulvio; Righetto, Roberto I racconti dell'Apocalisse.
      Pref. Ravasi, Gianfranco, Religione: T 1996, Società Edit. Interna-
      zionale ix; 186 pp. 88-05-05636-7.
5678 Richard, Pablo Apokalypse: das Buch von Hoffnung und Wider-
      stand: ein Kommentar. TLaube, Michael, Luzern 1996, Exodus
      254 pp. 3-905577-00-3 [NThAR 1997,37].
5679 Roloff, Jürgen Revelation. 1993, ⇒9,5692... 11/1,4333. RSJTh
      49 (1996) 374-375 (Barker, Margaret).
5680 Talbert, Charles H. The Apocalypse. 1994, ⇒10,5484;
      11/1,4339. RWThJ 58 (1996) 175-178 (Johnson, Dennis E.).
5681 Vers l'édition de l'Apocalypse. BVLI 40 (1996) 21-22.
5682 Visser, Derk Apocalypse as Utopian expectation (800-1500): the
      Apocalypse commentary of BERENGAUDUS of Ferrières and the
      relationship between exegesis, liturgy and iconography. SHCT 73:
      Lei 1996, Brill xiii; 239 pp. f130/$84. 90-04-10621-9.
5683 Wall, Robert W. Revelation. NIBC 18: 1991, ⇒7,5022...
      11/1,4341. RVJTR 60 (1996) 690-691 (Meagher, P.M.).
5684 Weyer-Menkhoff, Michael Sein Angesicht sehen: die Botschaft
      der 'Offenbarung'. Collab. Nonnenmann, Dagmar, Porta-Studien
      28: Marburg 1996, SMD 287 pp. Studentenmission in Deutschland
      [NThAR 1997,195].

G2.4 Apocalypsis, Revelation, topics

5685 Abir, P.A. A theology of protest in the book of Revelation. ITS 33
      (1996) 43-53.
5686 Adinolfi, Marco Cibi e bevande nell'Apocalisse. Atti del VI Sim-
      posio. 1996, ⇒264. 155-162.
5687 Adler, William Introduction. Apocalyptic heritage. CRI 3: 1996,
      ⇒5757. 1-31.
5688 Aukerman, Dale Reckoning with apocalypse: terminal politics and
      christian hope. 1993, ⇒10,5702. RInterp. 50 (1996) 98, 100
      (Jewett, Robert).
5689 Bauckham, Richard The climax of prophecy: studies in the book
      of Revelation. 1993, ⇒9,5702*... 11/1,4347. REvQ 68 (1996) 168-
      171 (Slater, Thomas B.);
5690 La teologia dell'Apocalisse. 1994 <1993>, ⇒10,5490. RPaVi
      41/2 (1996) 63-64 (Doglio, Claudio).
5691 Beckwith, Roger T. A time, times and half a time: the revelation of
      the prophet John and the three-and-a-half times. Calendar and chro-
      nology. AGJU 33: 1996, ⇒112. 297-309.
5692 Bedriñán, Claudio La dimensión socio-politica del mensaje teoló-
      gico del Apocalipsis. Diss. DVanni, Ugo, Tesi Gregoriana, Teolo-
      gia 11: R 1996, Gregorian Univ. Press 364 pp. L38.000. 88-7652-
      711-7.

5693 *Berlingieri, Giovanni* L'Apocalisse come 'teologia della storia': 'regno' e 'sacerdoti': l'impegno del cristiano nella storia. Vivarium 4 (1996) 219-246.

5694 **Biguzzi, Giancarlo** I settenari nella struttura dell'Apocalisse: analisi, storia della ricerca, interpretazione. SRivBib 31: Bo 1996, Dehoniane 411 pp. L57.000. 88-10-30219-2.

5695 *Biguzzi, Giancarlo* La sofferenza dei giusti nell'Apocalisse. Som. 239. PSV 34 (1996) 239-255.

5696 **Blondet, Maurizio** I fanatici dell'Apocalisse: l'ultimo assalto a Gerusalemme. La Bottega di Eraclito: Rimini 1995, Il Cerchio 155 pp. 88-86583-07-9.

5697 *Boismard, Marie-Émile* Le sort des impies dans l'Apocalypse. LV(L) 45/2 (1996) 69-79.

5698 *Borgen, Peder* Autobiographical ascent reports: PHILO and John the seer;

5699 Illegitimate invasion and proper ascent: a study of passages in PHILO's writings and the Revelation to John. Early christianity. 1996, ⇒116. 309-320/293-307;

5700 Moses, Jesus, and the Roman Emperor: observations on PHILO's writings and the Revelation of John. NT 38 (1996) 145-159;

5701 Polemic in the book of Revelation. Early christianity. 1996, ⇒116. 275-291.

5702 **Briggs, Robert Alan** A background investigation of the Jewish temple imagery in the book of Revelation. Diss. Southern Bapt. Theol. Sem. 1996, ᴰ*Borchert, G.L.*, 391 pp. [EThL 74,338*].

5703 **Carey, William Greg** Attention-seeking behavior, rhetoric, resistance and authority in the book of Revelation. Diss. Vanderbilt 1996, ᴰ*Segovia, Fernando F.*, 279 pp. [RTL 29,583].

5704 **Christe, Yves** L'Apocalypse de Jean: sens et développements de ses visions synthétiques. P 1996, Picard 271 pp. 170 ill. FF350 [HZ 266,474].

5705 **Collins, C.** Authority figures: metaphors of mastery from the *Iliad* to the *Apocalypse*. L 1996, Rowman & L. xiv; 202 pp. $52.50/$23. 0-8476-8238-2/9-0 [ClR 48/1,204—Goldhill, Simon].

5706 **Conninck, Frédéric** Quelques points de repère pour une lecture sociologique des discours apocalyptiques. Hokhma 62 (1996) 68-74.

5707 *Doglio, Claudio* Dio nell'Apocalisse. Dio—Signore nella bibbia. DSBP 13: 1996, ⇒328. 244-266.

5708 **Falbo, Giovanni** "L'Apocalisse": attualità della storia della salvezza. Vivere la parola, Itinerari Biblici per la comunità 3: R 1996, Coletti 262 pp.

5709 *Ford, Josephine Massyngbaerde* Visual art and the Apocalypse. BiTod 34 (1996) 366-373.

5710 *Giesen, Heinz* Das Römische Reich im Spiegel der Johannes-Apokalypse. Religion. ANRW II.26.3: 1996, ⇒183. 2501-2614.

5711 *Giroud, Jean-Claude* L'agneau égorgé et debout. LV(L) 45/2 (1996) 35-42.

5712 **Glonner, Georg** Die Bildersprache des Johannes von Patmos: Untersuchung der Bildersprache in der Johannes-Apokalypse anhand einer um bildinterpretatorische Elemente erweiterten historisch-kritischen Methode. Diss. Mü 1996-97, ᴰ*Gnilka, J.* [BZ 42,317].

5713 **Heinze, André** Johannesapokalypse und johanneische Schriften: geschichtliche und traditionsgeschichtliche Untersuchungen. Diss. Gö 1996-97, *DStegemann, H.*, 483 pp. [EThL 74,338*].

5714 *Hengel, M.* Die Throngemeinschaft des Lammes mit Gott in der Johannesapokalypse. ThBeitr 27 (1996) 159-175.

5715 **Keller, Catherine** Apocalypse now and then: a feminist approach to the end of the world. Boston 1996, Beacon 370 pp. $30. 0-8070-6778-4 [ThTo 54/2,243.

5716 *Kelly-Buccellati, Marilyn* Seals in ancient Mesopotamia and seals of God in Revelation. RTLu 1 (1996) 79-100.

5717 *Koch, Klaus* Einleitung zur Apokalyptik. Wende der Zeiten. 1996 <1982>, ⇒133. 109-134.

5718 **Koottappillil, George** The symbolism of thronos and its biblical-theological implications in the Apocalypse. Diss. excerpt Pont. Univ. Gregoriana 1996, vii; 84 pp.

5719 **Kraybill, J. Nelson** Imperial cult and commerce in John's Apocalypse. JSNT.S 132: Shf 1996, Academic 262 pp. £33/$49. 1-85075-616-3.

5720 *Kyrtatas, Dimitris J.* The Apocalypse: revelation and prophecy. BiTod 34 (1996) 353-358.

5721 **Malina, Bruce J.** On the genre and message of Revelation. 1995, ⇒11/1,4386. RBTB 26 (1996) 89-90 (*Barr, David L.*); ETR 71 (1996) 596-597 (*Campbell, Gordon*); RSR 84 (1996) 286-287 (*Morgen, Michèle*).

5722 **Manning, Don** Secrets of revelation: the Rosetta Stone of the Bible. Kalispell, Mont. 1996, William & J. xii; 161 pp. [NThAR 1998,98].

5723 *Martin, François* L'auteur identifié, l'auteur autorisé. LV(L) 45/2 (1996) 7-21.

5724 **McGinn, Bernard** Apocalypticism in the western tradition. CS 430: Aldershot 1994, Variorum 336 pp. 0-86078-396-0. RCHR 82 (1996) 528-530 (*Reeves, Marjorie*).

5725 **McLean, John Andrew** The seventieth week of Daniel 9:27 as a literary key for understanding the structure of the Apocalypse of John. Diss. Michigan, *DFreedman, David Noel*, Mellen 38: Lewiston, NY 1996, Mellen (8) i; 324 pp. $100. 0-7734-2434-2.

5726 **Metzger, Bruce M.** Breaking the code: understanding the book of Revelation. 1993, ⇒9,5727; 10,5512. RAThR 78/1 (1996) 165-166 (*Petersen, Rodney L.*).

5727 **Michaels, J. Ramsay** Interpreting the book of Revelation. 1992, ⇒8,5932... 11/1,4391. REvQ 68 (1996) 351-352 (*Beasley-Murray, G.R.*).

5728 **Moyise, Steve** The OT in the book of Revelation. JSNT.S 115: 1995, ⇒11/1,4393. RJBL 115 (1996) 772-773 (*Wilson, J. Christian*).

5729 **Muse, Robert L.** The book of Revelation: an annotated bibliography. Books of the Bible 2: NY 1996, Garland xxxvi; 352 pp. $58. 0-8240-7394-0 [NThAR 1997,100].

5730 **Naden, Roy C.** The lamb among the beasts. Hagerstown 1996, Review and H. 300 pp. $24 [AUSS 36,148s—Matak, Dragutin].

5731 **Nusca, Anthony Robert** Heavenly worship, ecclesial worship: a 'liturgical approach'. Diss. Pont. Univ. Gregoriana 1996, *DVanni, Ugo*, 515 pp. [EThL 74,339*].

5732 *Nützel, Johannes M.* Gottesvolk aus Juden und Heiden: zum Selbst-Verständnis der Christen in der Johannes-Apokalypse. [F]Kertelge K., 1996, ⇒48. 458-478.

5733 **O'Brien, Kevin John** An examination of the meaning, the purpose, and the function of the interlude within the sevenfold series of the book of Revelation. Diss. Union Theol. Sem. in Virginia 1996, 337 pp. [EThL 74,339*].

5734 *Paczkowski, Mieczyslaw Celestyn* La lettura cristologica dell'Apocalisse nella chiesa prenincena. SBFLA 46 (1996) 187-222.

5735 *Pani, Giancarlo* Ireneo di Lione e l'*Apocalisse*. Atti del VI Simposio. 1996, ⇒264. 173-198.

5736 **Pezzoli-Olgiati, Daria** Täuschung und Klarheit: zur Wechselwirkung zwischen Vision und Geschichte in der Johannesoffenbarung. Diss. Z 1995-96, [D]*Weder, H.* [RTL 27,537].

5737 *Prévost, Jean-Pierre* John, the seer of Patmos. BiTod 34 (1996) 347-351.

5738 *Ramos, Felipe Fernandez* El Apocalipsis: libro de la esperanza, 2;
5739 Comentario: el Apocalipsis, Beato y beatos. StLeg 37 (1996) 11-66/66-82.

5740 *Rand, Jan A. du* '...let him hear what the Spirit says...': the functional role and theological meaning of the Spirit in the book of Revelation. ExAu 12 (1996) 43-58.

5741 **Reichelt, Hansgünter** Angelus interpres—Texte in der Johannes-Apokalypse: Strukturen, Aussagen und Hintergründe. EHS.T 507: 1994, ⇒10,5521. [R]CBQ 58 (1996) 765-766 (*Bruns, J. Edgar*); RSR 84 (1996) 298-300 (*Morgen, Michèle*).

5742 **Richard, Pablo** Apocalipse: reconstrução da esperança. [T]*Brumetta, Attílio,* Petrópolis 1996, Vozes 294 pp. 85-326-1566-X [PerTeol 28,276].

5743 **Riley, William** The spiritual adventure of the Apocalypse. Mystic 1996, Twenty-Third 159 pp. $10 [DoLi 47,443s—*Greehy, J.J.*].

5744 *Ritt, Hubert* Rachephantasie, infantiles Weltbild, psychischer Konflikt?: Gewalt in der Offenbarung des Johannes. BiKi 51 (1996) 128-132.

5745 *Rowland, Christopher* Apocalyptic, God and the world: appearance and reality: early christianity's debt to the Jewish apocalyptic tradition. [F]Hooker M., 1996, ⇒43. 238-249.

5746 **Royalty, Robert M.** The streets of heaven: the imagery and ideology of wealth in the Apocalypse of John. Diss. Yale 1996, [D]*Garrett, S.R.* [EThL 74,339*].

5747 [E]**Rusconi, Roberto** Storia e figure de l'Apocalisse fra '500 e '600. Opere di Gioacchino da Fiore: testi e strumenti 7: R 1996, Viella 406 pp. Atti del 4º congresso internazionale di studi gioachimiti, San Giovanni in Fiore 14-17 settembre 1994. L76.000. 88-85669-53-0 [CFr 68,357ss—Bérubé, Camille].

5748 *Sagne, Jean-Claude* "Oui, je viens bientôt": le désir et l'espérance. LV(L) 45/2 (1996) 43-54.

5749 *Schürmann, Heinz* Das 'etabliert Böse' bedacht im Lichte der Apokalypse. [F]Feiereis K., EThSt 71: 1996, ⇒24. 43-59.

5750 *Selvidge, Marla J.* Reflections on violence and pornography: misogyny in the Apocalypse and ancient Hebrew prophecy. A feminist companion. 1996, ⇒170. 274-285.

5751 **Slater, Thomas Bowie** Christ and community: a socio-historical study of the christology of Revelation. Diss. King's College, L 1996, ᴰ*Stanton, G.N.*, 209 pp. [EThL 74,339*].

5752 **Sleeper, Charles Freeman** The victorious Christ: a study of the book of Revelation. LVL 1996, Westminster xi; 142 pp. $10. 0-664-25620-1.
      Smalley, Stephen S. 'The Paraclete': pneumatology in the... Apocalypse ⇒5475.

5753 **Stock, Klemens** L'ultima parola è di Dio: l'Apocalisse come buona notizia. Bibbia e Preghiera 21: R 1995, ADP 200 pp. L25.000. 88-7357-152-2.

5754 ᴱ**Strecker, Georg; Schnelle, Udo** Texte zur Briefliteratur und zur Johannesapokalypse, Teilbd. 1. Introd. *Seelig, Gerald,* Neuer Wettstein: Texte zum NT aus Griechentum und Hellenismus 2: B 1996, De Gruyter xxiii; 973 pp. DM498. 3-11-014507-3 [ThPQ 145,421].

5755 **Stuckenbruck, Loren T.** Angel veneration and... christology of the Apocalypse of John. WUNT 2/70: 1995, ⇒11/1,4422. ᴿThLZ 121 (1996) 363-366 (*Frenschkowski, Marco*); JThS 47 (1996) 248-253 (*Hurtado, Larry W.*); DSD 3/1 (1996) 76-77 (*Fletcher-Louis, Crispin*); SJTh 49 (1996) 227-229 (*Barker, Margaret*); CBQ 58 (1996) 777-778 (*Thompson, Leonard L.*).

5756 *Sweet, John* Revelation. ᶠHooker M., 1996, ⇒43. 160-173.

5757 **VanderKam, James C.; Adler, W.** The Jewish apocalyptic heritage in early christianity. CRI 3/4: Assen 1996, Van Gorcum xiii; 286 pp. 90-232-2913-4. ᴿCDios 209 (1996) 765-766 (*Gutiérrez, J.*).

5758 **Vanni, Ugo** Apocalisse. Archivi di arte antica: T 1996, Allemandi 222 pp. 75 pl. L150.000. 88-422-0491-9.

5759 *Vanni, Ugo* La chiesa in preghiera discerne la storia: lettura del libro dell'Apocalisse. Horeb 6/1 (1996) 34-47 [ZID 23,235];

5760 La liturgia della parola nell'Apocalisse. DSBP 12: 1996, ⇒327. 119-130.

5761 **Wainwright, A.W.** Mysterious Apocalypse. 1993, ⇒9,5698... 11/1,4432. ᴿAUSS 34 (1996) 347-348 (*Strand, Kenneth A.*).

G2.5 *Apocalypsis,* Revelation 1,1...

5762 **Synnes, Martin** Sju profetiske budskap til menighetene: en gjennomgåelse av sendebrevene i Johannes' Åpenbaring. Oslo 1996, Verbum 145 pp. NOK125 [1-3].

5763 **Julien, Jerome M.** What the spirit says to the churches. Neerlandia, Alberta 1996, Inheritance 107 pp. 0-921100-76-0 [1-3] [NThAR 1997,292].

5764 *Stuckenbruck, Loren T.* The Son of Man as the Old of Days. ᵀ*Abtze, Kikes,* DBM 15 (1996) 8-14 [1,13-18] G.

5765 *Slater, Thomas B.* More on Revelation 1.13 and 14.14. BiTr 47 (1996) 146-149.

5766 *Beale, G.K.* The Old Testament background of Rev 3.14. NTS 42 (1996) 133-152.

5767 **Contreras Molina, Francisco** Estoy a la puerta y llamo (Ap 3,20). 1995, ⇒11/1,4443. ᴿLumen 45/1 (1996) 87-89 (*Ortiz de Urtaran,*

Félix); Phase 36 (1996) 357-358 (*Vicent, R.*); Communio 29/2-3 (1996) 399-400 (*Burgos, M. de*).

5768 *Toribio Cuadrado, J.F.* Apocalipsis 4-5: díptico litúrgico de creación y redención. Mayéutica 22 (1996) 9-65.

5769 *Bredin, M.R.* The influence of the Aqedah on Revelation 5.6-9. IBSt 18 (1996) 26-43.

5770 **Stefanović, Ranko** The background and meaning of the sealed book of Revelation 5. Andrews University Seminary Doctoral Dissertations 22: Berrien Springs, Mich. 1996, Andrews University Press xi; 370 pp. ^D*Paulien, Jon*, 1-883925-13-4 [NThAR 1997,293].

5771 *Corsini, Eugenio* La bestia dalla terra dell'*Apocalisse*. Atti del VI Simposio. 1996, ⇒264. 111-126 [12-13].

5772 **Busch, Peter** Der gefallene Drache: Mythenexegese am Beispiel von Apokalypse 12. TANZ 19: Tü 1996, Francke xi; 276 pp. DM68. 3-7720-1870-X.

5773 *Guéry, Dominique-Emanuelle* Les signes de la femme et du dragon, Ap. 12. LV(L) 45/2 (1996) 23-33.

5774 *Biguzzi, Giancarlo* 'La terra' da cui sale la bestia di Ap 13,11. Atti del VI Simposio. 1996, ⇒264. 111-126.

5775 *Ford, J. Massyngbaerde* The physical features of the antichrist. JSPE 14 (1996) 23-41 [13; 1 John 2,18; 2 John 4. 11].

5776 **Mazzeo, Michele** La sequela di Cristo-Agnello in Apocalisse 14,1-5: la dimensione escatologico-apocalittica della sequela cristiana nel libro dell'Apocalisse. SBF, Thesis ad Doctoratum 348: Reggio Calabria 1996, Pont. Athenaeum Antonianum 102 pp. Diss. abstract [RB 104,315].

5777 *Giesen, Heinz* Evangelium und Paränese: zum Verständnis der Gerichtsaussagen in Offb 14,6-13. SNTU.A 21 (1996) 92-131.

5778 *Niccacci, Alviero* La grande prostituta e la sposa dell'agnello. Atti del VI Simposio. 1996, ⇒264. 137-154 [17-18].

5779 **Rissi, Mathias** Die Hure Babylon... Studie zur Apokalypse des Johannes. BWANT 136: 1995, ⇒11/1,4464. ^RThLZ 121 (1996) 554-555 (*Böcher, Otto*); SNTU.A 21 (1996) 278-279 (*Fuchs, A.*); CritRR 9 (1996) 258-260 (*Pippin, Tina*) [17].

5780 *Provan, Iain* Foul spirits, fornication and finance: Revelation 18 from an Old Testament perspective. JSNT 64 (1996) 81-100.

G2.7 **Millenniarismus,** *Apc 20...*

5781 *Coninck, Frédéric* Quelques points de repère pour une lecture sociologique des discours apocalyptiques. Hokhma 62 (1996) 68-74.

5782 **Delumeau, Jean** Mille ans de bonheur. Une histoire du paradis, 2. 1995, ⇒11/1,4468. ^RCRAI (1996/1) 385-386 (*Delumeau, Jean*).

5783 *Duquoc, Christian* "Apocalypse now?". LV(L) 45/2 (1996) 3-5.

5784 **Grosso, Michael** The millennium myth: love and death at the end of time. Wheaton, Ill. 1995, Quest 384 pp. 0-8356-0711-9/34-8 [NThAR 1998,97].

5785 *Kuri Camacho, Ramón* Del pelagianismo a la gnosis o la storia como mística y la fiebre milenarista. Anamnesis 6/2 (1996) 129-142 [2 Sam 22; Ps 18].

5786 Multiple Jérusalem: Jérusalem terrestre, Jérusalem céleste. Dédale 3-4 (1996) 624 pp. FF169.

5787 ^E**Nardi, Carlo** Il millenarismo: testi dei secoli I-II. BPat 27: 1995, ⇒11/1,4474. ^RVetChr 33 (1996) 237-238 (*Grasso, Cristina*).

5788 **O'Leary, Stephen D.** Arguing the Apocalypse: a theory of millennial rhetoric. 1994, ⇒10,5562; 11/1,4476. ^RHistory of European Ideas 22 (1996) 125-126 (*Laffey, John F.*); Numen 43 (1996) 316-317 (*Kippenberg, Hans G.*).

5789 *Rainbow, Paul A.* Millennium as metaphor in John's Apocalypse. WThJ 58 (1996) 209-221.

5790 **Sutton, Hilton** The book of Revelation revealed: understanding God's master plan for the end of the age. Tulsa ²1995, Harrison 278 pp. [=Revelation, God's grand finale] 1-57794-057-1 [NThAR 1999,6].

5791 **Sim, Unyong** Das himmlische Jerusalem in Apk 21,1-22,5 im Kontext biblisch-jüdischer Traditionen und antiken Städtebaus. Diss. ^D*Wengst, Kl.*, Bochumer Altertumswissenschaftliches Colloquium 25: Trier 1996, WVT 255 pp. 3-88476-199-4 [NThAR 1997,37].

5792 *Greinacher, Norbert* Christlicher Glaube und Utopie: Gedanken zu Offb 21,1-5. Diak. 27 (1996) 356-358.

5793 *Preez, Jannie du* All things new: notes on the church's mission in the light of Revelation 21:1-8. Missionalia 24 (1996) 372-382.

5794 *Nobile, Marco* La 'nuova Gerusalemme' in un documento di Qumran e in Apocalisse 21: genesi di una teologia. Atti del VI Simposio. 1996, ⇒264. 163-171.

5795 *Garrido, R.* Los enigmas del Apocalipsis: el Bien Supremo (Apoc 22,1-21). EvV 38 (1996) 24-26.

5796 **Maniscalco, Edward F.** Rhyme and reason in Erasmus' 1516 Greek text of Revelation 22:16-21. Diss. Marquette 1996, ^D*Hagen, Kenneth*, 214 pp. DAI-A 57/06, p. 2529; AAC 9634107.

XII. Paulus

G3.1 Pauli biographia

5797 **Anderson, R. Dean** Ancient rhetorical theory and Paul. Contributions to Biblical Exegesis and Theology 18: Kampen 1996, Kok 315 pp. *f*65. 90-390-0142-1 [NTAb 41,155].

5798 Association Catholique Française Pour l'Étude de la Bible: Paul de Tarse. LeDiv 165: P 1996, Cerf 376 pp. FF255.

5799 **Ball, Charles Ferguson** The life and times of the apostle Paul. Wheaton, Ill. 1996, Tyndale vii; 238 pp. 0-8423-3500-5 [NThAR 1997,291].

5800 *Barbaglio, Giuseppe* Il cammino sofferto di Paolo. Horeb 5/1 (1996) 26-31 [ZID 23/1,3].

5801 **Bony, Paul** Saint Paul... tout simplement. Tout Simplement: P 1996, L'Atelier 207 pp. F100. 2-7082-3233-9 [RTL 28,291].

5802 *Borse, Udo* Paulus in Jerusalem. ^FBORSE U., SBAB 21: 1996 <1981>, ⇒9. 251-276.

G3.1 Paul's biography 315

5803 **Burrow, Beverly Jean** Pauline autobiography: theological content, rhetorical function, and biblical antecedents. Diss. Baylor 1996, ᴰ*Sloan, R.B.*, 224 pp. [EThL 74,320*].

5804 **Buscemi, Alfio Marcello** Paolo: vita, opera e messaggio. ASBF 43: J 1996, Franciscan Printing Press vii; 335 pp. $25.

5805 **Dreyfus, Paul** Pablo de Tarso ciudadano del imperio. M 1996, Palabra 487 pp. [EphMar 47,313].

5806 *Flusser, David* Paulus, Apostel: II, aus jüdischer Sicht. TRE 26 (1996) 153-160.

5807 **Gnilka, Joachim** Paulus von Tarsus: Zeuge und Apostel. Herders Theol. Komm. zum NT.S 6: FrB 1996, Herder 332 pp. DM85. 3-451-26115-4.

5808 *Hübner, Hans* Paulus, Apostel: I, Neues Testament. TRE 26 (1996) 133-153.

5809 **Lo Magro, Raffaele** Paolo di Tarso: i viaggi e la dottrina. Storia Pioltello (MI) 1996, Laura Rangoni 91 pp. 88-86513-28-3.

5810 **Lohse, Eduard** Paulus: eine Biographie. Mü 1996, Beck 334 pp. 3-406-40949-0 [NThAR 1997,163].

5811 **Murphy-O'Connor, Jerome** Paul: a critical life. Oxf 1996, Clarendon xvi; 416 pp. £12/$35. 0-8146-5845-8 [NTAb 41,161]. ᴿTablet (29 June 1996) 860-861 (*Houlden, Leslie*); PIBA 19 (1996) 99-109 (*Nolan, Brian*).

5812 **Penna, Romano** Un cristianismo posible: Pablo de Tarso. 1993, ⇒9,5798. ᴿRevBib 58 (1996) 244-247 (*Levoratti, A.J.*).

5813 *Penna, Romano* Tre tipi di conversione raccontati nell'antichità. Atti del IV Simposio di Tarso. 1996, ⇒263. 73-92.

5814 **Riesner, Rainer** Die Frühzeit des Apostels Paulus. WUNT 2/71: 1994, ⇒10,5588; 11/1,4494. ᴿAnton. 71/1 (1996) 117-119 (*Nobile, Marco*); ThLZ 121 (1996) 274-278 (*Niebuhr, Karl-Wilhelm*); RB 103 (1996) 141-143 (*Murphy-O'Connor, Jerome*); Salm. 43 (1996) 119-123 (*Trevijano, Ramón*); ZKTh 188 (1996) 264-265 (*Oberforcher, Robert*); BZ 40 (1996) 275-278 (*Söding, Thomas*); EvQ 68 (1996) 47-58 (*Wenham, David*); ThGl 86 (1996) 629-630 (*Ernst, Josef*); StMon 38/1 (1996) 215-216 (*Roure, D.*).

5815 **Sánchez Bosch, Jordi** Nacido a tiempo: una vida de Pablo. 1994, ⇒10,5589; 11/1,4495. ᴿRB 103 (1996) 282-284 (*Quesnel, Michel*).

5816 **Saffrey, Henri Dominique** San Paolo apostolo: una biografia storica. 1995, ⇒11/1,4496. ᴿLat. 62 (1996) 671-672 (*Penna, Romano*).

5817 **Sandnes, Karl Olav** Paul—one of the prophets. WUNT 2/43: 1991, ⇒7,5149... 9,5801. ᴿJThS 47 (1996) 219-221 (*Aune, David E.*).

5818 *Schlosser, Jacques* Introduction. Paul de Tarse. LeDiv 165: 1996, ⇒273. 13-23.

5819 **Storm, Hans-Martin** Die Paulusberufung nach Lukas. ANTJ 10: 1995, ⇒11/1,4497. ᴿThLZ 121 (1996) 670-672 (*Ernst, Josef*).

5820 **Tajra, Harry W.** The martyrdom of St Paul. WUNT 2/67: 1994, ⇒11/1,4499. ᴿRB 103 (1996) 152-153 (*Taylor, Justin*); CBQ 58 (1996) 565-567 (*Pervo, Richard I.*); EE 71 (1996) 649 (*Muñoz León, Domingo*).

5821 *Taylor, Nicholas H.* Paolo: fariseo, cristiano e dissonante. ᵀ*Protopapa, Cornelia*, ReSo 11/1 (1996) 22-39.

5822 **Wansink, Craig S.** Chained in Christ: the experience and rhetoric of Paul's imprisonments. JSNT.S 130: Shf 1996, Academic 239 pp. £35.50. 1-85075-605-8 [NTS 43,622].

5823 **Wenham, David** Paul: follower of Jesus or founder of Christianity?. 1995, ⇒11/1,4500. ᴿTTK 67 (1996) 63-64 (*Kvalbein, Hans*); ETR 71 (1996) 440 (*Campbell, Gordon*); ThLZ 121 (1996) 672-674 (*Rese, Martin*); JETh 10 (1996) 255-257 (*Bayer, Hans F.*) [1 Cor 9; 1 Thess 4-5].

G3.2 Corpus paulinum; *generalia, technica epistularis*

5824 **Agosto, Efrain** Paul's use of Greco-Roman conventions of commendation. Diss. Boston Univ. 1996, ᴰ*Sampley, J. Paul*, 256 pp. AAC 9530617; DAI-A 56/05, p. 1825.

5825 *Aletti, Jean-Noël* Paul et la rhétorique: état de la question et propositions. Paul de Tarse. LeDiv 165: 1996, ⇒273. 27-50.

5826 **Ariarajah, S. Wesley** Did I betray the gospels?: the letters of Paul and the place of women. Geneva 1996, WCC xiv; 58 pp. $8. 2-8254-1183-3. ᴿVJTR 60 (1996) 689-690 (*Lobo Gajiwala, Astrid*).

5827 *Barr, G.K.* Contrasts in scale and genre in the letters of Paul and SENECA. IBSt 18 (1996) 16-25.

5828 **Baumert, Norbert** Woman and man in Paul: overcoming a misunderstanding. ᵀ*Madigan, Patrick; Maloney, Linda M.*, ColMn 1996, Liturgical. $35. 0-8146-5055-4 [NTAb 41,156].

5829 **Betz, Hans Dieter** Paulinische Studien. 1994, ⇒10,160. ᴿJR 76 (1996) 105-106 (*Roetzel, Calvin J.*).

5830 **Brossier, François** Vocabulario de las epístolas paulinas. ᵀ*Darrícal, Nicolás*, CuaBi 88: Estella 1996, Verbo Divino 68 pp. 84-8169-091-0.

5831 *Byrskog, Samuel* Co-senders, co-authors and Paul's use of the first person plural. ZNW 87 (1996) 230-250.

5832 **Clabeaux, John J.** A lost edition of the letters of Paul... Marcion. CBQ.MS 21: 1989, ⇒5,5788... 7,5164. ᴿThR 61 (1996) 279-281 (*Mühlenberg, Ekkehard*).

5833 **Cousar, Charles B.** The letters of Paul. Interpreting Biblical Texts: Nv 1996, Abingdon 212 pp. 0-687-00852-2.

5834 *Detering, Hermann* The Dutch radical approach to the Pauline epistles. JHiC 3 (1996) 163-193.

5835 *Dewey, Joanna* Textuality in an oral culture: a survey of the Pauline traditions. Semeia 65/2 (1994) 37-65.

5836 *Gryziec, Piotr R.* Specyfika paraklezy w listach Św. Pawła [De paraclesi in epistulis paulinis]. RBL 49 (1996) 85-90. **P.**

5837 **Holmstrand, Jonas** 'Jag vill att ni skall veta, bröder...': övergångsmarkörer, textstruktur och innehåll i första Thessalonikerbrevet, Filipperbrevet och Galaterbrevet. Diss. Uppsala 1996, 224 pp. [NThAR 1997,260].

5838 **Jaquette, James L.** Discerning what counts: the function of the adiaphora topos in Paul's letters. SBL.DS 146: 1995, ⇒11/1,4516. ᴿCBQ 58 (1996) 553-554 (*Newman, Carey C.*); RB 103 (1996) 631-632 (*Murphy-O'Connor, J.*); Neotest. 30 (1996) 465-466 (*Vorster, J.N.*); JBL 115 (1996) 758-760 (*Deming, Will*).

5839 ᴱ**Jervis, L. Ann; Richardson, Peter** Gospel in Paul: studies on Corinthians, Galatians and Romans. ᶠLONGENECKER R.,

JSNT.S 108: 1994, ⇒10,76a. ᴿSR 25 (1996) 502-504 (*Braun, Willi*); CBQ 58 (1996) 184-187 (*Harrill, J. Albert*).

5840 *Joseph, M.J.* Paul's understanding of 'economics' in social relations. BiBh 22/4 (1996) 190-199.

5841 **Lambrecht, Jan** Pauline studies. BEThL 115: 1994, ⇒10,195; 11/1,4517. ᴿRivBib 44 (1996) 240-242 (*De Lorenzi, Lorenzo*).

5842 *Liebert, Donald Hans* The "apostolic form of writing": group letters before and after 1 Corinthians. Corinthian correspondence. BEThL 125: 1996, ⇒6143. 433-440.

5843 *Mara, Maria Grazia* Paolo e il suo epistolario nella comunità antiochena del II secolo. Atti del IV Simposio di Tarso. 1996, ⇒263. 139-145.

5844 **Meißner, Stefan** Die Heimholung des Ketzers: Studien zur jüdischen Auseinandersetzung mit Paulus. WUNT 2/87: Tü 1996 Mohr ix; 359 pp. DM118. 3-16-146589-X.

5845 **Murphy-O'Connor, Jerome** Paul et l'art épistolaire. 1994, ⇒10,5606; 11/1,4523. ᴿLTP 52/1 (1996) 227-229 (*Racine, Jean-François*);

5846 Paul the letter-writer. 1995, ⇒11/1,4524. BTB 26 (1996) 56 (*Watson, Duane F.*); DoLi 46 (1996) 573-575 (*McConvery, Brendan*); JBL 115 (1996) 755-756 (*Stowers, Stanley K.*).

5847 **Müller, Markus** Vom Schluss zum Ganzen: zur Bedeutung des paulinischen Briefkorpusabschlusses. Diss. ⇒11/1,4525. FRLANT 172: Gö 1996, Vandenhoeck & R. 296 pp. DM98. 3-525-53855-3.

5848 *Nieuviarts, Jacques* Saint Paul: la bonne nouvelle dans toute la Méditerranée. BLE.S 1 (1996) 89-103.

5849 ᴱ**Padovese, Luigi** Atti del III Simposio di Tarso su S. Paolo. 1995, ⇒11/1,4528. ᴿOrph. 17 (1996) 232-234 (*Gallico, Antonino*).

5850 *Pani, Giancarlo* Le edizioni delle lettere di Paolo e i commenti: dall'invenzione della stampa alla fine del XVI secolo. Atti del IV Simposio di Tarso. 1996, ⇒263. 7-58.

5851 *Pitta, Antonio* Esortazione morale e kerygma paolino. La foi agissant. SMBen.BE 13: 1996, ⇒277. 219-240.

5852 **Reed, Jeffrey T.** Are Paul's thanksgivings "epistolary"?. JSNT 61 (1996) 87-99.

5853 **Reynier, Chantal** El evangelio del resucitado: una lectura de Pablo. Temas Bíblicos: Bilbao 1996, Desclée de B. 223 pp. [EstAg 32,340].

5854 **Richards, Randolph E.** The secretary in the letters of Paul. WUNT 2/42: 1991, ⇒7,5156... 11/1,4533. ᴿHeyJ 37 (1996) 87-89 (*Prior, Michael*).

5855 **Sacchi, Alessandro** Lettere paoline e altre lettere. Corso di Studi Biblici 6: Leumann 1996, LDC 632 pp. L60.000. 88-01-10475-8 [RdT 37,576].

5856 *Salles, Catherine* L'épistolographie hellénistique et romaine. Paul de Tarse. LeDiv 165: 1996, ⇒273. 79-97.

5857 **Schmid, Ulrich** Mᴀʀᴄɪᴏɴ und sein Apostolos: Rekonstruktion... der marcionitischen Paulusbriefausgabe. ANTT 25: 1995, ⇒11/1,4536. ᴿREAug 42 (1996) 305-307 (*Braun, René*).

5858 *Schmithals, Walter* Methodische Erwägungen zur Literarkritik der Paulusbriefe. ZNW 87 (1996) 51-82.

5859 *Tescaroli, Cirilo* Las huellas de San Pablo en Damasco y Tesalónica. AcPa 29 (1996) 251-253.

5860 **Thompson, Ian H.** Chiasmus in the Pauline letters. JSNT.S 111: 1995, ⇒11/1,4539. ᴿCBQ 58 (1996) 778-780 (*Paffenroth, Kim*); CritRR 9 (1996) 289-291 (*Weima, Jeffrey A.D.*) [Gal 5,13-6,2].

5861 **Trobisch, David** Paul's letter collection. 1994, ⇒10,5615; 11/1,4541. ᴿCBQ 58 (1996) 172-173 (*Bowe, Barbara E.*).

5862 *Verhoef, Eduard* Die holländische Radikale Kritik. The Corinthian correspondence. BEThL 125: 1996, ⇒6143. 427-432.

5863 **Vidal, Senén** Las cartas originales de Pablo. Estructuras y Proceso, Religión: M 1996, Trotta 489 pp. 84-8164-101-4. ᴿCommunio 29/1 (1996) 114-117 (*Burgos, M. de*); EstAg 31 (1996) 347-348 (*Cineira, D.A.*).

5864 **Weima, Jeffrey A.D.** Neglected endings: the significance of the Pauline letter closings. JSNT.S 101: 1994, ⇒10,5617; 11/1,4545. ᴿEvQ 68 (1996) 246-247 (*Marshall, Howard I.*); CBQ 58 (1996) 781-783 (*Fitzgerald, John T.*); JBL 115 (1996) 557-559 (*Sumney, Jerry L.*).

5865 **Wickert, Ulrich** Studien zu den Pauluskommentaren THEODOR von Mopsuestia. BZNW 27: 1962, ⇒45,3902d; 46,4602c. ᴿThR 61 (1996) 292-294 (*Mühlenberg, Ekkehard*).

5866 **Wiles, Maurice F.** The divine apostle: the interpretation of St. Paul's epistles in the early church. 1967, ⇒49,3621... 52,3632. ᴿThR 61 (1996) 299-300 (*Mühlenberg, Ekkehard*).

5867 **Winninge, Mikael** Sinners and the righteous: a comparative study of the Psalms of Solomon and Paul's letters. CB.NT 26: 1995, ⇒11/1,4547. ᴿSEÅ 61 (1996) 144-147 (*Holmberg, Bengt*).

5868 **Wolter, Hans-Jürgen** Die Zeit des Apostel Paulus: eine paulinische und frühchristliche Chronologie. Theorie und Forschung 415; Theologie 28: Rg 1996, Roderer 64 pp. 3-89073-888-5 [NThAR 1997,101].

G3.3 Pauli theologia

5869 **Adamopoulo, Themistocles Anthony** Endurance, Greek and early christian: the moral transformation of the Greek idea of endurance from Homeric battlefield to the apostle Paul. Diss. Brown 1996, ᴰ*Stowers, S.K.*, 377 pp. [EThL 74,321*].

5870 *Aletti, Jean-Noel* L'apôtre Paul et la parousie de Jésus Christ: l'eschatologie paulinienne et ses enjeux. RSR 84 (1996) 15-41.

5871 *Aune, David E.* Zwei Modelle der menschlichen Natur bei Paulus. ThQ 176 (1996) 28-39.

5872 **Barrett, Charles K.** Paul: an introduction to his thought. 1994, ⇒10,5618; 11/1,4551. ᴿHeyJ 37 (1996) 198-200 (*Way, David*); RB 103 (1996) 290-291 (*Murphy-O'Connor, Jerome*); HBT 18/1 (1996) 112-113 (*Ramsaran, Rollin A.*); JBL 115 (1996) 363-365 (*Soards, Marion L.*);

5873 La teologia di San Paolo: introduzione al pensiero dell'apostolo. Universa Teologia Biblica: CinB 1996, San Paolo 264 pp. L28.000 [RdT 37,719].

5874 **Bielecki, Stanislaw** Kairos chrześcijanina z ujęciu listów św. Pawła [Der Kairos des Christen in den Briefen des Apostels Paulus]. Diss.-Habil. Lublin 1996, Katolickiego Uniwersytetu Lubelskiego 412 pp. 83-228-0564-0 [RTL 29,583]. **P.**

5875 *Bossman, David M.* Paul's fictive kinship movement. BTB 26 (1996) 163-171 [Rom 4,16].

5876 *Chamakalayil, Jacob* Apostolic ministry in its relationship to the mystery of the crucified and risen Christ: a study in major Pauline letters. Laur. 37/1-2 (1996) 281-290 [< Diss. Pont. Inst. Biblicum 1995, ^D*Vanhoye, Albert*].

5877 **Davis, Christopher A.** The structure of Paul's theology. 1995, ⇒11/1,4560. ^RCritRR 9 (1996) 197-199 (*Sumney, Jerry L.*).

5878 *Dunn, James D.G.* Deutero-Pauline letters. ^FHOOKER M., 1996, ⇒43. 130-144.

5879 *Edwards, Gordon Elizabeth* Exploring the implications of Paul's use of Sarx (flesh). Biblical ethics and homosexuality [^E**Brawley, R.L.**]. 1996, ⇒H3.7. 69-86.

5880 **Fee, Gordon D.** God's empowering presence: the Holy Spirit in the letters of Paul. 1994, ⇒10,7529. ^RBibl.Interp. 4 (1996) 235-237 (*Summers, Stephen*); JPentec 8 (1996) 7-21 (*Schweizer, E.*) [NTAb 41,63]; WThJ 58 (1996) 343-347 (*Inman, Benjamin*);

5881 Paul, the Spirit and the people of God. Peabody, MASS 1996, Hendrickson xv; 208 pp. 1-56563-170-6. ^RChristToday 40 (1996) 18-24 (*Zoba, W.M.*) [NTAb 41,66].

5882 **Fitzmyer, Joseph A.** According to Paul: studies in the theology of the apostle. 1993, ⇒9,196... 11/1,4565. ^RAUSS 34 (1996) 120-123 (*Melbourne, Bertram*).

5883 **Gaukesbrink, Martin** Die Sühnetradition bei Paulus: Rezeption und theologischer Stellenwert. Diss. Müns 1996/97, ^D*Kertelge, K.* [BZ 42,317].

5884 *Gräbe, Petrus J.* Καινὴ διαθήκη in der paulinischen Literatur: Ansätze zu einer paulinischen Ekklesiologie. ^FKERTELGE K., 1996, ⇒48. 267-287.

5885 *Grech, Prospero* Formule trinitarie in San Paolo. Atti del IV Simposio di Tarso. 1996, ⇒263. 133-138.

5886 **Hagenow, Stephan** Heilige Gemeinde—sündige Gemeinde: paulinische Denkmodelle im Umgang mit postkonversionaler Sünde. Diss. Heidelberg 1996, ^D*Berger, K.*, 299 pp. [EThL 74,322*].

5887 **Hall, Sydney G.** Christian anti-Semitism and Paul's theology. 1993, ⇒9,5848... 11/1,4567. ^RJJS 47 (1996) 157-158 (*Oakes, Peter*); ThRv 92 (1996) 481-483 (*Mußner, Franz*).

5888 **Horn, Friedrich-Wilhelm** Das Angeld des Geistes: Studien zur paulinischen Pneumatologie. FRLANT 154: 1992, ⇒8,6078... 11/1,4569. ^RBijdr. 57/1 (1996) 83-84 (*Parmentier, Martin*).

5889 **Hübner, Hans** Die Theologie des Paulus. 1993, ⇒9,9650; 10,5636. ^RSEÅ 61 (1996) 159-161 (*Kieffer, René*).

5890 *Kertelge, Karl* Gottes Gerechtigkeit—das Evangelium des Paulus. ^FTHUESING W., NTA 31: 1996, ⇒94. 183-195.

5891 *Kieffer, R.* Teologoi och kristologi hos Paulus och Johannes. SvTK 72 (1996) 25-32.

5892 **Kim, Panim** Die Heilsgegenwart bei Paulus: eine religionsgeschichtlich-theologische Untersuchung zu Sündenvergebung und Geistgabe. Diss. Gö 1996, ^D*Stegemann, H.* [EThL 74,322*].

5893 **Kraus, Wolfgang** Das Volk Gottes: zur Grundelegung der Ekklesiologie bei Paulus. WUNT 2/85: Tü 1996, Mohr xii; 443 pp. DM148. 3-16-146432-X. ^RLuThK 20/2-3 (1996) 142-143 (*Stolle, Volker*).

5894 **Kucharski, Jacek** Religijno-semiotyczne tlo rzeczownikowych
synonimów: soteriologicznych listów sw. Pawla apostola [Pauline
soteriology, linguistic analysis]. Radom 1996, n.p. lxxviii; 453 pp.
Bibl. **P.**

5895 **Maggioni, Bruno** Il Dio di Paolo e il vangelo della grazia.
Cammini nello Spirito 2: Mi 1996, Paoline 232 pp. Bibl. 88-315-
1252-8. RPaVi 41/5 (1996) 56 (*Bagni, Arcangelo*).

5896 **Maleparampil, Joseph** The 'Trinitarian' formulae in St. Paul.
EHS.T 546: 1995, ⇒11/1,4578. REstTrin 30 (1996) 445-446
(*Pikaza, Xabier*).

5897 *Marshall, I.* Howard Salvation, grace and works in the later writings in the Pauline corpus. NTS 42 (1996) 339-358.

5898 *Martinez, Ernest R.* Paul and the Easter gospel. PrPe 10/4 (1996)
149-153.

5899 **McLean, Bradley Hudson** The cursed Christ: Mediterranean expulsion rituals and Pauline soteriology. Diss. D*Guenther, H.O.*,
JSNT.S 126: Shf 1996, Academic 263 pp. £39/$58.50. 1-85075-
589-2 [NTAb 41,160].

5900 *Merklein, Helmut* Der (neue) Bund als Thema der paulinischen
Theologie. ThQ 176 (1996) 290-308;

5901 Paulus und die Sünde. Sünde und Erlösung im NT. QD 161: 1996,
⇒181. 123-163.

5902 *Nardoni, Enrique* Justicia en las cartas paulinas. RevBib 58 (1996)
211-235.

5903 *Pacomio, Luciano* 'Servire' e lo Spirito Santo in San Paolo. Atti
del IV Simposio di Tarso. 1996, ⇒263. 125-132.

5904 **Penna, Romano** [v.1] Jew and Greek alike; [v.2] Wisdom and
folly of the cross. Paul the apostle: a theological and exegetical
study. T*Wahl, Thomas P.* ColMn 1996, Liturgical 2 vols. $35. 0-
8146-5835-0+-912-8.

5905 **Pitta, Antonio** Sinossi paolina. 1994, ⇒10,5644; 11/1,4585. RBib.
77 (1996) 124-128 (*Pastor-Ramos, Federico*); CivCatt 147 II
(1996) 526-527 (*Scaiola, D.*); CBQ 58 (1996) 353-354 (*Collins,
Raymond F.*); MF 96 (1996) 650-651 (*Fanin, Luciano*).

5906 *Pittner, Bertram* Die Gottlosigkeit und ihre Überwindung im Licht
der Paulusbriefe. FFEIEREIS K., EThSt 71: 1996, ⇒24. 19-27.

5907 *Punt, Jeremy* Paul, hermeneutics and the scriptures of Israel.
Neotest. 30 (1996) 377-425.

5908 *Reynier, Chantal* Le langage de la croix dans le corpus paulinien.
Paul de Tarse. LeDiv 165: 1996, ⇒273. 361-373;

5909 Le langage de la croix dans les écrits pauliniens. Spiritus 37 (1996)
60-68.

5910 **Richardson, Neil** Paul's language about God. JSNT.S 99: 1994,
⇒10,5645. RJThS 47 (1996) 221-224 (*Moule, C.F.D.*); JBL 115
(1996) 550-552 (*Sumney, Jerry L.*).

5911 *Riesner, Rainer* Chronologie und Theologie bei Paulus. JETh 10
(1996) 110-122.

5912 *Sanders, E.P.* Paul. FHOOKER M., 1996, ⇒43. 112-129.

5913 **Sandnes, Karl Olav** I tidens fylde: en innføring i Paulus' teologi.
Oslo 1996, Luther 317 pp. NOK248 [TTK 68,160].

5914 *Schlosser, Jacques* Théologie et christologie dans les lettres de
Paul. Paul de Tarse. LeDiv 165: 1996, ⇒273. 331-359.

5915 *Sellin, Gerhard* Die religionsgeschichtlichen Hintergründe der paulinischen "Christusmystik". ThQ 176 (1996) 7-27.

5916 Smith, Morton Pauline worship as seen by pagans. New Testament. 1996 <1980>, ⇒151. 95-102.

5917 Tamez, Elsa Gegen die Verurteilung zum Tod: Paulus oder die Rechtfertigung durch den Glauben aus der Perspektive der Unterdrückten und Ausgeschlossenen. FrS 1996, Exodus.

5918 Taubes, Jacob Die politische Theologie des Paulus: Vorträge, gehalten an der Forschungsstätte der evangelischen Studiengemeinschaft in Heidelberg 23.-27. Februar 1987 [<Tonband]. EAssmann, Aleida; Assmann, Jan, Mü 1993, Fink 200 pp. DM38. 3-7705-2844-1. RZKTh 188 (1996) 249-252 (Palaver, Wolfgang).

5919 Treiyer, Enrique B. Saint Paul et l'horizon de l'au-delà de la mort. Sum. diss. 1996, DSevrin, J.-M., TDL.T 16, Fasc. 1 sect. théologie.

5920 Trevijano Etcheverría, R. La evolución de la escatología paulina. Carthaginensia 12 (1996) 125-153.

5921 Vanni, U. La creazione in Paolo: una prospettiva di teologia biblica. La natura. 1996, ⇒189. 201-259.

5922 Wilt, Timothy 'Jesus' and 'Christ' in Paul's letters. BiTr 47 (1996) 230-232.

5923 Wischmeyer, Oda φύσις und κτίσις bei Paulus: die paulinische Rede von Schöpfung und Natur. ZThK 93 (1996) 352-375.

5924 Witherington, Ben Paul's narrative thought world. 1994, ⇒10,5591; 11/1,4596. RPSB 17/1 (1996) 103-104 (Reumann, John); RRT (1996/2) 62-64 (Chaplin, Doug); CBQ 58 (1996) 176-177 (Craffert, Pieter F.); JBL 115 (1996) 552-554 (Fisk, Bruce N.).

G3.4 Pauli stylus et modus operandi—Paul's image

5925 Blumenfeld, Bruno Classical and Hellenistic sources for the political Paul. Diss. NY, Union 1996-97 [RTL 29,583].

5926 Bollók, János The description of Paul in the Acta Pauli. Apocryphal Acts of Paul. 1996, ⇒450. 1-15.

5927 Cirignano, Giulio; Montuschi, Ferdinando La personalità di Paolo: un approccio psicologico alle lettere paoline. CSB 27: Bo 1996, Dehoniane 224 pp. L32.000. 88-10-40728-8 [BeO 39,63].

5928 Czachesz, István The Acts of Paul and the western text of Luke's Acts: Paul between canon and apocrypha. Apocryphal Acts of Paul. 1996, ⇒450. 107-125.

5929 Dewey, Arthur J. Spirit and letter in Paul. Studies in the Bible and early Christianity 33: Lewiston, NY 1996, Mellen xxii; 231 pp. 0-7734-9703-X.

5930 Dodd, B.J. The problem with Paul. DG 1996, IVP 180 pp. $13. 0-8308-1871-5 [NTAb 41,158].

5931 Eisenman, Robert Paul as Herodian. JHiC 3 (1996) 110-122.

5932 Elliott, Neil Liberating Paul: the justice of God and the politics of the apostle. BiSe 27: 1995, ⇒11/1,4600. R RRT (1996/1) 29-34 (Campbell, W.S.); Dialog 35/I (1996) 65-66 (Rieke, LuVern V.); CBQ 58 (1996) 546-547 (Mitchell, Margaret M.); JBL 115 (1996) 554-557 (Witherington III, Ben).

5933 EEngberg-Pedersen, Troels Paul in his Hellenistic context. 1995, ⇒11/1,4601. Pacifica 9 (1996) 215-216 (Byrne, Brendan).

5934. *Harnisch, Wolfgang* "Toleranz" im Denken des Paulus?: eine exegetisch-hermeneutische Vergewisserung. EvTh 56/1 (1996) 64-82.

5935 **Heininger, Bernhard** Paulus als Visionär: eine religionsgeschichtliche Studie. Herder's Biblical Studies 9: FrB 1996, Herder x; 343 pp. DM78. 3-451-26157-8.

5936 **Jewett, Robert** Saint Paul at the movies: the apostle's dialogue with American culture. 1993, ⇒9,5871... 11/1,4604. ᴿTJT 12 (1996) 101-102 (*Graham, Susan Lochrie*).

5937 *Kangas, R.* The pattern of Paul and the religion of James. Affirmation & Critique 1/3 (1996) 32-43 [NTAb 41,64].

5938 **Klumbies, Paul-Gerhard** Die Rede von Gott bei Paulus in ihrem zeitgeschichtlichen Kontext. FRLANT 155: 1992, ⇒8,6108; 10,5667. ᴿThLZ 121 (1996) 1156-1158 (*Holtz, Traugott*).

5939 *Livio, Jean-Bernard* Paul, misogyne?. Choisir 437 (1996) 13-16.

5940 **Malina, Bruce J.** Portraits of Paul: an archaeology of ancient personality. LVL 1996, Westminster xv; 271 pp. $23. 0-664-25681-3 [ET 108,314].

5941 *Mosetto, Francesco* La figura di Paolo nei panegirici di San Giovanni CRISOSTOMO. Atti del IV Simposio di Tarso. 1996, ⇒263. 205-218.

5942 *Neyrey, Jerome H.* Luke's social location of Paul: cultural anthropology and the status of Paul in Acts. History in Acts. 1996, ⇒5223. 251-279.

5943 **Palmer, Gesine** Ein Freispruch für Paulus: John TOLANDS Theorie des Judenchristentums. ᴱ*Palmer, Claus-Michael*, ANTZ 7: B 1996, Institut Kirche und Judentum 184 pp. Mit einer Neuausgabe von Tolands 'Nazarenus' von Claus-Michael Palmer. 3-923095-89-9.

5944 **Stanley, Christopher D.** Paul and the language of scripture: citation technique in the Pauline epistles and contemporary literature. MSSNTS 69: 1992, ⇒8,6127... 10,5674. ᴿEvQ 68 (1996) 360-362 (*Rosner, Brian S.*).

5945 ᴱ**Swüste, Gerard** De handelingen van Paulus: portret van een bevlogen gelovige. Zoetermeer 1996, Meinema 79 pp. *f*18.90. 90-211-3651-1.

5946 *Zeller, Dieter* Selbstbezogenheit und Selbstdarstellung in den Paulusbriefen. ThQ 176 (1996) 40-52.

5947 **Ziesler, John** Pauline Christianity. 1990, ⇒7,5248; 8,6132. ᴿRB 103 (1996) 139-140 (*Murphy-O'Connor, Jerome*).

G3.5 **Apostolus Gentium** [⇒G4.6, Israel et Lex / Jews & Law]

5948 **Adinolfi, Marco** Da Antiochia a Roma: con Paolo nel mondo greco-romano. CinB 1996, San Paolo 238 pp. L48.000. 88-215-3290-9 [RdT 38,141].

5949 *Barclay, John M.G.* "Neither Jew nor Greek": multiculturalism and the new perspective on Paul. Ethnicity. BiblInterp. 19: 1996, ⇒171. 197-214.

5950 **Baslez, Marie-Françoise** Paolo di Tarso: l'apostolo delle genti. 1993, ⇒9,5880; 10,5675. ᴿOrph. 17 (1996) 485-486 (*Milazzo, Vincenza*).

5951 **Becker, Jürgen** Paolo l'apostolo dei popoli. Introd. *Penna, R.*, BiBi(B) 20: Brescia 1996, Queriniana 478 pp. L75.000. 88-399-2020-X [RdT 37,427];

5952 Paul: l'apôtre des nations. 1995, ⇒11/1,4612. REeV 106 (1996) 276-277 (*Cothenet, Édouard*).

5953 Pablo: el apóstol de los paganos. Biblioteca de Estudios Bíblicos 83: S 1996, Sígueme 575 pp. 84-301-1276-6. RCommunio 29/1 (1996) 117-120 (*Burgos, M. de*); RevAg 37 (1996) 1183-1185 (*Sabugal, Santos*); EstAg 31 (1996) 578-579 (*Mielgo, C.*); EstTrin 30 (1996) 452-453 (*Pikaza, Xabier*).

5954 **Boyarin, Daniel** A radical Jew: Paul and the politics of identity. 1994, ⇒10,5677. RPSB 17/1 (1996) 101-103 (*Scroggs, Robin*); IBSt 18 (1996) 222-224 (*McCullough, J.C.*); HeyJ 37 (1996) 198-200 (*Way, David*); JJS 47 (1996) 372-374 (*Rowland, Christopher*); AJSR 21 (1996) 148-151 (*Himmelfarb, Martha*).

5955 **Carrillo Alday, Salvador** Pablo, apóstol de Cristo. EstB 13: 1995, ⇒11/1,4618. REfMex 14 (1996) 397-398 (*Lugo Rodríguez, Raúl H.*).
EDunn, J.D.G. Paul and the Mosaic law ⇒255.

5956 **Freed, Edwin D.** The apostle Paul, christian Jew: faithfulness and law. 1994, ⇒10,5682. RCBQ 58 (1996) 744-746 (*Boisclair, Regina A.*); CritRR 9 (1996) 202-204 (*Johnson, E. Elizabeth*).

5957 **Hollingsworth, R. Maurice** Eschatology: the bridge between Pauline thought and missionary methods. Diss. Southwestern Bapt. Theol. Sem. 1996, 266 pp. [EThL 74,322*].

5958 **Horie, Hildegard** Paulus: Apostel nach Gottes Willen. Bibel Live: Stu 1996, Hänssler 357 pp. 3-7751-2448-9 [NThAR 1997,260].

5959 *Ingelaere, Jean-Claude* Paul et l'exercice de l'autorité apostolique. Paul de Tarse. LeDiv 165: 1996, ⇒273. 119-138.

5960 *Smith, Morton* Paul's arguments as evidence of the christianity from which he diverged. New Testament. 1996 <1986>, ⇒151. 103-109.

5961 **Tomić, C.** Začetki Cerkva—Pavel, apostol narodov. 1995, ⇒11/1,4624. RBogoslovni Vestnik 56/2 (1996) 249-252 (*Rozman, Francè*). **Croatian.**

5962 **Wood, Edwin Jackson** The social world of the ancient craftsmen as a model for understanding Paul's mission. Diss. Southwestern Bapt. Theol. Sem. 1995, 238 pp. [EThL 74,321*].

G3.6 *Pauli fundamentum* **philosophicum** [G4.3] *et* **morale**

5963 *Alvarez Verdes, Lorenzo* La función de la "razón" en el pensamiento ético de S. Pablo. Sum. 41; rés. 42. StMor 34/1 (1996) 7-42.

5964 **Finsterbusch, Karin** Die Thora als Lebensweisung für Heidenschristen: Studien zur Bedeutung der Thora für die paulinische Ethik. Diss. DBurchard, C., StUNT 20: Gö 1996, Vandenhoeck & R. 221 pp. DM68. 3-525-53375-6.

5965 **Laato, Timo** Paul and Judaism: an anthropological approach. SFSHJ 115: 1995, ⇒11/1,4634. RRB 103 (1996) 623-624 (*Murphy-O'Connor, J.*).

5966 *Lee, Han S.* Ethics and charisma: a study of their relationship in Paul's letters. Chongshin Review 1 (1996) 31-67 [Amos 1,3-2,16].

5967 *Lichtenberger, Hermann* Das Tora-Verständnis im Judentum zur Zeit des Paulus: eine Skizze. Paul and the Mosaic law. WUNT 89: 1996, ⇒255. 7-23.
5968 *Mathewson, Dave* Verbal aspect in imperatival constructions in Pauline ethical injunctions. FgNT 9 (1996) 21-35.
5969 **Matlock, R. Barry** Unveiling the apocalyptic Paul: Paul's interpreters and the rhetoric of criticism. JSNT.S 127: Shf 1996, Academic 361 pp. £43. 1-85075-590-6.
5970 **O'Toole, Robert F.** Chi è cristiano?: saggio sull'etica paolina. 1995, ⇒11/1,4641. [R]StMor 34 (1996) 535-539 (*Alvarez Verdes, L.*).
5971 *Purvis, Sally B.* Following Paul: some notes on ethics then and now. Word and World 16 (1996) 413-419 [ZID 23,14].
5972 [E]**Rosner, Brian S.** Understanding Paul's ethics. 1995, ⇒11/1,110. [R]CThMi 23 (1996) 454 (*Linss, Wilhelm C.*).
5973 **Söding, Thomas** Das Liebesgebot bei Paulus. NTA 26: 1994, ⇒10,5705. Sal. 58 (1996) 382-383 (*Abbà, G.*); CBQ 58 (1996) 362-363 (*Perkins, Pheme*); RB 103 (1996) 625-627 (*Murphy-O'Connor, J.*); CritRR 9 (1996) 275-277 (*Siker, Jeffrey S.*) [1 Cor 8; 13].
5974 **Warne, Graham John** Hebrew perspectives on the human person in the Hellenistic era: PHILO and Paul. 1995, ⇒11/1,4653. [R]StPhilo 8 (1996) 205-207 (*Hay, David M.*).
5975 **Zürner, Bernhard** Paulus ohne Gott: eine charakterologische Untersuchung. Bonn 1996, Bouvier 826 pp. 3-416-02619-5 [NThAR 1997,70].

G3.7 *Pauli* communitates *et* spiritualitas

5976 **Ade, Annegret** Sklaverei und Freiheit bei PHILO von Alexandria als Hintergrund der paulinischen Aussagen zur Sklaverei. Diss. Heidelberg 1996, [D]*Theißen, G.*, 281 pp. [EThL 74,321*].
5977 **Ahiarajah, S.W.** Did I betray the gospel?: the letters of Paul and the place of women. Risk Book 70: Geneva 1996, WCC Publications xiv; 58 pp. FS9.90. 2-8254-1183-3 [NTAb 41,155].
5978 *Campbell, Douglas A.* A Reformational slogan on ministry and Paul's gospel of grace. [F]JAMIESON P., 1996, ⇒44. 51-72.
5979 **Carson, Donald** A call to spiritual reformation: priorities from Paul and his prayers. 1992, ⇒9,5905. [R]SBET 14/2 (1996) 172-173 (*McFarlane, Graham*).
5980 *Claudel, Gérard* L'héritage chrétien de Paul. Paul de Tarse. LeDiv 165: 1996, ⇒273. 243-266.
5981 *Destro, A.; Pesce, M.* "Liminality" and "wholeness": the church and those "outside" according to St. Paul (humano-sociological aspect). DBM 15/1 (1996) 38-51.
5982 *Franco, Ettore* Chiesa come koinōnía: immagini, realtà, mistero. Sum. 192. RivBib 44 (1996) 157-192.
5983 *Gnilka, Joachim* Die Kollekte der paulinischen Gemeinden für Jerusalem als Ausdruck ekklesialer Gemeinschaft. [F]KERTELGE K., 1996, ⇒48. 301-315.
5984 **Hagenow, Gabriele** Der Tempel der Christen: traditionsgeschichtliche Untersuchungen zur Aufnahme des Tempelkonzepts im

frühen Christentum. Diss. Heidelberg 1996, ᴰ*Berger, K.*, 277 pp. [EThL 74,287*].

5985 *Hahn, Ferdinand* Die Einheit der Kirche nach dem Zeugnis des Apostels Paulus. ᶠKᴇRTELGE K., 1996, ⇒48. 288-300.

5986 *Hu, Maria Teresa* The trinitarian spirituality of St. Paul. CTUF 108 (1996) 201-218 [ThIK 18/1,28]. C.

5987 **Kloppenborg, John S.** Egalitarianism in the myth and rhetoric of Pauline churches. ᶠMᴀCK B., 1996. 247-263.

5988 **MacDonald, Margaret Y.** Las comunidades paulinas. 1994, ⇒10,5711; 11/1,4668. ᴿREsp 55 (1996) 153-154 (*Martínez, Emilio*).

5989 *Marguerat, Daniel* La mystique de l'apôtre Paul. Paul de Tarse. LeDiv 165: 1996, ⇒273. 307-329.

5990 *Marshall, Christopher D.* 'For me to live is Christ': Pauline spirituality as a basis for ministry. ᶠJAMIESON P., 1996, ⇒44. 96-116.

5991 **Monga Ngoy, Gédéon** Language cultuel appliqué aux croyants chez Paul: significations théologiques et éthiques de la symbolique cultuelle paulinienne pour une église africaine. Diss. Bruxelles ᴰ*Lejeune, C.*, 1996, 368 pp. [EThL 74,323*].

5992 **Pesce, Mauro** Le due fasi della predicazione di Paolo: dall'evangelizzazione alla guida delle comunità. CSB 22: 1994, ⇒10,5712; 11/1,4670. ᴿRB 103 (1996) 294-295 (*Murphy-O'Connor, Jerome*); CritRR 9 (1996) 253-255 (*Zilonka, Paul*);

5993 As duas fases da pregação de Paulo. ᵀ*Bagno, Marcos*, Bíblica Loyola 20: São Paulo 1996, Loyola 254 pp. 85-15-01359-9 [PerTeol 29,134].

5994 *Pesce, Mauro; Destro, Adriana* Identità nella comunità paolina: santi e fratelli. Atti del IV Simposio di Tarso. 1996, ⇒263. 107-124.

5995 **Pinckaers, S.** La vita spirituale del cristiano secondo San Paolo e San TᴏᴍᴍᴀSᴏ d'Aquino. Mi 1996, Jaca 261 pp. [AnnTh 11,250ss—Bosch, Vicente].

5996 *Plymale, S.F.* Paul, prayer, and presence. Listening 31/2 (1996) 152-164 [NTAb 41,65].

5997 **Schmeller, Thomas K.** Hierarchie und Egalität: eine sozialgeschichtliche Untersuchung paulinischer Gemeinden und griechischrömischer Vereine. SBS 162: 1995, ⇒11/1,4676. ᴿThLZ 121 (1996) 837-839 (*Schenk, Wolfgang*); ITS 33 (1996) 164-166 (*Legrand, L.*); SNTU.A 21 (1996) 271-272 (*Niemand, Chr.*).

5998 *Theobald, Michael* "Allen bin ich alles geworden ..." (1 Kor 9,22b): Paulus und das Problem der Inkulturation des Glaubens. ThQ 176 (1996) 1-6.

5999 *Vidal Manzanares, César* El esoterismo: análisis desde los escritos de Pablo de Tarso. BiFe 22 (1996) 370-395.

6000 *Yount, W.R.* The pastor as teacher. SWJT 39 (1996) 15-23.

G3.8 *Pauli receptio*, history of research

6001 **Babcock, William S.** Paul and the legacies of Paul. 1990, ⇒6,510...11/1,4481. ᴿThR 61 (1996) 302-306 (*Mühlenberg, Ekkehard*).

6002 **Beker, J. Christiaan** Heirs of Paul: their legacy in the New Testament and the church today. GR 1996, Eerdmans 146 pp. $16. 0-8028-4256-9 [NTS 43,620].

6003 **Fabris, Rinaldo** La tradizione paolina. 1995, ⇒11/1,4681. REccl(M) 10 (1996) 342-343 (*Izquierdo, A.*); Asp. 43 (1996) 422-423 (*Rolla, A.*); Lat. 62 (1996) 632-634 (*Penna, Romano*).

6004 E**Feld, Helmut** Johannes CALVINUS: commentarii in Pauli epistolas ad Gal, Eph, Phil, Col. Ioannis Calvini opera 16. 1992, ⇒8,6187; 11/1,4682. RZwing. 23 (1996) 203-206 (*Saxer, Ernst*).

6005 **Jewett, Robert** Paul the apostle to America... Pauline scholarship. 1994, ⇒10,5719. RMid-Stream 35 (1996) 233-234 (*Baird, William R.*); CTJ 31 (1996) 254-257 (*DeBoer, Willis R.*); NewTR 9/2 (1996) 95-96 (*Reid, Barbara*); CBQ 58 (1996) 155-156 (*Getty, Mary Ann*); JSNT 63 (1996) 125-126 (*Reed, Jeffrey T.*).

6006 E**Martel, Gérard de** Expositiones Pauli Epistolarum ad Romanos, Galathas et Ephesios e codice Sancti Michaelis in periculo Maris. Avranches, Bibl. mun. 79. CChr.CM 151: Turnhout 1995, Brepols xli; 304 pp. 2-503-04511-1. RRHE 91 (1996) 541-544 (*Dolbeau, François*).

G3.9 *Themata particularia de Paulo*, details

6007 *Adinolfi, Marco* Le immagini militari nelle diatribe di EPITTETO: un confronto con l'epistolario paolino. Atti del IV Simposio di Tarso. 1996, ⇒263. 59-72.

6008 **Alves, Manuel Isidro** Sagrado e santidade: simbolismo da linguagem cultual em S. Paulo. Fundamenta 16: Lisboa 1996, Didaskalia 137 pp. = Did(L) 26/1 (1996) 3-115.

6009 *Beaude, Pierre-Marie* Psychologie et exégèse paulinienne;

6010 Le travail de Paul sur les modèles d'appartenance socioreligieux et sociopolitiques;

6011 *Boespflug, François* La conversion de Paul dans l'art médiéval. Paul de Tarse. LeDiv 165: 1996, ⇒273. 99-118/139-146/147-168.

6012 *Brossier, François* Chair et corps selon saint Paul. Alliance 106-107 (1996) 82-83.

6013 *Coulot, Claude* L'Esprit Saint et la connaissance. Paul de Tarse. LeDiv 165: 1996, ⇒273. 207-221.

6014 **Frazier, Charles David** A comparison of the function of cultic aim in the Pauline corpus with that of non-rabbinic Judaism and the mystery cults. Diss. New Orleans Bapt. Theol. Sem. 1996, D*Simmons, Billy*, 225 pp. DAI-A 57/07, p. 3075; AAC 9640216.

6015 *Gaventa, B.R.* Our mother St. Paul: toward the recovery of a neglected theme. PSB 17 (1996) 29-44.

6016 *Greisch, Jean* La facticité chrétienne: HEIDEGGER, lecteur de Saint Paul. RICP 60 (1996) 85-101.

6017 **Henderson, Walter Eugene, Jr.** Paul's use of athletic imagery. Diss. New Orleans Baptist Theol. Sem. 1996, D*Simmons, Billy E.*, 160 pp. DAI-A 57/07, p. 3076; AAC 9628015.

6018 *Ordon, Hubert* Pawłowa argumentacja na rzecz niesienia pomocy potrzebujacym [Die paulinische Argumentation für die Kollecte zum Besten der armen Christen]. Zsfg. 82. Vox Patrum 16 (1996) 75-83. **P.**

6019 *Pratscher, Wilhelm* Die Bewältigung von Leid bei Paulus. SNTU.A 21 (1996) 73-91.

6020 **Saß, Gerhard** Leben aus den Verheißungen... Paulus. FRLANT 164: 1995, ⇒11/1,4703. RThLZ 121 (1996) 1059-1061 (*Haufe, Günter*).

6021 *Thacker, A.* Was Paul a sexist?. EpworthRev 23/1 (1996) 85-94 [NTAb 40,441].

6022 *Troiani, Lucio* Giudei e greci. FMOSCATI S., 1996, ⇒67. 415-422.

6023 *Trumper, Tim* The metaphorical import of adoption: a plea for realisation I: the adoption metaphor in biblical usage. SBET 14 (1996) 129-145.

6024 **Van Spanje, Teunis Erik** Inconsistentie bij Paulus?: een confrontatie met het werk van Heikki RAEISAENEN. Diss. Kampen, DVan Bruggen, K., Kampen 1996, Kok xv; 237 pp. ƒ49.50. 90-242-7856-2.

G4.1 **Ad Romanos** *Textus, commentarii*

6025 EAland, Barbara; Jucket, Andreas Römer- und 1. Korintherbrief. NT syr, 2. ANTT 14: 1991, ⇒7,5249; 8,6204. RBiOr 53 (1996) 182-189 (*Brock, Sebastian P.*).

6026 **Bénétreau, Samuel** L'épître de Paul aux Romans. Commentaire Évangélique de la Bible 1: Vaux-sur-Seine 1996, Edifac 256 pp. 2-904407-16-2 [NThAR 1997,35].

6027 **Bence, Clarence L.** Romans: a bible commentary in the Wesleyan tradition. Indianapolis, Ind. 1996, Wesleyan 248 pp. 0-89827-157-6 [NThAR 1997,260].

6028 **Bowen, Roger** A guide to Romans. SPCK International Study Guide 11: L ²1996, SPCK xi; 244 pp. 0-281-04953-X.

6029 *Breen, Aidan* The biblical text and sources of the Würzburg Pauline glosses (Romans 1-6). Irland und Europa im früheren Mittelalter / Ireland and Europe in the early Middle Ages. ENí Chatáin, Próinséas; Richter, Michael, Stu 1996, Klett-Cotta. 9-16 [RBen 106,409].

6030 TEBruyn, Theodore de, PELAGIUS's commentary on... Romans. 1993, ⇒9,5940; 10,5731. RJEH 47/1 (1996) 131-133 (*Bammel, C.P.*); Gn. 68 (1996) 462-463 (*Kannengiesser, Charles*); Latomus 55 (1996) 665-667 (*Duval, Y.-M.*).

6031 **Byrne, Brendan** Romans. Sacra Pagina 6: ColMn 1996, Liturgical xix; 503 pp. $30. 0-8146-5808-3 [NTAb 41,157].

6032 EEymann, Hugo S. Einleitung. Epistula ad Romanos. BVLI 21: FrB 1996, Herder 80 pp. 1. Lief. 3-451-00181-0 [RB 104,472].

6033 **Fitzmyer, Joseph A.** Romans. AncB 33: 1993, ⇒9,5945... 11/1,4713. RPrPe 10 (1996) 164-165 (*Ashton, John*); AUSS 34 (1996) 123-124 (*Badenas, Roberto*).

6034 EFrede, Hermann Josef; Stanjek, Herbert SEDULII SCOTTI collectaneum in apostolum, I: in epistolam ad Romanos. Collectanea in omnes beati Pauli epistulas. AGLB 31: FrB 1996, Herder 57* (2) 346 pp. 3-451-21952-2.

6035 *Goudineau, H.* LUTHER et CALVIN: commentateurs de l'Épître aux Romains: une comparaison. PosLuth 44 (1996) 16-52.

6036 *Grayston, Kenneth* Reading the book 3: Paul's letter to the Romans. ET 108 (1996) 68-71.

6037 ᵀHeither, Theresia ORIGENES: commentari in epistolam ad Romanos: Römerbriefkommentar: fünftes und sechstes Buch: siebtes und achtes Buch: lateinisch und deutsch. ᴱ*Brox, Norbert,* FC 2-4 [3: ⇒9,5947]: FrB 1993-1994, Herder 340; 344 pp. 3-451-22208-6/109-8. ᴿZKTh 188 (1996) 298-299 (*Lies, Lothar*);

6038 ORIGENES: commentarii in epistulam ad Romanos, 5: liber nonus, liber decimus. Fontes Christiani 2: FrB 1996, Herder 312 pp. DM46. 3-451-22122-5/222-1.

6039 **Lémonon, Jean-Pierre** Romains, Galates. P 1996, Bayard 240 pp. FF125. 2-227-36606-0 [BCLF 583,1119].

6040 **Lee, Eun-Jae** Philipp Jakob SPENER als Bibelausleger: eine Untersuchung seiner Römerbrieferklärung (1677). Diss. Tü 1996, 258 pp.

6041 ᵀᴱMara, Maria Grazia AGOSTINO interprete di Paolo... Romani. LCPM 16: 1993, ⇒9,5949; 10,5737*. ᴿRSLR 32 (1996) 447-450 (*Mazzucco, Clementina*).

6042 ᴱMills, Watson Early Romans. Bibliographies for biblical research. NT 6: Lewiston, NY 1996, Mellen xix; 205 pp. 0-7734-2418-0.

6043 **Moo, Douglas J.** The epistle to the Romans. New Internat. Comment. on the NT: GR 1996, Eerdmans xxv; 1012 pp. $50. 0-8028-2317-3. ᴿCommunio 29/2-3 (1996) 393-395 (*Burgos, M. de*).

6044 **Osculati, Roberto** La lettera ai Romani: letture dal Nuovo Testamento. Spiritualità del nostro tempo: Mi 1996, Istituto di Propaganda Libraria 246 pp. 88-7836-350-2.

6045 **Perrella, Ettore** Lettera ai Romani. Trans. e commento; Introd. *Brena, Gian Luigi,* Arché 1: Padova 1996, Panda 126 pp.

6046 **Reller, Jobst** Mose BAR KEPHA und seine Paulinenauslegung nebst Edition und Übersetzung des Kommentars zum Römerbrief. GOF.S 35: 1994, ⇒10,5739. ᴿThLZ 121 (1996) 172-174 (*Wiefel, Wolfgang*).

6047 ᴱSider, Robert D. ERASMUS: annotations on Romans. Collected works of Erasmus 56. 1994, ⇒10,5741. ᴿSCJ 27 (1996) 281-283 (*Young, Archibald M.*); EHR 111 (1996) 971-972 (*Scribner, R.W.*); JThS 47 (1996) 755-758 (*Brooks, Peter Newman*).

6048 **Stendahl, Krister** Final account: Paul's letter to the Romans. 1995, ⇒11/1,4727. ᴿThTo 53 (1996) 396, 398 (*Pickett, Ray*); SvTK 72 (1996) 178-180 (*Grenholm, Cristina*).

6049 **Stuhlmacher, Peter** Paul's letter to the Romans. 1994, ⇒10,5743. ᴿVJTR 60 (1996) 482-483 (*Meagher, P.M.*); Interp. 50 (1996) 432, 434 (*Carlson, Richard*).

6050 *Tseng, Thomas* The motive for which Paul wrote *Romans.* CTUF 110 (1996) 531-542 [ThIK 18/2 (1997) 32]. C.

6051 **Wagner, Günter** Romans and Galatians. An exegetical bibliography of the NT, 4. Macon, GA 1996, Mercer Univ. Press xiv; 379 pp. $40. 0-86554-468-9.

6052 *Wengert, Timothy J.* Philip MELANCHTHON's 1522 Annotations on Romans and the Lutheran origins of rhetorical criticism. ᶠSTEINMETZ D., 1996, ⇒86. 118-140.

G4.2 *Ad Romanos: themata*, **topics**

6053 **Boers, Hendrikus** The justification of the gentiles... Gal, Rom.
1994, ⇒10,5748. [R]CBQ 58 (1996) 149-150 (*Morton, Russel*); ETR
71 (1996) 595-596 (*Campbell, Gordon*); JThS 47 (1996) 622-624
(*Dunn, James D.G.*).

6054 *Borse, Udo* Die geschichtliche und theologische Einordnung des
Römerbriefes. [F]Borse, U., SBAB 21: 1996 <1972>, ⇒9. 236-
250.

6055 [E]**Cipriani, S.** La lettera ai Romani ieri e oggi. 1995, ⇒11/1,74.
[R]Angelicum 73 (1996) 437-438 (*Jurič, Stipe*).

6056 [E]**Donfried, Karl P.** The Romans debate. [2]1991, ⇒7,298...
11/1,4733. [R]RTR 55 (1996) 44-45 (*Milne, Douglas J.W.*).

6057 **Garlington, Don B.** Faith, obedience and perseverance... Romans.
1994, ⇒10,5749. [R]CBQ 58 (1996) 787-788 (*Byrne, Brendan*);
CritRR 9 (1996) 207-209 (*deSilva, David A.*).

6058 **Guerra, Anthony J.** Romans and the apologetic tradition.
MSSNTS 81: 1995, ⇒11/1,4736. [R]JThS 47 (1996) 226-230 (*Bell,
Richard H.*); AThR 78 (1996) 503-504 (*Tobin, Thomas H.*); CBQ
58 (1996) 750-751 (*Crawford, Barry S.*); CritRR 9 (1996) 221-223
(*Ascough, Richard S.*).

6059 *Jervis, L. Ann* Becoming like God through Christ: discipleship in
Romans. Patterns of discipleship. 1996, ⇒188. 143-162.

6060 *Mattison, M.M.* Judaizers and justification: bridging the gap between contemporary Pauline studies and New Testament theology.
JournRadRef 5/2 (1996) 3-30 [NTAb 40,439].

6061 **Mosher, Steve** God's power, Jesus' faith, and world mission: a
study in Romans. Scottdale, PA 1996, Herald 360 pp. $20. 0-
8361-9031-9 [NTAb 41,161].

6062 **Nanos, Mark D.** The mystery of Romans: the Jewish context of
Paul's letter. Mp 1996, Fortress ix; 435 pp. $25. 0-8006-2937-X
[JSJ 28,345]. [R]BiRe 12/6 (1996) 16, 53-54 (*Walters, James C.*).

6063 *Pani, Giancarlo* Culto e purità rituale nella *Lettera ai romani*:
Lefevre d'Etaples, Erasmo e Lutero. ASE 13/1 (1996)
257-289.

6064 *Porter, C.L.* Romans and the reformation of community. Encounter
57/1 (1996) 1-21 [NTAb 40,442].

6065 *Raabe, P.R.* The law and christian sanctification: a look at Romans;

6066 *Raabe, P.R.; Voelz, J.W.* Why exhort a good tree?: anthropology
and parenesis in Romans. ConcJourn 22/2 (1996) 178-185/154-163
[NTAb 40,442].

6067 *Trakatellis, Dimitrios* Being transformed: Chrysostom's exegesis of the epistle to the Romans. Die Väter legen aus. 1996, ⇒153.
65-91. **G**.

G4.3 *Naturalis cognitio Dei*, **Rom 1-5**

6068 **Moores, John D.** Wrestling with rationality in Paul: Romans 1-8.
MSSNTS 82: 1995, ⇒11/1,4748. [R]JThS 47 (1996) 619-621
(*Thiselton, Anthony C.*); AThR 78 (1996) 664-665 (*Tobin, Thomas
H.*).

6069 Lloyd-Jones, David M. Il vangelo di Dio. Mantova 1994, Passag-
      gio/Om 319 pp. ^RSdT 8/1 (1996) 73 (*Ciniello, Nino*) [1,1-17].
6070 *Müller, Ulrich B.* "Sohn Gottes"—ein messianischer Hoheitstitel
      Jesu. ZNW 87 (1996) 1-32 [1,3-4].
6071 *Pedersen, Per Damgaard* Romerbrevet 1,18-32: skriftanvendelse,
      teologiske hovedlinjer og retorisk funktion. IXΘΤΣ 23/1 (1996) 4-
      14.
6072 **Smith, Richard Lester** The supremacy of God in apologetics:
      Romans 1:19-21 and the transcendental method of Cornelius VAN
      TIL. Diss. Westminster Theol. Sem. 1996, ^D*Edgar, William*, 310
      pp. DAI-A 57/06, p. 2530; AAC 9634685.
6073 *Smith, Mark D.* Ancient bisexuality and the interpretation of Ro-
      mans 1:26-27. JAAR 64 (1996) 223-256.
6074 *Rogers, Eugene F.* THOMAS and BARTH in convergence on Ro-
      mans 1?. MoTh 12 (1996) 57-84.

6075 *Mijoga, Hilary B.P.* An approach to Christian mission in Africa:
      Paul's approach in Rom 2:13 and 3:20a. JTSA 95 (1996) 55-62
      [ThIK 18/2,22].
6076 *Wright, N.T.* The law in Romans 2. Paul and the Mosaic law.
      WUNT 89: 1996, ⇒176. 131-150.
6077 *Boyarin, Daniel* The Jews in neo-Lutheran interpretations of Paul.
      Dialog 35 (1996) 193-198 [2].

6078 *Hays, Richard B.* Three dramatic roles: the law in Romans 3-4.
      Paul and the Mosaic law. WUNT 89: 1996, ⇒176. 151-164.
6079 *Stegemann, Wolfgang* Der Tod Jesu als Opfer?: anthropologische
      Aspekte seiner Deutung im Neuen Testament. Abschied von der
      Schuld?: zur Anthropologie und Theologie von Schuldbekenntnis,
      Opfer und Versöhnung [^E**Riess, Richard**]. Theologische Akzente
      1: Stu 1996, Kohlhammer. 120-139 [3,25].
6080 **Neubrand, Maria** Abraham—Vater von Juden und Nichtjuden:
      eine exegetische Studie zu Röm 4. Diss. Mü 1996/97, ^D*Laub* [BZ
      42,317].

6081 *Bammel, C.P.* Patristic exegesis of Romans 5:7. JThS 47 (1996)
      532-542.
6082 *Gómez Velasco, F.* Por un solo hombre: estudio exegético de Rm
      5,12-21. Mayéutica 22 (1996) 9-65 [ZID 22,451].
6083 *Hofius, Otfried* Die Adam-Christus-Antithese und das Gesetz:
      Erwägungen zu Röm 5,12-21. Paul and the Mosaic law. WUNT
      89: 1996, ⇒176. 165-206.
6084 *Poirier, John C.* Romans 5:13-14 and the universality of law. NT
      38 (1996) 344-358.
6085 **Reid, Marty L.** Augustinian and Pauline rhetoric in Romans five:
      a study of early christian rhetoric. Mellen 30: Lewiston, NY 1996,
      Mellen (8) vii; 200 pp. £50. 0-7734-2367-2.

G4.4 *Redemptio cosmica:* **Rom 6-8**

6086 *Bligh, John* Baptismal transformation of the gentile world. HeyJ 37
      (1996) 371-381.

6087 Fitte, Hernan 'Tierra nueva y cielo nuevo': entre ruptura y conti-
      nuidad (a propósito de la redacción del número 39 de la Gaudium
      et spes). Esperanza del hombre. 1996, ⇒173. 391-402.
6088 Maldamé, Jean-Michel Cristo e il cosmo: cosmologia e teologia.
      1995, ⇒11/1,4767. RIl Futuro dell'Uomo 23/2 (1996) 86-87
      (Bisio, Franco); Lat. 62 (1996) 644-646 (Ancona, Giovanni).
6089 Schlarb, Robert Wir sind mit Christus begraben... Römer 6,1-11.
      BGBE 31: 1990, ⇒6,6239... 9,5992. RRB 103 (1996) 294
      (Murphy-O'Connor, Jerome).

6090 Stepp, P.L. The believer's participation in the death of Christ:
      'corporate identification' and a study of Romans 6:1-14. Mellen
      49: Lewiston, NY 1996, Mellen xi; 112 pp. $60. 0-7734-2409-1
      [NTAb 41,162].
6091 Barber, Gerald Wayne The contribution of the concept 'upo
      nomon' in Romans 6:14-15 to the theology of Romans 5-8 and
      Paul's view of salvation history. Diss. Trinity Evang. Div. School
      1996, DMoo, Douglas J., 389 pp. DAI-A 57/05, p. 2080; AAC
      9631845.
6092 Borse, Udo "Abbild der Lehre" (Röm 6,17) im Kontext. FBORSE
      U., SBAB 21: 1996 <1968>, ⇒9. 225-235.
6093 Aageson, James W. "Control" in Pauline language and culture: a
      study of Rom 6. NTS 42 (1996) 75-89.

6094 Díaz-Rodelas, Juan Miguel Pablo y la ley... Rom 7,7-8,4. EMISJ
      28: 1994, ⇒10,5803; 11/1,4773. RRET 56 (1996) 261-263 (Pozo
      Abejón, G. del); Lat. 62 (1996) 373-375 (Penna, Romano); EstB
      54 (1996) 428-430 (Huarte, J.); Bib. 77 (1996) 570-573
      (Barbaglio, Giuseppe); ActBib 33/2 (1996) 173-174 (Boada, J.).
6095 Trudinger, Paul An autobiographical digression?: a note on Ro-
      mans 7:7-25. ET 107 (1996) 173-174.
6096 Khiok-Khing, Y. A Confucian reading of Romans 7:14-25: nomos
      (law) and li (propriety). Jian Dao 5 (1996) 127-141 [NTAb
      40,443].

6097 Hedin, Barbara Ann Romans 8:6-11. Interp. 50 (1996) 55-58.
6098 Giglioli, Alberto L'uomo o il creato?: Κρίσις in S. Paolo. 1994,
      ⇒10,5798. RCivCatt 147 II (1996) 423-424 (Scaiola, D.); Gr. 77
      (1996) 578-579 (Marconi, Gilberto) [8,19-22].
6099 Findeis, Hans-Jürgen Von der Knechtschaft der Vergänglichkeit
      zur Freiheit der Herrlichkeit: zur Hoffnungsperspektive der Schöp-
      fung nach Röm 8,19-22. FTHUESING W., NTA 31: 1996, ⇒94.
      196-225.
6100 Limburg, Klaus Rom 8,19-22: una perícopa controvertida. Espe-
      ranza del hombre. 1996, ⇒173. 379-389.
6101 Cocchini, Francesca Cosmologia e antropologia nell'interpreta-
      zione agostiniana di Rm 8,19-23 (De div. quaest. LXXXIII, q.67).
      Atti del IV Simposio di Tarso. 1996, ⇒263. 147-158.
6102 Ndiaye, Benjamin Jésus 'premier-né d'une multitude de frères':
      étude de Rm. 8,28-30. Diss. 1996 Institut Catholique de Paris,
      DQuesnel, Michel, 266 pp. [RICP 61,343s—Quesnel, Michel].
6103 Cabra, Giordano 'Chi ci separerà dall'amore di Cristo?' (Rm
      8,55). Presbyteri 30 (1996) 665-677.

6104 **Jacomb, Thomas** Romans 8. E 1996, Banner of Truth 381 pp. £13. 0-85151-702-2 [Evangel 17,26].

G4.6 *Israel et Lex;* **The Law and the Jews,** *Rom 9-11*

6105 *Adam, A.K.M.* According to whose law?: Aristobulus, Galilee and the νομοι των ιουδαιων. JSPE 14 (1996) 15-21.
6106 *Cosgrove, Charles H.* Rhetorical suspense in Romans 9-11: a study in polyvalence and hermeneutical election. JBL 115 (1996) 271-287.
      ᴱ**Dunn, J.D.G.** Paul and the Mosaic law ⇒176.
6107 *Dunn, James D.G.* Introduction;
6108 In search of common ground. Paul and the Mosaic law. WUNT 89: 1996, ⇒176. 1-5/309-334.
6109 **Elass, Mateen** Paul's understanding and use of the concept of election in Romans 9-11. Diss. Durham 1995, 303 pp. [EThL 74,326*].
6110 *Hahn, Ferdinand* Die Stellung des Apostels Paulus zum Judentum und zur Tora. ᶠHᴀʜɴ F., 1996, ⇒34. 85-98.
6111 *Hengel, Martin* Die Stellung des Apostels Paulus zum Gesetz in den unbekannten Jahren zwischen Damaskus und Antiochien. Paul and the Mosaic law. WUNT 89: 1996, ⇒176. 25-51.
6112 **Kruse, Colin G.** Paul, the law and justification. Leicester 1996, Apollos 320 pp. £15. 0-8028-0318-0.
6113 **Lodge, John G.** Romans 9-11: a reader-response analysis. Diss. Pont. Univ. Gregoriana, ᴰ*Aletti, Jean-Noël,* Univ. of South Florida: International Studies in Formative Christianity and Judaism 6: Atlanta, GA 1996, Scholars xvii; 243 pp. $85. 0-7885-0312-X.
6114 *Mindling, J.A.* Paul's people and passiontide preaching. NewTheolRev 9/1 (1996) 71-75 [NTAb 40,440].
6115 **Rothgangel, Martin** Antisemitismus als religionspädagogische Herausforderung... Röm 9-11. 1995, ⇒11/1,4790. ᴿFrRu 3 (1996) 134-135 (*Müller, Christiane*).
6116 **Sänger, Dieter** Die Verkündigung des Gekreuzigten und Israel... zum Verhältnis von Kirche und Israel bei Paulus. WUNT 2/75: 1994, ⇒10,5810. ᴿOrdKor 37 (1996) 132-133 (*Giesen, Heinz*); Bib. 77 (1996) 133-135 (*Penna, Romano*); JThS 47/1 (1996) 224-226 (*Dunn, James D.G.*); ETR 71 (1996) 287-288 (*Rakotoharintsifa, Andrianjatovo*); KeTh 47 (1996) 257-258 (*Noordegraaf, A.*).
6117 **Schreiner, Thomas R.** The law and its fulfilment. 1993, ⇒9,6023... 11/1,4792. ᴿEvQ 68 (1996) 72-73 (*Lacey, D.R. de*).
6118 *Stegemann, Ekkehard* Le sujet de l'épître aux Romains et Romains 9-11. ᵀ*Braunschweig-Lütolf, Ursula,* Le déchirement. MoBi 32: 1996, ⇒192. 113-125.
6119 **Stowers, Stanley K.** A rereading of Romans: justice, Jews and gentiles. 1994, ⇒10,5812. ᴿCBQ 58 (1996) 363-365 (*Byrne, Brendan*); Interp. 50 (1996) 431-432 (*Achtemeier, Paul J.*); JBL 115 (1996) 365-368 (*Bassler, Jouette M.*); CritRR 9 (1996) 27-44 (*Hays, Richard B.*).
6120 **Thielman, Frank** Paul and the law. 1994, ⇒10,5813; 11/1,4795. ᴿBS 153 (1996) 252-253 (*Pyne, Robert A.*).

6121 *Vreekamp, Henk* Paulus en die verzoening van Graz. ITBT 4/7 (1996) 15-18.

6122 *Westerholm, Stephen* Paul and the law in Romans 9-11. Paul and the Mosaic law. WUNT 89: 1996, ⇒176. 215-237.

6123 **Wright, N.T.** Climax of covenant. 1991, ⇒7,5364... 10,5818. RJJS 47 (1996) 161-162 (*Wansbrough, Henry*).

6124 *Edgar, C.F.* Paul and the law: a narrative analysis of the pentateuch and its significance for understanding Romans 9:30-10:4. Sewanee Theological Review 39 (1996) 269-284 [NTAb 41,68].

6125 *Westerholm, Stephen* Response to Heikki RAEISAENEN. Paul and the Mosaic law. WUNT 89: 1996, ⇒176. 247-249 [9].

6126 *Dewey, Arthur J.* A re-hearing of Romans 10:1-15. Semeia 65/2 (1994) 109-127.

6127 *Stowasser, Martin* Christus, das Ende welchen Gesetzes?: eine Problemanzeige. PzB 5 (1996) 1-18 [10,4].

6128 *Oegema, Gerbern S.* Versöhnung ohne Vollendung?: Römer 10,4 und die Tora der messianischen Zeit. Bund und Tora. WUNT 92: 1996, ⇒1645. 229-261.

6129 *Pidcock-Lester, Karen* Romans 10:5-15. Interp. 50 (1996) 288-292.

6130 **Keller, Winfrid** Gottes Treue—Israels Heil: eine Darstellung und Fortführung der Diskussion um Franz MUSSNERs Auslegung von Röm 11,25-27 auf einen Sonderweg zum Heil für Israel. Diss. FrB 1996/97, DOberlinner [BZ 42,316].

G4.8 Rom 12...

6131 **Borghi, Ernesto** La vita cristiana è davvero un sacrificio logica?: Romani 12-13: exegesi e linee ermeneutiche. Diss. Fribourg 1996, DRouiller, G., [EThL 74,326*].

6132 **Vollmer, Jochen** 'Jedermann sei untertan der Obrigkeit': ein nichtchristlicher Einschub in den Römerbrief: für eine glaubwürdigere Taufpraxis. FFCh 36: Stuttgart 1996, Tempel 20 pp. [13,1-7] [NThAR 1997,293].

6133 *Eckert, Jost* "Zieht den Herrn Jesus Christus an ...!" (Röm 13,14): zu einer enthusiastischen Metapher der neutestamentlichen Verkündigung. TThZ 105 (1996) 39-60.

6134 *Barclay, John M. G.* 'Do we undermine the law?': a study of Romans 14.1-15.6. Paul and the Mosaic law. WUNT 89: 1996, ⇒176. 287-308.

6135 **Schneider, Nélio** Die "Schwachen" in der christlichen Gemeinde Roms. Theologie 5: Müns 1996, Lit 175 pp. 3-8258-2762-3 [14,1-15,13].

6136 *Knight, G.W.* The scriptures were written for our instruction. JETS 39 (1996) 3-13 [15,4].

6137 *Fernández, Victor Manuel* 'La gran colecta para Jerusalen' o 'la gracia y el dinero' (Rom 15,25-31; 2 Cor 8-9). RevBib 58 (1996) 183-189.

6138 *Plisch, U.-K.* Die Apostelin Junia: das exegetische Problem in Röm 16.7 im Licht von Nestle-Aland27 und der sahidischen Überlieferung. NTS 42 (1996) 477-478.

6139 *North, J. Lionel* 'Good wordes and faire speeches' (Rom 16.18
AV): more materials and a Pauline pun. NTS 42 (1996) 600-614.
6140 *Meggitt, Justin J.* The social status of Erastus (Rom. 16:23). NT
38 (1996) 218-223.
6141 *Borse, Udo* Das Schlußwort des Römerbriefes: Segensgruß (16,24)
statt Doxologie (VV. 25-27). ᶠBORSE U., SBAB 21: 1996
<1994>, ⇒9. 39-59

G5.1 Epistulae ad Corinthios I, *textus, commentarii*

ᴱAland, B., *(al)*, Römer- und 1. Korintherbrief ⇒6025.
6142 **Barbaglio, Giuseppe** La prima lettera ai Corinzi. 1995,
⇒11/1,4829. LASBF 46 (1996) 465-470 (*Chrupcała, Lesław Daniel*).
6143 ᴱ**Bieringer, Reimund** The Corinthian correspondence. BEThL
125: Lv 1996, Peeters xxvii; 792 pp. Colloquium Biblicum Lova-
niense 1994. FB2.400. 90-6186-754-1.
6144 **Calvin, John** The first epistle to the Corinthians. ᴱ*Torrance,
David W.; Torrance, Thomas F.;* ᵀ*Fraser, John W.*, GR 1996,
Eerdmans vi; 370 pp. £15. 0-8028-0809-3 [EvQ 70,275—Rosner,
Brian S.].
6145 **Dowling, Robin; Dray, Stephen** 1 Corinthians. Crossway Bible
Guide: Leicester 1995, Crossway 197 pp. 1-85684-121-9.
6146 **Foulkes, Irene** Problemas pastorales en Corinto: comentario
exegético-pastoral a 1 Corintios. Lectura popular de la Biblia: San
José 1996, Seminario Bíblico Latino-americano 432 pp. [CBQ
59,204].
6147 ᴱ**Fröhlich, Uwe** Einleitung (Fortsetzung). Epistula ad Corinthios I,
2. Lief. Vetus Latina 22/1: FrB 1996, Herder. 3-451-00161-6. 81-
160 [RBen 106,409].
6148 **Frör, Hans** Jullie Korintiërs!: de briefwisseling van de gemeente in
Korinthe met Paulus. Baarn 1996, Ten Have 220 pp. ƒ39.90. 90-
259-4656-9.
6149 **Haykin, Michael A.G.** The Spirit of God: the exegesis of 1 and 2
Corinthians in the pneumatomachian controversy of the fourth century. SVigChr 27: 1994, ⇒10,5855. ᴿVigChr 50 (1996) 83-84
(*Van Oort, J.*); EThL 72 (1996) 463-465 (*Verheyden, J.*).
6150 **Hollander, H.W.** 1 Korintiërs. Een praktische bijbelverklaring 1:
Kampen 1996, Kok 137 pp. ƒ35. 90-242-7826-0.
6151 ᴱ**Mills, Watson E.** 1 Corinthians. Bibliographies for biblical research: NT 7: Lewiston 1996, Mellen xvi; 206 pp. 0-7734-2419-9
[NThAR 1998,132].
6152 **Roukema, Riemer** De uitleg van Paulus' eerste brief aan de Co-
rinthiërs: in de tweede en derde eeuw. Kampen 1996, Kok 303 pp.
ƒ60 [GThT 97/4,182].
6153 *Stewart-Sykes, Alistair* Ancient editors and copyists and modern
partition theories: the case of the Corinthian correspondence. JSNT
61 (1996) 53-64.
6154 **Surgy, Paul de; Carrez, Maurice** Corinthiens: commentaire pastoral. Les épîtres de Paul, 1. Commentaires: P 1996, Bayard 232
pp. FF125. 2-227-366-05-2.
6155 **Witherington III, Ben** Conflict and community in Corinth... 1-2
Cor. 1995, ⇒11/1,4839. ᴿTrinJ 17 (1996) 101-104 (*Lamp, Jeff S.*);

ETR 71 (1996) 439 (*Campbell, Gordon*); VJTR 60 (1996) 484-486 (*Meagher, P.M.*); Bib. 77 (1996) 445-448 (*Martin, Ralph P.*).
6156 **Wolff, Christian** Der erste Brief des Paulus an die Korinther. ThHK 7: B 1996, Evang. Verl.-Anst. xxix; 445 pp. DM49. 3-374-01622-7 [NThAR 1997,133].

G5.2 *1 & 1-2 ad Corinthios—themata*, topics

6157 *Belleville, Linda L.* "Imitate me, just as I imitate Christ": discipleship in the Corinthian correspondence. Patterns of discipleship. 1996, ⇒188. 120-142.
6158 ᴱ**Bianchi, E.**, (*al*), L'apostolo e la sua comunità: un "dialogo" con la prima lettera di Paolo ai cristiani di Corinto. 1995, ⇒11/1,4841. Presenza Pastorale 66 (1996) 243-244.
6159 *Bieringer, Reimund* Zwischen Kontinuität und Diskontinuität: die beiden Korintherbriefe in ihrer Beziehung zueinander nach der neueren Forschung. Corinthian correspondence. BEThL 125: 1996, ⇒6143. 3-38.
6160 *Borse, Udo* "Tränenbrief" und 1. Korintherbrief. ᶠB ᴏ ʀ s ᴇ U., SBAB 21: 1996 < 1984 >, ⇒9. 277-306.
6161 *Brodie, Thomas L.* The systematic use of the pentateuch in 1 Corinthians: an exploratory survey. Corinthian correspondence. BEThL 125: 1996, ⇒6143. 441-456.
6162 *Collins, Raymond F.* Reflections on 1 Corinthians as a Hellenistic letter. Corinthian correspondence. BEThL 125: 1996, ⇒6143. 39-61.
6163 **Doohan, Helen** Corinthian correspondance: ministering in the best and worst of times. Scripture for worship & education: San Jose, CA, 1996, Resource ix; 212 pp. 0-89390-361-2.
6164 *Dunn, Peter W.* The influence of 1 Corinthians on the Acts of Paul. SBL.SP 35: 1996, ⇒274. 438-454.
6165 *Fredrickson, David E.* No noose is good news: leadership as theological problem in the Corinthian correspondence. WaW 16 (1996) 420-426 [ZID 23,14].
6166 *Hickling, C.J.A.* Paul's use of Exodus in the Corinthian correspondence. Corinthian correspondence. BEThL 125: 1996, ⇒6143. 267-376.
6167 **Horrell, David G.** The social ethos of the Corinthian correspondence: interests and ideology from 1 Corinthians to 1 Clement. Studies of the NT and Its World: E 1996, Clark xvi; 395 pp. £24. 0-567-08528-7 [ET 108,281].
6168 *Hunt, Allen Rhea* The inspired body: Paul, the Corinthians, and divine inspiration. ᴿCBQ 60 (1998) 367-368 (*McDonald, Patricia M.*).
6169 *Koperski, Veronica* Knowledge of Christ and knowledge of God in the Corinthian correspondence. Corinthian correspondence. BEThL 125: 1996, ⇒6143. 377-396.
6170 *Krentz, Edgar* Preaching to an alien culture: resources in the Corinthian letters. WaW 16 (1996) 465-472.
6171 *Liebert, Donald Hans* The "apostolic form of writing": group letters before and after 1 Corinthians;

6172 *Lindemann, Andreas* Die paulinische Ekklesiologie angesichts der Lebenswirklichkeit der christlichen Gemeinde in Korinth. Corinthian correspondence. BEThL 125: 1996, ⇒6143. 433-440/63-86.

6173 *Maier, Harry 1 Clement*, 1 and 2 Corinthians, and the rhetoric of hubris. CSBS annual meeting 28 May 1996; Sum. BCSBS 55 (1995/1996) 17-18.

6174 **Martin, Dale B.** The Corinthian body. 1995, ⇒11/1,4849. [R]JThS 47 (1996) 624-629 (*Horrell, David*); ThTo 53 (1996) 540, 542-543 (*Waetjen, Herman C.*); TS 57 (1996) 740-741 (*Tobin, Thomas H.*).

6175 *Neirynck, Frans* The sayings of Jesus in 1 Corinthians. Corinthian correspondence. BEThL 125: 1996, ⇒6143. 142-176.

6176 **Quast, Kevin** Reading the Corinthian correspondence. 1994, ⇒10,5863. [R]CBQ 58 (1996) 354-355 (*Pattee, Stephen*).

6177 **Ramsaran, Rollin A.** Liberating words: Paul's use of rhetorical maxims in 1 Corinthians 1-10. Valley Forge 1996, Trinity 168 pp. $17. 1-563-38164-8 [BiTod 35,264].

6178 *Robbins, Jerry K.* The second thoughts of a captive intellect: pastoral reflections on Paul's letters to the Corinthians. WaW 16 (1996) 401-412 [ZiD 23/1, 14].

6179 **Rocchetta, Carlo** "Per il Signore": la verginità consacrata nella prima lettera ai Corinzi. Meditazioni bibliche 6: Mi 1996, OR 144 pp. L21.000. 88-8053-036-4. [R]PalCl 75/1-2 (1996) 152-153 (*Lavarda, Girolamo*).

6180 *Steyn, Gert J.* Reflections on τὸ ὄνομα τοῦ κυρίου in 1 Corinthians;

6181 *Tomson, Peter J.* La première épître aux Corinthiens comme document de la tradition apostolique de Halakha;

6182 *Verhoef, Eduard* The senders of the letters to the Corinthians and the use of "I " and "we". Corinthian correspondence. BEThL 125: 1996, ⇒6143. 459-470/479-490/417-425.

G5.3 1 Cor 1-7: *sapientia crucis...abusus matrimonii*

6183 *Brown, Alexandra R.* Apocalyptic transformation in Paul's discourse on the cross. WaW 16 (1996) 427-436 [ZiD 23/1, 14].

6184 *Heyer, C.J. den* Paulus over het schandaal van het kruis. ITBT 4/1 (1996) 29-30.

6185 *Reinmuth, Eckart* LAB 40,4 und die Krise der Weisheit im 1. Korintherbrief: ein Beitrag zu den hermeneutischen Voraussetzungen der Paulinischen Argumentation. Corinthian correspondence. BEThL 125: 1996, ⇒6143. 471-478.

6186 **Rotzetter, Anton** Im Kreuz ist Leben. FrS 1996, Paulusverlag 229 pp. DM38 [GuL 70,477].

6187 **Theis, Joachim** Paulus als Weisheitslehrer... 1 Kor 1-4. BU 22: 1991, ⇒7,5408... 11/1,4869. [R]CDios 209 (1996) 762-763 (*Gutiérrez, J.*).

6188 **Litfin, Duane** St Paul's theology of proclamation: 1 Cor 1-4. MSSNTS 79: 1994, ⇒10,5871; 11/1,4868. [R]EvQ 68 (1996) 161-162 (*Kern, Philip*); Bib. 77 (1996) 128-131 (*Watson, Duane F.*); CBQ 58 (1996) 160-162 (*Fiore, Benjamin*); JR 76 (1996) 106-108 (*Mitchell, Margaret M.*).

6189 **Pogoloff, Stephen** Logos and Sophia... 1 Cor 1-4. SBL.DS 134: 1992, ⇒8,6378; 11/1,4870. ^RRB 103 (1996) 143-144 (*Murphy-O'Connor, Jerome*).
6190 *Vos, Johan S.* Die Argumentation des Paulus in 1 Kor 1,10-3,4;
6191 *Sevrin, Jean-Marie* La gnose à Corinthe: questions de méthode et observations sur 1 Co 1,17-3,3. Corinthian correspondence. BEThL 125: 1996, ⇒6143. 87-119/122-139
6192 *Beintker, Michael* Das Wort vom Kreuz und die Gestalt der Kirche [The word of the cross and the form of the church]. Abstr. *Rossol, Heinz D.*, Luther Digest 4 (1996) 15-17 [1,18].
6193 *Keck, Leander E.* God the other who acts otherwise: an exegetical essay on 1 Cor 1:26-31. WaW 16 (1996) 437-443 [ZID 23,14].
6194 *Verheyden, Joseph* ORIGEN on the origin of 1 Cor 2,9. Corinthian correspondence. BEThL 125: 1996, ⇒6143. 491-511.
6195 **Müller, Christoph G.** Gottes Pflanzung... Gemeindetheologie in 1.Kor.3,5-17. FuSt 5: 1995, ⇒11/1,4879. ^RThPh 71 (1996) 273-274 (*Gruber, M.*); BZ 40 (1996) 282-284 (*Hainz, Josef*); CBQ 58 (1996) 351-352 (*Morton, Russell*).
6196 *Lambrecht, Jan* Paul as example: a study of 1 Corinthians 4,6-21. ^FKERTELGE K., 1996, ⇒48. 316-335.

6197 *Deming, Will* The unity of 1 Corinthians 5-6. JBL 115 (1996) 289-312.
6198 **Rosner, Brian S.** Paul, scripture and ethics... 1 Cor 5-7. AZ-GATU 22: 1994, ⇒10,5881; 11/1,4882. ^RETR 71 (1996) 116-117 (*Rakotoharintsifa, Andrianjatovo*); RB 103 (1996) 144-145 (*Murphy-O'Connor, Jerome*); JSJ 27 (1996) 88-91 (*Tomson, Peter*); Salm. 43 (1996) 126-129 (*Trevijano, Ramón*); CBQ 58 (1996) 560-562 (*Harrill, J. Albert*); WThJ 58 (1996) 313-316 (*Hays, Richard B.*); JBL 115 (1996) 155-157 (*Richardson, Peter*).
6199 *Rosner, Brian S.* The function of scripture in 1 Cor 5,13b and 6,16. Corinthian correspondence. BEThL 125: 1996, ⇒6143. 513-518;
6200 The origin and meaning of 1 Corinthians 6,9-11 in context. BZ 40 (1996) 250-253.
6201 **Smith, Jay E.** The interpretation of 1 Corinthians 6:12-20 and its contribution to Paul's sexual ethics. Diss. Trinity Evang. Div. School 1996, ^DMoo, D.J., 367 pp. [EThL 74,328*].
6202 *Fisk, Bruce N.* πορνευειν as body violation: the unique nature of sexual sin in 1 Corinthians 6.18. NTS 42 (1996) 540-558.
6203 **Clement, Olivier** Corps de mort et de gloire. 1995, ⇒11/1,4861. LV(L) 45/5 (1996) 88-90 (*Revellin, Louise*) [6].
6204 *Gravrock, Mark* Why won't Paul just say no?: purity and sex in 1 Corinthians 6. WaW 16 (1996) 444-455 [ZiD 23,14].
6205 *Caragounis, Chrys C.* "Fornication" and "concession"?: interpreting 1 Cor 7,1-7. Corinthian correspondence. BEThL 125: 1996, ⇒6143. 543-559.
6206 *Poirier, John C.; Frankovic, Joseph* Celibacy and charism in 1 Cor 7:5-7. HThR 89 (1996) 1-18.
6207 *Zimmermann, Mirjam; Zimmermann, Ruben* Zitation, Kontradiktion oder Applikation?: die Jesuslogien in 1 Kor 7,10 f. und 9,14: traditionsgeschichtliche Verankerung und paulinische Interpretation. ZNW 87 (1996) 83-100.

6208 *Gundry-Volf, Judith M.* Controlling the bodies: a theological profile of the Corinthian sexual ascetics (1 Cor 7). Corinthian correspondence. BEThL 125: 1996, ⇒6143. 519-541.

6209 **Deming, Will** Paul on marriage and celibacy... 1 Cor 7. MSSNTS 83: 1995, ⇒11/1,4893. ᴿRRT (1996/1) 89-90 (*Parker, D.C.*); Salm. 43 (1996) 129-132 (*Trevijano, Ramón*); CBQ 58 (1996) 544-545 (*Pelser, Gert*); Irén. 69 (1996) 429-430; RB 103 (1996) 628-630 (*Murphy-O'Connor, J.*).

G5.4 *Idolothyta...Eucharistia:* 1 Cor 8-11

6210 *Lambrecht, Jan* Universalism in 1 Cor 8:1-11:1?. Gr. 77 (1996) 333-339.

6211 *Barton, Stephen C.* 'All things to all people': Paul and the law in the light of 1 Corinthians 9.19-23. Paul and the Mosaic law. WUNT 89: 1996, ⇒176. 271-285.

6212 *Richter, Hans-Friedemann* Anstößige Freiheit in Korinth: zur Literarkritik der Korintherbriefe (1 Kor 8,1-13 und 11,2-16);

6213 *Smit, J.F.M.* 1 Cor 8,1-6: a rhetorical partitio: a contribution to the coherence of 1 Cor 8,1-11,1;

6214 *Denaux, Adelbert* Theology and christology in 1 Cor 8,4-6: a contextual-redactional reading. Corinthian correspondence. BEThL 125: 1996, ⇒6143. 561-575/577-591/593-606.

6215 *Stowers, Stanley K.* Elusive coherence: ritual and rhetoric in 1 Corinthians 10-11. ᶠMᴀᴄᴋ B., 1996, ⇒54. 68-83.

6216 *Schrage, Wolfgang* Einige Hauptprobleme der Diskussion des Herrenmahls im 1. Korintherbrief. Corinthian correspondence. BEThL 125: 1996, ⇒6143. 191-198 [10,3-4.16-17; 11,17-34; 16,20-22].

6217 *Enns, Peter E.* The "moveable well" in 1 Cor 10:4: an extrabiblical tradition in an apostolic text. BBR 6 (1996) 23-38.

6218 *Koet, Bart J* The Old Testament background to 1 Cor 10,7-8 [Exod 32];

6219 *Baumert, Norbert* ΚΟΙΝΩΝΙΑ ΤΟΥ ᾽ΑΙΜΑΤΟΣ ΤΟΥ ΧΡΙΣΤΟΥ (1 Kor 10,14-22). Corinthian correspondence. BEThL 125: 1996, ⇒6143. 607-615/617-622.

6220 *Pelletier, Anne-Marie* "Créée pour l'homme"?. Alliance 104 (1996) 4-8 [11,9].

6221 *MacGinn, S.E.* ἐξουσίαν ἔχειν ἐπὶ τῆς κεφαλῆς 1 Cor 11:10 and the ecclesial authority of women. Listening 31 (1996) 91-104 [NTAb 41,70].

6222 *Van Cangh, Jean Marie* Peut-on reconstituer le texte primitif de la cène? (1 Cor 11,23-26 par Mc 14,22-26). Corinthian correspondence. BEThL 125: 1996, ⇒6143. 623-637.

6223 *Chrupcala, Leslaw D.* Chi mangia indegnamente il corpo del Signore (1Cor 11,27). SBFLA 46 (1996) 53-86.

6224 *Schneider, Sebastian* Glaubensmängel in Korinth: eine neue Deutung der "Schwachen, Kranken, Schlafenden" in 1 Kor 11,30. FgNT 9 (1996) 3-19.

G5.5 1 Cor 12s...Glossolalia, charismata

6225 *Cattaneo, Enrico* Carisma e istituzione nella chiesa antica. RdT 37 (1996) 201-216.

6226 *Engelbrecht, E.A.* 'To speak in a tongue': the Old Testament and early rabbinic background of a Pauline expression. ConJ 22 (1996) 295-302 [NTAb 41,71].

6227 *Espinel, J.L.* Profetismo cristiano. Comunidades 89 (1996) 109-116.

6228 *Filoramo, Giovanni* La crisi del profetismo nella tradizione cristiana primitiva. Hum(B) 51 (1996) 836-853.

6229 *Grudem, Wayne* Le don de prophétie. ᵀ*Hirsch, Violaine,* Tychnique 119 (1996) 3-10.

6230 *Macchia, F.D.* Tongues and prophecy: a pentecostal perspective. Conc(USA) (1996/3) 63-69 [NTAb 41,97].

6231 *Nadeau, Gilles* Le discernement dans la Bible. Cahiers de Spiritualité Ignatienne 20 (1996) 239-249.

6232 *Pliya, Jean* Charismes et guérison;

6233 *Tardif, Emiliano* Ministère de délivrance. Séminaire sur la Guérison 3-7 Oct. 1995. Tychique 121 (1996) 55-67/68-72.

6234 *Reiling, J.* "Dit alles bewerkt één en dezelfde Geest": exegetische notities bij 1 Korintiërs 12:1-11. KeTh 47 (1996) 309-318.

6235 *Brandes, Orlando* Um dom do espírito: o discernimento. RCB 77/78 (1996) 106-112 [12,10].

6236 *Barbaglio, Giuseppe* Unità e pluralità della chiesa: una lettura di 1 Cor 12,12-27. ᶠDᴜᴘᴏɴᴛ J., 1996. 159-171.

6237 *Amphoux, Christian-B.* 'Toute la foi, jusqu'à déplacer les montagnes' (1 Co 13,2): une parole de Jésus citée par Paul?. ᶠLᴇɢᴀssᴇ S., LeDiv 166: 1996, ⇒51. 333-355.

6238 *Zani, Lorenzo* L'inno di Paolo alla carità: *1Cor* 13: 4, la carità non viene mai meno (*1Cor* 13,8-13). Presbyteri 30 (1996) 620-624.

6239 *Parmentier, M.* Die Unhaltbarkeit des Dispensationalismus. IKZ 86 (1996) 147-160 [13,8-13; 14,22].

6240 *Cooper, Stephen A.* Scripture at Cassiciacum: I Corinthians 13:13 in the Soliloquies. AugSt 27/2 (1996) 21-46.

6241 *Cox, Steven L.* 1 Corinthians 13: an antidote to violence: love. RExp 93 (1996) 529-536.

6242 *Focant, Camille* 1 Corinthiens 13: analyse rhétorique et analyse de structures. Corinthian correspondence. BEThL 125: 1996, ⇒6143. 199-245.

6243 *Jervis, L. Ann* The greatest of these is love (1 Corinthians 14.34-35). ᶠJᴀᴍɪᴇsᴏɴ P., 1996, ⇒44. 73-95.

6244 *Crüsemann, Marlene* Unrettbar frauenfeindlich: der Kampf um das Wort von Frauen in 1 Kor 14, (33b) 34-35 im Spiegel antijudaistischer Elemente der Auslegung. Von der Wurzel getragen. 1996, ⇒204. 199-223.

6245 *Lockwood,P.F.* Does 1 Corinthians 14:34-35 exclude women from the pastoral office?. LTJ 30/1 (1996) 30-38 [NTAb 41,71].

G5.6 **Resurrectio;** *1 Cor 15...* [ᶠ5.6]

6246 *Ayestarán, José C.* Reencarnación o resurrección?. Iter 7/1 (1996) 61-87.

6247 *Bagni, Arcangelo* La risurrezione della carne. Evangelizzare 22 (1996) 631-633.

6248 *Barth, Gerhard* Umstrittener Auferstehungsglaube. Neutestamentliche Versuche. 1996 <1994>, ⇒111. 363-383.

6249 **Blank, Renold J.** Auferstehung oder Reinkarnation. Mainz 1996, Grünewald 159 pp. DM29.80. 3-7867-1900-4 [ThRv 93,165].

6250 *Bruckner, J.K.* Resurrection or justification of the ungodly: what basis for a biblical theology?. WaW 16/1 (1996) 76-83.

6251 **Bynum, Caroline Walker** The resurrection of the body in western christianity. LHR 15: 1995, ⇒11/1,4940. [R]JR 76 (1996) 634-635 (*McGinn, Bernard*); TS 57 (1996) 350-352 (*Hayes, Zachary*); AsbTJ 51/2 (1996) 115-116 (*Bundy, David*).

6252 *Hertzberg, Arthur* Der Tod und die künftige Welt: jüdische Texte zur Auferstehung. Diak. 27 (1996) 175-179.

6253 *Puech, Émile* Die Erwartung der Toten. WUB 1 (1996) 16.

6254 **Sesboüé, Bernard** The resurrection and the life. [T]*Burton, Jane;* [E]*Heymans, Steven,* ColMn 1996, Liturgical 103 pp. $10. 0-8146-2267-4 [TD 44,87].

6255 *Tura, Ermanno Roberto* Morti e risorti con Cristo. RPLi 34 (1996) 11-17.

6256 *Barth, Gerhard* Zur Frage nach der in 1. Korinther 15 bekämpften Auferstehungsleugnung. Neutestamentliche Versuche. 1996 <1992>, ⇒111. 341-362.

6257 *Hollander, Harm W.; Van der Hout, Gijsbert E.* The apostle Paul calling himself an abortion: 1 Cor. 15:8 within the context of 1 Cor. 15:8-10. NT 38 (1996) 224-236.

6258 *Boer, Martinus C. de* Paul's use of a resurrection tradition in 1 Cor 15,20-28. Corinthian correspondence. BEThL 125: 1996, ⇒6143. 639-651.

6259 *Barth, Gerhard* Erwägungen zu 1. Korinther 15,20-28. Neutestamentliche Versuche. 1996 <1970>, ⇒111. 315-334.

6260 *Holleman, Joost* Jesus' resurrection as the beginning of the eschatological resurrection (1 Cor 15,20). Corinthian correspondence. BEThL 125: 1996, ⇒111. 653-660.

6261 *Johnson, Andy* Firstfruits and death's defeat: metaphor in Paul's rhetorical strategy in 1 Cor 15:20-28. WaW 16 (1996) 456-464 [ZID 23,14].

6262 **Teani, Maurizio** Corporeità e risurrezione... 1 Cor 15,35-49. Aloi. 24: 1994, ⇒10,5947; 11/1,4951. [R]Gr. 77 (1996) 115-117 (*Penna, Romano*); JThS 47 (1996) 230-232 (*Hickling, C.J.A.*); ThLZ 121 (1996) 562-564 (*Barbaglio, Giuseppe*); CBQ 58 (1996) 171-172 (*Marrow, Stanley B.*).

6263 **Smith, Morton** Transformation by burial (1 Cor 15:35-49; Rom 6:3-5 and 8:9-11). New Testament. 1996 <1983>, ⇒151. 110-129.

6264 **Brodeur, Scott** The Holy Spirit's agency in the resurrection of the dead: an exegetico-theological study of 1 Corinthians 15,44b-49 and Romans 8,9-13. Diss. Pont. Univ. Gregoriana, [D]*Aletti, Jean-Noël,* Tesi Gregoriana, Teologia 14: R 1996, Gregorian Univ. Press 300 pp. L30.000. 88-7652-720-6.

6265 *Schneider, Sebastian* 1 Kor 15,51-52: ein neuer Lösungsvorschlag zu einer alten Schwierigkeit. Corinthian correspondence. BEThL 125: 1996, ⇒6143. 661-669.

6266 E*Brecht, Martin* Martin LUTHER: sing mir das Lied gegen den Tod: LUTHERs Predigt über 1. Kor 15,54-57. Luther 67/2 (1996) 52-57.

6267 *Tuckett, Christopher M.* The Corinthians who say "There is no resurrection of the dead" (1 Cor 15,12). Corinthian correspondence. BEThL 125: 1996, ⇒6143. 247-275.

6268 *Toit, A.B. du* Encountering grace: towards understanding the essence of Paul's Damascus experience. Neotest. 30 (1996) 71-87 [15; Gal 1].

6269 **Verburg, Winfried** Endzeit und Entschlafene: syntaktisch-sigmatische, semantische und pragmatische Analyse von 1 Kor 15. FzB 78: Wü 1996, Echter 327 pp. DM48. 3-429-01778-5. RRevAg 37 (1996) 1188-1189 (*Sabugal, Santos*).

6270 *Fusco, Vittorio* La presenza e l'attesa: annotazioni sul *Maranathà*. FDUPONT J., 1996, ⇒21. 215-233 [16,22].

G5.9 Secunda epistula ad Corinthios

6271 **Bieringer, Reimund; Lambrecht, Jan** Studies on 2 Corinthians. BEThL 112: 1994, ⇒10,5954. RBZ 40 (1996) 140-142 (*Dautzenberg, Gerhard*); ThLZ 121 (1996) 354-356 (*Mitchell, Margaret M.*); JThS 47 (1996) 633-635 (*Hickling, C.J.A.*).

6272 **Boer, Cornelis den** De tweede brief van Paulus aan de Korinthiërs, 2: VII-XIII. Kampen 1996, Kok 231 pp. 90-297-1371-2 [NThAR 1998,335].

6273 E*Feld, Helmut* CALVIN: commentarii in 2 Cor. Opera exegetica 15: 1994, ⇒10,5952; 11/1,4958. RSCJ 27 (1996) 528-529 (*Furcha, Edward J.*).

6274 **Kreitzer, Larry Joseph** 2 Corinthians. NTGu: Shf 1996, Academic 146 pp. £7. 1-85075-789-5 [CBQ 59,422].

6275 **Thrall, Margaret E.** II Cor I-VII. ICC: 1994, ⇒10,5953; 11/1,4960. RNBl 77 (1996) 204-206 (*Barrett, C.K.*); Bib. 77 (1996) 285-289 (*Furnish, Victor P.*); JThS 47 (1996) 629-632 (*Hickling, C.J.A.*); JBL 115 (1996) 559-560 (*Fee, Gordon D.*).

6276 *Belleville, Linda L.* Paul's polemic and theology of the spirit in Second Corinthians. CBQ 58 (1996) 281-304.

6277 *DeSilva, D.A.* Meeting the exigency of a complex rhetorical situation: Paul's strategy in 2 Corinthians 1 through 7. AUSS 34 (1996) 5-22.

6278 *Hafemann, Scott* Paul's argument from the Old Testament and christology in 2 Cor 1-9: the salvation-history/restoration structure of Paul's apologetic. Corinthian correspondence. BEThL 125: 1996, ⇒6143. 177-303.

6279 **Harvey, Anthony Ernest** Renewal through suffering: a study of 2 Corinthians. Studies of the New Testament and Its World: E 1996, Clark xii; 148 pp. £19. 0-567-08508-2 [Theol. 100,298].

6280 *Myrick, A.A.* "Father" imagery in 2 Corinthians 1-9 and Jewish paternal tradition. TynB 47 (1996) 163-171.

6281 **Savage, Timothy B.** Power through weakness: Paul's understanding of the Christian ministry in 2 Corinthians. MSSNTS 86: C 1996, CUP xvi; 251 pp. £35. 0-521-49640-3 [TTh 36,113].

6282 *Watson, Nigel M.* "Physician, heal thyself"?: Paul's character as revealed in 2 Corinthians, and the congruence between word and deed. Corinthian correspondence. BEThL 125: 1996, ⇒6143. 671-678.

6283 **Wünsch, Hans-Michael** Der paulinische Brief 2Kor 1-9 als kommunikative Handlung: eine rhetorisch-literaturwissenschaftliche Untersuchung. Diss. Theologie 4: Müns 1996, LIT 349 pp. DM58.80. 3-8258-2603-1.

6284 *Welborn, L.L.* Like broken pieces of a ring: 2 Cor 1.1-2.13; 7.5-16 and ancient theories of literary unity. NTS 42 (1996) 559-583.

6285 *Hotze, Gerhard* Gemeinde als Schicksalsgemeinschaft mit Christus (2 Kor 1,3-11). ᶠKᴇʀᴛᴇʟɢᴇ K., 1996, ⇒48. 336-355.

6286 *Barth, Gerhard* Die Eignung des Verkündigers in 2Kor 2,14-3,6. Neutestamentliche Versuche. 1996 <1980>, ⇒111. 263-282.

6287 **Schröter, Jens** Der versöhnte Versöhner... 2Kor 2,14-7,4. TANZ 10: 1993, ⇒9,6151... 11/1,4974. ᴿCBQ 58 (1996) 562-564 (*Donfried, Karl P.*); JBL 115 (1996) 370-372 (*Hafemann, Scott J.*).

6288 *Oliveira, Anacleto de* 'Ihr seid ein Brief Christi' (2 Kor 3,3): ein paulinischer Beitrag zur Ekklesiologie des Wortes Gottes. ᶠKᴇʀᴛᴇʟɢᴇ K., 1996, ⇒48. 356-377.

6289 *Steinmetz, David C.* Cᴀʟᴠɪɴ and the irrepressible Spirit. ExAu 12 (1996) 94-107 [3,6].

6290 *Koch, Dietrich-Alex* Abraham und Mose im Streit der Meinungen: Beobachtungen und Hypothesen zur Debatte zwischen Paulus und seinen Gegnern in 2 Kor 11,22-23 und 3,7-18. Corinthian correspondence. BEThL 125: 1996, ⇒6143. 305-324.

6291 *Randrianarimalala, Roger* The Lord is the Spirit 2 Cor 3:17A. Hekima Review 15 (1996) 29-36.

6292 **Hafemann, Scott J.** Paul, Moses, and the history of Israel: the letter/spirit contrast and the arguments from scripture in 2 Corinthians 3. WUNT 2/81: 1995, ⇒11/1,4979. ᴿSalm. 43/1 (1996) 136-141 (*Trevijano, Ramón*); BZ 40 (1996) 284-286 (*Dautzenberg, Gerhard*); JETh 10 (1996) 232-235 (*Schnabel, Eckhard J.*); JBL 115 (1996) 760-762 (*Scott, James M.*).

6293 *Kertelge, Karl* Buchstabe und Geist nach 2 Kor 3. Paul and the Mosaic law. WUNT 89: 1996, ⇒ᶠKᴇʀᴛᴇʟɢᴇ K., 1996, ⇒48. 117-130.

6294 *Lebourlier, Jean* L'Ancien Testament, miroir de la gloire du seigneur Jésus: une lecture du chapitre 3 de la deuxième Épître aux Corinthiens. BLE 97 (1996) 321-329.

6295 *Schröter, Jens* Der Apostolat des Paulus als Zugang zu seiner Theologie: eine Auslegung von 2 Kor 4,7-12. Corinthian correspondence. BEThL 125: 1996, ⇒6143. 679-692.

6296 **Savundranayagam, Michael Angelo P.R.** Weakness and power of the apostle in 2Cor 4:7-12. Diss. extr. Pont. Univ. Urbaniana 1996, ᴰ*Biguzzi, Giancarlo*, xi; 69 pp.

6297 *Walter, Nikolaus* Hellenistische Eschatologie bei Paulus?: zu 2 Kor 5,1-10. ThQ 176 (1996) 53-64.

6298 *Smith, I.K.* Does 2 Corinthians 5:1-8 refer to an intermediate state?. RTR 55 (1996) 14-23.

6299 **Gloer, W. Hulitt** An exegetical and theological study of Paul's understanding of new creation and reconciliation in 2 Cor. 5:14-21.

Mellen 42: Lewiston, NY 1996, Mellen (8) xiii; 262 pp. $90. 0-7734-2411-3 [ThD 44,169].

6300 *Porter, Stanley E.* Reconciliation and 2 Cor 5,18-21. Corinthian correspondence. BEThL 125: 1996, ⇒6143. 693-705.

6301 *Sorg, Theo* Das Wort von der Versöhnung: 2 Korinther 5,19-21. Das Wort vom Kreuz. 1996, ⇒206. 61-66.

6302 *Lang, Manfred* Erwägungen zu 2Kor 5,19a. BN 84 (1996) 46-50.

6303 *Moore, Richard K.* 2 Cor 5,21: the interpretative key to Paul's use of δικαιοσύνη θεοῦ?. Corinthian correspondence. BEThL 125: 1996, ⇒6143. 707-715.

6304 **Webb, William J.** Returning home: new covenant and second exodus as the context for 2 Corinthians 6.14-7.1. JSNT.S 85: 1993, ⇒9,6168... 11/1,4985. Irén. 69 (1996) 289-290.

6305 *Heil, Christoph* Die Sprache der Absonderung in 2 Kor 6,17 und bei Paulus. Corinthian correspondence. BEThL 125: 1996, ⇒6143. 717-729 [6,14-7,1].

6306 *Ascough, Richard S.* The completion of a religious duty: the background of 2 Cor 8.1-15. NTS 42 (1996) 584-599.

6307 *Betz, Hans Dieter* 2 Korinther 8 und 9. 1992, ⇒8,6476... 11/1,4987. ᴿBiKi 51 (1996) 40-41 (*Schmitt, Christoph*).

6308 *Costen, James H.* Learning to give is basic to being a christian: II Corinthians 9:1-15. JITC 24 (1996-97) 189-197 [ZID 23,406].

6309 **Heckel, Ulrich** Kraft in Schwachheit... 2 Kor 10-13. WUNT 2/56: 1993, ⇒9,6173... 11/1,4989. ᴿCritRR 9 (1996) 223-226 (*Hafemann, Scott J.*).

6310 *Lambrecht, Jan* Dangerous boasting: Paul's self-commendation in 2 Corinthians 10-13. Corinthian correspondence. BEThL 125: 1996, ⇒6143. 325-346.

6311 **Peterson, Brian K.** Eloquence and the proclamation of the gospel in Corinth: social standards and eschatological crisis: a rhetorical and exegetical investigation of II Corinthians 10-13. Diss. Richmond 1996/97 [RTL 29,587].

6312 **Sundermann, Hans-Georg** Der schwache Apostel und die Kraft der Rede: eine rhetorische Analyse von 2 Kor 10-13. EHS.T 575: Fra 1996, Lang 279 pp. DM84 3-631-48572-7 [Diss. Marburg 1991].

6313 **Andrews, Scott** The politics of fools: Paul and the opponents in 2 Cor. 10-12. Diss. Duke 1996, ᴰ*Martin, D.* [RTL 29,582].

6314 *Lambrecht, Jan* Paul's appeal and the obedience to Christ: the line of thought in 2 Corinthians 10,1-6. Bib. 77 (1996) 398-416.

6315 **Merritt, H. Wayne** In word and deed: moral integrity in Paul. 1993, ⇒9,6176; 11/1,4991. ᴿNeotest. 30 (1996) 217-218 (*Thom, J.C.*) [10,11].

6316 *Atkins, R.* Pauline theology and shame affect: reading a social location. Listening 31 (1996) 137-151 [11,1-12,13] [NTAb 41,73].

6317 *Trakatellis, Dimitrios* Power in weakness: exegesis of 2 Cor 12,1-13. Die Väter legen aus. 1996, ⇒153. 195-231. G.

6318 *Costen, James H.* How to be a powerful church leader: II Corinthians 12,1-10. JITC 24 (1996) 167-173.

6319 *Jegher-Bucher, Verena* Der Pfahl im Fleisch: Überlegungen zu II Kor 12,7-10 im Zusammenhang von 12,1-13. ThZ 52 (1996) 32-41.

6320 *Thrall, Margaret E.* Paul's journey to paradise: some exegetical issues in 2 Cor 12,2-4. Corinthian correspondence. BEThL 125: 1996, ⇒6143. 347-363.
6321 *Russell, Ronald* Redemptive suffering and Paul's thorn in the flesh. JETS 39 (1996) 559-570 [12,7-10].
6322 *Thomas, J.C.* 'An angel from Satan': Paul's thorn in the flesh (2 Corinthians 12.7-10). JPentec 9 (1996) 39-52 [ZID 22,449].
6323 *North, J.L.* Paul's protest that he does not lie in the light of his Cilician origin. JThS 47 (1996) 439-463 [12,7-10].

G6.1 Ad Galatas

6324 **Boles, Kenneth L.** Galatians & Ephesians. College NIV Commentary: Joplin, Miss 1996, College 346 pp. 0-89900-627-2 [NThAR 1997,132].
6325 **Dunn, James D.G.** The epistle to the Galatians. BNTC: 1993, ⇒9,6180... 11/1,4997. RRB 103 (1996) 291-292 *(Murphy-O'Connor, Jerome)*.
6326 TGarzón Bosque, Isabel Juan CRISOSTOMO: comentario a la carta a los Gálatas. Introd., notas *Zincone, Sergio*, Biblioteca de Patrística 34: M 1996, Ciudad Nueva 200 pp. 84-89651-14-0.
6327 **George, Timothy** Galatians. NAC 30: 1994, ⇒10,5987; 11/1,5000. REvQ 68 (1996) 349-351 *(Ciampa, Roy)*.
6328 **Hagen, Kenneth** LUTHER's approach to Scripture as seen in his "Commentaries" on Galatians 1519-1538. 1993, ⇒8,6502... 10,5988. RJEH 47 (1996) 375-376 *(Trueman, Carl R.)*; JThS 47 (1996) 758-760 *(Morgan, Robert)*; KeTh 47/1 (1996) 78-79 *(Boendermaker, J.P.)*; NTT 97 (1996) 181 *(Lønning, Inge)*; RExp 93 (1996) 576-577 *(Seifrid, Mark A.)*.
6329 *Kolb, Robert* The influence of LUTHER's Galatians Commentary of 1535 on later sixteenth-century Lutheran commentaries on Galatians. Luther Digest 4 (1996) 119-124 [⇒9,6195].
    Lémonon, Jean-Pierre Romains, Galates ⇒6039.
6330 **Lührmann, Dieter** Galatians. 1992, ⇒8,6505... 11/1,5002. RSJTh 49 (1996) 513-515 *(Barclay, John)*.
6331 **Matera, Frank J.** Galatians. 1992, ⇒8,6507... 11/1,5003. RVJTR 60 (1996) 487-488 *(Meagher, P.M.)*.
6332 **Morris, Leon** Galatians: Paul's charter of christian freedom. Leicester 1996, Inter-Varsity 191 pp. £15. 0-85110-658-7.
6333 **Pitta, Antonio** Lettera ai Galati. Introd., versione, commento. SOCr 9: Bo 1996, EDB 459 pp. L64.000. 88-10-20616-9 [RdT 38,287].
6334 **Pohl, Adolf** Der Brief des Paulus an die Galater. WStB.NT: 1995, ⇒11/1,5005. RJETh 10 (1996) 240-242 *(Schröder, Michael)*.

6335 *Constantinou, Mitt.* Η΄ Σύναξη Ορθόδοξων Βιβλικών Θεολόγων Μεσημβρία (Nesebar), Βουλγαρία 10-15 Σεπτεμβρίου 1995: η προς Γαλατας επιστολη [The Conference of Orthodox Biblical Theologians (Nesebar, Bulgaria, 10-15 September 1995): the letter to the Galatians]. Collab. *Tsakona, M.B.*, DBM 15 (1996) 85-88.
6336 **Dunn, James D.G.** The theology of Paul's letter to the Galatians. 1993, ⇒9,6189... 11/1,4998. RInterp. 50 (1996) 190-192 *(Kellogg, Frederic R.)*; EstB 54 (1996) 282-283 *(León, L. de)*.

6337   *Elliott, S.M.* Paul and his gentile audiences: mystery-cults, Anatolian popular religiosity, and Paul's claim of divine authority in Galatians. Listening 31/2 (1996) 117-136 [NTAb 41,73].

6338   *Hall, Robert G.* Arguing like an apocalypse: Galatians and an ancient topos outside the Greco-Roman rhetorical tradition. NTS 42 (1996) 434-453.

6339   *Keesmaat, Sylvia C.* Paul and his story: exodus and tradition in Galatians. HBT 18/2 (1996) 133ss [ThD Index Feb. 1997,5].

6340   *Lemmer, Richard* Why should the possibility of rabbinic rhetorical elements in Pauline writings (e.g. Galatians) be reconsidered?. Rhetoric. JSNT.S 131: 1996, ⇒268. 161-179.

6341   *Lohse, Eduard* Das Gesetz Christi: zur theologischen Begründung christlicher Ethik im Galaterbrief. ᶠKᴇ ʀᴛ ᴇ ʟ ɢ ᴇ K., 1996, ⇒48. 378-389.

6342   *Meynet, Roland* Composition et genre littéraire de la première section de l'épître aux Galates. Paul de Tarse. LeDiv 165: 1996, ⇒273. 51-64.

6343   *Nobile, Marco* La torà al tempo di Paolo: alcuni riflessioni. Atti del IV Simposio di Tarso. 1996, ⇒263. 93-106.

6344   *Pitta, A.* Paolo, i gentili e la legge: percorso genetico a partire dalla Lettera ai Galati. RStB 8 (1996) 251-276.

6345   **Scott, James M.** Paul and the nations... Gal. WUNT 2/84: 1995, ⇒11/1,5026. ᴿJETh 10 (1996) 242-244 (*Baum, Armin Daniel*).

6346   **Silva, Moisés** Explorations in exegetical method: Galatians as a test case. GR 1996, Baker 236 pp. 0-8010-1123-X.

6347   *Vanhoye, Albert* Paraclèse et doctrine pauliniennes: désaccord ou accord?. La foi agissant. SMBen.BE 13: 1996, ⇒277. 200-218.

6348   ᴱ**Lambrecht, Jan** The truth of the gospel (Galatians 1:1-4:11). SMBen.BE 12: 1993, ⇒9,392... 11/1,5030. ᴿEstB 54 (1996) 563-565 (*Huarte, J.*).

6349   *Dodd, Brian J.* Christ's slave, people pleasers and Galatians 1.10. NTS 42 (1996) 90-104.

6350   *Hoerber, R.G.* Paul's conversion/call. ConJ 22/2 (1996) 186-188 [1,11-17] [NTAb 40,446].

6351   *Wright, N.T.* Paul, Arabia, and Elijah (Galatians 1:17). JBL 115 (1996) 683-692.

6352   *Viciano, Albert* Antike versus zeitgenössische Exegese: Tʜᴇᴏᴅᴏ ʀᴇᴛ von Kyros Kommentar zu Gal 1,19. FKTh 12 (1996) 285-289.

6353   **Hennings, Ralph** Der Briefwechsel zwischen Aᴜɢᴜꜱᴛɪɴᴜꜱ und Hɪᴇ ʀᴏɴʏᴍ ᴜꜱ und ihr Streit um den Kanon des AT... Gal. 2,11-14. SVigChr 21: 1994, ⇒10,6029; 11/1,5038. ᴿFZPhTh 43 (1996) 491-494 (*Schenker, Adrian*); JAC 39 (1996) 277-279 (*Heinberg, Barbara*).

6354   *Lambrecht, Jan* Paul's reasoning in Galatians 2:11-21. Paul and the Mosaic law. WUNT 89: 1996, ⇒176. 53-74.

6355   **Amadi-Azuogu, Chinedu Adolphus** Paul and the law in the arguments of Galatians: a rhetorical and exegetical analysis of Galatians 2,14-6,2. BBB 104: Bonn 1996, Beltz A. xv; 370 pp. DM98. 3-89547-104-6 [NTAb 41,155].

6356   **Eckstein, Hans-Joachim** Verheissung und Gesetz: eine exegetische Untersuchung zu Galater 2,15-4,7. Diss. ᴰ*Hofius, O.*, WUNT

2/86: Tü 1996, Mohr x; 297 pp. DM178. 3-16-146426-5 [NTAb 41,158].

6357 *Longenecker, Bruce W.* Defining the faithful character of the covenant community: Galatians 2.15-21 and beyond. Paul and the Mosaic law. WUNT 89: 1996, ⇒176. 75-97.

6358 *Smiga, George M.* Preaching at risk: interpreting Paul's statements on the law. NewTR 9/3 (1996) 74-95 [2,16].

6359 *Marín Heredia, F.* "Por pura gracia" (Gál 2,16). Sum. Carthaginensia 12 (1996) 155-163.

6360 **McGahey, James R.** 'No one is justified by works of the law' (Galatians 2:16a): the nature and rationale of Paul's polemic against 'works of the law' in the epistle to the Galatians. Diss. Dallas Theol. Sem. 1996, 392 pp. DAI-A 57/04, p. 1675; AAC 9627853.

6361 *Janzen, J. Gerald* COLERIDGE and *pistis Christou.* ET 107 (1996) 265-268 [2,20; Phil 3,9].

6362 *Stanton, Graham* The law of Moses and the law of Christ: Galatians 3:1-6:2. Paul and the Mosaic law. WUNT 89: 1996, ⇒176. 99-116.

6363 *Neuman, H.T.* Paul's appeal to the experience of the Spirit in Galatians 3.1-5: christian existence as defined by the cross and effected by the Spirit. JPentec 9 (1996) 39-52 [ZID 22,449].

6364 *Downing, F. Gerald* A Cynic preparation for Paul's gospel for Jew and Greek, slave and free, male and female. NTS 42 (1996) 454-462 [3,28].

6365 *Arnold, Clinton E.* Returning to the domain of the powers: στοιχεῖα as evil spirits in Galatians 4:3,9. NT 38 (1996) 55-76.

6366 *Martin, Troy* Pagan and Judeo-Christian time-keeping schemes in Gal 4.10 and Col 2.16. NTS 42 (1996) 105-119.

ᴱVanhoye, Albert La foi agissant... Gal 4,12-6,16 ⇒277.

6367 *Lambrecht, Jan* Like a mother in the pain of childbirth again: a study of Galatians 4:12-20. La foi agissant. SMBen.BE 13: 1996, ⇒277. 13-31 (Disc. 31-39).

6368 *Smith, Christopher C.* ἐκκλεῖσαι in Galatians 4:17: the motif of the excluded lover as a metaphor of manipulation. CBQ 58 (1996) 480-499.

6369 *Galitis, Georgios* Gesetz und Freiheit: die Allegorie von Hagar und Sara in Gal. 4,21-5,1;

6370 *Dunn, James D.G.* 'Neither circumcision nor uncircumcision, but...' (Gal 5.2-12; 6.12-16; cf. 1 Cor 7.17-20). La foi agissant. SMBen.BE 13: 1996, ⇒277. 41-69 (Disc. 70-78)/79-110 (Disc. 110-122).

6371 *Lambrecht, J.* Is Gal. 5:11b a parenthesis?: a response to T. BAARDA. NT 38 (1996) 237-241.

6372 *Perrot, Charles* La loi et son accomplissement selon Ga 5,13-26. La foi agissant. SMBen.BE 13: 1996, ⇒277. 123-142 (Disc. 142-154).

6373 **Wilder, William Nelson** Freed from the law to be led by the Spirit: echoes of the Exodus narrative in the context and background of Galatians 5:18. Diss. Union Theol. Sem. in Virginia 1996: 338 pp. [EThL 74,331*].

6374 *Hawkins, Charles S.* Galatians 5:22-23 and 2 Samuel 13: remembering Tamar. RExp 93 (1996) 537-542.

6375   *Campbell, R.A.* 'Against such things there is no law'?: Galatians 5:23b again. ET 107 (1996) 271-272.
6376   *Schrage, Wolfgang* Probleme paulinischer Ethik anhand von Gal 5,26-6,10. La foi agissant. SMBen.BE 13: 1996, ⇒277. 155-194 (Disc. 194-200).

G6.2 Ad Ephesios

6377   **Arnold, Clinton E.** Ephesians, 1992, 5,6213... 8,6565. REvangel 14/1 (1996) 30-31 (*Bigg, Howard C.*).
6378   **Barra, Domenico** L'epistola agli Efesini. Commentari biblici: Palermo 1996, Gesù vive 167 pp. [SdT 11,109s—Mattioli, Andrea].
6379   **Best, Ernest** Ephesians. 1993, ⇒9,6241; 11/1,5053. REvQ 68 (1996) 162-164 (*Hui, Archie*).
6380   **Hahn, Eberhard** Der Brief des Paulus an die Epheser. WStB: Wu 1996, Brockhaus 192 pp. DM32. 3-417-25025-0.
6381   **Howell, David B.** Ephesians: God calls a new people. Macon, Ga. 1996, Smyth & H. 112 pp. 1-57312-039-1 [NThAR 1997,194].
6382   **Klein, William Wade** The book of Ephesians: an annotated bibliography. Books of the Bible 8: GRLH 1466: NY 1996, Garland xxiii; 312 pp. $50. 0-8153-0364-5.
6383   **Layton, Richard Ashby** ORIGEN as a reader of Paul: a study of the 'Commentary on Ephesians'. Diss. Virginia 1996, 377 pp. [EThL 74,270*].
6384   **Liefeld, Walter L.** Ephesians. IVP NT Commentary: Leicester 1996, InterVarsity 178 pp. 0-85111-681-7.
6385   ENeri, **Umberto** Lettera agli Efesini. BIBLIA NT 9: 1995, ⇒11/1,5062. RLat. 62 (1996) 631-632 (*Penna, Romano*).
6386   *Newman, C.C.* An annotated bibliography of Ephesians. RExp 93 (1996) 271-275.
6387   *Pickering, Stuart R.* Readings in a papyrus text of Ephesians at Yale University. NTTRU 4 (1996) 108-116.
6388   *Polhill, J.B.* An overview of Ephesians;
6389   A teaching outline of Ephesians. RExp 93 (1996) 179-186/267-269.
6390   **Schnackenburg, Rudolf** Ephesians. 1991, ⇒7,5586... 10,6067. REvQ 68 (1996) 70-71 (*Marshall, I. Howard*).
6391   **Snodgrass, Klyne R.** Ephesians. NIV Application Commentary: GR 1996, Zondervan 384 pp. 0-310-49340-4.
6392   **Speyr, Adrienne von** The letter to the Ephesians. TWalker, *Adrian*, SF 1996, Ignatius 269 pp. $13. 0-89870-570-3.
6393   EUhlig, **Siegbert; Maehlum, Helge** NT aethiopice: die Gefangenschaftsbriefe. AthF 33: 1993, ⇒9,6239; 11/1,5064. RBSOAS 59/1 (1996) 203-205 (*Knibb, Michael A.*).

6394   *Arnold, Clinton E.* Introducing Ephesians: establishing believers in Christ. SWJT 39 (1996) 4-13.
6395   *Bailey, Raymond* Preaching Ephesians. RExp 93 (1996) 543-551.
6396   **Gese, Michael** Die Rezeption der paulinischen Theologie im Epheserbrief. Diss. Tü 1996, 242 pp. [NThAR 1997,36].
6397   **Kittredge, Cynthia Briggs** The language of obedience in the Pauline tradition: rhetorical analysis and historical reconstruction of

the letters to the Philippians and to the Ephesians. Diss. Harvard 1996, DFiorenza, E.S., 258 pp. [EThL 74,332*].

6398 Klein, William W. Reading Ephesians: the glory of Christ in the church. SWJT 39 (1996) 14-19.

6399 **Lincoln, Andrew T.; Wedderburn, A.J.M.** The theology of the later Pauline letters. 1993, ⇒9,6248; 11/1,5068. RSJTh 49 (1996) 504-506 (Best, Ernest).

6400 Marshall, M.T. The fullness of incarnation: God's new humanity in the body of Christ. RExp 93 (1996) 187-201.

6401 Martin, R.P. Reconciliation and unity in Ephesians. RExp 93 (1996) 203-235.

6402 **Moritz, Thorsten** A profound mystery: the use of the Old Testament in Ephesians. NT.S 85: Lei 1996, Brill xiii; 252 pp. f142/$91.75. 90-04-10556-5 [RB 104,316].

6403 Moritz, Thorsten Reasons for Ephesians. Evangel 14/1 (1996) 8-14.

6404 Mouton, Elna The communicative power of the epistle to the Ephesians. Rhetoric. JSNT.S 131: 1996, ⇒268. 280-307.

6405 Otero Lazaro, Tomas El objeto de la revelacion y el conocimiento en la carta a los Efesios. Burg. 37/1 (1996) 21-35.

6406 Qualls, P.; Watts, J.D. Isaiah in Ephesians. RExp 93 (1996) 249-259.

6407 Steinmetz, Franz-Josef Die Weisheit und das Kreuz: Marginalien zum Kolosser- und Epheserbrief. FTHUESING W., NTA 31: 1996, ⇒94. 226-240.

6408 **Strelan, Rick** Paul, Artemis, and the Jews in Ephesus. Diss. Queensland. BZNW 80: B 1996, De Gruyter xxi; 380 pp. DM168. 3-11-015020-4 [NTAb 41,162].

6409 Trites, Allison Proclaiming Ephesians: God's order in a needy world. SWJT 39 (1996) 43-50.

6410 **Vera Colona, Héctor Eduardo** La vocación como misterio en la epístola a los Efesios. Diss. Pamplona 1996, DChapa Prado, J., 262 pp. [EThL 74,331*].

6411 Capes, David B. Interpreting Ephesians 1-3: "God's people in the mystery of his will". SWJT 39 (1996) 20-31.

6412 Reynier, Chantal La bénédiction en Éphésiens 1,3-14: élection, filiation, rédemption. NRTh 118 (1996) 182-199.

6413 Newman, C.C. Election and predestination in Ephesians 1:4-6a: an exegetical-theological study of the historical, christological realization of God's purpose. RExp 93 (1996) 237-247.

6414 **Tosaus Abadía, José Pedro** Cristo y el universo: estudio... de Ef 1,10b en Ef. y en la obra de IRENEO. 1995, ⇒11/1,5077. RLumen 45 (1996) 236-239 (Gil Ortega, Urbano).

6415 MacMahan, C. The wall is gone! RExp 93 (1996) 261-266 [2,11-22].

6416 Stefani, Piero 'Ha riconciliato i due con Dio in un solo corpo' (Ef 2,16): la riconciliazione tra israele e le genti ['He has reconciled the two with God in one body': reconciliation between Israel and the gentiles]. Sum. 329. StEcum 14 (1996) 321-329.

6417 Roark, C.M. Interpreting Ephesians 4-6: God's people in a walk worthy of his calling. SWJT 39 (1996) 32-42.

6418 **Harris, W. Hall** The descent of Christ: Ephesians 4:7-11 and traditional Hebrew imagery. AGJU 32: Lei 1996, Brill xvii; 221 pp.
*f*115/$74.25. 90-04-10310-4.
6419 *Costen, James H.* Walk as children of light: Ephesians 5:6-14.
JITC 24 (1996) 157-165.
6420 *Costen, James H.* A second look at that "ole time religion": Ephesians 6:10-20. JITC 24 (1996) 199-206.
6421 *Searle, David* Ephesians 6:12: the true nature of the believer's
conflict;
6422 Ephesians 6:12: struggling against the rulers, against the authorities. Evangel 14 (1996) 4-8/68-71.

G6.3 Ad Philippenses

6423 **Bormann, Lukas** Philippi: Stadt und Christengemeinde zur Zeit
des Paulus. NT.S 78: 1995, ⇒11/1,5097. ᴿZKG 107 (1996) 112-
114 (*Wehr, Lothar*); ThLZ 121 (1996) 264-265 (*Rebell, Walter*);
JThS 47 (1996) 232-239 (*Bockmuehl, M.*); EThL 72 (1996) 241-
245 (*Verheyden, J.*); RB 103 (1996) 627-628 (*Murphy-O'Connor,
J.*).
6424 **Carson, D.A.** Basics for believers: an exposition of Philippians.
GR 1996, Baker 124 pp. $10. 0-8010-5494-X [NTAb 41,157].
6425 **Fee, Gordon D.** Paul's letter to the Philippians. NIC.NT: 1995,
⇒11/1,5089. ᴿWThJ 58/1 (1996) 165-167 (*Thielman, Frank*);
VJTR 60 (1996) 488-490 (*Meagher, P.M.*); Neotest. 30 (1996)
218-220 (*Pretorius, E.A.C.*); SNTU.A 21 (1996) 273-274 (*Fuchs,
A.*).
6426 **Kramer, Gerhard H.** Gegrepen door Christus: bijbel-studies bij
de brief van Paulus aan de Filippiërs. Vaassen 1996 Medema 168
pp. 90-6353-260-1 [NThAR 1997,194].
6427 **Pilhofer, Peter** Die erste christliche Gemeinde Europas. WUNT
2/87: 1995, ⇒11/1,5106. ᴿEThL 72 (1996) 241-245 (*Verheyden,
J.*).

6428 **Banker, John E.** A semantic and structural analysis of Philippians.
Dallas 1996, Summer Institute of Linguistics 199 pp. 1-55671-020-
8 [NThAR 1997,193].
6429 *Cuvillier, Élian* L'intégrité de l'épître aux Philippiens: état de la
question. Paul de Tarse. LeDiv 165: 1996, ⇒273. 65-77.
6430 *Fitzgerald, John T.* Philippians in the light of some ancient discussions of friendship. Friendship. NT.S 82: 1996, ⇒180. 141-160.
6431 *Hawthorne, Gerald F.* The imitation of Christ: discipleship in Philippians. Patterns of discipleship. 1996, ⇒188. 163-179.
    Kittredge, C. The language of obedience... Phil..⇒6397.
6432 *Luter, A.B.* Partnership in the gospel: the role of women in the
church at Philippi. JETS 39 (1996) 411-420.
6433 *Reumann, John* Philippians, especially chapter 4, as a "letter of
friendship": observations on a checkered history of scholarship.
Friendship. NT.S 82: 1996, ⇒180. 83-106.
6434 **Ware, James Patrick** 'Holding forth the word of life': Paul and
the mission of the church in the letter to the Philippians in the context of Second Temple Judaism. Diss. Yale 1996, ᴰ*Malherbe,
A.H.*, 366 pp. [EThL 74,332*].

6435   **Witherington III, Ben** Friendship and finances in Philippi: the letter of Paul to the Philippians. 1994, ⇒10,6098. RSBET 14/2 (1996) 158-159 (*Wilson, Alistair I.*).

6436   *Janzen, J. Gerald* Creation and new creation in Philippians 1:6. HBT 18 (1996) 27-54.
6437   *Barth, Gerhard* Phil. 1,23 und die paulinische Zukunftserwartung (Eschatologie). Neutestamentliche Versuche. 1996 <1979>, ⇒111. 335-340.
6438   *Treiyer, E.* S'en aller et être avec Christ: Philippiens 1:23. AUSS 34 (1996) 47-64.
6439   *Wortham, Robert A.* Christology as community identity in the Philippians hymn: the Philippians hymn as social drama (Philippians 2:5-11). PRSt 23 (1996) 269-287.
6440   *Manzi, Franco* Fil 2,6-11 ed Eb 5,5-10: due schemi cristologici a confronto. Sum. 64. RivBib 44 (1996) 31-64.
6441   *Navarro Cuervo, Horacio* La kenosis de Cristo: estudio exegético y teologico de Filipenses 2,6-11: el desprendimiento solidario de Jesus, un autodespojo que enriquece al hombre.   Mayéutica 22 (1996) 339-436 [Rev 4-5] [ZID 23,275].
6442   *Weber, Beat* Philipper 2,12-13: Text-Kontext-Intertext. BN 85 (1996) 31-37.
6443   *Reed, Jeffrey T.* Philippians 3:1 and the epistolary hesitation formulas: the literary integrity of Philippians, again. JBL 115 (1996) 63-90.
6444   **Koperski, Veronica** The knowledge of Christ Jesus my Lord: the high christology of Philippians 3:7-11. Contributions to Biblical Exegesis and Theology 16: Kampen 1996, Kok xviii; 368 pp. ƒ70. 90-390-0132-4. SNTU.A 21 (1996) 274-276 (*Schreiber, S.*).
6445   *Berry, Ken L.* The function of friendship language in Philippians 4:10-20. Friendship. NT.S 82: 1996, ⇒180. 107-124.
6446   *Malherbe, Abraham J.* Paul's self-sufficiency (Philippians 4:11). Friendship. NT.S 82: 1996, ⇒180. 107-124/125-139.

G6.4 Ad Colossenses

6447   **Aletti, Jean-Noël** Lettera ai Colossesi. 1994, ⇒10,6123. RCivCatt 147 I (1996) 297-298 (*Scaiola, D.*); StPat 43/1 (1996) 188-190 (*Leonardi, Giovanni*);
6448   **Arnold, Clinton E.** The Colossian syncretism. WUNT 2/77: 1995, ⇒11/1,5129. RJETh 10 (1996) 224-226 (*Schröder, Michael*).
6449   **Donelson, Lewis R.** Colossians, Ephesians, First and Second Timothy, and Titus. Westminster Bible companion: LVL 1996, Westminster viii; 192 pp. $16. 0-664-25264-8.
6450   **Dunn, James D.G.** The epistles to the Colossians and to Philemon: a commentary on the Greek text. NIGTC: GR 1996, Eerdmans xvii; 388 pp. $32. 0-8028-2441-2.
6451   *Knowles, Michael P.* "Christ in you, the hope of glory": discipleship in Colossians. Patterns of discipleship. 1996, ⇒188. 180-202.
6452   **Martin, Troy W.** By philosophy and empty deceit: Colossians as response to a Cynic critique. JSNT.S 118: Shf 1996, Academic 223 pp. £30/$45. 1-85075-559-0 [CBQ 59,386].

6453   *Olbricht, Thomas H.* The Stoicheia and the rhetoric of Colossians: then and now. Rhetoric. JSNT.S 131: 1996, ⇒268. 308-328.

   Steinmetz, F. Die Weisheit...zum Kolosser und Epheserbrief ⇒6407.

6454   **Thurston, Bonnie** Reading Col, Eph, and 2 Thess. 1995, ⇒11/1,5127. RCritRR 9 (1996) 291-293 (*Arnold, Clinton E.*).

6455   *Gunton, C.* Atonement and the project of creation: an interpretation of Colossians 1:15-23. Dialog 35/1 (1996) 35-41 [NTAb 40,450].

6456   *Campbell, Douglas A.* Unravelling Colossians 3.11b. NTS 42 (1996) 120-132.

G6.5 Ad Philemonem

6457   *Balz, Horst* Philemonbrief. TRE 26 (1996) 487-492.

   Dunn, J. The epistles to Col. and Philemon ⇒6450.

6458   *Kea, Perry V.* Paul's letter to Philemon: a short analysis of its values. PRSt 23 (1996) 223-232.

6459   *Taylor, N.H.* Onesimus: a case study of slave conversion in early christianity. RelT 3 (1996) 259-281 [ZID 23,10].

G6.6 Ad Thessalonicenses

6460   **Donfried, Karl P.; Marshall, I. Howard** The theology of the shorter Pauline letters. 1993, ⇒9,6346... 11/1,5164. RInterp. 50 (1996) 190-192 (*Kellogg, Frederic R.*).

6461   **Martin, D. Michael** 1,2 Thessalonians. NAC 33: Nv 1995, Broadman & H. 313 pp. 0-8054-0133-4 [RB 103,477].

6462   **Orsatti, Mauro** 1-2 Tessalonicesi. LoB.NT 10: Brescia 1996, Queriniana 134 pp. 88-399-1586-9.

6463   **Richard, Earl J.** First and Second Thessalonians. Sacra Pagina 11: ColMn 1995, Liturgical xv; 409 pp. $30. 0-8146-5813-X. RBTB 26 (1996) 173-174 (*Watson, Duane F.*).

6464   *Viray Mendoza, Jaime* Christian vocation in 1 and 2 Thessalonians. Diss. Navarra 1993, DBasevi, Claudio, Excerpta e dissertationibus in sacra theologia 28/1: Pamplona 1996, Facultad de Teología 11-91. 84-87146-66-X.

6465   **Weatherly, Jon A.** 1 & 2 Thessalonians. Joplin, Miss. 1996, College 302 pp. 1-89900-636-1 [NThAR 1997,164].

6466   **Bickmann, Jutta** Kommunikation gegen den Tod: Studien zur paulinischen Briefpragmatik am Beispiel des Ersten Thessalonicherbriefes. Diss. Münster 1996/97, DLöning [BZ 42,317].

6467   **Busch, Albrecht** Wachsende Hoffnung: 1. Thessalonicherbrief. ABC-Team: Neuk 1996, Aussaat 80 pp. 3-7615-3536-8 [NThAR 1997,68].

6468   *Demke, Christoph* Theology and literary criticism in 1 Thessalonians. JHiC 3 (1996) 194-214.

6469   *DeSilva, David A.* 'Worthy of his kingdom': honor discourse and social engineering in 1 Thessalonians. JSNT 64 (1996) 49-79.

6470 *Donfried, Karl P.* The assembly of the Thessalonians: reflections on the ecclesiology of the earliest christian letter. [F]KERTELGE K., 1996, ⇒48. 390-408.

6471 *Hester, James D.* The invention of 1 Thessalonians: a proposal. Rhetoric. JSNT.S 131: 1996, ⇒268. 251-279.

6472 **Smith, Abraham** Comfort one another: reconstructing the rhetoric...of 1 Thess. 1995, ⇒11/1,5168. [R]CritRR 9 (1996) 271-273 (*Jewett, Robert*).

6473 *Weima, Jeffrey A.D.* "How you must walk to please God": holiness and discipleship in 1 Thessalonians. Patterns of discipleship. 1996, ⇒188. 98-119.

6474 *Benson, G.P.* Note on 1 Thessalonians 1:6. ET 107 (1996) 143-144.

6475 *Perrot, Charles* 'La colère est tombée sur eux, à jamais' (1 Th 2,16). [F]LEGASSE S., LeDiv 166: 1996, ⇒51. 285-299.

6476 **Schlueter, Carol J.** Filling up the measure: polemical hyperbole in 1 Thessalonians 2:14-16. JSNT.S 98: 1994, ⇒10,6166; 11/1,5170. [R]Salm. 43/1 (1996) 123-126 (*Trevijano, Ramón*); JBL 115 (1996) 766-768 (*Grieb, A. Katherine*).

6477 *Stegemann, Ekkehard* Remarques sur la polémique antijudaïque dans 1 Thessaloniciens 2,14-16. [T]*Braunschweig-Lütolf, Ursula,* Le déchirement. MoBi 32: 1996, ⇒192. 99-112.

6478 *Manjaly, Thomas* Missionary as builder of communities: mission strategy in 1 Thess 2,1-12. IMR 18/3 (1996) 83-96.

6479 *Gundry, Robert H.* A brief note on "Hellenistic formal receptions and Paul's use of 'ἀπάντησις in 1 Thessalonians 4:17". BBR 6 (1996) 39-41.

6480 *Hughes, F.W.* The social world of 2 Thessalonians. Listening 31/2 (1996) 105-116 [NTAb 41,76].

6481 *Menken, Maarten J.J.* Christology in 2 Thessalonians: a transformation of Pauline tradition. EstB 54 (1996) 501-522.

6482 *Van Aarde, Andries G.* The second letter to the Thessalonians reread as pseudepigraph. JHiC 3 (1996) 237-266.

6483 *Berger, Martin* Die Katechon-Vorstellung 2Thess 2,6f: Dietrich BONHOEFFERs Interpretation im Kontext der Rezeptionsgeschichte. PzB 5 (1996) 33-56.

6484 *Newman, John Henry* Les jours de l'Antichrist. Le Christ au Monde 41/6 (1996) 429-440 [2].

G7.0 Epistulae pastorales

6485 **Bassler, Jouette M.** 1 Timothy, 2 Timothy, Titus. Abingdon NT Comm.: Nv 1996, Abingdon 223 pp. 0-687-00157-9.

6486 *Bassler, Jouette M.* A plethora of epiphanies: christology in the Pastoral Letters. PSB 17 (1996) 310-325.

6487 **Davies, Margaret** The Pastoral Epistles: I & II Timothy and Titus. Epworth Commentaries: L 1996, Epworth xxii; 119 pp. 0-7162-0504-1.

6488 *Goulder, Michael* The pastor's wolves: Jewish christian visionaries behind the Pastoral Epistles. NT 38 (1996) 242-256.

6489 **Griffiths, Michael** Timothy and Titus. Crossway Bible Guide: Leicester 1996, Crossway 223 pp. 1-85684-142-1 [NThAR 1997,292].

6490 **Johnson, Luke Timothy** Letters to Paul's delegates: 1 Timothy, 2 Timothy, Titus. The NT in Context: Valley Forge, PA 1996, Trinity viii; 263 pp. 1-56338-144-3.

Lau, A., Manifest in the flesh: the epiphany christology of the Pastoral Epistles ⇒6925.

6491 *Linnemann, Eta* Echtheitsfragen und Vokabelstatistik. JETh 10 (1996) 87-109.

6492 *Löning, Karl* 'Gerechtfertigt durch seine Gnade' (Tit 3,7): zum Problem der Paulusrezeption in der Soteriologie der Pastoralbriefe. F THUESING W., NTA 31: 1996, ⇒94. 241-257;

6493 'Säule und Fundament der Wahrheit' (1 Tim 3,15): zur Ekklesiologie der Pastoralbriefe. F KERTELGE K., 1996, ⇒48. 409-430.

6494 *Niemand, Christoph* "... damit das Wort Gottes nicht in Verruf kommt" (Titus 2,5): das Zurückdrängen von Frauen aus Leitungsfunktionen in den Pastoralbriefen—und was daraus heute für das Thema "Diakonat der Frauen" zu lernen ist. ThPQ 144 (1996) 351-361.

6495 *Porter, Stanley E.* Pauline authorship and the Pastoral Epistles: a response to R.W. WALL's response. BBR 6 (1996) 133-138.

6496 **Redalié, Yann** Paul après Paul: le temps, le salut, la morale selon les épîtres à Timothée et à Tite. MoBi 31: 1994, ⇒10,6185; 11/1,5186. R Bib. 77 (1996) 131-132 (*Fabris, Rinaldo*); CBQ 58 (1996) 355-357 (*Johnson, Luke Timothy*); JBL 115 (1996) 768-770 (*Kidd, Reggie M.*).

6497 *Roloff, Jürgen* Pastoralbriefe. TRE 26 (1996) 50-68.

6498 **Thompson, James W.** Equipped for change: studies in the Pastoral Epistles. Abilene, TX 1996, A.C.U. 147 pp. 0-89112-019-X.

6499 **Wagener, Ulrike** Die Ordnung des "Hauses Gottes": der Ort von Frauen in der Ekklesiologie und Ethik der Pastoralbriefe. WUNT 2/65: 1994, ⇒10,6188; 11/1,5188. R BZ 40 (1996) 144-148 (*Gielen, Marlis*); RB 103 (1996) 297-298 (*Murphy-O'Connor, Jerome*); ThLZ 121 (1996) 457-461 (*Sänger, Dieter*); SEA 61 (1996) 150-152 (*Stenström, Hanna*); JETh 10 (1996) 244-247 (*Haubeck, Wilfrid*) [1 Tim 2,9-3,1; 5,3-16].

G7.2 1-2 ad Timotheum

Borse, Udo Die Wir-Stellen der Apostelgeschichte und Timotheus ⇒5182.

6500 ET **Di Nola, Gerardo** Giovanni CRISOSTOMO: commento alla prima lettera a Timoteo. CTePa 124: 1995, ⇒11/1,5193. R Hum(B) 51 (1996) 989-990 (*Moreschini, Claudio*); Comp. 41 (1996) 257-258 (*Romero Pose, Eugenio*).

6501 *Gibson, Richard J.* The literary coherence of 1 Timothy. RTR 55 (1996) 53-66.

6502 **Oberlinner, Lorenz** 1. Tim. HThK 11/2: 1994, ⇒10,6183; 11/1,5195. R LebZeug 51 (1996) 154-155 (*Weiser, Alfons*); RB 103 (1996) 296-297 (*Murphy-O'Connor, Jerome*); BZ 40 (1996) 142-144 (*Roloff, Jürgen*); ThGl 86 (1996) 209-211 (*Ernst, Josef*); CivCatt 147 IV (1996) 307-309 (*Scaiola, D.*).

6503   *Green, Lowell C.* LUTHER's understanding of the freedom of God
       and the salvation of man: his interpretation of 1 Timothy 2:4. Zsfg.
       73. ArRefG 87 (1996) 57-73.
6504   *Stratton, Beverly* Eve through several lenses: truth in 1 Timothy
       2.8-15. A feminist companion. 1996, ⇒170. 258-274.
6505   ᴱKöstenberger, Andreas J., *(al)*, Women in the church... 1 Tim
       2:9-15. 1995, ⇒11/1,5200. ᴿJETh 10 (1996) 421-425
       (Stadelmann, Helge).
6506   *Köstenberger, Andreas J.* The crux of the matter: Paul's pastoral
       pronouncements regarding women's roles in 1 Tim 2:9-15. Faith &
       Mission 14/1 (1996) 24-48.
6507   *Testa, Emmanuele* L'inno sul "sacramentum pietatis" (1Tm 3,16).
       SBFLA 46 (1996) 87-100.
6508   *Goodwin, Mark J.* The Pauline background of the living God as
       interpretive context for 1 Timothy 4.10. JSNT 61 (1996) 65-85.

6509   **Oberlinner, Lorenz** 2. Tim. HThK 11/2: 1995, ⇒11/1,5196. ᴿBZ
       40 (1996) 288-289 *(Weiser, Alfons)*.
6510   **Ortiz, Félix** 2 Timoteo, Tito. Estudios bíblicos dinámicos: Ter-
       rassa 1996, Clie 122 pp. 84-7645-902-5 [NThAR 1998,336].

6511   *Gineste, Bernard Genomenos en rhômè (2 Tm 1, 17)*: Onésiphore
       a-t-il "été à Rome"?. RThom 96 (1996) 67-106.

G7.3 Ad Titum

6512   **Oberlinner, Lorenz** Kommentar zum Titusbrief. Die Pasto-
       ralbriefe, 3. HThK 11/2-3: FrB 1996, Herder x; 209 pp. DM74. 3-
       451-26114-6.

6513   *Stegemann, Wolfgang* Anti-Semitic and racist prejudices in Titus
       1:10-16. Ethnicity. 1996, ⇒171. 271-294.
6514   *Holman, C.L.* Titus 3:5-6: a window on worldwide pentecost.
       JPentec 8 (1996) 53-62 [NTAb 41,78].

G8 Epistula ad Hebraeos

6515   **Ellingworth, Paul** The epistle to the Hebrews. NIGTC: 1993,
       ⇒9,6399... 11/1,5215. ᴿAnton. 71 (1996) 119-121 *(Nobile,
       Marco)*.
6516   **Gench, Frances Taylor** Hebrews and James. Westminster Bible
       Companion: LVL 1996, Westminster x; 128 pp. $13. 0-664-
       25527-2.
6517   **Gräßer, Erich** Aufbruch und Verheißung: gesammelte Aufsätze
       zum Hebräerbrief. 1992, ⇒8,247a. ᴿThRv 92 (1996) 34-36
       (Backhaus, Knut); ThLZ 121 (1996) 527-528 *(Hegermann, Ha-
       rald)*;
6518   An die Hebräer, 2: Hebr 7,1-10,18. 1993, ⇒10,6208; 11/1,5217.
       ᴿBZ 40 (1996) 148-151 *(Theobald, Michael)*.
6519   **Hübner, Hans** Hebräerbrief. Biblische Theologie des NT, 3. 1995,
       ⇒11/1,5230. ActBib 33/2 (1996) 178-179 *(Boada, J.)*; ThLZ 121
       (1996) 937-940 *(Niederwimmer, Kurt)*.

6520 EParker, T.H.L. Ioannis CALVINI: opera exegetica: commentarius in epistolam ad Hebraeos. Genève 1996, Droz xvi; 268 pp. [SCJ 28,552ss Holder, R.W.].

6521 Segraves, Daniel L. A commentary on Hebrews 1-8. Hebrews—better things, 1. Hazelwood, Mo. 1996, Word Aflame 236 pp. 3-491-77017-3 [NThAR 1997,195].

6522 *Allen, David L.* The Lukan authorship of Hebrews: a proposal. JOTT 8 (1996) 1-22.

6523 Backhaus, Knut Der Neue Bund und das Werden der Kirche: die Diatheke-Deutung des Hebräerbriefs im Rahmen der frühchristlichen Theologiegeschichte. NTA 29: Müns 1996, Aschendorff xv; 414 pp. DM145. 3-402-04777-2.

6524 *Backhaus, Knut* Per Christum in Deum: zur theozentrischen Funktion der Christologie im Hebräerbrief. FTHUESING W., ⇒94. 258-284.

6525 *Benetreau, Samuel* La mort de Jésus et le sacrifice dans l'épître aux Hébreux. FV 95/4 (1996) 33-45.

6526 *Clark, Neville* Reading the book, 2: the letter to the Hebrews. ET 108 (1996) 37-40.

6527 *Colijn, Brenda B.* "Let us approach": soteriology in the epistle to the Hebrews. JETS 39 (1996) 571-586.

6528 *deSilva, David A.* Exchanging favor for wrath: apostasy in Hebrews and patron-client relationships. JBL 115 (1996) 91-116.

6529 *Frey, Jörg* Die alte und die neue διαθηκη nach dem Hebräerbrief. Bund und Tora. WUNT 92: 1996, ⇒1645. 263-310.

6530 Garuti, Paolo Alle origini dell'omiletica cristiana: la lettera agli Ebrei. ASBF 38: 1995, ⇒11/1,5228. RAng. 73 (1996) 306-309 (*Jurič, Stipe*); RevBib 58/3 (1996) 191-192 (*Ricciardi, Alberto*); CBQ 58 (1996) 746-747 (*Swetnam, James*).

6531 Guthrie, George H. The structure of Hebrews. NT.S 72: 1994, ⇒10,6222; 11/1,5229. RRExp 93 (1996) 139-141 (*Newman, Carey C.*).

6532 *Isaacs, Marie E.* Hebrews. FHOOKER M., 1996, ⇒43. 145-159.

6533 *Lane, William L.* Standing before the moral claim of God: discipleship in Hebrews. Patterns of discipleship. 1996, ⇒188. 203-224.

6534 Löhr, Hermut Umkehr und Sünde im Hebräerbrief. BZNW 73: 1994, ⇒10,6230; 11/1,5234. RJETh 10 (1996) 236-239 (*Schnabel, Eckhard J.*); CBQ 58 (1996) 162-163 (*Swetnam, James*).

6535 *Michaud, J.P.* Que reste-t-il des rites après Jésus?: une lecture de l'épître aux Hébreux. Théologiques 4 (1996) 33-35.

6536 *Mitchell, Alan C.* Holding on to confidence: παρρησία in Hebrews. Friendship. NT.S 82: 1996, ⇒180. 203-226.

6537 Niemirski, Zbigniew Listy Pawlowe oraz list do Hebrajczyków (wprowadzenie). Biblioteka Radomskiego Instytutu Teologicznego 1: Radom 1996, "AVE" 206 pp. P.

6538 *Pilhofer, Peter* ΚΡΕΙΤΤΟΝΟΣ ΔΙΑΘΗΚΗΣ ΕΓΓΥΟΣ: die Bedeutung der Präexistenzchristologie für die Theologie des Hebräerbriefs. ThLZ 121 (1996) 319-328.

6539 Schenck, Kenneth The setting of the sacrifice: eschatology and cosmology in the epistle to the Hebrews. Diss. Durham 1996, 240 pp. [EThL 74,335*].

6540   *Theobald, Michael* Zwei Bünde und ein Gottesvolk: die Bundest-
       heologie des Hebräerbriefs im Horizont des christlich-jüdischen
       Gesprächs. ThQ 176 (1996) 309-325.
6541   *Thompson, James W.* The hermeneutics of the epistle to the
       Hebrews. RestQ 38 (1996) 229-237.
6542   *Vanhoye, Albert* La "teleiosis" du Christ: point capital de la chri-
       stologie sacerdotale d'Hébreux. NTS 42 (1996) 321-338.
6543   *Weiss, Herold* Sabbatismos in the epistle to the Hebrews. CBQ 58
       (1996) 674-689.

6544   *Hedrick, Charles W.* A new Coptic fragment of the book of
       Hebrews. FYOUNG D., 1996, ⇒107. 243-246 [1,1-13].
6545   *März, Claus-Peter* '...Nur für kurze Zeit unter die Engel gestellt'
       (Hebr 2,7): Anthropologie und Christologie in Hebr 2,5-9.
       FFEIEREIS K., EThSt 71: 1996, ⇒24. 29-42.
6546   **Franco Martínez, César Augusto** Jesucristo... en la Carta a los
       Hebreos. StSem NT 1: 1992, ⇒8,6759... 11/1,5245. RLASBF 46
       (1996) 470-472 (*Bissoli, Giovanni*) [2,9-10].
6547   *Burns, Lanier* Hermeneutical issues and principles in Hebrews as
       exemplified in the second chapter. JETS 39 (1996) 587-607.
6548   **Niehof, Thomas Jay** Do not fall as they did: the wilderness gene-
       ration of Psalm 95 as a warning in Hebrews 3 and 4. Diss. Trinity
       Evang. Div. School 1996, DMood, D.J., 246 pp. [EThL 74,335*].
6549   *Van Kooten, Robert* Guarding the entrance to the place of rest:
       Hebrews 4:12-13. Kerux 11/3 (1996) 29-33 [Zech 6,1-8].
6550   *Compton, R.B.* Persevering and falling away: a reexamination of
       Hebrews 6:4-6. Detroit Baptist Seminary Journal 1 (1996) 135-167
       [NTAb 41,78].
6551   *Dieterlé, Christiane* Par-delà le voile: l'épître aux Hébreux et le
       sacrifice (Hébreux 6,13 à 10,21). FV 95/4 (1996) 47-51.
6552   *Sorg, Theo* Schaut auf das Kreuz! Hebräer 9,15.24-28. Das Wort
       vom Kreuz. 1996, ⇒206. 75-92.
6553   **Rose, Christian** Die Wolke der Zeugen... Heb 10,32-12,3.
       WUNT 2/60: 1994, ⇒10,6253. RBZ 40 (1996) 151-153 (*Theobald,
       Michael*); ThRv 92 (1996) 36-38 (*Backhaus, Knut*); CBQ 58
       (1996) 768-769 (*Davids, Peter H.*); JBL 115 (1996) 562-563
       (*Koester, Craig*).
6554   *Grässer, Erich* Das Schriftargument in Hebr 10,37f. FKERTELGE
       K., 1996, ⇒48. 431-439.
6555   *Swetnam, James* Hebrews 11,1-13,24: a suggested structure. MTh
       47/1 (1996) 27-40 [ThD Index Feb. 1997,8].
6556   *Van der Horst, Pieter W.* Sarah's seminal emission: Hebrews 11.11
       in the light of ancient embryology. A feminist companion. 1996,
       ⇒170. 112-134.
6557   *Bulley, Alan D.* Death and rhetoric in the Hebrews 'hymn to faith'.
       Sum. rés. 409. SR 25 (1996) 409-423 [11].

G9.1 1 Petri

6558   *Amphoux, Christian-Bernard* Hypothèses sur l'origine des Épîtres
       Catholiques. La lecture liturgique. 1996, ⇒6559. 308-332.
6559   E**Amphoux, Christian-Bernard; Bouhot, Jean-Paul** La lecture
       liturgique des épîtres catholiques dans l'église ancienne. Histoire

du texte biblique 1: Lausanne 1996, Zèbre 367 pp. FS49. 2-
9700088-1-5. ^RBLE 97 (1996) 406-408 (*Martimort, A.G.*).

6560 *Bouhot, Jean-Paul* Les lectionnaires latins;
6561 *Bouhot, Jean-Paul; Amphoux, Christian-B.* Lecture liturgique et
critique textuelle des Épîtres. La lecture liturgique. 1996, ⇒6559.
239-281/283-307.
6562 **Chester, Andrew; Martin, Ralph P.** The theology of the letters of
James, Peter, and Jude. 1994, ⇒10,6286. ^RJBL 115 (1996) 161-
163 (*Watson, Duane F.*); CBQ 58 (1996) 343-344 (*Winkler, Jude*).
6563 *Desreumaux, Alain* Les lectionnaires syro-palestiniens. La lecture
liturgique. 1996, ⇒6559. 87-103.
6564 *Fritsch, Emmanuel* Les lectionnaires éthiopiens. La lecture liturgique. 1996, ⇒6559. 197-219.
6565 ^EHofmann, Josef; Uhlig, Siegbert NT aethiopice: die katholischen Briefe. ÄthF 29: 1993, ⇒9,6435; 11/1,5267. ^RBSOAS 59/1
(1996) 203-205 (*Knibb, Michael A.*); JAOS 116 (1996) 297-298
(*Dombrowski, Franz Amadeus*).
6566 *Johannet, José* Les apostolaires slaves anciens. La lecture liturgique. 1996, ⇒6559. 47-52.
6567 **Knoch, Otto Bernhard** Le due lettere di Pietro: la lettera di
Giuda. ^T*Faini, Silvia*, Il Nuovo Testamento Commentato: Brescia
1996, Morcelliana 494 pp. L50.000. 88-372-1499-5.
6568 *Marconi, G.* La vita e l'ambiente nelle lettere di Giacomo, Pietro e
Giuda, I-II. La natura. 1996, ⇒189. 171-186, 187-199.
6569 *Outtier, Bernard* Les lectionnaires géorgiens. La lecture liturgique.
1996, ⇒6559. 75-85.
6570 **Perkins, Pheme** First and Second Peter, James, and Jude. 1995,
⇒11/1,5272. ^RCBQ 58 (1996) 764-765 (*Cahill, Michael*); CritRR
9 (1996) 251-253 (*Chester, Andrew*).
6571 *Renoux, Charles* Les lectionnaires arméniens. La lecture liturgique.
1996, ⇒6559. 53-74.
6572 *Richards, W.L.* A closer look: "Text und Textwert der griechischen
Handschriften des Neuen Testaments: die katholischen Briefe".
AUSS 34 (1996) 37-46.
6573 *Rouwhorst, Gerard* Les lectionnaires syriaques. La lecture liturgique. 1996, ⇒6559. 105-140.
6574 **Wachtel, Klaus** Der byzantinische Text der Katholischen Briefe.
ANTT 24: 1995, ⇒11/1,5273. ^RNT 38 (1996) 409-411 & ThLZ
121 (1996) 1162-1163 (*Elliott, J.K.*); CritRR 9 (1996) 297-299
(*Richards, W. Larry*).
6575 *Zanetti, Ugo* Les leçons du Paris, B.N., éthiopien 42;
6576 Les lectionnaires coptes. La lecture liturgique. 1996, ⇒6559. 220-
237/141-196.

6577 **Achtemeier, Paul J.** 1 Peter: a commentary on First Peter. Hermeneia: Mp 1996, Fortress xxxvi; 423 pp. $50. 0-8006-6030-7.
^RWThJ 58 (1996) 321-323 (*McCartney, Dan G.*).
6578 *Böcher, Otto* Petrus, Apostel: I, Neues Testament. TRE 26 (1996)
263-273.
6579 **Brox, Norbert** La primera Carta de Pedro. 1994, ⇒10,6258;
11/1,5262. ^RCDios 209 (1996) 496-497 (*Gutiérrez, J.*).
6580 *Brox, Norbert* Petrusbriefe. TRE 26 (1996) 308-319.

6581 **Casurella, Anthony** Bibliography of literature on First Peter. NTTS 23: Lei 1996, Brill xviii; 171 pp. ƒ90/$58.25. 90-04-10488-7 [NTAb 41,157].

6582 **Grudem, Wayne A.** La prima epistola di Pietro. 1995, ⇒11/1,5265. ᴿSdT 8/2 (1996) 176-177 (*Racca, Tonino*).

6583 **McKnight, Scot** 1 Peter. NIV Application Commentary: GR 1996, Zondervan 295 pp. 0-310-49290-4.

6584 **Bechtler, Steven Richard** Following in his steps: suffering, community, and christology in 1 Peter. Diss. Princeton Theol. Sem. 1996, 290 pp. DAI-A 57/05, p. 2080; AAC 9629090.

6585 *Bosetti, Elena* I cristiani come stranieri nella prima lettera di Pietro. RStB 8.1-2 (1996) 317-334.

6586 **Campbell, Barth Lynn** Honor, shame, and the rhetoric of 1 Peter. Diss. Fuller Theol. Sem. 1996, 366 pp. [EThL 74,336*].

6587 **Long, Mark Thomas** Holiness as a theme in 1 Peter. Diss. New Orleans Bapt. Theol. Sem. 1995, ᴰ*Simmons, B.E.*, 185 pp. [EThL 74,336*].

6588 **Metzner, Rainer** Die Rezeption des Matthäusevangeliums im 1. Petrusbrief. WUNT 2/74: 1995, ⇒11/1,5279. ᴿThLZ 121 (1996) 666-668 (*Schweizer, Eduard*).

6589 *Michaels, J. Ramsey* Going to heaven with Jesus: from 1 Peter to *Pilgrim's Progress*. Patterns of discipleship. 1996, ⇒188. 248-268.

6590 *Schumacher, Ferdinand* 'Laßt euch als lebendige Steine zu einem geistigen Haus aufbauen' (1 Petr 2,5). ᶠKᴇʀᴛᴇʟɢᴇ K., 1996, ⇒48. 440-457.

6591 *Skilton, John H.* A glance at some old problems in First Peter. WThJ 58 (1996) 1-9.

6592 **Stimpfle, Josef** Das christliche Leben als Verherrlichung Gottes: eine bibeltheologische Untersuchung zum ersten Petrusbrief. Augsburg 1996, Wissner xiv; 362 pp. 3-89639-026-0 [NThAR 1997,101].

6593 *Tite, P.L.* The compositional function of the Petrine prescript: a look at 1 Pet 1:1-3. JETS 39 (1996) 47-56.

6594 *Puig i Tàrrech, Armand* Une semence, une fraternité: lecture de 1P 1,22-2,3. ᶠDᴜᴘᴏɴᴛ J., 1996, 173-195.

6595 *Jossa, Giorgio* La sottomissione alle autorità politiche in 1Pt 2,13-17. RivBib 44 (1996) 205-211.

6596 *Slaughter, James R.* Submission of wives (1 Pet. 3:1a) in the context of 1 Peter. BS 153 (1996) 63-74.

6597 *Bosetti, Elena* 'Beati voi, se soffrite per la giustizia' (1Pt 3,14). Som. 223. PSV 34 (1996) 223-238.

G9.2 2 Petri

6598 **Arentsen, M.J.** De kracht en de komst van Christus: bijbelstudies bij de tweede brief van Petrus. Vaassen 1996, Medema 311 pp. 90-6353-253-9 [NThAR 1997,35].

6599 **Lloyd-Jones, David Martyn** 2 Pietro. Mantova 1996, Passaggio 256 pp. ᴿSdT 8 (1996) 177-178 (*Perboni, Alfio*).

6600 **Moo, Douglas J.** 2 Peter and Jude. NIV Application Commentary: GR 1996, Zondervan 316 pp. 0-310-20104-7 [NThAR 1997,261].

6601 *Tábet, Miguel Angel* Vida cristiana y esperanza del hombre en 2 Pt. Esperanza del hombre. 1996, ⇒173. 155-164.
6602 *Thurén, Lauri* Style never goes out of fashion: 2 Peter re-evaluated. Rhetoric. JSNT.S 131: 1996, ⇒268. 329-347.

6603 *Miller, Robert J.* Is there independent attestation for the transfiguration in 2 Peter?. NTS 42 (1996) 620-625 [1,16-18].
6604 *Sherwood, J.* The only sure word. MastJ 7/1 (1996) 53-74 [1,16-21] [NTAb 41,80].
6605 *Monforte, José María* Escatología y esperanza activa en 2 Pt 3,3-15. Esperanza del hombre. 1996, ⇒173. 165-179.

G9.4 Epistula Jacobi... data on both apostles James

6606 **Frankemölle, Hubert** Der Brief des Jakobus: Kapitel 1 [⇒11/1,5300], 2-5. ÖTBK 17/1-2: 1994, ⇒10,6278. [R]ZKTh 188 (1996) 268-270 (*Oberforcher, Robert*).
 Gench, F. Hebrews and James ⇒6516.
6607 **Holloway, Gary** James & Jude. College NIV Commentary: Joplin, Miss. 1996, College 203 pp. 0-89900-638-8 [NThAR 1997,292].
6608 **Johnson, Luke Timothy** The letter of James. AncB 37A: 1995, ⇒11/1,5303. [R]CV 38 (1996) 281-284 (*Segert, Stanislav*).
6609 **Vouga, François** A carta de Tiago. [T]*Bagno, Marcos,* Bíblica Loyola 7a: São Paulo 1996, Loyola 166 pp. 85-15-01384-3 [PerTeol 29,133].
6610 **Vries, E. de** Jakobus: een praktische bijbelverklaring. Tekst en Toelichting: Kampen 1996, Kok 90 pp. *f*25. 90-2427876-7 [ITBT 5/5,32].

6611 *Ahrens, Matthias* Vom Chaos zur Einheit: literarische oder historische Betrachtung des Jakobusbriefes?. PzB 5 (1996) 59-63.
6612 **Baker, William R.** Personal speech-ethics in the epistle of James. WUNT 2/68: 1995, ⇒11/1,5306. [R]CBQ 58 (1996) 339-340 (*Davids, Peter H.*); Bib. 77 (1996) 135-138 (*Wilson, R. McL.*).
6613 **Bernheim, Pierre-Antoine** Jacques, frère de Jésus. P 1996, Noêsis 387 pp. FF150. 2-911606-05-1 [RB 104,312].
6614 **Cargal, Timothy, B.** Restoring the diaspora: discursive structure and purpose in the epistle of James. SBL.DS 144: 1993, ⇒10,6285; 11/1,5308. [R]TJT 12/1 (1996) 96-98 (*Hartin, Patrick J.*).
 Chester, A., (*al*), The theology of... James ⇒6562.
6615 *Crotty, Robert* James the Just in the history of early christianity. ABR 44 (1996) 42-52.
6616 **Eisenman, Robert H.** James the brother of Jesus: the key to unlocking the secrets of early christianity and the Dead Sea Scrolls. NY 1996, Viking xxxvi; 1074 pp. 0-670-86932-5 [NThAR 1997,260].
6617 *Hartin, Patrick J.* "Who is wise and understanding among you?" (James 3:13): an analysis of wisdom, eschatology and apocalypticism in the epistle of James. SBL.SPS 35: 1996, ⇒274. 483-503.
6618 [E]**Herbers, Klaus; Bauer, Dieter R.** Der Jakobskult in Süddeutschland. Jakobus-Studien 7: 1995, ⇒11/1,5311. [R]HJ 116/1 (1996) 200-202 (*Flachenecker, Helmut*).

6619 *Jackson-McCabe, Matt A.* A letter to the twelve tribes in the diaspora: wisdom and 'apocalyptic' eschatology in the letter of James. SBL.SPS 35: 1996, ⇒274. 504-517.

6620 **Klein, Martin** "Ein vollkommenes Werk": Vollkommenheit, Gesetz und Gericht als theologische Themen des Jakobusbriefes. BWANT 139: 1995, ⇒11/1,5313. [R]BZ 40 (1996) 289-290 (*Hoppe, Rudolf*); ThLZ 121 (1996) 663-665 (*Karrer, Martin*).

6621 **Konradt, Matthias** Christliche Existenz nach dem Jakobusbrief: eine Studie zu seiner soteriologischen und ethischen Konzeption. Diss. Heidelberg 1996/97, [D]*Burchard, Ch.* [ThLZ 122,763].

6622 **Penner, Todd C.** The epistle of James and eschatology: re-reading an ancient christian letter. JSNT.S 121: Shf 1996, Academic 331 pp. £53/$80. 1-85075-574-4 [NTAb 41,162].

6623 *Rolland, Philippe* La date de l'épître de Jacques. NRTh 118 (1996) 839-851.

6624 *Starowieyski, Marek* La légende de Saint Jacques le Majeur. Sum. rés. 193. Apocrypha 7 (1996) 193-203.

6625 **Webber, Randall C.** Reader response analysis of the epistle of James. L 1996, International Scholars (4) iv; 125 pp. 1-57292-086-7.

G9.6 Epistula Judae

Chester, A., (*al*), The theology of...Jude ⇒6562.

6626 **Heiligenthal, Roman** Zwischen Henoch und Paulus: Studien zum theologiegeschichtlichen Ort des Judasbriefes. TANZ 6: 1992, ⇒8,6835; 9,6482. [R]JThS 47 (1996) 245-248 (*Bauckham, Richard*).

Holloway, G. James & Jude ⇒6607.

Knoch, O. ...La lettera di Giuda ⇒6567.

6627 [E]**Krieg, Matthias; Zangger-Derron, Gabrielle** Judas: ein literarisch-theologisches Lesebuch. Z 1996, TVZ 342 pp. 3-290-17145-0 [NThAR 1997,194].

6628 **Landon, Charles** A text-critical study of the epistle of Jude. Diss. Stellenbosch. JSNT.S 135: Shf 1996, Academic 172 pp. £30/$45. 1-85075-636-8 [CBQ 59,422].

6629 **Lyle, Kenneth Ralph** Ethical admonition in the epistle of Jude. Diss. Southern Bapt. Theol. Sem. 1995, [D]*Garland, D.E.*, 229 pp. [EThL 74,337*].

Moo, D. 2 Peter and Jude ⇒6600.

6630 *Reed, Jeffrey T.; Reese, Ruth A.* Verbal aspect, discourse prominence, and the letter of Jude. FgNT 9 (1996) 181-199.

Renoux, C. La chaîne sur...Jude ⇒5664.

6631 **Turner, J. David; Deibler, Ellis: Turner, Janet L.** Jude: a structural commentary. Mellen 44: Lewiston 1996, Mellen 128 pp. 0-7734-2415-6 [NThAR 1997,293].

6632 *Webb, Robert L.* The eschatology of the epistle of Jude and its rhetorical and social functions. BBR 6 (1996) 139-151.

XIII. Theologia Biblica

h1.1 Biblical Theology [OT] God

6633 *Adams, D.L.* The present God: a framework for biblical theology. ConJ 22 (1996) 279-294 [NTAb 41,84].

6634 **Armstrong, Karen** Una historia de Dios: 4000 años de búsqueda en el judaísmo, cristianismo y el Islam. Paidós Contextos: Barc 1993, Paidós 521 pp. REstFr 97 (1996) 194-195 (*Llimona, Jordi*);

6635 A history of God: the 4000-year quest of Judaism, Christianity, and Islam. 1993. ⇒9,7001... 11/2,2762. RJdm 45 (1996) 380-383 (*Hamel, Gildas*).

6636 **Baudler, Georg** El Jahwe Abba: wie die Bibel Gott versteht. Dü 1996, Patmos 263 pp. DM44.80. 3-491-77981-2 [ThLZ 122,324].

6637 *Deiana, Giovanni* Il Dio dell'Antico Testamento. Dio—Signore nella bibbia. DSBP 13: 1996, ⇒328. 19-75.

6638 *Dumas, André* L'insolence de Dieu: suite sans fin ⇒6644. FV 95/5 (1996) 45-46.

6639 **Friedman, Richard Elliott** The disappearance of God. 1995, ⇒11/2,2774. RTS 57 (1996) 735-736 (*Sklba, Richard J.*); BiRe 12/1 (1996) 17, 45 (*Hendel, Ronald S.*).

6640 **Gerstenberger, Erhard S.** Jahwe—ein patriarchaler Gott?. 1988, ⇒4,3117... 9,3010. RThR 61 (1996) 91-93 (*Reventlow, Henning Graf*).

6641 **Goodman, Lenn E.** God of Abraham. NY 1996, OUP xvii; 364 pp. $50.

6642 *Görg, Manfred* Der "schlagende" Gott in der "älteren" Bibel. BiKi 51 (1996) 94-100.

6643 *Gross, Walter* Das verborgene Gesicht Gottes—eine alttestamentliche Grunderfahrung und die heutige religiöse Krise. Gott—ein Fremder in unserem Haus?. EHünermann, Peter, QD 165: FrB 1996, Herder. 3-451-02165-X. 65-77.

6644 *Houziaux, Alain* L'insolence de Dieu. FV 95/1 (1996) 85-92.

6645 **Kaiser, Otto** Der Gott des Alten Testaments, 1: Grundlegung. 1993, ⇒9,7019; 11/2,2780. REvTh 56 (1996) 258-285 (*Dietrich, Walter*); JR 76 (1996) 328-337 (*Rendtorff, Rolf*); ThR 61 (1996) 56-58 (*Reventlow, Henning Graf*).

6646 *Klopfenstein, Martin A.* Die Gottesfrage im Alten Testament;
6647 Gott und Krieg im Alten Testament—ein vielschichtiges Problem;
6648 Im Spiegel Gottes;
6649 Vom Zorn Gottes im Alten Testament. Leben aus dem Wort. BEAT 40: 1996, ⇒132. 161-173/203-213/329-331/199-213.

6650 **Leeming, David Adams; Page, Jake** God: myths of the male divine. NY 1996, OUP xii; 196 pp. Bibl. 0-19-509306-2.

6651 **Lindström, Fredrik** God and the origin of evil. CB.OT 21: 1983, ⇒64,6192... 3,6351. RThR 61 (1996) 86-87 (*Reventlow, Henning Graf*).

6652 **Miles, Jack** God: a biography. 1995, ⇒11/2,2790. RRExp 93 (1996) 296-298 (*Watts, John D.W.*); Jdm 45 (1996) 376-380 (*Hamel, Gildas*);

6653 Dios: una biografía. TUdina, Dolors, Barc 1996, Planeta 491 pp. RActBib 33 (1996) 181-182 (*Boada, J.*).

6654 *Otto, Eckart* Der eine Gott—die eine Welt: biblische Fundamente politischer Einigungsprozesse in der Moderne: Grundsatzfragen zur Begründung des europäischen Einigungsprozesses. Kontinuum. Orientalia biblica et christiana 8: 1996 < 1992 >, ⇒2002. 304-316.

6655 *Panimolle, Salvatore A.* Il Signore Dio, centro e cuore della spiritualità biblica. Dio—Signore nella bibbia. DSBP 13: 1996, ⇒328. 7-18.

6656 *Rad, Gerhard von* La realidad de Dios. La acción de Dios. 1996 < 1958 >, ⇒144. 130-149.

6657 **Samuel, Michael** The Lord is my shepherd: the theology of a caring God. Northvale, NJ 1996, Aronson xii; 267 pp. Bibl. 1-568-21912-1 [NThAR 1998,99].

6658 **Scharbert, Josef** Mit Gott "Deutsch reden": der Dialog zwischen Mensch und Gott in der Bibel. St. Ottilien 1996, EOS 119 pp. 3-88096-416-5.

6659 *Schmitt, John J.* Gender correctness and biblical metaphors: the case of God's relation to Israel. BTB 26 (1996) 96-106 [Jer 3; Ezek 16; 23; Hos 2].

6660 **Soulen, R. Kendall** The God of Israel and christian theology. Mp 1996, Fortress xii; 195 pp. $16. 0-8264-0860-5 [ThTo 54,86].

6661 **Stolz, Fritz** Einführung in den biblischen Monotheismus. Die Theologie: 1996, Da:Wiss viii; 238 pp. 3-534-10512-5.

6662 **Streit, Judith Ann** The God of Abraham: a study in characterization. Diss. Iliff 1996, 233 pp. [EThL 74,194*].

6663 *Suh, Joong S.* The faithfulness of God and the destiny of Israel. Yonsei Journal of Theology 1 (1996) 55-66 [ZID 23,414].

6664 **Vanoni, Gottfried** "Du bist doch unser Vater" (Jes 63,16): zur Gottesvorstellung des Ersten Testaments. SBS 159: 1995, ⇒11/2,2863. [R]ITS 33 (1996) 185-187 (Ceresko, Anthony R.).

6665 *Vincent, Jean Marcel* Aspekte der Begegnung mit Gott im Alten Testament: die Erfahrung der göttlichen Gegenwart im Schauen Gottes. RB 103 (1996) 5-39.

6666 *Weinfeld, Moshe* Feminine features in the imagery of God in Israel: the sacred marriage and the sacred tree. VT 46 (1996) 515-529.

6667 *Whybray, R.N.* The immorality of God: reflections on some passages in Genesis, Job, Exodus and Numbers. JSOT 72 (1996) 89-120 [Gen 18,22-33; Exod 32,7-14; Num 11,11-25; Job 1-2].

H1.4 *Femininum in Deo*—God as father and mother

6668 **Alonso Schökel, Luis** Dio Padre: meditazioni bibliche. 1994, ⇒10,7045. [R]CivCatt 147 I (1996) 518-519 (*Scaiola, D.*).

6669 **Eilberg-Schwartz, Howard** God's phallus: and other problems for men and monotheism. 1994, ⇒10,7051. [R]AJSR 21 (1996) 164-166 (*Rosenbaum, Stanley N.*).

6670 **Galot, Jean** Père, qui es-Tu?: petite catéchisme sur le Père. Versailles 1996, Saint-Paul 174 pp. FF69. 2-85049-665-0. [R]EeV 106 (1996) 461 (*Oury, G.-M.*).

6671 *Grelot, Pierre* Dieu, le Père de Jésus Christ. 1994, ⇒10,7407; 11/2,3409. [R]RSR 84 (1996) 606-608 (*Sesboüé, Bernard*).

6672 **Johnson, Elizabeth A.** She who is: the mystery of God in feminist discourse. 1992, ⇒8,7065... 11/2,2854. [R]JR 76 (1996) 341-345 (*Lefebure, Leo D.*); KHÅ 96 (1996) 199-201 (*Blückert, Kjell*).

6673 *Kwame Kumi, George* God's image as equivalently father and mother: an African perspective. AfER 38 (1996) 203-228.
6674 *Mary Corona, Sr.* The compassionate God of the bible. Jeevadhara 26 (1996) 173-183.
6675 **Raschke, Carl A.; Raschke, Susan Doughty** The engendering God: male and female faces of God. 1995, ⇒11/2,2858. ^RAThR 78 (1996) 693-695 (*McDougall, Joy A.*).
6676 *Spencer, Aída B.* Father-rule: the meaning of the metaphor "father" for God in the bible. JETS 39 (1996) 433-442.
6677 ^E**Van Wijk-Bos, Johanna W.H.**, Reimagining God: the case for scriptural diversity. 1995, ⇒11/2,2867. ^RCBQ 58 (1996) 529 (*Green, Barbara*).
6678 **Widdicombe, Peter** The fatherhood of God from ORIGEN to ATHANASIUS. 1994, ⇒11/2,2866. ^RChH 65 (1996) 662-663 (*Kolp, Alan*); JThS 47 (1996) 292-295 (*McWilliam, Joanne*); REAug 42 (1996) 167-170 (*Kannengiesser, Charles*).

H1.7 Revelatio

6679 **Baccari, Luciano** La rivelazione nelle religioni. R 1996, Borla 140 pp. ^RUnitas 51/3-4 (1996) 177-178 (*Grossi, Vittorino*).
6680 *Bartholomew I, Patriarch* Revelation revisited. Parabola 21/1 (1996) 29-34.
6681 **Claverie, Pierre** Le livre de la foi: révélation et parole de Dieu dans la tradition chrétienne. Les éveques du Maghreb. P 1996, Cerf 157 pp. 2-204-05506-9.
6682 *González Montes, Adolfo* "Dei Verbum" sobre el fondo de "Dei Filius": explicitación, desarrollo y progreso en el concepto de revelación. Salm. 43 (1996) 341-364.
6683 **Gunton, Colin E.** A brief theology of revelation. 1995, ⇒11/2,2874. ^REE 71 (1996) 329-330 (*Madangi Sengi, Jean de Dieu*); ET 107 (1995-96) 33-34 (*Rodd, C.S.*); CTJ 31 (1996) 374-376 (*Feenstra, Ronald J.*); JThS 47 (1996) 780-782 (*Wiles, Maurice*).
6684 **Haught, John F.** Mystery and promise: a theology of revelation. 1993, ⇒10,7089*; 11/2,2876. ^RScrTh 28 (1996) 954-955 (*Odero, J.M.*); EThL 72 (1996) 476-477 (*Brito, E.*).
6685 *Levoratti, Armando J.* Historia e historicidad de la revelación. RevBib 58 (1996) 1-55.
6686 *McPake, John* John MCCONNACHIE as the original advocate of the theology of Karl BARTH in Scotland: the primacy of revelation. SBET 14/2 (1996) 101-114.
6687 *Nieuviarts, Jacques* La bible, la terre et le livre: incarnation et révélation. BLE.S 1 (1996) 61-73.
6688 Report of the joint commission between the Roman Catholic Church and the World Methodist Council: 'The word of life: a statement on revelation and faith'. 1996, ^ROiC 32/4 (1996) 363-377 (*Henn, William*).
6689 **Tillich, Paul** Teologia sistematica, 1: religione e rivelazione: l'essere di Dio. ^T*Bertalot, R.*, Claudiana 1996, T 364 pp. L49.000. 88-7016-226-5.
6690 *Wagner, Siegfried* 1. Sam. 9,15: 'Jahwe aber hatte das Ohr des Samuel geöffnet...': Bemerkungen zum Problem der Offenbarung

im Alten Testament. Ausgewählte Aufsätze. BZAW 240: 1996
<1971>, ⇒156. 47-56.

H1.8 Theologia fundamentalis

6691 **Korsmeyer, Jerry D.** God—creature—revelation: a neoclassical
framework for fundamental theology . 1995, ⇒11/2,2825.
RHorizons 23 (1996) 343-344 (*Whitney, Barry L.*).

6692 E**Latourelle, René; Fisichella, Rino** Dictionary of fundamental
theology. NY 1995, Crossroad xxxviii; 1222 pp. $75. [AUSS
35,286ss—Hasel, Frank M.].

6693 **Ohlig, Karl-Heinz** Fundamentalchristologie. 1986, ⇒2,5639...
7,7134. RThRv 92 (1996) 255-258 (*Schwager, Raymund*).

6694 **Placher, William C.** Narratives of a vulnerable God: Christ,
theology, scripture. 1994, ⇒10,7036; 11/2,2925. RSBET 14 (1996)
166-168 (*Francis, Denise*).

6695 **Waldenfels, Hans** Manuel de théologie fondamentale. 1990,
⇒7,7147... 10,7150. RTelema 22/3-4 (1996) 88-89 (*Haes, René
de*);

6696 Einführung in die Theologie der Offenbarung. 1996, Da:Wiss ix;
208 pp. DM39.80. 3-534-11864-2.

H2.1 Anthropologia theologica—VT & NT

6697 *Ausín, Santiago* Unidad del génere humano. Esperanza del hombre.
1996, ⇒173. 407-436.

6698 *Baltzer, Dieter* Anthropologische Aspekte alttestamentlicher Didaktik: Gottesebenbildlichkeit und Herrschaftsauftrag. Alttestamentliche Fachdidaktik. 1996, ⇒535. 143-167.

6699 *Botha, J. Eugene* Exploring gesture and nonverbal communication
in the bible and the ancient world: some initial observations.
Neotest. 30 (1996) 1-19.

6700 *Carr, Dhyanchand* Is there space for ethnic consciousness and cultural particularity within the one new humanity we hope and work
for?. IRM 85 (1996) 11-23.

6701 *Friedrich, Gerhard* Der Realismus des biblischen Menschenbildes.
Religion. ANRW II.26.3. 1996, ⇒183. 2715-2735.

6702 *Goldberg, Harvey E.* Cambridge in the land of Canaan: descent,
alliance, circumcision, and instruction in the bible. JANES 24
(1996) 9-34.

6703 *Golka, Friedemann W.* Sozialanthropologie und Altes Testament
am Beispiel biblischer und afrikanischer Sprichwörter. FMICHEL
D., BZAW 241: 1996, 65-89.

6704 *Kirchschläger, Walter* "Was ist zwischen dir und mir, Frau?" biblische Anregungen zum Paradigma der Generationenbeziehung.
Diak. 27 (1996) 366-372.

6705 *Klopfenstein, Martin A.* Aus der Stille;
6706 *Klopfenstein, Martin A.* Hunger-Menu;
6707 *Klopfenstein, Martin A.* Jeder Mensch ist Ebenbild Gottes;
6708 *Klopfenstein, Martin A.* Sorgfalt im Umgang mit Worten;

6709 *Klopfenstein, Martin A.* Zuhören Leben aus dem Wort. Leben aus dem Wort. BEAT 40: 1996, ⇒132. 327-328/333-335/253-254/323-324/325-326.

6710 *Loza, José* La dignidad y responsabilidad del hombre: perspectivas del Antiguo Testamento. Esperanza del hombre. 1996, ⇒173. 45-66.

6711 *Osiek, Carolyn* The family in early christianity: "family values" revisited. CBQ 58 (1996) 1-24.

6712 **Pastor Ramos, Federico** Antropología bíblica. Estella 1995, Verbo Divino 320 pp. ᴿEE 71 (1996) 480-482 (*Piñero, Antonio*).
  Ramírez, Guillermo The social location of the prophet Amos ⇒3715.

6713 *Ramos, Felipe F.* La metamorfosis del creyente. Salm. 43 (1996) 209-248.

6714 **Ribeiro, Hélcion** Ensaio de antropologia cristã: da imagem à semelhança com Deus. Petrópolis 1995, Vozes 222 pp. ᴿREB 56 (1996) 995-997 (*Lepargneur, Hubert*).

6715 *Scaiola, Donatella* La paura nell'Antico Testamento. PSV 33/1 (1996) 11-19 [Ps 127].

6716 *Schnelle, Udo* Neutestamentliche Anthropologie: ein Forschungsbericht. Religion. ANRW II.26.3. 1996, ⇒183. 2658-2714.

6717 *Schürmann, Heinz* Das drei-einige Selbst im Lichte paulinischer Anthropologie. ꜰTʜᴜᴇsɪɴɢ W., NTA 31: 1996, ⇒94. 389-429.

6718 *Segalla, Giuseppe* Cuatro modelos de 'hombre nuevo' en la literatura neotestamentaria. Esperanza del hombre. 1996, ⇒173. 83-135.

6719 **Tepe, Valfredo** Para que tanto sofrimento?. Petrópolis 1996, Vozes 204 pp. REB 56 (1996) 749-752 (*Garmus, Ludovico*).

6720 **Wénin, André** L'homme biblique: anthropologie et éthique dans le Premier Testament. 1995, ⇒11/2,3002. ᴿFV 95 (1996) 126-127 (*Flichy, Odile*); Cahiers de l'Atelier 470 (1996) 101-102 (*Durand, Xavier*); Synaxis 14/1 (1996) 373-376 (*Minissale, Antonino*).

6721 *Ziegenaus, Anton* Del Antiguo Testamento a la antropología cristiana: la importancia decisiva de los libros deuterocanónicos. Esperanza del hombre. 1996, ⇒173. 67-82.

H2.7 Œcologia VT & NT—saecularitas

6722 *Delfieux, Pierre-Marie* Argent-serviteur ou mammon-dictateur. Com(F) 21/4 (1996) 29-34.

6723 **Gustafson, James M.** A sense of the divine: the natural environment from a theocentric perspective. 1994, ⇒10,7216; 11/2,3047. ᴿInterp. 50 (1996) 90, 92 (*Cobb, John B.*).

6724 *Hiebert, Theodore* Re-imaging nature: shifts in biblical interpretation. Interp. 50 (1996) 36-46.

6725 *Klopfenstein, Martin A.* Plädoyer für eine wohnliche Welt. Leben aus dem Wort. BEAT 40: 1996, ⇒132. 259-260.

6726 *Lewis, J.M.* Servants of creation: reshaping a biblical theology of ecology. ModBelieving 37/1 (1996) 16-24 [NTAb 40,467].
  ᴱ**Lorenzani, Massimo** La natura e l'ambiente nella bibbia ⇒189.

6727 **Murray, Robert** The cosmic covenant: biblical themes of justice, peace and the integrity of creation. HeyM 7: 1992, ⇒8,7266... 10,7240. ᴿRSPT 80/1 (1996) 143-144 (*Fantino, J.*).

6728   *Nash, James A.* Toward the ecological reformation of christianity.
       Interp. 50 (1996) 5-15.
6729   *Nigossian, S.A.* Water in biblical literature. NESTThRev 17/1
       (1996) 33-51 [NTAb 41,98].
6730   **Page, Ruth** God and the web of creation. L 1996, SCM xix; 188
       pp. £15. 0-334-02653-9. [R]ET 108 (1996-97) 129-132 (*Rodd, C.S.;
       Page, Ruth*).
6731   *Perrot, Charles* Entre Dieu et mammon: l'argent dans les évangi-
       les. Com(F) 21/4 (1996) 13-28.
6732   **Primavesi, Anne** Del Apocalipsis al Génesis: ecología, feminismo,
       cristianismo. [T]*Martínez Riu, Antonio,* Barc 1995, Herder 384 pp.
       [R]Lumen 45 (1996) 244-246 (*Gil Ortega, Urbano*); Iter 7/2 (1996)
       151-152 (*Moracho, Félix*); Cart. 12 (1996) 507-509 (*Oliver Alcón,
       F.*).
6733   *Rolston, Holmes* The bible and ecology. Interp. 50 (1996) 16-26.
6734   *Torre, Jesús de la* La tierra en la biblia. NuMu 174-175 (1996) 51-
       66 [ThIK 18/1,78].
6735   *Towner, W. Sibley* The future of nature. Interp. 50 (1996) 27-35.

H3.1   *Foedus*—the Covenant; the Chosen People; Providence

6736   [E]**Avemarie, Friedrich; Lichtenberger, Hermann** Bund und Tora:
       zur theologischen Begriffsgeschichte in alttestamentlicher, frühjüdi-
       scher und urchristlicher-Tradition. WUNT 92: Tü 1996, Mohr x;
       346 pp. DM218. 3-16-146627-6. [R]OrdKor 39 (1998) 364-365
       (*Giesen, Heinz*).
6737   *Backhaus, Knut* Gottes nicht bereuter Bund: alter und neuer Bund
       in der Sicht des Frühchristentums < German >   Ekklesiologie des
       Neuen Testaments. [F]KERTELGE K., 1996, ⇒48. 33-55;
6738   Hat Jesus vom Gottesbund gesprochen?. ThGl 86 (1996) 343-356
       [Matt 26,28; Mark 14,24; Luke 22,20; 1 Cor 11,25].
6739   *Brewer, D.I.* Three weddings and a divorce: God's covenant with
       Israel, Judah and the church. TynB 47 (1996) 1-25.
6740   **Damrosch, David** The narrative covenant: transformations of
       genre in the growth of biblical literature. 1987, ⇒3,6734... 6,7280.
       [R]JNES 55 (1996) 143-144 (*Handy, Lowell K.*).
6741   *Groß, Walter; Theobald, Michael* Wenn Christen vom Neuen Bund
       reden... eine riskante Denkfigur auf dem Prüfstand. ThQ 176
       (1996) 257-258.
6742   **Holwerda, David E.** Jesus and Israel: one covenant or two?. 1995,
       ⇒11/2,3131. [R]BS 153 (1996) 112-114 (*Spencer, Stephen R.*);
       WThJ 58 (1996) 161-163 (*Otto, Randall E.*); RRT 3/2 (1996) 8-16
       (*Need, Stephen W.*); HBT 18 (1996) 205-208 (*Waldow, H. Eber-
       hard von*).
6743   *Kaimakis, Dimitris* The meaning of faith in the Old Testament.
       DBM 15/2 (1996) 3-9.
6744   *Klopfenstein, Martin A.* Der Staat Israel als Frage an uns Christen.
       Leben aus dem Wort. BEAT 40: 1996, ⇒132. 223-234.
6745   **Lippi, Adolfo** Elezione e passione: saggio de teologia in ascolto
       all'ebraismo. Religione e religioni: T 1996, Elle di Ci 152 pp.
       L15.000. [R]PalCl 75/1-2 (1996) 154-157 (*Lavarda, Girolamo*).
6746   **Millan, Armand Michael L.** The desert in the tradition of Israel:
       an analysis of some passages of Hosea, Amos, Isaiah, Jeremiah,

Ezekiel and the Psalms. Diss. Pamplona 1996, ^D*Caro Pineda, F.*, 266 pp. [EThL 74,237*].

6747 *Mondin, Battista* Le matrici della teologia cristiana. CiVi 51 (1996) 7-18.

6748 *Mußner, Franz* JHWH, der sub contrario handelnde Gott Israels. ^FTHUESING W., NTA 31: 1996, ⇒94. 25-33.

6749 **Novak, David** The election of Israel: the idea of the chosen people. 1995, ⇒11/2,3145. ^RFirst Things 62 (1996) 52-54 (*Pawlikowski, John T.*); MoTh 12/4 (1996) 491-493 (*Wyschogrod, Michael*).

6750 *Pawlikowski, John T.* Ein Bund oder zwei Bünde?: zeitgenössische Perspektiven. ThQ 176 (1996) 325-340.

6751 *Pike, Dana M.* The "Congregation of YHWH" in the Bible and at Qumran. RdQ 17 (1996) 233-240.

6752 **Poole, David N.J.** The history of the covenant concept from the Bible to Johannes CLOPPENBURG, *De foederi Dei*. Lewiston, NY 1992, Mellen 316 pp. 0-7734-9814-1. ^RRTR 95 (1996) 149-150 (*Milne, Douglas J.W.*).

6753 **Ran, Oh Kyong (Sr. Justina)** The new covenant in the NT as fulfilment of the OT covenant. Diss. extract Pont. Univ. Urbaniana. R 1995, xiii; 78 pp.

6754 *Rieger, Hans-Martin* Eine Religion der Gnade: zur "Bundesnomismus"-Theorie von E.P. SANDERS. Bund und Tora. WUNT 92: 1996, ⇒1645. 129-161.

6755 **Röhser, Günther** Prädestination und Verstockung. TANZ 14: 1994, 10,7286... 11/2,3148. ^RCritRR 9 (1996) 262-264 (*Hanges, James C.*).

6756 **Schmidt, Werner H.** Alttestamentlicher Glaube. Neuk ⁸1996, Neuk xiii; 495 pp. 3-7887-1585-5.

6757 *Schnabel, Eckhard J.* Die Gemeinde des Neuen Bundes in Kontinuität und Diskontinuität zur Gemeinde des Alten Bundes. Israel in Geschichte. 1996, ⇒632. 147-213.

6758 *Vanhoye, Albert* Discussioni sulla Nuova Alleanza. RTLu 1 (1996) 163-178 [Jer 31,31-34; 2 Cor 3,14].

6759 **Vogel, Manuel** Das Heil des Bundes: Bundestheologie im Frühjudentum und im frühen Christentum. Diss. TANZ 18: Tü 1996, Francke 392 pp. DM86. 3-7720-1869-6.

H3.5 *Liturgia, spiritualitas VT*—OT prayer

6760 **Aleixandre, Dolores** Compañeros en el camino: iconos bíblicos para un itinerario de oración. Santander 1995 Sal Terrae 231 pp. [MCom 54/1,239].

6761 *Bourgeois, H.* L'appel au pardon et son impact sur la violence. LumVie 45/1 (1996) 43-52 [NTAb 40,463].

6762 **Cimosa, Mario** La preghiera nella Bibbia greca: studi sul vocabolario dei LXX. 1992, ⇒9,10168; 10,7296. ^RBeO 38 (1996) 63-64 (*Jucci, Elio*).

6763 **Cocagnac, M.** L'énergie de la parole biblique. LiBi 109: P 1996, Cerf 280 pp. FF120.

6764 *Easton, M.* What does Scripture tell us?. Way.S 85 (1996) 98-106 [NTAb 41,94].

6765 *Fernandez, E.* Expressions in the liturgy—1, 'The Lord be with you'. Emmanuel 102 (1996) 196-199 [NTAb 41,94].

6766 **Feuillet, André** En prière avec la Bible. P 1995, Téqui 258 pp. FF99. [R]Miles Immacolatae 32 (1996) 721-723 (*Calkins, Arthur Burton*).

6767 **Ghidelli, Carlo** Preghiere della Bibbia: parlare a Dio con la parola di Dio. CinB 1995, San Paolo 259 pp. [R]Ter. 47 (1996) 354-355 (*Pasquetto, Virgilio*); Ang. 73 (1996) 305-306 (*Stancati, T.*).

6768 **Hill, Andrew E.** Enter his courts with praise!. GR 1996, Baker 335 pp. $20 [BS 154,380].

6769 **Juengst, Sara Covin** Like a garden: a biblical spirituality of growth. LVL 1996, Westminster 128 pp. $13 [Spiritual Life 42,250].

6770 *Kavanagh, Aidan J.* Scriptural word and liturgical worship. Reclaiming the Bible. 1996, ⇒596. 131-137.

6771 **Lagarde, Claude** Em nome dos pais: exegese e catequese hoje: a Bíblia como fonte para a oração. [T]*Estêvão Allgayer, António*, Petrópolis 1995, Vozes 158 pp. [R]REB 56 (1996) 748 (*Ribeiro Guimarães, Almir*).

6772 **Manns, Frédéric** La preghiera d'Israele al tempo di Gesù. CSB 28: Bo 1996, EDB 287 pp. 88-10-40729-6.

6773 **Masini, Mario** La 'lectio divina': teologia, spiritualità, metodo. CinB 1996, San Paolo 509 pp. L42.000. 88-215-3126-0. [R]Mar. 58 (1996) 565-569 (*Ciardi, Fabio*).

6774 **McKay, Heather A.** Sabbath and synagogue: the question of sabbath worship in ancient Judaism. 1994, ⇒10,7307; 11/2,3194. [R]Worship 70 (1996) 352-353 (*Sloyan, Gerard S.*); CBQ 58 (1996) 557-559 (*Saldarini, Anthony J.*); JAOS 116 (1996) 295-296 (*Harrington, Daniel J.*); JBL 115 (1996) 736-737 (*Cohen, Shaye J.D.*).

6775 *Milgrom, Jacob* The water libation in the festival of booths. BiRe 12/6 (1996) 18, 55-56.

6776 **Newman, Judith H.** Praying by the book: scripturalization of prayer in Second Temple Judaism. Diss. Harvard 1996, [D]*Kugel, J.L.*, 268 pp. [EThL 74,240*].

6777 *Nichols, Bridget* The bible in the liturgy: a hermeneutical discussion of faith and language. StLi 26 (1996) 200-216.

6778 *Panimolle, Salvatore A.* I quattro gradi della 'lectio divina' secondo GUIDO il Certosino. PaVi 41/6 (1996) 52-55.

6779 **Peltz, Carl F.** Minute meditations. Boston 1996, Pauline 127 pp. $5 [BiTod 34,393].

6780 **Rosenau, Hartmut** Fragen ist die Frömmigkeit des Denkens: biblische Themen aus philosophischer Sicht. Edition C: Paperback 456: Moers 1996, Brendow 94 pp. 3-87067-627-2.

6781 **Rossi de Gasperis, Francesco** La roca que nos ha engendrado (Dt 32,18): ejercicios en Tierra Santa. El pozo de Siquem 75: Santander 1996, Sal Terrae 182 pp. 84-293-1191-2 [ActBib 33,229—Rocafiguera, J.Mª].

6782 **Rossier, François** L'intercession entre les hommes dans la bible hébraïque: l'intercession entre les hommes aux origines de l'intercession auprès de Dieu. Diss. OBO 152: Gö 1996, Vandenhoeck & R. xiv; 380 pp. FS114. 3-525-53788-3. [R]ET 108 (1996-97) 364-365 (*Rogerson, J.W.*).

6783 [E]**Terrin, A.N.** Scriptura crescit cum orante: bibbia e liturgia. Caro salutis cardo, 2. Contributi 7: Padova 1994, Messagero 284 pp. L30.000. [R]Asp. 43 (1996) 587-588 (*Di Napoli, G.*).

6784 **Thompson, Michael E.W.** I have heard your prayer: the Old Testament and prayer. C 1996, Epworth x; 262 pp. £13. 0-7162-0509-2.
6785 *Towner, P.H.* The shape and motive of piety in Chinese religious tradition and the biblical tradition: *li* and *eusebeia.* Jian Dao 5 (1996) 95-126 [NTA 40,470].
6786 **Warnier, Philippe** Prier avec la bible. P 1996, Bayard 280 pp. [EeV 106,166].
6787 **Webber, Robert E.** Worship old and new: a biblical, historical, and practical introduction. GR [2]1994, Zondervan 272 pp. $20. 0-310-47990-8. [R]CTJ 31 (1996) 268-269 (*Witvliet, John D.*).

H3.7 *Theologia moralis VT*—OT moral theology

6788 *Albertz, Rainer* Macht Reichtum blind?: von der Schwierigkeit, als Wohlstandsbürger die Bibel zu lesen. Zorn. 1996, ⇒110. 9-23.
6789 *Allsopp, M.E.* The role of Sacred Scripture in Richard A. McCORMICK's ethics. ChiSt 35/2 (1996) 185-196 [NTAb 41,92].
6790 **Ashley, Benedict** Living the truth in love: a biblical introduction to moral theology. Staten Island, N.Y. 1996, Alba xiv; 558 pp. $25 [HPR 99/6,72—MacCarthy, Peter T.].
6791 Die biblische Moral und die Marktwirtschaft. Ungarische Ökumenische Studienhefte 11: Budapest 1995, Ungarisches Ökumenisches Studienzentrum 90 pp. [R]LuThK 19/1 (1996) 62-64 (*Scheerer, Reinhard*).
6792 *Bovati, Pietro* L'esercizio della giustizia nella bibbia. L'esercizio della giustizia e la bibbia. Atti del convegno nazionale di biblia, Milano 1994. Settimello 1996, BIBLIA. 31-65 [APIB 10,263].
6793 *Brawley, Robert L.* The power of God at work in the children of God. Biblical ethics. 1996, ⇒6794. 35-50.
6794 [E]**Brawley, Robert Lawson** Biblical ethics and homosexuality: listening to scripture. LVL 1996, Westminster x; 162 pp. $17. 0-664-25638-4.
6795 *Connor, Kimberly Rae* "Everybody talking about heaven ain't going there": the biblical call for justice and the postcolonial response of the spirituals. Semeia 75 (1996) 107-128.
6796 [E]**Füssel, Kuno; Segbers, Franz** '...so lernen die Völker des Erdkreises Gerechtigkeit': ein Arbeitsbuch zu Bibel und Ökonomie. Luzern 1995, Exodus. [R]PzB 5 (1996) 65-68 (*Arzt, Peter; Ernst, Michael*).
6797 *Gasque, W.W.* Prosperity theology and the New Testament. ERT 20/1 (1996) 40-46 [NTAb 41,95].
6798 *Gordon, Cyrus H.* The background of some distinctive values in the Hebrew bible. [F]YOUNG D., 1996, ⇒107. 57-68.
6799 *Homerski, Józef* Caritas w Starym Testamencie [Charity in the Old Testament]. Sum. 74. Vox Patrum 16 (1996) 65-74. **P.**
6800 *Hurtado, L.W.* The bible and same-sex erotic relations. Crux 32/2 (1996) 13-19 [NTAb 41,96].
6801 **Janzen, Waldemar** Old Testament ethics. 1994, ⇒10,7324; 11/2,3238. [R]CritRR 9 (1996) 150-152 (*Brown, William P.*).
6802 **Jones, David Clyde** Biblical christian ethics. GR 1994, Baker 216 pp. $15. 0-8010-5228-9. [R]CTJ 31 (1996) 257-258 (*Van Til, Kent*).

6803 *Klauck, Hans-Josef* Eine Frage von Leben und Tod: zur Metapho-
      rik von Sünde und Vergebung in der Bibel. Diak. 27 (1996) 86-94.
6804 *Klopfenstein, Martin A.* Flüchtlinge sind nicht unsere Feinde;
6805 Konflikte und ihre Lösung in biblischer Sicht;
6806 Politik und Mitverantwortung;
6807 Vergebung—nicht vergebens. Leben aus dem Wort. BEAT 40:
      1996, ⇒132. 249-251/235-249/285-293/337-338.
6808 *Krašovec, Jože* Punishment in the light of a teleological universe.
      Sum. 423; Zsfg. 445. Synthesis Philosophica 11 (1996) 423-445.
6809 *Lang, Bernhard* Die Fremden in der Sicht des Alten Testaments.
      Wahrnehmung des Fremden. 1996, ⇒218. 9-37.
6810 *Lienhard, F.* L'amour, Dieu et l'éthique. FV 95/1 (1996) 19-43
      [NTAb 40,467].
6811 *Lob-Hüdepohl, Andreas* Die eine Ethik vor dem Anspruch der vie-
      len: zum Universalitätsanspruch christlicher Ethik in moralisch
      vielstimmiger Welt. Wahrnehmung des Fremden. 1996, ⇒218.
      267-298.
6812 **Malchow, Bruce V.** Social justice in the Hebrew bible: what is
      new and what is old. Michael Glazier: ColMn 1996, Liturgical xv;
      83 pp. $9. 0-8146-5523-8.
6813 **Neri, Umberto** I fondamenti biblici dell'etica cristiana. Catechesi
      di Monteveglio 6: Bo 1996, EDB 156 pp. L18.000. 88-10-70956-
      X.
6814 **Otto, Eckart** Theologische Ethik des Alten Testaments. 1994,
      ⇒10,7238; 11/2,3253. ᴿSJOT 10 (1996) 148-151 (*Rosendal, Bent*);
      CBQ 58 (1996) 522-524 (*Janzen, Waldemar*); Sal. 68 (1996) 187-
      188 (*Abbà, G.*); RdT 37 (1996) 63-78 (*Prato, Gian Luigi*); CritRR
      9 (1996) 164-166 (*Gnuse, Robert*).
6815 *Otto, Eckart* Wirtschaftsethik im Alten Testament. Kontinuum.
      1996 <1994>, ⇒2002. 331-341.
6816 *Rad, Gerhard von* Hermano y prójimo en el Antiguo Testamento.
      La acción de Dios. 1996 <1970>, ⇒144. 218-229.
6817 **Rae, Scott B.** Brave new families: biblical ethics and reproductive
      technologies. GR 1996, Baker 247 pp. $17. 0-8010-2077-8 [BS
      154,234].
6818 *Rebić, Adalbert* Ćudoredna situacija čovjeka u Starome zavjetu
      [The ethical situation of man in the Old Testament]. Sum. 584.
      BoSm 66 (1996) 567-584.
6819 *Schroeder, Christoph* Macht und Gerechtigkeit: Ansätze des norda-
      merikanischen Forschungsprojekts "Bible and Theology" zur Neu-
      konzeption einer Biblischen Theologie. JBTh 11 (1996) 183-196.
6820 ᴱ**Seow, Choon-Leong** Homosexuality and christian community.
      LVL 1996, Westminster 159 pp. $15. 0-664-25664-3 [Interp.
      51,197].
6821 **Sheriffs, Deryck** The friendship of the Lord: an Old Testament
      spirituality. Carlisle 1996, Paternoster xiii; 363 pp. £15. 0-85364-
      646-5 [ET 108,280].
6822 **Silva, Rui Manuel Araújo Rosas da** A consciência moral uni-
      versal desde os livros hebraicos aos livros gregos do Antigo Testa-
      mento em comparação com a filosofia grega clássica e helenística.
      Diss. Pont. Athenæum Sanctae Crucis 1996, ᴰ*Livi, Antonio,* R
      1996, xxii; 412 pp.
6823 *Tiessen, Terrance* Peut-on définir une éthique universelle à partir
      de l'Écriture?. Hokhma 63 (1996) 19-44.

6824 **Vetter, Dieter** Die Gleichheit aller Menschen nach Israels Bibel: zur Erklärung der Menschenrechte vor zweihundert Jahren. Judentum. 1996 <1989>, ⇒154. 282-288.

6825 **Visotzky, Burton L.** The genesis of ethics. NY 1996, Crown (10) 211 pp. 0-517-70299-1.

6826 *Waetjen, Herman C.* Same-sex sexual relations in antiquity and sexuality and sexual identity in contemporary American society. Biblical ethics and homosexuality. 1996, ⇒6794. 103-116.

6827 **Weinfeld, Moshe** Social justice in ancient Israel and in the ancient Near East. 1995, ⇒11/2,3266. [R]ZAR 2 (1996) 222-226 (*Otto, Ekkart*).

6828 **Westing, Harold J.; Thome, Penny** Building biblical values. GR 1996, Kregel 253 pp. [Faith & Mission 14,121].

H3.8 *Bellum et pax VT-NT*—War and peace in the whole Bible

6829 **Barbaglio, Giuseppe** Dieu est-il violent?: une lecture des écritures juives et chrétiennes. 1994, ⇒10,7748; 11/2,3270. [R]RTL 27 (1996) 353-357 (*Wénin, André*).

6830 [E]**Burns, J. Patout** War and its discontents: pacifism and quietism in the Abrahamic traditions. Wsh 1996, Georgetown Univ. Press xi; 220 pp. $55. 0-87840-603-4 [ThD 44,93].

6831 **Cahill, Lisa Sowle** Love your enemies: discipleship, pacifism, and just war theory. 1994, ⇒11/2,3276. [R]Interp. 50 (1996) 192-194 (*Allen, Joseph L.*); JR 76 (1996) 487-488 (*Kelsay, John*); RStR 22/2 (1996) 129-134 (*Brown, Daniel A.*).

6832 **Dear, John** The God of peace. 1994, ⇒11/2,3282. [R]Interp. 50 (1996) 440 (*Grant, J. Jeremy M.*).

6833 *Dubreucq, Marc* La guerre et ses rites sacrés. DosB 62 (1996) 5-6.

6834 *Habgood, J.* On war. Theol. 99 (1996) 258-261.

6835 **Héritier, Françoise** De la violence. Opus 37: P 1996, Jacob 400 pp. 2-7381-0408-8.

6836 *Lang, B.* La violence au service de la religion: de quelques formes élémentaires d'agression dans la bible. De la violence [E]**Héritier, F.**, P 1996, Jacob]. 169-200 [Deut 13; 17; Ps 2; 149] [ZAW 111,296—Köckert, M.].

6837 *Le Saux, Madeleine* Shalom, la paix dans l'Ancien Testament. DosB 62 (1996) 9-10.

6838 **Longman III, Tremper; Reid, Daniel G.** God is a warrior. 1995, ⇒11/2,3293. [R]Evangel 14/3 (1996) 88-89 (*Cotton, Bill*); BS 153 (1996) 496-497 (*Chisholm, Robert B.*); JETh 10 (1996) 213-215 (*Möller, Karl*).

6839 **Mauser, Ulrich** The gospel of peace: a scriptural message for today's world. 1992, ⇒8,7395... 10,7348. [R]RStR 22/2 (1996) 129-134 (*Brown, Daniel A.*).

6840 *Otto, Eckart* Krieg und Religion im Alten Orient und im alten Israel. Glaubenskriege in Vergangenheit und Gegenwart [E]**Herrmann, J.** Veröffentlichung der Joachim-Jungius-Gesellschaft 83: Gö 1996, Vandenhoeck & R. 153 pp. DM42. 3-525-86272-5]. 37-47 [OTA 19,494].

6841 **Römer, Thomas** Dieu obscur: le sexe, la cruauté et la violence dans l'Ancien Testament. EssBib 27: Genève 1996, Labor et F.

122 pp. F98. 2-8309-0824-4. REeV 106 (1996) 418 (*Monloubou, Louis*).

6842 **Schlomit, Adam** Handelt Gott gewaltlos?: zum Problem der Gewalt in der Kirche und ihrer Wurzel. J 1996, 38 pp.

6843 **Swartley, Willard M.** The love of enemy and non-retaliation in the NT. 1992, ⇒8,4194... 10,7357*. RRStR 22/2 (1996) 129-134 (*Brown, Daniel A.*).

6844 *Swartley, Willard M.* War and peace in the New Testament   Religion. ANRW II.26.3. 1996, ⇒183. 2298-2408.

6845 **Williams, James G.** The bible, violence and the sacred: liberation from the myth of sanctioned violence. SF 1996, Harper Collins 288 pp. $27 [JRHe 36,297—Liechty, Daniel].

6846 EYoder, **Perry B.; Swartley, Willard M.** The meaning of peace: biblical studies. 1992, ⇒8,4194; 9,7533. RRStR 22/2 (1996) 129-134 (*Brown, Daniel A.*).

6847 **Zerbe, Gordon M.** Non-retaliation in early Jewish and New Testament texts: ethical themes in social contexts. JSPE.S 13: 1993, ⇒9,7534... 11/2,3313. RInterp. 50 (1996) 84-85 (*Ascough, Richard S.*).

6848 EZolt, **David** Holy war online: a debate in cyberspace. Lakewood, Ohio 1996, MMI iv; 308 pp. 0-9648968-1-8 [NThAR 1997,163].

H4.1 Messianismus

6849 *Beckwith, Roger T.* The year of the Messiah: Jewish and early Christian chronologies, and their eschatological consequences. Calendar and chronology. AGJU 33: 1996, ⇒112. 217-275.

6850 *Betz, Otto* The messianic idea in the 4Q fragments: its relevance for the christology of the New Testament. MBURGMANN H., 1996 <1993>, ⇒12. 61-75.

6851 **Collins, John Joseph** The scepter and the star: the messiahs of the Dead Sea scrolls and other ancient literature. 1995, ⇒11/2,3318. RTS 57 (1996) 339-341 (*Fitzmyer, Joseph A.*); CBQ 58 (1996) 506-508 (*Cook, Edward M.*); DSD 3 (1996) 335-336 (*Dunn, James D.G.*).

6852 *Coppens, Joseph* Le messianisme. 1989 <1974>, ⇒5,7363; 6,7383. RThR 61 (1996) 98-100 (*Reventlow, Henning Graf*).

6853 *Cortese, Enzo* Come sbloccare l'attuale esegesi messianica. SBFLA 46 (1996) 33-44.

6854 *Cousin, Hugues* Les textes messianiques de la Septante ont-ils aidé l'exégèse apostolique?: ont-ils été récusés par les sages?. Le déchirement. MoBi 32: 1996, ⇒192. 205-219.

6855 *Cross, Frank Moore* Notes on the doctrine of the two Messiahs at Qumran and the extracanonical Daniel Apocalypse (4Q246). Current research... on the Dead Sea Scrolls. StTDJ 20: 1996, ⇒293. 1-13.

6856 *Eltrop, Bettina* Du aber, Betlehem Efrata, ... aus Dir soll mir einer hervorgehen (Mi 5,1). BiKi 51 (1996) 168-171.

6857 *García Martínez, Florentino* Two messianic figures in the Qumran texts. Current research. StTDJ 20: 1996, ⇒293. 14-40.

6858 **Goodman-Thau, Eveline** Zeitbruch: zur messianischen Grunderfahrung in der jüdischen Tradition. B 1995, Akademie 216 pp.

DM78. 3-05-002511-5. ᴿThLZ 121 (1996) 38-39 (*Wiefel, Wolfgang*).

6859 *Halperin, David J.* The son of the Messiah: Ishmael ZEVI and the Sabbatian Aqedah. HUCA 67 (1996) 143-219.

6860 *Hengel, Martin* Die Bar Kokhba-Münzen als politisch-religiöse Zeugnisse;

6861 *Hengel, Martin* Messianische Hoffnung und politischer "Radikalismus" in der "jüdisch-hellenistischen Diaspora": zur Frage der Voraussetzungen des jüdischen Aufstandes unter Trajan 115-117 n. Chr. <1989>. Judaica et Hellenistica. WUNT 90: 1996, ⟹128. 344-350/314-343.

6862 **Hornung, Andreas** Messianische Juden zwischen Kirche und Israel: Entwicklung und Begründung ihres Selbstverständnisses. Giessen 1995, Brunnen 144 pp. DM24.80. ᴿJETh 10 (1996) 272-274 (*Kägi-Studer, Hansjörg*).

6863 *Hruby, Kurt* Das Leiden des Messias <1964>;

6864 Die Messiaserwartung in der talmudischen Zeit, mit besonderer Berücksichtigung des leidenden Messias <1964>;

6865 Die rabbinische Exegese messianischer Schriftstellen <1965>. Aufsätze [ᴱOsten-Sacken, P. von der]. ANTZ 5: 1996, ⟹K5. 281-297/267-280/298-317.

6866 Der Messias. JBTh 8 (1993). ᴿThR 61 (1996) 172-175 (*Reventlow, Henning Graf*).

6867 *Koch, Klaus* Messias und Menschensohn: die zweistufige Messianologie der jüngeren Apokalyptik. Wende der Zeiten. 1996 <1993>, ⟹133. 235-266.

6868 **Liebes, Yehuda** Studies in Jewish myth and Jewish messianism. 1993, ⟹11/2,3334. ᴿJQR 87 (1996) 245-250 (*Wolfson, Elliot R.*).

6869 **Lucrezi, Francesco** Messianismo regalità impero: idee religiose e idea imperiale nel mondo romano. F 1996, Giuntina xv; 163 pp. 88-8057-036-6.

6870 *Marcus, Joel* Modern and ancient Jewish apocalypticism. JR 76 (1996) 1-27.

6871 **Oegema, Gerbern S.** Der Gesalbte und sein Volk... von den Makkabäern bis Bar Koziba. 1994, ⟹10,7372; 11/2,3339. ᴿThLZ 121 (1996) 41-45 (*Niebuhr, Karl-Wilhelm*).

6872 *Ragacs, Ursula* Die Messiasfrage in jüdisch-christlichen Disputationen des Mittelalters. PzB 5 (1996) 19-30.

6873 **Ravitzky, Aviezer** Messianism, Zionism, and Jewish religious radicalism. Ch Studies in the History of Judaism: Ch 1996, Univ. of Chicago Press 280 pp. $48/$17. 0-226-70577-3/8-1 [Religion 28,417ss—Neusner, Jacob].

6874 *Romanides, John S.* Christ in the Old Testament and the ecumenical council. Theol(A) 67 (1996) 431-438 [Matt 22,21]. G.

6875 *Smith, Morton* Messiahs: robbers, jurists, prophets, and magicians. New Testament. 1996 <1977>, ⟹151. 39-46;

6876 What is implied by the variety of Messianic figures?. Studies in... method. 1996 <1959>, ⟹150. 161-167.

6877 *Stuckenbruck, Loren T.* "Messias" Texte in den Schriften von Qumran. ᴹBURGMANN H., 1996 <1993>, ⟹12. 129-139.

6878 **Thoma, Clemens** Das Messiasprojekt: Theologie jüdisch-christlicher Begegnung. 1994, ⟹10,7374; 11/2,3348. ᴿLebZeug 51 (1996) 312-313 (*Petzel, Paul*).

H4.3 *Eschatologia VT*—OT hope of future life

6879 EBremer, J.M.; Van den Hout, Th.P.J.; Peters, R. Hidden futures: death and immortality in the...ancient world. 1994, ⇒11/2,552. RBSOAS 59 (1996) 131-132 (*Katz, Dina*).

6880 *Day, John* The development of belief in life after death in ancient Israel. FMASON R., 1996, ⇒57. 231-257.

6881 García Cordero, Maximiliano La esperanza del más allá a través de la biblia. 1992, ⇒9,7548. REstB 54 (1996) 425-426 (*Mielgo, C.*).

6882 Lane, Dermot A. Keeping hope alive: stirrings in christian theology. Dublin 1996, Gill & M. £11. 0-7171-2460-6. DoLi 47/1 (1997) 28-34 (*Mills, John Orme*).

6883 Puech, Émile La croyance des esséniens en la vie future: immortalité, résurrection, vie éternelle?. 1993, ⇒9,7555... 11/2,3362. RBAEO 32 (1996) 426-427 (*Sen, Felipe*).

H4.5 *Theologia totius VT*—General Old Testament theology

6884 Aguiar Retes, Carlos El ayuno agradable a YHWH: discernimiento, abnegación, conmiseración, solidaridad fraterna y fidelidad en el sufrimiento. Diss. Pont. Univ. Gregoriana 1996, DSimian-Yofre, Horacio, 293 pp. [EThL 74,235*].

6885 Gunneweg, Antonius H.J. Biblische Theologie des AT. 1993, ⇒9,7560*... 11/2,3375. RLuThK 20/4 (1996) 199-200 (*Behrens, Achim*); EvTh 56 (1996) 258-285 (*Dietrich, Walter*); JR 76 (1996) 328-337 (*Rendtorff, Rolf*); ThR 61 (1996) 53-54 (*Reventlow, Henning Graf*).

6886 Helyer, Larry R. Yesterday, today and forever: the continuing relevance of the Old Testament. Salem, Wis. 1996, Shf xii; 459 pp. $20. 1-879215-31-4 [BBR 8,244s—Martens, Elmer A.].

6887 EHubbard, Robert L., (al), Studies in OT theology. FHUBBARD D., 1992, ⇒8,88. RThR 61 (1996) 126-130 (*Reventlow, Henning Graf*); EvQ 68 (1996) 62 (*Riggans, Walter*).

6888 Altes Testament und christlicher Glaube. JBTh 6 (1991). RThR 61 (1996) 170-171 (*Reventlow, Henning Graf*).
      Janowski, B. Gottes Gegenwart in Israel ⇒131.

6889 Kim, Wonil Toward a substance-critical task of Old Testament theology. Diss. Claremont 1996, DKnierim, R.P., 417 pp. [EThL 74,234*].

6890 Kittel, Gisela Der Name über alle Namen: biblische Theologie AT. 1989, ⇒6,9140... 8,9333. RThR 61 (1996) 61-62 (*Reventlow, Henning Graf*).

6891 Knierim, Rolf The task of Old Testament theology. 1995, ⇒11/2,3381. RBS 153 (1996) 493-494 (*Merrill, Eugene H.*); ET 107 (1995-96) 309 (*Coggins, Richard*); Horizons 23 (1996) 330-331 (*Laffey, Alice L.*); CBQ 58 (1996) 580-581 (*Brueggemann, Walter*).

6892 Perdue, Leo G. The collapse of history: reconstructing OT theology. 1994, ⇒10,7396. RJR 76 (1996) 349-353 (*Brueggemann, Walter*); RExp 93 (1996) 436-437 (*Block, Daniel I.*); ThR 61 (1996) 95-96 (*Reventlow, Henning Graf*).

6893 **Preuß, Horst Dietrich** Theologie des ATs. 1991-1992, ⇒7,7388...
11/2,3389. ᴿEvTh 56 (1996) 258-285 (*Dietrich, Walter*); JR 76
(1996) 328-337 (*Rendtorff, Rolf*); ThLZ 121 (1996) 649-653
(*Waschke, Ernst-Joachim*); ThR 61 (1996) 55-56 (*Reventlow, Henning Graf*);

6894 Old Testament theology, 2. ᵀ*Perdue, Leo G.*, E 1996, Clark x; 438
pp. £30. 0-567-08521-X [RB 104,316].

6895 Religionsgeschichte Israels oder Theologie des Alten Testaments?.
JBTh 10 (1995). ᴿThQ 176 (1996) 359-360 (*Niehr, Herbert*).

6896 *Rendtorff, Rolf* Recent German Old Testament theologies. JR 76
(1996) 328-337.

6897 **Sailhamer, John H.** Introduction to Old Testament theology: a
canonical approach. GR 1995, Zondervan 327 pp. $20. ᴿBS 153
(1996) 118-119 (*Merrill, Eugene H.*); JETh 10 (1996) 203-208
(*Renz, Thomas*).

6898 *Schmidt, Johann Michael* Rede von Gott. Altes Testament. 1996,
⇒169. 289-323.

6899 **Schmitt, Armin** Wende des Lebens: Untersuchungen zu einem
Situations-Motiv der Bibel. BZAW 237: B 1996, De Gruyter xi;
325 pp. DM168. 3-11-014757-2 [CBQ 59,424].

6900 **Schreiner, Josef** Theologie des AT. 1995, ⇒11/2,3394. ᴿJR 76
(1996) 328-337 (*Rendtorff, Rolf*); RivBib 44 (1996) 480-482
(*Nobile, Marco*); ThLZ 121 (1996) 653-655 (*Kaiser, Otto*); Cart.
12 (1996) 475-476 (*Sanz Valdivieso, R.*).

6901 **Schroven, Brigitte** Theologie des Alten Testaments zwischen Anpassung und Widerspruch: christologische Auslegung zwischen den
Weltkriegen. Neuk 1996, Neuk'er 300 pp. DM78 [BiKi 52,147].

6902 *Wagner, Siegfried* Zur Frage nach dem Gegenstand einer Theologie
des Alten Testaments. Ausgewählte Aufsätze. BZAW 240: 1996
<1970>, ⇒156. 25-46.

6903 *Wittenberg, Gunther H.* Old Testament theology, for whom?. Semeia 73 (1996) 221-240.

H5.1 *Deus—NT—God* [as Father ⇒H1.4]

6904 **Díaz Mateos, Manuel** La solidaridad de Dios. CEP 159: Lima
1996, Centro de Espiritualidad Ignaciana 177 pp. [NThAR
1997,132].

6905 *Hahn, Ferdinand* Das Bekenntnis zu dem einen Gott im Neuen Testament. ᶠHᴀʜɴ F., 1996 <1978>, ⇒34. 55-68.

6906 *Panimolle, Salvatore A.* Dio nel Nuovo Testamento. Dio—Signore
nella bibbia. DSBP 13: 1996, ⇒328. 142-243.

6907 **Schlosser, Jacques** El Dios de Jesús. 1995, ⇒11/2,3418. ᴿEE 71
(1996) 108-110 (*Piñero, Antonio*).

6908 *Zeller, Dieter* Der eine Gott und der eine Herr Jesus Christus: religionsgeschichtliche Überlegungen. ᶠTʜᴜᴇsɪɴɢ W., NTA 31:
1996, ⇒94. 34-49.

H5.2 **Christologia ipsius NT**

6909 *Amato, Angelo* Cristologia e mariologia: considerazioni teologico-spirituali. Ricerche Teologiche 7/1 (1996) 149-160.

6910 *Berger, Klaus* Jesus als Nasoräer/Nasiräer. NT 38 (1996) 323-335.
6911 **Brown, Raymond E.** An introduction to NT christology. 1994, ⇒10,7410; 11/2,3432. ᴿRivBib 44 (1996) 237-239 (*Fabris, Rinaldo*); CBQ 58 (1996) 537-539 (*Sloyan, Gerard S.*); Interp. 50 (1996) 314, 316 (*Chilton, Bruce*);
6912 Jésus dans les quatre évangiles: introduction à la christologie du Nouveau Testament. ᵀ*Degorce, Jean-Bernard; Barrios-Delgado, Dominique*, LiBi 111: P 1996, Cerf 311 pp. FF130. 2-204-05402-X [EThL 73,171].
6913 *Buckwalter, H.D.* The origin of christology—evolution or explosion?. EvJo 14/1 (1996) 9-24 [NTAb 41,86].
6914 **Casciaro, José María; Monforte, J.M.** Jesucristo, salvador de la humanidad. Pamplona 1996, EUNSA 668 pp. 84-313-1422-2 [Proyecció 44,319].
6915 **Davis, Carl J.** The name and way of the Lord: Old Testament themes, New Testament christology. JSNT.S 129: Shf 1996, Academic 227 pp. £30. 1-85075-604-X [NTS 43,620].
6916 **Dunn, James D.G.** Christology in the making. GR ²1996 <1989>, Eerdmans xlvi; 443 pp. $30. 0-8028-4257-7 [NTS 43,620].
6917 **Fredriksen, Paula** De Jésus aux Christs: les origines des représentations de Jésus dans le NT. 1992, ⇒9,4319; 11/2,3439. ᴿRTL 27 (1996) 102-103 (*Dermience, Alice*).
6918 **González, Sergio** Títulos cristológicos: 'Pimpollo, Pastor, Padre del siglo futuro, Esposo, Hijo de Dios, Jesús': estudio teológico - mistico: en *De los nombres de Cristo* de Fray Lᴜɪs de León. Valladolid 1995, EstAg 478 pp. ᴿRecollectio 19 (1996) 413-414 (*Caparrós, Antonio*); ScrTh 28 (1996) 653-654 (*Hervás, J.L.*).
6919 **Guillet, Jacques** Jésus dans la foi des premiers disciples. 1995, ⇒11/2,3440. ᴿNRTh 118 (1996) 417-422 (*Simoens, Yves*).
6920 *Hübner, Hans* Deus hermeneuticus. ᶠTʜᴜᴇsɪɴɢ W., NTA 31: 1996, ⇒94. 50-58.
6921 **Iammarrone, Giovanni** Gesù di Nazaret messia del regno e figlio di Dio: lineamenti di cristologia. Strumenti di Scienze Religiose: Padova 1996, Messaggero 406 pp. L29.000. ᴿTer. 47 (1996) 698-700 (*Pasquetto, Virgilio*).
6922 *Jonge, Marinus de* Monotheism and christology. ᶠHᴏᴏᴋᴇʀ M., 1996, ⇒43. 225-237.
6923 *Kieffer, René* Teologi och kristologi hos Paulus och Johannes. Sum. 32. SvTK 72 (1996) 25-32.
6924 **Koskenniemi, Erkki** Aᴘᴏʟʟᴏɴɪᴏs von Tyana in der neutestamentlichen Exegese. WUNT 2/61: 1994, ⇒10,4470; 11/2,2078. ᴿCBQ 58 (1996) 757-758 (*Danker, Frederick W.*).
6925 **Kuschel, Karl-Josef** Born before all time: the dispute over Christ's origin. 1992, ⇒8,7532... 11/2,3443. ᴿJR 76 (1996) 353-355 (*Hurtado, Larry W.*).
6926 **Lau, Andrew Y.** Manifest in flesh: the epiphany christology of the Pastoral Epistles. Diss. St Andrews. WUNT 2/86: Tü 1996, Mohr xi; 336 pp. DM98. 3-16-146302-1 [ThD 44,369—Heiser, W. Charles].
6927 ᵀ**Lemm, Robert** Luis de León: Over de namen van Christus: tweede en derde boek van *De los nombres de Cristo*. Kampen 1996, Kok 184 pp. ƒ35. 90-289-2205-9. ᴿStr. 63 (1996) 1062-1063 (*Van Herck, Walter*).

6928 *Notomhardio, R.* Jesus as lord (*kyrios*): a consideration of the development of the concept in the New Testament. Stulos 4/1 (1996) 75-87 [NTAb 41,88].

6929 **O'Collins, Gerald** Christology. 1995, ⇒11/2,3545. ᴿTS 57 (1996) 547-549 (*Heft, James L.*); ScrTh 28 (1996) 963-964 (*Riestra, J.A.*); Milltown Studies 37/1 (1996) 132-135 (*Moloney, Raymond*); JThS 47 (1996) 782-784 (*Newlands, George*); Theol. 99 (1996) 304-305 (*Parr, John*).

6930 **O'Collins, Gerald; Kendall, Daniel** Focus on Jesus: essays in christology and soteriology. Leominster 1996, Gracewing viii; 255 pp. £13. 0-85244-360-9.

6931 ᴱ**Ohlig, Karl-Heinz** Christologie, 1: des origines à l'antiquité tardive. ᵀ*Lauret, Bernard; Durand, Georges Matthieu de*, Textes en Main: P 1996, Cerf 289 pp. FF150. 2-204-05207-8;

6932 **Penna, Romano** I ritratti originali di Gesù il Cristo: inizi e sviluppi della cristologia neotestamentaria. Studi sulla Bibbia e il suo ambiente 1: CinB 1996, San Paolo 298 pp. L38.000. 88-215-3218-6. ᴿLat. 62 (1996) 680-681; RdT 37 (1996) 699-705 (*Barbaglio, Giuseppe*).

6933 **Pikaza, Xabier** Dios judío, Dios cristiano. Estella 1996, Verbo Divino 428 pp. ᴿComunidades 89 (1996) 123-124 (*Gómez, Enrique*).

6934 *Plessis, Isak J. du* The mystery of God and Jesus Christ—beyond agnosticism and foundationalism. Neotest. 30 (1996) 39-57.

6935 **Schnackenburg, Rudolf** Die Person Jesu Christi im Spiegel der vier Evangelien. 1993, ⇒9,7600; 10,7420. ᴿZM 80 (1996) 318-320 (*Kahl, Josef*).

6936 *Ska, Jean-Louis* Jésus et la Samaritaine (Jn 4): utilité de l'Ancien Testament. NRTh 118 (1996) 641-652.

6937 ᵀ**Velleda, Minelli; Bambilla, E.** Gesù il volto di Dio: riflessi di vangelo. Perché abbiate la vita 5: Mi 1994, Ancora 144 pp. Aut. anon. L15.000. 88-7610-473-9. ᴿBen. 43 (1996) 446-448 (*Valli, Annamaria*).

6938 **Wojciechowski, Michał** Jezus jako Święty w pismach Nowego Testamentu [Jesus as the Holy One in the New Testament]. Rozprawy i Studia Biblijne 2: Wsz 1996, Oficyna Wydawnicza 'Vocatio' 244 pp. Sum. 241-244. 83-7146-058-9. **P**.

6939 **Wright, Nicholas Thomas** Jesus and the victory of God. Christian origins and the question of God, 2. Mp 1996, Fortress xxi; 741 pp. $65. 0-8006-2682-6. ᴿET 108 (1996-97) 225-226 (Resp. 259) (*Rodd, C.S.*).

H5.3 *Christologia praemoderna*—patristic to Reformation

6940 *Argárate, Pablo* La encarnación come divinización en la liturgia y en los padres greco-orientales. ΕΠΙΜΕΛΕΙΑ 5 (1996) 9-28.

6941 **Benericetti, Ruggero** Il Cristo nei sermoni di S. Pier Cʀɪsoʟoɢo. StRav 6: Cesena 1995, Centro Studi e Ricerche sulla Antica Provincia Ecclesiastica Ravennate 351 pp. ᴿREAug 42/1 (1996) 185-186 (*Cantin, A.*); RSR 84 (1996) 615-616 (*Sesboüé, Bernard*).

6942 ᵀ**Congourdeau, M.-H.** Maxɪme le Confesseur: l'agonie du Christ. Introd. *Léthel, F.-M.*, CPF 64: P 1996, Migne 156 pp. FF90. 2-908587-25-4.

6943 **DeVries, Dawn** Jesus Christ in the preaching of CALVIN and SCHLEIERMACHER. LVL 1996, Westminster x; 115 pp. $15. 0-664-22067-3. ᴿCTJ 31 (1996) 603-607 (*Muller, Richard A.*).

6944 **Grillmeier, Aloys** L'église de Constantinople au VI siècle. Le Christ dans la tradition chrétienne, 2/2. 1993, ⇒9,7613... 11/2,3465. ᴿScrTh 28 (1996) 345-347 (*Mateo-Seco, L.F.*);

6945 The church of Constantinople in the sixth century. Christ in christian tradition, 2/2. 1995, ⇒11/2,3464. ᴿGOTR 41/1 (1996) 85-87 (*Gros, Jeffrey*); SJTh 49 (1996) 231-233 (*Wickham, L.R.*);

6946 The church of Alexandria with Nubia and Ethiopia after 451. ᵀ*Dean, O.C.*, Christ in Christian tradition, 2/4. L 1996, Mowbray xxiv; 431 pp. £45. 0-264-66018-8;

6947 L'église d'Alexandrie, la Nubie et l'Ethiopie après 451. Collab. *Hainthaler, Theresia*, Le Christ dans la tradition chrétienne, 2/4. CFi 192: P 1996, Cerf 603 pp. FF450. 2-204-05227-2. ᴿTelema 22/3-4 (1996) 71-73 (*Mpay, Kemboly*); EeV 106 (1996) 166-168 (*Jay, Pierre*).

6948 *Ihara, Shôichi* The significance of Jesus as a human being in classic christology. KaKe 65 (1996) 67-105 [ThIK 18/1,50]. **J.**

6949 *Kallarangatt, Joseph* The teaching of Addai: a Syriac christological masterpiece. COri 17/4 (1996) 190-202 [ThIK 18/2,35].

6950 **Leclercq, Jean** La contemplazione di Cristo nel monachesimo medievale. CinB 1994, San Paolo 210 pp. ᴿLat. 62 (1996) 413-414 (*Rava, Eva C.*).

6951 **Lyman, J. Rebecca** Christology and cosmology... ORIGEN. 1993, ⇒9,7620... 11/2,3474. ᴿJThS 47 (1996) 289-291 (*Young, Frances M.*).

6952 **McGuckin, J.A.** Saint CYRIL of Alexandria: the christological controversy. SVigChr 5/3: 1994, ⇒10,7446; 11/2,3475. ᴿVDI 217 (1996) 221-224 (*Muraviev, A.V.*).

6953 *Moloney, Raymond* Patristic approaches to Christ's knowledge, 1. Milltown Studies 37/1 (1996) 65-81.

6954 **Nguên-Van-Khanh, Norbert** The teacher of his heart: Jesus Christ in the thought and writings of St. FRANCIS. Franciscan Pathways: NY 1994, Franciscan Institute 253 pp. $15. 1-57659-066-6. ᴿCFr 66/1-2 (1996) 263-264 (*Schmucki, Oktavian*).

6955 ᵀPons Pons, Guillermo Juan DAMASCENO: homilías cristológicas y marianas. Biblioteca de Patrística 33: M 1996, Ciudad Nueva 227 pp. Introd., notas. [Proyección 44,162].

6956 **Rey Escapa, Jaime** La libertad de Cristo según el beato Juan DUNS ESCOTO. Diss. excerpt Pont. Univ. Gregoriana 1996, 136 pp.

6957 *Ribeiro, Ari Luís do Vale* A cristologia de São MÁXIMO Confessor. Teocomunicação 26 (1996) 45-61 [ThIK 18/1,70].

6958 **Rosenberger, M.** Der Weg des Lebens: zum Zusammenhang von Christologia und Spiritualität in der Verkündigung des hl. AUGUSTINUS. Regensburg 1996, Pustet 199 pp. [ArchTeolGran 59,339].

6959 **Schoot, H.J.M.** Christ the 'name' of God: THOMAS AQUINAS on naming Christ. 1993, ⇒10,7452. ᴿRSR 84 (1996) 617-618 (*Sesboüé, Bernard*).

6960 **Simonetti, Manlio** Studi sulla cristologia del II e III secolo. SEAug 44: R 1993, Institutum Patristicum Augustinianum 353 pp.

L55.000. ᴿRSR 84 (1996) 611-612 (*Sesboüé, Bernard*); JThS 47 (1996) 649-652 (*Slusser, Michael*).

6961 **Strutwolf, Holger** Demonstratio evangelica: die Trinitästheologie und Christologie des EUSEB von Caesarea und die Auseinandersetzung mit dem Platonismus in seiner apologetischen Theologie. Diss.-Habil. ᴰ*Aland, B.*, Müns 1996-1997 [ThLZ 122,764].

6962 **Suárez Rodriguez, J.L.** El Cristo antiguo. M 1996, Apis 167 pp. [BiFe 23/1,155].

6963 *Van den Broek, Roelof* The christian "school" of Alexandria in the second and third centuries;

6964 Juden und Christen in Alexandrien im 2. und 3. Jahrhundert. Studies in Gnosticism [**Van den Broek, R.**]. Nag Hammadi studies 39: 1996, ⇒M1.1. 197-205/181-196.

H5.4 (*Commentationes de*) *Christologia* moderna

6965 **Adam, Karl** Gesù il Cristo. Brescia ¹⁶1995 <1934>, Morcelliana 254 pp. ᴿLat. 62 (1996) 381-383 (*Ancona, Giovanni*).

6966 **Amato, Domenico** Cristo centro e respiro della storia: il pensiero cristologico di Vito FORNARI. R 1995, Pont. Univ. Lateranense 236 pp. L30.000. ᴿCivCatt 147 I (1996) 529-530 (*Ferraro, G.*).

6967 **Bérulle, Pierre de** Les grandeurs de Jésus: morceaux choisis. ᴱ*Boureau, René*, Epiphanie: P 1996, Cerf 128 pp. FF90. ᴿEeV 106 (1996) 457 (*Oury, G.-M.*);

6968 Discours de l'état et des grandeurs de Jésus: introduction historique et théologique. Introd. ᴱ*Lescot, Rémi*; collab. *Join-Lambert, Michel*, Œuvres complètes, 7. P 1996, Cerf lxxi; 514 pp. FF290. ᴿEeV 106 (1996) 301-303 (*Oury, G.-M.*).

6969 *Beckford, R.* Does Jesus have a penis?: black male sexual representation and christology. Theology and Sexuality 5 (1996) 10-21 [ZID 22,471].

6970 **Bousquet, François** Le paradoxe Jésus-Christ: devenir chrétien par passion d'exister: élements pour une christologie de KIERKEGAARD comme question aux contemporains. Diss. Institut Catholique de Paris 1996, ᴰ*Doré, Joseph*, 2 vols; 1000 + 602 pp. RICP 59 (1996) 305-309 (*Doré, Joseph*).

6971 *Braine, D.* What makes a christology into a christian theology?. NBl 77 (1996) 288-302 [NTAb 41,86].

6972 *Chung, Hyung-Kyung* Asian christologies and people's religions. VFTW 19/1 (1996) 214-227 [ThIK 18/1 (1997) 43].

6973 **Commissione theologica internazionale.** Cristo, verbo del padre. CinB 1996, San Paolo [Orientamenti Pastorali 45/1,30ss—Amato, Angelo].

6974 **Cowdell, Scott** Is Jesus unique?: a study of recent christology. Theological Inquiries: Mahwah 1996, Paulist viii; 456 pp. $25. 0-8091-3628-7 [NTAb 41,164].

6975 **Dalferth, Ingolf U.** Der auferweckte Gekreuzigte: zur Grammatik der Christologie. 1994, ⇒11/2,3500. ᴿThLZ 121 (1996) 1187-1190 (*Rössler, Martin*).

6976 **Danz, Christian** Die philosophische Christologie F.W.J. SCHELLINGS. Schellingiana 9: Stu 1996, Frommann [ArPh 60/1,155ss—Tilliette, Xavier].

6977 **De Marchi, Sergio** La cristologia in Italia (1930-1990). 1995, ⇒11/2,3502. RLat. 62 (1996) 184-186 (*Sanna, Ignazio*).
6978 *Dubois, Robert* Le moi malgache et le moi de Jésus. Aspects du Christianisme à Madagascar 6/6 (1996) 263-268 [ThIK 18/1,16].
6979 **Dupuis, Jacques** Homme de Dieu, Dieu des hommmes: introduction à la christologie. 1995, ⇒11/2,3504. REE 71 (1996) 127-127 (*Madangi Sengi, Jean de Dieu*); ScEs 48 (1996) 353-355 (*Archambault, Jean-Marie*); RSR 84 (1996) 628-630; RAT 20 (1996) 245-247 (*De Haes, René*).
6980 *Dupuis, Jacques* Religious plurality and the christological debate. SEDOS Bulletin 28/12 (1996) 329ff [ThD Index Feb. 1997,12].
6981 **Evdokimov, Michel** Le Christ dans la tradition et la littérature russes. Préf. *Doré, Joseph*, CJJC 67: P 1996, Desclée 354 pp. FF189. 2-7189-0689-8. REeV 106 (1996) 168-170 (*Jay, Pierre*) [BCLF 585,1728].
6982 *Evers, Georg* Asian, African and Latin American contributions towards christology. Jahrbuch für Kontextuelle Theologien 96 (1996) 174-196.
6983 **Falbo, G.** Gesù Cristo, figlio di Dio, salvatore. Vivere la Parola, Itinerari Biblici per la Comunità 2: R 1996, Coletti 222 pp.
6984 **Gabus, Jean-Paul** La nouveauté de Jésus Christ, témoin de Dieu pour le monde. P 1996, Les Bergers 187 pp. FF120. 2-85304-125-5.
      Genest, Hartmut Der Tod des Gottmenschen... HEGELs Christologie ⇒2823.
6985 **Godzieba, Anthony J.** Bernhard WELTE's fundamental theological approach to christology. AmUSt.TR 160: 1994, ⇒11/2,3510. REThL 72 (1996) 478-479 (*Brito, E.*).
6986 **Goedt, Michel de** Le Christ de JEAN de la Croix. CJJC 59: P 1996, Desclée 267 pp. [EeV 107/21,468];
6987 Le Christ de THERESE de Jésus. CJJC 58: P 1996, Desclée 268 pp. REeV 106 (1996) 445-446 (*Jay, Pierre*).
6988 **Gronchi, Maurizio** La cristologia di S. BERNARDINO da Siena. 1992, ⇒10,7484. RRSLR 32 (1996) 464-466 (*Visani, Oriana*).
6989 **Guillet, Jacques** Jésus-Christ dans notre monde. Christus Essais: P 1996, Desclée de B. 254 pp. FF130. 2-220-03832-7 [EeV 106,269].
6990 *Haight, R.* Jesus and world religions. MoTh 12/3 (1996) 321-344 [NTAb 41,87].
6991 EHart, **Trevor A.; Thimell, Daniel P.** Christ in our place: the humanity of God in Christ for the reconciliation of the world. FTORRANCE J., 1989, ⇒7,154*. RSBET 14/1 (1996) 78-79 (*McGowan, A.T.B.*).
6992 *Heijke, Jan P.* Christologie en historische Jezus bij EBOUSSI (Kameroen) en UDOH (Nigeria). WeZ 3 (1996) 22-33 [ThIK 18/1,81].
6993 **Honoré, Jean** La pensée christologique de NEWMAN. CJJC 68: P 1996, Desclée vi; 184 pp. [RThom 97,610].
6994 **Hünermann, Peter** Jesus Christus: Gottes Wort in der Zeit: eine systematische Christologie. 1994, ⇒10,7486; 11/2,3522. RRET 56 (1996) 125-126 (*Gesteira, Manuel*); RSR 84 (1996) 624-627 (*Sesboüé, Bernard*); ActBib 33 (1996) 210-211 (*Boada, J.*).
6995 JOHN PAUL II, POPE Only Christ can fulfill man's hopes. TSchindler, *David Louis*, Com(US) 23/1 (1996) 122-128 [Cf. OR (15 November 1995)].

6996 *Joos, André* Cristologia russa oggi: come coglierne l'originalità. Nicolaus 23/1-2 (1996) 5-71.

6997 **Karlić, Ivan** Il Gesù della storia nella teologia di J. MOLTMANN. Diss. Pont. Facoltà teologica S. Bonaventura. Cristologia: R 1996, Herder 248 pp. [Bog.Smo. 68,280ss—Dogan, Nikola].

6998 **Kasper, Walter** Jésus le Christ. [T]*Désigaux, J.; Liefooghe, A.*, CFi 88: P 1996, Cerf 421 pp. 2-204-01040-5.

6999 *Kavunkal, Jacob* The Indian church and an ecumenical christology. Verbum SVD 37 (1996) 431-449 [ThIK 18/2,79].

7000 **Kay, James F.** Christus praesens: a reconsideration of Rudolf BULTMANN's christology. 1994, ⇒11/2,3525. [R]CTJ 31 (1996) 554-557 (*Hagner, Donald A.*).

7001 *Kim, Yong B.* Jesus Christ among Asian minjung: a christological reflection. VFTW 19/2 (1996) 83-127.

7002 **Knitter, Paul F.** Jesus and the other names: christian mission and global responsibility. Oxf 1996, One World 193 pp. £15 [DoLi 47,509].

7003 *Krötke, Wolf* Die Christologie Karl BARTHs als Beispiel für den Vollzug seiner Exegese. Karl BARTHs Schriftauslegung. 1996, ⇒207. 1-21.

7004 **Kuschel, Karl-Josef** Generato prima di tutti i secoli?: la controversia sull'origine di Cristo. BTCon 84: Brescia 1996, Queriniana 778 pp. L120.000. 88-399-0384-4. [R]RSEc 14 (1996) 596-598 (*Morandini, Simone*); ActBib 33 (1996) 211-212 (*Boada, J.*).

7005 **Le Guillou, Marie-Joseph** Le visage du ressuscité. P 1996, Saint-Augustin 424 pp. FF98. [R]EeV 106 (1996) 672 (*Paillerets, M. de*).

7006 **Leatham, Robert** The work of Christ. Contours of christian theology: DG 1993, InterVarsity 288 pp. $16. 0-8308-1532-5. [R]TrinJ 17 (1996) 252-257 (*Fields, Bruce L.*).

7007 **Lethel, François-Marie** Théologie de l'amour de Jésus: écrits sur la théologie des saints. Vénasque 1996, Carmel 266 pp. [R]EeV 106 (1996) 569-571 (*Jay, Pierre*).

7008 *Magesa, Laurenti C.* Christology, African women and ministry. AfER 38/2 (1996) 66-88 [ThIK 18/1,15].

7009 *Martins, Florinda* 'C'est moi la vérité': para uma cristologia fenomenológica. Itin. 42 (1996) 475-480.

7010 **Masinganda, André Mungwatisio** Du discours christologique à l'emergence d'ecclésiologie en contexte négro-africain: pertinence doctrinale et contextuelle. Diss. Pont. Univ. Gregoriana 1996, [D]*Dupuis, Jacques*, 122 pp.

7011 **Maurice, Évelyne** La christologie de Karl RAHNER. CJJC 65: P 1995, Desclée 266 pp. [R]RSR 84 (1996) 621-622 (*Sesboüé, Bernard*); BLE 97 (1996) 211-213 (*Maldamé, J.M.*); ETR 71 (1996) 457-458 (*Bennahmias, Richard*).

7012 **McDermott, Brian O.** Word become flesh: dimensions of christology. 1993, ⇒10,7496; 11/2,3530. [R]EThL 72 (1996) 480-481 (*Brito, E.*).

7013 **Menacherry, Cheriyan** Christ: the mystery in history: a critical study of the christology of Raymond PANIKAR. Diss. Pont. Univ. Gregoriana, [D]*Dupuis, Jacques*, THEION 5: Fra 1996, Lang 311 pp. DM89. 3-631-48369-4. [R]VJTR 60 (1996) 899-900 (*Gispert-Sauch, G.*).

7014   **Menke, Karl-Heinz** Die Einzigkeit Jesu Christi im Horizont der Sinnfrage. Kriterien 94: Einsiedeln 1995, Johannes 180 pp. DM18. 3-89411-331-6. ᴿThGl 86 (1996) 640-642 (*Fuchs, Gotthard*).

7015   **Ntima, Kanza** Non: je ne mourrai pas, je vivrai: méditation sur le cheminement christologique en Afrique. Kinshasa 1996, Loyola 190 pp.

7016   **O'Collins, Gerald** Gesù oggi: linee fondamentali di cristologia. 1993, ⇒10,7509. ᴿCoTh 66/3 (1996) 214-218 (*Skierkowski, Marek*).

7017   **Ocáriz, F.; Mateo Seco, L.F.; Riestra, J.A.** The mystery of Jesus Christ: a christology and soteriology textbook. Dublin 1994, Four Courts v; 320 pp. 1-85182-127-9. ᴿMilltown Studies 37 (1996) 159-162 (*Kelly, David*).

7018   ᴱ**Ohlig, Karl-Heinz** Christologie, 2: du moyen âge à l'époque contemporaine. ᵀ*Van Hoa, B.*, Textes en Main: P 1996, Cerf 287 pp. FF150. 2-204-05240-X.

7019   **Olivieri Pennesi, Alessandro** Il Cristo del *New Age*: la cristologia neo-gnostica in alcuni esponenti di rilievo: una valutazione critica cattolica. Diss. sum. Pont. Univ. Gregoriana 1996, ᴰ*O'Collins, Gerald*, R 1996, 83 pp.

7020   **Parappally, Jacob** Emerging trends in Indian christology. Bangalore 1995, Indian Institute of Spirituality xiii; 312 pp. Rs120. 81-85812-12-8. ᴿVJTR 60 (1996) 566-568 (*Sebastian, A.*).

7021   **Patterson, Bob E.** Who is Jesus Christ?. Macon, Ga. 1996, Smyth & H. 131 pp. 1-57312-027-8 [NThAR 1997,195].

7022   *Pavlou, Teleosphora* Fare teologia e cristologia nella chiesa ortodossa oggi. Ricerche Teologiche 7/1 (1996) 7-28.

7023   **Peelman, Achiel** Christ is a native American. Maryknoll 1995, Orbis 253 pp. ᴿStudies in World Christianity 2/2 (1996) 223-225 (*Cox, James L.*).

7024   *Phan, Peter C.* The Christ of Asia (an essay on Jesus as the eldest son and ancestor). StMiss 45 (1996) 25-55;

7025   Jesus the Christ with an Asian face. TS 57 (1996) 399-430.

7026   **Pro, Bernard** Peut-on éviter Jésus-Christ?. P 1995, De Fallois/Saint-Augustin 312 pp. BEF690. ᴿColl. 26 (1996) 443-444 (*Vanden Berghe, Eric*).

7027   **Schleiermacher, Friedrich D.E.** La festa di Natale: un dialogo: interpretazioni di Friedrich W.J. SCHELLING e di Karl BARTH [Die Weihnachtsfeier]. Giornale di Teologia 231: Brescia 1994 <1806>, Queriniana 199 pp. L25.000. 88-399-0731-9. ᴿGr. 77 (1996) 580-581 (*Vercruysse, Jos*); Lat. 62 (1996) 402-407 (*Selvadagi, Paolo*).

7028   **Sesboüé, Bernard** Pédagogie du Christ: éléments de christologie fondamentale. 1994, ⇒11/2,3558. ᴿEThL 72 (1996) 479-480 (*Brito, E.*).

7029   **Sivadó, Csaba** John MEYENDORFF krisztológiája [Christologia John Meyendorff]. Budapest 1996-97, Diss. Univ. Catholica a Petro Pázmány [FolTh 8,232].

7030   **Stock, Alex** Schrift und Gesicht. Poetische Dogmatik: Christologie, 2. Pd 1996, Schöningh 292 pp. DM68 [LM 36,42].

7031   **Thompson, William H.** The struggle for theology's soul: contesting scripture in christology. NY 1996, Crossroad xii; 310 pp. $40. 0-8245-1543-9. ᴿHorizons 23 (1996) 306-330 (*Sloyan, Ge-*

rard S.; Kopas, Jane; Perkins, Pheme; Cooke, Bernard; Thompson, William M.); TS 57 (1996) 763-764 (*Krieg, Robert A.*).

7032 **Tilliette, Xavier** El Cristo de la filosofía: prolegómenos a una cristología filosófica. Bilbao 1994, Desclée de B. 285 pp. EfMex 14 (1996) 424-425 (*Monreal Maldonado, Sarah Arcelia*).

7033 *Tilliette, Xavier* Le Christ du philosophe. Com(F) 21/5 (1996) 94-99.

7034 **Torre, Giuseppe** La soteriologia nella riflessione cristologica di Bernard SESBOUE. Diss. Pont. Univ. Lateranense 1996, DBordoni, Marcello, R 1996, 331 pp.

7035 **Torres Queiruga, Andrés** Repensar la cristología. Estella 1996, Verbo Divino 386 pp. [REB 227,771].

7036 **Vass, George** God and Christ. A pattern of christian doctrines, 1. Understanding Karl Rahner 3: L 1996, Sheed & W. xvii; 206 pp. £25. 0-7220-9352-7.

7037 *Walk, J.* ...den böse Menschen getötet haben. GlLern 11/2 (1996) 105-106 [ZID 22,474].

7038 *Weinandy, Thomas* The human 'I' of Jesus. IThQ 62 (1996-97) 259-268.

7039 *Wolosky, Shira* An American-Jewish typology: Emma LAZARUS and the figure of Christ. Prooftexts 16/2 (1996) 113-125.

7040 *Wullung, F.X. Heryatno Wono* Christologische Reflexion im Kontext der multireligiösen Gesellschaft. Umat Baru 29 (1996) 23-33 [ThIK 18/1,46]. **Indonesian.**

H5.5 *Spiritus Sanctus; pneumatologia*—**The Holy Spirit**

7041 *Balter, L.* Le culte du Saint Esprit. RICP 59 (1996) 273-287.

7042 **Ferguson, Sinclair B.** The Holy Spirit. Contours of Christian Theology: Leicester 1996, Inter-Varsity 288 pp. 0-85111-895-X.

7043 *Goldingay, John* Was the Holy Spirit active in Old Testament times?: what was new about the christian experience of God;

7044 *Grenz, Stanley* The Holy Spirit: divine love guiding us home;

7045 *Haroutunian, Joseph* Spirit, Holy Spirit, spiritism. ExAu 12 (1996) 14-28/1-13/59-75.

7046 *Johnson, Luke Timothy* The Holy Spirit in the New Testament. PrPe 10 (1996) 138-142.

7047 *Johnston, Robert K.* God in the midst of life: the spirit and the Spirit. ExAu 12 (1996) 76-93.

7048 **Keener, Craig S.** 3 crucial questions about the Holy Spirit. GR 1996, Baker 214 pp. $12. 0-8010-5592-X [NTAb 41,165].

7049 *Land, Steven J.* Be filled with the Spirit: the nature and evidence of spiritual fullness. ExAu 12 (1996) 108-120.

7050 *Martins Terra, João Evangelista* A experiência do espírito ontem e hoje;

7051 O espírito, dom do fim dos tempos. RCB 77/78 (1996) 97-105/113-127.

7052 **Moreno García, Ardón** La sabiduría del Espíritu: sentir en Cristo: estudio de phrónēma-phronéō en Rom 8,5-8 y Flp 2,1-5. Pont. Univ. Gregoriana 1995, DVanhoye, Albert, Roma 1995, 371 pp. RMater Clementissima (1996) 97-100 (*Escamilla Romero, Gonzalo*).

7053 **Terra, João Evangelista Martins** Espirito Santo e Bíblia. RCB
20/77-78: São Paolo 1996, Loyola 157 pp. [NTAb 41,168].
7054 **Turner, Max** The Holy Spirit and spiritual gifts: then and now.
Carlisle 1996, Paternoster xiii; 374 pp. £18. 0-85364-758-5 [EvQ
70,287—Marshall, I. Howard].

H5.6 *Spiritus et Filius;* **'Spirit-Christology'**, Filioque

7055 **Bordoni, Marcello** La cristologia nell'orizzonte dello Spirito.
BTCon 82: Brescia 1995, Queriniana 315 pp. 88-399-0382-8.
^RRdT 37 (1996) 567-568 (*O'Collins, Gerald*).
7056 *Borgen, Peder* Jesus Christ, the reception of the spirit and a cross-
national community. Early christianity. 1996 <1994>, ⇒116.
253-272.
7057 *Breck, John* 'The two hands of God': Christ and the Spirit in Orthodox theology. SVTQ 40 (1996) 231-246.
7058 *Kloppenburg, Bonaventura* Jesus Cristo e a efusão do Espírito
Santo. RCB 77/78 (1996) 81-96.

H5.7 *Ssma Trinitas*—**The Holy Trinity**

7059 **Boulnois, Marie-Odile** Le paradoxe trinitaire chez CYRILLE d'A-
lexandrie. 1994, ⇒10,7559. ^RASEs 13 (1996) 655-656 (*Pazzini,
Domenico*).
7060 *Breuning, Wilhelm* Überlegungen zur neutestamentlichen Logik des
trinitarischen Bekenntnisses. ^FTHUESING W., NTA 31: 1996,
⇒94. 368-388.
7061 **Gunton, Colin E.** The one, the three and the many: God, creation
and the culture of modernity. 1993, ⇒9,7772; 10,7568. ^RCThMi
23/1 (1996) 50-51 (*Hütter, Reinhard*).
7062 *Humphrey, E.M.* Why we worship God as Father, Son and Holy
Spirit. Crux 32/2 (1996) 2-12 [NTAb 41,96].
7063 **Marsh, Thomas** The triune God. 1994, ⇒10,7577; 11/2,3623.
^RScEs 48 (1996) 359-361 (*Lison, Jacques*).
7064 *Müller, Gerhard Ludwig* Jesus Christus, der Sohn des Vaters: Zeu-
gung und Sohnschaft im dreifaltigen Gott. Anthropotes 12 (1996)
289-303.
7065 **Toon, Peter** Our triune God: a biblical portrayal of the Trinity.
Wheaton, IL 1996, Victor 271 pp. $18. [BS 154,488].
7066 *Wehr, Lothar* Das Heilswirken von Vater, Sohn und Geist nach den
Paulusbriefen und dem Johannesevangelium: zu den neutestamentlichen Voraussetzungen der Trinitätslehre. MThZ 47 (1996) 315-
324.

H5.8 *Regnum messianicum, Filius hominis*—
Messianic kingdom, Son of Man

7067 *Berk, Lucas* Zoon van de mens. ITBT 4/4 (1996) 16-17.
7068 *Chilton, Bruce* The Son of Man: who was he?. BiRe 12/4 (1996)
34-39, 45-47.

7069 **Christensen, Jens** Menneskesønnen: en bibelteologisk studie. Bibel og Historie 19: Aarhus 1996, Universitetsforlag 139 pp. [NTT 98,181].

7070 **Dupuy, Michel** La royauté du Christ. CJJC 46: 1990, ⇒7,7599*; 9,7800. ᴿScEs 48 (1996) 238-240 (*Archambault, Jean-Marie*).

7071 *Katz, Paul* Jesus als Vorläufer des Christus: mögliche Hinweise in den Evangelien auf Elia als den "Typos" Jesu. ThZ 52 (1996) 225-235.

7072 *Loba Mkole, J.-C.* Une synthèse d'opinions philologiques sur le Fils de l'homme. JNSL 22/1 (1996) 85-90.

7073 **Martin de Vivies, Pierre** Jésus et le fils de l'homme, emplois et significations de l'expression 'Fils de l'homme' dans les évangiles. Lyon 1995, Profac 173 pp. ᴿEeV 106 (1996) 363-365 (*Cothenet, Édouard*).

7074 **Mateos Juan; Camacho, Fernando** El hijo del hombre: hacia la plenitud humana. Cordoba 1995, El Almendro 360 pp. 84-8005-025-X. ᴿBLE 97/3 (1996) 291-292 (*Marchadour, A.*).

7075 *Rota Scalabrini, Patrizio* 'Regno di Dio': un'immagine da chiarire. RCI 77 (1996) 808-828.

7076 **Vögtle, Anton** Die "Gretchenfrage" des Menschensohnproblems. QD 152: 1994, ⇒10,7618; 11/2,3675. ᴿThPQ 144 (1996) 80-81 (*Stowasser, Martin*).

H6.1 *Creatio, sabbatum NT* [⇒E3.5]; **The Creation** [⇒E1.6; H2.8]

7077 *Alviar, José* Some anthropological aspects of creation theology. PhilipSac 31 (1996) 303-309.

7078 *Beckwith, Roger T.* The Sabbath and Sunday. Calendar and chronology. AGJU·33: 1996, ⇒112. 10-50.

7079 **Haffner, Paul** Mystery of creation. Leonminster 1995, Gracewing xvi; 224 pp. Eccl(M) 10/1 (1996) 187-188 (*Haffner, P.*).

7080 *Hahn, Ferdinand* Schabbat und Sonntag. ᶠHAHN F., 1996 <1986>, ⇒34. 69-84.

7081 Schöpfung und Neuschöpfung. JBTh 5 (1990). ᴿThR 61 (1996) 168-170 (*Reventlow, Henning Graf*).

7082 *Löning, Karl* Neutestamentliche Schöpfungstheologie in kanonischer Perspektive. BiLi 69 (1996) 216-227.

7083 *Mauser, Ulrich W.* Creation and human sexuality in the New Testament. Biblical ethics. 1996, ⇒6793. 3-15.

7084 **Mildenberger, Friedrich** Theologie als Ökonomie. Biblische Dogmatik: eine biblische Theologie in dogmatischer Perspektive, 3. Stu 1993, Kohlhammer 496 pp. DM59. 3-17-011083-7. ᴿProtest. 51 (1996) 355-356 (*Rostagno, Sergio*).

7085 *Muñoz León, Domingo* El universo creado y la encarnación redentora de Cristo. Esperanza del hombre. 1996, ⇒173. 287-329.

7086 **Noemi Callejas, Juan** El mundo: creación y promesa de Dios. Cultura y Religión 8: Santiago de Chile 1996, San Pablo 622 pp. 956-256-223-9 [Gr. 78,213].

7087 **Russell, David Michael** The "new heavens and new earth": hope for the creation in Jewish apocalyptic and the New Testament. Studies in Biblical Apocalyptic Literature 1: Ph 1996, Visionary (6) vi; 266 pp. $18.45. 1-896400-17-5.

H6.3 *Fides, veritas in NT*—**Faith and truth**

7088 ^E**Baldermann, Ingo** Glaube und Öffentlichkeit. JBTh 11: Neuk
      1996, Neuk'er viii; 264 pp. 3-7887-1605-3.
7089 **Barr, James** Biblical faith and natural theology. 1993, ⇒10,7639;
      11/2,3726. ^RJR 76 (1996) 338-341 (*Lefebure, Leo D.*); JThS 47
      (1996) 777-780 (*Barton, John*).
7090 **Kasper, Walter** La foi au défi. 1989, ⇒6,7677... 8,7723. ^RBLE
      97 (1996) 106-107 (*Péré, J.J.*).
7091 **Martini, Carlo Maria** ¿Todavía existe algo en qué creer?. Valen-
      cia 1996, Edicep 116 pp. [EfMex 15,406].
7092 **Middleton, J. Richard; Walsh, Brian J.** Truth is stranger than it
      used to be: biblical faith in a postmodern age. 1995, ⇒11/2,3754.
      ^RCTJ 31/1 (1996) 287-293 (*Cooper, John W.*); TrinJ 17 (1996) 95-
      98 (*Leffel, Jim*).
7093 *Piechota, Lech* Lacune puntualizzasioni sul concetto di 'virtù' in
      generale e su 'fede', 'speranza' e 'carità' in particolare, fino alle
      soglie del Nuovo Testamento. Ricerche Teologiche 7/1 (1996) 51-
      82.
7094 ^E**Van den Brink, G.** Gegrond geloof: kernpunten uit de ge-
      loofsleer: in bijbels, historisch en belijdend perspectief. Zoetermeer
      1996, Boekencentrum 605 pp. *f*89. 90-239-0832-5.
7095 **Vattimo, Gianni** Credere di credere. Mi 1996, Garzanti. ^RLa Sa-
      pienza della Croce 11 (1996) 371-386 (*Lippi, Adolfo*).
7096 **Wallis, Ian G.** The faith of Jesus Christ in early christian tradi-
      tions. MSSNTS 84: 1995, ⇒11/2,2218. ^RCBQ 58 (1996) 568-569
      (*deSilva, David A.*); RB 103 (1996) 630-631 (*Murphy-O'Connor,
      J.*); ChH 65 (1996) 658-659 (*Patrick, T. Hall*); ETR 71 (1996)
      285-287 (*Cuvillier, Elian*); ThLZ 121 (1996) 366-368 (*Schweizer,
      Eduard*).

H6.6 *Peccatum NT*—Sin, Evil [⇒E1.9]

7097 **Berger, Klaus** Wie kann Gott Leid und Katastrophen zulassen?.
      Stu 1996, Quell 244 pp. DM29.80. 3-7918-1951-8 [NTAb
      41,163].
7098 *Fiedler, Peter* Sünde und Sündenvergebung in der Jesustradition;
7099 *Frankemölle, Hubert* Sünde und Befreiung von der Sünde. Sünde
      und Erlösung im NT. QD 161: 1996, ⇒181. 76-91/9-17.
7100 Sünde und Gericht. JBTh 9 (1994). ^RThR 61 (1996) 175-176
      (*Reventlow, Henning Graf*).
7101 *Klauck, Hans-Josef* Heil ohne Heilung?: zu Metaphorik und Her-
      meneutik der Rede von Sünde und Vergebung im Neuen Testa-
      ment. Sünde und Erlösung im NT. QD 161: 1996, ⇒181. 18-52.
7102 **Mattioli, Anselmo** L'inquietante mistero del male: idee e prospet-
      tive nella bibbia. 1994, ⇒11/2,3836. ^RCivCatt 147 II (1996) 622-
      624 (*Scaiola, D.*).
7103 **Ratzinger, Card. Josef** In the beginning...: a catholic understan-
      ding of the story of creation and the fall. 1995, ⇒11/2,3851.
      ^RMonth 29 (1996) 163-164 (*O'Reilly, Paul*).

7104 *Schmeller, Thomas* Sünde und Befreiung von der Sünde im NT— befreiungstheologisch gelesen. Sünde und Erlösung im NT. QD 161: 1996, ⇒181. 185-201.

7105 **Sung, Chong-Hyon** Vergebung der Sünden: Jesu Praxis. WUNT 2/57: 1993, ⇒9,4439... 11/2,3864. ᴿCritRR 9 (1996) 284-286 (*Chilton, Bruce*).

7106 **Ulmer, Rivka** The evil eye in the bible and in rabbinic literature. 1994, ⇒11/2,3868. ᴿBiOr 53 (1996) 514-516 (*Van Bekkum, Wout Jac.*); AJSR 21 (1996) 151-153 (*Yuter, Alan J.*).

7107 *Werbick, Jürgen* Die biblische Rede von Sünde und Erlösung im Horizont der Grunderfahrungen des modernen Menschen. Sünde und Erlösung im NT. QD 161: 1996, ⇒181. 164-184.

H7.0 Soteriologia NT

7108 **Auer, Johann** Gesù il salvatore: soteriologia: mariologia. 1993, ⇒11/2,3876. ᴿTheotokos 4 (1996) 663-664 (*Fiores, Stefano de*).

7109 *Bammel, Caroline P.* Justification by faith in Augustine and Origen. JEH 47 (1996) 223-235.

7110 *Bucher, Anton A.* "Es liegt an jedem einzelnen zu verzeihen": psychologische Anmerkungen zur Rezeption biblischer Texte über Vergebung. Sünde und Erlösung im NT. QD 161: 1996, ⇒181. 202-218.

7111 ᴱ**Carson, D.A.** Right with God: justification in the bible and the world. 1992, ⇒11/2,3877. ᴿSBET 14 (1996) 165-166 (*Rowlands, Eryl*); EvQ 68 (1996) 267-269 (*Peck, John*).

7112 **Dunn, J.D.G.; Suggate, A.M.** The justice of God. 1993, ⇒10,7706*. ᴿEvangel 14/3 (1996) 91-93 (*Bray, Gerald*); RExp 93 (1996) 300-301 (*Seifrid, Mark*).

Frankemölle, Hubert Sünde und Erlösung im NT ⇒181.

7113 *Grayston, Kenneth* Atonement and martyrdom. ᶠHooker M., 1996, ⇒43. 250-263.

7114 *McIlhone, J.P.* Are you saved?: a fundamentalist view of Christ. ChicStud 35/1 (1996) 54-67 [NTAb 40,459].

7115 *Otto, Eckart* Gewaltvermeidung und -überwindung in Recht und Religion Israels: rechtshistorische und theologische Anmerkungen eines Alttestamentlers zu R. Schwagers Entwurf einer biblischen Erlösungslehre. Kontinuum. 1996 <1992>, ⇒2002. 246-264.

7116 *Smith, Morton* Salvation in the gospels, Paul, and the magical papyri. New Testament. 1996 <1986>, ⇒151. 130-139.

7117 **Ternant, Paul** Le Christ est mort 'pour tous': du serviteur Israël au serviteur Jésus. 1993, ⇒9,7962. ᴿRB 103 (1996) 616-618 (*Boismard, M.-É.*); RSR 84 (1996) 597-599 (*Sesboüé, Bernard*).

7118 **Van Dyk, Leanne** The desire of divine love: John McLeod Campbell's doctrine of the atonement. NY 1995, Lang 186 pp. ᴿSJTh 49 (1996) 124-127 (*Torrance, Thomas F.*).

7119 **VanGemeren, Willem** The progress of redemption. 1988, ⇒5,7732; 6,7750. ᴿSBET 14 (1996) 86-87 (*Grogan, G.W.*).

7120 **Winter, Michael** The atonement. 1995, ⇒11/2,3915. ᴿSJTh 49 (1996) 123-124 (*McIntyre, John*).

7121 *Yates, Roy* From christology to soteriology. ET 107 (1996) 268-270.

7122 *Zager, Werner* Wie kam es im Urchristentum zur Deutung des Todes Jesu als Sühnegeschehen?: eine Auseinandersetzung mit Peter STUHLMACHERs Entwurf einer "Biblischen Theologie des Neuen Testaments". ZNW 87 (1996) 165-186.

7123 **Zahl, Paul Francis Matthew** Die Rechtfertigungslehre Ernst KAESEMANNS. Diss. Tü 1994, ^D*Moltmann, J.*, CThM.ST 13: Stu 1996, Calwer xiii; 224 pp. 3-7668-3449-5.

H7.2 *Crux, sacrificium;* The Cross; the nature of sacrifice

7124 *Backhaus, Knut* Kult und Kreuz: zur frühchristlichen Dynamik ihrer theologischen Beziehung. ThGl 86 (1996) 512-533.

7125 **Bailie, Gil** Violence unveiled. 1995, ⇒11/2,3918. ^RMoTh 12,1 (1996) 113-115 (*Hauerwas, Stanley*).

7126 ^E**Balmary, Marie** Le sacrifice du fils dans les trois monothéismes. Pardès 22: P 1996, Cerf 262 pp. 2-204-05494-1.

7127 *Balthasar, Hans Urs von* Christ: alpha and omega. ^T*Walker, Adrian*, Com(US) 23 (1996) 465-471.

7128 *Barth, Gerhard* Für uns gestorben?: unsere Verlegenheit am Karfreitag. Neutestamentliche Versuche. 1996 <1990>, ⇒111. 441-454.

7129 **Bestul, Thomas H.** Texts of the Passion: Latin devotional literature and medieval society. Middle Ages: Ph 1996, Univ. of Pennsylvania xviii; 264 pp.

7130 **Bonnechère, Pierre** Le sacrifice humain en Grèce ancienne. 1994, ⇒10,7753*. ^RClR 46 (1996) 278-279 (*Dowden, Ken*); HR 36 (1996) 76-79 (*Baudy, Gerhard*).

7131 *Caillet, Jean-Pierre, (al)*, Des catacombes à l'art romain: l'évolution des représentations de la croix dans l'art chrétien. MoBi 97 (1996) 17-33.

7132 **Cantalamessa, Raniero** Nous prêchons un Christ crucifié: méditations pour le Vendredi-Saint [dans la basilique Saint-Pierre]. ^T*Macina, M.R.*, Nouan-le-Fuzelier 1996, Béatitudes 196 pp. FF69. ^REeV 106 (1996) 525 (*Oury, G.-M.*).

7133 **Chilton, Bruce** The temple of Jesus: his sacrificial program. 1992, ⇒8,4361... 11/2,3927. ^RBibl.Interp. 4 (1996) 227-230 (*Duling, Dennis C.*); SJTh 49 (1996) 361-362 (*Barker, Margaret*).

7134 *Frettlöh, M.L.* Wider die Halbierung des Wortes vom Kreuz: feministisch-theologische Kritik und Revision der Kreuzestheologie kritisch ins Bild gesetzt. GlLern 11/2 (1996) 107-112 [ZID 22,474].

7135 *Frey, C.* Das Kreuz—diffuses Symbol oder Anstoß zu Umkehr und Leben?. GlLern 11/2 (1996) 113-123 [ZID 22,474].

7136 *Galvin, J.P.* Jesus as scapegoat. Way 36/1 (1996) 61-68 [NTAb 40,459].

7137 **Hälbig, Klaus W.** Der Schlüssel zum Paradies: die Symbolik des Kreuzes Christi: zwölf Bildmeditationen. St. Ottilien 1996, Eos 180 pp. DM38. 3-88096-297-9 [EuA 87/1,167].

7138 **Levenson, Jon D.** The death and resurrection of the beloved son: the transformation of sacrifice in Judaism and christianity. 1993, ⇒9,7998... 11/2,3945. ^RRStR 22 (1996) 10-20 (*Strenski, Ivan*); AJSR 21 (1996) 129-132 (*Greenspahn, Frederick E.*); RExp 93 (1996) 571-572 (*Seifrid, Mark A.*).

7139 *Lippi, Adolfo* Incarnazione kenosi nichilismo: reflessioni sul libro *Credere di credere* di Gianni VATTIMO. La Sapienza della Croce 11 (1996) 371-386.

7140 *Lupande, Joseph M.; Healey, Joseph G.; Sybertz, Donald F.* The Sukuma sacrificial goat and christianity: an example of inculturation in Africa. Worship 70 (1996) 506-516.

7141 *Marx, Alfred* Les offrandes végétales dans l'AT. VT.S 57: 1994, ⇒10,7770. ᴿETR 71 (1996) 109-110 (*Smyth, Françoise*).

7142 *Milbank, John* Stories of sacrifice. MoTh 12/1 (1996) 27-56.

7143 *Moscati, Sabatino* Nuovi contributi sul 'sacrificio dei bambini'. Rés. 499. AANL.R 7 (1996) 499-504.

7144 ᴱ*Neusch, Marcel* Le sacrifice dans les religions. 1994, ⇒10,7772. ᴿScrTh 28 (1996) 319-321 (*Odero, J.M.*); RTL 27 (1996) 240-241 (*Scheuer, J.*).

7145 *Painadath, Sebastian* The vulnerable God: a meditation on the cross. Jeevadhara 26 (1996) 230-238.

7146 *Sassmann, Christiane Karin* Die Opferbereitschaft Israels: anthropologische und theologische Voraussetzungen des Opferkultes. Diss. Bochum 1994. EHS.T 529: Fra 1995, Lang 280 pp. [JQR 89,175s—Blum, Erhard].

7147 ᴱ*Schenk, Richard* Zur Theorie des Opfers: ein interdisziplinäres Gespräch. 1995, ⇒11/2,3956. ᴿThGl 86 (1996) 92-93 (*Hattrup, Dieter*); ZKTh 118 (1996) 71-74 (*Schwager, Raymund*); ThPh 71 (1996) 617-619 (*Splett, J.*).

7148 *Sesboüé, Bernard* Le mystère de la croix. MoBi 97 (1996) 12-16.

7149 *Smith, William Robertson* Sacrifice: preliminary survey. Community. 1996 <1894>, ⇒172. 43-64.

Sorg, T. Das Wort vom Kreuz ⇒206.

7150 *Stegemann, Wolfgang* Der Tod Jesu als Opfer?: anthropologische Aspekte seiner Deutung im Neuen Testament. Abschied von der Schuld?. Theologische Akzente 1: 1996, ⇒2116. 120-139 [Rom 3,25].

7151 *Teselle, Eugene* The cross as ransom. Sum. 147. JEarlyC 4 (1996) 147-170.

7152 *Vollenweider, S.* Diesseits von Golgatha: zum Verständnis des Kreuzestodes Jesu als Sühneopfer. GlLern 11/2 (1996) 124-137 [ZID 22,474].

H7.4 *Sacramenta, Gratia*

7153 *Antonini, Bernardo* Sin—penance—reconciliation in the bible and in the church. Sum. 147. Theol(M) 7 (1996) 11-29. *R.*

7154 *Barth, Gerhard* Taufe auf den Namen Jesu: Kurzbericht über den Stand neutestamentlicher Arbeiten zum Verständnis der Taufe im Urchristentum <1988>;

7155 *Barth, Gerhard* Zur Frage der Einzelbeichte <1957>;

7156 *Barth, Gerhard* Zwei vernachlässigte Gesichtspunkte zum Verständnis der Taufe im Neuen Testament <1973>. Neutestamentliche Versuche. 1996, ⇒111. 45-64/247-261/11-44.

7157 *Bożek, Ryszard* Ordo celebrandi matrimonium e l'uso della sacra scrittura: dallo scritto sacro alla celebrazione della parola di Dio: contributo per l'approfondimento del sacramento del matrimonio.

Thesis ad Lauream 341, Pont. Ateneo Sant'Anselmo 1996, ᴰ*Triacca, Achille Maria*, 132 pp. excerpt.

7158 *Castellano Cervera, Jesús* Il battesimo comunione con Cristo nel suo mistero di morte e di vita. Unità e Carismi 6/6 (1996) 10ss.

7159 *Coda, Piero* Uno in Cristo: il battesimo come evento trinitario. R 1996, Città Nuova 200 pp. L22.000. Unitas(R) 51/3-4 (1996) 176 (*Concetti, Gino*).

7160 ᴱ*Dudley, Martin; Rowell, Geoffrey* The oil of gladness: anointing in the christian tradition. ColMn 1993, Liturgical ix; 221 pp. $11. ᴿJEarlyC 4 (1996) 116-118 (*Shippee, Arthur*).

7161 *Goffi, Tullo* Fedeltà al battesimo: vivere nello Spirito. RPLi 34 (1996) 18-22.

7162 ᴱᵀ*Hunter, David G.* Marriage in the early church. Sources of Early Christian Thought: Mp 1994, Augsburg viii; 157 pp. $12. ᴿJEarlyC 4 (1996) 251-253 (*Walsh, Efthalia Makris*).

7163 *Légasse, Simon* Naissance du baptême. LeDiv 153: 1993, ⇒9,8047... 11/2,3993. ᴿEstB 54 (1996) 141-142 (*González García, F.*).

7164 *MacIlmoyle, Leslie* Baptism: let's face it. L 1996, Janus xiii; 230 pp. 1-85756-280-1 [NThAR 1998,101].

7165 *Magrassi, M.* Gesù e il malato: il sacramento che porta salvezza. Noci (Ba) 1996, La Scale.

7166 *Mathon, Gérard* Le mariage des chrétiens: des origines au concile de Trente. BHC 31: P 1993, Desclée 380 pp. ᴿRSR 84 (1996) 133-136 (*Bourgeois, Henri*).

7167 *McPartlan, Paul* Sacrament of salvation: an introduction to eucharistic ecclesiology. E 1995, Clark 144 pp. £20. 0-567-29299-1. ᴿAtK 126 (1996) 461-463 (*Małecki, Roman*).

7168 ᴱ*Orabona, Luciano* Guitmondo di Aversa: la 'verità' dell'eucaristia. Pref. *Chiarinelli, Lorenzo*, Fonti e Studi 6: N 1995, Ed. Scientifiche Italiane 315 pp. L60.000. ᴿBen. 43/2 (1996) 423-426 (*Bova, Giancarlo*).

7169 *Padoin, Giacinto* 'Il pane che io darò': il sacramento dell'Eucaristia. Ricerche teologiche: R 1993, Borla 320 pp. L36.000. 88-263-0980-9. ᴿAsp. 43 (1996) 580-581 (*Di Napoli, G.*).

7170 *Paprocki, Henryk* Le mystère de l'Eucharistie... la liturgie eucharistique byzantine. 1993, ⇒11/2,4008. ᴿEstTrin 30 (1996) 305-306 (*Miguel, José María de*).

7171 *Pohl, Adolf; Strübind, Kim* 'Also Exegese!...' oder: 'was man nicht versteht, soll man auch nicht praktizieren': ein Briefwechsel zwischen Adolf POHL und Kim STRUEBIND zum Taufverständnis im Neuen Testament (1). Zeitschrift für Theologie und Gemeinde 1 (1996) 145-209 [ZID 22,458].

7172 *Rudolph, Kurt* Antike Baptisten: zu den Überlieferungen über frühjüdische und frühchristliche Taufsekten <1981>;

7173 Jüdische und christliche Täufertraditionen im Spiegel des Kölner Mani-Kodex <1984>. Gnosis. 1996, ⇒147. 569-606/686-697.

ʜ7.6 *Ecclesiologia, theologia missionis, laici*—The Church

7174 *Aguirre, R.* La persecución en el cristianismo primitivo. RLAT 13 (1996) 11-42 [NTAb 41,88].

7175 *Amaladoss, Michael* The gospel, community and culture: becoming communities of the kingdom in Tamilnadu (India) today. ZMR 80 (1996) 243-254.

7176 *Anthonysamy, S.J.* Christian mission in the context of many religions today: a biblical perspective. IMR 19/2 (1996) 9-19 [ThIK 18/1,34].

7177 *Barnes, Elizabeth B.* The story of discipleship: Christ, humanity, and church in narrative perspective. 1995, ⇒11/2,4037. RFaith & Mission 13/2 (1996) 127-8 (*Bush, L. Russ III*).

7178 *Bauckham, Richard* Kingdom and church according to Jesus and Paul. HBT 18 (1996) 1-26.

7179 *Benn, W.* The Bible and the Church. ChM 110/2 (1996) 156-164 [NTAb 41,89].

7180 *Beyerhaus, Peter* Die Bibel in der Mission. Er sandte sein Wort: Theologie der christlichen Mission, 1. Wu 1996, Brockhaus 845 pp. DM68. 3-417-29412-6. RLuThK 20 (1996) 207-209 (*Stolle, Volker*).

7181 *Borgen, Peder* Militant and peaceful proselytism and christian mission. Early christianity. 1996, ⇒116. 45-69.

7182 *Bowman, Ann L.* Women, spiritual gifts, and ministry. Faith & Mission 14/1 (1996) 57-74.

7183 *Dal Covolo, Enrico* Laici e laicità nei primi secoli della chiesa. RdT 37 (1996) 359-375.

7184 *Denaux, A.* Heeft Jezus de kerk gesticht?. Coll. 25 (1996) 341-360.

7185 *Ferguson, Everett* The church of Christ: a biblical ecclesiology for today. GR 1996, Eerdmans xx; 443 pp. $35. 0-8028-4189-9 [ThD 44,168].

7186 *Filbeck, David* Yes, God of the gentiles, too: the missionary message of the Old Testament. BGCM Wheaton 1996, Billy Graham Center, Wheaton College 237 pp. 1-879089-14-9.

7187 *Goldsworthy, Graeme L.* The great indicative: an aspect of a biblical theology of mission. RTR 55 (1996) 2-13.

7188 *Goulder, M.D.* The Jewish-Christian mission, 30-130. Religion. ANRW II.26.3: 1996, ⇒183. 1979-2037.

7189 *Grech, Prosper* La iglesia, sacramento de unidad de todo el génere humano. Esperanza del hombre. 1996, ⇒173. 437-449.

7190 *Grossi, Vittorino* Dal 'sermo humilis' delle traduzioni latine della bibbia alla teologia agostiniana dell'evangelizzazione. Atti del VI Simposio di Efeso. 1996, ⇒264. 273-291.

7191 *Herlyn, O.* 'Prüfet alles, das Gute behaltet!': einige biblische Hinweise zum 'Proprium' kirchlich-diakonischen Handelns. RKZ 137 (1996) 406-410.

7192 *Holum, Kenneth G.* In the blinking of an eye: the christianizing of classical cities in the Levant. Religion and politics. 1996, ⇒212. 131-150.

7193 *Hu, Peter* The history of lay ministries in the church. CTUF 109-110 (1996) 333-338, 483-500 [ThIK 18/2,31s]. C.

7194 E*Karotemprel, S.*, (al), Following Christ in mission: a foundational course in missiology. Boston 1996, Pauline 477 pp. $20 [CBQ 59,206].

7195 *Kavunkal, Jacob* Pluriforming mission. Sum. 852. VJTR 60 (1996) 852-868.

7196 *Kee, Howard Clark* Who are the people of God?: early christian models of community. 1995, ⇒11/2,4093. RTablet (16 Aug. 1996)

1052 *(Cameron, Averil)*; TS 57 (1996) 523-525 *(Matera, Frank J.)*; ET 107 (1995-96) 26 *(Bockmuehl, M.)*; ThTo 53 (1996) 411-412, 414 *(Siker, Jeffrey S.)*; ThLZ 121 (1996) 660-663 *(Roloff, Jürgen)*.

7197 *Kirchschläger, Walter* Kath'olische Kirche: biblische Anmerkungen zu einer Kirchenvision. Diak. 27 (1996) 7-12;

7198 Kirche ist Freiheit!. ThPQ 144 (1996) 52-66.

7199 *Laghi, Card. Pio* Il regno di Dio è "in mezzo" a voi (Lc 17,21) (teoria dell'"intimismo" e struttura ecclesiale della fede). Seminarium 36 (1996) 738-748.

7200 *Lalu, Yos* Yesus, Kerejaan Allah Dan Gereja [Die Reich-Gottes-Verkündigung Jesu und das Verhältnis der Kirche zum Reich Gottes]. Umat Baru 172 (1996) 25-33 [ThIK 18/2,49]. *Indonesian*.

7201 *Lee, Pan-Seok* Straßenverkündigung als die Missionsmethode Jesu und der Apostel. Samok 209 (1996) 33-42 [ThIK 18/1,54]. *K.*

7202 *Lips, Hermann von* Neutestamentliche Aspekte zur Ekklesiologie. BThZ 13 (1996) 60-70.

7203 *Louis-Marie de Jésus, Frère* Quelques images de l'Église à travers la Bible et la liturgie. Carmel 82 (1996) 3-18.

7204 *Maggioni, Bruno* La parola si fa carne: itinerari biblici di spiritualità missionaria. Bo 1996, Ed. Missionaria Italiana 160 pp. L13.000. RClar. 36-37 (1996-97) 638 *(Pardilla, Angel)*.

7205 *Marriage, Alwyn* The people of God: a royal priesthood. 1995, ⇒11/2,4109. RScrTh 28 (1996) 966-967 *(Villar, J.R.)*.

7206 *Mims, Gene* Kingdom principles for church growth. Nv 1994, Convention 118 pp. Faith & Mission 14/1 (1996) 118-21 *(Schofield, James C.)*.

7207 *Nobile, Marco* Ecclesiologia biblica. CSB 30: Bo 1996, EDB 166 pp. L24.000. 88-10-40730-X [RdT 38,287].

7208 *Paget, James Carleton* Jewish proselytism at the time of Christian origins: chimera or reality?. JSNT 62 (1996) 65-103.

7209 *Ramachandra, Vinoth* Gods that fail: modern idolatry and christian mission. Carlisle 1996, Paternoster viii; 226 pp. 0-85364-755-0 [RB 105,158].

7210 *Roloff, Jürgen* Die Kirche im Neuen Testament. GNT 10: 1993, ⇒9,8174; 10,7895. RZKTh 118 (1996) 67-71 *(Marucci, Corrado)*.

7211 *Scanlon, R.* Women deacons: at what price?. HPR 96/10 (1996) 6-14 [NTAb 41,91].

7212 *Scheurer, Erich* Altes Testament und Mission: zur Begründung des Missionsauftrages. TVG: Gießen 1996, Brunnen 501 pp.

7213 E*Schreiner, Josef* Unterwegs zur Kirche: alttestamentliche Konzeptionen. QD 110: 1987, ⇒3,563... 5,7913. RThR 61 (1996) 100-102 *(Reventlow, Henning Graf)*.

7214 *Sieben, Hermann Josef* Vom Apostelkonzil zum Ersten Vatikanum: Studien zur Geschichte der Konzilsidee. KonGe.U: Pd 1996, Schöningh xii; 600 pp. DM148. 3-506-74726-6 [Sapienza 50,241].

7215 *Sievernich, Michael* Mission—mit welchem Recht?;

7216 *Stemberger, Günter* Von einer jüdischen Sekte zur Weltreligion. Wahrnehmung des Fremden. 1996, ⇒218. 245-266/73-85.

7217 *Thomas, J.C.* Women in the church: an experiment in pentecostal hermeneutics. RERT 20 (1996) 220-232 [NTAb 41,91].

7218 *Van Rheenen, Gailyn* Missions: biblical foundations and contemporary strategies. GR 1996, Zondervan 251 pp. $20 [Miss. 25,486].

7219 *Vanhoye, Albert* La chiesa di fronte alle leggi imperfette: fondamenti biblici. I cattolici e la società pluralista: il caso delle leggi
imperfette [EJoblin, J., (al), Civis 13: 1996 Studio Domenicano.
Atti del I Colloquio sui cattolici nella società pluralista]. 117-131
[APIB 10,270];

7220 La testimonianza del Nuovo Testamento circa la non-ammissione
delle donne all'ordinazione sacerdotale. Dall''inter insigniores'
all''ordinatio sacerdotalis'. Congregazione per la Dottrina della
Fede. Documenti e Studi 6: 1996 Libreria Editrice Vaticana. 159-
165 [APIB 10,270].

7221 *Walker, Andrew* Telling the story: gospel, mission and culture. L
1996, SPCK 239 pp. £15.

7222 *Weston, P.* Evangelism: some biblical and contemporary perspectives. ERT 20 (1996) 248-258 [NTAb 41,99].

7223 *Wright, Chris* The Old Testament and christian mission. Evangel
14/2 (1996) 37-43.

H7.7 *Œcumenismus*—The ecumenical movement

7224 *Alexander, Jean* Oecuménisme et mission, I: les Actes des Apôtres
et les épîtres de Paul. Mission de l'Église 110 (1996) 6-13.

7225 *Geisler, Norman L.; MacKenzie, Ralph E.* Roman catholics and
evangelicals: agreements and differences. GR 1995, Baker 538 pp.
$25. RBS 153 (1996) 373-374 (*Pyne, Robert A.*).

7226 *Golda, Manfred* Erfahrungsbericht über ökumenische Bibelkreise.
BiLi 69 (1996) 89-90.

7227 *Greeley, Andrew M.; Neusner, Jacob* Common ground: a priest
and a rabbi read Scripture together. Cleveland, OH ²1996, Pilgrim
xviii; 335 pp. $17. 0-8298-1120-6.

7228 *Haudel, Matthias* Die Bibel und die Einheit der Kirchen. 1993,
⇒9,8292... 11/2,4225. RBijdr. 57 (1996) 106-107 (*Parmentier,
Martin*).

7229 *Henn, William* One faith: biblical and patristic contributions toward understanding unity in faith. 1995, ⇒11/2,3740. RMid-
Stream 35 (1996) 350-351; 352-353 (*Gros, Jeffrey; Russell, Horace O.*); TS 57 (1996) 741-743 (*O'Keefe, John J.*); ChH 65
(1996) 670-671 (*Nassif, Bradley*).

7230 *Silva, Aldina da* Joseph face à ses frères: un appel pour mieux
dialoguer aujourd'hui. P 1996, Médiaspaul 79 pp. [EeV 107,7].

7231 *Tavard, George* The Bible in ecumenism. OiC 32 (1996) 310-322.

7232 *Toews, J.E.* Toward a biblical perspective on people of other
faiths. Conrad Grebel Review 14/1 (1996) 1-23 [NTAb 40,470].

H7.8 **Amt**—*Ministerium ecclesiasticum*

7233 *Balthasar, Hans Urs von* How weighty is the argument from 'unin-
terrupted tradition' to justify the male priesthood?. Com(US) 23/1
(1996) 185-192.

7234 **Beilner, Wolfgang** Dienst und Dienste in der Kirche. Vermittlung
32: Salzburg 1996, n.p. 219 pp.

7235 **Campbell, R. Alastair** The elders: seniority within earliest christianity. 1994, ⇒11/2,4342. RCTJ 31 (1996) 223-227 (*Moor,*

Henry de); CBQ 58 (1996) 742-743 (*Johnson, Luke Timothy*);
AUSS 34 (1996) 107-109 (*Itin, Rolando A.*); Theol. 99 (1996)
156-157 (*Franklin, Eric*).

7236 Currie, H.M. Lay presidency. ET 107 (1996) 334-335.
7237 **Dassmann, Ernst** Ämter und Dienste in den frühchristlichen Gemeinden. 1994, ⇒11/2,4351. ᴿRHE 91 (1996) 505-508 (*Faivre,
Alexandre*); ThLZ 121 (1996) 676-679 (*Strutwolf, Holger*).
7238 **Denzler, Georg** Die Geschichte des Zölibats. 1993, ⇒9,8438.
ᴿKHÅ 96 (1996) 179-184 (*Lawe, Kari*).
7239 *Dominic, A. Paul* Cliche and charism of authority as service. ITS
33/1 (1996) 17-27.
7240 **Eisen, Ute E.** Amtsträgerinnen im frühen Christentum: epigraphische und literarische Studien. FKDG 61: Gö 1996, Vandenhoeck &
R. 287 pp. DM88. 3-525-55170-3 [ThLZ 122,457].
7241 *Federici, Tommaso* Per una teologia biblico-liturgica sul "sacerdozio". RivLi 83 (1996) 345-368.
7242 **Greshake, Gisbert** Ser sacerdote: teología espiritualidad del mini-
sterio sacerdotal. 1995, ⇒11/2,4361. Lumen 45/1 (1996) 85-86
(*Ortiz de Urtaran, Félix*).
7243 *Guillemette, Nil* Is celibacy better?. Landas 10/1 (1996) 3-38 [ThIK
18/1,58].
7244 **Hammann, Gottfried** L'amour retrouvé, la diaconie chrétienne et
le ministère de diacre: du christianisme primitif aux réformateurs
protestants du XVIᵉ siècle. 1994, ⇒10,8086; 11/2,4364. ᴿMSR 53
(1996) 206-208 (*Heuclin, J.*).
7245 *Haucke, Manfred* Il sacerdozio femminile nel recente dibattito
teologico. RTLu 1 (1996) 257-281.
7246 **Häring, Bernhard** Priesthood imperiled: a critical examination of
ministry in the catholic church. Liguori 1996, Triumph xv; 175 pp.
$20. 0-89243-920-3 [ThD 44,171].
7247 *Hauser, Hermann* L'église à l'âge apostolique: structure et évolution des ministères. Préf. *Grelot, Pierre*, LeDiv 164: P 1996, Cerf
198 pp. FF150. 2-204-05332-5. ᴿRThom 96 (1996) 679-682
(*Rolland, Philippe*); BLE 97 (1996) 401-402 (*Dutheil, J.*).
7248 **Hermans, Theo** Origène: théologie sacrificielle du sacerdoce des
chrétiens. ThH 102: P 1996, Beauchesne xxxvi; 252 pp. FF180. 2-
7010-1331-3. ᴿIrén. 69 (1996) 430-431; EstTrin 30 (1996) 306-
307 (*Miguel, José María de*); ScEs 48 (1996) 350-351 (*Barry,
Catherine*).
7249 *Hofrichter, Peter* Diakonat und Frauen im kirchlichen Amt. HID
50 (1996) 140-158.
7250 **Illanes, José Luis; Belda-Plans, Manuel** Teología espiritual y sacerdocio. México 1995, Encuentros sacerdotales 231 pp. ᴿScrTh
28 (1996) 974-975 (*Simón, P.J.*).
7251 **Kaufman, Peter Ivan** Church, book, and bishop: conflict and authority in early Latin christianity. Explorations: Boulder 1996,
Westview ix; 166 pp. $61.50/$16 [AThR 79,440].
7252 *Leonardi, Giovanni* I fondamenti biblici della vita consacrata in tre
studi recenti. StPat 43 (1996) 153-167.
7253 *Marczewski, Marek* Posługa charytatywna diakona w kościele
pierwszych wieków [Caritative Tätigkeit des Diakons in der frühen
Kirche]. Zsfg. 227. Vox Patrum 16 (1996) 217-228. **P**.
7254 *Mayhue, R.L.* A biblical call to pastoral vigilance. MastJ 7/1
(1996) 31-52 [NTAb 41,90].

7255 *Montagnini, Felice* Il vescovo si affaccia sulla scena del Nuovo Testamento. [F]FORESTI B., 1996, ⇒25. 17-32.

7256 **Nelson, Richard D.** Raising up a faithful priest: community and priesthood in biblical theology. 1993, ⇒9,8498... 11/2,4392. [R]BiOr 53 (1996) 777-779 (*Hentschel, Georg*).

7257 *Niewiadomski, Józef* Notwendige, weil Not-wendende Diakoninnenweihe. ThPQ 144 (1996) 339-348.

7258 **Noll, Ray Robert** Christian ministerial priesthood: a search for its beginnings in the primary documents of the Apostolic Fathers. 1993, ⇒10,8109. [R]JEarlyC 4 (1996) 386-389 (*Jefford, Clayton N.*).

7259 *O'Grady, J.* Roman christianity and the church of Rome. ChiSt 35/2 (1996) 177-184 [NTAb 41,90].

7260 *Pasquato, Ottorino* L'istituzione formativa del presbitero nel suo sviluppo storico (sec. I-XVI). Sal. 58 (1996) 269-299.

7261 *Perrot, Charles* Service de l'évangile et genèse des ministères à l'origine. Spiritus 37 (1996) 173-185 [ThIK 18/1,83].

7262 *Pires, José Maria* "Tout a tous" (1 Co 9,22) ou pasteur authentique du troupeau (Mc 10,45; Jn 10,10; 1 Pi 5,2-4). Telema 22/2 (1996) 10-14.

7263 *Raberger, Walter* "Ordinationsfähigkeit" der Frau?: Anmerkungen zum Thema "Frauenpriestertum". ThPQ 144 (1996) 398-411.

7264 *Roloff, Jürgen* Kirchenleitung nach dem Neuen Testament: Theorie und Realität. KuD 42 (1996) 136-153.

7265 [E]**Schwörzer, Horst** Amt Eucharistie-Abendmahl: gelebte Ökumene. [F]GRILLMEIER Alois, Lp 1996, St. Benno 120 pp. DM16.80. 3-7462-1187-5 [ThRv 93,435].

7266 *Simonetti, Manlio* Presbiteri e vescovi nella chiesa del I e II secolo. VetChr 33 (1996) 115-132.

7267 *Sodi, Manlio* Temi biblici dei riti di ordinazione secondo il Pontificale Romano. RivLi 83 (1996) 600-613.

7268 *Stolle, V.* Im Dienst Christi und der Kirche: zur neutestamentlichen Konzeptualisierung kirchlicher Ämter. LuThK 20 (1996) 65-132.

7269 *Terra, João Evangelista Martins* O bom pastor;
7270 O sacerdócio na Bíblia;
7271 Sacerdócio profético. RCB 79/80 (1996) 109-127/57-75/128-149.

7272 **Thurian, Max** La identidad del sacerdote. Edelwis 33: M 1996, Atenas 127 pp. 84-7020-417-3 [Isidorianum 6,299].

7273 **Torrance, Thomas F.** Royal priesthood: a theology of ordained ministry. [2]1993, ⇒10,8133. [R]SJTh 49 (1996) 238-241 (*Wakefield, Gordon S.*).

7274 **Vogels, Heinz-Jürgen** Celibacy: gift or law?. 1992, ⇒9,8529. [R]VJTR 60 (1996) 700-702 (*Carapiet, Mervyn*).

7275 **Ysebaert, Joseph** Die Amtsterminologie im Neuen Testament und in der alten Kirche. 1994, ⇒10,8139; 11/2,4414. [R]JEarlyC 4 (1996) 382-384 (*Ferguson, Everett*); JThS 47 (1996) 265-266 (*Harvey, A.E.*); ThLZ 121 (1996) 687-689 (*Strutwolf, Holger*); CritRR 9 (1996) 314-316 (*Mullen, Roderic L.*).

H8.0 Oratio, *spiritualitas personalis*

7276 **Alphonso Liguori** Pratica di amar Gesù Cristo. [E]*Desideri, F.*; Introd. *Marcelli, E.*, Spiritualità nei Secoli 52: R 1996, Città Nuova 190 pp. L20.000.

7277 **Barry, William A.** Who do you say I am?: meeting the historical Jesus in prayer. Notre Dame 1996, Ave Maria 148 pp. $8. 0-87793-575-0. ᴿRfR 55 (1996) 651-652 (*Mueller, J.J.*).

7278 **Beilner, Wolfgang** Leben nach dem Willen Gottes. Vermittlung 50: Salzburg 1996, n.p. 259 pp.

7279 *Campbell, A.* Once more: is worship biblical?. ChM 110/2 (1996) 131-139 [NTAb 41,93].

7280 *Cheriavely, John F.* Priestly spirituality and pastoral charity. ITS 33/1 (1996) 28-42.

7281 **Cullmann, Oscar** Das Gebet im NT. 1994, ⇒10,168; 11/2,4429. ᴿJETh 10 (1996) 227-229 (*Haubeck, Wilfrid*); ThZ 52 (1996) 277-282 (*Braun, Dietrich*);

7282 La preghiera nel NT. PBT 39: 1995, ⇒11/2,4432. ᴿItin. 4 (1996) 237-238 (*Varagona, Francesco*); Lat. 62 (1996) 634-635 (*Penna, Romano*); Clar. 36-37 (1996-97) 623-626 (*Pardilla, Angel*);

7283 La prière dans le NT. 1995, ⇒11/2,4431. ᴿBLE 97 (1996) 191-192 (*Légasse, S.*); EeV 106 (1996) 366-368 (*Walter, Louis*); RB 103 (1996) 441-443 (*Tournay, R.J.*).

7284 **Delhez, Charles** Si tu veux... 40 méditations à la suite de Jésus de Nazareth. Foi Vivante, Étudiants 380: Namur 1996, Fidélité 148 pp. [EeV 107,329].

7285 *Gerhards, Albert* Der Schriftgebrauch in den altkirchlichen Liturgien. ᶠDassmann E., JAC.E 23: 1996, ⇒19. 177-190.

7286 **Hamman, Adalbert Gautier** La preghiera nella Chiesa antica. TC 6: 1994, ⇒11/2,4447. ᴿLat. 62 (1996) 169-172 (*Pasquato, Ottorino*); VetChr 33 (1996) 236-237 (*Grasso, Cristina*); Mar. 58 (1996) 570-574 (*Fusco, Roberto*); Sal. 58 (1996) 792-794 (*Pasquato, O.*).

7287 **Kakkanatt, Antony** Christological catechesis of the Malankara liturgy. Diss. Univ. Pont. Salesiana, R 1996, ᴰ*Amato, Angelo*, xx; 362 pp.

7288 **Ko, M; Cavaglia, P.; Colomer, J.** Da Gerusalemme a Mornese e a tutto il mondo: meditazioni sulla prima comunità cristiana e sulla prima comunità delle Figlie di Maria Ausiliatrice. Orizzonti 9: R 1996, LAS 223 pp. L25.000 [StPat 45,235—Lorenzin, Tiziano].

7289 **Manns, Frédéric** Lire la bible en église. Préf. *Sabbah, Michel*, P 1996, Médiaspaul 352 pp. 2-7122-0570-7.

7290 **Martini, Card. Carlo** La femme de la réconciliation. ᵀ*Rodembourg, André*, Versailles 1996, Saint-Paul 86 pp. FF50 [EeV 106,399].

7291 *Marucci, Corrado* La preghiera nel Nuovo Testamento. RdT 37 (1996) 113-123.

7292 **Mazza, Enrico** The origins of the eucharistic prayer. ᵀ*Lane, Ronald E.*, ColMn 1995, Liturgical x; 362 pp. $35. ᴿTS 57 (1996) 526-528 (*Baldovin, John F.*).

7293 **Michel, O.** Aufsehen auf Jesus: fünfzehn Bibelstudien. Einf. *Riesner, R.*, Giessen ⁵1996, Brunnen 200 pp. DM22.80. 3-7655-1080-7 [NTAb 41,166].

7294 **Miller, Patrick D.** They cried to the Lord: the form and theology of biblical prayer. 1994, ⇒10,8179; 11/2,4470. ᴿJR 76 (1996) 615-616 (*Kiley, Mark*).

7295 **Morrison, Geroge H.** Meditations on the gospels. Chattanooga, Tenn. 1996 AMG v; 713 pp. 0-89957-214-6 [NThAR 1997,195].

7296 **Neuner, J.** Walking with Him: a biblical guide through thirty days of spiritual exercises. [2]1987, ⇒3,8094. [R]BiBh 22 (1996) 158-159 (*George, Gabriel*).

7297 [E]**Ryan, Gregory** The burning heart: reading the New Testament with John MAIN. NY 1996, Paulist 91 pp. $9. 0-8091-3724-0. [R]ScrB 27 (1997) 89-90 (*Mills, Mary E.*).

7298 **Schaefer, Mary M.** Heavenly and earthly liturgies: patristic prototypes, medieval perspectives, and a contemporary application. Worship 70 (1996) 482-505.

7299 **Scharbert, Josef** Mit Gott "Deutsch reden": der Dialog zwischen Mensch und Gott in der Bibel. St. Ottilien 1996, EOS 119 pp. 3-88096-416-5.

7300 *Stuart, Streeter S.* A New Testament perspective on worship. Sum. 221. EvQ 68 (1996) 209-221.

7301 *Timm, Hermann* C'est la vie: das Evangelium als ABC religiöser Lebenskunst. PTh 85 (1996) 204-210.

7302 *Venetz, Hermann Josef* Vom Beten Jesu. LS 47 (1996) 5-10.

7303 **Whelan, Michael** Living strings: an introduction to biblical spirituality. 1994, ⇒10,8196. [R]CTJ 31 (1996) 269-270 (*Schwanda, Tom*).

H8.1 *Spiritualitas publica:* **Liturgia, vita communitatis, Sancti**

7304 **Bradshaw, Paul F.** La liturgie chrétienne en ses origines: sources et méthodes. 1995, ⇒11/2,4500. [R]EstTrin 30 (1996) 307-308 (*Miguel, José María de*); Mar. 58 (1996) 291-294 (*Mazza, Enrico*).

7305 **Brown, Peter** Le renoncement à la chair: virginité, célibat et continence dans le christianisme primitif. 1995, ⇒11/2,4545. [R]RHPhR 76 (1996) 329-330 (*Maraval, P.*).

7306 **Burton-Christie, Douglas** The word in the desert: scripture and the quest for holiness in early christian monasticism. 1993, ⇒9,8664... 11/2,4546. [R]JThS 47 (1996) 295-298 (*Gould, Graham*).

7307 **Dawn, Marva J.** Reaching out without dumbing down: a theology of worship for the turn-of-the-century culture. GR 1995, Eerdmans 316 pp. $17. [R]BS 153 (1996) 382-383 (*Ralston, Timothy J.*).

7308 **Dumm, Demetrius** Cherish Christ above all: the Bible in the Rule of Benedict. Mahwah, NJ 1996, Paulist 163 pp. $13 [AThR 80/1,98—Marr, Andrew].

7309 *Dumm, Manfred* "Nachahmung"—ein vergessenes Thema?. JETh 10 (1996) 33-86.

7310 **Durchholz, Evamaria; Knoepffler, Nikolaus** FRANZISKUS, IGNATIUS und die Nachfolge Jesu: eine theologische und psychologische Deutung. Innsbruck 1995, Tyrolia 150 pp. DM32.80. [R]CFr 66 (1996) 608-609 (*Meyer, Ruth*).

7311 *Faix, Wilhelm* "Geistliches Handeln" im Gemeindeaufbau: Pastoraltheologische Erwägungen zu einem umstrittenen Thema. JETh 10 (1996) 149-169.

7312 *Gubler, Marie L.* Das 'Dialogprinzip' in den neutestamentlichen Gemeinden. ThBer 22 (1996) 11-43 [ZID 23,450].

7313 **Hengel, Martin** The charismatic leader and his followers. [T]*Greig, James C.G.;* [E]*Riches, John,* E 1996 Clark xv; 111 pp. $24. 0-567-03001-6 [NTAb 41,146].

7314 **Keroloss, Heshmat** Virginity in the early church. Diss. Fordham 1996, [D]*Lienhard, J.,* [RTL 29,585].

7315 **Metzger, M.** Storia della liturgia: le grandi tappe. CinB 1996, San Paolo 224 pp. [R]EstTrin 30 (1996) 308-309 (*Miguel, José María de*).

7316 **Peterson, R.A.** Preservation, perseverance, assurance, and apostasy. Presbyterion 22/1 (1996) 31-41 [NTAb 41,98].

7317 [E]**Richter, Klemens; Kranemann, Benedikt** Christologie der Liturgie. QD 159: 1995, ⇒11/2,634. [R]BiLi 69 (1996) 185-186 (*Buchinger, Harald*); EO 13 (1996) 515-519 (*Neunheuser, Burkhard*); ZKTh 118 (1996) 407-409 (*Meyer, Hans Bernhard*).

7318 **Salzmann, Jorg Christian** Lehren und Ermahnen: zur Geschichte des christlichen Wortgottesdienstes in den ersten drei Jahrhunderten. WUNT 2/59: 1993, ⇒11/2,4531. [R]ThRv 92 (1996) 193-194 (*Thönnes, Dietmar*).

7319 **Tilliette, Guy** Mystère pascal et sainteté chrétienne. P 1996, Téqui 138 pp. FF49 [EeV 107,24].

н8.2 Theologia moralis NT

7320 *Armando, Augello* Poveri e povertà nel Nuovo Testamento. Vivarium 4 (1996) 187-217.

7321 **Bentue, Antonio** La gratuïtat, clau de l'ética bíblica. Cristianisme i cultura 18: Barc 1996, Curilla 141 pp. 84-8286-081-X [NThAR 1999,43].

7322 *Berger, Klaus* Glaubwürdigkeit und Unglaubwürdigkeit kirchlicher Praxis im Evangelium. LouvSt 21 (1996) 75-82.

7323 *Bockmuehl, Markus* Halakhah and ethics in the Jesus tradition. [F]HOOKER M., 1996, ⇒43. 264-278.

7324 **Brooten, Bernadette J.** Love between women: early christian responses to female homoeroticism. Sexuality, History, and Society: Ch 1996, Univ. of Ch Press xxii; 412 pp. $35 [ChH 68,138s—Hunter, David G.].

7325 *Cahill, Lisa Sowle* Kingdom and cross: christian moral community and the problem of suffering. Interp. 50 (1996) 156-168.

7326 **Dąbek, Tomasz M.** 'Nawracajcie się': metanoia w Nowym Testamencie. Katowice 1996, Księgarnia św. Jacka 275 pp. [R]RBL 49 (1996) 274-277 (*Grzybek, Stanisław*).

7327 *Dugandžic, Ivan* Kršćanski moral i Isusova etika: posebnost Isusove etike u usporedbi s opcom racionalnom etikom [Christliche Moral und Ethik Jesus: das spezifische der Ethik Jesu im Vergleich mit allgemeiner und rationaler Ethik]. Zsfg. 611. BoSm 66 (1996) 585-612. **Croatian**.

7328 **Dunn, J.D.G.** Christian liberty: a NT perspective. 1993, ⇒11/2,4607*. [R]Evangel 14/3 (1996) 89-90 (*Bray, Gerald*).

7329 **Dziuba, Andrzej Franciszek** Oredzie moralne Jezusa Chrystusa [Messaggio morale di Gesù Cristo]. Wsz 1996, Wydawnictwa Akademii Teologii Katolickiej 348 pp. 83-7072-063-3. [R]AtK 127 (1996) 472-474 (*Krawczyk, Roman*). **P**.

7330 EFerguson, Everett Christian life: ethics, morality, and discipline
      in the early church. 1993, ⇒9,8741. RAUSS 34 (1996) 118-120
      (Richardson, William).
7331 Gardner, E. Clinton Justice and christian ethics. 1995,
      ⇒11/2,4614*. RJThS 47 (1996) 813-814 (Gorringe, Tim).
7332 Gerhardsson, Birger 'Med hela ditt hjärta': om Bibelns ethos.
      Lund 1996, Novapress 159 pp. 91-7137-004-8 [NThAR
      1997,191].
7333 Grenz, Stanley Sexual ethics: a biblical perspective. 1990,
      ⇒10,8315; 11/2,4619. RSdT 8 (1996) 90-91 (Finch, Paul).
7334 Hays, Richard B. The moral vision of the New Testament: com-
      munity, cross, new creation: a contemporary introduction to New
      Testament ethics. SF 1996, HarperSanFrancisco xv; (2) 508 pp.
      $25. 0-06-063796-X [[TS 58,537].
7335 Hung-Kil, Chang Neuere Entwürfe zur Ethik des Neuen Testa-
      ments im deutschsprachigen Raum: ihre Sichtung und. kritische
      Würdigung. Diss. Erlangen 1995-1996, DMerk, O. [EThL
      74,286*].
7336 Jaquette, James L. Life and death, adiaphora, and Paul's rhetorical
      strategies. NT 38 (1996) 30-54 [Rom 8,38-39; 14,7-9; Phil 1,21-
      26.]
      EKea, P. Perspectives on New Testament ethics ⇒101.
7337 Keck, Leander E. Rethinking "New Testament ethics". JBL 115
      (1996) 3-16.
7338 Lacroix, Xavier Il corpo di carne: la dimensione etica estetica e
      spirituale dell'amore. Persona e psiche: Bo 1996, EDB 336 pp. 88-
      10-80775-8.
7339 Martin, Dale B. Ἀρσενοκοίτης and μαλακός: meanings and conse-
      quences. Biblical ethics and homosexuality. 1996, ⇒6794. 117-
      136.
7340 Marxsen, Willi NT foundations for christian ethics. 1993,
      ⇒9,8808... 11/2,4644. RInterp. 50 (1996) 68-70 (Verhey, Allen).
7341 Matera, Frank J. New Testament ethics: the legacies of Jesus and
      Paul. LVL 1996, Westminster vii; 325 pp. $30. 0-664-22069-X
      [Theol. 797,383].
7342 McDonald, J.I.H. Biblical interpretation and christian ethics.
      1993, ⇒10,8350; 11/2,4638*. RInterp. 50 (1996) 68-70 (Verhey,
      Allen); SJTh 49 (1996) 499-500 (Pattison, Stephen); JThS 47
      (1996) 809-813 (Torrance, Iain); EvQ 68 (1996) 250-251
      (Williams, Stephen).
7343 Meeks, Wayne A. The origins of Christian morality: the first two
      centuries. 1993, ⇒9,8809... 11/2,4647. RRHPhR 76 (1996) 119-
      120 (Vahanian, G.).
7344 Mejía, Jorge El compromiso por la paz y la justicia y la vocación
      escatológica de la iglesia. Esperanza del hombre. 1996, ⇒173. 553-
      569.
7345 Patte, Daniel New Testament ethics: envisioning its critical study
      in this day and age. PRSt 23 (1996) 175-198.
7346 Pedi, Umberto Anche Gesù ebbe problemi di coscienza. Presbyteri
      30 (1996) 287-292 [John 12,23-28].
7347 Pilch, John J. Forgiveness or forgoing revenge?. BiTod 34 (1996)
      383-387.

7348 **Pinckaers, Servais** The sources of christian ethics. 1995,
⇒11/2,4672. ᴿTS 57 (1996) 371-373 (*Bretzke, James T.*); Theol.
99 (1996) 395-396 (*Attfield, David*).

7349 *Reimer, David J.* The Apocrypha and biblical theology: the case of
interpersonal forgiveness. ᶠMASON R., 1996, ⇒57. 259-282.

7350 **Schenk-Ziegler, Alois** Correctio fraterna im Neuen Testament: die
'brüderliche Zurechtweisung' in biblischen, frühjüdischen und hellenistischen Schriften. Diss. Tü 1995, ᴰ*Theobald, M.*, 492 pp.
[RTL 29,588].

7351 **Schmidt, Thomas E.** Straight and narrow?: compassion and clarity
in the homosexuality debate. DG 1995, InterVarsity 240 pp. $11.
ᴿBS 153 (1996) 127 (*Pyne, Robert A.*).

7352 **Schnackenburg, Rudolf** El mansaje moral del Nuevo Testamento
II: los primeros predicadores cristianos. 1991, ⇒7,8365...
10,8381. ᴿRCatT 21 (1996) 251-255 (*Rubio, Anna*).

7353 *Seow, Choon-Leong* Textual orientation. Biblical ethics and homosexuality. 1996, ⇒6794. 17-34.

7354 *Sevrin, Jean-Marie* La réconciliation dans le Nouveau Testament.
Sum. 59. Irén. 69 (1996) 46-59.

7355 *Siker, Jeffrey S.* Gentile wheat and homosexual christians: New
Testament directions for heterosexual church. Biblical ethics and
homosexuality. 1996, ⇒6794. 137-151.

7356 *Smit, Dirk J.* Saints, disciples, friends?: recent South African
perspectives on Christian ethics and the New Testament. Neotest.
30 (1996) 169-185.

7357 *Šporčić, Ivan* Tko je kršćanin?: Novozavjetni vidici [Wer ist ein
Christ?: die neutestamentlichen Auslegungen und Auffassungen].
Zsfg. 199. BoSm 66 (1996) 179-199. **Croatian.**

7358 **Tremblay, R.** Cristo e la morale in alcuni documenti del magistero. R 1996, Dehoniane 208 pp. [RTM 29,146].

7359 **Vacek, Edward Collins** Love, human and divine: the heart of
Christian ethics. Wsh 1994, Georgetown Univ. Press xix; 352 pp.
0-87840-551-8. ᴿMilltown Studies 37/1 (1996) 136-141 (*Cronin,
Kieran*).

7360 *Venetz, Hermann Josef* Vom Zerbrechen der alten Ideale angesichts
der neuen Wirklichkeit: Anfragen des Neuen Testaments. LS 47
(1996) 70-75.

7361 **Wheeler, Sondra Ely** Wealth as peril and obligation... NT. 1995,
⇒11/2,4719. ᴿThTo 53 (1996) 404, 406, 408 (*Koenig, John*).

7362 **Wogaman, J. Philip** Christian ethics: a historical introduction.
1993, ⇒9,8846... 11/2,4723. ᴿInterp. 50 (1996) 71-73
(*Gunnemann, Jon P.*); Mid-Stream 35/1 (1996) 160-161 (*Fowler,
Newton B.*).

7363 *Ziegler, Josef Georg* "Wo der Geist des Herrn wirkt, da ist Freiheit" (2 Kor 3,17): die christliche Botschaft der Freiheit. TThZ 105
(1996) 139-150.

H8.4 *NT ipsum de reformatione sociali*—**Political action in Scripture**

7364 ᴱ**Cromartie, Michael** Caesar's coin revisited: christians and the
limits of government. GR 1996, Eerdmans ix; 197 pp. $16. 0-
8028-4202-X [ThD 44,159].

7365 **Dal Covolo, Enrico** Chiesa, società, politica: aree di 'laicità' nel cristianesimo delle origini. 1994, ⇒11/2,4749. RAug. 36/1 (1996) 271-272 (*Gori, Franco*); Aevum 70 (1996) 162-163 (*Barzanò, Alberto*); AtK 126/1 (1996) 149-151 (*Widok, Norbert*).

7366 *Debergé, Pierre* Le pouvoir politique est-il toujours mauvais?: regard sur quelques textes du Nouveau Testament. BLE 97 (1996) 331-348 [Rom 3,1-7; 1 Tim 2,1-4; 1 Pt 2,13-17].

7367 **Duchrow, Ulrich** Alternatives to global capitalism: drawn from biblical history, designed for political action. 1994, 10,8420... 11/2,4756. RCritRR 9 (1996) 381-383 (*Rumscheidt, Martin*).

7368 **O'Donovan, Oliver** The desire of the nations: rediscovering the roots of political theology. C 1996, CUP xii; 304 pp. £37.50/$60. 0-521-49677-2 [JThS 48,756].

7369 *Peterson, A.L.* Religious narratives and political protest. JAAR 64 (1996) 27-44.

7370 *Rowland, Christopher* What does the bible say?. PrPe 10 (1996) 176-180.

7371 *Terpstra, Marin; Wit, Theo de* Het 'uitzonderlijke' als messiaanse mogelijkheid: de negatieve politieke theologie van Jacob TAUBES. TTh 36 (1996) 365-386.

7372 **Walsh, Jerome P.M.** The mighty from their thrones. 1987, ⇒3,2608... 6,8487. RThR 61 (1996) 93-94 (*Reventlow, Henning Graf*).

7373 **Weber, Hans-Ruedi** Power: focus for a biblical theology. 1989, ⇒5,8563... 7,8485. RThR 61 (1996) 68-70 (*Reventlow, Henning Graf*).

H8.5 Theologia liberationis latino-americana

7374 *Antony Raja, E.* Biblical symbols of liberation. MaAr 20/3 (1996) 106-115 [ThIK 18/1,38]. **Tamil.**

7375 *Avalos, Hector* The gospel of Lucas GAVILAN as postcolonial biblical exegesis. Semeia 75 (1996) 87-105.

7376 *Carroll R., M. Daniel* The prophetic text and the literature of dissent in Latin America: Amos, GARCIA MAQUEZ, and CABRERA INFANTE dismantle militarism. Bibl.Interp. 4 (1996) 76-100.

7377 *Corrie, John* A new way of being the church?: liberation theology and the mission of the church in a postmodern context. Evangel 14/2 (1996) 50-54.

7378 *Dullas, Pampan* Jesus' message of liberation for today. MaAr 20/3 (1996) 116-125 [ThIK 18/1,38]. **Tamil.**

7379 *Dumas, Benoit A.* Teología de la liberación: ¿por qué esa desconfianza?. RF 234 (1996) 171-181.

7380 EEllacuria, Ignacio; Sobrino, Jan Mysterium liberationis: Grundbegriffe der Theologie der Befreiung. Luzern 1995-1996, Exodus 2 vols; 1316 pp. [LebZeug 52,315].

7381 *Girard, Marc* Une théologie biblique appliquée: le modèle latino-américain. ScEs 48 (1996) 289-305.

7382 *Hinkelammert, Franz-J.* Taking stock of Latin American liberation theology today. VFTW 19/2 (1996) 46-82 [ThIK 18/2,47].

7383 *Pixley, Jorge* Toward a militant biblical scholarship. Bibl.Interp. 4 (1996) 72-75.

7384   *Schönborn, Paul Gerhard* Bibelarbeit in Brasilien. Orien. 60/18 (1996) 189-190 [ThIK 18/2,82].
7385   *Siker, Jeffrey S.* Uses of the bible in the theology of Gustavo GUTIERREZ: liberating scriptures of the poor. Bibl.Interp. 4 (1996) 40-71.
7386   **Sobrino, Jon** Jesus the liberator. 1993, ⇒10,8550; 11/2,4930. ᴿPrPe 10 (1996) 395-396 (*McLoughlin, David*).

н8.6   *Theologiae emergentes*—**Theologies of emergent groups**

7387   *Abe, Gabriel Oyedele* Redemption, reconciliation, propitiation: salvation terms in an African milieu. JTSA 95 (1996) 3-12 [ThIK 18/2,22].
7388   *Kitshoff, Mike C.* Isaiah SHEMBE's views on the ancestors in biblical perspective. JTSA 95 (1996) 23-36 [ThIK 18/2,22].
7389   **Kwok Pui-lan** Discovering the Bible in the non-biblical world. 1995, ⇒11/2,5034. ᴿAJTh 10/2 (1996) 451-452 (*England, John C.*).
7390   *Lee-Linke, Sung-Hee* Jesus und Minjung (OCHLOS): Kontextualisierung des Evangeliums in der Minjung-Theologie. JBTh 11 (1996) 15-29.
7391   *Pobee, John S.* Nog éénmaal Christus onze voorvader. WeZ 3 (1996) 34-40 [ThIK 18/1,83].
7392   **Sanneh, Lamin** Translating the message: the missionary impact on culture. 1989, ⇒5,8669. ᴿREB 56 (1996) 1012-1014 (*Hoornaert, Eduardo*).

н8.7   *Mariologia*—**The mother of Jesus in the NT**

7393   ᴱ**Aparicio Rodríguez, Angel** María del evangelio: las primeras generaciones cristianas hablan de María. Monografías 2: M 1994, Claretianas 463 pp. ᴿMar. 58 (1996) 242-245 (*Fernández, Domiciano*);
7394   Eva-Maria. EphMar 46/1 (1996) 115-138 [NTAb 41,92].
7395   *Balthasar, Hans Urs von* Mary—church—office. Com(US) 23/1 (1996) 193-198.
7396   **Bartosik, Grzegorz M.** Z niej nrodzit siç Jezus: szkice z mariologii biblijnej [Da lei è nato Gesù: saggio di mariologia biblica]. Niepokalanów 1996, Wydawniotwo Ojców Franciszkanów 122 pp. [MF 97/1-2,346].
7397   **Bastero de Elizalde, Juan Luis** María, madre del redentor. Pamplona 1995, EUNSA 133 pp. 84-313-1360-9. ᴿEE 71 (1996) 489-490 (*Martínez Sierra, A.*); ScrTh 28 (1996) 266-268 (*Illanes, J.L.*).
7398   *Beattie, Tina* Mary, the virgin priest. Month 29 (1996) 485-493.
7399   ᴱ**Beinert, Wolfgang; Petri, Heinrich** Handbuch der Marienkunde, 1: theologische Grundlegung: geistliches Leben; 2, Gestaltetes Zeugnis: gläubiger Lobpreis. Regensburg ²1995-96, Pustet 695 + 650 pp. DM148 + DM148. 3-7917-1525-9.
7400   *Bengoechea, Ismael* Jesucristo, María y las mujeres del evangelio (n.12-16 de la 'Mulieris dignitatem'). EstMar 62 (1996) 155-174.

7401 **Benko, Stephen** The virgin goddess: studies in the pagan and christian roots of mariology. SHR 59: 1993, ⇒11/2,5108. [R]ThLZ 121 (1996) 369-374 (*Wyrwa, Dietmar*).

7402 *Bevilacqua, Gabriella* Maria ed Ecate: una nuova associazione magica. Rés. 505. AANL.R 7 (1996) 505-512.

7403 **Borgeaud, Philippe** La mère des dieux: de Cybèle à la Vierge Marie. P 1996, Seuil 264 pp. Bibl. FF140. 2-02-010903-4.

7404 *Boss, Sarah Jane* Mary at the margins: christology and ecclesiology in modernity. Month 29 (1996) 463-475.

7405 *Bou i Simó, Jordi* La maternidad de María y de la mujer (MD 17-19). EstMar 62 (1996) 175-198.

7406 *Brennan, Walter* The virginity of Mary in the theology of the new creation. Milltown Studies 38 (1996) 75-97.

7407 **Buby, Bertrand** Mary of Galilee, 3: the Marian heritage of the early church. NY 1996, Alba xxiv; 360 pp. $36/$20. [BiTod 35,260]. [R]Miles Immacolatae 32 (1996) 716-719 [also vols 1-2 ⇒10,8671; 11/2,5115s] (*Samaha, John M.*).

7408 **Colzani, G.** Maria: mistero di grazia e di fede. CinB 1996, San Paolo 336 pp. [Theotokos 5,738ss—De Fiores, Stefano].

7409 **Coyle, Kathleen** Mary in the christian tradition: from a contemporary perspective. Mystic, CT [2]1996, Twenty-Third xvi; 132 pp. $13 [CBQ 59,420].

7410 **Cunneen, Sally** In search of Mary: the woman and the symbol. NY 1996, Ballantine xxi; 403 pp. 0-345-38246-3.

7411 *Diez Merino, Luis* Eva-María y la mujer (Md 9.10.11): relación con las fuentes bíblicas. EstMar 62 (1996) 113-154.

7412 *Dupleix, André* 'Faites tout ce qu'il vous dira': Marie et l'appel à la sainteté. BLE.S 1 (1996) 117-130.

7413 *Elizondo, Felisa* María y la mujer: imagen y semejenza de Dios (MD 6-8). EstMar 62 (1996) 101-111.

7414 **Frison, Ferdinando** Il silenzio di Maria ai piedi della Croce. Rovigo 1996, Artestampa 60 pp. [R]PalCl 75 (1996) 862-863 (*Lavarda, Girolamo*).

7415 *Frost, Francis* Mother of God and mother of the church. Month 29 (1996) 500-506.

7416 *Galot, Jean* Marie corédemptrice: controverses et problèmes doctrinaux. EeV 106 (1996) 209-216.

7417 **García de Paredes, José Cristo Rey** Mariología. 1995, ⇒11/2,5123. [R]EE 71 (1996) 328-329 (*Martínez Sierra, A.*); Lumen 45 (1996) 239-241 (*Gil Ortega, Urbano*); Mar. 58 (1996) 258-261 (*Semeraro, Marcello*); NatGrac 43 (1996) 493-494 (*Villamonte, A.*).

7418 **Gaventa, Beverly R.** Mary: glimpses of the mother of Jesus. 1995, ⇒11/2,5124. [R]ThTo 53 (1996) 528, 530-531 (*Scholer, David M.*).

7419 **Gazzotti, E.** Maria fotografata dai vangeli. ABC della Fede 4: Bo 1996, Dehoniane 71 pp. [R]Miles Immacolatae 32/2 (1996) 701-702 (*Gal, Mary*).

7420 *Gironés, Gonzalo* María, la madre de Dios y la mujer. EstMar 62 (1996) 91-100.

7421 **Gottemoller, Bartholomew** Mary: God's supreme masterpiece. Santa Barbara, CA 1996 Queenship xiv; 191 pp. [R]Miles Immacolatae 32 (1996) 724-727 (*Calkins, Arthur Burton*).

7422 **Guilbert, Pierre** Marie des écritures. Racines: Montrouge 1995, Nouvelle Cité 274 pp. ^RMar. 58 (1996) 530-533 (*Masini, Mario*).

7423 **Haarmann, Harald** Die Madonna und ihre griechischen Töchter: Rekonstruktion einer kulturhistorischen Genealogie. Hildesheim 1996, Olms (6) 273 pp. 3-487-10163-7.

7424 *Hogan, William F.* Woman of compassion. Spiritual Life 42 (1996) 201-204.

7425 **John Paul II, Pope** Su Maria [documenti]. La catechesi del Papa 1.5-1.11.1996. Miles Immaculatae 32 (1996) 391-466.

7426 ^E**Kießig, M.** Maria, la madre di nostro Signore: un contributo della chiesa evangelico-luterana tedesca. Mi 1996, Paoline 159 pp. [Theotokos 5,358].

7427 **Laurentin, René** María, clave del misterio cristiano: la más cercana a los hombres porque es la más cercana a Dios. M 1996, San Pablo 164 pp. ^RRevAg 37 (1996) 1199-1200 (*Domínguez Sanabria, Jesús*).

7428 *Lizotte, Aline* Peut-on continuer à appeler Marie: 'la Sainte Vierge'?. EeV 106 (1996) 490-496; 497-509; 516-525.

7429 **Luisetto, Giovanni M.** Maria dalla quale è nato il Cristo. Spunti di mariologia: Conegliano, Treviso 1994, Ancilla 469 pp. L40.000. 88-85332-21-8. ^RMiles Immacolatae 32 (1996) 705-707 (*Bertazzo, Ludovico*).

7430 *Maunder, Chris* Mother or disciple: the quest for the historical Mary. Month 29 (1996) 494-499.

7431 *McPartlan, Paul* Mary and catholic-orthodox dialogue. Month 29 (1996) 476-484.

7432 **Mimouni, Simon Claude** Dormition et assomption de Marie: histoire des traditions anciennes. ThH 98: 1995, ⇒11/2,5142. ^REeV 106 (1996) 554-558 (*Cothenet, Édouard*).

7433 *Molina Prieto, Andres* La virginidad de María, paradigma bíblico de la consagración virginal femenina (MD 20-22). EstMar 62 (1996) 213-229.

7434 **Murad, Afonso** Quem é esta mulher?: Maria na Bíblia. São Paulo 1996, Paulinas 244 pp. 85-7311-544-0. ^RPerTeol 28 (1996) 407-409 (*Taborda, Francisco*).

7435 **Orozco, Antonio** Madre de Dios y madre nuestra: iniciación a la mariología. Biblioteca de Iniciación Teológica: M 1996, Rialp 124 pp. ^RScrTh 28 (1996) 964-965 (*Bastero, J.L.*).

7436 **Pedico, Maria Marcellina** Magnificate con me il Signore: celebrazioni biblico-liurgiche in lode a Maria. Mi 1996, Paoline 241 pp. L18.000. ^RUnitas(R) 51/3-4 (1996) 177 (*Pedrini, Arnaldo*).

7437 **Pelikan, Jaroslav** Mary through the centuries: her place in the history of culture. NHv 1996, Yale Univ. Press x; (2) 267 pp. $25. 0-300-06951-0.

7438 ^E**Peretto, Elio** L'immagine teologica di Maria, oggi: fede e cultura. R 1996, Marianum (4) xi; 5-428 pp. Atti del 10' Simposio Internazionale Mariologico (R, 4-7 ottobre 1994). L60.000. 88-87016-49-6.

7439 **Pikaza, Xabier** La amiga de Dios: el mensaje mariano del Nuevo Testamento. M 1996, San Pablo 229 pp. ^REstTrin 30 (1996) 475-476 (*Ofilada Mina, Macario*).

7440 *Pikaza, Xabier* María misterio de esperanza: lectura de Lc. 1-2. Isidorianum 5 (1996) 26-85.

7441 **Ponce Cuéllar, Miguel** María, madre del redentor y madre de la Iglesia. Manual de Mariología: Badajoz 1995, Los Santos de M. 409 pp. 84-605-2243-1. RMar. 58 (1996) 253-256 (*Fernández, Domiciano*).

7442 *Rocacher, Jean* Iconographie mariale. BLE.S 1 (1996) 51-55.

7443 **Schreiner, Klaus** Maria: Jungfrau, Mutter, Herrscherin. Mü 1994, Hanser 591 pp. DM78. 3-446-17831-7. RThRv 92 (1996) 323-326 (*Gössmann, Elisabeth*);

7444 María, virgen, madre, reina. TCherek, Annette, Barc 1996, Herder 599 pp. 84-254-1943-3 [PerTeol 30,468].

7445 **Ségalen, Jean-Marie** Orar con María. Collab. *Durrwell, François-Xavier; Prévot, René*, M 1996, Sociedad Educación Atenas 222 pp.

7446 **Sendler, Egon** Le icone bizantine della Madre di Dio. Dimensioni dello spirito 29: CinB 1995, San Paolo 284 pp. RMar. 58 (1996) 281-284 = 558-560 (*Gharib, Georges*).

7447 **Serra, Aristide** Nato da donna...(Gal 4,4): ricerche bibliche su Maria di Nazaret (1989-1992). 1992, ⇒8,309; 10,8709. RLASBF 46 (1996) 472-475 (*Chrupcała, Lesław Daniel*).

7448 **Tavard, George Henry** The thousand faces of the Virgin Mary. ColMn 1996, Liturgical viii; 275 pp. $20. 0-8146-5914-4. RRfR 55 (1996) 654-655 (*Morkovsky, Mary Christine*).

7449 La vergine madre nella chiesa delle origini: itinerari mariani dei due millenni. R 1996, Centro di Cultura Mariana 255 pp. [Theotokos 5,749ss—Bottino, Adriana].

7450 *Wansbrough, Henry* Mary in the mystery. Month 29 (1996) 455-462.

7451 *Wyler, Bea* Mary's call. A feminist companion. 1996, ⇒170. 136-148.

H8.8 *Feminae NT*—Women in the NT and church history

7452 *Amadu-Asuogu, Chinedu Adolphus* The place of women in the New Testament house codes: an exegetical analysis of 1 Tim 3,11-15 and 1 Cor 14,33b-35. Bulletin of Ecumenical Theology 8/1 (1996) 39-59 [ThIK 18/2,25].

7453 ETAmonville Alegría, Nicole d' El amor de Magdalena: l'amour de Madeleine: sermón anónimo francés del siglo XVII, descubierto por Rainer Maria RILKE en la tienda de un anticuario parisino. Barc 1996, Herder 70 pp. 84-254-1994-8. RFranciscanum 38 (1996) 368-369 (*Vargas Guillén, Germán*).

7454 **Arjava, Antti** Women and law in late antiquity. Oxf 1996, Clarendon xii; 304 pp. £35. 0-19-815033-4 [JThS 48,642].

7455 **Bernabé Ubieta, C.** María Magdalena: tradiciones en el cristianismo primitivo. 1994, ⇒10,8716; 11/2,5167. RCDios 209/1 (1996) 274-275 (*Gutiérrez, J.*).

7456 **Boer, Esther A. de** Maria Magdalena: de mythe voorbij: op zoek naar wie zij werkelijk is. Zoetermeer 1996, Meinema 175 pp. [NThAR 1997,132].

7457 **Bonanate, Mariapia** Il vangelo secondo una donna: ieri e oggi. Letteratura biblica 7: Mi 1996, Paoline 268 pp. L24.000. 88-315-1188-2.

7458 **Boxler, Madeleine** 'Ich bin ein predigerin und appostlorin': die deutschen Maria Magdalena-Legenden des Mittelalters (1300-

1550): Untersuchungen und Texte. Diss. Z 1995. DLAS 22: Bern 1996, Lang 619 pp. $73 [Spec. 74,134ss—Schleissner, Margaret].

7459 **Clark, Gillian** Women in late antiquity: pagan and christian life-styles. 1993, ⇒9,9323; 11/2,5183. ᴿRSLR 32 (1996) 643-645 (*Testa, Rita Lizzi*).

7460 **Coffey, Kathy** Hidden women of the gospels. NY 1996, Crossroad 179 pp. 0-8245-1561-7.

7461 **Cooper, Kate** The virgin and the bride: idealized womanhood in late antiquity. L 1996, Harvard Univ. Press xii; 180 pp. Bibl. 0-674-93949-2.

7462 *Emmanuelle-Marie, Sr.* Marie-Madeleine. Sources 22/1-2 (1996) 1-10.

7463 **Grelot, Pierre** La donna nel Nuovo Testamento. CinB 1996, San Paolo 134 pp. L20.000 [RdT 37,719];

7464 La condition de la femme d'après le NT. 1995, ⇒11/2,5199. ᴿNRTh 118 (1996) 430-431 (*Mattheeuws, A.*).

7465 **Grenz, Stanley J.** Women in the church: a biblical theology of women in ministry. 1995, ⇒11/2,5200. ᴿBS 153 (1996) 381-382 (*Sullivan, Christy T.*); TrinJ 17 (1996) 114-124 (*Schreiner, Thomas R.*).

7466 **Hamington, M.** Hail Mary?: the struggle for ultimate womanhood in catholicism. L 1995, Routledge x; 216 pp. £13. 0-415-91303-9/4-7. ᴿTTh 36 (1996) 426-427 (*Maeckelberghe, Els*).

7467 **Haskins, Susan** Mary Magdalen. 1993, ⇒9,9339... 11/2,5203. ᴿSCJ 27 (1996) 1189-1191 (*Terpstra, Nicholas*);

7468 María Magdalena: mito y metáfora. ᵀ*Amonville, Nicole d'*, Barc 1996, Herder 522 pp. 84-254-1931-X. ᴿFranciscanum 38 (1996) 370-372 (*Vargas Guillén, Germán*).

7469 *Hellwig, Monika Konrad* Jesus and the church tradition on women. CTUF 107 (1996) 21-27 [ThIK 18/1,27]. C.

7470 **Jensen, Anne** Gottes selbstbewußte Töchter. 1992, ⇒9,9342... 11/2,5211. ᴿJAC 39 (1996) 264-265 (*Bammel, Caroline P.*); IKZ 86 (1996) 126-128 (*Arx, Urs von*).

7471 *Lee, Dorothy A.* Women as "sinners": three narratives of salvation in Luke and John. ABR 44 (1996) 1-15 [Lk 7,36-50; Jn 4,1-42; 7,53-8,11].

7472 *Levine, Amy-Jill* Second Temple Judaism, Jesus, and women: yeast of Eden. A feminist companion. 1996 <1994>. 302-331.

7473 **Lindboe, Inger Marie** Women in the New Testament: a select bibliography. 1990, ⇒6,8864... 10,8739. ᴿSEÅ 61 (1996) 162-163 (*Stenström, Hanna*).

7474 **MacDonald, Margaret Y.** Early christian women and pagan opinion: the power of hysterical women. C 1996, CUP xiv; 276 pp. £37.50/£14. 0-521-56174-4/728-9 [NTS 43,622].

7475 **Marjanen, Atti** The woman Jesus loved: Mary Magdalene in the Nag Hammadi library and related dcouments. Diss. Helsinki 1996. NHS 40: Lei 1996, Brill 261 pp. ƒ136. 90-04-10658-8 [ThLZ 122,462].

7476 *Mary Corona, Sr.* Renewed commitment to gospel vision on women. Vaiharai 1/1 (1996) 7-17 [ThIK 18/1,39].

7477 *McKechnie, Paul* 'Women's religion' and second-century christianity. JEH 47 (1996) 409-431.

7478 **Mourlon-Beernaert, P.** Marthe, Marie et les autres: les visages féminins de l'évangile. 1992, ⇒8,9068. ᴿRTL 27 (1996) 103-104 (*Dermience, Alice*).

7479 *Reinhartz, Adele* From narrative to history: the resurrection of Mary and Martha. A feminist companion. 1996 <1991>, ⇒170. 197-224.

7480 **Ricci, Carla** Mary Magdalene and many others: women who followed Jesus. 1994, ⇒11/2,5230. ᴿCBQ 58 (1996) 357-358 (*Thompson, Mary R.*); Interp. 50 (1996) 430-431 (*Castelli, Elizabeth A.*) [Lk 8,1-3].

7481 **Ruckstuhl, Eugen** Jesus, Freund und Anwalt der Frauen: Frauenpräsenz und Frauenabwesenheit in der Geschichte Jesu. Diss. ᴰ*Kirchschläger, Walter*. Stu 1996, Kathol. Bibelwerk 208 pp. 3-460-33101-1.

7482 **Schottroff, Luise** Lydias ungeduldige Schwestern. 1994, ⇒10,8751; 11/2,5239. ᴿEvTh 56 (1996) 377-387 (*Eisen, Ute E.*); ZKTh 118 (1996) 252-255 (*Oberforcher, Robert*);

7483 Lydia's impatient sisters. 1995, ⇒11/2,5240. ᴿHBT 18/2 (1996) 203-204 (*Thurston, Bonnie*); TS 57 (1996) 525-526 (*Osiek, Carolyn*).

7484 **Sirago, Vito Antonio** Galla Placidia: la nobilissima. Donne d'Oriente e d'Occidente 1: Mi 1996, Jaca 159 pp. 88-16-43501-1.

7485 **Synek, Eva Maria** Heilige Frauen der frühen Christenheit. ÖC 43: 1994, ⇒11/2,5248. ᴿThLZ 121 (1996) 177-178 (*Strohmaier-Wiederanders, Gerlinde*).

7486 *Thorley, John* Junia, a women apostle. NT 38 (1996) 18-29 [Rom 16,7].

7487 *Trotzig, Aina* Den heliga Maria Magdalena i svensk medeltidskonst: en ikonografisk undersökning. 75 ill. KHÅ 96 (1996) 13-96.

7488 **Van Bremen, Riet** The limits of participation: women and civic life in the Greek east in the Hellenistic and Roman periods. Dutch Monographs on Ancient History and Archaeology 15: Amst 1996, Gieben xvii; 399 pp. *f*145. 90-5063-567-9 [AnCl 67,517ss— D'Hautcourt, Alexis].

7489 *Virgili, Rosanna* Le donne del vangelo. Firmana 12-13 (1996) 271-278.

7490 **Wind, Renate** Maria aus Nazareth, aus Bethanien, aus Magdala: drei Frauengeschichten. KT 145: Mü 1996, Kaiser 96 pp. DM20. 3-579-05145-8 [Lk 10,38-42].

H8.9 *Theologia feminae*—Feminist theology

7491 *Batmartha, Ina Johanne* Machen Geburt und Monatsblutung die Frau "unrein"?: zur Revisionsbedürftigkeit eines mißverstandenen Diktums. Von der Wurzel getragen. 1996, ⇒204. 43-60.

7492 *Bowen, Nancy R.* Canon and the community of women: a feminist response to canonical criticism. ᶠSANDERS J., JSOT.S 225: 1996, ⇒77. 237-252.

7493 *Bowman, Ann L.* Women, spiritual gifts, and ministry. Faith & Mission 14/1 (1996) 57-74.

7494 **Boyer, Mark G.** Biblical reflections on male spirituality. ColMn 1996, Liturgical 108 pp. 0-8146-2323-9.

7495 *Brekus, Catherine A.* Harriet LIVERMORE, the pilgrim stranger: female preaching and biblical feminism in early-nineteenth-century America. ChH 65 (1996) 389-404.
7496 *Brenner, Athalya* Introduction. A feminist companion. 1996, ⇒170. 15-29;
7497 Pornoprophetics revisited: some additional reflections. JSOT 70 (1996) 63-86 [Ezek 16; 21,8; 23; Hos 2];
7498 Women's traditions problematized: some reflections. ᴹVAN DIJK-HEMMES F., 1996, ⇒99. 53-66.
7499 *Brocke, Edna* Do the origins already contain the malady?. A feminist companion. 1996 <1993>, ⇒170. 349-354.
7500 **Cheney, Emily** She can read: feminist reading strategies for biblical narrative. Valley Forge, PA 1996, Trinity xiv; 192 pp. $18. 1-56338-167-2.
7501 **Cole, Susan; Ronan, Marian; Taussig, Hal** Wisdom's feast: sophia in study and celebration. Kansas City 1996, Sheed & W. 240 pp. $15 [BiTod 35,319].
7502 *Corley, Kathleen* Feminist myths of christian origins. ᶠMACK B., 1996, ⇒54. 51-67,
7503 *Dewey, Joanna* From storytelling to written text: the loss of early christian women's voices. BTB 26 (1996) 71-78.
7504 *Fiorenza, Elisabeth Schüssler* Challenging the rhetorical half-turn: feminist and rhetorical biblical criticism. Rhetoric. JSNT.S 131: 1996, ⇒268. 28-53.
7505 **Fiorenza, Elisabeth Schüssler** But she said: feminist practices of biblical interpretation. 1992, ⇒8,8173... 11/2,5352. ᴿRStR 22 (1996) 293-296 (*D'Angelo, Mary Rose*); RStR 22 (1996) 296-300 (*Castelli, Elizabeth*);
7506 Jesus: Miriam's child, Sophia's prophet: critical issues in feminist christology. 1994, ⇒11/2,5351. ᴿJR 76 (1996) 345-8 (*Lefebure, Leo D.*); TS 57 (1996) 167-169 (*Mayeski, Marie Anne*); RStR 22 (1996) 293-296 (*D'Angelo, Mary Rose*); RStR 22 (1996) 296-300 (*Castelli, Elizabeth*);
7507 Discipulado de iguais: uma ekklesia-logia feminista crítica da libertação. ᵀ*Toledo, Yolanda Steidel*, Petrópolis 1995, Vozes 404 pp. ᴿREB 56 (1996) 493-496 (*Lepargneur, Hubert*);
7508 Gesù figlio di Miriam, profeta di Sophía: questioni critiche di cristologia femminista. Sola Scriptura 17: T 1996, Claudiana 288 pp. L45.000 [RdT 38,287];
7509 Pero ella dijo: prácticas feministas de la interpretación bíblica. Estructuras y Procesos, Religión: M 1996, Trotta 283 pp. 84-8164-130-8.
7510 **Gerstenberger, Erhard S.** Yahweh, the patriarch: ancient images of God and feminist theology. Mp 1996, Fortress xv; 168 pp. $16. 0-8006-2843-8 [RExp 94/3,464].
7511 *Gnadt, Martina S.* "Abba isn't Daddy": Aspekte einer feministisch-befreiungstheologischen Revision des "Abba Jesu". Von der Wurzel getragen. 1996, ⇒204. 115-131.
7512 *Gosline, S.L.* Female priests: a sacerdotal precedent from ancient Egypt. JFSR 12/1 (1996) 25-39 [NTAb 41,100].
7513 **Gouëffic, Louise** Breaking the patriarchal code: the linguistic basis of sexual bias. Manchester, CT 1996, Knowledge I. & T. (18) 228 pp. 1-879198-17-7.

7514 *Hellwig, Monika Konrad* A revision of christology and soteriology. CTUF 107 (1996) 43-56 [ThIK 18/1,27]. C.

7515 **Hopkins, Julie** Feministische Christologie: wie Frauen heute von Jesus reden können. ^T*Dieckmann, Elisabeth*, Mainz 1996, Grünewald 311 pp. 3-7867-1897-0;

7516 Verso una cristologia femministica: Gesù di Nazareth, le donne europee e la crisi cristologica. GdT 243: Brescia 1996, Queriniana 198 pp. L27.000. 88-399-0743-2.

7517 **Jay, Nancy** Throughout your generations forever: sacrifice, religion and paternity. 1992, ⇒11/2,5314. ^RRStR 22 (1996) 10-20 (*Strenski, Ivan*).

7518 ^E**Jost, Renate; Valtink, Eveline** Ihr, aber, für wen haltet ihr mich?: auf dem Weg zu einer feministisch-befreiungstheologischen Revision von Christologie. Gü 1996 Kaiser 424 pp.

7519 **Kadel, Andrew** Martrology. a bibliography of writings by christian women from the first to the fifteenth centuries. 1995, ⇒11/2,965. ^RJEarlyC 4 (1996) 554-555 (*Shaw, Teresa M.*).

7520 *Kassian, Mary A.* The challenge of feminism. Faith & Mission 14/1 (1996) 14-23.

7521 **Key, Mary Ritchie** Male/female language: with a comprehensive bibliography. Lanham ²1996, Scarecrow xxxv; 324 pp. 0-8108-3083-3.

7522 *Klein, Lillian R.* On "anti-Judaism" in German feminist thought: some reflections by way of a response. A feminist companion. 1996, ⇒170. 355-362.

7523 *Lee, Archie C.C.* Feminist critique of the bible and female principle in culture. AJTh 10/2 (1996) 240-252 [ThIK 18/2,33].

7524 **Martin, Francis** The feminist question: feminist theology in the light of Christian tradition. 1994, ⇒11/2,5327. ^RMoTh 12/1 (1996) 115-117 (*Greene-McCreight, Kathryn*).

7525 *McKay, Heather A.* Gendering the discourse of display in the Hebrew Bible. ^MVAN DIJK-HEMMES F., 1996, ⇒99. 169-199.

7526 *McKay, Heather A.* "Old wine in new wineskins": the refashioning of male Hebrew Bible characters in New Testament texts. A feminist companion. 1996, ⇒170. 62-94.

7527 *Milgrom, Jo* Giving Eve's daughters their due. BiRe 12/1 (1996) 30-36.

7528 *Moltmann-Wendel, Elisabeth* Hagars Schwestern: biblische Gotteserfahrung aus der Perspektive afro-amerikanischer Frauen. EvTh 56/1 (1996) 168-170.

^E**Newsom, Carol A.** Da Genesi a Neemia ⇒1232.

7529 *Patterson, Dorothy* A biblically based women's studies program. Faith & Mission 14/1 (1996) 75-93.

7530 *Perroni, Marinella* Scienze umane e interpretazione della bibbia: una valutazione dell'esegesi femminista: verso un senso critico integrale. StPat 43 (1996) 67-92.

7531 **Primavesi, Anne** Do Apocalipse ao Gênesis: ecologia, feminismo e cristianismo. ^T*Costa, Alberto*, São Paulo 1996, Paulinas [Atualidade Teológica 1/1,85ss—*Corrêa Pinto, Maria Conceição*].

7532 *Rees-Hanley, Amanda* Un feminisme biblique. Telema 22/2 (1996) 17-20.

7533 ^E**Russell Letty, M.** Interpretación feminista de la Bíblia. Bilbao 1995, DDB 184 pp. ^REfMex 14 (1996) 413-414 (*Cepeda Salazar,*

Antonino); RevAg 37 (1996) 1187-1188 (*López, Luisa*); ScrTh 28 (1996) 923-924 (*Jarne, J.*);

7534 *Russell Letty, M.* Feministische Theologie heute: Reflexionen aus der Sicht einer weißen Amerikanerin. PTh 85 (1996) 178-189.

7535 **Rutledge, David** Reading marginally: feminism, deconstruction and the bible. Bibl.Interp. 21: Leiden 1996, Brill x; 234 pp. $76.25. 90-04-10564-6.

7536 ᴱ**Schmidt, Eva Renate; Korenhof, Mieke; Jost, Renate** Riletture bibliche al femminile. 1994, ⇒10,8822. ᴿClar. 36-37 (1996-97) 604-605 (*Alday, Josu M.*); RivBib 44 (1996) 376-377 (*Perroni, Marinella*); Laur. 37 (1996) 343-344 (*González, Manuel*).

7537 **Schneiders, S.M.** Le texte de la rencontre: l'interprétation du Nouveau Testament comme écriture sainte. LeDiv 161: P 1995, Cerf 332 pp. FF150. 2-204-05193-4. ᴿTTh 36 (1996) 410-411 (*Van Diemen, A.*); FV 95 (1996) 123-124 (*Flichy, Odile*).

7538 *Schottroff, Luise* "Gesetzesfreies Heidenchristentum"—und die Frauen?: feministische Analysen und Alternativen. Von der Wurzel getragen. 1996, ⇒204. 227-245.

7539 **Schottroff, Luise,** (*al*), Feministische Exegese. 1995, ⇒11/2,1766. YESW 4 (1996) 186-188 (*Schüngel-Straumann, Helen*); ThLZ 121 (1996) 1125-1128 (*Wischmeyer, Oda*).

7540 **Selvidge, Marla J.** Notorious voices: feminist biblical interpretation, 1500-1920. L 1996, SCM x; 246 pp. $30. 0-334-02642-3.

7541 *Selvidge, Marla J.* Reflections on violence and pornography: misogyny in the Apocalypse and ancient Hebrew prophecy;

7542 *Siegele-Wenschkewitz, Leonore* In the dangerous currents of old prejudices: how predominant thoughts have disastrous effects and what could be done to counter them <1993>. A feminist companion. 1996, ⇒170. 274-285/342-348.

7543 *Smiles, V.* Bible and church: obstacles to the progress of women. SiTo 68/2 (1996) 100-107 [NTAb 40,462].

7544 **Sölle, Dorothee; Schottroff, Luise** Den Himmel erden: eine öko-feministische Annäherung an die Bibel. Mü 1996, dtv 170 pp. DM16.90 [LM 36/7,40].

7545 **Straumann, Helen Schürgel** Denn Gott bin ich, kein Mann: Gottesbilder im Ersten Testament—feministisch betrachtet. Mainz 1996, Grünewald 221 pp. 3-7867-1904-7 [YESW 4,165].

7546 *Timmerman, Guus* Theologie zonder fundamenten?: Francis Schüssler FIORENZA en de opvatting van rationaliteit in het pragmatisme. TTh 36 (1996) 18-38.

7547 **Torjesen, Karen Jo** Cuando las mujeres eran sacerdotes: el liderazgo de las mujeres en la iglesia primitiva y el escándalo de su subordinación con el auge del cristianismo. Córdoba 1996, Almendro 258 pp. [Mayéutica 24,238—Moreno, José Alberto].

7548 *Valtink, Eveline* Feministisch-christliche Identität und Antijudaismus;

7549 *Wacker, Marie-Theres* Den/dem anderen Raum geben: feministisch-christliche Identität ohne Antijudaismus. Von der Wurzel getragen. 1996, ⇒204. 1-26/247-269.

7550 **Williams, Delores S.** Sisters in the wilderness. 1993, ⇒9,9535... 11/2,6367. ᴿEvTh 56/2 (1996) 166-170 (*Moltmann-Wendel, Elisabeth*).

7551 **Wondra, Ellen K.** Humanity has been a holy thing: toward a contemporary feminist christology. 1994, ⇒11/2,5369. RJR 76 (1996) 496-497 (*Sedgwick, Timothy F.*).

H9.0 Eschatologia NT, *spes*, hope

7552 **Erlemann, Kurt** Naherwartung und Parusierverzögerung im NT. TANZ 17: 1995, ⇒11/2,5426. RActBib 33 (1996) 8-14 (*Fàbrega, Valentí*); ThLZ 121 (1996) 45-48 (*Schmithals, Walter*).

7553 *Espinel, José Luis* Análisis del lenguaje simbólico del Nuevo Testamento para la esperanza. Esperanza del hombre. 1996, ⇒173. 481-488.

7554 **Faupel, David W.** The everlasting gospel: the significance of eschatology in the development of Pentecostal thought. JPentec.S 10: Shf 1996, Academic 326 pp. 1-85075-761-5.

7555 **Frosini, Giordano** Aspettando l'aurora: saggio di escatologia cristiana. 1994, ⇒11/2,5249. RCivCatt 147 I (1996) 203-206 (*Vanzan, P.*).

7556 **Gil Ribas, Josep** Escatología cristiana. CStP 50: 1994, ⇒11/2,5435. RRET 56 (1996) 531-532 (*Gesteira, Manuel*).

7557 *Glé, Jean-Marie* Le retour de l'eschatologie. RSR 84 (1996) 219-251.

7558 **González de Cardedal, Olegario** Raíz de la esperanza. 1995, ⇒11/2,5438. REE 71 (1996) 129-130 (*Uríbarri, Gabino*).

7559 **Gounelle, André; Vouga, François** Dopo la morte...?: i cristiani e l'aldilà. PBT 36: T 1995, Claudiana 202 pp. RLat. 62 (1996) 392-394 (*Sanna, Ignazio*).

7560 **Gozzelino, Giorgio** Nell'attesa della beata speranza: saggio di escatologia cristiana. 1993, ⇒10,8870; 11/2,5439. Anime e Corpi 187 (1996) 675-676 (*Casera, Antonio*).

7561 *Hahn, Ferdinand* Das irdische und das himmlische Jerusalem. FHAHN F., 1996, ⇒34. 130-143.

7562 EJeppesen, Knud, (*al*), In the last days: on Jewish and christian apocalyptic. FOTZEN B., 1994, ⇒10,89e. RSEÅ 61 (1996) 136-137 (*Hartman, Lars*).

7563 *Kim, Seyoon* Salvation and suffering according to Jesus. Sum. 207. EvQ 68 (1996) 195-207.

7564 EKlauck, Hans-Josef Weltgericht und Weltvollendung: Zukunftsbilder im NT. FSCHNACKENBURG R., QD 150: 1994, ⇒10,113. REE 71 (1996) 301-302 (*Uríbarri, Gabino*).

7565 **Lona, Horacio E.** Über die Auferstehung des Fleisches: Studien zur frühchristlichen Eschatologie. BZNT 66: 1993, ⇒9,9596. RZKG 107 (1996) 115-118 (*Vinzent, Markus*).

7566 **Martelet, Gustave** L'au-delà retrouvé. P [2]1995 <1974>, Desclée 169 pp. FF98. REeV 106 (1996) 571 (*Jay, Pierre*).

7567 *Marucci, Corrado* L'Inferno e le sue pene. RdT 37 (1996) 549-558.

7568 **Moltmann, Jürgen** Das Kommen Gottes: christliche Eschatologie. 1995, ⇒11/2,5477. REE 71 (1996) 487-489 (*Uríbarri, Gabino*).

7569 **Peterson, Robert A.** Hell on trial: the case for eternal punishment. Phillipsburg 1995, Presbyterean and R. RWThJ 58 (1996) 169-170 (*Hofstetter, N.E. Barry*).

7570 **Pozo, Cándido** La venida del Señor en la gloria: escatología. 1993, ⇒10,8895; 11/2,5496. ᴿDiálogo 3 n.s. (1996) 182-189 (*Lattanzio, Marcelo*).
7571 **Selby, Gary Steven** Apocalyptic and rhetoric in the epistles of the New Testament. Diss. Maryland College Park 1996, ᴰ*Gaines, Robert N.*, 310 pp. DAI-A 57/07, p. 3076; AAC 9640219.
7572 **Steiger, Johann Anselm** Bibel-Sprache und Jüngster Tag bei Johann Peter HEBEL. APTh 25: Gö 1994, Vandenhoeck & R. 380 pp. 3-525-62334-8. ᴿThLZ 121 (1996) 582-583 (*Adam, Gottfried*).
7573 **Susin, Luiz Carlos** Assim na terra como céu: brevilóquio sobre escatologia e criação. Petrópolis 1995, Vozes 196 pp. ᴿREB 56 (1996) 752-754 (*Libânio, J.B.*).
7574 **Tamayo-Acosta, Juan-José** L'escatologia cristiana. Ricerche teologiche: R 1996, Borla 580 pp. 88-263-1125-0.

H9.5 *Theologia totius [VT-] NT*—General [OT-] NT theology

7575 *Barth, Gerhard* Vielfalt und Einheit als Problem neutestamentlicher Theologie. Neutestamentliche Versuche. 1996, ⇒111. 423-440.
7576 **Beilner, Wolfgang; Ernst, Michael** Unter dem Wort Gottes. 1993, ⇒11/2,5643. ᴿBiLi 69 (1996) 187-188 (*Pichler, Josef*).
7577 **Berger, Klaus** Theologiegeschichte des Urchristentums: Theologie des Neuen Testaments. UTB.W: 1995 < 1994 >, ⇒11/2,5644. ᴿBib. 77 (1996) 278-281 (*Légasse, S.*); WiWei 59 (1996) 328-330 (*Kowalski, Beate*); ZKTh 118 (1996) 265-267 (*Oberforcher, Robert*).
7578 **Blank, Josef** Studien zur biblischen Theologie. SBAB 13: 1992, ⇒8,212. ᴿThRv 92 (1996) 31-32 (*Söding, Thomas*).
7579 **Caird, G.B.** NT theology. ᴱ*Hurst, L.D.*, 1994, ⇒10,8923; 11/2,5645. ᴿEvQ 68 (1996) 354-356 (*Marshall, I. Howard*); CBQ 58 (1996) 539-540 (*Bauer, David R.*); HeyJ 37 (1996) 200-202 (*Turner, Geoffrey*).
7580 *Cazelles, Henri* Sur les fondements de la recherche en théologie biblique. Études, 1996 < 1995 >, ⇒120. 13-24.
7581 **Childs, Brevard S.** Biblical theology of the OT and NT. 1992 [Reissued 1996, XPress, London 1-85931-046-X], ⇒8,9322... 11/2,5647. ᴿThR 61 (1996) 65-68 (*Reventlow, Henning Graf*); EvTh 56 (1996) 258-285 (*Dietrich, Walter*);
7582 Die Theologie der einen Bibel: (*a*) 1: Grundstrukturen. 1994, ⇒11/2,5648. ᴿBog.Smo. 66 (1996) 555-557 (*Dugandžić, Ivan*); LuThK 20 (1996) 201-202 (*Günther, Hartmut*); JETh 10 (1996) 200-203 (*Dreytza, Manfred*);
7583 (*b*) 2: Hauptthemen. ᵀ*Oeming, Ch.; Oeming, M.*, FrB 1996, Herder 495 pp. DM98. 3-451-23292-8 [ThLZ 122,647].
7584 *Donahue, John R.* The literary turn and New Testament theology: detour or new direction. JR 76 (1996) 250-275.
7585 **Espeja, Jesús** El evangelio en un cambio de época. Estella 1996, Verbo Divino 315 pp. ᴿCTom 123 (1996) 619-621 (*Lago Albo, Luis*).
7586 *Fuchs, Ottmar* Biblische Theologie und Öffentlichkeit. JBTh 11 (1996) 225-247.

7587 **Garrett, James Leo** Systematic theology: biblical, historical, and evangelical. 1995, ⇒11/2,5650. ᴿRTR 95 (1996) 155-156 *(Jensen, Peter F.)*.

7588 **Gnilka, Joachim** Theologie des NT. 1994, ⇒10,8929; 11/2,5653. ᴿActBib 33 (1996) 34-36 *(Boada, J.)*; ETR 71 (1996) 436-439 *(Siegert, Folker)*.

7589 **Haacker, Klaus** Biblische Theologie als engagierte Exegese. 1993, ⇒11/2,5656. ᴿThLZ 121 (1996) 1055-1059 *(Hübner, Hans)*.

7590 *Hasel, Frank* Algunas reflexiones sobre la relación entre la teología sistemática y la teología bíblica. Theologika 11/1 (1996) 102-123 [ZID 23,321].

7591 *Hasel, G.F.* Proposals for a canonical biblical theology. AUSS 34 (1996) 23-33.

7592 **Ingraffia, Brian D.** Postmodern theory and biblical theology. 1995, ⇒11/2,5663. ᴿThTo 53 (1996) 560, 562 *(Adam, A.K.M.)*.

7593 Einheit und Vielfalt biblischer Theologie. JBTh 1 (1986). ᴿThR 61 (1996) 159-162 *(Reventlow, Henning Graf)*.

7594 Der eine Gott der beiden Testamente. JBTh 2 (1987). ᴿThR 61 (1996) 162-163 *(Reventlow, Henning Graf)*.

7595 *Jeanrond, Werner G.* Criteria for new biblical theologies. ᴿJR 76 (1996) 233-249.

7596 *Kaiser, Walter C.* Biblical theology and the interpretation of messianic texts. AUSS 34 (1996) 195-209.

7597 **Klein, Hans** Leben neu entdecken: Entwurf einer biblischen Theologie. 1991, ⇒7,9036; 10,8938. ᴿThR 61 (1996) 63-65 *(Reventlow, Henning Graf)*.

7598 *Long, Burke O.* Ambitions of dissent: biblical theology in a postmodern future. JR 76 (1996) 276-289.

7599 **Łach, Jan** Błogosławiony, który przychodzi w imię Pańskie [Blessed is he who comes in the name of the Lord (NT)]. Wsz 1996, Akad. Teologii Katolickiej 253 pp. 83-7072-071-4 [NThAR 1997,194]. **P**.

7600 *Martens, Elmer A.* Accessing theological readings of a biblical book. AUSS 34 (1996) 223-237.

7601 *Mauser, U.* An anniversary for biblical theology. ThTo 53 (1996) 74-80.

7602 *Mondin, Battista* Nuovo Testamento e teologia. CiVi 51 (1996) 117-126.

7603 *Morgan, Robert* Can the critical study of scripture provide a doctrinal norm?. JR 76 (1996) 206-232.

7604 *Newsom, Carol A.* BAKHTIN, the bible, and dialogic truth. JR 76 (1996) 290-306.

7605 **Penchansky, David** The politics of biblical theology: a postmodern reading. SABH 10: 1995, ⇒11/2,5679. ᴿJR 76 (1996) 355-357 *(Schweiker, William)*.

7606 *Schwank, Benedikt* Das A und Ω einer "Biblischen Theologie". SNTU.A 21 (1996) 132-145.

7607 *Segalla, Giuseppe* Dieci anni di teologia (biblica) del Nuovo Testamento (1985-1995): tra la ricerca di un'unità teologico-biblica e la deriva verso una pluralità storico-religiosa. Teol(Br) 21 (1996) 67-127.

7608 **Strecker, Georg** Theologie des Neuen Testaments. ᴱHorn, Friedrich Wilhelm, De-Gruyter-Lehrbuch: B 1996, De Gruyter xiv; 741 pp. DM78. 3-11-014896-X [ZThK 119/2,230].

7609 **Stuhlmacher, Peter** Wie treibt man biblische Theologie?. BThSt 24: 1995, ⇒11/2,5688. ᴿJETh 10 (1996) 259-263 (*Gebauer, Roland*).

7610 **Thüsing, Wilhelm** Studien zur NT Theologie. WUNT 2/82: 1995, ⇒11/2,338. ᴿThRv 92 (1996) 500-502 (*Hübner, Hans*); ThLZ 121 (1996) 839-840 (*Schoenborn, Ulrich*).

7611 *Vogels, Walter* Cette impossible théologie biblique?: bilan et perspectives. ScEs 48 (1996) 251-271.

7612 *Vos, J.S.* De theologie van het Nieuwe Testament: een overzicht over recent verschenen werken (1). GThT 96 (1996) 103-116.

7613 *Wagner, Siegfried* 'Biblische Theologien' und 'Biblische Theologie'. Ausgewählte Aufsätze. BZAW 240: 1996 <1978>, ⇒156. 109-130.

7614 **Warzecha, Julian** Idżcie i wy: z zagadnień biblijnej teologii apostolstwa, "Apostolicum" [Andate anche voi: alcuni argomenti della teologia biblica dell'apostolato]. Ząbki 1996, 209 pp. [CoTh 67,228ss—Weron, Eugeniusz]. **P.**

XIV. Philologia biblica

Ј1.1 **Hebraica** *grammatica*

7615 *Aslanoff, Cyril* La réflexion linguistique hébraïque dans l'horizon intellectuel de l'Occident médiéval: essai de comparaison des traités de grammaire hébraïque et provençale dans la perspective de l'histoire des doctrines grammaticales. REJ 155 (1996) 5-32.

7616 **Auvray, Paul** Bibelhebräisch zum Selbststudium: Kurzgrammatik, erläuterte Texte, Vocabular. ᵀ*Knauer, Peter*, UTB.WG: Pd 1996, Schöningh. DM39.80. 3-506-98505-1.

7617 **Bartelmus, Rüdiger** Einführung in das biblische Hebräisch. 1994, ⇒10,8957*. ᴿThLZ 121 (1996) 431-433 (*Willi-Plein, Ina*).

7618 **Beisvåg, Ola** Hebraisk Førstehjelp til det Gamle Testamente i kirkens gudstjeneste. Oslo 1996, Hebraica 264 pp. [NTT 97,252—Brekke, Vidar].

7619 *Ben Menachem, David Sefer Ha-Eshel* by R. Yiẓhak BEN YEHUDAH. Sum. II. Leš. 59/4 (1996) 299-312. **H.**

7620 *Berg, Werner* Siebenerreihen von Verben und Substantiven. BN 84 (1996) 11-15 [Gn 22,9s; Ex 1,1-7; 2,23-25; 12,31-32; 20,9-10; Dt 5,21].

7621 ᴱ**Bergen, Robert D.** Biblical Hebrew and discourse linguistics. 1994, ⇒10,8959; 11/2,5698. ᴿHebStud 37 (1996) 136-138 (*Kedar-Kopfstein, Benjamin*); CBQ 58 (1996) 370-372 (*Biddle, Mark E.*).

7622 **Blau, Joshua** A grammar of Biblical Hebrew. PLO 12: Wsb ²1993, Harrassowitz xii; 220 pp. DM78. 3-447-03362-2. ᴿArOr 64 (1996) 142-143 (*Oliverius, Jaroslav*);

7623 עיונים בבלשנות עברית [Studies in Hebrew linguistics]. J 1996, Magnes 386 pp. [Leš. 61,217ss—Birnbaum, Gabriel]. **H.**

7624 ᴱ**Bodine, Walter** Linguistics and Biblical Hebrew. 1992, ⇒8,343 ... 11/2,5701. ᴿJNES 55 (1996) 208-209 (*Goerwitz, Richard L.*).

7625 **Bolozky, Shmuel** 501 Hebrew verbs: fully conjugated in all the tenses in a new easy-to-follow format alphabetically arranged by root. Happauge, NY 1996 Barron xvii; 910 pp. 0-8120-9468-9 [NThAR 1997,66].

7626 *DeCaen, Vincent* EWALD and DRIVER on Biblical Hebrew "aspect": anteriority and the orientalist framework. ZAH 9 (1996) 129-151.

7627 *Demichelis, Maria Sita* La racine hébraïque d'après le grammairien Abū 'l-Walīd Marwân IBN ĠANAH (XIe siècle). Henoch 18 (1996) 177-195.

7628 **Eskhult, Mats** Studies in verbal aspect. 1990, ⇒6,9158... 8,9352. RAcOr 55 (1994) 205-211 (*Toll, Chr.*).

7629 **Fassberg, Steven E.** Studies in biblical syntax. 1994, ⇒10,8965. RCBQ 58 (1996) 513-514 (*Greenspahn, Frederick E.*); JSSt 41 (1996) 331-333 (*Joosten, Jan*). **H**.

7630 *Fernández Tejero, Emilia* Masora or grammar revisited. Proceedings... Congress of Masoretic Studies. 1996, ⇒270. 11-23.

7631 *Fredericks, Daniel C.* A North Israelite dialect in the Hebrew Bible?: questions of methodology. Sum. 7. HebStud 37 (1996) 7-20.

7632 **Gai, Amikam** The twofold nature of the deverbal nouns in ancient Semitic languages. ZDMG 146 (1996) 278-316.

7633 **Garbini, Giovanni; Durand, Olivier** Introduzione alle lingue semitiche. 1994, ⇒10,8967. RJAOS 116 (1996) 279-281 (*Rosenthal, Franz*); Anton. 71 (1996) 115-116 (*Nobile, Marco*); PaVi 41/1 (1996) 55 (*Balzaretti, Claudio*).

7634 **García-Jalón de la Lama, Santiago** Inventario de las gramáticas hebreas del siglo XVI de la Biblioteca General de la Universidad de Salamanca. BSal.E 183: S 1996, Pub. Univ. Pontificia 190 pp. 84-7299-373-6 [EstB 55,568].

7635 *García-Jalón, Santiago* La gramática hebrea en la Península Ibérica en el siglo XVI. EstB 54 (1996) 349-359.

7636 *Gianto, Agustinus* Variations in Biblical Hebrew. Bib. 77 (1996) 493-508.

7637 *Goerwitz, Richard L.* Is Tiberian *səgôl* a phoneme?. Proceedings... Congress of Masoretic Studies. 1996, ⇒270. 155-170.

7638 EGoldman, Shalom Hebrew and the Bible in America: the first two centuries. 1993, ⇒9,276. RHebStud 37 (1996) 214-217 (*Noll, Mark A.*).

7639 **Groß, Walter** Die Satzteilfolge im Verbalsatz alttestamentlicher Prosa: untersucht an den Büchern Dtn, Ri und 2Kön. Collab. *Disse, Andreas; Michel, Andreas*, FAT 17: Tü 1996, Mohr xvi; 465 pp. 3-16-146634-9.

7640 **Hadas-Lebel, Mireille** Storia della lingua ebraica. 1994, ⇒10,8969. RSdT 8/1 (1996) 69-70 (*Guerra, Alberto*); Henoch 18 (1996) 211-213 (*Capelli, Piero*).

7641 *Hendel, Ronald S.* In the margins of the Hebrew verbal system: situation, tense, aspect, mood. ZAH 9 (1996) 152-181.

7642 *Herranz Pascual, Carmen* Las últimas teorías sintácticas sobre el verbo hebreo bíblico, II: los textos [Recent theories about the syntax of the Biblical Hebrew verb, II: texts]. Sum. res. 3. MEAH.H 45 (1996) 3-26.

7643 **Hildebrandt, Ted** Hebrew tutor for Windows. 1995 Parsons Technology. $49. RRExp 93 (1996) 429-430 (*Nogalski, James D.*).

7644 *Kedar-Kopfstein, Benjamin; Lichtenberger, Hermann; Müller, Hans-Peter* Lexikalisches und grammatisches Material. ZAH 9 (1996) 62-88; 204-217.

7645 **Kelley, Page H.** Biblical Hebrew: an introductory grammar. 1992, ⇒8,9363... 10,8976. ᴿJAOS 116 (1996) 281 (*Kaye, Alan S.*).

7646 *Khan, Geoffrey* Remarks on vowels represented by šewa and hatep signs in the Tiberian vocalization system. JSSt 41 (1996) 65-74;

7647 The Tiberian pronunciation tradition of Biblical Hebrew. ZAH 9 (1996) 1-23.

7648 **Lancellotti, Angelo** Grammatica dell'ebraico biblico. ASBF 24: J 1996, Franciscan Printing Press viii; 200 pp.

7649 **Lettinga, Jan P.** Grammatica van het Bijbels Hebreeuws. ᴱ*Muraoka, Takamitsu*; Collab. *Van Peursen, W.Th.*, Lei ⁹1996, Brill xiii, 218 pp. 90-04-10652-9;

7650 Hulpboek bij de grammatica van het bijbels Hebreeuws: oefeningen, stukken uit het Oude Testament en woordenlijsten. ᴱ*Muraoka, Takamitsu*; Collab. *Van Peursen, W.Th.*, Lei ⁸1996, Brill ix; 117 pp. 90-04-10653-7.

7651 **Martin, James D.** DAVIDSON's Introductory Hebrew Grammar. ²⁷1993, ⇒9,9689; 11/2,5732. ᴿSJTh 49 (1996) 375-376 (*Emmerson, Grace I.*).

7652 *McGurk, Patrick; Szerwiniack, Olivier* Des recueils d'interprétations de noms hébreux (suite). ⇒10,8994*. Scr. 50 (1996) 117-122.

7653 *Merwe, C.H.J. van der* A biblical Hebrew reference grammar for theological students: some theoretical considerations. JNSL 22/1 (1996) 125-141;

7654 From paradigms to texts: new horizons and new tools for interpreting the Old Testament. JNSL 22/2 (1996) 167-179.

7655 **Miller, Cynthia Lynn** The representation of speech in Biblical Hebrew narrative: a linguistic analysis. HSM 55: Atlanta 1996, Scholars xx; 466 pp. $45. 0-7885-0248-4 [NThAR 1997,99].

7656 **Morag, Shelomo** Studies on Biblical Hebrew. J 1995, Magnes 342 pp. 965-223-884-8. ᴿMEAH.H 45 (1996) 241-242 (*Sáenz-Badillos, A.*). **H.**

7657 ᴱ**Muraoka, Takamitsu** Studies in ancient Hebrew semantics. Abr-n.S 4: 1995, ⇒11/2,516. ᴿSJOT 10 (1996) 309-310 (*Ehrensvärd, Martin G.*); Lěš. 59 (1996) 253-256 **[H.]** (*Blau, Joshua*).

7658 *Naveh, Joseph* On formal and informal spelling of unpronounced gutturals. ICS 15 (1996) 263-267.

7659 *Niccacci, Alviero* Finite verb in the second position of the sentence: coherence of the Hebrew verbal system. ZAW 108 (1996) 434-440.

7660 **Putnam, Frederic Clarke** A cumulative index to the grammar and syntax of Biblical Hebrew. WL 1996, Eisenbrauns xii; 338 pp. $34.50/$24.50. 1-57506-001-9/7-8 [ET 108,319].

Regt, L.J. de Aspects of the syntax and rhetoric of participant reference in Exodus ⇒1788.

7661 *Regt, Leendert J. de* Domains of Biblical Hebrew discourse as a translation problem. JTrTL 8 (1996) 50-72 [ZID 23,168].

7662 *Riepl, Christian* Literatur—Sprache—Computer. ZAH 9 (1996) 24-41.

7663 **Sáens-Badillos, Angel** A history of the Hebrew language. 1993, ⇒10,8990; 11/2,5741. ᴿHebStud 37 (1996) 131-133 (*Hatav, Galia*).

7664 *Shapiro, Ophira* On methods of teaching Biblical Hebrew to non-native speakers. ^{M}VAN DIJK-HEMMES F., 1996, ⇒99. 217-229.

7665 ^{E}**Talstra, Eep** Narrative and comment: contributions to discourse grammar and Biblical Hebrew. ^{F}SCHNEIDER W., 1995, ⇒11/1,26. ^{R}ThLZ 121 (1996) 343-345 *(Beyse, Karl-Martin)*.

7666 *Tropper, Josef* Aramäisches *wyqtl* und hebräisches *wayyiqtol*. UF 28 (1996) 633-645.

7667 *Ullendorff, Edward* The demise of the Hebraist (principally in Great Britain). ICS 15 (1996) 289-292.

7668 *Van Dyke Parunak, H.* The discourse implications of resumption in Hebrew: אשר clauses: a preliminary assessment from Genesis. Literary structure. 1996, ⇒200. 101-116.

7669 **Volgger, David** Notizen zur Phonologie des Bibelhebräischen. ATSAT 36: 1992, ⇒9,9707... 11/2,5745. ^{R}ArOr 64 (1996) 141-142 *(Segert, Stanislav)*.

7670 **Weinberg, Werner** Essays on Hebrew. ^{E}*Citrin, Paul*, SFSHJ 46: 1993, ⇒11/2,5746. ^{R}JAOS 116 (1996) 281-282 *(Kaye, Alan S.)*.

7671 *Weitzman, Steven* The shifting syntax of numerals in Biblical Hebrew. JNES 55 (1996) 177-185.

7672 *Westermann, Claus* Bedeutung und Funktion des Imperativs in den Geschichtsbüchern des Alten Testaments. Das mündliche Wort. 1996, ⇒157. 98-112.

7673 **Wilson, Douglas Keyes** An investigation into the linguistic evidence and classification of dialect variation in Biblical Hebrew. Diss. Mid-America Bapt. Theol. Sem. 1996, 186 pp. [EThL 74,185*].

7674 *Zewi, Tamar* Subordinate nominal sentences involving prolepsis in Biblical Hebrew. JSSt 41 (1996) 1-20.

7675 **Zuber, Beat** Das Tempussystem des biblischen Hebräisch. 1986, ⇒1,8822... 4,a209. ^{R}VT 46 (1996) 143-144 *(Khan, G.A.)*.

J1.2 Lexica et inscriptiones hebraicae; later Hebrew

7676 **Ahituv, Shmuel** Handbook of ancient Hebrew inscriptions. 1992, ⇒9,9709. ^{R}Tarbiz 65 (1996) 529-533 [H. Sum. XI] *(Gai, Amikam)*.

7677 **Babut, Jean-Marc** Les expressions idiomatiques de l'hébreu biblique. CRB 33: 1995, ⇒11/2,5751. ^{R}RHPhR 76 (1996) 226-227 *(Joosten, J.)*.

7678 *Ben-Hayyim, Ze'ev* האקדמיה ללשון העברית – תפקידה והמילון ההיסטורי שלה [The Academy of the Hebrew language—its role and the Historical Dictionary project]. Leš. 59 (1996) 185-202. **H.**

7679 *Chiesa, Bruno* Nova et vetera: testi e studi di letteratura ebraica antica e medievale. Henoch 18 (1996) 365-382.

7680 ^{E}**Clines, David J.A.** The dictionary of classical Hebrew, *(a)*, 1: א. 1993, ⇒9,9718... 11/2,5755. ^{R}AJSR 21 (1996) 111-118 *(Rendsburg, Gary A.)*; JAOS 116 (1996) 283-285 *(Fitzmyer, Joseph A.)*; OLZ 91 (1996) 174-182 *(Lehmann, Reinhard G.)*; AUSS 34 (1996) 111-112 *(Gane, Roy E.)*;

7681 *(b)*, 2: ב-ו. Shf 1995, Academic 660 pp. £75. 1-85075-544-2. ^{R}EThL 72 (1996) 206-207 *(Lust, J.)*;

7682 *(c)*, 3: ז-ט. Shf 1996, Academic 424 pp. £75. 1-85075-634-1.

7683 **Davies, G.I.** Ancient Hebrew inscriptions: corpus and concordance. 1991, ⇒7,9097... 11/2,5757. ᴿJNES 55 (1996) 209-210 (*Pardee, Dennis*).

7684 **Deutsch, R.; Heltzer, M.** Forty new ancient West Semitic inscriptions. 1994, ⇒10,9008. ᴿPEQ 128 (1996) 172-173 (*Mitchell, T.C.*);

7685 New epigraphic evidence from the biblical period. 1995, ⇒11/2,5758b. OLoP 27 (1996) 243-245 (*Lipiński, E.*).

7686 *Díez Merino, Luis* Onomástica y toponimia: targum, midrás y Antiguo Testamento. ᶠMcNamara M., JSOT.S 230: 1996, ⇒58. 30-51.

7687 ᴱ**Doniach, N.S.; Kahane, A.** The Oxford English-Hebrew dictionary. Oxf 1996, OUP xxiii; 1091 pp. In collab. with The Oxford Centre for Hebrew and Jewish Studies. £40. 0-19-864322-5.

7688 *Dozio, Paolo* Alcune note sulla lingua ebraica in Ruggero Bacone. SBFLA 46 (1996) 223-244.

7689 *Ego, Beate; Kamlah, Jens, (al)*, Dokumentation neuer Texte. ZAH 9 (1996) 89-108, 218-232.

7690 *Florentin, Moshe* בידולים עיונים בתורת הצורות של עברית השומרונים סמנטיים באמצעים מורפולוגיים [Studies in the morphology of Samaritan Hebrew]. Leš. 59 (1996) 217-241. **H.**

7691 **Fohrer, Georg** Dizionario di ebraico e aramaico dell'Antico Testamento. CasM 1996, Piemme 362 pp. L60.000 [PaVi 42/3,58].

7692 *Hamilton, Gordon J.* A new Hebrew-Aramaic incantation text from Galilee: 'rebuking the sea'. JSSt 41 (1996) 215-249.

7693 *Hendel, Ronald S.* The date of the Siloam inscription: a rejoinder to Rogerson and Davies. BA 59 (1996) 233-237;

7694 Sibilants and šibbolet (Judges 12:6). BASOR 301 (1996) 69-75.

7695 **Hüttenmeister, Frowald-Gil** אוצר ראשי תיבות וקיצורים במצבות AHG: Abkürzungsverzeichnis hebräischer Grabinschriften. Fra 1996, Gesellschaft zur Förderung Judaistischer Studien in Fra iv; 349 pp. 3-922056-08-3 [JSJ 28,366].

7696 **Kaddari, Menaḥem Zevi** Post-Biblical Hebrew syntax and semantics. Ramat-Gan 1991-1995, Bar-Ilan Univ. Press 2 vols. ᴿLeš. 59 (1996) 151-174 [H. Sum. iii] (*Azar, Moshe*). **H.**

7697 (**Koehler-Baumgartner**) *Stamm, Johann J.; Hartmann, Benedikt* HALAT: Supplementband. Lei ³1996, Brill lxxvii; 131 pp. 90-04-10714-2.

7698 (**Koehler-Baumgartner,** *al.*) The Hebrew and Aramaic lexicon of the OT, 1. ᵀ*Richardson, Mervyn E.J., al.,* 1994, ⇒10,9012; 11/2,5766. ᴿJSSt 41 (1996) 137-142 (*Clines, David J.A.*); CBQ 58 (1996) 106-108 (*Segert, Stanislav*);

7699 The Hebrew and Aramaic lexicon of the OT, 2-3: ט–ע; פ–שׁ. ᵀ*Richardson, Mervyn E.J., al.,* Lei 1995-1996, Brill viii; vi pp. ƒ258.50/$162.50; ƒ270/$168.75. 90-04-09697-3/8-1. 367-906; 907-1364.

7700 *Lübbe, John* An Old Testament dictionary of semantic domains. ZAH 9 (1996) 52-57.

7701 *Mathys, Felix* Erwägungen zu einer neu edierten Inschrift, angeblich aus Hirbet el-Kom. BN 84 (1996) 51-53.

7702 **Mellon, Brad F.** Distinguishing Greek and Hebrew words in the semantic field 'servant': with special reference to 'Servant of the Lord' constructions. Diss. Westminster 1996, ᴰ*Silva, M.,* 253 pp. [EThL 74,184*].

7703 *Misgav, Hagay* An alphabetical sequence on an ossuary. Sum. 110. ͨAtiqot 29 (1996) 47*-49*. **H.**

7704 *Morag, Shelomo* Some notes (following Elisha QIM RON's paper, "The biblical lexicon in the light of the Dead Sea scrolls"). DSD 3 (1996) 152-156.

7705 **Murtonen, A.** Hebrew in its West Semitic setting. 1990, ⇒2,7306... 10,9014. RVT 46 (1996) 136-138 (*Khan, G.A.*).

7706 *Naveh, Joseph* Gleanings of some pottery inscriptions. IEJ 46 (1996) 44-51.

7707 *Nebe, Wilhelm* Zu Lachisch Ostracon, 2. ZAH 9 (1996) 48.

7708 **Noy, David** Jewish inscriptions of western Europe, 2: the city of Rome. C 1995, CUP. 6 maps; 20 pl. 592 pp. £85. 0-521-44202-8. RJThS 47 (1996) 256-259 (*Van der Horst, P.W.*).

7709 **Pierdominici, Nazario** Esame di alcuni aspetti pragmalinguistici dell'ebraico israeliano. Diss. F 1994/95, DZatelli, Ida [RivBib 46/3].

7710 **Renz, Johannes** Die althebräischen Inschriften 1-3. 1995, ⇒11/2,5774. RSEL 13 (1996) 128-130 (*Merlo, Paolo*); ATG 59 (1996) 408-409 (*Torres, A.*).

7711 **Reymond, Philippe** Dictionnaire d'hébreu et d'araméen bibliques. 1991, ⇒7,9120... 11/2,5775. RMEAH 43/2 (1994) 181-182 (*Torres, Antonio*).

7712 **Richler, B.** Guide to Hebrew manuscript collections. 1994, ⇒11/2,898. Henoch 18 (1996) 219-222 (*Perani, Mauro*).

7713 **Ridzewski, Beate** Neuhebräische Grammatik auf Grund der ältesten Handschriften und Inschriften. 1992, ⇒8,9417; 9,9736. RJAOS 116 (1996) 282-283 (*Malone, Joseph L.*).

7714 *Rocco, Benedetto* La sinagoga quattrocentesca di Agira: dedica in ebraico;

7715 Tre candelabri musulmani con iscrizioni ebraiche nella Galleria Regionale di Palazzo Abatellis in Palermo. Ho Theológos 14 (1996) 129-138/253-268.

7716 **Sciumbata, Maria Patrizia** Il campo lessicale dei sostantivi della 'conoscenza' in ebraico antico. Diss. F 1996/97, DZatelli, Ida [RivBib 46,3].

7717 *Talmon, Shemaryahu* Hebrew written fragments from Masada. DSD 3 (1996) 168-177.

7718 **Targarona Borrás, Judit** Diccionario hebreo-español. Barc 1995, Riopiedras 1433 pp. 84-7213-128-9. RMEAH.H 44 (1995) (1996) 180-181 (*Salvatierra Ossorio, Aurora*).

7719 *Tawil, Hayim* Hebrew סלף, Mishnaic Hebrew צלף Akkadian ṣḫlā̄-pu/ṣullupu: a lexicographical note II. Beit Mikra 146 (1996) 292-276.

7720 ETedghi, J. Les interférences de l'hébreu dans les langues juives. P 1995, INALCO 136 pp. Actes de la journée d'études, 1994, École des Hautes Etudes du Judaïsme. RHenoch 18 (1996) 393-396 (*Demichelis, Maria Sita*).

7721 *Tov, Emanuel* Scribal practices reflected in the Paleo-Hebrew texts from the Judean Desert. ICS 15 (1996) 268-273.

7722 EVian, Paolo La raccolta e la Miscellanea Visconti degli autografi Ferrajoli: introduzione, inventario e indice. StT 377: Cataloghi somari e inventari dei fondi manoscritti 5: Città del Vaticano 1996, Biblioteca Apostolica Vaticana cxxix; 781 pp. 88-210-0678-6.

7723 *Yardeni, Ada; Greenfield, Jonas C.* 13 צאלים נחל—כתובה של שובר [A receipt for a ketubba]. [F]Stern M., 1996, ⇒87. Sum. 147*. 197-208. H.

7724 *Zirlin, Yaël* Celui qui se cache derrière l'image: colophons des enlumineurs dans les manuscrits hébraïques. Sum. rés. 53. [R]REJ 155 (1996) 33-53.

j1.3 Voces *ordine alphabetico consonantium* hebraicarum

Aramaic

אַבָּא *Gnadt, M.* "Abba isn't Daddy' ⇒7511.

מֵתָא ;קרתא *Goldenberg, D.* Retroversion to Jesus' ipsissima verba ⇒3991.

Hebrew

7725 אַב *Willis, John T.* 'ab as an official term. SJOT 10 (1996) 115-136 [Is 22,21-22].

7726 אֲדָמָה *Aspesi, Francesco* Precedenti divini di 'adāmâ. SEL 13 (1996) 33-40.

אוֹת ;בְּרִית *Van Den Eynde, S.* Keeping God's Sabbath: 'wt and brjt ⇒2061.

7727 בטח *Pérez Fernández, Miguel* El verbo בטח en la literatura rabínica tannaítica: léxico y teología. Esperanza del hombre. 1996, ⇒173. 461-468.

7728 בָּכָא **Anderson, Gary A.** A time to mourn, a time to dance: the expression of grief and joy in Israelite religion. 1991, ⇒7,a725; 11/2,5805. [R]JNES 55 (1996) 213-215 (*Handy, Lowell K.*).

7729 בַּקְבֻּק *Rubiato Díaz, M.ª Teresa* Recipientes bíblicos VI: *Baqbuq*. Sum. res. 160. Sef. 56 (1996) 149-160 [1 Kgs 14,3; Jer 19,1.10].

7730 בְּרִית *Avemarie, Friedrich* Bund als Gabe und Recht: semantische Überlegungen zu berît in der rabbinischen Literatur. Bund und Tora. WUNT 92: 1996, ⇒1645. 163-216.

7731 גּוִיָּה *Toloni, Giancarlo* Un caso atipico di evoluzione semantica: il lessema ebraico gewiyyâ. StPat 43/3 (1996) 75-93.

7732 גלל *Jiménez Sánchez, Milagros* Un estudio comparativo de la raíz gll en los principales gramáticos medievales con Sĕ'adyah ibn Danan. Sum. res. 97. MEAH 43/2 (1994) 97-126.

7733 דָּבָר *Zuurmond, Rochus* The power of the word. [F]Zuurmond R., DBAT.B: 1996, ⇒109. 11-27 [OTA 19,499].

7734 הֶבֶל *Ehlich, Konrad* הבל—Metaphern der Nichtigkeit. [F]Michel D., BZAW 241: 1996, 49-64.

7735 הִנֵּה (וְהִנֵּה) *Zewi, Tamar* The particles הִנֵּה and וְהִנֵּה in Biblical Hebrew. Sum. 21. HebStud 37 (1996) 21-37.

7736 זוּ *Chiera, Giovanna* Il pronome zū in ebraico. [F]Moscati S., III, 1996, ⇒67. 1109-1115.

7737 חֵן *Grossfeld, Bernard* מצא חן בעיני—'Finding favor in someone's eyes: the treatment of this Biblical Hebrew idiom in the ancient Aramaic versions. [F]McNamara M., JSOT.S 230: 1996, ⇒58. 52-66.

חִנָּם *Klopfenstein, Martin A.* ḥnm (ḥinnam) im Hiobbuch ⇒2995.

7738 חֶסֶד Clark, Gordon R. The word *hesed* in the Hebrew bible. JSÖT.S 157: 1993, ⇒9,9766; 11/2,5821. ᴿBS 153 (1996) 695-696 (*Chisholm, Robert B.*); JSSt 41 (1996) 333-335 (*Davies, Eryl W.*).

7739 חַרְטֻמִּים Goedicke, Hans *ḥarṭummîm*. Or. 65 (1996) 24-30 [Gn 41,8.24].

7740 חַמָּנִים Cazelles, Henri Hammanîm-Hamon/humun et l'expansion phénicienne. Études. 1996 <1994>, ⇒120. 219-225.

7741 יָדִיד Toloni, Giancarlo L'interpretazione greca de *yādîd* nei profeti. Sum. 39. BeO 38 (1996) 3-40.

7742 יְדִידְיָה Toloni, Giancarlo La traduzione di *yᵉdîdᵉyāh* (2 Sam 12,25) in alcune versioni antiche. Aevum 70 (1996) 21-35.

7743 ידע Wagner, Siegfried ידע in den Lobliedern von Qumran. Ausgewählte Aufsätze. BZAW 240: 1996 <1968>, ⇒156. 1-24.

7744 כ Jenni, Ernst Die Präposition Kaph. 1994, ⇒10,9043*; 11/2,5831. ᴿETR 71 (1996) 592-594 (*Bauks, Michaela*); BiOr 53 (1996) 761-763 (*Muraoka, T.*).

7745 כתב Schaack, Thomas Die Ungeduld des Papiers: Studien zum alttestamentlichen Verständnis des Schreibens anhand des Verbums *ktb* im Kontext administrativer Vorgänge. Diss. Kiel 1996-97, ᴰ*Donner, H.*. [= BZAW 262].

7746 לב Hsu, Grace 'Heart' in the OT and the Analects of CONFUCIUS. CTUF 108 (1996) 167-177 [ThIK 18/1,28]. C.

7747 לקח Lange, Armin Kognitives *lqḥ* in Sap A, im Tenak und Sir. ZAH 9 (1996) 190-195.

7748 מֵם Emerton, John A. Are there examples of enclitic *mem* in the Hebrew Bible?. ᶠHARAN M., 1996, ⇒35. 321-338.

7749 נָא Wilt, Timothy A sociolinguistic analysis of *naʾ*. VT 46 (1996) 237-255.

7750 נגד Naeh, Shlomo "עזר כנגדו", "כנגד המשחיתים" משמעויות נשכחות ופתגם אבוד [Forgotten meanings and a lost proverb]. Sum. i. Leš. 59/1 (1996) 99-117.

7751 נכר Sciumbata, Maria Patrizia I lessemi a radicale *nkr* del campo lessicale dei verbi della conoscenza nella bibbia ebraica. Sum. 29. RivBib 44 (1996) 3-29.

7752 נקם Peels, Hendrik G.L. The vengeance of God: the meaning of the root NQM. OTS 31: 1995, ⇒11/2,5845. ᴿThLZ 121 (1996) 255-256 (*Körner, Juta*); EvQ 68 (1996) 281-282 (*Jenson, Philip*).

7753 סוד Neef, Heinz-Dieter Gottes himmlischer Thronrat... *sôd JHWH* im AT. AzTh 79: 1994, ⇒10,9046. ᴿThLZ 121 (1996) 148-149 (*Seidel, Bodo*).

7754 סוח; סנה Jiménez Bedman, Francisco Los términos סוח y סנה en el Rollo de Cobre (3Q15) [The lexical items סוח and סנה in the Copper Scroll (3Q15)]. Sum. res. 27. MEAH.H 45 (1996) 27-35.

7755 סוף; עתיד Girón Blanc, Luis F. Los usos de עתיד y de סוף en hebreo rabínico tardío (según Cantar de los Cantares Rabbá). MEAH 41/2 (1992) 35-51.

7756 פָּרִץ Harland, P.J. Robber or violent man?: a note on the word *pārîs*. VT 46 (1996) 530-534.

7757 צֶדֶק Krašovec, Jože La justice (ṢDQ) de Dieu dans la bible hébraïque. OBO 76: 1988, ⇒4,a307... 7,9181. ThR 61 (1996) 157-159 (*Reventlow, Henning Graf*).

7758 צֶדֶק Rosenberg, Roy A. Ṣedeq as divine hypostasis in Qumran texts and its link to the emergence of christianity. ᴹBURGMANN H., 1996 <1993>, ⇒12. 109-127.

צוּר **Kowalski, V.** Rock of ages ⇒1832.
7759 צלמות *Cohen, Chaim* The meaning of צלמות 'darkness': a study in philological method. ᶠHARAN M., 1996, ⇒35. 287-309.
7760 קרב **Schweizer, Harald** Sprachkritik als Ideologiekritik: zur Grammatikrevision am Beispiel von *QRB*. 1991, ⇒7,9188; 11/2,5865. ᴿEThL 72 (1996) 214-216 (*Vervenne, M.*).

רוּח *Schüngel-Straumann, Helen Ruah* und Gender-Frage am Beispiel der Visionen beim Propheten Ezechiel ⇒3552.
7761 רחק *Cross, Frank Moore* A papyrus recording a divine legal decision and the root *rhq* in biblical and Near Eastern legal usage. ᶠHARAN M., 1996, ⇒35. 311-320.
7762 שבּת *Rechenmacher, Hans* *šabbat[t]*—Nominalform und Etymologie. ZAH 9 (1996) 199-203.
7763 –שׁה *Fassberg, Steven E.* The orthography of the relative pronoun –שׁin the Second Temple and mishnaic periods. ICS 15 (1996) 240-250.

שלוֹם *Klopfenstein, M.* Friede (Schalom) im AT ⇒452.
7764 שקק *Greenberg, Moshe* Noisy and yearning: the semantics of שׁקק. ᶠHARAN M., 1996, ⇒35. 339-344.
7765 תמם *Bell, Robert D.* The Old Testament integrity principle. BVp 30 (1996) 15-18 [OTA 19,484].
7766 תמם *Egger-Wenzel, Renate* Der Gebrauch von *tmm* bei Ijob und Ben Sira. Freundschaft. BZAW 244: 1996, ⇒3224. 203-238.

Phoenician

7767 **Hggbʿl** *Peri, C.* Sul significato del nome fenicio *Hggbʿl*. RSFen 24 (1996) 99-102.

Ugaritic

7768 **d(h)rt; hdrt** *Tropper, Josef* Ugaritic dreams: notes on Ugaritic *d(h)rt* and *hdrt*. ᶠGIBSON J., 1996, ⇒31. 305-313.
7769 **qtn** *Vita, Juan-Pablo* La herramienta *katinnu* en el texto de Ugarit RS 19.23. Sum. res. 443. Sef. 56 (1996) 439-443.
7770 **šrd; trt; šrt** *Dietrich, Manfried; Loretz, Oswald* Ugaritisch *šrd* "dienen", *trt* und *šrt* "Sängerin". UF 28 (1996) 159-164.

ɪ1.5 *Phoenicia, ugaritica*—Northwest Semitic [ᴛ5.4]

7771 **Aartun, Kjell** Bäume... Studien zur ugaritischen Lexikographie, I. 1991, ⇒7,9202; 9,9819. JAOS 116 (1996) 134-135 (*Segert, Stanislav*); JNES 55 (1996) 205-208 (*Clemens, D.M.*).
7772 *Amadasi Guzzo, Maria Giulia* Remarques sur la terminaison du substantif féminin pluriel devant les pronoms suffixes en phénicien. JSSt 41 (1996) 203-213.
7773 *Avner, R.; Eshel, E.* A juglet with a Phoenician inscription from a recent excavation in Jaffa, Israel. TEuph 12 (1996) 59-63.
7774 **Beckman, Gary** Texts from the vicinity of Emar in the collection of Jonathan ROSEN. History of the Ancient Near East, Monographs 2: Padova 1996, Sargon 143 pp.; 177 pp. [pl.].
7775 *Cross, Frank Moore* A Philistine ostracon from Ashkelon. BArR 22/1 (1996) 64-65.

7776 *Cunchillos, Jesús-Luis; Galán, José Manuel* Filología e informática: epigrafía ugarítica. Sum. res. 170. Sef. 56 (1996) 161-170.

7777 *Dalix, Anne-Sophie* Exemples de bilinguisme à Ougarit: Iloumilkou: la double identité d'un scribe. Mosaïque de langues. 1996, ⇒284. 81-90.

7778 **Dietrich, Manfried; Loretz, Oswald** Analytic Ugaritic bibliography 1972-1988. AOAT 20/6: Neuk 1996, Neuk'er x; 1077 pp. [OLZ 92,455];

7779 Word-List of *The cuneiform alphabetic texts from Ugarit*. Collab. *Kisker, Hans-Werner*, Abhandlungen zur Literatur Alt-Syrien-Palästinas (ALASP) 12: Müns 1996, UGARIT ix; 232 pp. DM80. 3-927120-40-5.

7780 **Dietrich, Manfried; Loretz, Oswald; Sanmartín, Joaquín** The cuneiform alphabetic texts from Ugarit. ²1995, ⇒11/2,5891. RThLZ 121 (1996) 1128-1129 (*Hermann, Wolfram*); ArOr 64 (1996) 424-426 (*Segert, Stanislav*).

7781 *Dietrich, Manfried; Mayer, Walter* Hurritica Alalaḫiana (I). UF 28 (1996) 177-188.

7782 *Finkelberg, Margalit; Uchitel, Alexander; Ussishkin, David* A linear A inscription from Tel Lachish (Lach ZA 1). TelAv 23 (1996) 195-207.

7783 *Fox, Joshua* A sequence of vowel shifts in Phoenician and other languages. JNES 55 (1996) 37-47.

7784 *Frendo, Anthony J.* The particles *beth* and *waw* and the periodic structure of the Nora Stone inscription. PEQ 128 (1996) 8-11.

7785 *Garbini, G.* Evoluzione fonetica nel fenicio;

7786 Lessico militare fenicio a Sam'al. RSFen 24 (1996) 3-5/181-184.

7787 *Gianto, Agustinus* Kajian Antardisiplin Dialek-dialek Semit Barat [Interdisciplinary studies of West Semitic languages]. Linguistik Lapangan, Bahasa dan Politik, Evaluasi Kamus. E**Purwo, Bambang K.**, Pellba 9: Jakarta 1996, Lembaga Bahasa Unika Atmajaya. 177-202 [APIB 10,264];

7788 What's new in North-West Semitic lexicography and Palmyrene studies?. Or. 65 (1996) 440-449.

7789 *Gitin, Seymour; Dothan, Trude* Royal temple inscription found at Philistine Ekron. BA 59 (1996) 181-182.

7790 *Hess, Richard S.* A comparison of the Ugarit, Emar and Alalakh archives. FGIBSON J., 1996, ⇒31. 75-83.

7791 **Hoftijzer, Jean; Jongeling, K.** Dictionary of the North-West Semitic inscriptions: I-II. HO I/21-22: 1995, ⇒11/2,5895. RETR 71 (1996) 111-112 (*Macchi, Jean-Daniel*).

7792 **Lindenberger, James M.** Ancient Aramaic and Hebrew letters. 1994, ⇒11/2,5954. RJBL 115 (1996) 565-567 (*Bernstein, Moshe J.*); CBQ 58 (1996) 122-123 (*Moriya, Akio*).

7793 *Margalit, Baruch* Philological notes on a recently published Phoenician inscription from southern Anatolia. IOSOT 1992. BEAT 28: 1996, ⇒160. 119-129.

7794 **Olmo Lete, Gregorio del; Sanmartín, Joaquín** Diccionario de la lengua ugarítica, 1: (↑>i/u)-l. AulOr.S 7: Sabadell (Barc) 1996, AUSA xxvii; 250 pp. 84-88810-.

7795 *Pardee, Dennis* L'ougaritique et le hourrite dans les textes rituels de Ras Shamra-Ougarit. Mosaïque de langues. 1996, ⇒284. 63-80.

7796 *Peri, C.* A proposito dell'iscrizione di Tabnit. RSFen 24 (1996) 67-72.

7797 **Rin, Svi; Rin, Shifra** The third column of the Acts of the Gods: a revised paraphrase of the Ugaritic poetry with Tiberian vocalization. ²1992, ⇒8,9559. ᴿJSSt 41 (1996) 313-314 (*Wyatt, N.*).

7798 *Ruiz Cabrero, L.A.; López Pardo, F.* Ceramicas fenicias con *Graffiti* de la isla de Essaouira (antigua Mogador, Marruecos). RSFen 24 (1996) 153-179.

7799 *Schwemer, Daniel* Hethitisch *mad-* "widerstehen" und hieroglyphen-luwisch *mariianinzi* "Rebellen" in der Karatepe-Inschrift. WO 27 (1996) 30-35.

7800 **Sivan, Daniel** Ugaritic grammar. 1993, ⇒11/2,5906. ᴿPEQ 128 (1996) 80-81 (*Khan, Geoffrey*). **H.**

7801 **Smith, Mark S.** The Ugaritic Baal cycle, 1: KTU 1.1-1.2. VT.S 55: 1994, ⇒10,9107; 11/2,5907. ᴿETR 71 (1996) 281 (*Römer, Thomas*) AulOr 14 (1996) 269-277 (*Olmo Lete, Gregorio del*).

7802 *Sznycer, Maurice* Le bilinguisme punico-latin en Afrique du nord à l'époque romaine. Mosaïque de langues. 1996, ⇒284. 197-210.

7803 *Tidwell, N.L.* Mesha's *ḥmslt bᵓrnn*: what and where?. VT 46 (1996) 490-497.

7804 **Tropper, Josef** Die Inschriften von Zincirli. 1993, ⇒9,9833... 11/2,5979. ᴿArOr 64 (1996) 139-141 (*Segert, Stanislav*).

7805 *Watson, W.G.E.* Comments on some Ugaritic lexical items. JNSL 22/1 (1996) 73-84;

7806 Final -*m* in Ugaritic yet again. Sum. 259;

7807 Further comments on Ugaritic *wn*. AulOr 14 (1996) 259-268/285-287.

ᴊ1.6 Aramaica

7808 *Arnold, Bill T.* The use of Aramaic in the Hebrew Bible: another look at bilingualism in Ezra and Daniel. JNSL 22/2 (1996) 1-16.

7809 *Becking, Bob* The second Danite inscription: some remarks. BN 81 (1996) 21-30.

7810 **Beyer, Klaus** Die aramäischen Texte vom Toten Meer: Ergänzungsband. 1994, ⇒10,9114; 11/2,5920. ᴿFolOr 32 (1996) 174-178 (*Dombrowski, Bruno W.W.*); ThLZ 121 (1996) 439-445 (*Hoftijzer, Jacob*).

7811 *Cathcart, Kevin J.* The curses in Old Aramaic inscriptions. ᶠMᴄNᴀᴍᴀʀᴀ M., JSOT.S 230: 1996, ⇒58. 140-152.

7812 *Cryer, Frederick* Of epistemology, Northwest-Semitic epigraphy and irony: the "bytdwd/house of David" inscription revisited. JSOT 69 (1996) 3-17.

7813 ᴱ**Ephᶜal, Israel; Naveh, Joseph** Aramaic ostraca of the fourth century BC from Idumaea. J 1996, Magnes 100 pp. 965-223-958-5.

7814 *Eshel, Esther; Kloner, Amos* An Aramaic ostracon of an Edomite marriage contract from Maresha, dated 176 B.C.E. IEJ 46 (1996) 1-22.

7815 *Fassberg, Steven E.* The pronominal suffix of the second feminine singular in the Aramaic texts from the Judean desert. DSD 3 (1996) 10-19.

7816 **Fitzmyer, Joseph A.** The Aramaic inscriptions of Sefire. BibOr 19/A: ²1995, ⇒11/2,5934. ᴿBiOr 53 (1996) 794-796 (*Lipiński, E.*).

7817 *Garbini, Giovanni* Note lessicali palmirene. Summarium 495.
RANL 8 (1996) 495-498 ['mr; gmwt; mṣb; mgd].
7818 *Healey, John F.* 'May he be remembered for good': an Aramaic
formula. FMcNAMARA M., JSOT.S 230: 1996, ⇒58. 177-186.
7819 EHillers, Delbert R.; Cussini, Eleonora Palmyrene Aramaic texts.
Publ. of the CAL Project: Baltimore 1996, Johns Hopkins Univ.
Press xviii; 458 pp. $78. 0-8018-5278-1 [BiOr 54,468].
7820 Hug, Volker Altaramäische Grammatik der Texte des 7. und 6.
Jhs. v. Chr. 1993, ⇒11/2,5943. RBiOr 53 (1996) 796-798
(*Muraoka, T.*).
7821 *Hunter, Erica C.D.* Incantation bowls: a Mesopotamian phenomenon?. Or. 65 (1996) 220-233.
7822 Jobling, W.J. Nabataean-Aramaic: a provisional lexicon (Nablex).
Kensington, MD 1995, Dunwoody xi; 84 pp. 1-881265-20-X.
7823 *Layton, Scott C.* Leaves from an onomastician's notebook. ZAW
108 (1996) 608-620.
7824 Lemaire, André Nouvelles inscriptions araméennes d'Idumée au
Musée d'Israël. TEuph.S 3: P 1996, Gabalda 171 pp. 47 pl. 2-
85021-087-0.
7825 *MacDonald, Michael C.A.* Nabataean inscriptions copied by W.J.
BANKES in the Ḥawran. Syr. 73 (1996) 97-98.
7826 Martínez Borobio, Emiliano Gramática del arameo antiguo. Barc
1996, Univ. de Barc ix; 142 pp. 84-477-0563-3.
7827 *Moortgat-Correns, Ursula* Zwei unveröffentliche Fundstücke vom
Tell Fecherije aus den Jahren 1927 und 1929. Phil. Komm. *Böck,
Barbara*, AltOrF 23 (1996) 316-334.
7828 EMuraoka, Takamitsu Studies in Qumran Aramaic. Abr-n.S 3:
1992, ⇒8,9586; 9,9858. RBAEO 32 (1996) 423-425 (*Sen, Felipe*);
MEAH 43/2 (1994) 170-177 (*Torres, Antonio*).
7829 ETMüller-Kessler, Christa; Sokoloff, Michael The forty martyrs
of the Sinai Desert, Eulogios, the stoner-cutter, and Anastasia. A
corpus of Christian and Palestinian Aramaic 3: Groningen 1996,
Styx 138 pp. [LASBF 46,475s—Pazzini, Massimo].
7830 Porten, Bezalel; Yardeni, Ada <ed & trans> Textbook of Aramaic documents from ancient Egypt, 3: literature, accounts, lists.
1993, ⇒9,9866... 11/2,5967. RJSJ 27 (1996) 351-355 (*Grelot, P.*);
ArOr 64 (1996) 426-427 (*Segert, Stanislav*).
7831 Qimron, E. Biblical Aramaic. 1993, ⇒10,9868; 11/2,5969. RPEQ
128 (1996) 79-80 (*Khan, Geoffrey*). H.
7832 Rodrigues Pereira, Alphons S. Studies in Aramaic poetry (c.100
B.C.E.-c.600 C.E.): selected Jewish, Christian and Samaritan
poems. Diss. Rijksuniv. 1996, 279 pp. [NThAR 1997,99].
7833 *Sasson, Victor* Deir 'Alla smr—obscured, not re-evaluated and
other shady matters. ZAW 108 (1996) 258-262;
7834 Murderers, usurpers, or what?: Hazael, Jehu, and the Tell Dan Old
Aramaic inscription. UF 28 (1996) 547-554.
7835 *Sauer, Georg* Die assyrische Zeit und die Bilingue von Tell Fekhe-
rije. Religionsgeschichte Syriens. 1996, ⇒217. 122-127.
7836 *Schniedewind, William M.* Tel Dan stela: new light on Aramaic
and Jehu's revolt. BASOR 302 (1996) 75-90.
7837 *Segni, Leah di; Naveh, Joseph* A bilingual Greek-Aramaic inscription from Ḥ. Qastra, near Haifa. ʿAtiqot 29 (1996) 77-78.
7838 *Tropper, Josef* Aramäisches *wyqtl* und hebräisches *wayyiqtol*. UF
28 (1996) 633-645.

7839　Will, Ernest À propos de quelques inscriptions palmyréniennes: le cas de Septimus Vorôd. Syr. 73 (1996) 109-115.
7840　Zsengellér, József Personal names in the Wadi ed-Daliyeh papyri. ZAH 9 (1996) 182-189.

7841　Luke, K. East Semitic survivals in Syriac. BiBh 22 (1996) 139-155.

J2.1 Akkadica

7842　CAD 17/3: Š. 1994, ⇒11/2,6002. ᴿOLZ 91 (1996) 285-291 (Soden, Wolfram von).
7843　De Odorico, Marco The use of numbers and quantifications in the Assyrian royal inscriptions. 1995, ⇒11/2,6004. ᴿMes. 31 (1996) 263-264 (Saporetti, C.).
7844　Foster, Benjamin R. Before the Muses: an anthology of Akkadian literature. 1993, ⇒9,9892; 11/2,6009. ᴿJSSt 41 (1996) 301-303 (Livingstone, Alasdair).
7845　Malbran-Labat, Florence La version akkadienne de l'inscription trilingue de Darius à Behistun. 1994, ⇒11/2,6033. ᴿZA 86 (1996) 275-284 (Streck, M.P.).

J2.7 Arabica

7846　Bar-Asher, Moshe La composante hébraïque du judéo-arabe algérien: communautés de Tlemcen et Aïn-Temouchent. 1992, ⇒10,9168. ᴿHebStud 37 (1996) 217-221 (Hary, Benjamin).
7847　Kaltner, John The use of Arabic in Biblical Hebrew lexicography. CBQMS 28: Wsh 1996, Catholic Biblical Association 122 pp. $7.50. 0-915170-27-2.
7848　Testen, David On the Arabic of the ʿEn ʿAvdat inscription. JNES 55 (1996) 281-292.

J3.0 Aegyptia

7849　Assmann, Jan Kulturelle und literarische Texte;
7850　Assmann, Jan Verkünden und Verklären: Grundformen hymnischer Rede im Alten Ägypten;
7851　Baines, John Classicism and modernism in the literature of the New Kingdom;
7852　Blumenthal, Elke Die literarische Verarbeitung der Übergangszeit zwischen Altem und Mittlerem Reich;
7853　Burkard, Günter Metrik, Prosodie und formaler Aufbau ägyptischer literarischer Texte;
7854　Burstein, Stanley M. Images of Egypt in Greek historiography. Ancient Egyptian literature. 1996, ⇒230. 59-82/313-334/157-174/105-135/447-463/591-604.
7855　Caluwe, Albert de Un livre des morts sur bandelette de momie. 1991, ⇒7,9335*. ᴿOLZ 91 (1996) 412-413 (Luft, Ulrich).
7856　Collier, Mark The language of literature: on grammar and texture;
7857　Derchain, Philippe Auteur et société;

7858 *Derchain, Philippe* Théologie et littérature;
7859 *Eyre, Christopher J.* Is Egyptian historical literature "historical" or "literary"?;
7860 *Fischer-Elfert, Hans-W.* Die Arbeit am Text: altägyptische Literaturwerke aus philologischer Perspektive. Ancient Egyptian literature. 1996, ⇒230. 531-553/83-94/351-360/415-433/499-513.
7861 **Foster, John L.** Thought couplets in the Tale of Sinue. 1993, ⇒9,9953; 11/2,6126. ^RBiOr 53 (1996) 51-53 *(Burkard, G.).*
7862 *Gnirs, Andrea M.* Die ägyptische Autobiographie. Ancient Egyptian literature. 1996, ⇒230. 191-241.
7863 *Görg, Manfred* Edrei in ägyptischer Nebenüberlieferung. BN 84 (1996) 36-40.
7864 *Guglielmi, Waltraud* Die ägyptische Liebespoesie;
7865 Der Gebrauch rhetorischer Stilmittel in der ägyptischen Literatur;
7866 *Gumbrecht, Hans-Ulrich* Does Egyptology need a "theory of literature"?;
7867 *Haarmann, Ulrich* Medieval Muslim perceptions of pharaonic Egypt. Ancient Egyptian literature. 1996, ⇒230. 335-347/465-497/3-18/605-627.
7868 **Hoch, James E.** Semitic words in Egyptian texts of the New Kingdom and third intermediate period. 1994, ⇒10,9205; 11/2,6141. ^RWZKM 146 (1996) 507-514 *(Quack, Joachim Friedrich);* AcOr 56 (1995) 194-198 *(Pierce, Richard Holton).*
7869 **Jasnow, Richard** A late period hieratic wisdom text (P.Brooklyn 47.218.135). SAOC 52: 1992, ⇒10,9209. ^RBiOr 53 (1996) 409-412 *(Shirun-Grumach, I.).*
7870 *Loprieno, Antonio* Defining Egyptian literature: ancient texts and modern literary theory. Albright centennial conference. 1996, ⇒303. 209-232;
7871 Defining Egyptian literature: ancient texts and modern theories;
7872 The "king's novel";
7873 Linguistic variety and Egyptian literature;
7874 Loyalistic instructions. Ancient Egyptian literature. 1996, ⇒230. 39-58/277-295/515-529/403-414.
7875 *Parkinson, Richard B.* Individual and society in Middle Kingdom literature;
7876 Types of literature in the Middle Kingdom. Ancient Egyptian literature. 1996, ⇒230. 137-155/297-312.
7877 **Quack, Joachim Friedrich** Studien zur Lehre für Merikare. GOF.A 23: 1992, ⇒8,9724; 9,9983. ^RBiOr 53 (1996) 53-58 *(Goedicke, Hans).*
7878 *Quirke, Stephen G.* Archive;
7879 Narrative literature. Ancient Egyptian literature. 1996, ⇒230. 379-401/263-276.
7880 *Roccatti, Alessandro* La datazione di opere letterarie egizie. VO 10 (1996) 261-265.
7881 *Rochette, Bruno* Sur le bilinguisme dans l'Égypte gréco-romaine. CÉg 71 (1996) 153-168.
7882 *Schenkel, Wolfgang* Ägyptische Literatur und ägyptologische Forschung: eine wissenschaftliche Einleitung;
7883 *Simpson, William Kelly* Belles lettres and propaganda. Ancient Egyptian literature. 1996, ⇒230. 21-38/435-443.
7884 **Spalinger, Anthony John** The private feast lists of ancient Egypt. ÄA 57: Wsb 1996, Harrassowitz xi; 184 pp. 3-447-03873-X.

7885 *Tait, W. John* Demotic literature: forms and genres. Ancient Egyptian literature. 1996, ⟹230. 175-187.
7886 ᴱ**Tiradritti, Francesco** Informatica ed egittologia all'inizio degli anni '90. Informatica e Discipline Umanistiche 7: R 1996, Bulzoni 264 pp. Congresso Internazionale di Egittologia (6: 1991: T).
7887 *Vernus, Pascal* Langue littéraire et diglossie. Ancient Egyptian literature. 1996, ⟹230. 555-564.
7888 **Walker, James Harcourt** Studies in Ancient Egyptian anatomical terminology. The Australian Centre for Egyptology, Studies 4: Warminster 1996, Aris & P. ix; 347 pp. Bibl. 0-85668-803-7.
7889 *Ward, William A.* A new look at Semitic personal names and loanwords in Egyptian. CÉg 71 (1996) 17-47.
7890 ᴱᵀ**Wente, Edward F.** Letters from Ancient Egypt. 1990, ⟹6,9559... 9,9997. ᴿCÉg 71 (1996) 57-62 (*Winand, Jean*); JNES 55 (1996) 223-224 (*Redford, Donald*).

ᴊ5.1 Graeca *grammatica, onomastica*

7891 **Adrados, F.R.** Nueva sintaxis del griego antiguo. 1992, ⟹9,10083*. ᴿAt. 84 (1996) 656-660 (*Cuzzolin, Pierluigi*).
7892 **Brixhe, Claude** Phonétique et phonologie du grec ancien I: quelques grandes questions. BCILL 82: Lv(N) 1996, Peeters 162 pp. Bibl.
7893 **Brooks, James A.; Winbery, Carlton L.** A morphology of NT Greek. 1994, ⟹10,9285. ᴿJBL 115 (1996) 169-171 (*Schmidt, Daryl D.*).
7894 **Buzetti, Carlo** Nuovi studenti del Nuovo Testamento greco: proposte e strumenti per un corso-base. R 1995, LAS 109 pp. L20.000. 88-1213-0390-8. ᴿAng. 73 (1996) 589-590 (*De Santis, Luca*).
7895 **Chapman, Benjamin; Shogren, Gary Steven** Greek New Testament insert. Quakertown, PA ²1994, Stylus 63 pp. Faith & Mission 13/2 (1996) 112-114 (*Lanier, David E.*).
7896 ᴱ**Crespo, E.; García Ramón, J.L.; Striano, A.** Dialectologia graeca. M 1993, Univ. Autónoma de Madrid 397 pp. Actas del II Coloquio 1991. ᴿCIR 46 (1996) 67-69 (*Clackson, J.*).
7897 *Dean, Margaret E.* The grammar of sound in Greek texts: toward a method for mapping the echoes of speech in writing. ABR 44 (1996) 53-70.
7898 **Dickey, Eleanor** Greek forms of address: from Hᴇʀᴏᴅᴏᴛᴜs to Lᴜᴄɪᴀɴ. Oxf Classical Monographs: Oxf 1996, Clarendon xxi; 336 pp. 0-19-815054-7.
7899 ᴱ**Glare, P.G.W.** Lɪᴅᴅᴇʟʟ and Sᴄᴏᴛᴛ supplement. Collab. *Thompson, A.A.*, Oxf 1996, Clarendon xxxi; 320 pp. £50. 0-19-864223-7 [NT 39,205].
7900 *Heimerdinger, Jenny* Word order in Koine Greek: using a text-critical approach to study word order patterns in the Greek text of Acts. FgNT 9 (1996) 139-180.
7901 **Kitchell, K.F.** Greek 2000—crisis, challenge, deadline. CJ 91 (1996) 393-420 [NTAb 41,17].
7902 **Leivestad, Ragnar** Nytestamentlig gresk grammatikk. ᴱ*Sandvei, Bjørn Helge*, Oslo ²1996, Universitetsforlaget 312 pp. ᴿNTT 97 (1996) 169-170 (*Økland, Jorunn*).

7903 [E]**Lust, Johan,** (al), A Greek-English lexicon of the Septuagint: (a)
A-I. 1992, ⇒8,9839... 11/2,6296. [R]ThLZ 121 (1996) 917-920
(*Holtz, Traugott*);

7904 (b) K-Omega. Stu 1996, Dt. Bibelges. 218-528 + LXVI pp. 3-
438-05126-7.

7905 **Macnair, Ian** Discovering NT Greek. 1993, ⇒9,10114. [R]EvQ 68
(1996) 63-64 (*Edwards, Ruth B.*).

7906 *Margain, Jean* La Septante comme témoin de l'hébreu post-
exilique et michnique. Mosaïque de langues. 1996, ⇒284. 191-195.

7907 **McKay, Kenneth L.** A new syntax of the verb in NT Greek. 1994,
⇒11/2,6297. [R]CBQ 58 (1996) 163-164 (*Parunak, H. Van Dyke*).

7908 **Mounce, William D.** Basics of Biblical Greek: workbook. 1993,
⇒10,9307. [R]Neotest. 30 (1996) 224-225 (*Smit, Johannes A.*).

7909 News and notes: a Greek-English lexicon of the Septuagint.
BIOSCS 29 (1996) 7-10.

7910 **Osborne, Michael J.; Byrne, Sean G.** The foreign residents of
Athens: an annex to the Lexicon of Greek Personal Names: Attica.
StHell 33: Lv 1996, Peeters xxxvii; 479 pp. Bibl. 90-6831-883-7.

7911 **Palmer, Michael W.** Levels of constituent structure in NT Greek.
1995, ⇒11/2,6309. [R]FgNT 9 (1996) 220-222 (*Wong, Simon*);
[R]CritRR 9 (1996) 249-251 (*Wallace, Daniel B.*).

7912 **Pelaez, Jesús** Metodología del diccionario griego-español del
Nuevo Testamento. Estudios de filología neotestamentaria 6: Cordoba 1996, El Almendro 163 pp. 84-8005-027-6 [RTL 29,129].

7913 **Perpillou, Jean-Louis** Recherches lexicales en grec ancien: étymo-
logie, analogie, représentations. Bibliothèque d'Études Classiques:
Lv 1996, Peeters 220 pp. 90-6831-824-1.

7914 **Porter, Stanley E.** Idioms of the Greek New Testament. Biblical
Languages: Greek 2: Shf [2]1996, Academic 339 pp. Bibl. 1-85075-
379-2;

7915 Studies in the Greek New Testament: theory and practice. Studies
in Biblical Greek 6: NY 1996, Lang vii; 290 pp. $33. 0-8204-
2858-2 [NTAb 41,138].

7916 **Rusconi, Carlo** Vocabolario del greco del Nuovo Testamento. Bo
1996, EDB xiii; 385 pp. L52.000. 88-10-20587-1.

7917 **Spicq, Celas** Theological lexicon of the NT. 1994, ⇒10,9318;
11/2,6324. [R]BS 153 (1996) 249-250 (*Bock, Darrell L.*);

7918 Note di lessicografia neotestamentaria, 2. [E]*Viero, Franco Luigi*,
GLNT.S 4: 1994, ⇒10,9319. [R]Lat. 62 (1996) 371-373 (*Penna,
Romano*).

7919 **Stevens, Gerald L.** NT Greek workbook. 1994, ⇒11/2,6326.
[R]AUSS 34 (1996) 148-149 (*Reynolds, Edwin E.*);

7920 NT Greek. 1994, ⇒11/2,6326. [R]RExp 93 (1996) 299 (*Painter,
Jack*); AUSS 34 (1996) 147-148 (*Reynolds, Edwin E.*).

7921 **Swetnam, James** Il greco del NT, 1: morfologia. 1995,
⇒11/2,6329. [R]RivBib 44 (1996) 482-483 (*Buzetti, Carlo*).

7922 **Threatte, L.** The grammar of the Attic inscriptions, II: morphology. B 1996, De Gruyter xxv; 839 pp. [At. 86,608—Bertolini,
Francesco].

7923 **Verboomen, Alain** L'imparfait périphrastique dans l'évangile de
Luc et dans la Septante. 1992, ⇒8,9866; 10,9324. [R]EtCl 64 (1996)
382-383 (*Leclercq, H.*).

7924   **Wahlgren, Staffan** Sprachwandel im Griechisch der frühen römischen Kaiserzeit. SGLG 60: Göteborg 1995, 220 pp. RBAGB (1996) 191-192 (*Irigoin, Jean*).
7925   **Wallace, Daniel B.** Greek grammar beyond the basics: an exegetical syntax of the New Testament. GR 1996, Zondervan xxxii; 797 pp. $40. 0-310-37340-9.
7926   **Whittaker, Molly; Holtermann, Horst; Hänni, Andreas** Einführung in die griechische Sprache des Neuen Testaments: Grammatik und Übungsbuch: Ianua linguae graecae C. Gö ⁶1996, Vandenhoeck & R. 188; 35 pp. Beiheft: Schlüssel der Übersetzungsübungen. 3-525-52142-1.
7927   **Zerwick, Max; Grosvenor, Mary** A grammatical analysis of the Greek New Testament. R ⁵1996, Pont. Biblical Institute Press xxxviii; 778 pp. L50.000. 88-7653-588-8.
7928   **Zuntz, G.** Greek: a course in classical and post-classical Greek grammar. EPorter, S.E., 1994, ⇒11/2,6336. RCIR 46 (1996) 301-302 (*Randall, J.G.*).

ɹ5.2 Voces *ordine alphabetico consonantium* graecarum

7929   ἀβαναυσως *Lona, Horacio E.* Zur Bedeutung von ἀβαναυσως in 1 Clem 44,3. VigChr 50 (1996) 5-11.
7930   ἀποκαλύπτω; ἀποκάλυψις *Smith, Morton* On the history of ἀποκαλύπτω and ἀποκάλυψις. New Testament. 1996 <1983>, ⇒151. 194-205.
7931   διαθηκη; νόμος *Schwemer, Anna Maria* Zum Verhältnis von διαθηκη und νόμος in den Schriften der jüdischen Diaspora Ägyptens in hellenistisch-römischer Zeit. Bund und Tora. WUNT 92: 1996, ⇒1645. 67-109.
7932   δόξα **Raurell, Frederic** 'Doxa' en la teologia i antropologia dels LXX. CStP 59: Barc 1996, Herder 491 pp. 84-254-1989-1. RRCatT 21 (1996) 462-466 (*Bosch i Veciana, Antoni*).
7933   δόξα *Raurell, Frederic* Èxode i resurrecció διὰ τῆς δόξης θεοῦ. Sum. 17. RCatT 21 (1996) 1-17.
7934   ει *Burchard, Christoph* EI nach einem Ausdruck des Wissens oder Nichtwissens: Joh 09,25, Act 19,02, I Cor 01,16, 07,16 <1961>;
7935   ἐξουσία **Scholtissek, Klaus** Vollmacht im AT und Judentum. PaThSt 24: 1993, ⇒10,9342. RCritRR 9 (1996) 168-170 (*Smith-Christopher, Daniel L.*).
7936   ἔρχεσθαι **Toribio Cuadrado, José Fernando** "El Viniente:" estudio del verbo ἔρχεσθαι en la literatura joánica. 1993, ⇒9,10158; 10,9344. REE 71 (1996) 650-651 (*Benéitez, Manuel*); ScrTh 28 (1996) 897-900 (*Balaguer, Vincente*).
7937   εὐχαριστία *Longosz, Stanisław* Nazwa 'eucharistia' (ochres przedchrześcijański). Arg. 363. Vox Patrum 16 (1996) 349-363. P.
7938   καταλλάσσω **Porter, Stanley E.** Καταλλάσσω in ancient Greek literature. 1994, ⇒10,9328. REvQ 68 (1996) 248-249 (*Thrall, Margaret E.*).
7939   κοιμαομαι **Jackson, Paul Norman** An investigation of koimaomai in the New Testament: the concept of eschatological sleep. Mellen 45: Lewiston, NY 1996. Mellen (10) vii; 241 pp. 0-7734-2417-2.

7940 ναζαρηνός; ναζαραῖος Parente, Fausto Ναζαρηνός—Ναζαραῖος: an unsolved riddle in the synoptic tradition. ICS 15 (1996) 185-201.

7941 νοῦς Rudolph, Kurt Bemerkungen zur manichäischen Vorstellung vom νοῦς. Gnosis. NHS 42: 1996 <1991>, ⇒147. 714-723.

7942 νωθρός Campbell, John M. An analysis of the semantic domains of νωθρός with implications for the interpretation of Hebrews 5.11-6.12. Diss. New Orleans Baptist Theol. Sem. 1996, DRay, Charles A. Jr., 159 pp. DAI-A 57/07, p. 3074; AAC 9640217.

7943 παρρησία Fredrickson, David E. παρρησία in the Pauline epistles. Friendship. NT.S 82: 1996, ⇒180. 163-183.

7944 παρρησία Klassen, William παρρησία in the Johannine corpus. Friendship. NT.S 82: 1996, ⇒180. 227-254.
    παρρησία Mitchell, A. Hebrews ⇒6536.
    παρρησία Winter, S.C. παρρησία in Acts ⇒5222.

7945 πίστις Barth, Gerhard Pistis in hellenistischer Religiosität. Neutestamentliche Versuche. 1996 <1982>, ⇒111. 169-194.

7946 πίστις; πιστεύειν Lindsay, Dennis R. Josephus and faith... NT. AGJU 19: 1993, ⇒10,9358. RCBQ 58 (1996) 349-351 (Chesnutt, Randall D.).

7947 σπαργανον Kügler, Joachim Die Windeln Jesu (Lk 2)—Nachtrag: zum Gebrauch von σπαργανον bei PHILO von Alexandrien. BN 81 (1996) 8-14.

7948 συγκαταβασις Brändle, Rudolf συγκαταβασις als hermeneutisches und ethisches Prinzip in der Paulusauslegung des Johannes CHRYSOSTOMUS. FDASSMANN E., JAC.E 23: 1996, ⇒19. 297-307.

7949 σῶμα Toloni, G. Un'ulteriore accezione di σῶμα nei LXX. EstB 54 (1996) 145-164 [1 Sam 31,10.12; Nah 3,3].

7950 ῥῆμα Burchard, Christoph A note on ῥῆμα in JosAs 17:1f.; Luke 2:15,17; Acts 10:37 <1985>. Collab. Burfeind, Carsten, Gesammelte Studien. SVTP 13: 1996, ⇒119. 213-221/247-261.

7951 τελώνης Herrenbrück, Fritz Steuerpacht und Moral: zur Beurteilung des τελώνης in der Umwelt des Neuen Testaments. Religion. ANRW II.26.3: 1996, ⇒183. 2221-2297.

J5.4 Papyri et inscriptiones graecae—Greek epigraphy

7952 Alpi, Frédéric; Nordiguian, Lévon Les inscriptions de l'église de Blât: essai de relecture. Syr. 73 (1996) 5-14.

7953 Atallah, Nabil Nouvelles inscriptions grecques et latines du nord-est de la Jordanie. Syr. 73 (1996) 15-22.

7954 EBagnall, Roger S.; Obbink, Dirk D. Columbia Papyri X. ASP 34: Atlanta, GA 1996, Scholars xii; 234 pp. 50 pl. 0-7885-0275-1.

7955 Bernand, André Inscriptions historiques grecques. 1992, ⇒10,9374; 11/2,6426. RBiOr 53 (1996) 461-468 (Łajtar, Adam).

7956 EBetz, Hans Dieter The Greek magical papyri in translation inclu ding the demotic spells, 1: texts. Lei 21996, Brill lviii; 353 pp. $25. 0-226-04447-5 [JSJ 28,364].

7957 Bij de Vatte, Alice J.; Van Henten, Jan Willem Jewish or non-Jewish?: some remarks on the identification of Jewish inscriptions from Asia Minor. BiOr 53 (1996) 16-28.

7958 *Chausson, François; Nordiguian, Lévon* L'église de Maad et ses inscriptions. Syr. 73 (1996) 37-46.

7959 ᴱDe Lange, Nicholas Greek Jewish texts from the Cairo Genizah. TSAJ 51: Tü 1996, Mohr 473 pp. DM268. 3-16-146438-9.

7960 ᴱErnst, Michael Die Wüste spricht: Papyri beleuchten Literatur und Alltagsleben der Antike. Salzburg 1996, Inst. für Neutestamentl. Bibelwiss. 98 pp. Katalog zur Ausstellung in der Universitätsbibliothek, 1996; Exponate der Österreichischen Nationalbibliothek. 3-901636-01-3.

7961 *Figueras, Pau* New Greek inscriptions from the Negev. SBFLA 46 (1996) 265-284.

7962 *Gatier, Pierre-Louis* Gouverneurs et procurateurs à Gérasa. Syr. 73 (1996) 47-56.

7963 **Gregg, Robert C.; Urman, Dan** Jews, pagans, and christians in the Golan Heights: Greek and other inscriptions of the Roman and Byzantine eras. SFSHJ 140: Atlanta, GA 1996, Scholars xxi; 360 pp. $150. 0-7885-0314-6.

7964 **Hunger, H.** Katalog der griechischen Handschriften der Österreichischen Nationalbibliothek 4: Supplementum graecum. Collab. *Hannick, Christian*, Wien 1995, Hollinek xvii; 422 pp. ᴿOCP 62 (1996) 451-452 (*Pieralli, L.*).

7965 **Ioannidou, Grace** Catalogue of the Greek and Latin literary papyri in Berlin: (P. Berol. inv. 21101-21299, 21911). Phot. *Büsing, Margarete*, Berliner Klassikertexte 9: Mainz 1996, Von Zabern xviii; 269 pp. 3-8053-1721-2.

7966 **Johnson, Gary J.** Early-christian epitaphs from Anatolia. 1995, ⇒11/2,6462. ᴿCBQ 58 (1996) 756 (*Kraabel, A.T.*).

7967 **Malingrey, Anne-Marie** La littérature grecque chrétienne. Initiations aux Pères de l'Église: P 1996, Cerf 159 pp. 2-204-05304-X.

7968 ᴱPanciera, Silvio Iscrizioni greche e latine del Foro romano e del Palatino: inventario generale: inediti: revisioni. R 1996, Storia e Letteratura 445 pp. L150.000 [AnCl 67,428—Raepsaet-Charlier, Marie-Thérèse].

7969 ᴱPestman, P.W.; Rupprecht, H.-A. Berichtigungsliste der griechischen Papyrusurkunden aus Ägypten. Lei 1995, Brill x; 476 pp. *f*210. 90-04-10409-7. ᴿJAOS 116 (1996) 766-767 (*Bagnall, Roger S.*).

7970 **Rupprecht, Hans-Albert** Kleine Einführung in die Papyruskunde. Die Altertumswissenschaft: 1994, Da:Wiss xii; 272 pp. DM56. 534-04493-2. ᴿBiOr 53 (1996) 720-721 (*Kehoe, Dennis*).

7971 ᴱᵀShelton, J.C.; Whitehorne, J.E.G. The Oxyrhynchus papyri, 62. PEES.GR 82: L 1995, Egypt Exploration Society x; 182 pp. 12 pl. 0-85698-127-3. ᴿJJP 26 (1996) 216-218 (*Appel, W.*).

7972 ᴱVan Henten, Jan Willem; Van der Horst, Pieter Willem Studies in early Jewish epigraphy. AGJU 21: 1994, ⇒10,323b; 11/2,6456. ᴿJAOS 116 (1996) 772-774 (*Price, Jonathan J.*).

7973 **Wardy, Robert** The birth of rhetoric. L 1996, Routledge viii; 197 pp. [SCI 17,238ss—Winterbottom, Michael].

7974 **Weber, Thomas** Gadarenes in exile: two inscriptions from Greece reconsidered. ZDPV 112 (1996) 10-17.

7975 *Ziegler, Renate* Bemerkungen zur Datierung dokumentarischer Papyri und Ostraka. ZPE 114 (1996) 157-161.

J6.5 Latina

7976 E**Alföldi, Géza** Corpus inscriptionum latinarum 6.8.2: titulos imperatorum domusque eorum thesauro schedarum imaginumque ampliato. B 1996, De Gruyter 389 pp. 645 fig. DM890. 3-11-015194-4 [AJA 101,817].

7977 **Clarke, M.L.** Rhetoric at Rome: a historical survey. L 1996, Routledge 206 pp. [SCI 17,238—Winterbottom, Michael].

7978 *Eck, Werner* Zu lateinischen Inschriften aus Caesarea in Iudaea / Syria Palaestina. ZPE 113 (1996) 129-143.

7979 *Macías Villalobos, Cristóbal Caelum* en la Vulgata. Fortunatae 8 (1996) 235-265 [EThL 74,160*].

7980 *Moussy, Claude Ornamentum* et *ornatus*: de P L A U T E à la Vulgate. REL 74 (1996) 92-107 [EThL 74,160*].

7981 *Raurell, Frederic* 'Gloria' and 'maiestas' in the 'Veteres Versiones Latinae' of the bible. EstFr 97 (1996) 145-180 [Exod 20,1-17].

Wardy, R. The birth of rhetoric ⇒7973.

J8 Language, writing and the Bible

7982 *Atherton, C.* What every grammarian knows?. CQ 46 (1996) 239-260.

7983 E**Black, David Alan** Linguistics and NT interpretation... discourse analysis. 1992, ⇒11/2,6615. REvQ 68 (1996) 64-66 (*McComiskey, Douglas*).

7984 **Brox, Norbert** Terminologisches zur frühchristlichen Rede von Gott. Bayerische Akad. der Wiss., Phil.-hist. Kl. Sitzungsberichte 1996/1: Mü: Bayerische Akad. der Wiss. 1996, 46 pp. 3-7696-1585-9.

7985 *Chadwick, Robert* Introduction to cuneiform writing. Rés. 5. BCSMS 31 (1996) 5-14.

7986 **Chomsky, Noam** Probleme sprachlichen Wissens. T*Schiffmann, M.*, Weinheim 1996, Beltz A. 208 pp. DM68. 3-89547-098-8 [ThLZ 122,326].

7987 *Colless, Brian E.* The Egyptian and Mesopotamian contributions to the origins of the alphabet. Cultural interaction. Abr-n.S 5: 1996, ⇒285. 67-75.

7988 *Collon, Dominique; Walker, Christopher* Britisches Museum: die Anfänge der Schrift. WUB 2 (1996) 55-61.

7989 *Collon, Dominique; Walker, Christopher* Les débuts de l'écriture. MoBi 96 (1996) 57-63.

7990 E**Daniels, Peter T.; Bright, William** The world's writing systems. Oxf 1996, OUP xlv; 920 pp. $150. 0-19-507-993-0. RArOr 64 (1996) 405-410 (*Segert, Stanislav*).

7991 *Feldman, Louis H.* H O M E R and the Near East: the rise of the Greek genius. BA 59 (1996) 13-21.

7992 *Gai, Amikam* Adnominal and adverbial attributes in Semitic languages. Muséon 109 (1996) 369-393.

7993 **Hock, Hans Heinrich; Joseph, Brian, D.** Language history, language change, and language relationship: an introduction to historical and comparative linguistics. Trends in Linguistics, Studies and Monographs 93: B 1996, De Gruyter xv; 602 pp. Bibl. 3-11-014784-X.

7994 *Huehnergard, John* New directions in the study of Semitic languages. Albright centennial conference. 1996, ⇒303. 251-272.
7995 *Israel, Felice* Parole di origine fenicia o costiera nel lessico di Canaan?. ᶠMoscati S., III, 1996, ⇒67. 1171-1177.
7996 *Kaufman, Stephen A.* Semitics: directions and re-directions. Albright centennial conference. 1996, ⇒303. 273-282.
7997 ᴱLappin, Shalom The handbook of contemporary semantic theory. Handbooks in Linguistics: Oxf 1996, Blackwell xvii; 670 pp. 0-631-18752-9.
7998 Lehmann, Winfred Philipp Theoretical bases of Indo-European linguistics. L 1996, Routledge xii; 324 pp. 0-415-13850-7.
7999 *Lemaire, André; Lozachmeur, Hélène* Remarques sur le plurilinguisme en Asie Mineure à l'époque perse;
8000 *Malbran-Labat, Florence* Akkadien, bilingues et bilinguisme en Élam et à Ougarit;
8001 *Masson, Emilia* Le bilinguisme hittito-hatti au début du royaume. Mosaïque de langues. 1996, ⇒284. 91-123/33-61/23-32.
8002 Neville, Robert Cummings The truth of broken symbols. SUNY Religious Studies: Albany, NY 1996, State Univ. of NY Press xxv; 320 pp. 0-7914-2741-2.
8003 Nevis, Joel A., (al), Clitics: a comprehensive bibliography 1892-1991. Amst 1994, Benjamins 274 pp. ᴿBulletin de la Société de Linguistique de Paris 91/2 (1996) 110-111 (*Bader, Françoise*).
8004 Orel, Vladimir E.; Stolbova, Olga V. Hamito-Semitic etymological dictionary. HO 18: 1995, ⇒11/2,6604. ᴿSEL 13 (1996) 121-122 (*Watson, Wilfred G.E.*).
8005 *Pelikan, Jaroslav* Sacred philology. Reformation of the bible. 1996, ⇒730. 3-21.
8006 *Pilch, John J.* Altered states of consciousness: a "kitbashed" model. BTB 26 (1996) 133-138.
8007 *Rainey, A.F.* The imperative 'see' as an introductory particle: an Egyptian-West Semitic calque. ᶠYoung D., 1996, ⇒107. 309-316.
8008 *Robbins, Vernon K.* Narrative in ancient rhetoric and rhetoric in ancient narrative. SBL.SPS 35: 1996, ⇒274. 368-384.
8009 Schmandt-Besserat, Denise Before writing. 1992, ⇒8,a162... 11/2,6678. BCSMS 31 (1996) 35-43 (*Brown, Stuart C.*);
8010 How writing came about. Austin, TX 1996, Univ. of Texas Press xii; 193 pp. $20. 0-292-77704-3.
8011 Semerano, Giovanni Le origini della cultura europea. F 1984-1994, Olschki 2 vols; lxx; 956 pp. ᴿRivBib 44 (1996) 351-354 (*Balzaretti, Claudio*).
8012 ᴱSihler, Andrew L. New comparative grammar of Greek and Latin. 1995, ⇒11/2,6609. ᴿAJP 117 (1996) 670-675 (*Weiss, Michael*).
8013 Steiner, Deborah T. The tyrant's writ: myths and images of writing in ancient Greece. Princeton 1994, Princeton Univ. Press 294 pp. £30. 0-691-03238-6. ᴿAJP 117 (1996) 145-148 (*Cole, Thomas*).
8014 ᴱStone, Michael E. Rock inscriptions and graffiti project. SBL.RBS 28,29,31: Atlanta 1992-1994, Scholars 3 vols. $30/20 per vol. ᴿABR 44 (1996) 71-72 (*Jenkins, R.G.*).

8015 ᴱSwiggers, Pierre; Wouters, Alfons Ancient grammar: content and context. Orbis Supplementa 7: Lv 1996, Peeters xi; 220 pp. 90-6831-881-0.

8016 *Tropper, Josef* Ägyptisches, nordwestsemitisches und altsüdarabisches Alphabet. UF 28 (1996) 619-632.

8017 **Verkuyl, Henk J.** A theory of aspectuality: the interaction between temporal and atemporal structure. Cambridge Studies in Linguistics 64: C 1996 CUP xvii; 393 pp. Bibl. 0-521-56452-2.

8018 *Vetter, Dieter* Was leistet die biblische Erzählung?: Beobachtung einer Stilform als Lese- und Verstehenshilfe. Das Judentum und seine Bibel. 1996 <1986>, ⇒154. 473-496.

8019 **Yule, George** The study of language. C ²1996, CUP viii; 294 pp. 0-521-56851-X.

XV. Postbiblica

κ1.1 **Pseudepigrapha [=catholicis 'Apocrypha']** *VT generalia*

8020 Apocrypha and Pseudepigrapha, Jewish-Hellenistic literature, Dead Sea scrolls [bibliography]. QS 66 (1996) 323-327.

8021 **Aranda Pérez, Gonzalo; García Martínez, Florentino; Pérez Fernandez, Miguel** Literatura judía intertestamentaria. Introducción al estudio de la Biblia 9: Estella 1996, Verbo Divino 576 pp. 84-7151-910-0. ᴿMEAH.H 45 (1996) 223-226 (*Ayaso Martínez, José R.*).

8022 **Bernabé, Massimo** Pseudepigrapha and medieval illustrated manuscripts of the Septuagint: prolegomenous reflections. JSPE 14 (1996) 85-90.

8023 **Bernstein, Moshe** Re-arrangement, anticipation and harmonization as exegetical features in the Genesis Apocryphon. DSD 3 (1996) 37-57.

8024 ᴱ**Carracedo Fraga, J.** Liber de ortu et obitu patriarcharum. CChr.SL 108 E: Turnhout 1996, Brepols 67; 131 pp. FB3.000. 2-503-50511-2 [EstB 55,568].

8025 ᴱ**Charlesworth, James H.; Evans, Craig A.** The Pseudepigrapha and early biblical interpretation. JSPE.S 14: 1993, ⇒11/2,6731. ᴿCBQ 58 (1996) 378-380 (*Elliott, Neil*).

8026 **Cimosa, Mario** La letteratura intertestamentaria. 1992, ⇒8,a239... 11/2,6732. ᴿBeO 38 (1996) 205-208 (*Jucci, Elio*).

8027 *Díez Merino, Luis* La esperanza de los cielos nuevos y la tierra nueva en la literatura judaica intertestamental. Esperanza del hombre. 1996, ⇒173. 351-377.

8028 *Eshai, Hanan* A note on the recently published text: the 'Joshua Apocryphon'. The centrality of Jerusalem. 1996, ⇒236. 89-93 [OTA 19,501].

8029 **Evans, Craig A.** Noncanonical writings & NT. 1992, ⇒9,10436; 11/2,6735. ᴿSR 25 (1996) 360-362 (*Desjardins, Michel*).

8030 *Hengel, Martin* Anonymität, Pseudepigraphie und "literarische Fälschung" in der jüdisch-hellenistischen Literatur. Judaica et Hellenistica. WUNT 90: 1996 <1972>. 196-251.

8031 ^E**Kaestli, J.D.; Marguerat, D.** Il mistero degli apocrifi: introduzione a una letteratura da scoprire. Mi 1996, Massimo 188 pp.
L20.000 [RdT 38/1,143].

8032 *Kraft, Robert A.* Scripture and canon in Jewish Apocrypha and
Pseudepigrapha. Antiquity [^E**Sæbø, Magne**]. 1996, ⇒γ1. 199-216.

8033 *Leicht, Reimund* A newly discovered Hebrew version of the
apocryphal 'Prayer of Manasseh' [T-S K 1.144, T-S K 21.95P and
T-S K 95.T]. JSQ 3 (1996) 359-373 [IAJS 44,2].

8034 **Nieto Ibáñez, Jesús Maria** La historia del judaísmo de época romana en los Apócrifos del Antiguo Testamento: la adaptación del
pasado bíblico. Sum. res. 147. Sef. 56 (1996) 127-147.

8035 ^E**Reeves, John C.** Tracing the threads: studies in the vitality of
Jewish Pseudepigrapha. 1994, ⇒10,257d; 11/2,6742. ^RCBQ 58
(1996) 190-192 (*Bergren, Theodore A.*).

8036 **Schwemer, Anna Maria** Studien zu den frühjüdischen Prophetenlegenden: *Vitae prophetarum.* TSAJ 49-50: Tü 1995-1996,
Mohr 2 vols. [vol. 1 Jes, Jer, Ez und Dan ⇒11/2,6746; vol. 2 Die
Viten der kleinen Propheten und der Propheten aus den Geschichtsbüchern. xvii; 389; 76* pp. DM298. 3-16-146440-0].
^RSNTU.A 21 (1996) 281-282 (*Fuchs, A.*); ThLZ 121 (1996) 1145-
1148 (*Tilly, Michael*);

8037 Synopse zu den Vitae Prophetarum. Studien zu den frühjüdischen
Prophetenlegenden. Tü 1996, Mohr 76 pp. Beiheft.

8038 *Smith, Morton* The eighth book of Moses and how it grew. New
Testament. 1996 <1984>, ⇒151. 217-226;

8039 Pseudepigraphy in the Israelite literary tradition. Studies in...
method. 1996 <1972>, ⇒150. 55-72.

κ1.2 Henoch

8040 **Davidson, Maxwell J.** Angels at Qumran: a comparative study of
1 Enoch 1-36, 72-108 and sectarian writings from Qumran. JSPE.S
11: 1992, ⇒9,10444; 11/2,6755. ^RJSSt 41 (1996) 336-339
(*Dimant, Devorah*).

8041 *Gleßmer, Uwe* Horizontal measuring in the Babylonian astronomical compendium MUL.APIN and in the astronomical book of 1En.
Henoch 18 (1996) 259-282.

8042 *Knibb, M.* Isaianic traditions in the book of Enoch. ^FMASON R.,
1996, ⇒57. 217-229.

8043 *Puech, Émile* Notes sur les fragments grecs du manuscrit 7Q4 = 1
Hénoch 103 et 105. RB 103 (1996) 592-600.

8044 *VanderKam, James C.* 1 Enoch, Enochic motifs, and Enoch in
early christian literature. Apocalyptic heritage. CRI 3: 1996,
⇒5757. 33-101.

8045 **VanderKam, James C.** Enoch: a man for all generations. Studies
on personalities of the Old Testament: Columbia, SC 1996, Univ.
of South Carolina Press ix; 207 pp. 1-57003-060-X.

κ1.3 Testamenta

8046 *Kugler, Robert A.* Some further evidence for the Samaritan provenance of Aramaic Levi (1QTestLevi; 4QTestLevi). RdQ 17 (1996)
351-358.

8047 **Kugler, Robert A.** From patriarch to priest: the Levi-Priestly tradition from Aramaic Levi to Testament of Levi. SBL Early Judaism and its Literature 9: Atlanta 1996, Scholars 264 pp. $33/$22. 0-7885-0177-1/8-X.

к1.5 Salomonis Odae *et psalmi*

8048 **Azar, Éphrem** Les Odes de Salomon: présentation et traduction. Sagesses chrétiennes: P 1996, Cerf 258 pp. FF145. 2-204-05351-1.
8049 **Franzmann, Majella** The Odes of Solomon. NTOA 20: 1991, ⇒9,10457... 11/2,6782. ᴿOCP 62 (1996) 238-240 (*Yousif, P.*).
8050 **Pierre, Marie-Joseph** Les Odes de Salomon. 1994, ⇒10,9600; 11/2,6783. ᴿThLZ 121 (1996) 256-257 (*Lattke, Michael*).
8051 *Rudolph, Kurt* War der Verfasser der Oden Salomos ein "Qumran-Christ"?: ein Beitrag zur Diskussion um die Anfänge der Gnosis. Gnosis. NHS 42: 1996 <1964>, ⇒147. 503-537.

8052 **Ward, Grant** A philological analysis of the Greek and the Syriac texts of the Psalms of Solomon. Diss. Temple 1996, ᴰ*Wright, R.*, 305 pp. EThL 74,175*.

к1.6 Jubilaea, Adam, Aḥiqar, Asenet, Ezekiel

8053 *Bonneau, Guy; Duhaime, Jean* Angélologie et légitimation socio-religieuse dans le livre des Jubilés. EeT(O) 27 (1996) 335-349.
8054 *Doering, Lutz* Jub 2,24 nach 4QJuba VII,17 und der Aufbau von Jub 2,17-33. BN 84 (1996) 23-28.
8055 **Halpern-Amaru, Betsy** Rewriting the bible: land and covenant in post-biblical Jewish literature. 1994, ⇒11/2,6784. ᴿJAOS 116 (1996) 557-558 (*Attridge, Harold W.*).
8056 *Steck, Odil Hannes* Die getöten "Zeugen" und die verfolgten "Tora-Sucher" in Jub 1,12: ein Beitrag zur Zeugnis-Terminologie des Juiläenbuches (II). ZAW 108 (1996) 70-86.
8057 *VanderKam, James C.* Jubilees' exegetical creation of Levi the priest. RdQ 17 (1996) 359-373.

8058 ᴱ**Stone, Michael E.** Armenian apocrypha relating to Adam and Eve. SVTP 14: Lei 1996, Brill xviii; 225 pp. 90-04-10663-4;
8059 *Genesis 1-4*; *Penitence of Adam*; *Book of Adam*. Texts and concordances of the Armenian Adam literature, 1. SBLEJL 12: Atlanta 1996, Scholars ii; 334 pp. $50. 0-7885-0278-6 [CBQ 59,208].

8060 *Cazelles, Henri* Ahiqar, *umman* et *amûn*. Études. 1996 <1995>, ⇒120. 243-252.

8061 **Standhartinger, Angela** Das Frauenbild im Judentum der hellenistischen Zeit... 'Joseph und Aseneth'. 1995, ⇒11/2,6800. ᴿThLZ 121 (1996) 1149-1153 (*Sänger, Dieter*).
8062 **Wills, Lawrence M.** The Jewish novel in the ancient world. 1995, ⇒11/2,6801. ᴿJThS 47 (1996) 583-584 (*Schaper, Joachim*).

8063   **Mueller, James R.** The five fragments of the *Apocryphon of Eze-
       kiel.* JSPE.S 5: 1994, ⇒10,9608. ᴿJThS 47 (1996) 192-194
       (*Bauckham, Richard*).

κ1.7 Apocalypses, ascensiones

8064   **Frankfurter, David** Elijah in Upper Egypt: the Apocalypse of Eli-
       jah and early Egyptian christianity. 1993, ⇒9,10466; 11/2,6808.
       ᴿJAC 39 (1996) 287-289 (*Dehandschutter, Boudewijn*).
8065   *Frankfurter, David* The legacy of Jewish apocalypses in early Chri-
       stianity: regional trajectories. Apocalyptic heritage. CRI 3: 1996,
       ⇒5757. 129-200.
8066   **Harlow, Daniel C.** The Greek *Apocalypse of Baruch (3 Baruch)* in
       Hellenistic Judaism and early christianity. SVTP 12: Lei 1996,
       Brill xvi; 263 pp. $104.50. 90-04-10309-0 [OTA 19,552].
8067   **Himmelfarb, Martha** Ascent to heaven in Jewish and christian
       apocalypses. 1993, ⇒10,8873; 11/2,6803. ᴿAJSR 21 (1996) 153-
       157 (*Halperin, David J.*); JThS 47 (1996) 590-592 (*Rowland,
       C.C.*).
8068   ᴱ**Kapler, C.** Apocalypses et voyages dans l'au-delà. 1987,
       ⇒3,3625... 6,9977. ᴿRET 56 (1996) 121-122 (*Trebolle Barrera,
       J.*).
8069   **Knight, Jonathan** Disciples of the beloved one: the christology,
       social setting and theological context of the Ascension of Isaiah.
       JSPE.S 18: Shf 1996, JSOT 354 pp. 1-85075-558-2.
8070   *Nuvolone, Flavio G.* Apocalypse d'Esdras grecque et latine, rap-
       ports et rhétorique. Sum. rés. 81. Apocrypha 7 (1996) 81-108.
8071   *Staples, Peter* D.W. Rɪᴅᴅʟᴇ e la funzione sociale di apocalissi e
       martirologi: un recupero critico. ᵀ*Stein, Elisabeth*, ReSo 11/1
       (1996) 48-62.
8072   **Tardieu, Michel; Hadot, Pierre** Recherches sur la formation de
       l'Apocalypse de Zostrien et les sources de Marius Vɪᴄᴛᴏʀɪɴᴜs:
       "Porphyre et Victorinus": questions et hypothèses. Res Orientales
       9: Bures-sur-Yvette 1996, Groupe pour l'Étude de la Civilisation
       du Moyen-Orient 157 pp. Bibl. 2-9508266-3-6.

κ2.1 Philo judaeus alexandrinus

       Amir, Y. La letteratura giudeo-ellenistica... Fɪʟᴏɴᴇ ⇒1065.
8073   *Begg, Christopher T.* The golden calf episode according to
       Psᴇᴜᴅᴏ-Pʜɪʟᴏ. Studies in... Exodus. BEThL 126: 1996,
       ⇒1794. 577-594.
8074   **Birnbaum, Ellen** The place of Judaism in Pʜɪʟᴏ's thought:
       Israel, Jews, and proselytes. BJSt 290; StPhilo.M 2; Atlanta 1996,
       Scholars xviii; 262 pp. $40. 0-7885-0182-8 [JSJ 28,365].
8075   *Borgen, Peder* Autobiographical ascent reports: Pʜɪʟᴏ and John
       the seer;
8076   Illegitimate invasion and proper ascent: a study of passages in
       Pʜɪʟᴏ's writings and the Revelation to John. Early christianity.
       1996, ⇒92. 309-320/293-307;

8077 PHILO of Alexandria—a systematic philosopher or an eclectic editor: an examination of his *Exposition of the laws of Moses*. Sum. 115. SO 71 (1996) 115-134;
The Sabbath controversy in Jn 5:1-18 and PHILO's writings ⇒5544.

8078 *Carlier, Caroline* Sur un titre latin du *De Vita Contemplativa*. StPhilo 8 (1996) 58-72.

8079 *Cazeaux, Jacques* Être juif et parler grec: l'allégorie de PHILON. Les premières traditions. 1996, ⇒159. 165-204 [OTA 20,133].

8080 **Cohen, Naomi G.** PHILO Judaeus: his universe of discourse. BEAT 24: 1995, ⇒11/2,6818. RJQR 86 (1996) 510-515 (*Winston, David*); JSJ 27 (1996) 338-342 (*Fuglseth, Kaare Sigvald*).

8081 **Decharneux, Baudouin** L'ange, le devin et le prophète: chemins de la parole dans l'oeuvre de PHILON d'Alexandrie dit 'le juif'. Spiritualités et pensées libres 2: Bru 1994, Université de Bruxelles 160 pp. FB650/FF120. RCBQ 58 (1996) 704-705 (*Reeves, John C.*); VigChr 50 (1996) 428-429 (*Runia, D.T.*).

8082 *Dihle, Albrecht* Das Streben nach Vollkommenheit nach PHILON und GREGOR von Nyssa. FDASSMANN E., JAC.E 23: 1996, ⇒19. 329-335.

8083 *Feldman, Louis H.* JOSEPHUS' Jewish Antiquities and PSEUDO-PHILO's Biblical Antiquities. Studies in Hellenistic Judaism. AGJU 30: 1996 <1989>, ⇒124. 57-82.

8084 TEGraffigna, Paola FILONE d'Alessandria: *La vita contemplativa*. 1992, ⇒9,10475. RBeO 38 (1996) 269-270 (*Jucci, Elio*).

8085 *Hahn, Ferdinand* Die Gestalt Abrahams in der Sicht PHILOS. FHAHN F., 1996 <1993>, ⇒34. 160-171.

8086 *Jackson, H.M.* Echoes and demons in the Pseudo-Philonic *Liber Antiquitatum Biblicarum*. JSJ 27 (1996) 1-20.

8087 **Jacobson, Howard** A commentary on PSEUDO-PHILO's *Liber antiquitatum biblicarum*. AGJU 31: Lei 1996, Brill 2 vols; xvi; 1370 pp. Latin text, Eng. transl. *f*432. 90-04-10360-0. RJQR 86 (1996) 456-459 (*Harrington, Daniel J.*).

8088 **Laporte, Jean** Théologie liturgique de PHILON d'Alexandrie et d'ORIGENE. 1995, ⇒11/2,6835. RJThS 47 (1996) 646-648 (*Edwards, M.J.*).

8089 **Levison, John R.** Torah and covenant in PSEUDO-PHILO's *Liber antiquitatum biblicarum*. Bund und Tora. WUNT 92: 1996, ⇒1645. 111-127.

8090 *Mach, Michael* PHILO von Alexandrien. TRE 26 (1996) 523-531.

8091 **Mattila, Sharon Lea** Wisdom, sense perception, nature, and PHILO's gender gradient. HThR 89 (1996) 103-129.

8092 **Murphy, Frederick J.** PSEUDO-PHILO: rewriting the bible. 1993, ⇒9,10486... 11/2,6839. RAJSR 21 (1996) 134-139 (*Mathews, Susan F.*).

8093 *Nielsen, Donald A.* La misura divina: creazione e retribuzione nel libro della Sapienza in FILONE: aspetti dell'incontro fra giudaismo ed ellenismo. TStein, Elisabeth, Religioni e Società 11/1 (1996) 9-21.

8094 **Nikiprowetzky, Valentin** Études philoniennes. Patrimoines, Judaïsme: P 1996, Cerf 332 pp. FF120. 2-204-05235-3 [EThL 73,167].

8095 *Paul, André* De l'Intertestament à la christologie. FLEGASSE. LeDiv 166: 1996, ⇒51. 91-120.

8096 *Royse, James R.* YONGE's collection of fragments of PHILO. St-Philo 8 (1996) 107-121.
8097 *Runia, D.T. (al),* PHILO of Alexandria: an annotated bibliography 1993. StPhilo 8 (1996) 122-142.
8098 **Runia, David** PHILO of Alexandria and the church fathers: a collection of papers. VigChr.S 32: Lei 1995, Brill 300 pp. £64.25. 90-04-10355-4. RJJS 47 (1996) 164-165 (*Edwards, M.J.*);
8099 PHILO in early christian literature. 1993, ⇒9,10494... 11/2,6845. RRB 103 (1996) 310-311 (*Nodet, Étienne*).
8100 *Runia, David T.* A provisional bibliography 1994-96. StPhilo 8 (1996) 143-154.
8101 **Sly, Dorothy I.** PHILO's Alexandria. L 1996, Routledge xi; (7) 200 pp. 0-415-09679-0.
8102 *Sterling, Gregory E.* PHILO and mysticism. StPhilo 8 (1996) 73.
8103 *Strickert, Fred* PHILO on the cherubim. StPhilo 8 (1996) 40-57.
8104 *Whittaker, John* The terminology of the rational soul in the writings of PHILO of Alexandria. StPhilo 8 (1996) 1-20.
8105 *Winston, David* PHILO's mysticism. StPhilo 8 (1996) 74-82.

κ2.4 *Evangelia apocrypha*—Apocryphal Gospels

8106 *Autané, Maurice* Du bon usage des Apocryphes. DosB 65 (1996) 25-26.
8107 *Bauer, Johannes B.* Schriftrezeption in den neutestamentlichen Apokryphen. FDASSMANN E., JAC.E 23: 1996, ⇒19. 43-48.
8108 **Bovon, François** Révélations NT/apocryphe. 1993, ⇒9,186; 11/2,6861. RSEÅ 61 (1996) 149-150 (*Hartman, Lars*); EstB 54 (1996) 561-563 (*Urbán, A.*).
8109 *Chevillard, Jean; Gruson, Philippe* Le protévangile de Jacques. DosB 65 (1996) 15-18.
8110 **Cross, James E.** Two Old English apocrypha and their manuscript source: 'The gospel of Nicodemus' and 'The avenging of the Saviour'. CSASE 19: C 1996, CUP xi; 307 pp. $65 [JEarlyC 6,331—Smith, Clyde Curry].
8111 *Dubreucq, Marc* L'évangile de Pierre. DosB 65 (1996) 10-13.
8112 **Elliott, J.K.** The Apocryphal NT. 1993, ⇒9,10505... 11/2,6863. RBibl.Interp. 4 (1996) 233-235 (*Bauckham, Richard*).
8113 *Ghiberti, Giuseppe* La risurrezione di Gesù nell'*Evangelium Petri* in rapporto ai vangeli canonici. Atti del IV Simposio. 1996, ⇒263. 219-243.
8114 EGruson, Philippe Les évangiles apocryphes. DosB 65 (1996) 2-26.
8115 EHoffmann, R. Joseph The secret gospels: a harmony of apocryphal Jesus traditions. Westminster College-Oxford: critical studies in religion: Amherst, NY 1996, Prometheus 196 pp. $33. 1-57392-069-X [BiTod 35,262].
8116 EKaestli, Jean Daniel; Marguerat, Daniel Le mystère apocryphe. 1995, ⇒11/2,6869. RBLE 97 (1996) 296-298 (*Debergé, P.*); FV 95/5 (1996) 84-85 (*Carrez, Maurice*).
8117 *Le Saux, Madeleine* Les Apocryphes dans la foi des chrétiens. DosB 65 (1996) 22-24.
8118 *Paupert, Catherine* L'apocryphe, fable catéchétique. Sum. rés. 249. Apocrypha 7 (1996) 249-251.

8119 ᵀᴱRagg, Lonsdale; Ragg, Laura El evangelio de Bernabé. ᵀAnzaldúa-Morales, Mohammad Alí, Chihuahua, México 1994, Anzaldúa-Morales, Mohammad Alí ix; 124 pp. Ed. y trad. del manuscrito italiano de la Biblioteca Imperial de Viena. ᴿIslamochristiana 22 (1996) 302-303 (Bernabé-Pons, Luis F.).

8120 Rassart-Debergh, Marguerite Littérature apocryphe et art copte. Sum. rés. 253. Apocrypha 7 (1996) 253-259.

8121 Rebell, Walter Les apocryphes—textes concurrentiels du Nouveau Testament. Sum. rés. 243. Apocrypha 7 (1996) 243-247.

8122 Tescaroli, Livio Letteratura cristiana extracanonica del primo secolo. Saggi e testi storici 22: L'Aquila 1996, Japadre 567 pp. 88-7006-340-1.

8123 Turner, Martha Lee The gospel according to Philip: the sources and coherence of an early christian collection. NHMS 38: Lei 1996, Brill xi; 283 pp. $95. 90-04-10443-7 [JEarlyC 5,317].

8124 Van den Broek, Roelof Der Bericht des koptischen KYRILLOS von Jerusalem über das Hebräerevangelium. Studies in gnosticism [ᴱVan den Broek, R.]. Nag Hammadi studies 39: 1996, ⇒м1.1. 142-156.

8125 Van der Horst, P.W. Exegetische notities over Maria in het "Protevangelium Jacobi". NedThT 50 (1996) 108-121.

к2.7 Alia apocrypha NT—Apocryphal Acts of apostles

8126 ANDREAS: MacDonald, Dennis R. Christianizing HOMER... Acts of Andrew. 1994, ⇒11/2,6879. ᴿJBL 115 (1996) 163-165 (Burrus, Virginia).

8127 BARTHOLOMAEUS: Van den Berg-Onstwedder, Gonnie A new fragment of the Apocryphon of Bartholomew the Apostle. GöMisz 150 (1996) 37-41.

8128 JACOBUS: Nagel, Peter Hinab oder hinauf?: ein mißverstandenes Ortsadverb in der Epistula Jacobi apocrypha. GöMisz 152 (1996) 43-49.

8129 JOHANNES: Van den Broek, Roelof Autogenes and Adamas: the mythological structure of the Apocryphon of John;

8130 The creation of Adam's psychic body in the Apocryphon of John;

8131 Von der jüdischen Weisheit zum gnostischen Erlöser: zum Schlußhymnus des Apokryphons des Johannes. Studies in gnosticism [ᴱVan den Broek, R.]. Nag Hammadi studies 39: 1996, ⇒м1.1. 56-66/67-85/86-116.

8132 PAULUS: Adamik, Tamás The baptized lion in the Acts of Paul. Apocryphal Acts of Paul. 1996, ⇒8136. 60-74.

8133 ᴱᵀAmat Rousseau, Jacqueline Passion de Perpétue et de Félicité (suivi des) Actes. SC 417: P 1996, Cerf 318 pp. Introd., texte critique, tr., comm.; FF293. 2-204-05386-4 [RTL 29,385—Gryson, R.].

8134 Bolyki, János Events after the martyrdom: missionary transformation of an apocalyptical metaphor in Martyrium Pauli;

8135 Bremmer, Jan N. Magic, martyrdom and women's liberation in the Acts of Paul and Thecla. Apocryphal Acts of Paul. 1996, ⇒8136. 92-106/36-59.

8136 ^E**Bremmer, Jan Nicolaas** The apocryphal Acts of Paul and Thecla. Studies on the Apocryphal Acts of the Apostles 2: Kampen 1996, Kok (6) vi; 210 pp. ƒ59.80. 90-390-0152-9 [JSJ 28,365].

8137 **Carozzi, Claude** Eschatologie et au-delà: recherches sur l'*Apocalypse de Paul*. 1994, ⇒10,9639c; 11/2,6890. ^RRHR 213 (1996) 222-224 (*Delage, Étienne*).

8138 *Dunn, Peter W.* The influence of 1 Corinthians on the Acts of Paul. SBL.SPS 35: 1996, ⇒274. 438-454.

8139 *Herczeg, Pál* New Testament parallels to the apocryphal Acta Pauli documents. Apocryphal Acts of Paul. 1996, ⇒8136. 142-149.
      Lalleman, P. The resurrection in the Acts of Paul ⇒4740.

8140 *Lalleman, Pieter J.; Misset-Van de Weg, Magda* Bibliography of Acts of Paul;

8141 *Luttikhuizen, Gerard* The apocryphal correspondence with the Corinthians and the Acts of Paul. Apocryphal Acts of Paul. 1996, ⇒8136. 191-198/75-91.

8142 *McConvery, Brendan* The Acts of Thecla. BiTod 34 (1996) 183-187.

8143 *Misset-Van de Weg, Magda* A wealthy woman named Tryphaena: patroness of Thecla of Iconium. Apocryphal Acts of Paul. 1996, ⇒8136. 16-35.

8144 *Pervo, Richard I.* The "Acts of Titus": a preliminary translation with an introduction, notes, and appendices. SBL.SPS 35: 1996, ⇒274. 455-482.

8145 *Pesthy, Monika* Thecla among the Fathers of the church. Apocryphal Acts of Paul. 1996, ⇒8136. 164-178.

8146 ^{TE}**Sitarz, Eugen** Die Taten der Thekla: Geschichte einer Jüngerin des Apostels Paulus. Ill. *Broczkowska, Beata*, Ostfildern 1996, Schwaben 104 pp. DM36. 3-7966-0776-4 [NThAR 1997,70].

8147 *Stricher, Joseph* Les Actes de Paul et de Thècle. DosB 65 (1996) 19-21.

8148 PETRUS: *Matthews, Christopher R.* Nicephorus Callistus' physical description of Peter: an original component of the 'Acts of Peter'?. Sum. rés. 135. Apocrypha 7 (1996) 135-145.

8149 PHILIPPUS: ^E**Amsler, Frédéric** Actes de l'apôtre Philippe. ^T*Bovon, François; Bouvier, Bertrand*, Apocryphes 8: Turnhout 1996, Brepols 318 pp. 2-503-50422-1 [RB 104,469].

8150 *Amsler, Frédéric* The apostle Philip, the viper, the leopard, and the kid: the masked actors of a religious conflict in Hierapolis of Phrygia (Acts of Philip VIII-XV and Martyrdom);

8151 *Matthews, Christopher R.* Peter and Philip upside down: perspectives on the relation of the Acts of Philip to the Acts of Peter;

8152 *Painchaud, Louis* La composition de l'évangile selon Philippe (NH II,3): une analyse rhétorique. SBL.SPS 35: 1996, ⇒274. 432-437/23-34/35-66.

8153 *Beatrice, Pier Franco* Traditions apocryphes dans la 'Théosophie de Tübingen'. Sum. rés. 109. Apocrypha 7 (1996) 109-122.

8154 *Fleith, Barbara* Die 'Legenda aurea' und ihre dominikanischen Bruderlegendare: Aspekte der Quellenverhälnisse apokryphen Gedankenguts. Rés. Zsfg. 167. Apocrypha 7 (1996) 167-192.

8155 ^E**Pietersma, Albert** The Apocryphon of Jannes and Jambres... Chester Beatty XVI. Religions in the Greco-Roman World 119:

1994, ⇒10,9643*; 11/2,6902. ᴿJAOS 116 (1996) 562-563 (*Desjardins, Michel*); RHPhR 76 (1996) 242-244 (*Maraval, P.*).

8156 *Rey, André-Louis* 'Homerocentra' et littérature apocryphe chrétienne: quels rapports?. Sum. rés. 123. Apocrypha 7 (1996) 123-134.

8157 *Strus, Andrzej* La passione di Santo Stefano in due manoscritti greci. Sal. 58 (1996) 21-61.

8158 *Vicent, A.* La conversión de Caifás y el hallazgo de sus huesos. EstB 54 (1996) 35-78.

к3.1 Qumran—*generalia*

8159 Apocrypha and Pseudepigrapha, Jewish-Hellenistic literature, Dead Sea scrolls [bibliography]. QS 66 (1996) 323-327.

8160 *Bearman, Gregory; Spiro, Sheila* Imaging: clarifying the issues. DSD 3 (1996) 321-328.

8161 **Betz, O.; Riesner, R.** Gesù, Qumran e il Vaticano. Città del Vaticano 1996, LEV 271 pp. L30.000. ᴿTer. 47 (1996) 660-661 (*Borrell, Agustí*) [RdT 37,427].

8162 ᴱ**Brooke, George J.** New Qumran texts and studies. StTDJ 15: 1992, ⇒10,307. ᴿOLZ 91 (1996) 583-588 (*Fabry, Heinz-Josef*); ThLZ 121 (1996) 32-34 (*Betz, Otto*);

8163 Introduction and catalogue. Collab. *Bond, Helen K.*, The Allegro Qumran collection: supplement to the Dead Sea Scrolls on microfiche. Lei 1996, Brill 51 pp. + 30 microfiches. $613 ($499). 90-04-10558-1 [RdQ 18,149].

8164 **Campbell, Jonathan** Deciphering the Dead Sea Scrolls. L 1996, Fontana 220 pp. £8. 0-00-638466-8 [ET 108,383].

8165 **Charlesworth, J.H.** Graphic Concordance to the Dead Sea scrolls. 1991, ⇒7,9857... 11/2,6911. ᴿDSD 3 (1996) 66-68 (*Hempel, Charlotte*).

8166 **Cook, Edward M.** Solving the mysteries of the Dead Sea scrolls: new light on the bible. 1994, ⇒10,9650; 11/2,6914. ᴿCBQ 58 (1996) 108-109 (*Schuller, Eileen*).

8167 *Cook, Edward M.* What was Qumran?: a ritual purification center. BArR 22/6 (1996) 37, 39, 48-51, 73-75.

8168 **Cross, Frank Moore** The ancient library of Qumran. ³1995, ⇒11/2,6917. ᴿDSD 3 (1996) 68-70 (*Brooke, George J.*).

8169 *Dahmen, Ulrich* Weitere Nachträge zur Qumran-Konkordanz. ZAH 9 (1996) 109-128.

8170 *Davies, P.* Notes en marge: reflections on the publication of DJDJ 5. Qumranstudien. 1996, ⇒8176. 103-109.

8171 *Davies, Philip R.* How not to do archaelogy: the story of Qumran. Sects and scrolls. SFSHJ 134: 1996 <1988>, ⇒122. 79-87.

8172 *Dombrowski, Bruno W.W.* Qumranologica II, III. FolOr 32 (1996) 165-182, 183-199.

8173 **Dupont-Sommer, André** Les écrits esséniens découverts près de la Mer Morte. Préf. *Philonenko, Marc*, Histoire: P ²1996 <1959>, Payot vi; 468 pp. FF220. 2-228-89043-X [BCLF 580,2412].

8174 **Eisenman, Robert H.; Wise, Michael** Manoscritti segreti di Qumran. 1994, ⇒11/2,6926. ᴿCivCatt 147 III (1996) 434-436 (*Scaiola, D.*).

8175 *Fabry, Heinz-Josef* Theologisches Wörterbuch zu den Qumrantexten (ThWQ). ZAH 9 (1996) 49-51.

8176 ᴱ**Fabry, Heinz-Josef; Lange, Armin; Lichtenberger, Hermann** Qumranstudien: Vorträge und Beiträge der Teilnehmer des Qumranseminars auf dem internationalen Treffen der Society of Biblical Literature, Münster, 1993. SIJD 4: Gö 1996, Vandenhoeck & R. x; 252 pp. DM98. 3-525-54202-X.

8177 ᵀ**García Martínez, Florentino** The Dead Sea Scrolls translated: the Qumran texts in English. (*a*), 1994, ⇒10,9661; 11/2,6933. ᴿRB 103 (1996) 289-290 (*Murphy-O'Connor, J.*);

8178 (*b*), ²1996, lxvii; 519 pp. $30. 0-8028-4193-7. ᴿFolOr 32 (1996) 172-174; 184-189 (*Dombrowski, Bruno W.W.*);

8179 Textos de Qumrán. 1992, ⇒10,9659. ᴿMEAH 42/2 (1993) 227-228 (*Pérez Fernández, Miguel*).

8180 *García Martínez, Florentino* Nouveaux livres sur les manuscrits de la Mer Morte. JSJ 27 (1996) 46-74.

8181 **García Martínez, Florentino; Parry, Donald W.** A bibliography of the finds in the Desert of Judah 1970-1995. StTDJ 19: Lei 1996, Brill x; 561 pp. *f*250/$161.50. 90-04-10588-3 [JSOT 74,121].

8182 **García Martínez, Florentino; Trebolle Barrera, Julio** Os homens de Qumran: literatura, estrutura e concepções religiosas. ᵀ*Gonçalves Pereira, Fernando*, Petrópolis 1996, Vozes 300 pp. 85-326-1651-8 [PerTeol 29,284];

8183 Gli uomini di Qumran: letteratura, struttura sociale e concezioni religiose. ᴱ*Catastini, Alessandro*, StBi 113: Brescia 1996, Paideia 374 pp. L50.000. 88-394-0535-6 [Gr. 78,210].

8184 **Golb, Norman** Wer schrieb die Schriftrollen vom Toten Meer?. ᵀ*Rinne, Olga*, Hamburg 1994, Hoffmann u. C. 544 pp. DM58. 3-455-11024-X. ᴿFolOr 32 (1996) 165-171 (*Dombrowski, Bruno W.W.*);

8185 Who wrote the Dead Sea scrolls?. 1995, ⇒11/2,6935. ᴿFolOr 32 (1996) 165-172 (*Dombrowski, Bruno W.W.*).

8186 **Harrington, Daniel J.** Wisdom texts from Qumran. Literature of the Dead Sea Scrolls: L 1996, Routledge. $17. 0-415-13907-4 [NThAR 1997,131].

8187 **Humbert, Jean-Baptiste; Chambon, Alain** Fouilles de Khirbet Qumrân et de Aïn Feshkha 1: album et photographies. 1994, ⇒10,9663; 11/2,6939. ᴿOLZ 91 (1996) 532-540 (*Strobel, August*); ThLZ 121 (1996) 446-448 (*Maurer, Alexander*); RivAC 72 (1996) 426-427 (*Hamarneh, Basema*).

8188 *Kapera, Zdzisław J.* New research on Qumran in eastern Europe. Qumranstudien. 1996, ⇒8176. 165-189;

8189 Chirbet Qumran: osiedle mnichów czy villa rustica? [Chirbet Qumran: situs monachroum an villa rustica?]. RBL 49 (1996) 18-28. **P.**;

8190 Forty-eight years of Qumran studies;

8191 Hans Burgmann's bibliography on the Dead Sea Scrolls: addenda <1993>. ᴹBurgmann H., 1996, ⇒12. 141-167/209-212.

ᴱ**Kapera, Z.** Mogilany 1993: papers on the Dead Sea Scrolls. ᴹBurgmann H ⇒12.

8192 ᴱ**Kronholm, Tryggve** Qumranlitteraturen: fynden och forskningsresultaten: föreläsningar vid ett symposium i Stockholm.

Kungl. Vitterhets Historie och Antikvitets Akademien 35: Stockholm 1996, Almqvist & W. 163 pp. Arrangerat av Kungl. Vitterhets Historie och Antikvitets Akademien. Sum. 91-7402-260-1 [NThAR 1997,193].

8193 *Levine, Baruch A.* The contribution of Jonas GREENFIELD to the study of Dead Sea literature. DSD 3 (1996) 2-9.

8194 *Lichtenberger, H.* Das Rombild in den Texten von Qumran. Qumranstudien. 1996, ⇒8176. 221-231.

8195 *Magness, Jodi* What was Qumran?: not a country villa. BArR 22/6 (1996) 37-38, 40-47, 72-73.

8196 **Maier, Johann** Die Qumran-Essener: die Texte vom Toten Meer: Bd. 1, Die Texte der Höhlen 1-3 u. 5-11; Bd. 2, Die Texte der Höhle 4; Bd. 3, Einführung, Zeitrechnung, Register u. Bibl. UTB 1862, 1863, 1916: Tü 1995-1996, Mohr xxvi; 441; viii; 741; xvi; 478 pp. DM49.80+49.80+49.80. 3-8252-1862-7/3-5/1916-X. RFolOr 32 (1996) 183-189 (*Dombrowski, Bruno W.W.*).

8197 **Muchowski, Piotr** Rękopisy znad Morza Martwego: Qumran-Wadu Murabba'at-Masada. Biblioteka zwojów tlo Nowego Testamentu 5: Kraków 1996, Enigma xxxi; 477 pp. 16 pl. 83-86110-23-6 [JSJ 28,367]. **P**.

8198 *Muraoka, Takamitsu* Notae qumranicae philologicae. RdQ 17 (1996) 573-583.

8199 *Nir-El, Yoram; Broshi, Magen* The black ink of the Qumran scrolls. DSD 3 (1996) 157-167.

8200 *Parry, Donald W.; Booras, Steven W.* The Dead Sea scrolls CD-ROM database project. Current research... on the Dead Sea Scrolls. StTDJ 20: 1996, ⇒293. 239-250.

8201 E**Piñero, Antonio,** (*al*), Los manuscritos del Mar Muerto: balance de hallazgos y de cuarenta años de estudio. 1994, ⇒10,9671*. RRevBib 58 (1996) 117-119 (*Levoratti, A.J.*).

8202 **Price, Randall** Secrets of the Dead Sea scrolls. Eugene, Or. 1996, Harvest 535 pp. 1-56507-454-8 [NThAR 1997,226].

8203 *Puech, Émile* Du bilinguisme à Qumrân?. Mosaïque de langues. 1996, ⇒284. 171-189.

8204 E**Reed, Stephen A.** The Dead Sea scrolls catalogue. SBLRBS 32: 1994, ⇒10,9673... 11/2,6949. RHebStud 37 (1996) 187-190 (*Seely, David Rolph*).

8205 *Riesner, Rainer* Archäologische Neuigkeiten aus Qumran. BiKi 51 (1996) 184-185.

8206 **Rohrhirsch, Ferdinand** Wissenschaftstheorie und Qumran: die Geltungsbegründung von Aussagen in der Biblischen Archäologie am Beispiel von Chirbet Qumran und En Feschcha. NTOA 32: FrS 1996, Universitätsverlag xii; 408 pp. FS110. 3-7278-1076-9 [JSJ 28,368].

8207 *Sacchi, Paolo* I manoscritti del Mar Morto: bilancio di un fatto culturale. FMOSCATI S., I, 1996, ⇒67. 383-392.

8208 **Schiffman, Lawrence H.** Reclaiming the Dead Sea scrolls. 1994, ⇒10,9676; 11/2,6950. RJud. 52 (1996) 66-69 (*Lange, Armin*).

8209 *Schiffman, Lawrence H.* Jerusalem in the Dead Sea scrolls. The centrality of Jerusalem. 1996, ⇒236. 73-88 [OTA 19,505].

8210 *Segert, Stanislav* Access to the Dead Sea scrolls—2. CV 38 (1996) 131-173.

8211 ᴱShanks, Hershel L'aventure des manuscrits de la Mer Morte. P 1996, Seuil 371 pp. FF140. 2-02-021417-2. ᴿRSR 84 (1996) 482-483 (*Guillet, Jacques*); EeV 106 (1996) 545-547 (*Cothenet, E.*).

8212 Słowo Towarzystwa Biblijnego w Polsce na Święto Biblii 1996 [Edictum Societatis Biblicae Poloniae in Festum Bibliorum A.D. 1996]. RBL 49 (1996) 18-28. **P**.

8213 **Soggin, J. Alberto** I manoscritti del Mar Morto. ²1995, ⇒11/2,6957. ᴿHenoch 18 (1996) 385-387 (*Sacchi, Paolo*).

8214 *Stoll, D.* Die Schriftrollen vom Toten Meer—mathematisch oder wie kann man einer Rekonstruktion Gestalt verleihen?. Qumranstudien. 1996, ⇒8176. 205-218.

8215 **Thordson, Thord; Thordson, Maria** Qumran and the Samaritans. Ingaro, Sweden 1996, Thordson 262 pp. 91-86366-03-3 [DSD 6,94ss—Hjelm, Ingrid].

8216 ᴱ**Tov, Emanuel,** (*al*), The Dead Sea scrolls on microfiche. 1993, ⇒9,10583... 11/2,6960. ᴿJAOS 116 (1996) 549-550 (*Kaufman, Stephen A.*);

8217 Companion volume to the Dead Sea scrolls microfiche edition. Lei ²1995 <1993>, Brill 187 pp. Bibl.; 9 pl. ƒ140/$80. 90-04-10288-4(B). ᴿJJS 47 (1996) 363-365 (*Falk, Daniel K.*).

8218 *Tov, Emanuel* "Discoveries in the Judaean desert". RdQ 17 (1996) 613-621;

8219 Scribal practices reflected in the documents from the Judean desert and in the rabbinic literature. ᶠHARAN M., 1996, ⇒35. 383-403.

8220 ᴱ**Trebolle Barrera, Julio,** (*al*), The Madrid Qumran Congress, 1991. StTDJ 11: 1992, ⇒8,498... 11/2,6961. ᴿDSD 3 (1996) 79-84 (*Bernstein, Moshe J.*); JAOS 116 (1996) 140-142 (*Kampen, John*).

8221 ᴱ**Ulrich, Eugene; VanderKam, James** The community of the renewed covenant. CJAn 10: 1994, ⇒11/2,538. ᴿCBQ 58 (1996) 395-396 (*Wise, Michael O.*).

8222 *Valtschanov, Slavtscho* Qumran in der bulgarischen Forschung. ᴹBURGMANN·H., 1996 <1993>, ⇒12. 169-173.

8223 **VanderKam, James** Dødehavsrullerne—teorier og kendsgerninger. Frederiksberg 1995, Anis xviii; 225 pp. ᴿSEÅ 61 (1996) 130-131 (*Krantz, Eva Strömberg*).

8224 **VanderKam, James C.** The Dead Sea Scrolls today. 1994, ⇒10,9683; 11/2,6962. ᴿRThom 96 (1996) 337-341 (*Ramlot, Léon*); ScrTh 28 (1996) 294-295 (*Ausín, S.*); HebStud 37 (1996) 190-192 (*Crawford, Sidnie White*); Jud. 52 (1996) 63-65 (*Lange, Armin*);

8225 Manoscritti del Mar Morto: il dibattito recente oltre le polemiche. R 1995, Città Nuova 232 pp. L28.000. ᴿCivCatt 147 II (1996) 628-630 (*Prato, G.L.*).

8226 **Vaux, Roland de** Die Ausgrabungen von Qumran und Ein Feschka 1A: die Grabungstagebücher. ᵀᴱ*Rohrhirsch, Ferdinand; Hofmeir, Bettina,* NTOA.Archaeologica A1: FrS 1996, Universitätsverlag xii; 230 pp. FS90. 3-7278-1073-4 [JSJ 28,368].

8227 **Vermes, Geza** The Dead Sea scrolls in English. ⁴1995. ⇒11/2,6963. ᴿDSD 3 (1996) 214-217 (*VanderKam, James C.*).

8228 ᴱ**Wacholder, Ben Zion; Abegg, Martin G.; Bowley, James** A preliminary edition of the unpublished Dead Sea Scrolls: the Hebrew and Aramaic texts from cave four: concordance of fascicles

1-3. Wsh 1996, Biblical Archaeology Society xvi; 403 pp. 1-880317-45-1 [DSD 4,229].

8229 ᴱWise, Michael Owen, (al), Methods of investigation of the Dead Sea scrolls and the Khirbet Qumran site. 1994, ⇒11/2,540. ᴿJBL 115 (1996) 185-186 (Burkes, Shannon).

8230 ᵀWise, Michael Owen; Abegg, Martin G., Jr.; Cook, Edward M. The Dead Sea scrolls: a new translation. SF 1996, HarperSanFrancisco xiv; 513 pp. $35. 0-06-069200-6 [ThD 44,358—Heiser, W. Charles].

8231 Woodward, Scott R., (al), Analysis of parchment fragments from the Judean desert using DNA techniques. Current research... on the Dead Sea Scrolls. StTDJ 20: 1996, ⇒293. 215-238.

8232 Zuckerman, Bruce Bringing the Dead Sea scrolls back to life: a new evaluation of photographic and electronic imaging of the Dead Sea scrolls. DSD 3 (1996) 178-207.

к3.4 Qumran, libri biblici et parabiblici

8233 Attridge, H. Qumran Cave 4, VIII: parabiblical texts, 1. DJD 13: 1994, ⇒10,9687; 11/2,6966b. ᴿJThS 47 (1996) 589-590 (Lim, Timothy H.); JJS 47 (1996) 322-336 (Ullendorff, Edward).

8234 Beckwith, Roger T. The Qumran psalter: the courses of the Levites and the use of the Psalms at Qumran. Calendar and chronology. AGJU 33: 1996, ⇒112. 141-166.

8235 Berger, Klaus Salmos de Qumrán. BA 1996, Lumen 192 pp. [Revista de Teología 33,61s—Castiglioni, Mario].

8236 Brin, Gershon Studies in 4Q424, fragment 3. VT 46 (1996) 271-295.

8237 ᴱBrooke, George Qumran Cave 4, XVII: parabiblical texts, 3. Collab. VanderKam, James; Milik, Jozef T.; Strugnell, John, DJD 22: Oxf 1996, Clarendon xi; 351 pp. 29 pl. £80. 0-19-826936-6 [ZAW 109,446].

8238 Brooke, George J. 4Q252 as early Jewish commentary. RdQ 17 (1996) 385-401.

8239 Browning, Daniel C. Jr. The strange search for the ashes of the red heifer [3Q15]. BA 59 (1996) 74-89.

8240 Clayton, Ken Jesus and the scrolls: everyman's guide to christianity and the Dead Sea scrolls. Wilmslow, Cheshire 1992, Belvedere 256 pp. £6. 0-906463-01-7. ᴿDSD 3 (1996) 211-212 (Wright, N.T.).

8241 Collins, John J. Pseudo-Daniel revisited. RdQ 17 (1996) 111-135.

8242 Crawford, Sidnie White Has every book of the bible been found among the Dead Sea scrolls?. BiRe 12/5 (1996) 28-33, 56.

8243 Cross, Frank Moore Notes on the doctrine of the two Messiahs at Qumran and the extracanonical Daniel Apocalypse (4Q246). Current research... on the Dead Sea Scrolls. StTDJ 20: 1996, ⇒293. 1-13.

8244 Davies, Philip R.; Taylor, Joan E. On the testimony of women in 1QSa. DSD 3 (1996) 223-235.

8245 Davila, James R. The Hodayot hymnist and the four who entered paradise. RdQ 17 (1996) 457-478.

8246 Emerton, J.A. A note on two words in 4Q393. JJS 47 (1996) 348-351.

8247 *Fabry, Heinz-Josef* Methoden der Schriftauslegung in den Qumranschriften. [F]DASSMANN E., JAC.E 23: 1996, ⇒19. 18-33;

8248 Der Umgang mit der kanonisierten Tora in Qumran. Die Tora als Kanon. 1996, ⇒1308. 293-327.

8249 *Fletcher-Louis, Crispin* 4Q374: a discourse on the Sinai tradition: the deification of Moses and early christology. DSD 3 (1996) 236-252.

8250 *Flint, Peter W.* 4Qpseudo-Daniel ar/c (4Q245) and the restoration of the priesthood. RdQ 17 (1996) 137-150.

8251 *García Martínez, F.; Tigchelaar, Eibert J.C.* Psalms manuscripts from Qumran cave 11: a preliminary edition. RdQ 17 (1996) 73-107.

8252 [E]**García Martínez, Florentino** Testi di Qumran. [T]*Martone, Corrado,* Biblica: Studi e Testi 4: Brescia 1996, Paideia 796 pp. L98.000. 88-394-0540-2 [RTL 28,292].

8253 *Gleßmer, Uwe* Ein Psalmen-Fragment als Anfrage an exegetische Methodik. ZAH 9 (1996) 42-47.

8254 *Hamacher, E.* Die Sabbatopferlieder im Streit um Ursprung und Anfänge der jüdischen Mystik. JSJ 27 (1996) 119-154.

8255 *Hempel, Charlotte* The earthly Essene nucleus of 1QSa. DSD 3 (1996) 253-269.

8256 *Jack, Alison* An arboreal sign of the end-time (4Q385 2). JJS 47 (1996) 337-344.

8257 *Kallai, Zecharia* Samuel in Qumrân: expansion of a historiographical pattern (4QSam[a]). RB 103 (1996) 581-591 [1 Sam 10,27-11,3].

8258 *Lange, A.* 1QGenAp XIX10-XX32 as paradigm of the wisdom didactic narrative. Qumranstudien. 1996, ⇒8176. 191-204.

8259 *Lange, A.; Sieker, M.* Gattung und Quellenwert des Gebets des Nabonid. Qumranstudien. 1996, ⇒8176. 3-34.

8260 *Morgenstern, Matthew* A new cluse to the original length of the Genesis Apocryphon. JJS 47 (1996) 345-347.

8261 *Newsom, C.A.* 4Q378 and 4Q379: an Apocryphon of Joshua. Qumranstudien. 1996, ⇒8176. 35-85.

8262 **Nitzan, Bilhan** Qumran prayer and religious poetry. StTDJ 12: 1994, ⇒10,7309*; 11/2,6994. [R]AJSR 21 (1996) 389-392 (*Eshel, Hanan*); RSLR 32 (1996) 438-439 (*Martone, Corrado*).

8263 *Parry, Donald W.* 4QSam[a] and the tetragrammaton. Current research... on the Dead Sea Scrolls. StTDJ 20: 1996, ⇒293. 106-125.

8264 *Pfann, Stephen J.* 4QDaniel/d (4Q115): a preliminary edition with critical notes. RdQ 17 (1996) 37-71.

8265 *Pike, Dana M.* The book of Numbers at Qumran: texts and context. Current research... on the Dead Sea Scrolls. StTDJ 20: 1996, ⇒293. 166-193.

8266 *Puech, Emile* La prière de Nabonide (4Q242). [F]MCNAMARA M., JSOT.S 230: 1996, ⇒58. 208-227.

8267 **Qimron, Elisha; Strugnell, John** Miqsat Ma'aśeh Ha-Torah. Qumran Cave IV, 5. 1994, ⇒10,9693; 11/2,6968. [R]FolOr 32 (1996) 179-182 (*Dombrowski, Bruno W.W.*); AJSR 21 (1996) 145-148 (*Rendsburg, Gary A.*); HebStud 37 (1996) 119-125 (*Knohl, Israel*).

8268 *Ratzlaff, Richard* Prolegomena to a form-critical study of 1QS[b]. CSBS annual meeting 1996. Sum. BCSBS 55 (1995/1996) 18-19.

8269 **Skehan, P.W.**, (*al*), Qumran Cave 4—IV: Palaeo-Hebrew and Greek biblical manuscripts. DJD 9: 1992, ⇒8,a367... 10,9678. RBiOr 53 (1996) 798-800 (*Van der Kooij, A.*).

8270 **Steudel, Annette** Der Midrasch zur Eschatologie aus der Qumrangemeinde (4QMidrEschat[a.b]). 1994, ⇒10,9694; 11/2,7005. RRSLR 32 (1996) 435-437 (*Martone, Corrado*).

8271 *Stone, Michael E.* The Dead Sea scrolls and the Pseudepigrapha. DSD 3 (1996) 270-295.

8272 *Stone, Michael E.* The genealogy of Bilhah. DSD 3 (1996) 20-36;

8273 Testament of Naphtali. JJS 47 (1996) 311-321.

8274 *Stone, Michael E.; Greenfield, Jonas C.* The second manuscript of Aramaic Levi Document from Qumran (4QLevi[b] Aram);

8275 The third and fourth manuscripts of *Aramaic Levi Document* from Qumran (4QLevi[c] aram and 4QLevi[d] aram). Muséon 109 (1996) 1-15/245-259.

8276 *Talmon, Shemaryahu* Fragments of a Joshua Apocryphon—Masada 1039-211 (final photo 5254). JJS 47 (1996) 128-139.

8277 *Tov, Emanuel* Special layout of poetical units in the texts from the Judean desert. FVAN UCHELEN N., 1996, ⇒100. 115-128.

8278 E**Ulrich, Eugene**, (*al*), Qumran Cave 4 VII: Genesis to Numbers. DJD 12: 1994, ⇒11/2,6966a. RRT (1996/1) 98-99 (*Hempel, Charlotte*); JJS 47 (1996) 152-154 (*Herbert, Edward D.*); JThS 47 (1996) 190-192 (*Lim, Timothy H.*).

8279 *Ulrich, Eugene; Skehan, Patrick W.* An edition of 4QIsa/e including the former 4QIsa/l. RdQ 17 (1996) 23-36.

8280 *Van der Woude, A.S.* Once again: the wicked priests in the Habakkuk Pesher from cave 1 of Qumran. RdQ 17 (1996) 375-384.

8281 **Zdun, Pawel** PieŚni ofiary szabatoweij z Qumran i Masady [Songs of the sabbath sacrifice from Qumran and Masada]. Teksty z Pusyni Judznkiej 1: Kraków 1996, Enigma xxii; 198 pp. 83-86110-25-2 [Qumran Chronicle 7,253ss—Kapera, Zdzisław J]. **P.**

к3.5 *Qumran*—**varii rotuli et fragmenta**

8282 *Alexander, Philip S.* The redaction-history of Serekh ha-Yaḥad: a proposal. RdQ 17 (1996) 437-456.

8283 E**Baumgarten, Joseph** Qumran Cave 4 XIII: the Damascus Document (4Q266-273). Collab. *Milik, Józef T.; Pfann, Stephen; Yardeni, Ada*, DJD 18: Oxf 1996, Clarendon xix; 236 pp. 62 pl. £70. 0-19-826391-1.

8284 *Bernstein, Moshe J.* The employment and interpretation of scripture in 4QMMT: preliminary observations. Reading 4QMMT. 1996, ⇒8353. 29-51.

8285 TE**Charlesworth, James H.** The Dead Sea Scrolls: Hebrew, Aramaic, and Greek texts with English translations, (*a*), 1: Rule of the Community and related documents. 1994, ⇒10,9698. RJAC 39 (1996) 263-264 (*Maier, Johann*); AJS Review 21 (1996) 386-389 (*Rendsburg, Gary A.*); FolOr 32 (1996) 189-194 (*Dombrowski, Bruno W.W.*); ThLZ 121 (1996) 34-37 (*Maurer, Alexander*); RB 103 (1996) 288-289 (*Murphy-O'Connor, J.*); JJS 47 (1996) 361-363 (*Alexander, Philip S.*);

8286 (b), 2: Damascus Document, War Scroll, and related documents. Princeton Theological Seminary Dead Sea Scrolls Project 2: Tü 1994, Mohr xx; 229 pp. ᴿATG 59 (1996) 401-403 (Torres, A.).

8287 Charlesworth, James H.; Strawn, Brent A. Reflections on the text of Serek ha-Yaḥad found in cave IV. RdQ 17 (1996) 403-435.

8288 ᴱCharlesworth, James Hamilton; Rietz, Henry W.L. The Dead Sea Scrolls: Rule of the Community. 1996, $100. ⇒11/2,7018.

8289 Elman, Yaakov Some remarks on 4QMMT and the rabbinic tradition: or, when is a parallel not a parallel?. Reading 4QMMT. 1996, ⇒8353. 99-128.

8290 Eshel, Esther 4Q471b: a self-glorification hymn. RdQ 17 (1996) 175-203;

8291 4QMMT and the history of the Hasmonean period. Reading 4QMMT. 1996, ⇒8353. 53-65.

8292 Fröhlich, I. The biblical narratives in Qumran exegetical works (4Q252; 4Q180; the Damascus Document). Qumranstudien. 1996, ⇒8176. 111-124.

8293 García Martínez, Florentino 4QMMT in a Qumran context. Reading 4QMMT. 1996, ⇒8353. 15-27.

8294 Gmirkin, Russell The war scroll and Roman weaponry reconsidered. DSD 3 (1996) 89-129.

8295 Ibba, Giovanni Le lacune di 1QM I,3-5. Henoch 18 (1996) 251-258.

8296 Jiménez Bedman, Francisco Los términos סוח y סנה en el Rollo de Cobre (3Q15) [The lexical items סוח and סנה in the Copper Scroll (3Q15)]. Sum. res. 27. MEAH.H 45 (1996) 27-35.

8297 Kampen, John; Bernstein, Moshe J. Introduction. Reading 4QMMT. 1996, ⇒8353. 1-7.

8298 Kugler, Robert A note on 1QS 9:14: the sons of righteousness or the sons of Zadok?. DSD 3 (1996) 315-320.

8299 Lemaire, André Nouveaux fragments du Rouleau du Temple de Qumrân. RdQ 17 (1996) 271-274.

8300 Lundberg, Marilyn; Zuckerman, Bruce New Aramaic fragments from Qumran Cave One. CAL.N 12 (1996) 1-6.

8301 Maier, Johann Die Tempelrolle vom Toten Meer und das "Neue Jerusalem": 11Q19 und 11Q20; 1Q32, 2Q24, 4Q554-555, 5Q15 und 11Q18: Übersetzung und Erläuterung: mit Grundrissen der Tempelhofanlage und Skizzen zur Stadtplanung. UTB 829: Mü ³1996, Reinhardt lvi; 350 pp. 3-8252-0829-X.

8302 Martone, Corrado Hodayot e Regola della Guerra alla luce di un testo qumranico recentemente pubblicato. Henoch 18 (1996) 111-120.

8303 Metso, Sarianna The textual development of the Qumran Community Rule. Diss. Helsinki. Helsinki 1996, Yliopistopaino [StTh 51,87].

8304 Nitzan, Bilhah 4Q302/302a (Sap. A): Pap. praise of God and parable of the tree: a preliminary edition. RdQ 17 (1996) 151-173.

8305 Qimran, Elisha The nature of the reconstructed composite text of 4QMMT. Reading 4QMMT. 1996, ⇒8353. 9-13.

8306 Qimron, Elisha The Temple Scroll: a critical edition with extensive reconstructions. Judean Desert Studies: Beer Sheva 1996, Ben Gurion Univ. of the Negev Press 124 pp. $24. 965-21-030-7.

8307 Reed, Stephen A. Genre, setting and title of 4Q477. JJS 47 (1996) 147-148.

8308 *Schatzman, Israel* על הצבא במגילת מלחמת בני אור בבני חושך [The army of the sons of light in the War Scroll (1QM)]. 1996, [F]STERN M., 1996, ⇒87. Sum. 145*. 105-145. **H**.

8309 *Schiffman, Lawrence H.* The construction of the temple according to the Temple Scroll. RdQ 17 (1996) 555-571;

8310 The place of 4QMMT in the corpus of Qumran manuscripts. Reading 4QMMT. 1996, ⇒8353. 81-98.

8311 *Schuller, E.* The cave 4 Hodayot manuscripts: a preliminary description. Qumranstudien. 1996, ⇒8176. 87-100.

8312 *Schwartz, Daniel R.* MMT, JOSEPHUS and the Pharisees. Reading 4QMMT. 1996, ⇒8353. 67-80.

8313 *Seely, David Rolph* The Barki Nafshi texts (4Q434-439). Current research... on the Dead Sea Scrolls. StTDJ 20: 1996, ⇒293. 194-214.

8314 *Stegemann, Hartmut* Some remarks to 1QSa, to 1QSb, and to Qumran messianism. RdQ 17 (1996) 479-505.

8315 *Steudel, Annette* The eternal reign of the people of God—collective expectations in Qumran texts (4Q246 and 1QM). RdQ 17 (1996) 507-525.

8316 *Talmon, Shemaryahu; Knohl, Israel* A calendrical scroll from Qumran Cave 4: Mišmarot B[b] (4Q321[a]). [F]HARAN M., 1996, ⇒35. 65*-71*. **H**.

8317 [ET]**Wolters, Albert M.** The Copper Scroll: overview, text and translation. Shf 1996, Academic 55 pp. $20. 1-85075-793-4.

к3.6 Qumran et Novum Testamentum

8318 **Betz, Otto W.; Riesner, Rainer** Jezus, Qumran i Watykan: Kulisy Trzeciej Bitwy o Zwoje znad Morza Martwego. Biblioteka zwojów tlo NT 2: Kraków 1996, Enigma 237 pp. 83-86110-22-8. **P**.

8319 *Brooke, George J.* 4Q252 et le Nouveau Testament. [T]*Dunne, James*, Le déchirement. MoBi 32: 1996, ⇒192. 221-242.

8320 *Buchanan, George Wesley* 4Q246 and the political titles of Jesus. [M]BURGMANN H., 1996 <1993>, ⇒12. 77-87.

8321 [E]**Charlesworth, James H.** Jesus and the DSS. 1995, ⇒8,345... 11/2,7060. [R]DSD 3 (1996) 332-334 (*Brooke, George J.*).

8322 *Davies, Philip R.* Sadducees in the Dead Sea scrolls. Sects and scrolls. SFSHJ 134: 1996 <1990>, ⇒122. 127-138.

8323 *deSilva, David A.* The Dead Sea scrolls and early christianity. Sewanee Theological Review 39 (1996) 285-302 [OTA 19,501].

8324 *Di Palma, Gaetano* La papirologia e il Nuova Testamento. Asp. 43 (1996) 525-536 [Mk 6,52-53].

8325 *Eisenman, Robert H.* The Dead Sea scrolls and the first christians: essays and translations. Shaftesbury 1996, Element xxix; 449 pp. 1-85230-785-4 [NThAR 1997,260].

8326 *Kampen, John* 4QMMT and New Testament studies. Reading 4QMMT. 1996, ⇒8353. 129-144.

8327 *Paton, David M.* An evaluation of the hypothesis of Barbara THIERING concerning Jesus and the Dead Sea scrolls. [M]BURGMANN H., 1996 <1993>, ⇒12. 89-107.

8328 **Rosenberg, Roy A.** The veneration of divine justice: the Dead Sea scrolls and christianity. CSRel 40: 1995, ⇒11/2,7077. [R]JSJ 27

(1996) 85-87 (*Van der Woude, A.S.*); DSD 3 (1996) 72-76 (*Brooke, George J.*).

8329 *Rosenberg, Roy A.* Şedeq as divine hypostasis in Qumran texts and its link to the emergence of christianity. ᴹBURGMANN H., 1996 <1993>, ⇒12. 109-127.

8330 **Schick, Alexander; Betz, Otto; Cross, Frank M.** Jesus und die Schriftrollen von Qumran: wurde die Bibel verfälscht?: Jubiläumsband zur Entdeckung der Qumran-Rollen vor 50 Jahren. Berneck 1996, Schwengeler 263 pp. 3-85666-395-9 [NThAR 1997,193].

8331 **Stegemann, Hartmut** Die Essener, Qumran, Johannes der Täufer und Jesus. ⁴1994, ⇒10,9725; 11/1,2958. ᴿZAW 108 (1996) 322 (*Schmitt, H.-C.*); RB 103 (1996) 286-288 (*Murphy-O'Connor, J.*); Jud. 52 (1996) 65-66 (*Lange, Armin*);

8332 Los esenios, Qumrán, Juan Bautista y Jesús. ᵀ*Godoy, Rufino*, Estructuras y Procesos, Religión: M 1996, Trotta 315 pp. 84-8164-077-8;

8333 Gli Esseni, Qumran, Giovanni Battista e Gesù: una monografia. Studi religiosi: Bo 1996, EDB (4) xi; 397 pp. 88-10-40794-6.

8334 ᴱ**Strus, Andrzej** Tra giudaismo e cristianesimo: Qumran—giudeocristiani. 1995, ⇒11/2,7080. ᴿLASBF 46 (1996) 476-480 (*Cortese, Enzo*).

8335 *Thiering, Barbara E.* Jesus and the Dead Sea scrolls: the question of method. JHiC 3 (1996) 215-236.

k3.8 Historia et doctrinae Qumran

8336 *Beckwith, Roger T.* The perpetual calendar of the Dead Sea scrolls. Calendar and chronology. AGJU 33: 1996, ⇒112. 93-140.

8337 **Besch, Bernt** Der Dualismus in den Kernschriften von Qumran: ein Beitrag zur Diskussion über Wesen und Herleitung des qumranischen Dualismus. Diss. Pont. Univ. S. Thomae. R 1996, xiv; 247 pp.

8338 *Callaway, Phillip R.* 4QMMT and recent hypotheses on the origin of the Qumran community. ᴹBURGMANN H., 1996 <1993>, ⇒12. 15-29.

8339 *Caquot, André* Un exposé polémique de pratiques sectaires (4QMMT). RHPhR 76 (1996) 257-276.

8340 *Davies, Philip R.* Communities at Qumran and the case of the missing "teacher" <1991>;

8341 Halakhah at Qumran <1990>;

8342 Redaction and sectarianism in the Qumran scrolls <1992>;

8343 The teacher of righteousness and the "end of days" <1988>. Sects and scrolls. SFSHJ 134: 1996, ⇒122. 139-150/113-126/151-161/89-94.

Deiana, G. Lo straniero nel periodo qumranico ⇒2629.

8344 *Dimant, Devorah* Men as angels: the self-image of the Qumran community. Religion and politics. 1996, ⇒212. 93-103.

8345 *Dombrowski, Bruno W.W.* Preliminary remarks on ideological and sociostructural developments of the Qumran association as suggested by internal evidence of Dead Sea scrolls. ᴹBURGMANN H., 1996 <1993>, ⇒12. 31-43.

8346 *Elgvin, Torleif* Wisdom in the Yahad: 4QWays of righteousness. RdQ 17 (1996) 205-232.

García Martínez, F. Two messianic figures in the Qumran texts ⇒6857.

8347 **García Martínez, Florentino,** *(al),* Los hombres de Qumrán: literatura, estructura social y concepciones religiosas. 1993, ⇒9,10642... 11/2,7102. ᴿBAEO 32 (1996) 422 *(Sen, Felipe);* BiOr 53 (1996) 177-180 *(Lattke, Michael).*

8348 **García Martínez, Florentino; Trebolle Barrera, Julio** The people of the Dead Sea scrolls. 1995, ⇒11/2,7103. ᴿFolOr 32 (1996) 194-198 *(Dombrowski, Bruno W.W.);* ThLZ 121 (1996) 1142-1144 *(Bergmeier, Roland).*

8349 *García Martínez, Florentino* Calendarios en Qumrán. EstB 54 (1996) 327-348, 523-552.

8350 *Glessmer, U.* The Otot-Texts (4Q319) and the problem of intercalations in the context of the 364-day calendar. Qumranstudien. 1996, ⇒8176. 125-164.

8351 *Harrington, Daniel J.* The Raz nihyeh in a Qumran wisdom text (1Q26, 4Q415-418, 423). RdQ 17 (1996) 549-553.

8352 *Hengel, Martin* Qumran und der Hellenismus. Judaica et Hellenistica. WUNT 90: 1996 <1978>, ⇒128. 258-294.

8353 ᴱ**Kampen, John; Bernstein, Moshe J.** Reading 4QMMT: new perspectives on Qumran law and history. SBL Symposium 2: Atlanta 1996, Scholars xii; 169 pp. $40/$25. 0-7885-0222-0/3-9 [JSOT 74,121].

8354 *Klingbeil, Martin* El Qumran y el canon del Antiguo Testamento. Theologika 11/2 (1996) 238-261 [ZID 23,321].

8355 *Laperrousaz, Ernest-Marie* La protohistoire de la communauté essénienne du maître de justice: essai de synthèse. ᴹBᴜʀɢᴍᴀɴɴ H., 1996 <1993>, ⇒12. 45-59.

8356 *Le Morvan, Michael* Qumran: the community. ScrB 26 (1996) 20-33.

8357 *Lyons, William John* Possessing the land: the Qumran sect and the eschatological victory. DSD 3 (1996) 130-151.

8358 *Maier, Johann* Early Jewish biblical interpretation in the Qumran literature. Antiquity [ᴱSæbø, Magne]. 1996, ⇒ʏ1. 108-129;

8359 Messias oder Gesalbter?: zu einem Übersetzungs- und Deutungsproblem in den Qumrantexten. RdQ 17 (1996) 585-612.

8360 *Puech, Émile* Jonathan le prêtre impie et les débuts de la communauté de Qumrân: 4QJonathan (4Q523) et 4QPsAp (4Q448). RdQ 17 (1996) 241-270.

8361 **Schiffman, Lawrence H.** Law, custom and messianism in the Dead Sea sect. 1995, ⇒11/2,7120. ᴿJJS 47 (1996) 366-369 *(Schwartz, Joshua).*

8362 *Seely, David Rolph* The "circumcised heart" in 4Q434 Barki Nafshi. RdQ 17 (1996) 527-535.

8363 ᴱ**Shanks, H.** Understanding the Dead Sea scrolls. 1993, ⇒8,367b; 11/2,6954. ᴿVT 46 (1996) 573-574 *(Emerton, John A.E.).*

8364 *Sheres, Ita, (al),* The truth about the virgin: sex and ritual in the Dead Sea scrolls. 1995, ⇒11/2,7124. ᴿDSD 3 (1996) 219-221 *(Harrington, Hannah K.).*

8365 *Smith, Morton* The Dead Sea sect in relation to ancient Judaism Studies in... method. 1996 <1961>, ⇒150. 168-183.

8366 *Strugnell, John* More on wives and marriage in the Dead Sea scrolls: (4Q416 2 ii 21 [Cf. 1 Thess 4:4] and 4QMMT $ B). RdQ 17 (1996) 537-547.

8367 *Tenšek, Tomislav Zdenko* Židovski asketizam u sirijskom kršćiĭ -
kom anbijentu [Jews' asceticism in Syrian christian ambiance].
Riass. 44. BoSm 66 (1996) 37-44.

8368 **Widengren, Geo**, (*al*), Apocalyptique iranienne et dualisme
qoumrânien. 1995, ⇒11/2,7127. ᴿETR 71 (1996) 428-430
(*Léonard, Jeanne Marie*); ThLZ 121 (1996) 537-538 (*Hutter,
Manfred*); CritRR 9 (1996) 175 (*Sandgren, Leo*).

к4.1 Sectae jam extra Qumran notae: Esseni, Zelotae

8369 **Bergmeier, Roland** Die Essenerberichte des Flavius JOSEPHUS.
1993, ⇒9,10651... 11/2,7130. ᴿDSD 3 (1996) 61-63 (*Steudel,
Annette*).

8370 **Couvert, Étienne** Die Wahrheit über die Schriftrollen vom Toten
Meer: wer waren die Essener?. Durach 1996, Pro Fide Catholica
159 pp. 3-929170-88-4 [NThAR 1999,4].

8371 *Davies, Philip R.* The birthplace of the Essenes: where is "Damascus"?. 95-111.

8372 *Elgvin, Torleif* Early Essene eschatology: judgment and salvation
according to Sapiential Work A. Current research... on the Dead
Sea scrolls. StTDJ 20: 1996, ⇒293. 126-165.

8373 *Hengel, Martin* Zeloten und Sikarier. Judaica et Hellenistica.
WUNT 90: 1996 <1989>, ⇒128. 351-357.

8374 **Hengel, Martin** Gli zeloti: ricerche sul movimento di liberazione
giudaico dai tempi di Erode I al 70 d.C. BSSTB 11: Brescia 1996,
Paideia 538 pp. L112.000. 88-394-0536-4 [Gr. 79,759—Prato,
Gian Luigi].

8375 **Puech, Émile** La croyance des esséniens en la vie future: immortalité, résurrection, vie éternelle?. 1993, ⇒9,7555... 11/2,3362.
ᴿBAEO 32 (1996) 426-427 (*Sen, Felipe*).

8376 *Smith, Morton* Zealots and Sicarii, their origins and relation. Studies in... method. 1996 <1971>, ⇒150. 211-226.

8377 **Stemberger, Günter** Farisei, Sadducei, Esseni. SB 105: 1993,
⇒10,9753; 11/2,7140. ᴿProtest. 51 (1996) 72-73 (*Costabel,
Bruno*).

к4.3 Samaritani

8378 ᴱ**Crown, Alan D.**, (*al*), A companion to Samaritan studies. 1993,
⇒9,10655... 11/2,7145. ᴿThLZ 121 (1996) 37-38 (*Bergmeier,
Roland*).

8379 *Crown, Alan D.* The Samaritans, their literature and the codicology
of their manuscripts. BAIAS 15 (1996-1997) 87-104.

8380 **Crown, Alan David** A bibliography of the Samaritans. ²1993,
⇒9,10656; 11/2,7144. ᴿBiOr 53 (1996) 522-526 (*Bóid, I.R.M.*).

8381 *Dexinger, Ferdinand* Die Samaritaner in der Kreuzzugszeit. Hallesche Beiträge zur Orientwissenschaft 22 (1996) 94-115.

8382 *Fossum, Jarl; Arbor, Ann* Social and institutional conditions for
early Jewish and christian interpretation of the Hebrew Bible with
special regard to religious groups and sects. Antiquity [ᴱSæbø,
Magne]. 1996, ⇒Y1. 239-255.

8383 *Giles, Terry* Samaritan torah scroll cases. ProcGLM 16 (1996) 151-161.

8384 *Margain, Jean* Compléments à la bibliographie samaritaine. Rés. 162. REJ 155 (1996) 147-163;

8385 Les Samaritains et le texte du Pentateuque. Les premières traditions. 1996, ⇒159. 58-64.

8386 *Montevecchi, Orsolina* Samaria e samaritani in Egitto. Aeg. 76 (1996) 81-92.

8387 **Plummer, Reinhard** Samaritan marriage contracts and deeds of divorce, I. Wsb 1993, Harrassowitz xi; 380 pp. 37 pl. RJQR 87 (1996) 224-225 (*Sokoloff, Michael*).

8388 *Richter-Bernburg, Lutz* St. John of Acre—Nablus—Damascus: the Samaritan minority under crusaders and Muslims. Hallesche Beiträge zur Orientwissenschaft 22 (1996) 117-130.

8389 **Thordson, Thord & Maria** Qumran and the Samaritans. Ingaro, Sweden 1996, Thordson 262 pp. 91-86366-03-3 [DSD 6,94ss—Hjelm, Ingrid].

к4.5 *Sadoqitae, Qaraitae*—Cairo Genizah; Zadokites, Karaites

8390 EBroshi, **Magen** The Damascus Dcoument reconsidered. 1992, ⇒8,a440... 11/2,7154. RJNES 55 (1996) 144-146 (*Wise, Michael O.*).

8391 **Campbell, Jonathan G.** The use of scripture in the Damascus Document 1-8, 19-20. BZAW 228: 1995, ⇒11/2,7155. RJThS 47 (1996) 587-589 (*Falk, Daniel K.*); JJS 47 (1996) 154-156 (*Pearce, Sarah*).

8392 *Harviainen, Tapani* The Cairo *Genizot* and other sources of the second Firkovich collection in St. Petersburg. Proceedings 12th Congress of Masoretic Studies. 1996, ⇒270. 25-36.

8393 **Klein, Michael L.** Complementary fragments from the Cairo Genizah. FHARAN M., 1996, ⇒35. 95*-117*. **H.**

8394 **Lange, Nicholas de** Greek Jewish texts from the Cairo Genizah. TSAJ 51: Tü 1996, Mohr x; 473 pp. DM268. 3-16-146438-9.

8395 **Schäfer, Peter; Shaked, Shaul** Magische Texte aus der Kairoer Geniza, I. 1994, ⇒10,9769*. RJQR 87 (1996) 172-173 (*Davila, James R.*); JRAS 6 (1996) 229-231 (*Bos, Gerrit*).

8396 *Veltri, Giuseppe* Zur Überlieferung medizinisch-magischer Traditionen: das MATRA-Motiv in den Papyri Magicae und der Kairoer Geniza. Henoch 18 (1996) 157-175.

к5 **Judaismus prior vel totus**

8397 *Amit, Moshe* עולמות שלא נפגשו—יהדות ויוונות [Worlds which did not meet]. FSTERN M., 1996, ⇒87. Sum. 149*. 251-271. **H.**

8398 **Avemarie, Friedrich** Tora und Leben: Untersuchungen zur Heilsbedeutung der Tora in der frühen rabbinischen Literatur. TSAJ 55: Tü 1996, Mohr xiv; 664 pp. DM218. 3-16-146532-6. RHenoch 18 (1996) 376-377 (*Chiesa, Bruno*).

8399 **Azria, Régine** Le judaïsme. Repères 203: P 1996, Découverte 124 pp. FF49. 2-7071-2617-9 [BCLF 587-9,2053s].

8400 **Bar-Kochva, Bezalel** PSEUDO-HECATAEUS: on the Jews: legitimizing the Jewish diaspora. Hellenistic Culture and Society 21: Berkeley 1996, Univ. of California Press xii; 396 pp. Bibl. £45/$55. 0-520-20059-4.

8401 *Barclay, John* The Jews of the Diaspora. FHOOKER M., 1996, ⇒43. 27-40.

8402 **Baumgarten, Albert I.** מי היו הצדוקים?—הצדוקים בירושלים ובקומראן [Who were the Sadducees?: the Sadducees of Jerusalem and Qumran]. FSTERN M., 1996, ⇒87. Sum. 155*. 393-411. **H.**

8403 **Beckwith, Roger T.** Judaism between the testaments: the stages of its religious development. Calendar and chronology. AGJU 33: 1996, ⇒112. 167-216.

8404 **Boccaccini, Gabriele** Middle Judaism: Jewish thought 300 B.C.E. to 200 C.E. 1991, ⇒8,a450... 11/2,7174. RJSJ 27 (1996) 334-338 (*Neusner, Jacob*).

8405 *Borgen, Peder* Judaism in Egypt. Early christianity. 1996 <1992>, ⇒116. 71-102.

8406 *Botha, Pieter J.J.* History and point of view: understanding the Sadducees. Neotest. 30 (1996) 235-280.

8407 **Brewer, D.I.** Techniques and assumptions in Jewish exegesis before 70 CE. TSAJ 30: 1992, ⇒8,a451... 11/2,7177. ROTEs 9 (1996) 529-532 (*Cook, J.*).

8408 **Capelli, P.** La letteratura rabbinica dall'epoca di Gesù alla chiusura del talmud. Bo 1996, Studio Domenicano 152 pp. [RivBib 47,253s—Vanoli, Alessandro].

8409 **Caplan, Philip J.** The puzzle of the 613 commandments and why bother. Northvale, NJ 1996, Aronson xiv; 255 pp. Bibl. 1-56821-893-1.

8410 *Causse, Antonin* From an ethnic group to a religious community: the sociological problem of Judaism. Community. 1996, ⇒172. 95-118.

8411 **Cohn, Gabriel H.; Fisch, Harold** Prayer in Judaism: continuity and change. Northvale, NJ 1996, Aronson xii; 256 pp. 1-56821-501-0.

8412 *Davies, Philip R.* The "Damascus" sect and Judaism. Sects and scrolls. SFSHJ 134: 1996 <1994>, ⇒122. 163-177.

8413 **Dexinger, Ferdinand** Sondervorlesung zum Frühjudentum: die jüdische Religion vom Ende des Exils bis zur Redaktion der Mischna (538 v.Chr.-200 n.Chr.). Wien 1996, 127 pp. WS 1996/97.

8414 **Draï, Raphaël** La pensée juive et l'interrogation divine: exégèse et épistémologie. Thémis—Philosophie: P 1996, PUF 446 pp. FF158. 2-13-0477534 [RHPhR 78,468s—Pfrimmer, T.].

8415 *Feldman, Louis H.* Diaspora synagogues: new light from inscriptions and papyri. Studies in Hellenistic Judaism. AGJU 30: 1996, ⇒124. 577-602.

8416 EFeldman, Louis H.; Reinhold, Meyer Jewish life and thought among Greeks and Romans: primary readings. E 1996, Clark xxxiv; 436 pp. £17.50. 0-567-08525-2.

8417 **Fröhlich, Ida** 'Time and times and half a time': historical consciousness in the Jewish literature of the Persian and Hellenistic eras. JSJ.S 19: Shf 1996, Academic 248 pp. £39/$58.50. 1-85075-566-3 [CBQ 59,205].

8418 *Gafni, Isaiah M.* עונש, ברכה או שליחות—הפזורה היהודית בימי הבית
השני ובתקופת התלמוד [Punishment, blessing or mission—Jewish
dispersion in the Second Temple and Talmudic period]. FSTERN
M., 1996, ⇒87. Sum. 148*. 229-250. H.

8419 **Goldblatt, David** The monarchic principle: studies in Jewish self-
government in antiquity. TSAJ 38: Tü 1994, Mohr xii; 336 pp.
$137.50. RJJS 47 (1996) 167-169 (*Schwartz, Seth*).

8420 **Goodman, Martin** Mission and conversion: proselytizing in the
religious history of the Roman empire. 1994, ⇒11/2,7184. RJThS
47 (1996) 197-201 (*Niebuhr, K.-W.*); HeyJ 37 (1996) 214-215
(*Cameron, Averil*); JR 76 (1996) 464-466 (*Collins, John J.*); SCI
15 (1996) 303-307 (*Mendels, Doron*).

8421 *Goodman, Martin* The Roman identity of Roman Jews. FSTERN
M., 1996, ⇒87. 85*-99*.

8422 **Grabbe, Lester L.** An introduction to first century Judaism: Jewish religion and history in the Second Temple period. E 1996,
Clark xiv; 124 pp. £10. 0-567-08506-6 [Theol. 797,381].

8423 *Hengel, Martin* Die Begegnung von Judentum und Hellenismus im
Palästina der vorchristlichen Zeit < 1970 > ;

8424 Proseuche und Synagoge: jüdische Gemeinde, Gotteshaus und Got-
tesdienst in der Diaspora und in Palästina < 1971 > ;

8425 Die Synagogeninschrift von Stobi < 1966 > . Judaica et Hellenistica. WUNT 90: 1996, ⇒128. 151-170/171-195/91-130.

8426 *Hengel, Martin; Lichtenberger, Hermann* Die Hellenisierung des
antiken Judentums als Praeparatio Evangelica. Judaica et Hellenistica. WUNT 90: 1996 < 1981 > , ⇒128. 295-313.

8427 **Holladay, Carl R.** Orphica. Fragments from Hellenistic Jewish
authors, 1. SBL.TT 40; PS 14: Atlanta 1996, Scholars x; 301 pp.
$50. 0-7885-0143-7 [CBQ 59,819].

8428 **Hruby, Kurt** Aufsätze zum nachbiblischen Judentum und zum
jüdischen Erbe der frühen Kirche. EOsten-Sacken, Peter von der,
ANTZ 5: B 1996, Institut Kirche und Judentum 517 pp. 3-923095-
86-4 [NThAR 1997,99].

8429 *Hruby, Kurt* Einige Bemerkungen zum Tachanun und zum Platz des
individuellen Gebets in der synagogalen Liturgie;

8430 Geschichtlicher Überblick über die Anfänge der synagogalen Liturgie und ihre Entwicklung < 1962/63 > ;

8431 Gesetz und Gnade in der rabbinischen Überlieferung < 1969 > ;

8432 Die Nächstenliebe im jüdischen Denken < 1969 > ;

8433 Die Synagoge < 1971 > . Aufsätze. ANTZ 5: 1996, ⇒8427. 241-
264/203-240/71-99/100-124/127-200.

EIsaac, B., (*al*), Studies on the Jewish diaspora ⇒291.

8434 **Isaacs, Ronald H.** The Jewish book of numbers. Northvale, NJ
1996, Aronson xiv; 210 pp. 1-56821-951-2;

8435 Mitzvot: a sourcebook for the 613 commandments. Northvale, NJ
1996, Aronson xi; 265 pp. Bibl. 1-56821-900-8.

8436 *Ker, D.P.* Jewish missionary activity under review. IBSt 18 (1996)
205-216.

8437 **Klawans, Jonathan** Impurity and sin in ancient Judaism. Diss.
NY, Union, 1996-97 [RTL 29,581].

8438 **Kogut, Şimcha** [שמחה] המקרה בין טעמים לפרשנות: בחינה [קוגות,
לפרשנותטעמים פרשנות הלשונית ועניינית של זיקות ומחלקות בין
המסורתית [Correlations between biblical accentuation and tradi-

tional Jewish exegesis]. Perry Foundation for Biblical Research: J ²1996, Magnes 274 pp. [NThAR 1997,225]. **H.**

8439 *Langer, Gerhard* Das Judentum in Syrien vom 7. bis ins 20. Jahrhundert;

8440 Das Judentum in Syrien von den Hasmonäern bis um 700 n. Chr. Religionsgeschichte Syriens. 1996, ⇒217. 341-350/242-260.

8441 *Lichtenberger, Hermann* Das Tora-Verständnis im Judentum zur Zeit des Paulus: eine Skizze. Paul and the Mosaic law. WUNT 89: 1996, ⇒176. 7-23.

8442 ᴱ**Lucas, Franz D.** Geschichte und Geist: fünf Essays zum Verständnis des Judentums. 1995, ⇒11/2,116. ᴿJJS 47 (1996) 202-203 (*Brenner, Michael*).

8443 *Maier, Johann* Jüdisches Grundempfinden von Sünde und Erlösung in frühjüdischer Zeit. Sünde und Erlösung im NT. QD 161: 1996, ⇒181. 53-75.

8444 *Massonnet, Jean* Paul et la Torah. Paul de Tarse. LeDiv 165: 1996, ⇒273. 195-206.

8445 ᴱ**Mayer, Günter** Das Judentum. 1994, ⇒11/2,7211. ᴿZDMG 146 (1996) 521-522 (*Schlüter, Margarete*); ThLZ 121 (1996) 39-41 (*Maier, Johann*).

8446 *Menache, Sophia* Communication in the Jewish diaspora: a survey. Communication in the Jewish diaspora. 1996, ⇒232. 15-57.

8447 **Momigliano, Arnaldo** Essays on ancient and modern Judaism. 1994, ⇒10,207f. ᴿJR 76 (1996) 147-149 (*Foa, Anna*).

8448 **Munk, Reinier** The rationale of halakhic man: Joseph B. SOLOVEITCHIK's conception of Jewish thought. Amsterdam Studies in Jewish Thought 3: Amst 1996, Gieben ix; 144 pp. 90-5063-607-1.

8449 *Nebe, G. Wilhelm* Die beiden griechischen Briefe des Jonatan Archivs in Engedi aus dem zweiten jüdischen Aufstand 132-135 nach Chr. RdQ 17 (1996) 275-289.

8450 ᴱ**Neusner, Jacob** Judaism in late antiquity, I-II. HO 16-17: 1995, ⇒11/2,376. ᴿThLZ 121 (1996) 448-452 (*Niebuhr, Karl-Wilhelm*).

8451 **Neusner, Jacob** Introduction to rabbinic literature. 1994, ⇒10,9803; 11/2,7216. ᴿCritRR 9 (1996) 354-356 (*Sawyer, Deborah F.*).

8452 **Noethlichs, Karl Leo** Das Judentum und der römische Staat: Minderheitenpolitik im antiken Rom. Da:Wiss 1996, vi; 250 pp. DM68. 3-534-10091-3.

8453 **Ognibeni, Bruno** La seconda parte del Sefer ʾoklah weʾoklah. 1995, ⇒11/2,7225. ᴿSef. 56 (1996) 447-448 (*Azcárraga, M.J.*).

8454 *Paperon, Bernard* La femme dans le judaïsme. RDC 46/1 (1996) 99-104.

8455 *Quarles, Charles L.* The soteriology of R. AKIBA and E.P. SANDERS' *Paul and Palestinian Judaism*. NTS 42 (1996) 185-195.

8456 *Rappaport, Uriel* בחברה ריבוד חברתי, מבנה פוליטי ואידיאולוגיה היהודית ערב המרד הגדול [Social stratification, political structure and ideology on the eve of the destruction of the second temple]. ᶠSTERN M., 1996, ⇒87. Sum. 146*. 147-166. **H.**

8457 **Ravitzky, Aviezer** History and faith: studies in Jewish philosophy. Amsterdam Studies in Jewish Thought 2: Amst 1996, Gieben ix; 325 pp. 90-5063-597-0.

8458 *Rokéah, David* Ancient Jewish proselytism in theory and in practice. ThZ 52 (1996) 206-224.

8459 **Safrai, Ze'ev** The Jewish community in the talmudic period. J 1995, Zalman Shazar Center for Jewish History 395 pp. RJJS 47 (1996) 165-167 (*Goodblatt, David*). **H.**

8460 **Sanders, E.P.** Judaism...63 BCE-66 CE. 1992, ⇒8,4403... 11/2,7231. RBBR 6 (1996) 167-177 (*Neusner, Jacob*).

8461 **Schmidt, Francis; Rappaport, Uriel; Dimant, Devorah** L'Étranger, le temple et la loi dans le judaïsme ancien. Annales: P 1996, Colin 939-1182. FF98. 2-200-90802-4 [BCLF 598-599,1570].

8462 **Schwarzfuchs, Simon** A concise history of the rabbinate. 1993, ⇒9,10707; 11/2,7235. RJJS 47 (1996) 180-182 (*Shapiro, Marc B.*).

8463 EShanks, **Hershel** Christianity and rabbinic Judaism: a parallel history of their origins and early development. 1992, 1993, ⇒8,367a...11/2,7237. RScrB 26 (1996) 55-56 (*Need, Stephen, W.*).

8464 *Siegert, Folker* Early Jewish interpretation in a Hellenistic style. Antiquity [ESæbø, **Magne**]. 1996, ⇒γ1. 130-198.

ESierra, **Sergio J.** La lettura ebraica delle Scritture ⇒205.

8465 *Smith, Morton* The gentiles in Judaism 125 BCE-AD 66;

8466 The image of God: notes on the hellenization of Judaism, with especial reference to GOODENOUGH's work on Jewish symbols <1958>. Studies in... method. 1996, ⇒150. 263-319/116-149;

8467 The Jewish elements in the magical papyri. New Testament. 1996 <1986>, ⇒151. 242-256;

8468 Palestinian Judaism in the first century. Studies in... method. 1996 <1956>, ⇒150. 104-115.

8469 *Stemberger, Günter* Zum Verständnis der Tora im rabbinischen Judentum. Die Tora als Kanon. 1996, ⇒1308. 329-343.

8470 *Tassin, Claude* Paul dans le monde juif du 1er siècle. Paul de Tarse. LeDiv 165: 1996, ⇒273. 171-193.

8471 *Tuckett, Christopher* Les pharisiens avant 70 et le Nouveau Testament. TVoilley, *Pascale*, Le déchirement. MoBi 32: 1996, ⇒192. 67-95.

8472 *Van Bekkum, Wout Jac.* Deutung und Bedeutung in der hebräischen Exegese. FJB 23 (1996) 1-13.

8473 *Van den Broek, Roelof* Juden und Christen in Alexandrien im 2. und 3. Jahrhundert. Studies in gnosticism [EVan den **Broek, R.**]. Nag Hammadi studies 39: 1996, ⇒M1.1. 181-196.

8474 **Verman, Mark** The history and varieties of Jewish meditation. Northvale, NJ 1996, Aronson xv; 239 pp. Bibl. 1-56821-522-3.

8475 *Vetter, Dieter* Für Christen nur ein Schimpfwort: Rückbesinnung auf die Bedeutung der Pharisäer für das jüdische Volk <1967>;

8476 Religion als Ethik?: zur Problematik von Moses MENDELSSOHN Bestimmung des Judentums <1992>;

8477 "Wer keine Frau hat, lebt ohne Freude": das rabbinische Judentum zwischen Sinnbejahung und Enthaltsamkeit <1993>. Judentum. 1996, ⇒154. 229-231/289-316/163-195.

8478 **Vetter, Dieter** Die Wurzel des Ölbaums: das Judentum. Kleine Bibliothek der Religionen 5: FrB 1996, Herder 208 pp. DM24.80 [BiLi 70,244].

8479   **Vidal-Naquet, Pierre** The Jews: history, memory, and the present.
       T*Curtis, David Ames*; Foreword *Berman, Paul*; New Pref. by auth.
       NY ²1996, Columbia Univ. Press [Jdm 47/1,120].
8480   *Wahlde, Urban C. von* The relationships between pharisees and
       chief priests: some observations on the texts in Matthew, John and
       JOSEPHUS. NTS 42 (1996) 506-522.
8481   *Weiß, Hans-Friedrich* Pharisäer. TRE 26 (1996) 473-485.
8482   **Will, Edouard; Orrieux, Claude** 'Prosélytisme juif?': histoire
       d'une erreur. 1992, ⇒8,4938... 11/2,7244. ᴿGn. 68 (1996) 273-
       275 *(Cohen, Shaye J.D.)*.
8483   **Wise, Michael Owen** Thunder in Gemini and other essays on the
       history, language and literature of Second Temple Palestine.
       JSPE.S 15: 1994, ⇒10,231. ᴿCBQ 58 (1996) 738-740 *(Flint, Peter
       W.)*; DSD 3 (1996) 87-88 *(Lim, Timothy H.)*.

к6.0 Mišna, tosepta; Tannaim

8484   *Ditheil, Jacques* L'amour de la torah d'après les 'Pirqé Avoth'.
       ᶠLEGASSE S., LeDiv 166: 1996, ⇒51. 73-89.
8485   *Harris, Jay M.* From inner-biblical interpretation to early rabbinic
       exegesis. Antiquity [ᴱSæbø, Magne]. 1996, ⇒ʏ1. 256-269.
8486   T**Hirsch, Samson Raphael** Pirqei Avot: Sprüche der Väter. Basel
       1994, Morascha 123 pp. ᴿFrRu 3 (1996) 212-214 *(Franz-Klauser,
       Olivia)*.
8487   **Houtman, Alberdina** Mishnah and Tosefta: a synoptic comparison
       of the tractates Berakhot and Shebiit. TSAJ 59: Tü 1996, Mohr xi;
       255 pp. 3-16-146638-1.
8488   T**Hüttenmeister, Frowald G.; Larsson, Göran** Die Tosefta: Seder
       II: Moëd, 2: Schekalim - Jom ha-kippurim. RT I.2,2: Stu 1997,
       Kohlhammer vi; 361 pp. DM448. 3-17-013615-1. ᴿMEAH.H 45
       (1996) 243-244 *(Pérez Fernández, Miguel)*.
8489   **Kasher, Rimon** Targumic Toseftot to the Prophets. Sources for the
       Study of Jewish Culture 2: J 1996, World Union of Jewish Studies
       314 pp. Bibl. H.
8490   *Kraemer, David* Scriptural interpretation in the mishnah. Antiquity
       [ᴱSæbø, Magne]. 1996, ⇒ʏ1. 278-284.
8491   **Lapin, Hayim** Early rabbinic civil law and the social history of
       Roman Galilee: a study of the Mishnah tractate Babaʾ Mesiʿaʾ.
       Diss. Columbia. BJSt 307: Atlanta 1996, Scholars 210 pp. 0-7885-
       0204-2. ᴿJSJ 27 (1996) 345-350 *(Neusner, Jacob)*.
8492   *Lapin, Hayim* Rabbis and public prayers for rain in later Roman
       Palestine. Religion and politics. 1996, ⇒212. 105-129.
8493   *Neusner, Jacob* The hermeneutics of the law in rabbinic Judaism:
       mishnah, midrash, talmuds. Antiquity [ᴱSæbø, Magne]. 1996,
       ⇒ʏ1. 303-322.
8494   **Neusner, Jacob** Religion and law: how through halakhah Judaism
       sets forth its theology and philosophy. USF Studies in the History
       of Judaism 135: Atlanta 1996, Scholars 146 pp. [AcOr 58,202ss—
       Groth, Bente].
8495   *Pérez Fernández, Miguel* Tipología exegética en los Tannaítas.
       Sum. 53. MEAH 41/2 (1992) 53-62.

8496 *Vetter, Dieter* Das Studium der Überlieferung als gemeinschaftsbildendes Element im Zeitalter der Mischna und des Talmuds. Judentum. 1996, ⇒154. 13-80.

к6.5 Talmud; midraš

8497 **Agus, Aharon R.E.** Hermeneutic biography in rabbinic midrash: the body of this death and life. SJ 16: B 1996, De Gruyter 242 pp. DM168. 3-11-015067-0 [Numen 46,450s—Veltri, Giuseppe].

8498 **Alon, Gedaliah** The Jews in their land in the talmudic age (70-640 C.E.). ᵀᴱ*Levi, Gershon*, CM 1996, Harvard Univ. Press xii; 810 pp. 3rd printing.

8499 ᵀᴱ**Bokser, Baruch M.** Yerushalmi Pesaḥim. ᴱ*Schiffman, Lawrence H.*, The talmud of the land of Israel: a preliminary translation and explanation, 13. Ch 1994, Univ. of Chicago Press xxiii; 633 pp. ᴿProoftexts 16 (1996) 175-188 (*Jaffee, Martin S.*).

8500 *Bollag, Michel* Meine Bücher suche ich: die hebräische Bibel rabbinisch gelesen: ein Kurs im Zürcher Lehrhaus. BiKi 51 (1996) 73-74.

8501 ᵀ**Bulman, Yehudah** Nation of witnesses: anthology of commentaries and insights of the talmudic sages and Torah exegetes on the revelation at Sinai and the commandment to recall every detail of its greatness. Compiler *Rozner, Shlomo*, J 1996, Feldheim (12) 163 pp. 0-87306-759-2.

8502 *Büchner, D.* Midrash: a bibliographical essay. Sum. 49. JSem 8/1 (1996) 49-78.

8503 *Di Sante, Carmine* Il concetto di Dio negli scritti rabbinici. Dio— Signore nella bibbia. DSBP 13: 1996, ⇒328. 122-141.

8504 **Fraenkel, J.** Le monde spirituel des contes aggadiques. Patrimoines: P 1996, Cerf 229 pp. FF170 [NRTh 120,484—Ska, J.-L.].

8505 **Girón Blanc, Luis-Fernando** Seder ʿolam rabbah, el gran orden del universo: una cronología judía. Biblioteca Midrásica 18: Estella 1996, Verbo Divino 168 pp. 84-8169-115-1 [EstB 55,568].

8506 **Goldberg, Edwin C.** Midrash for beginners. Northvale, NJ 1996, Aronson xiv; 74 pp. 1-56821-599-1.

8507 **Haas, Peter J.** Responsa: literary history of a rabbinic genre. SBL Semeia studies: Atlanta, Ga. 1996, Scholars 320 pp. 0-7885-0244-1 0-7885-0245-X.

8508 **Hammer, Reuven** The classic midrash. NY 1995, Paulist 528 pp. $25/£19. ᴿJJS 47 (1996) 378-380 (*Jacobs, Irving*).

8509 *Hayes, C.E.* Response to Jacob NEUSNER. JSJ 27 (1996) 324-333.

8510 ᴱ**Hengel, Martin,** (*al*), Maaserot—Zehnte; Maaser Sheni—Zweiter Zehnt. ᵀ*Ulmer, Rivka,* Übersetzung des Talmud Yerushalmi, I/7-8. Tü 1996, Mohr vi; 315 pp. 3-16-146175-4.

8511 **Hoffman, Lawrence** A covenant of blood: circumcision and gender in rabbinic Judaism. Chicago Studies in the History of Judaism: Ch 1996 Univ. of Chicago Press 256 pp. $42.50/$17. 0-226-34783-4/4-2 [Gen 17] [ThD 44,70].

8512 *Hruby, Kurt* Kurze Einführung in die rabbinische Tradition und ihre Quellenschriften. Aufsätze. ANTZ 5: 1996, ⇒8427. 21-47.

8513 **Jacobs, Irving** The midrashic process: tradition and interpretation in rabbinic Judaism. 1995, ⇒11/2,7292. ROLZ 91 (1996) 42-44 (*Janssen, Enno*); JThS 47 (1996) 264 (*Horbury, William*); JR 76 (1996) 504-505 (*Fishbane, Michael*).

8514 *Kalmin, Richard* Genealogy and polemics in rabbinic literature of late antiquity. HUCA 67 (1996) 77-94;

8515 Patterns and developments in rabbinic midrash of Late Antiquity. Antiquity [ESæbø, Magne]. 1996, ⇒Y1. 285-302.

8516 *Kern-Ulmer, Brigitte (Rivka)* The depiction of magic in rabbinic texts: the rabbinic and the Greek concept of magic. JSJ 27 (1996) 289-303.

8517 *Kraemer, David* Local conditions for a developing rabbinic tradition. Antiquity [ESæbø, Magne]. 1996, ⇒Y1. 270-277.

8518 **Lachs, Samuel Tobias** Humanism in talmud and midrash. 1993, ⇒10,9856. RAJSR 21 (1996) 157-159 (*Freund, Richard A.*).

8519 *Lachs, Samuel Tobias* Talmudic and midrashic analecta. JSJ 27 (1996) 453-459.

8520 TELandesman, Dovid As the Rabbis taught: studies in the aggados of the Talmud: Tractate Megillah. Collab. *Gebhard, Chanoch,* Northvale, NJ 1996, Aronson 320 pp. 1-56821-949-0.

8521 TLangermmann, Y. Tzvi Yemenite midrash: philosophical commentaries on the torah. Sacred Literature: SF 1996, HarperSanFrancisco xxx; 351 pp. 0-06-065391-4.

8522 *Lawee, Eric* The "Ways of Midrash" in the biblical commentaries of Isaac ABARBANEL. HUCA 67 (1996) 107-142.

8523 *Levi, John S.* AKIBA. ABR 44 (1996) 16-31.

8524 **Levinas, Emmanuel** Cuatro lecturas talmùdicas. TGarcía-Baró, Miguel, Barc 1996, Riopiedras 148 pp. [EstFil 46,552-553—Luis Carballada, Ricardo de].

8525 **Levinson, Pnina Navé** Introduzione alla teologia ebraica. CinB 1996, San Paolo 246 pp. L37.000. 88-215-3121-X [Protest. 52,198].

8526 *Levinson, Pnina Navé* Einführung in die jüdische Schriftauslegung. BiKi 51 (1996) 54-62.

8527 **Limentani, Giacoma** Il midrash: come i maestri ebrei leggevano la bibbia. Letteratura biblica 8: Mi 1996, Paoline 168 pp. L20.000 88-315-1311-7 [RdT 38,143].

8528 *Llewelyn, S.R.* The introduction of Ḥazaqah into Jewish law. JSJ 27 (1996) 155-167.

8529 Midrashic and Halakhic literature, Jewish law [bibliography]. QS 66 (1996) 329-367.

8530 *Miller, Merrill P.* The authority and intelligibility of torah: reflections on a talmudic story. FSANDERS J., JSOT.S 225: 1996, ⇒77. 184-205.

8531 *Momigliano, Giuseppe* L'interpretazione omiletica: il Midrash-haggadah. La lettura ebraica. 1996, ⇒205. 127-145.

8532 **Neusner, Jacob** Scripture and midrash in Judaism, I. JudUm 47: 1994, ⇒11/2,7308. RivBib 44 (1996) 235-237 (*Perani, Mauro*);

8533 The talmud of Babylonia. 1994, ⇒10,9865. RCritRR 9 (1996) 19-25 (*Goldman, Edward A.*);

8534 Beyond catastrophe: the rabbis' reading of Isaiah's vision: Israelite messiah-prophecies in formative Judaism: an anthology of Pesiqta deRab Kahana for the Seven Sabbaths after the ninth of Ab. SFSHJ

131: Atlanta, GA 1996, Scholars x; 133 pp. 0-7885-0214-X. Pesikta de-Rav Kahana 16-22.

8535 *Neusner, Jacob* The end of an episteme: SATLOW's tasting the dish: rabbinic rhetorics of sexuality;

8536 German scholarship on rabbinic judaism: the GOLDBERG-SCHAEFER school. Formative Judaism. SFSHJ 133: 1996, ⇒142. 197-205/167-179;

8537 The hermeneutics of the law in rabbinic Judaism: mishnah, midrash, talmuds. Antiquity [ESæbø, Magne]. 1996, ⇒Y1. 303-322;

8538 Reason and the learning community of Israel, the holy people;

8539 TILLY's form-analysis of Yerushalmi Moed Qatan. Formative Judaism. SFSHJ 133: 1996, ⇒142. 27-36/189-192.

8540 ENeusner, Jacob; Neusner, Noam M.M. The book of Jewish wisdom: the talmud of the well-considered life. NY 1996, Continuum 324 pp. $27.50. 0-8264-0890-7 [ThD 44,158].

8541 *Niehoff, M.R.* The phoenix in rabbinic literature. HThR 89 (1996) 245-265.

8542 **Pérez Fernández, Miguel** El método exegético del midrás *Sifra* [The exegetical method of the midrash *Sifra*]. Sum. res. 37. MEAH.H 45 (1996) 37-50.

8543 *Rabello, Alfredo Mordechai* L'interpretazione del *Talmud* babilonese e del *Talmud* di ʾEreṣ Yiśraʾel: il *Midrash halakah*. La lettura ebraica. 1996, ⇒205. 103-125.

8544 *Rubenstein, Jeffrey L.* From mythic motifs to sustained myth: the revision of rabbinic traditions in medieval midrashim. HThR 89 (1996) 131-159.

8545 *Sagi, Avi* "He slew the Egyptian and hid him in the sand": Jewish tradition and the moral element. HUCA 67 (1996) 55-76.

8546 TSatlow, Michael L. "Try to be a man": the rabbinic construction of masculinity. HThR 89 (1996) 19-40.

8547 ESchäfer, Peter; Becker, Hans-Jürgen Berakhot und Peʾa. Synopse zum Talmud Yerushalmi: Ordnung Zeraʿim, 1/1-2. TSAJ 31: 1991, ⇒10,9869. RJAOS 116 (1996) 559-560 (*Sarason, Richard S.*);

8548 Demai, Kilʾayim and Sheviʿit. Synopse zum Talmud Yerushalmi: Ordnung Zeraʿim, 1/3-5. TSAJ 33: 1992, ⇒10,9870. RJAOS 116 (1996) 559-560 (*Sarason, Richard S.*);

8549 Terûmôt, Maʿaśerôt, Maʿaśer Shenî, Ḥalla, ʿOrla, und Bikkurim. Synopse zum Talmud Yerushalmi: Ordnung Zeraʿim, 1/6-11. TSAJ 35: 1992, ⇒8,a538. RJAOS 116 (1996) 559-560 (*Sarason, Richard S.*);

8550 Ordnung Neziqin, Ordnung Toharot: Nidda. Synopse zum Talmud Yerushalmi. TSAJ 47: 1995, ⇒11/2,7316. RFJB 23 (1996) 190-191 (*Tilly, Heinz-Peter*).

8551 *Silberman, Lou H.* Once again: the use of rabbinic material. NTS 42 (1996) 153-155.

8552 *Smith, Morton* GOODENOUGH's Jewish symbols in retrospect. Studies in... method. 1996 <1967>, ⇒150. 184-200.

8553 **Steinsaltz, Adin** Talmud für jedermann. TSeidler, M., Basel 1995, Morascha 383 pp. FrRu 3 (1996) 296-299 (*Käppeli, Silvia*).

8554 *Stemberger, G.* La investigación actual en torno al judaísmo rabínico: *status quaestionis*. Sum. res. 63. MEAH 41/2 (1992) 63-84.

8555 **Stemberger, Günter** Introduzione al Talmud e al Midrash. 1995,
⇒11/2,7319. RCivCatt 147 I (1996) 409-411 (*Prato, G.L.*).

8556 *Stemberger,   Günter* Grundzüge   rabbinischer   Hermeneutik.
FDASSMANN E., JAC.E 23. 1996, ⇒19. 34-42.

8557 **Stemberger, Günter** Introduction to the talmud and midrash. E
1996, Clark xii; 433 pp. £19. 0-567-29509-5 [EvQ 69,367].

8558 **Stern, David** Parables in midrash: narrative and exegesis in rabbinic literature. 1991, ⇒11/2,7320. RRStR 22 (1996) 119-123
(*Saldarini, Anthony J.*).

8559 **Strack, H.L.; Stemberger, G.** Introduction to the talmud and
midrash. 1991, ⇒7,a9*... 10,771*. RJAOS 116 (1996) 144-145
(*Goldman, Edward A.*).

8560 *Terbuyken, Peri* Rom in der rabbinischen Hermeneutik: die
Kompositionstechnik von j'Abodah Zarah 1,2 und Cant. Rabbah
1,35/42. JAC 39 (1996) 116-127.

8561 *Teugels, Lieve* Did Moses see the chariot?: the link between Exod
19-20 and Ezek 1 in early Jewish interpretation. Studies in... Exodus. BEThL 126: 1996, ⇒1794. 595-602.

8562 TThoma, Clemens Von Isaak bis zum Schilfmeer: BerR 63 - 100;
ShemR 1 - 22; Einleitung, Übersetzung mit Kommentar, Texte.
Die Gleichnisse der Rabbinen, 3. JudChr 16: Bern 1996, Lang 452
pp. 3-906756-68-8.

8563 *Touati, Charles* Israël LEVI et la recherche sur la littérature talmu-
dique: à propos d'un centenaire. REJ 155 (1996) 479-483.

8564 *Tsevat, Matitiahu* Three early rabbinic cardinal principles: reasons
of the commandments. Or. 65 (1996) 435-439.

8565 TUlmer, Rivka Maaserot, Zehnte: Maaser Sheni, Zweiter Zehnt.
Übersetzung des Talmud Yerushalmi I/7-8. Tü 1996, Mohr vi; 315
pp. DM198. 3-16-146175-4. RATG 59 (1996) 413-414 (*Torres,
A.*).

8566 **Van Loopik, Marcus** The ways of the sages... the minor tractates
of the Babylonian talmud. TSAJ 26: 1991, ⇒7,9998... 10,9860.
RBijdr. 57 (1996) 216-217 (*Poorthuis, Marcel*).

8567 *Vetter, Dieter* Krieg und Frieden: Weisungen und Erwartungen im
Judentum der talmudischen Zeit <1989>;

8568 Die Lehren vom Tod und von der "kommenden Welt" im talmudischen Schrifttum <1991>. Judentum. 1996, ⇒154. 135-162/196-
226.

8569 *Viterbi, Benedetto Carucci* Le regole ermeneutiche per
l'interpretazione del testo biblico: Torah scritta e Torah orale. La
lettura ebraica. 1996, ⇒205. 75-101.

8570 *Webber, Alan* Building regulation in the land of Israel in the talmudic period. JSJ 27 (1996) 263-288.

8571 *Wiesel, Elie* Talmud lesen. BiKi 51 (1996) 63-65.

к7.1 **Judaismus mediaevalis,** *generalia*

8572 *Dotan, Aron* Masoretic schools in the light of SAADIA's teaching.
Proceedings 12th Congress...for Masoretic Studies. 1996, ⇒270.
1-9.

8573 *Friedman, Mordechai A.* Babatha's Ketubba: some preliminary
observations. IEJ 46 (1996) 55-76.

8574 *Grabois, Aryeh* The use of letters as a communication medium among medieval European Jewish communities;

8575 *Grossman, Avraham* Communication among Jewish centers during the tenth to the twelfth centuries. Communication in the Jewish diaspora. Jewish studies 16: 1996, ⇒232. 93-105/107-126.

8576 **Hayoun, Maurice-Ruben** La science du judaïsme: die Wissenschaft des Judentums. Que sais-je?: P 1995, PUF 126 pp. ROLZ 91 (1996) 593-595 (*Wächter, Ludwig*).

8577 **Heschel, Abraham J.** Prophetic inspiration after the prophets: MAIMONIDES and other medieval authorities. Hoboken, NJ 1996, Ktav 157 pp. $23. 0-88125-346-4 [ET 108,286].

8578 *Menache, Sophia* Introduction: the "pre-history" of communication. Communication in the Jewish diaspora. Jewish studies 16: 1996, ⇒232. 1-13.

8579 *Reiner, Elchanan* בין יהושע לישוע: מסיעור מקראי למיתוס מקומי (פרק בעולמו הדתי של היהודי הגלילי) [From Joshua to Jesus—the transformation of a biblical story to a local myth (a chapter in the religious life of the Galilean Jew]. Sum. xxii. Zion 61 (1996) 281-316. H.

8580 **Saenz-Badillos, Ángel; Targarona Borras, Judit** Los judíos de Sefarad ante la Biblia: la interpretación de la Biblia en el medievo. Córdoba 1996, Almendro 279 pp. Pta2.800 [Mayéutica 24,253—Herrero, Manu].

8581 *Schein, Sylvia* Between east and west: the Latin kingdom of Jerusalem and its Jewish communities as a communication center (1099-1291). Communication in the Jewish diaspora. Jewish studies 16: 1996, ⇒232. 141-169.

8582 *Stemberger, Günter* Hermeneutik der Jüdischen Bibel. Hermeneutik. 1996, ⇒604. 22-132.

8583 *Stow Debenedetti, Sandra* A Judeo-Italian version of selected passages from CECCO d'Ascoli's *Acerba*. Communication in the Jewish diaspora. Jewish studies 16: 1996, ⇒232. 283-311.

8584 *Stow, Kenneth R.* By land or by sea: the passage of the Kalonymides to the Rhineland in the tenth century. Communication in the Jewish diaspora. Jewish studies 16: 1996, ⇒232. 59-72.

8585 *Zonta, Mauro* Gli influssi dei commentatori ebrei sugli esegeti cristiani. La lettura ebraica. 1996, ⇒205. 299-316.

к7.3 Magistri Judaismi mediaevalis

8586 *Laras, Giuseppe* La bibbia nell'esegesi del NAHAMANIDE;

8587 *Perez, Maaravi* Il metodo esegetico di rabbi David QIMHI;

8588 *Sierra, Sergio J.* Rabbi Shelomo' Yizhaqi (RASHI);

8589 *Simon, Uriel* Il metodo esegetico di rabbi Abraham ibn ʿEZRA. La lettura ebraica. 1996, ⇒205. 237-244/169-201/157-168/203-219.

8590 ETwersky, Isadore Studies in MAIMONIDES. Harvard Judaic Texts and Studies 7: CM 1992, Harvard Univ. Press 214 pp. $15. 0-674-85175-7. RZRGG 48 (1996) 182-183 (*Niewöhner, Friedrich*).

к7.4 Qabbalâ, Zohar, Merkabâ—Jewish mysticism

8591 *Abrams, Daniel* Recent translations of kabbalistic texts. Henoch 18 (1996) 197-204.

8592 ^EBusi, Giulio, (al), Mistica ebraica: testi della tradizione segreta del giudaismo dal III al XVIII secolo. 1995, ⇒11/2,7427. ^RHenoch 18 (1996) 203-204 (Abrams, Daniel).
8593 Evangelische Akademie Baden. Der Chassidismus: Leben zwischen Hoffnung und Verzweiflung. Herrenalper Forum 15: Karlsruhe 1996, Evangelischer Presseverband 135 pp.
8594 Fisdel, Steven A. The practice of kabbalah: meditation in Judaism. Northvale, NJ 1996, Aronson viii; (2) 222 pp. Bibl. 1-56821-508-8.
8595 Guetta, Alessandro Elia BENAMOZEGH, l'unione di qabbalah e modernità. La lettura ebraica. 1996, ⇒205. 409-428.
8596 Horowitz, Isaiah The generations of Adam. ^{ET}Krassen, Miles, ClWS 85: Mahwah, NJ 1996, Paulist xiv; 449 pp. $35/$25. 0-8091-0474-1/3590-6 [ThD 44,71].
8597 Idel, Mosheh Cabbalà: nuove prospettive. F 1996, Giuntina 344 pp. L48.000 [Hum(B) 53,908—Menestrina, Giovanni].
8598 Idel, Mosheh Zohar: la Bibbia e la sua esegesi. La lettura ebraica. 1996, ⇒205. 245-260.
8599 Kuyt, Annelies The 'descent' to the chariot: towards a description of the terminology, place, function and nature of the Yeridah in Hekhalot literature. TSAJ 45: 1995, ⇒11/2,7443. ^RJJS 47 (1996) 376-378 (Halperin, David J.).
8600 Lemmer, Richard Early Jewish mysticism, Jewish apocalyptic and writings of the New Testament—a triangulation. Neotest. 30 (1996) 359-376.
8601 Matt, Daniel The essential Kabbalah: the heart of Jewish mysticism. SF 1995, HarperSanFrancisco 221 pp. ^RHenoch 18 (1996) 198-199 (Abrams, Daniel).
8602 Mysticism, Kabbalah and Hasidism [bibliography]. QS 66 (1996) 379-388.
8603 ^ESchäfer, Peter; Herrmann, Klaus Übersetzung der Hekhalot-Literatur, I: # 1-80. TSAJ 46: 1995, ⇒7,a65... 11/2,7453. ^RThLZ 121 (1996) 1144-1145 (Schreiner, Stefan); Henoch 18 (1996) 199-202 (Abrams, Daniel).
8604 Scholem, G. Las grandes tendencias de la mística judía. Árbol del Paraíso 6: M 1996, Siruela 476 pp. [CDios 111,336—Gutiérrez, J.].
8605 Scott, J.M. The triumph of God in 2 Cor 2.14: additional evidence of Merkabah mysticism in Paul. NTS 42 (1996) 260-281.
8606 Segal, Alan F. Some observations about mysticism and the spread of notions of life after death in Hebrew thought. SBL.SPS 35: 1996, ⇒274. 385-399.
8607 Swartz, Michael D. Scholastic magic: ritual and revelation in early Jewish mysticism. Princeton 1996, Princeton Univ. Press xii; 263 pp. $35.
8608 Wolfson, Elliott R. Through the speculum that shines: vision and imagination in medieval Jewish mysticism. 1994, ⇒11/2,7460. ^RTS 57 (1996) 146-148 (Gendler, Everett); JR 76 (1996) 506-509 (Tirosh-Rothschild, Hava).

κ7.5 Judaismus saec. 14-18

8609 Barnai, Jacob The spread of the sabbatean movement in the seventeenth and eighteenth centuries;

8610 *Ben-Shalom, Ram* Communication and propaganda between Provence and Spain: the controversy over extreme allegorization (1303-1306). Communication in the Jewish diaspora. Jewish studies 16: 1996, ⇒232. 313-338/171-225.

8611 *Bonfil, Roberto* Il Rinascimento: la produzione esegetica di ʿO. Servadio SFORNO. La lettura ebraica. 1996, ⇒205. 261-277.

8612 **Chamla, Mino** SPINOZA e il concetto della tradizione ebraica. Mi 1996, FrancoAngeli 222 pp. [Filosofia Politica 12,310].

8613 *Gertwagen, Ruthi* Geniza letters: maritime difficulties along the Alexandria-Palermo route;

8614 *Goldin, Simha* "Companies of disciples" and "companies of colleagues": communication in Jewish intellectual circles;

8615 *Gutwirth, Eleazar* Hebrew letters, Hispanic mail: communication among fourteenth-century Aragon Jewry. Communication in the Jewish diaspora. Jewish studies 16: 1996, ⇒232. 73-91/126-139/257-282.

8616 *Horowitz, Riwka* MENDELSSOHN e la scienza dell'ebraismo;

8617 *Piperno, Umberto* Grandezza e decadenza nell'esegesi di don Yizhaq ABRAVANEL. La lettura ebraica. 1996, ⇒205. 353-379/279-297.

8618 ᴱTimm, Erika; Turniansky, Chava Yiddish in Italia: carte ritrovate: manoscritti e antiche edizioni e stampa yiddish di area italiana. Mi 1996, Biblioteca Nazionale Braidense 76 pp.

8619 *Yovel, Yrmiahu* L'interpretazione eterodossa della bibbia in SPINOZA. La lettura ebraica. 1996, ⇒205. 317-327.

κ7.7 Hasidismus et Judaismus saeculi XIX

8620 **Dalfin, Chaim** To be Chasidic: a contemporary guide. Northvale, NJ 1996, Aronson xxviii; 250 pp. Bibl. 1-56821-905-9.

8621 **Goldstein, Niles Elliot** Forests of the night: the fear of God in early Hasidic thought. Northvale, NJ 1996, Aronson xii; 150 pp. Bibl. 1-56821-945-8.

8622 ᴱLevin, Meyer Classic Chassidic tales. Northvale, NJ 1996, Aronson xvii; 357 pp. 1-56821-911-3.

8623 Mysticism, Kabbalah and Hasidism [bibliography]. QS 66 (1996) 379-388.

8624 ᴱRapoport-Albert, Ada Hasidism reappraised. Oxf 1996, Littman 528 pp. $87.50. 1-874774-20-X.

8625 *Sierra, Sergio J.* Samuel David LUZZATTO. La lettura ebraica. 1996, ⇒205. 401-408.

κ7.8 Judaismus contemporaneus

8626 **Bernstein, Michael André** Foregone conclusions: against apocalyptic history. 1994, ⇒11/2,7527. ᴿHebStud 37 (1996) 221-223 (*Garber, Zev*).

8627 *Chetrit, Joseph* Tradition du discours et discours de la tradition dans les communautés juives du Maroc: étude socio-pragmatique. Communication in the Jewish diaspora. Jewish studies 16: 1996, ⇒232. 339-407.

8628 *Falk, Ze²ev W.* Euthanasia and Judaism. ZEE 40 (1996) 170-174.
8629 *Gutwein, Daniel* Traditional and modern communication: the Jewish context. Communication in the Jewish diaspora. Jewish studies 16: 1996, ⇒232. 409-426.
8630 *Meir, Ephraim* La presenza biblica nella cultura ebraica contemporanea: M. BUBER—F. ROSENZWEIG—E. LEVINAS. La lettura ebraica. 1996, ⇒205. 465-495.
8631 *Neusner, Jacob* Looking backward, looking forward. Formative Judaism. SFSHJ 133: 1996, ⇒142. 209-232.
8632 **Stemberger, Günter** La religione ebraica. Bo 1996, EDB 111 pp. 88-10-60412-1.
8633 *Vetter, Dieter* Der politische Zionismus: Werden—Wesen—Entwicklung. Judentum. 1996 <1992>, ⇒154. 317-336.
8634 **Vries, Simon Ph.** de Jüdische Riten und Symbole. Rororo 8758: Reinbek bei Hamburg ¹⁹⁻²¹1996, Rowohlt 344 pp. 3-499-18758-2.
8635 *Wyschogrod, Michael* A Jewish perspective on incarnation. MoTh 12 (1996) 195-209.

κ8 *Philosemitismus*—**Judeo-Christian rapprochement**

8636 *Abulafia, Anna Sapir* Twelfth-century humanism and the Jews;
8637 *Albert, Bat-Sheva* Adversus Iudaeos in the Carolingian empire. Contra Iudaeos. TSMJ 10: 1996, ⇒8676. 161-175/119-142.
8638 *Banon, David* Kritik und Tradition: jüdische und christliche Lektüre der Bibel. Jud. 52 (1996) 23-39.
8639 **Beck, Norman A.** Mature christianity in the 21st century: the recognition and repudiation of the anti-Jewish polemic of the NT. ²1994, ⇒11/2,7581. ᴿOTEs 9 (1996) 527-528 (*Bezuidenhout, L.C.*).
8640 *Bey, Horst von der* Dunkles Erinnern: Juden und Franziskaner. WiWei 59 (1996) 287-296.
8641 *Bouman, Johan* Die Shoah (Holocaust)—die Katharsis des gottlosen Heidentums. Israel in Geschichte [ᴱMaier, Gerhard]. 1996, ⇒Q1. 251-254.
8642 ᴱᵀ**Bradbury, Scott** SEVERUS of Minorca: letter on the conversion of the Jews. Oxf 1996, Clarendon x; 144 pp. [ChH 67,354—Wilken, Robert Louis].
8643 ᴱ**Brändle, Rudolf** Johannes CHRYSOSTOMUS: acht Reden gegen Juden. BGrL 41: 1995, ⇒11/2,7587. ᴿFrRu 3 (1996) 97-99 (*Thoma, Clemens*).
8644 *Brändle, Rudolf; Stegemann, Ekkehard* Die Entstehung der ersten "Christlichen Gemeinde" Roms im Kontext der Jüdischen Gemeinden. NTS 42 (1996) 1-11.
8645 *Cunz, Martin* Na'asè we-nishma' - faremo e asolteremo (Es 24,7): ridare al cristianesimo una prospettiva ebraica. Studi, Fatti, Ricerche 75 (1996) 3-6.
8646 *Dahan, Gilbert* Der erste Kreuzzug: die Beziehungen zwischen Juden und Christen. Jud. 52 (1996) 221-236.
8647 *Delgado, Mariano* Zwischen Duldung und Verfolgung: das Schicksal der Juden im christlichen Spanien. Wahrnehmung des Fremden. 1996, ⇒218. 155-189.

8648 **Dunn, James D.G.** Jews and christians: the parting of the ways A.D. 70 to 135. WUNT 66: 1992, ⇒8,467... 11/2,7609. ᴿRHE 91 (1996) 282-283 (*Haelewyck, Jean-Claude*).

8649 Early christianity in connection with Judaism [bibliography]. QS 66 (1996) 327-329.

Ehrlich, Carl Stephan "Anti-Judäismus" in der Hebräischen Bibel: der Fall: Ezechiel ⇒3544.

8650 *Fishman-Duker, Rivkah* Anti-Jewish arguments in the Chronicon Paschale;

8651 *Ginio, Alisa Meyuhas* The fortress of faith at the end of the west: Alonso de Espina and his *Fortalitium Fidei*;

8652 *Gutwirth, E.* Gender, history and the Judeo-christian polemic. Contra Iudaeos. TSMJ 10: 1996, ⇒8676. 105-117/215-237/257-278.

8653 *Hahn, Ferdinand* Die Bedeutung der alttestamentlich-jüdischen Traditionen für die christliche Theologie;

8654 Das frühjüdische Traditionsgut und das Neue Testament < 1993 > ;

8655 Theologie nach Auschwitz: ihre Bedeutung für die neutestamentliche Exegese: eine Thesenreihe;

8656 Die Verwurzelung des Christentums im Judentum < 1988 > ;

8657 Warum die Christen nicht Juden geblieben sind. ᶠHahn F., 1996, ⇒4634. 34-48/172-189/49-54/1-19/20-33.

8658 *Hardwick, Michael E.* Contra Apionem and Christian apologetics. Josephus' Contra Apionem [ᴱ**Feldman, L.**]. AGJU 34: 1996, ⇒q7. 369-402.

8659 **Harvey, Graham** The true Israel: uses of the names Jew, Hebrew and Israel in ancient Jewish and early Christian literature. Diss. Newcastle 1991, ᴰ*Sawyer, John F.A.*, AGJU 35: Lei 1996, Brill xvii; 303 pp. ƒ165/$106.50. 90-04-10617-0.

8660 *Hruby, Kurt* Juden und Judentum bei den Kirchenvätern < 1970 > ;

8661 Die Stellung der jüdischen Gesetzeslehrer zur werdenden Kirche. Aufsätze. ANTZ 5: 1996 < 1971 > , ⇒8428. 415-481/349-414.

8662 *Irshai, Oded* Cyril of Jerusalem: the apparition of the cross and the Jews. Contra Iudaeos. TSMJ 10: 1996, ⇒8676. 85-104.

8663 **Jochum, Herbert** Kirche und Synagoge: im Dialog. ᴱ*Neumüller, Gebhard*, Mü 1996, Kösel 123 pp. Kurs Religion; für die Sekundarstufe II; Bd. 4 [FrRu 6,141s—Trutwin, Werner].

8664 *Kaestli, Jean-Daniel* Où en est le débat sur le judéo-christianisme?. Le déchirement. MoBi 32: 1996, ⇒192. 243-272.

8665 *Klein, Lillian R.* On "anti-judaism" in German feminist thought: some reflections by way of a response. A feminist companion. 1996, ⇒170. 355-362.

8666 ᴱ**Klenicki, Leon; Wigoder, Geoffrey** A dictionary of the Jewish-Christian dialogue. Studies in Judaism and Christianity: Ann Arbor ²1995, Books Demand 222 pp. $63.30. 0-8357-2702-5. ᴿCoTh 66/2 (1996) 173-175 (*Chrostowski, Waldemar*).

8667 *Kofsky, Aryeh* Eusebius of Caesarea and the Christian-Jewish polemic. Contra Iudaeos. TSMJ 10: 1996, ⇒8676. 59-83.

8668 **Krauss, Samuel** The Jewish-Christian controversy from the earliest times to 1789, 1: History. ᴱ*Horbury, William*, TSAJ 56: Tü 1996, Mohr xiv; 310 pp. $137.50. 3-16-146473-7.

8669 *Lasker, Daniel J.* Jewish-christian polemics at the turning point: Jewish evidence from the twelfth century. HThR 89 (1996) 161-173;

8670 Jewish philosophical polemics in Ashkenaz. Contra Iudaeos. TSMJ 10: 1996, ⇒8676. 195-213.

8671 *Laytner, Anson* Christianity and Judaism: old history, new beginnings. Sum. 187. JES 33 (1996) 187-203.

8672 *Lichtenberger, Hermann* Jews and Christians in Rome in the time of Nero: JOSEPHUS and Paul in Rome. Religion. ANRW II.26.3. 1996, ⇒183. 2142-2176.

8673 **Lieu, Judith M.** Image and reality: the Jews in the world of the christians in the second century. E 1996, Clark 348 pp. £25. 0-567-08529-5. RET 108 (1996-97) 290-291 (*Rodd, C.S.*).

8674 *Limor, Ora* The epistle of Rabbi SAMUEL of Morocco: a bestseller in the world of polemics. Contra Iudaeos. TSMJ 10: 1996, ⇒8676. 178-194;

8675 יהודית סמכות—נוצרית קרושה [Christian tradition—Jewish authority]. Sum. 238. Cathedra 80 (1996) 31-62. **H.**

8676 E**Limor, Ora; Stroumsa, Guy G.** Contra Iudaeos: ancient and medieval polemics between christians and Jews. TSMJ 10: Tü 1996, Mohr viii; 290 pp. DM198. 3-16-146482-6 [ThD 44,162].

8677 *Lindner, Helgo* Israel, Judentum und Christentum in ihrem Verhältnis zueinander in der modernen Systematik. Israel in Geschichte [EMaier, G.]. 1996, ⇒Q1. 215-250.

8678 **Lucas, Leopold** The conflict between christianity and Judaism... fourth century. 1993, ⇒10,10111. RJEarlyC 4 (1996) 391-392 (*Frizzell, Lawrence E.*).

8679 **Maccoby, Hyam** A pariah people: the anthropology of antisemitism. L 1996, Constable 236 pp. 0-09-475450-0.

8680 *Mach, Michael* JUSTIN Martyr's *Dialogus cum Tryphone Iudaeo* and the development of christian anti-Judaism. Contra Iudaeos. TSMJ 10: 1996, ⇒8676. 27-47.

8681 *Macina, Menahem R.* L'"antijudaïsme" néotestamentaire: entre doctrine et polémique. NRTh 118 (1996) 410-416.

      EMarguerat, D. Le déchirement: juifs et chrétiens au premier siècle ⇒192.

8682 *Marguerat, Daniel* Ebrei e cristiani nel I secolo: la separazione. TSciumbata, M. Patrizia, Bollettino Amicizia Ebraico-Cristiana 31/3-4 (1996) 122-132.

8683 **Mayer, Reinhold** Zeit ist's: zur Erneuerung des Christseins durch Israel-Erfahrung. Gerlingen ²1996, Bleicher 263 pp. 3-88350-615-X. RJud. 52 (1996) 203-205 {*Triebel, Lothar*}.

8684 *Mulder, D.C.* Jewish-Christian relations: the complexity of an intra-christian discussion. ER 48 (1996) 513-519.

8685 *Neusner, Jacob* Judisk-kristen dialog: trosuppfattningar i konflikt, trohet i fred. SEÅ 61 (1996) 105-116.

8686 **Nicholls, William** Christian anti-Semitism: a history of hate. 1993, ⇒9,11055. RJdm 45 (1996) 368-373 (*Goldberg, Michael*).

8687 *Orfali, Moises* The Portuguese edition (1565) of HIERONYMUS de Sancta Fide's *Contra Iudaeos*. Contra Iudaeos. TSMJ 10: 1996, ⇒8676. 239-256.

8688 **Paul, André** Leçons paradoxales sur les juifs et les chrétiens. 1992, ⇒8,a775; 10,10132. RRivBib 44 (1996) 468-473 (*Perani, Mauro*);

8689 Il giudaismo antico e la bibbia. 1993, ⇒11/2,7699. RRivBib 44 (1996) 455-468 (*Perani, Mauro*).

8690 **Petersen, Birte** Theologie nach Auschwitz?: jüdische und christliche Versuche einer Antwort. VIKJ 24: B 1996, Institut Kirche und Judentum. 143 pp. 3-923095-25-2.

8691 *Petzel, Paul* Aspekte jüdischer Diasporaerfahrung—in christlicher Sicht. LebZeug 51 (1996) 137-151.

8692 **Quinzio, Sergio** Die Niederlage Gottes. ᵀ*Hausmann, Ulrich*; Nachwort *Kallscheuer, Otto*. Hamburg 1996, Rotbuch 120 pp. [FrRu 6,145s—Gorbauch, Horst].

8693 *Reichrath, Hans L.* Der christlich-jüdische Dialog: "die Geschichtlichkeit der Kirche war und ist eine Israelgeschichtlichkeit": Ekklesiologisches in Friedrich-Wilhelm MARQUARDTS Dogmatik. Jud. 52 (1996) 40-58.

8694 *Rokéhah, David* -הערות על היהודים והי—הערות על ישראל מקורות לתולדות עם ישראל
הדות בספרות הנוצרית [Christian Greek and Latin authors on Jews and Judaism]. ᶠSTERN M., 1996, ⇒87. Sum. 147*. 167-195. **H**.

8695 *Rosenkranz, Simone* Judentum, Christentum und Islam in der Sicht des Ibn KAMMUNA. Jud. 52 (1996) 4-22.

8696 ᴱ**Rothschild, Fritz A.** Jewish perspectives on christianity. NY 1996, Continuum x; 368 pp. $25.

8697 **Sanders, Jack T.** Schismatics, sectarians, dissidents, deviants: the first one hundred years of Jewish-Christian relations. 1993, ⇒9,11073... 11/2,7714. ᴿCBQ 58 (1996) 769-771 (*Frizzell, Lawrence E.*).

8698 *Sanders, Jack T.* The first decades of Jewish-Christian relations: the evidence of the New Testament (Gospels and Acts). Religion. ANRW II.26.3: 1996, ⇒183. 1937-1978.

8699 *Satran, David* Anti-Jewish polemic in the *Peri Pascha* of MELITO of Sardis: the problem of social context. Contra Iudaeos. TSMJ 10: 1996, ⇒8676. 49-58.

8700 *Schnabel, Eckhard J.* Die Gemeinde des Neuen Bundes in Kontinuität und Diskontinuität zur Gemeinde des Alten Bundes. Israel in Geschichte [ᴱMaier, G.]. 1996, ⇒Q1. 147-213.

8701 **Schreckenberg, Heinz** Die Juden in der Kunst Europas: ein historischer und theologischer Bildatlas. FrB 1996, Herder 408 pp. 658 ill. DM168. 3-451-26144-8 [BiLi 70,245].

8702 *Siegele-Wenschkewitz, Leonore* In the dangerous currents of old prejudices: how predominant thoughts have disastrous effects and what could be done to counter them. A feminist companion. 1996 <1993>, ⇒170. 342-348.

8703 *Stemberger, Günter* Exegetical contacts between Christians and Jews in the Roman empire. Antiquity [ᴱSæbø, Magne]. 1996, ⇒γ1. 569-585.

8704 *Stroumsa, Guy G.* Dall'antigiudaismo all'antisemitismo nel cristianesimo primitivo?. ᵀ*Perrone, L.*, Sum. 45. CrSt 17 (1996) 13-46;

8705 From anti-Judaism to antisemitism in early christianity?. Contra Iudaeos. TSMJ 10: 1996, ⇒8676. 1-26.

8706 **Taylor, Miriam S.** Anti-Judaism and early christian identity. StPB 46: 1995, ⇒11/2,7732. ᴿCritRR 9 (1996) 286-289 (*McKnight, Scot*).

8707 *Theißen, G.* Neutestamentliche Überlegungen zu einer jüdisch-christlichen Lektüre des Alten Testaments. JK 57 (1996) 115-136.

8708 *Vetter, Dieter* Hebräische Bibel—antisemitischer Mißbrauch <1989>;

8709 Relativierung des frühchristlichen Antijudaismus als Historie?: Plädoyer für eine Umkehr von den bösen Wegen der Geschichte und Kirchengeschichte <1989>;

8710 Das theozentrische Ziel und der spezifische Weg: Ausschließlichkeitsanspruch und Weitherzigkeit in der Tradition des Judentums als Anstoß zur theologischen Besinnung von Christen <1994>;

8711 *Vetter, Dieter* Wurzeln judenfeindlicher Auslegung der Hebräischen Bibel: kritische Anmerkungen aus Anlaß des 9./10. November 1988 <1988>. Judentum. 1996, ⇒154. 454-472/249-255/515-525/238-248.

8712 **Wander, Bernd** Trennungsprozesse zwischen Frühem Christentum und Judentum im 1. Jahrhundert n.Chr. TANZ 16: 1994, ⇒11/2,7747. RBZ 40 (1996) 131-135 (*Mußner, Franz*); CritRR 9 (1996) 300-302 (*Christiansen, Ellen Juhl*).

8713 *Watson, Francis* Bible, theology and the university: a response to Philip DAVIES. JSOT 71 (1996) 3-16.

8714 **Wilson, Stephen G.** Related strangers: Jews and christians 70-170 CE. 1995, ⇒11/2,7752. RBiRe 12/2 (1996) 14, 40 (*Saldarini, Anthony J.*).

8715 **Wohlmuth, Josef** Im Geheimnis einander nahe: theologische Aufsätze zum Verhältnis von Judentum und Christentum. Pd 1996, Schöningh 250 pp. [Ist. 43,350ss—Dupuy, B.].

8716 **Zenger, Erich** Am Fuß des Sinai: Gottesbilder des ersten Testaments. Dü 1993, Patmos 174 pp. RThR 61 (1996) 82-83 (*Reventlow, Henning Graf*).

XVI. Religiones parabiblicae

M1.1 Gnosticismus classicus

8717 *Albrile, Ezio* Zurvan tra i Mandei?: un excursus sulle origini dello Gnosticismo. Ter. 47 (1996) 193-244.

8718 *Conick, April D. de* The dialogue of the savior and the mystical sayings of Jesus. VigChr 50 (1996) 178-199.

8719 *Guerra Gómez, Manuel* El Gnosticismo antiguo y moderno. BiFe 22 (1996) 216-272.

8720 **Logan, Alastair H.B.** Gnostic truth and christian heresy: a study in the history of Gnosticism. E 1996, Clark xxiv; 373 pp. $25. 0-5670-9733-1. RSNTU.A 21 (1996) 280-281 (*Oberforcher, R.*).

8721 *Painchaud, Louis* The use of scripture in Gnostic literature. Sum. 129. JEarlyC 4 (1996) 129-146.

8722 **Perkins, Pheme** Gnosticism and the NT. 1993, ⇒9,11121... 11/2,7788. RInterp. 50 (1996) 86-88 (*Attridge, Harold W.*).

8723 *Rudolph, Kurt* Bibel und Gnosis: zum Verständnis jüdisch-biblischer Texte in der gnostischen Literatur, vornehmlich aus Nag Hammadi <1993> 190-209;

8724 "Christlich" und "Christentum" in der Auseinandersetzung zwischen "Kirche" und "Gnosis": Gedanken zur Terminologie und zum Verhältnis von "Selbstverständnis und "Fremdverständnis" <1993> 256-277;

8725 Erkenntnis und Heil: die Gnosis <1992> 14-33;
8726 Das frühe Christentum in Ägypten: zwischen Häresie und Orthodoxie <1993> 278-290;
8727 "Gnosis" and "gnosticism"—the problems of their definition and their relation to the writings of the New Testament <1983> 34-52;
8728 Gnosis und Gnostizismus: Forschung und Wirkungsgeschichte <1984> 3-13;
8729 Gnosis und Manichäismus nach den koptischen Quellen <1965> 629-654;
8730 Gnosis—Weltreligion oder Sekte <1979> 53-65;
8731 Der gnostische "Dialog" als literarisches Genus <1968> 103-122;
8732 Gnostische Reisen: im Diesseits und ins Jenseits <1994> 244-255;
8733 Ein Grundtyp gnostischer Urmensch-Adam-Spekulation <1957> 123-143;
8734 Intellektuelle, Intellektuellenreligion und ihre Repräsentation in Gnosis und Manichäismus <1989> 90-102;
8735 Jüdische und christliche Täufertraditionen im Spiegel des Kölner Mani-Kodex <1984> 686-697;
8736 Loyalitätskonflikte in der Gnosis <1990> 210-219;
8737 Mani und die Gnosis <1988> 655-666;
8738 Das Problem der "islamischen Gnosis" <1981> 291-298;
8739 Das Problem einer Soziologie und "sozialen Verortung" der Gnosis <1977> 66-79;
8740 Randerscheinungen des frühen Judentums und das Problem der Entstehung des Gnostizismus: einige Erwägungen <1975> 144-169;
8741 Sophia und Gnosis: Bemerkungen zum Problem "Gnosis und Frühjudentum" <1980> 170-189;
8742 Zur Soziologie, sozialen "Verortung" und Rolle der Gnosis in der Spätantike <1979> 80-89. Gnosis. NHS 42: 1996, ⇒147.
8743 *Smith, Morton* The history of the term "Gnostikos". New Testament. 1996 <1981>, ⇒151. 183-193.
8744 *Trumbower, Jeffrey A.* Traditions common to the primary Adam and Eve books and on the origin of the world (NHC II.5). JSPE 14 (1996) 43-54.
8745 *Van den Broek, Roelof* APULEIUS, gnostics and magicians on the nature of God 42-55;
8746 The Cathars: medieval gnostics? 156-177;
8747 EUGNOSTUS and ARSTIDES on the ineffable God 22-41;
8748 Gnosticism and hermetism in antiquity: two roads to salvation 3-21;
8749 Jewish and Platonic speculations in early Alexandrian theology: EUGNOSTUS, PHILO, VALENTINUS, and ORIGEN 117-130;
8750 Juden und Christen in Alexandrien im 2. und 3. Jahrhundert 181-196;
8751 The shape of Eden according to JUSTIN the gnostic 131-141;
8752 **Van den Broek, Roelof** Studies in Gnosticism and Alexandrian christianity. NHMS 39: Lei 1996, Brill ix; 300 pp. $106.50. 90-04-10654-5 [JEarlyC 5,317].
8753 ᴱ**Wallis, Richard T.** Neoplatonism and gnosticism. 1992, ⇒10,10173*. ᴿPhoen. 42 (1996) 163-165 (*Kalvelagen, R.E.M.*).

8754 **Williams, Michael Allen** Rethinking 'Gnosticism': an argument for dismantling a dubious category. Princeton 1996, Princeton Univ. Press xix; 335 pp. $49.50 [JEarlyC 6,684s—Smith, Carl B.].

m1.5 Mani, *dualismus;* Mandaei

8755 **Böhlig, Alexander; Markschies, Christoph** Gnosis und Manichäismus. BZNW 72: 1994, ⇒10,10181; 11/2,7810. ᴿThLZ 121 (1996) 168-171 (*Rudolph, Kurt*).

8756 *Burkert, Walter* Zum Umgang der Religionen mit Gewalt: das Experiment des Manichäismus. BThZ 13 (1996) 184-199.

8757 *Gardner, I.M.F.; Lieu, S.N.C.* From Narmouthis (Medinet Madi) to Kellis (Ismant el-Kharab): Manichaean documents from Roman Egypt. JRS 86 (1996) 146-169.

8758 **Gardner, Iain** The Kephalaia of the Teacher: the edited Coptic Manichaean texts in translation with commentary. NHMS 37: 1995, ⇒11/2,7815. ᴿREAug 42 (1996) 194-195 (*Dubois, Jean-Daniel*).

8759 *Hutter, Manfred* Die Bedeutung des syrischen Christentums für die gnostische Religion Manis. Religionsgeschichte Syriens. 1996, ⇒217. 261-272.

8760 *Klimkeit, Hans-Joachim* Der Gebrauch heiliger Schriften im Manichäismus. ꟳDᴀssᴍᴀɴɴ E., JAC.E 23: 1996, ⇒19. 191-199;

8761 Manichaean art on the silk road: old and new discoveries;

8762 The use of scripture in Manichaeism. NHMS 46: Lei 1996, Brill. 300-313/111-122.

8763 **Lieu, Samuel N.C.** Manichaeism in the later Roman empire and medieval China. ²1992, ⇒8,a887... 10,10189. ᴿOLZ 91 (1996) 540-541 (*Reck, Christiane*).

8764 **Lieu, Samuel N.C.** Manichaeism in Mesopotamia and the Roman east. 1994, ⇒10,10190. ᴿJAC 39 (1996) 289-291 (*Hutter, Manfred*); BSOAS 59 (1996) 377-378 (*Sundermann, Werner*).

8765 **Mayer, Gabriele** Und das Leben ist siegreich: ein Kommentar zu den Kapiteln 18-33 des Johannesbuches der Mandäer: der Traktat über Johannes den Täufer. Diss. Heidelberg 1996-1997, ᴰ*Berger, K.* [ThLZ 122,763].

8766 **Polotsky, Hans-Jacob** Il manicheismo: gnosi di salvezza tra Egitto e Cina. ᴱ*Leurini, C.; Panaino, A.; Piras, A.*, Rimini 1996, Il Cerchio 111 pp. L24.000 [RSO 71,275ss—Contini, Riccardo].

8767 *Rudolph, Kurt* Die Bedeutung des Kölner Mani-Codex für die Manichäismusforschung: vorläufige Anmerkungen. Gnosis. 1996 <1974>, ⇒147. 667-685;
       Bemerkungen zur manichäischen Vorstellung vom νοῦς ⇒7941;

8768 Das Christentum in der Sicht der mandäischen Religion <1975/58> 458-477;

8769 Coptica-Mandaica: zu einigen Übereinstimmungen zwischen koptisch-gnostischen und mandäischen Texten <1975> 433-457;

8770 Die Dämonisierung des "Anderen" in der mandäischen Überlieferung: ein Kapitel des Umganges von Religionen untereinander 478-491;

8771 Ergebnisse einer literarkritischen und traditionsgeschichtlichen Untersuchung der mandäischen Schriften <1962> 363-369;

Gnosis und Manichäismus nach den koptischen Quellen ⇒8729;
8772 Die Mandäer heute: eine Zwischenbilanz ihrer Erforschung und
ihres Wandels in der Gegenwart <1994> 538-568;
8773 Die mandäische Literatur: Bemerkungen zum Stand ihrer Textaus-
gaben <1977> 339-362;
8774 Der Mandäismus in der neueren Gnosisforschung <1978> 301-
338;
8775 Mani und der Iran <1991> 698-713;
Mani und die Gnosis ⇒8737;
8776 Probleme der mandäischen Religionsgeschichte <1973> 370-401;
8777 Quellenprobleme zum Ursprung und Alter der Mandäer <1975>
402-432;
8778 Stand und Aufgaben der Manichäismusforschung: einige Überlegungen <1992> 724-741;
8779 Das Verhältnis der Mandäer zum Manichäismus <1994> 607-
626. Gnosis. 1996, ⇒147.
8780 **Runciman, Steven** The medieval Manichee: a study of the christian dualist heresy. C 1996, CUP x; 214 pp. Bibl. 0-521-28926-2.
8781 **Villey, André** Psaumes des errant: écrits manichéens de Fayyūm.
1994, ⇒10,10198; 11/2,7834. [R]JEarlyC 4 (1996) 380-382 (*Doran,
Robert*).
8782 **Wurst, Gregor** Die Bêma-Psalmen. Corpus Fontium Mani-
chaeorum, Coptica: 1. Liber Psalmorum 2.1; The Manichaean coptic papyri in the Chester Beatty Library, Psalm Book 2.1: Turnhout
1996 Brepols x; 140 pp. 2-503-50526-0.

м2.1 Nag Hammadi, *generalia*

8783 **Charron, Régine** Concordance des textes de Nag Hammadi: le
Codex VII. 1992, ⇒8,a849... 11/2,7837. [R]JAOS 116 (1996) 561-
562 (*Good, Deirdre*).
8784 **Franzmann, Majella M.** Jesus in the Nag Hammadi writings. E
1996, Clark xxv; 293 pp. £24. 0-567-08526-0. [R]RSO 70 (1996)
466-469 (*Garbini, Giovanni*); Vox Patrum 30-31 (1996) 488-491
(*Myszor, Wincenty*).
8785 **Khosroyev, Alexander** Die Bibliothek von Nag Hammadi. 1995,
⇒11/2,7841. [R]JThS 47 (1996) 266-268 (*Wilson, R. McL.*).
8786 [E]**Pearson, Birger A.** Nag Hammadi Codex VII. NHMS 30: Lei
1996, Brill xxviii; 479 pp. *f*208. 90-0410-4518 [NT 39,208].
8787 **Reeves, John C.** Heralds of the good realm: Syro-Mesopotamian
Gnosis and Jewish traditions. NHMS 41: Lei 1996, Brill xiii; 251
pp. *f*145. 90-04-10459-3 [JSJ 28,367].
8788 **Richter, Siegfried** Exegetisch-literarkritische Untersuchungen von
Herakleidespsalmen des koptisch-manichäischen Psalmenbuches.
1994, ⇒10,10193; 11/2,7827. [R]AcOr 57 (1996) 163-165
(*Thomassen, Einar*).
8789 [E]**Robinson, James M.** The Nag Hammadi library in English. Lei
[4]1996, Brill xiv; 549 pp. *f*68/$44. 90-04-08856-3.
8790 **Scholer, D.M.** Nag Hammadi bibliography 1970-1994. NHMS 32:
Lei 1996, Brill 450 pp. *f*162/$105. 90-04-09473-3.
8791 **Slavenburg, J.**, (*al*), 50 jaar Nag Hammadi en nu?. Symposium-
bundel: Deventer 1996, Ankh-Hermes 71 pp. *f*19.50 [GThT 97/4,
181].

M2.2 *Evangelium etc. Thomae*—The Gospel of Thomas

8792 **Conink, April D. de** Seek to see him: ascent and vision mysticism in the gospel of Thomas. SVigChr 33: Lei 1996, Brill 200 pp. ƒ125/$80.75. 90-0410-4011.

8793 *Germond, Paul* A rhetoric of gender in early christianity: sex and salvation in the Acts of Thomas. Rhetoric. JSNT.S 131: 1996, ⇒268. 350-368.

       Horman, J. Is there a common Greek source for Thomas and Mark? ⇒4776.

8794 **Poirier, Paul-Hubert** La version copte de la Prédication et du Martyre de Thomas. SHG 67: Bru 1994, Bollandistes 124 pp. Contribution codicologique au corpus copte des *Acta apostolorum apocrypha* par Enzo Lucchesi. RJEarlyC 4 (1996) 593 (*Pervo, Richard I.*).

8795 *Poirier, Paul-Hubert* 'Évangile de Thomas', 'Actes de Thomas', 'Livre de Thomas': une tradition et ses transformations. Sum. rés. 9. Apocrypha 7 (1996) 9-26.

M2.3 *Singula scripta*—Various titles [⇒K3.4]

8796 EMahé, **Annie; Mahé, Jean-Pierre** Le témoignage véritable (NH IX,3): gnose et martyre. BCNH.T 23: Lv 1996, Peeters xvii; 250 pp. Bibl. 90-6831-834-9.

8797 TEOrlandi, **Tito** Evangelium veritatis. 1992, ⇒8,a877... 10,10217. RRSLR 32 (1996) 180-183 (*Iacopino, Giuliana*).

8798 TEPlisch, **Uwe-Karsten** Die Auslegung der Erkenntnis (Nag Hammadi Codex XI,1). TU 142: B 1996, Akademie xvi; 174 pp. DM220. 3-05-003008-9 [ThLZ 122,788].

8799 *Van den Broek, Roelof* The teachings of SILVANUS and the Greek gnomic tradition. Studies in gnosticism. 1996, ⇒8752. 259-283.

8800 EWaldstein, **Michael; Wisse, Frederik** The Apocryphon of John. NHMS 33: 1995, ⇒11/2,7865. RJBL 115 (1996) 775-776 (*Ehrman, Bart D.*).

8801 TEZandee, **J.** The teachings of SILVANUS (NH VII,4). 1991, ⇒7,a324... 10,10219. RJAOS 116 (1996) 560-561 (*Good, Deirdre*).

M3.5 Religiones mundi cum christianismo comparatae

8802 **Beers, William** Women and sacrifice: male narcissism and the psychology of religion. 1992, ⇒11/2,8057. RRStR 22/1 (1996) 10-20 (*Strenski, Ivan*).

8803 **Burke, Thomas Patrick** The major religions: an introduction with texts. CM 1996, Blackwell xxiii; 348 pp. 1-55786-714-3/5-1.

8804 **Dalai Lama** The good heart: a Buddhist perspective on the teachings of Jesus. Boston 1996, Wisdom 207 pp. [Buddhist-Christian Studies 18,240s—Steele, Springs].

8805 **Drummond, Richard Henry** A broader vision: perspectives on the Buddha and the Christ. Virginia Beach 1995, A.R.E. Press 341 pp. RSvTK 72/4 (1996) 182-183 (*Eilert, Håkan*).

8806 **Edwards, Douglas R.** Religion & power: pagans, Jews, and christians in the Greek East. NY 1996, OUP x; 234 pp. $40. 0-19-508263-X [CBQ 59,420].

8807 **Gruber, Elmar R.; Kersten, Holger** Der Ur-Jesus: die buddhistischen Quellen des Christentums. Üllstein-Buch 35590, Sachbuch: Fra 1996, Ullstein 366 pp. 3-548-35590-0.

8808 **Hanh, Thich Nhat** Bouddha vivant, Christ vivant. ᵀ*Coulin, Marianne* Voyageurs immobiles: P 1996, Lattès 189 pp. 2-7096-1686-6.

8809 **Lambert, Jean** Le Dieu distribué: une anthropologie comparée des monothéismes. 1995, ⇒11/2,8090. ᴿETR 71 (1996) 427-428 (*Smyth, Françoise*); FV 95/5 (1996) 85-86 (*Gabus, Jean-Paul*).

8810 **Smith, Wilfred Cantwell** What is scripture?: a comparative approach. 1993, ⇒9,11418... 11/2,8113. ᴿJR 76 (1996) 519-520 (*Droge, A.J.*).

8811 **Sonô Fazion, G.**, (*al*), Dharma e Vangelo: due progetti di salvezza a confronto. Introd. *Fitzgerald, Michael L.*, Religioni e dialogo: Assisi 1996, Cittadella 175 pp. 88-308-0597-1.

м3.6 *Sectae*—Cults

8812 **Dane, J.** 'De vrucht van bijbelsche opvoeding': populaire leescultuur en opvoeding in protestants-christelijke gezinnen, circa 1880-1940. Hilversum 1996, Verloren 255 pp. 90-6550-539-3. Diss. Groningen 1996 [BMGN 113,577ss—Sturm, Johan].

8813 ᴱ**Dillon, Matthew** Religion in the ancient world: new themes and approaches. Amst 1996, Hakkert x; 547 pp. 90-256-1094-3.

8814 El fenómeno de la 'New Age';

8815 El fenómeno de las sectas;

8816 El fenómeno del ocultismo. Auct. var. BiFe 22 (1996) 3-160/167-343/347-476.

8817 *Flemming, Dean* Biblical theological foundations for a response to religious pluralism. ATA Journal 4/2 (1996) 3-29 [ZID 23,153].

8818 *Gil, Juan Carlos* La 'New Age': visión de Cristo. BiFe 22 (1996) 107-129.

8819 ᴱ**Mager, Johannes** Die Gemeinde und ihr Auftrag. Studies in Adventist Ecclesiology 2: Lüneburg 1994, Saatkorn. ᴿAUSS 34 (1996) 345-346 (*Kiesler, Herbert*).

8820 *Quelle Parra, Constantino* La 'New Age': ¿reencarnación o resurrección?. BiFe 22 (1996) 38-71.

8821 **Rhodes, Ron; Bodine, Marian** Reasoning from the scriptures with the Mormons. Arrowsmith, Eugene, OR 1995, Harvest. $12. 1-56507-328-2. ᴿBS 153 (1996) 242-243 (*Woychuk, Jim; Zuck, Roy B.*).

8822 *Rudolph, Kurt* Antike Baptisten: zu den Überlieferungen über frühjüdische und frühchristliche Taufsekten. Gnosis. 1996 <1981>, ⇒147. 569-606.

8823 *Salas, Antonio* La 'New Age': nexos y discrepancias con la doctrina bíblica;

8824 El ocultismo: fundamentación bíblica;

8825 La religiosidad sectaria ante la biblia. BiFe 22 (1996) 5-37/349-369/169-184.

8826 *Smith, Morton* The common theology of the ancient Near East. Studies in...method. 1996 <1952>, ⇒150. 15-27.
8827 *Vidal Manzanares, César* La Iglesia de Unificación: un acercamiento desde el Nuevo Testamento. BiFe 22 (1996) 207-215.

M3.8 Mythologia

8828 *Arnaud, Daniel* Le fœtus et les dieux au Proche-Orient sémitique ancien: naissance de la théorie épigénétique. RHR 213 (1996) 123-142.
8829 E**Billington, Sandra; Green, Miranda** The concept of the goddess. L 1996, Routledge xiv; 192 pp. 0-415-14421-3.
8830 **Bottéro, Jean; Herrenschmidt, Clarisse; Vernant, Jean-Pierre** L'Orient ancien et nous: l'écriture, la raison, les dieux. Diss. D*Zabbal, François*, La Chaire de l'IMA: P 1996, Albin M. 229 pp. FF120. 2-226-08729-X [RB 105,466—Tarragon, J.-M. de].
8831 *Gasbarro, Nicola* Il linguaggio dell'idolatria: per una storia delle religioni culturalmente soggettiva. SMSR 62 (1996) 189-219.
8832 **Mander, Pietro; Durand, J.-M.** Mitología y religión del Oriente Antiguo, 2/1: semitas occidentales (Ebla, Mari). Estudios Orientales 8: Sabadell 1995, AUSA 576 pp. PTA5.300. [JAOS 119,135—Castillo, Jorge Silva].
8833 **Rohl, David M.** The bible: from myth to history. A test of time, 1. 1995, ⇒11/1,290. R*DiscEg 35 (1996) 151-152 (*Raisman, Vivien*).
8834 **Steuernagel, Dirk** Menschenopfer und Mord am Altar: Untersuchungen zu Darstellungen grausamer Episoden des griechischen Mythos in der etruskischen Grabkunst des 4. bis 1. Jhs. v. Chr. Diss Münster 1996 [AA (1997/1) 106].
8835 *Stietencron, Heinrich von* La pluralità del divino: costellazioni politeistiche. SMSR 62 (1996) 667-675.
8836 T**Tandy, David W.; Neale, Walter C.** HESIODUS: opera et dies: HESIOD's *Works and Days:* a translation and commentary for the social sciences. Berkeley 1996, University of California Press xiv; 149 pp. bibl. 0-520-20383-6.
8837 **Walker, Steven F.** JUNG and the Jungians on myth: an introduction. Theorists of Myth 4: 1995, ⇒11/2,8346. R*Religion 26/1 (1996) 91-93 (*Noel, Daniel C.*).
8838 **Wölfel, Claudia** Mythos und Allegorie auf Tafelsilber der römischen Kaiserzeit. Diss. Freie Universität B 1996 [AA (1997/1) 107].

M4.0 Religio romana

8839 *Belloni, Gian Guido* Divinità e culti in Roma: fonti scritte monumenti e monete. F*BELLONI G.*, 1996, ⇒5. 211-286.
8840 *Borgen, Peder* "Yes", "no", "how far?": the participation of Jews and christians in pagan cults. Early christianity. 1996 <1994>, ⇒116. 15-43.
8841 *Clauss, Manfred* Deus praesens: der römische Kaiser als Gott. Klio 78 (1996) 400-433.

8842 **Dumézil, Georges** Archaic Roman religion I-II. ᵀ*Krapp, Phillip*, Baltimore 1996, Johns Hopkins University Press 745 pp. $19+$19. 0-8018-5480-6/1-4 [AJA 101,818].

8843 **Grenier, Albert** The Roman spirit: in religion, thought and art. The History of Civilization: L 1996, Routledge xvi; 423 pp. Bibl. 0-415-15582-7.

8844 **Hirte, Hartwig** Römische Steindenkmäler der Pfalz: Denkmäler des Götterkultes. Diss. Mannheim 1996 [AA (1997/1) 102].

8845 **Klauck, Hans-Josef** Stadt- und Hausreligion, Mysterienkulte, Volksglaube. Die religiöse Umwelt des Urchristentums, 1. KStTh 9/1: 1995, ⇒11/2,8396. ᴿThLZ 121 (1996) 1154-1156 (*Sänger, Dieter*); SNTU.A 21 (1996) 216-218 (*Schreiber, S.*).

8846 **Magini, Leonardo** Le feste di Venere: fertilità femminile e configurazioni astrali nel calendario di Roma antica. R 1996, L'Erma di B. 117 pp. 88-7062-941-4.

8847 **Marco Simn, Francisco** Flamen dialis: el sacerdote de Júpiter en la religión romana. M 1996, Clásicas x; 254 pp. [EM 66,420ss—Delgado Delgado, José A.].

8848 ᴱ**Moreau, Alain** L'initiation. 1992, ⇒8,670... 11/2,8410. ᴿCIR 46 (1996) 113-115 (*Dowden, Ken*).

8849 **Rives, J.B.** Religion and authority in Roman Carthage from AUGUSTUS to CONSTANTINE. 1995, ⇒11/2,8415. ᴿJThS 47 (1996) 666-668 (*Barnes, T.D.*).

8850 **Sacchetti, Laura** Prodigi e cronaca religiosa: uno studio sulla storiografia latina arcaica. AANLR 8/2: R 1996, Accademia Nazionale dei Lincei. Bibl. 153-259.

8851 **Takács, Sarolta A.** Isis and Sarapis in the Roman world. 1995, ⇒11/2,8433. ᴿCIR 46 (1996) 284-285 (*Griffiths, J. Gwyn*).

8852 **Turcan, Robert** The cults of the Roman Empire. Oxf 1996, Blackwell 412 pp. 39 fig. $65. 0-631-20056-0 [AJA 101,821].

8853 **Versnel, H.S.** Transition and reversal in myth and ritual. Inconsistencies in Greek and Roman religion. 1994, ⇒9,11689... 11/2,8437. ᴿJR 76 (1996) 462-464 (*Betz, Hans Dieter*).

8854 **Wickop, Anke** Studien zum römischen Vestakult. Diss. Bonn 1996 [AA (1997/1) 107].

M4.5 Mithraismus

8855 **Brashear, William M.** A Mithraic catechism from Egypt. 1992, ⇒8,b226... 11/2,8445.ᴿ BiOr 53 (1996) 723-725 (*Horsley, G.H.R.*).

8856 **Gordon, Richard** Image and value in the Graeco-Roman world: studies in Mithraism and religious art. Collected Studies CS 551: Brookfield, VT 1996, Variorum xii; 338 pp. $113. 0-86078-608-0 [ThD 44,363—Heiser, W. Charles].

8857 *Pena, Ignacio* Las grutas de El-Magara: ¿un mithraeum?. SBFLA 46 (1996) 301-306.

M5.1 *Divinitates Graeciae*—Greek gods and goddesses

8858 **Ahlberg-Cornell, G.** Myth and epos in early Greek art. 1992, ⇒9,11710. ᴿRAr (1996/2) 419-421 (*Rolley, Claude*).

8859 ^E**Alcock, Susan E.; Osborne, Robin** Placing the gods: sanctuaries and sacred space in ancient Greece. 1994, ⇒10,259. ^RAJA 100 (1996) 618-619 (*Jameson, Michael H.*); CamArch 6 (1996) 314-317 (*Whitley, James*).

8860 **Bermejo Barrera, J.C.; González García, F.J.; Reboreda Morillo, S.** Los orígenes de la mitología griega. Universitaria-Serie Interdisciplinar 179: M 1996, Akal 430 pp. FF258 [RHR 215,511s—Bruit Zaidman, Louise].

8861 **Bremmer, Jan N.** Götter, Mythen und Heiligtümer im antiken Griechenland. Da:Wiss 1996, x; 163 pp. DM39.80. 3-89678-018-2.

8862 **Calame, C.** Thésée et l'imaginaire athénien: légende et culte en Grèce. Sciences Humaines: Lausanne ²1996, Payot 491 pp. FS50. 2-601-03175-1 [ClR 48,342s—Harrison, Thomas];

8863 Mythe et histoire dans l'Antiquité grecque: la création symbolique d'une colonie. Lausanne 1996, Payot 185 pp. FS36.70. 2-601-03189-1 [AnCl 67,450s—Constancio, Patrick].

8864 ^E**Carpenter, Thomas H.**, (*al*), Masks of Dionysus. 1993, ⇒9,354a. ^RHR 36 (1996) 73-76 (*Bremmer, Jan N.*).

8865 **Forsén, Björn** Griechische Gliederweihungen: eine Untersuchung zu ihrer religions- und sozialgeschichtlichen Bedeutung. Papers and Monographs of the Finnish Institute at Athens 4: Helsinki 1996, Finnish Institute at Athens 227 pp. 54 pl. FIM250. 951-95295-5-1 [AJA 101,818].

8866 *Frost, Frank J.* Faith, authority, and history in early Athens;

8867 *Garland, Robert* Strategies and religious intimidation and coercion in classical Athens. Religion and power. 1996, ⇒290. 83-89/91-99.

8868 **Georgoudi, Stella; Vernant, Jean-Pierre** Mythes grecs au figuré: de l'antiquité au baroque. Le temps des images: P 1996, Gallimard 240 pp. 48 figs. FF160. 2-07-73910-4 [AJA 102,457—Lyons, Deborah].

8869 **Halm-Tisserant, M.** Cannibalisme et immortalité: l'enfant dans le chaudron en Grèce ancienne. 1993, ⇒10,10599*. ^RRSFen 24 (1996) 185-193 (*Ribichini, S.*).

8870 *Kahil, Lilly* Cults in Hellenistic Alexandria. Alexander and Alexandrianism. 1996, ⇒311. 75-84.

8871 *Kron, Uta* Priesthoods, dedications and euergetism: what part did religion play in the political and social status of Greek women;

8872 *Linders, Tullia* Ritual display and the loss of power;

8873 *Malkin, Irad* Territorial domination and the Greek sanctuary;

8874 *Montgomery, Hugo* Piety and persuasion mythology and religion in fourth-century Athenian oratory;

8875 *Morgan, Catherine* From palace to polis?: religious developments on the Greek mainland during the Bronze Age/Iron Age transition. Religion and power. 1996, ⇒290. 139-182/121-124/75-81/125-132/41-57.

8876 **Osanna, Massimo** Santuari e culti dell'Acaia antica. Aucnus 5: Perugia 1996, Università degli Studi 326 pp. 29 fig.; 5 plans; 4 maps; 88-8114-371-2 [AJA 101,820].

8877 *Otto, B.* The sacrificed god. VDI 217 (1996) 103-119. **R**.

8878 **Parker, Robert** Athenian religion: a history. Oxf 1996, Clarendon xxx; 370 pp. £40. 0198-149794 [Prudentia 30/2,73s—Stevenson, Tom].

8879 **Penglase, Charles** Greek myths and Mesopotamia. 1994, ⇒10,10614. RGn. 68 (1996) 657-662 (*West, Martin L.*).
8880 *Polignac, François de* Offrandes, mémoires et compétition ritualisée dans les sanctuaires grecs à l'époques géométrique. Religion and power. 1996, ⇒290. Sum. 59. 59-66.
8881 **Ruud, I.M.** Minoan religion: a bibliography. Studies in Mediterranean Archaeology and Literature, Pocket-book 141: Jonsered 1996, Åström vi; 124 pp. 91-7081-162-8 [ClR 48/1,214—Mee, Christopher].
8882 *Semina, K.A.* On the phenomenon of the early Greek temple. Sum. 132. VDI 219 (1996) 124-132. R.
8883 *Shapiro, H.A.* Athena, Apollo, and the religious propaganda of the Athenian empire;
8884 *Sinn, Ulrich* The influence of Greek sanctuaries on the consolidation of economic power. Religion and power. 1996, ⇒290. 101-113/67-74.
8885 **Van Straten, F.T.** Hiera Kala: images of animal sacrifice in archaic and classical Greece. 1995, ⇒11/2,8508. RAJA 100 (1996) 619-620 (*Schachter, A.*); REG 109 (1996) 735-736 (*Samama, E.*).

M5.2 *Philosophorum critica religionis*—**Greek philosopher religion**

8886 **Rist, John Michael** Man, soul and body: essays in ancient thought from PLATO to DIONYSIUS. Collected Studies. CS 549: Aldershot 1996, Variorum x; 298 pp. £47.50. 0-86078-547-5.
8887 *Seeley, David* Jesus and the Cynics: a response to Hans Dieter BETZ. JHiC 3 (1996) 284-290 [Cf. JR 74 (1994) 453-474] [ZID 23,168].
8888 **Tilgher, Adriano** La visione greca della vita. Prospettive 3: Cosenza 1996, Lionello G. 106 pp. 88-86919-04-2.
8889 *Turcan, Robert* Attis Platonicus. MVERMASEREN M., 1996, ⇒219. 387-403.
ELane, Eugene N. Cybele, Attis and related cults ⇒219.

M5.3 *Mysteria eleusinia; Hellenistica*—**Mysteries; Hellenistic cults**

8890 *Bengisu, Rose Lou* Lydian mount Karios. MVERMASEREN M., 1996, ⇒219. 1996, ⇒219. 1-36.
8891 *Borgen, Peder* "Yes", "no", "how far?": the participation of Jews and christians in pagan cults. Early christianity. 1996 <1994>, ⇒116. 15-43.
8892 ETChuvin, P. NONNOS de Panopolis: les dionysiaques: Tome III, chants VI-VIII. P 1992, Belles Lettres 208 pp. RREG 109 (1996) 765-768 (*Fournet, J.-L.*).
8893 **Chuvin, Pierre** Mythologie et géographie dionysiaque: recherches sur l'œuvre de NONNOS de Panopolis. 1991, ⇒8,b368; 11/2,8586. RGn. 68 (1996) 295-299 (*Casadio, Giovanni*).
8894 **Damaskos, Dimitris** Untersuchungen zu hellenistischen Kultbildern. Diss. Freie Universität B 1996 [AA (1997/1) 102].
8895 *Fear, A.T.* Cybele and Christ. MVERMASEREN M., 1996, ⇒219. 37-50.

8896 *Frankemölle, Hubert* Die frühen Christen und die hellenistisch-römische Religion: eine Problemskizze. Wahrnehmung des Fremden. 1996, ⇒218. 39-72.

8897 *Green, Tamara* The presence of the goddess in Harran. ᴹVERMASEREN M., 1996, ⇒219. 87-100.

8898 *Hammerstaedt, Jürgen* Die Vergöttlichung unwürdiger Menschen bei den Heiden als apologetisches Argument in Schriften des SOKRATES, THEODORET, CYRILL von Alexandrien und Johannes CHRYSOSTOMUS. JAC 39 (1996) 76-101.

8899 ᴱ**Hopkinson, Neil** Studies in the *Dionysiaca* of NONNUS. Cambridge Philological Society, Suppl. 17: C 1994, Cambridge Philological Society 187 pp. ᴿREG 109 (1996) 318-320 (*Frangoulis, Hélène*).

8900 *Johnston, Patricia A.* Cybele and her companions on the northern littoral of the Black Sea. ᴹVERMASEREN M., 1996, ⇒219. 101-116.

8901 **Klauck, Hans-Josef** Herrscher- und Kaiserkult, Philosophie, Gnosis. Die religiöse Umwelt des Urchristentums, 2. KStTh 9/2. Stu 1996, Kohlhammer 205 pp. DM34. 3-17-013781-6.

8902 *Lane, Eugene N.* The name of Cybele's priests the "Galloi";

8903 *Metropoulou, Elpis* The goddess Cybele in funerary banquets and with an equestrian hero;

8904 *Naumann-Steckner, Friederike* Privater Dank-Silbervotive aus Nordafrika;

8905 *Pachis, Panayotis* "Γαλλαιον κυβελης ὀλολυγμα" (Anhol. Palat. VI,173): l'élément orgiastique dans le culte de Cybèle. ᴹVERMASEREN M., 1996, ⇒219. 117-133/135-165/167-191/193-222.

8906 **Pakkanen, Petra** Interpreting early Hellenistic religion: a study based on the mystery cult of Demeter and the cult of Isis. Papers and monographs of the Finnish Institute at Athens 3: Helsinki 1996, Finnish Institute at Athens (8) 175; (12) pp. Bibl. FIM180. 951-95295-4-3.

8907 *Rein, Mary Jane* Phrygian Matar: emergence of an iconographic type;

8908 *Robertson, Noel* The ancient mother of the gods;

8909 *Roller, Lynn* Reflections of the mother of the gods in Attic tragedy;

8910 *Sfameni Gasparro, Giulia* Per la storia del culto di Cibele in Occidente: il santuario rupestre di Akrai;

8911 *Smith, James O.* The high priests of the temple of Artemis at Ephesus. ᴹVERMASEREN M., 1996, ⇒219. 223-237/239-304/305-321/51-86/323-335.

8912 *Smith, Morton* The Jewish elements in the magical papyri. New Testament. 1996 <1986>, ⇒151. 242-256.

8913 *Summers, Kirk* LUCRETIUS' Roman Cybele;

8914 *Takacs, Sarolta A.* Magna Deum Mater Idaea, Cybele, and CATULLUS' Attis;

8915 *Ubiña, Robert* Magna Mater, Cybele and Attis in Roman Spain. ᴹVermaseren,ᴹVERMASEREN M., 1996, ⇒219. 337-365/367-386/405-433.

8916 ᵀᴱ**Vian, Francis** NONNOS de Panopolis: les dionysiaques: tome IX, chants XXV-XXIX. P 1990, Belles Lettres 368 pp. ᴿREG 109 (1996) 316-318 (*Frangoulis, Hélène*).

M5.5 Religiones anatolicae

8917 *Anabolu, Mükerrem (Usman)* Sfenks motifi ve Edirne ve Edincik altliklarinda almiş olduğu şekil [Le motif de Sphinx et ses différents formes sur les socles qui se trouvent à Edirne et Edincik]. BTTK 60 (1996) 251-254.

8918 *Haas, Volkert* Marginalien zu hethitischen Orakelprotokollen. AltOrF 23 (1996) 76-94.

8919 **McMahon, Gregory** The Hittite state cult of the tutelary deities. 1991, ⇒7,a716... 9,11872. ᴿJESHO 39 (1996) 183-185 (*Hazenbos, Joost J.M.; Van den Hout, Theo P.J.*).

8920 **Neu, Erich** Das hurritische Epos der Freilassung I: Untersuchungen zu einem hurritisch-hethitschen Textensemble aus Ḫattuša. StBT 32: Wsb 1996, Harrassowitz xix; 596 pp. 3-447-03487-4.

8921 **Singer, Itamar** Muwatalli's prayer to the assembly of gods through the storm-god of lightning (CTH 381). Atlanta, GA 1996, Scholars ix; 193 pp. 0-7885-0281-6.

8922 *Van den Hout, Theo P.J.* Een dodenrijk voor een koning een Hettitisch hiernamaals. Phoe. 42 (1996) 104-112.

8923 **Yoshida, Daisuke** Untersuchungen zu den Sonnengottheiten bei den Hethitern. Heidelberg 1996, Winter xviii; 391 pp. DM128. 3-8253-0402-7 [BiOr 55,475—Hutter, Manfred].

M6.0 Religio canaanaea, syra

8924 **Ackerman, Susan** Under every green tree: popular religion in sixth-century Judah. HSM 46: 1992, ⇒8,b411... 11/2,8633. ᴿJNES 55 (1996) 212-213 (*Edelman, Diana*).

8925 **Albertz, Rainer** Religionsgeschichte Israels in alttestamentlicher Zeit. 1992, ⇒8,b412... 10,10688. ᴿEvTh 56 (1996) 258-285 (*Dietrich, Walter*); ETR 71 (1996) 584-587 (*Macchi, Jean-Daniel*);

8926 A history of Israelite religion in the OT period, (*a*), 1:...to the end of the monarchy. 1994, ⇒10,10690; 11/2,8635. ᴿBiRe 12/3 (1996) 12, 14 (*Lewis, Theodore J.*); ETR 71 (1996) 584-585 (*Macchi, Jean-Daniel*); JR 76 (1996) 97-99 (*Knoppers, Gary N.*); HebStud 37 (1996) 148-150 (*Gillingham, Susan E.*);

8927 (*b*), 2: From the exile to the Maccabees. 1994, ⇒8,b412... 11/2,8635. ᴿETR 71 (1996) 585-587 (*Macchi, Jean-Daniel*).

8928 *Baltzer, Dieter* Der Gott und die Götter. Alttestamentliche Fachdidaktik. 1996, ⇒535. 127-141.

8929 **Bergmann, Martin S.** In the shadow of Moloch: the sacrifice of children and its impact on western religions. 1992, ⇒8,7809... 11/2,8640. ᴿRStR 22/1 (1996) 10-20 (*Strenski, Ivan*).

8930 *Bonnet, Corinne; Xella, Paolo* L'identité d'Astarté-ḥr. ᶠMOSCATI S., I, 1996, ⇒67. 29-46.

8931 **Cornelius, Izak** The iconography of the Canaanite gods Reshef and Baʿal. OBO 140: 1994, ⇒10,10699; 11/2,8650. ᴿOLoP 27 (1996) 239-240 (*Lipiński, E.*); CBQ 58 (1996) 508-509 (*Fulco, William J.*); AcOr 57 (1996) 161-163 (*Groth, Bente*).

8932 *Dever, William G.* Archaeology and the religions of Israel. BASOR 301 (1996) 83-90.

8933 *Dicou, Bert* YHWH and the gods of the nations. ^FZUURMOND R., YHWH, DBAT.B: 1996, ⇒109. 89-96 [OTA 19,486].

8934 ^E**Edelman, Diana Vikander** The triumph of Elohim: from Yahwisms to Judaisms. 1995, ⇒11/2,362. ^RJQR 86 (1996) 504-507 (*Smith, Mark S.*).

8935 *Engelken, Karen Ba'alšamem*: eine Auseinandersetzung mit der Monographie von H. NIEHR. ZAW 108 (1996) 233-248, 391-407.

8936 *Erniakulathil, John* Religion in the period of monarchy. BiBh 22 (1996) 85-107.

8937 ^E**Fine, Steven** Sacred realm: the emergence of the synagogue in the ancient world. NY 1996, OUP xix; 203 pp. $25. 0-195-102258 [Worship 71,376].

8938 *Fleming, Daniel* The Emar festivals: city unity and Syrian identity under Hittite hegemony. Emar [^E**Chavalas, M.**] 1996, ⇒T5.8. 81-121.

8939 **Fleming, Daniel E.** The installation of Baal's high priestess at Emar. HSSt 42: 1992, ⇒8,b421... 11/2,8666. ^RBZ 40 (1996) 315-318 (*Niehr, Herbert*); ZA 86 (1996) 140-147 (*Sallaberger, W.*).

8940 **Frevel, Christian** Aschera und der Ausschliesslichkeitsanspruch YHWHs. BBB 94/1-2: 1995, ⇒11/2,8667. ^RThQ 176 (1996) 79-80 (*Groß, Walter*); BiLi 69 (1996) 192-193 (*Hutter, Manfred*).

8941 **Garbini, Giovanni** Milkashtart, il re dell'Eliseo fenicio. SMSR 62 (1996) 179-187.

8942 **Geller, Stephen A.** Sacred enigmas: literary religion in the Hebrew Bible. L 1996, Routledge viii; 224 pp. £40. 0-415-12771-8.

8943 *Hadley, Judith M.* The fertility of the flock?: the de-personalization of Astarte in the Old Testament. ^MVAN DIJK-HEMMES F., 1996, ⇒99. 115-133.

^E**Haider, P.** Religionsgeschichte Syriens ⇒217.

8944 *Haider, Peter W.* Arados, Gabala, Baitokaike und weitere Kultzentren. 237-241;

8945 Eine christliche Hauskirche in Dura Europos. 284-288;

8946 Damaskus und Umgebung. 189-194;

8947 Edessa, Carrhae, Doliche. 228-237;

8948 Hellenistische und römische Neugründungen. 147-188;

8949 Die Religion in den Städten des 3. und 2. Jahrtausends v. Chr.: Allgemeines. 29-30;

8950 Religiöse Vorstellungen und Praktiken in der Jungsteinzeit und in der Stein-Kupferzeit. 13-28;

8951 Synkretismus zwischen griechisch-römischen und orientalischen Gottheiten: Allgemeines. 145-147. Religionsgeschichte Syriens. 1996, ⇒217.

8952 **Handy, Lowell K.** Among the host of the heavens. 1994, ⇒10,10712; 11/2,8675. ^ROLZ 91 (1996) 571-573 (*Heltzer, Michael*).

8953 *Healey, J.F.* Grain and wine in abundance: blessings from the ancient Near East. ^FGIBSON J., 1996, ⇒31. 65-74.

8954 *Houtman, Cornelis* Säkularisation im alten Israel?. ZAW 108 (1996) 408-425.

8955 *Hutter, Manfred* Grundzüge der phönizischen Religion;

8956 Die Religion nomadisierender Gruppen vom 3. bis zum 1. Jahrtausend v. Chr. Religionsgeschichte Syriens. 1996, ⇒217. 128-144/91-100.

8957 **Jones, Charles Vincent** Who was Jeroboam's God?: an investigation of syncretism in the northern cult. Diss. Westminster 1996, ^D*Longman, T.*, 315 pp. [EThL 74,190*].

8958 **Kletter, Raz** The Judean pillar-figurines and the archaeology of Asherah. BAR international series 636: Oxf 1996, Tempus Reparatum (2) 292 pp. £37. 0-86054-818-X.

8959 *Kreuzer, Siegfried* Die Religion der Aramäer auf dem Hintergrund der frühen aramäischen Staaten. Religionsgeschichte Syriens. 1996, ⇒217. 101-115.

8960 *Lang, Bernard* Neue Probleme in der Erforschung des biblischen Monotheismus. ^FZUURMOND R., YHWH, DBAT.B: 1996, ⇒109. 29-41 [OTA 19,490].

8961 *Lewis, Theodore J.* The disappearance of the goddess Anat: the 1995 West Semitic research project on Ugaritic epigraphy. BA 59 (1996) 115-121.

8962 **Lipiński, Edward** Dieux et déesses de l'univers phénicien et punique. OLA 64: 1995, ⇒11/2,8694. ^RSEÅ 61 (1996) 126-128 (*Mettinger, Tryggve N.D.*).

8963 *Lloyd, J.B.* Anat and the 'double' massacre of KTU 1.3 ii;

8964 *Mayer, Walter* The Hurrian cult at Ugarit;

8965 *Naccache, Albert F.H.* El's abode in his land. ^FGIBSON J., 1996, ⇒31. 151-165/205-211/249-271.

8966 **Niehr, Herbert** Der höchste Gott. BZAW 190: 1990, ⇒6,b3... 10,10727. ThR 61 (1996) 88-89 (*Reventlow, Henning Graf*).

8967 *Oden, Robert* Historical understanding and understanding the religion of Israel. Community. 1996 <1987>, ⇒172. 201-229.

8968 *Oesch, Josef* Die Religion Alalachs;

8969 Die religiösen Zeugnisse von Tell Chuera. Religionsgeschichte Syriens. 1996, ⇒217. 49-68/30-39.

8970 *Otto, Eckart* Krieg und Religion im Alten Orient und im alten Israel. Kontinuum. 1996, ⇒2002. 49-58.

8971 *Pardee, D.* Marziḥu, kispu, and the Ugaritic funerary cult: a minimalist view. ^FGIBSON J., 1996, ⇒31. 273-287.

8972 *Pisano, G.* Varia *iocalia* III: la falsa dea dell'uva. RSFen 24 (1996) 21-26.

8973 *Pratscher, Wilhelm* Das Christentum in Syrien in den ersten zwei Jahrhunderten;

8974 Das Pantheon von Palmyra. Religionsgeschichte Syriens. 1996, ⇒217. 273-284/217-227.

8975 **Prechel, Doris** Die Göttin Ishara: ein Beitrag zur altorientalischen Religionsgeschichte. Abhandlungen zur Literatur Alt-Syrien-Palästinas 11: Müns 1996, Ugarit-Verl. xii; 248 pp. 3-927120-36-7.

8976 *Ribichini, Sergio* Su alcuni aspetti del Kronos fenicio. ^FMOSCATI S., I, 1996, ⇒67. 371-381.

8977 *Ro, He-Won* Folklore and Yahwism in the Old Testament. Christian Thought 456 (1996) 19-33 [ThIK 18/2,52]. K.

8978 *Salje, Beate* Bankettszene im Totenkult: zur szenischen Darstellung auf dem Steingefäß Miron 399. Kamid el-Loz [^E**Kühne, H.**]. 1996, ⇒T2.7. 175-182.

8979 **Schmidt, Brian B.** Israel's beneficent dead: ancestor cult and necromancy in ancient Israelite religion and tradition. FAT 11: 1994, ⇒10,10730. ^RJThS 47 (1996) 169-172 (*Johnston, Philip S.*);

ThLZ 121 (1996) 437-439 (*Wächter, Ludwig*); BiOr 53 (1996) 508-510 (*Spronk, Klaas*); SEL 13 (1996) 126-128 (*Niehr, Herbert*); CBQ 58 (1996) 724-725 (*Smith, Mark S.*) [1 Sam 28].

8980 **Schmidt, Brian B.** The gods and the dead of the domestic cult at Emar: a reassessment. Emar [ᴱChavalas, M.] 1996, ⇒ᴛ5.8. 141-163.

8981 *Smith, Mark S.* Melqart, Baal of Tyre and Dr. BONNET. UF 28 (1996) 773-775.

8982 *Smith, Morton* Helios in Palestine <1982>;

8983 On the wine God in Palestine <1975>. Studies in... method. 1996, ⇒150. 238-262/227-237 [Gen 18; John 2].

8984 *Spronk, Klaas* Ideeën over de doden in het leven na de dood in het Bijbelse Israël. Phoe. 42 (1996) 78-90.

8985 **Stuckrad, Kocku von** Frömmigkeit und Wissenschaft: Astrologie in Tanach, Qumran und frührabbinischer Literatur. EHS.T 572: Fra 1996, Lang 220 pp. 3-631-49641-9.

8986 **Taylor, J. Glen** Yahweh and the sun: the biblical and archaeological evidence. JSOT.S 111: 1993, ⇒9,11925... 11/2,8724. ᴿTJT 12 (1996) 90-92 (*Miller, Patrick D.; Vaughn, Andrew G.*); SR 25 (1996) 508-509 (*Day, Peggy*).

8987 *Tropper, Josef* Auch Götter haben Angst: Anmerkungen zu den ugaritischen Texten KTU 1.5.II:6-7 und 1.6.VI:30-32 sowie zum Wortfeld 'Angst haben' im Semitischen. AulOr 14 (1996) 136-139.

8988 *Ward, W.A.* The goddess within the facade of a shrine: a Phoenician clay plaque of the 8th century B.C. RSFen 24 (1996) 7-19.

8989 *Watson, W.G.E.* An antecedent to Atirat and 'Anat?;

8990 *Wiggins, Steve A.* Shapsh, lamp of the gods. ᶠGIBSON J., 1996, ⇒31. 315-326/327-350.

м6.5 Religio aegyptia

8991 **Assmann, Jan** Egyptian solar religion in the New Kingdom. 1995, ⇒11/2,8736. ᴿJR 76 (1996) 671-673 (*Darnell, John Coleman*).

8992 *Bosse-Griffiths, Kate* The papyrus of Hapi-ankh. ZÄS 123 (1996) 97-102.

8993 **Broze, Michèle** Mythe et roman en Égypte ancienne: les aventures d'Horus et Seth dans le Papyrus Chester Beatty I. OLA 76: Lv 1996, Peeters 304 pp. 90-6831-890-X.

8994 *Chegodaev, Michael A.* The Great God ʾIlu and the Field of Ialu. DiscEg 36 (1996) 15-20.

8995 *Cozi, Massimo* La déesse Khefethernebes. GöMisz 153 (1996) 17-31.

8996 *DuQuesne, Terence* Anubis master of secrets (*hry-sšt3*) and the Egyptian conception of mysteries. DiscEg 36 (1996) 25-38.

8997 **Duquesne, Terence** Black and gold god: colour symbolism of the god Anubis with observations on the phenomenology of colour in Egyptian and comparative religion. Oxfordshire Communications in Egyptology 5: L 1996, Da'th 111 pp. [DiscEg 40,169—Kákosy, László].

8998 *Egberts, Arno* Van kisten en kalveren: twee Oudegyptische riten nader bekeken. Phoe. 42 (1996) 120-135.

8999 *Ferrari d'Occhieppo, Konradin; Krauss, Rolf; Schmidt-Kaler, Theodor* Die Gefilde der altägyptischen Unterwelt: Spiegelbild der Sonnenbahnen im Jahreslauf. ZÄS 123 (1996) 103-110.

9000 **Forman, Werner; Quirke, Stephen** Hieroglyphs and the afterlife in ancient Egypt. Norman 1996, Univ. of Oklahoma Press 192 pp. 174 fig. $40. 0-8061-2751-1.

9001 *Goedicke, Hans* Ancient Egyptian vision of eschatology. Sum. 38. JSSEA 25 (1995) 38-45.

9002 *Griffiths, J. Gwyn* The phrase *ḥr mw.f* in the Memphite theology. ZÄS 123 (1996) 111-115.

9003 ᴱ**Haase, Wolfgang** Heidentum: die religiösen Verhältnisse in den Provinzen. Religion. ANRW 2.18/5: 1995, ⇒11/2,755. ᴿNumen 43 (1996) 307-315 (*Frankfurter, David*).

9004 **Hermsen, Edmund** Die zwei Wege des Jenseits. OBO 112: 1991, ⇒7,a794. ᴿBiOr 53 (1996) 666-674 (*Waitkus, W.*).

9005 *Hermsen, Edmund* Perspektiven zum Verstehen der altägyptischen Religion. DiscEg 34 (1996) 5-16.

9006 *Hoffmann, Nadette* Reading the Amduat. ZÄS 123 (1996) 26-40.

9007 *Iversen, Erik* The reform of Akhenaten. GöMisz 155 (1996) 55-59.

9008 *Jaritz, Horst, (al),* Der Totentempel des Merenptah in Qurna. MDAI.K 52 (1996) 201-232.

9009 **Johnson, Sally B.** The cobra goddess of Ancient Egypt. 1990, ⇒7,a800; 8,b486. ᴿBiOr 53 (1996) 417-418 (*Lacovara, Peter*); CÉg 71 (1996) 67-73 (*Franco, Isabelle*).

9010 **Koch, Klaus** Geschichte der ägyptischen Religion. 1993, ⇒9,11967; 11/2,8782. ᴿArOr 64 (1996) 135-137 (*Bareš, Ladislav*).

9011 **Kristensen, W. Brede** Life out of death: studies in the religions of Egypt and of Ancient Greece. 1992, ⇒9,11969. ᴿBiOr 53 (1996) 415-416 (*Van Voss, M. Heerma*).

9012 **Kurth, Dieter** Treffpunkt der Götter: Inschriften aus dem Tempel des Horus von Edfu. 1994, ⇒11/2,8785. ᴿWO 27 (1996) 159-162 (*Derchain-Urtel, Maria-Theresia*); BiOr 53 (1996) 412-415 (*Labrique, Françoise*).

9013 *Kügler, Joachim* Die Wahrheit der Religionen und das Problem der 'mittleren Distanz': zur Frage eines gemeinsamen Anliegens von Ägyptologie und Theologie. GöMisz 154 (1996) 49-55.

9014 *Leitz, Christian* Die Schlangensprüche in den Pyramidentexten. Or. 65 (1996) 381-427.

9015 **Merkelbach, Reinhold** Isis regina—Zeus Sarapis: die griechisch-ägyptische Religion nach den Quellen dargestellt. 1995, ⇒11/2,8792. ᴿCÉg 71 (1996) 383-386 (*Malaise, Michel*).

9016 *Onstine, Suzanne* The relationship between Osiris and Re in the Book of Caverns. Sum. 66. JSSEA 25 (1995) 66-77.

9017 *Patanè, Massimo* A propos du passage du paganisme au monothéisme. DiscEg 34 (1996) 83-86.

9018 **Perpillou-Thomas, Françoise** Fêtes d'Égypte ptolémaïque et romaine. StHell 31: 1993, ⇒10,10771; 11/2,8797. ᴿNumen 43 (1996) 303-307 (*Frankfurter, David*).

9019 **Pinch, Geraldine** Votive offerings to Hathor. 1993, ⇒9,11980. ᴿOLZ 91 (1996) 547-551 (*Romano, James F.*).

9020 **Quirke, Stephen** Altägyptische Religion. Stu 1996, Reclam 274 pp. 3-15-010419-X.

9021 **Roberts, Alison** Hathor rising: the serpent power of Ancient Egypt. Totnes, Devon 1995, NorthGate 186 pp. 182 ill. £12.50. 0-952-4233-08. ᴿDiscEg 35 (1996) 147-150 (*Matthews, Valerie*).

9022 ᵀ**Roulin, Gilles** Le livre de la nuit: une composition égyptienne de l'au-delà: 1, traduction et commentaire; 2, copie synoptique. OBO 147/1-2: FrS 1996, Éd. Universitaires 409 + 169 pp. 21 pl. FS180. 3-7278-1054-8.

9023 *Sherkova, T.A.* 'The eye of Horus': the symbolism of the eye in pre-dynastic Egypt. Sum. 115. VDI 219 (1996) 96-115. **R**.

9024 **Smith, M.** The liturgy of opening the mouth for breathing. 1993, ⇒10,10780; 11/2,8811. ᴿBiOr 53 (1996) 678-682 (*Hoffmann, Friedhelm*); Or. 65 (1996) 171-173 (*Goyon, J.-Cl.*).

9025 **Snape, Steven R.** Egyptian temples. Shire Egyptology 24: Princes Risborough, Bucks. 1996, Shire 64 pp. £5. 0-7478-0327-7.

9026 *Spalinger, Anthony* Sovereignty and theology in New Kingdom Egypt: some cases of tradition. Saec. 47 (1996) 217-238.

9027 *Störk, L.* Die Flucht der Götter. GöMisz 155 (1996) 105-108.

9028 *Van Dijk, Jacobus* Hymnen aan Re en Osiris in Memphitische graven van het Nieuwe Rijk. Phoe. 42 (1996) 3-22.

9029 *Way, Thomas von der* Überlegungen zur Jenseitsvorstellung in der Amarnazeit. ZÄS 123 (1996) 157-164.

9030 *Wilkinson, Richard H.* The motif of the path of the sun in Ramesside royal tombs: an outline of recent research. Sum. 78. JSSEA 25 (1995) 78-84.

9031 *Willems, Harco* Verlieden en andere onaangename personen in het Egyptische hiernamaals. Phoe. 42 (1996) 60-77.

9032 **Zecchi, Marco** A study of the Egyptian god Osiris Hemag. Archeologia e storia della civiltà egiziana e del vicino Oriente antico, Materiali e studi 1: Imola, Bo 1996, La mandragora ix; 145 pp. Bibl. 88-86123-59-0. ᴿAeg. 76 (1996) 187-189 (*Davoli, Paola*).

м7.0 Religio mesopotamica

9033 *Abusch, Tzvi* Some reflections on Mesopotamian witchcraft. Religion and politics. 1996, ⇒212. 21-33.

9034 *Böck, Barbara* 'Wenn du zu Nintinuga gesprochen hast,...': Untersuchungen zu Aufbau, Inhalt, Sitz-im-Leben und Funktion sumerischer Gottesbriefe. AltOrF 23 (1996) 3-23.

9035 *Braun-Holzinger, Eva Andrea* Altbabylonische Götter und ihre Symbole: Benennung mit Hilfe der Siegellegenden. BaghM 27 (1996) 235-359.

9036 **Cohen, Mark E.** The cultic calendars of the ancient Near East. 1993, ⇒9,11888; 11/2,8831. ᴿJAOS 116 (1996) 776-777 (*Hunger, Hermann*); BiOr 53 (1996) 89-95 (*Reynolds, Fran*).

9037 *Cohen, Mark E.* The sun, the moon, and the city of Ur;

9038 *Dandamayev, Muhammad* State gods and private religion in the Near East in the first millennium B.C.E. Religion and politics. 1996, ⇒212. 7-20/35-45.

9039 *Deller, Karlheinz* Der Tempel des Gottes Bêl-eprija/aprija in der Stadt Aššur. ᶠBERAN T., 1996, ⇒6. 115-130.

9040 **Di Vito, Robert** Studies in 3rd millennium Sumerian and Akkadian personal names: the designation and conception of the personal god. StP.SM 16: 1993, ⇒9,12011; 11/2,8835. ^RBiOr 53 (1996) 113-116 (*Limet, Henri*); OLZ 91 (1996) 133-151 (*Archi, Alfonso*).

9041 *Dietrich, Manfried* Altbabylonische Omina zur Sonnenfinsternis. WZKM 86 (1996) 99-105.

9042 *Galter, Hannes D.* Religion und Kult in Mari am Euphrat. Religionsgeschichte Syriens. 1996, ⇒217. 69-79.

9043 *Guinan, Ann K.* Left/right symbolism in Mesopotamian divination. SAA Bulletin 10/1 (1996) 5-10.

9044 *Hess, Richard S.* Asherah or Asherata?. Or. 65 (1996) 209-219.

9045 *Hoskisson, Paul Y.* The scission and ascendancy of a goddess: *dīlī-tum* at Mari. ^FYOUNG D., 1996, ⇒107. 261-266.

9046 *Hruska, Blahoslav* Zum "Heiligen Hügel" in der altmesopotamischen Religion. WZKM 86 (1996) 161-175.

9047 *Hruška, Blahoslav* Kultovní život starého Sumeru [The religious life of ancient Sumer]. Praha 1995, Orientální ústav AV ČR 140 pp. ^RArOr 64 (1996) 138 (*Pečírkova, Jana*).

9048 **Hunger, Hermann** Astrological reports to Assyrian kings. 1992, ⇒10,12588. ^RWO 27 (1996) 176-177 (*Soden, W. von*); BiOr 53 (1996) 130-134 (*Watanabe, K.*); JNES 55 (1996) 241-242 (*Biggs, Robert D.*).

9049 *Hunger, Hermann* Ein astrologisches Zahlenschema. WZKM 86 (1996) 191-196.

9050 **Hutter, Manfred** Babylonier, Syrer, Perser. Religionen in der Umwelt des Alten Testaments, 1. Kohlhammer Studienbücher Theologie 4/1: Stu 1996, Kohlhammer 256 pp. DM40. 3-17-012041-7.

9051 **Jonker, Gerdien** The topography of remembrance: the dead, tradition and collective memory in Mesopotamia. SHR 68: 1995, ⇒11/2,8841. ^RRA 90 (1996) 186-190 (*Charpin, D.*).

9052 *Katz, Dina* Het Sumerische dodenrijk. ^T*Van Soldt, Wilfred*, Phoe. 42 (1996) 91-103.

9053 **Lawson, Jack N.** The concept of fate in ancient Mesopotamia of the first millennium: toward an understanding of *šimtu*. 1994, ⇒10,10798 [*šimtu*]. ^RJSSt 41 (1996) 311-313 (*Livingstone, Alasdair*).

9054 **Maul, Stefan M.** 'Herzberuhigungsklagen': die sumerisch-akkadischen Eršahunga-Gebete. 1988, ⇒6,b91... 9,12021. ^RJNES 55 (1996) 59-61 (*Farber, Walter*);

9055 Zukunftsbewältigung: eine Untersuchung altorientalischen Denkens anhand der babylonisch-assyrischen Löserituale (Namburbi). 1994, ⇒11/2,10799. ^RMes. 31 (1996) 264-266 (*De Martino, S.*).

Otto, E. Krieg und Religion im Alten Orient... ⇒8970.

9056 **Pongratz-Leisten, Beate** Ina Šulmi Īrib: die kulttopographische und ideologische Programmatik der akītu-Prozession in Babylonien und Assyrien im 1. Jahrtausend v. Chr. 1994, ⇒10,10801. ^RBiOr 53 (1996) 363-395 (*George, A.R.*).

9057 *Powell, Marvin A.* The sin of Lugalzagesi. WZKM 86 (1996) 307-314.

9058 ^T**Roemer, Willem H.Ph.; Hecker, Karl** Lieder und Gebete I. Religiöse Texte, Lfg. 5. TUAT: 1989, ⇒11/2,773. ^ROLZ 91 (1996) 165-167 (*Groneberg, Brigitte*).

9059 **Sallaberger, Walther** Der kultische Kalender der Ur III-Zeit, I-II. UAVA 7: 1993, ⇒9,12027; 11/2,8848. ^RJSSt 41 (1996) 306-310 (*Livingstone, Alasdair*).

9060   *Sanmartín, Joaquín* Götter, die in Zelten wohnten?. WZKM 86 (1996) 391-397.

9061   *Sigrist, Marcel; Westenholz, Joan Goodnick* The Neo-Sumerian empire: its history, culture and religion. Royal cities. 1996, ⇒248. 31-52.

9062   **Tinney, Steve** The Nippur lament: royal rhetoric and divine legitimation in the reign of Isme-Dagon of Isin (1953-1935 B.C.). Occasional Publications of the S.N. Kramer Fund 16: Ph 1996, University Museum xxii; 297 pp. 28 fig. 0-924171-39-1.

9063   *Van der Toorn, K.* Domestic religion in ancient Mesopotamia. Houses and households. UNHAII 78: 1996, ⇒299. 69-78.

9064   *Vanstiphout, H.L.J.* De heilige Lugalbanda. Phoe. 42 (1996) 35-53.

9065   *Veenhof, Klaas R.* An old Assyrian incantation against a black dog (kt a/k 611). WZKM 86 (1996) 425-433.

9066   *Venco Ricciardi, R.* Parthian domestic architecture at Hatra. Houses and households. UNHAII 78: 1996, ⇒299. 309-321.

9067   *Vivante, Anna* Cult furnishings of Mesopotamia from Ubaid to the end of early dynastic periods. CMAO 6 (1996) 71-170.

9068   *Waetzoldt, H.* Privathäuser: ihre Größe, Einrichtung und die Zahl der Bewohner. Houses and households. UNHAII 78: 1996, ⇒299. 145-152.

9069   *Wakeman, Mary K.* Religious conservatism and political invention in ancient Sumer. [F]YOUNG D., 1996, ⇒107. 363-370.

9070   **Zettler, Richard L.** The Ur III temple of Inanna at Nippur. 1992, ⇒8,b599... 10,10808. [R]BiOr 53 (1996) 528-531 (*Sigrist, M.*); Syria 73 (1996) 218-219 (*Lafont, Bertrand*).

M7.5 *Religio persiana*—Iran

9071   **Boyce, M.** Zoroastrism, its antiquity and constant vigour. 1992, ⇒9,12034... 11/2,8861. [R]WO 27 (1996) 183-185 (*Gaube, Heinz*).

9072   A history of Zoroastrianism, 1: the early period. HO 1/8.2A: Lei 1996, Brill xvi; 350 pp 3. impr. with corr. 90-04-10474-7.

9073   **Panaino, Antonio** Tištrya part II: the Iranian myth of the star Sirius. Orientale Roma 68/2: R 1995, IsMEO xvi; 148 pp 10 pl. [R]SEL 13 (1996) 136-138 (*Piras, Andrea*).

M8   Islam; Religions of Africa and Asia

9074   **Adang, Camilla** Muslim writers on Judaism and the Hebrew Bible: from Ibn RABBAN to Ibn HAZM. IPTS 22: Lei 1996, Brill vi; 324 pp. ƒ140. 90-04-10034-2.

9075   **Al-Assiouty, Sarwat Anis** Recherches comparées sur le christianisme primitif et l'Islâm Premier. P 1987-1994, Letouzey & Ané 4 vols. [R]RivBib 44 (1996) 213-218 (*Balzaretti, Claudio*).

9076   **Bonanate, Ugo** Bibbia e Corano. 1995, ⇒11/2,8999. [R]ThLZ 121 (1996) 15-17 (*Antes, Peter*).

9077   *Cazelles, Henri* Un bibliste interroge le Coran. Études. 1996 <1992>, ⇒120. 25-34.

9078   **Gil, Moshe** A history of Palestine, 634-1099. 1992, ⇒8,b591... 11/2,8907. [R]JNES 55 (1996) 70-73 (*Harrison, Timothy P.*).

9079 *Hoheisel, Karl* Jonas im Koran. ᶠDᴀssᴍᴀɴɴ E., JAC.E 23: 1996, 611-621.

9080 **Kuschel, Karl-Josef** Streit um Abraham: was Juden, Christen und Muslime trennt—und was sie eint. 1994, ⇒11/2,9036. ᴿActBib 33 (1996) 91-92 (*Boada, J.*);

9081 Abraham: sign of hope for Jews, christians and muslims. 1995, ⇒11/2,4245. ᴿOCP 62 (1996) 455-461 (*Troll, Ch.W.*);

9082 La controversia su Abramo: ciò che divide—e ciò che unisce ebrei, cristiani e musulmani. ᵀ*Danna, Carlo*, Giornale di teologia 245: Brescia 1996, Queriniana 444 pp. L55.000. 88-399-0745-9;

9083 Discordia en la casa de Abrahán: lo que separa y los que une a judíos, cristianos y musulmanes. ᵀ*Ruiz-Garrido, Constantino*, Estella 1996, Verbo Divino 347 pp. Ptas3.500. 84-8169-099-6 [Gen 16].

9084 **Lazarus-Yafeh, Hava** Intertwined worlds: medieval Islam and bible criticism. 1992, ⇒8,b702; 9,12179. ᴿJRAS 6 (1996) 240-241 (*Khan, Geoffrey*).
Otto, Eckart "Wir wollen den Wald... Beobachtungen zur Rezeption des AT in Melanesien ⇒639.

9085 *Raja, Jesu R.* La Biblia y los libros sagrados de las religiones nocristianas. RevBib 58 (1996) 173-182.

9086 *Reichmuth, Stefan* Bild und Gegenbild: der Islam als Faszination und Herausforderung in Vergangenheit und Gegenwart. Wahrnehmung des Fremden. 1996, ⇒218. 125-154.

9087 **Schimmel, Annemarie** Jesus und Maria in der islamischen Mystik. Mü 1996, Kösel 192 pp. DM38. 3-466-20417-8 [ThRv 93,258].

9088 **Twesigye, Emmanuel K.** African religion, philosophy, and christianity in Logos-Christ: common ground revisited. AmUSt.TR 188: NY 1996, Lang xvi; 394 pp. 0-8204-3069-2.

9089 **Dalaï-Lama XIV** Le Dalaï-lama parle de Jésus: une perspective bouddhiste sur les enseignements de Jésus. ᵀ*Lablanche, Dominique*; Préf. *Ribes, Jean-Paul*; Afterword *Freeman, Laurence*; Foreword *Kiely, Robert*, P 1996, Brepols 300 pp. FF120. 2-503-83105-2 [BCLF 587-9,2056].

9090 ᴱ**Greef, Théo de** Pierre JOHANNS: to Christ through the Vedânta. The writings of Reverend P. Johanns, S.J. Bangalore 1996, United Theological College 2 vols; 596 pp. [LV.F 52,457].

9091 **Lefebure, Leo D.** The Buddha and the Christ: explorations in Buddhist and christian dialogue. 1993, ⇒9,12285... 11/2,9140. ᴿVJTR 60 (1996) 629-631 (*Sebastian, A.*).

9092 **Staffner, Hans** Jesus Christ and the Hindu community. 1988, ⇒5,b280... 9,12304. ᴿITS 33 (1996) 293-295 (*Marceau, William C.*).

XVII. Historia Medii Orientis Biblici

Q1 *Syria prae-islamica, Canaan* Israel Veteris Testamenti

9093 **Ahlström, Gösta W.** The history of ancient Palestine. 1993, ⇒9,12326... 11/2,9186. ᴿAUSS 34 (1996) 97-99 (*Storfjell, J. Bjørnar*); SJTh 49 (1996) 359-360 (*Johnstone, William*).

9094 *Astour, Michael C.* Who was the king of the Hurrian troops at the siege of Emar?. Emar [^E**Chavalas, M.**]. 1996, ⇒т5.8. 25-56.

9095 **Barstad, Hans** The myth of the empty land: a study in the history and archaeology of Judah during the 'exilic' period. SO.S 28: Oslo 1996, Scandinavian Univ. Press 113 pp. NOK178/$25. 82-00-22756-1 [EThL 73,148].

9096 *Beckman, Gary* Emar and its archives;
9097 Family values on the middle Euphrates in the thirteenth century B.C.E.;
9098 Select Emar bibliography. Emar [^E**Chavalas, M.**]. 1996, ⇒т5.8. 1-12/57-79/165-172.

9099 *Beit-Arieh, Itzhaq* Edomites advance into Judah: Israelite defensive fortresses inadequate. BArR 22/6 (1996) 28-36.

9100 *Bondì, S.F.* Aspetti delle relazioni tra la Fenicia e le colonie d'Occidente in età persiana. TEuph 12 (1996) 73-83.

9101 ^E**Boyer, Frédéric** Damas. MoBi 98 (1996) 1-40.

9102 *Briquel-Chatonnet, Françoise* Arwad cité phénicienne. Alle soglie della classicità: il Mediterraneo tra tradizione e innovazione. ^FMoscati S., I, 1996, ⇒67. 63-72.

9103 **Brown, John Pairman** Israel and Hellas. BZAW 231: 1995, ⇒11/2,9197. ^ROLoP 27 (1996) 240-243 (*Lipiński, E.*).

9104 *Capelli, Piero* Cronologie normative e razionalità della storia nell'antico Israele. Henoch 18 (1996) 1-2.

9105 *Cazelles, Henri* Clans, état monarchique, et tribus <1993>;
9106 L'état: nécessité et limites selon la bible <1986>;
9107 La guerre syro-ephraïmite dans le contexte de la politique internationale <1991>. Études. 1996, ⇒120. 139-152/75-88/227-241.

9108 *Chavalas, Mark* Terqa and the kingdom of Khana. BA 59 (1996) 90-103.

9109 ^E**Chavalas, Mark W.; Hayes, John L.** New horizons in the study of ancient Syria. 1992, ⇒8,705*; 9,559. ^RRA 90 (1996) 81-84 (*Ziegler, Nele*).

9110 *Colbi, Paolo S.* Chi erano i Filistei?. TS(I) 72 (maggio-giugno 1996) 29-30.

9111 *Crüsemann, Frank* Human solidarity and ethnic identity: Israel's self-definition in the genealogical system of Genesis. Ethnicity. 1996, ⇒171. 57-76.

9112 **Davies, Philip R.** In search of 'Ancient Israel'. JSOT.S 148: 1992, ⇒8,b818... 11/2,9200. ^RVT 46 (1996) 567-568 (*Williamson, H.G.M.*).

9113 *Davies, Philip R.* Introduction to the origins of the ancient Israelite states. Origins. JSOT.S 228: 1996, ⇒9122. 11-21.

9114 *Dever, William G.* Revisionist Israel revisited: a rejoinder to Niels Peter Lemche. CurResB 4 (1996) 35-50.

9115 *Dietrich, Walter* The 'ban' in the age of the early kings. Origins. JSOT.S 228: 1996, ⇒9122. 196-210.

9116 *Edelman, Diana* Ethnicity and early Israel. Ethnicity. ⇒171. 25-55.

9117 **Ehrlich, Carl S.** The Philistines in transition: a history from ca. 1000-730 B.C.E. Studies in the History and Culture of the Ancient Near East 10: Lei 1996, Brill xii; 235 pp. ƒ112/$66. 90-04-10426-7 [RB 104,471].

9118 *Finkelstein, Israel* The archaeology of the United Monarchy: an alternative view. Sum. 177. Levant 28 (1996) 177-187;

9119 The territorial-political system of Canaan in the late Bronze Age. UF 28 (1996) 221-255.

9120 *Frick, Frank S.* Religion and socio-political structure in early Israel: an ethno-archaeological approach. Community. 1996, ⇒172. 448-470.

9121 *Fritz, Volkmar* Philister und Israel. ⇒334. TRE 26 (1996) 518-523.

9122 E**Fritz, Volkmar O.; Davies, Philip R.** The origins of the ancient Israelite states. JSOT.S 228: Shf 1996, Academic 219 pp. £33/$49; £14/$20. 1-85075-629-5 [CBQ 59,421].

9123 **Hallo, William W.** Origins: the ancient Near Eastern background of some modern Western institutions. Studies in the history and culture of the ancient Near East 6: Lei 1996, Brill xvii; 362 pp. ƒ116/$68.50. 90-04-10328-7. R RSO 70 (1996) 463-466 (*Peri, Chiara*).

9124 *Hentschel, Georg* Die politische Macht aus der Sicht des Ersten Testaments. F FEIEREIS K., EThSt 71: 1996, ⇒24. 11-18.

9125 *Herion, Gary A.* The impact of modern and social science assumptions on the reconstruction of Israelite history. Community. 1996 <1986>, ⇒172. 230-257.

9126 **Herrmann, Siegfried; Klaiber, Walter** Die Geschichte Israels: von Abraham bis Bar-Kochba. Bibelwissen: Stu 1996, Dt. Bibelges. 197 pp. 3-438-06206-2.

9127 *Hoftijzer, J.* Koninklijk bestuur in Oud-Israël. Phoe. 42 (1996) 136-151.

9128 **Hoglund, Kenneth G.** Achaemenid imperial administration in Syria-Palestine and the missions of Ezra and Nehemiah. SBL.DS 125: 1992, ⇒8,3044; 11/2,9216. R BiOr 53 (1996) 790-794 (*Dombrowski, Bruno W.W.*).

9129 *Hoglund, Kenneth G.* Edomites. Peoples. 1996, ⇒226. 335-347.

9130 *Hopkins, David* Bare bones: putting flesh on the economics of ancient Israel. Origins. JSOT.S 228: 1996, ⇒9122. 121-139.

9131 **Jullien, C. & F.** La bible en exil. Préf. *Stève, M.-J.*, Neuchâtel 1995, Recherches et Publications ix; 158 pp. FS38. 2-940032-02-5. R RB 103 (1996) 601-602 (*Tournay, R.J.*).

9132 *Klement, Herbert H.* Die neueren literaturwissenschaftlichen Methoden und die Historizität des Alten Testaments. Israel in Geschichte. 1996, ⇒9139. 81-101.

9133 **Klengel, Horst** Syria 3000 to 300 B.C.: a handbook of political history. 1992, ⇒8,b825; 9,12343. R BiOr 53 (1996) 157-161 (*Roos, J. de*).

9134 *Knight, Douglas A.* Political rights and powers in monarchic Israel. Semeia 66 (1994) 93-117.

9135 *Lehmann, Gustav Adolf* Umbrüche und Zäsuren im östlichen Mittelmeerraum und Vorderasien zur Zeit der "Seevölker"-Invasionen um und nach 1200 v. Chr.: neue Quellenzeugnisse und Befunde. HZ 262 (1996) 1-38.

9136 *Lemche, Niels Peter* Clio is also among the Muses!: Keith W. WHITELAM and the history of Palestine: a review and a commentary. SJOT 10 (1996) 88-114;

9137 Early Israel revisited. CurResB 4 (1996) 9-34;

9138 Where should we look for Canaan?: a reply to Nadav NAʾAMAN. UF 28 (1996) 767-772.

9139 E**Maier, Gerhard** Israel in Geschichte und Gegenwart: Beiträge zur Geschichte Israels und zum jüdisch-christlichen Dialog. Bericht von der 9. Theologischen Studienkonferenz des Arbeitskreises für evangelikale Theologie (AfeT) vom 20.-23. August 1995 in Bad Blankenburg. Wu 1996, Brockhaus 276 pp. 3-417-29415-0.

9140 **Maier, Johann** Entre los dos testamentos: historia y religión en la época del segundo templo. BEB 89: M 1996, Sigueme 365 pp. [Ef-Mex 15,404].

9141 *Mantovani, Piera Arata* L'età persiana in Palestina: 538-332 A.C. PaVi 41/2 (1996) 50-52;

9142 Il regno di Giuda nel VII e VI sec a.C. PaVi 41/1 (1996) 51-53.

9143 **Margueron, Jean-Claude; Pfirsch, Luc** Le Proche-Orient et l'Égypte antiques. Histoire université, histoire de l'humanité: P 1996, Hachette 416 pp. 2-01-016799-6 [RB 104,475].

9144 *Mazar, Amihai; Miroschedji, Pierre de* Hartuv, an aspect of the Early Bronze I culture of southern Israel. BASOR 302 (1996) 1-40.

9145 **Merrill, Eugene H.** Kingdom of priests: a history of Old Testament Israel. GR 1996, Baker 546 pp. 0-8010-2103-0.

9146 *Milevski, Ianir* Settlement patterns in northern Judah during the Achaemenid period, according to the Hill Country of Benjamin and Jerusalem surveys. BAIAS 15 (1996-1997) 7-29.

9147 *Millard, Alan* Die Geschichte Israels auf dem Hintergrund der Religionsgeschichte des alten Vorderen Orients. Israel in Geschichte. 1996, ⇒9139. 25-42.

9148 **Olmo Lete, Gregorio del** El *continuum* cultural cananeo: pervivencias cananeas en el mundo fenicio-púnico. AulOr.S 14: Sabadell 1996, AUSA 188 pp. Apéndices: *Historia Phoenicia* de FILON de Biblos, trad. de *J. Cors i Meya*; *De Dea Syria*, de LUCIANO de Samosata, trad. de *M. Camps i Gaset*. 84-88810-20-2.

9149 *Otto, Eckart* Gibt es Zusammenhänge zwischen Bevölkerungswachstum, Staatsbildung und Kulturentwicklung im eisenzeitlichen Israel? <1986>;

9150 Interdependenzen zwischen Geschichte und Rechtsgeschichte des antiken Israels <1988>. Kontinuum. 1996, ⇒2002. 3-15/75-93.

9151 *Pehlke, Helmuth* Das Verhältnis der Archäologie zur Exegese, dargestellt an drei Beispielen. JETh 10 (1996) 7-32.

9152 **Peterca, Vladimir** De la Abraham la Iosua. Bucuresti 1996, Institutul Teologic Romano-Catolic 187 pp. 973-97299-8-3. **Rumanian.**

9153 *Rainey, Anson F.* Who is a Canaanite?: a review of the textual evidence. BASOR 304 (1996) 1-15.

9154 **Redford, Donald B.** Egypt, Canaan and Israel in ancient times. 1992, ⇒8,b836... 11/2,9235. ᴿJSSt 41 (1996) 121-126 (*Kitchen, K.A.*).

9155 *Redford, Donald B.* A response to Anson RAINEY's "Remarks on Donald REDFORD's Egypt, Canaan, and Israel in ancient times". BASOR 301 (1996) 77-81.

9156 *Rendtorff, Rolf* Welche Folgerungen hat der Wandel in der Pentateuchforschung für unsere Sicht der Geschichte Israels?. Israel in Geschichte. 1996, ⇒9139. 43-59.

9157 *Ro, He W.* Hellenism in Hebraism: origin and history of the Philistines in the history of ancient Israel. Yonsei Journal of Theology 1 (1996) 1-34 [ZID 23,414].

9158 **Sacchi, Paolo** Storia del secondo tempio: Israele tra il IV secolo a.C. ed il I d.C. 1994, ⇒11/2,9237. ᴿProtest. 51 (1996) 73-74 (*Noffke, Eric*); RSLR 32 (1996) 178-180 (*Martone, Corrado*).

9159 **Schams, Christine** The status and functions of Jewish scribes in the Second-Temple period. Diss. Oxf 1996, ᴰ*Goodman, M.D.*, [TynB 49,377ss].

9160 *Schaper, Joachim* Die religionsgeschichtlichen Wurzeln des frühisraelitischen Stämmebundes. VT 46 (1996) 361-375.

9161 *Schäfer-Lichtenberger, Christa* Sociological and biblical views of the early state. Origins. JSOT.S 228: 1996, ⇒9122. 78-105.

9162 *Schmidt, Johann Michael* Rückkehr und Neuaufbau: die Persische Zeit;

9163 Die Zeit des Exils. Altes Testament. 1996, ⇒169. 74-87/58-74.

9164 **Soggin, J. Alberto** An introduction to the history of Israel and Judah. ²1993 <1984>, ⇒10,11007; 11/2,9246. ᴿJAOS 116 (1996) 546-548 (*Rainey, Anson F.*).

9165 **Sturm, Josef** La guerre de Ramsès II contre les hittites. ᵀ*Vandersleyen, Claude*, Connaissance de l'Égypte Ancienne 6: ᴿOLZ 93 (1998) 448-450 (*Kitchen, Kenneth A.*).

9166 **Thompson, Thomas L.** Early history of the Israelite people from the written and archaeological sources. 1994, ⇒8,b848... 11/2,9254. ᴿAUSS 34 (1996) 149-151 (*Merling, David*).

9167 *Vella, Nicholas* Elusive Phoenicians. Antiquity 70 (1996) 245-250.

9168 *Weinstein, James* A wolf in sheep's clothing: how the high chronology became the middle chronology. BASOR 304 (1996) 55-63.

9169 **Wellhausen, Julius** Prolegomena to the history of Israel. 1994 <1885>, ⇒10,11011. ᴿJSSt 41 (1996) 316-318 (*Smend, Rudolf*).

9170 **Westermann, Claus** Une histoire d'Israël—mille ans et un jour. Foi Vivante, Bible: P 1996, Cerf 2 vols; 140+ 220 pp. [LV(L) 47/3,107].

9171 *Westermann, Claus* Kirchengeschichte und Geschichte Israels. Das mündliche Wort. 1996, ⇒157. 196-201.

9172 **Whitelam, Keith W.** The invention of ancient Israel: the silencing of Palestinian history. L 1996, Routledge viii; 281 pp. £40. 0-415-10758-X. ᴿIEJ 46 (1996) 284-288 (*Levine, Baruch A.; Malamat, Abraham*); SJOT 10 (1996) 88-114 (*Lemche, Niels Peter*).

9173 *Whybray, R.N.* What do we know about ancient Israel?. ET 108 (1996) 71-74.

9174 *Yon, Marguerite* Les derniers rois phéniciens de Kition: état des recherches. ᶠMoscati S., I, 1996, ⇒67. 441-450.

9175 *Younker, Randall W.* Ammonites. Peoples. 1996, ⇒226. 293-316.

9176 *Zaccagnini, Carlo* Tyre and the cedars of Lebanon. ᶠMoscati S., I, 1996, ⇒67. 451-466.

9177 *Zadok, Ran* Notes on Syro-Palestinian history, toponymy and anthroponymy. UF 28 (1996) 721-749.

Q2 **Historiographia**—*theologia historiae*

9178 **Bagnall, Roger S.** Reading papyri, writing ancient history. 1995, ⇒11/2,9268. ᴿAeg. 76 (1996) 195-196 (*Lama, Mariachiara*); CÉg 71 (1996) 365-366 (*Huß, Werner*).

9179 **Bakker, Nico** Geschiedenis in opspraak: over de legitimatie van het concept geschiedenis: een theologische verhandeling. Kampen 1996, Kok [ITBT 5/3,24-27—*Boer, Dick*].

9180 *Balentine, Samuel E.* The politics of religion in the Persian period. ᶠMason R., 1996, ⇒57. 129-146.

9181 *Benoist, Jocelyn* L'écriture de la contingence: sur le sens et l'objet du discours historique. RSR 84 (1996) 253-265.
9182 ᴱ**Borobio, Emiliano Martínez** Literatura e historia en el Próximo Oriente Antiguo. n.p. 1996, Museo Sefardí 155 pp. Ciclo de conferencias pronunciadas en el curso "El Próximo Oriente Antiguo II" (Textos históricos y literarios en el Antiguo Oriente y en la Biblia), Toledo, Noviembre 1995-Junio 1996. 84-922145-0-3.
9183 **Brettler, Marc Zvi** The creation of history in ancient Israel. 1995, ⇒11/2,9276. ᴿJSSt 41 (1996) 318-320 (*Lemche, Niels Peter*).
9184 *Cazelles, Henri* Historiographies bibliques et prébibliques. Études. 1996, ⇒120. 253-279.
9185 *Detienne, Marcel* Pour un débat sur les historicités comparées. Israël construit son histoire. 1996, ⇒199. 153-166 [OTA 19,399].
9186 *Dever, William G.* Archaeology and the current crisis in Israelite historiography. ꟳAᴠɪʀᴀᴍ J., ErIs 25: 1996, ⇒2. 18*-27*.
9187 *Halpern, Baruch* The construction of the Davidic state: an exercise in historiography. Origins. JSOT.S 228: 1996, ⇒9122. 44-75.
9188 ᴱ**Hornblower, S.** Greek historiography. 1994, ⇒10,425*; 11/2,9307. ᴿJHS 116 (1996) 210 (*Alonso-Núñez, J.M.*).
9189 *Japhet, Sara* L'historiographie post-exilique: comment et pourquoi. Israël construit son histoire. 1996, ⇒199. 123-152 [OTA 19,436].
9190 *Krivouchine, Ivan* L'époque préchrétienne dans L'Histoire Ecclésiastique d'Eᴜsᴇʙᴇ de Césarée. Tr. 51 (1996) 287-294.
9191 *Liverani, Mario* Ancient propaganda and historical criticism. Albright centennial conference. 1996, ⇒303. 283-289.
9192 **Long, V. Philips** The art of biblical history. 1994, ⇒10,11045; 11/2,9314. ᴿSBET 14 (1996) 159-161 (*Wilson, Alistair I.*).
9193 *Maier, Gerhard* Wahrheit und Wirklichkeit im Geschichtsverständnis des Alten Testaments. Israel in Geschichte. 1996, ⇒9139. 9-23 [OTA 19,401].
9194 *McConville, J.G.* Faces of exile in Old Testament historiography. ꟳMᴀsᴏɴ R., 1996, ⇒57. 27-44.
9195 ᴱ**Millard, A.R.**, (*al*), Faith, tradition, and historiography: OT historiography in its ancient Near Eastern context. 1994, ⇒10,326*; 11/2,9319. ᴿCBQ 58 (1996) 389-391 (*Viviano, Pauline A.*).
9196 *O'Mara, Patrick F.* Was there an Old Kingdom historiography?: is it datable?. Or. 65 (1996) 197-208.
9197 *Rad, Gerhard von* Historiografía teologica en el Antiguo Testamento <1948>;
9198 Palabra de Dios e historia en el Antiguo Testamento <1941>. La acción de Dios. 1996, ⇒144. 160-172/173-195.
9199 *Rosica, Thomas M.* Holy ground and holy people. BiTod 34 (1996) 107-111.
9200 **Schillebeeckx, Edward** História humana: revelação de Deus. 1995, ⇒11/2,9338. ᴿREB 56 (1996) 236-239 (*Bombonatto, Ir. Vera*).
9201 *Thompson, Thomas L.* Historiography of ancient Palestine and early Jewish historiography: W.G. Dᴇᴠᴇʀ and the not so new biblical archaeology. Origins. JSOT.S 228: 1996, ⇒9122. 26-43.
9202 *Yavetz, Zvi* Cᴀʟɪɢᴜʟᴀ, imperial madness and modern historiography. Klio 78 (1996) 105-129.

Q3 *Historia Ægypti*—Egypt

9203 **Aḥituv, Shmuel** מינהל הגבול בין מצרים לכנען [The border administration between Egypt and Canaan]. Aviram J., ErIs 25: 1996,
⇒2. Sum. 87*. 27-30. H.

9204 **Assmann, Jan** Ägypten: eine Sinngeschichte. Da:Wiss 1996, 549
pp.

9205 *Baines, John* Contextualizing Egyptian representations of society
and ethnicity. Albright centennial conference. 1996, ⇒303. 339-
384.

9206 *Baud, Michel* Les formes du titre de 'mère royale' à l'Ancien Empire. 1996, Sum. 620. BIFAO 96 (1996) 51-71.

9207 **Beckerath, Jürgen von** Chronologie des ägyptischen Neuen Reiches. HÄB 39: 1994, ⇒10,11078. ROr. 65 (1996) 453-457 (*Luft,
Ulrich*).

9208 **Bowman, Alan K.** Egypt after the pharaohs: 332 BC-AD 642 from
Alexander to the Arab conquest. L ²1996, British Museum
Press 270 pp. £15. 0-7141-0992-4 [DiscEg 38,135].

9209 **Bridges, Marilyn** Egypt: antiquities from above. Essay *Lively,
Penelope,* Boston 1996, Bulfinch 128 pp. Bibl. 0-8212-2257-0.

9210 **Cervelló Autuori, Josep** Egipto y África: origen de la civilización
y la monarquía faraónicas en su contexto africano. AulOr.S 13:
Barc 1996, Ausa 281 pp. 52 fig. 84-88810-23-7 [DiscEg 41,75—
DuQuesne, Terence].

9211 EChauprade, Aymeric Histoires d'Égypte. P 1996, Sortilèges 349
pp. 2-251-49117-1.

9212 *Coleman, John E.* Did Egypt shape the glory that was Greece?.
Black Athena 1996, ⇒229. 280-302.

9213 *Collombert, Philippe* Les 'fils royaux de Ramses': une nouvelle
hypothèse. GöMisz 151 (1996) 23-35.

9214 **Cribiore, Raffaella** Writing, teachers, and students in Graeco-
Roman Egypt. ASP 36: Atlanta, GA 1996, Scholars xiv; 316 pp.
80 pl. 0-7885-0277-8.

9215 **Curl, James Stevens** Egyptomania: the Egyptian revival: a recur-
ring theme in the history of taste. Manchester ²1994, Manchester
University Press xxii; 298 pp. 0-7190-4126-0/7-9. RBiOr 53
(1996) 714-718 (*Fitzenreiter, Martin*).

9216 *Depuydt, Leo* The function of the Ebers calendar concordance.
Or. 65 (1996) 61-88.

9217 **Desroches Noblecourt, Christiane** Ramsès II: la véritable histoire.
P 1996, Pygmalion 428 pp. 2-85704-481-X.

9218 EEide, T., (*al*), Fontes Historiae Nubiorum (*a*), 1: from the eighth
to the mid-fifth century B.C. 1994, ⇒10,11088; 11/2,9376. RClR
46 (1996) 332-333 (*Alston, Richard*).

9219 (*b*), 2: from the mid-fifth to the first century BC. Bergen 1996,
Univ. of Bergen 400 pp. 82-91626-01-4.

9220 **Ellis, Walter M.** Ptolemy of Egypt. 1994, ⇒11/2,9378. RBiOr 53
(1996) 726-733 (*Hauben, Hans*); JAOS 116 (1996) 767-768
(*Delia, Diana*).

9221 *Görg, Manfred* Ofir und Punt. BN 82 (1996) 5-8.

9222 *Hagens, Graham* A critical review of dead-reckoning from the 21st
dynasty. JARCE 33 (1996) 153-163.

9223 *Haider, Peter W.* Menschenhandel zwischen dem ägyptischen Hof
und der minoisch-mykenischen Welt?. Ä&L 6 (1996) 137-156.

9224 *Higginbotham, Carolyn* Elite emulation and Egyptian governance in Ramesside Canaan. TelAv 23 (1996) 154-169.

9225 *Hoffmeier, James K.* Egyptians. Peoples. 1996, ⇒226. 251-290.

9226 **Husson, Geneviève; Valbelle, Dominique** L'état et les institutions en Égypte des premiers pharaons aux empereurs romains. 1992, ⇒8,b951; 11/2,9396. ᴿCÉg 71 (1996) 263-265 (*Héral, Suzanne*).

9227 **James, T.G.H.** A short history of ancient Egypt. NY 1996, Sterling 167 pp. 159 col. pl. $22. 0-304-34711-6 [AJA 101,199].

9228 **Janssen, Rosalind M.; Janssen, Jac J.** Getting old in ancient Egypt. L 1996, Rubicon xviii; 167 pp. £20/£15. 0-948695-46-3/7-1 [DiscEg 39,125].

9229 **Kamil, J.** The ancient Egyptians—life in the Old Kingdom. Cairo 1996, American University in Cairo. 977-424-392-7 [EgArch 12,27—Hart, George].

9230 *Kitchen, Kenneth A.* The historical chronology of ancient Egypt: a current assessment. AcAr 67/1 (1996) 1-13.

9231 **Lalouette, Claire** Au royaume d'Égypte: le temps des rois-dieux. P 1991, Fayard 390 pp. 2-213-02690-4. ᴿCÉg 71 (1996) 269-270 (*Broze, Michèle*).

9232 *Leahy, Anthony* The adoption of Ankhnesneferibre at Karnak. Sum. 145. JEA 82 (1996) 145-165.

9233 *Leprohon, Ronald J.* The programmatic use of the royal titulary in the twelfth dynasty. JARCE 33 (1996) 165-171.

9234 **Luft, Ulrich** Die chronologische Fixierung des ägyptischen Mittleren Reiches... Illahun. 1992, ⇒9,12456; 10,11102. ᴿZDMG 146 (1996) 176-182 (*Hotabi-Sternberg, Heike El; Müller, Matthias*); BiOr 53 (1996) 683-685 (*Simpson, William Kelly*).

9235 *Manuelian, Peter Der* Living in the past: studies in archaism of the Egyptian twenty-sixth dynasty. 1994, ⇒10,11094; 11/2,9373. ᴿBiOr 53 (1996) 662-666 (*Graefe, Erhart*); DiscEg 36 (1996) 137-143 (*Ray, John*).

9236 ᴱ**Martina, Minas**, (*al*), Aspekte spätägyptischer Kultur. ᶠWₙₜₑₙ E., 1994, ⇒10,145. ᴿBiOr 53 (1996) 644-649 (*Kákosy, László*).

9237 **Montserrat, Dominic** Sex and society in Graeco-Roman Egypt. L 1996, Kegan P. $76.50. 0-7103-0530-3 [AJA 101,619s—Meskell, Lynn].

9238 *Moreno García, Juan Carlos* Administration territoriale et organisation de l'espace en Egypte au troisième millénaire avant J.-C.: grgt et le titre ᶜ(n)d-mr grgt. ZÄS 123 (1996) 116-138.

9239 *O'Connor, David* Egypt and Greece: the Bronze Age evidence. Black Athena 1996, ⇒229. 49-61.

9240 *Pérez Lagarcha, Antonio* Megiddo y Kadesh: realidad e ideología de dos victorias militares en el antiguo Egipto. BAEO 32 (1996) 23-30.

9241 *Read, John G.* Chronological placements for Thutmose III, Amenhotep II Ramesses II and the third dynasty. DiscEg 36 (1996) 103-117.

9242 **Rohl, David** Pharaonen und Propheten: das Alte Testament auf dem Prüfstand. Mü 1996, Droemer K. [JETh 11,195—Fischer, Stefan].

9243 *Scheidel, Walter* What's in an age?: a comparative view of bias in the census returns of Roman Egypt. BASPap 33 (1996) 25-59.

9244 *Seidlmayer, Stephan J.* Town and state in the early Old Kingdom: a view from Elephantine. Aspects of early Egypt. ⇒9245. 108-127.

9245 ᴱSpencer, Jeffrey Aspects of early Egypt. L 1996, British Museum Press 216 pp. 4 col. pl.; 28 pl.; 26 fig.; 26 tables; 9 maps; £30. 0-7141-0999-1 [AJA 101,432].

9246 ᴱThomas, Nancy The American discovery of ancient Egypt: essays. LA 1996, LA Country Museum of Art 188 pp. 0-8109-6313-2.

9247 Vandersleyen, Claude L'Égypte et la vallée du Nil, 2: de la fin de l'Ancien Empire à la fin du Nouvel Empire. 1995, ⇒11/2,9427. ᴿJEA 82 (1996) 221-222 (*Taylor, John H.*).

9248 Vercoutter, Jean L'Égypte et la vallée du Nil, 1: des origines à la fin de l'Ancien Empire. 1992, ⇒8,b975... 11/2,9428. ᴿCÉg 71 (1996) 265-269 (*Trigger, Bruce G.*).

9249 Weslby, Derek A. The kingdom of Kush: the Napatan and Meroitic empires. L 1996, British Museum 240 pp. £20. 0-7141-0986-X [BiOr 55,147—Zach, Michael H.].

9250 Wilkinson, Toby A.H. State formation in Egypt: chronology and society. Cambridge Monographs in African Archaeology 40: BAR International 651: Oxf 1996, Tempus R. vi; 180 pp. £32. 0-86054-838-4 [Antiquity 71,778].

9251 *Woodward, Scott* Genealogy of New Kingdom pharaohs and queens. Arch. 49/5 (1996) 45-47.

9252 *Yamauchi, Edwin* Cambyses in Egypt. ᶠYOUNG D., ⇒107. 371-392.

Q4.0 Historia Mesopotamiae

9253 Algaze, Guillermo The Uruk world system: the dynamics of expansion of early Mesopotamian civilization. 1993, ⇒9,12476; 10,11127. ᴿJAOS 116 (1996) 147-148 (*Postgate, J.N.*).

9254 *Arnold, Bill T.* Babylonians. Peoples. 1996, ⇒226. 43-75.

9255 *Battini, Laura* Un exemple de propagande néoassyrienne: les défenses de Dur-Sharrukin. CMAO 6 (1996) 217-235.

9256 Bär, Jürgen Der assyrische Tribut und seine Darstellung: eine Untersuchung zur imperialen Ideologie im neuassyrischen Reich. AOAT 243: Neuk 1996, Neuk'er xiii; 362 pp. Num. ill. [Or. 68,128ss—Braun-Holzinger, Eva A.].

9257 *Bodine, Walter R.* Sumerians. Peoples. 1996, ⇒226. 19-42.

9258 Crawford, Harriet Sumer and the Sumerians. 1991, ⇒7,b156... 11/2,9439. ᴿJESHO 39 (1996) 180-183 (*Neumann, Hans*).

9259 *D'Agostino, Franco* Da Neriglissar a Nabonedo e oltre (considerazioni sulla storia economica neo-babilonese). ᶠMOSCATI S., I, 1996, ⇒67. 117-127.

9260 Dandamayev, Muhammad A. Iranians in Achaemenid Babylonia. 1992, ⇒9,12483. ᴿJRAS 6 (1996) 113-114 (*Schramm, Wolfgang*).

9261 Forest, Jean-Daniel Mésopotamie: l'apparition de l'état VIIe-IIIe millénaires. P 1996, Méditerranée 272 pp. [NEA(BA) 61,69s—Schwartz, Glenn M.].

9262 Frame, Grant Rulers of Babylonia from the second dynasty of Isin to the end of Assyrian domination (1157-612 B.C.). 1995, ⇒11/2,9447. ᴿBSOAS 59 (1996) 553-555 (*George, A.R.*).

9263 **Freydank, Helmut** Beiträge zur mittelassyrischen Chronologie und Geschichte. 1991, ⇒7,b181; 10,11133. RBiOr 53 (1996) 123-125 (*Galter, Hannes D.*).

9264 *Gallagher, William* The Istanbul stela of Nabonidus. WZKM 86 (1996) 119-126.

9265 *Glassner, Jean-Jacques* Les temps de l'histoire en Mésopotamie. Israël construit son histoire. 1996, ⇒199. 167-189 [OTA 19,377].

9266 **Grayson, Albert Kirk** Assyrian rulers of the early first millennium BC II (858-745 BC). Royal Inscriptions of Mesopotamia, Assyrian Periods 3: Toronto 1996, Univ. of Toronto Press xxiii; 265 pp. $150/£110. 0-8020-0886-0.

9267 *Horowitz, Wayne* The 360 and 364 day year in ancient Mesopotamia. Sum. 35. JANES 24 (1996) 35-44.

9268 **Janssen, Caroline** Bābil, the city of witchcraft and wine: the name and fame of Babylon in medieval Arabic geographical texts. Memoirs: WL 1995, Eisenbrauns x; 263 pp. $65. 0-614-96323-0. RMes. 31 (1996) 236-238 (*Invernizzi, A.*).

9269 *Jursa, Michael* Akkad, das Eulmas und Gubaru. WZKM 86 (1996) 197-211.

9270 **Lamberg-Karlovsky, Carl C.** Beyond the Tigris and the Euphrates Bronze Age civilizations. Studies by the Dept of Bible and ancient Near East 9: J 1996, Ben-Gurion Univ. of the Negev Press 286 pp. 0334-2255 [Antiquity 72,935—Sinclair, Anthony].

9271 *Lanfranchi, Giovanni B.* Assyrian culture. Royal cities. 1996, ⇒248. 171-196.

9272 **Larsen, Mogens Trolle** The conquest of Assyria: excavations in an antique land 1840-1860. L 1996, Routledge xiv; 390 pp. 8 col. pl.; 56 fig. £40. 0-415-14356-X [AJA 101,819].

9273 *Liebig, Michael* Nochmals zur Geographie des 8. Feldzuges Sargons II. von Assyrien. ZA (1996) 207-210.

9274 *Matthews, Victor H.* Messengers and the transmission of information in the Mari kingdom. FYOUNG D., 1996, ⇒107. 267-274.

9275 **Nemet-Nejat, Karen Rhea** Cuneiform mathematical texts as a reflection of everyday life in Mesopotamia. AOS 75: 1993, ⇒11/2,b385. RJNES 55 (1996) 317-318 (*Young, Dwight W.*).

9276 **Oded, Bustenay** War, peace, and empire: justifications for war in Assyrian royal inscriptions. 1992, ⇒8,7398; 11/2,9437(!). RBiOr 53 (1996) 128-130 (*Van der Spek, R.J.*).

9277 **Ponchia, Simonetta** L'Assiria e gli stati transeufratici nella prima meta dell'VIII sec. a.C. 1991, ⇒8,d14. RBiOr 53 (1996) 489-490 (*Schramm, Wolfgang*).

9278 **Porter, Barbara Nevling** Images, power and politics: figurative aspects of Esarhaddon's Babylonian policy. 1993, ⇒11/2,9472. RBiOr 53 (1996) 200-202 (*Postgate, J.N.*).

9279 *Reiner, Erica* Wie man sich bettet... WZKM 86 (1996) 351-354.

9280 **Rollinger, Robert** HERODOTS babylonischer Logos. 1993, ⇒10,11146; 11/2,9473. ROLZ 91 (1996) 525-532 (*Dalley, Stephanie*).

9281 **Sachs, Abraham J.; Hunger, Hermann** Astronomical diaries and related texts from Babylonia, 2: diaries from 261 B.C. to 165 B.C. 1989, ⇒6,e462. RZA 86 (1996) 274-275 (*Van Soldt, W.H.*).

9282 **Shifra, Shin; Klein, Jacob** In those distant days: anthology of Mesopotamian literature in Hebrew. TA 1996, Am Oved 744 pp. IS103 [JAOS 119,142s—Katz, Dina]. **H.**

9283 **Soden, Wolfram von** The Ancient Orient: an introduction to the study of the ancient Near East. 1994, ⇒10,11149. ᴿOTEs 9 (1996) 169-171 (*Fourie, L.C.H.*).

9284 *Soden, Wolfram von* Die babylonischen Königsinschriften 1157-612 v.Chr. und die Frage nach der Planungszeit und dem Baubeginn von Etemenanki. ZA 86 (1996) 80-88.

9285 *Stager, Lawrence E.* The fury of Babylon: Ashkelon and the archaeology of destruction. BArR 22/1 (1996) 56-69, 76-77.

9286 ᴱᵀ**Tadmor, Hayim** The inscriptions of Tiglath-pileser III, king of Assyria. 1994, ⇒10,11149*. ᴿArOr 64 (1996) 283-284 (*Pečírková, Jana*).

9287 *Tyborowski, Witold* The third year of Nebuchadnezzar II (602 B.C.) according to the Babylonian Chronicle BM 21946—an attempt at an interpretation. ZA 86 (1996) 211-216.

9288 *Vallat, François* L'Élam à l'époque paléo-babylonienne et ses relations avec la Mésopotamie. Amurru 1. 1996, ⇒306. 297-319.

9289 *Watkins, T.* The origins of the household in North Mesopotamia. Houses and households. UNHAII 78: 1996, ⇒299. 79-88.

9290 *Weisberg, David* The culture of the Neo-Babylonian empire. Royal cities. 1996, ⇒248. 221-236.

Q4.5 *Historia Persiae*—Iran

9291 **Briant, Pierre** Histoire de l'empire perse: de Cyrus à Alexandre. P 1996, Fayard 1248 pp. FF280. 2-213-59667-0.

9292 **Dandamayev, Muhammad** A political history of the Achaemenid empire. 1989, ⇒5,b503... 10,11150*. ᴿWO 27 (1996) 181-182 (*Gaube, Heinz*).

9293 **Frei, Peter; Koch, Klaus** Reichsidee und Reichsorganisation im Perserreich. OBO 55: FrS ²1996, Universitätsverlag 337 pp. FS95. 3-7278-1045-9 [NThAR 1997,225].

9294 **Högemann, Peter** Das alte Vorderasien und die Achämeniden: ein Beitrag zur Herodot-Analyse. 1992, ⇒8,d38; 10,11151. ᴿZDMG 146 (1996) 183-198 (*Koch, Heidemarie*).

9295 *Jacobs, Bruno* Die Verwandten des Königs' und die 'Nachkommen der Verschwörer': Überlegungen zu Titeln, Ämtern und Insignien am Achämenidenhof. ᶠBoᴿCHARDT J., 1996, ⇒8. 273-284.

9296 **Koch, Heidemarie** Achämeniden-Studien IV. 1993, ⇒11/2,9504. ᴿZDMG 146 (1996) 198-199 (*Schramm, Wolfgang*).

9297 **Petit, Thierry** Satrapes et satrapies dans l'empire achéménide de Cyrus le Grand à Xerxès 1ᵉʳ. 1990, ⇒7,b196... 11/2,9508. ᴿGn. 68 (1996) 225-228 (*Wiesehöfer, Josef*).

9298 *Vallat, F.* Nouvelle analyse des inscriptions néo-elamites. ᶠSᴘʏcᴋᴇᴛ A., 1996, ⇒83. 385-395.

9299 **Vogelsang, W.J.** The rise and organization of the Achaemenid empire. 1992, ⇒8,d47... 11/2,9512. ᴿBiOr 53 (1996) 150-157 (*Koch, Heidemarie*).

9300 **Weber, Ursula; Wiesehöfer, Josef** Das Reich der Achaimeniden: eine Bibliographie. AMI.E 15: B 1996, Reimer xxi; 756 pp. DM198. 3-496-00813-X [OLZ 92,228].

Yamauchi, Edwin Cambyses in Egypt ⇒9252.

9301 *Yamauchi, Edwin M.* Persians. Peoples. 1996, ⇒226. 107-124.

Q5 *Historia Anatoliae*—**Asia Minor, Hittites [T8.2]**

9302 **Beckman, Gary** Hittite diplomatic texts. SBL Writings from the Ancient World 7: Atlanta 1996, Scholars xx; 206 pp. $45/$30. 0-7885-0153-4 0-7885-0154-2 [OTA 19,525].

9303 *Hawkins, David* The Hittites and their empire. Royal cities. 1996, ⇒248. 69-82.

9304 *Hoffner, Harry A. Jr.* Hittites. Peoples. 1996, ⇒226. 127-155.

9305 *Houwink ten Cate, Philo H.J.* The Hittite dynastic marriages of the period between ca. 1258 and 1244 B.C. AltOrF 23 (1996) 40-75.

9306 **Jasink, Anna Margherita** Gli stati neo-ittiti. 1995, ⇒11/2,9520. ᴿOLZ 91 (1996) 564-566 (*De Martino, Stefano*).

9307 **MacQueen, J.G.** The Hittites and their contemporaries in Asia Minor. NY ²1996, Thames & H. 176 pp. 118 fig.; 28 plans. $16. 0-500-27887-3 [AJA 101,431].

9308 **Popko, Maciej** Zippalanda: ein Kultzentrum im hethitischen Kleinasien. 1994, ⇒10,11164. ᴿOLZ 91 (1996) 34-38 (*Haas, Volkert*).

9309 *Steiner, Gerd* Muršili I: Sohn oder Enkel Labarna-Ḫattušilis I?. UF 28 (1996) 561-618.

9310 **Strobel, Karl** Die Galater: Geschichte und Eigenart der keltischen Staatenbildung auf dem Boden des hellenistischen Kleinasien. Untersuchungen zur Geschichte und historischen Geographie des hellenistischen und römischen Kleinasien, 1: B 1996 Akademie 269 pp. DM280. 3-05-002543-3.

9311 *Sürenhagen, Dietrich* Politischer Niedergang und kulturelles Nachleben des hethitischen Großreiches im Lichte neuerer Forschung. ᶠBᴇʀᴀɴ T., 1996, ⇒6. 283-293.

9312 *Wilhelm, Gernot* L'état actuel et les perspectives des études hourrites. Amurru 1. 1996, ⇒306. 175-187.

Q6.1 **Historia Graeciae classicae**

9313 **Catenacci, Carmine** Il tiranno e l'eroe: per un'archeologia del potere nella Grecia antica. Testi e pretesti: Mi 1996, Mondadori ix; 309 pp. Bibl. 88-424-9604-9.

9314 **Coulet, C.** Communiquer en Grèce ancienne: écrits, discours, information, voyages. P 1996, Belles Lettres 237 pp. FF125. 2-251-33815-2 [JHS 118,243—Greenwood, Emily].

9315 **Demand, N.** History of ancient Greece. NY 1996, Overture xviii; 397 pp. 0-07-016207-7 [ClR 48,371s—Bowden, Hugh].

9316 **Doblhofer, Georg** Vergewaltigung in der Antike. Beiträge zur Altertumskunde 46: Stu 1994, Teubner x; 134 pp. DM48. 3-519-07495-8. ᴿClR 46 (1996) 327-329 (*Harris, Edward M.*).

9317 ᴱ**Fiaccadori, Gianfranco; Eleuteri, Paolo** I greci in occidente: la tradizione filosofica, scientifica e letteraria dalle collezioni della Biblioteca Marciana. F 1996, Il Cardo lxxv; 92 pp. 88-8079-087-0.

9318 **Fitton, Lesley J.** The discovery of the Greek Bronze Age. CM 1996, Harvard Univ. Press 212 pp. $30. 0-674-21188-X [AJA 101,198].

9319 **Garland, Robert** The eye of the beholder: deformity and disability in the Graeco-Roman world. Ithaca 1995, Cornell Univ. Press 272 pp. $42.50. 0-8014-3144-1. ᴿCIR 46 (1996) 329-330 (*Parkin, Tim*); JHS 116 (1996) 225-226 (*Montserrat, Dominic*).

9320 *Hannestad, Lise* Absolute chronology: Greece and the Near East c.1000-500 BC. AcAr 67/1 (1996) 39-49.

9321 **Lewis, Sian** News and society in the Greek polis. Chapel Hill 1996, Univ. of North Carolina Press 206 pp. $17. 0-8078-4621-X [AJA 101,819].

9322 **Martin, Thomas R.** Ancient Greece: from prehistoric to Hellenistic times. NHv 1996, Yale Univ. Press 252 pp. 45 fig.; 8 maps. $16. 0-300-06596-1 [AJA 101,432].

9323 **Osborne, Robin** Greece in the making, 1200-490 B.C. Routledge History of the Ancient World: NY 1996, Routledge xx; 396 pp. 88 fig.; 7 tables. $25. 0-415-03583-X [AJA 102,629s—Thomas, Carol G.].

9324 **Reden, Sitta von** Exchange in ancient Greece. L 1995, Duckworth 244 pp. ᴿREG 109 (1996) 727-729 (*Samama, E.*).

Q6.5 Alexander, Seleucidae; historia Hellenismi

9325 *Bar-Kochva, Bezalel* פרק—אנטיוכוס החסיד והורקנוס הטיראן בהיסטוריוגרפיה של מדינת החשמונאים [Antiochus the pious and Hyrcanus the tyrant: a chapter in the historiography of the Hasmonaean state]. Sum. v. Zion 61 (1996) 7-44. **H.**

9326 **Barclay, John M.G.** Jews in the Mediterranean diaspora from Alexander to Trajan (323 BCE-117 CE). E 1996, Clark xvi; 522 pp. £35/$50. 0-567-08500-7 [OTA 19,550].

9327 ᴱ**Bilde, Per**, (*al*), Aspects of Hellenistic kingship. Studies in Hellenistic civilization 7: Aarhus 1996, Univ. Press 147 pp. DKK198/$30. 87-7288-474-6.

9328 *Boccaccini, Gabriele* Il Dio unico, padre e creatore nel giudaismo di età ellenistico-romana. Dio—Signore nella bibbia. DSBP 13: 1996, ⇒328. 102-121.

9329 [Auct. var.] Cultural transitions in Athens and the eastern Mediterranean in the Hellenistic Age. ᶠBADIAN E., 1996, ⇒3. 191-269.

9330 *Engberg-Pedersen, Troels* PLUTARCH to Prince PHILOPAPPUS on how to tell a flatterer from a friend. Friendship. NT.S 82: 1996, ⇒180. 61-79.

9331 *Feldman, Louis H.* The Jews as viewed by PLUTARCH < 1990 >;

9332 Torah and secular culture: challenge and response in the Hellenistic period < 1987 >. Studies in Hellenistic Judaism. AGJU 30: 1996, 529-552/487-503.

9333 *Glad, Clarence E.* Frank speech, flattery, and friendship in PHILODEMUS. Friendship. NT.S 82: 1996, ⇒180. 21-59.

9334 **Green, Peter** Alexander to Actium: the Hellenistic age. 1990, ⇒6,653... 11/2,9631. ᴿGn. 68 (1996) 420-427 (*Dobesch, Gerhard*).

9335 **Hengel, Martin** L''ellenizzazione' della Giudea nel I secolo d.C. 1993, ⇒9,12713; 11/2,9636. ᴿPaVi 41/2 (1996) 58 (*Rolla, Armando*).

9336 *Hengel, Martin* Die Begegnung von Judentum und Hellenismus im Palästina der vorchristlichen Zeit < 1970 >;

9337 Zum Problem der "Hellenisierung" Judäas im 1. Jahrhundert nach Christus;

9338 *Hengel, Martin; Lichtenberger, Hermann* Die Hellenisierung des antiken Judentums als Praeparatio Evangelica <1981>. Judaica et Hellenistica. WUNT 90: 1996, ⇒128. 151-170/1-90/295-313.

9339 *Joubert, Stephan; Van Henten, Jan Willem* Two a-typical Jewish families in the Greco-Roman period. Neotest. 30 (1996) 121-140.

9340 **Meissner, B.** Historiker zwischen Polis und Königshof: Studien zur Stellung der Geschichtsschreiber in der griechischen Gesellschaft in spätklassischer und frühhellenistischer Zeit. 1992, ⇒9,12628; 10,11250. ᴿJHS 116 (1996) 208-209 (*Spawforth, A.J.S.*).

9341 **Reader, William W.** The severed hand and the upright corpse: the declamations of Marcus Antonius POLEMO. SBL.TT 42; Graeco-Roman religion 12: Atlanta, Ga. 1996, Scholars xxv; 540 pp. 0-7885-0282-4.

9342 **Rigsby, Kent J.** Asylia: territorial inviolability in the Hellenistic world. Hellenistic Culture and Society 22: Berkeley 1996, Univ. of California Press xvii; 672 pp. £65. 0-520-20098-5.

9343 *Roth-Gerson, Leah* שנאת-ישראל בסוריה בתקופה ההלניסטית והרומית [Anti-Semitism in Syria in the Hellenistic and Roman period]. ᶠSTERN M., 1996, ⇒87. Sum. 151*. 301-321. **H.**

9344 *Schremer, Adiel* גיל הנישואים של גברים יהודים בארץ ישראל בתקופת הבית השני, המשנה והתלמוד [Men's age at marriage in Jewish Palestine of the Hellenistic and Roman periods]. Sum. vi. Zion 61 (1996) 45-66. **H.**

9345 *Schwartz, Daniel R.* על מסעו הפרתי של אנטיוכוס סידטס ובעיית הפיצול בחקר ההיסטוריה [On Antiochus VII Sidetes' Parthian expedition and the fragmentation of historical research]. ᶠSTERN M., 1996, ⇒87. Sum. 144*. 83-102. **H.**

9346 *Shimoff, Sandra R.* Banquets: the limits of Hellenization. JSJ 27 (1996) 440-452.

9347 *Siegert, Folker* Early Jewish interpretation in a Hellenistic style. Antiquity [ᴱSæbø, Magne]. 1996, ⇒ʏ1. 130-198.

9348 **Stewart, Andrew** Faces of power: Alexander's image and Hellenistic politics. 1993, ⇒9,12636; 11/2,9654. ᴿGn. 68 (1996) 693-697 (*Will, Édouard*).

9349 **Striker, Gisela** Essays on Hellenistic epistemology and ethics. C 1996, CUP xviii; 335 pp. £37.50/$55; £14/$20. 0-521-47051-X/641-0.

9350 **Swain, Simon** Hellenism and empire: language, classicism, and power in the Greek world AD 50-250. Oxf 1996, Clarendon xii; 499 pp. 0-19-814772-4.

9351 ᴱ**Virgilio, Biagio** Studi ellenistici VIII. Biblioteca di studi antichi 78; Studi ellenistici 8: Pisa 1996, Istituti Editoriali e Poligrafici Internazionali 7-245 pp. 88-8147-005-5.

9352 *Warrior, Valerie* Evidence in LIVY on Roman policy prior to war with Antiochus the Great. ᶠBADIAN E., 1996, ⇒3. 356-375.

9353 *Wikander, Charlotte* Religion, political power and gender—the building of a cult-image. Religion and power. BOREAS 24: 1996, ⇒290. Sum. 183. 183-188.

9354 **Will, Ernest** De l'Euphrate au Rhin: aspects de l'hellénisation et de la romanisation du Proche-Orient. BAH 135: Beyrouth 1995, Institut Français d'Archéologie du Proche-Orient viii; 977 pp. FF500. 2-7053-0672-2. ᴿMes. 31 (1996) 292-293 (*Invernizzi, A.*).

Q7 Josephus Flavius

Amir, Yehoshua La letteratura giudeo-ellenistica ⇒1065.

9355 *Bar-Kochva, Bezalel* איש והקטאיוס היוונית המנטיקה היהודי, משולם אברירה [Mosollamus the Jew, Greek mantics and Hecataeus of Abdera]. ᶠSTERN M., 1996, ⇒87. Sum. 152*. 323-344. **H.**

Bar-Kochva, Bezalel An ass in the Jerusalem Temple ⇒2491.

Bauckham, Richard JOSEPHUS' account of the temple in *Contra Apionem* 2.102-109 ⇒2492.

9356 *Begg, Christopher* Ahaz, King of Judah according to JOSEPHUS. SJOT 10 (1996) 28-52;

9357 Elisha's great deeds according to JOSEPHUS (AJ 9,47-94). Henoch 18 (1996) 69-110 [2 Kgs 4,1-8,15];

9358 The execution of the Saulides according to JOSEPHUS. Sum. 17. Sef. 56/1 (1996) 3-17 [2 Sam 21,1-14];

9359 Jotham and Amon: two minor kings of Judah according to JOSEPHUS. BBR 6 (1996) 1-13 [2 Kgs 15,32-38; 21,19-26; 2 Chr 33,21-25;

9360 Samuel's anointing of David in JOSEPHUS and PSEUDO-PHILO. RSLR 32 (1996) 491-529 [1 Sam 16,1-13];

9361 Saul's war with Amalek according to JOSEPHUS. Laur. 37 (1996) 387-415 [1 Sam 15];

9362 The Abigail story (1 Samuel 25) according to JOSEPHUS. EstB 54 (1996) 5-34;

9363 Abimelech, king of Shechem according to JOSEPHUS;

9364 The ark in Philistia according to JOSEPHUS [1 Sam 5];

9365 The last six kings of Israel according to JOSEPHUS. EThL 72 (1996) 46-64/385-397/371-384;

9366 The loss of the ark according to JOSEPHUS. SBFLA 46 (1996) 167-186;

9367 The rape of Tamar (2 Samuel 13) according to JOSEPHUS. EstB 54 (1996) 465-500;

9368 The 'royal lottery' according to JOSEPHUS. Res. 288. RCatT 21 (1996) 273-288;

9369 Solomon's two "Satans" according to JOSEPHUS. BN 85 (1996) 44-55.

9370 *Bilde, Per Contra Apionem* 1.28-56: an essay on JOSEPHUS' view of his own work in the context of the Jewish canon. JOSEPHUS' *Contra Apionem*. AGJU 34: 1996, ⇒9384. 94-114.

9371 *Feldman, Louis H.* Asinius POLLIO and Herod's sons <1985>. 52-56;

9372 Asinius POLLIO and his Jewish interests <1953>. 37-44;

9373 Bibliography: JOSEPHUS' portrayal of the Hasmoneans as compared with 1 Maccabees. 603-605;

9374 The identity of POLLIO, the Pharisee, in JOSEPHUS <1958/59>. 45-51;

9375 The influence of JOSEPHUS on Cotton MATHER's Biblia Americana: a study in ambiguity <1993>. 237-273;

9376 JOSEPHUS' attitude toward the Samaritans: a study in ambivalence <1992>. 114-136;

JOSEPHUS' *Jewish Antiquities* and PSEUDO-PHILO's *Biblical Antiquities* ⇒8083;

9377 JOSEPHUS' portrait of Jephthah. FSTERN M., 1996, ⇒87. 67*-84*;

9378 JOSEPHUS' portrayal of the Hasmoneans compared with 1 Maccabees <1994>;

9379 Pro-Jewish intimations in anti-Jewish remarks cited in JOSEPHUS against Apion. Studies in Hellenistic Judaism <1987/88>. AGJU 30: 1996, ⇒124. 137-163/177-236;

9380 Reading between the lines: appreciation of Judaism in anti-Jewish writers cited in *Contra Apionem*. JOSEPHUS' *Contra Apionem*. AGJU 34: 1996, ⇒9384. 250-270;

9381 The sources of JOSEPHUS' *Antiquities*, Book 19 <1962>. 164-176;

9382 The term "Galileans" in JOSEPHUS <1981/82>. 111-113;

9383 *Feldman, Louis H.; Gibbs, John G.* JOSEPHUS' vocabulary for slavery <1985/86>. 83-110. Studies in Hellenistic Judaism. AGJU 30: 1996, ⇒124.

9384 EFeldman, Louis H; Levinson, John R. JOSEPHUS' *Contra Apionem*. AGJU 34: Lei 1996, Brill x; 517 pp. *f*254/$164. 90-04-10325-2 [JSJ 28,365].

9385 Gnuse, Robert Karl Dreams and dream reports in the writings of JOSEPHUS: a traditio-historical analysis. AGJU 36: Lei 1996, Brill vii; 320 pp. *f*173. 90-04-10616-2 [JSJ 28,366].

9386 Gray, Rebecca Prophetic figures in late Second Temple Jewish Palestine: the evidence from JOSEPHUS. 1993, ⇒9,12648... 11/2,9686. RJQR 87 (1996) 219-222 (*Schwartz, Daniel R.*).

9387 *Hall, Robert G.* JOSEPHUS, *Contra Apionem* and historical inquiry in the Roman rhetorical schools. JOSEPHUS' *Contra Apionem*. AGJU 34: 1996, ⇒9384. 229-249.

9388 *Kasher, Aryeh* נגר" [בחיבור] היוונית ההיסטוריוגרפיה בגנות יוספוס ["אפיון [JOSEPHUS' reproach of Greek historiography in *Contra Apionem*]. FSTERN M., 1996, ⇒87. Sum. 150*. 273-299. H.;

9389 Polemic and apologetic methods of writing in *Contra Apionem*. JOSEPHUS' *Contra Apionem*. AGJU 34: 1996, ⇒9384. 143-186.

9390 *Lamour, Denis* L'organisation du récit dans l'*Autobiographie* de Flavius JOSEPHE. BAGB 2 (1996) 141-150.

9391 *Levison, John R.* JOSEPHUS' interpretation of the divine spirit. JJS 47 (1996) 234-255.

9392 *Levison, John R.; Wagner, J. Ross* The character and context of JOSEPHUS' *Contra Apionem*. JOSEPHUS' *Contra Apionem*. AGJU 34: 1996, ⇒9384. 1-48.

9393 Lindsay, Dennis R. JOSEPHUS and faith: Πίστις and Πιστεύειν as faith terminology in... JOSEPHUS and in the NT. AGJU 19: 1993, ⇒10,9358. RCBQ 58 (1996) 349-351 (*Chesnutt, Randall D.*).

9394 Mason, Steve JOSEPHUS & NT. 1992, ⇒8,d187... 11/2,9698. RCoTh 66/1 (1996) 193-195 (*Wojciechowski, Michał*).

9395 *Mason, Steve* The *Contra Apionem* in social and literary context: an invitation to Judean philosophy. JOSEPHUS' *Contra Apionem*. AGJU 34: 1996, ⇒9384. 187-228.

9396 *Mason, Steve; Kraft, Robert A.* JOSEPHUS on canon and scriptures. Antiquity [ESæbø, Magne]. 1996, ⇒y1. 217-235.

9397 *Moessner, David P.* "Eyewitnesses," "informed contemporaries," and "unknowing inquirers": JOSEPHUS' criteria for authentic historiography and the meaning of παρακολουθέω. NT 38 (1996) 105-122.

9398 *Niehoff, Maren R.* Two examples of JOSEPHUS' narrative technique in his "Rewritten Bible". JSJ 27 (1996) 31-45.

9399 [E]**Parente, Fausto; Sievers, Joseph** JOSEPHUS and the history of the Greco-Roman period. [F]SMITH M., 1994, ⇒10,123. [R]Sef. 56 (1996) 213-216 (*Spottorno, M.ª Victoria*).

9400 *Pucci Ben Zeev, Miriam* POLYBIUS, JOSEPHUS, and the Capitol in Rome. JSJ 27 (1996) 21-30;

9401 Who wrote a letter concerning Delian Jews?. RB 103 (1996) 237-243.

9402 *Schreckenberg, Heinz* A concordance to the Latin text of *Contra Apionem*;

9403 Text, Überlieferung und Textkritik von *Contra Apionem*. JOSEPHUS' *Contra Apionem*. AGJU 34: 1996, ⇒9384. 453-517/49-82.

9404 **Schröder, Bernd** Die 'väterlichen Gesetze': Flavius JOSEPHUS als Vermittler von Halachah an Griechen und Römer. Diss. TSAJ 53: Tü 1996, Mohr x; 313 pp. DM178. 3-16-146481-8.

9405 *Spilsbury, Paul Contra Apionem* and *Antiquitates Judaicae:* points of contact. JOSEPHUS' *Contra Apionem*. AGJU 34: 1996, ⇒9384. 348-368.

9406 *Taran, Anat* התלמודית בספרות החורבן ותיאורי פלוויוס יוספוס [Remarks on JOSEPHUS Flavius and the destruction of the Second Temple]. Sum. xiii. Zion 61 (1996) 141-157. **H**.

9407 *Van Henten, Jan Willem; Abusch, Ra'anan* The depiction of the Jews as Typhonians and JOSEPHUS' strategy of refutation in *Contra Apionem*. JOSEPHUS' *Contra Apionem*. AGJU 34: 1996, ⇒9384. 271-309.

Q8.1 *Roma Pompeii et Caesaris*—**Hyrcanus to Herod**

9408 *Atkinson, Kenneth* Herod the Great, Sosius, and the siege of Jerusalem (37 B.C.E.) in Psalm of Solomon 17. NT 38 (1996) 313-322.

9409 [E]**Fittschen, Klaus; Foerster, Gideon** Judaea and the Greco-Roman world in the time of Herod in the light of archaeological evidence. AAWG.PH 215: Gö 1996, Vandenhoeck & R. 251 pp. Acts of a symposium organized by the Institute of Archaeology, the Hebrew University of Jerusalem, and the Archaeological Institute, Georg-August-University of Göttingen at Jerusalem, November 3rd-4th 1988. DM160. 3-525-82359-2 [NThAR 1997,68].

9410 *Geiger, Joseph* היבטים—הורדוס ורומא חדשים [Herod and Rome: new aspects]. [F]STERN M., 1996, ⇒87. Sum. 146*. 133-145. **H**.

9411 **Richardson, Peter** Herod: king of the Jews and friend of the Romans. Columbia, SC 1996, Univ. of South Carolina Press xxv; 360 pp. $35. 1-57003-136-3 [JSJ 28,367].

Q8.4 **Zeitalter Jesus Christ**: particular/general

9412 *Chester, Andrew* The Jews of Judaea and Galilee. [F]HOOKER M., 1996, ⇒43. 9-26.

9413 **Galinsky, Karl** Augustan culture: an interpretive introduction. Princeton, NJ 1996, Princeton Univ. Press xi; 474 pp. $39.50. 0-691-04435-X. [R]Prudentia 28/2 (1996) 52-57 (*Stevenson, T.R.*).

9414 **Horsley, Richard A.; Hanson, John S.** Banditi, profeti e messia: movementi popolari al tempo di Gesù. 1995, ⇒11/2,9764. RAnton. 71 (1996) 359-361 (*Nobile, Marco*); PaVi 41/3 (1996) 60-61 (*Rolla, Armando*).

9415 **Roth, Paul** In jener Zeit: Alltag im Lande Jesu. Graz 1996, Styria 221 pp. 3-222-12379-9.

9416 *Siegert, Folker* Le judaïsme au premier siècle et ses ruptures intérieures. Le déchirement. MoBi 32: 1996, ⇒192. 25-65.

9417 **Udoh, Fabian** Tribute and taxes in early Roman Palestine (63 BCE-70 CE). Diss. Duke 1996, D*Sanders, E.P.* [RTL 29,582].

9418 **Vidal Manzanares, César** El judeo-cristianismo palestino en el siglo 1. 1995, ⇒11/2,9775. RActBib 33 (1996) 30-31 (*Borràs, Antonio*); Cart. 12 (1996) 482-483 (*Marín Heredia, F.*).

9419 **Vouga, François** Geschichte des frühen Christentums. 1994, ⇒10,11335. RBZ 40 (1996) 125-128 (*Roloff, Jürgen*).

9420 **Wilcke, Hans-Alwin** Neutestamentliche Umwelt und Zeitgeschichte. ABC des NT 3: Essen 1996, Blaue Eule 273 pp. 3-89206-765-1 [NThAR 1997,101].

Q8.7 *Roma et Oriens*, prima decennia post Christum

9421 **Botermann, Helga** Das Judenedikt des Kaisers Claudius: römischer Staat und *Christiani* im 1. Jahrhundert. Hermes.E 71: Stut 1996, Steiner 200 pp. DM88. 3-515-06863-5.

9422 *Eshel, Hanan* The contribution of documents and other remains found in the Judean Desert between 1979 and 1993 to the understanding of the Bar Kokhba Revolt. BAIAS 15 (1996-97) 108-110.

9423 *Hengel, Martin* Hadrians Politik gegenüber Juden und Christen. Judaica et Hellenistica. WUNT 90: 1996 <1984/85>, ⇒128. 358-391.

9424 **Mendels, Doron** The rise and fall of Jewish nationalism. 1992, ⇒9,287*; 11/2,9810. RJAOS 116 (1996) 292-294 (*Attridge, Harold W.*).

9425 **Price, Jonathan** Jerusalem under siege: the collapse of the Jewish state 66-70 C.E. 1992, ⇒8,d292... 11/2,9818. RJQR 86 (1996) 496-497 (*Schwartz, Seth*).

9426 **Reznick, Leibel** The mystery of Bar Kokhba: an historical and theological investigation of the last king of the Jews. Northvale, NJ 1996 Aronson xi; 186 pp. 1-56821-502-9.

9427 *Rosen, Klaus* Marc Aurel und das Ideal des Civilis Princeps. FDASSMANN E., JAc.E 23: 1996, ⇒19. 154-160.

Q9.1 *Historia Romae generalis et* post-christiana

9428 EBarzano, A. Il cristianesimo nelle leggi di Roma imperiale. Letture cristiane del primo millennio 24: Mi 1996, Paoline 415 pp. L48.000 [Asp. 45,429ss—Longobardo, Luigi].

9429 **Bauman, Richard A.** Crime and punishment in ancient Rome. L 1996, Routledge xii; 228 pp. £40. 0-415-11375-X [AnCl 67,526—Jones, Huguette].

9430 **Bowersock, G.W.** Martyrdom and Rome. 1995, ⇒11/2,9847. RJThS 47 (1996) 275-279 (*Mühlenberg, Ekkehard*); SCI 15 (1996) 308-309 (*Schwartz, Seth*).

9431 **Butterweck, Christel** 'Martyriumssucht' in der Alten Kirche?: Studien zur Darstellung und Deutung frühchristlicher Martyrien. BHTh 87: Tü 1995, Mohr 288 pp. RVigChr 50 (1996) 212-215 (*Buschmann, G.*).

9432 CAH 10: the Augustan empire, 43 B.C.-A.D. 69. C ^{2}1996, CUP xxii; 1193 pp. 0-521-26430-8.

9433 *Colpe, Carsten* Civilitas Graeca und Eupistia hellenike: Kennworte zur Religionspolitik des Kaisers Julian. FDASSMANN E., JAC.E 23: 1996, ⇒19. 308-328.

9434 **Crook, J.A.** Legal advocacy in the Roman world. 1995, ⇒11/2,9860. RPrudentia 28/1 (1996) 51-53 (*Lacey, W.K.*); ClR 46 (1996) 89-90 (*Gardner, Jane F.*); JRS 86 (1996) 192-193 (*Burton, G.P.*).

9435 **Demandt, Alexander** Das Privatleben der römischen Kaiser. Beck' Archäologischer Bibliothek: Mü 1996, Beck 287 pp. DM58/DM48. 3-406-40524-X/5-8 [AnCl 67,497—Van Langenhoven, Paul].

9436 **Doblhofer, Georg** Vergewaltigung in der Antike. Beiträge zur Altertumskunde 46: Stu 1994, Teubner x; 134 pp. DM48. 3-519-07495-8. RClR 46 (1996) 327-329 (*Harris, Edward M.*).

9437 **Domenicucci, Patrizio** Astra Caesarum: astronomia, astrologia e catasterismo da Cesare a Domiziano. Testi e studi di cultura classica 16: Pisa 1996, ETS 191 pp. 88-7741-932-6.

9438 **Feldman, Louis H.** Jew and gentile in the ancient world. 1993, ⇒10,12786; 11/2,9869. REtCl 64/1 (1996) 100-101 (*Leclercq, H.*); BiOr 53 (1996) 807-810 (*Henten, J.W.*); JHS 116 (1996) 224-225 (*McGing, Brian*);

9439 *Feldman, Louis H.* Abba Kolon and the founding of Rome. Studies in Hellenistic Judaism. AGJU 30: 1996 < 1990/91 >, ⇒124. 411-437.

9440 EFeldmeier, R.; Heckel, U. Die Heiden: Juden, Christen und das Problem des Fremden. 1994, ⇒11/2,9977. RThLZ 121 (1996) 48-50 (*Lindemann, Andreas*).

9441 **Feldtkeller, Andreas** Identitätssuche des syrischen Urchristentums. NTOA 25: 1993, ⇒9,12785b. REstB 54 (1996) 276-279 (*López Fernández, E.*); JBL 115 (1996) 347-349 (*Tyson, Joseph B.*).

9442 *Fick, Sabine* Emesa, Heliopolis und Hierapolis. Religionsgeschichte Syriens. 1996, ⇒217. 194-216.

9443 **Flower, Harriet I.** Ancestor masks and aristocratic power in Roman culture. Oxf 1996, Clarendon xvii; 410 pp. £50. 0-19-815018-0 [AJA 102,448—Saller, Richard].

9444 **Forbis, Elizabeth** Municipal virtues in the Roman empire: the evidence of Italian honorary inscriptions. Beiträge zur Altertumskunde 79: Stu 1996, Teubner vi; 299 pp. DM110 [HZ 267,736s—Andermahr, Anna Maria].

9445 **Fox, Matthew** Roman historical myths: the regal period in Augustean literature. Oxf Classical Monographs: Oxf 1996, Clarendon viii; 269 pp. £35. 0-19-815020-2 [AnCl 67,485s—Poucet, Jacques].

9446 ^{TE}**Gerlaud, Bernard** NONNOS de Panopolis: les dionysiaques: tome VI, chants XIV-XVII. 1994, ⇒11/2,9882. ^RREG 109 (1996) 315-316 (*Jouan, François*).

9447 *Harland, Philip A.* Honours and worship: emperors, imperial cults and associations at Ephesus (first to third centuries C.E.). Sum. rés. 319. SR 25 (1996) 319-334.

9448 **Inglebert, Hervé** Les romains chrétiens face à l'histoire de Rome: histoire, christianisme et romanités en Occident dans l'Antiquité tardive (IIIe-Ve siècles). Collection des Études Augustiniennes, Antiquité 145: P 1996, Institut d'Études Augustiniennes 744 pp. FB1400. 2-85121-149-8 [AnCl 67,508ss—Wankenne, Jules].

9449 **Krause, Jens-Uwe** Gefängnisse im Römischen Reich. Heidelberger Althistorische Beiträge und Epigraphische Studien 23: Stu 1996, Steiner vi; 365 pp. [ZSSR.R 115,615ss—Klingenberg, Georg].

9450 **Le Glay, Marcel; Vousin, Jean-Louis; Le Bohec, Yann,** (*al*), A history of Rome. ^T*Nevill, Antonia,* Oxf 1996, Blackwell xxiii; 608 pp. £15.

9451 **Löhr, Winrich Alfried** Basilides und seine Schule: eine Studie zur Theologie- und Kirchengeschichte des zweiten Jahrhunderts. WUNT 2/83: Tü 1996, Mohr x; 414 pp. 3-16-146300-5.

9452 *Martin, Dale B.* The construction of the ancient family: methodological considerations. JRS 86 (1996) 40-60.

9453 **Morley, Neville** Metropolis and hinterland: the city of Rome and the Italian economy 200 B.C. - A.D. 200. C 1996, CUP xi; 211 pp. $50. 0-521-56006-3 [AJA 102,451—Peña, J. Theodore].

9454 **Nippel, W.** Public order in ancient Rome. 1995, ⇒11/2,9918. ^RClR 46 (1996) 318-320 (*Alston, Richard*).

9455 **Ratti, Stéphane** Les empereurs romains d'Auguste à Dioclétien dans le Bréviaire d'Europe: les livres 7 à 9: introduction, traduction et commentaire. Besançon 1996, Université de Besançon 453 pp. 2-251-60604-1 [AnCl 67,357s—Chausson, François].

9456 *Ricci, Cecilia* Principes et reges externi (e loro schiavi e liberti) a Roma e in Italia: testimonianze epigrafiche di età imperiale. Sum. 561. AANL.R 7 (1996) 561-592.

9457 [Auct. var.] The rise of Rome. ^FBADIAN E.,. 1996, ⇒3. 271-461.

9458 *Ritter, Adolf Martin* Constantin und die Christen. ZNW 87 (1996) 251-268.

9459 ^E**Sordi, Marta** Roma dalle origini ad Azio. R 1994, Coletti 400 pp. L45.000. 88-7826-705-8. ^RAevum 70 (1996) 174-175 (*Landucci Gattinoni, Franca*).

9460 *Stanley, Christopher D.* 'Neither Jew or Greek': ethnic conflict in Graeco-Roman society. JSNT 64 (1996) 101-124.

9461 *Ulrich, Jörg* EUSEB, HistEccl III,14-20 und die Frage nach der Christenverfolgung unter Domitian. ZNW 87 (1996) 269-289.

9462 **Vielberg, Meinolf** Untertanentopik: zur Darstellung der Führungsschichten in der kaiserzeitlichen Geschichtsschreibung. Zetemata H.5: Mü 1996, Beck 172 pp. DM72 [HZ 267,736—Urban, Ralf].

9463 **Watson, Alan** The spirit of Roman law. Spirit of the Laws: Athens, GA 1995, Univ. of Georgia Press 272 pp. $45. 0-8203-1669-5. ^RClR 46 (1996) 292-294 (*Johnston, D.E.L.*).

XVIII. Archaeologia terrae biblicae

T1.1 General biblical-area archaeologies

9464 *Atkinson, Kenneth* Two dogs, a goat and a partridge: an archaeologist's best friends. BArR 22/1 (1996) 42-43, 74.

9465 **Bahn, Paul** Archaeology: a very short introduction. Oxf 1996, OUP 110 pp. $8. 0-19-285325-2 [AJA 101,631].

9466 [E]**Bahn, Paul G.** The Cambridge illustrated history of archaeology. C 1996, CUP 399 pp. 92 col. fig.; 124 fig. $40. 0-521-45498-0 [AJA 101,430].

9467 *Banning, E.B.* Highlands and lowlands: problems and survey frameworks for rural archaeology in the Near East. BASOR 301 (1996) 25-45.

9468 **Biers, William R.** Art, artefacts and chronology in classical archaeology. 1992, ⇒8,d431; 10,11485. [R]Gn. 68 (1996) 566-567 (*Raeck, Wulf*).

9469 [E]**Briese, C.; Docter, R.F.; Mansel, K.** Interactions in the Iron Age. Hamburger Beiträge zur Archäologie 19-20: Mainz 1996, Von Zabern 322 pp. 89 ill.; 10 maps. DM168. 3-8053-1765-4.

9470 *Davidson, Lawrence* Biblical archaeology and the press: shaping American perceptions of Palestine in the first decade of the Mandate. BA 59 (1996) 104-114.

9471 **Davis, Whitney** Replications: archaeology, art history, psychoanalysis. Collab. *Quinn, Richard W.*, University Park, PA 1996, Pennsylvania State Univ. Press xvi; 352 pp. 0-271-01524-1.

9472 *Dever, W.G.* Recent archaeological discoveries and biblical research. 1990, ⇒6,b908... 11/2,a038. [R]AcOr 55 (1994) 200-205 (*Skjeggestad, Marit*).

9473 *Dever, William G.* The tell: microcosm of the cultural process. [F]VAN BEEK G., 1996, ⇒96. 37-45.

9474 Excavations and surveys of Israel, 15. J 1996, Israel Antiquity Authority xii; 139 pp. [ZAW 110,464—Zwickel, W.].

9475 *Finkelstein, Israel* Toward a new periodization and nomenclature of the archaeology of the southern Levant. Albright centennial conference. 1996, ⇒303. 103-123.

9476 **Frend, William H.C.** The archaeology of early christianity: a history. L 1996, Chapman xx; 412 pp. 26 pls; 8 maps; 3 plans. £39.50/$39. 0-8006-2811-X [CBQ 59,421].

9477 [E]**Levy, Thomas E.** The archaeology of society in the Holy Land. 1995, ⇒11/2,a054. [R]AJA 100 (1996) 174-176 (*Falconer, Steven E.*); Antiquity 70 (1996) 214-217 (*Wright, Katherine I.*).

9478 *Margueron, Jean-Claude* Le prestige de l'Orient ancien: les grandes missions archéologiques françaises. CRAI (1996) 1003-1011.

9479 *Rebić, Adalbert* Arheološka iskapanja u Palestini i njihov prinos boljem poznavanju Biblije [Archaeological excavations in Palestine and their contribution to better knowledge of the bible]. Sum. 130. BoSm 66 (1996) 107-130.

9480 [E]**Shanks, Hershel** Biblical archaeology: from the ground down. Video on 2 cassettes. Wsh 1996, Biblical Archaeology Society 90 minutes. $70. 1-880317-47-8 [RExp 94,13].

9481   *Shanks, Hershel* Archaeological hot spots: a roundup of digs in Israel. BArR 22/6 (1996) 52-56, 77;
9482   Is the bible right after all?. BArR 22/5 (1996) 30-37, 74-77.
9483   **Sichtermann, Hellmut** Kulturgeschichte der klassischen Archäologie. Mü 1996, Beck 439 pp. DM78. 3-406-40392-1 [AJA 102,429—Hauser, Stefan R.].
9484   **Stiebing, William H.** Uncovering the past: a history of archaeology. 1994, ⇒10,11513. ᴿAJA 100 (1996) 605 (*Murray, Tim*).
9485   **Van Wyk, Koot** Archaeology in the bible and text in the tel. Berrien Springs 1996, Louis Hester Publications ix; 397 pp. 0-9635837-1-9 [RB 104,479].
9486   *Wolff, Samuel R.* Archaeology in Israel. AJA 100 (1996) 725-768.

т1.2 Musea, organismi, exploratores

9487   **Berman, Lawrence Michael; Letellier, Bernadette** Pharaohs: treasures of Egyptian art from the Louvre. Oxf 1996, OUP 100 pp. 0-19-521235-5.
9488   ᴱ**Budde, Hendrik; Lewy, Mordechai** Von Halle nach Jerusalem: Halle, ein Zentrum der Palästinakunde im 18. und 19. Jahrhundert. Halle 1994, Ministerium für Wissenschaft und Forschung des Landes Sachsen-Anhalt in Zusammenarbeit mit dem Generalkonsulat des Staates Israel 125 pp. ᴿOLZ 91 (1996) 187-190 (*Simon, Heinrich*).
9489   ᴱ**Donati, Angela** Dalla terra alle genti: la diffusione del cristianesimo nei primi secoli. Mi 1996, Electa 342 pp. Mostra, Rimini 1996. L65.000. ᴿPaVi 41/3 (1996) 45-48 (*Mantovani, Piera Arata*).
9490   **Fiechter, Jean-Jacques** La moisson des dieux: la constitution des grandes collections égyptiennes, 1815-1830. P 1994, Julliard 288 pp. 2-260-01131-4. ᴿJEA 82 (1996) 244-246 (*Ridley, R.T.*).
9491   **Fischer, Henry George** Varia Nova. Egyptian studies 3: NY 1996, The Metropolitan Museum of Art xxxiii; 264 pp. 0-87099-755-6.
9492   **Fortin, Michel** Les collections d'antiquités de l'Université Laval et du Musée de l'Amérique française (Québec, Canada). Corpus of Cypriote Antiquities 16; SIMA 20: Jonsered 1996, Åström 279 pp. 62 pl. $83. 91-7081-087-7 [AJA 101,431].
9493   **Grafman, Rafi** Crowning glory: silver Torah ornaments of the Jewish Museum, NY. ᴱ*Mann, Vivian B.*, NY 1996, Jewish Museum xv; 398 pp. Bibl. 1-56792-068-3.
9494   **Greenfield, Jeanette** The return of cultural treasures. C ²1996, CUP xxii; 351 pp. 0-521-47746-8.
9495   **Jørgensen, Mogens** Catalogue Egypt I (3000-1550 B.C.). Phot. *Haupt, Ole*, Copenhagen 1996, Ny Carlsberg Glyptotek 214 pp. [ArOr 66,176—Bárta, Miroslav].
9496   Das Jüdische Museum New York. Museen der Welt. Mü 1996, Beck 128 pp. num. ill. 3-406-38352-1.
9497   Palermo punica: guida breve. Palermo 1996, Museo Archeologico "A. Salinas" 27 pp. 6 dic. 1995 al 30 sett. 1996.
9498   ᴱ**Quirke, Stephen; Spencer, Jeffrey** The British Museum Book of Ancient Egypt. 1992, ⇒8,d517. ᴿCÉg 71 (1996) 279-281 (*Affholder-Gérard, Brigitte*).

9499 *Thomas, Nancy; Lacovara, Peter* American archaeology on the Nile. LA County Museum of Art, Nov. 1995-Jan 1996. EgArch 8 (1996) 23-26.

9500 E**Westenholz, Joan M. Goodnick** Royal cities of the biblical world. J 1996, Bible Lands Museum xxii; 334 pp. 965-7027-01-2.

T1.3 *Methodi*—Science in archaeology

9501 *Baillie, M.G.L.* The chronology of the Bronze Age 2354 BC to 431 BC. AcAr 67/1 (1996) 291-298.

9502 **Baillie, M.G.L.** A slice through time: dendrochronology and precision dating. L 1996, Batsford 176 pp. 64 fig. $50. 0-7134-7654 [AJA 101,198].

9503 *Bass, George F.* Underwater archaeology in the Near East: past, present, and future. Albright centennial conference. 1996, ⇒303. 125-138.

9504 *Bearman, Gregory H.; Spiro, Sheila I.* Archaeological applications of advanced imaging techniques. BA 59 (1996) 56-66.

9505 *Bellia, Giuseppe* La "nuova archeologia biblica": dalla svolta epistemologica all'antropologia storica. Ho Theológos 14 (1996) 205-252, 369-419.

9506 **Buck, C.E.; Cavanagh, W.G.; Litton, C.D.** Bayesian approach to interpreting archaeological data. Chichester 1996, Wiley 395 pp. 116 fig.; 39 tables. $50. 0-471-96197-3 [AJA 101,631].

9507 *Curto, Silvio* I raggi X al servizio dell'archeologia. Aeg. 76 (1996) 3-6.

9508 *Dentzer, Jean-Marie* Les perspectives d'avenir. CRAI (1996) 1019-1026.

9509 **Drennan, Robert D.** Statistics for archaeologists: a commonsense approach. Interdisciplinary contributions to archaeology: NY 1996, Plenum 278 pp. 33 fig.; 69 tables. $42.50. 0-306-45327-4 [AJA 101,431].

9510 *Goren, Y.* Petrographic study of archaeological artifacts and its application in the archaeology of Israel. Qad. 29 (1996) 107-114. **H.**

9511 *Jull, A.J. Timothy, (al)*, Radiocarbon dating of scrolls and linen fragments from the Judean Desert. ʿAtiqot 28 (1996) 85-91.

9512 *Lass, Egon H.* Lost in the maze: an alternative method of designing matrix diagrams. BAIAS 15 (1996-97) 41-49.

9513 *Misgav, Hagay* קטע מרצף אלפביתי על גלוסקמה [An alphabetical sequence on an ossuary]. Sum. 110. ʿAtiqot 29 (1996) 47*-49*.

9514 *Pigott, Vincent C.* Near Eastern archaeometallurgy: modern research and future directions. Albright centennial conference. 1996, ⇒303. 139-176.

9515 **Pollard, A. Mark; Heron, Carl** Archaeological chemistry. C 1996, Royal Society of Chemistry 375 pp. 103 fig.; tables; map. $39. 0-85404-523-6 [AJA 101,199].

9516 *Segal, D.; Carmi, I.; Szabo, J.* ^{14}C age calibration. Qad. 29 (1996) 115-117. **H.**

9517 *Segal, Dror; Carmi, Israel* Reḥovot radiocarbon date list V. ʿAtiqot 29 (1996) 79-106.

9518 *Warren, Peter* The Aegean and the limits of radiocarbon dating. AcAr 67/1 (1996) 283-290.

T1.4 *Exploratores*—Excavators, pioneers

9519 *Barag, D.* Judith MARQUET-KRAUSE—the first excavator of Ai.
Qad. 29 (1996) 118-119. **H.**

9520 **Baruffa, Antonio** Giovanni Battista DE ROSSI: l'archeologo
esploratore delle catacombe. 1994, ⇒10,11549; 11/2,a138. RLat.
62 (1996) 198-200 (*Dattrino, Lorenzo*).

9521 *Gardin, Jean-Claude* Une archéologie moderne: les initiatives
d'Henri SEYRIG. CRAI (1996) 1013-1018.

9522 **Kettel, Jeannot** Jean-François CHAMPOLLION le Jeune. 1990,
⇒6,d37... 11/2,a150. ROLZ 91 (1996) 284-285 (*Luft, Ulrich*).

T1.5 *Materiae primae*—metals, glass; stone

9523 *Adler, Wolfgang; Kiefer, Sabine* Die Metallgefässe aus dem
'Schatzhaus'. Kamid el-Loz [EKühne, H.]. 1996, ⇒T2.7. 119-131.

9524 *Archi, Alfonso* Les comptes rendus annuels de métaux (CAM).
Amurru 1. 1996, ⇒306. 73-99.

9525 *Avilova, L.J.* Mesopotamian metal in the Early and Middle Bronze
Age. Sum. 81. VDI 219 (1996) 68-81. **R.**

9526 *Bachmann, Hans-Gert* Zum Kenntnisstand der frühen Metallurgie
in ASIA MINOR. FBERAN T., 1996, ⇒6. 15-24.

9527 **Barkóczi, László** Antike Gläser. Bibliotheca archaeologica 19: R
1996, Bretschneider 124 pp. 74 pl. 88-7062-931-7 [AJA 101,198].

9528 **Connan, Jacques; Deschesne, Odile** Le bitume à Suse: collection
du Musée du Louvre. P 1996, Réunion des Musées Nationaux 444
pp. Num. ill. FF300. 2-901026-43-5. RMes. 31 (1996) 210-213
(*Negro, F.*).

9529 **Dercksen, Jan Gerrit** The Old Assyrian copper trade in Anatolia.
Publications de l'Institut historique-archéologique de Stamboul 75:
Lei 1996, Nederlands Historisch-Archaeologisch Instituut te Istan-
bul x; 279 pp. ƒ85. 90-6258-076-9 [AJA 101,631].

9530 **Lilyquist, C.; Brill, R.H.** Studies in Early Egyptian glass. 1993,
⇒9,13042... 11/2,a187. RBiOr 53 (1996) 70-74 (*Bulté, Jeanne*).

9531 **Liritzis, Veronica McGeehan** The role and development of metal-
lurgy in the Late Neolithic and Early Bronze Age of Greece.
SIMA-PB 122: Jonsered 1996, Åström 417 pp. 144 fig.; 88 maps;
37 tables. 91-781-088-5 [AJA 101,199].

9532 *Pigott, Vincent C.* Near Eastern archaeometallurgy: modern research and future directions. Albright centennial conference. 1996,
⇒303. 139-176.

9533 *Rossoni, Gabriele* L'uso del ferro in Palestina durante l'Età del
Ferro I-II. CMAO 6 (1996) 235-280.

9534 *Schlick-Nolte, Birgit* Kostbare Glasgefässe aus dem 'Schatzhaus'.
Kamid el-Loz [EKühne, H.]. 1996, ⇒T2.7. 183-202.

9535 **Treister, Michail Y.** The role of metals in ancient Greek history.
Lei 1996, Brill 481 pp. 20 fig.; 8 plans; 45 maps. $159. 90-04-
10473-9 [AJA 101,771—Muhly, J.D.].

9536 *Rosen, Steven A.* Flint implements. City of David excavations
[EAriel, D.]. Qedem 35: 1996, ⇒T4.3. 257-267.

9537 ^EYon, Marguerite Arts et industries de la pierre. Ras Shamra-Ougarit 6: 1991, ⇒7,b637. ^RSyria 73 (1996) 211-213 (*Collon, Dominique*).

T1.7 Technologia antiqua

9538 **Aberbach, Moshe** Labor, crafts and commerce in ancient Israel. 1994, ⇒11/2,a206. ^RAJS Review 21 (1996) 381-384 (*Corbett, John H.*).

9539 **Heltzer, Michael** Die Organisation des Handwerks im 'Dunklen Zeitalter' und im 1. Jahrtausend v.u.Z. im östlichen Mittelmeergebiet. 1992, ⇒9,13072; 10,11601. ^ROLZ 91 (1996) 562-564 (*Thiel, Winfried*);

9540 *Heltzer, Michael* Crafts in the West (Syria, Phoenicia, Palestine, ca. 1500-331 BCE). AltOrF 23 (1996) 278-283.

9541 *Hovers, Erella* The groundstone industry. City of David excavations [^EAriel, D.]. Qedem 35: 1996, ⇒T4.3. 171-189.

9542 *Kayani, P.I.* Formative pyrotechnology in northern Mesopotamia. Sum. rés. 133. Paléorient 22/2 (1996) 133-141.

9543 *Klengel, Horst* Handwerker im hethitischen Anatolien. AltOrF 23 (1996) 265-277.

9544 **Moorey, P.R.S.** Ancient Mesopotamian materials and industries: the archaeological evidence. 1994, ⇒11/2,a220. ^RAJA 100 (1996) 176-177 (*Potts, D.T.*); Antiquity 70 (1996) 225-227 (*Oates, Joan*).

9545 **Moscati, Sabatino** Artigianato a Monte Sirai. Studia punica 10: R 1996, Università degli Studi di Roma 'Tor Vergata' 122 pp. 22 pl. [CBQ 60,196].

9546 **Shepherd, Robert** Ancient mining. 1993, ⇒10,11607; 11/2,a228. ^RJHS 116 (1996) 227-228 (*Jones, John Ellis*).

9547 ^E**Wartke, Ralf-B.** Handwerk und Technologie im Alten Orient. 1994, Tagung B, 1991, ⇒10,11608*; 11/2,a232. ^RBiOr 53 (1996) 531-534 (*Moorey, P.R.S.*).

T1.8 Architectura

9548 **Arnold, Dieter** Building in Egypt. 1991, ⇒7,b651... 11/2,a236. ^RJNES 55 (1996) 225-226 (*Teeter, Emily*).

9549 *Aurenche, O.* Famille, fortune, pouvoir et architecture domestique dans les villages du Proche Orient. Houses and households. UNHAII 78: 1996, ⇒299. 1-16.

9550 **Balty, Jean Ch.** Curia ordinis: recherches d'architecture et d'urbanisme antiques sur les curies provinciales du monde romain. 1991, ⇒11/2,a237. ^RAnCl 65 (1996) 574-575 (*Trousset, Pol*).

9551 **Bretschneider, Joachim** Architekturmodelle in Vorderasien... AOAT. 1991, ⇒8,d636*; 9,13088. ^RBiOr 53 (1996) 204-209 (*Margueron, Jean-Claude*).

9552 *Briend, Jacques* Das Haus in biblischer Zeit. WUB 1 (1996) 53-55.

9553 Bulletin analytique d'architecture du monde grec. RAr 2 (1996) 293-410.

9554 *Calvet, Y.* Maisons privées paléo-babyloniennes à Larsa: remarques d'archtecture. Houses and households. UNHAII 78: 1996, ⇒299. 197-209.

9555 ED'Andria, Francesco; Mannino, Katia Ricerche sulla casa in
      Magna Graecia e in Sicilia. Università di Lecce, archeologia e sto-
      ria 5: Galatina (LE) 1996, Congedo 451 pp. 123 fig.; 108 plans;
      17 maps. 88-80861-506 [AJA 101,818].

9556 Donderer, Michael Die Architektur der späten römischen Republik
      und der Kaiserzeit: epigraphische Zeugnisse. ErF 69: Erlangen
      1996, Universitätsbibliothek Erlangen-Nürnberg 355 pp. 72 pl.; 3-
      930-357-08-9 [AJA 101,632].

9557 Dosch, G. Houses and households in Nuzi: the inhabitants, the
      family and those dependent on it. Houses and households. UNHAII
      78: 1996, ⇒299. 301-308.

9558 Endruweit, Albrecht Städtischer Wohnbau in Ägypten: klimage-
      rechte Lehmarchitektur in Amarna. 1994, ⇒10,12730; 11/2,a247.
      RJESHO 39 (1996) 50-52 (Spence, Kate).

9559 Enea, Alessandra Per una rilettura delle abitazioni palestinesi a
      pianta curvilinea del Bronzo Antico. VO 10 (1996) 85-103.

9560 Fisher, Moshe L. Das korinthische Kapitell im Alten Israel in der
      hellenistischen und römischen Periode. 1990, ⇒7,b695a; 9,13100.
      RBiOr 53 (1996) 225-227 (Waele, J.A.K.E. de).

9561 Frankfort, Henri The art and architecture of the ancient Orient.
      Collab. Roaf, Michael; Matthews, Donald, The Pelican History of
      Art: NHv 51996, Yale Univ. Press 483 pp. Bibl. 0-300-06470-5.

9562 Goell, Theresa; Sanders, Donald H. Affiliations of the architecture
      at Nemrud Daği. Nemrud Daği [ESanders, D.]. 1996, ⇒T6.5.
      133-151.

9563 Gros, Pierre L'architecture romaine du début du IIIe siècle av. J.-
      C. à la fin du haut-empire: les monuments publics. Les manuels
      d'art et d'archéologie antiques: P 1996, Picard 503 pp. 19 pl.; 531
      fig.;   7   maps.   FF650.   2-7084-0500-4   [AJA   102,614ss—
      MacDonald, William].

9564 Guinan, A.K. Social constructions and private designs: the house
      omens of šumma alu. Houses and households. UNHAII 78: 1996,
      ⇒299. 61-68.

9565 Japp, Sarah Die Architektur Herodes des Großen. Diss. Köln
      1996 [AA (1997/1) 103.

9566 Kalla, G. Das altbabylonische Wohnhaus und seine Struktur nach
      philologischen Quellen. Houses and households. UNHAII 78:
      1996, ⇒299. 247-256.

9567 EKempinsky, Aharon; Reich, Ronny The architecture of ancient
      Israel from the prehistoric to the Persian periods. FDUNAYEVSKY
      I., 1992, ⇒8,48... 11/2,a246. RJNES 55 (1996) 228-230 (Hallote,
      Rachel S.).

9568 Kleiss, Wolfram Orientalische Kastenmauern und europäische Holz-
      Erde-Mauern. FBERAN T., 1996, ⇒6. 149-158.

9569 Kohlmeyer, K. Houses in Habuba Kabira South: spatial organisa-
      tion and planning of Late Uruk residential archtecture. Houses and
      households. UNHAII 78: 1996, ⇒299. 89-103.

9570 Kolbus, Susanne Zur Funktion der frühbronzezeitlichen umwallten
      Plätze Palästinas. Diss. Müns 1996 [AA (1997/1) 103].

9571 Koliński, R. Building a house in third millennium northern Meso-
      potamia: when vision collides with reality. Houses and households.
      UNHAII 78: 1996, ⇒299. 137-144.

9572 Lawrence, A.W. Greek architecture. Rev. Tomlinson, R.A., L
      51996, Yale Univ. Press xiv; 243 pp. 0-300-06492-6.

9573 *Margueron, J.C.* La maison orientale. Houses and households. UNHAII 78: 1996, ⇒299. 17-38.

9574 *Miglus, P.A.* Die räumliche Organisation des altbabylonischen Hofhauses. Houses and households. UNHAII 78: 1996, ⇒299. 211-220.

9575 **Murray, Peter & Linda** The Oxford companion to christian art and architecture. NY 1996, OUP xii; 596 pp. $55 [JEarlyC 6,686ss—Jensen, Robin].

9576 *Neumann, H.* Der sumerische Baumeister (šidim). Houses and households. UNHAII 78: 1996, ⇒299. 153-169.

9577 **Nielsen, Inge** Hellenistic palaces: tradition and renewal. 1994, ⇒11/2,a273. [R]Mes. 31 (1996) 284-287 (*Invernizzi, A.*); BAIAS 15 (1996-97) 81-83 (*Jacobson, David M.*).

9578 *Nigro, Lorenzo* Le residenze palestinesi del Bronzo Tardo—i modelli planimetrici e strutturali. CMAO 6 (1996) 1-69.

9579 *Novák, Mirko* Der Landschaftsbezug in der orientalischen Palastarchitektur. AltOrF 23 (1996) 335-379.

9580 [E]**Pearson, Michael Parker; Richards, Colin** Architecture and order: approaches to social space. Material Cultures: L 1994, Routledge 264 pp. $23. 0-415-15743-9. [R]AJA 100 (1996) 416-417 (*Rapoport, Amos*).

9581 **Pilgrim, Cornelius von** Elephantine XVIII: Untersuchungen in der Stadt des Mittleren Reiches und der Zweiten Zwischenzeit. Mainz 1996, Von Zabern 364 pp. 41 charts. DM260. 3-8053-1746-8 [BiOr 55,411—Aston, D.A.].

9582 *Robson, E.* Building with bricks and mortar: quantity surveying in the Ur III and Old Babylonian periods. Houses and households. UNHAII 78: 1996, ⇒299. 181-190.

9583 **Rykwert, Joseph** The dancing column: on order in architecture. CMS 1996, MIT Press xviii; 598 pp. Bibl. 0-262-18170-3.

9584 **Segal, Arthur** Theatres in Roman Palestine and Provincia Arabia. Mn.S 140: 1995, ⇒11/2,a287. [R]Mes. 31 (1996) 287-288 (*Invernizzi, A.*).

9585 *Stone, E.C.* Houses, households and neighbourhoods in the Old Babylonian period: the role of extended families. Houses and households. UNHAII 78: 1996, ⇒299. 229-235.

9586 *Turnheim, Yehudit* Formation and transformation of the entablature in northern Eretz Israel and the Golan in the Roman and Byzantine periods. ZDPV 112 (1996) 122-138.

9587 **Wallace-Hadrill, Andrew** Houses and society in Pompeii and Herculaneum. 1994, ⇒10,11639. [R]Prudentia 28/1 (1996) 77-83 (*Stevenson, T.R.*).

9588 **Werner, Peter** Die Entwicklung der Sakralarchitektur in Nordsyrien und Südostkleinasien vom Neolithikum bis in das 1. Jt. v.Chr. 1994, ⇒10,11642. [R]Mes. 31 (1996) 214-219 (*Mazzoni, S.*).

[E]**Winter, Nancy A.** Proceedings of the international conference on Greek architectural terracottas ⇒320.

9589 **Wulf-Rheidt, Ulrike** Die hellenistischen und römischen Wohnhäuser von Pergamon. Diss. Technische Hochschule Karlsruhe 1996 [AA (1997/1) 107].

9590 *Yakar, Jak* Hattuša-Boğazköy: aspects of Hittite architecture. Royal cities. 1996, ⇒248. 53-68.

T1.9 *Supellex*—furniture; objects of daily life

9591 **Daviau, P.M. Michèle** Houses and their furnishings in Bronze Age
Palestine. JSOT.MS 8: 1993, ⇒9,13137... 11/2,a298. ᴿSyria 73
(1996) 213-214 (*Braemer, F.*).
9592 *Futato, Eugene M.* Early Bronze III Canaanean blade/scraper cores
from Tell Halif, Israel. ᶠVᴀɴ Bᴇᴇᴋ G., 1996, ⇒96. 61-74.
ᴱ**Herrmann, Georgina** The furniture of western Asia ⇒313.

T2.1 *Res militaris*—weapons, army activities

9593 *Ben-Dov, Rachel* ראש־דומח סורי מחפירות תל דן [A Syrian socketed
spearhead from Tel Dan]. ᶠAᴠɪʀᴀᴍ J., ErIs 25: 1996, ⇒2. Sum.
89*. 65-66. **H.**
9594 *David, Israel* Lanchester modeling and the biblical account of the
battles of Gibeah. Naval Research Logistics 42 (1995) 579-584
[IAJS 42,29].
9595 **Eph³al, Israel** Siege and its ancient Near Eastern manifestations.
Perry: J 1996, Hebrew University 194 pp. $13. ᴿUF 28 (1996)
785-787 (*Heltzer, M.*). **H.**
9596 **Goldsworthy, Adrian Keith** The Roman army at war 100 B.C.-
A.D. 200. Oxf Classical Mon.: Oxf 1996, OUP 315 pp. 11 fig.; 5
tables. $72. 0-19-815057-1 [AJA 101,818].
9597 ᴱ**Kennedy, David L.** The Roman army in the east. AA 1996, Journal of Roman Archaeology 320 pp. 18 fig.; 34 plans; 19 maps; 13
tables. $89.50. 1-887829-18-0 [AJA 101,431].
9598 *Littauer, M.A.; Crouwel, J.H.* The origin of the true chariot. Antiquity 70 (1996) 934-939.
9599 **Polito, Eugenio** Fulgentibus armis: introduzione allo studio dei
fregi d'armi antichi. Diss. Freie Univ. B 1996 [AA 1997/1, 105].
9600 ᴱ**Rich, John; Shipley, Graham** War and society in the Roman
world. 1993, ⇒9,361; 11/2,a340b. ᴿAt. 84 (1996) 299-303 (*Noè,
Eralda*).
9601 **Shatzman, Israel** The armies of the Hasmonaeans and Herod.
1991, ⇒7,b728... 9,13185. ᴿJQR 86 (1996) 446-451 (*Gichon,
Mordechai*); Gn. 68 (1996) 648-649 (*Clauss, Manfred*).

T2.3 **Nautica**

9602 **Göttlicher, Arvid** Kultschiffe und Schiffskulte im Altertum. 1992,
⇒8,d765. ᴿGn. 68 (1996) 62-63 (*Wachsmuth, Dietrich*).
9603 **Hornig, Karin** Nutzungsweisen von Wasserfahrzeugen im antiken
Mittelmeerraum. Diss. FrB 1996 [AA (1997/1) 102].
9604 **Kingsley, Seun A.; Raveh, Kurt** The ancient harbour and anchorage at Dor, Israel: results of the underwater surveys 1976-1991.
BAR International 626: Oxf 1996, Tempus R. ii; xiii; 123 pp. 53
figures; 94 pl. Dor Maritime Archaeology Project. £34. 0-86054-
807-4 [RB 104,314].
9605 **Morrison, J.S.** Greek and Roman oared warships. Collab. *Coates,
J.F.*, Oxf 1996, Oxbow xviii; 403 pp. $120. 0-900188-07-4.

9606 **Wachsmann, Shelley** The Sea of Galilee boat: an extraordinary 2000 year old discovery. 1995, ⇒11/2,a395. [R]BA 59 (1996) 245-246 (*DeVries, LaMoine*); BArR 22/5 (1996) 67-68 (*Hohlfelder, Robert L.*).
9607 **Wallinga, H.T.** Ships and sea-power before the Great Persian War. 1993, ⇒9,13225... 11/2,a394. [R]BiOr 53 (1996) 238-240 (*Meijer, F.J.A.M.*).

T2.4 *Athletica*—sport, games

9608 **Fortuin, Rigobert W.** Der Sport im augusteischen Rom: philologische und sporthistorische Untersuchungen (mit einer Sammlung, Übersetzung und Kommentierung der antiken Zeugnisse zum Sport in Rom). Palingenesia 57: Stu 1996 Steiner 440 pp. DM144 [HZ 265,752].
9609 **Hübner, Ulrich** Spiele und Spielzeug im antiken Palästina. OBO 121: 1992, ⇒8,d797; 11/2,a404. [R]JAOS 116 (1996) 534-535 (*Meier, Samuel A.*).
9610 **Sinn, Ulrich** Sport in der Antike: Wettkampf, Spiel und Erziehung im Altertum. Wü 1996, Ergon 168 pp. 105 fig. 3-928034-98-7 [AJA 101,432].
9611 **Wacker, Christian** Das Gymnasium in Olympia und seine Funktion. Diss. Wü 1996 [AA (1997/1) 106].
9612 **Yegül, Fikret** Baths and bathing in classical antiquity. 1992, ⇒9,13267; 10,11751. [R]Gn. 68 (1996) 50-53 (*Nielsen, Inge*).

T2.5 **Musica**, dance

9613 **Blumenberg, Hans** La passion selon saint Matthieu. [T]*Baatsch, Henri-Alexis; Cassagnau, Laurent*. P 1996, L'Arche 366 pp. FF165. 2-85181-381-1 [BCLF 598-599,1557].
9614 *Caubet, Annie* La musique à Ougarit: nouveaux témoignages matériels. [F]GIBSON J., 1996, 9-31.
9615 **Foley, Edward** Foundations of christian music: the music of pre-Constantinian christianity. American Essays in Liturgy: Collegeville 1996, Liturgical 111 pp. [ProEc 7,501s—Joncas, Jan].
9616 [E]**Krenzer, Rolf; Horn, Reinhard** Wenn wir us die Hände reichen: Spiellieder zur Bibel. Stu 1996, Kath. Bibelwerk 112 pp. DM30 [BiLi 69,190—Ebenbauer, Melitta].
9617 **Manniche, Lise** Music and musicians in Ancient Egypt. 1991, ⇒8,d844; 11/2,a449. [R]CEg 71 (1996) 281-283 (*Careddu, Giorgio*).
9618 *Piovano, Attilio* Dalle tradizioni locali al canto gregoriano. PaVi 41/3 (1996) 51-52;
9619 Forme e strutture del canto gregoriano. PaVi 41/4 (1996) 54-56;
9620 L'innesto della polifonia: dalle primitive forme dell'*Ars antiqua* alla fioritura dell'*Ars nova*. PaVi 41/6 (1996) 59-60;
9621 Le principali novità nella monodia sacra (a partire dai sec. IX-X). PaVi 41/5 (1996) 52-54;
9622 Radici storiche del canto giudaico-cristiano. PaVi 41/1-2 (1996) 45-46/41-42.

9623 *Rashid, Subhi Anwar* Mesopotamische Musikinstrumente im Spiegel der Glyptik. [F]BERAN T., 1996, ⇒6. 257-273.
9624 **Remmert, Sönke** Bibeltexte in der Musik: ein Verzeichnis ihrer Vertonungen. Dienst am Wort 74: Gö 1996, Vandenhoeck & R. 231 pp. DM34. 3-525-59338-4 [NThAR 1997,66].
9625 *Shelt, Christopher* Toward a biblical theology of music in worship. RTR 55 (1996) 67-80.

T2.6 Textilia, *vestis*, clothing

9626 **Germer, Renate** Die Textilfärberei. ÄA 53: 1992, ⇒8,d865... 10,11766. [R]BiOr 53 (1996) 442-445 (*Granger-Taylor, Hero*).
9627 **Vogelsang-Eastwood, Gillian** Pharaonic Egyptian clothing. 1993, ⇒9,13325... 11/2,a480. [R]BiOr 53 (1996) 445-450 (*Bochi, Patricia A.*).

T2.7 *Ornamenta corporis*, jewellry

9628 [E]**Calinescu, Adriana** Ancient jewelry and archaeology. Bloomington 1996, Indiana Univ. Press 288 pp. 190 fig.; 7 maps. $60. 0-253-329-93-0 [AJA 101,631].
9629 [E]**Demakopoulou, Katie** The Aidonia treasure: seals and jewellery of the Aegean Late Bronze Age. Athens 1996, Ministry of Culture 120 pp. 163 col. fig.; 11 fig. 960-214-646-X [AJA 101,818].
9630 *Echt, Rudolf; Thiele, Wolf-Rüdiger* Werkstoffkundliche Untersuchungen an Goldschmuck aus dem 'Schatzhaus'. Kamid el-Loz 16. 1996, ⇒9940. 289-299,
9631 **Effinger, Maria** Minoischer Schmuck. BAR-IS 646: Oxf 1996, Reparatum 367 pp. 7 col. pl.; 61 pl.; 174 fig.; 42 plans; 6 tables. £46. 0-86054-831-7 [AJA 101,818].
9632 *Goldman, Bernard* Nabataean / Syro-Roman lunate earrings. IEJ 46 (1996) 77-99.
9633 [E]**Kühne, Hartmut; Salje, Beate** Kamid el-Loz 15: die Glyptik. Saarbrücker Beiträge zur Altertumskunde 56: Bonn 1996, Habelt 194 pp. Bibl. 3-7749-2766-9.
9634 **Rehm, Ellen** Der Schmuck der Achämeniden. 1992, ⇒10,11796*; 11/2,a490. [R]WO 27 (1996) 253-259 (*Koch, Heidemarie*); BiOr 53 (1996) 545-546 (*Moorey, P.R.S.*).
9635 *Swersky, Ann* Gemstones;
9636 *Zuckerman, Sharon* Beads and pendants. City of David excavations [E]**Ariel, D.**]. Qedem 35: 1996, ⇒T4.3. 268-275/276-290.

T2.8 Utensilia

9637 *Barag, Dan* מסורות קדומות בכלי־אבן פיניקיים מן המאות הח'/הז—לפסה"נ [Early traditions in Phoenician stone vessels of the eighth-seventh centuries BCE]. [F]AVIRAM J., ErIs 25: 1996, ⇒2. Sum. 90*. 82-93. H.
9638 *Gill, Dan; Shimron, Arieh* Appendix B: petrographic description of selected stone implements and specimens.   City of David excavations [E]**Ariel, D.**]. Qedem 35: 1996, ⇒T4.3. 193-203.

9639 *Lilyquist, Christine* Stone vessels at Kamid el-Loz, Lebanon: Egyptian, Egyptianizing, or non-Egyptian?: a question at sites from the Sudan to Iraq to the Greek mainland;

9640 *Rost, Franz* Petrographische Untersuchungen der Steingefäße Miron 404, 406 und 416. Kamid el-Loz 16. 1996, ⇒9941. 133-173/301-303.

9641 *Schaub, R. Thomas* Pots as containers. FVAN BEEK G., 1996, ⇒96. 231-243.

9642 **Siebert, Anne-Viola** Instrumenta sacra: Untersuchungen zu römischen Opferkult- und Priestergeräten. Diss. Müns 1996 [AA 1997/1,105].

9643 *Sparks, Rachael* Egyptian stone vessels in Syro-Palestine during the second millennium B.C. and their impact on the local stone vessel industry. Cultural interaction. Abr-n.S 5: 1996, ⇒285. 51-66.

9644 *Venturi, Fabrizio* Una 'fiasca del pellegrino' da Tell Afis: l'evoluzione dei 'pilgrim flasks' cananaici nel passaggio tra Bronzo Tardo e Ferro I. VO 10 (1996) 147-161.

T2.9 *Pondera et mensurae*—weights and measures

9645 *Barkay, Gabriel* A balance beam from Tel Lachish. TelAv 23 (1996) 75-82.

9646 *Eran, Abraham* Weights and weighing in the city of David: the early weights from the Bronze Age to the Persian period. City of David excavations [EAriel, D.]. Qedem 35: 1996, ⇒T4.3. 204-256.

9647 *Girndt, Uwe* Einige Untersuchungen zur altägyptischen Grundeinheit der Längenmessung. GöMisz 151 (1996) 53-66.

9648 **Hitzi, Konrad** Die Gewichte griechischer Zeit aus Olympia: eine Studie zu den vorhellenistischen Gewichtssystemen in Griechenland. OlFrosch 25: B 1996, De Gruyter 278 pp. 43 pl. DM280. 3-11-014606-1 [AJA 101,633].

9649 *Imhausen, Annette* Das Zahlensystem der Ägypter—(k)ein Dezimalsystem. DiscEg 36 (1996) 49-51.

9650 *Legon, John A.R.* The quest for the true *nbj* measure. DiscEg 36 (1996) 69-78.

9651 *Ronen, Yigal* The enigma of the shekel weights of the Judean kingdom. BA 59 (1996) 122-125.

9652 *Shamir, Orit* Loomweights and whorls. City of David excavations [EAriel, D.]. Qedem 35: 1996, ⇒T4.3. 135-170.

9653 *Spalinger, Anthony* Some times. RdE 47 (1996) 67-77.

T3.0 **Ars antiqua**, *motiva, picturae* [icones ⇒T3.1 infra]

9654 *Albenda, Pauline* The beardless winged genies from the northwest palace at Nimrud. SAA Bulletin 10/1 (1996) 67-78.

9655 *Amiet, P.* Alliance des hommes, alliance des dieux dans l'iconographie orientale. FSPYCKET A., 1996, ⇒83. 1-6.

9656 **Amyx, D.A.; Lawrence, Patricia** Studies in archaic Corinthian vase painting. Hesp.S 28: Princeton 1996, American School of Classical Studies at Athens 172 pp. 64 pl.; 5 fig. $65. 0-87661-528-0 [AJA 101,631].

9657 **Arafat, K.W.** PAUSANIAS' Greece: ancient artists and Roman rulers. C 1996, CUP 261 pp. $60. 0-521-55340-7 [AJA 101,430];
9658 Classical Zeus. 1990, ⇒6,814... 8,d931. ᴿGn. 68 (1996) 378-380 (*Simon, Erika*).
9659 *Azria, Régine* L'art juif. ASSR 41 (1996) 13-17.
9660 **Bachmann, Manuel** Die strukturalistische Artefakt- und Kunstanalyse: Exposition der Grundlagen anhand der vorderorientalischen, ägyptischen und griechischen Kunst. OBO 148: FrS 1996, Universitäsverlag 80 pp. FS25. 3-7278-1077-7 [RB 104,469].
9661 **Balensiefen, Lilian** Die Bedeutung des Spiegelbildes als ikonographisches Motiv in der antiken Kunst. TFAK 10: Tü 1990, Wasmuth xiii; 252 pp. ᴿGn. 68 (1996) 630-40 (*Schmidt, Margot*).
9662 **Belting, Hans** Likeness and presence: a history of the image before the era of art. 1994, ⇒10,11831*; 11/2,a522. ᴿJThS 47 (1996) 705-709 (*Louth, Andrew*); JR 76 (1996) 680-681 (*Brubaker, Leslie*).
9663 *Berlejung, Angelika* Die Macht der Insignien: Überlegungen zu einem Ritual der Investitur des Königs und dessen königsideologischen Implikationen. UF 28 (1996) 1-35.
9664 *Bleibtreu, Erika* Akkadische Zweikampfszenen. WZKM 86 (1996) 53-63.
9665 **Boardman, John** The diffusion of classical art in antiquity. 1993, ⇒11/2,a523. ᴿAJA 100 (1996) 190-191 (*Pollitt, J.J.*).
9666 **Borg, Barbara** Mumienporträts: Chronologie und kultureller Kontext. Mainz 1996, Von Zabern xv; 263 pp. 87 pl. 3-8053-1742-5.
9667 *Bouffartigue, Jean* Le corps d'argile: quelques aspects de la représentation de l'homme dans l'antiquité grecque. RevSR 70 (1996) 204-223.
9668 *Bryan, Betsy M.* Art, empire, and the end of the late Bronze Age. Albright centennial conference. 1996, ⇒303. 33-79.
9669 *Di Paolo, Silvana* Per una proposta di interpretazione dell'avorio A 22249 di Megiddo: l'assunzione tra gli antenati regali divinizzati e l'attraversamento del deserto lugubre. UF 28 (1996) 189-220.
9670 *Elsner, John* Image and ritual: reflections on the religious appreciation of classical art. CQ 46 (1996) 515-531.
9671 **Eschweiler, Peter** Bildzauber im alten Ägypten: die Verwendung von Bildern und Gegenständen in magischen Handlungen nach den Texten des Mittleren und Neuen Reiches. Diss. Heidelberg 1991, ᴰ*Assmann, Jan*, OBO 137: FrS 1994, Universitätsverlag x; 372 pp. 3-7278-0957-4. ᴿBiOr 53 (1996) 692-697 (*Raven, Maarten J.*); Or. 65 (1996) 357-360 (*Kákosy, László*).
9672 *Fay, Biri* The "Abydos princess". MDAI.K 52 (1996) 115-141.
9673 ᴱᵀ**Garzya Romano, Chiara** ERACLIUS Romanus: De coloribus et artibus romanorum: i colori e le arti dei romani: e la compilazione pseudo-eracliana: introduzione, testo latino e traduzione, commentario. Istituto italiano per gli studi storici. Testi storici, filosofici e letterari 6: Bo 1996, Il Mulino lxi; 137 pp. 88-15-05533-9.
9674 **Hackländer, Nele** Der archaistische Dionysos: eine archäologische Untersuchng zur Bedeutung archaistischer Kunst in hellenistischer und römischer Zeit. EHS.Archäologie 57: Fra 1996, Lang 224 pp. 35 pl. $55. 3-631-49065-8 [AJA 101,431].
9675 **Havelock, Christine Mitchell** The Aphrodite of Knidos and her successors: a historical review of the female nude in Greek art. AA

1995, Univ. of Michigan Press. $47.50. 0-472-10585-X. ᴿAJA 100 (1996) 794-795 (*King, Helen*).

9676 *Hiller, Stefan* Zur Rezeption ägyptischer Motive in der minoischen Freskenkunst. Ä&L 6 (1996) 83-105.

9677 *Hrouda, Barthel* Westlicher Einfluß in der altorientalischen Kunst der mittanisch-mittelassyrischen Zeit?. ᶠBᴇʀᴀɴ T., 1996, ⇒6. 139-147.

9678 *Keel, Othmar* Bibliographie. I. Zu den Sammlungen.-II. Corpus der Stempelsiegel und Amulette aus Palästina/Israel.-III Ikonographisch-exegetische Arbeiten aus dem Biblischen Institut der Universität Freiburg Schweiz;

9679 Warum Sammlungen altorientalischer Miniaturkunst an einem Biblischen Institut?. Altorientalische Miniaturkunst. 1996, ⇒9681. 181-187/9-24;

9680 Ein weiterer Skarabäus mit einer Nilpferdjagd, die Ikonographie der sogenannten Beamtenskarabäen und der ägyptische König auf Skarabäen vor dem Neuen Reich. Ä&L 6 (1996) 119-136; Die Welt der altorientalischen Bildsymbolik... Psalmen ⇒2753.

9681 **Keel, Othmar; Uehlinger, Christoph** Altorientalische Miniaturkunst: die ältesten visuellen Massenkommunikationsmittel: ein Blick in die Sammlungen des Biblischen Instituts der Universität Freiburg Schweiz. Collab. *Gasser, Madeleine*, FrS ²1996, Universitäsverlag 192 pp. 3-7278-1053-X [OLZ 92,531].

9682 *Keel, Othmar; Uehlinger, Christoph* Nachtrag zur Neuauflage: der Ausbau der Sammlungen zwischen 1990 und 1995. Altorientalische Miniaturkunst. 1996, ⇒9681. 147-167.

9683 *Klingbeil, Martin* Nombres y funciones de las deidades en la iconografía del antiguo cercano oriente y su importancia para los estudios bíblicos. Theologika 11/1 (1996) 160-183 [ZID 23,321].

9684 **Koch, Nadia** De picturae initiis: die Anfänge der griechischen Malerei im 7. Jahrhundert v. Chr. Studien zur antiken Malerei und Farbegung 3: Mü 1996, Biering und B. 218 pp. 29 col. pl.; 8 pl. DM158. 3-930609-09-6 [AJA 101,633].

9685 **Kontorli-Papadopoulou, Litsa** Aegean frescoes of religious character. SIMA 117: Jonsered 1996, Åström 186 pp. 27 col. pl.; 133 pl. 91-7081-118-0 [AJA 101,199].

9686 *Levy, Thomas E.; Golden, Jonathan* Syncretistic and mnemonic dimensions of chalcolithic art: a new human figurine from Shiqmim. BA 59 (1996) 150-159.

9687 *Lipiński, E.* Egypto-Canaanite iconography of Reshef, Baᶜal, Ḥ-ron, and Anat. CÉg 71 (1996) 254-262.

9688 **Lippolis, Enzo** Arte e artigianato in Magna Grecia. I greci in Occidente: N 1996, Electa 541 pp. Bibl. 88-435-5234-1.

9689 *Markoe, Glenn* The emergence of orientalizing in Greek art: some observations on the interchange between Greeks and Phoenicians in the eighth and seventh centuries B.C. BASOR 301 (1996) 47-67.

9690 **Matthiae, Paolo** La storia dell'arte dell'Oriente Antico: i grandi imperi 1000-330 a.C. Mi 1996, Electa 282 pp. 88-435-5347-X.

9691 *Minas, Martina* Die Dekorationstätigkeit von Ptolemaios VI. Philometor und Ptolemaios VIII. Euergetes II. an ägyptischen Tempeln (Teil 1). OLoP 27 (1996) 51-78.

9692 *Moscati, S.* La 'scuola' di Villaricos. RSFen 24 (1996) 57-66.

9693 **Niemeyer, Hans Georg** Semata: über den Sinn griechischer Standbilder. Sitzungen der J. Jungius-Ges. der Wiss. 14/1: Hamburg

1996, Joachim Jungius-Ges. der Wiss. 83 pp. 6 fig.; 8 pl. DM24.
3-525-86288-1 [AJA 101,432].

9694 **Nowicka, Maria** Le portrait dans la peinture antique. Bibliotheca
Antiqua 22: Varsovie 1993, Académie polonaise des Sciences 206
pp. 69 fig. $30. 83-85463-10-0. [R]AnCl 65 (1996) 539-540 (*Balty,
Jean Ch.*).

9695 *Ovadiah, Asher; Mucznik, Sonia* A fragmentary Roman zodiac and
horoscope from Caesarea Maritima. [R]SBFLA 46 (1996) 375-380.

9696 *Pittman, Holly* Constructing context: the Gebel el-Arak knife:
Greater Mesopotamian and Egyptian interaction in the late fourth
millennium B.C.E. Albright centennial conference. 1996, ⇒303.
9-32.

9697 *Rashad, Mahmoud* Die Bedeutung der Jagd für die Herrscherdar-
stellungen bei den Achämeniden, Parthern und Sasaniden.
[F]BERAN T., 1996, ⇒6. 241-255.

9698 *Schmandt-Besserat, D.* Art, writing and narrative in Mesopotamia.
[F]SPYCKET A., 1996, ⇒83. 315-321.

9699 **Svenson, Dominique** Darstellungen hellenistischer Könige mit
Götterattributen. Archäologische Studien 10: Fra 1996, Lang 373
pp. 65 pl; 9 fig. $77. 3-631-48351-1 [AJA 101,200].

9700 **Tassignon, Isabelle** Iconographie et religion dionysiaques en Gaule
belgique et dans les deux Germanies. Genève 1996, Droz 378 pp.
2-87019-265-7 [AnCl 67,584—Raepsaet-Charlier, Marie-Thérèse].

9701 **Teissier, B.** Egyptian iconography on Syro-Palestinian cylinder
seals of the Middle Bronze Age. OBO.A 11: FrS 1996, University
Press xii; 224 pp. 5 pl. FS85. 3-525-53892-8 [Levant 29,260].
[R]AulOr 14 (1996) 295-297 (*Mangado Alonso, M.L.*).

9702 **Turcan, Robert** L'art romain dans l'histoire: six siècles
d'expression de la romanité. 1995, ⇒11/2,a552. [R]RAr (1996/2)
253-268 (*Picard, Gilbert Charles*).

9703 **Vollenweider, Marie-Louise** Camées et intailles, tome 1: les
portraits grecs du Cabinet des Médailles. Collab. *Avisseau-
Broustet, Mathilde*, P 1995, Bibliothèque Nationale de France 2
vols. Vol. textes + vol. pl. 2-7177-1915-6. [R]Mes. 31 (1996) 277-
282 (*Invernizzi, A.*).

9704 **Wilkinson, Richard H.** Symbol and magic in Egyptian art. L
1994, Thames H. 224 pp. $25. 0-500-23663-1. [R]JARCE 33 (1996)
207-208 (*Kákosy, László*).

9705 *Zissu, Boaz* 'מערת הרוכב'—זכרי חורבת [H. Zikhri—'the rider's
cave']. Sum. 126. ʿAtiqot 30 (1996) 17*-21*;

9706 A graffito depicting a horseman from the Judaean foothills. PEQ
128 (1996) 52-56.

T3.1 *Theologia iconis*—ars postbiblica

9707 *Aurenhammer, Hans H.* Das Christuskind als tragischer Held?: eine
antike Pathosformel in Giovanni BELLINIS 'Lochis-Madonna'.
[F]BORCHARDT J., 1996, II, ⇒8. 377-394.

9708 *Avner-Levy, Rina* A note on the iconography of the personifications
in the "Hippolytos mosaic" at Madaba, Jordan. SBFLA 46 (1996)
363-374.

9709 **Barbagallo, Salvatore** Iconografia liturgica del Pantokrator. Diss. Pont. Ateneo Sant'Anselmo, ᴰ*Valenziano, Crispino*, Thesis ad lauream 227: R 1996, 272 pp.

9710 *Besgen, Achim* Das biblische Werk Marc CHAGALLs. StZ 214 (1996) 845-856.

9711 *Boespflug, François* La conversion de Paul dans l'art médiéval. Paul de Tarse. LeDiv 165: 1996, ⇒273. 147-168.

9712 *Caillet, Jean-Pierre, (al),* Des catacombes à l'art romain: l'évolution des représentations de la croix dans l'art chrétien. MoBi 97 (1996) 17-33.

9713 *Cartlidge, David R.* An electronic database of pictorial images paralleled in christian apocrypha. Sum. rés. 301. Apocrypha 7 (1996) 301-303.

9714 *De Spirito, Giuseppe* L'annonciation de Sainte-Marie-Majeure: image apocryphe?. Sum. rés. 273. Apocrypha 7 (1996) 273-292.

9715 *Delenda, Odile* L'enfance du Christ dans l'art, présage de la Rédemption. Sedes Sapientiae 14/1 (1996) 37-48.

9716 **Derbes, Anne** Picturing the Passion in late medieval Italy: narrative paintings, Franciscan ideologies, and the Levant. C 1996, CUP xvi; 270 pp. £16/$23. 0-521-63926-3 [CFr 69,369s—Gieben, Servus].

9717 *Dillenberger, Jane Daggett* Jesus as pop icon: the unknown religious art of Andy WARHOL. BiRe 12/5 (1996) 22-27, 54.

9718 *Domagalski, Bernhard* Zur biblischen Ikonographie im frühchristlichen Deutschland. ᶠDASSMANN E., JAC.E 23: 1996, ⇒19. 526-542.

9719 **Duwe, Gert** Die Anbetung der Heiligen Drei Könige in der niederländischen Malerei des 15. und 16. Jahrhunderts. Fra 1994, Lang 253 pp. ᴿMar. 58 (1996) 278-281 *(Ferraris, Giovannella).*

9720 **Elsner, Jaś** Art and the Roman viewer: the transformation of art from the pagan world to christianity. Cambridge Studies in New Art History and Criticism: C 1995, CUP 375 pp. $25. 0-521-59952-0. ᴿAJA 100 (1996) 805-807 *(Kellum, Barbara)*; Antiquity 70 (1996) 711-712 *(Janes, Dominic).*

9721 *Engemann, Josef* Biblische Themen im Bereich der frühchristlichen Kunst. ᶠDASSMANN E., JAC.E 23: 1996, ⇒19. 543-556.

9722 **Erffa, Hans Martin von** Ikonologie der Genesis: die christlichen Bildthemen aus dem Alten Testament und ihre Quellen Bd. II. Mü 1995, Deutscher Kunstverlag 533 pp. DM198. 3-422-06114-2. ᴿJThS 47 (1996) 560-563 *(Murdoch, Brian).*

9723 **Finney, Paul Corby** The invisible God: the earliest christians on art. 1994, ⇒11/2,a574. ᴿBiRe 12/2 (1996) 40-41 *(Jensen, Robin M.)*; JEarlyC 4 (1996) 263-265 *(Snyder, Graydon F.).*

9724 *Goranson, Stephen* 7 vs 8: the battle over the holy day at Dura-Europos. BiRe 12/4 (1996) 22-33, 44.

9725 ᴱ**Grierson, Roderick** African Zion: the sacred art of Ethiopia. NHv 1996, Yale Univ. Press xi; 272 pp. Catalogue by *Marilyn E. Heldman; Stuart C.H. Munro-Hay.* 0-300-05915-9.

9726 *Jiménez Martel, Germán* La sagrada escritura como fuente de inspiración religiosa en la obra de José ARENCIBIA Gil: analisis iconografico e icnologico del mural de la capilla mayor de la iglesia de San Francisco de Asis de Las Palmas de Gran Canaria. Almogaren 18 (1996) 109-115.

9727 **Koch, Guntram** Frühchristliche Kunst: eine Einführung. UB 453: Stu 1995, Kohlhammer 168 pp. RThR 61 (1996) 475-477 (*Mühlenberg, Ekkehard*);

9728 Early christian art and architecture: an introduction. L 1996, SCM vii; 184 pp. Bibl. 0-334-02632-6.

9729 *Korol, Dieter* Ein frühes Zeugnis für ein mit einer neutestamentlichen Szene geschmücktes "Templon": die Darstellung der Magierhuldigung aus einer Kirche des 5. Jh. in Trani. JAC 39 (1996) 200-224.

9730 *Lambert, Chiara* Il miracolo della guarigione del cieco su una pisside eburnea del VI secolo. PaVi 41/4 (1996) 53-54;

9731 Il miracolo della moltiplicazione dei pani in alcuni manufatti paleocristiani. PaVi 41/3 (1996) 49-50.

9732 **Langener, Lucia** Isis lactans—Maria lactans: Untersuchungen zur koptischen Ikonographie. Arbeiten zum spätantiken und koptischen Agypten 9: Altenberge 1996, Oros xvii; 190 pp. DM90. 3-89375-131-9 [ThLZ 122,959].

9733 **Lazarev, Viktor Nikititch** Icones russes. P 1996, Desclée 403 pp. [Contacts 49,275].

9734 *Mariaux, Pierre-Alain* Figurer l'apocryphe, ou la vérité dévoilée par la peinture: quelques iconographes du XIXe siècle face à l'image chrétienne. Sum. rés. 293. Apocrypha 7 (1996) 293-300.

9735 *Mata, Ángela Franco* La naturaleza en la escultura gótica española: un paseo por la Biblia. VyV 54 (1996) 295-313.

9736 **Mathews, Thomas F.** The clash of gods: a reinterpretation of early christian art. 1993, ⇒9,13453... 11/2,a594. RJThS 47 (1996) 703-705 (*Murray, Sister Charles*).

9737 **May, Sigmund; Mülling, Christina** Von Gott geheilt: Holzschnitte zur Bibel. Mü 1996, Don Bosco 96 pp. DM29.80. 3-7698-0835-5 [OrdKor 38,506].

9738 *McKenzie, A. Dean* MICHELANGELO's masterpiece reclaimed. BiRe 12/6 (1996) 42-50.

9739 **Murray, Peter & Linda** The Oxford companion to christian art and architecture. NY 1996, OUP xii; 596 pp. $55 [JEarlyC 6,686ss—Jensen, Robin.

9740 *Nichols, Aidan* Icons: more than art. PrPe 10 (1996) 30-31.

9741 *Nieddu, Anna Maria* La pittura paleocristiana in Sardegna: nuove acquisizioni. RivAC 72 (1996) 245-283.

9742 **Onasch, Konrad** Ikone: Kirche, Gesellschaft. Pd 1996, Schöningh 129 pp. DM48. 3-506-78332-9 [OrdKor 38,505].

9743 **Onasch, Konrad; Schnieper, Annemarie** Ikonen: Faszination und Wirklichkeit. FrB 1995, Herder 301 pp. ÖS765. 3-451-23533-1. RZKTh 118 (1996) 546-547 (*Meyer, Hans Bernhard*).

9744 **Parry, Kenneth** Depicting the word: Byzantine iconophile thought of the eighth and ninth centuries. The Medieval Mediterranean 12: Lei 1996, Brill x; 216 pp. $74.25 [CTJ 33,515ss—Payton, James].

9745 *Prigent, Pierre* Images chrétiennes, images sacrées: un problème historico-théologique du paléo-christianisme. RHPhR 76 (1996) 179-193.

9746 *Quacquarelli, Antonio* Il mito soggetto di culto e mezzo di comunicazione sociale nella iconografia paleocristiana dei secoli II-IV. VetChr 33 (1996) 5-24.

9747 *Rein, Mary Jane* Phrygian Matar: emergence of an iconographic type. MVERMASEREN M., 1996, ⇒219. 223-237.

9748 **Schrenk, Sabine** Typos und Antitypos in der frühchristlichen Kunst. JAC.E 21: 1995, ⇒11/2,a611. ᴿZKTh 118 (1996) 544-545 (*Meyer, Hans Bernhard*).

9749 **Schurr, Eva** Die Attribute in der frühchristlichen Kunst. Diss. Erlangen 1996 [AA (1997/1) 105].

9750 ᴱ**Schwebel, Horst** Die Bibel in der Kunst: die Renaissance. Stu 1996, Dt. Bibelges. 144 pp. Bildauswahl, Einf. u. Erl. von *Manfred Wundram*, 3-438-04463-3 [NThAR 1998,267].

9751 *Schwelien, Maria* Mit Krone, Helm und Lorbeerkranz: die Gestalt des Pilatus in der Kunst. Pontius zu Pilatus. 1996, ⇒196. 69-81.

9752 **Sepière, Marie-Christine** L'image d'un Dieu souffrant: aux origines du crucifix. 1994, ⇒11/2,a613. ᴿRHPhR 76 (1996) 328-329 (*Prigent, P.*).

9753 **Smith, David R.; Guenther, Liz** Realism and invention in the prints of Albrecht DÜRER. Hanover 1996, Univ. Press of New England 78 pp. $19. 0-9648953-0-7 [ETR 74,129s—Clerc, F.].

9754 **Sörries, Reiner** Christlich-antike Buchmalerei: im Überblick. Wsb 1993, Reichert 2 vols. Textband + Tafelband. DM198. ᴿJAC 39 (1996) 294-299 (*Zimmermann, Barbara*).

9755 *Spatharakis, Ioannis; Klinkenberg, Emanuel* The pictorial cycle of the life of St. John the evangelist in Crete. ByZ 89 (1996) 420-440.

9756 *Stäps, Detlef* "Er ist der Herr" (Joh 21,7): zur ältesten Pantokrator-Ikone. GuL 69 (1996) 137-140.

9757 *Thierry, Nicole* L'iconographie cappadocienne de l'affront fait à Anne d'après le 'Protoévangile de Jacques'. Sum. rés. 261. Apocrypha 7 (1996) 261-272.

9758 ᴱ**Van der Horst, Koert; Noel, William; Wüstefeld, Wilhelmina C.M.** The Utrecht psalter in medieval art: picturing the psalms of David. L 1996, Miller xii; 271 pp. plates. 1-872501-69-9 [JEH 49,524—Marner, Dominic].

9759 ᴱ**Widmann, Gertrud** Die Bilder der Bibel von Sieger KOEDER: erschließende und meditative Texte. Ostfildern 1996, Schwabenverlag 220 pp. DM58. 3-7966-0791-8 [ThRv 93,438].

T3.2 Sculptura

9760 **Amberger-Lahrmann, Mechthild** Anatomie und Physiognomie in der hellenistischen Plastik: dargestellt am Pergamonaltar. AAWLM.G 1996/10: Mainz 1996, Akad. der Wiss. 63 pp. Bibl. 3-515-06978-X.

9761 **Berger, Ernst; Gisler-Huwiler, Madeleine** Der Parthenon in Basel: Dokumentation zum Fries I-II. Studien der Skulpturhalle Basel 3: Mainz 1996, Von Zabern 239 pp. 5 tables; 161 pl. DM198. 3-8053-0781-0 [AJA 101,774s—Jenkins, Ian].

9762 *Caubet, A.* L'ivoire et la coquille dans la statuaire du Proche-Orient ancien. ᶠSPYCKET A., 1996, ⇒83. 65-69.

9763 **Dreyfus, Renée; Schraudolph, Ellen** Pergamon: the Telephos frieze from the great altar. Austin 1996, Univ. of Texas Press 120 pp. 27 col. fig.; 68 fig. $30. 0-88401-089-9 [AJA 101,818].

9764 *Fehr, Burkhard* The Laocoon group or the political exploitation of a sacrilege. Religion and power. 1996, ⇒290. Sum. 189. 189-204.

9765 *Franco Mata, Maria A.* La naturaleza en la escultura gotica espa-
nola: un paseo por la biblia. VyV 54 (1996) 295-313 [ZID 23,-
414].

9766 **Grenier, Jean-Claude** Les statuettes funéraires du Museo Gregoriano Egizio. Museo Gregoriano Egizio Aegyptiaca Gregoriana 2:
Città del Vaticano 1996, Monumenti, Musei e Gallerie Pontificie
130 pp. 66 pl.

9767 *Hamilton, Naomi (al),* Can we interpret figurines?. CamArch 6
(1996) 281-307.

9768 *Hrouda, B.* Einige Bemerkungen zur Rundplastik im alten Orient.
FSPYCKET A., 1996, ⇒83. 137-143.

9769 *Kaptan, Deniz* The Great King's audience. FBORCHARDT J.,
1996, I, ⇒8. 1996, 259-271 [Apadana reliefs, Persepolis].

9770 **Kreilinger, Ulla** Römische Bronzeappliken: historische Reliefs im
Kleinformat. Archäologie und Geschichte 6: Heidelberg 1996,
Archäologie und Geschichte 224 pp. 56 pl. DM148. 3-9801-863-6-
9 [AJA 101,199].

9771 **Marcadé, Jean** Sculptures déliennes. P 1996 De Boccard 225 pp.
104 fig. FF150. 2-7018-0100-1 [AJA 101,633].

9772 **Mattusch, Carol C.** Classical bronzes: the art and craft of Greek
and Roman statuary. Ithaca 1996, Cornell Univ. Press xvii; 280
pp. 9 col. pl.; 172 fig. $45. 0-8014-3182-4 [AJA 101,587s—
Hurwitt, Jeffrey M.].

9773 **Mattusch, Carol C.,** *(collab.),* The fire of Hephaistos: large classical bronzes from North American collections. CM 1996, Harvard
Univ. Art Museums 359 pp. 16 col. pl.; 415 fig.; 11 drawings; 45
tables. $25. 0-916724-89-1 [AJA 101,806s—Dillon, Sheila].

9774 **Paliompeis, Stefanos** Studien zur Innenausstattung griechischer
Tempel: Skulptur und Malerei. Diss. Mainz 1996 [AA (1997/1)
104].

9775 **Pollitt, J.J.; Palagia, O.** Personal styles in Greek sculpture. C
1996, CUP xi; 187 pp. 131 pl. £37.50/$60. 0-521-55187-0 [ClR
48,426ss—Arafat, K.W.].

9776 *Rolley, Claude* Les bronzes grecs et romains: recherches récentes.
RAr (1996/2) 269-291.

9777 *Rosen, Steven A.* The chipped stone assemblage from Hartuv.
BASOR 302 (1996) 41-50.

9778 *Sackler, Arthur M.* Statues from ʿAin Ghazal at the Smithsonian.
BA 59 (1996) 180-181.

9779 **Spivey, Nigel** Understanding Greek sculpture: ancient meanings,
modern readings. L 1996, Thames & H. 240 pp. 141 ill. $35. 0-
500-23710-7. RAntiquity 70 (1996) 989-991 (*Gill, David*).

9780 **Tunca, Ö.** Une statuette d'adorant de l'âge du Bronze ancien pro-
venant de Tell Amarna (Syrie). FSPYCKET A., 1996, ⇒83. 381-
384.

9781 **Webb, Pamela A.** Hellenistic architectural sculpture:; figural motifs in western Anatolia and the Aegean islands. Wisconsin Studies
in Classics: Madison 1996, Univ. of Wisconsin Press xiv; 225 pp.
142 figs. $60. 0-299-14980-3 [AJA 102,446—Roccos, Linda Jo-
nes].

9782 *Winter, I.J.* Artists' trial pieces from Susa?. FSPYCKET A., 1996,
⇒83. 397-406.

т3.3 *Glyptica;* stamp and cylinder seals, scarabs, amulets

9783 *Aharoni, Miriam* An Iron Age cylinder seal. IEJ 46 (1996) 52-54.
9784 *Barkay, Gabriel; Vaughn, Andrew G.* Lmlk and official seal impressions from Tel Lachish. TelAv 23 (1996) 61-74;
9785 New readings of Hezekian official seal impressions. BASOR 304 (1996) 29-54.
9786 *Beit-Arieh, Itzhaq* חותם נושא כתובת מחורבת קיטמית [A seal bearing an inscription from the Edomite shrine at Ḥorvat Qitmit]. ᶠAᴠɪʀᴀᴍ J., ErIs 25: 1996, ⇒2. Sum. 89*. 59-64. H.
9787 **Blocher, Felix** Siegelabrollungen auf frühaltbabylonischen Tontafeln in der Yale Babylonian Collection. Katalog. 1992, ⇒9,13545; 11/2,a692. ᴿOLZ 91 (1996) 307-309 (*Bleibtreu, Erika*).
9788 *Brandl, Baruch* A 'Hyksos' scarab and a Syrian cylinder seal from a burial cave at Moẓa ᶜIllit;
9789 A 'Hyksos' scarab from a burial cave on Mt. Canaan, Ẓefat (Wadi Ḥamra). ᶜAtiqot 29 (1996) 7-14/1-5.
9790 *Buccellati, Giorgio; Kelly-Buccellati, Marilyn* The seals of the king of Urkesh: evidence from the western wing of the royal storehouse AK. WZKM 86 (1996) 65-98.
9791 *Cahill, Jane M.* 'Horus eye' amulets. City of David excavations [ᴱAriel, D.]. Qedem 35: 1996, ⇒т4.3. 291-297.
9792 **Collon, Dominique** First impressions: cylinder seals in the ancient Near East. 1987, ⇒3,d739... 9,13552. ᴿJAOS 116 (1996) 271-273 (*Bleibtreu, Erika*).
9793 *Cornelius, Izak* Some additional representations of the God Baal-Seth on seal-amulets. JNSL 22/2 (1996) 157-166.
9794 ᴱ**Demakopoulou, Katie** The Aidonia treasure: seals and jewellery of the Aegean Late Bronze Age. Athens 1996, Ministry of Culture 120 pp. 163 col. fig.; 11 fig. 960-214-646-X [AJA 101,818].
9795 *Dempsey, Deirdre* Ostraca and a seal impression from Tell Nimrîn, Jordan. BASOR 303 (1996) 73-78.
9796 *Eggler, Jürg* Escarabajos provenientes de excavaciones realizadas en Palestina/Transjordania de la época de hierro I (ca. 1200-1000 AC): su distribución local, lugar y caracteristicas, y contexto arqueológico. Theologika 11/1 (1996) 184-214 [ZID 23,321].
9797 **Ferioli, Piera; Fiandra, Enrica** Archives before writing. 1994, ⇒11/2,680. ᴿCamArch 6 (1996) 165-173 (*Oates, Joan*).
9798 *Ferioli, Piera; Fiandra, Enrica* The continuance of more ancient bureaucratic-administrative criteria in the age of writing. Administration in ancient societies. 1996, ⇒308. 87-97 (disc. 99-111).
9799 *Garrison, Mark B.* A Persepolis fortification seal on the tablet MDP 11 308 (Louvre Sb 130 78). JNES 55 (1996) 15-35.
9800 **Garrison, Mark B.; Root, Margaret Cool** Persepolis seal studies: an introduction with provisional concordances of seal numbers and associated documents on Fortification Tablets 1-2087. Achaemenid history 9: Lei 1996, Nederlands Instituut voor het Nabije Oosten 141 pp. 7 fig. *f*57. 90-6258-409-8 [AJA 101,632].
9801 *Gasser, Madeleine; Keel, Othmar; Müller-Winkler, Claudia* Die Sammlung ägyptischer Amulette und Bronzen. Altorientalische Miniaturkunst. 1996, ⇒9681. 93-118.
9802 **Gorton, Andrée Feghall** Egyptian and Egyptianizing scarabs: a typology of steatite, faience and paste scarabs from Punic and other

Mediterranean sites. Oxf 1996, Oxf Univ. Committee for Archaeology 191 pp. 90 fig.; 48 maps; 7 tables. $48. 0-947816-43-7 [AJA 101,819].

9803 *Görg, Manfred* Zu einigen Schutzsymbolen auf palästinischen Skarabäen. BN 83 (1996) 9-12.

9804 **Herbordt, Suzanne** Neuassyrische Glyptik des 8.-7. Jh. v.Chr. 1992, ⇒8,e131... 11/2,a702. ᴿOLZ 91 (1996) 424-432 *(Hausleiter, Arnulf)*; Or. 65 (1996) 184-187 *(Collon, Dominique)*.

9805 **Herrmann, Christian** Ägyptische Amulette aus Palästina/Israel. OBO 138: 1994, ⇒10,11978; 11/2,a703. ᴿBiOr 53 (1996) 456-460 *(Ward, William A.)*; CÉg 71 (1996) 289-295 *(Gubel, Eric)*; AcOr 57 (1996) 153-157 *(Pierce, Richard Holton)*.

9806 *Horowitz, Wayne* An inscribed clay cylinder from Amarna Age Beth Shean. IEJ 46 (1996) 208-218.

9807 **Keel, Othmar** Studien zu den Stempelsiegeln aus Palästina/Israel, 4. OBO 135: 1994, ⇒10,11981; 11/2,a707. ᴿJAOS 116 (1996) 535-537 *(Ward, William A.)*; AcOr 56 (1995) 220-222 *(Groth, Bente)*;

9808 Corpus der Stempelsiegel-Amulette aus Palästina/Israel: Von den Anfängen bis zur Perserzeit: Einleitung. OBO.A 10: 1995, ⇒11/2,a706. ᴿAUSS 34 (1996) 342-345 *(Klingbeil, Gerald A.)*; AcOr 57 (1996) 157-160 *(Groth, Bente)*.

9809 *Keel, Othmar* Siegel und Siegeln in der Bibel;

9810 *Keel, Othmar; Keel-Leu, Hildi* Die Sammlung vorderasiatischer Stempel- und Rollsiegel (ehemals Sammlung R. Schmidt). Altorientalische Miniaturkunst. 1996, ⇒9681. 87-92/25-57.

9811 **Kotansky, R.** Greek magical amulets, I: the inscribed gold, silver, copper, and bronze lamellae: part I: published texts of known provenance (Pap. Colon, XXII.1). Opladen 1994, Westdeutscher xxx; 415 pp. ᴿJHS 116 (1996) 233-235 *(Jordan, David R.)*.

9812 *Levin, Adina* A newly discovered Ammonite seal. IEJ 46 (1996) 243-247.

9813 *Malek, Jaromir* The Egyptian text on the seal impression from Alalakh (Tell Atchana). Sum. 173. Levant 28 (1996) 173-176.

9814 *Marchetti, Nicolò* L'aquila anzu: nota su alcuni amuletti mesopotamici. VO 10 (1996) 105-121.

9815 **Marcus, Michelle I.** Emblems of identity and prestige: the seals and sealings from Hasanlu, Iran. University Museum Monograph 84; Hasanlu Special Studies 3: Ph 1996, Univ. Museum, Univ. of Pennsylvania xxviii; 171 pp. 45 pl.; 118 fig.; 6 tables. $50. 0-924171-26-X [AJA 102,623s—Aruz, Joan].

9816 **Matthews, Donald M.** The Kassite glyptic of Nippur. OBO 116: 1992, ⇒8,e143... 11/2,a713*. ᴿOr. 65 (1996) 180-184 *(Collon, Dominique)*.

9817 *Matthiae, Gabriella Scandone* A cylinder seal in the 'Hyksos' style (MB II) from Ebla. CMAO 6 (1996) 181-190.

9818 *McCollough, C. Thomas; Glazier-McDonald, Beth* An Aramaic bronze amulet from Sepphoris. ᶜAtiqot 28 (1996) 161-165.

9819 **Otten, Heinrich** Zu einigen Neufunden hethitischer Königssiegel. AAWLM.G 13: 1993, ⇒9,13577. ᴿBiOr 53 (1996) 136-138 *(Sürenhagen, Dietrich)*.

9820 *Özgüç, N.* Seal impressions on Kültepe documents notarized by native rulers. ᶠSᴘʏᴄᴋᴇᴛ A., 1996, ⇒83. 267-278.

9821 *Pinnock, Frances* Su alcuni sigilli paleosiriani di probabile produzione eblaita. CMAO 6 (1996) 171-180.

9822 **Pittman, Holly** The glazed steatite glyptic style. 1994, ⇒11/2,a721. ᴿOLZ 91 (1996) 566-571 (*Osten-Sacken, Elisabeth von der*).

9823 **Popham, Mervyn R.; Gill, Margaret A.V.** The latest sealings from the palace and houses at Knossos. BSA Studies 1: L 1996, British School at Athens 65 pp. 47 pl.; 49 tables; 2 plans. £24. 0-904887-24-3 [AJA 101,199].

9824 *Puech, E.* Deux amulettes palestiniennes, une en grec et une bilingue en grec-christo-palestinien. ᶠSPYCKET A., 1996, ⇒83. 299-310.

9825 **Richards, Fiona V.** Scarab seals from a Middle to Late Bronze Age tomb at Pella in Jordan. OBO 117: 1992, ⇒8,e151... 11/2,a724. ᴿJEA 82 (1996) 223-224 (*Martin, Geoffrey T.*).

9826 **Rova, Elena** Ricerche sui sigilli a cilindro vicino-orientali del periodo di Uruk/Jemdet Nasr. Nota methodologica *Camiz, Sergio, Orientis Antiqui Collectio 20*: R 1994, Istituto per l'Oriente C.A. Nallino x; 331 pp. 59 pl. L80.000. ᴿRA 90 (1996) 185-186 (*Huot, Jean-Louis*); Mes. 31 (1996) 240-244 (*Mollo, P.*).

9827 ᴱ**Sass, Benjamin; Uehlinger, Christoph** Studies in the iconography of Northwest Semitic inscribed seals. OBO 125: 1993, Proc. symposium, FrS 1991. ᴿAcOr 56 (1995) (1996) 214-215 (*Barstad, H.M.*).

9828 *Stoof, Magdalena* Siegelamulette in den Gräbern von Mostagedda (Mittelägypten). Hallesche Beiträge zur Orientwissenschaft 21 (1996) 43-79.

9829 **Teissier, Beatrice** Sealing and seals on texts from Kültepe kārum level 2. 1994, ⇒11/2,a736. ᴿBSOAS 59 (1996) 129-130 (*Matthews, D.M.*); BiOr 53 (1996) 202-204 (*Collon, Dominique*).

9830 *Uehlinger, Christoph* Die Sammlung ägyptischer Siegelamulette (Skarabäensammlung Fouad S. Matouk). Altorientalische Miniaturkunst. 1996, ⇒9681. 58-86.

9831 *Urman, Dan* A signet ring of Bar-Kokhba (?) from the vicinity of Quneitra in the Golan. BAIAS 15 (1996-97) 51-54.

9832 **Van Wyk, Koot** Squatters in Moab: a study in iconography, history, epigraphy, orthography, ethnography, religion and linguistics of the ANE. Berrien Springs 1996, Louis Hester vi; 193 pp. [CBQ 59,424].

9833 **Wallenfels, Ronald** Uruk: Hellenistic seal impressions in the Yale Babylonian collection, I: cuneiform tablets. 1994, ⇒10,12002. ᴿAJA 100 (1996) 177-178 (*Garrison, Mark B.*).

9834 **Wiese, André B.** Die Anfänge der ägyptischen Stempelsiegel-Amulette: eine typologische und religionsgeschichtliche Untersuchung zu den "Knopfsiegeln" und verwandten Objekten der 6. bis frühen 12. Dynastie. OBO.A 12: FrS 1996, University Press xxi; 196 pp. 93 pl. ill. FS138. 3-7278-1091-2.

T3.4 Mosaica

9835 ᴱ**Alexander, Margaret A.; Ennaifer, Mongi** Corpus des mosaïques de Tunisie, 2. Fasc. 1-3. 1980-87. ⇒6,d707... 8,e168. ᴿGn. 68 (1996) 84-85 (*Donderer, Michael*).

9836   *Lambert, Chiara* Le figure e i simboli degli evangelisti in alcuni mosaici ravennati (con particolare riferimento a S. Marco). PaVi 41/5 (1996) 51-52.

9837   **Osborne, J.; Claridge, A.** Mosaics and wallpaintings in Roman churches. Paper Museum of Cassiano dal Pozzo, A. Antiquities and Architecture, II, Early Christian and Medieval Antiquities: L 1996, Harvey M. 2 vols; 384 + 334 pp. £150. 1-872501-62-1 [RivAC 74,616ss—Minasi, Mara].

9838   **Piccirillo, Michele** The mosaics of Jordan. 1993, ⇒10,12016; 11/2,a745. RIEJ 46 (1996) 140-142 (*Talgam, Rina*).

9839   *Rey-Coquais, Jean-Paul* Mosaïques inscrites paléochrétiennes de la Syrie du Nord-Ouest. Syr. 73 (1996) 101-107.

9840   *Said, Dorreya* Die Mosaiken der Bibliothek von Alexandria. WUB 1 (1996) 44-45.

9841   VI coloquio internacional sobre mosaico antiguo. Guadalajara 1994, Associación española del mosaico 438 pp. Palencia-Mérida 1990; ill. Ptas8.000. 84-7846-286-4. RAnCl 65 (1996) 586-587 (*Balty, Janine*).

9842   *Vitto, Fanny* Byzantine mosaics at Bet She'arim: new evidence for the history of the site. 'Atiqot 28 (1996) 115-146.

9843   *Wisskirchen, Rotraut* Zum Apsismosaik der Kirche Hosios David/Thessalonike. FDASSMANN E., JAC.E 23: 1996, ⇒19. 582-594.

т3.5 *Ceramica*, pottery

9844   **Adan-Bayewitz, D.** Common pottery in Roman Galilee. 1993, ⇒9,13610... 11/2,a748. RIEJ 46 (1996) 270-272 (*Magness, Jodi*).

9845   *Ariel, Donald T.* Appendix F: a ceramic two-faced figurine. City of David excavations [EAriel, D.]. Qedem 35: 1996, ⇒т4.3. 109-134.

9846   EArnold, Dorothea; Bourriau, Janine An introduction to Ancient Egyptian pottery. Fasc. 1-2. 1993, ⇒9,13612. RBiOr 53 (1996) 437-442 (*Aston, D.A.*).

9847   **Aston, David A.** Egyptian pottery of the late New Kingdom and third Intermediate Period (twelfth - seventh centuries BC): tentative footsteps in a forbidding terrain. Studien zur Archäologie und Geschichte Altägyptens 13: Heidelberg 1996, Heidelberger Orientverlag x; 350 pp. fig. 2 pl. 3-927552-24-0.

9848   EBarnett, William K.; Hoopes, John W. The emergence of pottery: technology and innovation in ancient societies. Wsh 1996, Smithsonian Institution Press 285 pp. 50 fig. 17 maps; 17 tables. $30. 1-56098-517-8 [AJA 101,198].

9849   *Bartoloni, P.* Appunti sulla ceramica fenicia tra Oriente e Occidente dall'VIII al VI sec. A.C. TEuph 12 (1996) 85-95.

9850   *Bunimovitz, Shlomo; Yasur-Landau, Asaf* Philistine and Israelite pottery: a comparative approach to the question of pots and people. TelAv 23 (1996) 88-101.

9851   *Deitsch-Van der Meulen, W.* An archaeological background for the Iron Age grey ware pottery from Northwest Iran in the RMO Collection. OMRM 76 (1996) 85-92.

9852   *Eiland, Murray L.* Some technological and petrographic observations on post-Assyrian pottery from Nineveh in Iraq. Continuity and change. Berliner Beiträge zum Vorderen Orient 17: 1996, ⇒296. 23-53.

9853 *Ellis-Lopez, Susan* Analytical techniques in Near Eastern archaeology: ethnography and pottery study. BA 59 (1996) 183-184.

9854 **Eriksson, Kathryn O.** Red lustrous wheel-made ware. 1993, ⇒9,13624... 11/2,a762. ᴿOLZ 91 (1996) 301-307 (*Meyer, Jan-Waalke*).

9855 *Gerritsen, Fokke A.* Hellenistic and Roman-Parthian pottery from the Balikh Valley, northern Syria. OMRM 76 (1996) 93-108.

9856 *Gilbert-Peretz, Diana* Appendix A: Catalogue;
9857 Ceramic figurines. City of David excavations [ᴱ**Ariel, D.**]. Qedem 35: 1996, ⇒T4.3. 42-84/29-41.

9858 *Gitin, Seymour* Formulating a ceramic corpus: the Late Iron II, Persian and Hellenistic pottery at Tell Gezer. ᶠVᴀɴ Bᴇᴇᴋ G., 1996, ⇒96. 75-101.

9859 *Gopher, Avi Dan*: the pottery Neolithic levels. Dan [ᴱ**Biran, A.**]. 1996, ⇒T4.6. 65-81.

9860 *Goren, Yuval; Kamaiski, Elisheva; Kletter, Raz* Appendix C: the technology and provenience of the figurines from the city of David: petrographic analysis. City of David excavations [ᴱ**Ariel, D.**]. Qedem 35: 1996, ⇒T4.3. 87-89.

9861 *Greenberg, Raphael; Porat, Naomi* A third millennium Levantine pottery production center: typology, petrography, and provenance of the metallic ware of northern Israel and adjacent regions. BASOR 301 (1996) 5-24.

9862 **Hausmann, Ulrich** Hellenistische Keramik: eine Brunnenfüllung nördlich von Bau C und Reliefkeramik verschiedener Fundplätze in Olympia. OlForsch 27: B 1996, De Gruyter 125 pp. 50 pl. 3-11-014972-9 [AJA 101,632].

9863 **Hayes, J.W.** The Hellenistic and Roman pottery. Nicosia 1991, 223 pp. Paphos III; Contrib. *L.L. Neuru;* pref. by *Ino Nicolaou;* num. ill. 9963-36-417-9. ᴿSyria 73 (1996) 223-224 (*Peignard-Giros, Annette*).

9864 **Heesen, P.** The J.L. Tʜᴇᴏᴅᴏʀ collection of Attic black-figure vases. Amst 1996, Allard Pierson Museum 210 pp. 51 pl. *f*249. 90-7121-126-6 [JHS 118,250—Sparkes, Brian A.].

9865 **Hendrix, Ralph E.; Drey, Philip R.; Storfjell, J. Bjornar** Ancient pottery of Transjordan: an introduction utilizing published whole forms, late Neolithic through late Islamic. Berrien Springs 1996, Institute of Archaeology xii; 342 pp. $19. 0-964-2060-1-3. ᴿLASBF 46 (1996) 422-424 (*Schick, Robert*).

9866 *Henrickson, R.C.; Blackman, M.J.* Large-scale production of pottery at Gordion: comparison of the Late Bronze and Early Phrygian industries. Sum. rés. 67. Paléorient 22/1 (1996) 67-81.

9867 ᴱ**Herfort-Koch, Marlene; Mandel, Ursula; Schädler, Ulrich** Hellenistische und kaiserzeitliche Keramik des östlichen Mittelmeergebietes: Kolloquium Fra 24.-25. April 1995. Schriften des Arbeitskreises Frankfurt und die Antike: Frankfurt 1996, Archäologisches Institut der Goethe-Universität 151 pp. 30 pl. 5 fig. 3-9803946-3-8 [AJA 101,632].

9868 **Herr, Larry G.; Trenchard, Warren C.** Published pottery of Palestine. Atlanta 1996, Scholars 309 pp. $35. 0-7885-0280-8 [CBQ 59,205].

9869 *Herrmann, Christian* Die Sammlung von Modeln für ägyptische Fayencen. Altorientalische Miniaturkunst. 1996, ⇒9681. 119-123.

9870 *Ilan, David* Middle Bronze Age painted pottery from Tel Dan. Sum. 157. Levant 28 (1996) 157-172.

9871 **Jenkins, Ian; Sloan, Kim** Vases and volcanoes: Sir William HAMILTON and his collection. L 1996, British Museum 320 pp. 100 col. fig. 170 fig. £25. 0-7141-1766-8 [AJA 101,199].

9872 **Karstens, Karsten** Allgemeine Systematik der einfachen Gefäßformen. 1994, ⇒10,12035. ROr. 65 (1996) 37-40 (*Nagel, Wolfram*).

9873 **Karvonen-Kannas, Kerttu** The Seleucid and Parthian terracotta figurines from Babylon in the Iraq Museum, the British Museum and the Louvre. Monografie di Mesopotamia 4: F 1995, Lettere 228 pp. Num. ill. L290.000. 88-7166-220-2. RMes. 31 (1996) 274-276 (*Negro, F.*).

9874 **Lehmann, Gunnar** Untersuchungen zur späten Eisenzeit in Syrien und Libanon: Stratigraphie und Keramikformen zwischen ca. 720 bis 300 v. Chr. Altertumskunde des Vorderen Orients 5: Müns 1996, Ugarit-Verl. x; 548+218 pp. 3-927120-33-2.

9875 **Loffreda, St.** La ceramica di Macheronte e dell'Herodion (90 a.C.-135 d.C.). SBF.CMa 39: J 1996, Franciscan Printing Press 227 pp. 70 fig. 67 phot. [ZAW 110,472—Zwickel, W.].

9876 **Magness, Jodi** Jerusalem ceramic chronology: circa 200-800 C.E. 1993, ⇒9,13643; 11/2,a767. RIEJ 46 (1996) 137-40 (*Geva, Hillel*).

9877 *Marchand, Sylvie; Baud, Michel* La céramique miniature d'Abou Rawash: un dépôt à l'entrée des enclos orientaux. BIFAO 96 (1996) 255-288.

9878 *Mayerson, Philip* Another unreported Ascalonian jar: the Sabitha / Sapation. IEJ 46 (1996) 258-261.

9879 **Samuelson, Anna-Greta** Bronze Age white painted I ware in Cyprus. 1993, ⇒9,13653. RBiOr 53 (1996) 554-555 (*Maguire, Louise*).

9880 **Schwarz, Shirley J.** Greek vases in the National Museum of Natural History, Smithsonian Institution, Washington, DC. Bibliotheca archaeologica 17: R 1996, Bretschneider 176 pp. 87 pl. 88-7062-928-7 [AJA 101,200].

9881 EShapiro, H. Alan; Picón, Carlos; Scott, Gerry D. Greek vases in the San Antonio Museum of Art. Austin 1996, Univ. of Texas Press 248 pp. 16 col. fig. 390 fig. $40. 1-883502-04-7 [AJA 101,634].

9882 *Sharon, Ilan* Appendix E: analysis of homogeneity of the distribution of figurines in strata 13-10. City of David excavations [EAriel, D.]. Qedem 35: 1996, ⇒T4.3. 100-108.

9883 **Shelton, Kim S.** The Late Helladic pottery from Prosymna. SIMA-PB 138: Jonsered 1996, Åström 365 pp. 73 fig. 102 tables; 8 maps. 91-7081-114-8 [AJA 101,200].

9884 **Sidorova, Nalalya** Corpus vasorum antiquorum: Pushkin State Museum of Fine Arts: fasc. 1: Attic black-figured vases. R 1996, Bretschneider 64 pp. 66 pl. 4 fig. 88-7062-937-6 [AJA 101,634].

9885 **Sparkes, Brian A.** The red and the black: studies in Greek pottery. L 1996, Routledge 230 pp. 105 fig. $19. 0-415-12661-4. RAntiquity 70 (1996) 988-989 (*Gill, David*).

9886 **Stiehler-Alegria Delgado, Giesela** Die kassitische Glyptik. München: Vorderasiat. Stud. 18: Mü 1996, Herold 316 pp. 41 pl. DM128. 3-89019-377-3.

9887 *Tsuneki, A.; Miyake, Y.* The earliest pottery sequence of the Levant: new data from Tell el-Kerkh 2, Northern Syria. Sum. rés. 109. Paléorient 22/1 (1996) 109-123.

9888 **Vickers, Michael; Gill, David** Artful crafts: ancient Greek silverware and pottery. Oxf 1994, Clarendon viii; 254 pp. $55. 0-198-13226-3. ᴿAJA 100 (1996) 422-423 (*Elia, Ricardo J.*); RAr (1996/2) 227-252 (*Williams, Dyfri*); ClR 46 (1996) 123-126 (*Boardman, John*); JHS 116 (1996) 230-231 (*Simon, Erika*).

9889 *Yamauchi, Edwin M.* Magic bowls: Cyrus H. GoʀᴅoɴNordon and the ubiquity of magic in the pre-modern world. BA 59 (1996) 51-55.

9890 *Yellin, Joseph* Appendix D: chemical characterization of the city of David figurines and inferences about their origin. City of David excavations [ᴱAriel, D.]. Qedem 35: 1996, ⇒T4.3. 90-99.

9891 *Zorn, Jeffrey R.* The date of a bronze vase from Tell en-Naṣbeh. TelAv 23 (1996) 209-212.

T3.6 Lampas

9892 **Bailey, Donald M.** A catalogue of the lamps in the British Museum IV: lamps of metal and stone, and lampstands. L 1996, British Museum 205 pp. 192 pl. £70. 0-7141-2206-8 [AJA 101,198].

9893 *Magness, Jodi* Blessings from Jerusalem: evidence for early christian pilgrimage;

9894 *Rosenthal-Heginbottom, Renate* A Jewish lamp depicting the sacrifice of Isaac. ᶠAᴠɪʀᴀᴍ J., ErIs 25: 1996, ⇒2. 37*-45*/52*-60*.

9895 **Trost, Catherine; Hellmann, Marie-Christine** Lampes antiques du Département des monnaies, médailles et antiques 3: fonds général: lampes chrétiennes. P 1996, Bibliothèque nationale de France 163 pp. 40 pl. FF490. 2-7177-1956-3 [AJA 101,200].

9896 **Voss, Jens** Die Menora: Gestalt und Funktion des Leuchters im Tempel zu Jerusalem. OBO 128: 1993, ⇒9,13685... 11/2,8730. ᴿAcOr 56 (1995) (1996) 218-220 (*Groth, Bente*).

9897 *Wexler, Lior; Gilboa, Gabi* Oil lamps of the Roman period from Apollonia-Arsuf. TelAv 23 (1996) 115-131.

T3.7 Cultica

9898 *Beck, Pirhiya* Ḥorvat Qitmit revisited via ʿEn Ḥazeva. TelAv 23 (1996) 102-114.

9899 *Brenk, Beat; Jäggi, Carola; Meier, Hans-Rudolf* Neue Forschungen zur Kathedrale von Gerasa: Probleme der Chronologie und der Vorgängerbauten. ZDPV 112 (1996) 139-155.

9900 **Cooper, Frederick A.** The temple of Apollo Bassitas I: architecture; II: illustrations. Princeton 1996, American School of Classical Studies at Athens 472 pp.; 2 vols 215 pl. $110 + $90. 0-87661-946-4/8-0.

9901 **Dräger, Olaf** *Religionem significare*: Studien zu reich verzierten römischen Altären und Basen aus Marmor. 1994, ⇒11/2,a797. RAJA 100 (1996) 801-802 (*Varner, Eric R.*).

9902 *Felten, Florens* Griechische Heiligtümer in hellenistischer Zeit. FBORCHARDT J., II, 1996, ⇒8. 139-158.

9903 **Hoppe, Leslie J.** The synagogues and churches of ancient Palestine. 1994, ⇒10,12073. RCHR 82 (1996) 493-494 (*Strange, James F.*).

9904 *Levine, Lee I.* של העדות—העתיקה בעת ביהדות ורב־גוניות אחידות בתפוצות בתי־הכנסת [Unity and diversity in ancient Judaism: the case of the Diaspora synagogue]. FSTERN M., 1996, ⇒87. Sum. 154*. 379-392. H.

9905 *MacLennan, Robert S.* In search of the Jewish diaspora: a first-century synagogue in Crimea?. BArR 22/2 (1996) 44-51, 69.

9906 **Platon, Lefteris; Pararas, Yannis** Pedestalled offering tables in the Aegean world. 1991, ⇒8,e264. RBiOr 53 (1996) 240-242 (*Bennet, John*).

9907 **Siebenmorgen, Harald** Delphi: Orakel am Nabel der Welt. Archäologische Veröffentlichungen des Badischen Landesmuseums 1: Sigmaringen 1996, Thorbecke 216 pp. 82 col. fig. 217 fig. 9 plans. DM58. 3-7995-0304-8 [AJA 101,200].

9908 ETsafrir, **Yoram** Ancient churches revealed. 1993, ⇒9,13683... 11/2,a811. RAJA 100 (1996) 194-195 (*Branham, Joan R.*).

9909 EUrman, **Dan; Flesher, Paul V.M.** Ancient synagogues: historical analysis and archaeological discovery. StPB 47/1: 1995, ⇒11/2,a812. RJAOS 116 (1996) 540-541 (*Magness, Jodi*).

T3.8 **Funeraria**; *Sindon*, the Shroud

9910 *Abd el-Gelil, Mohammed; Saadani, Adel; Raue, Dietrich* Some inscriptions and reliefs from Matariya. MDAI.K 52 (1996) 143-156.

9911 **Abdalla, Aly** Graeco-Roman funerary stelae from Upper Egypt. 1992, ⇒8,e270*; 10,12083. RJEA 82 (1996) 239-24 (*Parlasca, Klaus*).

9912 *Assmann, Jan* Der literarische Aspekt des ägyptischen Grabes und seine Funktion im Rahmen des "monumentalen Diskurses". Ancient Egyptian literature. 1996, ⇒230. 97-104.

9913 **Avni, Gideon; Greenhut, Zvi** The Akeldama tombs: three burial caves in the Kidron valley, Jerusalem. IAA Reports 1: J 1996, Israel Antiquities Authority (12) 129 pp. 965-406-018-3.

9914 *Barbet, Alix* Die römischen Gräber von Constanza. WUB 2 (1996) 44-45.

9915 **Barbet, Alix; Vibert-Guigue, Claude** Les peintures des nécropoles romaines d'Abila et du nord de la Jordanie I-II. 1994, ⇒10,12362. RAJA 100 (1996) 629-630 (*Downey, Susan B.*).

9916 *Beck, Pirhiya; Zevulun, Uza* Back to square one. BASOR 304 (1996) 64-75.

9917 **Bloch-Smith, Elizabeth** Judahite burial practices and beliefs about the dead. JSOT.S 123; JSOT/ASOR.MS 7: 1992, ⇒8,e275... 11/2,a821. RJAOS 116 (1996) 537-538 (*Carter, Charles E.*).

9918 **Boehmer, Rainer Michael; Pedde, Friedhelm; Salje, Beate** Uruk: die Gräber. ADFGUW: Endberichte 10: Mainz 1996, Von Zabern xx; 237 pp. 271 pl. DM300. 3-8053-1590-2.

9919 *Brock, Edwin* A puzzle of Pharaonic proportions. EgArch 9 (1996) 31-32.

9920 *Chappaz, Jean-Luc* Répertoire annuel des figurines funéraires, 9. BSÉG 20 (1996) 85-94.

9921 *Ciampini, Emanuele Marcello* Testi funerari del Medio Regno in contesto 'anomalo': il caso di formule su stele. VO 10 (1996) 267-295.

9922 *Collon, Dominique* Britisches Museum: die Königsgräber von Ur. WUB 1 (1996) 57-63.

9923 *Covello-Paran, Karen* Middle Bronze Age burial caves at Hagosherim, Upper Galilee. ʿAtiqot 30 (1996) 71-83.

9924 *Cozi, Massimo* La nécropole de Kheferthernebes. GöMisz 151 (1996) 37-47.

9925 **Cremer, Marielouise** Hellenistisch-römische Grabstelen im nordwestlichen Kleinasien. 1991-1992, ⇒11/2,a827. ᴿGn. 68 (1996) 178-179 (*Rémy, Bernard*).

9926 *Damati, Emanuel; Stepansky, Yosef* מערת קבורה מתקופת הברונזה הבורונזה 2 במורדות הר כנען, צפת [ואדי חמרה] [A Middle Bronze Age II burial cave on Mt. Canaan, Zefat (Wadi Ḥamra)]. Sum. 107. ʿAtiqot 29 (1996) 1*-29*. **H.**

9927 *Darcque, Pascal* Trois inhumations simultanées du Bronze récent I à Bassit (Syrie). Syr. 73 (1996) 129-140.

9928 **Dodson, Aidan** The canopic equipment of the kings of Egypt. 1994, ⇒10,12094. ᴿDiscEg 34 (1996) 125-128 (*DuQuesne, Terence*); JEA 82 (1996) 215-216 (*Aston, D.A.*).

9929 *Dodson, Aidan* A canopic jar of Ramesses IV and the royal canopic equipment of the Ramesside period. GöMisz 152 (1996) 11-17.

9930 *Dresken-Weiland, Jutta* Zwei Fragmente eines frühchristlichen Säulensarkophags in Bonn und Berlin. JAC 39 (1996) 165-169.

9931 *Dreyer, Günter, (al)*, Umm el-Qaab: Nachuntersuchungen im frühzeitlichen Königsfriedhof: 7./8. Vorbericht. MDAI.K 52 (1996) 11-81.

9932 **Elayi, Josette; Haykal, M.R.** Nouvelles découvertes sur les usages funéraires des Phéniciens d'Arwad. TEuph.S 4: P 1996, Gabalda 177 pp. 37 pl. 2-85021-094-3.

9933 *Feig, Nurit* מערת קבורה בטבעון [A burial cave at Tivʿon]. Sum. 129. ʿAtiqot 30 (1996) 61*-65*. **H.**

9934 *Ferron, J.* Contacts et échanges culturels attestés par les sept sarcophages à scènes en relief phéniciens sculptés entre le début du VIe et la fin du IVe siècle av. J.-C. TEuph 12 (1996) 41-57.

9935 *Frerich, Stefan* Zur Deutung der Szene "Frau vor Christus" auf frühchristlichen Sarkophagen. ᶠDASSMANN E., JAC.E 23: 1996, ⇒19. 557-574.

9936 *Gershuny, Lili; Zissu, Boaz* מערות קבורה מימי הבית השני בגבעת שפירא, ירושלים [Tombs of the Second Temple period at Givʿat Shapira, Jerusalem]. Sum. 128. ʿAtiqot 30 (1996) 45*-59*. **H.**

9937 *Geus, C.H.J. de* Graven en sociale verhoudingen tijdens de Israëlitische monarchie. Phoe. 42 (1996) 23-34.

9938 *Golani, Amir* A Persian period cist tomb on the Ashqelon coast. ʿAtiqot 30 (1996) 115-119.

9939 **Gonen, Rivka** Burial patterns and cultural diversity in Late Bronze Age Canaan. ASOR.DS 7: 1992, ⇒8,e286; 9,13694. [R]JAOS 116 (1996) 538-539 (*Liebowitz, Harold*); JNES 55 (1996) 297-300 (*Joffe, Alexander H.*).

9940 *Grajetzki, Wolfram* Ein Sargtyp des Neuen Reiches und sein möglicher Ursprung in der Amarnazeit. GöMisz 150 (1996) 65-70.

9941 [E]**Hachmann, Rolf** Kāmid el-Lōz 16: 'Schatzhaus'-Studien. [F]VENTZKE Walter, Saarbrücker Beiträge zur Altertumskunde 59: Bonn 1996, Habelt 321 pp. 40 pl. 3-7749-2767-7 [ZAW 109,457].

9942 *Hachmann, Rolf* Das Königsgrab von Kamid el-Loz und die Königsgräber der mittleren und späten Bronze- und frühen Eisenzeit im Küstengebiet östlich des Mittelmeers und in Mesopotamien. Kamid el-Loz 16. 1996, ⇒9941. 203-288.

9943 **Herdejürgen, Helga** Die antiken Sarkophagreliefs VI: die dekorativen Sarkophage 2:1: stadtrömische und italische Girlandensarkophage 1: die Sarkophage des ersten und zweiten Jahrhunderts. B 1996, Mann 188 pp. 112 pl. DM198. 3-7861-1890-6 [AJA 101,632].

9944 **Huskinson, Janet** Roman children's sarcophagi: their decoration and social significance. Oxf Monographs on Classical Archaeology: Oxf 1996, Clarendon 135 pp. 16 pl. £50. 0-19-814086-X [AJA 101,199].

9945 *Ilan, David Dan*: the Middle Bronze Age tombs. Dan [E]**Biran, A.**]. 1996, ⇒T4.6. 161-329.

9946 *Jánosi, Peter* Die Grabanlagen der Königin Hetepheres II. ZÄS 123 (1996) 46-62.

9947 *Janot, Francis* Les instruments et la pratique des prêtres-embaumeurs. Sum. 622. BIFAO 96 (1996) 245-253.

9948 **Kanawati, Naguib; McFarlane, Ann** Deshasha: the tombs of Inti, Shedu and others. Reports 5: Sydney 1993, Australian Centre for Egyptology 76 pp. 61 pl. 1-86408-064-7. [R]DiscEg 34 (1996) 129-133 (*Harpur, Y.M.*).

9949 *Kareem, Juam²a* A newly discovered tombstone from North Shuneh, Jordan. PEQ 128 (1996) 125-130.

9950 **Khanzadian, Emma** Les tombes du Bronze Moyen et Récent. Metsamor 2: la nécropole, 1. Civilisations du Proche-Orient, Hors-série 1: Neuchâtel 1995, Recherches et Publications xi; 111 pp. Num. ill. FS90. 2-940032-04-01. [R]Mes. 31 (1996) 228-231 (*Biscione, R.*); ZA 86 (1996) 293-294 (*Orthmann, Winfried*).

9951 *Kloner, Amos* A tomb with inscribed ossuaries in East Talpiyot, Jerusalem. ʿAtiqot 29 (1996) 15-22.

9952 **Koch, Guntram** Sarkophage der römischen Kaiserzeit. Da:Wiss 1993, 259 pp. 122 ill. DM79. 3-534-10401-3. [R]AnCl 65 (1996) 581-582 (*Evers, Cécile*).

9953 **Kockel, Valentin** Porträtreliefs stadtrömischer Grabbauten. 1993, ⇒11/2,a838. [R]GGA 248 (1996) 70-91 (*Borg, Barbara*).

9954 **Koortbojian, Michael** Myth, meaning and memory on Roman sarcophagi. 1995, ⇒11/2,a839. [R]AJA 100 (1996) 434 (*Elsner, Jaś*).

9955 **Lapp, Günther** Typologie der Särge und Sarkgammern von der 6. bis 13. Dynastie. 1993, ⇒9,13701; 11/2,a840. [R]OLZ 91 (1996) 407-412 (*Hölzl, Regina*).

9956 *Le Goff, Isabelle* Étude des restes humains. Syr. 73 (1996) 141-152.

9957 *Leach, Stephany; Rega, Elizabeth* Interim report on the human ske-
letal material recovered from the 1995 Tell Es-Sa'idiyeh excavations, areas BB and DD. PEQ 128 (1996) 131-138.

9958 *Leclère, François* A cemetery of Osirid figurines at Karnak.
EgArch 9 (1996) 9-12.

9959 **Lüscher, Barbara** Untersuchungen zu ägyptischen Kanopenkästen:
vom Alten Reich bis zum Ende der Zweiten Zwischenzeit. 1990,
⇒6,d835; 10,12102. RCÉg 71 (1996) 101-104 (*Kettel, Jeannot*).

9960 **Lyons, Claire L.** The archaic cemeteries. Morgantina studies 5:
Princeton 1996, Princeton Univ. Press xxix; 263 pp. 96 ill. $90. 0-
691-04016-8.

9961 **Marinelli, Emanuela** La sindone: un'immagine 'impossibile'.
CinB 1996, San Paolo 238 pp. L22.000.

9962 **McDonald, John K.** House of eternity: the tomb of Nefertari.
Conservation and cultural heritage: LA 1996, Getty Conservation
Inst. and Getty Museum 116 pp. $25. 0-89236-415-7.

9963 *Menu, Bernadette* Le tombeau de Pétosiris (3): culpabilité et re-
sponsabilité. Sum. 623. BIFAO 96 (1996) 343-357.

9964 *Messika, Natalie* קברים מן התקופה הפרסית בקרבת תל אל־סמרייה
[לוחמי הגטאות] [Persian period tombs and graves near Tell es-
Sumeiriya (Lohamé Hageta'ot). Sum. 108. 'Atiqot 29 31*-39*.

9965 *Misgav, Hagay* קטע מרצף אלפביתי על גלוסקמה [An alphabetical
sequence on an ossuary]. Sum. 110. 'Atiqot 29 (1996) 47*-49*.

9966 **Mrogenda, Ute** Die Terrakottafiguren von Myrina: eine Untersuchung ihrer möglichen Bedeutung und Funktion im Grabzusam-
menhang. EHS.A 63: Fra 1996, Lang vii; 200 pp. 8 pl. DM53. 3-
631-30962-7 [Mes. 33,394ss—Menegazzi, R.].

9967 *Nur ed-Din, Abd el-Halim; Kessler, Dieter* Das Priesterhaus am
Ibiotapheion von Tuna el-Gebel: Vorberichte über die Grabungen
in Tuna 1989-1994 (I). MDAI.K 52 (1996) 263-293.

9968 *Pitard, Wayne T.* Care of the dead at Emar. Emar [EChavalas,
M.]. 1996, ⇒T5.8. 123-140.

9969 *Porat, Pinhas* Tombs at Tell el-Hammam (H. Haman). 'Atiqot 29
(1996) 29-33.

9970 *Rausa, Federico* Disegni di monumenti funerari romani in alcuni
mss. di Pirro LIGORIO. Rés. 505; Sum. 693. AANL.R 7 (1996)
513-559; 693-740.

9971 **Reeves, Nicholas; Wilkinson, Richard H.** The complete Valley of
the Kings: tombs and treasures of Egypt's greatest pharaohs. L
1995, Thames & H. 224 pp. 532 ill. $30. 0-500-05080-5 [JAOS
119,162s—Leprohon, Ronald J].

9972 *Rocchi, Federico* Two observations on the sarcophagus in KV 62.
DiscEg 34 (1996) 87-90.

9973 *Roquette, Jean-Maurice* Au musée de l'Arles antique: les premiers
sarcophages chrétiens. MoBi 99 (1996) 51-57.

9974 **Schneider, Hans Diederik** The Memphite tomb of Horemheb II: a
catalogue of the finds: sixtieth excavation memoir. Lei 1996,
Rijksmuseum van Oudheden xx; 114 pp. 108 pl. 0-85698-131-1
[BiOr 55,415—Chappaz, Jean-Luc].

9975 **Schneider, Hans Diederik** The Memphite tomb of Horemheb,
commander-in-chief of Tut'ankhamun, 2: a catalogue of the finds.
Excavation Memoir 60: L 1996, Egypt Exploration Society xxi;
115 pp. 108 pl. fig. Contrib. by *C.J. Eyre, Y.M. Harpur,* phot. by
C.J. Eyre . 0-85698-131-1.

9976 *Sevin, Veli; Kavakli, Ersin* Van/Karagündüz Erken demir çaği
nekropolü [La nécropole des débuts de l'Âge de Fer à
Van/Karagündüz]. BTTK 60 (1996) 1-20. **Turkish**.
9977 *Shanks, Hershel* Death knell for Israel archaeology?. BArR 22/5
(1996) 48-53.
9978 *Shaw, Brent D.* Seasons of death: aspects of mortality in imperial
Rome. JRS 86 (1996) 100-138.
9979 *Siegelmann, Azriel* קברים בכרמל [Carmel tombs]. Sum. 196.
ʿAtiqot 28 (1996) 13*-15*.
9980 *Skupinska-Løvset, Ilona* Funerary busts from Tell el-Hammam.
ʿAtiqot 29 (1996) 35-41.
9981 **Strudwick, N.; Strudwick, H.M.** The tombs of Amenhotep, Kh-
numose, and Amenmose at Thebes. Griffith Institute Monographs:
La Haule 1996, La Haule xx; 212 pp.; 2 vols. 108 pl. £120; $240
0-900416-58-0 [BiOr 55,119—Dziobek, Eberhard].
9982 *Taʿani, Hikmat* Archaeological tomb at the adh-Dhunayba/Irbid,
1994. ADAJ 40 (1996) 5*-9*. **A**.
9983 *Thill, Florence* Coutumes funéraires égyptiennes en Nubie au
Nouvel Empire. RdE 47 (1996) 79-106.
9984 *Van Haarlem, Willem M.* A tomb of the First Dynasty at Tell Ibra-
him Awad. 21 pl. OMRM 76 (1996) 7-34.
9985 *Vasiljević, Vera* Eine Darstellung des Aufstehens von der Toten-
bahre?. GöMisz 152 (1996) 89-92.
9986 *Wilkinson, Toby* A re-examination of the early dynastic necropolis
at Helwan. MDAI.K 52 (1996) 337-354.
9987 **Willems, Harco** The coffin of Heqata (Cairo JdE 36418): a case
study of Egyptian funerary culture of the Early Middle Kingdom.
OLA 70: Lv 1996, Peeters xxxvi; 551 pp. 51 pl. BEF2.900. 90-
6831-769-5 [OLZ 93,438ss—Grajetzki, Wolfram].
9988 *Wolff, Samuel* A Second Temple period tomb on the Shuʿafat ridge,
North Jerusalem. ʿAtiqot 29 (1996) 23-28.
9989 *Yannai, Eli* קבר מתקופות הברונזה הקדומה 1 והברונזה הביניימית ליד
תל אסור [אסויר] [A tomb of the Early Bronze Age I and Intermediate Bronze Age near Tel Esur (Assawir)]. Sum. 125. ʿAtiqot 30
(1996) 1*-16*.

т3.9 *Numismatica*, **coins**

9990 *Abramzon, M.G.* The emperor and the army in Roman coinage.
Sum. 137. VDI 218 (1996) 122-137. **R**.
9991 *Acquaro, Enrico; Manfredi, Lorenza-Ilia* Rassegna di numismatica
punica 1992-1994. SEAP 15 (1996) 43-139.
9992 *Arslan, Ermanno A.* Monete axumite di imitazione nel deposito del
cortile della sinagoga di Cafarnao. SBFLA 46 (1996) 307-316.
9993 **Ashton, Richard** Studies in ancient coinage from Turkey. Royal
Numismatic Society Special Publication 29: British Institute of
Archaeology at Ankara, Mon. 17: L 1996, Royal Numismatic Society and British Institute of Archaeology at Ankara 160 pp. 68 pl.
8 fig. 8 tables. $75. 0-901405-33-7 [AJA 101,631].
9994 **Bastien, Pierre** Le buste monétaire des empereurs romains I-III.
1992-1994, ⇒10,12126; 11/2,a866. ʀAJA 100 (1996) 798-799
(*Levy, Brooks Emmons*).

9995 *Belloni, Gian Guido* Monete romane e propaganda: impostazione di una problematica complessa. FBELLONI G., 1996, ⇒5. 387-415.

9996 *Bond, Helen K.* The coins of Pontius Pilate: part of an attempt to provoke the people or to integrate them into the empire?. JSJ 27 (1996) 241-262.

9997 *Elayi, J. & A.G.* Nouveaux trésors de monnaies phéniciennes (CH VIII) (Pls. IV-VIII). TEuph 11 (1996) 95-114.

9998 *Gitler, Haim* A comparative study of numismatic evidence from excavations in Jerusalem. SBFLA 46 (1996) 317-362.

9999 *Goell, Theresa; Sanders, Donald H.* Coins. Nemrud Daği [ESanders, D.]. 1996, ⇒T6.5. 472-474.

10000 EHackens, T.; Moucharte, Gh. Studia Phoenicia IX: numismatique et histoire économique phéniciennes et puniques. 1992, ⇒9,564. RSEL 13 (1996) 131-132 (*Xella, Paolo*).

10001 **Harl, Kenneth W.** Coinage in the Roman economy: 300 B.C. to A.D. 700. Baltimore 1996, Johns Hopkins Univ. Press 533 pp. 32 pl. 30 tables. $50. 0-8018-5291-9 [AJA 101,431].

10002 **Herbert, K.** Roman imperial coins: Augustus to Hadrian and Antonine selections, 31 BC-AD 180. Wulfing Collection in Washington Univ. 3: Wauconda 1996, Bolchazy-Carducci xxii; 92 pp. 42 pl. $80/$50. 0-86516-322-7/32-4 [ClR 48,559—Williams, J.].

10003 **Karayotov, Ivan** The coinage of Mesambria I: silver and gold coinage of Mesambria. Sozopol 1994, Center of Underwater Archaeology iv; 134 pp. 48 pl. RAJA 100 (1996) 191-192 (*Stolyarik, Elena*).

10004 EKing, Cathy E.; Wigg, David G. Coin finds and coin use in the Roman world: Thirteenth Oxford Symposium on Coinage and Monetary History 25.-27.3.1993. Studien zu Fundmünzen der Antike 10: B 1996, Mann 460 pp. A Nato advanced research workshop. DM174. 3-7861-1628-8 [Latomus 57,705s—Zehnacker, H.].

10005 **Kreitzer, Larry J.** Striking new images: Roman imperial coinage and New Testament world. JSNT.S 134: Shf 1996, Academic 258 pp. $45. 1-85075-623-6 [BTB 27,120].

10006 **Lummel, Peter** 'Zielgruppen' römischer Staatskunst: die Münzen der Kaiser Augustus bis Trajan und die trajanischen Staatsreliefs. Quellen und Forschungen zur antiken Welt 6: Mü 1991, Tuduv 203 pp. 30 pl. RGn. 68 (1996) 728-730 (*Hannestad, Niels*).

10007 *Manfredi, L.-I.* Un'edicola votiva punica su due serie monetali di Lixus. RSFen 24 (1996) 47-56.

10008 *Manfredi, Lorenza Ilia* Tipi monetali a Malta e Biblo. Sum. 302. RSO 70 (1996) 289-302.

10009 *Powell, Marvin A.* Money in Mesopotamia. Sum. 224. JESHO 39 (1996) 224-242.

10010 **Rebuffat, François** La monnaie dans l'Antiquité. P 1996, Picard 304 pp. FF300. 2-7084-0495-4 [AnCl 67,440s—Kayser, François].

10011 *Weiser, Wolfram; Cotton, Hannah M.* 'Gebt dem Kaiser, was des Kaisers ist...': die Geldwährungen der Griechen, Juden, Nabatäer und Römer im syrisch-nabatäischen Raum. ZPE 114 (1996) 237-287.

T4.2 *Situs effossi*, syntheses

10012 *Grossmann, Peter; Jones, Michael; Reichert, Andreas* Report on the season in Firan-Sinai (February-March 1992). ByZ 89 (1996) 11-36.

10013 ᴱBienkowski, Piotr Early Edom and Moab: the beginning of the Iron Age in southern Jordan. 1992, ⇒8,340... 11/2,a918. ᴿBiOr 53 (1996) 550-552 (*Geus, C.H.J. de*).

10014 ᴱLaperrousaz, Ernest-Marie; Lemaire, André La Palestine à l'époque perse. 1994, ⇒10,252; 11/2,a937. ᴿCBQ 58 (1996) 187-188 (*Cody, Aelred*).

10015 Noort, Ed Die Seevölker in Palästina. 1994, ⇒10,12196; 11/2,a942. ᴿCBQ 58 (1996) 521-522 (*Matthews, Victor H.*).

ᴛ4.3 Jerusalem, *archaeologia* et historia

10016 ʿ*Ad, Uzi* Jerusalem, Binyane Haʾumma. ESI 15 (1996) 71-72.

10017 Acquaviva, Giorgio La chiesa-madre di Gerusalemme: storia e risurrezione del giudeocristianesimo. 1994, ⇒10,12200. ᴿCivCatt 147 II (1996) 624-626 (*Cremascoli, G.*).

10018 ᴱAriel, Donald T.; De Groot, Alon Excavations at the City of David, 1978-1985: final report IV: various reports. ᴰ*Shiloh, Yigal*, Qedem 35: J 1996, Hebrew University x; 342 pp. $52. 0333-5844 [RB 104,469].

10019 Armstrong, Karen Jerusalem: one city, three faiths. Borzoi NY 1996, Knopf xxi; 471 pp. 0-679-43596-4.

10020 Auld, A. Graeme; Steiner, Margreet Jerusalem, 1: from the Bronze Age to the Maccabees. Cities of the Biblical World: Macon 1996, Mercer Univ. Press xii; 100 pp. £11. 0-86554-520-0.

10021 *Avni, Gideon* Jerusalem as textbook. BArR 22/3 (1996) 36-45, 65.

10022 *Bahat, Dan* Jerusalem—capital of Israel and Judah;

10023 *Bahat, Dan; Hurvitz, Gila* Jerusalem—First Temple period: archaeological exploration. Royal cities. 1996, ⇒248. 307-326/287-306.

10024 *Barkay, Gabriel* A late Bronze Age Egyptian temple in Jerusalem?. IEJ 46 (1996) 23-43.

10025 *Baumgarten, Albert I.* City lights: urbanization and sectarianism in Hasmonean Jerusalem;

10026 *Beentjes, Panc* Jerusalem in the book of Chronicles. Centrality of Jerusalem. 1996, ⇒236. 50-64/15-28.

10027 *Bieberstein, Klaus* Die Grabeskirche im Wandel der Zeiten. WUB 1 (1996) 35-43.

10028 Bieberstein, Klaus; Bloedhorn, Hanswulf Jerusalem, 1-3: Grundzüge der Baugeschichte vom Chalkolithikum bis zur Frühzeit der osmanischen Herrschaft. BTAVO B 100/1-3: 1994, ⇒10,12209; 11/2,a957. ᴿZDPV 112 (1996) 67-69 (*Weippert, Helga*).

10029 Bieberstein, Klaus; Burgoyne, M. Hamilton Jerusalem—Baugeschichte: Karten I-IV. TAVO B IV 7: Wsb 1992, Reichert. ᴿZDPV 112 (1996) 66-67 (*Weippert, Helga*).

10030 *Billig, Yaʿakov* Jerusalem, Arnona. ESI 15 (1996) 80-81;

10031 Jerusalem, the lower aqueduct. ESI 15 (1996) 78-79.

10032 Bissoli, Giovanni Gerusalemme: realtà, sogni e speranze. J 1996, Franciscan Printing Press 173 pp.

10033 Blok, Hanna; Steiner, Margreet Jerusalem: Ausgrabungen in der Heiligen Stadt. ᵀ*Damen, Ulrich*; Nachtrag ᴱ*Riesner, Rainer*, Studien zur Biblischen Archäologie und Zeitgeschichte 4: Gießen 1996, Brunnen 176 pp. DM29.80. 3-7655-9805-4.

10034 *Breuning, Wilhelm* Jerusalem: seine Aktualität für die biblischen Religionen. [F]DASSMANN E., JAC.E 23: 1996, ⇒19. 602-610.

10035 **Cuënot, Michel** Jerusalém: alegria para toda a terra. São Paulo 1996, Loyola 188 pp. 85-15-01339-8 [PerTeol 30,145].

10036 **Davies, W.D.; Meyers, Eric, M.; Schroth, Sarah W.** Jerusalem and the Holy Land rediscovered: the prints of David ROBERTS (1796-1864). Foreword *Mezzatesta, Michael P.*, Durham, NC 1996, Duke Univ. Museum of Art xi; 379 pp. $90. 0-938989-15-4 [TD 44,173].

10037 *De-Groot, Alon* Jerusalem, City of David. ESI 15 (1996) 75-77.

10038 *Dujardin, Jean* Das Herz des jüdischen Volkes. WUB 1 (1996) 21-24.

10039 **Elad, A.** Medieval Jerusalem & Islamic worship: holy places, ceremonies, pilgrimage. Lei 1995, Brill xxiii; 196 pp. [R]Henoch 18 (1996) 390-392 (*Tottoli, Roberto*).

10040 *Eshel, Hanan* A note on a recently published text: the "Joshua Apocryphon". Centrality of Jerusalem. 1996, ⇒236. 89-93.

10041 [E]**Eshel, Itzak; Prag, Kay** Excavations by K.M. KENYON in Jerusalem 1961-1967, 4. 1995, ⇒11/2,a966. [R]BArR 22/4 (1996) 17-18 (*Shanks, Hershel*).

10042 *Fabris, Franca Ciccolo* Storie di pellegrinaggi a Gerusalemme. Studi, Fatti, Ricerche 75 (1996) 8-16.

10043 *Feig, Nurit* New discoveries in the Rephaim Valley, Jerusalem. PEQ 128 (1996) 3-7.

10044 *Feig, Nurit; Rabu, Omar Abd* Jerusalem, Khirbet er-Ras. ESI 15 (1996) 74-75.

10045 *France, John* The destruction of Jerusalem and the first crusade. JEH 47 (1996) 1-17.

10046 *Friedman, Yvonne* The city of the King of Kings: Jerusalem in the crusader period. Centrality of Jerusalem. 1996, ⇒236. 190-216.

Gibson, S. Below the Temple Mount in Jerusalem ⇒2496.

10047 **Gibson, Shimon; Taylor, Joan E.** Beneath the church of the Holy Sepulchre: the archaeology and early history of traditional Golgatha. 1994, ⇒10,12218*; 11/2,a971. [R]RB 103 (1996) 301-303 (*Murphy-O'Connor, J.*).

10048 *Gill, Dan* The geology of the city of David and its ancient subterranean waterworks. Excavations... City of David. Qedem 35: 1996, ⇒10018. 1-28.

10049 *Goren, Haim; Rubin, Rehav* Conrad SCHICK's models of Jerusalem and its monuments. PEQ 128 (1996) 103-124.

10050 *Görg, Manfred* Zu zwei angeblichen Belegen für Jerusalem. BN 85 (1996) 5-7.

10051 **Grabar, Oleg,** (*al*), The shape of the holy: early Islamic Jerusalem. Princeton 1996, Princeton Univ. Press xiv; 232 pp. 84 fig. $65/£45. 0-691-03653-5 [RB 105,266—Murphy-O'Connor, J.].

10052 *Greenbut, Zvi* Jerusalem, Reḥavya. ESI 15 (1996) 72-73;

10053 שתי מערות קבורה מימי הבית השני ברחביה, ירושלים [Two burial caves of the Second Temple period in Reḥavia, Jerusalem]. Sum. 109. ʿAtiqot 29 (1996) 41*-46*.

10054 *Gruson, Philippe* Die Geschichte einer Stadt. WUB 1 (1996) 8-11;

10055 Tre mila anni tra le sue mura. Il Mondo della Bibbia 7/2 (1996) 8-11.

10056 ^EHaan, W.; Van Harskamp, A.; Jansen, Y. Jeruzalem: beeld en realiteit. Interacties: Kampen 1996, Kok 111 pp. f24.90 [GThT 97/2,99].

10057 The Holy Sepulchre. Holy Land 16 (1996) 10-14.

10058 *Hovers, Erella* Appendix A: raw data. Excavations... City of David. Qedem 35: 1996, ⇒10018. 189-192.

10059 ^EJenner, K.D.; Wiegers, G.A. Jeruzalem als heilige stad: religieuze voorstelling en geloofspratijk. Leidse Studiën van de Godsdienst 1: Kampen 1996, Kok 263 pp. f45. 90-242-7971-2 [Streven 64,670].

10060 *Kaswalder, Pietro* La settima stazione della Via Crucis. TS(I) 72 (mar.-apr. 1996) 25-30.

10061 *Kletter, Raz* Jerusalem, Har Ḥozevim. ESI 15 (1996) 70-71.

10062 *Kopciowski, Elia* Gerusalemme nel midrash e nella liturgia ebraica. Studi, Fatti, Ricerche 76 (1996) 5-7.

10063 ^EKörner, Irmela; Paffenholz, Alfred Jerusalem: Stadt des Friedens: ein Streifzug durch 3000 Jahre. Phot. *Sydow, Günther,* Z 1996, Benziger 183 pp. [FrRu 4,289].

10064 *Krochmalnik, Daniel* Der Nabel der Welt: über die Sonderstellung Jerusalems in der jüdischen Tradition. BiKi 51 (1996) 66-72.

10065 *Ligato, Giuseppe* La torre di David. TS(I) 72 (lug.-ago. 1996) 29-31.

10066 **Mazar, Eilat; Mazar, Benjamin** Excavations in the south of the Temple Mount: the Ophel of biblical Jerusalem. 1989, ⇒6,d962... 11/2,a992. ^RBiOr 53 (1996) 511-512 (*Blok, Hanna*).

10067 *Mazor, Gaby* מערת קולומבריום בראס א׳־שייח׳ ענבר, ממזרח לירושלים [A columbarium cave at Ras esh-Sheikh ʿAnbar, east of Jerusalem]. Sum. 110. ʿAtiqot 29 (1996) 51*-55*.

10068 *Mora, Vinzenz* Christliches Gedächtnis. WUB 1 (1996) 25-29.

10069 *Mullins, Robert A.* Jerusalem through the ages. Holy Land 16 (1996) 62-77:

10070 The Muristan. Holy Land 16 (1996) 90-91.

10071 *Murphy-O'Connor, Jerome* The City of David. Holy Land 16 (1996) 59-61.

10072 *Murphy-O'Connor, Jerome* The geography of faith: tracing the Via Dolorosa. BiRe 12/6 (1996) 32-41, 52-53.

10073 *Naʾaman, Nadav* The contribution of the Amarna letters to the debate on Jerusalem's political position in the tenth century B.C.E. BASOR 304 (1996) 17-27.

10074 **Peters, F.E.** The distant shrine: the Islamic centuries in Jerusalem. 1993, ⇒10,12231. ^RJNES 55 (1996) 73-74 (*Rood, Judith Mendelsohn*).

10075 *Platti, Emilio* Die islamische Verehrung. WUB 1 (1996) 30-34.

10076 *Potin, Jacques* Gerusalemme: l'alto luogo della passione. Il Mondo della Bibbia 7/2 (1996) 31-41.

10077 ^EPrawer, Joshua The history of Jerusalem: early Muslim period (638-1009). Exec. ed. *Ben-Shammai, Haggai,* Sefer Yerushalayim: NY 1996 <1987>, NY Univ. Press xvii; 443 pp. $75. 0-8147-6639-0 [TD 44,87].

10078 *Provera, Mario* Jerusalem in the thought and writing of St. Jerome. ^ELewitt, George, Holy Land 16 (1996) 86-88.

10079 *Regev, Eyal* מקוואות טהרה של מעמדות וכתות בישראל בימי בית שני [Ritual baths of Jewish groups in the Second Temple period]. Sum. 203. Cathedra 79 (1996) 3-21. **H.**

10080 *Rodríguez Carballo, José* Jerusalén, patria espiritual de todos los creyentes. VyV 54 (1996) 415-431.
10081 *Rogerson, John; Davies, Philip R.* Was the Siloam tunnel built by Hezekiah?. BA 59 (1996) 138-149.
10082 [E]**Rosovsky, Nitza** City of the great king: Jerusalem from David to the present. CM 1996, Harvard Univ. Press xiv; 562 pp. £23.50.
10083 *Safrai, Shmuel* Jerusalem in the Halacha of the Second Temple period;
10084 *Safrai, Zeev* The role of the Jerusalem elite in national leadership in the late Second Temple era;
10085 *Schiffman, Lawrence H.* Jerusalem in the Dead Sea scrolls;
10086 *Schwartz, Daniel R.* Temple or city: what did Hellenistic Jews see in Jerusalem?;
10087 *Seybold, Klaus* Jerusalem in the view of the psalms. Centrality of Jerusalem. 1996, ⇒236. 94-113/65-72/73-88/114-127/7-14.
10088 *Sowers, Sidney G.* Did Xerxes wage war on Jerusalem?. HUCA 67 (1996) 43-53.
10089 *Stefani, Piero* Ebrei, cristiani e musulmani guardano a Gerusalemme. Studi, Fatti, Ricerche 74 (1996) 3-6.
10090 *Tottoli, Roberto* La santità di Gerusalemme nell'Islam. Henoch 18 (1996) 327-355.
10091 **Walker, Peter W.L.** Jesus and the Holy City: New Testament perspectives on Jerusalem. GR 1996, Eerdmans xiii; (2) 370 pp. £17. 0-8028-4287-9.
10092 **Ze'evi, D.** An Ottoman century: the district of Jerusalem in the 1600s. Albany 1996, State University of New York Press 258 pp. [R]RSO 70/1-2 (1996) 259-261 (*Amoretti, Biancamaria S.*).

т4.4 **Judaea, Negeb**; *Situs alphabetice*

10093 *Elliott, Jack D.* The Nabatean synthesis of Avraham NEGEV: a critical appraisal. [F]VAN BEEK G., 1996, ⇒96. 47-60.
10094 *Goren, Yuval* The southern Levant in the Early Bronze Age IV: the petrographic perspective. BASOR 303 (1996) 33-72.
10095 *Haiman, Mordechai* Early Bronze Age IV settlement pattern of the Negev and Sinai deserts: view from small marginal temporary sites. BASOR 303 (1996) 1-32.
10096 *Lehmann, Gunnar; Niemann, Hermann Michael; Zwickel, Wolfgang* Zora und Eschtaol: ein archäologischer Oberflächensurvey im Gebiet nördlich von Bet Schemesch. UF 28 (1996) 343-442.
10097 *Levy, Thomas E.; Witten, Alan J.; Alon, David* Denizens of the desert. Arch. 49/2 (1996) 36-40.
10098 *Mayerson, Philip* Some observations on the Negev archaeological survey. IEJ 46 (1996) 100-107.
10099 *Rubin, Rehav* Urbanization, settlement and agriculture in the Negev desert—the impact of the Roman-Byzantine empire on the frontier. ZDPV 112 (1996) 49-60.

10100 **Abu Ġoš**: *Ehrlich, Michael* The identification of Emmaus with Abu Goš in the Crusader period reconsidered. ZDPV 112 (1996) 165-169.

10101 *'Ein Hazeva/Tamar*: *Cohen, R.; Yisrael, Y.* The excavations at 'Ein Hazeva / Israelite and Roman Tamar. Qad. 29 (1996) 78-92. H.

10102 *'En Gedi*: *Liphschitz, Nili* Timber analysis of 'En Gedi wooden coffins: a comparative study. 'Atiqot 28 (1996) 93-97.

10103 *'En Hazeva*: *Cohen, Rudolph; Israel, Yigal* 'En Hazeva—1990-1994. ESI 15 (1996) 110-116.

10104 *'En Hatzeva*: *Cohen, Rudolf; Yisrael, Yigal* Smashing the idols: piecing together an Edomite shrine in Judah. BArR 22/4 (1996) 40-51, 65.

10105 *Arad*: *Amiran, Ruth* Early Arad, 2: sixth to eighteenth seasons of excavation, 1971-1978, 1980-1984. J 1996, xiii; 174; 67 pp. 30 maps. $80. 965-221-031-5;

10106 *Ilan, Ornit; Sebbane, Michael* מפעל־המים מתקופת־הברזל בערד [The Iron Age water system at Tel Arad]. F Aviram J., ErIs 25: 1996, ⇒2. Sum. 88*. 31-40. H.

10107 *Ashdod*: *Dothan, Moshe; Porath, Yosef* Ashdod V: excavation of Area G: the fourth-sixth seasons of excavations, 1968-1970. 1993, ⇒9,13821. RJAOS 116 (1996) 278-279 *(Jacobs, Paul F.)*.

10108 *Ashkelon*: *Stager, Lawrence E.* Ashkelon and the archaeology of destruction: Kislev 604 BCE. F Aviram J., ErIs 25: 1996, ⇒2. 61*-74*;

10109 *Perrot, Jean; Gopher, Avi* A late neolithic site near Ashkelon. IEJ 46 (1996) 145-166.

10110 *Bat 'Ayin*: *Barukh, Yuval* Bat 'Ayin. ESI 15 (1996) 90-92.

10111 *Be'er Reseq*: *Khalaily, Hamoudi; Sagiv, Nachum* Be'er Reseq. ESI 15 (1996) 93-94.

10112 *Be'er Sheva'*: *Fabian, Peter; Rabin, Dan* Be'er Sheva'. ESI 15 (1996) 105-106.

10113 *Elat*:*Avner, Rina* Elat. ESI 15 (1996) 119-121.

10114 *el-Meharret*: *Timm, Stefan* 'Gott kommt von Teman, der Heilige vom Berg Paran' (Habakuk 3:3)—und archäologisch Neues aus dem äußersten Süden (Tell el-Meharret). OTEs 9 (1996) 308-333.

10115 *Horvat Hamoza*: *Billig, Ya'akov* Horvat Hamoza. ESI 15 (1996) 81-82.

10116 *Horvat Raqiq*: *Dagan, Yehuda* Horvat Raqiq. ESI 15 (1996) 103-104.

10117 *Har Karkom*: *Anati, Emmanuel* Har Karkom, survey—1993/1994. ESI 15 (1996) 116-119.

10118 *Haror*: *Oren, Eliezer D.; Yekutieli, Yuval* מערכת הביצורים מתקו־ פת־הברונזה התיכונה [The Middle Bronze Age defence system at Tel Haror]. F Aviram J., ErIs 25: 1996, ⇒2. Sum. 87*. 15-26. H.

10119 *Hebwa*: *Dorner, Josef* Vorbericht über die Grabungskampagnen 1993/94 auf Tell Hebwa IV/Süd am Nordsinai. A&L 6 (1996) 167-177.

10120 *Hurvat Shilhah*: *Mazar, Amihai; Amit, David; Ilan, Zvi* Hurvat Shilhah: an Iron Age site in the Judean Desert. F Van Beek G., 1996, ⇒96. 193-211.

10121 *Jemmeh*: *Van Beek, Gus W.* Ancient methods for minimizing earthquake damage at Tell Jemmeh. F Aviram J., ErIs 25: 1996, ⇒2. 1*-8*.

10122 *Jericho*:*Riklin, Shim'on* Jericho (Tell es-Sultan). ESI 15 (1996) 68-70.

10123 *Mamshit (Mampsis)*: *Erickson-Gini, Talli* Mamshit (Mampsis).
ESI 15 (1996) 108-110.

10124 *Masada*: [E]**Barag, Dan; Hershkovitz, Malka** Masada IV: the
Yigael YADIN excavations 1963-1965: final reports: lamps...
1994, ⇒10,12272. [R]JAOS 116 (1996) 539-540 *(Dever, W.G.)*;

10125 **Foerster, Gideon** Masada V: the Yigael YADIN excavations 1963-
1965: final report: art and architecture. 1995, ⇒11/2,b047. [R]Bib.
77 (1996) 582-584 *(North, Robert)*;

10126 **Hadas-Lebel, Mireille** Masada: der Untergang des jüdischen
Königreichs oder die andere Geschichte von Herodes. [T]*Till, Hans,*
B 1995, Wagenbach 143 pp. [R]FrRu 3 (1996) 282-283 *(Starobinski-
Safran, Esther)*;

10127 *Magness, Jodi* Masada 1995: discoveries at camp F. BA 59 (1996)
181-182;

10128 **Soscia, Geremia** L'olocausto di Masada: [esiste un limite al pote-
re]. Padova 1996, CECC 203 pp. 88-7974-134-9.

10129 *Moẓa*: *De-Groot, Alon; Greenbut, Zvi* Moẓa. ESI 15 (1996) 83-84.

10130 *Murabbaat*: *Mendecki, Norbert* Prace archeologiczne w grotach
Murabbaat i w grotach pomiędzy Masadą a En-Gedi [De repertioni-
bus archaeologicis in cavernis Murabbaat nec non inter Massadam
et En-Gedi]. RBL 49 (1996) 230-235. **P.**

10131 *Naḥal Barqai*: *Givon, Shmuel* Naḥal Barqai—1993. ESI 15 (1996)
88-90.

10132 *Oboda*: *Negev, Avraham* Oboda: a major Nabatean caravan halt.
Aram 8 (1996) 67-87.

10133 *Ramat Avishur*: *Gudovitch, Shlomo* Ramat Avishur. ESI 15 (1996)
92-93.

10134 *Shiqmim*: *Levy, Thomas E.*, *(al)*, Shiqmim—1993. ESI 15 (1996)
106-108.

10135 *Timnah*: **Kelm, George L.; Mazar, Amihai** Timnah, a biblical
city in the Sorek valley. 1995, ⇒11/2,b055. [R]BA 59 (1996) 246
(Zorn, Jeffrey R.).

10136 *Yarmut*: **Miroschedji, Pierre de** Tel Yarmut—1993. ESI 15 (1996)
85-88.

T4.5 Samaria, Sharon

10137 ʿ*Akko:Muqari, Abdallah* ʿAkko. ESI 15 (1996) 27-28.

10138 ʿ*Aleq; Abu Ḥof*: *Zissu, B.* Two Herodian Columbarium towers at
Khirbet ʿAleq and Khirbet Abu Ḥof. Qad. 29 (1996) 100-106. **H**.

10139 ʿ*Amal*: *Feig, Nurit* Tel ʿAmal. ESI 15 (1996) 47-48.

10140 ʿ*Ein ez-Zeituna (Naḥal*: *Glick, Don* ʿEin ez-Zeituna (Naḥal ʿIron
Road). ESI 15 (1996) 50-51.

10141 *Ashqelon*: *Baumgarten, Yaʿaqov* Ashqelon, Haṭayyasim Street;

10142 *Braun, Eliot; Gophna, Ram* Ashqelon, Afridar;

10143 *Kogan-Zehavi, Elena* Migdal Ashqelon. ESI 15 (1996) 99-100/97-
98/94-96.

10144 *Bet Sheʾan*: *Seligman, Jon* Bet Sheʾan, the citadel. ESI 15 (1996)
43-47.

10145 *Caesarea Maritima*: *Porath, Y.* Herod's 'amphitheatre' at Caesarea. Qad. 29 (1996) 93-99. **H;**

10146 ᴱ**Raban, Avner; Holum, Kenneth G.** Caesarea Maritima: a retrospective after two millennia. DMOA 21: Lei 1996, Brill xliv; 694 pp. ƒ412/$242.50. 90-04-10378-3 [RB 104,477];

10147 *Dalit*: **Gophna, Ram** Excavations at Tel Dalit: an Early Bronze Age walled town in central Israel. TA 1996, Ramot 224 pp. 965-274-225-2.

10148 *Dor*: **Kingsley, Seun A.; Raveh, Kurt** The ancient harbour and anchorage at Dor, Israel: results of the underwater surveys 1976-1991. BAR Internat. 626: Oxf 1996, Tempus R. ii; xiii; 123 pp. 53 fig. 94 pl. Dor Maritime Archaeology Project. £34. 0-86054-807-4 [RB 104,314];

10149 Areas A and C. - B: the finds Excavations at Dor: final report. Qedem reports 2: J 1996, Israel Exploration Society 503 pp.;

10150 **Stern, Ephraim** Dor—ruler of the seas: twelve years of excavations at the Israelite-Phoenician harbour town on the Carmel coast. 1994, ⇒11/2,b063. ᴿRB 103 (1996) 468-469 *(Axe, Tony).*

10151 *Ekron*: **Rosenberg, Stephen** An Assyrian temple in Ekron of the Philistines. BAIAS 15 (1996-97) 115-117.

10152 *el Farᶜah*: **Amiet, Pierre; Briend, Jacques; Courtois, Liliane** Tell el Farᶜah: histoire, glyptique et céramologie. Diss. ᴰ*Contenson, Henri de*, OBO.A 14: FrS 1996, Universitaires iv; 91 pp. FS36. 3-525-53895-2 [RB 104,468].

10153 *Gerisa*: **Herzog, Zeᵓev; Tsuk, Tsvika** Tel Gerisa—1991/1992. ESI 15 (1996) 60-62.

10154 *Ḥ. Qastra*: **Siegelmann, Azriel** 1988 קסטרה, חפירת בדיקה בח' [Soundings at Ḥ. Qastra, 1988]. Sum. 113. ᶜAtiqot 29 (1996) 77*-92*.

10155 *Ḥalas*: **Sion, Ofer** Khirbet Ḥalas. ESI 15 (1996) 57-58.

10156 *Ḥorvat Ḥermeshit*: **Yron-Lubin, Michal** Ḥorvat Ḥermeshit (Neᵓot Qedumim)—1993. ESI 15 (1996) 66-68.

10157 *Ḥorvat Raᶜash*: **Ayalon, Etan, (al)**, Ḥorvat Raᶜash;

10158 *Naḥal Tanninim*: **Siegelmann, Azriel; Rawak, Yehoshua** Upper Naḥal Tanninim, aqueducts. ESI 15 (1996) 55-56/51-52.

10159 *Naḥal Tut*: **Alexandre, Yardenna** Naḥal Tut (Site 8);

10160 *Or ᶜAqiva*: **Neeman, Yehuda** Or ᶜAqiva, Byzantine road. ESI 15 (1996) 49-50/52-54.

10161 *Samaria*: **Tappy, Ron E.** The archaeology of Israelite Samaria: Early Iron Age through the ninth century BCE. HSS 44: 1992, ⇒8,e500... 11/2,b086. ᴿPEQ 128 (1996) 82-84 *(Isserlin, B.S.J.).*

10162 *Shalem*: **Eisenberg, Emanuel** Tel Shalem—soundings in a fortified site of the Early Bronze Age IB. ᶜAtiqot 30 (1996) 1-24.

10163 *Shoham*: **Nadelman, Yonatan** Shoham—1993;

10164 *Tabun Cave*: **Ronen, Avraham** Tabun Cave;

10165 *Tel Aviv*: **Gorzalczany, Amir** Tel Aviv, Khirbet el-Ḥadra. ESI 15 (1996) 63-64/35-36/58-59.

10166 *Yehud*: **Shemueli, Oren** Tel Yehud. ESI 15 (1996) 64-65.

10167 *Ziqim*: **Zissu, Boaz** Ziqim. ESI 15 (1996) 100-101.

ᴛ4.6 **Galilaea;** *Golan*

10168 *Ben-David, Chaim* גאולוגיה והתיישבות עתיקה בגולן [Geology and ancient settlement in the Golan]. Cathedra 81 (1996) 171-175. **H.**

10169 **Gal, Z.** Lower Galilee during the Iron Age. ASOR 8: 1992,
⇒10,12185; 11/2,a930. ᴿJNES 55 (1996) 295-297 *(Joffe, Alexander H.)*.
10170 **Horsley, Richard A.** Archaeology, history, and society in Galilee.
Valley Forge, PA 1996, Trinity xiii; 240 pp. $20. 1-56338-182-6.

10171 *ʿAfula*: *Gal, Zvi; Covello-Paran, Karen* Excavations at ʿAfula,
1989. ʿAtiqot 30 (1996) 25-67.
10172 *ʿAmud Cave*: *Hovers, Erella; Rak, Yoel* ʿAmud Cave—1993/1994.
ESI 15 (1996) 22-25.
10173 *Banias*: *Maʿoz, Zvi* Banias, temple of Pan—1993;
10174 *Tzafgeris, Vassilios; Israeli, Shoshana* Banias—1993. ESI 15
(1996) 1-5/5-7.
10175 *Bet Sheʿarim*: *Vitto, Fanny* Byzantine mosaics at Bet Sheʿarim:
new evidence for the history of the site. ʿAtiqot 28 (1996) 115-146.
10176 *Beth Shan*: **James, Frances W.; McGovern, Patrick E.** The Late
Bronze Egyptian garrison at Beth Shan...levels VII and VIII. 1993,
⇒10,12311; 11/2,b086. ᴿAJA 100 (1996) 787-788 *(Dessel, J.P.)*;
10177 *Mazar, Amihai* The excavations at Tel Beth Shean between 1989
and 1885. BAIAS 15 (1996-97) 110-114;
10178 **Ovadiah, Asher; Turnheim, Yehudit** 'Peopled' scrolls in Roman
architectural decoration in Israel: the Roma theatre at Beth
Shean/Scythopolis. 1994, ⇒11/2,b091. ᴿAJA 100 (1996) 436-437
(Sturgeon, Mary C.); AnCl 65 (1996) 585-586 *(Baratte, François)*;
10179 *Yannai, Eli* A new approach to levels VI-V at Tel Beth-shan.
TelAv 23 (1996) 185-194.
10180 *Bethsaida*: **Arav, Rami; Freund, Richard A.** Bethsaida: a city by
the north shore of the Sea of Galilee. The Bethsaida Excavations
Project: Reports and Contextual Studies, 1. Kirksville, Miss. 1995,
Jefferson 337 pp. $35/$20. 0-943549-30-2/-37-X. ᴿBA 59 (1996)
242-243 *(Matthews, Victor H.)*;
10181 *Pixner, Bargil* Betsaida—zehn Jahre später. HlL 128/3 (1996) 6-9.
10182 *Bira*: *Stern, Edna J.* Tel Bira. ESI 15 (1996) 28-29.
10183 *Capernaum*: *Loffreda, Stanislao* La casa di Pietro a Cafarnao.
TS(I) 72 (sett.-ott. 1996) 14-18.

10184 *Dan*:**Biran, Avraham** Biblical Dan. 1994, ⇒10,12319; 11/2,b098.
ᴿOLZ 91 (1996) 316-320 *(Niemann, Michael)*;
10185 *Biran, Avraham Dan*: a chronicle of the excavations, 1966-1992.
Dan. 1996, ⇒10187. 7-63;
10186 ?ברן "במות שערים" [High places at the gates of Dan?]. ᶠAVIRAM
J., ErIs 25: 1996, ⇒2. Sum. 89*. 55-58;
10187 **Biran, Avraham; Ilan, David; Greenberg, Raphaël** Dan I: a
chronicle of the excavations, the pottery Neolithic, the Early
Bronze Age and the Middle Bronze Age tombs. Collab. *Gopher,
Avi; Horwitz, Liora Kolska; Porat, Naomi*, Annual of the Nelson
Glueck School of Biblical Archaeology: J 1996, Hebrew Union
College. $52. 0-8782-0307-9 [RB 104,312;
10188 *Biran, Abraham* Tel Dan—1993. ESI 15 (1996) 7-10;
10189 *Gopher, Avi Dan*: the pottery Neolithic levels;
10190 *Greenberg Raphael Dan*: the Early Bronze Age levels. Dan. 1996,
⇒10187. 65-81/83-160;
   Ilan, David Middle Bronze Age painted pottery... Dan ⇒9870;

10191 The Middle Bronze Age tombs. Dan. 1996, ⇒10187. 161-329.

10192 *El-ᶜOreme*: *Fritz, Volkmar; Vieweger, Dieter* Vorbericht über die Ausgrabungen in Kinneret (Tell el-ᶜOreme) 1994 und 1995;

10193 *Rabe, Norbert* Perforierte Tonkugeln vom Tell el-ᶜOreme. ZDPV 112 (1996) 81-99/100-121.

10194 *El-Wawiyat*: *Onn, Alexander*, (*al*), Tell el-Wawiyat (Tel Tannim)—1993. ESI 15 (1996) 10-12.

10195 *Esh-Shubeika*: *Tatcher, Ayelet; Syon, Danny* Khirbet esh-Shubeika—1993. ESI 15 (1996) 21-22.

10196 *Ḥazor*: *Ben-Tor, Amnon; Rubiato, M.T.* The renewed excavations of Tel Hazor, 1990-1995. Qad. 29 (1996) 2-18.

10197 *Ben-Tor, Amnon* חפירות חצור לזכר יגאל ידין—מטרות ותוצאות ראשוניות [The Yigael Yadin memorial excavations at Hazor: aims and preliminary results of 1990-1992 seasons]. [F]AVIRAM J., ErIs 25: 1996, ⇒2. Sum. 89*. 67-81. **H**.

10198 *Ben-Tor, Amnon* Excavations and surveys. IEJ 46 (1996) 262-268; id., Tel Ḥazor—1993. ESI 15 (1996) 12-14.

10199 *Rubiato Díaz, M.ª Teresa* Nuevos hitos en la arqueología de Canaán VI: campaña de excavaciones en Tel Hatsor. Sum. res. 197. Sef. 56 (1996) 189-197 [1 Kgs 14,3; Jer 19,1.10].

10200 *Horvat ᶜOvesh*: *Aviᶜam, Mordechai; Getzov, Nimrod* Ḥorvat ᶜOvesh. ESI 15 (1996) 17-18.

10201 *Horvat Kenes*: *Avshalom-Gorni, Dina; Aviᶜam, Mordechai* Ḥorvat Kenes. ESI 15 (1996) 25-27.

10202 *Jezreel*: *Ussishkin, David* המיתחם המבוצר של מלכי בית עמרי ביזרעאל [The fortified enclosure of the kings of the house of Omri at Jezreel]. [F]AVIRAM J., ErIs 25: 1996, ⇒2. Sum. 87*. 1-14. **H**;

10203 *Williamson, H.G.M.* Tel Jezreel and the dynasty of Omri. PEQ 128 (1996) 41-51;

10204 *Woodhead, John* [Report on the 1995 season at Tel Jezreel]. Levant 28 (1996) 209-210.

10205 *Meᶜona*:*Braun, Eliot* Salvage excavations at the early Bronze Age site of Meᶜona: final report. ᶜAtiqot 28 (1996) 1-31;

10206 *Horwitz, Liora Kolska* The faunal remains from Meᶜona. ᶜAtiqot 28 (1996) 37-39;

10207 *Marder, Ofer* The flint assemblage from Meᶜona. ᶜAtiqot 28 (1996) 32-36.

10208 *Megiddo*: *Di Paolo, Silvana* Gli avori di Megiddo: un esempio di arte siriana?. VO 10 (1996) 163-208;

10209 *Finkelstein, Israel* The stratigraphy and chronology of Megiddo and Beth-shan in the 12th-11th centuries B.C.E. TelAv 23 (1996) 170-184;

10210 *Fritz, Volkmar* Erwägungen zum Palast 3177 in Megiddo. [F]BERAN T., 1996, ⇒6. 131-138;

10211 **Kempinski, A.** Megiddo: a city-state and royal centre in north Israel. 1989, ⇒5,d927... 10,12342. PEQ 128 (1996) 57-62 *(Bourke, Stephen)*;

10212 *Ruderman, Abraham* A visit to Armageddon. JBQ 24 (1996) 199-200.

10213 *Migdal Haᶜemeq*: *Shalem, Dina* Migdal Haᶜemeq;

10214 *Nahal ᶜEn Gev*: *Belfer-Cohen, A.*, (*al*), Nahal ᶜEn Gev I;

10215 *Qiryat Ata*: *Golani, Amir* Qiryat Ata. ESI 15 (1996) 36-41/30-31/31-33.

10216 **Ruğm el-Heri**: *Lev-Yadun, Simcha; Mizrachi, Yonathan; Kochavi, Moshe* Lichenometric studies of cultural formation processes at Rogem Hiri. IEJ 46 (1996) 196-207;

10217 *Mizrachi, Yonathan*, (*al*), The 1988-1991 excavations at Rogem Hiri, Golan Heights. IEJ 46 (1996) 167-195.

10218 *Sasa*: *Cohen-Weinberger, Anat; Goren, Yuval* Petrographic analysis of Iron Age I pithoi from Tel Sasa. ʿAtiqot 28 (1996) 77-83;

10219 *Golani, Amir; Yogev, Ora* The 1980 excavations at Tel Sasa;

10220 *Horwitz, Liora Kolska* Fauna from Tel Sasa, 1980;

10221 *Stepansky, Yosef; Segal, Dror; Carmi, Israel* The 1993 soundings at Tel Sasa: excavation report and radiometric dating. ʿAtiqot 28 (1996) 41-58/59-61/63-76.

10222 *Sepphoris*: [E]**Nagy, Rebecca Martin; Meyers, Carol L.; Weiss, Zeev** Sepphoris in Galilee: crosscurrents of culture. Raleigh, NC 1996, North Carolina Museum of Art 240 pp. $30 [BArR 25/1, 66s—Levine, Lee I.];

10223 **Weiss, Ze'ev; Netzer, Ehud** Promise and redemption: a synagogue mosaic from Sepphoris. J 1996, Israel Museum 47 + 49 pp. 965-278-184-3. **H**.

10224 *Tiberias*: St. Peter's Church in Tiberias. Holy Land 16 (1996) 103-104.

10225 *Yoqneʿam*: *Avissar, Miriam* Tel Yoqneʿam, the Crusader acropolis. ESI 15 (1996) 41-42;

10226 **Ben-Tor, A.; Avissar, M.; Portugali, Y.** Yoqneʿam, 1: the late periods. Qedem Reports 3: J 1996, Institute of Archaeology, The Hebrew University 262 pp. $52. 0793-4289 [NThAR 1997,191].

T4.8 *Transjordania;* **(East-) Jordan**

10227 *Daviau, P.M. Michèle* New project announcement: excavations in the land of Moab. BA 59 (1996) 179-180.

10228 [E]**Edelman, Diana Vikander** You shall not abhor an Edomite...: Edom and Seir. Archaeology and Biblical Studies 3: 1995, ⇒11/2,500. [R]LASBF 46 (1996) 484-485 *(Cortese, Enzo)*.

10229 [E]**Ghazi Bin Mohammed** The holy sites of Jordan. Amman 1996, Turab 141 pp. Contrib. Sheikh *Hassan Saqaf* (Islamic sites) and Father *Michele Piccirillo* (Christian sites) [Levant 29,258].

10230 **Henry, Donald O.** Prehistorical cultural ecology and evolution: insights from southern Jordan. Interdisciplinary Contributions to Archaeology: NY 1995, Plenum 450 pp. $49.50. 0-306-45048-8. [R]Antiquity 70 (1996) 473-475 *(Baird, Douglas)*.

10231 Jordan: tracing 4000 years of history. Phot. *Polimeni, Bruna*; text *Darwish, Nazmieh Rida Tawfiq*. Amman 1996, Jordan Distribution Agency 95 pp. New ed. 88-7280-188-5 [NThAR 1998,362].

10232 *Kennedy, David; Gader al-Husan, Abdel* New milestones from northern Jordan, 1992-1995. ZPE 113 (1996) 257-262.

10233 **MacDonald, Burton** Ammon, Moab and Edom: early states/nations of Jordan in the biblical period. 1994, ⇒11/2,12356*. [R]BA 59 (1996) 241-242 *(Cresson, Bruce C.)*.

10234 *Mattingly, Gerald L.* The King's Highway, the desert highway, and central Jordan's Kerak plateau. Aram 8 (1996) 89-99.

10235 *Piccirillo, Michele* Ricerca storico-archeologica in Giordania XVI—1996. SBFLA 46 (1996) 391-424.

10236 *Sapin, J.* Réflexions sur des stratégies et des techniques d'adaptation dans la Transjordanie du Ier Millénaire. TEuph 11 (1996) 45-61.

10237 *Van der Steen, Eveline J* The central east Jordan valley in the Late Bronze and Early Iron Ages. BASOR 302 (1996) 51-74.

10238 **Willeitner, J.** Jordanien. Mü 1996, Hirmer 222 pp. Aufnahmen von H. Dollhopf. DM98. 3-7774-7110-0 [ZAW 109,460].

10239 *ʿAmman*: **Northedge, Alastair** Studies on Roman and Islamic ʿAmman. 1992, ⇒9,13942... 11/2,b141. ᴿLevant 28 (1996) 221-224 *(Ward-Perkins, Bryan)*.

10240 *Aqaba*: *Parker, S. Thomas* The Roman 'Aqaba project: the 1994 campaign. ADAJ 40 (1996) 231-257.

10241 *Edom*:**Dicou, Bert** Edom, Israel's brother and antagonist: the role of Edom in biblical prophecy and story. JSOT.S 169: 1994, ⇒11/2,b152. ᴿThLZ 121 (1996) 819 *(Hübner, Ulrich)*.

10242 *El-Kheleifeh*: **Pratico, Gary D.** Nelson Glueck's 1938-1940 excavations at Tell el-Kheleifeh. 1993, ⇒9,13968... 11/2,b144. ᴿWO 27 (1996) 266-269 *(Weippert, Helga)*; IEJ 46 (1996) 280-282 *(Stern, Ephraim)*.

10243 *En-Nahas*: *Fritz, Volkmar* Ergebnisse einer Sondage in Hirbet en-Nahas, Wadi el-ʿAraba (Jordanien). ZDPV 112 (1996) 1-9.

10244 *Es-Saʿidiyeh*: *Tubb, Jonathan N.; Dorrell, Peter G.; Cobbing, Felicity J.* Interim report on the eighth (1995) season of excavations at Tell Es-Saʿidiyeh. PEQ 128 (1996) 16-40.

10245 *Gerasa*: *Sear, Frank* The south theatre at Jarash, 1994 campaign. ADAJ 40 (1996) 217-230.

10246 *Ghassul, Teleilat*: *Bourke, Stephen J.* Teleilat Ghassul 1995: a second season of renewed excavations by the University of Sydney. OrExp (1996) 41-43.

10247 *Hesban*:ᴱMerling, David; **Geraty, Lawrence T.** Hesban after 25 years. Berrien Springs 1994, Institute of Archaeology xxiv; 379 pp. $15. 0-9642060-0-5. ᴿAUSS 34 (1996) 134-136 *(Hasel, Michael G.)*.

10248 **Mitchel, Larry A.** Hellenistic and Roman strata: a study of the stratigraphy of Tell Hesban from the 2d century B.C. to the 4th century A.D. 1992, ⇒10,12378. ᴿJAOS 116 (1996) 277-278 *(Magness, Jodi)*.

10249 *Iktanu*: *McCartney, Carole* A report on the chipped stone assemblage from Tell Iktanu, Jordan. Sum. 131. Levant 28 (1996) 131-155.

10250 *Johfiyeh*: *Lamprichs, Roland* Some notes on Tell Johfiyeh: an Iron Age site in northern Jordan. UF 28 (1996) 325-342.

10251 *Machaerus*: *Loffreda, Stanislao* La fortezza di Macheronte. TS(I) 72 (lug.-ago. 1996) 11-15.

10252 *Majouthous*: *Suleiman, Emsaytif* A short note on the excavations of Yajuz 1994-1995. ADAJ 40 (1996) 457-462.

10253 *Pella*: *Bourke, Stephen J.* Report on the seventeenth season of excavations at Pella in Jordan by the University of Sydney, 1995. OrExp (1996) 3-5;

10254 **McNicoll, Anthony W.** Pella in Jordan 2: the second interim report of excavations 1982-1985. 1992, ⇒9,13990. ᴿGn. 68 (1996) 142-145 *(Weber, Thomas)*;

10255 *Watson, Pamela* Pella hinterland survey 1994: preliminary report. Sum. 63. Levant 28 (1996) 63-76;
10256 *Watson, Pamela; Tidmarsh, John* Pella/Tell Al-ḥuṣn excavations 1993: the University of Sydney—15th season. ADAJ 40 (1996) 293-313.

10257 **Petra**: *Al-Muheisen, Zeidoun; Tarrier, Dominique* Menace des eaux et mesures préventives à Pétra à l'époque nabatéenne. Syr. 73 (1996) 197-204;
10258 **Bignasca, A.**, (*al*), Petra—Ez. Zantur I: Ergebnisse der Schweizerisch-Liechtensteinischen Ausgrabungen 1988-1992. Terra Achaeologica 2: Mainz 1996, Von Zabern ix; 411 pp. 1027 ill. DM180 [ZAW 110,460—Zwickel, W.];
10259 **Lacerenza, Giancarlo** Il viaggio a Petra di Giammartino Arconati VISCONTI (1865). AION.S 88: N 1996, Istituto Universitario Orientale xi; 51 pp.;
10260 **McKenzie, J.** The architecture of Petra. 1990, ⇒6,e235... 10,12406. RPEQ 128 (1996) 63-70 *(Parr, Peter)*;
10261 *Meza, Alicia I.* The Egyptian statuette in Petra and the Isis cult connection. ADAJ 40 (1996) 167-176;
10262 *Mildenberg, Leo* Once again, Petra on the frankincense road?. Aram 8 (1996) 55-65;
10263 *Peterman, Glen; Schick, Robert* The monastery of Saint Aaron. ADAJ 40 (1996) 473-480;
10264 *Sharp Joukowsky, Martha* 1995 archaeological excavation of the southern temple at Petra, Jordan. ADAJ 40 (1996) 177-206;
10265 EZayadine, Fawzi Petra and the caravan cities. 1990, ⇒9,579*. RSEL 13 (1996) 133-135 *(Lacerenza, Giancarlo)*.

10266 **Ras en-Naqb**: *Waheeb, Mohammad* Archaeological excavation at Ras An-Naqab - 'Aqaba road 339-348 alignment: preliminary report (1995). ADAJ 40 (1996) 339-348.
10267 **Umm al-Rasas**: **Piccirillo, Michele; Alliata, Eugenio** Umm al-Rasas: Mayfaʿah I: gli scavi del complesso di Santo Stefano. SBF.CMa 28: 1994, ⇒11/2,b205. RRB 103 (1996) 464-465 *(Axe, Tony)*.
10268 **Wadi Faynan**: *Ruben, Isabelle* [Report on Wadi Faynan Project];
10269 **Wadi Hasa**: *Bienkowski, Piotr* [Report on Wadi Hasa];
10270 **Wadi Kafrain**: *Prag, Kay; Barnes, Hugh* Three fortresses on the Wadi Kafrain, Jordan. Levant 28 (1996) 213-214/214-215/41-61.
10271 **Yaşileh**: *Al-Muheisen, Zeidoun; Tarrier, Dominique* Les fouilles de Yasileh (Jordanie du Nord): le site et la nécropole dans une perspective régionale. Syr. 73 (1996) 185-196.

T5.1 Phoenicia—*Libanus*, **Lebanon**

10272 **Briquel-Chatonnet, Françoise** Les relations entre les cités de la côte phénicienne et les royaumes d'Israël et de Juda. 1992, ⇒8,e636... 11/2,b207. RSyria 73 (1996) 207-208 *(Bron, François)*.
10273 **El-Ghassil**: **Doumet-Serhal, Claude** Les fouilles de Tell el-Ghassil de 1972 à 1974: étude du matériel. BAHI 146: Beyrouth 1996, Institut Français d'Archéologie du Proche-Orient 304 pp. 27 ill. 2-7053-0562-9 [OLZ 93,652—Kulemann-Ossen, Sabina].

10274 *Sidon*: **Stucky, Rolf A.** Die Skulpturen aus dem Eschmun-Heiligtum bei Sidon. 1993, ⇒10,12424*; 11/2,b222. ᴿRAr (1996/2) 434-435 *(Fourrier, Sabine)*.
10275 *Tyre*: **Bikai, Patricia Maynor; Fulco, William J.; Marchand, Jeannie** Tyre: the shrine of Apollo. Amman 1996, National Press ix; 85 pp. [CBQ 61,326s—Hauer, C.E.].
10276 *Lacerenza, Giancarlo* Echi biblici in una leggenda: Tiro in Beniamin da Tudela. AION 56 (1996) 462-470.

τ5.2 *Situs mediterranei* **phoenicei et punici**

10277 *Acquaro, E.*, (*al*), Tharros XXIII. 18 pl. RSFen.S 24 (1996) 5-166.
10278 **Baurain, C.; Bonnet, C.** Les phéniciens: marins des trois continents. 1992, ⇒8,e655... 11/2,b226. ᴿRSFen 24 (1996) 88-92 *(Garbini, Giovanni)*.
10279 **Ferjaoui, Ahmed** Recherches sur les relations entre l'Orient phénicien et Carthage. OBO 124: 1993, ⇒9,14066; 10,12460. ᴿBiOr 53 (1996) 161-162 *(Lipiński, E.)*.
10280 Libya Antiqua: Annual of the Department of Antiquities of Libya. R 1996, Bretschneider 174 pp. 84 pl. 11 fig. 8 tables. 88-7062-934-1 [AJA 101,431].
10281 *Manzo, Andrea* Culture ed ambiente: l'Africa nord-orientale nei dati archeologici e nella letteratura geografica ellenistica. AION.S 87: N 1996, Istituto Universitario Orientale 86 pp.
10282 *Pellicer Catalán, M.* Huelva Tartesia y Fenicia. RSFen 24 (1996) 119-140.
10283 *Pisano, Giovanna* Nuove ricerche puniche in Sardegna. Studia punica 11: R 1996, Univ. 'Tor Vergata' 144 pp. [CBQ 60,197].
10284 **Riis, P.J.**, (*al*), Sukas X: the Bronze and Early Iron Age remains at the southern harbour. Publications of the Carlsberg Expedition to Phoenicia 12: Historisk-filosofiske Skrifter 17: Copenhagen 1996, 65 pp. 43 fig. 5 pl. DKK130. 0023-3307. ᴿRSFen 24 (1996) 195-196 *(Bartoloni, Piero)*.
10285 *Tsirkin, Ju.B.* The downfall of Tartessos and the Carthaginian establishment on the Iberian Peninsula. RSFen 24 (1996) 141-152.
10286 **Vidal González, Pablo** La isla de Malta en época fenicia y punica. Oxf 1996, Tempus R. 176 pp. 63 figs. 28 tables. £36. 0-86054-842-2 [AJA 102,437—Gomez Bellard, Carlos].
10287 **Webster, Gary S.** A prehistory of Sardinia 2300-500 B.C. Monographs in Mediterranean Archaeology 5: Shf 1996, Academic 224 pp. 35 fig. 34 plans. 10 tables. 12 maps. 1-85075-508-6 [AJA 101,433].

τ5.4 **Ugarit**—*Ras Šamra*

10288 **Baldacci, Massimo** La scoperta di Ugarit: la città-stato ai primordi della bibbia. CasM 1996, Piemme 414 pp. L48.000. 88-384-2530-2 [NThAR 1997,98].
10289 **Bordreuil, Pierre** Une bibliothèque au sud de la ville (Ras Shamra-Ougarit VII). 1991, ⇒8,e708... 10,12779*. ᴿOLZ 91 (1996) 558-562 *(Klengel, Horst)*.

10290 **Brooke, George J.** Ugarit and the Bible. UBL 11: 1994, ⇒10,308. RThQ 176 (1996) 82-83 *(Niehr, Herbert)*.

10291 **Callot, Olivier** La tranchée 'ville sud': études d'architecture domestique. Ras Shamra-Ougarit 10: 1994, ⇒10,12480; 11/2,b260. RRA 90 (1996) 80-81 *(Amiet, P.)*; BiOr 53 (1996) 821-824 *(Wright, G.R.H.)*.

10292 *Cazelles, Henri* Archives de Syrie-Palestine. Études. 1996 <1989>, ⇒120. 89-95.

10293 **Contenson, Henri de** Préhistoire de Ras Shamra: les sondages stratigraphiques de 1955 à 1976. 1992, ⇒10,12480*. RIEJ 46 (1996) 273-277 *(Garfinkel, Yosef)*.

10294 *Dietrich, Manfried* Aspects of the Babylonian impact on Ugaritic literature and religion. FGIBSON J., 1996, ⇒31. 33-47.

10295 EDietrich, Manfried; Loretz, Oswald Ugarit und seine altorientalische Umwelt. Ugarit: ein ostmediterranes Kulturzentrum im Alten Orient: Ergebnisse und Perspektiven der Forschung. 1995, ⇒11/2,b262. RUF 28 (1996) 783-784 *(Niehr, Herbert)*.

10296 *Dietrich, Manfried; Mayer, Walter* Festritual für die Palastgöttin Pidray: der hurro-ugaritische Opfertext KTU 1.132. UF 28 (1996) 165-176.

10297 **Ekschmitt, Werner** Ugarit—Qumran—Nag Hammadi: die großen Schriftfunde zur Bibel. 1993, ⇒9,14083. RThLZ 121 (1996) 244-245 *(Stegemann, Wolfgang)*.

10298 *Gachet, Jacqueline* Le "centre de la ville" d'Ougarit: la maison C. Syr. 73 (1996) 153-184.

10299 *Herrmann, Wolfram* Göttergruppen erneut bezeugt und bestätigt. UF 28 (1996) 275-276.

10300 *Lloyd, J.B.; Wyatt, N.* The Edinburgh Ras Shamra Project: an introduction. FGIBSON J., 1996, ⇒31. 423-430.

10301 *Mallet, Joël* Ras Shamra-Ougarit (Syrie): la chronologie de la période du Bronze moyen (fin du IIIe millénaire av. J.-C. et 1re moitié du second). UF 28 (1996) 443-451.

10302 *Margalit, Baruch* atrt. ṣrm. ... ṣdynm (KTU 1.14:IV:35-39): exit 'Sidon'. UF 28 (1996) 453-455.

10303 *Márquez Rowe, I.* Syllabic and alphabetic texts—a further note on scribal education at Ugarit. UF 28 (1996) 457-462.

10304 *Mazzini, Giovanni* Miserable Daniel: notes for a reading of KTU 1.17 I 16. UF 28 (1996) 485-490.

10305 *Merlo, Paolo* Über die Ergänzung <št> in KTU 1.23:59. UF 28 (1996) 491-494.

10306 *Moor, Johannes C. de* Fishes in KTU 4.427:23-29. UF 28 (1996) 155-157.

10307 *Olmo Lete, Gregorio del* Once again on the 'divine names' of the Ugaritic kings: a reply. Sum. 11. AulOr 14 (1996) 11-16.

10308 *Sauer, Georg* Ugarit und Byblos. Religionsgeschichte Syriens. 1996, ⇒217. 79-90.

10309 *Schmidt, Brian B.* A re-evaluation of the Ugaritic king list (KTU 1.113). FGIBSON J., 1996, ⇒31. 289-304.

10310 *Sivan, Daniel* A note on the use of the ʾu-sign in Ugaritic roots with first ʾaleph. UF 28 (1996) 555-559.

10311 *Tropper, Josef* Nachträge zum letzten Zeichen des ugaritischen Alphabets. UF 28 (1996) 651-652.

10312 Ugarit-Forschungen 28. Müns 1996, Ugarit-Verlag vi; 837 pp. 3-927120-56-1.

10313 *Van Soldt, Wilfred* Studies in the topography of Ugarit (1): the spelling of the Ugaritic toponyms. UF 28 (1996) 653-692.
10314 *Veldhuis, Niek* The Ugarit lexical text RS 13.53. WO 27 (1996) 25-29.
10315 *Vita, Juan-Pablo* Una nueva interpretación del documento administrativo ugarítico 00-4.392. UF 28 (1996) 693-699.
10316 *Watson, Wilfred G.E.* Non-Semitic words in the Ugaritic lexicon (2). UF 28 (1996) 701-719;
10317 Ugaritic onomastics (5). Sum. 93. AulOr 14 (1996) 93-106.
10318 *Wyatt, Nick* The vocabulary and neurology of orientation: the Ugaritic and Hebrew evidence. ^FGIBSON J., 1996, ⇒31. 351-380 [aḫr; qdm; ymn; šmal].
10319 *Xella, Paolo* Les pouvoirs du dieu ʿAttar: morphologie d'un dieu du panthéon ugaritique. ^FGIBSON J., 1996, ⇒31. 381-404.
10320 *Yon, Marguerite* The temple of the Rhytons at Ugarit. ^FGIBSON J., 1996, ⇒31. 405-422.
10321 ^E**Yon, Marguerite; Sznycer, Maurice; Bordreuil, Maurice** Le pays d'Ougarit autour de 1200 av. J.-C.: histoire et archéologie. Ras Shamra-Ougarit 11: 1995 (Actes du Colloque, P 1993), ⇒11/2,753. ^ROLZ 91 (1996) 558-562 *(Klengel, Horst).*

T5.5 **Ebla**

10322 **Archi, Alfonso** Testi amministrativi: registrazioni di metalli e tessuti. ARET 7: 1988, ⇒4,e77; 5,e111. ^RBiOr 53 (1996) 474-479 *(Selz, Gebhard J.).*
10323 *Archi, Alfonso* Bulle e cretule iscritte da Ebla. VO 10 (1996) 29-35;
10324 Chronologie relative des archives d'Ébla;
10325 Les femmes du roi Irkab-Damu;
10326 *Biga, Maria Giovanna* Prosopographie et datation relative des textes d'Ébla. Amurru 1. 1996, ⇒306. 11-28/101-124/29-72.
10327 **D'Agostino, Franco** Testi amministrativi di Ebla, Archivio L. 2769, 3A. Materiali per il vocabolario sumerico 3: Materiali epigrafici di Ebla 7A: R 1996, Herder lvi pp. pl.
10328 *Fronzaroli, Pelio* Notes sur la syntaxe éblaïte. Amurru 1. 1996, ⇒306. 125-134;
10329 Il serpente dalle sette teste a Ebla. ^FMOSCATI S., III, 1996, ⇒67. 1135-1144.
10330 *Krebernik, Manfred* The linguistic classification of Eblaite: methods, problems, and results. Albright centennial conference. 1996, ⇒303. 233-249;
10331 Neue Beschwörungen aus Ebla. VO 10 (1996) 7-28.
10332 *Matthiae, Paolo* Tell Mardikh-Ebla (Siria), campagna di scavi 1995. OrExp (1996) 84-87.
10333 **Milano, Lucio** Testi amministrativi: assegnazioni di prodotti alimentari. ARET 9: R 1990, Missione Archeologica Italiana in Siria xviii; 418 pp. Archivio L.2712, parte I. ^RBiOr 53 (1996) 479-489 *(Selz, Gebhard J.).*
10334 *Milano, Lucio* Ébla: gestion des terres et gestion des ressources alimentaires. Amurru 1. 1996, ⇒306. 135-171.
10335 *Oesch, Josef* Die Religion Eblas. Religionsgeschichte Syriens. 1996, ⇒217. 39-48.

10336 *Pettinato, Giovanni* Religione ed economia ad Ebla: appunti di lessicografia eblaita, II. Zsfg. 13. RSO 70 (1996) 1-13.

10337 **Pettinato, Giovanni** Testi amministrativi di Ebla: archivio L. 2752. Materiali Epigrafici di Ebla 5: Materiali per il Vocabolario Sumerico 2: R 1996, Università degli Studi di Roma xvi; 476 pp. [BiOr 54,397].

10338 *Seminara, Stefano* Il 'lugalato' da Ebla a Emar: sopravvivenze emarite della terminologia e della prassi eblaite della gestione del potere. Sum. 79. AulOr 14 (1996) 79-92.

10339 *Sjöberg, Åke W.* The Ebla list of animals MEE 4, no.116. WO 27 (1996) 9-24.

10340 *Urioste Sanchez, Ignacio de* Aspetti della circolazione di metalli preziosi ad Ebla: catene di distribuzione e restituzione parziale. VO 10 (1996) 73-82.

10341 **Vigano, Lorenzo** On Ebla: an accounting of third millennium Syria. AulOr.S 5: Barca 1996, Ausa vii; 208 pp. 84-88810-21-0 [NThAR 1998,362].

τ5.8 Situs effossi Syriae in ordine alphabetico

10342 *Foss, Clive* Dead cities of the Syrian hill country. Arch. 49/5 (1996) 48-53.

10343 *Tate, G.* Les campagnes de la Syrie du Nord du IIe au VIIe siècle, I. 1992, ⇒9,14117. RJESHO 39 (1996) 170-179 *(Doukellis, Panagiotis N.)*.

10344 **Abu Snesleh**: *Lamprichs, Roland; Kerner, Susanne* Abu Snesleh: erste Ergebnisse der Ausgrabungen 1990 und 1992: Fundortbeschreibung-Stratigraphie-Architektur. UF 28 (1996) 287-323.

10345 **Alalakh**: *Mendecki, Norbert* Alalach—zapomniane królestwo [Alalach—regnum oblitum]. RBL 49 (1996) 49-51. **P**.

10346 **Baricha**: **Peña, I.; Castellana, R. Fernandez** Inventaire du Jébel Baricha: recherches archéologiques dans la région des Villes Mortes de la Syrie du Nord. SBF.CMi 33: 1987, ⇒3,e455; 4,g28. RBiOr 53 (1996) 199-200 *(Innemée, K.C.)*.

10347 **Bderi**: *Engel, T.* Archeobotanical analysis of timber and firewood used in third millennium houses at Tell Bderi (Northeast-Syria). Houses and households. UNHAII 78: 1996, ⇒299. 105-115.

10348 **Brak**: *Oates, David & Joan* Excavations in Tell Brak (Syria) in 1976-1991. Sum. 164. VDI 218 (1996) 148-165. **R**.

10349 **El Umbaši**: *Braemer, Frank; Echallier, Jean-Claude; Taraqji, Ahmed* Khirbet el Umbashi (Syrie): rapport préliminaire sur les campagnes 1993 et 1994. Syr. 73 (1996) 117-127.

10350 **Emar**: EChavalas, Mark W. Emar: the history, religion, and culture of a Syrian town in the late Bronze Age. Bethesda 1996, CDL xvii; 179 pp. 1-883053-18-8;

10351 *Margueron, Jean-Claude* Emar: a Syrian city between Anatolia, Assyria and Babylonia. Cultural interaction. Abr-n.S 5: 1996, ⇒285. 77-90.

10352 *Pitard, Wayne T.* The archaeology of Emar ⇒10350. 13-23.

10353 *Fecherije*: *Moortgat-Correns, Ursula* Zwei unveröffentliche Fundstücke vom Tell Fecherije aus den Jahren 1927 und 1929. Philolog. Komm. v. Barbara *Böck*. AltOrF 23 (1996) 316-334.

10354 *Haut-Khabur*: *Lyonnet, Bertille* La prospection archéologique de la partie occidentale du Haut-Khabur (Syrie du Nord-Est) : méthodes, résultats et questions autour de l'occupation aux IIIe et IIe millénaires av. n. è. Amurru 1. 1996, ⇒306. 363-376.

10355 *Jerablus-Tahtani*: *Peltenburg, Edgar*, (*al*), Jerablus-Tahtani, Syria, 1995: preliminary report. Sum. 1. Levant 28 (1996) 1-25.

10356 *Kamid el-Loz*: *Hachmann, Rolf* Zur absoluten Chronologie des 'Schatzhauses'. Kamid el-Loz 16. 1996, ⇒9941. 17-26.

10357 *Mari*: **Anbar, Moshê** Les tribus amurrites de Mari. OBO 108: 1991, ⇒7,d669... 11/2,b339. [R]RA 90 (1996) 91-93 *(Villard, Pierre)*;

10358 *Margueron, Jean-Claude* Mari: campagne 1995. OrExp (1996) 35-38.

10359 *Palmyra*: **Sadurska, Anna; Bounni, Adnan** Les sculptures funéraires de Palmyre. 1994, ⇒11/2,b348. [R]AJA 100 (1996) 437-438 *(Gawlikowski, Michal)*.

10360 *Rad Shaqrad*: *Kolinski, Rafal* Tell Rad Shaqrad 1991-1995. OrExp (1996) 67-69.

10361 *Sūkās*:**Oldenburg, Evelyn** Sūkās IX: the Chalcolithic and Early Bronze periods. Historisk-filosofiske Skrifter 14: 1991, ⇒7,d691. [R]JNES 55 (1996) 63-65 *(Joffe, Alexander H.)*.

10362 *Wadi al-ʿAjib*: *Betts, Alison*, (*al*), Studies of Bronze Age occupation in the Wadi al-ʿAjib, southern Hauran. Sum. 27. Levant 28 (1996) 27-39.

т6.1 Mesopotamia, *generalia*

10363 **Huot, Jean-Louis** Les premiers villageois de Mésopotamie. 1994, ⇒11/2,b379. [R]Syria 73 (1996) 215-218 *(Contenson, Henri de)*.

10364 **Kuklick, Bruce** Puritans in Babylon: the ancient Near East and American intellectual life, 1880-1930. Princeton 1996, Princeton Univ. Press 266 pp. $30 [IJMES 30,584s—Maidman, M.P.].

10365 **Potts, Timothy** Mesopotamia and the east: an archaeological and historical study of foreign relations ca. 3400-2000 BC. Oxf Univ. Committee for Archaeology Monograph 37: Oakville, CT 1994, David Brown 340 pp. £48. 0-947816-37-2. [R]Antiquity 70 (1996) 472-473 *(Crawford, Harriet)*.

10366 **Sack, Ronald H.** Cuneiform documents from the Chaldean and Persian periods. 1994, ⇒10,12598. [R]BSOAS 59 (1996) 338 *(George, A.R.)*.

10367 **Wilkinson, T.J.; Tucker, D.J.** Settlement development in the north Jazira, Iraq. 1995, ⇒11/2,b395. [R]Mes. 31 (1996) 222-225 *(Fiorina, P.)*.

т6.5 Situs effossi Iraq *in ordine alphabetico*

10368 *Assur*:**Miglus, Peter A.** Das Wohngebiet von Assur: Stratigraphie und Architektur. WVDOG 93: B 1996, Mann 2 vols. Anhang von

St. Heidemann und *P.A. Miglus;* num. pl. DM400. 3-7861-1731-4 [Mes. 33,364ss—Fiorina, P.];

10369 **Preusser, Conrad** Die Paläste in Assur. WVDOG 66: B [2]1996 <1955>, Mann viii; 36 pp. 26 pl. DM360. 3-7861-2004-8 [Mes. 33,363—Fiorina, P.].

10370 *Babylon*: **Schmid, Hansjörg** Der Tempelturm Etemenanki in Babylon. 1995, ⇒11/2,b403. [R]Mes. 31 (1996) 233-235 *(Invernizzi, A.)*; ZA 86 (1996) 294-301 *(Miglus, P.A.)*;

10371 *Westenholz, Joan Goodnick* Babylon—place of the creation of the great gods. Royal cities. 1996, ⇒248. 197-220.

10372 *Drehem*: **Sigrist, Marcel** Drehem. 1992, ⇒9,14237; 11/2,b408. [R]JESHO 39 (1996) 185-189 *(Maaijer, R. de)*.

10373 *Ḥabuba Kabira*: *Kohlmeyer, K.* Houses in Ḥabuba Kabira South: spatial organisation and planning of Late Uruk residential archtecture;

10374 *Haradum*: *Kepinski-Lecomte, C.* Spacial occupation of a new town: Haradum (Iraqi Middle Euphrates, 18th-17th centuries B.C.). Houses and households. UNHAII 78: 1996, ⇒299. 89-103/191-196.

10375 *Hatra*:**Vattioni, Francesco** Hatra. AION.S 81: 1994, ⇒11/2,b415. [R]Henoch 18 (1996) 383-384 *(Bertolino, Roberto)*.

10376 *Isin-Išān-Baḥrīyāt*: **Hrouda, B.** Isin-Išān-Baḥrīyāt, IV: die Ergebnisse der Ausgrabungen 1986-1989. 1992, ⇒11/2,b416. [R]JAOS 116 (1996) 131-133 *(Dunham, Sally)*.

10377 *Kalḫu (Nimrūd)*: **Paley, Samuel M.; Sobolewski, Richard P.** The reconstruction of the relief representations...in the northwest palace at Kalḫu (Nimrūd), III: principal entrances...courtyards. 1992, ⇒9,14246; 10,12622. [R]JAOS 116 (1996) 273-274 *(Porter, B.N.)*.

10378 *Karrana*: **Wilhelm, Gernot; Zaccagnini, Carlo** Tell Karrana 3: Tell Jikan, Tell Khirbet Salih. Baghdader Forschungen 15: Mainz 1993, Von Zabern xiv; 239 pp. DM180. 3-8053-1543-0. [R]Mes. 31 (1996) 225-228 *(Mollo, P.)*.

10379 *Nemrud Daği*: **Sanders, Donald H.** Nemrud Daği: the hierothesion of Antiochus I of Commagene: vol. 1: text; vol. 2: illustrations. WL 1996, Eisenbrauns xliv + 528; xxiv + 332 pp. 0-931464-89-7/90-0:

10380 *Bachmann, Hans-Gert; Brown, Thomas E.; Chase, W.T.* Mineralogy ⇒10379. 12-15;

10381 *Bachmann, Hans-Gert* Geology. ⇒10379. 5-12;

10382 Geography: introduction ⇒10379. 1-2;

10383 *Bachmann, Hans-Gert; Sanders, Donald H.* Flora and fauna ⇒10379. 15-16;

10384 *Goell, Theresa; Sanders, Donald H.; Young, John H.* Detailed site description: east terrace, west terrace, north terrace ⇒10379. 100-130;

10385 *Goell, Theresa; Sanders, Donald H.* The mound: approaches, site circulation, tumulus construction ⇒10379. 91-100;

10386 Investigations and excavations of the 1970s and 1980s ⇒10379. 79-80;

10387 Affiliations of the architecture at Nemrud Daği ⇒10379. 133-151;

10388 Coins ⇒10379. 472-474;

10389 *Goell, Theresa; Neugebauer, Otto* Dating of Nemrud Daği and of the life of Antiochus I, king of Commagene ⇒10379. 87-91;

10390 *Goell, Theresa* Topography ⇒10379. 4-5;
10391 Investigations and excavations of the 1950s and 1961 ⇒10379. 36-52;
10392 Ancient sources and previous scholarship ⇒10379. 17-34;
10393 Bibliography ⇒10379. 485-504.
10394 *Hutt, Jeremy R.* Investigations and excavations of 1963 and 1964, geophysical explorations ⇒10379. 52-79.

10395 *Nimroud: Collon, Dominique* Nimrud: ville royale assyrienne. MoBi 98 (1996) 55-61.
10396 *Nineveh: Russell, John* Nineveh. Royal cities. 1996, ⇒248. 153-170.
10397 *Nippur:* **Cole, Steven William** Nippur in late Assyrian times, c. 755-612 BC. State Archives of Assyria Studies 4: Helsinki 1996, The Neo-Assyrian Text Corpus Project xx; 138 pp. $29.50. 951-45-7286-6;
10398 Nippur IV: the early Neo-Babylonian governor's archive from Nippur. The University of Chicago. OIP 114: Ch 1996, Oriental Institute xliii; 458 pp. 1-885923-03-1;
10399 **Zettler, Richard L.** Nippur III. 1993, ⇒11/2,b426. ᴿOLZ 91 (1996) 417-424 *(Van Ess, Margarete)*.
10400 *Nuzi:* ᴱ**Morrison, Martha A.; Owen, David I.** The eastern archives of Nuzi. 1993, ⇒9,14250; 11/2,b429. ᴿOLZ 91 (1996) 555-558 *(Jankowska, Ninel B.)*.
10401 *Ur: Janssen, C.* When the house is on fire and the children are gone. Houses and households. UNHAII 78: 1996, ⇒299. 237-246;
10402 *Westenholz, Joan Goodnick* Ur—capital of Sumer. Royal cities. 1996, ⇒248. 3-30.

т6.9 **Iran,** *Persia,* Asia centralis

10403 [Accademia Nazionale dei Lincei:] La Persia e l'Asia centrale da ALESSANDRO al X secolo. Atti dei Convegni Lincei 127: R 1996, Accademia Nazionale dei Lincei 711 pp. collab. l'Istituto Italiano per il Medio ed Estremo Oriente. Convegno internazionale, Roma, 9-12 nov. 1994.
10404 AMI 26 (1993). ᴿMes. 31 (1996) 204-207 *(Lippolis, C.)*.
10405 AMI 28 (1995-1996).
10406 ᴱ**Kleiss, Wolfram; Calmeyer, Peter** Bisutun: Ausgrabungen und Forschungen in den Jahren 1963-1967. TF 7: B 1996, Mann 267 pp. Dt. Archäologisches Institut. Abt. Teheran. 3-7861-1860-4.
10407 *Perrot, Jean; Ladiray, Daniel* The palace of Susa;
10408 *Ziffer, Irit* Achaemenid. Royal cities. 1996, ⇒248. 237-254/255-286.

т7.1 **Ægyptus,** *generalia*

10409 **Arnaudiès, Alain; Boutros, Wadie** Lexique pratique des chantiers de fouilles et de restauration. Bibliothèque générale 15: Le Caire 1996, Institut français d'Archéologie Orientale 219 pp. FF77.50 [CÉg 73,96—Mekhitarian, A.].

10410 **Aufrère, Sydney H.; Golvin, J.-Cl.; Goyon, J.-Cl.** L'Égypte restituée: sites et temples de Haute Égypte (1650 av.J.-C.-300 ap.J.-C.). 1991, ⇒7,d828. ᴿCÉg 71 (1996) 271-273 *(Van Essche, Éric)*.

10411 **Behlmer, Heike; Alcock, Anthony** A piece of Shenoutiana from the Department of Egyptian Antiquities (EA 71005). British Museum. Occasional Paper 119: L 1996, British Museum (4) 40 pp. 16 pl. 0-86159-119-4.

10412 ᴱ**Falck, Martin von; Lichtwark, Friedericke** Ägypten: Schätze aus dem Wüstensand: Kunst und Kultur der Christen am Nil. Wsb 1996, Reichert 420 pp. DM49. 3-88226-872-7 [Phoenix 43/1,50].

10413 *Giddy, Lisa, (al),* Fieldwork, 1995-6 [Memphis, Saqqara, el-Amarna, Buto, Gebel Dokhan, Qasr Ibrim). JEA 82 (1996) 1-22.

10414 *Grimal, Nicolas* Travaux de l'Institut français d'archéologie orientale en 1995-1996. BIFAO 96 (1996) 489-610.

10415 **Hancock, Graham** Fingerprints of the gods: a quest for the beginning and the end. L 1995, Heinemann 578 pp. 32 pl. £17. ᴿDiscEg 34 (1996) 135-142 *(Malek, Jaromir)*.

10416 **Herbin, François René** Le livre de parcourir l'éternité. OLA 58: 1994, ⇒10,12675. ᴿOLZ 91 (1996) 151-158 *(Quack, Joachim F.)*.

10417 **Jaros-Deckert, Brigitte; Rogge, Eva** Statuetten des alten Reiches. Corpus antiquitatum aegyptiacarum: Ägyptisch-Orientalische Sammlung 15: Mainz 1993, Von Zabern 107 pp. Kunsthistorisches Museum Wien. 204 ill. Lose-Blatt-Katalog ägyptischer Altertümer. DM78. 3-8053-1497-3. ᴿBiOr 53 (1996) 435-437 *(Tefnin, R.)*.

10418 *Leclant, Jean; Clerc, Gisèle* Fouilles et travaux en Égypte et au Soudan, 1994-1995 (TAB. V-XXXIV). Or. 65 (1996) 234-356.

10419 ᴱ**Rose, Jerome C.** Bioarchaeology of ancient Egypt and Nubia: a bibliography. British Museum. Occasional Paper 112: L 1996, British Museum v; 110 pp. £7.50. 0-86159-112-7.

10420 **Scott, Gerry D.** Temple, tomb and dwelling: Egyptian antiquities from the HARER family trust collection. 1992, ⇒8,g42. ᴿBiOr 53 (1996) 74-79 *(Pamminger, Peter)*.

T7.2 **Luxor,** *Karnak* [East Bank]—**Thebae** [West Bank]

10421 *Deir el Medina*: ᴱ**Lesko, Leonard H.** Pharaoh's workers: the villagers of Deir el Medina. 1994, ⇒10,12719; 11/2,b565. JESHO 39 (1996) 433-434 *(Eyre, Christopher J.)*; OLZ 91 (1996) 280-284 *(Endesfelder, Erika)*.

10422 *Thebes*: **Barthelmess, Petra** Der Übergang ins Jenseits in den thebanischen Beamtengräbern der Ramessidenzeit. 1992, ⇒8,g83... 11/2,b555. ᴿBiOr 53 (1996) 58-60 *(Milde, H.)*.

10423 ᴱ**Baines, John** Stone vessels, pottery and sealings from the tomb of Tutʿankhamūn. 1993, ⇒11/2,b549. ᴿBiOr 53 (1996) 701-705 *(Nicholson, Paul T.)*;

10424 **Eaton-Krauss, M.** The sarcophagus in the tomb of Tutankhamun. 1993, ⇒9,14362; 11/2,b551. ᴿJEA 82 (1996) 224-226 *(Dodson, Aidan)*;

10425 ᴱ**Seyfried, Karl-Joachim** Das Grab des Paenkhemenu. 1991, ⇒7,d871*. ᴿBiOr 53 (1996) 433-435 *(Taylor, John H.)*.

т7.3 **Amarna**

10426 *Cruz-Uribe, Eugene* Atum, Shu, and the gods during the Amarna period. Sum. 15. JSSEA 25 (1995) 15-22.
      Endruweit, A. Städtischer Wohnbau in... Amarna ⇒9558.
10427 *Heintz, Jean-Georges; Millot, Lison* Bibliographie d'El-Amarna: Suppl. II [1995-96] [= Suppl. à I.D.E.A., 2 (1995) 1-119] [Addenda & Corrigenda—Éd. du 31 Déc. 1996]. UF 28 (1996) 257-274.
10428 **Hess, Richard S.** Amarna personal names. ASOR.DS 9: 1993, ⇒9,14392... 11/2,b577. ᴿJAOS 116 (1996) 270-271 *(Izre'el, Shlomo)*; OLZ 91 (1996) 51-57 *(Tropper, Josef)*; SEL 13 (1996) 9-17 *(Bonechi, Marco)*.
10429 *Janssen, Rosalind M.* Recollections of 'a golden boy': John PENDLEBURY at el-Amarna. DiscEg 36 (1996) 53-67.
10430 *Johnson, W. Raymond* Amenhotep III and Amarna: some new considerations. Sum. 65. JEA 82 (1996) 65-82.
10431 *Rainey, A.F.* CAT "Tails". UF 28 (1996) 513-526.
10432 **Rainey, Anson F.** Canaanite in the Amarna tablets: a linguistic analysis of the mixed dialect used by the scribes from Canaan. HO, 1 Abt.: der Nahe und Mittlere Osten 25: Lei 1996, Brill 4 vols. $371. 90-04-10503-4 [OLZ 92,358].
10433 *Shaw, Ian* Akhetaten (Tell el-Amarna). Royal cities. 1996, ⇒248. 83-112.

т7.4 **Memphis,** *Saqqara*—**Pyramides,** *Giza* (Cairo)

10434 *Cook, R.J.* A note on the geometry of the star-shafts in the pyramid of Khufu. DiscEg 36 (1996) 21-23.
10435 **Cook, Robin** The horizon of Khufu: the pyramids of Giza and the geometry of heaven. L 1996, Seven Islands 206 pp. Num. ill. 0-951-85762-2 [DiscEg 37,119ss—Legon, John A.R.].
10436 *Formicone, Luigi* Das Gerät für die Konstruktion der Pyramide. GöMisz 153 (1996) 33-43.
10437 **Giddy, Lisa L.** The Anubieion at Saqqara II: the cemeteries. 1992, ⇒9,1405... 11/2,b606. ᴿBiOr 53 (1996) 427-430 *(Kessler, Dieter)*; JNES 55 (1996) 226-228 *(Patch, Diana Craig)*.
10438 **Hart, George** Pharaohs and pyramids: a guide through Old Kingdom Egypt. 1991, ⇒8,g147. ᴿJNES 55 (1996) 66-68 *(Roth, Ann Macy)*.
10439 **Hodges, Peter** How the pyramids were built. Modern Egyptology: Warminster 1993, Aris & P. xiv; 154 pp. £15. 0-85668-600-X. ᴿBiOr 53 (1996) 430-433 *(Legon, John A.R.)*.
10440 *Hönig, Werner* Cheopspyramide: der Sonnenweg an 12 Stunden des Tages. DiscEg 36 (1996) 45-47.
10441 **Kanawati, Naguib; Hassan, A.** The Teti cemetery at Saqqara, 1. Reports 8: Sydney 1996, Australian Centre for Egyptology 77 pp. 1-86408-259-3.
10442 **Labrousse, Audran** Mission archéologique de Saqqara III: l'architecture des pyramides à textes: I-Saqqara Nord. Bibliothèque d'Étude 114: Cairo 1996, Institut Français 2 vols. 132 fig. 25 pl. 0259-3823.

10443 *Labrousse, Audran* The pyramids of Pepi I and his queens at Saqqara. EgArch 8 (1996) 3-6.
10444 ᴱ**Lambert, Phyllis** Fortifications and the synagogue: the fortress of Babylon and the Ben Ezra synagogue, Cairo. 1994, ⇒11/2,b630. ᴿBArR 22/3 (1996) 6, 8 *(Khan, Geoffrey)*.
10445 *Martin, Geoffrey T.* Preliminary report on the Saqqara excavations, 1995. OMRM 76 (1996) 35-39.
10446 *O'Mara, Patrick F.* Can the Gizeh pyramids be dated astronomically?: logical foundations for an Old Kingdom astronomical chronology II, III. DiscEg 34, 35 (1996) 65-82, 97-112.
10447 **Raven, Maarten J.** The tomb of Iurudef a Memphite official in the reign of Ramesses II. 1991, ⇒7,d913... 10,12754. ᴿBiOr 53 (1996) 324-363 *(Niwiński, Andrzej)*; CÉg 71 (1996) 278-279 *(Meulenaere, Herman de)*.
10448 ᴱ**Schmitz, Bettina** Untersuchungen zu Idu II: Giza: ein interdisziplinäres Projekt. HÄB 38: Hildesheim 1996, Gerstenberg x; 86 pp. 30 tables. 3-8067-8135-4 [BiOr 55,409—Bolshakov, Andrey O.].
10449 **Verner, Miroslav** The Pyramid complex of Khentkaus. Excavations of the Czech Institute of Egyptology, Abusir III. Praha 1995, Univ. Carolina Pragensis 184 pp. 32 pl. 80-7066-909-8. ᴿDiscEg 36 (1996) 123-128 *(Malek, Jaromir)*.
10450 *Wier, Stuart Kirkland* Insight from geometry and physics into the construction of Egyptian Old Kingdom pyramids. CamArch 6 (1996) 150-163.

T7.5 **Delta Nili**

10451 **Fernández Sangrador, Jorge Juan** Los orígenes de la comunidad cristiana de Alejandría. 1994, ⇒10,12777; 11/2,b644. ᴿScrTh 28 (1996) 253-258 *(Chapa, J.)*.
10452 **Kolataj, Wojciech** Imperial baths at Kom el-Dikka = Laznie Cesarskie na Kom el-Dikka. 1992, ⇒11/2,b640. ᴿBiOr 53 (1996) 733-735 *(Nielsen, Inge)*.
10453 **Pensabene, Patrizio** Elementi architettonici di Alessandria e di altri siti egiziani. 1993, ⇒11/2,b642. ᴿSyria 73 (1996) 220-222 *(Dentzer-Feydy, Jacqueline)*.

T7.6 *Alii situs Ægypti* **alphabetice**

10454 *Alexandria*: *Empereur, Jean-Yves* Alexandria: the underwater site near Qaitbay Fort. EgArch 8 (1996) 7-10.
10455 *Berenike*: ᴱ*Sidebotham, Steven E.; Wendrich, Willemina Z.* Berenike 1995: preliminary report of the 1995 excavations at Berenike (Egyptian Red Sea Coast) and the survey of the Eastern Desert. CNWS publications, special ser. 2: Lei 1996, CNWS 483 pp. 90-73782-70-8.
10456 *Dair Abu Fana*: *Buschhausen, Helmut,(al)*, Die Ausgrabungen von Dair Abu Fana in Ägypten in den Jahren 1991, 1992 und 1993. Ä&L 6 (1996) 13-73.
10457 *Douch*: **Bousquet, Bernard** Tell-Douch et sa région: géographie d'une limite de milieu à une frontière d'empire. Collab. *Robin,*

Marc, DFIFAO 31: Le Caire 1996, Institut Français d'Archéologie Orientale du Caire 368 pp. 2-7247-0180-1.

10458 *El-Ashmunein*: **Spencer, A.J.** Excavations at El-Ashmunein, 2: the temple area. 1989, ⇒5,e445. ᴿBiOr 53 (1996) 425-426 *(Lacovara, Peter).*

10459 *El-Balamun*: **Spencer, A.J.** Excavations at Tell el-Balamun 1991-1994. L 1996, British Museum 100 pp. 100 pl. £50 [ArOr 66, 173—Smoláriková, Květa].

10460 *El-Dabᶜa*: **Bietak, M.** Avaris: the capital of the Hyksos. L 1996, British Museum Press ix; 98 pp. Recent excavations at Tell el-Dabᶜa; the first Sackler Foundation Distinguished Lecture in Egyptology; 62 ill. 34 charts. £15. 0-7141-0968-1 [OLZ 92,479].

10461 *El-Faraᶜin/Buto*: **Faltings, Dina; Köhler, Christiana E.** Vorbericht über die Ausgrabungen des DAI in Tell el-Faraᶜin/Buto 1993 bis 1995. MDAI.K 52 (1996) 87-114.

10462 *El-Hagarsa*: **Kanawati, Naguib** The tombs of El-Hagarsa. 1993, ⇒10,12802; 11/2,b685. ᴿJEA 82 (1996) 216-218 *(Strudwick, Nigel).*

10463 *Elephantine*: **Gempeler, Robert D.** Elephantine X: die Keramik römischer bis frühsrabischer Zeit. 1992, ⇒9,14442; 11/2,b665. ᴿBiOr 53 (1996) 705-710 *(Köhler, E. Christiana).*

10464 *Hebwa* **Aston, David A.** Tell Hebwa IV: preliminary report on the pottery. Ä&L 6 (1996) 179-197.

10465 *Heliopolis*: *Shaker, Mohammed; Raue, Dietrich; Abd el-Gelil, Mohammed* Recent excavations at Heliopolis. Or. 65 (1996) 136-146.

10466 *Hierakonpolis/Nekhen*:   **Adams,   Barbara**   Ancient   Nekhen: GARSTANG in the city of Hierakonpolis. Egyptian Studies Association Publication no. 3: New Malden, UK 1995, SIA. ᴿDiscEg 36 (1996) 129-131 *(Midant-Reynes, B.).*

10467 *Pelusium*: **Jaritz, Horst,**(al)**,** Pelusium: prospection archéologique et topographique de la région de Kanaʾis, 1993 et 1994. BÁBFA 13: Stu 1996, Steiner 222 pp. 61 pl. 4 fig. 10 plans. DM136. 3-515-06804-X [AJA 101,819].

10468 *Tanis*: *Brissaud, Philippe* Tanis (Tell San el-Hagar). Royal cities. 1996, ⇒248. 113-152.

ᴛ7.7 *Antiquitates Nubiae et alibi;* **Egypt outside Egypt**

10469 *Llagostera, Esteban* La momia de una hija del faraon Ramses II en Madrid. BAEO 32 (1996) 325-345.

10470 **O'Connor, David B.** Ancient Nubia. 1993, ⇒10,12839. ᴿOLZ 91 (1996) 551-555 *(Zach, Michael H.)*; AJA 100 (1996) 783-784 *(Smith, Stuart T.).*

10471 **Otto, Karl-Heinz; Buschendorf-Otto, Gisela** Felsbilder aus dem sudanesischen Nubien. 1993, ⇒11/2,b718. ᴿBiOr 53 (1996) 450-452 *(Huyge, Dirk).*

10472 **Säve-Söderbergh, Torgny; Troy, Lana** New Kingdom pharaonic sites: the finds and the sites. 1991, ⇒7,d972... 9,14505. ᴿJNES 55 (1996) 147-149 *(Williams, Bruce)*; CÉg 71 (1996) 284-285 *(Meulenaere, Herman de).*

10473 **Shinnie, Peter L.** Ancient Nubia. L 1996, Kegan Paul xviii; 145 pp. ill. pl. £45/$76.50. 0-7103-0517-6.

10474 **Welsby, Derek A.** The kingdom of Kush, the Napatan and Meroitic empires. L 1996, British Museum Press 240 pp. 81 fig. 12 col. pl. £25 [JNES 58,309s—Williams, Bruce].

10475 *Hamra Dom (El-Qasr wa es-Saiyad)*: **Säve-Söderbergh, Torgny** The Old Kingdom cemetery at Hamra Dom (El-Qasr wa es-Saiyad). 1994, ⇒10,12831. RBiOr 53 (1996) 418-420 *(Müller-Wollermann, Renate)*; JEA 82 (1996) 219-221 *(Strudwick, Nigel)*.

10476 *Serra*: **Williams, Bruce B.** Excavations at Serra East 1-5. 1993, ⇒10,12844. RBiOr 53 (1996) 452-456 *(Bietak, Manfred)*.

10477 *Taffeh*: *Raven, Maarten J.* The temple of Taffeh: a study of details. OMRM 76 (1996) 41-62.

т8.1 Anatolia *generalia*

10478 *Bayram, Sebahattin; Çeçen, Salih* The institution of slavery in ancient Anatolia in the light of new documents [=Yeni Belgelerin Işlǧlnda Eski Anadolu'da Kölelik Müessesesi, 579-604] BTTK 60 (1996) 605-630.

10479 *Hopkins, Liza* The rise of social complexity in East Central Anatolia in the early Bronze Age. Cultural interaction. Abr-n.S 5: 1996, ⇒285. 17-26.

10480 **Ivantchik, Askold I.** Les cimmériens au Proche-Orient. OBO 127: 1993, ⇒10,12862. ROr. 65 (1996) 46-49 *(Zawadzki, Stefan)*.

10481 **Joukowsky, Martha Sharp** Early Turkey: Anatolian archaeology from prehistory through the Lydian period. Dubuque 1996, Kendall/Hunt 493 pp. 350 fig.; 28 plans; 17 maps; 6 tables. 0-7872-2141-4 [AJA 101,633].

10482 Lykien. FBORCHARDT J., I, 1996, ⇒8. 19-258 [auct. var.].

10483 EMikasa, Takahito Essays on Anatolian archaeology. 1993, ⇒9,358. RJAOS 116 (1996) 778-780 *(Gorny, Ronald L.)*.

10484 *Sever, Hüseyin* Die Urformen der Börse und Inflation in Anatolien und ein Gestein, dessen Ausfuhr in der Zeit der Kolonie aus Anatolien verboten ist (1970-1750 v.Chr.). BTTK 60 (1996) 237-242.

т8.2 Boğazköy—*Hethaei*, the Hittites

10485 **Neve, Peter** Ḫattuša. 1993, ⇒10,12886; 11/2,b774. ROLZ 91 (1996) 582-583 *(Börker-Klähn, Jutta)*.

10486 *Yakar, Jak* Hattuša-Boğazköy: aspects of Hittite architecture. Royal cities. 1996, ⇒248. 53-68.

т8.3 Ephesus; Pergamum

10487 *Carile, Antonio* Efeso bizantina: struttura ed evoluzione di una città dell'Anatolia bizantina. VI Simposio di Efeso. 1996, ⇒264. 293-310.

Smith, J. The high priests of the temple of Artemis at Ephesus. MVermaseren, M.J., ⇒8911.

10488 **Hübner, Gerhild** Die Applikenkeramik von Pergamon. 1993, ⇒10,12903. ᴿBiOr 53 (1996) 246-249 *(Yntema, Douwe)*; Gn. 68 (1996) 356-361 *(Rotroff, Susan I.)*.

т8.6 *Situs Anatoliae*—Turkey sites; Urartu

10489 *Gil Fuensanta, Jesús,* (al), Trabajos de la misión arqueológica española en Turquía (I): una exploración y prospección en los márgenes del Eufrates en las provincias de Antep y Urfa. BAEO 32 (1996) 7-22.

10490 *Apameia*: Balty, Janine; Balty, Jean-Charles Spaziergang in den Ruinen Apameias. WUB 1 (1996) 46-51.
10491 *Pamukkale*: **Kekeç, Tevhit** Pamukkale: "Hierapolis". Istanbul 1996, Hitit Color 80 pp. 975-7487-23-6.
10492 *Sardis; Idalion; el-Handaquq*: ᴱ**Dever, William G.** Preliminary excavations reports: Sardis, Idalion, and Tell el-Handaquq North. AASOR 53: Atlanta 1996, Scholars 154 pp. fig. $85. 0-7885-0315-4.
10493 *Side*:**Nollé, Johannes** Side im Altertum: Geschichte und Zeugnisse, 1: Geographie—Geschichte—Testimonia—griechische und lateinische Inschriften (1-4). 1993, ⇒11/2,b862. ᴿGn. 68 (1996) 697-701 *(Brixhe, Glaude)*.

10494 **Wartke, Ralf-Bernhard** Urartu. 1993, ⇒9,14641; 11/2,b899. ᴿBiOr 53 (1996) 211-216 *(Van Loon, Maurits N.)*.

т9.1 Cyprus

10495 ᴱ**Åström, Paul** Acta Cypria. 1991-2. ⇒9,552d. ᴿSyria 73 (1996) 209-210 *(Cook, Valérie)*.
10496 ᴱ**Åström, Paul; Herscher, Ellen** Late Bronze Age settlement in Cyprus: function and relationship. SIMA-PB 126: Jonsered 1996, Åström 80 pp. 12 fig., 5 maps. SEK100. 91-7081-120-2 [AJA 101,631].
10497 *Frankel, David; Webb, Jennifer M.; Eslick, Christine* Anatolia and Cyprus in the third millennium B.C.E.: a speculative model of interaction. Cultural interaction. Abr-n.S 5: 1996, ⇒285. 37-50.
10498 **Karageorghis, Vassos** The coroplastic art of ancient Cyprus, 6: the Cypro-archaic period: monsters, animals and miscellanea. Nicosia 1996, Leventis xii; 111 pp. 50 pl.; 75 fig.; map. 9963-560-27-X [Levant 29,258].
10499 ᴱ**Karageorghis, Vassos; Michaelides, Demetrios** The development of the Cypriot economy from the prehistoric period to the present day. Nicosia 1996, University of Cyprus viii; 260 pp. charts; tables; Greek summaries. 9963-607-10-1 [Levant 29,258].
10500 ᴱ**Knapp, A.B.** Sources for the history of Cyprus, 2: Near Eastern and Aegean texts from the third to the first millennia BC. Altamont, NY 1996 Greece and Cyprus Research Center ix; 92 pp. $30. 0-9651704-0-3 [Levant 29,259].

10501 *Mayer, Walter* Zypern und Ägäis aus der Sicht der Staaten Vorderasiens in der 1. Hälfte des 1. Jahrtausends. UF 28 (1996) 463-484.
10502 **Reyes, A.T.** Archaic Cyprus: a study of the textual and archaeological evidence. 1994, ⇒10,12999. ^RJAOS 116 (1996) 261-262 *(Fortin, Michel).*
10503 ^E**Yon, Marguerite** Kinyras: l'archéologie française à Chipre. 1993, ⇒10,494; 11/2,b911. ^RBiOr 53 (1996) 828-830 *(Hekman, Jan Jaap).*

10504 *Amathonte: Petit, T.* Religion et royauté à Amathonte de Chypre. TEuph 12 (1996) 97-120.
10505 *Marki Alonia:* **Frankel, David; Webb, Jennifer M.** Marki Alonia, an Early and Middle Bronze Age town in Cyprus: excavations 1990-1994. SIMA 123.1: Jonsered 1996, Åström 359 pp. 35 pl.; 105 fig.; 21 plans; 15 maps; 93 tables. 91-7081-170-9 [AJA 101,632].
10506 *Palaipaphos:* ^E**Sørensen, Lone Wriedt; Rupp, David W.** The land of the Paphian Aphrodite, 2: the Canadian Palaipaphos survey project: artifact and ecofactual studies. 1993, ⇒9,14674. ^RBiOr 53 (1996) 235-238 *(Baxevani, Evi).*

T9.3 *Graecia,* Greece—mainland

10507 **Biers, William R.** The archaeology of Greece: an introduction. Ithaca, NY ²1996, Cornell Univ. Press 350 pp. 0-8014-3173-5.
10508 *Blackman, David J.* Archaeology in Greece 1996-97. ArRep 43 (1996) 1-125;
10509 Archaeology in Greece 1997-1998. Collab. *Baker, Julian; Hardwick, Nicholas.* Numismatic appendix 129-136. ArRep 44 (1996) 1-128.
10510 **Engels, Donald** Roman Corinth. 1990, ⇒7,e164... 9,14707. ^RGn. 68 (1996) 523-530 *(Quaß, Friedemann).*
10511 **Shanks, Michael** Classical archaeology of Greece: experiences of the discipline. L 1996, Routledge 212 pp. 42 fig. $50. 0-415-08521-7. ^RAntiquity 70 (1996) 712-714 *(Whitley, James).*
10512 *Tomlinson, R.A.* Archaeology in Greece 1995-96. ArRep 42 (1996) 1-47.

T9.4 Creta

^E**Everly, D.** Minotaur. ^FPOPHAM M., 1996, ⇒72.
10513 **Rackham, Oliver; Moody, Jennifer** The making of the Cretan landscape. Manchester 1996, Manchester Univ. Press 237 pp. 4 col. pl.; 37 fig.; 35 maps. £20. 0-7190-3647-X [AJA 101,820].
10514 **Rutkowski, Bogdan; Nowicki, Krzysztof** The Psychro Cave and other sacred grottoes in Crete. Studies and Monographs in Mediterranean Archaeology and Civilization 2.1: Wsz 1996, Art and Archaeology 83 pp. 6 fig.; 20 plans. 1233-6246 [AJA 101,432].

T9.5 Insulae graecae

10515   *Bacchielli, Lidiano* Kyrene, das Athen Afrikas. WUB 2 (1996) 46-51.

10516   **Brun, Patrice** Les archipels égéens dans l'antiquité grecque: Ve-IIe siècles de notre ère. Institut de recherches d'histoire ancienne 157: P 1996, Annales littéraires de l'Université de Franche-Comté 255 pp. 9 col. pl.; 5 maps. 2-251-60616-5 [AJA 101,818].

10517   **Dickinson, O.T.P.K.** The Aegean Bronze Age. 1994, ⇒11/2,a923. RJHS 116 (1996) 211-212 *(Rutter, Jeremy)*.

10518   EKardulias, P. Nick Beyond the site: regional studies in the Aegean area. 1994, ⇒10,13129. RAJA 100 (1996) 178-179 *(Wagstaff, Malcolm)*.

10519   *Kuniholm, Peter Ian* The prehistoric Aegean: dedrochronological progress as of 1995. AcAr 67/1 (1996) 327-335.

10520   ELaffineur, Robert; Niemeier, Wolf-Dietrich Politeira: society and state in the Aegean Bronze Age. Aegeum 12: Liège 1995, Univ. de Liège 2 vols. Proceedings of the 5th International Aegean Conference, Heidelberg 1994. FB5.500/$180. RAJA 100 (1996) 612-614 *(Rutter, Jeremy B.)*.

10521   **Lemos, Anna A.** Archaic pottery of Chios: the decorated styles. 1991, ⇒8,g578; 11/2,b992. RGn. 68 (1996) 145-149 *(Möller, Astrid)*.

10522   *Manning, Stuart W.* Dating the Aegean Bronze Age: without, with, and beyond, radiocarbon. AcAr 67/1 (1996) 15-37.

10523   **Manning, Stuart W.** The absolute chronology of the Aegean Early Bronze Age. 1995, ⇒11/2,a768. RAJA 100 (1996) 784-785 *(Kuniholm, Peter Ian)*; Antiquity 70 (1996) 232-234 *(Whitelaw, Todd)*.

10524   **Sakellarakis, Yannis** Digging for the past. Athens 1996, Ammos 253 pp. 358 col. figs. $149.50. 960-202-144-6 [AJA 102,430—Shanks, Michael].

10525   *Warren, Peter* The Aegean and the limits of radiocarbon dating. AcAr 67/1 (1996) 283-290.

T9.6 Urbs Roma

10526   **Caerols Pérez, J.J.** Sacra vía: (I. a.c.-I d.C.): estudio de las fuentes escritas. M 1995, Clásicas xii; 283 pp. 2 maps. RCIR 46 (1996) 135-137 *(Smith, Christopher)*.

10527   **Castriota, David** The ara pacis augustae and the imagery of abundance in later Greek and early Roman imperial art. 1995, ⇒11/2,c011. RAJA 100 (1996) 799-800 *(Galinsky, Karl)*.

10528   **Darwall-Smith, Robin Haydon** Emperors and architecture: a study of Flavian Rome. CollLat 231: Bruxelles 1996, Latomus 339 pp. 69 pl.; Bibl. BF2.200. 2-87031-171-0.

10529   **Favro, Diane** The urban image of Augustan Rome. New York 1996, CUP 362 pp. 80 fig.; 21 plans; 13 maps; 6 tables. $80. 0-521-45083-7 [AJA 101,632].

10530   **Richardson, Lawrence** A new topographical dictionary of ancient Rome. 1992, ⇒9,14801...11/2,c029. RGn. 68 (1996) 53-56 *(Ziolkowski, Adam)*.

10531 ᴱ**Steinby, Eva Margareta** Lexicon topographicum urbis Romae: I (A-C); II (D-G). 1993-1995, ⇒9,14803; 11/2,c032. ᴿAnCl 65 (1996) 572-573 *(Raepsaet-Charlier, Marie-Thérèse)*;

10532 II (D-G). ⇒11/2,c032. AnCl 65 (1996) 354-356 *(Edwards, Catharine)*;

10533 III (H-O). Roma 1996, Quasar 503 pp. 221 fig. L240.000 [AnCl 67,552—Raepsaet-Charlier, Marie-Thérèse].

T9.7 Catacumbae; Pompei

10534 Giovanni Battista de Rossi e le catacombe romane: mostra fotografica; catalogo mostra. Città del Vaticano 1994, 183 pp. Auct. var.; 125 fig. ᴿRivAC 72 (1996) 448-451 *(Ramieri, Anna Maria)*.

10535 *Giuliani, Raffaella* Il restauro del cubicolo detto "delle stagioni" nella catacomba dei SS. Marcellino e Pietro sulla Via Labicana. RivAC 72 (1996) 35-64.

10536 *Griesheimer, Marc* Nouvelles inscriptions funéraires de la catacombe Saint-Jean. RivAC 72 (1996) 115-132.

10537 *Sgarlata, Mariarita* Le stagioni della rotonda di Adelfia (Indagini 1988 e 1993 nella catacomba di S. Giovanni a Siracusa). RivAC 72 (1996) 75-113.

10538 *Tomasello, Francesco* La rotonda di Antiochia a Siracusa: una nuova lettura. RivAC 72 (1996) 133-163.

10539 **Köhler, Jens** Pompai: Untersuchungen zur hellenistischen Festkultur. EHS.A 61: Fra 1996, Lang 195 pp. DM53. 3-631-30293-2 [Mes. 33,402ss—Conti, M.C.].

10540 **Laurence, Ray** Roman Pompeii: space and society. 1994, ⇒10,13199; 11/2,c051. ᴿAJA 100 (1996) 430 *(Small, David B.)*; ClR 46 (1996) 140-141 *(Davies, Alison)*.

XIX. Geographia biblica

U1.0 Geographica

10541 *Feldman, Louis H.* Some observations on the name of Palestine. Studies in Hellenistic Judaism. AGJU 30: 1996 <1990>, ⇒124. 553-576.

10542 *Finkelstein, Israel* The Philistine countryside. IEJ 46 (1996) 225-242.

10543 *Gitay, Yehoshua* Geography and theology in the biblical narrative: the question of Genesis 2-12. ᶠTUCKER G., JSOT.S 229: 1996, ⇒95. 205-216.

10544 **Karmon, Yehuda** Israel: eine geographische Landeskunde. Wissenschaftliche Länderkunden 22: Da:Wiss ²1994 <1983>, 300 pp. ᴿThR 61 (1996) 348-349 *(Perlitt, Lothar)*.

10545 **Patton, Mark** Islands in time: island sociogeography amd Mediterranean prehistory. L 1996, Routledge 223 pp. 16 plans; 15 maps; 19 tables. $70. 0-415-12659-2 [AJA 101,432].

10546   **Schyle, D.; Uerpmann, H.-P.** Das Epipaläolithikum des Vorderen Orients. BTAVO 85 1-2: Wsb 1996, Harrassowitz xii; 392; vi; 366 pp. DM252 [ZAW 110,478—Zwickel, W.].

u1.2 Historia geographiae

10547   *Burger, J.* Historical geography and textual interpretation: an idealistic approach. OTEs 9 (1996) 191-203.
10548   *Dearman, J. Andrew* The 'border' area between Ammon, Moab and Israel in the Iron Age. OTEs 9 (1996) 204-212.
10549   *Domeris, William R.* The interface between historical geography and archaeology. OTEs 9 (1996) 213-223.
10550   *Olivier, Hannes* Putting the Holy Land on the map;
10551   Spatial awareness: an essential element of historical understanding in Old Testament studies. OTEs 9 (1996) 237-248/249-260.
10552   *Otto, Eckart* Stadt und Land im spätbronzezeitlichen und früheisenzeitlichen Palästina: zur Methodik der Korrelierung von Geographie und antiker Religionsgeschichte. Kontinuum. 1996 <1989>, ⇒2002. 16-29.
10553   *Scheffler, Eben* The interface between historical geography and the holistic history of Ancient Israel. OTEs 9 (1996) 294-307.
10554   *Wittenberg, G.H.* The relevance of historical geography for Old Testament theology with special reference to Exodus 34:10-26. OTEs 9 (1996) 334-346.

u1.4 Atlas—maps; *photographiae*; Guide-books, *Führer*

10555   Atlante di archeologia. T 1996, UTET 569 pp. L270.000. 88-02-05021-X [StPat 45,230—Abbà, Maurizio].
10556   **Avi-Yonah, Michael** Eretz-Israel in the Madaba Map. [E]*Barkay, G.; Schiller, E.*, Ariel 116: J [2]1996, Ariel 127 pp. 13 col. pl.; ill.; photos. NIS38 [IEJ 48,298—Katzenstein, Hannah].
10557   **Donner, Herbert** The mosaic map of Madaba. 1992, ⇒8,g712... 11/2,c103. [R]DSD 3 (1996) 212-214 (*Alexander, Philip S.*).
10558   **Gazit, Dan** Archaeological survey of Israel: map of Urim (125). J 1996, Israel Antiquities Authority 83*; 140 pp. 965-406-023-X.
10559   [E]**Keel, Othmar; Küchler, Max** Herders großer Bibelatlas. FrB [3]1996, Herder 255 pp. DM49.80. 3-451-26138-3 [NTS 43,621].
10560   **Manley, Bill** The Penguin historical atlas of ancient Egypt. L 1996, Penguin 144 pp. 0-14-0-51331-0.
10561   *Piccirillo, Michele* La carta musiva di Madaba. TS(I) 72 (nov.-dic. 1996) 20-23.
10562   **Rova, Elena** Atlante storico del vicino oriente antico, 3: Alta Mesopotamia, 1: la preistoria fino al 2000. R 1996, Università La Sapienza 60 pp.
10563   *Stepansky, Yosef* Map of Rosh Pinna, survey—1993. ESI 15 (1996) 14-17.
10564   **Thrower, N.J.W.** Maps & civilization: cartography in culture and society. Ch 1996, Univ. of Chicago Press 326 pp. 0-226-79972-7 [[NeoTest. 32,413].

10565 *Chapman, Rupert L. III; Gibson, Shimon* A note on T.E. LAWRENCE as photographer in the wilderness of Zin. PEQ 128 (1996) 94-102.

10566 **Murphy-O'Connor, Jerome** La Terra Santa: guida storico-archeologica. Bo 1996, Dehoniane 498 pp. L42.000. 89-20583-9 [BeO 39,63].

10567 **Robertson, O. Palmer** Understanding the land of the bible: a biblical-theological guide. Phillipsburg, NJ 1996, P&R x; 158 pp. 0-87552-399-4 [NThAR 1997,257].

U1.7 Onomastica

10568 **Frayne, D.R.** The early dynastic list of geographical names. 1992, ⇒8,g789...11/2,c153. [R]BiOr 53 (1996) 110-113 *(Kessler, K.)*.

10569 **George, A.R.** Babylonian topographical texts. OLA 40: 1992, ⇒8,g790... 11/2,c154. [R]JNES 55 (1996) 61-63 *(Biggs, Robert D.)*; OLZ 91 (1996) 415-417 *(Groneberg, Brigitte)*.

10570 **Liverani, Mario** Studies on the annals of Ashurnasirpal II,2: topographical analysis. 1992, ⇒8,g796.... 11/2,c158. [R]BiOr 53 (1996) 125-127 *(Zimansky, Paul)*.

10571 *Sapin, J.* Symbiose ethno-linguistique: considérations géographiques et historiques sur la toponymie de la Trouèe de Homs. TEuph 12 (1996) 13-39.

10572 **Thompson, Th.L.; Goncalves, F.J.; Van Cangh, J.M.** Toponomie palestinienne; plaine de St-Jean d'Arc et Corridor de Jérusalem. PIOL 37: 1988, ⇒4,g963... 7,e389. [R]BiOr 53 (1996) 512-514 *(Blok, Hanna)*.

U2.1 Geologia: soils, mountains, volcanoes, earthquakes

10573 **Ambraseys, N.N.; Mellville, C.P.; Adams, R.D.** The seismicity of Egypt, Arabia and the Red Sea: a historical review. C 1994, CUP xix; 181 pp. 68 maps, 9 pl. £60. [R]JRAS 6 (1996) 231-233 *(Smith, Rex)*.

10574 *Amiran, D.* Earthquakes in Eretz-Israel. Qad. 29 (1996) 53-61. **H.**

10575 Location index for earthquakes in Israel since 100 B.C.E. IEJ 46 (1996) 120-130.

10576 *Bachmann, Hans-Gert* Geology;

10577 *Bachmann, Hans-Gert; Brown, Thomas E.; Chase, W.T.* Mineralogy. Nemrud Daǧi. 1996, ⇒10379. 5-12/12-15.

10578 [E]**Niemi, Tina M.; Ben-Avraham, Zvi; Gat, Joel R.** The Dead Sea: the lake and its setting. Oxf 1996, OUP ix; 286 pp. 2 pl. 188 fig. 39 tables. $75. 0-19-508703-8 [AJA 103,584s—Donahue, J.].

10579 [E]**Stiros, S.; Jones, R.E.** Archaeoseismology. Fitch Laboratory Occasional Paper 7: Athens 1996, British School at Athens 268 pp. 115 fig. 19 plans, 27 maps. £35. 0-904887-26-X [AJA 101,821].

υ2.2 *Hydrographia;* rivers, seas, salt; *Clima*

10580 **Crouch, Dora P.** Water management in ancient Greek cities. 1993, ⇒9,14961... 11/2,c186. ᴿGn. 68 (1996) 280-282 *(Garbrecht, Günther).*

10581 **Marín Heredia, Francisco** Torrente: temas bíblicos. 1994, ⇒10,13324. ᴿTer. 47 (1996) 332-333 *(Borrell, Agustí).*

10582 **McCann, Anna Marguerite; Freed, Joann** Deep water archaeology: a late-Roman ship from Carthage and an ancient trade route. Journal of Roman Archaeology, Suppl. 13: AA 1994, Journal of Roman Archaeology xviii; 145 pp. $64.50. 1-887829-13-X. ᴿAJA 100 (1996) 438-439 *(Sherwood, Andrew N.).*

10583 **Meshel, Zeev; Tsuk, Tvvika; Fahlbusch, Henning; Peleg, Yehuda** The water-supply system of Susita. TA 1996, Institute of Archaeology 131 pp. [BAR 24/3,60—Meyers, Eric].

10584 *Pace, James H.* The cisterns of the Al-Karak plateau. ADAJ 40 (1996) 369-374.

10585 *Pienaar, D.N.* The impact of exposure to the land of the Bible. OTEs 9 (1996) 261-272.

10586 *Porath, Yosef* המנהרה של אמת המים הגבוהה לקיסריה ברכס הכורכר [ג'סר א־זרקא] [The tunnel of Caesarea Maritima's high level aqueduct at the Kurkar Ridge (Jisr ez-Zarqa)]. Sum. 126. ʿAtiqot 30 (1996) 23*-43*.

10587 *Rogerson, John; Davies, Philip R.* Was the Siloam tunnel built by Hezekiah?. BA 59 (1996) 138-149.

10588 **Said, Rushdi** The river Nile. 1993, ⇒11/2,c201. ᴿBiOr 53 (1996) 41-43 *(De Putter, Thierry).*

10589 *Stepansky, Yosef* תעלות חצובות בקרבת תל חצור: אמת המים הקדומה ביותר בארץ ישראל? [Rock-hewn channels near Tel Hazor: the earliest water conduit in Eretz Israel?]. Sum. 195. ʿAtiqot 28 (1996) 1*-7*.

10590 ᴱ**Bar-Yosef, Ofer; Kra, Renee S.** Late quaternary chronology and paleoclimates of the eastern Mediterranean. 1994, ⇒11/2,c207. ᴿAJA 100 (1996) 417-418 *(Perlès, Catherine).*

υ2.5 *Fauna,* animalia

10591 *Adler, Wolfgang* Die spätbronzezeitlichen Pyxiden in Gestalt von Wasservögeln. Kamid el-Loz 15. 1996, ⇒9633. 27-117.

10592 *Bakon, Shimon* Not to inflict hurt on animals. JBQ 24 (1996) 149-155.

10593 *Burney, Charles* "The highland sheep are sweeter...". Cultural interaction. Abr-n.S 5: 1996, ⇒285. 1-15.

10594 *Hesse, Brian; Wapnish, Paula* Pig's feet, cattle bones and bird's wings. BArR 22/1 (1996) 62.

10595 *Hongo, H.* Faunal remains from Tell Aray 2, Northwestern Syria. Sum. rés. 125. Paléorient 22/1 (1996) 125-144.

10596 *Horwitz, Liora Kolska* Faunal remains from areas A, B, D, H and K. City of David excavations. Qedem 35: 1996, ⇒10018. 302-317.

10597 *Horwitz, Liora Kolska; Tchernov, Eitan* Bird remains from areas A, D, H and K. City of David excavations. Qedem 35: 1996, ⇒10018. 298-301.

10598 **Houlihan, Patrick F.** The animal world of the pharaohs. NY 1996, Thames & H. xv; 245 pp. 153 fig. $40 [JAOS 119,170— Robins, Gay].

10599 **Kessler, Dieter** Die heiligen Tiere und der König I. 1989, ⇒5,e989...9,15016. RBiOr 53 (1996) 60-62 *(Meulenaere, H.J.A. de)*; CÉg 71 (1996) 79-81 *(Van Rinsveld, Bernard)*.

10600 *Luke, K.* The animal world in the light of the bible. BiBh 22 (1996) 62-80.

10601 **Panayides, Aliki** Vom Affe bis Zebu: Tierdarstellungen und Tierverständnis im Hellenismus. Diss. Bern 1996 [AA (1997/1) 104].

10602 *Strommenger, E.; Bollweg, J.* Onager und Esel im alten Zentralvorderasien. FSPYCKET A., 1996, ⇒83. 349-366.

10603 *Tchernov, E.* Appendix B: the faunal world of the city of David as represented by the figurines. City of David excavations. Qedem 35: 1996, ⇒10018. 85-86.

10604 *Uval, Beth* The earth is full of your creations (Ps. 104:24). JBQ 24 (1996) 251-254.

10605 *Zeder, Melinda A.* The role of pigs in Near Eastern subsistence: a view from the southern Levant. Retrieving the past. FVAN BEEK G., 1996, ⇒96. 297-312.

U2.6 *Flora;* plantae biblicae et antiquae

10606 *Bisset, Norman G.*, *(al)*, Was opium known in 18th dynasty ancient Egypt?: an examination of materials from the tomb of the chief royal architect Kha. Ä&L 6 (1996) 199-201.

10607 *Bisset, Norman G.; Bruhn, Jan G.; Zenk, Meinhart H.* The presence of opium in a 3.500 year old Cypriote base-ring juglet. Ä&L 6 (1996) 203-204.

10608 **Brewer, Douglas J.; Redford, B. Donald** Domestic plants and animals: the Egyptian origins. 1994, ⇒11/2,c295. ROr. 65 (1996) 451-453 *(Germer, Renate)*.

10609 *Briend, Jacques* Das Öl und seine vielfältige Verwendung in den Königreichen Israel und Juda. WUB 2 (1996) 52-54.

10610 *Briend, Jacques; Quesnel, Michel* L'huile, aux multiples usages. MoBi 96 (1996) 50-52.

10611 *Quesnel, Michel* Das Öl in neutestamentlicher Zeit. WUB 2 (1996) 54.

10612 *Tyree, E. Loeta; Stefanoudaki, Evangelia* The olive pit and Roman oil making. BA 59 (1996) 171-178.

10613 **Walsh, Carey Ellen** The fruit of the vine: viticulture in ancient Israel and the Hebrew Bible. Diss. Harvard 1996, 287 pp. [EThL 74,242*].

10614 **Ylla-Català, Miquel** Les plantes en la bíblia: a la recerca de símbols. Els Daus Barc 1995, Claret 142 pp. Pròleg de *Raurell, F..* REstFr 97 (1996) 187-188 *(Llimona, Jordi)*.

u2.8 **Agricultura, alimentatio**

10615 **Bonacossi, Daniele Morandi** Tra il fiume e la steppa: inse-
diamento e uso del territorio nella bassa valle del fiume Habur in
epoca neo-assira I-II. HANE Monographs 1: Padova 1996, Sargon 2 vols. tables; maps; plans; figs. L90.000 [AJA 101,198].

10616 **Christensen, Peter** The decline of Iranshahr: irrigation and envi-
ronments in the history of the Middle East, 500 B.C. to A.D.
1500. Copenhagen 1993, Museum Tusculanum 352 pp. £47.50.
87-7289-295-5. ᴿJESHO 39 (1996) 432-433 *(Vogelsang, Willem)*.

10617 **Civil, Miguel** The farmer's instructions: a Sumerian agricultural
manual. 1994, ⇒10,13427; 11/2,c341. ᴿBiOr 53 (1996) 471-474
(Katz, Dina).

10618 ᴱ**Eitam, David; Heltzer, Michael** Olive oil in antiquity: Israel
and neighbouring countries from the neolithic to the early Arab
period. History of the Ancient Near East, Studies 7: Padova
1996, Sargon xxxiv; 315 pp. 39 pl.

10619 **Frankel, Rafael,** *(al)*, History and technology of olive oil in the
Holy Land. 1994, ⇒11/2,c351. ᴿAntiquity 70 (1996) 475-476
(Forbes, Hamish).

10620 *Geyer, B; Besançon, J.* Environnement et occupation du sol dans
la vallée de l'Euphrate syrien durant le Néolithique et le Chalcoli-
thique. Sum. rés. 5. ᴿPaléorient 22/2 (1996) 5-15.

10621 **Habbe, Joachim** Palästina zur Zeit Jesu: die Landwirtschaft in
Galiläa als Hintergrund der synoptischen Evangelien. Neuk.
Theol. Diss. und Habil. 6: Neuk 1996, Neuk x; 126 pp.
DM39.80. 3-7887-1579-0 [ZDPV 115,96ss—Zangenberg, Jür-
gen].

10622 *Hopkins, David C.* Life on the land: the subsistence struggles of
early Israel. Community. 1996 < 1987 >, ⇒172. 471-488.

10623 *Jouanna,. Jacques* Le vin et la médecine dans la Grèce ancienne.
Sum., rés. 410. REG 109 (1996) 410-434.

10624 *Litvinenko, Yu.N.* 'Colonial' agriculture in Ptolemaic Egypt.
Sum. 28. VDI 219 (1996) 17-28. **R**.

10625 *Liverani, Mario* Reconstructing the rural landscape of the ancient
Near East. Sum. 1. JESHO 39 (1996) 1-41.

10626 ᴱ**McGovern, Patrick E.; Fleming, Stuart J.; Katz, Solomon
H.** The origins and ancient history of wine. Langhorne, PA 1995,
Gordon & B. xxiii; 409 pp. $85 [JNES 58,298—Biggs, R.D.].

10627 ᴱ**Milano, Lucio** Drinking in ancient societies. 1994, ⇒10,480;
11/2,c379. ᴿZA 86 (1996) 285-287 *(Krebernik, M.)*.

10628 ᴱ**Murray, Oswyn; Tecuşan, Manuela** In vino veritas. L 1995,
British School at Rome xviii; 317 pp. £40 [JNES 58,299s—
Biggs, Robert D].

10629 **Zeder, Melinda A.** Feeding cities: specialized animal economy
in the ancient Near East. 1991, ⇒7,e552... 10,13474. ᴿJNES 55
(1996) 127-132 *(Joffe, Alexander H.)*.

u2.9 **Medicina** biblica et antiqua

10630 **Amundsen, Darrel W.** Medicine, society and faith in the ancient
and medieval worlds. Baltimore, MD 1996, Johns Hopkins Univ.
Press xv, 391 pp. £33. 0-8018-5109-2.

10631 **Avalos, Hector I.** Illness and health care in the ancient Near East: the role of the temple in Greece, Mesopotamia, and Israel. HSM 54: 1995, ⇒11/2,c408. ᴿJThS 47 (1996) 592-594 *(Hunter, Erica C.D.)*.

10632 **Bardinet, Thierry** Les papyrus médicaux de l'Égypte pharaonique: traduction intégrale et commentaire. Penser la médicine: P 1995, Fayard 591 pp. FF180. ᴿOr. 65 (1996) 360-365 *(Westendorf, Wolfhart)*. () () () () () () () ()

10633 **Brown, Michael L.** Israel's divine healer. 1995, ⇒11/2,c419. ᴿJETh 10 (1996) 208-211 *(Renz, Thomas)* () () () () () () () ()

10634 **Dodds, Eric R.** Parapsicologia nel mondo antico. Quadrante 43: Bari 1991, Laterza xxxii; 107 pp. Introd. di *G. Cambiano.* ᴿRSLR 32 (1996) 701-702 *(Gramaglia, Pier Angelo)*.

10635 **Filer, Joyce** Disease: Egyptian bookshelf. 1995, ⇒11/2,c441. Discussions in Egyptology 36 (1996) 121-122 *(McEvedy, B.)*.

10636 **Jori, Alberto** Medicina e medici nell'antica Grecia: saggio sul Perí téchnes ippocratico. Istituto italiano per gli studi storici in Napoli 39: Bo 1996, Mulino xxi; 452 pp. 88-15-05792-7.

10637 *Jouanna, Jacques* Le vin et la médecine dans la Grèce ancienne. Sum., rés. 410. REG 109 (1996) 410-434.

10638 **Nunn, John F.** Ancient Egyptian medicine. Norman 1996, Univ. of Oklahoma Press 240 pp. 77 fig. 28 tables. $39.99. 0-8061-2831-3. ᴿAntiquity 70 (1996) 486-488 *(Rowling, John Thompson)*.

10639 **Speert, Harold** Scripture and science: a physician's reflections on Judaic doctrine. Austin, Tex. 1995, Landes 246 pp. 1-57059-256-X [NThAR 1997,193].

10640 *Westendorf, Wolfhart* Beiträge aus und zu den medizinischen Texten. GöMisz 153 (1996) 107-112.

10641 **Wilmanns, Juliane G.** Der Sanitätsdienst im römischen Reich. Medizin der Antike 2: Hildesheim 1995, Olms 314 pp. ᴿArOr 64 (1996) 423-424 *(Strouhal, Eugen)*.

U3 *Duodecim tribus;* Israel tribes; land ideology

10642 *Chinitz, Jacob* The listing of the tribes of Israel. JBQ 24/1 (1996) 36-42.

10643 *Halpern, Baruch* Sybil, or the two nations?: archaism, kinship, alienation, and the elite redefinition of traditional culture in Judah in the 8th-7th centuries B.C.E. Albright centennial conference. 1996, ⇒303. 291-338.
     Halpern-Amaru, B. Rewriting the Bible: land and covenant in post-biblical Jewish literature ⇒8055.

10644 *Milgrom, Jacob* The land from Jewish perspective. Al-Liqa' 9-10 (1996) 85-88.

10645 *Vetter, Dieter* Die Bedeutung des Landes in der jüdischen Überlieferung. Judentum. 1996 <1992>, ⇒154. 256-272.

U4 *Limitrophi,* adjacent lands; *Viae,* roads, routes

10646 **Fischer, Moshe; Isaac, Benjamin; Roll, Israel** The Jaffa-Jerusalem roads. Roman roads in Judaea II. BAR International

Ser. 628: Oxf 1996, Tempus R. iii; vii; 434 pp. £49. 0-86054-809-0 [RB 104,313].

10647   *Kloner, Amos* Stepped roads in Roman Palestine. Aram 8 (1996) 111-137.

10648   *MacDonald, Burton* The route of the Via Nova Traiana immediately south of Wadi al Hasa. PEQ 128 (1996) 12-15.

10649   *Olivier, H.* The relationship between landscape resources and human occupation in Jordan in the nineteenth century. Sum. 96. JSem 8/1 (1996) 96-110.

10650   *Piccirillo, Michele* La strada romana Esbus-Livias. SBFLA 46 (1996) 285-300.

u5.0 *Ethnographia,* sociologia; servitus

10651   *Adamthwaite, Murray R.* Ethnic movements in the thirteenth century B.C. as discernible from the Emar texts. Cultural interaction. Abr-n.S 5: 1996, ⇒285. 91-112.

10652   *Agnati, Ulrico* Alcune correlazioni tra mestiere e *status libertatis* nella Roma tardo-repubblicana e imperiale. Sum. 601. AANL.R 7 (1996) 601-624.

10653   **Aguirre, Rafael** La mesa compartida: estudios del NT desde las ciencias sociales. Presencia teológica 77: 1994, ⇒11/2,c562. ᴿCBQ 58 (1996) 369-370 *(Malina, Bruce J.).*

10654   ᴱ**Bail, Ulrike; Jost, Renate** Gott an den Rändern: sozialgeschichtliche Perspektiven auf die Bibel. Gü 1996, Gü'er 168 pp. [FrRu 4,289s—Schwendemann, Wilhelm].

10655   *Barth, Gerhard* Kirche und Sklavenfrage im Neuen Testament: Unzeitgemäße Bemerkungen zu einem modernen Trend. Neutestamentliche Versuche. 1996 <1994>, ⇒111. 299-313.

10656   *Ben-Gurion, David* The bible: Israel's spiritual and national roots. JBQ 24 (1996) <1964> 143-148.

10657   **Benetti, Santos** Política, poder y corrupción en la Biblia. BA 1996, San Pablo 432 pp. [REB 227,768].

10658   **Bernbeck, Reinhard** Die Auflösung der häuslichen Produktionsweise. 1994, ⇒11/2,c574. ᴿJESHO 39 (1996) 52-54 *(Thuesen, Ingolf).*

        Bird, P. Poor man or poor woman: gendering the poor in prophetic texts. ᴹVᴀɴ Dɪᴊᴋ-Hᴇᴍᴍᴇs F., 1996, ⇒3252.

10659   *Bisconti, Fabrizio; Quesnel, Michel* La bain et la toilette aux temps bibliques. MoBi 98 (1996) 52-54.

10660   **Bradley, Keith R.** Slavery and society at Rome. 1994, ⇒11/2,c583. ᴿAAW 49 (1996) 221-223 *(Weiler, Ingomar).*

10661   *Brett, Mark G.* Interpreting ethnicity: method, hermeneutics, ethics. Ethnicity and the bible. 1996, ⇒171. 3-22.

10662   *Bunimovitz, Shlomo* ־בעיית משאבי־האנוש בארץ־ישראל בתקופת הברונזה המאוחרת והשלכותיה החברתיות־הכלכליות [The problem of human resources in Late Bronze Age Palestine and its socioeconomic implications]. ᶠAᴠɪʀᴀᴍ J., ErIs 25: 1996, ⇒2. Sum. 88*. 45-54. H.;

10663   ביצורי תקופת הברונזה התיכונה בארץ־ישראל כתופעה חברתית [Middle Bronze Age fortifications in Palestine as a social phenomenon]. Sum. 185. Cathedra 81 (1996) 7-22. **H.**

10664 *Cameron, Ron* Mythmaking and intertextuality in early christianity. ^FMACK B., 1996, ⇒54. 37-50.

10665 *Carter, Charles E.* A discipline in transition: the contributions of the social sciences to the study of the Hebrew Bible. Community. 1996, ⇒172. 3-36.

10666 *Castilla y Cortázar, Blanca* Familia e instituciones sociales: la restauración de la dignidad del ser humano: varón y mujer. Esperanza del hombre. 1996, ⇒173. 527-539.

10667 *Cazelles, Henri* Le salut par les institutions divines dans la bible. Études. 1996 <1965>, ⇒120. 97-107.

10668 *Clarke, Graeme W.* Cultural interaction. Cultural interaction. Abr-n.S 5: 1996, ⇒285. 129-143.

10669 *Craffert, Pieter F.* On New Testament interpretation and ethnocentrism. Ethnicity and the bible. 1996, ⇒171. 449-468.

10670 *Dearman, J. Andrew* Marriage in the Old Testament. Biblical ethics and homosexuality. 1996, ⇒6794. 53-67.

10671 **Del Signore, Gabriella** Vivere come stranieri: l'estraneità nell'Antico Testamento. Pref. *Nogaro, Raffaele*, Molfetta 1996, La Meridiana 176 pp. L22.000. 88-85221-74-2.

10672 **Destro, Adriana; Pesce, Mauro** Antropologia delle origini cristiane. 1995, ⇒11/2,c615. ^RLat. 62 (1996) 376-377 *(Penna, Romano)*; VetChr 33/1 (1996) 234-235 *(Aulisa, Immacolata)*; PaVi 41/2 (1996) 60-61 *(Rolla, Armando)*.

10673 *Diakonoff, I.M.* Extended family households in Mesopotamia (III-II millennia B.C.). Houses and households. 1996, ⇒299. 55-60.

10674 *Dunnhill, John* Methodological rivalries: theology and social science. JSNT 62 (1996) 105-119.

10675 ^EEck, Werner; **Heinrichs, Johannes** Sklaven und Freigelassene in der Gesellschaft der römischen Kaiserzeit. TzF 61: 1993, ⇒9,6326; 11/2,c622. ^RGn. 68 (1996) 232-235 *(Bradley, K.R.)*.

10676 **Elliott, John H.** What is social-scientific criticism?. 1993, ⇒9,15276; 11/2,c625. ^RBTB 26 (1996) 57-58 *(Oakman, D.E.)*.
 Ellis-Lopez, S. Analytical techniques in Near Eastern archaeology: ethnography and pottery study ⇒9853.

10677 *Feldmeier, Reinhard* The "nation" of strangers: social contempt and its theological interpretation in ancient Judaism and early christianity. Ethnicity and the bible. 1996, ⇒171. 241-270.

10678 *Finkelstein, Israel* Ethnicity and origin of the Iron I settlers in the highlands of Canaan: can the real Israel stand up?. BA 59 (1996) 198-212.

10679 *Fossum, Jarl; Arbor, Ann* Social and institutional conditions for early Jewish and christian interpretation of the Hebrew Bible with special regard to religious groups and sects. Antiquity [^ESæbø, **Magne**]. 1996, ⇒Y1. 239-255.

10680 **Garnsey, Peter** Ideas of slavery from ARISTOTLE to AUGUSTINE. C 1996, CUP xv; 269 pp. W.B. Stanford Memorial Lectures. £37.50/£14. 0-521-57433-X -03-X [AnCl 67,468s—Straus, Jean A.].

10681 *Glancy, Jennifer A.* The mistress-slave dialectic: paradoxes of slavery in three LXX narratives. JSOT 72 (1996) 71-87.

10682 **Greenspahn, Frederick E.** When brothers dwell together: the preeminence of younger siblings in the Hebrew Bible. 1994,

⇒11/2,c645. ᴿPSB 17/1 (1996) 93-95 *(Miller, Patrick D.)*; AJS
Review 21 (1996) 372-375 *(Brin, Gershon)*; JQR 87 (1996) 212-
215 *(Schwartz, Baruch J.)*; JBL 115 (1996) 117-118 *(Bailey,
Randall C.)*.

10683 *Greenspahn, Frederick E.* Primogeniture in ancient Israel.
ᶠYOUNG D., 1996, ⇒107. 69-79.

10684 **Grimm, Veronika E.** From feasting to fasting, the evolution of a
sin: attitudes to food in late antiquity. L 1996, Routledge x; 294
pp. £40. 0-416-13595-8.

10685 **Harrill, J. Albert** The manumission of slaves in early chri-
stianity. HUTh 32: 1995, ⇒11/1,4889. ᴿRHE 91 (1996) 891-893
(Faivre, Alexandre); CBQ 58 (1996) 751-753 *(Craffert, Pieter
F.)*; JThS 47 (1996) 640-642 *(Meggitt, Justin)* [1 Cor 7,21].

10686 *Hawley, Susan* Does God speak Miskitu?: the bible and ethnic
identity among the Miskitu of Nicaragua. Ethnicity and the bible.
1996, ⇒171. 315-342.

10687 *Herion, Gary A.* The impact of modern and social science assumptions on the reconstruction of Israelite history. Community.
1996 <1986>, ⇒172. 230-257.

10688 **Herrmann-Otto, Elisabeth** Ex ancilla natus: Untersuchungen zu
den 'hausgeborenen' Sklaven und Sklavinnen im Westen des
römischen Kaiserreiches. FASk 24: 1994. ⇒11/2,c659. ᴿSDHI
62 (1996) 618-630 *(Doria, Carla Masi)*; Epig. 58 (1996) 263-
264 *(Susini, Giancarlo)*; AAW 49 (1996) 234-237 *(Petermandl,
Werner)*.

10689 *Hnuni, Thanzauva; Hnuni, R.L.* Ethnicity, identity and hermeneutics: an Indian tribal perspective. Ethnicity and the bible.
1996, ⇒171. 343-357.

10690 **Holmberg, Bengt V.** Historia social del cristianismo primitivo:
la sociología y el Nuevo Testamento. 1995, ⇒11/2,c662. ᴿRLAT
13 (1996) 199-203 *(Rosa Borjas, German Ramón)*; RevBib 58
(1996) 58-60 *(Miguez, Néstor O.)*.

10691 ᴱ**Hultgren, Arland J.; Haggmark, Steven A.** The earliest christian heretics: readings from their opponents. Mp 1996, Fortress
xvi; 199 pp. $24. 0-8006-2963-9 [CBQ 59,421].

10692 *Hume, Lynne* The rainbow serpent, the cross, and the fax ma-
chine: Australian Aboriginal responses to the bible. Ethnicity and
the bible. 1996, ⇒171. 359-379.

10693 **Ilan, Tal** Jewish women in Greco-Roman Palestine: an inquiry
into images and status. Peabody, MA 1996, Hendrickson xiii;
270 pp. $20. 1-56563-240-0 [ThD 44,71].

10694 **Iverson, Cheryl Lynn** Restoration: a semantic domain study of
restoration and recovery as it relates to persons in the ancient
Israelite community. Diss. Drew 1996, ᴰ*Huffmon, H.B.*, 304 pp.
[EThL 74,185*].

10695 Volk Gottes, Gemeinde und Gesellschaft. JBTh 7 (1992). ᴿThR
61 (1996) 171-172 *(Reventlow, Henning Graf)*.

10696 *Je'Adayibe, Gwamna D.* The "poor" in biblical perspective: a
challenge to diakonia. CV 38 (1996) 232-246.

10697 *Jobling, David; Rose, Catherine* Reading as a Philistine: the ancient and modern history of a cultural slur. Ethnicity and the
bible. 1996, ⇒171. 381-417.

10698 **Keßler, Rainer** Staat und Gesellschaft im vorexilischen Juda. VT.S 47: 1992, ⇒8,k207; 10,13618. RBZ 40 (1996) 311-314 *(Mommer, Peter)*.

10699 *Klopfenstein, Martin A.* Jahweglaube und Gesellschaftsordnung: Aspekte der sozial- und wirtschaftsgeschichtlichen Erforschung Israels und ihre Bedeutung für die Interpretation alttestamentlicher Texte. Leben aus dem Wort. BEAT 40: 1996, ⇒132. 59-74.

10700 ᴱ**Kloppenborg, John S.; Wilson, Stephen G.** Voluntary associations in the Graeco-Roman world. L 1996, Routledge xvii; 333 pp. 23 fig. £50. 0-415-13593-1 [AnCl 67,502—D'Hautcourt, Alexis].

10701 **Krause, Jens-Uwe** Witwen und Waisen im römischen Reich I-IV. 1994-5, ⇒10,13621. RAAW 49 (1996) 216-221 *(Weiler, Ingomar)*.

10702 *Lemche, Niels Peter* On the use of "system theory", "macro theories", and "evolutionistic thinking" in modern Old Testament research and biblical archaeology. Community. 1996 <1990>, ⇒172. 273-286.

10703 *Levenson, Jon D.* The universal horizon of biblical particularism. Ethnicity and the bible. 1996, ⇒171. 143-169.

10704 **Lüdemann, Gerd** Heretics: the other side of early christianity. L 1996, SCM xiv; 335 pp. £17.50. 0-334-02616-4. RET 108 (1996-97) 35-36 *(Rodd, C.S.)*;

10705 Das Unheilige in der Heiligen Schrift: die andere Seite der Bibel. Stu 1996, Radius 136 pp. 3-87173-092-0.

10706 **Malina, B.J.** Die Welt des Neuen Testaments: kulturanthropologische Einsichten. 1993, ⇒9,15341. SNTU.A 21 (1996) 218-220 *(Niemand, Chr.)*.

10707 **Malina, Bruce; Joubert, S.; Van der Watt, J.** Vensters wat die woord laat oopgaan. Halfway House 1995, Orion. RNeotest. 30/1 (1996) 228-230 *(Craffert, Pieter F.)*.

10708 **Matthews, Victor H.; Benjamin, Don C.** Social world of ancient Israel 1250-587 BCE. 1993, ⇒9,15342... 11/2,c712. RJAOS 116 (1996) 291-292 *(Evans, Carl D.)*.

10709 *Meyers, Carol L.* Procreation, production, and protection: male-female balance in early Israel. Community. 1996 <1983>, ⇒172. 489-514.

10710 **Mödritzer, Helmut** Stigma und Charisma im Neuen Testament und seiner Umwelt: zur Soziologie des Urchristentums. NTOA 28: 1994, ⇒10,13643; 11/2,c717. RJBL 115 (1996) 742-744 *(Holmberg, Bengt)*.

10711 *Pfälzner, P.* Activity and the social organisation of third millennium B.C. households. Houses and households. 1996, ⇒299. 117-127.

10712 *Pieszczoch, Szczepan* Wczesnochrześcijańska caritas wobec niewolników [La charité chrétienne antique envers les esclaves]. Rés. 246. Vox Patrum 16 (1996) 241-247. **P**.

10713 *Pilch, John J.* Poczucie humoru biblii [The bible's sense of humor]. ᵀ*Sawicki, Bernard*, RBL 49 (1996) 255-260. **P**.

10714 *Rodinò, Nerina* La bibbia e la festa. RdT 37 (1996) 92-98.

10715 ᴱ**Rohrbaugh, Richard L.** The social sciences and New Testament interpretation. Peabody, MASS 1996, Hendrickson ix; 240 pp. $19. 1-56563-239-7 [RExp 94,467].

10716   *Rousselle, Aline* Famille antique et modèle chrétien. MoBi 101 (1996) 29-32.

10717   *Sagona, Claudia* Red to blue: colour symbolism and human societies. Cultural interaction. Abr-n.S 5: 1996, ⇒285. 145-155.

10718   **Saller, R.P.** Patriarchy, property and death in the Roman family. 1994, ⇒11/2,c746. ᴿClR 46 (1996) 106-107 *(Gardner, Jane F.)*.

10719   *Schäfer-Lichtenberger, Christa* Sociological and biblical views of the early state. Origins. JSOT.S 228: 1996, ⇒9122. 78-105.

10720   *Segovia, Fernando F.* Racial and ethnic minorities in biblical studies. Ethnicity and the bible. 1996, ⇒171. 469-492.

10721   *Smith-Christopher, Daniel L.* Between Ezra and Isaiah: exclusion, transformation and inclusion of the "foreigner" in post-exilic biblical theology. Ethnicity and the bible. 1996, ⇒171. 117-142.

10722   *Snyman, Gerrie* Carnival in Jerusalem: power and subversiveness in the early Second Temple period. OTEs 9 (1996) 88-110.

10723   **Solin, Heikki** Die stadtrömischen Sklavennamen: ein Namenbuch I. Lateinische Namen, II. Griechische Namen, III. Barbarische Namen. Forschungen zur antiken Sklaverei 2: Stu 1996, Steiner xxiv, xvi, xvi, 727 pp. DM196. 3-515-07002-8.

10724   **Sparks, Kenton Lane** Ethnicity and identity in Ancient Israel: prolegomena to the study of ethnic sentiments and their expression in the Hebrew bible. Diss. North Carolina 1996, ᴰ*Van Seters, J.* [JQR 87,266].

10725   **Stegemann, Ekkehard W.; Stegemann, Wolfgang** Urchristliche Sozialgeschichte: die Anfänge im Judentum und die Christusgemeinde in der mediterranen Welt. 1995, ⇒11/2,c756. ᴿFrRu 3 (1996) 216-218 *(Reichrath, Hans L.)*.

10726   *Sugirtharajah, R.S.* Orientalism, ethnonationalism and transnationalism: shifting identities and biblical interpretation. Ethnicity and the bible. 1996, ⇒171. 419-429.

10727   **Theissen, Gerd** Social reality and the early christians. 1992, ⇒8,k258...11/2,c764. ᴿScrB 26 (1996) 94-96 *(Robinson, B.P.)*;

10728   Histoire sociale du christianisme primitif: Jésus—Paul—Jean. ᵀ*Jaillet, Ira; Fink, Anne-Lise;* Préf. *Marguerat, Daniel*, MoBi 33: Genève 1996, Labor et Fides 297 pp. FF198. 2-8309-0814-7. ᴿEeV 106 (1996) 551-554 *(Cothenet, E.)*.

10729   *Thompson, Leonard L.* Social location of early christian apocalyptic. Religion. ANRW II.26.3: 1996, 2615-2656.

10730   *Tsengele, Marie-Rose* La pauvreté-richesse: à l'ecoute de la bible: de la dimension socio-économique à la liberté spirituelle. Telema 22/3-4 (1996) 60-68.

10731   ᴱ**Wagner-Hasel, Beate** Matriarchatstheorien der Altertumswissenschaft. 1992, ⇒10,13678. ᴿGn. 68 (1996) 63-65 *(Guyot, Peter)*.

10732   **Weber, Max** Ancient Judaism. Community. 1996 <1952>, ⇒172. 65-94.

10733   *Wimbush, Vincent L.* '...not of this world...': early christianities as rhetorical and social formation. ᶠMACK B., 1996, ⇒54. 23-36.

U5.3 Commercium, oeconomica

10734 **Aubert, Jean-Jacques** Business managers in ancient Rome... Institores, 200 B.C.-A.D. 250. 1994, ⇒11/2,c792. RAJP 117 (1996) 501-504 *(Rauh, Nicholas K.)*.

10735 *Brennan, Peter V.* Obsidian in the Bayburt-Erzurum Area, eastern Anatolia. Cultural interaction. Abr-n.S 5: 1996, ⇒285. 27-36.

10736 ECharpin, D.; Joannès, F.** La circulation des biens, des personnes et des idées dans le Proche-Orient ancien. 1991, ⇒8,683; 10,1369. ROLZ 91 (1996) 291-293 *(Prechel, Doris)*.

10737 **Duncan-Jones, R.** Money and government in the Roman empire. 1994, ⇒11/2,c806. RAt. 84 (1996) 637-638 *(Foraboschi, Daniele)*; JRS 86 (1996) 208-209 *(Howgego, Christopher)*.

10738 *Fales, Frederick Mario* Prices in Neo-Assyrian sources. SAA Bulletin 10/1 (1996) 11-53.

10739 *Frayn, Joan M.* Aspects of trade on the Judaean coast in the Hellenistic and Roman periods. Aram 8 (1996) 101-109.

10740 *Gophna, Ram; Liphschitz, Nili* The Ashkelon trough settlements in the early Bronze Age I: new evidence of maritime trade. TelAv 23 (1996) 143-153.

10741 *Guri-Rimon, Ofra* ייעודם העיקרי של מבצרי מנהל—מרכזי ומרכזי אוצר בתי המדבר [Treasure houses and administrative centers: the primary purpose of the desert strongholds]. Sum. 191. Cathedra 82 (1996) 7-12. **H**.

10742 EGyselen, Rika** Circulation des monnaies...marchandises... 1993, ⇒10,13710. RBiOr 53 (1996) 39-41 *(Van der Vliet, E. Ch.L.)*.

10743 *Homès-Fredericq, D.* Influences diverses en Transjordanie à l'époque achéménide. TEuph 11 (1996) 63-76.

EHudson, M.** Privatization in the ancient Near East ⇒315.

10744 **Knapp, A. Bernard; Cherry, John F.** Provenience studies and Bronze Age Cyprus: production, exchange and politico-economic change. Monographs in World Archaeology 21: Prehistory 1994, Madison xiv; 280 pp. $27.50. 1-881094-10-3. RAJA 100 (1996) 418-419 *(Manning, Stuart W.)*; Antiquity 70 (1996) 718-719 *(Day, Peter M.)*.

10745 *Koshurnikov, S.* Prices and types of constructed city lots in the Old Babylonian period. Houses and households. 1996, ⇒299. 257-260.

10746 **McCann, Anna Marguerite; Freed, Joann** Deep water archaeology: a late-Roman ship from Carthage and an ancient trade route. Journal of Roman Archaeology Suppl. 13: AA 1994, Journal of Roman Archaeology xviii; 145 pp. $64.50. 1-887829-13-X. RAJA 100 (1996) 438-439 *(Sherwood, Andrew N.)*.

10747 *Michel, C.* Propriétés immobilières dans les tablettes paléo-assyriennes. Houses and households. 1996, ⇒299. 285-300.

10748 *Michel, Cécile* Le commerce dans les textes de Mari. Amurru 1. 1996, ⇒306. 385-426.

10749 **Moscati, Sabatino** La bottega del mercante: artigianato e commercio fenicio lungo le sponde del Mediterraneo. Storia: T 1996, Società Editrice Internazionale x; 166 pp. 88-05-05557-3.

Neumann, Hans Zum privaten Werkvertrag im Rahmen der neusumerischen handwerklichen Produktion ⇒2023.

10750 *Olivier, J.P.J.* Money matters: some remarks on the economic situation in the kingdom of Judah during the seventh century BC. OTEs 9 (1996) 451-464.

10751 *Powell, Marvin A.* Money in Mesopotamia. Sum. 224. JESHO 39 (1996) 224-242.

10752 *Renger, Johannes* Handwerk und Handwerker im alten Mesopotamien: eine Einleitung. AltOrF 23 (1996) 211-231.

10753 **Safrai, Ze'ev** The economy of Roman Palestine. 1994, ⇒10,13739; 11/2,c845. ᴿJSJ 27 (1996) 95-98 *(Rutgers, L.V.)*.

10754 **Skaist, Aaron** The Old Babylonian loan contract: its history and geography. 1994, ⇒11/2,c847. ᴿOLZ 91 (1996) 293-295 *(Jakobson, Vladimir A.)*.

10755 *Steinkeller, Piotr* The organization of crafts in third millennium Babylonia: the case of potters. AltOrF 23 (1996) 232-253.

ᴜ5.7 **Nomadismus**, ecology

10756 *Akkermans, P.M.M.G.; Duistermaat, K.* Of storage and nomads: the sealings from late Neolithic Sabi Abyad, Syria. Comments 33-44; Sum. rés. 17. Paléorient 22/2 (1996) 17-44.

10757 **Avni, Gideon** Nomads, farmers, and town-dwellers: pastoralist-sedentist interaction in the Negev Highlands, sixth-eighth centuries CE. Suppl. to the Archaeological Survey of Israel: J 1996, Israel Antiquities Authority 108 pp. 965-406-022-1 [NThAR 1998,362].

10758 *Frendo, Anthony J.* The capabilities and limitations of ancient Near Eastern nomadic archaeology. Or. 65 (1996) 1-23.

10759 *Gal, Z.* Ecological aspects of archaeology in Israel. Qad. 29 (1996) 120-122. **H**.

10760 **Gitau, Samson** African and biblical understanding of the environment. Diss. Nairobi 1996, ᴰ*Waruta, Douglas W.* [NAOTS 1 (1996) 5—Holter, Knut].

10761 *Pitard, Wayne T.* An historical overview of pastoral nomadism in the central Euphrates valley. ᶠYᴏᴜɴɢ D., ⇒107. 293-308.

ᴜ5.8 **Urbanismus**

10762 *Bunnens, Guy* Syro-Anatolian influence on Neo-Assyrian town planning. Cultural interaction. Abr-n.S 5: 1996, ⇒285. 113-128.

10763 *Castel, C.* Un quartier de maisons urbaines du Bronze Moyen à Tel Mohammed Diyab (Djezireh Syrienne). Houses and households. 1996, ⇒299. 273-283.

10764 **Cohen, Getzel M.** The Hellenistic settlements in Europe, the islands and Asia Minor. Berkeley 1996, University of California Press 468 pp. 11 maps. $65. 0-520-08329-6 [AJA 101,631].

10765 **Foucault-Forest, Chantal** L'habitat privé en Palestine au Bronze Moyen et au Bronze Récent. BAR International Ser. 625: Oxf 1996, Tempus R. v; ii; 147 pp. 115 pl. £34. 0-86054-806-6 [RB 104,313].

10766 *Hirschfeld, Yizhar* שינויים בדפוסי ההתיישבות של האוכלוסייה היהודית הכפרית לפני המרידות ברומאים [Changes in settlement patterns of the Jewish rural populace before and after the rebellions against Rome]. Sum. 239. Cathedra 80 (1996) 3-18. **H.**

10767 **Hoepfner, Wolfram; Schwandner, Ernst-Ludwig** Haus und Stadt im klassischen Griechenland. ²1994, ⇒10,13763. ᴿAnCl 65 (1996)·544-547 *(Grandjean, Yves)*.

10768 *Koshurnikov, S.* Prices and types of constructed city lots in the Old Babylonian period. Houses and households. 1996, ⇒299. 257-260.

10769 *Meyer, Jan-Waalke* Offene und geschlossene Siedlungen: ein Beitrag zur Siedlungsgeschichte und historischen Topographie in Nordsyrien während des 3. und 2. Jts. v. Chr. AltOrF 23 (1996) 132-170.

10770 *Oppenheimer, Aharon* עיור ותחומי ערים בארץ־ישראל הרומית [Urbanisation and city territories in Roman Palestine]. ᶠSTERN M., 1996, ⇒87. Sum. 148*. 209-226. **H.**

10771 **Saliou, Catherine** Le traité d'urbanisme de Julien d'Ascalon: droit et architecture en Palestine au VIᵉ siècle. TravMém 8: P 1996, De Boccard 160 pp. 12 fig. 8 tables. 2-7018-0097-8 [AJA 101,432].

10772 *Vallet, R.* Habuba Kebira (Syrie) ou la naissance de l'urbanisme. Sum. rés. 45. Paléorient 22/2 (1996) 45-76.

10773 **Winter, Bruce W.** Seek the welfare of the city: christians as benefactors and citizens. 1994, ⇒11/2,c908. ᴿJR 76 (1996) 622 *(Gebhard, Elizabeth R.)*; CBQ 58 (1996) 569-570 *(Willis, Wendell)*; JThS 47 (1996) 259-262 *(Edwards, Ruth B.)*; JBL 115 (1996) 536-538 *(Walters, James C.)*.

U5.9 *Demographia*, **population statistics**

10774 **Bagnall, Roger S.; Frier, Bruce W.** The demography of Roman Egypt. 1994, ⇒10,13788; 11/2,c910. ᴿAJP 117 (1996) 341-343 *(Whitehorne, John)*; At. 84 (1996) 638-640 *(Foraboschi, Daniele)*.

Otto, E. Gibt es Zusammenhänge zwischen Bevölkerungswachstum, Staatsbildung und Kulturentwicklung im eisenzeitlichen Israel? ⇒9149.

10775 **Scheidel, Walter** Measuring sex, age and death in the Roman empire: explorations in ancient demography. Journal of Roman Archaeology, Suppl. 21: Ann Arbor 1996 Cushing-Malloy 184 pp. [CÉg 74,188ss—Straus, Jean A.].

10776 *Tsafrir, Yoram* Some notes on the settlement and demography of Palestine in the Byzantine period: the archaeological evidence. ᶠVAN BEEK G., 1996, ⇒96. 269-283.

U6 **Narrationes peregrinorum et exploratorum;** *Loca sancta*

10777 **Artola, Antonio María** La tierra, el libro, el Espíritu. Bilbao 1996, Desclée de B. 569 pp. 84-330-0671-3 [ScrTh 30,982s—Jarne, Javier].

10778 **Bermejo Cabrera, Enrique** La proclamación de la Escritura en la liturgia de Jerusalén: estudio terminológico del *Itinerarium*

Egeriae. SBF.CMa 37: 1993, ⇒10,13816; 11/2,c921. RCTom 123 (1996) 614-615 *(Espinel, J.L.).*

10779 **Davis, J.** The landscape of belief: encountering the Holy Land in nineteenth-century American art and culture. Princeton 1996, Princeton Univ. Press 264 pp. £42.50 [PEQ 130,74s— Thompson, Jason].

10780 EGyselen, **Rika** Sites et monuments disparus d'après les témoignages de voyageurs. Res Orientales 8: Bures-sur-Yvette 1996, Groupe pour l'Étude de la Civilisation du Moyen-Orient 205 pp. 2-9509266-2-B.

10781 **Külzer, Andreas** Peregrinatio graeca in Terram Sanctam: Studien zu Pilgerführern und Reisebeschreibungen über Syrien, Palästina und den Sinai aus byzantinischer und metabyzantinischer Zeit. Studien und Texte zur Byzantinistik 2: Fra 1994, Lang xvi; 284 pp. DM138. 3-631-46784-2. RZDPV 112 (1996) 187-190 *(Bieberstein, Klaus).*

10782 *Lewis, Norman N.; Sartre-Fauriat, Annie; Sartre, Maurice* William John BANKES: travaux en Syrie d'un voyageur oublié. Syr. 73 (1996) 57-95.

10783 TMaraval, **Pierre** Récits des premiers pèlerins chrétiens au Proche Orient (IVe-VIIe siècle). P 1996, Cerf 300 pp. FF150. 2-204-05299-X. RREG 109 (1996) 320-321 *(Malingrey, Anne-Marie).*

10784 *Mulzer, Martin* Mit der Bibel in der Hand?: Egeria und ihr 'Codex'. ZDPV 112 (1996) 156-164.

10785 *Olivier, J.P.J.* Armoede in die Heilige Land volgens die negentiende-eeuse reisberigte (met spesifieke verwysing na die el-Kerak-plato). Sum. Annale Universiteit van Stellenbosch 1 (1996) 1-28.

10786 **Rüger, Hans Peter** Syrien und Palästina nach dem Reisebericht des BENJAMIN von Tudela. ADPV 12: 1990, ⇒6,g889. RBiOr 53 (1996) 578-580 *(Van Leeuwen, Richard).*

10787 **Taylor, Joan E.** Christians and the holy places: the myth of Jewish-Christian origins. 1993, ⇒9,15533... 11/2,c953. RJSSt 41 (1996) 148-150 *(Prag, Kay).*

υ7 *Crucigeri*—**The Crusades**; *Communitates Terrae Sanctae*

10788 *Beltz, Walter* Kreuzzüge—religionswissenschaftliche Anmerkungen. Hallesche Beiträge zur Orientwissenschaft 22 (1996) 7-11.

10789 **Flori, Jean** La première croisade: l'occident chrétien contre l'Islam. P 1996, Complexe 287 pp. FF56 [EHR 112,968—Keats-Rohan, K.S.B.].

10790 ETHousley, **Norman** Documents on the later crusades, 1274-1580. L 1996, Macmillan xiv; 204 pp. $40 [IHR Review 20,151ss—Cole, Penny J.].

10791 *Ligato, Giuseppe* Le crociate. TS(I) 72 (gen.-feb. 1996) 50-53.

10792 TELundquist, **Eva Rodhe** SALADIN and the crusaders. 1992, ⇒10,13836*. RZDMG 146 (1996) 573-575 *(Hillenbrand, Carole).*

10793 **Maier, Christoph T.** Preaching the crusades. 1994, ⇒11/2,c977. RHeyJ 37 (1996) 229-230 *(Swanson, R.N.).*

10794 *Passerat, Georges* Mare nostrum: l'idée de croisade: le fil des événements. BLE.S 1 (1996) 21-41.

10795 **Pringle, R. Denys** The churches of the Crusader Kingdom of Jerusalem: a corpus I: A-K (exclud. Acre & Jerusalem). 1993, ⇒7,e902... 11/2,c982. ᴿLevant 28 (1996) 225 *(Zeitler, Barbara)*.

10796 **Richard, Jean** Histoire des Croisades. P 1996, Fayard 544 pp. FF170 [CHR 84/1,80—Powell, James M.].

10797 *Schein, Sylvia* Between east and west: the Latin kingdom of Jerusalem and its Jewish communities as a communication center (1099-1291). Communication. 1996, ⇒232. 141-169.

10798 *Thoma, Clemens* Reflexionen über den ersten Kreuzzug vor 900 Jahren. FrRu 3 (1996) 161-167.

10799 *Zöllner, Walter* Die Kreuzzüge—Strukturen und Probleme. Hallesche Beiträge zur Orientwissenschaft 22 (1996) 13-27.

10800 **Schick, Robert** The christian communities of Palestine from Byzantine to Islamic rule: a historical and archaeological study. Studies in Late Antiquity and Early Islam 2: Princeton, NJ 1995, Darwin. $60. 0-87850-081-2 [[JSSt 44,326ss—Bosworth, C. Edmund].

XX. Historia scientiae biblicae

γ1.1 History of exegesis: General

10801 ᴱ**Aland, Kurt; Rosenbaum, Hans-Udo** Kirchenväter-Papyri, 1: Beschreibungen. PTS 42: 1995, ⇒11/2,g053. ᴿCÉg 71 (1996) 185-186 *(Martin, Alain)*.

10802 ᴱ**Bosio, Guido; Dal Covolo, Enrico; Maritano, Mario** Introduzione ai Padri della Chiesa: secoli III e IV. 1993, ⇒9,15618... 11/2,g069. ᴿAug. 36 (1996) 276-278 *(Bergamelli, Ferdinando)*.

10803 **Callan, Terrance** The origins of christian faith. 1994, ⇒11/2,g072. ᴿCBQ 58 (1996) 537-539 *(Sloyan, Gerard S.)*.

10804 *Colpe, Carsten* Formen der Intoleranz: altkirchliche Autoren und ihre antipagane Polemik. Wahrnehmung des Fremden. 1996, ⇒218. 87-123.

10805 **Daniélou, Jean** Etudes d'exégèse judéo-chrétienne. 1966, ⇒48,4346b. ᴿThR 61 (1996) 287 *(Mühlenberg, Ekkehard)*.

10806 *Felber, Anneliese* Syrisches Christentum und Theologie vom 3.-7. Jahrhundert. Religionsgeschichte Syriens. 1996, ⇒217. 288-304.

10807 ᴱ**Felici, Sergio** Esegesi e catechesi nei Padri (secc. IV-VII). 1994, ⇒9,448*; 11/2,g089. ᴿCivCatt 147 III (1996) 317-318 *(Cremascoli, G.)*; ATG 59 (1996) 320-322 *(Granado, C.)*.

10808 **Gamble, Harry Y.** Books and readers in the early Church. 1995, ⇒11/2,g094. ᴿVigChr 50 (1996) 426-428 *(Treter, Timothy M.)*; JThS 47 (1996) 652-655 *(Thomas, J. David)*.

10809 **Gibert, Pierre** Breve storia dell'esegesi biblica. ᵀ*Crespi, P.*, Giornale di Teologia 238: Brescia 1995, Queriniana 236 pp. L.30.000. 88-399-0738-6. ᴿActBib 33 (1996) 176-177 *(O'Callaghan, Josep)*.

10810   **Gibert, Pierre** Pequena história da exegese bíblica. [T]*Da Rosa Cândido, Edinei,* Petrópolis 1995, Vozes 206 pp. [R]RCB 77 (1996) 148-149 *(Ribeiro, Ari L. do V.).*

10811   [E]**Gros, Gérard** La bible et ses raisons: diffusion et distorsions du discours religieux (XIVe siècle-XVIIe siècle). Saint-Etienne 1996, Publications de l'Université de Saint-Etienne 270 pp. [ASSR 44/2,65s—Chédozeau, Bernard].

10812   **Karpp, Heinrich** Schrift, Geist und Wort Gottes. 1992, ⇒8,k565; 9,15647. [R]ThR 61 (1996) 148-151 *(Reventlow, Henning Graf).*

10813   **Kinzig, Wolfram** Novitas christiana: die Idee des Fortschritts in der Alten Kirche. 1994, ⇒10,13921; 11/2,g108. [R]JThS 47 (1996) 271-274 *(Wilken, Robert L.).*

10814   **Laporte, Jean** La bible et les origines chrétiennes (initiations). P 1996, Cerf 523 pp. F195. 2-204-05317-1 [RB 104,315].

10815   **Lüdemann, Gerd** Die Ketzer: die andere Seite des frühen Christentums. 1995, ⇒11/2,g115. [R]ThLZ 121 (1996) 454-455 *(Müller, Ulrich B.).*

10816   **Muller, Richard A.** Post Reformation reformed dogmatics 2: holy scripture. GR 1993, Baker xvi; 543 pp. 0-8010-6299-3. [R]EvQ 68 (1996) 81-82 *(Trueman, Carl R.).*

10817   *Muller, Richard A.; Thompson, John L.* The significance of precritical exegesis: retrospect and prospect. [F]STEINMETZ D., 1996, ⇒86. 335-345.

10818   *Müller, C. Detlef G.* Charakteristika koptischer Exegese an ausgewählten Beispielen. [F]DASSMANN E., JAC.E 23: 1996, ⇒19. 200-209.

10819   *Ribeiro, Ari Luís do Vale* Leitura da Bíblia na igreja primitiva e a exegese patrística. RCB 77/78 (1996) 128-147.

10820   *Ritter, Adolf Martin* Ist Dogmengeschichte Geschichte der Schrifttauslegung?. [F]DASSMANN E., JAC.E 23: 1996, ⇒19. 1-17.

10821   [E]**Sæbø, Magne** Hebrew Bible/Old Testament: the history of its interpretation 1: from the beginnings to the Middle Ages 1: Antiquity. Gö 1996, Vandenhoeck & R. 847 pp. DM210. 3-525-53636-4 [CBQ 59,207].

10822   *Scholten, Clemens* Titel-Gattung-Sitz im Leben: Probleme der Klassifizierung antiker Bibelauslegung am Beispiel der griechischen Hexaemeronschriften. [F]DASSMANN E., JAC.E 23: 1996, ⇒19. 254-269.

10823   *Studer, Basil* Die patristische Exegese, eine Aktualisierung der Heiligen Schrift (zur hermeneutischen Problematik der frühchristlichen Bibelauslegung). REAug 42 (1996) 71-95.

10824   *Uthemann, Karl-Heinz* Was verraten Katenen über die Exegese ihrer Zeit?: ein Beitrag zur Geschichte der Exegese in Byzanz. [F]DASSMANN E., JAC.E 23: 1996, ⇒19. 284-296.

10825   *Viciano, Albert* Das formale Verfahren der antiochenischen Schriftauslegung: ein Forschungsüberblick. [F]DASSMANN E., JAC.E 23: 1996, ⇒19. 370-405.

10826   *Vogt, Hermann-J.* Unterschiedliche Exegese der Alexandriner und der Antiochener: cyrillische Umdeutung christologischer Texte des Theodor von Mopsuestia. [F]DASSMANN E., JAC.E 23: 1996, ⇒19. 357-369.

Y1.4 *Patres apostolici et saeculi II*—First two centuries

10827 *Barbieri, Edoardo* Lo 'Ps. Marcellus brevior' in una traduzione italiana del trecento. Som. rés. 205. Apocrypha 7 (1996) 205-224.

10828 **Culdaut, Francine**, *(al)*, En el origen de la palabra cristiana: tradición y escrituras en el siglo II. Documentos en torno a la Biblia 22: Estella 1993, Verbo Divino 201 pp. 84-7151-850-3. RRET 56 (1996) 259-260 *(Barrado Fernández, P.)*.

10829 *Dal Covolo, Enrico* 'Regno di Dio': eclissi di una formula sinottica da Paolo agli apologisti greci del II secolo. Atti del IV Simposio di Tarso. 1996, ⇒263. 187-203.

10830 *Drijvers, Han J.W.* Early Syriac christianity: some recent publications. VigChr 50 (1996) 159-177.

10831 **Feiertag, Jean Louis** Questions d'un païen à un chrétien (Consultationes Zacchaei christiani et Apollonii philosophi): tomes I-II. SC 401-402: P 1994, Cerf 224 + 277 pp. FF94 + 97. 2-204-05125-X/6-8. REThL 72 (1996) 254-256 *(Verheyden, J.)*.

10832 **Jefford, Clayton, N.; Harder, Kenneth J.; Amezaga, Louis D.** Reading the Apostolic Fathers: an introduction. Peabody 1996, Hendrickson xvi; 192 pp. [OCP 64,238—Farrugia, E.G.].

10833 **Jones, F. Stanley** An ancient Jewish christian source on the history of christianity: Pseudo-Clementine *Recognitions* 1.27-71. SBL.TT 27: CA 2: Atlanta 1995, Scholars xiv; 208 pp. $40. RCBQ 58 (1996) 555-556 *(Adler, William)*.

10834 *Le Boulluec, Alain* L'écriture comme norme hérésiologique dans les controverses des IIe et IIIe siècles (Domaine grec). FDASSMANN E., JAC.E 23: 1996, ⇒19. 66-76.

10835 **Orbe, Antonio** La teologia de secoli II e III: il confronto della grande chiesa con lo gnosticismo I-II. 1995, ⇒11/2,g161. RLat. 62 (1996) 379-380 *(Pasquato, Ottorino)*.

10836 **Osborn, Eric** The emergence of christian theology. 1993, ⇒9,15740...11/2,g162. RJEarlyC 4 (1996) 119-120 *(Grant, R.M.)*.

10837 **Ridings, Daniel** The Attic Moses: the dependency theme in some early Christian writers. SGLG 59: 1995, ⇒11/2,g164. RRHE 91 (1996) 517-518 *(Zeegers, Nicole)*.

10838 *Skarsaune, Oskar* The development of scriptural interpretation in the second and third centuries—except CLEMENT and ORIGEN. Antiquity. 1996, ⇒10821. 373-442.

10839 *Stanton, Graham* Other early christian writings: 'Didache', Ignatius, 'Barnabas', Justin Martyr. FHOOKER M., 1996, ⇒ 43. 174-190.

10840 **Wagner, Walter H.** After the apostles: christianity in the second century. 1994, ⇒10,13959; 11/2,g169. RCBQ 58 (1996) 365-366 *(Siker, Jeffrey S.)*.

10841 BARNABAS: TDe Capitani, Giorgio Lettera di Barnaba; Lettera a Diogneto. Padri apostolici 3: Mi 1996, Mimep D. 160 pp. Pref. di *Giovanni Saldarini;* Bibl. 88-86242-43-3.

10842   *Derry, Kken* One stone on another: towards an understanding of symbolism in *The Epistle of Barnabas.* Sum. 515. JEarlyC 4 (1996) 515-528.

10843   *Henne, Philippe* Barnabé, le temple et les pagano-chrétiens. RB 103 (1996) 257-276.

10844   **Hvalvik, Reidar** The struggle for scripture and covenant: the purpose of the epistle of Barnabas and Jewish-Christian competition in the second century. WUNT 2/82: Tü 1996, Mohr xiii; 415 pp. DM118. 3-16-146534-2. ᴿHenoch 18 (1996) 374-375 *(Chiesa, Bruno).*

10845   **Paget, James Carleton** The Epistle of Barnabas. WUNT 2/64: 1994, ⇒10,13962*; 11/2,g175. ᴿThLZ 121 (1996) 357-358 *(Koch, Dietrich-Alex)*; HeyJ 37 (1996) 528-529 *(Hall, Stuart G.).*

10846   *Paget, James Carleton* Paul and the Epistle of Barnabas. NT 38 (1996) 359-381.

10847   **Urbán, Angel** Barnabae epistulae concordantia. AlOm.A 165; Concordantia in Patres Apostolicos 4: Hildesheim 1996, Olms 227 pp. 3-487-10256-0.

10848   CELSUS: *Rouger, Denise* La critique du texte biblique au IIe siècle: CELSE lecteur de l'évangile. Les premières traditions. 1996, ⇒159. 207-240.

10849   CLEMENS A: ᵀMerino Rodríguez, Marcelo Clemens Alexandrinus: Stromata I, II-III: cultura y religión: conoscimiento religioso y continencia auténtica. Fuentes Patrísticas 7, 10: M 1996-1998, Ciudad Nueva 2 vols. 88-89651-.

10850   **Rizzerio, Laura** Clemente di Alessandria e la "physiologia veramente gnostica": saggio sulle origini e sulle implicazioni di un'epistemologia e di un'ontologia "cristiane". BRThAM 6: Lv 1996, Peeters x; 344 pp. Bibl. 90-6831-794-6.

10851   *Van den Hoek, Annewies* Divergent gospel traditions in CLEMENT of Alexandria and other authors of the second century. Sum. rés. 43. Apocrypha 7 (1996) 43-62;

10852   Techniques of quotation in Clement of Alexandria: a view of ancient literary working methods. VigChr 50 (1996) 223-243.

10853   CLEMENS R. *Peterlin, D.* CLEMENT's answer to the Corinthian conflict in A.D. 96. JETS 39 (1996) 57-69.

10854   *Pouderon, Bernard* Flavius CLEMENS et le proto-Clément juif du roman pseudo-clémentin. Sum. rés. 63. Apocrypha 7 (1996) 63-79.

10855   DIDACHE: *Alon, Gedaliah* The halacha in the teaching of the twelve apostles. Didache. AGJU 37: 1996 <1958>, ⇒10857. 165-194.

10856   *Audet, Jean-Paul* Literary and doctrinal affinities of the "Manual of Discipline". AGJU 37: 1996 <1952>, ⇒10857. 129-147.

10857   *Bammel, Ernst* Pattern and prototype of Didache 16. Didache. AGJU 37: 1996 <1961>, ⇒10857. 364-372.

10858   *Betz, Johannes* The eucharist in the Didache. Didache. AGJU 37: 1996 <1969>, ⇒10857. 244-275.

10859   *DeHalleux, André* Ministers in the Didache. Didache. AGJU 37: 1996 <1980>, ⇒10857. 300-320.

10860 EDraper, Jonathan A. The Didache in modern research. AGJU 37: Lei 1996, Brill xviii; 445 pp. ƒ238.50/$149.50. 90-04-10375-9 [NThAR 1997,68].

10861 Draper, Jonathan Christian self-definition against the "hypocrites" in Didache VIII. Didache. 1996 <1992>, ⇒10857. 223-243;

10862 The Didache in modern research: an overview. Didache. AGJU 37: 1996, ⇒10857. 1-42;

10863 Torah and troublesome apostles in the Didache community. Didache. AGJU 37: 1996 <1991>, ⇒10857. 340-363;

10864 The Jesus tradition in the Didache. Didache. AGJU 37: 1996 <1985>, ⇒10857. 72-91.

10865 Flusser, David Paul's Jewish-christian opponents in the Didache. Didache. AGJU 37: 1996 <1987>, ⇒10857. 195-211.

10866 EJefford, Clayton N. The Didache in context: essays on its text, history and transmission. NT.S 77: 1995, ⇒10,248; 11/2,g201. RJThS 47 (1996) 268-270 (Trevett, Christine).

10867 Mazza, Enrico Didache 9-10: elements of a eucharistic interpretation. Didache. AGJU 37: 1996 <1979>, ⇒10857. 276-299.

10868 Niederwimmer, Kurt An examination of the development of itinerant radicalism in the environment and tradition of the Didache. Didache. AGJU 37: 1996 <1977>, ⇒10857. 321-339.

10869 Rordorf, Willy An aspect of the Judeo-christian ethic: the two ways. Didache. AGJU 37: 1996 <1972>, ⇒10857. 148-164;

10870 Baptism according to the Didache. Didache. AGJU 37: 1996 <1972>, ⇒10857. 212-222.

10871 Schöllgen, Georg The Didache as a church order: an examination of the purpose for the composition of the Didache and the consequences for its interpretation. Didache. AGJU 37: 1996 <1986>, ⇒10857. 43-71.

10872 Seeliger, Hans Reinhard Considerations on the background and purpose of the apocalyptic conclusion of the Didache. Didache. AGJU 37: 1996 <1989>, ⇒10857. 373-382.

10873 Tuckett, Christopher M. Synoptic tradition in the Didache. Didache. AGJU 37: 1996 <1989>, ⇒10857. 92-128.

10874 HERMAS: Ayán Calvo, Juan José Hermas: el pastor. Fuentes Patrística 6: 1995, ⇒11/2,g205. RAng. 73 (1996) 596-598 (Degórski, Bazyli).

10875 Carlini, Antonio Papyrus Bodmer XXXVIII: Erma: Il Pastore (Ia-IIIa visione). 1991, ⇒7,g47; 8,k636. RVigChr 50 (1996) 417-419 (Hilhorst, A.).

10876 Wilson, C. Christian Five problems in the interpretation of the Shepherd of Hermas: authorship, genre, canonicity, apocalyptic, and the absence of the name 'Jesus Christ'. Mellen 34: Lewiston, NY 1996, Mellen 100 pp. $60. 0-7734-2392-3 [ThD 44,94].

10877 HIPPOLYTUS: TPeretto, Elio HIPPOLYTUS Romanus: Traditio apostolica: Tradizione apostolica. CTePa 133: R 1996, Città Nuova 151 pp. 88-311-3133-8.

10878 IGNATIUS: Rius-Camps, Josep L'espistolari d'IGNASI d'Antioquia (VI): traducció, notes i comentari: carta espúria als

Esmirnesos, segona part de la primitiva carta d'Ignasi als Efesis. Sum. 55. RCatT 21 (1996) 19-55.

10879   IRENAEUS: **Hoffman, Daniel L.** The status of women and Gnosticism in IRENAEUS and TERTULLIAN. 1995, ⇒11/2,g279. RCBQ 58 (1996) 551-552 *(Timbie, Janet A.)*.

10880   **Noormann, Rolf** IRENAEUS als Paulus Interpret. WUNT 2/66: 1994, ⇒10,5721. RBLE 97 (1996) 195-196 *(Légasse, S.)*; CBQ 58 (1996) 762-764 *(Perkins, Pheme)*.

10881   TERousseau, **Adelin** IRENEE de Lyon: démonstration de la prédication apostolique. SC 406: 1995, ⇒11/2,g226. RBib. 77 (1996) 580-582 *(Gargano, Guido Innocenzo)*.

10882   JUSTINUS: EMarcovich, **Miroslav** Iustini Martyris Apologiae pro christianis. 1994, ⇒10,14002*. RVigChr 50 (1996) 81-82 *(Van Winden, J.C.)*.

10883   ETMunier, **Charles** Saint Justin: Apologie pour les chrétiens. 1995, ⇒11/2,g236. RRHE 91 (1996) 512-513 *(Zeegers, Nicole)*; ThLZ 121 (1996) 1065-1066 *(Bartelink, G.J.M.)*.

10884   **Munier, Charles** L'Apologie de Saint Justin. 1994, ⇒10,14003; 11/2,g236. RRHE 91 (1996) 138-139 *(Zeegers, Nicole)*; ThLZ 121 (1996) 685-687 *(Wickert, Ulrich)*.

10885   *Tanzarella, Sergio* GIUSTINO e il millenarismo. BeO 38 (1996) 117-128.

10886   PAPIAS: *Oberweis, Michael* Das Papias-Zeugnis vom Tode des Johannes Zebedäi. NT 38 (1996) 277-295.

10887   POLYCARPUS: TBauer, **Johannes B.** Die Polykarpbriefe. 1995, ⇒11/2,g238. RJThS 47 (1996) 642-645 *(Maier, H.O.)*; ThLZ 121 (1996) 1061-1063 *(Löhr, Hermut)*.

10888   *Baumeister, Theofried* Die Norm des evangeliumgemässen Blutzeugnisses: das Martyrium Polycarpi als vorsichtige Exhortatio ad Martyrium. FDASSMANN E., JAC.E 23: 1996, ⇒19. 122-128.

10889   **Buschmann, Gerd** Martyrium Polycarpi: eine formkritische Studie. BZNW 70: 1994, ⇒10,14006; 11/2,g239. RCrSt 17 (1996) 635-637 *(Ruggiero, Fabio)*.

Y1.6 **Origenes**

10890   **Bammel, Caroline P. Hammond** Origeniana et Rufiniana. AGLB 29: FrB 1996, Herder 254 pp. DM145. 3-451-21943-3.

10891   **Crouzel, Henri** Bibliographie critique d'Origène: supplément II. Turnhout 1996, Brepols 363 pp. [BLE 97,395].

10892   EDaly, **Robert J.** Origeniana Quinta. BEThL 105: 1992, ⇒8,532... 11/2,g249. RJEarlyC 4 (1996) 594-596 *(Turcescu, Lucian)*.

  Doignon, Jean "Rengaines" origéniennes dans les Homélies sur Job d'Hilaire de Poitiers ⇒2946.

10893   EDorival, **Gilles; Le Boulluec, Alain** Origeniana Sexta: Origène et la Bible / Origen and the Bible. BEThL 118: 1995, ⇒11/2,571. RBLE 97 (1996) 396-398 [contents].

10894 **Fédou, Michel** La sagesse et le monde: essai sur la christologie d'Origène. 1995, ⇒11/2,g251. ^RREAug 42 (1996) 166-167 *(Bochet, Isabelle)*; RSR 84 (1996) 612-615 *(Sesboüé, Bernard)*.

10895 ^E**Geerlings, Wilhelm; König, Hildegard** Origenes: vir ecclesiasticus. ^FVOGT H.-J., 1995, ⇒11/2,539. ^RVetChr 33 (1996) 239-241 *(Veronese, Maria)*.

10896 **Hanson, R.P.C.** Allegory and event: a study of... Origen's interpretation of scripture. 1959, ⇒40,747. ^RThR 61 (1996) 285-288 *(Mühlenberg, Ekkehard)*.

10897 *Heither, Theresia* Origines als Exeget: ein Forschungsüberblick. ^FDASSMANN E., JAC.E 23: 1996, ⇒19. 141-153.

10898 *Jacob, Christoph* The reception of the Origenist tradition in Latin exegesis. Antiquity. 1996, ⇒10821. 682-700.

10899 **Lubac, Henri de** Geist aus der Geschichte: das Schriftverständnis des Origenes. 1968 <1950>, ⇒50,7575. ^RThR 61 (1996) 281-285 *(Mühlenberg, Ekkehard)*.

10900 **Neri, Umberto** Origene: testi ermeneutici. Epifania della Parola 7: Bo 1996, EDB 283 pp. 88-10-40229-4.
    Quacquarelli, Antonio Il genere omiletico in Origene: le *Omelie su Geremia* ⇒3468.

10901 *Restrepo Restrepo, Gonzalo* El método exegético de Orígenes. Cuestiones teológicas y filosóficas 59 (1996) 33-40 [EThL 74,164*].

10902 **Strutwolf, Holger** Gnosis als System: zur Rezeption der valentinianischen Gnosis bei Origenes. FKDG 56: 1993, ⇒9,15783; 11/2,g267. ^RThLZ 121 (1996) 174-176 *(Lattke, Michael)*.

Y1.8 **Tertullianus**

10903 **Daly, Cahal B.** Tertullian the Puritan and his influence. 1993, ⇒9,15795; 11/2,g274. ^RIBSt 18 (1996) 221-222 *(Kirkpatrick, L.)*.

10904 *Hilhorst, A.* Tertullian on the Acts of Paul. Apocryphal Acts of Paul. 1996, ⇒8136. 150-163.

10905 **Munier, Charles** Petite vie de Tertullien. P 1996, Desclée de B. 136 pp. [REAug 43/1,206].

10906 *Speigl, Jakob* Tertullian als Exeget. ^FDASSMANN E., JAC.E 23: 1996, ⇒19. 161-176.

10907 *Turek, Waldemar* L'influsso di Paolo su Tertulliano nell'evoluzione del concetto di speranza. Atti del IV Simposio di Tarso. 1996, ⇒263. 169-186.

Y2.0 *Patres graeci*—**The Greek Fathers**

10908 ^T**Grant, Robert M.; Menzies, Glen W.** Joseph's bible notes (Hypomnestikon): introduction, translation, and notes. SBL.TT 41.9: Atlanta 1996, Scholars. $45. 0-7885-0195-X. ^RJJS 47 (1996) 375-376 *(Edwards, M.J.)*.

10909 *Hidal, Sten* Exegesis of the Old Testament in the Antiochene school with its prevalent literal and historical method. Antiquity. 1996, ⇒10821. 543-568.

10910   *Paget, James N.B. Carleton* The Christian exegesis of the Old Testament in the Alexandrian tradition. Antiquity. 1996, ⇒10821. 478-542.
10911   *Procopé, J.F.* Greek philosophy, hermeneutics and Alexandrian understanding of the Old Testament. Antiquity. 1996, ⇒10821. 451-477.

10912   ATHANASIUS: *Canévet, Mariette* La théologie au secours de l'herméneutique biblique: l'exégèse de Phil. 2 et du Ps. 44 dans le Contra Arianos I,37-52 d'Athanase d'Alexandrie. OCP 62 (1996) 185-195.
10913   *Kannengiesser, Charles* Athanasius von Alexandrien als Exeget. ᶠDASSMANN E., JAC.E 23: 1996, ⇒19. 336-343.
10914   BASILIUS: **Rousseau, Philip** Basil of Caesarea. 1994, ⇒10,14085; 11/2,g333. ᴿJThS 47 (1996) 688-691 *(Van Dam, Raymond)*; TS 57 (1996) 344-346 *(Fedwick, Paul J.)*; JRS 86 (1996) 240-241 *(Clark, Gillian)*; HeyJ 37 (1996) 219-221 *(Meredith, Anthony)*.
10915   *Torchia, N. Joseph Sympatheia* in Basil of Caesarea's *Hexameron*: a Plotinian hypothesis. Sum. 359. JEarlyC 4 (1996) 359-377.

10916   CHRYSOSTOMUS: *Brottier, Laurence* L'actualisation de la figure de Job chez Jean Chrysostome. Livre de Job chez les Pères. 1996, ⇒2918. 63-110.
10917   **Kelly, J.N.D.** Golden Mouth: the story of John Chrysostom, ascetic, preacher, bishop. 1995, ⇒11/2,g337. ᴿGOTR 41 (1996) 393-395 *(Fotopoulos, John)*; JThS 47 (1996) 693-695 *(Young, Frances M.)*; TS 57 (1996) 346-347 *(Dennis, George T.)*.
10918   **Rau, Eckhard** Von Jesus zu Paulus: Entwicklung und Rezeption der antiochenischen Theologie im Urchristentum. 1994, ⇒10,14092. ᴿLebZeug 51 (1996) 153-154 *(Weiser, Alfons)*; TZ 52 (1996) 283-284 *(Rese, Martin)*; ThLZ 121 (1996) 669-670 *(Mell, Ulrich)*.

10919   DIONYSIUS: ᵀᴱ**Witakowski, Witold** Pseudo-Dionysius of Tel-Mahre. Dionysius (Telmahrensis): Chronicle (known also as the Chronicle of Zuqnin), 3. Translated Texts for Historians 22: Liverpool 1996, Liverpool University Press xxxii; 149 pp. 0-85323-760-3.
10920   EPHREM: *McCarthy, Carmel* Allusions and illusions: St Ephrem's verbal magic in the *Diatesseron* commentary. ᶠMc-NAMARA M., JSOT.S 230: 1996, ⇒58. 187-207.

10921   GREGORIUS Naz.: **Trisoglio, Francesco** San Gregorio di Nazianzo e il Christus Patiens: il problema dell'autenticità gregoriana del dramma. Filologia, Testi e studi 7: F 1996, Le Lettere 319 pp. 88-7166-280-6.
10922   ᵀ**Sieben, Hermann Josef** Gregorius Nazianzenus: orationes: orationes theologicae: theologische Reden. FC 22: FrB 1996, Herder 397 pp. Bibl. 3-451-23800-4.
10923   *Stains, David* Gregory Nazianzen's ascetic interpretation of Ecclesiastes 2 as a precedent for Gregory of Nyssa's condemna-

tion of slavery in his *Homily IV, on Ecclesiastes*. ProcGLM 16 (1996) 85-93 [EThL 74,178*].

10924 *Trisoglio, Francesco* San Gregorio Nazianzeno 1966-1993. Lustrum 38 (1996) 7-361.

10925 **Trisoglio, Francesco** Gregorio di Nazianzo: il teologo. SPMed 20: Mi 1996. Vita e Pensiero ix; 228 pp. 88-243-0182-X.

10926 **Demoen, Kristoffel** Pagan and biblical exempla in Gregory Nazianzen: a study in rhetoric and hermeneutica. CChr.LP II: Turnhout 1996, Brepols 498 pp. 2-503-50481-7 [VigChr 51,329].

GREGORIUS Nyssa: *Dihle, A.* Das Streben nach Vollkommenheit nach Philon und Gregor von Nyssa ⇒8082.

10927 *Gargano, Guido Innocenzo* I presupposti della mia 'lectio divina': una nota sull'esegesi biblica di Gregorio di Nissa padre della chiesa indivisa. F Dupont J., 1996, 235-239.

10928 **Böhm, Thomas** Theoria, Unendlichkeit, Aufstieg: philosophische Implikationen zu 'De vita Moysis' von Gregor von Nyssa. SVigChr 35: Lei 1996, Brill xii; 348 pp. 90-04-10560-3.

10929 ISIDORUS: **Évieux, Pierre** Isidore de Péluse. ThH 99: 1995, ⇒11/2,g386. R ScEs 48 (1996) 126-128 *(Pelland, Gilles)*; ThLZ 121 (1996) 374-375 *(Bartelink, G.J.M.)*.

10930 MAXIMUS C.: **Louth, Andrew** Maximus the Confessor. L 1996, Routledge ix; 230 pp. $60/$17 [AThR 80,275—Constas, Nicholas].

10931 *Yeago, David S.* Jesus of Nazareth and cosmic redemption: the relevance of St. Maximus the Confessor. MoTh 12/2 (1996) 163-193.

10932 **Blowers, Paul M.** Exegesis and spiritual pedagogy in Maximus the Confessor: an investigation of the *Quaestiones ad Thalassium*. CJAn 7: 1992, ⇒8,k821...10,14128. R SJTh 49 (1996) 378-379 *(Louth, Andrew)*.

10933 MELITO Sardensis: **Cohick, Lynn Harrison** Re-assessing the use of scriptural material and interpretations in the Περὶ Πασχά attributed to Melito of Sardes. Diss. Pennsylvania 1996, D Kraft, R.A., 336 pp. [EThL 74,163*].

10934 THEODORETUS: **Guinot, Jean-Noël** L'exégèse de Théodoret de Cyr. ThH 100: 1995, ⇒11/2,g403. R NRTh 118 (1996) 930-931 *(Leclair, G.)*.

10935 *Guinot, Jean-Noël* Regard sur l'utilisation du Livre de Job dans l'oeuvre de Théodoret de Cyr. Le Livre de Job chez les Pères. 1996, ⇒2918. 111-140.

10936 THEOPHILUS: *Zeegers, Nicole* Théophile d'Antioche est-il millénariste?. RHE 91 (1996) 743-784.

Y2.4 Augustinus

10937 **Delaroche, Bruno** Saint Augustin lecteur et interprète de Saint Paul: dans le *De peccatorum meritis et remissione* (hiver 411-412). EAug, Antiquité 146: P 1996, Institut d'Études Augustiniennes 408 pp. 2-85121-151-X. R RSR 84 (1996) 468-470 *(Duval, Y.-M.)*.

10938   *Delaroche, Bruno* Sauvés du péché: apologie pour Augustin. Com(F) 21 (1996) 63-73.
10939   ᴱ**Dolbeau, François** Augustin d'Hippone: vingt-six sermons au peuple d'Afrique. Retrouvé à Mayence, édités et commentés. EAug, Antiquité 147: P 1996, Institut d'Études Augustiniennes 756 pp. 2-85121-152-8.
        Doucet, Dominique Job: l'église et la tribulation: Augustin Adnotationes in Job 29-31 ⇒3004.
10940   *Folliet, Georges* La double citation de 1 Rois ou Samuel 2,9 par Saint Augustin (Confessions XIII,18,22, et Cité de Dieu XVII,4). RBen 106 (1996) 246-254.
        Fournier, C. Augustin, Adnotationes in Job I, 29-31 ⇒3005.
10941   **Guschewski, Petra** Das sog. Evangeliar des heiligen Augustinus [Bibliothek des Corpus Christi College]. Diss. Mü 1996 [AA (1997/1) 102].
        Marin, Marcello L'*elocutio* della scrittura nei due primi commenti agostiniani alla *Genesi* ⇒1326.
10942   ᴱ**Mayer, Cornelius** Augustinus-Lexikon, 1. Basel 1986-1994, Schwabe lx; 1294 pp. ᴿThQ 176 (1996) 155-157 *(Vogt, H.J.)*;
10943   Corpus Augustinianum Gissense auf CD-ROM. CAG. Basel 1996, Schwabe. ᴿREAug 42 (1996) 324-326 *(Madec, Goulven)*.
10944   **Stock, Brian** Augustine the reader: meditations, self-knowledge, and the ethics of interpretation. CM 1996, Harvard Univ. Press xi; 463 pp. 0-674-05276-5.
10945   **Studer, Basil** Gratia Christi—gratia Dei bei Augustinus. SEAug 40: 1993, ⇒9,16013; 11/2,g479. ᴿJAC 39 (1996) 279-280 *(Flasch, Kurt)*.
10946   *Studer, Basil* Die Kirche als Schule des Herrn bei Augustinus von Hippo. ᶠDASSMANN E., JAC.E 23: 1996, ⇒19. 485-498.
10947   *Studer, Basil* Le lettere paoline nella teologia trinitaria di Agostino. Atti del IV Simposio di Tarso. 1996, ⇒263. 159-168.
10948   *Weber, Dorothea* Adam, Eva und die Schlange: Überlegungen zu Augustins Interpretation des Sündenfalls in *De Genesis contra Manichaeos*. L'etica cristiana. 1996, ⇒279. 401-412.
10949   **Wiles, James W.** A scripture index to the works of St Augustine in English translation. 1995, ⇒11/2,g493. ᴿCTJ 31 (1996) 301-302 *(Muller, Richard A.)*.
10950   *Wohlmuth, Josef* Theophanietexte in der Exegese des Augustinus: ein systematisch orientiertes Gespräch zwischen Augustinus und der Phänomenologie. ᶠDASSMANN E., JAC.E 23: 1996, ⇒19. 512-525.
10951   *Wright, David F.* Augustine: his exegesis and hermeneutics. Antiquity. 1996, ⇒10821. 701-730.

ʏ2.5 Hieronymus

10952   *Clausi, Benedetto* La parola stravolta: polemica ed esegesi biblica nell'*Adversus Iovinianum* di Gerolamo. Retorica ed esegesi biblica. QVetChr 24: 1996, ⇒259. 87-126.
10953   ᵀᴱ**Donalson, Malcolm D.** A translation of Jerome's *Chronicon* with historical commentary. Lewiston 1996, Mellen x; 176 pp. $80. 0-7734-2258-7 [ThD 44,173].

10954 ^E**Hilberg, Isidorus** Sancti Eusebii Hieronymi epistulae, I-III. CSEL 54, 55, 56/1: W ²1996, Verlag der Österreichischen Akademie der Wissenschaften viii + 708; iv + 516; vi + 368 pp. AUS2.856. 3-7001-2602-6 [JThS 50,335ss—Scourfield, J.H.D.].

10955 ^E**Kamptner, Margit** Sancti Eusebii Hieronymi epistulae, IV: indexes and addenda. CSEL 56/2: W 1996, Verlag der Österreichischen Akademie der Wissenschaften 312 pp. AUS952. 3-7001-2603-4 [JThS 50,335—Scourfield, J.H.D.].

10956 *Kieffer, René* Jerome: his exegesis and hermeneutics. Antiquity. 1996, ⇒10821. 663-681.

10957 *Laurence, Patrick* Marcella, Jérôme et Origène. REAug 42 (1996) 267-293.

10958 *Provera, Mario* Jerusalem in the thought and writing of St. Jerome. Adapted by *Lewitt, George,* Holy Land 16 (1996) 86-88.

10959 *Quacquarelli, Antonio* L'uomo e la sua appartenenza alle due città nell'esegesi biblica di Gerolamo. VetChr 33 (1996) 275-288.

10960 **Rebenich, Stefan** Hieronymus und sein Kreis. 1992, ⇒9,16040... 11/2,g521. ^RJThS 47 (1996) 695-698 *(Clark, Elizabeth A.).*

Y2.6 **Patres Latini** *in ordine alphabetico*

10961 **Dekkers, E.** Clavis patrum latinorum. Steenbrugis ³1995. ^RRHE 91 (1996) 479-483 *(Gryson, R.);* RBen 106 (1996) 204-206; *(Bogaert, P.-M.).*

10962 *Gryson, R.* Nouveaux instruments de travail en patristique latine. RHE 91 (1996) 465-483.

10963 ^E**Odahl, Charles M.** Early christian Latin literature. 1993, ⇒10,14214. ^RClR 46 (1996) 66-67 *(Knott, B.I.).*

10964 *Piccinini, Elissa* La sirene nella patristica latina. VetChr 33 (1996) 353-370.

10965 *Schulz-Flügel, Eva* The Latin Old Testament tradition. Antiquity. 1996, ⇒10821. 642-662.

10966 AMBROSIASTER: *Geerlings, Wilhelm* Zur exegetischen Methode des Ambrosiaster. ^FDASSMANN E., JAC.E 23: 1996, ⇒19. 444-449.

10967 AMBROSIUS M.: *Ramos-Lisson, Domingo* En torno al alegorismo bíblico del tratado De Virginitate de San Ambrosio: los préstamos de los autores clásicos y cristianos. ^FDASSMANN E., JAC.E 23: 1996, ⇒19. 450-463.

10968 **Pasini, Cesare** Ambrogio di Milano: azione e pensiero di un vescovo. Mi 1996, San Paolo 272 pp. [REAug 43/1,214].

10969 CASSIANUS: *Frank, Karl Suso* Asketischer Evangelismus: Schriftauslegung bei Johannes Cassian. ^FDASSMANN E., JAC.E 23: 1996, ⇒19. 435-443.

10970 CYPRIANUS: *Burini, Clara* 'Innocente nelle mani e puro di cuore' (Ps. Cipriano, *I due monti* 9,3-5). Som. 275. PSV 34 (1996) 275-287.

10971 *Deléani, Simone* La syntaxe des titres dans les recueils scripturaires de saint Cyprien. RechAug 29 (1996) 91-112.

10972 CYRILLUS J.: *Saxer, Victor* Cyrill von Jerusalem und die Heilige Schrift: was er von ihr lernt und wie er sie gebraucht.
FDASSMANN E., JAC.E 23: 1996, ⇒19. 344-356.

10973 GREGORIUS M.: *Recchia, Vincenzo* I moduli espressivi
dell'esperienza contemplativa nelle *Omelie su Ezechiele* di Gregorio Magno: schemi tropi e ritmi. Retorica ed esegesi biblica.
QVetChr 24: 1996, ⇒259. 163-200.

10974 **Recchia, Vincenzo** Gregorio Magno papa ed esegeta biblico.
Quaderni di "Invigilata Lucernis" 4: Bari 1996, Dipartimento di
studi classici e cristiani xxxvii; 839 pp.

10975 TCremascoli, Giuseppe San Gregorio Magno: omelie sui vangeli. R 1994, Città Nuova 608 pp. L90.000. RCivCatt 147 IV
(1996) 193-194 *(Cremascoli, G.)*.
HILARIUS P.: *Doignon, Jean* Versets de Job sur le péché de
notre origine selon Hilaire de Poitiers ⇒2993.
Doignon, Jean "Rengaines" origéniennes dans les Homélies sur
Job d'Hilaire de Poitiers ⇒2946.

10976 *Durst, Michael* Nizäa als "autoritative Tradition" bei Hilarius von
Poitiers. FDASSMANN E., JAC.E 23: 1996, ⇒19. 406-422.

10977 HIPPOLYTUS: *Frickel, Josef* Hippolyt von Rom: als Prediger
verkannt. FDASSMANN E., JAC.E 23: 1996, ⇒19. 129-140.

10978 ISIDORUS: *Fontaine, Jacques* Isidore de Seville pédagogue et
théoricien de l'exégèse. FDASSMANN E., JAC.E 23: 1996,
⇒19. 423-434.

10979 MAXIMUS: TPlazanet-Siarri, Nadine Maxime de Turin prêche
l'année liturgique: 42 homélies. CPF: P 1996, Migne 208 pp.
[REAug 43/1,219].

10980 NOVITIANUS: ETGranado, Carmelo Novatianus: De Trinitate:
La Trinidad. Fuentes Patrísticas 8: M 1996, Ciudad Nueva 313
pp. 84-89651-13-2.
ZENON: *Maraval, Pierre* Job dans l'oeuvre de Zénon de Vérone
⇒2959.

10981 *Van Rompay, Lucas* The christian Syriac tradition of interpretation. Antiquity. 1996, ⇒10821. 612-641.

Y3.0 **Medium aevum,** *generalia*

10982 EBischoff, Bernhard; Lapidge, Michael Biblical commentaries
from the Canterbury school of Theodore and Hadrian. CSASE
10: 1994, ⇒10,14273*. RJThS 47 (1996) 336-338 *(Smith,
Lesley)*; JR 76 (1996) 631-632 *(Szarmach, Paul E.)*.

10983 **Buc, Philippe** L'ambiguité du livre: prince, pouvoir, et peuple
dans les commentaires de la bible au Moyen Age. ThH 95: 1994,
⇒10,14279; 11/2,g652. RMSR 53/4 (1996) 83-85 *(Cannuyer,
Christian)*; ScEs 48 (1996) 121-122 *(Pelland, Gilles)*.

10984 *Muller, Richard A.* Biblical interpretation in the era of the Reformation: the view from the Middle Ages. FSTEINMETZ D.,
1996, ⇒86. 3-22.

10985 **Nodes, D.J.** Doctrine and exegesis in biblical Latin poetry. 1993,
⇒10,14342. RJEarlyC 4 (1996) 585-587 *(Sider, Robert D.)*; Gn.
68 (1996) 160-162 *(Kirsch, Wolfgang)*.

10986 **Rubin, Miri** Corpus Christi: the eucharist in late medieval culture. 1991, ⇒9,16226; 10,14352. ᴿCThMi 23/2 (1996) 142-143 *(Killinger, Keith)*.
10987 *Zonta, Mauro* Gli influssi dei commentatori ebrei sugli esegeti cristiani. La lettura ebraica. 1996, ⇒205. 299-316.

Y3.4 **Exegetae mediaevales** [Hebraei ⇒κ7]

10988 AQUINAS: *Mongillo, Dalmazio* La 'testimonianza della coscienza' nella 'Lectura super epistolam ad Romanos' di S. Tommaso (CRO). Atti del IV Simposio. 1996, ⇒263. 255-274.
ERIUGENA: ᴱVan Riel, G. Eriugena...bible...hermeneutics ⇒276.
10989 FIORE: *Laffranchi, Marco* Giocacchino da Fiore: esegesi e storia. Florensia 10 (1996) 193-197.
10990 PETRICIS: *Xaranauli, Ana* Die Bibel in den Kommentaren Ioane Petricis. Georgica 19 (1996) 71-76.
10991 TRITHEMIUS: *Froehlich, Karlfried* Johannes Trithemius on the fourfold sense of scripture: the *Tractatus de inuestigatione sacrae scripturae* (1486). ᶠSTEINMETZ D., 1996, ⇒86. 23-60.

Y4.1 **Luther**

10992 ᵀBüttgen, Philippe De la liberté du chrétien: préfaces à la bible. Essais 338: P 1996, Seuil 163 pp. Edition bilingue allemand-français. FF45. 2-02-026285-1.
10993 *Cottin, Jérôme* Loi et évangile chez Luther et CRANACH. RHPhR 76 (1996) 293-314.
10994 **Sander-Gaiser, M.H.** Lernen als Spiel bei Martin Luther. Diss. Fra 1996, Haag & H. 302 pp.

Y4.3 **Exegesis et controversia saeculi XVI**

10995 *Corsani, Bruno* Lettura storica e lettura di fede della bibbia nei Riformatori. Sum. 7. AScRel 1 (1996) 189-201.
10996 ᴱMarianne, Ruel Robins Paroles d'évangile: quatre pamphlets allemands des années 1520. P 1996, Publications de la Sorbonne 247 pp. Traductions revues par Catherine Dejeumont [RHPhR 77,366].
10997 *Schreiner, Susan E.* 'The spiritual man judges all things': CALVIN and the exegetical debates about certainty in the Reformation. ᶠSTEINMETZ D., 1996, ⇒86. 189-215.
10998 **Shuger, Debora Kuller** The Renaissance bible: scholarship, sacrifice, and subjectivity. 1994, ⇒11/2,k011. ᴿBiRe 12/4 (1996) 17 *(Hendel, Ronald S.)*.

Y4.4 **Periti aetatis reformatoriae**

10999 BULLINGER: *Kok, Joel E.* Heinrich Bullinger's exegetical method: the model for Calvin?. ᶠSTEINMETZ D., 1996, ⇒86. 241-254.

11000 CALVIN **Battles, Ford Lewis** Interpreting John Calvin. GR 1996, Baker 377 pp. $30 [ThTo 55/1,108—Leith, John H.].

11001 *Godfrey, W. Robert* 'Beyond the sphere of our judgment': Calvin and the confirmation of scripture. WThJ 58 (1996) 29-39.

11002 **Puckett, David L.** John Calvin's exegesis of the Old Testament. Columbia Series in Reformed Theology. 1995, ⇒11/2,k067. ᴿWThJ 58 (1996) 324-327 *(Enns, Peter)*.

11003 **Thompson, John Lee** John Calvin and the daughters of Sarah. 1992, ⇒9,16471...11/2,k072. ᴿCTJ 31 (1996) 209-212 *(Pitkin, Barbara)*.

11004 **Steinmetz, David C.** Calvin in context. Oxf 1995, OUP 256 pp. $45/$16. 0-19509-164-7/5-5.

11005 CARLSTADT: ᵀᴱ**Furcha, E.J.** The essential Carlstadt: fifteen tracts by Andreas Bodenstein von Karlstadt. Classics of the Radical Reformation 8: Scottdale, PA 1995, Herald 432 pp. £38/$50. 0-8361-3116-9.

11006 ERASMUS: **Augustijn, Cornelis** Erasmus: his life, works, and influence. ᵀ*Grayson, J.C.*, Toronto ²1995 <1991>, Univ. of Toronto Press 272 pp. £13. 0-8020-7177-5.

11007 ᴱ**Sider, Robert D.** New Testament scholarship. ᵀ*Bateman, John J.*, Coll. Works of Erasmus 44: Toronto 1993, Univ. of Toronto xviii; 413 pp. ᴿSR 25 (1996) 362-363 *(Shantz, Douglas H.)*.

11008 LAS CASAS: **Gutiérrez, Gustavo** Alla ricerca dei poveri di Gesù Cristo: il pensiero di Bartolomé de Las Casas. 1995, ⇒11/2,k122. ᴿRdT 37 (1996) 253-268 *(Gaggioli, Luca)*.

11009 LUIS de León: *Hervás, José Luis* Nuestra unidad en Adán y en Cristo según Fray Luis de León. Esperanza del hombre. 1996, ⇒173. 503-510.

11010 TYNDALE: **Daniell, David** William Tyndale: a biography. 1994, ⇒10,14568; 11/2,k147. ᴿBibl.Interp. 4 (1996) 230-233 *(Coxon, Peter W.)*.

11011 VERMIGLI: *Thompson, John L.* The survival of allegorical argumentation in Peter Martyr Vermigli's Old Testament exegesis. ᶠSTEINMETZ D., 1996, ⇒86. 255-271.

11012 ZWINGLI: **Hoburg, Ralf** Seligkeit und Heilsgewißheit: Hermeneutik und Schriftauslegung bei Huldrych Zwingli bis 1522. CThM.ST 11: Stu 1994, Calwer 308 pp. FS106. 3-7668-0798-6 [Zwing. 25,184ss—Schindler, Alfred].

Υ4.5 *Exegesis post-reformatoria*—**Historical criticism to 1800**

11013 **Armogathe, Jean-Robert** Le grand siècle et la bible. 1989, ⇒6,k767...8,m410. ᴿRThom 96 (1996) 341-342 *(Fabre, Jean-Michel)*.

11014 **Baird, William** From deism to Tübingen. History of New Testament research 1: 1992, ⇒8,4110... 11/2,k158. ᴿChH 65 (1996) 733-735 *(Jodock, Darrell)*; ThR 61 (1996) 153-155 *(Reventlow, Henning Graf)*.

11015 **Breuer, Edward** The limits of enlightenment: Jews, Germans, and the eighteenth-century study of Scripture. HJM 7: CM 1996, Harvard Univ. Press 332 pp. 0-674-53426-3.

Y4.7 Auctores 1600-1800 alphabetice

11016 BUXTORF: **Burnett, Stephen G.** From christian Hebraism to
Jewish studies: Johannes Buxtorf (1564-1629) and Hebrew learning in the seventeenth century. SHCT 68: Lei 1996, Brill xii; 317
pp. $110.50. 90-04-10346-5.

11017 MENGDEN: *Zimmermann, Christian von* 'Er stehet unbewegt,
und achtet alles nicht': Notizen zu Leben und Werk des livländi-
schen Psalmdichters Gustav von Mengden (1627-1688). Daphnis
24 (1995) 401-425 [IAJS 42,45].

11018 SEMLER: **Lüder, Andreas** Historie und Dogmatik: ein Beitrag
zur Genese und Entfaltung von Johann Salomo Semlers Verständnis des AT. BZAW 233: 1995, ⇒11/2,k267. ᴿThLZ 121 (1996)
641-644 *(Reventlow, Henning Graf)*.

11019 SPINOZA: **Strauss, Leo** La critique de la religion chez Spinoza
ou les fondements de la science spinoziste de la bible: recherches
pour une étude du 'traité théologique-politique'. ᵀ*Almaleh,
Gérard; Baraquin, Albert; Depadt-Eichenbaum, Mireille,* Foreword *Krüger, Gerhard,* Afterword *Guttmann, Julius,* La Nuit
Surveillée: P 1996, Cerf xvi; 394 pp. FF240. 2-204-05308-0
[BCLF 580,2417].

Y5.0 *Saeculum XIX*—Exegesis—19th century; *Modernism*

11020 *Adriányi, Gabriel* Ein Exegetenstreit an der Theologischen Fa-
kultät der Universität zu Budapest 1806-1820. ᶠDASSMANN E.,
JAC.E 23: 1996, ⇒19. 595-601.

11021 **Bechtoldt, Hans-Joachim** Die jüdische Bibelkritik im 19. Jahrhundert. 1995, ⇒11/2,k288b. ᴿSNTU.A 21 (1996) 283-285
(Fuchs, A.).

11022 **Hauzenberger, Hans** Basel und die Bibel: die Bibel als Quelle ö-
kumenischer, missionarischer, sozialer und pädagogischer Impulse in der ersten Hälfte des 19. Jahrhunderts. Neujahrsblatt 174:
Basel 1996, Gesellschaft für das Gute und Gemeinnützige 260 pp.
Jubliäumsschrift der Basler Bibelgesellschaft. FS30/DM34.50. 3-
7190-1429-0 [ThZ 54,84s—Kuhn, Thomas K.].

11023 *Thuesen, Peter J.* Some scripture is inspired by God: late-nine-
teenth-century Protestants and the demise of a common bible.
ChH 65 (1996) 609-623.

11024 DELITZSCH: **Lehmann, Reinhard G.** Friedrich Delitzsch und
der Bibel—Babel—Streit. OBO 133: 1994, ⇒10,14651. ᴿWZKM
87 (1997) 296-299 *(Leonhard, Clemens)*; AcOr 58 (1997) 201-
202 *(Barstad, H.M.)*.

11025 DIESTEL: *Wagner, Siegfried* Ludwig Diestel—Notizen zu Leben
und Werk. Ausgewählte Aufsätze. BZAW 240: 1996 <1981>,
⇒156. 191-198.

11026 MOORE: *Smith, Morton* The work of George Foot Moore.
Studies in... method. 1996 <1967>, ⇒150. 201-210.

11027 SMITH: ᴱ**Johnstone, William** William Robertson Smith: essays
in reassessment. JSOT.S 189: 1995, ⇒11/2,k377. ᴿBTB 26
(1996) 90-91 *(Simkins, Ronald A.)*.

11028 **Diggins, John Patrick** The promise of pragmatism: Modernism and the crisis of knowledge and authority. Ch 1994, University of Chicago Press xiv; 515 pp. ᴿMoTh 12,2 (1996) 262-265 *(Quirk, Michael J.)*.
Montagnes, Bernard Le père Lagrange, 1855-1938: l'exégèse catholique dans la crise moderniste ⇒11062.

11029 **Renan, Ernest** L'antéchrist; les évangiles; l'église chrétienne; Marc-Aurèle. Histoire des origines du christianisme 2. ᴱ*Rétat, Laudyce*, P 1995, Laffont 1300 pp. 2-221-05806-2.

ʏ6.0 *Saeculum XX*—20th Century Exegesis

11030 *Doré, Joseph* Chemins de l'exégèse chrétienne d'aujourd'hui: une relecture théologique. ꜰLᴇɢᴀssᴇ S., LeDiv 166: 1996, ⇒51. 415-435.

11031 **Grelot, Pierre** Il rinnovamento biblico nel ventesimo secolo: memorie di un protagonista. CinB 1996, San Paolo 376 pp. L48.000 [RdT 37,849].

11032 **Harrisville, Roy A.; Sundberg, Walter** The bible in modern culture: theology and historical-critical method from Sᴘɪɴᴏᴢᴀ to Kᴀᴇsᴇᴍᴀɴɴ. 1995, ⇒11/2,k460. ᴿWThJ 58 (1996) 159-161 *(Silva, Moisés)*; SNTU.A 21 (1996) 220-222 *(Stimpfle, A.)*; CritRR 9 (1996) 137-139 *(Adam, A.K.M.)*.

11033 **Lehmkühler, Karsten** Kultus und Theologie: Dogmatik und Exegese in der religionsgeschichtlichen Schule. FSOTh 76: Gö 1996, Vandenhoeck & R. 327 pp. Diss. Erlangen-Nürnberg. DM98. 3-525-56283-7 [ThLZ 124,205ss—Schilson, Arno].

11034 *Marchadour, Alain* Un siècle d'exégèse critique. ꜰLᴇɢᴀssᴇ S., LeDiv 166: 1996, ⇒51. 7-21.

11035 Aʟʙʀɪɢʜᴛ: *Adams, Robert McC.* Epilogue;
11036 *Cooper, Jerrold S.; Schwartz, Glenn M.* Prologue. Albright centennial conference. 1996, ⇒303. 405-411/1-8.

11037 *Long, Burke O.* W.F. Albright as prophet-reformer: a theological paradigm inscribed in scholarly practice. ꜰTᴜᴄᴋᴇʀ G., JSOT.S 229: 1996, ⇒95. 152-172.

11038 *Machinist, Peter* William Foxwell Albright: the man and his work. Albright centennial conference. 1996, ⇒303. 385-403.

11039 Bᴀʀᴛʜ: *Schmithals, Walter* Zu Karl Barths Schriftauslegung: die Problematik des Verhältnisses von 'dogmatischer' und historischer Exegese. Karl Barths Schriftauslegung. 1996, ⇒207. 23-52.

11040 *Trowitzsch, Michael* "Nachkritische Schriftauslegung": Wiederaufnahme und Fortführung einer Fragestellung. Karl Barths Schriftauslegung. 1996, ⇒207. 73-109.

11041 Bᴀᴜᴍɢᴀʀᴛɴᴇʀ: *Smend, Rudolf* Der Exeget und der Dogmatiker—anhand des Briefwechsels zwischen W. Baumgartner und K. Barth. Karl Barths Schriftauslegung. 1996, ⇒207. 53-72.

11042 Bᴇɴ-Cʜᴏʀɪɴ: *Hahn, Ferdinand* Laudatio anläßlich des 75. Geburtstages von Schalom Ben-Chorin. ꜰHᴀʜɴ F., 1996 <1989>, ⇒34. 190-195.

11043 Bᴜʙᴇʀ:*Habbel, Torsten* Martin Bubers Werk bleibt interessant. ThRv 92 (1996) 477-482.

11044 **Kepnes, Steven** The text as thou: Martin Buber's dialogical hermeneutics and narrative theology. 1992, ⇒9,16776; 11/2,k479. RJR 76 (1996) 149-150 *(Smith, Ray Steinhoff)*.

11045 BULTMANN: **Gagey, Henri-Jérome**: Jésus dans la théologie de Bultmann. CJJC 57: 1993, ⇒10,14791. RRSR 84 (1996) 618-621 *(Sesboüé, Bernard)*.

11046 **Jaspert, Bernd** Sachgemässe Exegese: die Protokolle aus Rudolf Bultmanns neutestamentlichen Seminaren 1921-1951. MThSt 43: Marburg 1996, Elwert x; 275 pp. DM48. 3-7708-1062-7 [ThLZ 122,1023].

11047 **Valerio, Karolina de** Altes Testament und Judentum im Frühwerk Rudolf Bultmanns. BZNW 71: 1994, ⇒10,14798; 11/2,k492. RThRv 92 (1996) 300-304 *(Hübner, Hans)*.

11048 BURGMANN: *Callaway, Phillip R.* The writings and views of Hans Burgmann on the Dead Sea Scrolls;

11049 *Kapera, Zdzisław J.* Hans Burgmann's bibliography on the Dead Sea Scrolls: addenda. MBURGMANN H., 1996 <1993>, ⇒12. 187-198/209-212.

11050 CLAUDEL: *Saward, John* Regaining paradise: Paul Claudel and the renewal of exegesis. DR 114 (1996) 79-95.

11051 DEVER: *Shanks, Hershel* Is this man a biblical archaeologist [William G. Dever]?. BArR 22/4 (1996) 30-39, 62.

11052 DREYFUS: *Franco, Francesco* L'esegesi tra fede e scienza: l'ermeneutica ecclesiale di François Dreyfus. Asp. 43 (1996) 383-396.

11053 GIRARD: EWilliams, James G. The Girard reader. NY 1996, Crossroad xii; 303 pp. £14.

11054 GORDON: *Lubetski, Meir; Gottlieb, Claire* "Forever Gordon": portrait of a master scholar with a global perspective. BA 59 (1996) 2-12.

11055 *Marblestone, Howard* A "Mediterranean synthesis": Professor Cyrus H. Gordon's contributions to the classics. BA 59 (1996) 22-30.

11056 *Morrison, Martha A.* A continuing adventure: Cyrus Gordon and Mesopotamia. BA 59 (1996) 31-35.

11057 *Yamauchi, Edwin M.* Magic bowls: Cyrus H. Gordon and the ubiquity of magic in the pre-modern world. BA 59 (1996) 51-55.

11058 GOULDER: **Goodacre, Mark S.** Goulder and the gospels: an examination of a new paradigm. JSOT.S 133: Shf 1996, Academic 416 pp. $70. 1-85075-631-7 [BTB 27,120].

11059 GRELOT: **Grelot, Pierre** Combats pour la bible en église. 1994, ⇒10,14802; 11/2,k495. RScEs 48 (1996) 119-120 *(Pelland, Gilles)*.

11060 GUNKEL: *Wagner, A.* Gattung und 'Sitz im Leben': zur Bedeutung der formgeschichtlichen Arbeit Hermann Gunkels (1862-1932) für das Verstehen der sprachlichen Größe 'Text'. Texte-Konstitution, Verarbeitung, Typik. EMichaelis, S.; Thopinke, D., Linguistik 13: Mü 1996, Lincom. 117-163 [ZAW 110,480—Köckert, M.].

11061 KAESEMANN: *Gräßer, Erich* Ernst Käsemann zum neunzigsten Geburtstag. ZNW 87 (1996) 143-145.

11062 LAGRANGE: **Montagnes, Bernard** Le père Lagrange, 1855-1938: l'exégèse catholique dans la crise moderniste. 1995, ⇒11/2,k502. RRB 103 (1996) 304-306 *(Viviano, B.T.)*.

11063 Lubac:**Lubac, Henri** de Meine Schriften im Rückblick. ThRom 21: Einsiedeln 1996, Johannes 591 pp. Vorwort von Erzbischof *Christoph Schönborn*. DM67. 3-89411-337-5 [ThRv 94,627s— Müller, Gerhard L.].

11064 Luzzi: **Dür-Gademann, Hans-Peter** Giovanni Luzzi traduttore della bibbia e teologo ecumenico. T*Cunz, Marina Sartorio;* Pref. *Campi, Emilio*, CFVT 19: T 1996, Claudiana 270 pp. 88-7016-234-6 [EThL 74,166*].

11065 Mackenzie: *Momigliano, Nicoletta* Duncan Mackenzie and the Palestine Exploration Fund. PEQ 128 (1996) 139-170.

11066 Mason: *Barton, John* Rex Mason. F MASON R., 1996, ⇒57. 1-2.

11067 Massignon: **Rizzardi, Giuseppe** L. Massignon (1883-1962): un profilo dell'orientalista cattolico. Quodlibet 6: Mi 1996, Glossa 178 pp. 88-7105-060-6.

11068 Mesters: *Pereira, Antônio da Silva* Leitura da bíblia em Carlos Mesters: uma interpretação equivocada. REB 56 (1996) 945-955.

11069 Michel: *Wagner, Andreas; Lehmann, Reinhard G.* Verzeichnis der Veröffentlichungen Diethelm Michels. F MICHEL D., BZAW 241: 1996, ⇒64. 253-259.

11070 Milik: *García Martínez, Florentino* Bibligraphie qumrânienne de Jósef Tadeusz Milik. RdQ 17 (1996) 11-20.

11071 *Puech, Émile* Józef Tadeusz Milik. RdQ 17 (1996) 5-10.

11072 Muntingh: *Cloete, W.T.W.* Lukas Marthinus Muntingh. JNSL 22/2 (1996) V-VIII.

11073 Mussner: *Hoppe, Rudolf* Professor Dr.theol. Franz Mußner zum 80. Geburtstag. FrRu 3 (1996) 236-237.

11074 Rad: *Rad, Gerhard von* Meditación sobre sí mismo. La acción de Dios. 1996 <1966>, ⇒144. 291-293.

11075 Reisner: *Atkinson, Kenneth* An archaeologist before his time: George Reisner and the first American dig in the Holy Land. BArR 22/6 (1996) 68-69, 76.

11076 Schlatter: **Neuer, Werner** Adolf Schlatter: ein Leben für Theologie und Kirche. Stu 1996, Calwer xviii; 937 pp. DM88. 3-7668-3390-1.

11077 Schweitzer: E**Luz, Ulrich,** (*al*), Reich Gottes und Christentum. 1995, ⇒11/2,k512. R ThR 61 (1996) 118-119 *(Zager, Werner)*.

11078 **Schweitzer, Albert** Conversations sur le Nouveau Testament. T*Kemner, Pierre;* Pref. *Sorg, J.-P.;* Afterword *Döbertin, W.*, P 1996, Brepols 185 pp. FF85. 2-503-830-24-2.

11079 Smith:*Kysar, Robert* The contribution of D. Moody Smith to Johannine scholarship. F SMITH D., 1996, ⇒82. 3-17.

11080 Van Beek: *Van Beek, Ora* A biography of Gus W. Van Beek. Retrieving the past. F VAN BEEK G., 1996, ⇒96. xi-xvii.

11081 Vittorino: *Raspanti, Giacomo* Il significato storico dell'esegesi di Mario Vittorino. Ho Theológos 14 (1996) 103-128.

11082 **Raspanti, Giacomo** Mario Vittorino exegeta di S. Paolo. Pref. *Duval, Yves Marie*, Bibliotheca Philologica 1: Palermo 1996, L'epos 179 pp. L32.000 [CBQ 59,423].

11083 Watts: *House, Paul R.* The formation of a scholar. F WATTS J., JSOT.S 235: 1996, ⇒105. 13-20.

11084 WERFEL: **Eggers, Frank Joachim** 'Ich bin ein Katholik mit jüdischem Gehirn': Modernitätskritik und Religion bei Joseph Roth und Franz Werfel: Untersuchungen zu den erzählerischen Werken. Beiträge zur Literatur und Literaturwissenschaft des 20. Jahrhunderts 13: Fra 1996, Lang 300 pp. 3-631-48649-9.

Theologian-exegetes

11085 ALTHAUS: **Meiser, Martin** Paul Althaus als Neutestamentler. CThM 15: 1993, ⇒8,m638... 11/2,k739. ᴿSEÅ 61 (1996) 153-155 *(Bell, Richard)*.

11086 BARTH: **Kraege, Jean-Denis** L'écriture seule: pour une lecture dogmatique de la bible: l'exemple de Luther et de Barth. 1995, ⇒11/2,k764. ᴿETR 71 (1996) 455-456 *(Ansaldi, Jean)*; RThPh 128 (1996) 309-310 *(Cornu, Silke)*.

11087 BONHOEFFER: **Marsh, Charles** Reclaiming Dietrich Bonhoeffer: the promise of his theology. 1994, ⇒10,14996; 11/2,k788. ᴿMoTh 12,1 (1996) 121-123 *(Hunsinger, George)*.

11088 WITTGENSTEIN: **Malcolm, Norman** Wittgenstein: a religious point of view?. ᴱWinch, Peter, 1994, ⇒10,15128. ᴿMoTh 12,1 (1996) 123-7 *(Churchill, John)*.

Y7.2 *(Acta) Congressuum* Biblica: **nuntii,** rapports, Berichte

11089 *Ahl, Ruth* BUBER/ROSENZWEIGS Verdeutschung der Schrift—was bedeutete sie damals—was bedeutet sie heute?. Notizen von einem Studientag 1995. FrRu 3 (1996) 68-71.

11090 *Augustin, Matthias; Schunck, Klaus-Dietrich* Bericht zum 14. Kongreß der International Organization for the Study of the Old Testament (IOSOT) vom 19.-24. Juli 1992. Collected communications. BEAT 28: 1996, ⇒160. 9-10.

11091 *Bauer, Dieter* Ein Mann kommt nach oben: Bericht von einer Männer-Bibelarbeit auf dem Dresdner Katholikentag. BiKi 51/1 (1996) 28-32.

11092 *Božja, Riječ; Života, Izvor* Završna izjava V. plenarne skupštine Katoličke biblijske federacije Hong Kong, 2.-12.srpnja 1996 [Word of God—the source of life: final statement of the fifth general assembly of the Catholic Biblical Federation]. Bog.Smo. 66 (1996) 715-722.

11093 *Brzegowy, Tadeusz* XIII Międzynarodowe spotkanie Society of Biblical Literature (Budapeszt 1995) [De XIII conventu internationi 'Society of Biblical Literature' (Budapestini 1995)]. RBL 49 (1996) 51-52. **P**.

11094 *Casalini, Nello* La Settimana Biblica Abruzzese. TS(I) 72 (mag.-giu. 1996) 47-49.

11095 *Ceresko, Anthony R.* The 17th national conference of the Society for Biblical Studies. ITS 33 (1996) 156-159;

11096 Report of the XIX annual meeting of the Indian Theological Association at the N.B.C.L.C., Bangalore, May 4-8, 1996. ITS 33 (1996) 159-163.

11097 *Chmiel, Jerzy* 50. Zjazd Studiorum Novi Testamenti Societatis (Praga 1995) [The 50th General Meeting of the Studiorum Novi Testamenti Societas (Prague 1995)]. RBL 49 (1996) 124-126. **P**.;

11098   51. zjazd Studiorum Novi Testamenti Societatis (Strasburg 1996)
         [51ème congrès SNTS (Strasbourg 1996)]. RBL 49 (1996) 268-
         269. **P**.
11099   *Constantinou, Mitt.* Η´ Σύναξη Ορθόδοξων Βιβλικών Θεολόγων
         Μεσημβρία (Nesebar), Βουλγαρία 10-15 Σεπτεμβρίου 1995: η
         προς Γαλατας επιστολη [The Conference of Orthodox Biblical
         Theologians (Nesebar, Bulgaria, 10-15 September 1995): the let-
         ter to the Galatians]. Collab. *Tsakona, M.B.*, DBM 15 (1996) 85-
         88. **G**.
11100   *Eltrop, Bettina* 5. Vollversammlung der Katholischen Bibelföde-
         ration in Hongkong. BiKi 51 (1996) 186-187.
11101   *Fietta, Pietro* Quinta Assemblea della FEBICA (Federazione
         Biblica Cattolica) Hong Kong, 2-12 luglio 1996. PaVi 41/5
         (1996) 57-58.
11102   *Hałas, Stanisław* XXXIII sympozjum biblistów Polskirch w Szc-
         zecinie (1995) [De XXXIII symposio biblistarum polonorum (Ste-
         tini 1995)]. RBL 49 (1996) 53-54. **P**.
11103   *Hohnjec, Nikola* Međunarodni i međukonfesionalni susret o
         Bibliji (Toronto 26.IX.-4.X.1996) [General Assembly of the Uni-
         ted Bible Societies: international and interconfessional convention
         about the Bible (Toronto 26.IX.-4.X.1996)];
11104   Međunarodni simpozij o tumačenju Biblije (Lujubljana 17-
         21.IX.1996) [International Symposium on the Interpretation of
         the Bible (Lujubljana 17-21.IX.1996)];
11105   Peto zborovanje Katoličke biblijske federacije (Hong Kong, 2.-
         12.VII.1996) [The fifth general assembly of the Catholic Biblical
         Federation (Hong Kong, 2-12.VII.1996)]. BoSm 66 (1996) 726-
         727/724-725/713-714. **Croatian**.
11106   *Kanagaraj, Jey* The 17th national conference of the Society for
         Biblical Studies: a review. BiBh 22 (1996) 165-166.
11107   *Lopasso, Vincenzo* Qumrân e le origini cristiane: convegno ABI
         1995. Vivarium 4 (1996) 129-135.
11108   *Pisarek, Stanisław* IX colloquium biblicum (Weideń 1996) [De
         IX colloquio biblico Vindobonae (1996)]. RBL 49 (1996) 269-
         271. **P**.
11109   *Ruiz, Jean-Pierre* Report on the Fifty-ninth general meeting of
         the Catholic Biblical Association of America. 10-13 Aug. 1996,
         St.Paul, Minn. CBQ 58 (1996) 690-697.
11110   *Silva, Eunice da* XX semana bíblica nacional. São Paulo 1994.
         RCB 77/78 (1996) 11-36.
11111   *Tremolada, Pierantonio* Assemblea plenaria della *Catholic Bibli-*
         cal Federation a Hong Kong. PaVi 41/3 (1996) 52-54;
11112   La bibbia nella comunicazione della fede: seminario di studio.
         22-23.II.1996, Roma, promosso dalla Commissione Episcopale
         per la dottrina della fede e la catechesi. PaVi 41/2 (1996) 47-49.
11113   *Tuckett, Christopher M.* The scriptures in the gospels: Collo-
         quium Biblicum Lovaniense XLV (1996). EThL 72 (1996) 509-
         517.
11114   *Wodecki, Bernard* Kongres biblijny w Ljubljanie (1996) [De
         congressu biblico Labaci (Ljubljana 1996)];
11115   Międzynarodowy kongres w Jerozolimie z okazji 3000-lecia Jero-
         zolimy jako stolicy (1996) [Jerusalem—city of law and justice:
         international conference in Jerusalem (1996)]. RBL 49 (1996)
         263-267/261-263. **P**.

11116 *Wojciechowski, Michał* Międzynarodowy zjazd Society of Biblical Literature. Budapeszt 1995. CoTh 66/1 (1996) 183-187. **P.**

11117 *Xavier, A. Aloysius* Catholic Biblical Federation: V plenary assembly. 2-12 July 1996. ITS 33 (1996) 276-279.

11118 *Zovkić, Mato* Simpozij njemačkih bibličara o grijehu i oslobođenju u Novom zavjetu [Symposium of German biblicists about sin and redemption in the New Testament]. Arbeitsgemeinschaft deutschsprachiger katholischer Neutestamentler, Straßburg 1995. BoSm 66 (1996) 135-138. **Croatian.**

Y7.6 *(Acta) congressuum philologica:* **nuntii**

11119 *Litvinenko, Yu.N.* XXI International Congress of Papyrologists. Berlin 13-19.8.1995. VDI 218 (1996) 238-242. **R.**

Y7.8 *(Acta) congressuum orientalistica et archaeologica,* **nuntii**

11120 *Sen, Felipe* 5.º congreso internacional de Mogilany sobre los manuscritos del Mar Muerto. BAEO 32 (1996) 396-397.

11121 The twenty-second archaeological congress in Israel. Qad. 29 (1996) 63-64. **H.**

Y8.0 *Periti;* **Scholars, personalia, organizations**

11122 E**Étienne, Roland** Cent cinquantenaire 1846-1996: École française d'Athènes. BCH 120 (1996) 1-555.

11123 **Fogarty, Gerald P.F.** American catholic biblical scholarship: a history from the early republic to Vatican II. 1989, ⇒5,k816. R RHE 91 (1996) 990-993 *(Aubert, Roger).*

11124 *Fritz, Volkmar* Das Deutsche Evangelische Institut für Altertumswissenschaft des Heiligen Landes in den Jahren 1992-1994. ZDPV 112 (1996) 70-73.

11125 Giovanni Battista de Rossi e le catacombe romane: mostra fotografica; catalogo mostra. Città del Vaticano 1994, 183 pp. Auct. var.; 125 fig. R RivAC 72 (1996) 448-451 *(Ramieri, A.M.).*

11126 *Gitin, Seymour* W.F. Albright Institute of Archaeological Research, Jerusalem: project descriptions of Albright appointees 1995-1996. BASOR 303 (1996) 79-93.

11127 **Martin, Paul-Aimé** Le mouvement biblique au Canada: l'association catholique des études bibliques au Canada dans les années 1940 et 1950. Montréal 1996, Fides 58 pp. 2-7621-1864-6 [Études d'histoire religieuse 64,82—Lacroix, Benoît].

11128 *Serwint, Nancy* Cyprus American Archaeological Research Institute, Nicosia, Cyprus: project descriptions of CAARI appointees 1995-1996. BASOR 303 (1996) 95-96.

Y8.5 *Periti;* **in memoriam**

11129 Aland, Kurt 28.3.1915-13.4.1994. Gn. 68 (1996) 92-94 *(Mühlenberg, Ekkehard).*

11130 Bright, John 1908-26.3.1996. EThL 72 (1996) 290.
11131 Burgmann, Hans 1914-1992. ᴹBuʀɢᴍᴀɴɴ H., 1996, ⇒12.
       199-201 (Lichtenberger, Hermann); 203-207 (Van der Woude,
       A.S.).
11132 Calmeyer, Peter 5.9.1930-22.11.1995 ⇒11/2,q218. ZA 86
       (1996) 161-162 (Edzard, Dietz Otto).
11133 Chéhab, Maurice Hafez 27.12.1904-22.12.1994 ⇒11/2,q221.
       Syr. 73 (1996) 205-206 (Will, Ernest); RSFen 24 (1996) i-iv
       (bibl.) (Pisano, Giovanna).
11134 Frankfort, Hans 1897-1954. Van Loon, Maurits 'Hans' Frank-
       fort's earlier years, based on his letters to 'Bram' van Regteren
       Altena. Lei 1995, Ned. Inst. v.h. Nabije Oosten 65 pp. f32. 90-
       6831-676-1. ᴿBiOr 53 (1996) 818-821 (Moorey, P.R.S.).
11135 Gaster, Theodor H. 1906-1992. Hiers, Richard H.; Stahmer,
       Harold M. Theodor H. Gaster: biographical sketch and bibliogra-
       phy—a supplemental note. UF 28 (1996) 277-285.
11136 Hamilton, Robert aet. 89, 25.9.1995. Levant 28 (1996) iii-v
       (Moorey, Roger).
11137 Hasel, Gerhard Franz 1935-1994 ⇒10,15293. Theologika 11/1
       (1996) 2-7 (Alomía, K.M.) [ZID 23,320]; AUSS 34 (1996) 165-
       168 (Maxwell, C. Mervyn), bibl. 169-186 (Hasel, Michael G.).
11138 Hruby, Kurt 27.5.1921-5.9.1992 ⇒9,17356. ANTZ 5 (1996) 13-
       18 (Willi, Thomas).
11139 Kammenhuber, Annelies 19.3.1922-24.12.1995. Or. 66,86-88
       (Archi, Alfonso).
11140 Karusu, Semni 1898-8.12.1994 ⇒11/2,q288. Gn. 68 (1996) 476-
       479 (Hausmann, Ulrich).
11141 Kempinski, Aharon 26.1.1939-2.7.1994 ⇒10,15309. Henoch 18
       (1996) 205 (Soggin, J. Alberto).
11142 Kuschke, Arnulf, aet. 83, 2.11.1995 ⇒11/2,q299. ZDPV 112
       (1996) 74-76 (Weippert, Helga).
11143 Leanza, Sandro 1940-15.12.1996. ASEs 14/1,221-228 (Barbàra,
       Maria Antonietta).
11144 Lloyd, Seton 1902-1.1996. BiOr 53 (1996) 317-324 (Wright,
       G.R.H.).
11145 Luke, John Tracy 19.2.1935-11.10.1995. AfO 44-45,583-584
       (Robertson, John F.).
11146 Marchel, Witold 1922-1990. RBL 49 (1996) 271-274 (Rybacki,
       Kajetan). P.
11147 Mazar, Benjamin 28.6.1906-8.9.1995 ⇒11/2,q325. BASOR 301
       (1996) 1-3 (Cross, Frank Moore).
11148 Ostrasz, Antoni 23.6.1929-9.10.1996. ADAJ 40 (1996) 9-10
       (Macdonald, Michael; McQuitty, Alison; Goguel, Anne).
11149 Picard, Jean-Claude ob. 1996. Apocrypha 8,303-304 (Geoltrain,
       Pierre).
11150 Quaegebeur, Jan 14.12.1943-10.8.1995. RdE 47 (1996) 5-7
       (Traunecker, Claude).
11151 Rosłon, Józef Wiesław Leon. 1929-1993. RBL 49 (1996) 58-60
       (bibl. 60-62) (Salomon, Adam).
11152 Rost, Leonhard 30.11.1896-5.12.1979. ThLZ 121 (1996) 1106-
       1108 (Sauer, Georg).
11153 Rusche, Helga 1913-21.9.1996. BZ 41,313-314 (Nützel, Johan-
       nes M.).

11154   Salvador, Joaquim 1920-1995. RCB 77/78 (1996) 3, 7-10 *(Terra, João Evangelista Martins)*.
11155   Segundo, Juan Luís 1925-17.1.1996. REB 56 (1996) 699-701 *(Hoornaert, Eduardo)*, 449-451; MCom 54 (1996) 193-197 *(Medina Ylla, Elbio)*.
11156   Shalit, Leon 1905-1996. BAIAS 15 (1996-97) 84-86 *(Barnett, Barbara)*.
11157   Soden, Wolfram von 19.6.1908-6.10.1996. AfO 44-45,588-594 *(Borger, R.)*.
11158   Sparks, Hedley ob. 22.11.1996. JThS 48/1 [unnumbered page] *(Chadwick, Henry)*.
11159   Stanley, David Michael 17.10.1914-30.12.1996. SR 25 (1996) 489-491 *(Plevnik, Joseph)*.
11160   Starr, Richard Francis Strong 1900-9.3.1994 ⇒11/2,q380. ^{M}STARR R., 1996, ⇒85. 3-7 *(Owen, David I.)*.
11161   Van Dijk, Johannes Jacobus Adrianus 28.1.1915-14.5.1996. VO 10 (1996) 3-6 *(Archi, Alfonso)*; Phoenix 42 (1996) 114-117 *(Römer, W.H.Ph.)*.
11162   Vögtle, Anton 17.12.1910-17.3.1996. BZ 41,154-156 *(Broer, Ingo)*.
11163   Wasserstein, Abraham 5.10.1921-20.7.1995. SCI 15 (1996) 1-6 (Bibl. 7-15) *(Wasserstein, David J.; Geiger, J.)*.

Index Alphabeticus

Auctorum

^{D}dir. dissertationis ^{E}editor ^{F}Festschrift ^{M}mentio ^{R}recensio ^{T}Translator/vertens

Aageson J 6093
Aaron C 3612
Aartun K 7771
Abū 'l-Walīd ^{M}7627
Abadie P 2584 2626
Abarbanel I ^{M}8522
Abbà G ^{R}5973 6814 4098
Abbolito Simonetti G ^{T}5173
Abd el-Gelil M 9910 10465
Abdalla A 9911
Abe G 7387
Abécassis A 1656
Abegg M ^{E}8228 ^{T}8230
Aberbach M 9538

Abir P 2433 5685
Abma R 3417 ^{E}490
Abrams D 8591
Abramzon M 9990
Abravanel Y ^{M}8617
Abrego de Lacy J 3247
Abtze K ^{T}5764
Abulafia A 8636
Abusch R 9407 T 9033
Accorinti D ^{ET}5328
Achenbach R ^{R}2166 2167 2168
Achermann D 1254
Achtemeier E 789 3647 3696 P 6577 ^{R}6119

Ackerman J ^{D}2205 S 8924 ^{R}889
Acquaro E 402 9991 10277 ^{E}67
Acquaviva G 10017
Adam A 942 6105 3938 6965 ^{R}4443 P 743
Adamik T 8132
Adamopoulo T 5869
Adams B 10466 D 6633 E ^{R}3913 R 10573 11035
Adamthwaite M 10651
Adan-Bayewitz D 9844
Adang C 9074

Ade A 5976
Ademiluka S 1489
Adinolfi M 5686
5948 6007
Adler J 2458 **W**
3613 5687 5757
9523 10591 R252
Adrados F 7891
Adriányi G 11020
Aejmelaeus A 1064
2172 **L** 5373
Aers D 3939
Afanasieva V 1580
Agius J D3393
Agnati U 10652
Agosto E 5824
Agua A del 4981
Aguiar Retes C 6884
Aguirre R 3940s
7174 10653
Aguirre Monasterio
R E3855s
Agurides S 5374
Agus A 8497
Aharoni M 9783
Ahiarajah S 5977
Ahl R 11089 R4101
Ahlberg-Cornell G
8858
Ahlström G 9093
Ahn B-C 3857
Ahrens M 2880
6611
Ahuis F 1853
Aichele G 4792
R942
Aitken A-M 491
Aizin J T4002
Aizpurúa F 5636
Ajamian J E250
Akiba R. M8455
Akkermans P 10756
Aland B D6961
E1024 6025 **K**
4190 11129
E10801
Al-Assiouty S 9075
Albenda P 9654
Alberigo G F1
Albert B-S 8637
Alberto S E3927
Albertz R 110 981
1363 1426 2254

2816 2877 3778
6788 8925-8927
R2029 2684
Albrecht R 1255
Albrektson B 3011
Albright W M303
11035-8
Albrile E 8717
Alcock S E8859
Alegre X 5326
Aleixandre D 853
4720 6760
Aletti J-N 4185
4982 5303 5825
5870 6447 D4934
4967 6113 6264
Alexander J 5241
7224 **M** E9835
3036 8282 **T**
R2838 **Y** 10159
Alexeev A 3037
Alföldi G E7976
Alfonso de L 4114
4650 7276
Alfonso Sabio 3032
Alfsvag K R2697
Algaze G 9253
Aliotta M R1361
Allaire N 1683
Allam S E295
Allchin A 1364
Allen D 6522 **L**
3531 D2232 **R** 744
Alliata E 10267
Allison D 3942 4291
4583 R3964
Allsopp M 6789
Almaleh G T11019
Al-Muheisen Z
10257 10271
Alobaidi J ET2695
Alon D 10097 **G**
8498 10855
Alonso Alonso F
5519 **Schökel L**
414 1114 1606
1763 2664s 2696
2717 2780s 3213
6668
Alpi F 7952
Alroth B E290
Alt F 3943
Alter R 1310 2641

Altner H 1490
Alunno L 4115
Alvarez Barredo M
2521 3707 R4272
5645 **Gómez J**
4518 **Valdés A**
1564 Verdes L
5963 R5970
Alves H R2039 **M**
6008
Alviar J 7077
Amadasi Guzzo M
7772
Amadi-Azuogu C
6355 7452
Amador J 4146
Amaladoss M 4116
7175
Amat Rousseau J
8133
Amata B R4729
Amato A 6909 **C**
5508 **D** 6966
Amberger-Lahrmann
M 9760
Ambraseys N 10573
Ambrosius M 3689
R2641
Amezaga L 10832
Amiet P 9655 10152
Amir Y 1065
Amiran D 10574s R
E10105
Amisi K 5133
Amit D 10120 **M**
8397 **Y** 1697 2298
Amitzur H 2489
Ammassari A 5329
E1025 4262 4765
5028
Amonville Alegría N
d' TE7453
Amphoux C-B 1026
6237 6558 ET4263
E159 191 265 6559
R4421
Amsler F 8149s **S**
1365 3820
Amundsen D 10630
Amyx D 9656
Anabolu M (Usman)
8917
Anati E 1764 10117

Azar É [T]8048
Azria R 854 8399
   9659

Baarda T 5564
   [M]6371
Baatsch H-A [T]9613
Babcock W [E]6001
Babut J-M 1179
   7677
Baccari L 6679
Bacchielli L 10515
Bach A 528-531
   [R]2339
Bachmann H-G 9526
   10380-83 10576s
   M 9660
Backhaus K 6523s
   6737s 7124 [E]23
   [R]6517 6553
Backhouse R 2490
Backus I 5543
Bacon J 2678 [M]7688
Badenas R [R]6033
Bader G 2719 W
   2317 [E]3629
Badian E [F]3
Baecher C 4948
Baehrens W [E]2143
Baena B G 943
Bär J 9256
Báez S [R]1547
Bagnall R 9178
   10774 [E]7954
Bagni A 4868 4918
   4920 4960 6247
   [R]4783 5895
Bagno M [T]5993
   6609
Bagot J-P [T]1506
Bahat D 10022-23
Bahn P 9465
Bahn P [E]9466
Baik W 4204
Bail U 2853 3644
   [E]81 162 10654
Bailey D 9892 J
   4148 K 681 3351
   L 1565 R 1181s
   6395 [E]163 1180
Bailie G 7125
Baillie M 9501s

Baines J 1428 7851
   9205 [E]10423
Baird W 11014
   [R]6005
Baker W 6612
Bakhtin M [M]7604
Bakker H 1159 N
   9179
Bakon S 10592
   [T]2591
Balabán M 1160
Balaguer V [R]5056
Balch D [R]4247 4580
Balconi C 403
Baldacci M 10288
Baldermann I 492
   533s [E]7088
Balensiefen L 9661
Balentine S 9180
   [R]1823
Balestier-Stengel G
   [R]454
Ball C 5799 D 5376
Ballabio F [R]4174
Ballard H 2720
Balmary M [E]7126
Balter L 7041
Balthasar H von
   4723 7127 7233
   7395 [M]4687
Balty J 9550 10490
Baltz F 5578
Baltzer D 535s 3250
   4793 6698 8928 K
   [D]2750 3836
Balz H 6457 [E]335s -
   Cochois H [R]3485
Bambilla E [T]6937
Bammel C 1429
   6081 7109 10890
   [R]4278 6030 E
   4949 10857
Bammer A 1183
Bang S 5526
Banker J 6428
Bankes W [M]7825
   10782
Banning E 9467
Banon D 1857 8638
Banz C 1125
Barag D 9519 9637
   [E]10124
Baraquin A [T]11019

Bar-Asher M 7846
Baraúna J [T]3304
Barbagallo S 9709
Barbaglio G 5800
   6142 6236 6829
   [R]6094 6262
Barber G 6091
Barberá C 416
Barbet A 9914 9915
Barbi A 5267
Barbieri E 10827
Barbiero G 1965s
Barbour I 1459s R
   [E]164
Barbuto G 5658
Barclay J 5949 6134
   8401 9326 [E]43
   [R]6330
Bardinet T 10632
Bar-Efrat S 2349
Barišić M 4724
Barkay G 9645
   9784-85 10024
   [E]10556
Barker K 1126 4725
   [R]5679 5755 W
   [E]1905
Bar-Kochva B 2491
   8400 9325 9355
Barkóczi L 9527
Barnai J 8609
Barnard W 5377
Barnes E 7177 H
   10270 J 5293 M
   [R]1472
Barnett W [E]9848
Barnhart B 5357
Barnouin M 4974
Baroffio B 4448
Barr D [E]73 [R]5721 G
   5827 J 586 1493
   7089 [R]963
Barra D 6378
Barraclough R 4939
Barrado P [R]3518
   Fernández P [R]352
   496 903 1114 1493
   4536 5084 5411
Barré M 2857 [R]2758
Barrett C 4985-86
   5176-78 5872-73
   [R]6275
Barrick W 2466

Bohatcová M 1161
Bohlen R 829
Böhm T 10928 R3017
Böhmisch F R931
Böcher O 6578 R5779
Böck B 9034 R1588
Böhlig A 8755
Bösen W 4655
Böttge B 4386
Bohuytrón Solano J 5048
Bóid I R1022
Boira Sales J 3149
Boisclair R R5956
Boismard M-E 4462 4727s 4768 4796 4880 5181 5308 5333s 5697 E5545 R5449 5541
Boitani P 3643 M3641
Boiten G 3193
Božja R 11092
Bokser B TE8499
Boles K 6324
Bolewski J 4356
Bolin T 422
Böll H M4137
Bollag M 8500
Bollók J 5926
Bollweg J 10602
Bolognesi P 761
Bolozky S 7625
Bolt P 4975
Bolyki J 8134
Bombeck S 3616
Bommel J 2935
Bona E R175
Bonacossi D 10615
Bonanate M 7457 U 9076
Bonato V T3014
Bonaventura S. M1687 4358
Bond H 9996
Bondì S 9100
Bonfil R 8611
Bonhoeffer D 115 2783 M11087
Bonino S-T R840
Bonnafé A 1432s

Bonneau G 8053
Bonnechère P 7130
Bonner G R5350
Bonnet C 8930 10278 M8981 L R4559
Bonola G 1498
Bonora A 2916 3150
Bons E 2835 3664 3727
Bonte N 4118
Bony P 3253 5801
Bonz M 4990
Booij T 2884
Boomershine T 3952
Booras S 8200
Boorer S 1235 2936
Booth S 5385
Booy G 3419
Borchert G D5482 5702
Borchhardt J F8
Bordoni M 7055 D7034
Bordreuil M E10321 P 10289
Borg B 9666 M 3954s E3953
Borgeaud P 7403
Borgen P 116 3863 4175 4205s 5291 5386 5544 5556 5698-5701 7056 7181 8075ss 8405 8840 8891 E252
Borghi E 5137 6131
Borgonovo G 2937 E253
Bori P 1499 E5539
Boring M 3956
Bormann L 6423 E30
Borobio E E9182
Borrel i Viader A 4967 R4679 5124 3856 4678
Borrmans M 4131
Börschel R E9
Borse U 983 4970 5170 5182 5255 5290 5631 5802 6054 6092 6141 6160 F9

Boschi B R2699
Bosco G R205
Bose M 2475
Bosetti E 4991 6585 6597
Boshoff W R1945
Bosinski G 1462
Bosio G E10802
Bosman P R4932
Boss S 7404
Bossard F 1370 P 1370
Bosse-Griffiths K 8992
Bosshard-Nepustil E 3040
Bossman D 5875
Bossuyt P 5183
Botermann H 9421
Botha C T4099 J 4928 6699 P 3214 3244 4150 8406 R2896 4291
Bottéro J 1434s 8830
Bottigheimer R 495
Bottini G 4915
Bou i Simó J 7405
Boud'hors A 1088
Bouffartigue J 9667
Bouhot J-P 6560 6561 E6559
Boulnois M-O 7059
Bouman J 8641
Bounni A 10359
Boureau R E6967
Bourgeois D 5584 H 6761
Bourke S 10246 10253
Bourquin Y 4951
Bourriau, J E9846
Bousquet B 10457
Bousquet F 6970
Bouthors J-F 3744
Boutros, W 10409
Bouvier B T8149
Bouzard W 2725
Bovati P 2163 3254 3702s 3708 6792 R2257
Bovon F 5031-5033 8108 T8149

Cortese E 6853 2078
  R190 1778 2125
Corti G E429
Cosgrove C 6106
Costa A T7531 F
  R2671 J T2665
Silva C da 5236
Costacurta B D1557
Coste R F17
Costen J 2454 2909
  3422 3488 3578
  5157 5166 6308
  6317 6419s
Cothenet E   3961
  E325 R4 192 1063
  4422 5332 5415
  4186 5952
Cotter J 2732 W
  R4337
Cottereau P E501
Cotterell P 3015
Cottin J 10993
Cotton B R6838 H
  10011 E104
Couch M E345
Couffignal R 4897
Coulet C 9314
Coulie B R254 5651
Coulin M T8808
Coulot C 6013
Course J 2942
Courthial P 502
Courtois L 10152
Cousar   C   5833
  R4563 4672 5309
Cousin H 3423 5034
  6854
Cousins P E4586
Couto A R1319
Coutsoumpos P
  R5191
Couture A 1683
Couturier G F18
Couvert É 8370
Covello-Paran K
  9923 10171
Cowdell S 6974
Cowton C 5247
Cox C 984 R1082
  2920 S 6241
Coyle K 7409
Cozi M 8995 9924
Craffert P 600-602
  10669 R5924

Craghan J 2602
Craig K 2617 3746
  3822 R3758
Cramarossa L 4924
Cranach L M10993
Cratzius B 503
Craven T 3534
Crawford B R6058
  H 9258 S 8242
  R8224
Creach J 2733 2903
  R2588
Cremascoli G E787
  R2769 3549
  T10975
Cremer M 9925
Crenshaw J 121
  3698 D3565 R3062
  3065 3121 3124
Crespi P T10809
Crespo E E7896
Cribiore R 9214
Cristiani M 1502
Croatto J 1585
  R1327
Cromartie M E7364
Crook J 9433
Cross F 6855 7761
  7775 8168 8243
  8330 J 8110
Crossan J D 3962-6
  4209 4660 M4697
Crotty R 3967 6615
Crouch D 10580 F
  5301 5395
Crouwel J 9598
Crouzel H 10891
  TE2840
Crow L 2899
Crown A 8379-80
  E8378 R1009
Crump D 4996
Crüsemann F 1237
  1684 1910 1989
  2813 3788 9111 M
  6244
Cruz Hernández M
  1735
Cruz-Uribe E 10426
Cryer F 2437 7812
Cuenca Molina J
  R505 1840
Cuënot M 2902
  10035

Culbertson P 4523
  R4721
Culdaut F 10828
Culley R R1446
Cullmann O 7281ss
Culpepper R 5309
  5396s E82
Cunchillos J-L 7776
Cunneen S 7410
Cunz   M   8645
  T11064
Cuomo L 1115
Cureton R 2646
  M2642s
Curl J 9215
Currie H 7236 J
  1226
Curtis A 2273 R697
  D T8479
Curto S 9507
Curzon D 1685
Cussini E E7819
Custer J 2734
Cuvillier   E   4269
  4895 4952 5534
  6429 R275 4679
Cyprianus M10970s
Cyrillus A M3848
  6952 7059 J
  M8662 10972
Czachesz I 5928
Czerny M 4551
Czerski J 3868

Dagan Y 10116
D'Agostino F 9259
  10327
Dahan G 8646
Dahmen U 2180
  8169
Dailey T 2943 2992
Dalai Lama 8804
  9089
D'Alario V 3060
  3151 3156 R3206
Dalbesio A 5398
  5645 R2337 5205
Dalbosco H T2665
Dal Covolo E 861
  7183 7365 10829
  E10802
Dale R 3869

7379
Dumézil G 8842
Dumm D 7308 **M**
7309
Dumoulin P 3204
3206
Duncan-Jones R
10737
Dunderberg I 5359
Dungan D ^R4250
Dunkov D ^E2460
2534
Dunnhill J 10674
Dunn J 4306 4398
5188 5400 5878
6107s 6325 6336
6370 6450 6916
7112 7328 8648
^E176 255 ^R6053
6116 6851 **P** 6164
8138
Duns Scotus ^M6956
Dünzl F 3018 ^T3017
Dupleix A 5401
7412
Dupont J 2890 ^F21 -
Sommer A 8173
Dupuis J 6979-80
^D7010 7013
Dupuy M 7070
^E3973
Duquesne J 3974s **T**
8996s
Duquoc C 5783
^R4029
Durack J ^R4992
Durand A 5121 **G**
de 410 ^T6931 **J-M**
8832 ^E306 **O** 7633
X ^R6720
Duranti G 1297
Durchholz E 7310
Dürer A ^M9753
Dür-Gademann H-P
11064
Durlesser J ^R2999
Durst M 10976
Dutcher-Walls P
2535
Dutourd J 1346
Duval Y-M ^R3323
6030
Duwe G 9719

Dwyer T 2091 4804
Dyck J 2556
Dyk J 3141 ^E100
Dziuba A 7329
^R1921

Eakins J ^D2070
Easton M 6764
Easwaran E 4450
Eaton-Krauss M
10424
Ebach J 1913 2872
2947 3780 ^E905
Ebner M 3976
^R4858
Ebo D ^D1447
Eboussi Boulaga F
^M6992
Echallier J-C 10349
Echlin E 3977
Echt R 9630
Eck W 7978 ^E10675
Eckert J 6133
Eckstein H-J 4926
6356
Eco U ^M4853
Economou C 5272
Eddy P 3978
Edelman D 2384
9116 ^R685 ^E8934
10228
Edgar C 6124
Edgar W ^D6072
Edwards D 8806
^R358 **G** 5879 **M**
766 ^R1350 **R** 5402
5641 **S** ^R1324
Effinger M 9631
Egberts A 8998
Egeria ^M1727 10784
Eggenberger C 2408
Egger W 4153
Eggers F 11084
Egger-Wenzel R
2996 7766
Eggler J 9796
Ego B 1610 7689
^T2618
Egron A 353 461
Ehlich K 7734
Ehrlich C 1914 3544
9117 ^R1272 **M**

10100
Ehrman B 1032s ^E59
^R1131
Eid V 3575
Eide T ^E9218s
Eidevall G 3691
Eiland M 9852
Eilberg-Schwartz H
6669
Eisen U 7240
Eisenberg E 10162
Eisenman R 5931
6616 8325 8174
Eitam D ^E10618
Eitz A 1611s
Ejrnæs B 1162
Ekschmitt W 10297
Elad A 10039
Elas J 4507
Elass M 6109
Elayi A 9997 **J** 9932
9997
Elazar D 1646
Elbert P 1466
Elder L ^E73
Elders L 767
Eldridge D 543
Eleuteri P ^E9317
Elgvin T 8346 8372
Eliezer C 1467
Elizondo F 7413
Ellacuria I ^E7380
Ellens H 927 1508
Elliger K 433 ^E990
Ellington J 3384
^R3884 3884
Ellingworth P 1034
2038 6515 ^R1036
Elliott J 801 1035
4805 5189 8112
10093 10676
^E4136 ^R1220 1221
6574 6574 **K** 1036
M 3042 **N** 5932 **S**
6337
Ellis C 1770 **E** 802
^R4213 **M** 1647 **W**
9220 -**Lopez S**
9853
Elman Y 8289
Elnes E 2183
Els P ^D2322

Fritz V 2244 2274
2462 2476 9121
10192 10210
10243 11124
D2276 E9122
Frizzell L R2000
Fröehlich K 4558
10991
Fröhlich I 8292
8417 R302 U
E6147
Frolov S 1830 2376
2446
Fronzaroli P 10328s
Frör H 6148
Frosini G 7555
Frost F 7415 8866 R
1487
Frymer-Kensky T
R1362
Fuchs A R23 88 114
322 4221 4260
4318 4498 4510
4959 5347 5588
5600 5673 5779
6425 G 2949 4617
E214 O 547 7586
Fudge E 4586
Fuellenbach J 4587
Fuentes i Grau J
R468
Fuhs H 2227
Fulco W 10275
Fuller D 4177 R
R4743
Funk R 3985 T3986
Furcha E R6273
ET11005
Furnish V F27
R6275
Fusco V 4998 6270
R91
Füssel K E6796
Futato M 9592 M
R1605
Futterlieb H 1614
Fyall R 2950

Gabel J 890
Gabriel A 4891 K
548 4311
Gabus J-P 6984

Gachet J 10298
Gadecki S 5361
Gader al-Husan A
10232
Gafni I 8418 E87
Gagey H-J 11045
Gagnon R R4657
Gai A 7632 7992
Gaines R D7571
Gal Z 10169 10759
10171
Galán J 7776
Galbiati E 1070 G
3987
Galil G 2467
Galileo M1475
Galinsky K 9413
Galitis G 6369
Galizzi M 4270
4963
Gallagher E R4490
W 9264
Gallas A 951
Gallico A R5849
Galot J 4571 5536
5580 6670 7416
Galter H 9042 E297
Galvin J 3988 7136
Gamba G 4876
Gamberoni J 3504
Gamble H 10808
Gameson R E1100
Gammie J E3061
Gancho C T862
Gangemi A 5594
Gangloff F 3679
Garbini G 7633
7785s 7817 8941
R1437 3086
García -Baró M
T8524 Bazán F
3989 R3899 Cor-
dero M 2739 6881
de Fleury M 1688
de la Fuente O
1112 de Paredes J
7417 -Jalón de la
Lama S 7634-35
López F E1265
Márquez G M3709
Martínez F 6857
8180-3 8251 8293
8347ss 11070 E65

8177s 8252 T8179
Matamoros A
M3178 Moreno A
5337 5411s R4679
5326 5336 5490
5522 Pérez J 5056
Plaza E T3688
Recio J R1601
Santos A R2478
2514 -Treto F
3811
Gardin J-C 9521
Gardner E 7331 I
8757s
Gargano I 952 5087
10927
Garhammer E 906
Garland D 4573s
D6629 R 8867
9319
Garlington D 6057
Garmus L R6719
Garnsey P 10680
Garrett D 1702 J
7587 S D5746
Garrido R 5795
Garrison M 9799s
Garrone D 718 1570
1960
Garske V 4137
Garsky A 4208
Garstang J M10466
Garuti A 4559 P
6530
Garzetti A F28
Garzón Bosque I
T6326
Garzya A 953 Ro-
mano C ET9673
Gasbarro N 8831
Gasque W 6797
Gasser M 9801
Gaster T M11135
Gat J E10578
Gathercole P R912
Gatier P-L 7962
Gatti E T5052
Gaudemet J 1958
Gaukesbrink M 5883
Gaventa B 5639
6015 7418 R33
Gavilán L M7375
Gavron D 2410

Given M ^{R}5277
Giversen S ^{E}252 ^{F}32
Givon S 10131
Glad C 9333
Gladson J ^{R}118 2942
  2999
Glancy J 549 10681
Glare P ^{E}7899
Glassner J-J 9265
Glatt D 684 -**Gilad**
  D 2559
Glazier-McDonald B
  9818
Glé J-M 7557
Glenn E ^{R}914
Glessmer U 1018
  8041 8253 8350
  ^{E}133
Glick D 10140
Gloer W 3875 6298
Glonner G 5712
Glueck N ^{M}10242
Gmirkin R 8294
Gnadt M 7511
Gnilka J 3990 5807
  5983 7588 ^{D}5019
  5712
Gnirs A M 7862
Gnuse R 9385 ^{R}1654
  2185 6814
Godfrey W 11001
  ^{E}1905
Godoy R ^{T}8332
Godzieba A 6985
Goedicke H 7739
  9001
Goedt M de 6986s
Goell T 9562 9999
  10384-93
Goerwitz R 992
  2120 7637
Goffer Z 377
Goffi T 7161
Gögler R ^{R}4289
Goins K 4808
Golani A 9938
  10215 10219
Golb N 8184-85 V
  ^{E}1131
Golda M 7226
Goldberg A ^{E}289 **E**
  8506 **H** 6702 **M**
  ^{R}4080

Goldblatt D 8419
Golden J 9686
Goldenberg D 3991
Goldin P 2951 **S**
  8614
Goldingay J 769
  3416 7043
Goldman B 9632 **S**
  ^{E}7638
Goldstein N 8621
Goldsworthy A 9596
  G 7187 ^{R}272
Golitzin A ^{E}369
Golka F 3062s 6703
Gomà Civit I 4467
Gomes P 442
Gómez E ^{R}4613
  6933 **Aranda M**
  3159 ^{TE}3153 **Ve-
  lasco F** 6082
Goncalves F 10572
  Pereira F ^{T}8182
Gonen R 9939
Gonsalves M 3576
Gonzales Silva S
  ^{R}4518 **de C O**
  ^{R}3974 **García F**
  ^{R}4215
González de Carde-
  dal O 907 7558
  Echegaray J
  ^{ET}5669 **García F**
  8860 **J** 2040 2842
  2844 4312 4516
  Montes A 6682 **S**
  6918
Good D ^{R}1137 **E**
  2921
Goodacre M 11058
Goodblatt D 2386
Goodenough E
  ^{M}8466 8552
Goodhart S 1873
Goodman D 4216 **H**
  ^{E}215 **L** 6641 **M**
  8420s ^{D}9159 -
  Thau E 6858
Goodnick B 2157
Goodrick E 1220s
Goodwin M 6508
Goosen D 616
Gopher A 9859
  10109 10189

Gophna R 10142
  10147 10740
Goranson S 9724
Gordon C 1317
  6798 ^{M}9889
  11054-7 ^{R}2478
  2514 **R** 2354 3650
  8856
Goren H 10049 **Y**
  9510 9860 10094
  10218
Gorenberg G ^{E}1242
Görg M 1513 1739
  2275 2885 6642
  7863 9221 9803
  10050 ^{E}331s
Gorman F 1298 **M**
  1243
Gorton A 9802
Gorzalczany A
  10165
Goshen-Gottstein M
  ^{D}4275 ^{TE}3321
Gosline S 7512
Gosling F ^{R}3606
Gossa H 1615 ^{R}2500
Gosse B 1643 2041
  2331 2560 3376
  3489 3500 3571
Gottardo R ^{R}1332
  1761
Gottemoller B 7421
Gottfried R 1512
Göttlicher A 9602
Gottlieb C 11054 **I**
  ^{R}685
Göttling-Fuchs M
  1612
Gottwald N 2245
  3274
Goudineau H 6035
Gouëffic L 7513
Goulder M 2746
  4217 5229 6488
  7188 ^{M}11058
  ^{R}3042 4257
Gounelle A 7559 **R**
  3009
Gourgues M 2456
  ^{E}182 ^{R}5309
Gous I 3147 3514
Gow M 404
Gowan D 1776 3705

Hruby K 1992 6863-
65 8428-33 8512
8660s 11138
Hruška B 9046s
Hsu G 7746
Hu M 5986 **P** 7193
Huarte J R6094 6348
Hubbard D 456 **R**
E6887
Hubeňák F 3619
R4091 4681
Huber K 4815 4933
4938 R267 4932
Hubmann F R487
3281 3799
Hübner G 10488 **H**
130 5808 5889
6519 6920 E3190
U 9609
Hudson D 1384 **M**
3395 E315
Hueckel S 446
Huehnergard J 7994
Huffmon H D2960
3109 10694
Hug J 3195 **V** 7820
Hughes F 6480 **P**
R2404 1808 2413
Hui A R6379
Huidekoper E 4673
Huizing K 5059
Hüllstrung W R2684
Hultgren A E10691
Human D 2871
Humbert J-B 8187
Hume D M4493 **L**
10692
Humphrey E 7062
Humphries M 5567
Hünermann P 6994
E6643
Hunger H 7964
9048s 9281
Hung-Kil C 7335
Hunt A 6168 **H**
D3574 **P** 3054
Hüntelmann R
R1370
Hunter D ET7162 **E**
7821 **J** 3516 R4528
Hunziker-Rodewald
R 3791
Huot J-L 10363

Hurault B T1119 **L**
T1119
Hurowitz V 447
1268 1680 2018
2499 R2043 2145
2515
Hurst L E7579
R2353 5029
Hurtado L 4816
6800 R4795 5755
6925
Hurth E 4138
Hurvitz A 448 **G**
10023
Huskinson J 9944
Husson G 9226
Hutchinson R 4220
Hutt J 10394
Hüttenmeister F-G
7695 T8488
Hutter M 8759
8955s 9050
Huwyler B 3511
Hvalvik R 10844
Hynniewta M 3668
Hynson D E870

Iacopino G 4549
Iammarrone G 6921
Ibañez Arana A
1269s **Ramos M**
3591
Ibba G 8295
Ibn Ezra A 1333
3153 M8589
Idel M 8597s
Ignatius A M10878
L M7310
Ihara S 6948
Ilan D 9870 9945
10187 10191 **O**
10106 **T** 4459
10693 **Z** 10120
Ilgen K M1291
Illanes J 7250
Imbach J 4494
Imhausen A 9649
Imkamp W R4562
Immich D 553
Infante R 5422 5529
R343 3927 5231
Ingelaere J-C 5959

Inglebert H 9447
Ingraffia B 7592
Inman B R5880
Intrigillo G 4737
Ioannidou G 7965
Irenaeus L M794
6414 10879-81
Irigoin J 1042
Ironside H 5672
Irshai O 8662
Irwin W R2986
Isaac B 10646 E291
G 2874
Isaacs M 6532 **R**
8434s
Iser W M4853
Ishikawa R 2750
Isidorus P M10929 **S**
M10978
Ismail F E316
Israel F 7995 **Y**
10101 10103s
Israeli S 10174
Isserlin B R60
Iuvencus M4664
Ivantchik A 10480
Iversen E 3070 9007
Iverson C 10694
Izquierdo A R4680
6003
Izre'el S 227
Izumi Y 3536

Jack A 8256
Jackson B 1993
2093 **H** 8086 -
McCabe M 6619
P 7939
Jacob C 10898
Jacobi E 3881
Jacobs B 9295 **I**
8513 **M** 4001
Jacobson A 4221
R4612 **D** 773 2496
H 2400 8087
Jacomb T 6104
Jacomuzzi S 4139
Jacquet P 4453
Jaffee M R2089
Jaffin D 1622
Jagersma H 1321s
Jäggi C 9899

Langlamet F 2416
Langley W 4594
Lanier D R1031
Lannert B 4011
Lanpher J R4506
Laperrousaz E-M 8355 E10014
Lapide P 4677
Lapidge M E10982
Lapin H 8491s
Laporte J 8088 10814
Lapp G 9955
Lappin S E7997
Laras G 3283 8586
Lardon S E2790
Larkin K 2334 3828
Larsen F T517 M 9272
Larsson E 5196 G T8488
Las Casas B de M11008
Lasker D 8669s
LaSor W 456
Lass E 9512
Lasserre G 1996 4196
Lassner J 2485
Lategan B 628
Latourelle R 4499 E364 6692
Lattea K E4823
Lattis J 1475
Lau A 6926 W 3449
Laub D6080
Laube M T5678
Laudert-Ruhm G 4012
Laughlin J R49
Laurence P 10957 R 10540
Laurentin R 1524 4013 7427
Lauret B T6931
Lauwers M 1681
Lavarda G R3970 4465 6179 6745
Lavatori R 1525
LaVerdiere E 4625 4953 5089 5091s
Lavilla Martín 3435

Lavoie J-J 3164 3187 R1106 2702 3032
Law G 3284 P 3887
Lawee E 8522
Lawler J 870
Lawless G 5571
Lawrence A 9572
Lawrie D 2322
Lawson J 9053
Laytner A 8671
Layton R 6383 S 7823
Lázár I T4266 M E1120
Lazarev V 9733
Lazarus-Yafeh H 9084
Le Bohec Y 9449
Le Boulluec A 4824 4919 10834 E266 962 10893
Le Glay M 9449
Le Goff I 9956
Le Guillou M-J 7005
Le Morvan M 8356
Le Saux M 2136 3586 4531 4607 6837 8117
Lea T 3888
Leach S 9957
Leahy A 9232
Leal Salazar G 4921
Leanza S 11143
Leatham R 7006
Lebourlier J 6292
Leclant J 10418
Leclercq J 6950 E3051
Leclère F 9958
Ledrus M 5162
Leduc-Fayette D 2957
Lee A 629 2867 7523 R500 D 7471 R4629 E-J 6040 H 5966 J 1574 K-R 3364 -Linke S-H 7390 P-S 7201 Y-H 839 5344
Leeman S 2828

Leeming D 6650
Leene H 2852 3396
Lefebure L 3074 9091 R6672
Leff G R5666
Lefkowitz M 1443 E229
Légasse S 4678-81 4714 7163 F51 R3899 4727 5415
Legon J 9650
Legrand L 4015 5540 R5997
Lehane T 1834
Lehmann G 9135 9874 10096 H R3324 P 1922 R 11024 11069 E64 W 7998
Lehmkühler K 11033
Lehnart B 3285
Leicht R 8033
Leick G 365
Leiner M 932 R929
Leitner R 4425
Leitz C 9014
Leiva-Merikakis E 4321
Leivestad R 7902
Lejeune C D5991
Lelièvre A 3103 3140
Lemaire A 3286 3837 7824 7999 8299 E10014
Lemche N 2247 2417 9136ss 10702
Lemke W R1246 2683
Lemm R T6927
Lemmelijn B 1849s 1877
Lemmer R 6340 8600
Lémonon J-P 4014 6039
Lemos A 10521 I E72
Lenhardt P 1624
Lentini S 4682
Lenz J 4426

Lively P 9209
Liverani M 9191
10570 10625
Livi A D6822
Livingston M 2418
Livio J-B 5939
Lizotte A 7428
Llagostera E 10469
Llewelyn S 8528
Llimona J R6634
Lloyd J 8963 10300
E31 -Jones D 6069
6599 S 11144
Lo C 631
Lo Magro R 5809
Loader J 3115
D3158 W 4825
Loba Mkole J-C
7072
Lob-Hüdepohl A
6811
Lobo Gajiwala A
4016 R5826
Lockwood P 6245
Lockyer H 1710
Lodge J 6113
Lodu Kose L 4763
Loew J 4017
Loewe R R3153
Loewenstamm S
1781
Loffreda S 9875
10183 10251
Logan A 8720 M
871
Lohfink N 1275
2191s 2217 2235
2791 3189 3327
D3285 F52 R1997
2163 2166 2195
2274
Lohmeyer M 4510
Löhr H 6534 E257
W 1998 9450
Lohse E 1148 5810
6341
Lohwasser A R310
Lona H 7565 7929
Long B 7598 11037
G 3056 E751 M
6587 T 705 E13
185s V 9192
Longeaux J de 840

Longenecker B 5008
6357 E188
Longman T 6838
D3556 8957 E902
Longosz S 7937
Löning 6492s 7082
D6466
Lønning I R6328
Lopasso V 11107
R2369
López Pardo F 7798
Loprieno A 7870-74
E230
Lorenzani M E189
Lorenzen T 2566
3889
Lorenzini E 5436
Loretz O 2864 7770
7778-80 E10295
R3681
Loski T 4277
Loughlin G 687
Louis-Marie de
Jésus 7203
Louth A 10930
Louw L 557
Louyot Y 1591
Love M R3828 S
R4819
Lovering E E27
Lövestam E 4018
Lovik G 1043
Lowery R 2536
Loy D E281
Loza J 6710 Vera J
1592 3287
Lozachmeur H 7999
Lozada-Smith F
5547
Lozupone F 4627
Lubac H de 10899
11063 M11063
Lübbe J 7700
Lubetski M 11054
Lubszyk H 1388
Lucas F E8442 L
8678
Luciani D R275
1996 F 2552
Lücking S 4959
Lucrezi F 6869
Lüdemann G 3891 G
4741-5 10704-5

10815 E220 F53
M4757
Lüder A 11018
Ludolf v. Sachsen
3993
Luft U 9234
Lugo Rodríguez R
R5955
Lührmann D 6330
Luis de León M6918
11009 P de R3497
Luisetto G 7429
Luisier P 4683
Luke J 11145 K
3143 7841 10600
Lummel P 10006
Lund J R467 1760
Lundager J E76
Lundberg M 8300
Lundbom J 2193
Lunde J 4604
Lundquist E
TE10792
Luomanan P 4322
Lupande J 7140
Lurker M 350s
Lüscher B 9959
Lust J 1837 3546s
7904 E386 7903
R1082 2438 2768
3584 3627 3653
Luter A 2335 6432
B 3890
Lütgehetmann W
5517
Luther M 4378
10992 M1149 6328
10993s 11086
Luttikhuizen G 809
8141
Lutz R R323
Lutzky H 3560
Lux R 3738 D3842
Luz U 4323s 4600
4610 E11077
Ojeda J M2951
Luzzatto S M8625
Luzzi G 5198
M11064
Lyke L 2453
Lyle K 6629
Lyman J 6951
Lyonnet B 10354

McLean B 5899 **J**
5725
McLelland J D3522
McMahon G 8919
McMichael S 3328
McNamara M 1760
E1013 F58
McNicol A 4606
10254 E4227
McPake J 6686
McPartlan P 7167
7431
McQueen L 3699
McReynolds K 3890
McVann M R4774
McWilliam J R6678
Meadors E 4831
Meadowcroft T 3693
Meagher P 4024
R2645 2756 3538
4785 5313 5683
6049 6155 6331
6425
Mealand D 5010
Meeks W 5442 7343
D4847
Mees M 5368
Meester P de 4689
Meggitt J 6140
Méhat A R4560
4562
Meier H-R 9899 **J**
4025 4094 **S** 690
Meijboom H T4222
Meinhold A 3782
R3121
Meir A 1302 **E** 8630
Meiser M 11085
Meisinger H 4601
Meissner B 9340 **J**
R5078 **S** 5844
Mejía J 7344
Melanchthon P M46
Melbourne B R5882
Melcher S 2100
Mele G 2671
Melito S M10933
Mell U 4865 4873
4932 R4834
Mello A 1741 3478
4279
Mellon B 7702
Melloni A E1 1958

Meltzer T R2253
Melugin R 3290
3330 3358 E3331
R3403
Men' A 4026
Menache S 8446
8578 E232
Menacherry C 7013
Mencej M 460
Mendecki N 1593
3580 10130 10345
Mendel M M1283
Mendels D 9424
Mendenhall G 2248
Mendoza C R1840 **G**
2197
Mendt D 4690
Mengden G von
M11017
Menichelli E 5040
Menke K-H 7014
Menken M 5443-45
5512 5521 5550
5553 5558s 5581
5598 5608 5629s
6481
Menn E R858
Menninger R 4328
Menozzi D E1 1958
Mense J 558
Mensing R 2338
Menu B 9963 R319
Menzies G T10908
Meredith A R2680
3018
Merino L R990
Rodríguez M
T10849
Merk O D4254 7335
Merkelbach R 4512
9015
Merklein H 3895
4256 5446 5503
5900s
Merling D 2289
E10247
Merlo B E4465 **P**
10305
Merrill E 2165 9145
R6891 6897
Merritt H 6315
Merwe C van der
2873 7653s

Merz A 4068
Meshel Z 10583
Messadié G 1528
Messika N 9964
Messina J 1594
Mesters C 4027
5532 M11068
Metropoulou E 8903
Metso S 8303
Mettinger T 1840
1941 1944
Metzger B 1047
1091 5726 F59
R4647 **M** 7315 F60
Metzner R 6588
Meulenaere H De
F61
Meurer S E1149
Meves C 2961
Meyendorff J F62
M7029
Meyer H R892 1158
-**Blank M** 933 **J-**
W 10769 **L** de F63
P 5447 R1351
Meyers C 2048 2377
10709 D2173 E172
10222 **E** 3829
10036
Meynet R 513 3702s
3708 4160 6342
Meza A 10261
Michael T R3473 **T**
R3888
Michaelides D
E10499
Michaelis S E11060
Michaels J 5727
5448 6589
Michálek E 1169
Michaud J 6535
R4727
Michel C 10747s D
3077 3777 F64
M11069 O 7293
Mickiewicz F 4870
Middleton J 7092
R3332
Midgley M 1477
Miegge M 3626
Mielcarek K 5105
Mielgo C R52 2144
2166 5953 6881

Niemand C 5601
6494 R4214 4746
5997
Niemann H 2392
10096 R68 R 4692
E196
Niemeier W-D
E10520
Niemeyer H 9693
Niemi T E10578
Niemirski Z 6537
Nieto Ibáñez J 8034
Nietzsche F 5663
Nieuviarts J 692
4719 5848 6687
Nieuwenhuis J 5642
Niewiadomski J
7257
Nigosian S 2230
6729
Nigro L 9578
Nikiprowetzky V
8094
Nikolakopoulos K
4633 R153
Nilus A 3023
Nippel W 9453
Nir-El Y 8199
Nissinen M 3292
R2437
Nitzan B 8262 8304
Nkulu-Kankote K
5315
Nobel P E915
Nobile M 5794 6343
7207 R165 2140
3535 3990 4056
5814 6515 6900
Noble P 706 814
1712 3711 T
T3982
Noce C R92 5234
Nodes D 10985
Nodet É E1250
Noegel S 1814 2965
2966 2967 3487
3490 3507 R684
Noel F 5064 W
E9758
Noemi Callejas J
7086
Noethlichs K 8452
Nogalski J 3655ss

Nohrnberg J 1815
Nolan A 637 4034s
B R5358 5811
Noll M 46931 R
7258
Nolland J 4377
4381ss 5041
Nollé J 10493
Nonnos P 5328 8892
8916 9445 M8893
8899
Noordegraaf A
R6116
Noormann H 537 R
10880
Noort E 10015
R2275 2288 3418
Nordiguian L 7958
Norin S R2281
North J 6139 6323
Northedge A 10239
Nortjé S 5513
Norton D 897 G
R2301
Noss P 1202
Notomhardio R
6928
Nouailhat R 5231
Novak D 6749 M
9579
Novatianus M10980
Nowicka M 9694
Nowicki K 10514
Noy D 7708
Ntima K 7015
Nugel W T874
Nugent D R2834
Nun M 4481s
Nunn J 10638
Nur ed-Din A 9967
Nurmela R 3831
Nusca A 5731
Nützel J 5732
Nuvolone F 8070
Nysse R D1871

Oakes P R5887
Oates D 10348 J
10348
Obbink D E7954
Obeid M 4695

Oberforcher R 3768s
R929 3962 4655
5814 6606
Oberlinner L 6502
6509 6512 D6130
Obermann A 5453
Oberweis M 10886
O'Brien D 2544 J
R3655 3656 K
4634 4694 5599
5733 M 1259 2261
O'Callaghan J 1048
Ocáriz F 7017
O'Collins G 6929s
7016 D7019 R4731
4743 4743
O'Connell R 2303
3712
O'Connor D 2968
9239 10470 K
3479
Odahl C E10963
O'Day G D4930
Oded B 2306 9276
Odell M 3672s
Oden R 8967
Odendaal D R2033
Odero J R4144 6684
O'Donovan O 7368
Oegema G 2423
6128 6871
Oeming C T7583 M
800 R7 1804 2555
2913 2999 3006
3327 M 638 2523
3007 T7583
Oesch J 3849 8968s
10335 R2607 3652
3655 3656
O'Fearghail F 5080
Ofer Y 998
Ofilada Macario M
R1420 4128 Mina
M R5409
Ogden G 2146 3053
Ognibeni B 999s
8453
O'Grady J 7259
Oh D-ho 5150
Ohler A 842 2424
Ohlig K-H 6693
E6931 7018
Ohnuki T T5312

Pires J 7262
Piryns E 4429
Pisano G 8972
10283 S 2444
R2461
Pisarek S 11108
Pitard W 9968
10352 10761
Pitta A 5851 5905
6333 6344 E5052
Pittman H 9696
9822
Pittner B 5906
Pitzele P 1449
Pixley J 7383
Pixner B 4044 4099
10181
Pizzolato L 2892
Placher W 6694
Platon L 9906
Platti E 10075
Plazanet-Siarri N
T10979
Pledel A 3049
Pleins J 2849
Plessis I du 5066
6934
Plisch U-K 6138
TE8798
Pliya J 6232
Plummer R 8387
Plünnecke E R2931
Plymale S 5996
Pobee J 647 7391
Pochon M 1541
Podella T 1946
Poets K 4751
Poggi V R2525
Poggia S 405
Pogoloff S 6189
Pohl A 6334 7171
Pohlmann K-F 3539
Pöhlmann W 1673
Pohl-Patalong U 566
Poirier J 4903 5566
6084 6206 P-H
8794s R355 3177
4499
Poirot S 2525
Pokorný P R4414
Polag A 4639
Polak F 694 1787
2970

Polan G 3360 R3352
Polemo M M9341
Polhill J 6388-89
D4989s
Polignac F de 8880
Poling J E1138
Polito E 9599
Pollack A 2346
Pollard A 9515
Polley M R3413
Polliack M 1095
R3321
Pollitt J E9775
Polotsky H F71
8766
Polycarp St.
M10887s
Pomorska M 412
Pomykala K 2426
Ponce Cuéllar M
7441
Ponchia S 3086
9277
Pongratz-Leisten B
9056
Ponizy B 3207 3210
Pons Pons G T6955
Ponthot J R4727
Poole D 6752
Poorthuis M 880
1542 1851 E236
2765
Pope K 1209 R3013
Popham M 9823 F72
Popkes W 3900
Popko M 9308
Poppi A 4233 R4231
Porat N 9861 P
9969
Porath Y 10107
10145 10586
Porsch F R4251
Porten B 2009
ET7830
Porter B 9278 C
6064 J 466 517s S
6299 6495 7914s
7938 E197s 268
7928
Portugali Y 10226
Postgate J R9253
Potestà G 3295
Potin J 4100 10076

Pottier B 1543
R1494
Potts T 10365
Pouderon B 10854
Poupard P Card.
1481
Powell E 5322 I
4564 M 4332s
4456 9057 10009
10751 E4265
R4858 5058 R
4045
Powelson M E4234
Powery E R4018
Poythress V D4480
Pozo C 7570 Abe-
jón G del 1396
R6094
Prag K 10270
E10041
Prandi C 1597
Pratico G 10242
Prato G R178 425
1245 2144 3021
3703 6814 8225
Pratscher W 6019
8973s
Pratt R 695
Prawer J E10077
Precedo J R441 2351
Prechel D 8975
Preez J du 5793
Pregeant R 4334
Preiser W 2010
Premstaller V 3197
Pressler C R857
Prete B 4923 5164
Pretorius E R6425
Preucel R E237
Preuss H 6893s
Preusser C 10369
Prévost J-P 3296s
5737
Price D E730 J 1252
9425 E104 R7972
R 4199 8202 S
R1692
Prickett S 696
Priebe D 3680
Priest J F73 P R4529
Prieur A 5067
Prigent P 9745
Prijs L 1004

Rashkow I 1353
Raske M 2526
Raspanti G 11081s
Rassart-Debergh M 8120
Ratti S 9454
Ratzinger J Card. 731 7103 E269
Ratzlaff R 8268
Ratzsch D 1482
Rau E 10918
Raue D 10465
Raurell F 468 2655 3166 3529 5592 7932s 7981 R1084
Rausa F 9970
Rava E R6950
Ravasi G 1332 1629 2568 2686 2973 3903 5369 R7 440 4561 T2925
Raveh K 9604 10148
Raven M 10447 10477
Ravindra R 5461
Ravitzky A 6873 8457
Rawak Y 10158
Ray C D7942 J 5012
Rayan S 4124s
Read J 9241
Reader W 9341
Reardon B R2653
Reasoner M R98
Rebell W 8121 R4552 6423
Rebenich S 10960
Rebera R 2340
Rebić A 6818 9479 R4200s
Reboreda Morillo S 8860
Rebuffat F 10010
Recchia V 3550 10973s E3549
Rechenmacher H 7762
Redalié Y 6496
Redditt P 3659 3825 R3270
Reden S von 9324
Redford B 10608 D 9154s

Redmont J 2795
Reed J T 4236 5852 6443 6630 S 8307 E8204 R5518 6005
Reese R 6630
Rees-Hanley A 7532
Reetnitz P von T780
Reeves J 8787 E8035 R1696 M R5724 N 9971
Rega E 9957
Regev E 10079
Regt L de 1210 1788 7661 E200 901
Rehm E 9634
Reho C E69
Reich R 3119 E9567
Reichelt H 5741
Reichert A 10012
Reichmuth S 9086
Reichrath H 8693
Reid B 4537 5070 R4529 6005 D 6838 M 6085 S 651 2850 E95
Reiling J 6234
Reim G R5494
Reimer D 7349 E57
Reimer H 3800
Rein M 5569 8907 9747
Reinbold W 4700
Reiner E 2291 8579 9279
Reinhardt W 5013
Reinhartz A 7479
Reinhold M E8416
Reinmuth E 5014 6185
Reisner G M11075
Reiterer F 3241 E3224
Reller J 6046
Remaud M 1747 1887 3439
Remley P 1139
Remmert S 9624
Rems R 2025
Remus H 1818
Renan E 11029 M11029
Renaud B 1400 1928 F74

Rendsburg G 1354 D2966 R2619
Rendtorff R 145 818 1279s 1654 2102 2569 2763 3334 6896 9156 R6645 6885 6893 6900
Renger J 10752
Renn S R3013
Renoux C 2974 5651 5664 6571
Renz J 7710 T R6897
Rese M 5462 R5823
Resnick I T1545
Restrepo Restrepo G 10901
Rétat L E11029
Rettig J TE5350
Reumann J 6433 R1228 5924
Reuter E 2218 R3768
Revell E 469 E270
Revellin L R6203
Reventlow H 652 3299 E201 R16 103 131 139 145 269 431 488 506 691 800 802 805 818 820 1796 1941 1994 2425 4177 4183 6640 6645 6651 6852 6866 6885 6887s 6890 6892s
Rey A-L 8156 - Coquais J-P 9839
Escapa J 6956 F T4088
Reyes AT 10502
Reymond P 7711 S 5265
Reynier C 5853 5908s 6412
Reynolds R 1104
Reznick L 9426
Rhoads D 3904
Rhodes R 8821
Ri J 4046s
Ribeiro A R5063 A do Vale 6957 10819 Guimarães

Röhser G 6755
Rokéah D 8458
Rokéhah D 8694
Roll I 10646
Rolla A ^{R}3301 5366
    6003
Rolland P 4186
    4899 6623
Roller L 8909
Rolley C 9776
Röllig W ^{R}1601
Rollinger R 9280
Rollins W 935
Roloff J 5679 6497
    7210 7264 ^{R}6502
Rolston H 6733
    ^{R}1512
Romanides J 6874
Romaniuk K 5043
Romano M ^{T}1528
Römer T 1282 1820
    2263 3469 6841
    ^{E}199 ^{R}1613 2142
    2933
Romero C ^{R}2768
    Pose E ^{R}5173
    6500
Ronan M 7501
Ronen A 10164 Y
    9651
Rooke D 2054
Rooker M 3398
Root M 9800
Rooze E 1889
Roquette J-M 9973
Rordorf W 4640
    10869s ^{R}4729
Rose A 2687 C 6553
    10697 J ^{E}10419 M
    2167s 2262
Rösel M 523 1334
    1890
Rosen J ^{M}7774 K
    9427 S 9536 9777
Rosenau H 6780
Rosenbaum S ^{R}6669
Rosenberg D ^{E}1355
    M ^{R}15 R 7758
    8328s S 10151
Rosenberger M 6958
Rosenblatt J 921
    ^{E}697 M-E 5277
Rosendal B ^{F}76
    ^{R}6814

Rosenkranz S 8695
Rosenthal-Hegin-
    bottom R 9894
Rosenzweig F 1184
    ^{M}187 1147 11089
Rosica T 9199
Röslin H ^{M}1470
Rosłon J 11151
Rosner B 6198ss
    ^{E}5972 ^{R}897 902
    5944
Rosovsky N ^{E}10082
Ross A 1356 L 1211
Rossé G 4641 5015
    5323
Rossi de Gasperis F
    6781 Ferrini D
    ^{T}4501
Rossier F 6782
Rossin E 819
Rössler M ^{R}6975
Rossoni G 9533
Rost F 9640 L
    11152
Rota Scalabrini P
    1546 7075
Roth E 1004 P 9415
Rothe H ^{E}1170
Rothgangel M 6115
Roth-Gerson L 9343
Rothmann C ^{M}1470s
Rothschild F ^{E}8696
    J-P ^{E}413
Rottzoll D 3716
    ^{T}1333
Rotzetter A 6186
Rouet A 4642
Rouger D 1061
    10848
Rougier S 2796
Rouillard-Bonraisin
    H 3624 ^{R}2351
Rouiller G ^{D}5423
    6131
Roukema R 6152
Roulin G 9022
Roure D ^{R}5814
Rousseau A ^{TE}10881
    J 358 P 10914
Rousselle A 10716
Rouvière J-M 5577
Rouwhorst G 6573
Roux M le 2304
    ^{R}2300

Rova E 9826 10562
Rowell G ^{E}7160
Rowland C 5745
    7370 ^{R}5104 5954
Rowlett L 2292
Royalty R 5746
Royer M ^{T}5355
Royse J 8096
Royster D 4538
Rozman F 4200s
    ^{R}5961
Rozner S ^{E}8501
Ruben I 10268
Rubenstein J 2055
    3846 8544
Rubiato Díaz M
    7729 10199
Rubiato M 10196
Rubin M 10986 R
    10049 10099
Ruckstuhl E 5371
    7481
Ruderman A 10212
Rudolph K 147-148
    7172s 7941 8051
    8723-42 8767-79
    8822 W ^{E}990
Rue V 569
Rüger H 10786
Ruggieri G ^{E}1 1958
    V ^{R}50
Ruggiero A ^{TE}2711
Ruiz J-P 11109
    Cabrero L 7798 -
    Garrido C ^{T}336
    4128 9083
Rumscheidt M
    ^{R}1184
Runciman S 8780
Runia D 8097-8100
    ^{R}252
Rupp D ^{E}10506
Ruppert L 732-733
    1335 3335s 3440
    ^{D}3356
Rupprecht H-A 7970
    ^{E}7969
Ruprecht E 3477
Rusch W ^{R}5057
Rusche H 11153
Rusconi C 7916 R
    ^{E}5747
Russell A ^{R}1459-60
    1477 1485 D 3600

Saye S 658
Scaiola D 6715 ^{R}177
 419   1312   1336
 2337   3972   5011
 5199   5227   5364
 5905   6098   6447
 6502 6668
Scanlin H 1005
Scanlon R 7211
Scarpat G ^{ET}3191
Schaack T 7745
Schaberg J 570 4380
Schabert T ^{E}1452
Schachl-Raber U
 4338
Schädler U ^{E}312
 9867
Schaefer M 7298
Schäfer P 352 1789
 ^{E}39 8395 8547-50
 8603 -Lichtenber-
 ger C 2215 2293
 9161 10719 ^{R}2139
 2356 2436
Schäffer D 3803
Schams C 9159
Schaper J 2764 9160
 ^{R}1334 3226
Scharbert J 973 6658
 7299 ^{R}1235 1301
 2092
Schart A ^{R}193 3655
 3656
Schat A 1150
Schatkin M ^{R}2922
Schatz K 4565s
Schaub R 9641
Scheerer R ^{R}6791
Scheffler E 10553
Scheidel W 9243
 10775
Schein A ^{R}1686 S
 8581 10797
Schelling F ^{M}6976
 7027
Schenck K 6539
Schenk R ^{E}7147 W
 2656 ^{R}5997
Schenke H-M 2675
 L 5574
Schenkel W 7882
Schenker A 1006
 1790 1892s 2150

 2486s 3209 3383
 ^{R}6353
Schenk-Ziegler A
 7350
Scheuermann G
 4339 ^{E}5368
Scheurer E 7212
Schibler D 2294
Schick A 8330 R
 10263 10800
Schiefer F 571
Schierse F 1222
Schiffman L 8208s
 8309s 8361 10085
 ^{E}305 ^{E}8499   M
 ^{T}7986
Schillebeeckx E
 9200
Schiller E ^{E}10556
Schimmel A 9087
Schindler D 524
 1403
Schippers A 2676
Schlageter J ^{R}3512
Schlarb R 6089
Schlatter A ^{M}11076
Schlegelberger B
 ^{E}218
Schleiermacher F
 7027 ^{M}1395 2821
 6943
Schley D ^{R}684
Schlichting W 1675
Schlick-Nolte B
 9534
Schloemann M 1151
Schlomit A 6842
Schlosser J 4238
 4702   5818   5914
 6907 ^{E}273
Schlueter C 6476
Schlütter A 5466
Schmahl G 4843
Schmandt-Besserat
 D 8008s 9698
Schmeling G ^{E}238
Schmeller T 5997
 7104
Schmid H 1284
 10370 K 3495 U
 5857
Schmidt A ^{R}2697 B
 2439 8979s 10309

E ^{E}7536 F 2505
 8461 G ^{F}80 J 3302
 3603 6898 9162s L
 659   1285s   1404
 2264 ^{R}1294 2391
 T 3604 7351 W
 1852 1930 6756 -
 Kaler T 8999
Schmithals W 5858
 11039
Schmitt A 2608
 6899 C ^{R}6307 H-
 C ^{D}1276 ^{E}399 J
 6659
Schmitz B ^{E}10448 P
 ^{R}1410
Schmucki O ^{R}6954
Schnabel E ^{R}6294
 6534 6757 8700
Schnackenburg R
 4056   4340   6390
 6935 7352
Schneck R 2804
 4844
Schneider D 2712s
 G ^{E}335s H 5096
 9974s N 6135 S
 6224 6265 T 1212
Schneiders S 5632
 7537
Schnelle U 707
 3909s 5520 6716
 ^{E}5754 ^{R}5388 5484
Schnider F 1894
Schniedewind W
 2471   2581   7836
 ^{R}2261   2270   2470
 2478 2514 2539
Schnieper A 9743
Schnocks J 3559
Scholem G 8604
Scholer D 4239
 8790
Schöllgen G 660
 10871 ^{E}19
Scholten C 1405s
 10822 ^{E}19
Scholtissek K 4845
 5467 7935 ^{E}4058
 ^{R}4890
Scholz F ^{E}1170 S
 1716
Schönborn P 7384

Walsh B 7092 **C**
10613 **J** 2465 4965
7372 R1815
Walter L R3296 **N**
6297 R4058 4250
Walters J R6062
Waltke B 3123
Wanamaker C 4076
Wander B 8712
Wang A 2839
Wanke G 3476 E399
Wansbrough H 4856
7450 R4854 6123
Wansink C 5822
Wapnish P 10594
Ward G 8052 **W**
7889 8988
Wardy R 7973
Ware J 6434
Warne G 5974
Warnier P 6786
Warns E 581
Warren H T1175 **P**
9518 10525 **T**
R744
Warrington K R56
Warrior R 670 **V**
9352
Wartenberg G E46 -
Potter B 1936
Wartke R-B 10494
E9547
Waruta D D10760
Warzecha J 7614
R2770
Waschke E-J R3338
6893
Washington H 1637
3124
Wasserberg G 5074
Wasserstein A 1086
11163 F104 **D**
E104
Waters K 3370
Watkin J R1665
Watkins T 9289
Watson A 4435
4857 5253 9461 **D**
R964 5846 6188
6463 6562 **F** 8713
N 6282 **P** 10255s
W 2662s 7805ss

8989 10316s E31
2650 R2510 2718
Wattles J 4447
Watts J 1307 3819
6406 E105 F105
M11083 R2229
6652 **R** R4844
Way D R5872 5954
T von der 9029
Weatherly J 5027
6465 R5041
Weaver D 4349
R4580 **J** 671
Webb B 3349 **J**
10497 10505 **P**
9781 **R** 4412 6632
R4858 **W** 6304
Webber A 8570 **R**
6625 6787
Weber B 2866 6442
D 2858 10948 **H-**
R 582 7373 **K**
3238 4350 **L** 5611
M 10732 **T** 7974
U 9300
Webers T 4711
Webster E R3413 **G**
10287
Wedderburn A 6399
Weder H 672 5492
D5736
Weeks S 3096
Weems A 2773 **R**
673
Wegner A-C R3403
Wehr L 4567 7066
R6423
Wehrle J 3125
Weigl M 3798s
Weil D 1012
Weima J 5864 6473
R5860
Weimar P 1824
Weinandy T 7038
Weinberg J 2509
2573 **W** 7670
Weinfeld M 2170
2207 6666 6827
Weinstein J 9168
Weis R 1662 E77
Weisberg D 9290
R2589

Weiser A 4077
R6502 6509 **W**
10011
Weisman Z 485
Weiss H 4351 6543
8481 **I** 1638 **M**
2865 2904 **Z**
10223 E10222
Weitzman M 1096
R2928 **S** 2609
7671
Welborn L 6284
Welck C 5493
Welker M 4645
4758
Wellhausen J 9169
Wells G 4078 **R**
3452
Wellum S 783
Welsby D 10474
Welte B M6985
Wendland E 1176
1218 3759 3785
5144
Wendrich W E10455
Wengert T 6052
Wengst K D5791
Wenham D 5823
R5814 **G** 1340
Wénin A 1902 2374
6720 R6829
Wente E TE7890
Wenz A 784
Wenzel K 700
Werbick J 7107
Weren W 4290 4352
5613
Werfel F M11084
Werlitz J 3371s
Werner P 1088 9588
Werrell R R1128
Wescoat B R320
Weslby D 9249
Wesselius J 1639
1753
Wessels J 2268 4173
West G 674s 1293
3685 E211
Westbrook R R2011
V R380
Westendorf W
10640

Witvliet J R6787
Wodecki B 1655
　11114s
Wogaman J 7362
Wohlmuth　J　158
　8715 10950
Wojciechowski M
　4083　6938　11116
　R3864 3936
Wolf J de 2297
Wölfel C 8838
Wolfers D 2991
Wolff　C　6156　K
　2694 S 9486 9988
Wolfson　E　8608
　R6868
Wolinski J R2698
Wolosky S 7039
Wolter H-J 5868
Wolters　A　3845
　8317　R3623　3655
　3824s
Wondra E 7551
Wong G 3388 K-C
　4353 T 3925
Wood C 785 D777 D
　360 E 5962
Woodhead J 10204
Woodmorappe J
　1604
Woods F 2531
Woodward K 4761 S
　8231 9251
Wortham R 6439
Worthing M 1488
Worthington I E980
Wotling P R5663
Woungly-Massaga L
　4646
Wouters A 4354
　E8014
Wrede G 2825
Wright　A　2776　B
　3227　C 2114 2171
　7223　D 1561 2854
　10951 E272 R2977
　4618 J 3525 R102
　2488 N 4084 4110
　4479　6076　6123
　6351　6939　R
　D8052　E249　T
　4085

Wucherpfennig A
　R5053
Wujek J T1177
Wulf-Rheidt U 9589
Wullung F 7040
Wündrich R 3557
Wünsch H-M 6283
Wurst G 8782
Würthwein E 2270
Wüstefeld W E9758
Wyatt N 1454 2394s
　10300 10318 E31
Wyk K van E38 W
　van 2594 R2085
Wylen S 4111
Wyler B 7451
Wyller E 5657
Wyschogrod M 8635
　R6749
Wyse R 3128
Wysny A 3646
Wyssenbach　J　527
　729 R2280 3329

Xaranauli A 10990
Xavier　A　5496
　11117
Xella　P　2128　8930
　10319

Yadin Y F106
Yakar J 9590 10486
Yamada K 5226
Yamauchi　E　9252
　9301 9889 11057 I
　4086 E226
Yancey P 4112
Yang K 2070
Yannai　E　9989
　10179
Yardeni A 7723
　ET7830
Yasuda H 1423
Yasur-Landau A
　9850
Yates R 7121
Yavetz Z 9202
Yeager J 2992
Yeago D 10931
Yee G 3678

Yegül F 9612
Yekutieli Y 10118
Yellin J 9890
Yifrach E 3228
Yildiz E 4413
Yilibuw D 1178
Ylla-Català M 10614
Yoder P E6846
Yogev O 10219
Yon M 9174 10320
　E9537 10321
　10503
Yoo S 4480 5292
York A 890 1562
Yoshida D 8923
Young　B　4113　D
　1605 F107 J 10384
　P 4087
Younger K 2253
Younker R 9175
Yount W 6000
Yovel Y 8619
Yoyotte J 1455s
Yron-Lubin M
　10156
Ysebaert J 7275
Yu S 2208
Yuen S-C 3526
Yule G 8017

Zabbal F D8830
Zaccagnini　C　9176
　10378
Zaccaria G 741
Zadok R 9177
Zager W 4859 7122
　R3923 4035
Zahl P 7123
Zahrnt H 4088 5619
Zakovitch Y 1796
　1985
Zamagni C 2777
Zamora P R2459
　2919
Zandee J ET8801
Zanetti U 6575s
Zangger-Derron G
　E6627
Zani L 6238
Zapff B 3380
Zatelli I D908 7709

Situs

Voces

Ναζαρηνός /
  Ναζαραῖος 7940
νοῦς 7941
νόμος 7931
νωθρός 7942
οἰκουμένη 5056
παρακολουθέω 9397
παρρησία 5222
  6536 7943 7944
πίστις 7945s 9393
πιστεύειν 7946 9393
πορνεία 6202
ῥῆμα 7950
σάρξ 5879
σπαργανον 7947
στοιχεῖα 6365
συγκαταβασις 7948
σῶμα 7949
τελώνης 7951
υἱοθεσία 6023
φύσις 5923

Hebraicae

ab 7725
adamah 7726
ahab 2181
'ot 2061
berit 2061 7730
bth 7727
bkh 7728
baqbuq 7729
brk 2994
gebiyyah 3812 7731
goyim 2221
gll 7732

dabar 7733
hbl 3165 7734
hinneh 7735
zu 7736
hammanim 7740
hatta't 1859
hayot 1821
hen 7737
hinnam 2995
hesed 7738
hartummim 7739
yadid 7741
yedidyah 7742
yd' 7743
k 7744
kippur 2125
ktb 7745
leb 7746
lqh 7747
mem 7748
na 7749
neged 7750
nkr 7751
nqm 7752
sod 7753
suh 7754 8296
sup 7755
snh 7754 8296
'qb 1690
'tid 7755
prs 7756
sedeq 7757s 8329
sur 1832
salmawet 7759
qrb 7760
qrs 3510

ra'ah 3170
ruah 3552
rhq 7761
rš' 7668
šqq 7764
šabbat 7762
šh- 7763
šalom 452
tmm 7765s

Latinae

caelum 7979
gloria 7981
maiestas 7981
ornamentum/ornatus
  7980

Phoeniciae

Hggbʿl 7767

Ugariticae

ahr 10318
d(h)rt 7768
hdrt 7768
ymn 10318
marzihu 8971
kispu 8971
qdm 10318
qtn 7769
šmal 10318
šrd 7770
šrt 7770
trt 7770

Sacra Scriptura

Genesis	1,26: 1375 1403 1411 1413 1422	2,2-3: 1385	3,15: 1515
		2,4-5: 1419	3,16: 1559
1-2: 1366 1379		2,4-7: 1461	3,20-24: 1548
1,1-3: 1461	1,28: 1386	2,7: 1409	3,20: 1526
1,1-5: 1371	1401	2,16-17: 1490	1531
1,20: 1394	1: 1423	3,1-9: 1514	3: 1521 1552
1,26-27: 1378	2-3: 6504	3,6-13: 1532	4,1-4: 1548
1392 1416	2-12: 1347	3,8-9: 1551	4,17-24: 1576
1,26-28: 1399	10543	3,10: 1546	4: 1564 1566

5,14-19: 2117
8,2: 2118
8: 2119
10,6: 2120
11: 2089 2092
 2121
12,5: 2122
13,46: 2123
15,8: 2124
16: 2125s 2128
17-26: 1966
 2095
17,3-7: 2129
18,22: 2005
18: 2130
19,17-18: 1965
19,18: 2131
19,19: 2132
19,20-26: 2133
19: 843 1956
 2134
20,13: 2005
21,24: 2127
23,44: 2127
24,19-20: 2135
25,39-46: 1982
25: 2136
26: 2137

Numeri

5,11-31: 2660
6,1-21: 2660
6: 2139
8,1-4: 2060
9,12: 5629
9,15-23: 4385
11,10-15: 2660
11,11-25: 6667
11: 2151
13-14: 2152
15: 2139
16,15: 2153
17,16-26: 3477
17: 2154
20,9: 2154
21,3: 4473
22-24: 2156
 2159-62
24,17: 2155
 4385
26,47: 1747
30: 2139

Deuteronom.

1-11: 2209
4: 2210s 2216
5,6: 1937
5,16: 843 1956
5,21: 7620
5,25-6: 2127
6,4-5: 2212s
6,5: 2214
7: 2206 2215
9,7-10,11:
 8073
9: 2216
10,1-11: 2216
10,4: 1934
12,2-28: 2179
12: 2217s
13,9: 2219
13: 6836
14,1-17,13:
 2220
14: 2092
15,1-11: 2206
15,6: 2221
15,12-18: 1982
 2217
16,1-8: 2222
17,14-20: 2189
17: 6836
19-25: 2074
 2223
22,1-4: 1965
22,22-29: 2224
23,4-9: 1801
24,4-6: 2156
24,16: 2225
25,9: 2226
26,1-11: 2227
27,5-6: 1974
 1979
28,12: 2221
28: 2228
31,9: 1934
31,14-30: 2216
31,24: 1934
32,18: 6781
32: 2229-32
33,2: 2234
33,28: 2234
33: 2233
34,10-12: 2236
34: 2235

Josue

3-4: 1901
4,21-24: 1870
9: 2282
13-21: 2286
24,10: 2156
24,28-31: 2287

Judices

2,6-9: 2287
3,8-11: 2306
3,12-30: 2307s
4-5: 2309
4: 2310
5,1-31: 2311
5: 2312s
11: 2314
12,5-7: 2315
12,6: 7694
12: 2314
13-16: 2316s
13,2: 2381
16,28: 2318
17-18: 2319
17,1-6: 2320
19-21: 2307
 2321s
19,1: 2323
19,22: 2005

Ruth

1,1-6: 2342
2,1-23: 2343
2,14: 2344
3,1-4,22: 2345
4,1-6: 2346
4,11: 2347
4,17: 2348

1 Samuel

1-12: 2368
1,1: 2381
1,4-8: 2375
1,24: 2376
1: 2377
2,1-10: 2378
2,9: 10940
2,12-26: 2379
5,1-7,1: 2387

5: 9364
9,1: 2381
9,24: 2397
10,27-11,3:
 8257
10,27-11,1:
 2398
13,1: 2399
14,4: 2400
14,18: 2401
15-17: 2432
 5399
15,6: 2402
15,24: 2403
15: 9361
16,1-13: 9360
17: 520 2433s
20: 2435
21: 2436
22: 2436
25: 9362
28,8: 2437
28: 2438s 8979
31,3: 2419
31,10: 7949
31,12: 7949

2 Samuel

1,19-27: 2443
1,26: 2429
4: 2435
5-8: 2444
6: 2411 2445
7,1-17: 1650
7,13: 2446
7: 2447
9: 2435
10-12: 2448
11,2-26: 2428
11: 2449
12,1-15: 2428
 2450
12,6: 2451
12,25: 7742
12: 689
13,1-21: 2452
13: 6374 9367
14,1-20: 2453
16: 2435
18,9-33: 2454
19: 2435
20,14-22: 2455

2885
110: 2808
2886s
113: 1382 2888
115: 2723
116: 2889
118,116: 2890
118,22-23: 2891
118: 2892s
119,89: 2894
119,126: 2895
119: 2896ss
120-134: 2899-2902
121: 2903
127: 6715
130: 2904s
131: 2906
132: 2907
138: 2908
139,1-18: 2909
139,1-18: 5157
139: 2910s
145: 2912
147: 2913s
148: 2915
149: 6836

Job

1-2: 2993 6667
1,5: 2994
1,9: 2995
9-10: 2996
19,26: 2997
21-27: 2998s
22: 3000
26,5-14: 3001
26: 3002
28: 3003
29-31: 3004s
32-37: 3006
38-42: 3007
38: 3008s
42,7-9: 3010
42,10-17: 2993

Canticum,
Song

1,5: 3052s
1,12-2,16: 3054
4,8: 3055
6,4: 3056
6,10: 3056
7,6: 2652

Proverbia

1-9: 2936 3129-32 3134
1,8-19: 3133
2,16-22: 3139
5,1-23: 3139
6,20-35: 3139
7,1-27: 3139
7: 3135s
8,20: 3137
8,22-31: 1461
8,30: 3138
9,13-18: 3139
10,1-18,24: 3140
10: 9474
14,2: 3141
15,16: 3142
19,26: 843 1956
26,16: 3143
30,1: 3145
30,1-4: 3144
31,10-31: 3146ss
31: 1067

Eces, **Qohelet**

1,4-7: 3180
2,1-11: 3181
2,24: 3182
4,17-5,6: 3183
7,1-4: 3764
7,25-29: 3184
7,26-28: 3185
8,16-9,10: 3186
9,1-10: 3764

9,9: 3185
9,11-12: 3187
12,5: 3188
12,9: 3189
12,12: 711 3189

Sapientia Sal.

1,13-15: 3199
2-5: 3200
2,10-20: 3201
4,7-20: 3202
7: 3203
11-19: 3204
11,24: 3205
16,15-17,1: 3206
16,20-28: 3207
17,1-18,4: 3208
18,9: 3209
18,14-16: 3210

Ecus, **Sirach**

1,1-2,23: 3229
3,1-4,10: 3230
3,1-16: 843 1956
4,1-10: 3231
5,9-6,1: 3232
5,14-6,1: 3233
6,5-17: 3234s
12,8-12: 3236
19,6-19: 3237
19,20-30: 3238
20,21-23: 3233
22,19-26: 3239
22,25: 3233
24: 3240
25,1-11: 3241
27,16-21: 3242
29,14: 3233
37,1-6: 3243
41,14-42,8: 3244
41,18: 3233
41,22: 3233
48,1-49,16: 3245

50: 3246

Isaias

1-11: 3359
1,1-2,4: 3325
1,10-20: 3360
1,18: 1181
1: 3316 3358
2-12: 3362
2: 3361
5,1-7: 3363 4938
5,1-30: 3364
5,1: 3365
5,7: 3366
5,18: 3367
5: 3368
6,1-13: 3369
6,10: 5581
6: 3370
7,1-17: 3371s
7,6: 3373
7,14: 3374 4380
8,23: 3375s
9,1-6: 3375 3377
9,1-8: 3371
10,1-6: 3368
11: 3378
13-14: 3379
13: 3380
15-16: 3381s
19,16-25: 3383
22,15-25: 2041
22,21-2: 7725
25,11: 3384
26,17-18: 3385
27,2-6: 4938
28-33: 3386
28,1-6: 3387
29,1-8: 3371
31,1-3: 3388
36-37: 3389s
36-39: 3391s
37,3: 3390
40,1-11: 3406s
40,3: 5512
40,9: 3408
41,17-20: 3409

Micheas **Micah**

1,6: 3772
2: 3773
3,9-12: 3774
4,1-5: 3775
4,5: 3776
4,14: 3777
5,1: 6856
5,2: 3372
6,1-8: 3778
6,4: 3779
6,8: 3780

Nahum

3,3: 3812 7949

Habakkuk

1,1-4: 3814
3,3: 10114
3,9: 3816
3: 3817 3819

Soph. **Zephan.**

1-2: 3800
1,14-16: 3801
1: 3802
2,1-3: 3803
3,1-13: 1599
3,10: 3804
3,12-13: 3805
3,12: 3806
3,14-18: 3807
3,19: 3808
3: 3808

Zechariah

1-8: 3836
1,4: 3279
3,8: 3837 9159
5,5-11: 3559 3838
6,1-7,14: 3840
6,1-8: 3839 6549
6,9-15: 9159
6,12: 3837
7,12: 3279
8: 3841

9-10: 3842
9-14: 3828 3843s 3659
12,9-13,1: 3428
12,10: 5630
13,7: 3428
14,8: 5558
14,20: 3845
14: 3846

Malachi

1,2-5: 3851
2,3: 3852
3,13-21: 3853
3,16-17: 5171
3,22-24: 3854

Matthaeus

1-2: 4355-94
1,1-17: 4377-80
1,1: 4381
1,16: 4382
1,18-25: 4383
1: 4384
2,1-12: 4385s 9729
2,11: 4387
2,13-23: 4388
2,16-18: 4389
2,16: 4390
2: 4391-4
3,11: 4396
4,1-11: 4415s 7471
4,23-7,29: 4424
5-7: 4417-47
5,3-7,27: 4418
5,8: 4448
5,13: 4436
5,21-22: 4437
5,21-26: 4438
5,21-48: 4439
5,33-37: 4437 4440s
5,38-48: 4219
5,48: 4442
6,9: 4467
6,19-21: 4444

6,25-34: 4445
6,33: 4446
7,12: 4447
8,1-4: 971 4483
8,5-13: 5541
8,14-15: 4473
8,28-34: 4480s 4484
8,28: 4482
9,9-13: 4507
9,18-26: 4508
10,1-11,1: 4895
10,4: 4509
10: 4510
11,7: 4511
11,16-17: 4512
11,16-30: 4513
11,25-30: 4514
11,28-30: 4515
12,6: 4516
12,28: 4235
12,38-42: 5127
12,39-41: 4517
13,10-13: 4544
13,24-30: 4545s
13,52: 4547
15,11: 4548s
15,21-28: 4550 4552ss
15,22-28: 4907
15,30: 4518
15,34: 4555
16,1-4: 4568
16,17-19: 4305
16,18-19: 4569
16,19: 4570
17,1-9: 4571
17,22-20,19: 4572
17,24-25: 4573
17,24: 4574
18,3: 4575s
18,12-14: 5546
18: 4577ss
19-20: 4580
19,16-30: 4581
19: 4582
20-25: 4591
20,1-16: 4592
20,17-28: 747

20,21-28: 4305
20: 4593
21,28-31: 4594
21,33-46: 4595s
22,1-10: 5131
22,1-14: 4597
22,2-14: 4598 5132
22,16-17: 4939
22,21: 4599 6874
22,34-40: 4600
22,35-40: 4601
22,37: 4602 4786
23,9: 4603
24-25: 4604
24,40-41: 4605
24: 4606
25,1-12: 4607
25,14-30: 4608s
25,31-46: 4610
26,6-7: 4647
26,28: 6738
26,36-46: 4713
26,50-51: 4714
26: 4648s
27,19: 4715
27,33-54: 4716
27,37: 4717
27,46: 4555 4718s
28,1: 4762
28,16-20: 4305 4763
28,18-20: 4764
28,34: 4305

Marcus

1-3: 4860
1,1-15: 4861
1,2: 4786
1,4: 4775
1,9-11: 4862s
1,9-13: 4414 4864
1,9-15: 4865
1,16-20: 4866
1,21-28: 4867
1,29-31: 4868

22,14-38: 3418
22,20: 6738
22,24-30: 5165
22,28-30: 5056
23,13-25: 3422
5166
23,33-46: 5167
23,39-43: 5056
23,43: 5168
24,12: 5169
24,13-35:
5170ss
24,50-53: 5242

Johannes

1-9: 5359
1,1-2,12: 5333
1,1-18: 5501
5507
1,1: 1122 5508
1,6-8: 5509
1,14: 5510
1,18: 5511
1,19-28: 5509
1,23: 5512
1,29: 5513
1,35-51: 5514
1,48: 5515
1,51: 1691
2,1-11: 5463
5516s
2,6: 5518
2,13-4,54:
5334
2,13-22: 5519s
2,17: 5521
2,23-3,21:
5446
2,23-3,36 5522
2: 8983
3,1-15: 5523
3,1-21: 5524
3,13: 5525
3,14-21: 5526
3,14: 5527
3,16: 5528
3,29: 5529
10992
3: 5530
4,1-42: 747
929 5531ss
7471

4,1: 5534
4,3-42: 5535
4,10: 5536
4,21: 5537
4,22: 5538
4,23-24: 5539
4,41-42: 5540
4,46-54: 5463
5541
4: 5542 6936
5-7: 5543
5-12: 5342
5,1-18: 5544
5,1-47: 5545
5,6: 5546
5,8: 4871
5: 5547s
6,22-71: 5549
6,31: 5550
6,37: 5551
6,44: 5552
6,45: 5553
6,60-71: 5554
6,63: 5555
6: 1722 5375
5556s
7,38: 5558s
7,53-8,11:
5560 7471
7: 5530 5561
8,6: 5562
8,8: 5562
8,31: 5563
8,57: 5564
8: 5561 5565
9,1-41: 747
9,3: 5566
9,29: 7934
9: 5567-71
10,1-18: 5572
10,10: 5573
7262
10: 5574
11,1-53: 747
11: 5575-8
12,20-36: 5446
5579
12,23-28: 7346
12,27: 5580
12,40: 5581
13,1-5: 5594
13,1-11: 5595
13,1-20: 5596

13,2-20: 5597
13,18: 5598
13,25: 4634
5599
13,31-16,33:
5600
13: 5601s
15,1-6: 5603
15,1-17: 5604
15,3: 5605
15,12: 5606s
15,25: 5608
16,10: 5609
17,1-26: 5610
17,21-23: 5611
17: 5612
18-19: 5613
18-19: 5614
18-21: 5615
18,28-19,16:
5616-9
19,16-30: 5620
19,23-24: 5621
19,25-27:
5622ss
19,26-27: 5625
19,28-30: 5626
19,28-37: 5627
19,30: 5628
19,36: 5629
19,37: 5630
19: 5530
20,1-10: 929
20,8: 5631
20,11-18:
5632s
20,17: 5634
20,19-23: 5635
20,19: 5636
20,30-31: 5637
20: 5638
21,1-14: 929
21,7: 9756
21: 5493 5638s

Actus Apostol.

1-2: 5240
1,1: 5241
1,9-11: 5242
1,14: 5243
2,1-3: 1599
2,1-21: 5244

2,14-41: 5022
2,22-24: 5180
2,32-33: 5180
2,33: 5245
2,38: 5246
3,1-26: 5208
3,2: 5247
3,12-26: 3418
3,13-15: 5180
3,19-26: 5248
4,1-6,7: 5249
4,1-22: 5208
4,23-31: 3418
4,24-31: 5250
5,17-21: 5251
6-7: 5252s
6,1-8,4: 5254
6,1-11,26:
5255
6,1-7: 5256
6,8-7,60: 5072
6: 5257
7,3: 5258
8,9-24: 5259
8,26-32: 1037
8,26-40: 2483
3418 5260ss
8: 5263
9,1-22: 5264
9,22: 5265
9,26: 5265
9: 5266
10-11: 5267
10,26-31: 1037
10,34-43: 5268
10,36-42: 5180
10,37: 7950
10: 1887
12: 5269
13,1-18,23:
5207
13,16-41: 5022
13,23-31: 5180
15,13-21: 5283
15: 5284-92
16,11-40: 5293
17,18-20: 5294
17: 5295s
18,1-18: 5297
18,18: 5298
19,2: 7934
20: 5299
21,15-36: 5072

2,15-21: 6357
2,16: 6358ss
2,20: 6361
3,1-6,2: 6362
3,1-5: 6363
3,28: 6364
4,3: 6365
4,9: 6365
4,10: 6366
4,12-6,16: 277
4,12-20: 6367
4,17: 6368
4,21-5,1: 6369
5,2-12: 6370
5,11: 6371
5,13-6,2: 5860
5,13-26: 6372
5,18: 6373
5,22-23: 6374
5,23: 6375
5,26-6,10: 6376
6,12-16: 6370

Ad Ephesios

2,14-16: 3883
2,16: 6416
4-6: 6417
4,7-11: 6418
4,16-29: 1037
4,31-5,13: 1037
5,6-14: 6419
6,10-20: 6420
6,12: 6421s

Philippenses

1,6: 6436
1,21-26: 7336
1,23: 6437s
2,1-5: 7052
2,5-11: 3883 6439
2,6-11: 6440s
2,12-13: 6442
2: 10912
3,1: 6443

3,7-11: 6444
3,9: 6361
4,10-20: 6445
4,11: 6446

Colossenses

1,15-20: 3883
1,15-23: 6455
2,16: 6366
3,11: 6456

1 Thess.

1,6: 6474
2,1-12: 6478
2,14-16: 6476s
2,16: 6475
4-5: 5823
4,17: 6479

2 Thess.

2,6-7: 6483
2: 6484

1 ad Timotheum

2,1-4: 7366
2,4: 6503
2,8-15: 6504
2,9-3,1: 6499
2,9-15: 6505s
3,11-15: 7452
3,16: 3883 6507
4,10: 6508
5,3-16: 6499

2 ad Timotheum

1,17: 6511
2,11-13: 3883

Ad Titum

1,10-16: 6513

3,4-7: 3883
3,5-6: 6514

Ad Hebraeos

1,1-13: 6544
2,5-9: 6545
2,9-10: 6546
2: 6547
3: 6548
4,12-13: 6549
4: 6548
5,5-10: 6440
5,11-6,12: 7942
6,4-6: 6550
6,13-10,21: 6551
7,1-10,18: 6518
9,15: 6552
9,24-28: 6552
10,32-12,3: 6553
10,37-38: 6554
11,1-13,24: 6555
11,11: 6556
11: 6557

Jacobi, **James**

1,2-4: 4442
1: 6606
3,13: 6617
5,12: 4441

1 Petri

1,1-3: 6593
1,22-2,3: 6594
2,13-17: 6595 7366
3,1: 6596
3,14: 6597
3,18-22: 3883

2 Petri

1,16-18: 6603
1,16-21: 6604
3,3-15: 6605

1 Johannis

2,18: 5660 5775
4,8: 5652
4,16: 5652

2 Johannis

4: 5775
11: 5775

Apocalypsis
Revelation

1-3: 5762s
1,13-18: 5764
1,13: 5765
3,14: 5766
3,20: 5767
4-5: 5768 6441
5,6-9: 5769
5: 5770
12-13: 5771
12,14: 5691
12: 1642 5772s
13,11: 5774
13: 5775
14,1-5: 5776
14,6-13: 5777
14,14: 5765
17-18: 5778
17: 5779
18: 5780
21-22: 1424
21,1-22,5: 5791
21,1-5: 5792
21,1-8: 5793
21: 5794
22,1-21: 5795
22,16-21: 5796